Statistical Record of the Environment

Third Edition

GALE ENVIRONMENTAL LIBRARY

Statistical Record of the Environment

Third Edition

Compiled and Edited by
Charity Anne Dorgan

Gale Research Inc.

An International Thomson Publishing Company

I(T)P

Changing the Way the World Learns

NEW YORK · LONDON · BONN · BOSTON · DETROIT · MADRID
MELBOURNE · MEXICO CITY · PARIS · SINGAPORE · TOKYO
TORONTO · WASHINGTON · ALBANY NY · BELMONT CA · CINCINNATI OH

Charity Anne Dorgan, *Editor*

Editorial Code & Data Inc. Staff

Marlita A. Reddy, *Research Director*
Helen S. Fisher and Robert S. Lazich, *Contributing Editors*
Sherae R. Carroll and Nancy A. Ratliff, *Data Entry Associates*
Gary Alampi, *Programmer/Analyst*

Gale Research Inc. Staff

Christine B. Jeryan, *Managing Editor*
Deborah Milliken, *Production Assistant*
Cynthia Baldwin, *Product Design Manager*
Barbara J. Yarrow, *Graphic Services Manager*
Bernadette Gornie, *Cover Designer*
Cover photograph by Robert J. Huffman

Table of Contents

CHAPTER 4 - LAND AND LAND USE continued:

Forest Insects and Disease 170
    Table 202   Forestland Damage, by Insect: 1968-1993 170
    Table 203   Gypsy Moth Defoliation: 1988-1992 171
    Table 204   Mountain Pine Beetle Damage: 1988-1992 171
    Table 205   Southern Pine Beetle Outbreak: 1988-1992 172
    Table 206   Spruce Budworm Defoliation: 1988-1992 173
    Table 207   Western Spruce Budworm Defoliation: 1988-1992 173
Forests and Trees 174
    Table 208   Forest and Timberland Area: 1952-1992 174
    Table 209   National Forest System 175
    Table 210   National Forest System – Forests and Land: 1891-1993 176
    Table 211   National Forest System Land, by State: 1990-1991 177
    Table 212   Timberland, by Owner: 1952-1992 178
    Table 213   Tree Planting – Federal Land, by State: 1992-1993 179
    Table 214   Tree Planting – Non-Federal Land, by State: 1992-1993 180
    Table 215   Tree Planting – Private Land, by State: 1992-1993 182
    Table 216   Tropical Rainforest's Medicinal Plants 183
Land Area 183
    Table 217   Elevations – Highest Points, by State 183
    Table 218   Elevations – Lowest Points, by State 185
    Table 219   Elevations – Mean Elevations, by State 187
    Table 220   Land Area: 1990 188
    Table 221   Land Expansion of the United States 190
    Table 222   Land Ownership: 1900-1991 191
Land Area: Federal 192
    Table 223   Federal Land and Buildings: 1970-1991 192
    Table 224   Federal Offshore Activities: 1975-1992 193
    Table 225   Federal Public Domain Acquisitions 194
    Table 226   Federal Public Domain Area: 1978-1991 195
    Table 227   Federally Owned Land, by State: 1960-1991 196
Land Use 198
    Table 228   Land Cover and Use, by State 198
    Table 229   Land Cover and Use – Percent Distribution, by State 200
    Table 230   Land Trusts 201
    Table 231   Land Use: 1900-1991 202
    Table 232   Rangeland: 1936-1992 203
Mineral and Metal Production 203
    Table 233   Industrial Mineral Production: 1980-1993 203
    Table 234   Industrial Mineral Production Values: 1980-1993 205
    Table 235   Metal Production: 1980-1993 206
    Table 236   Metal Production Values: 1980-1993 207
    Table 237   Mineral and Metal Products: 1980-1992 208
    Table 238   Mineral Fuel Production: 1980-1993 209
    Table 239   Mineral Fuel Production Values: 1980-1993 210
    Table 240   Mining and Primary Metal Production Indexes: 1970-1993 210
    Table 241   Nonfuel Mineral Commodities: 1993 211
    Table 242   Nonfuel Mineral Production, by State or Area: 1980-1993 213
    Table 243   Principal Fuel, Nonmetal, and Metal Production: 1980-1993 . . . 214
    Table 244   World Mineral Production: 1985-1993 215

Introduction

Statistical Record of the Environment (SRE), now in its third edition, is a comprehensive presentation of statistical materials drawn from governmental and private sources. The third edition of *SRE* features—

- All new or completely updated materials.

- 60 original graphics.

- New chapter on climate and weather conditions.

- More than 880 tables.

- Broad coverage of environmental subjects with a focus on data available for the United States.

- Selected presentations on environmental data worldwide.

- Consolidated chapters that provide expanded coverage of subject areas.

- Detailed keyword index.

- Comprehensive source listings.

ORGANIZATION

Organization by Chapter

Statistical Record of the Environment is divided into 11 chapters that present environmental statistics on major topics. The chapters are:

Chapter 1 Summary Indicators
Chapter 2 Air and Water
Chapter 3 Climate and Weather Conditions
Chapter 4 Land and Land Use
Chapter 5 Wildlife and Habitat
Chapter 6 Energy
Chapter 7 Toxic and Hazardous Substances
Chapter 8 Wastes and Resource Recovery
Chapter 9 Costs and Expenditures
Chapter 10   Markets and Companies
Chapter 11 Politics, Opinion, Law

An attempt was made in this edition to bring together into a single chapter all the materials presented on a single subject. Many related topics—such as waste and recycling—have been combined into one chapter with expanded coverage of major issues and concerns. Areas for which new or updated data from previous editions could not be located have been omitted from this edition. Tables were not reprinted for the sake of covering a specific topic; for example, noise pollution. Other topics such as radioactive material did not offer enough new data to warrant an exclusive chapter. Tables on these topics have been incorporated into chapters on related issues.

For the most part, all the tables that deal with air quality and air pollution are in Chapter 2. Similarly, substantially all statistics that deal with costs, expenditures, and budgets are placed in Chapter 9. Needless to say, some exceptions exist. For example, all data on toxic and hazardous materials are presented in Chapter 7. Some tables show releases of these substances to the air, to bodies of water, and to the land. Thus at least some tables on air pollution are excluded from Chapter 2.

In order to help the user find all pertinent materials, chapter notes have again been included. These notes provide an indication of where, in addition to the given chapter, materials on the subject may be found.

Organization Within Chapters

Each table is assigned to a broad topic within subject-based chapters. Topic headers are placed above groups of tables between distinctive rules. On succeeding pages, the name of the topic appears in italic type beneath the table number and above the table title so that the user is always able to determine the topic under which the table appears. Topics are arranged alphabetically within each chapter.

Tables are numbered and may be located from the Table of Contents, the Keyword Index, or the Sources appendix by table number. Page numbers are also provided in the Table of Contents and in the Keyword Index.

Tables

The table title follows the topic designation. Whenever possible, a brief headnote is presented to explain the contents of the table. Please be aware that these notes, unless within quotes, were prepared by the editors and are not taken from the source unless that is expressly stated. To the extent possible, the headnotes provide information needed to understand unusual terminology.

A general discussion following this Introduction, titled Guide to the Subject Matter, presents a brief outline of the major environmental subject areas. The Guide to the Subject Matter presents contextual information so that the user unfamiliar with some topic may obtain a briefing on the issues.

Source notes have been added to each table, indicating material in which the table was found or from which data were gleaned. If the author of the source material took data from another reference or resource, that primary source is identified as well.

Footnotes or other explanatory notes are placed after the source information. Wherever possible, we have attempted to define abbreviations used in the source note of the table

itself. These may be explicitly stated in footnotes or shown in the Abbreviations and Acronyms list that follows the Source appendix.

A good number of tables display graphical presentations such as bar charts or pie charts. If the table has more than one column of data, the number of the column from which the data were drawn for charting is identified on the graphic. Tabular data follow whatever graphic is used.

SCOPE

SRE covers a wide range of environmental conditions, facts, and issues from a statistical vantage point. The major categories (air and water pollution, energy, solid waste generation and management, hazardous wastes and toxic substances) are covered from various perspectives. *SRE* also assembles information on special problems and wastes (oil spills, global warming, soil erosion), provides profiles of the pollution control industry and legislation, and presents background information of the sort required to place environmental information into a broader context.

Since *SRE* is drawn from today's report and periodicals literature, it tends to reflect current concerns, thrusts, and emphasis. Although care was taken to present as balanced a view as possible, the depth of coverage is admittedly uneven; it mirrors the current preoccupations of agencies and the media and should not be interpreted as judgment by the editors of the importance of subjects apparently slighted.

The majority of tables show data for the year 1990 or later. Some major series, found in previous editions, appear again in the third edition but in updated formats; for example, detailed coverage of the Toxic Release Inventory.

SOURCES

Data for *SRE* were drawn from national and state government publications and data bases and from the periodical literature. Numerous sources were consulted and at least 170 were used in this edition. All materials used in the compilation of tables are listed in the appendix titled Sources. Table references are provided in this list so that the user can access the tables by way of their sources if desired.

A statistical book, of course, omits an important element of information—the knowledgeable interpretation of the data, the extraction of significance. Almost invariably, tables were drawn from reports and articles that carried valuable commentary. If *SRE* serves as an introduction to the rich report literature on the environment and to the vigorous journalism that reports on the environment, one of its aims will have been realized.

APPENDED MATERIALS

Sources

Material used to compile tables are shown in this appendix, arranged alphabetically by last name of author, agency, publication, or article title. Full bibliographic citations are shown. Table references are provided, indicating all tables that cite the source.

Abbreviations and Acronyms

Many abbreviations and acronyms are used in the environmental field. In addition, many chemical names are used routinely in abbreviated forms. While efforts have been made to provide the user with explanations of abbreviations within each table, a general listing of all abbreviations is also provided. Abbreviations appear in the list in alphabetical order followed by an explanation.

Keyword Index

SRE features a Keyword Index by means of which the user may locate all subjects, companies, institutions, agencies, and geographical entities mentioned in *SRE*. Items are followed by table and page numbers. Cross-references are provided to facilitate the location of related or alternate terms. Page references do not necessarily identify the page on which the table begins. When a table spans two or more pages, index references will point to the page on which the item appears within the table—whether the second or a subsequent page.

ACKNOWLEDGMENTS

The editors are grateful for numerous comments and suggestions from users of earlier editions. We would like to thank government agencies, associations, publishers, and organizations that provided special materials for this edition. We thank all those who continue to advise and support *SRE,* in particular: Mr. William Franklin of Franklin Associates, LTD., unquestionably *the* authority on solid waste generation, composition, and recovery; and Dr. Thomas Bath, of the Solar Energy Research Institute, an authority on the future of renewable energy resources.

COMMENTS AND SUGGESTIONS

Comments on *SRE* or suggestions for improvement of its usefulness, format, and coverage are always welcome. Although every effort is made to maintain accuracy, errors may occur occasionally; the editors will be grateful if these are called to our attention. Please contact:

Statistical Record of the Environment
Gale Research Inc.
825 Penobscot Building
Detroit, MI 48226-4094
Phone: (313) 961-2241 or (800) 347-GALE
Fax: (313) 961-6815

Guide to the Subject Matter

This section presents a brief introduction to the subject of *SRE*. The subject matter of this work is as all-encompassing as the environment itself. The intent, therefore, is not to provide a comprehensive primer on such a vast subject; rather, we offer a minimal context for those users who can benefit from a thumbnail sketch. Of necessity, this summary leaves out much more than it shows; we hope that it will motivate the reader to delve further into the subject.

THE MEDIA

The term "medium" is used in the environmental field to mean air, water and land—the "media" to which pollutants are emitted or on which they are placed for disposal. Air, water, and land are also called "sinks"; the word signifies a medium capable of absorbing wastes. None of the media is truly a permanent sink for pollutants. Airborne particles settle out; airborne chemicals interact with one another and with components of the air and come down again (for example, as acid rain). Wastes placed on or under the land may come in contact with seeping precipitation and release pollutants to aquifers. Contaminants in water may evaporate, may be taken up by organisms and enter the human food chain, or can cause changes in water bodies with consequences for the other media. The interaction of media, their give-and-take of life-sustaining and endangering substances, the impossibility of isolating these great systems one from the other—the irreducible connectivity of everything to everything else—is at the very heart of environmental concern. There is no ultimate burial place for pollutants and wastes.

Each of the major media will be covered briefly in the following paragraphs. Interactions between the media—and between pollution, technology, economics, and institutional/political factors—will be highlighted.

AIR POLLUTION

Among the chief sources of air pollution is transportation; the use of automobiles and trucks causes the emission of carbon monoxide, nitrogen oxides, hydrocarbons (in the form of gasoline and diesel fumes), and lead. Hydrocarbons and nitrogen oxides, in combination, produce smog and are responsible for respiratory ailments; and carbon monoxide is toxic. Another major source of pollution is power generation; it results in flyash, dust, and the emission of sulfur oxides—implicated in the formation of acid rain. A third major source is represented by the process industries (steel, petroleum, cement, chemicals, pulp and paper); they are responsible for large quantities of particulate emissions (ashes, dust) and chemicals of various kinds. While these are the major source categories, virtually all other production activities emit some air pollutants from the combustion of fuels and the handling of raw materials, solvents, and other chemicals.

Control strategies are many and various and may be classified as technical, preventive, and social/institutional in mechanism.

Technical solutions include removal of *particulates* by—

- Filtering them out of effluent air streams or combustion gases in baghouses;

- Removing them by electrostatic precipitators: This process causes particles to be charged electrically and then collected on electrodes, a technology particularly well suited for capturing very fine particulates; and

- Spinning or knocking them from air or combustion streams mechanically in cyclones and similar devices.

The management of *chemicals* takes many forms depending on the character of the pollutant. Methods include combustion of waste hydrocarbons, the distillation of pollutants in specialized towers, their transformation by catalytic conversion (as in automobiles), their capture in adsorption columns (a type of filtering), and their removal by similar processing methods usually built into refining and chemicals production plants. The removal of sulfur oxides from coal-burning power plant off-gases presents a special and difficult problem. Sulfur removal requires scrubbers in which the hot gases are contacted with lime in a water medium. Vast amounts of sludge occur.

All of these technical procedures, in fact, tend merely to *transform* air pollutants into solid wastes, sludges, or waterborne wastes that require further handling. If a polluting substance is extracted as a product—elemental sulfur, for example, from utility flue gases—the product must be sold on the open market. Air pollution control is rarely the last step in the process.

In recent decades, a great many so-called "upstream" methods have been discovered, tried, and even mandated by legislation. The objective of these strategies is—

- To exchange potentially polluting with more suitable raw materials (low-sulfur coal in place of high-sulfur coal, unleaded gasoline in place of leaded);

- To introduce more efficient processing technology (more complete combustion of waste gases in after burners, for instance); and

- To promote recycling/reuse of what waste products remain.

Social/institutional strategies also are used or are in planning stages. These include:

- Reducing the magnitude of a polluting activity (auto use by car pooling or by parking restrictions);

- Land use controls for locating factories;

- Regulating the content of fuels or type of fuel used;

- Mandating inspection of vehicles; and

- Requiring more fuel-efficient vehicles.

The dominant issues in air pollution control have not changed significantly in the last twenty years—to pick a benchmark—but the public perception of the problem and the methods of remediation have. Auto use and electric power have the highest visibility. Methods for controlling automotive pollution have converged on fuel changes, fuel efficiency requirements, and technical controls. In electric generation, growing awareness of acid rain—in part a consequence of sulfur emissions—has galvanized political energy; the chief solution remains, as twenty years before, the installation of scrubbers that remove sulfur in a slurry of lime; scrubbers are costly and produce very large quantities of paste-like solid wastes; thus scrubbers are not an ideal or ultimate solution. Other alternatives have serious political or economic drawbacks: Nuclear power is politically opposed in this post-Chernobyl age; natural gas is a costly if clean substitute for coal; and coal desulfurization appears to require massive federal investments in research and demonstration in an age of towering deficits.

Although an air pollution issue, *global warming*—thought to be due to an increase in carbon dioxide production by human activity—is discussed under a separate heading.

WATER POLLUTION

The water medium may be viewed as having distinct parts—the oceans, surface waters on land (rivers, streams, lakes), and deep-lying aquifers that hold groundwater. Pollution enters the "water sink" as a consequence of human habitation, industry, and the pollutants carried by rain from cities and farms (runoff).

Municipal Sewage

The largest single impact on water is dense human population—cities. Organic human waste, if discharged untreated, can overwhelm the ability of bodies of water to absorb the waste. Microorganisms attempting to decompose the waste require oxygen for this "combustion" process; they use the oxygen naturally dissolved in the water. At a high enough level of biological oxygen demand (usually abbreviated BOD), oxygen levels are exhausted; fish and other oxygen-consuming (aerobic) organisms die out; the waters become septic; only anaerobic organisms survive; the water is now putrid and dangerous for man and beast.

Industrial Waste Water

Industry uses large amounts of water for generating energy, cooling, processing, transporting, and cleaning. Boiler feedwater must be very clean and free of minerals before use and must remain pure during use. Cooling waters are generally recycled and are not polluted; in some applications, fungicides are injected into the water to keep cooling towers clean.

The other industrial uses of water—for processing, transport, and cleaning—invariably cause water to become contaminated with organic materials (functionally similar to human waste), with chemicals and hydrocarbons, suspended particles, dissolved minerals, and so on. Typical processing applications include

water used in pulping wood, cooking food, or tanning leather. Water is used to transport many raw materials as slurries, suspensions, or emulsions in mining and manufacturing. In addition, water has long been the universal cleanser virtually in all industrial activities. When the water is no longer useful for the process, transport, or cleaning step, it is said to be "spent" and must be treated for recycling or disposal. In its spent state, water may be highly acidic or alkaline.

The most important sources of organic water pollutants are the pulp and paper, meat packing, food processing, textile, pharmaceuticals, leather tanning, and related industries that harvest and transform organic materials for human consumption. The petroleum refining, organic chemicals, and steel industries (steel by way of coking facilities) introduce hydrocarbons in various forms. The metals industries produce wastes with high acidity and alkalinity, oily waters, rusty waters. Inorganic chemicals, mining, and related operations emit water wastes heavy with suspended solids and dissolved minerals.

Urban and Agricultural Runoff

Pollutants also enter the water medium when rainfall runs off into lakes, rivers, and oceans carrying with it organics, solids, and chemicals occurring on land. Urban runoff is typically collected in storm sewers; in many cities, these sewers are permitted to bypass waste water treatment plants in whole or in part during storms. Storm sewer discharges introduce organics, debris, salt, and toxics. Agricultural runoff has similar characteristics but may include larger quantities of fertilizers and pesticides. Fertilizers in water can overstimulate the growth of aquatic plants and thus contribute to the eutrophication of bodies of water: They gradually turn into swamps. Diversion of urban runoff into long-term holding lagoons and careful grading of agricultural lands (fields, feedlots) are methods of minimizing the impact of runoff.

Treatment Technology

Waste water treatment is usually divided into three stages of advancing technical complexity—aptly named primary, secondary, and tertiary treatment.

- *Primary treatment* involves rough filtration to remove large solids; this may be followed by lagooning of the waste waters for whatever period is required for the natural oxidation of organics and for the settling out of fine solids.

- *Secondary treatment* calls for the introduction of oxygen into the waste at whatever rate is required to satisfy the waste stream's biological oxygen demand, meaning the extra oxygen required to help microorganisms to consume the waste rapidly. Since air is typically used as the source of oxygen, this process is also called aeration. Secondary treatment methods differ in the manner in which oxygen is introduced, the degree to which the waste is agitated mechanically during entrainment, and the capital/operating costs of the facility. Secondary treatment is applied to organic wastes.

- *Tertiary treatment* is a collective name for a host of different methods, each specific to a particular pollutant or a class of pollutants. Processes may be relatively simple—such as the adjustment of the waste stream's pH[1] (which, in addition to rendering the stream harmless, may also cause pollutants to be precipitated out), or processes may be complex. An example is carbon black treatment to remove difficult-to-process organic chemicals in specialized adsorption towers.

A difficult waste stream may require primary and secondary treatment and one or more tertiary steps. Costs of treatment tend to go up with the level of technology. Control strategies, therefore, tend to be a compromise between the competing goals of pure water and its affordability.

Waste water treatment produces residues in the form of sludge or solids that must be handled again for disposal. Depending on the nature of the waste, sludges may have to be handled as toxic wastes or may be disposed of by landspreading, incineration, composting, and landfilling. The costs of sludge management may be as much as or more than the costs of the treatment processes that produced them.

Drinking Water

Our drinking water comes from wells or is pumped from surface waters and treated before distribution. The purification of drinking water is called *water* treatment; *waste* water treatment applies to sewage or industrial waste water streams. Water treatment always involves filtration (to remove silt) and chlorination (to kill bacteria); it may involve many other steps, including removal of iron and desalination of brackish waters; the water may also be treated to control odors.

Drinking water is threatened by pollution of rivers and lakes and the contamination of aquifers. Aquifers are permeable stone formations capable of retaining water; next to oceans and polar ice caps, they hold most of the earth's water. But the water in aquifers is not stationary. It is replenished by precipitation and depleted by use; and it moves, albeit slowly, under the impetus of gravity and pressure; this movement is measured in inches per year. The slow movement of water in aquifers can produce surprises. The burial of toxic wastes may produce well water contamination five, ten,

---

1　pH is a symbol used to denote acidity and alkalinity on a scale of 0 to 14. Pure water has a pH of 7. Lower values indicate acidity, higher values alkalinity.

thirty years later: the time required by the very slow-moving underground river to carry its poisons to a well. The burial of waste may have been forgotten, records of it lost, by the time its consequences surface.

Ocean Pollution

Oceans are threatened by massive accidental oil spills, illegal dumping of chemical and oily wastes at sea, ocean dumping of garbage, and the introduction of toxic substances and organics by polluted rivers and rain. Like the vegetative cover of the continents, so the ocean's phytoplankton are a major source of oxygen in the water and in the atmosphere. Any diminution of the organic life in the ocean by pollution invariably affects the ecosystems on land as well. Toxic metals dumped into the oceans will be taken up by small marine organisms and may eventually be ingested by humans as harvested fish; the metals are cumulated and retained in tissue. Contaminated fish, of course, lead to fishing restrictions, harming those engaged in the fishing and processing industries.

The Regulatory Environment

A major part of waste water management is the responsibility of public bodies—cities, counties, independent sewerage districts, and other agencies. These institutions, collectively, are a political force of significant dimensions. In the evolution of water pollution control, therefore, the public sector has been prominent; federal funding for water treatment systems has long been a reality, and the federal water programs represent the largest single federal expenditure on environmental cleanup and maintenance. Since the federal government both funds waste water treatment by cities and also regulates, it tends to balance regulatory fervor by budgetary realism. Industrial water pollution is regulated much as air pollution is regulated; however, the presence of a large public sector with water pollution facilities leads, in this field, to many joint ventures be-

tween industry and local government to process wastes in common facilities designed for that purpose.

ENERGY

In this edition, the subject of *energy* is featured in a chapter of its own in an acknowledgment of the fact that the use of energy by modern man is one of the chief causes of environmental degradation.

Energy production and use invariably causes disruption to the environment and is often associated with the production of pollutants as well. The chief sources of energy are:

- **Coal**. Coal is mined from underground shafts, producing disturbances of aquifers or stripped from the surface of the land, causing at least temporary changes to ecosystems. The combustion of coal produces particulates, carbon monoxide, and sulfur dioxide; SO_2 is implicated in acid rain, harmful to forests.

- **Hydrocarbons**. Hydrocarbons, usually abbreviated as HC, are petroleum and its products and natural gas. The combustion of hydrocarbons in vehicles (as gasoline, diesel fuel, or aviation fuel), in power plants, and in furnaces of all kinds produces pollutants in the form of uncombusted volatile chemicals, toxic carbon monoxide, and nitrogen oxides (autos).

- **Hydroelectric power**. This category is familiar as electricity from dammed rivers; water is released from the dams to drive turbines. This "clean" form of energy nevertheless disrupts the ecology of river systems and is therefore no more environmentally "innocent" than any other form of energy.

- **Nuclear fission**. Nuclear power does not produce the familiar pollutants associated with coal and hydrocarbon burning. But in its place, radioactive spent nuclear fuels, solid wastes, gases, and waters must be managed—sometimes in perpetuity. Nuclear mishaps can have global, profound consequences as shown by the Chernobyl disaster in Russia.

Other sources of energy represent a minute fraction of total demand. Some of these—the burning of wood, waste, or crops (biomass, corn-based alcohols)—produce more or less pollutants depending on the "fuel" and the conversion technology.

Solar, wind, ocean, and geothermal energy are potentially low-disruption forms of power in the future. Solar energy comes in two forms. **Thermal solar energy** is obtained by heating water (or some other intermediary substance) with sunlight (which may be concentrated by reflectors). **Photovoltaic energy** makes use of semiconductor materials that convert sunlight directly into the electricity. Solar energy has its own drawbacks (beyond economic barriers): It would demand very large areas to produce energy on the scale needed by technical civilization; and, if implemented on a large scale, solar energy production would compete with agriculture for land surface.

Wind power is a special case of solar energy because it depends in part on atmospheric movements produced by the heating and cooling of the atmosphere as the earth rotates.

The **energy of the oceans** (tides, currents such as the Gulf Stream) may be exploitable in the future. Tides can be contained when at the full and released to drive turbines when at the ebb. Tide-based energy is analogous to hydroelectric power and has similar aspects: Ecosystems are invariably disrupted.

The energy of ocean currents—produced by the heat of the sun and the rotation of the earth—may be exploitable by placing large arrays of equipment into currents in order to capture the energy of the currents' movements and to store it in batteries. Again, any large-scale use of this technology would interfere in unpredictable ways with the ecosystems of the oceans and potentially also with global climate.

Geothermal energy—used now where volcanic heat is accessible near the surface—could be used widely in the future by tapping the heat at the center of the earth's core by specially drilled shafts. Aside from the formidable economic and technical barriers that now impede geothermal energy, this form of power production would also have environmental costs.

The broad conclusion is that all energy use at high levels per capita has adverse effects on the environment. Consequently, a long-term strategy made up of energy conservation through more intelligent use, less use, and a movement toward *relatively* less disruptive forms of energy will eventually be required to bring technical civilization into balance with a sustaining environment.

SOLID WASTE

Solid and semi-solid wastes (sludges) are produced by all human activities—including, of course, air and water pollution control. The largest categories of solid wastes are mining wastes, municipal solid waste (which is further subdivided), and industrial wastes resulting from processing and distribution.

As a general rule, the larger the solid waste category (usually measured in tons), the more it is likely to be benign. Mining waste, in the form of overburden removed in strip mining or excavated rock, is essentially harmless—although careless treatment can cause the leaching out of metals and minerals into groundwater and, to be sure, surface mining represents a disturbance of established ecosystems. Most municipal waste is miscellaneous organics and paper. Many large industrial waste streams (utility ashes, metallurgical slags) are largely inert. At the same time, relatively small waste streams may be disproportionately dangerous; examples are certain hospital wastes and toxic sludges from industrial processes.

Terminology

Wastes are said to be generated, discarded, reused or salvaged, converted, recycled, reduced at the source, and avoided—giving rise to phrases like "recyclables," "source reduction," and "waste avoidance." The mixture of discarded wastes is referred to as the waste stream, sometimes written as wastestream. Some terms, current in the past, are no longer widely used. "Refuse," "trash," and "garbage" are becoming obsolete terms.

The *generation* of waste is the act of producing a waste. The total waste generated may not be equivalent to the total waste *discarded*. Discarded waste is the generated waste less that portion of it which has been reused, converted, or recycled.

Wastes are *reused* when they are put back into use in much the same applications from which they were generated; for example, bricks salvaged from construction rubble and placed into service in a wall. *Conversion* implies a transformation—yard waste into compost, waste into energy. *Recycling* means the return of a material to industry for reprocessing—aluminum cans back into aluminum ingot, old newspapers back into newsprint by way of a deinking plant. In many cases, material recycled reaches a lesser use. Bleached, white paper may be recycled as dark, grey board used in packaging or as backing for writing pads. It should be noted that reuse, conversion, and recycling invariably produce additional wastes; these may be solid, airborne, or in water. Recycling is often labeled more generically as *resource recovery* to include any and all methods of recovering values from the waste.

Source reduction means the elimination of waste at the source; *waste avoidance* has the same meaning and is used by some because source reduction has an inelegant sound. Ex-

amples are purchasing products known to have less packaging, using returnable rather than disposable containers or washable rather than disposable diapers. Source reduction goes beyond personal acts by private individuals and may be mandated by government.

Municipal Solid Waste

Municipal Solid Waste, also called urban solid waste, is usually divided into residential, commercial and office, medical, and construction components, generated, respectively, by households, retail businesses and office buildings, hospitals/clinics, and demolition activities (construction rubble).

Within the residential waste category, distinctions have always been made between ordinary and "bulky" wastes (old furniture, dead refrigerators, and like objects). In recent years, residential waste has been further subdivided in many communities into household waste, recyclable materials, and yard waste—each of the three being collected and managed by separate systems.

Commercial waste is similar to household waste; it tends to have less organic content (food and yard waste) and more paper; much of the paper is in the form of corrugated board.

Industrial Solid Wastes

A portion of industrial solid waste is identical to commercial urban waste (packaging, miscellaneous paper, and such items). In some industries (food processing), solids are very similar to those that result from municipal waste water treatment. All other solid wastes tend to be specific to the industrial activity. Some of these wastes are homogeneous (sawdust, wood bark, rust) and occur in large quantities in one place. If they are recyclable physically, they tend to be recycled if the economics so warrant: Wood wastes are burned to provide process heat, metal-rich sludges are reintroduced into furnaces.

Major problems are presented by large quantities of essentially useless inerts—such as ash—and by small quantities of toxic or hazardous residues of processing, pollution control, or manufacturing. Flyash from electrical utilities has been shown to be an excellent paving additive; however, there is a disproportion between the quantities of flyash produced each year and the demand for paving materials. Therefore flyash is deposited on land. At the other end of the spectrum, industry generates highly contaminated and toxic wastes; these may be residuals of chemicals processing or spent solvents and lubricants in mechanical production facilities. The quantities generated at any one location may be relatively small—prohibiting economic resource recovery. And disposal requires special management because of the waste's toxicity or hazard. This subject is discussed more fully below.

Methods of Management

Solid wastes must be (1) collected, (2) optionally processed, and (3) disposed. Resource recovery may be accomplished as part of collection or processing.

Waste Collection. Waste collection is a labor-intensive and unpleasant activity. For that reason, technological effort has been devoted to improve the productivity of waste collection teams while, at the same time, reducing occupational exposure to waste. Residential collection systems have evolved over the past two decades. Labor requirements have been radically reduced, allowing, for instance, for a single operator to drive a truck and to discharge waste from appropriately configured containers into the truck without leaving the cab. Such techniques are not universally used, however. Reducing labor forces is politically difficult in some communities; new systems call for capital expenditures; and political pressure to increase recycling has caused communities to go in the other direction in recent years. Separate collection of household waste, recyclables, and yard wastes has called for more labor

rather than less. Periodic "bulky waste" collection, of course, has long been a routine aspect of municipal waste collection systems.

Commercial establishments normally place waste in large containers; these are mechanically emptied into collection trucks.

In communities where disposal sites are far away, wastes may be delivered to transfer stations and reloaded into larger trucks for long hauls. Transfer stations sometimes serve as processing sites for the removal of recyclable components.

Land Disposal. The most common method of solid waste disposal is to place it on land in a more or less disciplined manner. Open dumping is the least satisfactory of these approaches; wastes are simply discharged into a gully and left to lie—a breeding ground for rats, a haven for birds, and a source of polluted runoff. These dumps can catch on fire and produce air pollution.

Sanitary landfilling is the systematic placement of waste on land; waste deposited each day is covered by earth; the site is planned, engineered, and graded (to guide runoff away from the waste); after completion, it is converted to some public use (park, ballfield). Advanced sanitary landfills will, in addition, be equipped with liners—which may be of plastic or clay—designed to prevent rainwater from percolating through the waste and then into the groundwater. A lined fill requires, of course, that water accumulated at the bottom be pumped out and treated before release to bodies of water. Decomposing waste produces methane gas; a well-designed sanitary landfill will be equipped with appropriate vents to release gases to the atmosphere. Uncontrolled gases from landfills can seep into the basements of adjacent buildings and present a fire hazard.

The principal environmental impact of landfills is "leachate"—water contaminated by waste that enters aquifers (see above) or flows on the surface. Over time, leachate will seep out of all landfills, lined or not. Liners deteriorate; clay liners shift.... Thus even final resting places for waste are not final.

Solid Waste Processing and Recycling. Solid wastes are also composted, incinerated, and co-fired with coal to generate electricity (see below). Modern versions of these technologies tend to have a recycling facility at the front end for the diversion of "recyclables"— paper, metals, and glass. Waste is dumped on a moving belt from which people pick items for recycling (large pieces of cardboard, certain metals, glass). The waste is then shredded; more metals are removed by magnets. The residue is composted or burned. Technology for separating virtually every kind of material has been developed, including, for instance, machinery capable of sorting glass particles by color. Such hi-tech solutions, however, are rarely justified by the system's overall economics. The desirable components—corrugated board, aluminum, steel—are removed; these have well-established markets. Composting, incineration, and co-firing are not widely practiced because substantial capital investments are required, high disposal fees ("dump fees") are necessary, and the institutional arrangements for selling the waste as compost or as fuel are often very difficult to realize; public opposition to such ventures is always certain; the economics are rarely attractive.

Separate collection of recyclable waste is gaining recognition as an alternative to capital-intensive solutions. In these programs, the public is asked to separate components of the waste so that they can be assembled for shipment to a recycler with minimal mechanical processing. Direct recycling depends for its economic success on the volatile market for secondary products, where demand and prices fluctuate sharply in response to economic conditions. Yard waste composting is less problematical. If these materials are separately collected, they are largely uncontaminated by the products of industrial civilization and are easy to compost; the resulting product can be used in urban landscaping by the city itself.

Waste-to-Energy. Municipal and commercial waste has a high energy content. When appropriately handled, refuse-derived fuel (RDF) can be burned directly or in combination with another fuel such as coal. One method of turning waste into energy is in electric utilities. Shredded waste, with metals, glass, and other heavy objects removed, is injected into furnaces with powdered coal. The technology has been shown to work; institutional arrangements are more difficult to bring about. Large amounts of waste must be collected at predictable dump fees before electric utilities are willing to make furnace modifications and to build the required fuel delivery systems. "Control of the waste stream" tends to become a political issue with municipal and commercial waste management agencies pulling in different directions, interest groups opposing any form of burning, and utilities, generally shy of adverse publicity, growing lukewarm as controversy escalates.

Other waste-to-energy projects involve generating steam in specially designed incinerators and selling the steam to utilities, an industrial complex, or for internal use (for example, in waste water treatment). Solid waste may also be turned into a type of fuel oil by pyrolysis (combustion in an oxygen-poor atmosphere); the oil is then burned as fuel. Yet another method of combustion and energy recovery is in special fluid bed furnaces; the waste is introduced into a furnace filled with swirling hot sand held suspended by the incoming combustion air.

Medical Waste Management. Infectious medical wastes are normally incinerated in the hospital's own special incinerators; toxics are handled as hazardous wastes (see below); and normal housekeeping wastes are handled as commercial wastes.

Industrial Waste Management. With the exception of hazardous and toxic wastes, discussed below, industrial wastes are managed in the same way as urban wastes. Because waste streams are often homogeneous and large, much more recycling is often feasible.

Special Wastes

A number of wastes or obsolete products have special characteristics that require unusual management arrangements. A brief capsule of some of these wastes, and how they are handled, follows:

Municipal Sludges. Municipal waste water sludges are a special category of municipal solid wastes; they are usually managed within the institutional framework of municipal waste water treatment. Since waste water sludges are organic, they can be used as fertilizers. Intensive use of sludges to "manure" farmland is restricted by economics on the one hand (synthetic fertilizers are relatively cheap) and by health concerns. Sludges contain trace metals that cumulate in tissue, most notably cadmium; people who eat vegetables grown on sludge-fertilized land are somewhat at risk; the risk is low—a lifetime of eating such vegetables exclusively, combined with heavy smoking, describe a person at risk; but while there is risk, health authorities are disinclined to promote the solution. There is also cultural bias in the United States against using human waste on food crops.

For these reasons, sludges are typically placed on land or burned. The most effective land disposal method appears to be landfarming—a process whereby the sludge is plowed into the earth and the land is given time to process the waste. The method has also been used on oily sludges; sludges, however, are also landfilled with municipal waste. The most sophisticated sludge combustion methods involve the digestion of sludges, the combustion of the methane evolved, and the use of the heat to aid in the burning of digestor residues; and the residual heat is then used in the waste water treatment plant as steam.

Household waste is typically managed by the local government using either its own forces, one or more contractors, or a combination of both. Commercial waste is handled by private-sector waste management firms; many gener-

ators and waste management firms separate valuable paper components, especially corrugated board, for recycling before land disposal of the rest. Construction rubble is usually managed by the construction industry, using sites of its own, or by commercial waste haulers.

Tires. Old tires are difficult to bury. Unless cut into pieces, they have a tendency to rise to the top of a landfill after some period of months or years. For this reason, they are prohibited at some landfills or (if accepted) are placed into piles—where they represent a fire hazard. They burn very hot and may damage the refractory lining of incinerators. Management methods include tire shredding, combustion in special furnaces, pyrolysis, and remelting of the rubber portion of tires for use as an asphalt admixture. The technologies required for such hi-tech solutions are costly in relation to the value of the rubber. The aesthetic pollution of large accumulations of tires has led some to propose and to implement novel schemes, including disposal of tires under water to create fish habitats.

Waste Oil. Oil drained from the crankshaft by members of the public is normally taken to filling stations. From there, the oil is handled as hazardous waste or sent to waste oil rerefineries. The heavy residues of these operations are handled like other hazardous wastes.

White Goods. Obsolete refrigerators, freezers, and stoves hold some sheet metal and much else (insulation, wiring, electric motors, and the like). The metal is not much in demand by secondary metal dealers. Old white goods have mineral glazes and require extensive demolition and cleanup before they are suitable for remelting.

HAZARDOUS AND TOXIC WASTES

Hazardous wastes are highly acidic, alkaline, or explosive; contact with the waste causes burns or damages equipment and structures. Toxic wastes contain chemicals toxic to man, animals, and vegetation. Wastes labeled "toxic" may also be hazardous, and hazardous wastes may also be toxic. In what follows, the term "hazardous waste" will be used to mean either or both. Radioactive wastes are discussed separately.

Although hazardous wastes occur in the household (paints, cleansers, pesticides, pharmaceuticals), the bulk of such wastes is generated by the chemicals and petroleum industries. Careless disposal of these wastes in past decades has produced—and continues to produce—massive groundwater contamination. Since the early 1970s, the collection, transport, storage, and disposal of hazardous wastes has come under strict federal regulation:

CERCLA and SARA. Hazardous wastes are managed by the federal government under three sets of legislation. The Comprehensive Environmental Response, Compensation and Liability Act of 1980 (CERCLA) and the Superfund Amendments and Reauthorization Act of 1986 (SARA) together govern old, abandoned hazardous waste sites and dumps. These are usually referred to as Superfund sites; there are approximately 37,920 such sites.

RCRA. Currently operating hazardous waste treatment and disposal facilities are managed under the Resource Conservation and Recovery Act of 1976 (RCRA). There are 4,300 such sites.

EPCRA. The reporting of toxic materials releases and transfers is governed by the Emergency Planning and Community Right-to-Know Act (EPCRA). Under this legislation, the Environmental Protection Agency obtains annually data from emitters of toxics known as the Toxics Release Inventory.

Characteristics of Hazardous Waste Management

The most important aspect of hazardous waste management is the ultimate disposal of waste on land—which must be handled in such a manner that wastes will be isolated from the water and air media. Before strict regulation came into force, these wastes were typically dumped on land or buried in drums; the gradual deterioration of the containers resulted in the release of toxics into the soil and, by way of the soil, into ground and surface waters. Wastes held in lagoons also found their way into groundwater and, eventually, into wells—producing poisonings, cancer, nervous disorders, learning disabilities, and other health problems in the populations thus exposed.

Ultimate containment of such wastes presents technically and socially formidable challenges similar to the problem presented by radioactive wastes. Containers used must last for long periods of time and must themselves be protected from damage by water, erosion, and the shifting of the earth. The burial site must be appropriately constructed and constantly monitored. As containers age, they must be replaced. And institutional structures must be maintained to manage the waste in perpetuity. Ideal disposal sites—deep salt caverns, for example—are few; their capacity is limited. The costs of long term care are high.

For these reasons, it is desirable to reduce the tonnage of waste requiring ultimate disposal to a minimum. This is accomplished by treatment processes as varied as the hazardous wastes themselves. Organic wastes can be rendered harmless by burning them in specially designed incinerators. Treatment processes include a variety of chemical processes in which harmful chemicals are recovered, combined into harmless substances by chemical reaction, neutralized, or distilled from streams.

Despite all of the above, many hazardous wastes are routinely disposed of by conventional means—discharge to sewers, surface waters, land disposal, injection into the ground. This is permissible when the wastes have been treated, for instance, or they are diluted to such an extent that the concentration of toxic components in the waste stream is very low.

Clean Up of Old Sites

Poor waste management in the past has left an unsavory legacy of abandoned hazardous waste sites—many of them forgotten, covered, and the land reused for housing and other activities. These sites are gradually being identified and eliminated.

Many offending hazardous waste disposal sites are on federal facilities under the control of the Department of Defense or the Department of Energy. Federal actions to clean up its own house have always been sluggish at best; bureaucratic inertia, the sheer size and complexity of defense activities, and budgetary constraints are some of the reasons why. Groundwater contamination has spread from federal sites as from others; in recent years, under Congressional prodding, the Department of Defense has begun to plan a massive, 30-year program to bring itself in compliance with national standards.

Clean up of old sites is technically complex and invariably costs more than appropriate waste handling would have cost. Uncontrolled dumping of waste oil, to take a case, contaminates large quantities of soil, thus increasing the total tonnage of waste that must later be handled. Contaminated aquifers must be pumped, the dirty water treated, until the pool or pocket of pollution has been removed. Sinking wells for aquifer clean up is very costly. If wastes were dumped in barrels, new barrels must be acquired and the waste repackaged before they can be shipped to controlled disposal sites.

RADIOACTIVE WASTE

Radioactive/nuclear wastes occur in the mining of uranium, in nuclear power plants, in many industrial activities, in medical facilities, in academic laboratories, and in defense establishments. Wastes are classified as high- and low-level nuclear wastes as measured by the emission of alpha, beta, and gamma particles released by radioactive substances. The radioactive waste stream is made up of low-level

uranium mining and processing residues, low-level wastes from commercial and defense establishments, high-level wastes from the same sources, spent fuel, and other defense wastes. In form this waste ranges from mineral piles of low radioactivity all the way to highly toxic and "hot" chemical solids and liquids.

Nuclear wastes must be handled like hazardous wastes—with the added proviso that radiation must be contained. Radioactive materials decay as they emit particles. The rate of decay is determined by the elemental composition of the waste and may be minutes, hours, years or many thousands of years; decay rate is usually expressed as a substance's half-life, the amount of time required for half of the substance to decay. Since the half-life of some waste components is longer than the age of the earth, ultimate solutions to the radioactive waste problem are not forseeable unless ways are found to export such wastes into some remote corner of the solar system.

The principal method of managing nuclear wastes is concentration followed by permanent storage deep underground or in closely guarded and monitored sites. High-level wastes produce heat and require that their containers be cooled; low-level wastes require relatively less intensive management; most are managed on-site by those who generate the waste.

Measurement. The measurement of radioactivity is expressed in Curies (Ci); a Curie represents 37 billion atomic disintegrations per second. The nuclei of atoms are disintegrating and producing ionising radiation (alpha and beta particles, fission neutrons and protons, and the like). Ionising radiation can interfere with living cells.

The level of radioactivity, measured in Curies, is not in itself indicative of the degree of danger to which humans are exposed. Danger is present if the energy of the ionising radiation is high enough and exposure time is long enough. An absorbed "dose" of radiation is defined in rads. One rad is equal to 100,000 ergs of energy per kilogram of absorbing mass; by way of perspective, one calorie is equal to nearly 41.84 million ergs. The electrical energy of the radiation, in turn, is dependent on the mix of particles (alpha, beta, gamma, fission neutrons, protons) that make up a particular radiation source. The lethal dose of radiation is between 500 and 1500 rads. Annual safe exposure in the United States is 5 rads; a limit of 2 rads is urged by specialists. Another and related measure is in rems. A rem is equivalent to 83,300 ergs per kilogram of tissue; a dose of 450 rems will kill half those exposed to the radiation. Maximum exposure permitted in the workplace is 5,000 milirems (5 rems).

NOISE

Noise is measured in decibels (dB), a unit that shows the power required to create a sound; an alternative measure is based on air pressure produced by the sound (not discussed here). The loudness of noise measured in dB, as perceived by a hearer, is also dependent on the pitch of the sound (its frequency); high-pitched sounds appear louder than low pitched sounds—one reason why sirens whine rather than growl. Sound levels, for this reason, are sometimes expressed in dB(A), indicating an established average frequency.

A sound level of dB(A) 10 is audible; conversation is 60 dB(A); a rock concert is 100 dB(A). People perceive noise as irritating above 65 dB(A). Damage occurs at 80-90 dB(A) and prolonged exposure to noise above 90 dB(A) produces hearing loss. Noise perception, however, is highly subjective; one person's noise is another person's radio turned up a little.

The sources of unwelcome noise are machinery, machine operations, and the sounds of surface and air traffic. Areas of particular national emphasis have been aircraft noise, noise in the workplace, and noisy equipment (transportation and construction machinery).

Noise is controlled:

- Mechanically by shielding equipment with material that absorbs sounds;

- Architecturally by shielding living and working areas using acoustical surfaces or by constructing shielding walls along freeways to protect housing areas;

- Administratively through arrangements such as a rerouting of air traffic from corridors where people live; and

- Defensively with protective gear worn at work.

GLOBAL ISSUES

Global Warming

A potentially significant consequence of fossil fuel use may be a gradual warming of the earth, referred to as "global warming." Once clearly established, this conjectured outcome of oil, gas, wood, and coal combustion could lead to dramatic changes in climate, hence in agricultural productivity, and even in the size and the shape of the continents: Melting polar ice caps would cause a rise in the level of the oceans. There is no consensus that global warming is in fact taking place; long periods of warming and cooling appear to be a part of historical climate patterns; however, average temperatures have been rising since the late 19th century.

The mechanism thought to be responsible for global warming is the accumulation of carbon dioxide (CO_2) and other gases in the atmosphere. The amount of carbon in the atmosphere is regulated by the earth's carbon cycle. Plants and phytoplankton consume carbon dioxide in their cycles of growth; they "exhale" oxygen into the air; oxygen-breathing life forms consume oxygen to create body heat and exhale carbon dioxide; and decaying plant matter also releases carbon dioxide into the air. Thus a cycle is established. The burning of fossil fuels—which, ultimately, are vegetable matter long buried underground—add carbon dioxide to the cycle. If the earth's plant life cannot use all of the carbon in the atmosphere, carbon dioxide will build up. Deforestation, road building, expansion of urban space, and climate changes are reducing the amount of land available for plants; and use of fossil fuels increases the amount of carbon emitted. The circumstantial evidence is there.

Carbon dioxide—together with such other gases as methane (the chief component of natural gas), nitrous oxide, chlorofluorocarbons (used as refrigerants and aerosol propellants)—increases the atmosphere's ability to retain radiant heat while permitting sunlight to come in. For this reason, global warming is also known as the Greenhouse Effect.

If the earth is warming, the solution, ultimately, is to re-establish the balance between CO_2 emitted and carbon fixed by plants. This may be possible if other forms of energy are developed—solar power, nuclear power (which has environmental consequences of its own), and fuels derived from crops. The choices, however, will be between different kinds of disruptions of the status quo: Global warming will affect sea levels, forests, agriculture, and wildlife; it may cause major migrations and displacements; kicking the fossil fuel habit, however, is likely to have similar consequences. If the processes of change are slow; that is, if warming increases very slowly and new technologies and other measures have time to be adopted gradually, we may avoid the worst consequences of either route.

Ozone Depletion

In the highest levels of the atmosphere, the stratosphere, a band extending from 9 miles above the earth to 30 miles above, ozone acts as a filter to reduce the amount of harmful ultraviolet (UV) radiation that reaches the earth. UV splits normal oxygen molecules (O_2) into free oxygen atoms. These atoms then combine with other molecules to form ozone (O_3). UV also acts on ozone, breaking it into an oxygen atom and a molecule of O_2. The free oxygen again strives to combine with a molecule. The energy of UV radiation is consumed in this dance of oxygen atoms and molecules, shielding us from radiation that causes skin diseases, cancer, cataracts, retinal damage, corneal tumors, nutritional deficiencies, and infectious diseases.

When chlorine and other reactive gases are present in the stratosphere, they interfere with ozone creation and breakdown; harmful UV radiation increases. A number of chemicals used in modern life cause ozone depletion in the atmosphere. Among these are chlorofluorocarbons (CFCs) used as refrigerants, propellants (for aerosols), and as solvents; others include methyl chloroform (a solvent), carbon tetrachloride (used in CFC production), halons (fire extinguisher compounds), and nitrogen oxides. These products of modern industrial life have caused measurable reductions in the stratospheric ozone layer; an ozone "hole" has been detected over Antarctica. Corresponding increases in UV radiation have also been detected.

Approaches to halt ozone depletion include a search for substitute refrigerants, propellants, and solvents combined with controlling the release of such reactive substances to the atmosphere.

A Word About Gale and the Environment

We at Gale would like to take this opportunity to publicly affirm our commitment to preserving the environment. Our commitment encompasses not only a zeal to publish information helpful to a variety of people pursuing environmental goals, but also a rededication to creating a safe and healthy workplace for our employees.

In our effort to make responsible use of natural resources, we're publishing all books in the Gale Environmental Library on recycled paper. Our Production Department is continually researching ways to use new environmentally safe inks and manufacturing technologies for all Gale books.

In our quest to become better environmental citizens, we've organized a task force representing all operating functions within Gale. With the complete backing of Gale senior management, the task force reviews our current practices and, using the Valdez Principles[1] as a starting point, makes recommendations that will help us to: reduce waste, make wise use of energy and sustainable use of natural resources, reduce health and safety risks to our employees, and finally, should we cause any damage or injury, take full responsibility.

We look forward to becoming the best environmental citizens we can be and hope that you, too, have joined in the cause of caring for our fragile planet.

The Employees of Gale Research, Inc.

---

[1] The Valdez Principles were set forth in 1989 by the Coalition for Environmentally Responsible Economies (CERES). The principles serve as guidelines for companies concerned with improving their environmental behavior. For a copy of the Valdez Principles, write to CERES at 711 Atlantic Avenue, 5th Floor, Boston, MA 02111.

Thank you...

ALA TASK FORCE ON THE ENVIRONMENT (TFOE)

In developing this and other environment-related publications, Gale Research Inc. seeks to work closely with members of the Task Force on the Environment of the American Library Association. Of primary concern to us as publishers is designing publications to best meet the user's needs for useful and timely environmental reference information. We appreciate the availability of the members of TFOE and their willingness to answer questions and provide advice on our environmental publications. At the same time, we recognize that the ultimate responsibility for these publications is ours as publisher, and that the TFOE and the ALA are in no way officially involved in their preparation or endorse their purchase.

Statistical Record of the Environment

Third Edition

Chapter 1
SUMMARY INDICATORS

This chapter presents extracts from other chapters in *Statistical Record of the Environment* in the form of summary tables. The information presented is of the "frequently requested" variety: Facts and figures that offer quick insight into the magnitude of problems, issues, and expenditures related to the environment.

Tables are organized alphabetically by major topic. Columns labeled "Item" show the name of the category covered. Categories are followed by a "Value" column, a "Denomination" column, a "Date" column, and finally a "Table" column indicating the original table from which the item was extracted.

★ 1 ★

Air

Item	Value	Denomination	Date	Table
Carbon monoxide emissions				
Fuel combustion	5.433	Million short tons	1993	21
Industrial processes	5.219	Million short tons	1993	21
Transportation	75.261	Million short tons	1993	21
Lead emissions				
Fuel combustion	0.497	Million short tons	1993	24
Industrial processes	2.281	Million short tons	1993	24
Transportation	1.589	Million short tons	1993	24
Nitrogen oxide emissions				
Fuel combustion	11.690	Million short tons	1993	26
Industrial processes	0.911	Million short tons	1993	26
Transportation	10.423	Million short tons	1993	26
PM-10 fugitive dust emissions (total)	42.826	Million short tons	1993	27
PM-10 particulate emissions				
Fuel combustion	1.212	Million short tons	1993	28
Industrial processes	0.610	Million short tons	1993	28
Transportation	0.592	Million short tons	1993	28
Sulfur dioxide emissions				
Fuel combustion	19.266	Million short tons	1993	29
Industrial processes	1.868	Million short tons	1993	29

[Continued]

★1★

Air
[Continued]

Item	Value	Denomination	Date	Table
Transportation	0.718	Million short tons	1993	29
Volatile organic compound emissions				
Fuel combustion	0.648	Million short tons	1993	32
Industrial processes	11.201	Million short tons	1993	32
Transportation	8.301	Million short tons	1993	32

Source: Data are drawn from tables elsewhere in *Statistical Record of the Environment.*

★2★

Climate and Weather Conditions

Item	Value	Denomination	Date	Table
Country with most global warming gas emissions:				
United States	18.4	Percent of total emissions	NA	60
U.S. natural disasters				
Tornadoes	1,303	Number	1992	63
Floods	87	Number	1992	63
Hurricanes	1	Number	1992	63
U.S. city with highest normal annual precipitation:				
Mobile, Alabama	64.96	Inches	1961-1990	68

Source: Data are drawn from tables elsewhere in *Statistical Record of the Environment.* Note: "NA" indicates data not available or not provided in source material.

★3★

Energy

Item	Value	Denomination	Date	Table
Energy consumption				
Total consumption	33.08	Quadrillion Btu	1950	324
Total consumption	83.96	Quadrillion Btu	1993	324
Renewable energy resource consumption				
Hydroelectric power	2.90	Quadrillion Btu	1992	335
Geothermal power	0.26	Quadrillion Btu	1992	335
Biofuels	2.79	Quadrillion Btu	1992	335

[Continued]

★3★

Energy
[Continued]

Item	Value	Denomination	Date	Table
Solar energy	0.07	Quadrillion Btu	1992	335
Wind energy	0.03	Quadrillion Btu	1992	335
Energy production				
Total energy production	33.98	Quadrillion Btu	1950	362
Total energy production	65.81	Quadrillion Btu	1993	362
Electricity production				
Total production	329	Billion kilowatt hours	1950	359
Total production	2,882	Billion kilowatt hours	1993	359
Nuclear energy production				
Net generation of electricity	0.2	Billion kilowatt hours	1958	349
Net generation of electricity	610.3	Billion kilowatt hours	1993	349

Source: Data are drawn from tables elsewhere in *Statistical Record of the Environment.*

★4★

Environmental Markets

Item	Value	Denomination	Date	Table
Environmental consumer products markets				
Cleaning product sales	4,500	Million dollars	1992	822
Health and beauty product sales	4,300	Million dollars	1992	822
Nondurable sporting good and toy sales	2,100	Million dollars	1992	822
Stationery and school supply sales	880	Million dollars	1992	822
Wheel good sales	228	Million dollars	1992	822
Environmental goods and services market revenues				
Water and wastewater	60	Billion dollars	NA	823
Services	48	Billion dollars	NA	823
Waste management	40	Billion dollars	NA	823
Air quality control	22	Billion dollars	NA	823
Environmental technology markets				
North America	84.0	Billion dollars	1990	825
Europe	54.0	Billion dollars	1990	825
Eastern Europe/Commonwealth of Independent States	15.0	Billion dollars	1990	825

Source: Data are drawn from tables elsewhere in *Statistical Record of the Environment. Note:* "NA" indicates data not available or provided in source material.

★ 5 ★

Land

Item	Value	Denomination	Date	Table
Land area (total United States)	3,536,338	Square miles	1990	220
Cropland				
Cropland used for crops	332	Million acres	1993	182
Cropland harvested	299	Million acres	1993	184
Cropland diverted from production	60.0	Million acres	1993	184
Farms and farmland				
Number	5.74	Million	1900	185
Number	1.93	Million	1992	185
Area	0.84	Billion acres	1900	185
Area	0.95	Billion acres	1992	185
Irrigated farmland	51.3	Million acres	1993	186
Forest and timberland area	737	Million acres	1992	208
Forestland insect damage				
Eastern spruce budworm	0.1	Million acres	1993	208
Western spruce budworm	0.4	Million acres	1993	208
Gypsy moth	1.4	Million acres	1993	208
Mountain pine beetle	0.8	Million acres	1993	208
Southern pine beetle	10.4	Million acres	1993	208
Rangeland conditions				
Excellent	2	Percent	1936	232
Excellent	5	Percent	1992	232
Poor	36	Percent	1939	232
Poor	13	Percent	1992	232
Timberland (total)	489.6	Million acres	1992	212

Source: Data are drawn from tables elsewhere in *Statistical Record of the Environment.*

★ 6 ★

Pollution Abatement and Control Costs and Expenditures

Item	Value	Denomination	Date	Table
Expenditures for all media	91,456	Million dollars	1991	633
Air	28,060	Million dollars	1991	633
Water	37,310	Million dollars	1991	633
Solid waste	26,640	Million dollars	1991	633

[Continued]

★6★

Pollution Abatement and Control Costs and Expenditures
[Continued]

Item	Value	Denomination	Date	Table
Expenditures for all industries	7,866.9	Million dollars	1992	639
Operating costs for all industries	17,466.4	Million dollars	1992	673

Source: Data are drawn from tables elsewhere in *Statistical Record of the Environment.*

★7★

Public Opinion

Item	Value	Denomination	Date	Table
Status of local air quality:				
Very good or good	86	Percent	1993	872
Fair or poor	14	Percent	1993	872
Status of local water quality:				
Very good or good	86	Percent	1993	872
Fair or poor	14	Percent	1993	872
Status of local solid waste management:				
Very good or good	77	Percent	1993	872
Fair or poor	23	Percent	1993	872
Industrialized nation with "greatest" concern about environment among its citizens: Portugal	46	Percent	1993	869
Developing nation with "greatest" concern about environment among its citizens: Philippines	55	Percent	1993	869

Source: Data are drawn from tables elsewhere in *Statistical Record of the Environment.*

★8★

Toxic Release Inventory

Item	Value	Denomination	Date	Table
Chemical with largest air, water, and land releases:				
Methanol	214,541,828	Pounds	1992	386
Chemical with largest emissions to air:				
Methanol	194,790,687	Pounds	1992	385

[Continued]

★8★

Toxic Release Inventory
[Continued]

Item	Value	Denomination	Date	Table
Chemical with largest discharges to surface water: Phosphoric acid	158,674,836	Pounds	1992	384
Chemical with largest land releases: Zinc compounds	76,540,392	Pounds	1992	387
Chemical with largest underground injection: Ammonia	251,783,10	Pounds	1992	389
Chemical with largest total releases: Ammonia	463,857,411	Pounds	1992	388
State with most air, water, and land releases: Louisiana	277,878,454	Pounds	1992	464
State with most toxic chemical accidents: California	4,820	Number	1988-1992	391
Parent company with largest air, water, and land releases: Freeport-McMoran	155,3396,061	Pounds	1992	475
Parent company with largest total releases: DuPont	239,614,292	Pounds	1992	476
Facility with largest air, water, and land releases: Agrico Chemical Co. (Saint James, Louisiana)	90,800,120	Pounds	1992	473
Facility with greatest decrease in air, water, and land releases: BASF Corp. (Lowland, Tennessee)	-20,951,105	Pounds	1991-1992	469
Facility with greatest increase in air, water, and land releases: Lenzing Fibers Corp. (Lowland, Tennessee)	20,428,265	Pounds	1991-1992	471
Facility with greatest decrease in underground injection: BASF Corp. (Geismar, Louisiana)	-12,000,036	Pounds	1991-1992	470
Facility with greatest increase in underground injection: Vulcan Chemicals (Wichita, Kansas)	14,675,852	Pounds	1991-1992	472
Facility with largest total releases: American Cyanamid Co. (Westwego, Louisiana)	147,088,590	Pounds	1992	474

Source: Data are drawn from tables elsewhere in *Statistical Record of the Environment.*

★9★

Wastes and Resource Recovery

Item	Value	Denomination	Date	Table
Hazardous waste				
Largest source of hazardous waste: Organic solvents	70,000,000	Thousand metric tons	1989-1991	521
Largest source of industrial hazardous waste: Chemicals	33.8	Percent	1991	523
Municipal solid waste				
Generation	222.1	Million tons	2000	526

[Continued]

★ 9 ★

Wastes and Resource Recovery
[Continued]

Item	Value	Denomination	Date	Table
Recovery	66.8	Million tons	2000	526
Discards	155.4	Million tons	2000	526
Municipal solid waste management				
Gross discards	195.7	Million tons	1990	530
Net discards	162.3	Million tons	1990	530
Waste generation				
Largest source of nonhazardous industrial waste: Mining waste	1,500	Million tons	1992	571
Waste handling				
Most common method of waste handling: Landfills	62.5	Percent	1960	564
Most common method of waste handling: Landfills	49.3	Percent	2000	564
Recycling				
Most often recycled waste stream: Aluminum cans	63	Percent	1993	545

Source: Data are drawn from tables elsewhere in *Statistical Record of the Environment.*

★ 10 ★

Water

Item	Value	Denomination	Date	Table
Water area (total United States)	181,184	Square miles	1990	40
Inland	78,641	Square miles	1990	40
Coastal	42,491	Square miles	1990	40
Great Lakes	60,052	Square miles	1990	40
Water Use				
Source				
Ground water	80.6	Billion gallons per day	1990	55
Surface water	327.2	Billion gallons per day	1990	55
End-use sector				
Public supply	38.5	Billion gallons per day	1990	55
Rural and domestic livestock	7.9	Billion gallons per day	1990	55
Irrigation	137.0	Billion gallons per day	1990	55
Thermoelectric utility	195.0	Billion gallons per day	1990	55
Other industrial	29.9	Billion gallons per day	1990	55
Water withdrawals (total)	408	Billion gallons	1990	58
Water pollution				
Largest sources of surface water pollution:				
Rivers – Agriculture	159,353	Impaired miles	1992	51

[Continued]

★ 10 ★

Water

[Continued]

Item	Value	Denomination	Date	Table
Lakes and reservoirs – Agriculture	3,091,585	Impaired acres	1992	51
Estuaries – Municipal	4,383	Impaired square miles	1992	51

Source: Data are drawn from tables elsewhere in *Statistical Record of the Environment.*

★ 11 ★

Wildlife and Habitat

Item	Value	Denomination	Date	Table
Endangered species				
Threatened wildlife and plants	49	Number	1980	278
Threatened wildlife and plants	155	Number	1993	278
Endangered wildlife and plants	234	Number	1980	276
Endangered wildlife and plants	572	Number	1993	276
National Wild and Scenic River System				
Cumulative length	773	Miles	1968	313
Cumulative length	10,516	Miles	1993	313
National Wilderness Preservation System				
Land area	9.24	Million acres	1964	314
Land area	95.44	Million acres	1993	314
National Wildlife Refuge System				
Land area	17.5	Million acres	1946	315
Land area	89.2	Million acres	1993	315

Source: Data are drawn from tables elsewhere in *Statistical Record of the Environment.*

Chapter 2
AIR AND WATER

This chapter presents a variety of material on the media of air and water. The chapter is arranged alphabetically by subject category. Coverage intends to show information on the general status of air and water. Topics include air pollution, air quality, rivers, water area, water pollution, water quality, and water use.

The principal air pollutants are particulates (such as dust and flyash), various products of combustion—hydrocarbons, carbon monoxide, lead, and sulfur—and emissions from chemical synthesis, refining, and manufacturing operations. These last are of many kinds: Some are relatively benign; others are quite toxic.

In recent years the emission of carbon dioxide has come under scrutiny because excess levels are believed to cause a gradual warming of the earth's atmosphere. Several tables offer data on carbon dioxide emissions and concentrations. Further information on global warming is presented in the Climate and Weather Conditions chapter. Air pollution is linked fundamentally to energy consumption, so the Energy chapter also presents additional, indirect information about air.

Much of the material on water profiles its quantity, quality, and usage. Other information in the chapter offers an overview of water pollution. Wetlands are covered in the Land and Land Use chapter. Wilderness-related water concerns may be found in the Wildlife and Habitat chapter.

Additional information on air and water pollution will be found in the Toxic and Hazardous Substances chapter. Economic aspects of both media are covered in the Costs and Expenditures chapter; legal issues are handled in the Politics, Opinion, Law chapter.

Air Pollution

★ 12 ★

Air Pollutant Emission Changes, by Type of Pollutant: 1940-1992

Table shows the percent change from prior year (or for 1940 from 1930) for national air pollutant emissions. See also table on emissions by type of pollutant.

[In million metric tons, except lead which is in thousand metric tons]

Year	PM-10	PM-10, fugitive dust[1]	Sulfur doxide	Nitrogen dioxides	Volatile organic compounds	Carbon monoxide	Lead
1940	(NA)	(NA)	-5.8	-6.0	-6.8	(NA)	(NA)
1950	4.7	(NA)	12.2	37.6	21.8	8.7	(NA)
1960	-14.3	(NA)	-0.6	40.1	16.6	5.1	(NA)
1970	-12.7	(NA)	40.8	43.0	22.3	14.4	(NA)
1975	-40.0	(NA)	-10.2	6.9	-15.5	-14.0	-27.8
1980	-3.0	(NA)	-6.8	6.1	12.8	26.3	-52.7
1981	-6.3	(NA)	-5.3	-0.7	-6.5	-4.7	-21.4
1982	-18.3	(NA)	-5.8	-3.5	-6.2	-5.6	-2.1
1983	12.2	(NA)	-2.8	-2.9	2.2	-0.2	-14.6
1984	5.5	(NA)	4.1	2.8	2.9	-2.6	-14.2
1985	-3.0	(NA)	-1.2	-0.9	-4.3	-4.5	-52.3
1986	-6.0	11.7	-3.9	-0.6	1.4	-2.8	-63.7
1987	4.0	-15.8	0.6	2.4	-2.5	-5.3	-6.2
1988	6.6	42.3	2.1	3.6	1.2	-0.2	-5.6
1989	-3.6	-11.2	0.4	-0.7	-4.4	-5.7	-5.6
1990[2]	-2.1	-15.8	-1.6	0.3	-1.0	-1.1	-7.6
1991[2]	-4.4	10.7	-0.2	-0.6	-1.2	-1.8	-11.0
1992[2]	2.1	-8.2	-0.2	-1.1	-2.9	-3.9	3.3

Source: 1994 Statistical Abstract of the United States on CD-ROM [machine-readable datafiles]. CD-8A-94. Washington, DC: U.S. Department of Commerce, Economics and Statistics Administration, Bureau of the Census, Data User Services Division, January 1995. *Notes:* "NA" represents "not available." PM-10 indicates particulate matter of less than 10 microns. Metric ton equals 1.1023 short tons. 1. Sources such as agricultural tilling, construction, mining and quarrying, paved roads, unpaved roads, and wind erosion. 2. Preliminary.

★ 13 ★

Air Pollution

Air Pollutant Emissions, by Pollutant and Source: 1990-1992

Table shows total, controllable, and uncontrollable emissions by sources.

[In million metric tons, except lead which is in thousand metric tons]

| Year and pollutant | Total emissions | Controllable emissions | | | | | | Misc. uncon-trol-lable | Percent of total | | |
| | | Transportation | | Fuel combustion | | Indus-trial proc-esses | Solid waste dis posal | | Trans-porta-tion | Fuel combus tion | Indus-trial |
		Total	Road vehicles	Total	Electric utilities						
1990:											
Carbon monoxide	83.8	67.5	54.3	6.1	0.3	4.7	1.5	3.9	80.5	7.3	5.6
Sulfur oxides	20.7	0.9	0.7	17.8	14.4	2.0	0.0	0.0	4.3	86.0	9.7
Volatile organic compounds	21.5	8.3	6.3	0.7	0.0	10.0	2.1	0.5	38.6	3.3	46.5
Particulates[1]	46.1	1.6	1.3	1.1	0.2	1.8	0.2	41.5	3.5	2.4	3.9
Nitrogen oxides	21.4	9.7	7.1	10.7	6.8	0.8	0.1	0.1	45.3	50.0	3.7
Lead	5.1	1.7	1.5	0.5	0.1	2.2	0.7	0.0	33.3	9.8	43.1
1991:											
Carbon monoxide	82.3	66.3	53.4	6.0	0.3	4.7	1.5	3.8	80.6	7.3	5.7
Sulfur oxides	20.7	0.9	0.7	17.7	14.3	2.0	0.0	0.0	4.3	85.5	9.7
Volatile organic compounds	21.2	8.0	6.2	0.7	0.0	10.0	2.0	0.5	37.7	3.3	47.2
Particulates[1]	50.2	1.6	1.4	1.0	0.1	1.7	0.2	45.6	3.2	2.0	3.4
Nitrogen oxides	21.2	9.5	7.0	10.7	6.8	0.8	0.1	0.1	44.8	50.5	3.8
Lead	4.5	1.5	1.4	0.4	0.1	2.0	0.5	0.0	33.3	8.9	44.4
1992:											
Carbon monoxide	79.1	63.5	50.2	5.6	0.3	4.6	1.5	3.9	80.3	7.1	5.8
Sulfur oxides	20.6	1.0	0.7	17.7	14.4	1.9	0.0	0.0	4.9	85.9	9.2
Volatile organic compounds	20.6	7.5	5.5	0.6	0.0	9.9	2.1	0.5	36.4	2.9	48.1
Particulates[1]	46.7	1.7	1.4	1.0	0.1	1.8	0.2	42.0	3.6	2.1	3.9
Nitrogen oxides	21.0	9.4	6.8	10.6	6.8	0.8	0.1	0.1	44.8	50.5	3.8
Lead	4.7	1.4	1.3	0.4	0.1	2.1	0.7	0.0	29.8	8.5	44.7

Source: 1994 Statistical Abstract of the United States on CD-ROM [machine-readable datafiles]. CD-8A-94. Washington, DC: U.S. Department of Commerce, Economics and Statistics Administration, Bureau of the Census, Data User Services Division, January 1995. Primary source: U.S. Environmental Protection Agency. *National Air Pollutant Emission Trends, 1900-1992. Notes:* Metric ton equals 1.1023 short tons. 1. PM-10 indicates particulate matter of less than 10 microns. Represents both PM-10 and PM-10 fugitive dust.

★ 14 ★
Air Pollution

Air Pollutant Emissions, by Type of Pollutant: 1940-1992

Table shows national emissions for various types of pollutants. See also related table showing percent changes for emissions by pollutants.

[In million metric tons, except lead which is in thousand metric tons]

Year	PM-10	PM-10, fugitive dust[1]	Sulfur doxide	Nitrogen dioxides	Volatile organic compounds	Carbon monoxide	Lead
1940	14.04	(NA)	18.10	6.86	15.53	82.43	(NA)
1950	14.71	(NA)	20.31	9.44	18.92	89.62	(NA)
1960	12.60	(NA)	20.18	13.23	22.06	94.15	(NA)
1970	11.00	(NA)	28.42	18.92	26.98	107.68	199.10
1975	6.60	(NA)	25.51	20.23	22.81	92.63	143.83
1980	6.40	(NA)	23.78	21.47	25.72	117.03	68.00
1981	6.00	(NA)	22.51	21.32	24.04	111.58	53.42
1982	4.90	(NA)	21.21	20.57	22.56	105.37	52.31
1983	5.50	(NA)	20.62	19.97	23.05	105.20	44.66
1984	5.80	(NA)	21.47	20.53	23.71	102.49	38.30
1985	5.62	40.66	21.22	20.34	22.69	97.88	18.26
1986	5.29	45.41	20.39	20.21	23.00	95.16	6.62
1987	5.50	38.26	20.52	20.69	22.43	90.09	6.21
1988	5.86	54.45	20.95	21.44	22.70	89.87	5.86
1989	5.65	48.38	21.04	21.30	21.69	84.73	5.53
1990[2]	5.53	40.74	20.70	21.37	21.48	83.81	5.11
1991[2]	5.29	45.08	20.66	21.24	21.23	82.27	4.55
1992[2]	5.40	41.41	20.62	21.00	20.62	79.09	4.70

Source: 1994 Statistical Abstract of the United States on CD-ROM [machine-readable datafiles]. CD-8A-94. Washington, DC: U.S. Department of Commerce, Economics and Statistics Administration, Bureau of the Census, Data User Services Division, January 1995. *Notes:* "NA" represents "not available." PM-10 indicates particulate matter of less than 10 microns. Metric ton equals 1.1023 short tons. 1. Sources such as agricultural tilling, construction, mining and quarrying, paved roads, unpaved roads, and wind erosion. 2. Preliminary.

★ 15 ★

Air Pollution

Air Pollutants From Gasoline: 1984-1993

Table shows the decrease in air pollutants from cleaner burning gasoline. Data are for gasoline developed between 1984 and 1993.

[In percentages]

Pollutant	Reduction
Airborne lead	89
Carbon monoxide	37
Sulfur dioxide	26
Ozone	12
Nitrogen dioxide	12

Source: "Clearing the Air." *USA TODAY,* 4 January 1995, p. 1A. Primary source: American Petroleum Institute.

★ 16 ★

Air Pollution

Carbon Dioxide Concentrations: 1973-1992

Table shows concentrations of carbon dioxide above U.S. monitoring stations. Annual mean concentration is reported only when all 12 monthly average concentrations are available.

[In parts per million by volume]

Year	Mauna Loa, Hawaii	South Pole	American Samoa	Point Barrow, Alaska
1973	329.51	327.44	NA	NA
1974	330.08	328.29	NA	NA
1975	330.99	329.35	NA	333.19
1976	330.98	330.46	NA	334.01
1977	333.73	331.87	NA	NA
1978	335.34	NA	NA	NA
1979	336.78	334.84	NA	NA
1980	338.52	NA	NA	NA
1981	339.76	338.07	NA	340.87
1982	340.96	NA	340.43	342.40
1983	342.61	341.02	341.82	343.73
1984	344.25	NA	343.66	345.53
1985	345.73	343.63	NA	346.74
1986	346.99	345.19	NA	348.51
1987	348.79	346.85	347.88	349.76
1988	351.34	348.80	349.96	353.05
1989	352.75	350.30	351.44	355.11
1990	353.99	351.59	352.73	355.82

[Continued]

★ 16 ★

Carbon Dioxide Concentrations: 1973-1992
[Continued]

Year	Mauna Loa, Hawaii	South Pole	American Samoa	Point Barrow, Alaska
1991	355.42	NA	354.21	357.29
1992	356.24	354.08	355.06	357.63

Source: Executive Office of the President of the United States. *Environmental Quality 24: The Twenty-fourth Annual Report of the Council on Environmental Quality.* Prepared by Ray Clark. Written by Carroll Curtis. Edited by Barry Walsh. Washington, DC: U.S. Government Printing Office, 1994, p. 445. Primary source: Keeling, C. D., and T. P. Whorf. "Atmospheric CO_2 Records From Sites in the SIO Air Sampling Network." In *Trends '93: A Compendium of Data on Global Change.* Edited by T.A. Boden, D. P. Kaiser, R. J. Sepanski, and P. Y. Hughes. ORNL/CDIAC-65. Oak Ridge, TN: U.S. Department of Energy, Oak Ridge National Laboratory, Carbon Dioxide Information Analysis Center, 1994, pp. 16-26. *Note:* "NA" stands for "not available."

★ 17 ★

Air Pollution

Carbon Dioxide Emissions for Fuel Sources

Table compares the environmental dangers of various fuel sources. Data show tons of carbon emitted per quad of thermal energy produced.

[In millions]

Fuel sources	Emissions
Shale oil	50.2
Synthetic gas	42.9
Synthetic oil	40.7
Coal	28.3
Conventional oil	20.8
Natural gas	14.6
Natural geothermal energy	1.5
Nuclear energy	<1
Solar, hydro, and HDR geothermal energy	-0

Source: "Carbon Dioxide Emissions for Different Fuel Sources." *Technology Review* (January 1995), p. 44.

★ 18 ★

Air Pollution

Carbon Dioxide Emissions From Anthropogenic Sources: 1950-1991

Table shows U.S. emissions of carbon dioxide from anthropogenic sources such as the combustion of fossil fuels, human exhalations, and the decay of vegatable matter. Data do not include fuel bunkers used in international trade.

[In million metric tons of carbon, except as noted]

Year	Solid	Liquids	Gases	Cement	Gas flaring	Total	Per capita[1]
1950	347.1	244.8	87.1	5.3	11.8	696.1	4.57
1951	334.5	262.2	102.7	5.7	11.7	716.7	4.63
1952	296.6	273.2	109.9	5.8	12.5	697.9	4.44
1953	294.3	286.6	115.5	6.1	11.9	714.5	4.46
1954	252.2	290.2	121.2	6.3	10.6	680.5	4.18
1955	283.3	313.3	130.8	7.2	11.4	746.0	4.50
1956	295.0	328.5	138.1	7.6	12.7	781.9	4.63
1957	282.7	325.8	147.6	7.2	11.9	775.1	4.51
1958	245.3	333.0	155.8	7.5	9.3	750.8	4.29
1959	251.5	343.5	169.9	8.1	8.4	781.4	4.40
1960	253.4	349.8	180.4	7.6	8.3	799.5	4.43
1961	245.0	354.1	187.4	7.7	7.7	801.9	4.37
1962	254.2	364.3	198.7	8.0	6.3	831.5	4.46
1963	272.5	378.9	210.3	8.4	5.6	875.6	4.63
1964	289.7	389.7	219.8	8.8	5.0	912.9	4.76
1965	301.1	405.6	228.0	8.9	4.7	948.3	4.88
1966	312.7	425.9	246.4	9.1	5.5	999.7	5.08
1967	321.1	443.6	258.5	8.8	7.2	1,039.2	5.23
1968	314.8	471.9	277.4	9.4	7.6	1,081.0	5.38
1969	319.7	497.4	297.8	9.5	7.7	1,132.0	5.58
1970	322.4	514.8	312.1	9.0	7.2	1,165.5	5.68
1971	305.7	530.5	323.3	9.7	4.2	1,173.2	5.66
1972	310.4	575.5	327.6	10.2	3.6	1,227.4	5.86
1973	334.0	605.4	321.7	10.6	3.6	1,275.4	6.03
1974	330.1	580.7	307.9	10.0	2.4	1,231.1	5.76
1975	317.6	565.1	286.0	8.4	1.9	1,179.0	5.46
1976	351.6	608.9	291.3	9.0	2.0	1,262.8	5.78
1977	355.6	642.7	260.5	9.7	2.0	1,270.6	5.76
1978	361.2	655.5	264.7	10.4	2.2	1,294.0	5.80
1979	378.7	637.5	274.8	10.4	2.4	1,303.8	5.78
1980	394.6	583.5	272.5	9.3	1.8	1,261.8	5.54
1981	403.0	535.8	264.3	8.9	1.4	1,213.3	5.28
1982	390.1	507.8	245.4	7.8	1.4	1,152.4	4.97
1983	408.5	500.1	233.8	8.7	1.4	1,157.9	4.94
1984	427.8	513.8	241.5	9.6	1.6	1,194.2	5.05
1985	448.0	523.7	236.7	9.6	1.4	1,217.6	5.11
1986	439.6	544.4	242.2	9.7	1.4	1,237.4	5.14
1987	454.2	561.4	256.4	9.7	1.8	1,283.4	5.28
1988	491.7	585.8	268.0	9.5	2.1	1,357.1	5.54
1989	497.9	584.2	276.2	9.5	2.1	1,369.9	5.53

[Continued]

★ 18 ★

Carbon Dioxide Emissions From Anthropogenic
Sources: 1950-1991
[Continued]

Year	Solid	Liquids	Gases	Cement	Gas flaring	Total	Per capita[1]
1990	498.6	562.7	273.7	9.5	2.2	1,346.7	5.39
1991	492.3	555.1	287.2	9.3	2.0	1,346.0	5.33

Source: Executive Office of the President of the United States. *Environmental Quality 24: The Twenty-fourth Annual Report of the Council on Environmental Quality.* Prepared by Ray Clark. Written by Carroll Curtis. Edited by Barry Walsh. Washington, DC: U.S. Government Printing Office, 1994, p. 442. Primary source: Marland, G., R. J. Andres, and T. A. Boden. "Global, Regional, and Natural CO_2 Emmissions." In *Trends '93: A Compendium of Data on Global Change.* Edited by T.A. Boden, D. P. Kaiser, R. J. Sepanski, and P. Y. Hughes. ORNL/CDIAC-65. Oak Ridge, TN:U.S. Department of Energy, Oak Ridge National Laboratory, Carbon Dioxide Information Analysis Center, 1994, pp. 505-584. *Note:* 1. Metric tons.

★ 19 ★

Air Pollution

Carbon Dioxide Emissions Growth: 1990-2000

United States - 4,957

Japan - 1,173

Germany - 1,012

United Kingdom - 584

Canada - 457

Australia - 289

Spain - 261

Czech Republic - 170

Netherlands - 168

Sweden - 61

Austria - 59

Denmark - 52

Switzerland - 44

Norway - 36

New Zealand - 26

Chart shows data from column 1.

Table show the anticipated growth in carbon dioxide emissions for most developed nations.

[In million metric tons, except as noted]

Country	CO_2 emissions		
	1990[1]	2000[2]	Percent change
United States	4,957	5,163	4
Japan	1,173	1,200	2
Germany[3]	1,012	NA	NA
United Kingdom	584	587	1
Canada	457	510	12
Australia	289	336	16
Spain	261	277	6
Netherlands	168	168	0
Czech Republic	170	136	-20
Austria	59	66	12
Sweden	61	64	5
Denmark	52	54	4
Switzerland	44	44	0
Norway	36	40	11
New Zealand	26	30	15

Source: "Most Developed Countries Say CO_2 Emissions to Grow." *C&EN,* 13 March 1995, p. 29. Primary source: United Nations compilation of national communications. *Notes:* "NA" indicates "not available." 1. Reported inventory. 2. Projected. 3. Germany projects a 3 percent decrease by 2005.

★ 20 ★
Air Pollution

Carbon Emissions, by Country: 1990-2010

United States - 1,483	
China - 907	
Former Soviet Union - 868	
Japan - 395	
Latin America - 353	
Germany - 292	
Africa - 245	
Britain - 207	
Canada - 158	

Chart shows data from column 3.

Industrialized countries met for an Earth Summit in 1992. At the meeting, they agreed to a ceiling on "greenhouse gases" to avert their dangerous impact on the global climate system. Table shows carbon emissions and projections for selected countries.

[In million metric tons]

Country	1990	1992	2000	2005	2010
United States	1,338	1,341	1,483	1,553	1,632
Canada	130	134	158	164	168
Japan	310	320	395	425	443
Britain	164	174	207	218	230
Germany	265	254	292	311	325
China	649	678	907	1,040	1,170
Former Soviet Union	1,014	868	868	950	1,037
Africa	193	216	245	263	280
Latin America	275	286	353	395	434

Source: Stevens, William K. "Climate Talks Enter Harder Phase of Cutting Back Emissions." *New York Times,* 11 April 1995, p. B7. Primary source: U.S. Department of Energy.

★ 21 ★

Air Pollution

Carbon Monoxide Emissions, by Source: 1970-1993

Table shows U.S. emissions of carbon monoxide air pollutants for selected sources. Carbon monoxide is one of the six leading air pollutants.

[In million short tons]

Source	1970	1980	1984	1985	1986	1987	1988	1989	1990	1991	1992	1993
Fuel combustion	4.632	7.302	7.808	7.648	7.512	7.287	7.153	6.934	6.697	6.579	6.017	5.433
Electric utilities	0.237	0.322	0.316	0.292	0.291	0.300	0.313	0.319	0.314	0.314	0.313	0.322
Industrial	0.770	0.750	0.732	0.670	0.650	0.649	0.669	0.672	0.677	0.682	0.671	0.667
Other	3.625	6.230	6.760	6.686	6.571	6.338	6.172	5.942	5.726	5.583	5.033	4.444
Industrial processes	9.840	6.950	5.107	5.224	5.194	5.043	5.271	5.311	5.275	5.200	5.170	5.219
Chemical industries	3.397	2.151	2.082	1.845	1.853	1.798	1.917	1.925	1.940	1.953	1.964	1.998
Metals processing industries	3.644	2.246	1.734	2.223	2.079	1.984	2.101	2.132	2.080	1.992	2.044	2.091
Petroleum industries	2.197	1.723	0.383	0.462	0.451	0.455	0.441	0.436	0.435	0.410	0.403	0.398
Other industries	0.620	0.830	0.908	0.694	0.715	0.713	0.711	0.716	0.717	0.711	0.719	0.732
Solvent utilization	NA	NA	NA	NA	NA	NA	NA	NA	NA	NA	NA	NA
Storage and transport	NA	NA	NA	NA	NA	NA	NA	NA	NA	NA	NA	NA
Transportation	89.260	104.108	92.308	61.093	87.331	84.776	85.581	80.568	77.500	76.695	74.763	75.261
Highway vehicles	79.258	87.991	78.881	77.387	73.347	70.645	71.081	66.050	62.858	62.074	59.859	59.989
Off-highway vehicles	10.001	16.117	13.427	13.706	13.984	14.131	14.500	14.518	14.642	14.621	14.904	15.272
Other sources												
Waste disposal and recycling	7.059	2.300	2.028	1.941	1.916	1.850	1.806	1.747	1.686	1.644	1.717	1.732
Miscellaneous	7.909	8.344	7.011	6.116	6.161	6.203	6.332	6.290	12.623	9.826	8.679	9.506

Source: Executive Office of the President of the United States. *Environmental Quality 24: The Twenty-fourth Annual Report of the Council on Environmental Quality.* Prepared by Ray Clark. Written by Carroll Curtis. Edited by Barry Walsh. Washington, DC: U.S. Government Printing Office, 1994, p. 438. Primary source: U.S. Environmental Protection Agency. Office of Air Quality Planning and Standards. *National Air Quality and Emissions Trends Report, 1993.* EPA-454/R-94-026. Research Triangle Park, NC: U.S. Environmental Protection Agency, Office of Air Quality Planning and Standards, 1994, pp. 29, 35, 41, 46, 52-53, 57, tables 3-1 through 3-7. *Notes:* "NA" represents "not applicable." Totals may not agree with detail because of independent rounding.

★ 22 ★

Air Pollution

Criteria Air Pollutants: 1984-1993

Table shows the national ambient concentrations of criteria air pollutants. Data represent composite averages from all sites in the nationwide monitoring network. Sulfur dioxide and nitrogen dioxide records are arithmetic means. Carbon monoxide and ozone records are second maximum readings over 8- and 24-hour periods, respectively. PM-10 records are weighted arithmetic means. Lead records are maximum quarterly recordings.

Year	Sulfur dioxide[1]	Carbon monoxide[1]	Ozone[1]	Nitrogen dioxide[1]	PM-10 particulates[2]	Lead[2]
1984	0.0098	7.69	0.1252	0.0220	NA	0.423
1985	0.0093	6.97	0.1237	0.0220	NA	0.291
1986	0.0091	7.11	0.1197	0.0220	NA	0.180
1987	0.0089	6.69	0.1261	0.0220	NA	0.156
1988	0.0091	6.38	0.1364	0.0223	33.2	0.103
1989	0.0088	6.34	0.1169	0.0219	33.0	0.080
1990	0.0081	5.87	0.1143	0.0207	29.8	0.079
1991	0.0079	5.55	0.1155	0.0206	29.6	0.058

[Continued]

★ 22 ★

Criteria Air Pollutants: 1984-1993
[Continued]

Year	Sulfur dioxide[1]	Carbon monoxide[1]	Ozone[1]	Nitrogen dioxide[1]	PM-10 parti- culates[2]	Lead[2]
1992	0.0074	5.18	0.1071	0.0199	27.2	0.050
1993	0.0073	4.88	0.1097	0.0194	26.4	0.045

Source: Executive Office of the President of the United States. *Environmental Quality 24: The Twenty-fourth Annual Report of the Council on Environmental Quality.* Prepared by Ray Clark. Written by Carroll Curtis. Edited by Barry Walsh. Washington, DC: U.S. Government Printing Office, 1994, p. 444. Primary source: U.S. Environmental Protection Agency. Office of Air Quality Planning and Standards. *National Air Quality and Emissions Report, 1991.* EPA-450/R-94-026. Research Triangle Park, NC: U.S. Environmental Protection Agency, 1994. *Notes:* "NA" represents "not available." 1. Parts per million. 2. Micrograms per cubic meter.

★ 23 ★

Air Pollution

Hydrocarbon Emissions From Transportation: 1991

Table below shows the hydrocarbon emissions from the transportation sectors around the world. One way to reduce emissions is by using an alternate fuel. Compressed natural gas (CNG) vehicles were mass produced by Chrysler, Ford, and General Motors in 1992. Data from this initial fleet suggest that reducing annual emissions by 1 ton would require 14.4 CNG vehicles.

[In percentages]

Transportation sector	Percent of total hydrocarbon emissions
Mexico City, Mexico	77
Latin America	36
Canada	31
Western Europe	31
Australia	30
Japan	30
United States	30

Source: Baker, George, and Bart van Aardenne. "CNG: A Fuel for the Future." *Business Mexico* (1993), p. 48.

★ 24 ★

Air Pollution

Lead Emissions, by Source: 1970-1993

Table shows U.S. emissions of lead air pollutants for selected sources. Lead is one of the six leading air pollutants.

[In million short tons]

Source	1970	1980	1984	1985	1986	1987	1988	1989	1990	1991	1992	1993
Fuel combustion	10.616	4.299	0.541	0.515	0.516	0.510	0.511	0.505	0.500	0.495	0.491	0.497
Electric utilities	0.327	0.129	0.088	0.064	0.069	0.064	0.066	0.067	0.064	0.059	0.062	0.062
Industrial	0.237	0.060	0.029	0.030	0.025	0.022	0.019	0.018	0.018	0.018	0.018	0.018
Other	10.052	4.111	0.424	0.421	0.422	0.425	0.426	0.420	0.418	0.416	0.414	0.417
Industrial processes	26.354	3.938	2.535	2.531	2.128	2.143	2.224	2.461	2.443	2.238	2.189	2.281
Chemical industries	0.103	0.104	0.133	0.118	0.108	0.123	0.136	0.136	0.136	0.132	0.093	0.109
Metals processing industries	24.224	9.923	1.919	2.097	1.820	1.818	1.917	2.153	2.138	1.939	2.042	2.118
Petroleum industries	0.000	0.000	0.000	0.000	0.000	0.000	0.000	0.000	0.000	0.000	0.000	0.000
Other industries	2.208	0.808	0.483	0.316	0.199	0.202	0.172	0.173	0.169	0.167	0.054	0.054
Solvent utilization	0.000	0.000	0.000	0.000	0.000	0.000	0.000	0.000	0.000	0.000	0.000	0.000
Storage and transport	0.000	0.000	0.000	0.000	0.000	0.000	0.000	0.000	0.000	0.000	0.000	0.000
Transportation	180.301	65.509	38.240	16.207	3.808	3.343	2.911	2.368	1.887	1.705	1.645	1.589
Highway vehicles	171.961	62.189	35.930	15.978	3.589	3.121	2.700	2.161	1.690	1.519	1.542	1.383
Off-highway vehicles	8.340	3.320	2.310	0.229	0.219	0.222	0.211	0.207	0.197	0.186	0.193	0.206
Other sources												
Waste disposal and recycling	2.200	1.210	0.901	0.871	0.844	0.844	0.817	0.765	0.804	0.582	0.416	0.518
Miscellaneous	NA	NA	NA	NA	NA	NA	NA	NA	NA	NA	NA	NA

Source: Executive Office of the President of the United States. *Environmental Quality 24: The Twenty-fourth Annual Report of the Council on Environmental Quality.* Prepared by Ray Clark. Written by Carroll Curtis. Edited by Barry Walsh. Washington, DC: U.S. Government Printing Office, 1994, p. 439. Primary source: U.S. Environmental Protection Agency. Office of Air Quality Planning and Standards. *National Air Quality and Emissions Trends Report, 1993.* EPA-454/R-94-026. Research Triangle Park, NC: U.S. Environmental Protection Agency, Office of Air Quality Planning and Standards, 1994, pp. 29, 35, 41, 46, 52-53, 57, tables 3-1 through 3-7. *Notes:* "NA" represents "not applicable." Totals may not agree with detail because of independent rounding.

★ 25 ★

Air Pollution

National Ambient Air Pollutant Concentrations: 1982-1992

Data represent annual composite averages of pollutants based on daily 24-hour averages of monitoring stations—except carbon monoxide, which is based based on the second-highest, nonoverlapping, 8-hour average; ozone, average of the second-highest daily maximum one hour value; and lead, quarterly average of ambient lead levels. Based on data from the Aerometric Retrieval System.

Pollutant	Unit	Number of monitoring stations	Air quality standard[1]	1982	1984	1986	1988	1990	1992
Carbon monoxide	ppm	313	9[2]	7.98	7.78	7.15	6.39	5.85	5.19
Ozone	ppm	495	.12[3]	0.126	0.126	0.119	0.137	0.114	0.107
Sulfur dioxide	ppm	479	.03	0.010	0.010	0.009	0.009	0.008	0.007
PM-10 particulates[4]	micrograms of pollutant per cubic meter of air	682	50	(X)	(X)	(X)	33.6	30.6	27.8

[Continued]

★ 25 ★

National Ambient Air Pollutant Concentrations: 1982-1992

[Continued]

Pollutant	Unit	Number of monitoring stations	Air quality standard[1]	1982	1984	1986	1988	1990	1992
Nitrogen dioxide	ppm	172	.053	0.023	0.023	0.024	0.024	0.022	0.021
Lead	micrograms of pollutant per cubic meter of air	209	1.5[5]	0.488	0.392	0.149	0.088	0.062	0.043

Source: 1994 Statistical Abstract of the United States on CD-ROM [machine-readable datafiles]. CD-8A-94. Washington, DC: U.S. Department of Commerce, Economics and Statistics Administration, Bureau of the Census, Data User Services Division, January 1995. Primary source: U.S. Environmental Protection Agency. *National Air Quality and Emissions Trends Report* (annual). *Notes:* "ppm" represents "parts per million." "X" stands for "not applicable." 1. Refers to the primary National Ambient Air Quality Standard that protects the public health. 2. Based on 8-hour standard of 9 ppm. 3. Based on 1-hour standard of .12 ppm. 4. The particulates (PM-10) standard replaced the previous standard for total suspended particulates in 1987. 5. Based on 3-month standard of 1.5 micrograms of pollutant per cubic meter of air.

★ 26 ★

Air Pollution

Nitrogen Oxide Emissions, by Source: 1970-1993

Table shows U.S. emissions of nitrogen oxide air pollutants for selected sources. Nitrogen oxide is one of the six leading air pollutants.

[In million short tons]

Source	1970	1980	1984	1985	1986	1987	1988	1989	1990	1991	1992	1993
Fuel combustion	10.062	11.318	11.353	10.826	10.667	10.901	11.454	11.546	11.504	11.536	11.414	11.690
Electric utilities	4.900	7.023	7.268	6.916	6.909	7.128	7.530	7.607	7.516	7.482	7.493	7.782
Industrial	4.326	3.554	3.415	3.209	3.066	3.063	3.187	3.209	3.256	3.309	3.206	3.176
Other	0.836	0.741	0.670	0.701	0.694	0.710	0.737	0.730	0.732	0.745	0.735	0.732
Industrial processes	0.775	0.558	0.488	0.684	0.916	0.873	0.900	0.891	0.890	0.885	0.898	0.911
Chemical industries	0.271	0.216	0.161	0.374	0.381	0.371	0.398	0.395	0.399	0.401	0.411	0.414
Metals processing industries	0.077	0.065	0.054	0.087	0.080	0.076	0.082	0.083	0.081	0.079	0.080	0.082
Petroleum industries	0.240	0.072	0.070	0.124	0.109	0.101	0.100	0.097	0.100	0.103	0.096	0.096
Other industries	0.187	0.205	0.203	0.327	0.328	0.320	0.315	0.311	0.306	0.398	0.305	0.314
Solvent utilization	NA	NA	0.000	0.002	0.003	0.003	0.003	0.003	0.002	0.002	0.003	0.003
Storage and transport	NA	NA	0.000	0.002	0.002	0.002	0.002	0.002	0.002	0.002	0.003	0.003
Transportation	9.252	11.429	11.031	10.823	10.550	10.326	10.575	10.526	10.331	10.169	10.325	10.423
Highway vehicles	7.427	8.705	8.387	8.089	7.773	7.662	7.661	7.682	7.488	7.373	7.440	7.437
Off-highway vehicles	1.825	2.724	2.644	2.734	2.777	2.664	2.914	2.844	2.843	2.796	2.885	2.296
Other sources												
Waste disposal and recycling	0.440	0.111	0.090	0.087	0.087	0.085	0.084	0.084	0.082	0.081	0.083	0.084
Miscellaneous	0.330	0.248	0.210	0.201	0.202	0.203	0.206	0.205	0.384	0.305	0.272	0.296

Source: Executive Office of the President of the United States. *Environmental Quality 24: The Twenty-fourth Annual Report of the Council on Environmental Quality.* Prepared by Ray Clark. Written by Carroll Curtis. Edited by Barry Walsh. Washington, DC: U.S. Government Printing Office, 1994, p. 435. Primary source: U.S. Environmental Protection Agency. Office of Air Quality Planning and Standards. *National Air Quality and Emissions Trends Report, 1993.* EPA-454/ R-94-026. Research Triangle Park, NC: U.S. Environmental Protection Agency, Office of Air Quality Planning and Standards, 1994, pp. 29, 35, 41, 46, 52-53, 57, tables 3-1 through 3-7. *Notes:* "NA" represents "not applicable." Totals may not agree with detail because of independent rounding.

★ 27 ★
Air Pollution
PM-10 Fugitive Dust Emissions, by Source: 1985-1993

Total fugitive dust - 42.826

Unpaved - 14.404

Construction and mining - 11.368

Paved - 8.164

Crop tillage - 6.842

Wind erosion - 0.628

Fires and other burning - 1.026

Livestock - 0.394

Chart shows data from column 9.

Table shows U.S. emissions of PM-10 fugitive dust air pollutants for selected sources. PM-10 refers to particulates with aerodynamic diameter smaller than 10 micrometers. These smaller particles are likely to be responsible for most adverse health effects of particulates because of their ability to reach the thoracic or lower regions of the respiratory tract. PM-10 fugitive dust is one of the six leading air pollutants.

[In million short tons]

Source	1985	1986	1987	1988	1989	1990	1991	1992	1993
Agriculture									
Crop tillage	6.833	6.899	7.008	7.090	6.937	6.999	6.965	6.852	6.842
Livestock	0.275	0.285	0.330	0.376	0.397	0.381	0.363	0.386	0.394
Construction and mining	13.009	12.139	12.499	12.008	11.662	10.306	10.042	10.899	11.368
Roads									
Paved	6.299	6.555	6.877	7.365	7.155	7.299	7.437	7.621	8.164
Unpaved	14.719	14.672	13.960	15.626	15.346	15.661	14.267	14.540	14.404
Wind erosion	3.565	9.390	1.457	17.509	11.826	4.192	10.054	4.655	0.628
Fires and other burning	0.724	0.731	0.737	0.756	0.750	1.322	1.053	0.947	1.026
Total fugitive dust	45.424	50.671	42.868	60.730	54.073	46.250	50.181	45.900	42.826

Source: Executive Office of the President of the United States. *Environmental Quality 24: The Twenty-fourth Annual Report of the Council on Environmental Quality.* Prepared by Ray Clark. Written by Carroll Curtis. Edited by Barry Walsh. Washington, DC: U.S. Government Printing Office, 1994, p. 441. Primary source: U.S. Environmental Protection Agency. Office of Air Quality Planning and Standards. *National Air Quality and Emissions Trends Report, 1993.* EPA-454/R-94-026. Research Triangle Park, NC: U.S. Environmental Protection Agency, Office of Air Quality Planning and Standards, 1994, pp. 29, 35, 41, 46, 52-53, 57, tables 3-1 through 3-7. *Note:* Totals may not agree with detail because of independent rounding.

★ 28 ★

Air Pollution

PM-10 Particulate Emissions, by Source: 1985-1993

Table shows U.S. emissions of PM-10 particulates for selected sources. PM-10 refers to particulates with aerodynamic diameter smaller than 10 micrometers. These smaller particles are likely to be responsible for most adverse health effects of particulates because of their ability to reach the thoracic or lower regions of the respiratory tract. PM-10 particulates are one of the six leading air pollutants.

[In million short tons]

Source	1985	1986	1987	1988	1989	1990	1991	1992	1993
Fuel combustion	1.414	1.422	1.418	1.426	1.429	1.449	1.424	1.297	1.212
Electric utilities	0.284	0.289	0.282	0.278	0.278	0.291	0.253	0.255	0.270
Industrial	0.234	0.231	0.226	0.230	0.229	0.228	0.229	0.223	0.219
Other	0.896	0.902	0.910	0.918	0.922	0.930	0.942	0.819	0.723
Industrial processes	0.622	0.615	0.599	0.613	0.608	0.604	0.591	0.597	0.610
Chemical industries	0.067	0.068	0.068	0.073	0.074	0.074	0.072	0.075	0.075
Metals processing industries	0.147	0.137	0.131	0.141	0.142	0.140	0.136	0.137	0.141
Petroleum industries	0.032	0.031	0.030	0.029	0.028	0.028	0.028	0.027	0.026
Other industries	0.317	0.321	0.314	0.314	0.308	0.306	0.300	0.303	0.311
Solvent utilization	0.002	0.002	0.002	0.002	0.002	0.002	0.002	0.002	0.002
Storage and transport	0.057	0.056	0.054	0.054	0.054	0.054	0.053	0.053	0.055
Transportation	0.639	0.637	0.611	0.643	0.625	0.611	0.590	0.589	0.592
Highway vehicles	0.271	0.265	0.261	0.256	0.253	0.239	0.223	0.210	0.197
Off-highway vehicles	0.368	0.372	0.350	0.387	0.372	0.372	0.367	0.379	0.395
Other sources									
Waste disposal and recycling	0.279	0.275	0.265	0.259	0.251	0.242	0.245	0.246	0.248
Miscellaneous	0.000	0.000	0.000	0.000	0.000	0.000	0.000	0.000	0.000

Source: Executive Office of the President of the United States. *Environmental Quality 24: The Twenty-fourth Annual Report of the Council on Environmental Quality.* Prepared by Ray Clark. Written by Carroll Curtis. Edited by Barry Walsh. Washington, DC: U.S. Government Printing Office, 1994, p. 440. Primary source: U.S. Environmental Protection Agency. Office of Air Quality Planning and Standards. *National Air Quality and Emissions Trends Report, 1993.* EPA-454/R-94-026. Research Triangle Park, NC: U.S. Environmental Protection Agency, Office of Air Quality Planning and Standards, 1994, pp. 29, 35, 41, 46, 52-53, 57, tables 3-1 through 3-7. *Note:* Totals may not agree with detail because of independent rounding.

★ 29 ★

Air Pollution

Sulfur Dioxide Emissions, by Source: 1970-1993

Table shows U.S. emissions of sulfur dioxide air pollutants for selected sources. Sulfur dioxide is one of the six leading air pollutants.

[In million short tons]

Source	1970	1980	1984	1985	1986	1987	1988	1989	1990	1991	1992	1993
Fuel combustion	23.456	21.405	19.473	19.990	19.428	19.445	19.761	19.921	19.574	19.532	18.964	19.266
Electric utilities	17.398	17.483	16.023	16.273	15.701	15.715	15.990	16.218	15.898	15.784	15.417	15.836
Industrial	4.568	2.951	2.723	3.169	3.116	3.068	3.111	3.086	3.106	3.139	2.947	2.830
Other	1.490	0.971	0.728	0.578	0.611	0.663	0.660	0.623	0.597	0.608	0.600	0.600
Industrial processes	7.093	3.773	3.246	2.433	2.221	1.909	2.011	1.937	1.865	1.827	1.828	1.868
Chemical industries	0.591	0.280	0.229	0.456	0.432	0.425	0.449	0.440	0.440	0.442	0.447	0.460

[Continued]

★ 29 ★

Sulfur Dioxide Emissions, by Source: 1970-1993

[Continued]

Source	1970	1980	1984	1985	1986	1987	1988	1989	1990	1991	1992	1993
Metals processing industries	4.775	1.842	1.387	1.042	0.888	0.616	0.702	0.657	0.578	0.544	0.557	0.580
Petroleum industries	0.881	0.734	0.707	0.505	0.469	0.445	0.443	0.429	0.440	0.444	0.417	0.409
Other industries	0.846	0.918	0.923	0.425	0.427	0.418	0.411	0.405	0.401	0.391	0.401	0.413
Solvent utilization	0.000	0.000	0.000	0.001	0.001	0.001	0.001	0.001	0.001	0.001	0.001	0.001
Storage and transport	0.000	0.000	0.000	0.004	0.004	0.004	0.005	0.005	0.005	0.005	0.005	0.005
Transportation	0.658	0.989	0.643	0.654	0.670	0.690	0.721	0.747	0.745	0.744	0.756	0.718
Highway vehicles	0.279	0.458	0.445	0.446	0.449	0.457	0.468	0.480	0.480	0.478	0.483	0.438
Off-highway vehicles	0.379	0.531	0.198	0.208	0.221	0.233	0.253	0.267	0.265	0.266	0.273	0.278
Other sources												
Waste disposal and recycling	0.008	0.033	0.025	0.034	0.035	0.035	0.036	0.036	0.036	0.036	0.037	0.037
Miscellaneous	0.010	0.011	0.009	0.007	0.007	0.007	0.007	0.007	0.014	0.011	0.010	0.011

Source: Executive Office of the President of the United States. *Environmental Quality 24: The Twenty-fourth Annual Report of the Council on Environmental Quality.* Prepared by Ray Clark. Written by Carroll Curtis. Edited by Barry Walsh. Washington, DC: U.S. Government Printing Office, 1994, p. 435. Primary source: U.S. Environmental Protection Agency. Office of Air Quality Planning and Standards. *National Air Quality and Emissions Trends Report, 1993.* EPA-454/ R-94-026. Research Triangle Park, NC: U.S. Environmental Protection Agency, Office of Air Quality Planning and Standards, 1994, pp. 29, 35, 41, 46, 52-53, 57, tables 3-1 through 3-7. *Note:* Totals may not agree with detail because of independent rounding.

★ 30 ★
Air Pollution
Sulfur Emission Targets, by European Country: 1980-2010

Germany - 83
Finland - 80
Austria - 80
Denmark - 80
Sweden - 80
Netherlands - 77
Norway - 76
France - 74
Belgium - 70
Italy - 65
European Community - 62
Luxembourg - 58
Switzerland - 52
United Kingdom - 50
Spain - 35
Ireland - 30
Greece - 0
Portugal - 0

Chart shows data from column 6.

Table shows the targeted levels to the year 2010 for sulfur emissions in European countries. The push to reduce emissions has precipitated a change from oil and solid fuels to gas, threatening the closure of European refineries. Increased use also may necessitate importing gas at increasing prices.

[In 1,000 metric tons/year, except as noted]

Country	SO$_2$ emission level		SO$_2$ emission ceiling			Percent reduction from 1980		
	1980	1990	2000	2005	2010	2000	2005	2010
European Community	25,513	-	9,598	-	-	62	-	-
Austria	397	90	78	-	-	80	-	-
Belgium	828	443	248	232	215	70	72	74
Denmark	451	180	90	-	-	80	-	-
Finland	584	260	116	-	-	80	-	-
France	3,348	1,202	868	770	737	74	77	78
Germany	7,494	5,803	1,300	990	-	83	87	-
Greece	400	510	595	580	570	0[1]	3	4
Ireland	222	168	155	-	-	30	-	-
Italy	3,800	-	1,330	1,042	-	65	73	-
Luxembourg	24	-	10	-	-	58	-	-
Netherlands	466	207	106	-	-	77	-	-
Norway	142	54	34	-	-	76	-	-
Portugal	266	284	304	294	-	0[1]	3	-
Spain	3,319	2,316	2,143	-	-	35	-	-
Sweden	507	130	100	-	-	80	-	-

[Continued]

★ 30 ★

Sulfur Emission Targets, by European Country: 1980-2010

[Continued]

Country	SO$_2$ emission level		SO$_2$ emission ceiling			Percent reduction from 1980		
	1980	1990	2000	2005	2010	2000	2005	2010
Switzerland	126	62	60	-	-	52	-	-
United Kingdom	4,898	3,780	2,449	1,470	980	50	70	80

Source: "Warning Sounded on European Emissions Cutback." *Oil & Gas Journal*, 1 August 1994, p. 24. Primary source: Europia. *Notes:* "-" indicates data not available in source material. 1. Base year is 2000.

★ 31 ★

Air Pollution

Toxic Chemical Air Emissions, by Substance: 1991

Table shows the top 10 toxic chemical air emissions for the United States in 1991.

[In million pounds]

Chemical	Amount released
Methanol	199.7
Toluene	198.6
Ammonia	188.6
Acetone	160.2
Methyl chloroform	137.5
Xylenes	155.6
Carbon disulfide	89.3
Hydrochloric acid	82.9
Methylena chloride	79.3

Source: "Top 10 U.S. Toxic Chemical Air Emissions." *Water Environment & Technology* (March 1995), p. 15. Primary source: 1991 EPA Toxic Release Inventory. *Note:* 1 pound equals 2.7 kilograms.

★ 32 ★

Air Pollution

Volatile Organic Compound Emissions, by Source: 1970-1993

Table shows U.S. emissions of volatile organic compounds air pollutants for selected sources. Volatile organic compounds are one of the six leading air pollutants.

[In million short tons]

Source	1970	1980	1984	1985	1986	1987	1988	1989	1990	1991	1992	1993
Fuel combustion	0.722	1.050	1.118	0.788	0.787	0.765	0.778	0.755	0.739	0.732	0.691	0.648
Electric utilities	0.030	0.045	0.045	0.032	0.034	0.034	0.037	0.037	0.036	0.036	0.035	0.036
Industrial	0.150	0.157	0.156	0.248	0.254	0.249	0.271	0.266	0.266	0.270	0.271	0.271
Other	0.541	0.848	0.917	0.508	0.499	0.482	0.470	0.452	0.437	0.426	0.385	0.341
Industrial processes	12.326	12.103	11.402	10.506	10.399	10.637	10.657	10.938	10.982	11.000	11.051	11.201
Chemical industries	1.341	1.595	1.620	1.579	1.640	1.633	1.752	1.748	1.771	1.778	1.799	1.811
Metals processing industries	0.394	0.273	0.182	0.076	0.073	0.070	0.074	0.074	0.072	0.069	0.072	0.074
Petroleum industries	1.194	1.440	1.253	0.797	0.764	0.752	0.733	0.731	0.737	0.745	0.729	0.720
Other industries	0.270	0.237	0.227	0.439	0.445	0.460	0.479	0.476	0.478	0.475	0.482	0.486
Solvent utilization	7.174	6.584	6.309	5.779	5.710	5.828	6.034	6.053	6.063	6.064	6.121	6.249
Storage and transport	1.954	1.975	1.810	1.836	1.767	1.893	1.948	1.856	1.861	1.868	1.848	1.861
Transportation	13.611	13.305	11.414	11.384	10.913	10.239	10.396	9.295	9.397	8.622	8.232	8.301
Highway vehicles	12.219	10.990	9.441	9.376	8.874	8.201	8.290	7.192	6.854	6.499	6.072	6.094
Off-highway vehicles	1.392	2.315	1.973	2.008	2.039	2.038	2.106	2.103	2.120	2.123	2.160	2.207
Other sources												
Waste disposal and recycling	1.984	0.758	0.687	2.310	2.293	2.256	2.310	2.290	2.262	2.217	2.266	2.271
Miscellaneous	1.101	1.134	0.951	0.428	0.435	0.440	0.458	0.453	1.320	0.937	0.780	0.893

Source: Executive Office of the President of the United States. *Environmental Quality 24: The Twenty-fourth Annual Report of the Council on Environmental Quality.* Prepared by Ray Clark. Written by Carroll Curtis. Edited by Barry Walsh. Washington, DC: U.S. Government Printing Office, 1994, p. 435. Primary source: U.S. Environmental Protection Agency. Office of Air Quality Planning and Standards. *National Air Quality and Emissions Trends Report, 1993.* EPA-454/R-94-026. Research Triangle Park, NC: U.S. Environmental Protection Agency, Office of Air Quality Planning and Standards, 1994, pp. 29, 35, 41, 46, 52-53, 57, tables 3-1 through 3-7. *Note:* Totals may not agree with detail because of independent rounding.

Air Quality

★ 33 ★

Air Quality Levels Above National Ambient Air Quality Standards: 1984-1993

Ozone - 51.3

Carbon monoxide - 11.6

Particulates - 9.4

Lead - 5.5

Sulfur dioxide - 1.4

Nitrogen oxide - 0.0

Chart shows data from column 10.

Table shows the number of people living in counties with air quality levels above the National Ambient Air Quality Standards. Particulates for 1984 through 1986 refer to total suspended particulates. After 1986, particulates refer to PM-10; that is, particulates less than 10 micrometers in diameter.

[In million persons]

Pollutant	1984	1985	1986	1987	1988	1989	1990	1991	1992	1993
Sulfur dioxide	1.7	2.2	0.9	1.6	1.7	0.1	1.4	5.2	0.0	1.4
Nitrogen oxide	7.5	7.5	7.5	7.5	8.3	8.5	8.5	8.9	0.0	0.0
Carbon monoxide	61.3	39.6	41.4	29.4	29.5	33.6	21.7	19.9	14.3	11.6
Ozone	79.2	76.4	75.0	88.6	111.9	66.7	62.9	69.7	44.6	51.3
Lead	4.7	4.5	4.5	1.7	1.6	1.6	5.3	14.7	4.7	5.5
Particulates	32.6	47.8	41.7	21.5	25.6	27.4	18.8	21.5	25.8	9.4

Source: Executive Office of the President of the United States. *Environmental Quality 24: The Twenty-fourth Annual Report of the Council on Environmental Quality.* Prepared by Ray Clark. Written by Carroll Curtis. Edited by Barry Walsh. Washington, DC: U.S. Government Printing Office, 1994, p. 447. Primary sources: U.S. Environmental Protection Agency. Office of Air Quality Planning and Standards. *National Air Quality and Emissions Trends Report, 1993.* EPA-454/R-94-026. Research Triangle Park, NC: U.S. Environmental Protection Agency, Office of Air Quality Planning and Standards, October 1994; and earlier reports.

★ 34 ★
Air Quality

Air Quality Trends, by Major Urban Area: 1980-1993

Total - 275

Los Angeles, California - 169

Houston, Texas - 30

San Diego, California - 19

El Paso, Texas - 11

Phoenix, Arizona - 8

Denver, Colorado - 7

Chicago, Illinois - 6

Atlanta, Georgia - 4

Baltimore, Maryland - 4

New York, New York - 4

Philadelphia, Pennsylvania - 3

St. Louis. Missouri - 2

Dallas, Texas - 2

Washington, District of Columbia - 2

Boston, Massachusetts - 1

Pittsburgh, Pennsylvania - 1

Kansas City, Missouri - 1

Minneapolis-St. Paul, Minnesota - 1

Miami, Florida - 0

Detroit, Michigan - 0

Seattle, Washington - 0

Cleveland, Ohio - 0

San Francisco, California - 0

Chart shows data from column 9.

The PSI [Pollutant Standards Index] integrates information from many pollutants across an entire monitoring network into a single number that represents the worst daily air quality experienced in the urban area. Only carbon monoxide and ozone monitoring sites with adequate historical data are included in the PSI trend analysis, except for Pittsburgh, where sulfur dioxide contributed a significant number of days in the PSI high range. PSI index ranges and health effect descriptor words are as follows: 0 to 50 (good); 51 to 100 (moderate); 101 to 199 (unhealthful); 200 to 299 (very unhealthful); and 300 and above (hazardous). The table above shows the number of days when the PSI was greater than 100 (unhealthy or worse days).

PMSA	PSI days greater than 100									
	1984	1985	1986	1987	1988	1989	1990	1991	1992	1993
Atlanta, Georgia	8	9	17	19	15	3	16	5	4	14
Baltimore, Maryland	46	21	24	28	41	7	12	20	4	12
Boston, Massachusetts	7	3	2	5	12	2	1	3	1	3
Chicago, Illinois	12	8	9	15	21	3	3	8	6	1
Cleveland, Ohio	4	1	2	7	20	4	1	5	0	1
Dallas, Texas	11	15	5	8	3	3	5	0	2	4
Denver, Colorado	62	38	47	36	19	11	7	7	7	3

[Continued]

★ 34 ★

Air Quality Trends, by Major Urban Area: 1980-1993
[Continued]

PMSA	PSI days greater than 100									
	1984	1985	1986	1987	1988	1989	1990	1991	1992	1993
Detroit, Michigan	7	2	5	9	17	10	3	7	0	2
El Paso, Texas	20	24	34	27	13	29	20	8	11	5
Houston, Texas	49	48	45	55	48	34	48	40	30	26
Kansas City, Missouri	12	3	4	3	3	2	2	1	1	2
Los Angeles, California	204	194	211	134	226	212	163	157	169	131
Miami, Florida	2	5	4	4	4	4	1	2	0	0
Minneapolis-St. Paul, Minnesota	21	21	13	7	1	5	1	0	1	0
New York, New York	96	61	53	41	43	16	17	22	4	6
Philadelphia, Pennsylvania	31	25	21	36	34	19	11	24	3	20
Phoenix, Arizona	107	84	85	40	22	30	8	4	8	6
Pittsburgh, Pennsylvania	15	9	8	13	23	9	11	3	1	5
San Diego, California	51	54	45	41	49	61	39	25	19	14
San Francisco, California	2	5	4	1	1	0	1	0	0	0
Seattle, Washington	4	24	10	10	6	4	2	0	0	0
St. Louis, Missouri	22	10	13	14	17	12	8	6	2	5
Washington, District of Columbia	30	15	12	25	36	7	5	16	2	12
Total	853	679	673	578	674	487	385	363	275	272

Source: Executive Office of the President of the United States. *Environmental Quality 24: The Twenty-fourth Annual Report of the Council on Environmental Quality.* Prepared by Ray Clark. Written by Carroll Curtis. Edited by Barry Walsh. Washington, DC: U.S. Government Printing Office, 1994, p. 446. Primary source: U.S. Environmental Protection Agency. Office of Air Quality Planning and Standards. *National Air Quality and Emissions Trends Report, 1993.* EPA-450/R-94-026. Research Triangle Park, NC: U.S. Environmental Protection Agency, Office of Air Quality Planning and Standards, October 1992. *Note:* "PMSA" stands for "primary metropolitan statistical area."

★ 35 ★
Air Quality

National Ambient Air Quality Standard Excesses for Carbon Monoxide, by Metropolitan Area: 1987-1992

Table shows the number of days that selected metropolitan areas exceeded national ambient air quality standards for carbon monoxide. Areas generally represent the officially defined metropolitan area, but may, in some cases, not have all the counties identified as part of the area. Nonattainment status was as of November 2, 1993.

Metropolitan area	1987	1988	1989	1990	1991	1992
Albuquerque, New Mexico	14	5	6	3	2	0
Anchorage, Alaska	4	2	3	12	3	2
Baltimore, Maryland	1	2	0	1	0	0
Boston, Massachusetts; Lawrence, Massachusetts; Salem, Massachusetts[1]	2[2]	2[2]	0	0	0	0
Chico, California	0	2	1	1	0	0
Cleveland, Ohio; Akron, Ohio; Lorain, Ohio[1]	2[2]	2[2]	1	0	0	0
Colorado Springs, Colorado	1	2	1	0	0	0

[Continued]

★ 35 ★

National Ambient Air Quality Standard Excesses for Carbon Monoxide, by Metropolitan Area: 1987-1992
[Continued]

Metropolitan area	1987	1988	1989	1990	1991	1992
Denver, Colorado; Boulder, Colorado[1]	24	10	6	3	4	7
Duluth, Minnesota	(NA)	0	2	0	0	0
El Paso, Texas	11	3	5	4	3	3
Fairbanks, Alaska[3]	18	10	3	2	3	2
Fort Collins, Colorado	5	3	1	0	2	0
Fresno, California	3	4	13	1	1	0
Grant Pass, Oregon	(NA)	(NA)	(NA)	1	0	0
Greensboro, North Carolina; Winston-Salem, North Carolina	(NA)	(NA)	(NA)	0	0	0
Hartford, Connecticut[1]	7	3	1	0	1	1
Klamath County, Oregon[3]	(NA)	3	2	0	1	0
Lake Tahoe South Shore, California[3]	(NA)	(NA)	(NA)	5	0	1
Las Vegas, Nevada	4	26	26	17	6	2
Longmont, Colorado[3]	(NA)	(NA)	(NA)	0	0	0
Los Angeles, California; Anaheim, California; Riverside, California[1]	48	71	72	47	41	35
Medford, Oregon	3	2	15	0	3	0
Memphis, Tennessee	3	0	2	1	0	1
Minneapolis, Minnesota; St. Paul, Minnesota	5	8	2	1	2	0
Missoula County, Montana[3]	4	2	2	1	5	0
Modesto, California	0	2	8	2	1	0
New York, New York; Northern New Jersey; Long Island, New York[1]	69	26	16	4	2	2
Ogden, Utah	(NA)	(NA)	(NA)	3	0	0
Philadelphia, Pennsylvania Wilmington, Delaware; Trenton, New Jersey[1]	(NA)	0	2	0	0	0
Phoenix, Arizona	24[2]	11	9	4	3	5
Portland, Oregon; Vancouver, Washington[1]	4	3	2	2	2	0
Provo, Utah; Orem, Utah	20	5	12	11	6	3
Raleigh, North Carolina; Durham, North Carolina	2	2	2	2	0	0
Reno, Nevada	1	3	2	7	2	0
Sacramento, California	12	6	18	11	5	0
San Diego, California	0	2	4	0	0	0
San Francisco, California; Oakland, California; San Jose, California[1]	1	2	6	2	4	0
Seattle, Washington; Tacoma, Washington[1]	9	3	2	2	1	1

[Continued]

★ 35 ★

National Ambient Air Quality Standard Excesses for Carbon Monoxide, by Metropolitan Area: 1987-1992

[Continued]

Metropolitan area	1987	1988	1989	1990	1991	1992
Spokane, Washington	66	37	11	6	13	6
Stockton, California	(NA)	1	4	2	1	0
Washington, District of Columbia	2	2[4]	1	0	0	0

Source: 1994 Statistical Abstract of the United States on CD-ROM [machine-readable datafiles]. CD-8A-94. Washington, DC: U.S. Department of Commerce, Economics and Statistics Administration, Bureau of the Census, Data User Services Division, January 1995. *Notes:* "NA" indicates "not available." 1. Consolidated metropolitan statistical area (CMSA). 2. 1986 data. 3. Not a metropolitan area. 4. 1987 data.

★ 36 ★

Air Quality

National Ambient Air Quality Standard Excesses for Ozone, by Metropolitan Area: 1987-1992

Table shows the number of days that selected metropolitan areas exceeded national ambient air quality standards for ozone. Areas generally represent the officially defined metropolitan area, but may, in some cases, not have all the counties identified as part of the area. Nonattainment status was as of November 2, 1993.

Metropolitan area	1990-1992 average	1988	1989	1990	1991	1992[1]
Albany, New York Schenectady, New York; Troy, New York	0.6	4.0	0.0	0.0	1.1	0.0
Allentown, Pennsylvania; Bethlehem, Pennsylvania	0.3	10.1	0.0	0.0	0.0	0.0
Altoona, Pennsylvania	0.0	4.0	0.0	0.0	0.0	0.0
Atlanta, Georgia	4.4	13.2	0.0	11.3	4.0	2.2
Atlantic City, New Jersey	2.8	6.0	1.1	5.3	2.1	1.0
Baltimore, Maryland	4.9	19.3	2.7	5.6	8.2	2.0
Baton Rouge, Louisiana	5.1	6.3	3.0	6.1	2.0	2.0
Beaumont, Texas; Port Arthur, Texas	3.6	6.8	7.9	3.2	6.0	2.1
Birmingham, Alabama	2.1	2.0	0.0	4.1	0.0	0.0
Boston, Massachusetts; Lawrence, Massachusetts; Salem, Massachusetts[2]	2.9	11.4	2.0	2.0	7.6	2.2
Buffalo, New York; Niagra Falls, New York[3]	0.0	8.3	1.0	0.0	0.0	0.0
Canton, Ohio	0.3	5.2	0.0	0.0	1.0	0.0
Charleston, West Virginia	0.3	7.0	0.0	0.0	1.0	0.0
Charlotte, North Carolina; Gastonia, North Carolina; Rock Hill, South Carolina[4]	0.3	7.1	2.2	1.0	1.0	0.0

[Continued]

★ 36 ★

National Ambient Air Quality Standard Excesses for Ozone, by Metropolitan Area: 1987-1992

[Continued]

Metropolitan area	1990-1992 average	1988	1989	1990	1991	1992[1]
Chicago, Illinois; Gary, Indiana; Lake County, Illinois[3]	4.7	16.2	4.7	2.3	11.8	2.4
Cincinnati, Ohio; Hamilton, Ohio[3]	2.3	14.1	1.1	4.0	3.0	0.0
Cleveland, Ohio; Akron, Ohio; Lorain, Ohio[3]	2.0	13.3	4.0	1.2	2.0	2.0
Columbus, Ohio	0.7	4.0	0.0	1.0	1.0	0.0
Dallas, Texas; Fort Worth, Texas[3]	3.1	4.3	2.3	4.0	4.2	2.7
Dayton, Ohio; Springfield, Ohio	0.0	6.2	2.0	0.0	0.0	0.0
Detroit, Michigan; Ann Arbor, Michigan[3]	1.0	4.1	4.0	0.0	3.0	0.0
Door County, Wisconsin[5]	2.7	(NA)	0.0	3.5	4.0	0.0
Edmonson County, Kentucky[5]	0.0	5.2	(NA)	0.0	0.0	0.0
El Paso, Texas	3.7	5.4	7.2	4.1	3.2	5.1
Erie, Pennsylvania	0.0	6.1	0.0	0.0	0.0	0.0
Essex County, New York[5]	2.1	5.4	0.0	0.0	3.7	0.0
Evansville, Indiana	0.0	2.1	1.1	0.0	0.0	0.0
Grand Rapids, Michigan	3.4	7.0	2.0	2.0	2.0	0.0
Greater Connecticut, Connecticut[6]	8.3	10.0	5.1	6.1	17.3	4.0
Greenbrier County, West Virginia[5]	0.4	4.1	0.0	0.0	1.1	0.0
Hancock and Waldo County, Maine[5]	1.3	12.0	1.0	0.0	2.5	0.0
Harrisburg, Pennsylvania; Lebanon, Pennsylvania; Carlisle, Pennsylvania	0.3	6.9	0.0	1.0	0.0	0.0
Houston, Texas; Galveston, Texas; Brazoria, Texas[3]	13.0	8.3	14.2	24.0	16.6	6.9
Huntington, West Virginia; Ashland, Kentucky	1.5	10.4	1.0	4.6	3.1	0.0
Indianapolis, Indiana	0.3	2.1	1.0	1.0	0.0	0.0
Jefferson County, New York[5]	0.0	6.1	0.0	0.0	0.0	0.0
Jersey County, Illinois[5]	0.7	7.4	0.0	2.0	0.0	0.0
Johnstown, Pennsylvania	0.0	7.4	0.0	0.0	0.0	0.0
Kent County and Queen Anne's County, Maryland[5]	2.4	(NA)	2.2	1.0	6.3	0.0
Kewaunee County, Wisconsin[5]	0.8	10.6	0.0	0.0	2.1	0.0
Knox County and Lincoln County, Maine[5]	2.8	15.6	1.2	1.3	7.0	0.0
Lake Charles, Louisiana	1.5	3.0	2.0	2.0	1.0	1.3
Lancaster, Pennsylvania	0.0	3.0	0.0	0.0	0.0	0.0
Lewiston, Maine; Auburn, Maine	0.5	1.5	1.0	0.0	1.0	0.0

[Continued]

★ 36 ★

National Ambient Air Quality Standard Excesses for Ozone, by Metropolitan Area: 1987-1992
[Continued]

Metropolitan area	1990-1992 average	1988	1989	1990	1991	1992[1]
Lexington, Kentucky;						
Fayette, Kentucky	0.3	5.0	0.0	1.0	0.0	0.0
Louisville, Kentucky	1.8	7.3	1.0	2.1	3.4	0.0
Los Angeles South Coast						
Air, California[7]	106.1	148.0	121.7	103.6	91.0	124.4
Manchester, New Hampshire	1.0	2.0	0.0	1.0	(NA)	0.0
Manitowoc County, Wisconsin	2.8	15.5	1.2	2.3	5.1	0.0
Memphis, Tennessee	0.0	4.1	1.0	0.0	0.0	0.0
Miami, Florida;						
Fort Lauderdale, Florida[3]	0.3	3.0	0.0	1.0	0.0	0.0
Milwaukee, Wisconsin;						
Racine, Wisconsin[3]	4.7	14.2	7.1	2.3	10.2	2.4
Monterey Bay, California[8]	0.4	1.0	1.1	0.0	1.1	0.0
Muskegon, Michigan	3.0	12.1	5.1	3.1	4.8	1.0
Nashville, Tennessee	2.3	11.7	2.0	5.8	1.1	0.0
New York, New York;						
Northern New Jersey;						
Long Island, New York[9]	3.4	19.4	10.4	5.1	13.3	2.0
Norfolk, Virginia;						
Virginia Beach, Virginia;						
Newport News, Virginia	0.7	4.0	0.0	0.0	1.0	2.0
Owensboro, Kentucky	1.0	10.2	0.0	3.0	0.0	0.0
Paducah, Kentucky[5]	0.0	3.3	0.0	0.0	0.0	0.0
Parkersburg, West Virginia;						
Marietta, Ohio	0.0	17.0	0.0	0.0	1.0	0.0
Philadelphia, Pennsylvania;						
Wilmington, Delaware;						
Trenton, New Jersey[3]	8.4	18.2	3.1	5.0	10.3	4.1
Phoenix, Arizona	9.4	1.1	2.0	6.0	0.0	9.6
Pittsburgh, Pennsylvania;						
Beaver Valley, Pennsylvania[3]	0.6	14.8	2.0	0.0	0.0	0.0
Portland, Oregon;						
Vancouver, Washington[3]	2.4	2.4	0.0	4.2	1.4	1.5
Portland, Maine	4.5	11.2	4.0	6.3	4.8	2.3
Portsmouth, New Hampshire;						
Dover, New Hampshire;						
Rochester, New Hampshire	2.1	11.1	2.0	1.0	3.2	0.0
Poughkeepsie, New York	1.1	4.0	0.0	0.0	2.1	0.0
Providence, Rhode Island[10]	5.5	8.5	2.6	6.0	9.5	1.0
Raleigh, North Carolina;						
Durham, North Carolina	0.0	10.2	3.0	0.0	0.0	0.0
Reading, Pennsylvania	0.3	9.2	0.0	0.0	1.0	0.0
Reno, Nevada	1.4	0.0	0.0	4.1	0.0	0.0
Richmond, Virginia;						
Petersburg, Virginia	0.7	9.2	0.0	1.0	0.0	1.1

[Continued]

★ 36 ★

National Ambient Air Quality Standard Excesses for Ozone, by Metropolitan Area: 1987-1992
[Continued]

Metropolitan area	1990-1992 average	1988	1989	1990	1991	1992[1]
Sacramento, California	6.1	15.5	9.8	6.1	15.7	7.1
St. Louis, Missouri	1.4	7.3	2.1	2.1	1.0	2.0
Salt Lake City, Utah; Ogden, Utah	0.3	2.2	2.9	1.0	0.0	0.0
San Diego, California	7.3	7.1	16.5	26.0	7.1	6.1
San Joaquin Valley, California	22.6	2.0	0.0	24.5	33.9	17.5
San Francisco, California; Oakland, California; San Jose, California[3]	2.8	4.1	2.0	1.0	1.0	0.0
Santa Barbara, California; Santa Maria, California; Lompoc, California	1.3	0.0	2.0	2.0	4.1	2.0
Scranton, Pennsylvania; Wilkes-Barre, Pennsylvania	0.6	8.1	0.0	0.0	2.0	0.0
Seattle, Washington; Tacoma, Washington	1.1	0.0	0.0	3.3	0.0	0.0
Sheboygan, Wisconsin	3.2	15.5	1.2	0.0	7.5	0.0
Smyth County, Virginia[5]	(NA)	4.8	0.0	(NA)	(NA)	(NA)
South Bend, Indiana; Mishawaka, Indiana	0.0	3.2	0.0	0.0	0.0	0.0
Southeast Desert Modified Air Quality Management District (AQMD), California[11]	52.9	64.9	60.8	43.0	32.1	57.8
Springfield, Massachusetts	3.6	13.4	3.0	3.0	5.7	2.0
Sussex County, Delaware[5]	1.4	9.9	0.0	1.1	3.1	0.0
Tampa, Florida; St. Petersburg, Florida; Clearwater, Florida	0.5	0.0	0.0	0.0	0.0	0.0
Toledo, Ohio	0.0	6.2	1.0	0.0	0.0	0.0
Ventura County, California	17.6	53.0	40.3	14.0	32.6	6.2
Walworth County, Wisconsin	0.3	3.0	1.0	0.0	1.0	0.0
Washington, District of Columbia	2.4	13.8	2.0	3.4	6.1	1.1
York, Pennsylvania	0.3	4.6	0.0	1.0	0.0	0.0
Youngstown, Ohio; Warren, Ohio[12]	0.3	5.4	0.0	0.0	1.0	0.0

Source: *1994 Statistical Abstract of the United States on CD-ROM* [machine-readable datafiles]. CD-8A-94. Washington, DC: U.S. Department of Commerce, Economics and Statistics Administration, Bureau of the Census, Data User Services Division, January 1995. Primary source: U.S. Environmental Protection Agency. *Notes:* "NA" indicates "not available." 1. May represent a different monitoring location than one used to calculate average. 2. Consolidated metropolitan statistical area (CMSA). Includes both the Worcester, Massachusetts, and New Bedford, Massachusetts, metropolitan statistical areas (MSAs). 3. Consolidated metropolitan statistical area (CMSA). 4. Excludes York County, South Carolina. 5. Not a metropolitan area. 6. Primarily represents Hartford-New Haven area. 7. Primarily represents Los Angeles and Orange counties. 8. Primarily represents Monterey, Santa Cruz, and San Benito counties. 9. Consolidated metropolitan statistical area (CMSA). Excludes the Connecticut portion. 10. Covers entire State of Rhode Island. 11. Represents primarily San Joaquin, Turlock, Merced, Madera, Fresno, Kings, Tulare, and Kern counties. 12. Includes Sharon, Pennsylvania.

★ 37 ★

Air Quality

Unhealthy Air Pollution Levels, by City

Los Angeles, California - 70

Houston, Texas - 36

San Diego, California - 14

New York, New York - 13

Baton Rouge, Louisiana - 10

Fresno, California - 10

Phoenix, Arizona - 8

Sacramento, California - 6

Dallas-Fort Worth, Texas - 5

El Paso, Texas - 4

Philadelphia, Pennsylvania - 4

Table shows the cities reporting the most days of unhealthy air pollution levels.

City	Days
Los Angeles, California	70
Houston, Texas	36
San Diego, California	14
New York, New York	13
Baton Rouge, Louisiana	10
Fresno, California	10
Phoenix, Arizona	8
Sacramento, California	6
Dallas-Fort Worth, Texas	5
El Paso, Texas	4
Philadelphia, Pennsylvania	4

Source: "Cities That Failed to Meet Air Quality Standards for Ozone." *Philadelphia Business Journal* 12, no. 18 (5 July 1993), p. 38B. Primary source: *1993 Information Please Environmental Almanac.*

Rivers

★ 38 ★

River Flows

Table shows the flows of the largest U.S. rivers. Data include length, discharge, and drainage area for each river.

River	Location of mouth	Name and location of source stream	Length (miles)[1]	Average discharge at mouth (1,000 cubic feet per square per second)	Drainage area (1,000 square miles)
Mississippi River	Louisiana	Mississippi River (Minnesota)	2,340[2]	593[3]	1,150[4]
St. Lawrence River	Canada	North River (Minnesota)	1,900	348	396[5]
Ohio River	Illinois-Kentucky	Allegheny River (Pennsylvania)	1,310	281	203
Columbia River	Oregon-Washington	Columbia River (Canada)	1,240	265	258[5]
Yukon River	Alaska	McNeil River (Canada)	1,980	225	328[5]
Missouri River	Missouri	Red Rock Creek (Montana)	2,540	76.2	529[5]
Tennessee River	Kentucky	Courthouse Creek (North Carolina)	886	68	40.9
Mobile River	Alabama	Tickanetley Creek (Georgia)	774	67.2	44.6
Kuskokwim River	Alaska	South Fork Kuskokwim River (Alaska)	724	67	48
Copper River	Alaska	Copper River (Alaska)	286	59	24.4
Atchafalaya River[6]	Louisiana	Tierra Blanca Creek (New Mexico)	1,420	58	95.1
Snake River	Washington	Snake River (Wyoming)	1,040	56.9	108
Red River	Louisiana	Tierra Blanca Creek (New Mexico)	1,290	56	93.2
Stikine River	Alaska	Stikine River (Canada)	379	56	20[5]
Susitna River	Alaska	Susitna River (Alaska)	313	51	20
Tanana River	Alaska	Nabesna River (Alaska)	659	41	44.5
Arkansas River	Arkansas	East Fork Arkansas River (Colorado)	1,460	41	161
Susquehanna River	Maryland	Hayden Creek (New York)	447	38.2	27.2
Willamette River	Oregon	Middle Fork Williamette River (Oregon)	309	37.4	11.4
Nushagak River	Alaska	Nushagak River (Alaska)	285	36	13.4
Alabama River	Alabama	Tickanetley Creek (Georgia)	729	34.6	22.8
Wabash River	Indiana-Illinois	Wabash River (Ohio)	512	31	32.9
White River	Arkansas	White River (Arkansas)	722	30.5	27.8
Pend Oreille River	Canada	Blacktail Creek (Montana)	531	30.4	26.3[5]
Alsek River	Alaska	Aishihik River (Canada)	290	30	10.7[5]

Source: 1994 Statistical Abstract of the United States on CD-ROM [machine-readable datafiles]. CD-8A-94. Washington, DC: U.S. Department of Commerce, Economics and Statistics Administration, Bureau of the Census, Data User Services Division, January 1995. Primary source: U.S. Geological Survey. *Largest Rivers in the United States: Open File Report 87-242* (August 1987). *Notes:* 1. From source to mouth. 2. The length from the source of the Missouri River to the Mississippi River and thence to the Gulf of Mexico is about 3,710 miles. 3. Includes about 167,000 cubic feet per second diverted from the Mississippi into the Atchafalaya rivers but excludes the flow of the Red River. 4. Excludes the drainage areas of the Red and Atchafalaya rivers; drainage area includes both the U.S. and Canada. 5. Drainage area includes both the U.S. and Canada. 6. In east-central Louisiana, the Red River flows into the Atchafalaya River, a distributary of the Mississippi River. Data on average discharge, length, and drainage area include the Red River, but exclude all water diverted into the Atchafalaya from the Mississippi River.

★ 39 ★
Rivers

River Impairment

There are approximately 3.5 million miles of rivers in the United States. Of the 642,881 river miles assessed, 221,871 were found to be impaired. Table shows U.S. sources of river impairment.

[In percentages]

Source	Assessed river miles impaired
Agriculture	72
Municipal discharges	15
Urban runoff/storm sewers	11
Mining	11
Industrial discharges	7
Silviculture	7
Hydrologic/habitat modification	7

Source: "U.S. Sources of River Impairment." *Water Environment & Technology* (September 1994), p. 18. Primary source: U.S. Environmental Protection Agency. *1992 National Water Quality Inventory.*

Water Area

★ 40 ★

Water Area, by State and Other Area: 1990

Table shows the water area of U.S. states and other entities. Excludes territorial water.

Region division, state, and other area	Total		Inland square miles	Coastal square miles	Great Lakes square miles
	Square miles	Square kilometers			
United States	181,184	469,267	78,641	42,491	60,052
Northeastern United States	14,344	37,151	6,145	3,549	4,650
New England	5,844	15,136	3,696	2,148	0
Maine	2,876	7,449	2,263	613	0
New Hampshire	314	813	314	0	0
Vermont	366	948	366	0	0
Massachusetts	1,403	3,634	424	979	0
Rhode Island	186	482	168	18	0
Connecticut	699	1,810	161	538	0

[Continued]

★ 40 ★

Water Area, by State and Other Area: 1990
[Continued]

Region division, state, and other area	Total		Inland square miles	Coastal square miles	Great Lakes square miles
	Square miles	Square kilometers			
Middle Atlantic United States	8,500	22,015	2,449	1,401	4,650
New York	6,765	17,521	1,888	976	3,901
New Jersey	796	2,062	371	425	0
Pennsylvania	939	2,432	190	0	749
Midwestern United States	70,245	181,935	14,843	0	55,402
East North Central United States	57,832	149,785	4,976	0	52,856
Ohio	3,875	10,036	376	0	3,499
Indiana	550	1,425	315	0	235
Illinois	2,325	6,022	750	0	1,575
Michigan	39,896	103,331	1,704	0	38,192
Wisconsin	11,186	28,972	1,831	0	9,355
West North Central United States	12,413	32,150	9,867	0	2,546
Minnesota	7,326	18,974	4,780	0	2,546
Iowa	401	1,039	401	0	0
Missouri	811	2,100	811	0	0
North Dakota	1,710	4,429	1,710	0	0
South Dakota	1,225	3,173	1,225	0	0
Nebraska	481	1,246	481	0	0
Kansas	459	1,189	459	0	0
Southern United States	36,167	93,673	27,354	8,813	0
South Atlantic United States	17,925	46,426	12,557	5,368	0
Delaware	442	1,145	71	371	0
Maryland	2,522	6,532	680	1,842	0
District of Columbia	7	18	7	0	0
Virginia	2,728	7,066	1,000	1,728	0
West Virginia	145	376	145	0	0
North Carolina	3,954	10,241	3,954	0	0
South Carolina	1,078	2,792	1,006	72	0
Georgia	1,058	2,740	1,011	47	0
Florida	5,991	15,517	4,683	1,308	0
East South Central United States	4,464	11,562	3,354	1,110	0
Kentucky	679	1,759	679	0	0
Tennessee	926	2,398	926	0	0
Alabama	1,487	3,851	968	519	0
Mississippi	1,372	3,553	781	591	0
West South Central United States	13,778	35,685	11,443	2,335	0
Arkansas	1,107	2,867	1,107	0	0
Louisiana	6,084	15,758	4,153	1,931	0
Oklahoma	1,224	3,170	1,224	0	0
Texas	5,363	13,890	4,959	404	0
Western United States	60,428	156,509	30,299	30,129	0
Mountain	7,493	19,407	7,493	0	0
Montana	1,490	3,859	1,490	0	0
Idaho	823	2,132	823	0	0

[Continued]

★ 40 ★

Water Area, by State and Other Area: 1990

[Continued]

Region division, state, and other area	Total		Inland square miles	Coastal square miles	Great Lakes square miles
	Square miles	Square kilometers			
Wyoming	714	1,849	714	0	0
Colorado	371	961	371	0	0
New Mexico	234	606	234	0	0
Arizona	364	943	364	0	0
Utah	2,736	7,086	2,736	0	0
Nevada	761	1,971	761	0	0
Pacific United States	52,935	137,102	22,806	30,129	0
Washington	4,056	10,505	1,545	2,511	0
Oregon	1,091	2,826	1,050	41	0
California	2,896	7,501	2,674	222	0
Alaska	44,856	116,177	17,501	27,355	0
Hawaii	36	93	36	0	0
Other areas:					
Puerto Rico	81	210	65	16	0
American Samoa	13	34	7	6	0
Guam	7	18	7	0	0
Northern Mariana Islands	10	26	2	8	0
Palau	64	166	40	24	0
Virgin Islands of the United States	37	96	17	20	0

Source: 1994 Statistical Abstract of the United States on CD-ROM [machine-readable datafiles]. CD-8A-94. Washington, DC: U.S. Department of Commerce, Economics and Statistics Administration, Bureau of the Census, Data User Services Division, January 1995. Primary sources: U.S. Bureau of the Census. *1990 Census of Population and Housing.* Series CPH-1, unpublished data. *Note:* One square mile equals 2.59 square kilometers.

★ 41 ★
Water Area

Water Areas for Alaskan Water Bodies: 1990

Table shows the areas of selected water bodies in Alaska. Includes only that portion of a body of water under the jurisdiction of the United States.

Body of water	Area	
	Square miles	Square kilometers
Chatham Strait	1,559	4,039
Prince William Sound	1,382	3,579
Clarence Strait	1,199	3,107
Iliamna Lake	1,022	2,646
Frederick Sound	792	2,051
Sumner Strait	791	2,048
Stephens Passage	702	1,819
Kvichak Bay	640	1,659

[Continued]

★ 41 ★

Water Areas for Alaskan Water Bodies: 1990

[Continued]

Body of water	Area	
	Square miles	Square kilometers
Montague Strait	463	1,198
Becharof Lake	447	1,158
Icy Strait	436	1,130
Hotham Inlet	433	1,120
Selawik Lake	403	1,044
Nushagak Bay	393	1,018
Baird Inlet	348	902
Yakutat Bay	345	894
Teshekpuk Lake	324	839
Behm Canal	324	839
Turnagain Arm	322	834
Kachemak Bay	310	803
Glacier Bay	310	803
Stefansson Sound	301	780
Revillagigedo Channel	295	764
Kasegaluk Lagoon	293	759
Cordova Bay	241	623
Sitka Sound	229	593
Naknek Lake	225	582
Eschscholtz Bay	210	543
Stepovak Bay	206	534
Keku Strait	206	534
Port Clarence	187	486
Orca Bay	184	476
Knik Arm	169	437
Dall Lake	167	433
Knight Island Passage	167	432
Scammon Bay	163	423
Port Moller	159	412
Ernest Sound	158	410
Spafarief Bay	157	405
Pavlov Bay	153	396
Shishmaref Inlet	153	395
Smith Bay	140	363
Seymour Canal	140	361
Sitkalidak Strait	135	349
Tlevak Strait	135	349
Lake Clark	130	336
Lynn Canal	130	336
Chignik Bay	119	309
Elson Lagoon	119	309
Bucareli Bay	119	307
Hinchinbrook Entrance	118	306
Unga Strait	117	304
Tustumena Lake	115	297

[Continued]

★ 41 ★

Water Areas for Alaskan Water Bodies: 1990
[Continued]

Body of water	Area	
	Square miles	Square kilometers
Admiralty Bay	110	286
Port Wells	109	282
Cold Bay	109	281
Icy Bay	105	271
Peril Strait	102	265
Alitak Bay	98	254
Resurrection Bay	97	252
Peard Bay	95	247
Herendeen Bay	95	245
Izembek Lagoon	93	242
Golovnin Bay	88	228
Port Heiden	88	227
Cross Sound	87	224
Bechevin Bay	86	224
Imuruk Basin	84	217
Gulf of Esquibel	83	215
Felice Strait	83	214
Chinak Bay	81	209
Upper Ugashik Lake	80	208
Kujulik Bay	79	204
Morzhovoi Bay	79	204
Controller Bay	75	195

Source: 1994 Statistical Abstract of the United States on CD-ROM [machine-readable datafiles]. CD-8A-94. Washington, DC: U.S. Department of Commerce, Economics and Statistics Administration, Bureau of the Census, Data User Services Division, January 1995. Primary source: U. S. Bureau of the Census. Unpublished data. *Note:* One square mile equals 2.59 square kilometers.

★ 42 ★

Water Area

Water Areas for Atlantic Coast Water Bodies: 1990

Table shows the areas of selected water bodies and their states. Includes only that portion of a body of water under the jurisdiction of the United States, excluding Hawaii.

Body of water	State	Area	
		Square miles	Square kilometers
Chesapeake Bay	Maryland; Virginia	2,747	7,115
Pamlico Sound	North Carolina	1,622	4,200
Long Island Sound	Connecticut; New York	914	2,368
Delaware Bay	Delaware; New Jersey	614	1,591
Cape Cod Bay	Massachusetts	598	1,548

[Continued]

★ 42 ★

Water Areas for Atlantic Coast Water Bodies: 1990
[Continued]

Body of water	State	Area Square miles	Area Square kilometers
Albemarle Sound	North Carolina	492	1,274
Biscayne Bay	Florida	218	565
Buzzards Bay	Massachusetts	215	558
Tangier Sound	Maryland; Virginia	172	445
Currituck Sound	North Carolina	116	301
Pocomoke Sound	Maryland; Virginia	111	286
Chincoteague Bay	Maryland; Virginia	105	272
Great South Bay	New York	94	243
Core Sound	North Carolina	88	229

Source: 1994 Statistical Abstract of the United States on CD-ROM [machine-readable datafiles]. CD-8A-94. Washington, DC: U.S. Department of Commerce, Economics and Statistics Administration, Bureau of the Census, Data User Services Division, January 1995. Primary source: U. S. Bureau of the Census. Unpublished data. Note: One square mile equals 2.59 square kilometers.

★ 43 ★
Water Area

Water Areas for Gulf Coast Water Bodies: 1990

Table shows the areas of selected water bodies and their states. Includes only that portion of a body of water under the jurisdiction of the United States, excluding Hawaii.

Body of water	State	Area Square miles	Area Square kilometers
Mississippi Sound	Alabama; Louisiana; Mississippi	813	2,105
Laguna Madre	Texas	733	1,897
Lake Pontchartrain	Louisiana	631	1,635
Florida Bay	Florida	616	1,596
Breton Sound	Louisiana	511	1,323
Mobile Bay	Alabama	310	802
Lake Borgne	Louisiana; Mississippi	271	702
Matagorda Bay	Texas	253	656
Atchafalaya Bay	Louisiana	245	635
Galveston Bay	Texas	236	611
Tampa Bay	Florida	212	549
Vermilion Bay	Louisiana	189	489
Corpus Christi Bay	Texas	151	392
West Cote Blanche Bay	Louisiana	146	378
Trinity Bay	Texas	129	335
Choctawhatchee Bay	Florida	122	315
San Antonio Bay	Texas	118	306
Timbalier Bay	Louisiana	112	291
Charlotte Harbor	Florida	112	291

[Continued]

★ 43 ★

Water Areas for Gulf Coast Water Bodies: 1990
[Continued]

Body of water	State	Area Square miles	Area Square kilometers
Aransas Bay	Texas	104	268
Apalachicola Bay	Florida	101	262
Terrebonne Bay	Louisiana	99	256
East Cote Blanche Bay	Louisiana	94	243
St. George Sound	Florida	93	240
Sabine Lake	Louisiana; Texas	89	229
White Lake	Louisiana	85	221
Old Tampa Bay	Florida	83	214
Bon Secour Bay	Alabama	79	204
Pine Island Sound	Florida	75	194

Source: 1994 Statistical Abstract of the United States on CD-ROM [machine-readable datafiles]. CD-8A-94. Washington, DC: U.S. Department of Commerce, Economics and Statistics Administration, Bureau of the Census, Data User Services Division, January 1995. Primary source: U. S. Bureau of the Census. Unpublished data. *Note:* One square mile equals 2.59 square kilometers.

★ 44 ★

Water Area

Water Areas for Interior Water Bodies: 1990

Table shows the areas of selected U.S. interior water bodies and their states. Includes only that portion of a body of water under the jurisdiction of the United States, excluding Hawaii.

Body of water	State	Area Square miles	Area Square kilometers
Lake Michigan	Illinois; Indiana; Michigan; Wisconsin	22,342	57,866
Lake Superior[1]	Michigan; Minnesota; Wisconsin	20,557	53,243
Lake Huron[1]	Michigan	8,800	22,792
Lake Erie[1]	Michigan; New York; Ohio; Pennsylvania	5,033	13,036
Lake Ontario[1]	New York	3,446	8,926
Great Salt Lake	Utah	1,836	4,756
Green Bay	Michigan; Wisconsin	1,396	3,617
Lake Okeechobee	Florida	663	1,717
Lake Sakakawea	North Dakota	563	1,459
Lake Oahe	North Dakota; South Dakota	538	1,394
Lake of the Woods[1]	Minnesota	462	1,196
Lake Champlain[1]	New York; Vermont	414	1,072
Fort Peck Lake	Montana	379	981
Salton Sea	California	364	944
Toledo Bend Reservoir	Louisiana; Texas	268	694
Lower Red Lake	Minnesota	257	666
Lake Powell	Arizona; Utah	250	649
Kentucky Lake	Kentucky; Tennessee	234	605
Lake Mead	Arizona; Nevada	233	603

[Continued]

★ 44 ★

Water Areas for Interior Water Bodies: 1990

[Continued]

Body of water	State	Area	
		Square miles	Square kilometers
Lake Winnebago	Wisconsin	206	535
Mille Lacs Lake	Minnesota	200	518
Flathead Lake	Montana	191	495
Lake Tahoe	California; Nevada	187	486
Upper Red Lake	Minnesota	186	483
Pyramid Lake	Nevada	170	440
Leech Lake	Minnesota	162	419
Lake St. Clair[1]	Michigan	161	416
Eufaula Lake	Oklahoma	157	407
Sam Rayburn Resevoir	Texas	150	389
Goose Lake	California; Oregon	147	381
Utah Lake	Utah	139	361
Lake Marion	South Carolina	139	360
Lake Francis Case	South Dakota	134	346
Lake Pend Oreille	Idaho	133	343
Lake Texoma	Oklahoma; Texas	132	342
Yellowstone Lake	Wyoming	131	339
Livingston Reservoir	Texas	127	330
Franklin D Roosevelt Lake	Washington	124	322
Moosehead Lake	Maine	116	301
Clark Hill Lake	Georgia; South Carolina	105	272
Lake Maurepas	Louisiana	91	235
Lake Moultrie	South Carolina	89	230
Lake Winnibigoshish	Minnesota	87	225
Hartwell Lake	Georgia; South Carolina	86	224
Upper Klamath Lake	Oregon	85	221
Harry S. Truman Reservoir	Missouri	84	217
Oneida Lake	New York	80	207
Malheur Lake	Oregon	75	195

Source: 1994 Statistical Abstract of the United States on CD-ROM [machine-readable datafiles]. CD-8A-94. Washington, DC: U.S. Department of Commerce, Economics and Statistics Administration, Bureau of the Census, Data User Services Division, January 1995. Primary source: U. S. Bureau of the Census. Unpublished data. *Notes:* One square mile equals 2.59 square kilometers. 1. Area measurements for Lake Champlain, Lake Erie, Lake Huron, Lake Ontario, Lake St. Clair, Lake Superior, and Lake of the Woods include only those portions under the jurisdiction of the United States.

★ 45 ★

Water Area

Water Areas for Pacific Coast Water Bodies: 1990

Table shows the areas of selected water bodies and their states. Includes only that portion of a body of water under the jurisdiction of the United States, excluding Hawaii.

Body of water	State	Area	
		Square miles	Square kilometers
Puget Sound	Washington	808	2,092
San Francisco Bay	California	264	684
Willapa Bay	Washington	125	325
Hood Canal	Washington	117	303

Source: 1994 Statistical Abstract of the United States on CD-ROM [machine-readable datafiles]. CD-8A-94. Washington, DC: U.S. Department of Commerce, Economics and Statistics Administration, Bureau of the Census, Data User Services Division, January 1995. Primary source: U. S. Bureau of the Census. Unpublished data. *Note:* One square mile equals 2.59 square kilometers.

Water Pollution

★ 46 ★

Heavy Metal Contributions From Washing Products

Powder laundry detergent - 6.1

Liquid laundry detergent - 4.3

Liquid bleach - 4.4

Liquid fabric softener - 2.2

Liquid hand dishwashing detergent - 2.4

Powder bleach - 0.7

Powder automatic dishwashing detergent - 1.0

Liquid automatic dishwashing detergent - 0.4

Chart shows data from column 1.

According to a study of wastewater treatment plants in the southern San Francisco Bay area, household washing products are not significant contributors of major heavy metals to wastewater. Table shows the daily per capita heavy metals contributions from using household washing products.

Product	Product consumption[1]	Estimated heavy metal contribution[2]								
		Arsenic	Cadmium	Chromium	Copper	Lead	Nickel	Mercury	Silver	Zinc
Powder laundry detergent	6.1	0.23	0.0043	0.0085	0.0082	0.00165	0.0042	0.00021	0.0042	0.12
Liquid laundry detergent	4.3	0.00027	0.0012	0.006	0.0025	0.0012	0.00295	0.000145	0.00295	0.014
Liquid bleach	4.4	0.00006	0.0012	0.006	0.0012	0.0012	0.003	0.00015	0.003	0.035
Powder bleach	0.7	0.037	0.0013	0.00095	0.00056	0.000185	0.00045	0.000025	0.000465	0.0093
Liquid fabric softener	2.2	0.00007	0.0006	0.003	0.0006	0.0006	0.0015	0.000075	0.0015	0.0015
Liquid hand dishwashing detergent	2.4	0.00009	0.00065	0.0033	0.00065	0.00065	0.00165	0.00008	0.00165	0.00165
Liquid automatic dishwashing detergent	0.4	0.0073	0.00041	0.00055	0.00059	0.00041	0.000275	0.000015	0.00275	0.0086
Powder automatic dishwashing detergent	1.0	0.052	0.0029	0.00135	0.0066	0.000275	0.0007	0.000035	0.0007	0.025
Product total		0.33	0.013	0.030	0.021	0.0062	0.015	0.00074	0.017	0.22

Source: Jenkins, David, and Larry L. Russell. "Heavy Metals Contribution of Household Washing Products to Municipal Wastewater." *Water Environment Research* 66, no. 6 (September/October 1994), p. 809. *Notes:* 1. Kilograms/capita/year. 2. Milligrams/cap/year.

★ 47 ★

Water Pollution

Ocean Pollution, by Source

```
┌─────────────────────────────────────────────────┐
│  ┌─────────────────────────────────────────┐     │
│  │ Land runoff - 44                         │     │
│  └─────────────────────────────────────────┘     │
│  ┌──────────────────────────────────┐            │
│  │ Atmospheric pollution - 33       │            │
│  └──────────────────────────────────┘            │
│  ┌──────────────┐                                 │
│  │ Boating - 12 │                                 │
│  └──────────────┘                                 │
│  ┌───────────┐ Dumped waste - 10                  │
│  └───────────┘                                    │
│  ▯ Offshore oil production - 1                    │
│                                                   │
└─────────────────────────────────────────────────┘
```

Table shows sources of ocean pollution.

[In percentages]

Source	Pollution
Land runoff[1]	44
Atmospheric pollution	33
Boating	12
Dumped waste[2]	10
Offshore oil production	1

Source: "Sources of Ocean Pollution." *ScienceWorld,* 9 December 1994, p. 13. Primary source: World Resources Institute. *Notes:* 1. Includes fertilizers, gutter trash, and chemicals spilled on land. 2. All kinds.

★ 48 ★

Water Pollution

Oil Polluting Incidents: 1973-1992

Table shows oil polluting incidents and gallons per incident reported in and around U.S. waters.

Year	Incidents	Gallons	Gallons per incident
1973	11,054	15,289,188	1,383
1974	12,083	15,739,792	1,303
1975	10,998	21,528,444	1,957
1976	11,066	18,517,384	1,673
1977	10,979	8,188,398	746
1978	12,174	11,035,890	907
1979	11,556	10,051,271	870
1980	9,886	12,638,848	1,278
1981	9,589	8,919,789	930
1982	9,416	10,404,646	1,105
1983	10,530	8,378,719	796
1984	10,089	19,007,332	1,884
1985	7,740	8,465,055	1,094

[Continued]

★ 48 ★

Oil Polluting Incidents: 1973-1992
[Continued]

Year	Incidents	Gallons	Gallons per incident
1986	6,330	4,427,544	699
1987	6,083	3,759,983	618
1988	6,155	6,617,278	1,075
1989	7,923	13,506,643	1,705
Tankships	255	11,272,134	44,204
Tank barges	578	752,451	1,302
Other vessels	2,957	712,012	241
Non-vessels	4,133	770,046	186
1990	9,600	11,375,576	1,185
Tankships	312	4,977,710	15,954
Tank barges	530	1,001,742	1,890
Other vessels	3,493	483,989	139
Non-vessels	5,265	4912135	933
1991	9,850	1,452,103	147
Tankships	254	91,794	361
Tank barges	498	246,441	495
Other vessels	3,664	502,074	137
Non-vessels	5,434	611,794	113
1992	8,790	1,503,862	171
Tankships	198	117,899	595
Tank barges	328	73,559	224
Other vessels	4,893	400,296	82
Non-vessels	3,371	912,108	271

Source: 1994 Statistical Abstract of the United States on CD-ROM [machine-readable datafiles]. CD-8A-94. Washington, DC: U.S. Department of Commerce, Economics and Statistics Administration, Bureau of the Census, Data User Services Division, January 1995. Primary source: U.S. Coast Guard. Based on unpublished data from the Marine Safety Information System.

★ 49 ★

Water Pollution

Phosphorus Loadings to the Great Lakes: 1976-1991

Table shows the estimated phosphorus loading to each of the Great Lakes. The 1978 Great Lakes Water Quality Agreement set target loadings for each lake. They are: Lake Superior, 3,400 metric tons per year; Lake Michigan, 5,600 metric tons per year; Lake Huron, 4,360 metric tons per year; Lake Erie, 11,000 metric tons per year; and Lake Ontario, 7,000 metric tons per year.

[In metric tons]

Year	Lake Superior	Lake Michigan	Lake Huron	Lake Erie	Lake Ontario
1976	3,550	6,656	4,802	18,480	12,695
1977	3,661	4,666	3,763	14,576	8,935
1978	5,990	6,245	5,255	19,431	9,547
1979	6,619	7,659	4,881	11,941	8,988
1980	6,412	6,574	5,307	14,855	8,579
1981	3,412	4,091	3,481	10,452	7,437
1982	3,160	4,084	4,689	12,349	8,891
1983	3,407	4,515	3,978	9,880	6,779
1984	3,642	3,611	3,452	12,874	7,948
1985	2,864	3,956	5,758	11,216	7,083
1986	3,059	4,981	4,210	11,118	9,561
1987	1,949	3,298	2,909	8,381	7,640
1988	2,067	2,907	3,165	7,841	6,521
1989	2,323	4,360	3,227	8,568	6,728
1990	1,750	3,006	2,639	12,899	8,542
1991	2,709	3,478	4,460	11,113	10,475

Source: Executive Office of the President of the United States. *Environmental Quality 24: The Twenty-fourth Annual Report of the Council on Environmental Quality.* Prepared by Ray Clark. Written by Carroll Curtis. Edited by Barry Walsh. Washington, DC: U.S. Government Printing Office, 1994, p. 430. Primary source: Great Lakes Water Quality Board. *Great Lakes Water Quality Surveillance Subcommittee Report to the International Joint Commission, United States and Canada.* Windsor, Ontario, Canada: International Joint Commission (biennial).

★ 50 ★
Water Pollution

Surface Water Pollution – Causes: 1992

Table shows the causes of pollution in U.S. rivers, lakes, reservoirs, and estuaries. Data are for 1992.

Cause	Rivers (impaired miles)	Lakes and reservoirs (impaired acres)	Estuaries (impaired square miles)
Siltation	99,125	1,744,319	1,044
Nutrients	81,640	3,222,661	4,752
Organic enrichment	54,478	1,882,145	2,911
Pathogens	60,804	625,670	3,599
Metals	42,007	3,702,022	304
Salinity	26,434	560,729	580
Habitat modification	25,175	102,951	5
Pesticides	58,081	715,666	615
Priority organics	9,977	1,586,640	402
Suspended solids	29,296	1,290,076	910
Flow alteration	17,456	787,808	192
pH	10,845	291,830	120

Source: Executive Office of the President of the United States. *Environmental Quality 24: The Twenty-fourth Annual Report of the Council on Environmental Quality.* Prepared by Ray Clark. Written by Carroll Curtis. Edited by Barry Walsh. Washington, DC: U.S. Government Printing Office, 1994, p. 427. Primary source: U.S. Environmental Protection Agency. *National Water Quality Inventory: 1992 Report to Congress.* EPA 841-R-94-001. Washington, DC: U.S. Environmental Protection Agency, 1994.

★ 51 ★
Water Pollution

Surface Water Pollution – Sources: 1992

Table shows the sources of pollution in U.S. rivers, lakes, reservoirs, and estuaries. Data are for 1992.

Source	Rivers (impaired miles)	Lakes and reservoirs (impaired acres)	Estuaries (impaired square miles)
Agriculture	159,353	3,091,585	3,539
Municipal	32,359	1,149,606	4,383
Habitat modification	15,119	1,275,583	457
Resource extraction	23,697	343,915	998
Storm sewers/runoff	24,407	1,510,796	3,587
Industrial	16,339	387,784	1,902
Silviculture	16,236	217,350	310

[Continued]

★ 51 ★

Surface Water Pollution – Sources: 1992

[Continued]

Source	Rivers (impaired miles)	Lakes and reservoirs (impaired acres)	Estuaries (impaired square miles)
Construction	5,448	158,624	664
Land disposal	7,446	307,176	390
Combined sewers	5,984	229,904	448

Source: Executive Office of the President of the United States. *Environmental Quality 24: The Twenty-fourth Annual Report of the Council on Environmental Quality.* Prepared by Ray Clark. Written by Carroll Curtis. Edited by Barry Walsh. Washington, DC: U.S. Government Printing Office, 1994, p. 427. Primary source: U.S. Environmental Protection Agency. *National Water Quality Inventory: 1992 Report to Congress.* EPA 841-R-94-001. Washington, DC: U.S. Environmental Protection Agency, 1994.

Water Quality

★ 52 ★

Herbicide-Tainted Water

Missouri - 2,100,000	
Ohio - 1,700,000	
Louisiana - 1,500,000	
Illinois - 1,400,000	
Indiana - 1,300,000	
Maryland - 1,100,000	
Minnesota - 930,000	
Kansas - 830,000	
Iowa - 760,000	
	District of Columbia - 700,000
Kentucky - 650,000	
	Nebraska - 450,000
	Pennsylvania - 325,000
	Virginia - 300,000
	Michigan - 30,000

According to the Environmental Working Group, 14 million people drink herbicide-tainted water. The table below shows number affected by state.

State	People
Missouri	2,100,000
Ohio	1,700,000
Louisiana	1,500,000
Illinois	1,400,000
Indiana	1,300,000
Maryland	1,100,000
Minnesota	930,000
Kansas	830,000
Iowa	760,000
District of Columbia	700,000
Kentucky	650,000
Nebraska	450,000
Pennsylvania	325,000
Virginia	300,000
Michigan	30,000

Source: "It's Bad for Weeds—and for Drinking Water." *U.S. News & World Report,* 31 October 1994, p. 30. Primary source: Environmental Working Group.

★ 53 ★

Water Quality

National Ambient Water Quality in Rivers and Streams: 1975-1993

Table shows violation rates for national ambient water quality in U.S. rivers and streams. Violation levels are based on U.S. Environmental Protection Agency water quality criteria: Above 200 cells per 100 milliliter for fecal coliform bacteria; below 5 milligrams per liter for dissolved oxygen; above 1.0 milligrams per liter for total phosphorus; above 10 micrograms per liter for dissolved cadmium; and above 50 micrograms per liter for dissolved lead.

[Percent of all measurements exceeding water quality criteria]

Year	Fecal coliform bacteria	Dissolved oxygen	Total phosphorus	Total cadmium, dissolved	Total lead, dissolved
1975	36	5	5	1	1
1976	32	6	5	1	1
1977	34	11	5	1	1
1978	35	5	5	1	1
1979	34	4	3	4	13
1980	31	5	4	1	5
1981	30	4	4	1	3
1982	33	5	3	1	2
1983	34	4	3	1	5
1984	30	3	4	<1	<1
1985	28	3	3	<1	<1
1986	24	3	3	<1	<1
1987	23	2	3	<1	<1
1988	22	2	4	<1	<1
1989	30	3	2	<1	<1
1990	26	2	3	<1	<1
1991	15	2	2	<1	<1
1992	28	2	2	<1	<1
1993	31	1	2	NA	NA

Source: Executive Office of the President of the United States. *Environmental Quality 24: The Twenty-fourth Annual Report of the Council on Environmental Quality.* Prepared by Ray Clark. Written by Carroll Curtis. Edited by Barry Walsh. Washington, DC: U.S. Government Printing Office, 1994, p. 428. Primary source: U.S. Geological Survey. National-level unpublished data derived from state-level data reported in *Water Data Reports,* an annual series prepared in cooperation with state governments. *Notes:* "NA" indicates "not available." 1. Base figure too small to meet statistical standards for reliability of derived figures.

★ 54 ★

Water Quality

River and Stream Water Quality Violation Rate: 1980-1993

Table shows the National Ambient Water Quality in rivers and streams. Violation level based on U.S. Environmental Protection Agency water quality criteria. Violation rate represents the proportion of all measurements of a specific water quality pollutant that exceed the "violation level" for that pollutant. "Violation" does not necessarily imply a legal violation. Data based on U.S. Geological Survey's National Stream Quality Accounting Network (NASQAN) data system. Years refer to water years, which begin in October and end in September.

[In percentages]

Pollutant	Violation level	1975	1980	1985	1990	1991	1992	1993
Fecal coliform bacteria	Above 200 cells per 100 milliliters	36	31	28	26	15	28	31
Dissolved oxygen	Below 5 milligrams per liter	5	5	3	2	2	2	1
Phosphorus, total as phosporous	Above 1.0 milligrams per liter	5	4	3	3	2	2	2
Lead, dissolved	Above 50 micrograms per liter	(NA)	(Z)	(Z)	(Z)	(Z)	(Z)	(NA)
Cadmium, dissolved	Above 10 micrograms per liter	(NA)	1	(Z)	(Z)	(Z)	(Z)	(NA)

Source: 1994 Statistical Abstract of the United States on CD-ROM [machine-readable datafiles]. CD-8A-94. Washington, DC: U.S. Department of Commerce, Economics and Statistics Administration, Bureau of the Census, Data User Services Division, January 1995. Primary sources: U.S. Geological Survey. National-level data from unpublished material. State-level data from *Water-Data Report,* an annual series prepared in cooperation with state governments. *Note:* "Z" represents less than 1. "NA" stands for "not available."

Water Use

★ 55 ★

Offstream Water Use, by Source and End-Use Sector: 1900-1990

Table shows the sources and users of offstream water in the United States.

[In billion gallons per day]

Year	Source		End-use sector					
	Ground water	Surface water	Public supply	Rural domestic and livestock	Irrigation	Thermo-electric utility	Other industrial	Total
1900	NA	NA	3.0	2.0	20.0	5.0	10.0	40.0
1910	NA	NA	5.0	2.2	39.0	7.0	14.0	67.2
1920	NA	NA	6.0	2.4	56.0	9.0	18.0	91.4
1930	NA	NA	8.0	2.9	60.0	18.0	21.0	109.9
1940	NA	NA	10.0	3.1	71.0	23.0	29.0	136.1
1945	NA	NA	12.0	3.4	80.0	31.5	35.0	161.9
1950	34.0	150.0	14.0	3.6	89.0	40.0	37.0	183.6
1955	47.6	198.0	17.0	3.6	110.0	72.0	39.0	241.6

[Continued]

★ 55 ★

Offstream Water Use, by Source and End-Use Sector: 1900-1990

[Continued]

Year	Source		End-use sector					
	Ground water	Surface water	Public supply	Rural domestic and livestock	Irrigation	Thermo-electric utility	Other industrial	Total
1960	50.4	221.0	21.0	3.6	110.0	100.0	38.0	272.6
1965	60.5	253.0	24.0	4.0	120.0	130.0	46.0	324.0
1970	69.0	303.0	27.0	4.5	130.0	170.0	47.0	378.5
1975	83.0	329.0	29.0	4.9	140.0	200.0	45.0	418.9
1980	83.9	361.0	34.0	5.6	150.0	210.0	45.0	444.6
1985	73.7	320.0	37.0	7.8	140.0	190.0	31.0	405.8
1990	80.6	327.2	38.5	7.9	137.0	195.0	29.9	408.8

Source: Executive Office of the President of the United States. *Environmental Quality 24: The Twenty-fourth Annual Report of the Council on Environmental Quality.* Prepared by Ray Clark. Written by Carroll Curtis. Edited by Barry Walsh. Washington, DC: U.S. Government Printing Office, 1994, p. 425. Primary sources: U.S. Department of Commerce. Bureau of the Census. *Historical Statistics of the United States: Colonial Times to 1970.* Series J 92-103. Washington, DC: U.S. Department of Commerce, Bureau of the Census, 1976; Solley, W. B., R. R. Pierce, and H. A. Perlman. *Estimated Water Use in the United States.* Geological Survey Circular 1081. Reston, VA: U.S. Department of the Interior, U.S. Geological Survey, 1993; earlier reports. *Note:* "NA" represents "not available."

★ 56 ★

Water Use

Surface Water Designated-Use Support

Table shows designated-use support in surface waters of the United States. Data are provided for rivers, lakes and reservoirs, and estuaries.

Designated-use support	Rivers (miles)	Lakes and reservoirs (acres)	Estuaries (square miles)
Fully supporting	360,283	7,905,576	15,208
Threatened	41,066	2,304,321	3,353
Partially supporting	161,025	6,381,821	6,132
Not supporting	80,382	1,689,439	2,463
Not attainable	125	2,409	71
Total surface waters assessed	642,881	18,283,566	27,227
Total surface waters not assessed	2,908,366	21,638,871	9,663
Total surface waters	3,551,247	39,922,437	35,890

Source: Executive Office of the President of the United States. *Environmental Quality 24: The Twenty-fourth Annual Report of the Council on Environmental Quality.* Prepared by Ray Clark. Written by Carroll Curtis. Edited by Barry Walsh. Washington, DC: U.S. Government Printing Office, 1994, p. 426. Primary source: U.S. Environmental Protection Agency. *National Water Quality Inventory: 1992 Report to Congress.* EPA 841-R-94-001. Washington, DC: U.S. Environmental Protection Agency, 1994.

★ 57 ★
Water Use

Water Withdrawals and Consumptive Use, by State: 1990

Withdrawal signifies water physically withdrawn from source. Includes fresh and saline water.

[In million gallons per day, except as noted]

| State or other area | Water withdrawn | | | | Consumptive use[1], fresh water |
| | Total | Per capita (gallons per day), fresh water | Source | | |
			Ground water	Surface water	
United States[2]	407,900	1,340	80,640	327,260	93,980
Alabama	8,090	2,000	403	7,680	454
Alaska	641	517	112	529	26
Arizona	6,570	1,790	2,740	3,830	4,350
Arkansas	7,840	3,330	4,710	3,130	4,140
California	46,800	1,180	14,900	31,900	20,900
Colorado	12,700	3,850	2,800	9,910	5,250
Connecticut	4,840	325	165	4,680	103
Delaware	1,370	1,540	89	1,280	59
District of Columbia[3]	9	15	1	8	16
Florida	17,900	582	4,660	13,200	3,130
Georgia	5,350	816	996	4,360	822
Hawaii	2,740	1,070	590	2,150	627
Idaho	19,700	19,600	7,590	12,100	6,090
Illinois	18,000	1,570	945	17,100	750
Indiana	9,430	1,700	621	8,810	451
Iowa	2,860	1,030	495	2,370	271
Kansas	6,080	2,460	4,360	1,720	4,410
Kentucky	4,320	1,170	247	4,070	309
Louisiana	9,350	2,200	1,340	8,010	1,590
Maine	1,140	433	85	1,060	51
Maryland[3]	6,420	307	239	6,180	126
Massachusetts	5,520	338	338	5,180	195
Michigan	11,600	1,250	707	10,900	738
Minnesota	3,270	748	797	2,480	872
Mississippi	3,640	1,290	2,670	963	1,800
Missouri	6,930	1,150	728	6,200	529
Montana	9,320	11,600	218	9,100	2,090
Nebraska	8,940	5,660	4,800	4,150	4,230
Nevada	3,350	2,780	1,070	2,280	1,690
New Hampshire	1,310	378	64	1,250	26
New Jersey	12,800	287	566	12,200	211
New Mexico	3,480	2,300	1,760	1,720	2,060
New York	19,000	583	840	18,100	562
North Carolina	8,940	1,350	435	8,510	390
North Dakota	2,680	4,190	141	2,540	228
Ohio	11,700	1,080	904	10,800	901
Oklahoma	1,670	452	905	760	659

[Continued]

★ 57 ★

Water Withdrawals and Consumptive Use, by State: 1990
[Continued]

State or other area	Water withdrawn				Consumptive use[1], fresh water
	Total	Per capita (gallons per day), fresh water	Source		
			Ground water	Surface water	
Oregon	8,430	2,970	767	7,660	3,160
Pennsylvania	9,830	827	1,020	8,810	581
Rhode Island	526	132	25	501	18
South Carolina	6,000	1,720	282	5,720	293
South Dakota	592	851	251	341	345
Tennessee	9,190	1,880	503	8,690	252
Texas	25,200	1,180	7,880	17,300	9,020
Utah	4,480	2,540	971	3,510	2,230
Vermont	632	1,120	45	587	29
Virginia	6,860	762	443	6,420	224
Washington	7,940	1,630	1,450	6,490	2,830
West Virginia	4,580	2,560	728	3,860	509
Wisconsin	6,510	1,330	681	5,830	461
Wyoming	7,600	16,700	403	7,200	2,730

Source: 1994 Statistical Abstract of the United States on CD-ROM [machine-readable datafiles]. CD-8A-94. Washington, DC: U.S. Department of Commerce, Economics and Statistics Administration, Bureau of the Census, Data User Services Division, January 1995. Primary source: U.S. Geological Survey. Largest Rivers in the United States: Open File Report 87-242 (August 1987). Notes: Figures may not add due to rounding. 1. Includes self-supplied withdrawals for commercial use (1.2 mil. and 2.4 mil. gallons per day) and livestock (4.4 mil. and 4.5 mil. gallons per day) that are not shownper day) that are not shown separately under "major uses" in 1985 and 1990, respectively. 2. Includes Puerto Rico and Virgin Islands. 3. Data for 1990 are not entirely comparable with 1985 as public supply thermoelectric uses for the District of Columbia were included with Maryland.

★ 58 ★

Water Use

Water Withdrawals and Consumptive Use Per Day, by End Use: 1940-1990

Table shows daily water withdrawals and consumptive use in the United States, including Puerto Rico. Withdrawal signifies water physically withdrawn from a source. Includes fresh and saline water, but excludes water used for hydroelectric power.

Year	Total (billion gallons)	Per capita[1] (gallons)	Irrigation (billion gallons)	Public supply[2]		Rural[4] (billion gallons)	Industrial and miscella-neous[5] (billion gallons)	Steam electric utilities (billion gallons)
				Total (billion gallons	Per capita[3] (gallons)			
Withdrawals								
1940	140	1,027	71	10	75	3.1	29	23
1950	180	1,185	89	14	145	3.6	37	40
1955	240	1,454	110	17	148	3.6	39	72
1960	270	1,500	110	21	151	3.6	38	100

[Continued]

★ 58 ★

Water Withdrawals and Consumptive Use Per Day, by End Use: 1940-1990
[Continued]

| Year | Total (billion gallons) | Per capita[1] (gallons) | Irrigation (billion gallons) | Public supply[2] | | Rural[4] (billion gallons) | Industrial and miscella-neous[5] (billion gallons) | Steam electric utilities (billion gallons) |
				Total (billion gallons	Per capita[3] (gallons)			
1965	310	1,602	120	24	155	4.0	46	130
1970	370	1,815	130	27	166	4.5	47	170
1975	420	1,972	140	29	168	4.9	45	200
1980	440	1,953	150	34	183	5.6	45	210
1985	399	1,650	137	38	189	7.8	31	187
1990	408	1,620	137	41	195	7.9	30	195
Consumptive use								
1960	61	339	52	3.5	25	2.8	3.0	0.2
1965	77	403	66	5.2	34	3.2	3.4	0.4
1970	87	427	73	5.9	36	3.4	4.1	0.8
1975	96	451	80	6.7	38	3.4	4.2	1.9
1980	100	440	83	7.1	38	3.9	5.0	3.2
1985	92	380	74	(6)	(6)	9.2	6.1	6.2
1990	94	370	76	(6)	(6)	8.9	6.7	4.0

Source: 1994 Statistical Abstract of the United States on CD-ROM [machine-readable datafiles]. CD-8A-94. Washington, DC: U.S. Department of Commerce, Economics and Statistics Administration, Bureau of the Census, Data User Services Division, January 1995. Primary sources: For 1940-1960—U.S. Bureau of Domestic Business Development, based principally on committee prints, *Water Resources Activities in the United States,* for the Senate Committee on National Water Resources, U.S. Senate; after 1960—U.S. Geological Survey. *Estimated Use of Water in the United States in 1990.* Circular l081, and previous quinquennial issues. *Notes:* 1. Based on Bureau of the Census resident population as of July 1. 2. Includes commercial water withdrawals. 3. Based on population served. 4. Rural farm and nonfarm household and garden use, and water for farm stock and dairies. 5. For l940-l960, includes manufacturing and mineral industries, rural commercial industries, air-conditioning, resorts, hotels, motels, military and other state and federal agencies, and micscellaneous; thereafter, includes manufacturing, mining, and mineral processing, ordnance, construction, and miscellaneous. 6. Public supply consumptive use included in end-use categories.

Chapter 3
CLIMATE AND WEATHER CONDITIONS

Many environmental issues and concerns are directly related to climate and weather conditions. The ozone depletion, for example, exposes humans to more solar radiation, and "greenhouse gases" such as carbon dioxide and nitrous oxide contribute to global warming. According to the *1993 Information Please Environmental Almanac*, warmer climates have the potential to change ecosystems: Oceans may expand from the absorption of heat, thus raising sea level. Precipitation may increase or decrease. Levels of moisture in soil will be altered, interrupting agricultural production and markets, affecting the very food supply. Sea ice of arctic regions will thin, releasing additional greenhouse gases and adding to global warming (World Resources Institute, *1993 Information Please Environmental Almanac*, New York, NY: Houghton Mifflin Co., 1992, p. 317).

The tables in this chapter profile current weather conditions and trends. In particular, coverage is provided on global warming, natural disasters, precipitation (including cations and anions in precipitation), snow and ice, temperatures, and miscellaneous weather conditions such as humidity, sunshine, and wind speed.

Related data on greenhouse gases are included in the Air and Water chapter. Cost of natural disasters in lives lost and dollars is covered in the Costs and Expenditures chapter. Public opinion on environmental issues are profiled in the Politics, Opinion, Law chapter.

Global Warming

★ 59 ★

Fluorinated Compounds

Sulfur hexafluoride	
Perfluoroethane	
	Perfluorohexane
	Perfluoromethane
Carbon dioxide	

A World Resources Institute report suggested that fluorinated compounds contribute more to global warming than many other greenhouse gases. The table below shows the global warming potential and sources of fluorinated compounds.

Compound	Global warming potential[1]
Carbon dioxide (CO_2)	1
Perfluoromethane (CF_4)	6,300
Perfluoroethane (C_2F_6)	12,500
Sulfur hexafluoride (SF_6)	24,900
Perfluorohexane (C_6F_{14})	6,800

Source: Lucas, Allison. "Report Airs Concerns About Fluorinated Compounds." *ChemicalWeek*, 8 February 1995, p. 12. Primary source: World Resources Institute. *Note:* 1. Index: Carbon dioxide (CO_2) = 1.

★ 60 ★

Global Warming

Global Warming Gas Emissions, by Country

Gases such as carbon dioxide, methane, and chlorofluorocarbons add to global warming. The table below shows the emissions of the 5 nations with the most gas emissions.

Nation	Percent of total emissions
USA	18.4
Former Soviet Union	13.5
China	8.4
Japan	5.6
Brazil	3.8

Source: Kanamine, Linda. "Gas-Reduction Plan Rooted in Voluntary Efforts." *USA TODAY,* 19 October 1993, p. 3A. Primary source: World Resources Institute.

★ 61 ★

Global Warming

Greenhouse Gas Emissions, by Type and Source: 1985-1992

Table shows emission of greenhouse gases by selected sources. Emission estimates were mandated by Congress through Section 1605(a) of the Energy Policy Act of 1992 (title XVI). Gases that contain carbon can be measured either in terms of the full molecular weight of the gas or just in terms of of their carbon content.

Type and source	Unit	1985	1986	1987	1988	1989	1990	1991
Carbon dioxide:								
Gas	Million metric tons	4,667.1	4,662.1	4,806.3	5,031.6	5,067.5	5,012.4	(NA)
Carbon content	Million metric tons	1,272.9	1,271.5	1,310.8	1,372.3	1,382.1	1,367.0	1,351.7
Energy sources	Million metric tons	1,240.6	1,239.0	1,277.6	1,339.8	1,352.0	1,338.0	1,317.2
Cement production	Million metric tons	9.6	9.7	9.6	9.5	9.5	9.5	8.8
Gas flaring	Million metric tons	1.3	1.3	1.7	1.9	1.9	2.0	2.3
Other industrial	Million metric tons	6.1	5.7	6.2	6.8	6.9	6.9	6.8
Other, adjustments	Million metric tons	15.3	15.8	15.7	14.3	11.8	10.6	16.6
Methane:								
Gas	1,000 metric tons	29,486	29,179	29,134	29,263	28,891	29,109	(NA)
Energy sources	1,000 metric tons	7,442	7,436	7,665	7,865	8,039	8,446	8,190
Landfills	1,000 metric tons	11,310	11,360	11,240	11,220	10,980	10,720	(NA)
Agricultural sources	1,000 metric tons	10,734	10,383	10,229	10,178	9,852	9,933	10,046
Carbon content	Million metric tons	22.1	21.9	21.8	22.0	21.7	21.8	(NA)
Nitrous oxide	1,000 metric tons	303	304	316	334	334	343	354
Fertilizer	1,000 metric tons	124	108	106	107	108	109	117
Adipic acid production[1]	1,000 metric tons	51[2]	54	56	57	53	55	57
Transportation	1,000 metric tons	81	93	106	121	127	133	136
Stationary combustion	1,000 metric tons	47	49	48	49	46	46	44
Chlorofluorocarbons (CFC) gases[3]	1,000 metric tons	(NA)	(NA)	(NA)	(NA)	(NA)	222	(NA)

[Continued]

★ 61 ★

Greenhouse Gas Emissions, by Type and Source: 1985-1992
[Continued]

Type and source	Unit	1985	1986	1987	1988	1989	1990	1991
Carbon monoxide:								
Gas	Million metric tons	83.12	76.03	75.05	75.53	68.32	67.74	62.10
Energy related	Million metric tons	69.81	64.93	62.38	59.72	55.70	52.78	48.17
Industrial processes	Million metric tons	4.38	4.20	4.33	4.60	4.58	4.64	4.69
Solid waste disposal	Million metric tons	1.85	1.70	1.70	1.70	1.70	1.70	2.06
Other	Million metric tons	7.09	5.15	6.44	9.51	6.34	8.62	7.18
Carbon content	Million metric tons	35.62	32.58	32.16	32.37	29.28	29.03	26.61
Nitrogen oxide	Million metric tons	19.39	18.83	19.03	19.65	19.29	19.38	18.76
Energy related	Million metric tons	18.53	18.04	18.19	18.71	18.44	18.46	17.85
Industrial processes	Million metric tons	0.56	0.56	0.56	0.58	0.59	0.59	0.60
Solid waste disposal	Million metric tons	0.08	0.08	0.08	0.08	0.08	0.08	0.10
Other	Million metric tons	0.21	0.16	0.19	0.28	0.19	0.26	0.21
Nonmethane volatile organic compounds (VOCs)	Million metric tons	19.80	18.45	18.64	18.61	17.35	17.58	16.88
Energy related	Million metric tons	8.37	7.77	7.49	7.15	6.36	6.16	5.75
Industrial processes	Million metric tons	8.35	7.92	8.17	8.00	7.97	8.02	7.86
Solid waste disposal	Million metric tons	0.60	0.58	0.58	0.58	0.58	0.58	0.69
Other	Million metric tons	2.49	2.19	2.40	2.88	2.44	2.82	2.59

Source: 1994 Statistical Abstract of the United States on CD-ROM [machine-readable datafiles]. CD-8A-94. Washington, DC: U.S. Department of Commerce, Economics and Statistics Administration, Bureau of the Census, Data User Services Division, January 1995. Primary source: U.S. Energy Information Administration (EIA). *Emissions of Greenhouse Gases in the United States, 1985-1990* (September 1993). *Notes:* "NA" represents "not available." 1. A common industrial chemical that is an intermediate product in the production of nylon. 2. 1985 data not available; EIA estimate is an average of 1984 and 1986 data. 3. Covers only CFC-11, CFC-12, and CFC-113.

Natural Disasters

★ 62 ★

Earthquakes

```
Anchorage, Alaska - 9.2

San Francisco, California - 8.3

Charleston, South Carolina - 7.7

San Francisco, California - 6.9
```
Chart shows data from column 2.

Table shows the locations, dates, Richter Scale ratings, and loss of life associated with major U.S. earthquakes.

Location	Year	Richter scale	Deaths
Anchorage, Alaska	1964	9.2	131
New Madrid, Missouri	1811-1812[1]	8.4-8.8	[2]
San Francisco, California	1906	8.3	2,500
Charleston, South Carolina	1886	7.7	110
San Francisco, California	1989	6.9	62

Source: Allman, William F. "Rumblings Coast to Coast." *U.S. News & World Report,* 31 January 1994, p. 41. *Notes:* 1. Three quakes. 2. Unknown.

★ 63 ★

Natural Disasters

Tornadoes, Floods, and Tropical Storms: 1976-1993

Table shows number of incidents and loss of life and property from tornadoes, floods, and tropical storms.

Item	1976	1980	1985	1990	1991	1992	1993, preliminary
Tornadoes, number[1]	835	866	684	1,133	1,132	1,303	(NA)
Lives lost, total	44	28	94	53	39	39	(NA)
Most in a single tornado	5	5	18	29	13	10	(NA)
Property loss of $500,000 and over	46	92	69	91	64	(NA)	(NA)
Floods: Lives lost	187	97	304	147	63	87	(NA)
Property loss (million dollars)	1,000	1,500	3,000	2,058	1,416	800	(NA)
North Atlantic tropical storms and hurricanes:[2]							
Number reaching U.S. coast	(NA)	11	11	14	8	6	8
Hurricanes only	(NA)	1	6	0	1	1	1

[Continued]

★ 63 ★

Tornadoes, Floods, and Tropical Storms: 1976-1993
[Continued]

Item	1976	1980	1985	1990	1991	1992	1993, preliminary
Lives lost in U.S.	(NA)	2	30	13	15	24	3
Property loss (million 1990 dollars)[3]	213	411	4,457	57	1,500	25,000	35

Source: 1994 Statistical Abstract of the United States on CD-ROM [machine-readable datafiles]. CD-8A-94. Washington, DC: U.S. Department of Commerce, Economics and Statistics Administration, Bureau of the Census, Data User Services Division, January 1995. Primary sources, except as noted: U.S. National Oceanic and Atmospheric Administration. *Climatological Data, 1966-1980: National Summary* (monthly); U.S. National Oceanic and Atmospheric Administration (NOAA). *Storm Data* (monthly). *Notes:* "NA" represents "not available." 1. A violent, rotating column of air descending from a cumulonimbus cloud in the form of a tubular- or funnel-shaped cloud, usually characterized by movements along a narrow path and wind speeds from 100 to over 300 miles per hour. Also known as a "twister" or "waterspout." 2. Source: National Hurricane Center (Coral Gables, Florida), unpublished data. Tropical storms have maximum winds of 39 to 73 miles per hour; hurricanes have maximum winds of 74 miles per hour or higher. 3. Source: Hebert, Jarrell, & Mayfield. "The Deadliest, Costliest, and Most Intense U.S. Hurricances of This Century." NHC-31. NOAA Technical Memo (February 1993).

Precipitation

★ 64 ★

Cations and Anions in Precipitation in the Eastern United States: 1985-1993

Table shows the average concentrations of cations and anions in precipitation in the eastern United States. Data are from 77 sites. Sites included in the computations are those where precipitation amounts are available for at least 90 percent of the summary period and where at least 60 percent of the precipitation during the summary period is represented by valid samples.

Year	pH (units)	Hydrogen ion (micrograms per liter)	Sulfate ion (milligrams per liter)	Nitrate ion (milligrams per liter)	Ammonium ion (milligrams per liter)	Calcium ion (milligrams per liter)	Precip- itation (centi- meters)
1985	4.42	37.91	2.04	1.25	0.23	0.15	107.1
1986	4.42	38.14	2.14	1.29	0.24	0.13	102.5
1987	4.42	38.32	2.10	1.32	0.26	0.14	100.7
1988	4.43	37.07	2.14	1.33	0.21	0.17	96.4
1989	4.46	34.35	2.01	1.34	0.31	0.15	110.8
1990	4.48	32.82	1.80	1.17	0.27	0.12	122.6
1991	4.47	34.07	1.87	1.27	0.26	0.14	111.0
1992	4.49	32.29	1.78	1.22	0.25	0.12	108.2
1993	4.47	33.90	1.79	1.28	0.26	0.11	113.8

Source: Executive Office of the President of the United States. *Environmental Quality 24: The Twenty-fourth Annual Report of the Council on Environmental Quality.* Prepared by Ray Clark. Written by Carroll Curtis. Edited by Barry Walsh. Washington, DC: U.S. Government Printing Office, 1994, p. 443. Primary source: National Trends Network of the National Atmospheric Deposition Program (Fort Collins, Colorado; 1994). *Notes:* "pH" represents Pouvoir Hydrogene (hydrogen power), a measure of acidity or alkalinity.

★ 65 ★

Precipitation

Cations and Anions in Precipitation in the United States: 1985-1993

Table shows the average concentrations of cations and anions in precipitation in the entire United States. Data are from 116 sites. Sites included in the computations are those where precipitation amounts are available for at least 90 percent of the summary period and where at least 60 percent of the precipitation during the summary period is represented by valid samples.

Year	pH (units)	Hydrogen ion (micrograms per liter)	Sulfate ion (milligrams per liter)	Nitrate ion (milligrams per liter)	Ammonium ion (milligrams per liter)	Calcium ion (milligrams per liter)	Precip- itation (centi- meters)
1985	4.56	27.66	1.63	1.07	0.21	0.17	91.9
1986	4.56	27.53	1.68	1.09	0.21	0.15	92.4
1987	4.55	28.07	1.67	1.16	0.25	0.15	87.7
1988	4.56	27.27	1.73	1.16	0.19	0.20	83.0
1989	4.61	24.77	1.62	1.20	0.30	0.18	92.6
1990	4.62	23.88	1.47	1.07	0.27	0.15	103.7
1991	4.61	24.74	1.50	1.11	0.25	0.16	96.7
1992	4.63	23.41	1.44	1.09	0.26	0.14	93.7
1993	4.64	24.32	1.38	1.11	0.25	0.13	100.6

Source: Executive Office of the President of the United States. *Environmental Quality 24: The Twenty-fourth Annual Report of the Council on Environmental Quality.* Prepared by Ray Clark. Written by Carroll Curtis. Edited by Barry Walsh. Washington, DC: U.S. Government Printing Office, 1994, p. 443. Primary source: National Trends Network of the National Atmospheric Deposition Program (Fort Collins, Colorado; 1994). *Note:* "pH" represents Pouvoir Hydrogene (hydrogen power), a measure of acidity or alkalinity.

★ 66 ★

Precipitation

Cations and Anions in Precipitation in the Western United States: 1985-1993

Table shows the average concentrations of cations and anions in precipitation in the western United States. Data are from 39 sites. Sites included in the computations are those where precipitation amounts are available for at least 90 percent of the summary period and where at least 60 percent of the precipitation during the summary period is represented by valid samples.

Year	pH (units)	Hydrogen ion (micrograms per liter)	Sulfate ion (milligrams per liter)	Nitrate ion (milligrams per liter)	Ammonium ion (milligrams per liter)	Calcium ion (milligrams per liter)	Precip- itation (centi- meters)
1985	5.13	7.41	0.82	0.71	0.18	0.23	62.0
1986	5.18	6.57	0.78	0.68	0.17	0.19	72.4
1987	5.11	7.82	0.83	0.83	0.24	0.19	62.2
1988	5.10	7.93	0.93	0.83	0.16	0.27	56.6
1989	5.23	5.84	0.87	0.91	0.29	0.25	56.7
1990	5.21	6.22	0.80	0.87	0.29	0.22	66.2
1991	5.20	6.31	0.77	0.80	0.24	0.21	68.4

[Continued]

★ 66 ★

Cations and Anions in Precipitation in the Western United States: 1985-1993

[Continued]

Year	pH (units)	Hydrogen ion (micrograms per liter)	Sulfate ion (milligrams per liter)	Nitrate ion (milligrams per liter)	Ammonium ion (milligrams per liter)	Calcium ion (milligrams per liter)	Precip-itation (centi-meters)
1992	5.23	5.86	0.77	0.83	0.28	0.18	65.1
1993	5.27	5.41	0.71	0.76	0.23	0.18	74.4

Source: Executive Office of the President of the United States. *Environmental Quality 24: The Twenty-fourth Annual Report of the Council on Environmental Quality.* Prepared by Ray Clark. Written by Carroll Curtis. Edited by Barry Walsh. Washington, DC: U.S. Government Printing Office, 1994, p. 443. Primary source: National Trends Network of the National Atmospheric Deposition Program (Fort Collins, Colorado; 1994). *Note:* "pH" represents Pouvoir Hydrogene (hydrogen power), a measure of acidity or alkalinity.

★ 67 ★

Precipitation

Drought and Wetness: 1896-1993

The Palmer Drought Severity Index (PDSI) is used to measure long-term drought and wet conditions. The PDSI is calculated for each climate division in the conterminous United States. This table presents the percent area of the country experiencing severe to extreme long-term drought and wet conditions in the conterminous United States.

Year	Severe/ extreme drought	Severe/ extreme wetness
1896	5.39	7.91
1900	15.68	5.43
1905	6.90	17.68
1910	14.17	5.41
1915	3.84	24.13
1920	1.43	18.43
1925	16.68	0.69
1930	13.88	1.98
1935	23.38	3.06
1940	22.18	2.23
1945	2.72	16.97
1950	8.36	9.59
1955	29.44	1.53
1960	12.28	7.14
1965	7.58	13.72
1970	0.88	4.43
1975	1.23	22.51
1980	6.92	11.82
1985	4.39	20.68
1990	20.70	31.50
1991	12.22	22.14

[Continued]

★ 67 ★

Drought and Wetness: 1896-1993
[Continued]

Year	Severe/ extreme drought	Severe/ extreme wetness
1992	12.28	19.00
1993	1.95	34.80

Source: Executive Office of the President of the United States. *Environmental Quality 24: The Twenty-fourth Annual Report of the Council on Environmental Quality.* Prepared by Ray Clark. Written by Carroll Curtis. Edited by Barry Walsh. Washington, DC: U.S. Government Printing Office, 1994, p. 424. Primary source: U.S. Department of Commerce. National Oceanic and Atmospheric Administration. National Climatic Data Center (Ashville, North Carolina; 1994).

★ 68 ★

Precipitation

Precipitation – Annual, by City

Table shows normal annual precipitation for selected U.S. cities. Figures are airport data, except as noted. Based on standard 30-year period, 1961 through 1990. Cities are arranged alphabetically by state.

[In inches]

City	Annual
Mobile, Alabama	63.96
Juneau, Alaska	54.31
Phoenix, Arizona	7.66
Little Rock, Arkansas	50.86
Los Angeles, California	12.01
Sacramento, California	17.52
San Diego, California	9.90
San Francisco, California	19.70
Denver, Colorado	15.40
Hartford, Connecticut	44.14
Wilmington, Delaware	40.84
Washington, District of Columbia	38.63
Jacksonville, Florida	51.32
Miami, Florida	55.91
Atlanta, Georgia	50.77
Honolulu, Hawaii	22.02
Boise, Idaho	12.11
Chicago, Illinois	35.82
Peoria, Illinois	36.25
Indianapolis, Indiana	39.94
Des Moines, Iowa	33.12
Wichita, Kansas	29.33
Louisville, Kentucky	44.39
New Orleans, Louisiana	61.88
Portland, Maine	44.34
Baltimore, Maryland	40.76

[Continued]

★ 68 ★

Precipitation – Annual, by City

[Continued]

City	Annual
Boston, Massachusetts	41.51
Detroit, Michigan	32.62
Sault Ste. Marie, Michigan	34.23
Duluth, Minnesota	30.00
Minneapolis-St. Paul, Minnesota	28.32
Jackson, Mississippi	55.37
Kansas City, Missouri	37.62
St. Louis, Missouri	37.51
Great Falls, Montana	15.21
Omaha, Nebraska	29.86
Reno, Nevada	7.53
Concord, New Hampshire	36.37
Atlantic City, New Jersey	40.29
Albuquerque, New Mexico	8.88
Albany, New York	36.17
Buffalo, New York	38.58
New York, New York[1]	47.25
Charlotte, North Carolina	43.09
Raleigh, North Carolina	41.43
Bismarck, North Dakota	15.47
Cincinnati, Ohio	41.33
Cleveland, Ohio	36.63
Columbus, Ohio	38.09
Oklahoma City, Oklahoma	33.36
Portland, Oregon	36.30
Philadelphia, Pennsylvania	41.41
Pittsburgh, Pennsylvania	36.85
Providence, Rhode Island	45.53
Columbia, South Carolina	49.91
Sioux Falls, South Dakota	23.86
Memphis, Tennessee	52.10
Nashville, Tennessee	47.30
Dallas-Fort Worth, Texas	33.70
El Paso, Texas	8.81
Houston, Texas	46.07
Salt Lake City, Utah	16.18
Burlington, Vermont	34.47
Norfolk, Virginia	44.64
Richmond, Virginia	43.16
Seattle-Tacoma, Washington	37.19
Spokane, Washington	16.49
Charleston, West Virginia	42.53
Milwaukee, Wisconsin	32.93

[Continued]

★ 68 ★

Precipitation – Annual, by City

[Continued]

City	Annual
Cheyenne, Wyoming	14.40
San Juan, Puerto Rico	52.34

Source: 1994 Statistical Abstract of the United States on CD-ROM [machine-readable datafiles]. CD-8A-94. Washington, DC: U.S. Department of Commerce, Economics and Statistics Administration, Bureau of the Census, Data User Services Division, January 1995. Primary source: U.S. National Oceanic and Atmospheric Administration. *Climatography of the United States.* No. 81. *Note:* 1. City office data.

★ 69 ★

Precipitation

Precipitation in Alabama, by Selected City

Table shows the average number of days with precipitation of .01 inch or more. Figures are airport data for period of record through 1992, except as noted.

City	January	February	March	April	May	June	July	August	September	October	November	December
Birmingham	11	10	11	9	10	10	13	10	8	6	9	11
Birmingham[1]	10	10	11	9	10	9	12	10	9	8	10	9
Huntsville	11	10	12	10	11	9	10	9	9	7	10	11
Mobile	11	10	10	7	9	11	16	14	10	6	8	10
Montgomery	11	9	10	8	9	9	12	9	8	6	8	10

Source: 1994 Statistical Abstract of the United States on CD-ROM [machine-readable datafiles]. CD-8A-94. Washington, DC: U.S. Department of Commerce, Economics and Statistics Administration, Bureau of the Census, Data User Services Division, January 1995. Primary source: U.S. National Oceanic and Atmospheric Administration. *Comparative Climatic Data* (annual). *Note:* 1. City office data.

★ 70 ★

Precipitation

Precipitation in Alaska, by Selected City

Table shows the average number of days with precipitation of .01 inch or more. Figures are airport data for period of record through 1992, except as noted.

City	January	February	March	April	May	June	July	August	September	October	November	December
Anchorage	8	8	8	6	7	8	12	14	14	12	9	11
Annette	20	19	20	18	17	15	14	15	18	24	22	23
Barrow	4	4	4	4	4	5	9	11	11	11	6	5
Barter Island	5	5	5	6	6	6	8	12	10	12	8	5
Bethel	8	7	9	9	10	13	15	18	16	13	11	11
Bettles	7	7	7	5	6	10	11	13	11	11	10	10
Big Delta	6	4	4	4	7	12	14	12	9	9	7	6
Cold Bay	19	17	18	16	17	16	16	20	21	23	22	21
Fairbanks	7	7	6	5	7	11	12	12	9	11	10	9

[Continued]

★ 70 ★

Precipitation in Alaska, by Selected City
[Continued]

City	January	February	March	April	May	June	July	August	September	October	November	December
Gulkana	7	6	5	3	5	9	13	11	11	8	7	8
Homer	14	11	11	9	10	9	11	13	15	15	12	15
Juneau	18	17	18	17	17	15	17	18	20	23	20	21
King Salmon	11	10	11	10	12	13	15	17	16	13	12	12
Kodiak	17	16	16	16	18	15	15	14	16	16	17	17
Kotzebue	8	7	8	7	6	6	11	14	12	10	10	9
McGrath	10	8	9	7	9	13	15	17	14	12	12	12
Nome	11	8	10	9	8	9	13	16	14	11	12	10
St. Paul Island	18	15	16	14	14	13	15	19	20	22	21	20
Talkeetna	9	9	9	7	11	13	15	16	16	13	10	12
Unalakleet	5	6	6	7	6	8	13	17	12	10	7	8
Valdez	17	14	16	14	16	15	17	17	20	20	16	18
Yakutat	19	18	19	18	19	17	18	19	21	24	21	22

Source: 1994 Statistical Abstract of the United States on CD-ROM [machine-readable datafiles]. CD-8A-94. Washington, DC: U.S. Department of Commerce, Economics and Statistics Administration, Bureau of the Census, Data User Services Division, January 1995. Primary source: U.S. National Oceanic and Atmospheric Administration. *Comparative Climatic Data* (annual).

★ 71 ★

Precipitation

Precipitation in Arizona, by Selected City

Table shows the average number of days with precipitation of .01 inch or more. Figures are airport data for period of record through 1992, except as noted.

City	January	February	March	April	May	June	July	August	September	October	November	December
Flagstaff	7	7	9	6	4	3	12	11	6	5	5	7
Phoenix	4	4	4	2	1	1	4	5	3	3	3	4
Tucson	4	4	4	2	2	2	10	9	5	3	3	5
Winslow	4	4	5	3	3	2	7	9	5	4	3	5
Yuma	2	2	2	1	(Z)	(Z)	1	2	1	1	1	3

Source: 1994 Statistical Abstract of the United States on CD-ROM [machine-readable datafiles]. CD-8A-94. Washington, DC: U.S. Department of Commerce, Economics and Statistics Administration, Bureau of the Census, Data User Services Division, January 1995. Primary source: U.S. National Oceanic and Atmospheric Administration. *Comparative Climatic Data* (annual). *Note:* "Z" represents less than 1/2 day.

★ 72 ★

Precipitation

Precipitation in Arkansas, by Selected City

Table shows the average number of days with precipitation of .01 inch or more. Figures are airport data for period of record through 1992, except as noted.

City	January	February	March	April	May	June	July	August	September	October	November	December
Fort Smith	8	8	9	10	11	8	8	7	8	7	7	7
Little Rock	9	9	10	10	10	8	8	7	7	7	8	9
North Little Rock	9	10	10	10	12	9	9	7	8	8	9	10

Source: 1994 Statistical Abstract of the United States on CD-ROM [machine-readable datafiles]. CD-8A-94. Washington, DC: U.S. Department of Commerce, Economics and Statistics Administration, Bureau of the Census, Data User Services Division, January 1995. Primary source: U.S. National Oceanic and Atmospheric Administration. *Comparative Climatic Data* (annual).

★ 73 ★

Precipitation

Precipitation in California, by Selected City

Table shows the average number of days with precipitation of .01 inch or more. Figures are airport data for period of record through 1992, except as noted.

City	January	February	March	April	May	June	July	August	September	October	November	December
Bakersfield	6	6	7	4	2	(Z)	(Z)	(Z)	1	2	3	5
Bishop	4	3	3	2	3	2	2	2	2	2	3	3
Blue Canyon	12	11	13	10	7	3	1	1	3	6	11	12
Eureka	16	14	16	12	8	5	2	3	4	9	13	15
Fresno	7	7	7	4	2	1	(Z)	(Z)	1	2	5	7
Long Beach	5	5	5	3	1	(Z)	(Z)	(Z)	1	2	3	5
Los Angeles	6	6	6	3	1	(Z)	1	(Z)	1	2	3	5
Los Angeles[1]	6	5	6	4	1	1	(Z)	1	1	2	3	5
Mount Shasta	12	11	12	9	7	5	2	2	3	6	10	12
Redding	11	8	13	6	6	4	1	1	3	4	7	9
Sacramento	10	9	9	5	3	1	(Z)	(Z)	1	3	7	9
San Diego	7	6	7	4	2	1	(Z)	1	1	2	5	6
San Francisco	11	10	10	6	3	1	(Z)	(Z)	1	4	7	10
San Francisco[1]	11	10	11	6	3	1	1	1	2	4	8	10
Santa Barbara	4	5	6	2	1	(Z)	1	(Z)	1	2	3	5
Santa Maria	7	7	8	5	2	1	(Z)	(Z)	1	2	5	6
Stockton	9	8	8	5	2	1	(Z)	(Z)	1	3	6	6

Source: 1994 Statistical Abstract of the United States on CD-ROM [machine-readable datafiles]. CD-8A-94. Washington, DC: U.S. Department of Commerce, Economics and Statistics Administration, Bureau of the Census, Data User Services Division, January 1995. Primary source: U.S. National Oceanic and Atmospheric Administration. *Comparative Climatic Data* (annual). *Notes:* "Z" represents less than 1/2 day. 1. City office data.

★ 74 ★

Precipitation

Precipitation in Colorado, by Selected City

Table shows the average number of days with precipitation of .01 inch or more. Figures are airport data for period of record through 1992, except as noted.

City	January	February	March	April	May	June	July	August	September	October	November	December
Alamosa	4	4	5	5	6	5	9	10	6	4	4	4
Colorado Springs	5	5	8	7	10	9	13	12	7	5	4	5
Denver	6	6	9	9	11	9	9	9	6	5	6	5
Grand Junction	7	6	8	6	6	4	5	7	6	5	6	6
Pueblo	4	4	6	6	8	7	10	9	5	4	4	4

Source: 1994 Statistical Abstract of the United States on CD-ROM [machine-readable datafiles]. CD-8A-94. Washington, DC: U.S. Department of Commerce, Economics and Statistics Administration, Bureau of the Census, Data User Services Division, January 1995. Primary source: U.S. National Oceanic and Atmospheric Administration. *Comparative Climatic Data* (annual).

★ 75 ★

Precipitation

Precipitation in Connecticut, by Selected City

Table shows the average number of days with precipitation of .01 inch or more. Figures are airport data for period of record through 1992, except as noted.

City	January	February	March	April	May	June	July	August	September	October	November	December
Bridgeport	11	10	11	11	11	10	9	9	9	7	10	11
Hartford	11	10	11	11	12	11	10	10	9	8	11	12

Source: 1994 Statistical Abstract of the United States on CD-ROM [machine-readable datafiles]. CD-8A-94. Washington, DC: U.S. Department of Commerce, Economics and Statistics Administration, Bureau of the Census, Data User Services Division, January 1995. Primary source: U.S. National Oceanic and Atmospheric Administration. *Comparative Climatic Data* (annual).

★ 76 ★

Precipitation

Precipitation in Delaware, by Selected City

Table shows the average number of days with precipitation of .01 inch or more. Figures are airport data for period of record through 1992, except as noted.

City	January	February	March	April	May	June	July	August	September	October	November	December
Wilmington	11	9	11	11	11	10	9	9	8	8	9	10

Source: 1994 Statistical Abstract of the United States on CD-ROM [machine-readable datafiles]. CD-8A-94. Washington, DC: U.S. Department of Commerce, Economics and Statistics Administration, Bureau of the Census, Data User Services Division, January 1995. Primary source: U.S. National Oceanic and Atmospheric Administration. *Comparative Climatic Data* (annual).

★ 77 ★

Precipitation

Precipitation in District of Columbia, by Selected Location

Table shows the average number of days with precipitation of .01 inch or more. Figures are airport data for period of record through 1992, except as noted.

Washington, DC	January	February	March	April	May	June	July	August	September	October	November	December
Dulles Airport	10	9	10	10	12	10	11	10	9	8	9	10
Washington National Airport	10	9	11	10	11	9	10	9	8	7	9	9

Source: 1994 Statistical Abstract of the United States on CD-ROM [machine-readable datafiles]. CD-8A-94. Washington, DC: U.S. Department of Commerce, Economics and Statistics Administration, Bureau of the Census, Data User Services Division, January 1995. Primary source: U.S. National Oceanic and Atmospheric Administration. *Comparative Climatic Data* (annual).

★ 78 ★

Precipitation

Precipitation in Florida, by Selected City

Table shows the average number of days with precipitation of .01 inch or more. Figures are airport data for period of record through 1992, except as noted.

City	January	February	March	April	May	June	July	August	September	October	November	December
Apalachicola	9	8	8	6	5	10	15	14	11	5	6	8
Daytona Beach	7	8	8	6	8	12	13	14	13	10	7	7
Fort Myers	5	6	6	5	8	15	18	18	15	8	4	5
Gainesville	10	8	8	6	8	13	15	17	13	7	7	6
Jacksonville	8	8	8	7	8	12	14	15	13	8	6	8
Key West	6	6	5	5	8	12	12	15	16	11	7	7
Miami	7	6	6	6	10	15	16	17	17	14	9	6
Orlando	6	7	8	6	9	14	17	16	14	8	6	6
Pensacola	10	9	9	6	8	10	14	13	9	5	8	9
Tallahassee	10	9	9	7	9	13	16	15	9	5	7	8
Tampa	6	7	7	5	6	12	16	17	13	7	6	6
Vero Beach	9	7	8	7	9	13	14	13	15	12	10	7
West Palm Beach	8	7	8	7	11	14	15	16	17	13	9	8

Source: 1994 Statistical Abstract of the United States on CD-ROM [machine-readable datafiles]. CD-8A-94. Washington, DC: U.S. Department of Commerce, Economics and Statistics Administration, Bureau of the Census, Data User Services Division, January 1995. Primary source: U.S. National Oceanic and Atmospheric Administration. *Comparative Climatic Data* (annual).

★ 79 ★

Precipitation

Precipitation in Georgia, by Selected City

Table shows the average number of days with precipitation of .01 inch or more. Figures are airport data for period of record through 1992, except as noted.

City	January	February	March	April	May	June	July	August	September	October	November	December
Athens	11	9	11	9	9	9	11	9	8	6	8	10
Atlanta	11	10	11	9	9	10	12	10	8	6	8	10
Augusta	10	9	10	8	9	9	11	10	7	6	7	9
Columbus	10	10	10	8	8	9	13	10	8	5	8	10
Macon	11	10	10	7	9	10	13	11	8	6	7	9
Savannah	9	9	9	7	9	11	14	13	10	6	6	8

Source: 1994 Statistical Abstract of the United States on CD-ROM [machine-readable datafiles]. CD-8A-94. Washington, DC: U.S. Department of Commerce, Economics and Statistics Administration, Bureau of the Census, Data User Services Division, January 1995. Primary source: U.S. National Oceanic and Atmospheric Administration. *Comparative Climatic Data* (annual).

★ 80 ★

Precipitation

Precipitation in Hawaii, by Selected City

Table shows the average number of days with precipitation of .01 inch or more. Figures are airport data for period of record through 1992, except as noted.

City	January	February	March	April	May	June	July	August	September	October	November	December
Hilo	17	17	23	25	25	24	27	27	24	24	23	21
Honolulu	10	9	9	9	7	6	7	6	7	9	9	10
Kahului	11	10	11	10	6	5	6	6	6	7	10	11
Lihue	15	14	17	17	16	16	19	18	16	18	18	17

Source: 1994 Statistical Abstract of the United States on CD-ROM [machine-readable datafiles]. CD-8A-94. Washington, DC: U.S. Department of Commerce, Economics and Statistics Administration, Bureau of the Census, Data User Services Division, January 1995. Primary source: U.S. National Oceanic and Atmospheric Administration. *Comparative Climatic Data* (annual).

★ 81 ★
Precipitation

Precipitation in Idaho, by Selected City

Table shows the average number of days with precipitation of .01 inch or more. Figures are airport data for period of record through 1992, except as noted.

City	January	February	March	April	May	June	July	August	September	October	November	December
Boise	12	10	10	8	8	6	2	3	4	6	10	11
Lewiston	11	9	10	10	9	8	5	4	5	8	11	11
Pocatello	12	10	10	8	9	7	4	4	5	5	9	11

Source: 1994 Statistical Abstract of the United States on CD-ROM [machine-readable datafiles]. CD-8A-94. Washington, DC: U.S. Department of Commerce, Economics and Statistics Administration, Bureau of the Census, Data User Services Division, January 1995. Primary source: U.S. National Oceanic and Atmospheric Administration. *Comparative Climatic Data* (annual).

★ 82 ★
Precipitation

Precipitation in Illinois, by Selected City

Table shows the average number of days with precipitation of .01 inch or more. Figures are airport data for period of record through 1992, except as noted.

City	January	February	March	April	May	June	July	August	September	October	November	December
Cairo	10	9	12	11	11	9	9	8	7	7	9	10
Chicago	11	9	12	13	11	10	10	9	10	9	11	11
Moline	9	8	11	11	12	10	10	9	9	8	9	9
Peoria	9	8	11	12	11	9	9	8	9	8	9	10
Rockford	9	8	11	12	11	10	10	9	9	9	9	10
Springfield	9	9	12	12	10	10	9	8	8	8	9	10

Source: 1994 Statistical Abstract of the United States on CD-ROM [machine-readable datafiles]. CD-8A-94. Washington, DC: U.S. Department of Commerce, Economics and Statistics Administration, Bureau of the Census, Data User Services Division, January 1995. Primary source: U.S. National Oceanic and Atmospheric Administration. *Comparative Climatic Data* (annual).

★ 83 ★

Precipitation

Precipitation in Indiana, by Selected City

Table shows the average number of days with precipitation of .01 inch or more. Figures are airport data for period of record through 1992, except as noted.

City	January	February	March	April	May	June	July	August	September	October	November	December
Evansville	10	9	12	12	11	10	9	7	7	8	10	10
Fort Wayne	12	11	13	13	12	10	10	9	9	9	11	13
Indianapolis	12	10	13	12	12	10	10	9	8	8	10	12
South Bend	15	12	14	13	11	10	9	9	9	10	13	15

Source: 1994 Statistical Abstract of the United States on CD-ROM [machine-readable datafiles]. CD-8A-94. Washington, DC: U.S. Department of Commerce, Economics and Statistics Administration, Bureau of the Census, Data User Services Division, January 1995. Primary source: U.S. National Oceanic and Atmospheric Administration. *Comparative Climatic Data* (annual).

★ 84 ★

Precipitation

Precipitation in Iowa, by Selected City

Table shows the average number of days with precipitation of .01 inch or more. Figures are airport data for period of record through 1992, except as noted.

City	January	February	March	April	May	June	July	August	September	October	November	December
Des Moines	7	7	10	11	11	11	9	9	9	8	7	8
Dubuque	9	8	11	12	11	10	10	9	9	9	9	10
Sioux City	7	6	9	10	11	11	9	9	8	6	6	7
Waterloo	7	6	9	10	11	10	9	8	9	7	7	8

Source: 1994 Statistical Abstract of the United States on CD-ROM [machine-readable datafiles]. CD-8A-94. Washington, DC: U.S. Department of Commerce, Economics and Statistics Administration, Bureau of the Census, Data User Services Division, January 1995. Primary source: U.S. National Oceanic and Atmospheric Administration. *Comparative Climatic Data* (annual).

★ 85 ★

Precipitation

Precipitation in Kansas, by Selected City

Table shows the average number of days with precipitation of .01 inch or more. Figures are airport data for period of record through 1992, except as noted.

City	January	February	March	April	May	June	July	August	September	October	November	December
Concordia	5	5	8	9	11	10	8	9	8	6	5	5
Dodge City	5	5	7	7	10	9	8	8	6	5	4	4
Goodland	4	5	6	7	10	9	9	8	5	4	4	4
Topeka	6	6	9	10	11	10	9	8	8	7	6	6
Wichita	5	5	8	8	11	9	7	8	8	6	5	6

Source: 1994 Statistical Abstract of the United States on CD-ROM [machine-readable datafiles]. CD-8A-94. Washington, DC: U.S. Department of Commerce, Economics and Statistics Administration, Bureau of the Census, Data User Services Division, January 1995. Primary source: U.S. National Oceanic and Atmospheric Administration. *Comparative Climatic Data* (annual).

★ 86 ★

Precipitation

Precipitation in Kentucky, by Selected City

Table shows the average number of days with precipitation of .01 inch or more. Figures are airport data for period of record through 1992, except as noted.

City	January	February	March	April	May	June	July	August	September	October	November	December
Jackson	14	13	13	11	14	11	13	10	9	9	12	14
Lexington	12	11	13	12	12	10	11	9	8	8	11	12
Louisville	11	11	13	12	12	10	11	8	8	8	10	11
Paducah	8	10	10	11	11	8	9	7	7	8	10	10

Source: 1994 Statistical Abstract of the United States on CD-ROM [machine-readable datafiles]. CD-8A-94. Washington, DC: U.S. Department of Commerce, Economics and Statistics Administration, Bureau of the Census, Data User Services Division, January 1995. Primary source: U.S. National Oceanic and Atmospheric Administration. *Comparative Climatic Data* (annual).

★ 87 ★

Precipitation

Precipitation in Louisiana, by Selected City

Table shows the average number of days with precipitation of .01 inch or more. Figures are airport data for period of record through 1992, except as noted.

City	January	February	March	April	May	June	July	August	September	October	November	December
Baton Rouge	10	9	9	7	8	10	13	12	9	5	8	10
Lake Charles	10	8	8	7	8	9	11	11	9	6	8	9
New Orleans	10	9	9	7	8	11	15	13	10	6	7	10
Shreveport	10	8	9	9	9	8	8	7	7	7	8	9

Source: 1994 Statistical Abstract of the United States on CD-ROM [machine-readable datafiles]. CD-8A-94. Washington, DC: U.S. Department of Commerce, Economics and Statistics Administration, Bureau of the Census, Data User Services Division, January 1995. Primary source: U.S. National Oceanic and Atmospheric Administration. *Comparative Climatic Data* (annual).

★ 88 ★

Precipitation

Precipitation in Maine, by Selected City

Table shows the average number of days with precipitation of .01 inch or more. Figures are airport data for period of record through 1992, except as noted.

City	January	February	March	April	May	June	July	August	September	October	November	December
Caribou	15	12	13	13	13	14	14	13	12	13	14	15
Portland	11	10	11	12	12	11	10	10	8	9	12	11

Source: 1994 Statistical Abstract of the United States on CD-ROM [machine-readable datafiles]. CD-8A-94. Washington, DC: U.S. Department of Commerce, Economics and Statistics Administration, Bureau of the Census, Data User Services Division, January 1995. Primary source: U.S. National Oceanic and Atmospheric Administration. *Comparative Climatic Data* (annual).

★ 89 ★

Precipitation

Precipitation in Maryland, by Selected City

Table shows the average number of days with precipitation of .01 inch or more. Figures are airport data for period of record through 1992, except as noted.

City	January	February	March	April	May	June	July	August	September	October	November	December
Baltimore	10	9	11	11	11	9	9	10	8	7	9	9

Source: 1994 Statistical Abstract of the United States on CD-ROM [machine-readable datafiles]. CD-8A-94. Washington, DC: U.S. Department of Commerce, Economics and Statistics Administration, Bureau of the Census, Data User Services Division, January 1995. Primary source: U.S. National Oceanic and Atmospheric Administration. *Comparative Climatic Data* (annual).

★ 90 ★

Precipitation

Precipitation in Massachusetts, by Selected City

Table shows the average number of days with precipitation of .01 inch or more. Figures are airport data for period of record through 1992, except as noted.

City	January	February	March	April	May	June	July	August	September	October	November	December
Blue Hill	12	11	13	12	12	11	11	10	9	10	11	12
Boston	11	10	12	11	12	11	9	10	9	9	11	12
Worcester	12	11	12	11	12	11	10	10	9	9	12	13

Source: 1994 Statistical Abstract of the United States on CD-ROM [machine-readable datafiles]. CD-8A-94. Washington, DC: U.S. Department of Commerce, Economics and Statistics Administration, Bureau of the Census, Data User Services Division, January 1995. Primary source: U.S. National Oceanic and Atmospheric Administration. *Comparative Climatic Data* (annual).

★ 91 ★

Precipitation

Precipitation in Michigan, by Selected City

Table shows the average number of days with precipitation of .01 inch or more. Figures are airport data for period of record through 1992, except as noted.

City	January	February	March	April	May	June	July	August	September	October	November	December
Alpena	14	11	12	12	11	11	10	11	12	13	13	16
Detroit	13	11	13	13	11	10	9	9	10	10	12	14
Flint	13	11	13	13	11	10	9	9	10	9	12	13
Grand Rapids	16	12	13	13	10	10	9	9	11	11	14	16
Houghton Lake	15	11	12	12	10	10	9	10	12	12	14	15
Lansing	15	12	14	13	11	10	10	9	10	9	13	15
Marquette	18	13	15	13	10	12	11	13	15	16	16	18
Muskegon	17	14	13	12	11	9	8	8	10	11	14	16
Sault Sainte Marie	19	15	13	11	11	11	10	11	13	13	17	19

Source: 1994 Statistical Abstract of the United States on CD-ROM [machine-readable datafiles]. CD-8A-94. Washington, DC: U.S. Department of Commerce, Economics and Statistics Administration, Bureau of the Census, Data User Services Division, January 1995. Primary source: U.S. National Oceanic and Atmospheric Administration. *Comparative Climatic Data* (annual).

★ 92 ★

Precipitation

Precipitation in Minnesota, by Selected City

Table shows the average number of days with precipitation of .01 inch or more. Figures are airport data for period of record through 1992, except as noted.

City	January	February	March	April	May	June	July	August	September	October	November	December
Duluth	12	10	11	10	12	13	11	11	12	9	11	12
International Falls	12	9	10	9	11	13	11	12	12	10	11	12
Minneapolis-St. Paul	9	7	10	10	11	12	10	10	10	8	9	9
Rochester	8	8	10	12	11	11	10	10	11	9	9	10
Saint Cloud	9	7	9	9	11	11	10	10	9	7	8	9

Source: 1994 Statistical Abstract of the United States on CD-ROM [machine-readable datafiles]. CD-8A-94. Washington, DC: U.S. Department of Commerce, Economics and Statistics Administration, Bureau of the Census, Data User Services Division, January 1995. Primary source: U.S. National Oceanic and Atmospheric Administration. *Comparative Climatic Data* (annual).

★ 93 ★

Precipitation

Precipitation in Mississippi, by Selected City

Table shows the average number of days with precipitation of .01 inch or more. Figures are airport data for period of record through 1992, except as noted.

City	January	February	March	April	May	June	July	August	September	October	November	December
Jackson	11	9	10	8	10	8	10	10	8	6	8	10
Meridian	11	9	10	9	9	8	11	9	8	5	8	10
Tupelo	10	10	9	9	11	10	8	8	7	7	8	11

Source: 1994 Statistical Abstract of the United States on CD-ROM [machine-readable datafiles]. CD-8A-94. Washington, DC: U.S. Department of Commerce, Economics and Statistics Administration, Bureau of the Census, Data User Services Division, January 1995. Primary source: U.S. National Oceanic and Atmospheric Administration. *Comparative Climatic Data* (annual).

★ 94 ★

Precipitation

Precipitation in Missouri, by Selected City

Table shows the average number of days with precipitation of .01 inch or more. Figures are airport data for period of record through 1992, except as noted.

City	January	February	March	April	May	June	July	August	September	October	November	December
Columbia	7	8	11	11	12	8	8	8	9	9	10	9
Kansas City	7	7	10	11	11	10	8	9	8	8	8	8
Springfield	8	8	10	11	11	10	8	8	8	8	8	9
St. Louis	8	8	11	11	11	9	9	8	8	8	10	9

Source: 1994 Statistical Abstract of the United States on CD-ROM [machine-readable datafiles]. CD-8A-94. Washington, DC: U.S. Department of Commerce, Economics and Statistics Administration, Bureau of the Census, Data User Services Division, January 1995. Primary source: U.S. National Oceanic and Atmospheric Administration. *Comparative Climatic Data* (annual).

★ 95 ★

Precipitation

Precipitation in Montana, by Selected City

Table shows the average number of days with precipitation of .01 inch or more. Figures are airport data for period of record through 1992, except as noted.

City	January	February	March	April	May	June	July	August	September	October	November	December
Billings	8	7	9	10	11	11	7	6	7	6	6	7
Glasgow	8	7	7	7	10	10	8	7	6	5	6	8
Great Falls	9	8	9	9	11	12	7	8	7	6	7	8
Helena	8	6	9	8	11	11	7	7	7	6	7	8
Kalispell	15	12	12	10	11	12	7	8	8	9	13	15
Missoula	14	10	12	10	12	11	7	7	8	8	12	13

Source: 1994 Statistical Abstract of the United States on CD-ROM [machine-readable datafiles]. CD-8A-94. Washington, DC: U.S. Department of Commerce, Economics and Statistics Administration, Bureau of the Census, Data User Services Division, January 1995. Primary source: U.S. National Oceanic and Atmospheric Administration. *Comparative Climatic Data* (annual).

★ 96 ★

Precipitation

Precipitation in Nebraska, by Selected City

Table shows the average number of days with precipitation of .01 inch or more. Figures are airport data for period of record through 1992, except as noted.

City	January	February	March	April	May	June	July	August	September	October	November	December
Grand Island	5	6	8	9	11	10	9	8	7	5	5	5
Lincoln	6	5	9	9	11	8	8	9	8	6	6	6
Norfolk	6	6	8	9	11	10	9	8	8	6	5	6
North Platte	5	5	7	8	11	10	10	8	6	5	5	4

[Continued]

★ 96 ★

Precipitation in Nebraska, by Selected City

[Continued]

City	January	February	March	April	May	June	July	August	September	October	November	December
Omaha (Eppley Airport)	6	7	9	10	12	11	9	9	8	6	6	6
Omaha (north)	5	6	10	10	12	10	9	8	8	7	6	7
Scottsbluff	6	5	8	8	12	11	9	7	7	5	5	5
Valentine	4	5	7	8	11	10	9	8	6	4	4	5

Source: 1994 Statistical Abstract of the United States on CD-ROM [machine-readable datafiles]. CD-8A-94. Washington, DC: U.S. Department of Commerce, Economics and Statistics Administration, Bureau of the Census, Data User Services Division, January 1995. Primary source: U.S. National Oceanic and Atmospheric Administration. *Comparative Climatic Data* (annual).

★ 97 ★

Precipitation

Precipitation in Nevada, by Selected City

Table shows the average number of days with precipitation of .01 inch or more. Figures are airport data for period of record through 1992, except as noted.

City	January	February	March	April	May	June	July	August	September	October	November	December
Elko	9	9	9	7	8	6	3	4	4	5	7	8
Ely	7	7	9	7	7	5	6	5	4	5	5	6
Las Vegas	3	3	3	2	1	1	3	3	2	2	2	3
Reno	6	6	6	4	4	3	2	2	2	3	5	6
Winnemucca	8	7	8	6	6	5	2	3	3	4	7	8

Source: 1994 Statistical Abstract of the United States on CD-ROM [machine-readable datafiles]. CD-8A-94. Washington, DC: U.S. Department of Commerce, Economics and Statistics Administration, Bureau of the Census, Data User Services Division, January 1995. Primary source: U.S. National Oceanic and Atmospheric Administration. *Comparative Climatic Data* (annual).

★ 98 ★

Precipitation

Precipitation in New Hampshire, by Selected City

Table shows the average number of days with precipitation of .01 inch or more. Figures are airport data for period of record through 1992, except as noted.

City	January	February	March	April	May	June	July	August	September	October	November	December
Concord	11	10	11	12	12	11	10	10	9	9	11	11
Mt. Washington	19	18	19	18	17	16	16	16	15	15	19	20

Source: 1994 Statistical Abstract of the United States on CD-ROM [machine-readable datafiles]. CD-8A-94. Washington, DC: U.S. Department of Commerce, Economics and Statistics Administration, Bureau of the Census, Data User Services Division, January 1995. Primary source: U.S. National Oceanic and Atmospheric Administration. *Comparative Climatic Data* (annual).

★ 99 ★

Precipitation

Precipitation in New Jersey, by Selected City

Table shows the average number of days with precipitation of .01 inch or more. Figures are airport data for period of record through 1992, except as noted.

City	January	February	March	April	May	June	July	August	September	October	November	December
Atlantic City	11	10	11	11	10	9	9	9	8	7	9	10
Atlantic City[1]	10	10	10	10	10	9	9	9	8	7	9	10
Newark	11	10	11	11	12	10	10	9	8	8	10	11

Source: *1994 Statistical Abstract of the United States on CD-ROM* [machine-readable datafiles]. CD-8A-94. Washington, DC: U.S. Department of Commerce, Economics and Statistics Administration, Bureau of the Census, Data User Services Division, January 1995. Primary source: U.S. National Oceanic and Atmospheric Administration. *Comparative Climatic Data* (annual). *Note:* 1. City office data.

★ 100 ★

Precipitation

Precipitation in New Mexico, by Selected City

Table shows the average number of days with precipitation of .01 inch or more. Figures are airport data for period of record through 1992, except as noted.

City	January	February	March	April	May	June	July	August	September	October	November	December
Albuquerque	4	4	5	3	5	4	9	9	6	5	3	4
Clayton	4	3	5	5	8	8	10	9	6	4	3	3
Roswell	5	4	3	3	4	5	6	9	7	4	3	4

Source: *1994 Statistical Abstract of the United States on CD-ROM* [machine-readable datafiles]. CD-8A-94. Washington, DC: U.S. Department of Commerce, Economics and Statistics Administration, Bureau of the Census, Data User Services Division, January 1995. Primary source: U.S. National Oceanic and Atmospheric Administration. *Comparative Climatic Data* (annual).

★ 101 ★

Precipitation

Precipitation in New York, by Selected City

Table shows the average number of days with precipitation of .01 inch or more. Figures are airport data for period of record through 1992, except as noted.

City	January	February	March	April	May	June	July	August	September	October	November	December
Albany	12	11	12	12	13	11	10	10	10	9	12	12
Binghamton	17	15	15	14	13	12	11	11	10	12	15	17
Buffalo	20	17	16	14	12	10	10	11	11	12	16	20
Islip	10	9	10	12	10	10	10	8	8	8	11	10
New York (Central Park)	11	10	11	11	11	10	11	10	8	8	9	10
New York (John F. Kennedy Airport)	10	10	11	11	11	10	10	9	8	7	10	11
New York (La Guardia Airport)	11	10	11	11	11	10	10	9	8	8	10	11

[Continued]

★ 101 ★

Precipitation in New York, by Selected City

[Continued]

City	January	February	March	April	May	June	July	August	September	October	November	December
Rochester	18	16	15	13	12	11	10	10	11	12	15	18
Syracuse	19	16	17	14	13	11	11	11	11	12	16	19

Source: 1994 Statistical Abstract of the United States on CD-ROM [machine-readable datafiles]. CD-8A-94. Washington, DC: U.S. Department of Commerce, Economics and Statistics Administration, Bureau of the Census, Data User Services Division, January 1995. Primary source: U.S. National Oceanic and Atmospheric Administration. *Comparative Climatic Data* (annual).

★ 102 ★

Precipitation

Precipitation in North Carolina, by Selected City

Table shows the average number of days with precipitation of .01 inch or more. Figures are airport data for period of record through 1992, except as noted.

City	January	February	March	April	May	June	July	August	September	October	November	December
Asheville	10	9	11	10	12	11	12	13	10	8	10	10
Cape Hatteras	11	10	11	9	10	9	12	11	9	9	9	10
Charlotte	10	10	11	9	10	10	11	10	7	7	8	10
Greensboro/Winston-Salem/High Point	10	10	11	9	10	10	12	11	8	7	8	9
Raleigh	10	10	10	9	10	9	11	10	8	7	8	9
Wilmington	11	10	10	8	10	10	13	12	9	7	8	9

Source: 1994 Statistical Abstract of the United States on CD-ROM [machine-readable datafiles]. CD-8A-94. Washington, DC: U.S. Department of Commerce, Economics and Statistics Administration, Bureau of the Census, Data User Services Division, January 1995. Primary source: U.S. National Oceanic and Atmospheric Administration. *Comparative Climatic Data* (annual).

★ 103 ★

Precipitation

Precipitation in North Dakota, by Selected City

Table shows the average number of days with precipitation of .01 inch or more. Figures are airport data for period of record through 1992, except as noted.

City	January	February	March	April	May	June	July	August	September	October	November	December
Bismarck	8	7	8	8	10	11	9	8	7	6	6	8
Fargo	8	7	8	8	10	11	10	9	8	6	6	8
Williston	8	6	8	8	10	10	9	7	7	5	6	8

Source: 1994 Statistical Abstract of the United States on CD-ROM [machine-readable datafiles]. CD-8A-94. Washington, DC: U.S. Department of Commerce, Economics and Statistics Administration, Bureau of the Census, Data User Services Division, January 1995. Primary source: U.S. National Oceanic and Atmospheric Administration. *Comparative Climatic Data* (annual).

★ 104 ★

Precipitation

Precipitation in Ohio, by Selected City

Table shows the average number of days with precipitation of .01 inch or more. Figures are airport data for period of record through 1992, except as noted.

City	January	February	March	April	May	June	July	August	September	October	November	December
Akron	16	15	16	14	13	11	11	10	10	10	14	16
Greater Cincinnati	12	11	13	13	12	10	10	9	8	8	11	12
Cleveland	16	14	15	14	13	11	10	10	10	11	15	16
Columbus	13	11	14	13	13	11	11	9	8	9	12	13
Dayton	13	11	13	13	12	10	10	9	8	9	11	12
Mansfield	13	12	15	14	13	11	10	10	9	10	13	14
Toledo	13	11	13	13	12	10	10	9	10	9	12	14
Youngstown	17	15	15	14	13	11	11	10	10	11	15	17

Source: 1994 Statistical Abstract of the United States on CD-ROM [machine-readable datafiles]. CD-8A-94. Washington, DC: U.S. Department of Commerce, Economics and Statistics Administration, Bureau of the Census, Data User Services Division, January 1995. Primary source: U.S. National Oceanic and Atmospheric Administration. *Comparative Climatic Data* (annual).

★ 105 ★

Precipitation

Precipitation in Oklahoma, by Selected City

Table shows the average number of days with precipitation of .01 inch or more. Figures are airport data for period of record through 1992, except as noted.

City	January	February	March	April	May	June	July	August	September	October	November	December
Oklahoma City	5	6	7	8	10	9	6	7	7	6	5	6
Tulsa	6	7	8	9	11	9	6	7	7	7	6	7

Source: 1994 Statistical Abstract of the United States on CD-ROM [machine-readable datafiles]. CD-8A-94. Washington, DC: U.S. Department of Commerce, Economics and Statistics Administration, Bureau of the Census, Data User Services Division, January 1995. Primary source: U.S. National Oceanic and Atmospheric Administration. *Comparative Climatic Data* (annual).

★ 106 ★

Precipitation

Precipitation in Oregon, by Selected City

Table shows the average number of days with precipitation of .01 inch or more. Figures are airport data for period of record through 1992, except as noted.

City	January	February	March	April	May	June	July	August	September	October	November	December
Astoria	22	19	20	18	15	13	7	8	10	16	21	22
Burns	8	10	12	7	8	7	3	3	5	7	13	11
Eugene	18	15	17	13	10	7	2	4	6	11	16	18
Medford	13	11	12	9	8	5	2	2	4	8	12	14
Pendleton	12	11	11	9	8	7	3	3	4	7	11	12
Portland	18	16	17	14	12	9	4	5	8	12	18	19
Salem	18	16	17	14	11	8	3	4	7	12	18	19
Sexton Summit	16	15	17	12	9	6	2	3	5	10	16	17

Source: 1994 Statistical Abstract of the United States on CD-ROM [machine-readable datafiles]. CD-8A-94. Washington, DC: U.S. Department of Commerce, Economics and Statistics Administration, Bureau of the Census, Data User Services Division, January 1995. Primary source: U.S. National Oceanic and Atmospheric Administration. *Comparative Climatic Data* (annual).

★ 107 ★

Precipitation

Precipitation in Pennsylvania, by Selected City

Table shows the average number of days with precipitation of .01 inch or more. Figures are airport data for period of record through 1992, except as noted.

City	January	February	March	April	May	June	July	August	September	October	November	December
Allentown	11	10	11	12	12	11	10	10	9	8	10	11
Erie	18	15	15	14	12	10	10	11	11	13	17	19
Harrisburg	11	10	11	13	13	11	10	9	9	9	10	10
Middletown/Harrisburg International Airport	10	10	11	13	13	11	10	9	9	9	10	10
Philadelphia	11	9	11	11	11	10	9	9	8	8	9	10
Pittsburgh	16	14	16	14	13	11	11	10	9	10	13	16
Williamsport	12	11	13	13	13	12	12	11	10	10	12	12

Source: 1994 Statistical Abstract of the United States on CD-ROM [machine-readable datafiles]. CD-8A-94. Washington, DC: U.S. Department of Commerce, Economics and Statistics Administration, Bureau of the Census, Data User Services Division, January 1995. Primary source: U.S. National Oceanic and Atmospheric Administration. *Comparative Climatic Data* (annual).

★ 108 ★

Precipitation

Precipitation in Rhode Island, by Selected City

Table shows the average number of days with precipitation of .01 inch or more. Figures are airport data for period of record through 1992, except as noted.

City	January	February	March	April	May	June	July	August	September	October	November	December
Providence	11	10	12	11	11	11	9	9	8	9	11	12

Source: *1994 Statistical Abstract of the United States on CD-ROM* [machine-readable datafiles]. CD-8A-94. Washington, DC: U.S. Department of Commerce, Economics and Statistics Administration, Bureau of the Census, Data User Services Division, January 1995. Primary source: U.S. National Oceanic and Atmospheric Administration. *Comparative Climatic Data* (annual).

★ 109 ★

Precipitation

Precipitation in South Carolina, by Selected City

Table shows the average number of days with precipitation of .01 inch or more. Figures are airport data for period of record through 1992, except as noted.

City	January	February	March	April	May	June	July	August	September	October	November	December
Charleston	10	9	10	8	9	11	13	13	9	6	7	8
Charleston[1]	10	8	9	7	8	10	10	12	10	5	8	9
Columbia	10	10	10	8	9	10	12	11	8	6	7	9
Greenville-Spartanburg Airport	11	9	11	9	11	10	12	10	8	7	9	10

Source: *1994 Statistical Abstract of the United States on CD-ROM* [machine-readable datafiles]. CD-8A-94. Washington, DC: U.S. Department of Commerce, Economics and Statistics Administration, Bureau of the Census, Data User Services Division, January 1995. Primary source: U.S. National Oceanic and Atmospheric Administration. *Comparative Climatic Data* (annual). *Note:* 1. City office data.

★ 110 ★

Precipitation

Precipitation in South Dakota, by Selected City

Table shows the average number of days with precipitation of .01 inch or more. Figures are airport data for period of record through 1992, except as noted.

City	January	February	March	April	May	June	July	August	September	October	November	December
Aberdeen	6	6	7	8	9	10	8	8	6	5	6	6
Huron	6	7	8	9	10	11	9	8	7	6	6	6
Rapid City	7	7	9	9	12	12	9	8	6	5	6	6
Sioux Falls	6	6	9	9	11	11	10	9	8	6	6	6

Source: *1994 Statistical Abstract of the United States on CD-ROM* [machine-readable datafiles]. CD-8A-94. Washington, DC: U.S. Department of Commerce, Economics and Statistics Administration, Bureau of the Census, Data User Services Division, January 1995. Primary source: U.S. National Oceanic and Atmospheric Administration. *Comparative Climatic Data* (annual).

★ 111 ★

Precipitation

Precipitation in Tennessee, by Selected City

Table shows the average number of days with precipitation of .01 inch or more. Figures are airport data for period of record through 1992, except as noted.

City	January	February	March	April	May	June	July	August	September	October	November	December
Bristol-Johnson City-Kingsport	14	12	13	11	12	11	12	11	8	8	10	11
Chattanooga	12	11	12	10	10	10	12	10	8	7	9	11
Knoxville	12	11	13	11	11	10	11	10	8	8	10	11
Memphis	10	10	11	10	9	8	9	8	7	6	9	10
Nashville	11	11	12	11	11	9	10	9	8	7	9	11
Oak Ridge	12	11	12	11	11	11	12	10	8	8	10	11

Source: 1994 Statistical Abstract of the United States on CD-ROM [machine-readable datafiles]. CD-8A-94. Washington, DC: U.S. Department of Commerce, Economics and Statistics Administration, Bureau of the Census, Data User Services Division, January 1995. Primary source: U.S. National Oceanic and Atmospheric Administration. *Comparative Climatic Data* (annual).

★ 112 ★

Precipitation

Precipitation in Texas, by Selected City

Table shows the average number of days with precipitation of .01 inch or more. Figures are airport data for period of record through 1992, except as noted.

City	January	February	March	April	May	June	July	August	September	October	November	December
Abilene	5	5	5	6	8	6	5	6	6	6	4	5
Amarillo	4	4	5	5	8	8	8	8	6	5	3	4
Austin	8	8	7	7	9	6	5	5	7	6	7	8
Brownsville	8	6	4	4	5	6	5	7	10	6	6	7
Corpus Christi	8	7	5	5	7	6	5	6	9	6	6	7
Dallas-Fort Worth	7	6	7	8	9	7	5	5	7	6	6	7
Del Rio	5	5	5	6	7	5	4	4	7	5	4	6
El Paso	4	3	2	2	3	3	8	8	5	4	3	4
Galveston	10	9	8	6	6	7	9	9	9	6	8	10
Houston	11	9	9	7	8	9	10	9	9	7	9	9
Lubbock	4	4	4	4	8	7	7	7	6	5	3	4
Midland-Odessa	4	4	3	3	6	5	5	6	6	4	3	3
Port Arthur	10	9	8	7	7	8	11	12	10	6	8	9
San Angelo	5	5	4	5	7	5	5	5	6	5	4	4
San Antonio	8	8	7	7	9	6	4	5	7	6	6	8
Victoria	8	7	7	6	7	7	8	8	10	6	7	8
Waco	7	7	7	7	9	6	4	5	6	6	6	6
Wichita Falls	5	6	6	7	9	7	5	6	6	6	5	5

Source: 1994 Statistical Abstract of the United States on CD-ROM [machine-readable datafiles]. CD-8A-94. Washington, DC: U.S. Department of Commerce, Economics and Statistics Administration, Bureau of the Census, Data User Services Division, January 1995. Primary source: U.S. National Oceanic and Atmospheric Administration. *Comparative Climatic Data* (annual).

★ 113 ★

Precipitation

Precipitation in the Upper Mississippi River Basin and Southeastern United States, 1896-1993

Precipitation in the Upper Mississippi River Basin refers to cumulative total for the April-August period. Precipitation in the Southeastern United States refers to the cumulative total for the May-August period.

[In inches]

Year	Upper Mississippi River Basin	South- eastern United States
1896	21.48	20.16
1900	18.19	19.02
1905	21.74	22.15
1910	13.94	22.86
1915	22.14	20.91
1920	17.24	21.15
1925	15.56	13.69
1930	12.96	14.91
1935	21.08	20.10
1940	18.10	22.15
1945	21.27	21.33
1950	18.61	20.55
1955	17.15	19.98
1960	20.14	19.46
1965	20.59	19.91
1970	19.65	19.74
1975	18.81	22.64
1980	17.79	15.41
1985	17.56	21.85
1990	24.14	16.73
1991	19.79	23.96
1992	15.93	22.00
1993	28.58	13.52

Source: Executive Office of the President of the United States. *Environmental Quality 24: The Twenty-fourth Annual Report of the Council on Environmental Quality.* Prepared by Ray Clark. Written by Carroll Curtis. Edited by Barry Walsh. Washington, DC: U.S. Government Printing Office, 1994, p. 423. Primary source: U.S. Department of Commerce. National Oceanic and Atmospheric Administration. National Climatic Data Center (Ashville, North Carolina; 1994).

★ 114 ★

Precipitation

Precipitation in Utah, by Selected City

Table shows the average number of days with precipitation of .01 inch or more. Figures are airport data for period of record through 1992, except as noted.

City	January	February	March	April	May	June	July	August	September	October	November	December
Milford	7	7	8	6	5	3	5	6	4	4	5	6
Salt Lake City	10	9	10	9	8	5	5	6	5	6	8	9

Source: 1994 Statistical Abstract of the United States on CD-ROM [machine-readable datafiles]. CD-8A-94. Washington, DC: U.S. Department of Commerce, Economics and Statistics Administration, Bureau of the Census, Data User Services Division, January 1995. Primary source: U.S. National Oceanic and Atmospheric Administration. *Comparative Climatic Data* (annual).

★ 115 ★

Precipitation

Precipitation in U.S. Territories and Administered Areas

Table shows the average number of days with precipitation of .01 inch or more. Figures are airport data for period of record through 1992, except as noted.

Location	January	February	March	April	May	June	July	August	September	October	November	December
Guam	21	18	19	20	20	24	26	26	25	26	25	23
Johnston Island	11	12	15	14	13	12	12	13	14	16	15	16
Koror	22	19	20	19	24	25	24	23	21	23	22	24
Majuro, Marshall Islands	17	15	18	21	23	24	25	23	23	23	23	22
Pago Pago, American Samoa	25	22	23	22	21	19	19	18	17	22	21	23
Pohnpei, Caroline Islands	22	20	23	24	27	27	27	27	24	25	25	25
San Juan, Puerto Rico	17	13	12	13	16	15	19	18	17	17	18	19
Wake Island	11	10	12	14	15	16	19	19	19	19	15	13
Yap, West Caroline Islands	21	18	18	17	21	24	25	24	23	24	23	22

Source: 1994 Statistical Abstract of the United States on CD-ROM [machine-readable datafiles]. CD-8A-94. Washington, DC: U.S. Department of Commerce, Economics and Statistics Administration, Bureau of the Census, Data User Services Division, January 1995. Primary source: U.S. National Oceanic and Atmospheric Administration. *Comparative Climatic Data* (annual).

★ 116 ★

Precipitation

Precipitation in Vermont, by Selected City

Table shows the average number of days with precipitation of .01 inch or more. Figures are airport data for period of record through 1992, except as noted.

City	January	February	March	April	May	June	July	August	September	October	November	December
Burlington	14	12	13	12	14	12	12	13	12	12	14	15

Source: 1994 Statistical Abstract of the United States on CD-ROM [machine-readable datafiles]. CD-8A-94. Washington, DC: U.S. Department of Commerce, Economics and Statistics Administration, Bureau of the Census, Data User Services Division, January 1995. Primary source: U.S. National Oceanic and Atmospheric Administration. *Comparative Climatic Data* (annual).

★ 117 ★

Precipitation

Precipitation in Virginia, by Selected City

Table shows the average number of days with precipitation of .01 inch or more. Figures are airport data for period of record through 1992, except as noted.

City	January	February	March	April	May	June	July	August	September	October	November	December
Lynchburg	11	10	11	10	12	10	11	10	8	8	9	10
Norfolk	11	10	11	10	10	9	11	11	8	8	8	9
Richmond	10	9	11	9	11	9	11	10	8	7	8	9
Roanoke	10	10	11	10	12	10	12	11	8	8	9	9
Wallops Island	11	10	11	10	10	9	11	9	8	8	9	10

Source: 1994 Statistical Abstract of the United States on CD-ROM [machine-readable datafiles]. CD-8A-94. Washington, DC: U.S. Department of Commerce, Economics and Statistics Administration, Bureau of the Census, Data User Services Division, January 1995. Primary source: U.S. National Oceanic and Atmospheric Administration. *Comparative Climatic Data* (annual).

★ 118 ★

Precipitation

Precipitation in Washington, by Selected City

Table shows the average number of days with precipitation of .01 inch or more. Figures are airport data for period of record through 1992, except as noted.

City	January	February	March	April	May	June	July	August	September	October	November	December
Olympia	20	17	18	15	11	9	5	6	8	14	19	21
Quillayute	22	20	21	19	17	14	11	10	12	18	22	23
Seattle[1]	19	16	17	14	11	9	5	6	9	11	18	19
Seattle-Tacoma Airport	19	16	17	14	10	9	5	6	9	13	18	19
Spokane	14	11	11	9	9	8	4	5	6	8	13	15

[Continued]

★ 118 ★

Precipitation in Washington, by Selected City

[Continued]

City	January	February	March	April	May	June	July	August	September	October	November	December
Walla Walla	13	11	12	9	8	7	3	3	5	8	12	14
Yakima	9	7	7	5	5	5	2	3	3	5	9	10

Source: 1994 Statistical Abstract of the United States on CD-ROM [machine-readable datafiles]. CD-8A-94. Washington, DC: U.S. Department of Commerce, Economics and Statistics Administration, Bureau of the Census, Data User Services Division, January 1995. Primary source: U.S. National Oceanic and Atmospheric Administration. *Comparative Climatic Data* (annual). *Note:* 1. City office data.

★ 119 ★

Precipitation

Precipitation in West Virginia, by Selected City

Table shows the average number of days with precipitation of .01 inch or more. Figures are airport data for period of record through 1992, except as noted.

City	January	February	March	April	May	June	July	August	September	October	November	December
Beckley	16	15	15	15	14	12	13	11	11	10	13	15
Charleston	15	14	15	14	13	11	13	11	10	9	12	14
Elkins	18	16	17	15	14	13	14	12	11	11	14	17
Huntington	14	13	14	13	13	11	12	9	9	9	11	13

Source: 1994 Statistical Abstract of the United States on CD-ROM [machine-readable datafiles]. CD-8A-94. Washington, DC: U.S. Department of Commerce, Economics and Statistics Administration, Bureau of the Census, Data User Services Division, January 1995. Primary source: U.S. National Oceanic and Atmospheric Administration. *Comparative Climatic Data* (annual).

★ 120 ★

Precipitation

Precipitation in Wisconsin, by Selected City

Table shows the average number of days with precipitation of .01 inch or more. Figures are airport data for period of record through 1992, except as noted.

City	January	February	March	April	May	June	July	August	September	October	November	December
Green Bay	10	8	11	11	11	10	10	10	10	9	10	11
La Crosse	8	7	10	10	11	11	10	10	10	8	8	9
Madison	10	8	11	12	11	10	10	9	9	9	10	10
Milwaukee	11	10	12	12	12	11	10	9	9	9	11	11

Source: 1994 Statistical Abstract of the United States on CD-ROM [machine-readable datafiles]. CD-8A-94. Washington, DC: U.S. Department of Commerce, Economics and Statistics Administration, Bureau of the Census, Data User Services Division, January 1995. Primary source: U.S. National Oceanic and Atmospheric Administration. *Comparative Climatic Data* (annual).

★ 121 ★

Precipitation

Precipitation in Wyoming, by Selected City

Table shows the average number of days with precipitation of .01 inch or more. Figures are airport data for period of record through 1992, except as noted.

City	January	February	March	April	May	June	July	August	September	October	November	December
Casper	7	8	9	10	11	9	8	6	6	6	7	8
Cheyenne	6	6	9	10	12	11	11	10	7	6	6	6
Lander	4	5	8	8	9	6	6	5	5	5	5	5
Sheridan	9	9	11	11	12	11	7	6	7	7	8	9

Source: 1994 Statistical Abstract of the United States on CD-ROM [machine-readable datafiles]. CD-8A-94. Washington, DC: U.S. Department of Commerce, Economics and Statistics Administration, Bureau of the Census, Data User Services Division, January 1995. Primary source: U.S. National Oceanic and Atmospheric Administration. *Comparative Climatic Data* (annual).

Snow and Ice

★ 122 ★

Snow and Ice Pellets in East North Central United States, by City

Table shows snow and ice for period of record through 1992. Figures are airport data, except as noted.

[In inches]

City and state	January	February	March	April	May	June	July	August	September	October	November	December
Cairo, Illinois	3.8	2.5	2.1	0	0	0	0	0	0	0	0.4	1.4
Chicago, Illinois	10.5	8.1	6.8	1.7	0.1	T	T	T	T	0.4	1.9	8.5
Moline, Illinois	7.8	5.9	6	1	0	T	0	0	0	0.2	2.2	7.1
Peoria, Illinois	6.6	5.3	4.1	0.9	0	0	T	0	T	0.1	2	6
Rockford, Illinois	8.5	6.6	6.4	1.3	0	0	T	T	0	0.1	2.7	9.4
Springfield, Illinois	5.7	6.2	4.1	0.7	T	0	0	0	0	0	1.7	5
Evansville, Indiana	4.1	3.4	2.5	0.3	0	0	0	0	T	0	0.6	2.4
Fort Wayne, Indiana	8	7.4	5.2	1.4	T	T	0	T	0	0.3	3.2	7.1
Indianapolis, Indiana	6.1	5.6	3.4	0.5	0	T	0	T	0	0.2	1.8	4.9
South Bend, Indiana	19.1	14.5	8.9	2	0	T	T	T	0	0.7	8.1	17.9
Alpena, Michigan	21.5	15.6	13.5	4.7	0.3	0	0	T	T	0.6	8.2	21
Detroit, Michigan	10.2	8.9	6.7	1.6	T	0	0	0	T	0.2	3	10.4
Flint, Michigan	11.6	9.6	7.5	2.4	0	T	T	0	T	0.2	3.9	9.8
Grand Rapids, Michigan	20.5	11.7	10	3	0	0	T	0	T	0.8	7.9	18.1
Houghton Lake, Michigan	19.3	12.9	11.6	4.1	0.3	0	T	0	0	0.8	9.8	17
Lansing, Michigan	11.9	9.9	8.4	2.7	0.2	T	0	0	0	0.4	4.5	10.8
Marquette, Michigan	26.8	23	21.2	8.7	1.4	T	0	T	0.2	3.9	16.6	26.8
Muskegon, Michigan	31.3	17.3	11.3	2.7	0	0	T	0	T	0.5	9	24.9
Sault Sainte Marie, Michigan	28.7	19	15.1	5.5	0.5	T	0	T	0.1	2.4	15.4	30
Akron, Ohio	11.3	9.3	8.8	2.6	0.1	T	0	0	T	0.5	4.6	10
Greater Cincinnati Airport	6.8	5.2	4.2	0.5	0	0	T	0	0	0.2	2.1	3.9
Cleveland, Ohio	12.6	11.8	10.3	2.3	0.1	0	0	0	T	0.6	5.1	11.8
Columbus, Ohio	8.3	6.1	4.4	0.9	0	T	0	0	T	0	2.3	5.5
Dayton, Ohio	7.8	6	5.1	0.7	T	0	T	0	0	0.2	2.1	5.5
Mansfield, Ohio	11.2	10	6.7	1.9	0.1	0	0	0	T	0.2	2.4	8.7
Toledo, Ohio	9.4	8.1	6	1.6	0	0	T	0	T	0.1	2.9	8.5

[Continued]

★ 122 ★

Snow and Ice Pellets in East North Central United States, by City
[Continued]

City and state	January	February	March	April	May	June	July	August	September	October	November	December
Youngstown, Ohio	12.9	10.8	10.6	2.5	0.1	0	T	0	T	0.5	5.7	12.5
Green Bay, Wisconsin	10.5	8.3	9	2.3	0.2	T	0	T	T	0.2	4.7	11.2
La Crosse, Wisconsin	9.9	7.8	9.1	1.6	0	0	0	0	T	0.1	4.4	9.3
Madison, Wisconsin	9.7	7.2	8.1	2.1	0.1	T	T	T	T	0.2	3.7	11.2
Milwaukee, Wisconsin	12.8	9.6	8.6	1.7	0.1	T	T	T	T	0.3	2.9	10.6

Source: 1994 Statistical Abstract of the United States on CD-ROM [machine-readable datafiles]. CD-8A-94. Washington, DC: U.S. Department of Commerce, Economics and Statistics Administration, Bureau of the Census, Data User Services Division, January 1995. Primary source: U.S. National Oceanic and Atmospheric Administration. *Comparative Climatic Data* (annual). *Note:* "T" denotes trace.

★ 123 ★

Snow and Ice

Snow and Ice Pellets in East South Central United States, by City

Table shows snow and ice for period of record through 1992. Figures are airport data, except as noted.

[In inches]

City and state	January	February	March	April	May	June	July	August	September	October	November	December
Birminghan, Alabama	0.7	0.2	0.1	0.1	T	T	T	0	T	T	0	0.3
Birmingham, Alabama[1]	0.8	0.1	0.5	0.5	0	0	0	0	0	0	T	T
Huntsville, Alabama	1.5	0.8	0.2	T	0	0	0	T	0	T	0	0.2
Mobile, Alabama	0.1	0.2	0	T	T	0	T	0	0	0	T	0.1
Montgomery, Alabama	0.2	0.1	T	0	0	0	0	0	0	0	T	0
Lexington, Kentucky	5.5	4.7	2.6	0.3	T	0	T	T	0	0	0.6	1.8
Louisville, Kentucky	5.2	4.3	3.2	0.2	T	0	0	0	0	0	1.1	2.1
Paducah, Kentucky	3	3.6	0.5	T	0	T	T	0	0	T	T	2.5
Jackson, Mississippi	0.5	0.2	0.2	0	0	0	0	0	0	0	0	0
Meridian, Mississippi	0.5	0.2	0	0.1	T	0	T	0	0	0	T	0.4
Tupelo, Mississippi	1.5	0.9	0.2	0	T	0	T	0	0	0	0	0.4
Bristol/Johnson City/Kingsport, Tennessee	5.2	4.4	2.1	0.4	T	0	0	0	0	0	1	2.7
Chattanooga, Tennessee	1.8	1.2	0.4	0.1	T	0	0	0	0	T	0.1	0.6
Knoxville, Tennessee	4	3.6	1.5	0.4	T	0	0	0	0	T	0.6	1.6
Memphis, Tennessee	2.4	1.4	0.9	T	T	0	0	0	0	T	0.1	0.7
Nashville, Tennessee	3.9	3	1.4	0	0	0	0	T	0	T	0.5	1.5
Oak Ridge, Tennessee	3.3	3	1.1	0.2	T	0	T	T	0	T	0.3	1.8

Source: 1994 Statistical Abstract of the United States on CD-ROM [machine-readable datafiles]. CD-8A-94. Washington, DC: U.S. Department of Commerce, Economics and Statistics Administration, Bureau of the Census, Data User Services Division, January 1995. Primary source: U.S. National Oceanic and Atmospheric Administration. *Comparative Climatic Data* (annual). *Notes:* "T" denotes trace. 1. City office data.

★ 124 ★

Snow and Ice

Snow and Ice Pellets in Middle Atlantic United States, by City

Table shows snow and ice for period of record through 1992. Figures are airport data, except as noted.

[In inches]

City and state	January	February	March	April	May	June	July	August	September	October	November	December
Atlantic City, New Jersey	5.3	5.4	2.6	0.3	T	0	T	0	0	T	0.4	2.2
Newark, New Jersey	7.6	7.8	4.6	0.7	T	0	0	0	0	0	0.5	5.5
Albany, New York	16.1	13.9	10.6	2.7	0.1	T	T	0	T	0.2	4.2	15.1
Binghamton, New York	19.7	17.1	13.5	4.8	0.3	0	0	0	T	0.5	7.4	17.9
Buffalo, New York	23.5	18.2	11.3	3.2	0.3	T	0	T	T	0.2	11.6	22.6
Islip, New York	6.6	4.1	3.9	0.3	T	0	0	0	0	0	1	3.7
New York, New York (Central Park)	7.6	8.4	4.9	0.9	T	0	T	0	0	0	0.9	5.4
New York, New York (John F. Kennedy Airport)	7.2	7.6	3.6	0.4	T	0	0	0	0	0	0.3	3.4
New York, New York (La Guardia Airport)	6.8	8	4.2	0.6	T	0	0	0	0	0	0.5	4.7
Rochester, New York	22.7	22.2	13.9	3.6	0.3	0	T	T	T	0.1	6.7	19.7
Syracuse, New York	29.2	25.6	16.6	3.8	0.1	T	T	0	T	0.6	9.1	26.6
Allentown, Pennsylvania	8.5	8.9	5.5	0.7	T	0	0	0	0	0.1	1.3	6.2
Erie, Pennsylvania	23.1	15.6	10	2.7	0	T	0	T	T	0.3	10.5	22.8
Harrisburg, Pennsylvania	9.7	9.2	6.1	0.5	T	0	0	0	0	0	2	6.8
Middletown/Harrisburg International Airport	9.5	9.2	6.2	0.5	T	T	0	0	0	0	2	6.7
Philadelphia, Pennsylvania	6.5	6.3	3.6	0.3	T	0	0	0	0	0	0.7	3.5
Pittsburgh, Pennsylvania	11.5	9.1	8	1.7	0.1	T	T	0	T	0.2	3.3	8.2
Avoca, Pennsylvania	11.4	10.8	8.8	3.1	0.1	0	0	0	T	0.2	3.4	8.9
Williamsport, Pennsylvania	10.6	9.8	7.9	1.2	0	T	0	T	0	0	3	8.3

Source: 1994 Statistical Abstract of the United States on CD-ROM [machine-readable datafiles]. CD-8A-94. Washington, DC: U.S. Department of Commerce, Economics and Statistics Administration, Bureau of the Census, Data User Services Division, January 1995. Primary source: U.S. National Oceanic and Atmospheric Administration. *Comparative Climatic Data* (annual). *Note:* "T" denotes trace.

★ 125 ★

Snow and Ice

Snow and Ice Pellets in New England, by City

Table shows snow and ice for period of record through 1992. Figures are airport data, except as noted.

[In inches]

City and state	January	February	March	April	May	June	July	August	September	October	November	December
Bridgeport, Connecticut	7.4	7.2	4.6	0.5	T	0	T	T	0	0	0.6	4.5
Hartford, Connecticut	12	11.3	9.3	1.6	0	0	0	0	0	0.1	2	10.4
Caribou, Maine	23.7	21.6	19.1	8.4	0.7	T	T	0	0	1.7	12.1	23.1
Portland, Maine	19	17.1	12.3	2.9	0.2	0	0	0	T	0.2	3	14.6
Blue Hill, Massachusetts	15.3	15.9	11.2	3	0.1	T	0	0	0	0.2	2.8	10.8
Boston, Massachusetts	12	11.2	7.4	0.9	0	0	0	0	0	0	1.3	7.4
Worcester, Massachusetts	16.2	15.8	13.3	3.8	0.4	0	0	0	T	0.5	3.7	13.4
Concord, New Hampshire	17.7	14.4	10.4	2.3	0.1	0	0	0	T	0.1	3.9	13.6
Mt. Washington, New Hampshire	40.1	40.7	42.5	31.5	10.5	1.1	0	0.2	1.9	11.8	31.9	42.8
Providence, Rhode Island	9.5	9.5	7.4	0.8	0.2	0	0	0	0	0.1	1	6.9
Burlington, Vermont	18.7	16.5	11.9	3.6	0.2	0	T	0	0	0.2	6.6	18.3

Source: 1994 Statistical Abstract of the United States on CD-ROM [machine-readable datafiles]. CD-8A-94. Washington, DC: U.S. Department of Commerce, Economics and Statistics Administration, Bureau of the Census, Data User Services Division, January 1995. Primary source: U.S. National Oceanic and Atmospheric Administration. *Comparative Climatic Data* (annual). *Note:* "T" denotes trace.

★ 126 ★

Snow and Ice

Snow and Ice Pellets in Pacific United States, by City

Table shows snow and ice for period of record through 1992. Figures are airport data, except as noted.

[In inches]

City and state	January	February	March	April	May	June	July	August	September	October	November	December
Anchorage, Alaska	10.6	11.3	9	4.9	0.4	0	0	0	0.3	7.3	10.6	15
Annette, Alaska	12.7	11.1	9	2.3	0.1	T	0	0	0	0.2	3.2	11.2
Barrow, Alaska	2.1	2.1	1.8	2.1	1.8	0.6	0.5	0.7	3.5	6.7	3.4	2.5
Barter Island, Alaska	4.6	2.5	2.5	2.3	2.9	1.6	0.5	1.6	5.7	9.5	5.1	3.3
Bethel, Alaska	5.5	5.4	5.4	2	0.1	T	0	0.3	4.2	8.5	9.6
Bettles, Alaska	11.8	9.3	10.1	7.4	1.2	T	0	0.1	1.6	11.9	12.8	15
Big Delta, Alaska	5.7	4.4	4.3	3	0.7	T	0	T	1.6	9.1	7.4	6
Cold Bay, Alaska	10.6	11.5	10.5	6	1.8	0	T	0	0	3	7.8	10.1
Fairbanks, Alaska	10.1	8.7	6.6	3.5	0.8	T	T	T	1.5	10.9	13.5	14
Gulkana, Alaska	7.3	6.9	5.1	2.7	0.5	0	0	0.1	1.1	7.5	8.6	10.5
Homer, Alaska	10.4	12.2	9.5	3.3	0.4	T	0	0	0	2.2	7.4	13.1
Juneau, Alaska	25.8	18.6	15.2	3.6	0	T	0	0	T	1.1	12	22.8
King Salmon, Alaska	7.8	6.8	7.4	4.6	0.9	0	0	0	0	3	6.3	8.6
Kodiak, Alaska	15.7	18.3	13.3	8.2	0.7	T	0	0	0	2.3	7.9	13.5
Kotzebue, Alaska	6.1	5	5.9	4.9	1.6	0.1	0	0	1	6.6	8.2	7.7
McGrath, Alaska	13.9	12.1	12.5	7.1	0.9	0	T	T	1.1	10.2	17	18.9
Nome, Alaska	9.2	6.4	7.2	6.7	2.2	0.2	0	0	0.4	4.7	10.6	9
St. Paul Island, Alaska	11.8	9.5	9.1	5.6	2.1	0.1	0	0	0.1	2.6	6.6	9.4
Talkeetna, Alaska	19.4	18.8	18	8	0.8	T	0	T	0.2	10.3	16.8	22
Unalakleet, Alaska	5.1	6	5.9	3.8	1	0	0	0	0.9	4.1	7.3	5.5
Valdez, Alaska	64.3	56.1	54.7	22.7	0.6	0	0	0	0.2	10.9	40.5	75.7
Yakutat, Alaska	38.9	39.4	39	17.9	1.5	T	0	0	0	5.4	22	39.4
Bakersfield, California	T	T	0	0	0	0	0	0	0	0	0	T
Bishop, California	3.8	1.4	0.8	0.3	0.1	0	0	0	T	0	0.3	1.3
Blue Canyon, California	46.7	42.2	50.7	27.8	7.6	0.5	0	0	0.3	2.6	23.6	38.8
Eureka, California	0.2	0.1	0	T	0	0	0	0	0	0	0	0
Fresno, California	0.1	T	T	0	0	0	0	0	0	T	0	0
Long Beach, California	T	0	0	0	0	0	0	0	0	0	0	0
Los Angeles, California	T	T	T	0	0	0	0	0	0	0	0	T
Los Angeles, California[1]	0	T	0	0	0	0	0	0	0	0	0	T
Mount Shasta, California	29.9	16.9	17.1	8.9	0.8	T	0	0	0	0.4	9	21.9
Redding, California	0.5	0.2	0.3	T	0.3	T	0	0	0	0	T	2.5
Sacramento, California	T	0	T	0	0	0	0	0	0	0	0	T
San Diego, California	T	0	T	0	0	0	0	0	0	0	T	T
San Francisco, California	0	T	T	0	0	0	0	0	0	0	0	0
San Francisco, California[1]	T	T	T	0	0	0	0	0	0	0	0	T
Santa Barbara, California	0	0	0	0	0	0	0	0	0	0	0	0
Santa Maria, California	T	T	T	0	0	0	0	0	0	0	T	T
Stockton, California	0	0	T	T	0	0	0	0	0	0	0	0
Hilo, Hawaii	0	0	0	0	0	0	0	0	0	0	0	0
Honolulu, Hawaii	0	0	0	0	0	0	0	0	0	0	0	0
Kahului, Hawaii	0	0	0	0	0	0	0	0	0	0	0	0
Lihue, Hawaii	0	0	0	0	0	0	0	0	0	0	0	0
Astoria, Oregon	2.1	0.3	0.6	0	T	T	0	0	T	T	0.2	1.2
Burns, Oregon	6.4	8	4.8	0.8	0.3	0.1	0	0	T	0.8	7.1	13.3
Eugene, Oregon	3.6	0.7	0.5	T	T	T	0	0	T	T	0.3	1.3
Medford, Oregon	3.3	1.2	0.8	0.2	0	T	T	0	0	0	0.5	1.4
Pendleton, Oregon	7	3.3	0.9	0.1	T	0	0	0	0	0.1	1.7	4.1
Portland, Oregon	3.3	0.9	0.4	T	0	T	0	T	T	0	0.4	1.4
Salem, Oregon	2.8	1.1	0.6	0	T	T	0	0	T	T	0.3	1.6
Sexton Summit, Oregon	21.3	15.4	18.6	8.8	2.1	0.1	0	T	0.1	1.5	9.7	20.2
Olympia, Washington	7.3	3.3	1.8	0.1	T	T	0	0	T	T	1.4	3.5
Quillayute, Washington	5.1	2.9	1.6	0.4	T	T	0	0	T	T	1	2.9
Seattle, Washington[1]	3.1	0.9	0.7	0	T	0	0	0	0	T	0.7	1.9
Seattle-Tacoma Airport, Washington	5	1.7	1.4	0.1	T	0	T	0	T	0	1.2	2.6
Spokane, Washington	16.1	7.5	4.1	0.7	0.1	T	0	0	T	0.4	6.3	15.3
Walla Walla, Washington	7.5	3.9	1.2	0.2	T	0	0	0	0	0.1	2	5
Yakima, Washington	8.3	3.2	1.5	T	T	0	0	0	0	0.1	2.2	8.5

Source: 1994 Statistical Abstract of the United States on CD-ROM [machine-readable datafiles]. CD-8A-94. Washington, DC: U.S. Department of Commerce, Economics and Statistics Administration, Bureau of the Census, Data User Services Division, January 1995. Primary source: U.S. National Oceanic and Atmospheric Administration. *Comparative Climatic Data* (annual). *Notes:* "T" denotes trace. 1. City office data.

★ 127 ★

Snow and Ice

Snow and Ice Pellets in South Atlantic United States, by City

Table shows snow and ice for period of record through 1992. Figures are airport data, except as noted.

[In inches]

City and state	January	February	March	April	May	June	July	August	September	October	November	December
Wilmington, Delaware	6.7	5.9	3.1	0.2	T	T	T	0	0	0.1	0.9	3.3
Washington, District of Columbia (Dulles Airport)	7.3	6.7	2.9	0.3	T	0	0	0	0	0	1.2	3.9
Washington National Airport (District of Columbia)	5.4	5.3	2	0	T	0	T	T	0	0	0.9	3.1
Apalachicola, Florida	0	0	T	0	0	0	0	0	0	0	0	T
Daytona Beach, Florida	T	T	0	0	0	T	0	0	0	0	0	T
Fort Myers, Florida	0	0	0	0	0	0	0	0	0	0	0	0
Gainesville, Florida	0	T	T	0	0	0	0	T	0	0	0	T
Jacksonville, Florida	T	0	0	0	0	0	T	0	0	0	0	0
Key West, Florida	0	0	0	0	0	0	0	0	0	0	0	0
Miami, Florida	0	0	0	0	0	0	0	0	0	0	0	0
Orlando, Florida	T	0	T	T	0	0	T	T	0	0	0	0
Pensacola, Florida	0.1	0.1	T	0	0	0	0	0	0	0	0	T
Tallahassee, Florida	T	0	T	0	0	T	0	0	T	0	0	T
Tampa, Florida	0	T	T	0	0	0	0	0	0	0	0	0
Vero Beach, Florida	0	0	0	0	0	T	T	0	0	0	0	0
West Palm Beach, Florida	T	0	0	0	0	0	0	0	0	0	0	0
Athens, Georgia	1	0.7	0.4	0	0	0	0	0	0	0	0.1	0.2
Atlanta, Georgia	0.9	0.5	0.4	T	0	0	0	0	0	0	0	0.2
Augusta, Georgia	0.3	0.8	0	T	0	0	0	0	0	0	T	0
Columbus, Georgia	0.1	0.3	0	T	0	0	0	0	0	0	T	T
Macon, Georgia	0.3	0.6	0	0	T	0	0	0	0	0	0	0
Savannah, Georgia	0.1	0.2	0	0	0	T	0	0	0	0	0	0.1
Baltimore, Maryland	6	6.4	3.5	0.1	T	0	T	0	0	0	1	3.5
Asheville, North Carolina	4.8	4.6	2.5	0.7	T	T	0	T	0	T	0.8	1.8
Cape Hatteras, North Carolina	0.4	0.6	0.5	T	0	0	0	0	0	0	T	0.6
Charlotte, North Carolina	2.1	1.7	1.2	0	0	0	0	0	0	0	0.1	0.5
Greensboro/Winston-Salem/High Point, North Carolina	3.2	2.5	1.7	T	0	0	0	0	0	0	0.1	1.2
Raleigh, North Carolina	2.3	2.6	1.3	0	0	0	0	0	0	0	0.1	0.7
Wilmington, North Carolina	0.4	0.5	0.5	T	0	T	0	0	0	0	T	0.6
Charleston Airport, South Carolina	0.1	0.2	0.1	T	0	T	0	0	0	0	T	0.3
Columbia, South Carolina	0.5	0.8	0.2	T	0	0	0	0	0	0	T	0.2
Greenville-Spartanburg Airport, South Carolina	2.5	2	0.9	0	T	0	T	0	0	0	0.1	0.6
Lynchburg, Virginia	5.4	5.3	3.3	0.3	0	0	0	0	0	0.1	0.8	2.8
Norfolk, Virginia	2.7	2.9	1	0	0	T	0	T	0	0	0	0.9
Richmond, Virginia	4.9	4.1	2.4	0.1	T	0	0	0	0	T	0.4	2
Roanoke, Virginia	6.4	6.9	3.5	0.5	T	T	0	0	T	0	1.6	3.8
Wallops Island, Virginia	2.6	3.6	0.7	0.1	0	0	0	0	0	0	0.3	1.4
Beckley, West Virginia	17	16.1	8.1	2.8	0	0	0	0	T	0.3	3.8	10.9
Charleston, West Virginia	10.3	8.6	4.7	0.9	0	T	T	T	T	0.1	2.3	4.9
Elkins, West Virginia	21	17.7	11	4.5	0	0	0	0	0	0.5	6.1	14.2
Huntington, West Virginia	8.6	7.1	3.7	0.7	0	T	0	T	0	0	1.3	3.7

Source: 1994 Statistical Abstract of the United States on CD-ROM [machine-readable datafiles]. CD-8A-94. Washington, DC: U.S. Department of Commerce, Economics and Statistics Administration, Bureau of the Census, Data User Services Division, January 1995. Primary source: U.S. National Oceanic and Atmospheric Administration. *Comparative Climatic Data* (annual). *Note:* "T" denotes trace.

★ 128 ★

Snow and Ice

Snow and Ice Pellets in West North Central United States, by City

Table shows snow and ice for period of record through 1992. Figures are airport data, except as noted.

[In inches]

City and state	January	February	March	April	May	June	July	August	September	October	November	December
Des Moines, Iowa	8.1	7.1	6.2	1.9	0	0	T	0	T	0.2	3.1	6.7
Dubuque, Iowa	9.2	7.8	9.5	2.3	0.1	0	0	0	T	0.2	3.8	10.6
Sioux City, Iowa	6.2	5.4	7.6	1.5	0.1	T	T	0	0	0.7	3.7	6
Waterloo, Iowa	6.8	6.4	5.9	1.5	0	T	0	0	0	0.1	3.7	7.3
Concordia, Kansas	5.2	5.3	3.6	0.7	T	T	T	0	T	0.3	2.2	4.5

[Continued]

★ 128 ★

Snow and Ice Pellets in West North Central United States, by City

[Continued]

City and state	January	February	March	April	May	June	July	August	September	October	November	December
Dodge City, Kansas	4.5	3.6	4.8	0.9	0	T	T	T	T	0.2	2.2	3.4
Goodland, Kansas	6.2	5	9.3	4.2	0.5	0.1	T	T	0.2	1.9	4.7	5.8
Topeka, Kansas	5.7	4.5	3.8	0.6	T	T	T	0	0	0	1.3	4.9
Wichita, Kansas	4.5	4.2	2.5	0.3	T	T	0	0	T	0	1.3	3.3
Duluth, Minnesota	16.6	11.2	13.4	6.5	0.8	0	T	T	0.1	1.4	12.2	15.4
International Falls, Minnesota	12.4	9.5	9.6	5.8	0.8	0	T	T	0.1	1.7	11.9	12.2
Minneapolis-St. Paul, Minnesota	9.7	8.5	10.8	2.9	0.1	T	0	T	0	0.5	7.9	9.4
Rochester, Minnesota	9.9	7.8	9.6	3.8	0	T	0	T	0	0.8	5.7	10.8
Saint Cloud, Minnesota	8.7	7.4	9.7	2.5	0.1	0	0	0	0	0.5	7.4	8
Columbia, Missouri	5.6	6.1	4.4	0.7	T	T	0	0	0	0	1.8	4.2
Kansas City, Missouri	5.7	4.3	3.6	0.8	T	T	T	0	T	0	1.1	4.4
Springfield, Missouri	4.4	4.2	3.3	0.4	T	T	T	0	0	0	1.6	3
St. Louis, Missouri	5.3	4.4	4.3	0.4	T	T	0	0	0	T	1.4	3.9
Grand Island, Nebraska	5.6	6	6.3	1.7	0.2	T	T	T	0.1	0.5	3.5	6.3
Lincoln, Nebraska	5.8	5.6	5.7	1.3	0.1	0	T	T	0	0.4	2.9	5.2
Norfolk, Nebraska	5.7	5.7	6.6	1.9	0.1	T	T	T	0	0.5	3.8	6
North Platte, Nebraska	5.3	4.9	6.9	2.7	0.1	T	T	T	0.1	1.4	4	4.7
Omaha Eppley Airport, Nebraska	7.3	6.6	6.4	1	0.1	T	0	0	T	0.4	2.6	5.5
Omaha, Nebraska[1]	7.0	6.4	6.9	1.4	0	0	T	0	0	0.5	3.4	5.3
Scottsbluff, Nebraska	6.5	5.3	9	4.8	0.9	0	T	0	0.3	2.4	5.3	6.5
Valentine, Nebraska	4.5	5.3	7.7	3.6	0.1	T	0	T	0.5	1.1	5	4.6
Bismarck, North Dakota	7.1	6.7	8.2	3.8	0.9	T	T	T	0.3	1.8	5.9	6.8
Fargo, North Dakota	8.4	5.9	6.7	3.1	0.1	T	0	T	0	0.7	5.5	7
Williston, North Dakota	7.2	4.8	6.7	4.9	0.8	T	T	T	0.4	1.7	4.6	7.4
Aberdeen, South Dakota	6.6	6.8	6.8	3.5	0.2	T	T	T	0	0.7	4.8	6
Huron, South Dakota	6.6	8.7	9.3	2.2	0.1	T	T	0	T	0.7	5.1	6.3
Rapid City, South Dakota	4.8	6.4	9	6	0.8	0.1	T	T	0.1	1.6	4.9	5
Sioux Falls, South Dakota	6.4	8	9.5	2.2	0	T	0	0	0	0.7	5.3	7.3

Source: 1994 Statistical Abstract of the United States on CD-ROM [machine-readable datafiles]. CD-8A-94. Washington, DC: U.S. Department of Commerce, Economics and Statistics Administration, Bureau of the Census, Data User Services Division, January 1995. Primary source: U.S. National Oceanic and Atmospheric Administration. *Comparative Climatic Data* (annual). *Notes:* "T" denotes trace. 1. North.

★ 129 ★

Snow and Ice

Snow and Ice Pellets in West South Central United States, by City

Table shows snow and ice for period of record through 1992. Figures are airport data, except as noted.

[In inches]

City and state	January	February	March	April	May	June	July	August	September	October	November	December
Fort Smith, Arkansas	2.6	1.8	0.6	T	T	0	0	0	0	0	0.5	0.9
Little Rock, Arkansas	2.4	1.4	0.5	T	0	0	0	0	0	0	0.2	0.7
North Little Rock, Arkansas	3.2	2.6	0.5	T	T	T	0	0	0	T	0.4	0.5
Baton Rouge, Louisiana	0	0.2	T	0	T	0	0	0	0	0	T	T
Lake Charles, Louisiana	0.2	0.1	T	T	T	0	0	0	0	0	T	0
New Orleans, Louisiana	0	0.1	T	T	T	0	0	0	0	0	T	0.1
Shreveport, Louisiana	0.8	0.5	0.2	0	T	0	0	0	0	T	0	0.2
Oklahoma City, Oklahoma	3.1	2.5	1.4	0	T	T	0	0	T	T	0.5	1.8
Tulsa, Oklahoma	3.3	2.4	1.5	0	T	0	0	0	T	T	0.4	1.6
Abilene, Texas	1.9	1.1	0.7	T	T	T	T	0	0	T	0.4	0.7
Amarillo, Texas	3.9	3.6	2.6	0.6	0	T	0	0	0	0.3	1.8	2.7
Austin, Texas	0.5	0.3	0	0	T	0	0	0	0	0	0.1	T
Brownsville, Texas	T	T	T	0	0	0	0	T	0	0	T	T
Corpus Christi, Texas	0.1	0	T	0	0	0	0	0	0	0	T	T
Dallas-Fort Worth, Texas	1.2	1	0.2	T	T	0	0	0	0	0	0.1	0.2
Del Rio, Texas	0.7	0.2	0.1	T	T	0	0	0	0	T	T	T
El Paso, Texas	1.4	0.8	0.4	0.3	T	T	T	0	0	0	1	1.7
Galveston, Texas	0	0.2	T	T	T	0	0	0	0	0	0	0

[Continued]

★ 129 ★

Snow and Ice Pellets in West South Central United States, by City

[Continued]

City and state	January	February	March	April	May	June	July	August	September	October	November	December
Houston, Texas	0.2	0.2	0	0	T	T	0	0	0	0	T	0
Lubbock, Texas	2.5	2.9	1.5	0.2	0	T	T	0	0	0.2	1.2	1.9
Midland-Odessa, Texas	1.8	0.9	0.4	0	T	T	0	T	0	0	0.5	0.8
Port Arthur, Texas	0.1	0.2	0	0	T	0	T	0	0	0	T	0
San Angelo, Texas	1.5	0.7	0.2	T	T	T	T	0	T	T	0.5	0.2
San Antonio, Texas	0.5	0.2	T	T	T	T	0	0	0	0	0	0
Victoria, Texas	0.1	0	T	0	0	0	0	0	0	0	0	T
Waco, Texas	0.8	0.4	0.1	T	T	0	0	T	0	T	0	0.1
Wichita Falls, Texas	2.1	1.7	0.8	0	T	T	0	0	0	T	0.3	1

Source: 1994 Statistical Abstract of the United States on CD-ROM [machine-readable datafiles]. CD-8A-94. Washington, DC: U.S. Department of Commerce, Economics and Statistics Administration, Bureau of the Census, Data User Services Division, January 1995. Primary source: U.S. National Oceanic and Atmospheric Administration. *Comparative Climatic Data* (annual). *Note:* "T" denotes trace.

★ 130 ★

Snow and Ice

Snow and Ice Pellets in Western United States, by City

Table shows snow and ice for period of record through 1992. Figures are airport data, except as noted.

[In inches]

City and state	January	February	March	April	May	June	July	August	September	October	November	December
Flagstaff, Arizona	19.9	17.9	22.5	9.7	1.8	T	T	0	0.1	2.1	9.9	16
Phoenix, Arizona	T	0	T	T	T	0	0	0	0	T	0	0
Tucson, Arizona	0.3	0.2	0.3	0.1	T	0	0	T	T	T	0.1	0.3
Winslow, Arizona	2.6	1.9	2	0.4	0	0	0	0	T	0.2	0.7	3.1
Yuma, Arizona	0	0	0	0	0	0	0	0	0	0	0	T
Alamosa, Colorado	4.5	4.2	6.1	4.4	1.6	0	T	0	0.2	3.2	4.3	5.7
Colorado Springs, Colorado	5	5.1	9.4	6.3	1.5	0	T	T	1.1	3.3	5.5	5.7
Denver, Colorado	8.3	7.3	12.7	9	1.6	0	T	T	1.6	3.7	8.8	7.4
Grand Junction, Colorado	7.3	4.1	3.9	1.1	0.1	0	0	0	0.1	0.6	2.8	5.3
Pueblo, Colorado	5.9	4.3	6.9	3.5	0.7	T	T	T	0.5	1.3	4.6	5.3
Boise, Idaho	6.6	3.5	1.7	0.7	0.1	T	T	T	0	0.1	2.2	5.9
Lewiston, Idaho	6	2.4	1.4	0.1	T	0	T	0	0	0.1	1.7	4.3
Pocatello, Idaho	9.5	5.9	6	4.3	0.6	0	0	T	0.1	1.9	5.3	9
Billings, Montana	9.1	7.9	10.2	7.9	1.6	0	T	T	1.1	3.6	6.8	8.6
Glasgow, Montana	6.3	4.1	3.8	2.5	0.7	T	T	T	0.2	1.3	3	5.5
Great Falls, Montana	9.8	8.3	10.5	7.2	1.8	0.3	T	0.2	1.5	3.4	7.4	8.8
Helena, Montana	8.7	5.9	7.5	4.9	1.5	0.1	T	0.1	1.5	2.3	6.4	8.6
Kalispell, Montana	17.9	10.4	6.1	2.5	0.8	0	T	T	0.1	1.4	8.3	17
Missoula, Montana	12.3	7.5	6	2.1	0.7	T	T	T	0	0.9	6	10.9
Elko, Nevada	9.4	6	5.3	2.4	0.8	T	T	T	0.1	0.8	4.6	8.2
Ely, Nevada	8.7	6.7	9.6	5.8	2.4	0.2	T	T	0.3	2.4	5.2	7.4
Las Vegas, Nevada	1	0.1	0	T	0	0	0	T	0	T	0.1	0.1
Reno, Nevada	5.6	5.1	4.5	1.3	0.9	0	0	0	0	0.3	2.2	4.5
Winnemucca, Nevada	5.1	3.7	4.5	2.3	0.6	T	0	T	0	0.4	2.3	4.7
Albuquerque, New Mexico	2.6	2.2	1.9	0.6	0	T	T	T	T	0.1	1.2	2.7
Clayton, New Mexico	3.8	3.4	5	1.9	0.4	T	0	T	0.1	0.7	3	3.7
Roswell, New Mexico	2.8	2.7	1.3	0.3	0	0	0	0	0	0.1	1.3	3
Milford, Utah	8.7	6.8	9.5	5.3	1.5	0	0	0	0.3	1.5	4.7	6.8
Salt Lake City, Utah	13	9.3	9.6	5	0.6	T	T	T	0.1	1.3	6.6	12
Casper, Wyoming	9.9	10.3	14.2	12.5	3.8	0.2	T	T	1.1	5.2	10.7	10.8
Cheyenne, Wyoming	6.4	5.8	12.2	8.9	3.4	0.2	T	T	0.7	3.7	7.2	6.2

[Continued]

★ 130 ★

Snow and Ice Pellets in Western United States, by City

[Continued]

City and state	January	February	March	April	May	June	July	August	September	October	November	December
Lander, Wyoming	8.9	11.1	17.7	20.4	7.1	1.2	T	T	2.5	9	14.1	10.5
Sheridan, Wyoming	10.6	10.6	12.9	9.9	2	0.1	T	0	1.4	4.3	9.3	11

Source: 1994 Statistical Abstract of the United States on CD-ROM [machine-readable datafiles]. CD-8A-94. Washington, DC: U.S. Department of Commerce, Economics and Statistics Administration, Bureau of the Census, Data User Services Division, January 1995. Primary source: U.S. National Oceanic and Atmospheric Administration. *Comparative Climatic Data* (annual). *Note:* "T" denotes trace.

Temperatures

★ 131 ★

Below Freezing Temperatures in East North Central United States, by City

Table shows the mean number of days during which the minimum temperature was 32 Fahrenheit degrees or less in selected cities. Figures are airport data, except as noted. For period of record through 1991, except as noted.

City and state	Length of record (year)	Mean number (days)
Cairo, Illinois	45	6.7
Chicago, Illinois	33	13.3
Moline, Illinois	31	13.5
Peoria, Illinois	32	12.9
Alpena, Michigan	32	17.7
Detroit, Michigan	33	13.6
Flint, Michigan	28	13.9
Grand Rapids, Michigan	28	14.5
Houghton Lake, Michigan	27	17.1
Lansing, Michigan	28	14.9
Marquette, Michigan	13	19.6
Muskegon, Michigan	31	14.0
Sault Sainte Marie, Michigan	50	18.1
Akron, Ohio	28	12.5
Greater Cincinnati Airport	29	10.8
Cleveland, Ohio	31	12.3
Columbus, Ohio	32	11.9
Dayton, Ohio	28	11.7
Mansfield, Ohio	26	12.6
Toledo, Ohio	36	14.2
Youngstown, Ohio	48	13.4
Green Bay, Wisconsin	30	16.2

[Continued]

★ 131 ★

Below Freezing Temperatures in East North Central United States, by City

[Continued]

City and state	Length of record (year)	Mean number (days)
La Crosse, Wisconsin	39	15.1
Madison, Wisconsin	32	16.3
Milwaukee, Wisconsin	31	14.1

Source: 1994 Statistical Abstract of the United States on CD-ROM [machine-readable datafiles]. CD-8A-94. Washington, DC: U.S. Department of Commerce, Economics and Statistics Administration, Bureau of the Census, Data User Services Division, January 1995. Primary source: U.S. National Oceanic and Atmospheric Administration. Comparative Climatic Data (annual).

★ 132 ★

Temperatures

Below Freezing Temperatures in East South Central United States, by City

Table shows the mean number of days during which the minimum temperature was 32 Fahrenheit degrees or less in selected cities. Figures are airport data, except as noted. For period of record through 1991, except as noted.

City and state	Length of record (year)	Mean number (days)
Birminghan, Alabama	28	5.9
Birmingham, Alabama[1]	11	5.3
Huntsville, Alabama	24	6.5
Mobile, Alabama	29	2.2
Montgomery, Alabama	28	4.0
Jackson, Kentucky	8.1	10
Lexington, Kentucky	28	9.5
Louisville, Kentucky	31	8.9
Paducah, Kentucky	8	8.5
Jackson, Mississippi	28	5.0
Meridian, Mississippi	27	5.3
Tupelo, Mississippi	8	5.3
Bristol/Johnson City/Kingsport, Tennessee	30	9.6
Chattanooga, Tennessee	51	7.4
Knoxville, Tennessee	31	7.4
Memphis, Tennessee	50	5.7

[Continued]

★ 132 ★

Below Freezing Temperatures in East South Central United States, by City

[Continued]

City and state	Length of record (year)	Mean number (days)
Nashville, Tennessee	26	7.6
Oak Ridge, Tennessee	43	8.7

Source: 1994 Statistical Abstract of the United States on CD-ROM [machine-readable datafiles]. CD-8A-94. Washington, DC: U.S. Department of Commerce, Economics and Statistics Administration, Bureau of the Census, Data User Services Division, January 1995. Primary source: U.S. National Oceanic and Atmospheric Administration. *Comparative Climatic Data* (annual). *Note:* 1. City office data.

★ 133 ★

Temperatures

Below Freezing Temperatures in Middle Atlantic United States, by City

Table shows the mean number of days during which the minimum temperature was 32 Fahrenheit degrees or less in selected cities. Figures are airport data, except as noted. For period of record through 1991, except as noted.

City and state	Length of record (year)	Mean number (days)
Atlantic City, New Jersey	27	11.0
Atlantic City, New Jersey[1]	7.2	(NA)
Newark, New Jersey	26	8.5
Albany, New York	26	14.9
Binghamton, New York	40	14.5
Buffalo, New York	31	13.2
Islip, New York	8	9.8
New York, New York (Central Park)	78	7.9
New York, New York (John F. Kennedy Airport)	30	7.9
New York, New York (La Guardia Airport)	29	7.3
Rochester, New York	28	13.4
Syracuse, New York	28	13.6
Allentown, Pennsylvania	48	12.3
Erie, Pennsylvania	36	12.8
Harrisburg, Pennsylvania	26	12.6
Middletown/Harrisburg International Airport	53	10.6
Philadelphia, Pennsylvania	53	10.6
Pittsburgh, Pennsylvania	32	9.7

[Continued]

★ 133 ★

Below Freezing Temperatures in Middle Atlantic United States, by City

[Continued]

City and state	Length of record (year)	Mean number (days)
Avoca, Pennsylvania	32	12.3
Williamsport, Pennsylvania	47	12.8

Source: 1994 Statistical Abstract of the United States on CD-ROM [machine-readable datafiles]. CD-8A-94. Washington, DC: U.S. Department of Commerce, Economics and Statistics Administration, Bureau of the Census, Data User Services Division, January 1995. Primary source: U.S. National Oceanic and Atmospheric Administration. *Comparative Climatic Data* (annual). *Notes:* "NA" represents "not available.." 1. City office data.

★ 134 ★

Temperatures

Below Freezing Temperatures in New England, by City

Table shows the mean number of days during which the minimum temperature was 32 Fahrenheit degrees or less in selected cities. Figures are airport data, except as noted. For period of record through 1991, except as noted.

City and state	Length of record (year)	Mean number (days)
Bridgeport, Connecticut	26	9.9
Hartford, Connecticut	32	13.5
Caribou, Maine	52	18.7
Portland, Maine	51	15.7
Blue Hill, Massachusetts	106	13.1
Boston, Massachusetts	27	9.8
Worcester, Massachusetts	36	14.3
Concord, New Hampshire	26	17.3
Mt. Washington, New Hampshire	59	24.3
Providence, Rhode Island	28	11.8
Burlington, Vermont	27	15.5

Source: 1994 Statistical Abstract of the United States on CD-ROM [machine-readable datafiles]. CD-8A-94. Washington, DC: U.S. Department of Commerce, Economics and Statistics Administration, Bureau of the Census, Data User Services Division, January 1995. Primary source: U.S. National Oceanic and Atmospheric Administration. *Comparative Climatic Data* (annual).

★ 135 ★
Temperatures

Below Freezing Temperatures in Pacific United States, by City

Table shows the mean number of days during which the minimum temperature was 32 Fahrenheit degrees or less in selected cities. Figures are airport data, except as noted. For period of record through 1991, except as noted.

City and state	Length of record (year)	Mean number (days)
Anchorage, Alaska	27	19.1
Annette, Alaska	31	7.4
Barrow, Alaska	71	32.3
Barter Island, Alaska	41	31.0
Bethel, Alaska	33	22.4
Bettles, Alaska	39	24.0
Big Delta, Alaska	48	22.3
Cold Bay, Alaska	48	15.5
Fairbanks, Alaska	28	22.1
Gulkana, Alaska	43	23.8
Homer, Alaska	51	18.7
Juneau, Alaska	47	14.1
King Salmon, Alaska	28	19.9
Kodiak, Alaska	29	13.4
Kotzebue, Alaska	48	24.9
McGrath, Alaska	49	22.9
Nome, Alaska	25	23.8
St. Paul Island, Alaska	74	18.8
Talkeetna, Alaska	51	22.6
Unalakleet, Alaska	29	23.6
Valdez, Alaska	19	17.5
Yakutat, Alaska	27	16.3
Bakersfield, California	28	1.2
Bishop, California	44	14.3
Blue Canyon, California	44	9.7
Eureka, California	81	0.5
Fresno, California	28	2.3
Long Beach, California	31	0.1
Mount Shasta, California	42	13.7
Redding, California	5	4.2
Sacramento, California	41	1.7
San Francisco, California	32	0.2
Santa Barbara, California	8	1.0
Santa Maria, California	28	2.0
Stockton, California	32	2.2
Hilo, Hawaii	46	0.0
Honolulu, Hawaii	22	0.0
Kahului, Hawaii	27	0.0
Lihue, Hawaii	42	0.0

[Continued]

★ 135 ★

Below Freezing Temperatures in Pacific United States, by City

[Continued]

City and state	Length of record (year)	Mean number (days)
Astoria, Oregon	38	3.7
Burns, Oregon	7	20.7
Eugene, Oregon	49	5.5
Medford, Oregon	30	8.5
Pendleton, Oregon	56	8.3
Portland, Oregon	51	4.3
Salem, Oregon	29	6.6
Sexton Summit, Oregon	44	10.9
Olympia, Washington	32	8.6
Quillayute, Washington	25	6.4
Seattle, Washington[1]	41	1.8
Seattle-Tacoma Airport, Washington	32	3.1
Spokane, Washington	32	13.9
Walla Walla, Washington	73	6.5
Yakima, Washington	45	14.8

Source: 1994 Statistical Abstract of the United States on CD-ROM [machine-readable datafiles]. CD-8A-94. Washington, DC: U.S. Department of Commerce, Economics and Statistics Administration, Bureau of the Census, Data User Services Division, January 1995. Primary source: U.S. National Oceanic and Atmospheric Administration. Comparative Climatic Data (annual). Note: 1. City office data.

★ 136 ★

Temperatures

Below Freezing Temperatures in South Atlantic United States, by City

Table shows the mean number of days during which the minimum temperature was 32 Fahrenheit degrees or less in selected cities. Figures are airport data, except as noted. For period of record through 1991, except as noted.

City and state	Length of record (year)	Mean number (days)
Wilmington, Delaware	44	10.0
Washington, District of Columbia (Dulles Airport)	29	11.6
Washington National Airport (District of Columbia)	31	7.0
Apalachicola, Florida	62	0.7
Daytona Beach, Florida	48	0.6
Fort Myers, Florida	31	0.1
Gainesville, Florida	8	1.4
Jacksonville, Florida	50	1.5

[Continued]

★ 136 ★

Below Freezing Temperatures in South Atlantic United States, by City
[Continued]

City and state	Length of record (year)	Mean number (days)
Key West, Florida	43	0.0
Miami, Florida	27	0.0
Orlando, Florida	28	0.3
Pensacola, Florida	28	1.6
Tallahassee, Florida	30	3.6
Tampa, Florida	28	0.4
Vero Beach, Florida	8	0.2
West Palm Beach, Florida	27	0.1
Athens, Georgia	48	5.2
Atlanta, Georgia	31	5.3
Augusta, Georgia	27	5.6
Columbus, Georgia	46	4.3
Macon, Georgia	27	4.6
Savannah, Georgia	27	3.0
Baltimore, Maryland	41	9.7
Asheville, North Carolina	27	10.0
Cape Hatteras, North Carolina	34	3.1
Charlotte, North Carolina	31	6.6
Greensboro/Winston-Salem/High Point, North Carolina	28	8.3
Raleigh, North Carolina	27	7.8
Wilmington, North Carolina	28	4.3
Charleston, South Carolina	49	3.4
Columbia, South Carolina	25	6.0
Greenville-Spartanburg Airport, South Carolina	29	6.5
Lynchburg, Virginia	28	9.1
Norfolk, Virginia	43	5.4
Richmond, Virginia	62	8.5
Roanoke, Virginia	27	9.1
Wallops Island, Virginia	18	7.2
Beckley, West Virginia	28	11.3
Charleston, West Virginia	44	10.0
Elkins, West Virginia	47	14.4
Huntington, West Virginia	30	9.7

Source: 1994 Statistical Abstract of the United States on CD-ROM [machine-readable datafiles]. CD-8A-94. Washington, DC: U.S. Department of Commerce, Economics and Statistics Administration, Bureau of the Census, Data User Services Division, January 1995. Primary source: U.S. National Oceanic and Atmospheric Administration. *Comparative Climatic Data* (annual).

★ 137 ★

Temperatures

Below Freezing Temperatures in West North Central United States, by City

Table shows the mean number of days during which the minimum temperature was 32 Fahrenheit degrees or less in selected cities. Figures are airport data, except as noted. For period of record through 1991, except as noted.

City and state	Length of record (year)	Mean number (days)
Des Moines, Iowa	30	13.5
Dubuque, Iowa	24	14.8
Sioux City, Iowa	32	15.0
Waterloo, Iowa	32	15.8
Concordia, Kansas	29	12.6
Dodge City, Kansas	28	12.4
Goodland, Kansas	25	15.4
Topeka, Kansas	27	12.0
Wichita, Kansas	38	11.1
Duluth, Minnesota	30	18.5
International Falls, Minnesota	52	19.8
Minneapolis-St. Paul, Minnesota	32	15.6
Rochester, Minnesota	31	16.4
Saint Cloud, Minnesota	51	17.8
Columbia, Missouri	22	10.8
Kansas City, Missouri	19	11.0
Springfield, Missouri	31	10.2
St. Louis, Missouri	31	10.0
Grand Island, Nebraska	30	14.8
Lincoln, Nebraska	20	14.4
Norfolk, Nebraska	46	15.5
North Platte, Nebraska	27	17.6
Omaha Eppley Airport, Nebraska	27	14.1
Omaha, Nebraska[1]	37	13.7
Scottsbluff, Nebraska	27	17.0
Valentine, Nebraska	36	17.7
Bismarck, North Dakota	32	18.6
Fargo, North Dakota	32	18.0
Williston, North Dakota	30	18.7
Aberdeen, South Dakota	30	17.8
Huron, South Dakota	32	17.1
Rapid City, South Dakota	49	16.8
Sioux Falls, South Dakota	28	16.8

Source: 1994 Statistical Abstract of the United States on CD-ROM [machine-readable datafiles]. CD-8A-94. Washington, DC: U.S. Department of Commerce, Economics and Statistics Administration, Bureau of the Census, Data User Services Division, January 1995. Primary source: U.S. National Oceanic and Atmospheric Administration. *Comparative Climatic Data* (annual). *Note:* 1. City office data.

★ 138 ★

Temperatures

Below Freezing Temperatures in West South Central United States, by City

Table shows the mean number of days during which the minimum temperature was 32 Fahrenheit degrees or less in selected cities. Figures are airport data, except as noted. For period of record through 1991, except as noted.

City and state	Length of record (year)	Mean number (days)
Fort Smith, Arkansas	27	7.8
Little Rock, Arkansas	31	6.0
North Little Rock, Arkansas	14	5.3
Baton Rouge, Louisiana	32	2.4
Lake Charles, Louisiana	27	1.5
New Orleans, Louisiana	45	1.3
Shreveport, Louisiana	39	3.7
Oklahoma City, Oklahoma	26	7.7
Tulsa, Oklahoma	31	7.8
Abilene, Texas	28	5.3
Amarillo, Texas	30	11.1
Austin, Texas	30	2.1
Brownsville, Texas	25	0.3
Corpus Christi, Texas	27	0.7
Dallas-Fort Worth, Texas	28	4.0
Del Rio, Texas	28	1.7
El Paso, Texas	31	6.5
Galveston, Texas	121	0.4
Houston, Texas	22	2.1
Lubbock, Texas	44	9.4
Midland-Odessa, Texas	28	6.5
Port Arthur, Texas	31	1.6
San Angelo, Texas	31	5.3
San Antonio, Texas	49	2.3
Victoria, Texas	30	1.2
Waco, Texas	28	3.5
Wichita Falls, Texas	31	6.7

Source: 1994 Statistical Abstract of the United States on CD-ROM [machine-readable datafiles]. CD-8A-94. Washington, DC: U.S. Department of Commerce, Economics and Statistics Administration, Bureau of the Census, Data User Services Division, January 1995. Primary source: U.S. National Oceanic and Atmospheric Administration. *Comparative Climatic Data* (annual).

★ 139 ★
Temperatures

Below Freezing Temperatures in Western United States, by City

Table shows the mean number of days during which the minimum temperature was 32 Fahrenheit degrees or less in selected cities. Figures are airport data, except as noted. For period of record through 1991, except as noted.

City and state	Length of record (year)	Mean number (days)
Flagstaff, Arizona	42	21.0
Phoenix, Arizona	31	0.8
Tucson, Arizona	51	1.8
Winslow, Arizona	31	13.5
Yuma, Arizona	27	0.2
Alamosa, Colorado	46	22.7
Colorado Springs, Colorado	31	16.1
Denver, Colorado	31	15.7
Grand Junction, Colorado	28	13.3
Pueblo, Colorado	26	15.6
Boise, Idaho	52	12.4
Lewiston, Idaho	45	8.9
Pocatello, Idaho	28	16.8
Billings, Montana	32	14.8
Glasgow, Montana	27	17.7
Great Falls, Montana	30	15.7
Helena, Montana	28	18.2
Kalispell, Montana	32	18.9
Missoula, Montana	31	18.3
Elko, Nevada	27	19.1
Ely, Nevada	53	21.8
Las Vegas, Nevada	31	3.2
Reno, Nevada	28	17.4
Winnemucca, Nevada	42	18.8
Albuquerque, New Mexico	31	11.9
Clayton, New Mexico	46	14.1
Roswell, New Mexico	19	8.9
Milford, Utah	41	18.1
Salt Lake City, Utah	32	12.5
Casper, Wyoming	27	18.3
Cheyenne, Wyoming	32	17.2
Lander, Wyoming	45	18.5
Sheridan, Wyoming	27	18.6

Source: 1994 Statistical Abstract of the United States on CD-ROM [machine-readable datafiles]. CD-8A-94. Washington, DC: U.S. Department of Commerce, Economics and Statistics Administration, Bureau of the Census, Data User Services Division, January 1995. Primary source: U.S. National Oceanic and Atmospheric Administration. *Comparative Climatic Data* (annual).

★ 140 ★

Temperatures

Temperature Anomalies: 1901-1991

Anomalies are based on a 30-year reference period (1961-1990). Calendar year mean is for January-December. Seasonal year mean is calculated from four seasons in the following sequence: winter (December-February); spring (March-May); summer (June-August); and fall (September-November).

[In degrees celsius]

Year	Calendar year mean	Seasonal year mean
1901	-0.21	-0.05
1905	-0.45	-0.44
1910	-0.14	-0.39
1915	-0.11	-0.35
1920	-0.37	-0.61
1925	0.20	-0.06
1930	-0.21	-0.04
1935	0.12	0.20
1940	0.06	0.05
1945	-0.02	0.04
1950	-0.37	-0.34
1955	-0.25	-0.16
1960	-0.27	0.56
1965	-0.03	-0.19
1970	-0.12	-0.09
1975	-0.09	-0.08
1980	0.18	0.22
1985	-0.26	0.07
1990	0.72	0.55
1991	0.77	0.48

Source: Executive Office of the President of the United States. *Environmental Quality 24: The Twenty-fourth Annual Report of the Council on Environmental Quality.* Prepared by Ray Clark. Written by Carroll Curtis. Edited by Barry Walsh. Washington, DC: U.S. Government Printing Office, 1994, p. 448. Primary source: Karl, R., D.R. Easterling, R.W. Knight, and P.Y. Hughes. "U.S. National and Regional Temperature Anomalies." In *Trends '93: A Compendium of Data on Global Change.* Edited by T.A. Boden, D.P. Kaiser, R.J. Sepanski, and P.Y. Hughes. ORNL/CDIAC-65. Oak Ridge, TN: U.S. Department of Energy, Oak Ridge National Laboratory, Carbon Dioxide Information Analysis Center, 1994.

★ 141 ★
Temperatures

Temperatures, by City

Table shows the normal daily mean temperatures for selected cities. Figures are airport data except as noted. Based on standard 30-year period, 1961 through 1990. Data are presented alphabetically by state.

[In Fahrenheit degrees]

City	January	February	March	April	May	June	July	August	September	October	November	December
Mobile, Alabama	49.9	53.2	60.5	67.8	74.5	80.4	82.3	81.8	77.9	68.4	59.8	53.0
Juneau, Alaska	24.2	28.4	32.7	39.7	47.0	53.0	56.0	55.0	49.4	42.2	32.0	27.1
Phoenix, Arizona	53.6	57.7	62.2	69.9	78.8	88.2	93.5	91.5	85.6	74.5	61.9	54.1
Little Rock, Arkansas	39.1	43.6	53.1	62.1	70.2	78.4	81.9	80.6	74.1	63.0	52.1	42.8
Los Angeles, California	56.8	57.6	58.0	60.1	62.7	65.7	69.1	70.5	69.9	66.8	61.6	56.9
Sacramento, California	45.2	50.7	53.6	58.3	65.3	71.6	75.7	75.1	71.5	64.2	53.3	45.3
San Diego, California	57.4	58.6	59.6	62.0	64.1	66.8	71.0	72.6	71.4	67.7	62.0	57.4
San Francisco, California	48.7	52.2	53.3	55.6	58.1	61.5	62.7	63.7	64.5	61.0	54.8	49.4
Denver, Colorado	29.7	33.4	39.0	48.2	57.2	66.9	73.5	71.4	62.3	51.4	39.0	31.0
Hartford, Connecticut	24.6	27.5	37.5	48.7	59.6	68.5	73.7	71.6	63.3	52.2	41.9	29.5
Wilmington, Delaware	30.6	33.4	42.7	52.2	62.5	71.5	76.4	75.0	68.0	56.2	46.3	35.8
Washington, District of Columbia	34.6	37.5	47.2	56.5	66.4	75.6	80.0	78.5	71.3	59.7	49.8	39.4
Jacksonville, Florida	52.4	55.2	61.1	67.0	73.4	79.1	81.6	81.2	78.1	69.8	61.9	55.1
Miami, Florida	67.2	68.5	71.7	75.2	78.7	81.4	82.6	82.8	81.9	78.3	73.6	69.1
Atlanta, Georgia	41.0	44.8	53.5	61.5	69.2	76.0	78.8	72.7	62.3	53.1	44.5
Honolulu, Hawaii	72.9	73.0	74.4	75.8	77.5	79.4	80.5	81.4	81.0	79.6	77.2	74.1
Boise, Idaho	29.0	35.9	42.4	49.1	57.5	66.5	74.0	72.5	62.6	51.8	39.9	30.1
Chicago, Illinois	21.0	25.4	37.2	48.6	58.9	68.6	73.2	71.7	64.4	52.8	40.0	26.6
Peoria, Illinois	21.6	26.3	39.0	51.4	61.9	71.5	75.5	73.1	66.1	54.0	41.2	27.0
Indianapolis, Indiana	25.5	29.6	41.4	52.4	62.8	71.9	75.4	73.2	66.6	54.7	43.0	30.9
Des Moines, Iowa	19.4	24.7	37.3	50.9	62.3	71.8	76.6	73.9	65.1	53.5	39.0	24.4
Wichita, Kansas	29.5	34.8	45.4	56.4	65.6	75.7	81.4	79.3	70.3	58.6	44.7	33.0
Louisville, Kentucky	31.7	35.7	46.3	56.3	65.3	73.2	77.2	75.8	69.5	57.6	47.1	36.9
New Orleans, Louisiana	51.3	54.3	61.6	68.5	74.8	80.0	81.9	81.5	78.1	69.1	61.1	54.5
Portland, Maine	20.8	23.3	33.0	43.3	53.3	62.4	68.6	67.3	59.1	48.5	38.7	26.5
Baltimore, Maryland	31.8	34.8	44.1	53.4	63.4	72.5	77.0	75.6	68.5	56.6	46.8	36.7
Boston, Massachusetts	28.6	30.3	38.6	48.1	58.2	67.7	73.5	71.9	64.8	54.8	45.3	33.6
Detroit, Michigan	22.9	25.4	35.7	47.3	58.4	67.6	72.3	70.5	63.2	51.2	40.2	28.3
Sault Ste. Marie, Michigan	12.9	14.0	24.0	38.2	50.5	58.0	63.8	62.6	55.1	45.3	33.0	19.0
Duluth, Minnesota	7.0	12.3	24.4	38.6	50.8	59.8	66.1	63.7	54.2	43.7	28.4	12.8
Minneapolis-St. Paul, Minnesota	11.8	17.9	31.0	46.4	58.5	68.2	73.6	70.5	60.5	48.8	33.2	17.9
Jackson, Mississippi	44.1	47.9	56.7	64.6	72.0	78.8	81.5	80.9	75.9	64.7	55.8	47.8
Kansas City, Missouri	25.7	31.2	42.7	54.5	64.1	73.2	78.5	76.1	67.5	56.6	43.1	30.4
St. Louis, Missouri	29.3	33.9	45.1	56.7	66.1	75.4	79.8	77.6	70.2	58.4	46.2	33.9
Great Falls, Montana	21.2	27.4	33.3	43.6	53.1	61.6	68.8	66.9	56.6	47.5	33.9	23.9
Omaha, Nebraska	21.1	26.9	38.6	51.9	62.4	72.1	76.9	74.1	65.1	53.4	39.0	25.1
Reno, Nevada	32.9	38.0	42.8	48.6	56.5	65.1	71.6	69.6	60.4	50.8	40.3	32.7
Concord, New Hampshire	18.6	21.8	32.4	43.9	55.2	64.2	69.5	67.3	58.8	47.8	37.1	24.3
Atlantic City, New Jersey	30.9	33.0	41.5	50.0	60.4	69.4	74.7	73.4	66.1	54.9	45.8	35.8
Albuquerque, New Mexico	34.2	40.0	46.9	55.2	64.2	74.2	78.5	75.9	68.6	57.0	44.3	35.3
Albany, New York	20.6	23.5	34.3	46.4	57.6	66.9	71.8	69.6	61.3	50.2	39.7	26.5
Buffalo, New York	23.6	24.5	33.8	45.2	56.6	65.9	71.1	69.0	61.9	51.1	40.5	29.1
New York, New York[1]	31.5	33.6	42.4	52.5	62.7	71.6	76.8	75.5	68.2	57.5	47.6	36.6
Charlotte, North Carolina	39.3	42.5	50.9	59.4	67.4	75.7	79.3	78.3	72.4	61.3	52.1	42.6
Raleigh, North Carolina	38.9	42.0	50.4	59.0	67.0	74.3	78.1	77.1	71.1	60.1	51.2	42.6
Bismarck, North Dakota	9.2	15.7	28.2	43.0	55.0	64.4	70.4	68.3	57.0	45.7	28.6	14.0
Cincinnati, Ohio	28.1	31.8	43.0	53.2	62.9	71.0	75.1	73.5	67.3	55.1	44.3	33.5
Cleveland, Ohio	24.8	27.2	37.3	47.6	58.0	67.6	71.9	70.4	63.9	52.8	42.6	30.9
Columbus, Ohio	26.4	29.6	40.9	51.0	61.2	69.2	73.2	71.5	65.5	53.7	42.9	31.9
Oklahoma City, Oklahoma	35.9	40.9	50.3	60.4	68.4	76.7	82.0	81.1	73.0	62.0	49.6	39.3
Portland, Oregon	39.6	43.6	47.3	51.0	57.1	63.5	68.2	68.6	63.3	54.5	46.1	40.2
Philadelphia, Pennsylvania	30.4	33.0	42.4	52.4	62.9	71.8	76.7	75.5	68.2	56.4	46.4	35.8
Pittsburgh, Pennsylvania	26.1	28.7	39.4	49.6	59.5	67.9	72.1	70.5	63.9	52.4	42.3	31.5
Providence, Rhode Island	27.9	29.7	37.4	47.4	57.3	66.9	72.7	71.3	64.1	53.6	44.0	32.8
Columbia, South Carolina	43.8	46.8	55.2	63.0	70.9	77.4	80.9	79.7	74.2	63.3	54.6	46.9
Sioux Falls, South Dakota	13.8	19.7	32.5	46.9	58.4	68.3	74.3	71.4	60.9	48.6	33.0	18.3
Memphis, Tennessee	39.7	44.2	53.1	62.9	71.2	79.1	82.6	81.0	74.2	63.1	52.5	43.7
Nashville, Tennessee	36.2	40.4	50.2	59.2	67.7	75.6	79.3	78.1	71.8	60.4	50.0	40.5
Dallas-Fort Worth, Texas	43.4	47.9	56.7	65.5	72.8	81.0	85.3	84.9	77.4	67.2	56.2	46.9
El Paso, Texas	42.8	48.1	55.1	63.4	71.8	80.4	82.3	80.1	74.4	64.0	52.4	44.1
Houston, Texas	50.4	53.9	60.6	68.3	74.5	80.4	82.6	82.3	78.2	69.6	61.0	53.5
Salt Lake City, Utah	27.9	34.1	41.8	49.7	58.8	69.1	77.9	75.6	65.2	53.2	40.8	29.7
Burlington, Vermont	16.3	18.2	30.7	43.9	56.3	65.2	70.5	67.9	58.9	47.8	36.8	23.0

[Continued]

113

★ 141 ★

Temperatures, by City

[Continued]

City	January	February	March	April	May	June	July	August	September	October	November	December
Norfolk, Virginia	39.1	41.0	48.6	57.0	66.1	74.1	78.2	77.2	71.9	61.2	52.5	43.8
Richmond, Virginia	35.7	38.7	48.0	57.3	66.0	73.9	78.0	76.8	70.0	58.6	49.6	40.1
Seattle-Tacoma, Washington	40.1	43.5	45.6	49.2	55.1	60.9	65.2	65.5	60.6	52.8	45.3	40.5
Spokane, Washington	27.1	33.3	38.7	45.9	53.9	62.0	68.8	68.4	58.9	47.3	35.1	27.8
Charleston, West Virginia	32.1	35.5	45.9	54.8	63.5	71.4	75.1	73.9	67.7	56.2	46.8	37.0
Milwaukee, Wisconsin	18.9	23.0	33.3	44.4	54.6	65.0	70.9	69.3	61.7	50.3	37.7	24.4
Cheyenne, Wyoming	26.5	29.3	33.6	42.5	52.0	61.3	68.4	66.4	57.4	47.0	35.2	27.8
San Juan, Puerto Rico	77.0	77.1	78.0	79.4	80.9	82.3	82.6	82.7	82.5	81.9	80.0	78.1

Source: 1994 Statistical Abstract of the United States on CD-ROM [machine-readable datafiles]. CD-8A-94. Washington, DC: U.S. Department of Commerce, Economics and Statistics Administration, Bureau of the Census, Data User Services Division, January 1995. Primary source: U.S. National Oceanic and Atmospheric Administration. *Climatography of the United States.* No. 81. *Note:* 1. City office data.

★ 142 ★

Temperatures

Temperatures – Highest, by Selected City

Table shows the highest temperatures of record for selected cities. Figures are airport data, except as noted, for period of record through 1992. Data are presented alphabetically by state.

[In Fahrenheit degrees]

City	January	February	March	April	May	June	July	August	September	October	November	December
Mobile, Alabama	84	82	90	94	100	102	104	102	99	93	87	81
Juneau, Alaska	57	57	59	71	82	86	90	83	72	61	56	54
Phoenix, Arizona	88	92	100	105	113	122	118	116	118	107	93	88
Little Rock, Arkansas	83	85	91	95	98	105	112	108	106	97	86	80
Los Angeles, California	88	92	95	102	97	104	97	98	110	106	101	94
Sacramento, California	70	76	88	93	105	115	114	109	108	101	87	72
San Diego, California	88	88	93	98	96	101	95	98	111	107	97	88
San Francisco, California	72	78	85	92	97	106	105	98	103	99	85	75
Denver, Colorado	73	76	84	90	96	104	104	101	97	89	79	75
Hartford, Connecticut	65	73	87	96	97	100	102	101	99	91	81	74
Wilmington, Delaware	75	78	86	94	95	99	102	101	100	91	85	74
Washington, District of Columbia	79	82	89	95	99	101	104	103	101	94	86	75
Jacksonville, Florida	85	88	91	95	100	103	105	102	100	96	88	84
Miami, Florida	88	89	92	96	95	98	98	98	97	95	89	87
Atlanta, Georgia	79	80	85	93	95	101	105	102	98	95	84	79
Honolulu, Hawaii	87	88	88	89	93	92	92	93	94	94	93	89
Boise, Idaho	63	71	81	92	98	109	111	110	102	94	74	65
Chicago, Illinois	65	71	88	91	93	104	102	101	99	91	78	71
Peoria, Illinois	70	72	86	92	93	105	103	103	100	90	81	71
Indianapolis, Indiana	71	74	85	89	93	102	104	102	100	90	81	74
Des Moines, Iowa	65	73	91	93	98	103	105	108	101	95	76	69
Wichita, Kansas	75	84	89	96	100	110	113	110	107	95	85	83
Louisville, Kentucky	77	77	86	91	95	102	105	101	104	92	84	76
New Orleans, Louisiana	83	85	89	92	96	100	101	102	101	92	87	84
Portland, Maine	64	64	86	85	94	98	99	103	95	88	74	69
Baltimore, Maryland	75	79	87	94	98	100	104	105	100	92	83	77
Boston, Massachusetts	63	70	81	94	95	100	102	102	100	90	78	73
Detroit, Michigan	62	65	81	89	93	104	102	100	98	91	77	68
Sault Ste. Marie, Michigan	45	47	75	85	89	93	97	98	95	80	67	60
Duluth, Minnesota	52	55	78	88	90	93	97	97	95	86	70	55
Minneapolis-St. Paul, Minnesota	58	60	83	95	96	102	105	102	98	89	75	63
Jackson, Mississippi	82	85	89	94	99	105	106	102	104	95	88	84
Kansas City, Missouri	69	76	86	93	92	105	107	109	102	92	82	70
St. Louis, Missouri	76	85	89	93	93	102	107	107	104	94	85	76
Great Falls, Montana	67	70	78	89	93	101	105	106	98	91	76	69
Omaha, Nebraska	69	78	89	97	99	105	114	110	104	96	80	72
Reno, Nevada	70	75	83	89	96	103	104	105	101	91	77	70
Concord, New Hampshire	68	66	85	95	97	98	102	101	98	90	80	68

[Continued]

★ 142 ★

Temperatures – Highest, by Selected City
[Continued]

City	January	February	March	April	May	June	July	August	September	October	November	December
Atlantic City, New Jersey	78	75	87	94	99	106	104	102	99	90	84	75
Albuquerque, New Mexico	69	76	85	89	98	105	105	101	100	91	77	72
Albany, New York	62	67	86	92	94	99	100	99	100	89	82	71
Buffalo, New York	72	65	81	94	90	96	97	99	98	87	80	74
New York, New York[1]	72	75	86	96	99	101	106	104	102	94	84	72
Charlotte, North Carolina	78	81	90	93	100	103	103	103	104	98	85	77
Raleigh, North Carolina	62	69	81	93	98	107	109	109	105	95	75	65
Bismarck, North Dakota	79	84	92	95	97	104	105	105	104	98	88	79
Cincinnati, Ohio	69	73	84	89	93	102	103	102	98	88	81	75
Cleveland, Ohio	73	69	83	88	92	104	103	102	101	90	82	77
Columbus, Ohio	74	73	85	89	94	102	100	101	100	90	80	76
Oklahoma City, Oklahoma	80	84	93	100	104	105	109	110	102	96	87	86
Portland, Oregon	63	71	80	87	100	100	107	107	105	92	73	64
Philadelphia, Pennsylvania	74	74	87	94	97	100	104	101	100	96	81	72
Pittsburgh, Pennsylvania	69	69	82	89	91	98	103	100	97	87	82	74
Providence, Rhode Island	66	72	80	98	94	97	102	104	100	86	78	70
Columbia, South Carolina	84	84	91	94	101	107	107	107	101	101	90	83
Sioux Falls, South Dakota	66	70	87	94	100	110	108	108	104	94	76	61
Memphis, Tennessee	78	81	85	94	99	104	108	105	103	95	85	81
Nashville, Tennessee	78	84	86	91	97	106	107	104	105	94	84	79
Dallas-Fort Worth, Texas	88	88	96	95	103	113	110	108	106	102	89	88
El Paso, Texas	80	83	89	98	104	111	112	108	104	96	87	80
Houston, Texas	84	91	91	95	97	103	104	107	102	96	89	83
Salt Lake City, Utah	62	69	78	86	93	104	107	104	100	89	75	67
Burlington, Vermont	63	62	84	91	93	97	99	101	94	85	75	65
Norfolk, Virginia	78	81	88	97	100	101	103	104	99	95	86	80
Richmond, Virginia	80	83	93	96	100	104	105	102	103	99	86	80
Seattle-Tacoma, Washington	64	70	75	85	93	96	99	99	98	89	74	63
Spokane, Washington	59	61	71	90	96	101	103	108	98	86	67	56
Charleston, West Virginia	79	78	89	94	93	98	104	101	102	92	85	80
Milwaukee, Wisconsin	62	65	82	91	93	101	101	103	98	89	77	63
Cheyenne, Wyoming	66	71	74	83	90	100	100	96	93	83	73	69
San Juan, Puerto Rico	92	96	96	97	96	97	95	97	97	98	96	94

Source: 1994 Statistical Abstract of the United States on CD-ROM [machine-readable datafiles]. CD-8A-94. Washington, DC: U.S. Department of Commerce, Economics and Statistics Administration, Bureau of the Census, Data User Services Division, January 1995. Primary source: U.S. National Oceanic and Atmospheric Administration. *Comparative Climatic Data* (annual). *Note:* 1. City office data.

★ 143 ★

Temperatures

Temperatures – Lowest, by Selected City

Table shows the lowest temperatures of record for selected cities. Figures are airport data, except as noted, for period of record through 1992. Data are presented alphabetically by state.

[In Fahrenheit degrees]

City	January	February	March	April	May	June	July	August	September	October	November	December
Mobile, Alabama	3	11	21	32	43	49	60	59	42	32	22	8
Juneau, Alaska	-22	-22	-15	6	25	31	36	27	23	11	-5	-21
Phoenix, Arizona	17	22	25	32	40	50	61	60	47	34	25	22
Little Rock, Arkansas	-4	-5	11	28	40	46	54	52	37	29	17	-1
Los Angeles, California	23	32	34	39	43	48	49	51	47	41	34	32
Sacramento, California	23	23	26	32	36	41	48	49	43	36	26	18
San Diego, California	29	36	39	41	48	51	55	57	51	43	38	34
San Francisco, California	24	25	30	31	36	41	43	42	38	34	25	20
Denver, Colorado	-25	-30	-11	-2	22	30	43	41	17	3	-8	-25
Hartford, Connecticut	-26	-21	-6	9	28	37	44	36	30	17	1	-14
Wilmington, Delaware	-14	-6	2	18	30	41	48	43	36	24	14	-7
Washington, District of Columbia	-5	4	11	24	34	47	54	49	39	29	16	1
Jacksonville, Florida	7	19	23	34	45	47	61	63	48	36	21	11

[Continued]

★ 143 ★

Temperatures – Lowest, by Selected City

[Continued]

City	January	February	March	April	May	June	July	August	September	October	November	December
Miami, Florida	30	32	32	46	53	60	69	68	68	51	39	30
Atlanta, Georgia	-8	5	10	26	37	46	53	55	36	28	3	0
Honolulu, Hawaii	53	53	55	57	60	65	66	67	66	64	57	54
Boise, Idaho	-17	-15	6	19	22	31	35	34	23	11	-3	-25
Chicago, Illinois	-27	-17	-8	7	24	36	40	41	28	17	1	-25
Peoria, Illinois	-25	-18	-10	14	25	39	47	41	26	19	-2	-23
Indianapolis, Indiana	-22	-21	-7	16	28	37	44	41	28	17	-2	-23
Des Moines, Iowa	-24	-20	-22	9	30	38	47	40	26	14	-4	-22
Wichita, Kansas	-12	-21	-2	15	31	43	51	48	31	21	1	-16
Louisville, Kentucky	-20	-19	-1	22	31	42	50	46	33	23	-1	-15
New Orleans, Louisiana	14	19	25	32	41	50	60	60	42	35	24	11
Portland, Maine	-26	-39	-21	8	23	33	40	33	23	15	3	-21
Baltimore, Maryland	-7	-3	6	20	32	40	50	45	35	25	13	0
Boston, Massachusetts	-12	-4	6	16	34	45	50	47	38	28	15	-7
Detroit, Michigan	-21	-15	-4	10	25	36	41	38	29	17	9	-10
Sault Ste. Marie, Michigan	-36	-35	-24	-2	18	26	36	29	25	16	-10	-25
Duluth, Minnesota	-39	-33	-29	-5	17	27	35	32	22	8	-23	-34
Minneapolis-St. Paul, Minnesota	-34	-28	-32	2	18	34	43	39	26	15	-17	-29
Jackson, Mississippi	2	11	15	27	38	47	51	55	35	29	17	4
Kansas City, Missouri	-17	-19	-10	12	30	42	52	43	33	21	1	-23
St. Louis, Missouri	-18	-10	-5	22	31	43	51	47	36	23	1	-16
Great Falls, Montana	-37	-35	-29	-6	15	31	40	30	21	-11	-25	-43
Omaha, Nebraska	-23	-21	-16	5	27	38	44	43	25	13	-9	-23
Reno, Nevada	-16	-16	-2	13	18	25	33	24	20	8	1	-16
Concord, New Hampshire	-33	-37	-16	8	21	30	35	29	21	10	-5	-22
Atlantic City, New Jersey	-10	-11	5	12	25	37	42	40	32	20	10	-7
Albuquerque, New Mexico	-17	-5	8	19	28	40	52	50	37	21	-7	-7
Albany, New York	-28	-21	-21	10	26	36	40	34	24	16	5	-22
Buffalo, New York	-16	-20	-7	12	26	35	43	38	32	20	9	-10
New York, New York[1]	-6	-15	3	12	32	44	52	50	39	28	5	-13
Charlotte, North Carolina	-5	5	4	24	32	45	53	53	39	24	11	2
Raleigh, North Carolina	-44	-39	-31	-12	15	30	35	33	11	-10	-30	-43
Bismarck, North Dakota	-9	5	11	23	31	38	48	46	37	19	11	4
Cincinnati, Ohio	-25	-11	-11	17	27	39	47	43	33	16	1	-20
Cleveland, Ohio	-19	-15	-5	10	25	31	41	38	32	19	3	-15
Columbus, Ohio	-19	-13	-6	14	25	35	43	39	31	20	5	-17
Oklahoma City, Oklahoma	-4	-3	3	20	37	47	53	51	36	22	11	-8
Portland, Oregon	-2	-3	19	29	29	39	43	44	34	26	13	6
Philadelphia, Pennsylvania	-7	-4	7	19	28	44	51	44	35	25	15	1
Pittsburgh, Pennsylvania	-18	-12	-1	14	26	34	42	39	31	16	-1	-12
Providence, Rhode Island	-13	-7	1	14	29	41	48	40	33	20	6	-10
Columbia, South Carolina	-1	5	4	26	34	44	54	53	40	23	12	4
Sioux Falls, South Dakota	-36	-31	-23	5	17	33	38	34	22	9	-17	-28
Memphis, Tennessee	-4	-11	12	29	38	48	52	48	36	25	9	-13
Nashville, Tennessee	-17	-13	2	23	34	42	51	47	36	26	-1	-10
Dallas-Fort Worth, Texas	4	7	15	29	41	51	59	56	43	29	20	-1
El Paso, Texas	-8	8	14	23	31	46	57	56	41	25	1	5
Houston, Texas	12	20	22	31	44	52	62	60	48	32	19	7
Salt Lake City, Utah	-22	-30	2	14	25	35	40	37	27	16	-14	-21
Burlington, Vermont	-30	-30	-20	2	24	33	39	35	25	15	-2	-26
Norfolk, Virginia	-3	8	18	28	36	45	54	49	45	27	20	7
Richmond, Virginia	-12	-10	11	23	31	40	51	46	35	21	10	-1
Seattle-Tacoma, Washington	0	1	11	29	28	38	43	44	35	28	6	6
Spokane, Washington	-22	-17	-7	17	24	33	37	35	24	10	-21	-25
Charleston, West Virginia	-15	-6	0	19	26	33	46	41	34	17	6	-12
Milwaukee, Wisconsin	-26	-19	-10	12	21	33	40	44	28	18	-5	-20
Cheyenne, Wyoming	-29	-34	-21	-8	16	25	38	36	8	-1	-14	-28
San Juan, Puerto Rico	61	62	60	64	66	69	69	70	69	67	66	63

Source: 1994 Statistical Abstract of the United States on CD-ROM [machine-readable datafiles]. CD-8A-94. Washington, DC: U.S. Department of Commerce, Economics and Statistics Administration, Bureau of the Census, Data User Services Division, January 1995. Primary source: U.S. National Oceanic and Atmospheric Administration. *Comparative Climatic Data* (annual). *Note:* 1. City office data.

★ 144 ★

Temperatures

Temperatures – Maximum, by City

Table shows normal daily maximum temperatures for selected U.S. cities. Figures are airport data except as noted. Based on standard 30-year period, 1961 through 1990. Data are presented alphabetically by state.

[In Fahrenheit degrees]

City	January	February	March	April	May	June	July	August	September	October	November	December
Mobile, Alabama	59.7	63.6	70.9	78.5	84.6	90.0	91.3	90.5	86.9	79.5	70.3	62.9
Juneau, Alaska	29.4	34.1	38.7	47.2	55.1	60.9	63.9	62.7	55.9	47.1	36.7	31.6
Phoenix, Arizona	65.9	70.7	75.5	84.5	93.6	103.5	105.9	103.7	98.3	88.1	74.9	66.2
Little Rock, Arkansas	49.0	53.9	64.0	73.4	81.3	89.3	92.4	91.4	84.6	75.1	62.7	52.5
Los Angeles, California	65.7	65.9	65.5	67.4	69.0	71.9	75.3	76.6	76.6	74.4	70.3	65.9
Sacramento, California	52.7	60.0	64.0	71.1	80.3	87.8	93.2	92.1	87.3	77.9	63.1	52.7
San Diego, California	65.9	66.5	66.3	68.4	69.1	71.6	76.2	77.8	77.1	74.6	69.9	66.1
San Francisco, California	55.6	59.4	60.8	63.9	66.5	70.3	71.6	72.3	73.6	70.1	62.4	56.1
Denver, Colorado	43.2	46.6	52.2	61.8	70.8	81.4	88.2	85.8	76.9	66.3	52.5	44.5
Hartford, Connecticut	33.2	36.4	46.8	59.9	71.6	80.0	85.0	82.7	74.8	63.7	51.0	37.5
Wilmington, Delaware	38.7	41.9	52.1	62.6	72.9	81.4	85.6	84.1	77.7	66.6	55.5	43.9
Washington, District of Columbia	42.3	45.9	56.5	66.7	76.2	84.7	88.5	86.9	80.1	69.1	58.3	47.0
Jacksonville, Florida	64.2	67.0	73.0	79.1	84.7	89.3	91.4	90.7	87.2	80.2	73.6	66.8
Miami, Florida	75.2	76.5	79.1	82.4	85.3	87.6	89.0	89.0	87.8	84.5	80.4	76.7
Atlanta, Georgia	50.4	55.0	64.3	72.7	79.6	85.8	88.0	87.1	81.8	72.7	63.4	54.0
Honolulu, Hawaii	80.1	80.5	81.6	82.8	84.7	86.5	87.5	88.7	88.5	86.9	84.1	81.2
Boise, Idaho	36.4	44.2	52.9	61.4	71.0	80.9	90.2	88.1	77.0	64.6	48.7	37.7
Chicago, Illinois	29.0	33.5	45.8	58.6	70.1	79.6	83.7	81.8	74.8	63.3	48.4	34.0
Peoria, Illinois	29.9	34.9	48.1	62.0	72.8	82.2	85.7	83.1	76.9	64.8	49.8	34.6
Indianapolis, Indiana	33.7	38.3	50.9	63.3	73.8	82.2	85.5	83.6	77.6	65.8	51.9	38.5
Des Moines, Iowa	28.1	33.7	46.9	61.8	73.0	82.2	86.7	84.2	75.6	64.3	48.0	32.6
Wichita, Kansas	39.8	45.9	57.2	68.3	76.9	86.8	92.8	90.7	81.4	70.6	55.3	43.0
Louisville, Kentucky	40.3	44.8	56.3	67.3	76.0	83.5	87.0	85.7	80.3	69.2	56.8	45.1
New Orleans, Louisiana	60.8	64.1	71.6	78.5	84.4	89.2	90.6	90.2	86.6	79.4	71.1	64.3
Portland, Maine	30.3	33.1	41.4	52.3	63.2	72.7	78.8	77.4	69.3	58.7	47.0	35.1
Baltimore, Maryland	40.2	43.7	54.0	64.3	74.2	83.2	87.2	85.4	78.5	67.3	56.5	45.2
Boston, Massachusetts	35.7	37.5	45.8	55.9	66.6	76.3	81.8	79.8	72.8	62.7	52.2	40.4
Detroit, Michigan	30.3	33.3	44.4	57.7	69.6	78.9	83.3	81.3	73.9	61.5	48.1	35.2
Sault Ste. Marie, Michigan	21.1	23.2	32.8	48.0	62.6	70.5	76.3	73.8	65.9	54.3	40.0	26.2
Duluth, Minnesota	16.2	21.7	32.9	48.2	61.9	71.0	77.1	73.9	63.8	52.3	35.2	20.7
Minneapolis-St. Paul, Minnesota	20.7	26.6	39.2	56.5	69.4	78.8	84.0	80.7	70.7	58.8	41.0	25.5
Jackson, Mississippi	55.6	60.1	69.3	77.4	84.0	90.6	92.4	92.0	88.0	79.1	69.2	59.5
Kansas City, Missouri	34.7	40.6	52.8	65.1	74.3	83.3	88.7	86.4	78.1	67.5	52.6	38.8
St. Louis, Missouri	37.7	42.6	54.6	66.9	76.1	85.2	89.3	87.3	79.9	68.5	54.7	41.7
Great Falls, Montana	30.6	37.5	43.7	55.3	65.2	74.6	83.3	81.6	69.6	59.3	43.5	33.1
Omaha, Nebraska	31.3	37.1	49.4	63.8	74.0	83.7	87.9	85.2	76.5	65.6	49.3	34.6
Reno, Nevada	45.1	51.7	56.3	63.7	72.9	83.1	91.9	89.6	79.5	68.6	53.8	45.5
Concord, New Hampshire	29.8	33.0	42.8	56.3	68.9	77.3	82.4	79.8	71.6	60.7	47.1	34.2
Atlantic City, New Jersey	40.4	42.5	51.6	60.7	71.2	80.0	84.5	83.3	76.6	66.0	55.7	45.3
Albuquerque, New Mexico	46.8	53.5	61.4	70.8	79.7	90.0	92.5	89.0	81.9	71.0	57.3	47.5
Albany, New York	30.2	33.2	44.0	57.5	69.7	79.0	84.0	81.4	73.2	61.8	48.7	34.9
Buffalo, New York	30.2	31.6	41.7	54.2	66.1	75.3	80.2	77.9	70.8	59.4	47.1	35.3
New York, New York[1]	37.6	40.3	50.0	61.2	71.7	80.1	85.2	83.7	76.2	65.3	54.0	42.5
Charlotte, North Carolina	49.0	53.0	62.3	71.2	78.3	85.8	88.9	87.7	81.9	72.0	62.6	52.3
Raleigh, North Carolina	48.9	52.6	62.1	71.7	78.6	85.0	88.0	86.8	81.1	71.6	62.6	52.7
Bismarck, North Dakota	20.2	26.4	38.5	54.9	67.8	77.1	84.4	82.7	70.8	58.7	39.3	24.5
Cincinnati, Ohio	36.6	40.8	53.0	64.2	74.0	82.0	85.5	84.1	77.9	66.0	53.3	41.5
Cleveland, Ohio	31.9	35.0	46.3	57.9	68.6	78.3	82.4	80.5	73.6	62.1	50.0	37.4
Columbus, Ohio	34.1	38.0	50.5	62.0	72.3	80.4	83.7	82.1	76.2	64.5	51.4	39.2
Oklahoma City, Oklahoma	46.7	52.1	62.0	71.9	79.1	87.3	93.4	92.5	83.8	73.6	60.4	49.9
Portland, Oregon	45.4	51.0	56.0	60.6	67.1	74.0	79.9	80.3	74.6	64.0	52.6	45.6
Philadelphia, Pennsylvania	37.9	41.0	51.6	62.6	73.1	81.7	86.1	84.6	77.6	66.3	55.1	43.4
Pittsburgh, Pennsylvania	33.7	36.9	49.0	60.3	70.6	78.9	82.6	80.8	74.3	62.5	50.4	38.6
Providence, Rhode Island	36.6	38.3	46.1	57.0	67.3	76.9	82.1	80.7	74.3	64.1	53.0	41.2
Columbia, South Carolina	55.3	59.3	68.2	76.5	83.5	88.8	91.6	90.1	85.1	76.3	67.8	58.8
Sioux Falls, South Dakota	24.3	29.6	42.3	59.0	70.7	80.5	86.3	83.3	73.1	61.2	43.4	28.0
Memphis, Tennessee	48.5	53.5	63.2	73.3	81.0	89.3	92.3	90.8	83.9	74.3	62.3	52.5
Nashville, Tennessee	45.9	50.8	61.2	70.8	78.8	86.5	89.5	88.4	82.5	72.5	60.4	50.2
Dallas-Fort Worth, Texas	54.1	58.9	67.8	76.3	82.9	91.9	96.5	96.2	87.8	78.5	66.8	57.5
El Paso, Texas	56.1	62.2	69.9	78.7	87.1	96.5	96.1	93.5	87.1	78.4	66.4	57.5
Houston, Texas	61.0	65.3	71.1	78.4	84.6	90.1	92.7	92.5	88.4	81.6	72.4	64.7
Salt Lake City, Utah	36.4	43.6	52.2	61.3	71.9	82.8	92.2	89.4	79.2	66.1	50.8	37.8
Burlington, Vermont	25.1	27.5	39.3	53.6	67.2	75.8	81.2	77.9	69.0	57.0	44.0	30.4

[Continued]

★ 144 ★

Temperatures – Maximum, by City

[Continued]

City	January	February	March	April	May	June	July	August	September	October	November	December
Norfolk, Virginia	47.3	49.7	57.9	66.9	75.3	82.9	86.4	85.1	79.6	69.5	61.2	52.2
Richmond, Virginia	45.7	49.2	59.5	70.0	77.8	85.1	88.4	87.1	80.9	70.7	61.3	50.2
Seattle-Tacoma, Washington	45.0	49.5	52.7	57.2	63.9	69.9	75.2	75.2	69.3	59.7	50.5	45.1
Spokane, Washington	33.2	40.6	47.7	57.0	65.8	74.7	83.1	82.5	72.0	58.6	41.4	33.8
Charleston, West Virginia	41.2	45.3	56.7	66.8	75.5	83.1	85.7	84.4	78.8	68.2	57.3	46.0
Milwaukee, Wisconsin	26.1	30.1	40.4	52.9	64.3	74.9	79.9	77.8	70.6	58.7	44.7	31.2
Cheyenne, Wyoming	37.7	40.5	44.9	54.7	64.6	74.4	82.2	80.0	71.1	60.0	46.8	38.8
San Juan, Puerto Rico	83.2	83.6	84.4	85.8	87.2	88.6	88.5	88.7	88.8	88.3	85.9	83.8

Source: 1994 Statistical Abstract of the United States on CD-ROM [machine-readable datafiles]. CD-8A-94. Washington, DC: U.S. Department of Commerce, Economics and Statistics Administration, Bureau of the Census, Data User Services Division, January 1995. Primary source: U.S. National Oceanic and Atmospheric Administration. *Climatography of the United States.* No. 81. *Note:* 1. City office data.

★ 145 ★

Temperatures

Temperatures – Minimum, by City

Table shows the normal daily minimum temperatures for selected cities. Figures are airport data, except as noted. Based on standard 30-year period, 1961 through 1990. Data are presented alphabetically by state.

[In Fahrenheit degrees]

City	January	February	March	April	May	June	July	August	September	October	November	December
Mobile, Alabama	40.0	42.7	50.1	57.1	64.4	70.7	73.2	72.9	68.7	57.3	49.1	43.1
Juneau, Alaska	19.0	22.7	26.7	32.1	38.9	45.0	48.1	47.3	42.9	37.2	27.2	22.6
Phoenix, Arizona	41.2	44.7	48.8	55.3	63.9	72.9	81.0	79.2	72.8	60.8	48.9	41.8
Little Rock, Arkansas	29.1	33.2	42.2	50.7	59.0	67.4	71.5	69.8	63.5	50.9	41.5	33.1
Los Angeles, California	47.8	49.3	50.5	52.8	56.3	59.5	62.8	64.2	63.2	59.2	52.8	47.9
Sacramento, California	37.7	41.4	43.2	45.5	50.3	55.3	58.1	58.0	55.7	50.4	43.4	37.8
San Diego, California	48.9	50.7	52.8	55.6	59.1	61.9	65.7	67.3	65.6	60.9	53.9	48.8
San Francisco, California	41.8	45.0	45.8	47.2	49.7	52.6	53.9	55.0	55.2	51.8	47.1	42.7
Denver, Colorado	16.1	20.2	25.8	34.5	43.6	52.4	58.6	56.9	47.6	36.4	25.4	17.4
Hartford, Connecticut	15.8	18.6	28.1	37.5	47.6	56.9	62.2	60.4	51.8	40.7	32.8	21.3
Wilmington, Delaware	22.4	24.8	33.1	41.8	52.2	61.6	67.1	65.9	58.2	45.7	37.0	27.6
Washington, District of Columbia	26.8	29.1	37.7	46.4	56.6	66.5	71.4	70.0	62.5	50.3	41.1	31.7
Jacksonville, Florida	40.5	43.3	49.2	54.9	62.1	69.1	71.9	71.8	69.0	59.3	50.2	43.4
Miami, Florida	59.2	60.4	64.2	67.8	72.1	75.1	76.2	76.7	75.9	72.1	66.7	61.5
Atlanta, Georgia	31.5	34.5	42.5	50.2	58.7	66.2	69.5	69.0	63.5	51.9	42.8	35.0
Honolulu, Hawaii	65.6	65.4	67.2	68.7	70.3	72.2	73.5	74.2	73.5	72.3	70.3	67.0
Boise, Idaho	21.6	27.5	31.9	36.7	43.9	52.1	57.7	56.8	48.2	39.0	31.1	22.5
Chicago, Illinois	12.9	17.2	28.5	38.6	47.7	57.5	62.6	61.6	53.9	42.2	31.6	19.1
Peoria, Illinois	13.2	17.7	29.8	40.8	50.9	60.7	65.4	63.1	55.2	43.1	32.5	19.3
Indianapolis, Indiana	17.2	20.9	31.9	41.5	51.7	61.0	65.2	62.8	55.6	43.5	34.1	23.2
Des Moines, Iowa	10.7	15.6	27.6	40.0	51.5	61.2	66.5	63.6	54.5	42.7	29.9	16.1
Wichita, Kansas	19.2	23.7	33.6	44.5	54.3	64.6	69.9	67.9	59.2	46.6	33.9	23.0
Louisville, Kentucky	23.2	26.5	36.2	45.4	54.7	62.9	67.3	65.8	58.7	45.8	37.3	28.6
New Orleans, Louisiana	41.8	44.4	51.6	58.4	65.2	70.8	73.1	72.8	69.5	58.7	51.0	44.8
Portland, Maine	11.4	13.5	24.5	34.1	43.4	52.1	58.3	57.1	48.9	38.3	30.4	17.8
Baltimore, Maryland	23.4	25.9	34.1	42.5	52.6	61.8	66.8	65.7	58.4	45.9	37.1	28.2
Boston, Massachusetts	21.6	23.0	31.3	40.2	49.8	59.1	65.1	64.0	56.8	46.9	38.3	26.7
Detroit, Michigan	15.6	17.6	27.0	36.8	47.1	56.3	61.3	59.6	52.5	40.9	32.2	21.4
Sault Ste. Marie, Michigan	4.6	4.8	15.3	28.4	38.4	45.5	51.3	51.3	44.3	36.2	25.9	11.8
Duluth, Minnesota	-2.2	2.8	15.7	28.9	39.6	48.5	55.1	53.3	44.5	35.1	21.5	4.9
Minneapolis-St. Paul, Minnesota	2.8	9.2	22.7	36.2	47.6	57.6	63.1	60.3	50.3	38.8	25.2	10.2
Jackson, Mississippi	32.7	35.7	44.1	51.9	60.0	67.1	70.5	69.7	63.7	50.3	42.3	36.1
Kansas City, Missouri	16.7	21.8	32.6	43.8	53.9	63.1	68.2	65.7	56.9	45.7	33.6	21.9
St. Louis, Missouri	20.8	25.1	35.5	46.4	56.0	65.7	70.4	67.9	60.5	48.3	37.7	26.0
Great Falls, Montana	11.6	17.2	22.8	31.9	40.9	48.6	53.2	52.2	43.5	35.8	24.3	14.6
Omaha, Nebraska	10.9	16.7	27.7	39.9	50.9	60.4	65.9	62.9	53.6	41.2	28.7	15.6
Reno, Nevada	20.7	24.2	29.2	33.3	40.1	46.9	51.3	49.6	41.3	32.9	26.7	19.9
Concord, New Hampshire	7.4	10.4	22.1	31.5	41.4	51.2	56.5	54.7	46.0	34.9	27.0	14.4

[Continued]

★ 145 ★

Temperatures – Minimum, by City
[Continued]

City	January	February	March	April	May	June	July	August	September	October	November	December
Atlantic City, New Jersey	21.4	23.5	31.3	39.3	49.6	58.7	64.8	63.5	55.5	43.7	35.8	26.3
Albuquerque, New Mexico	21.7	26.4	32.2	39.6	48.6	58.3	64.4	62.6	55.2	43.0	31.2	23.1
Albany, New York	11.0	13.8	24.5	35.1	45.4	54.6	59.6	57.8	49.4	38.6	30.7	18.2
Buffalo, New York	17.0	17.4	25.9	36.2	47.0	56.5	61.9	60.1	53.0	42.7	33.9	22.9
New York, New York[1]	25.3	26.9	34.8	43.8	53.7	63.0	68.4	67.3	60.1	49.7	41.1	30.7
Charlotte, North Carolina	29.6	31.9	39.4	47.5	56.4	65.6	69.6	68.9	62.9	50.6	41.5	32.8
Raleigh, North Carolina	28.8	31.3	38.7	46.2	55.3	63.6	68.1	67.5	61.1	48.4	39.7	32.4
Bismarck, North Dakota	-1.7	5.1	17.8	31.0	42.2	51.6	56.4	53.9	43.1	32.5	17.8	3.3
Cincinnati, Ohio	19.5	22.7	33.1	42.2	51.8	60.0	64.8	62.9	56.6	44.2	35.3	25.3
Cleveland, Ohio	17.6	19.3	28.2	37.3	47.3	56.8	61.4	60.3	54.2	43.5	35.0	24.5
Columbus, Ohio	18.5	21.2	31.2	40.0	50.1	58.0	62.7	60.8	54.8	42.9	34.3	24.6
Oklahoma City, Oklahoma	25.2	29.6	38.5	48.8	57.7	66.1	70.6	69.6	62.2	50.4	38.6	28.6
Portland, Oregon	33.7	36.1	38.6	41.3	47.0	52.9	56.5	56.9	52.0	44.9	39.5	34.8
Philadelphia, Pennsylvania	22.8	24.8	33.2	42.1	52.7	61.8	67.2	66.3	58.7	46.4	37.6	28.1
Pittsburgh, Pennsylvania	18.5	20.3	29.8	38.8	48.4	56.9	61.6	60.2	53.5	42.3	34.1	24.4
Providence, Rhode Island	19.1	20.9	28.8	37.7	47.3	56.8	63.2	61.9	53.8	43.0	34.9	24.4
Columbia, South Carolina	32.1	34.2	42.2	49.4	58.2	66.0	70.0	69.2	63.2	50.1	41.5	34.9
Sioux Falls, South Dakota	3.3	9.7	22.6	34.8	45.9	56.1	62.3	59.4	48.7	36.0	22.6	8.6
Memphis, Tennessee	30.9	34.8	43.0	52.4	61.2	68.9	72.9	71.1	64.5	51.9	42.7	34.8
Nashville, Tennessee	26.5	29.9	39.1	47.5	56.6	64.7	68.9	67.7	61.1	48.3	39.6	30.9
Dallas-Fort Worth, Texas	32.7	36.9	45.6	54.7	62.6	70.0	74.1	73.6	66.9	55.8	45.4	36.3
El Paso, Texas	29.4	33.9	40.2	48.0	56.5	64.3	68.4	66.6	61.6	49.6	38.4	30.7
Houston, Texas	39.7	42.6	50.0	58.1	64.4	70.6	72.4	72.0	67.9	57.6	49.6	42.2
Salt Lake City, Utah	19.3	24.6	31.4	37.9	45.6	55.4	63.7	61.8	51.0	40.2	30.9	21.6
Burlington, Vermont	7.5	8.9	22.0	34.2	45.4	54.6	65.2	70.0	64.2	52.9	43.8	15.5
Norfolk, Virginia	30.9	32.3	39.3	47.1	56.8	65.2	70.0	69.4	64.2	52.9	43.8	35.4
Richmond, Virginia	25.7	28.1	36.3	44.6	54.2	62.7	67.5	66.4	59.0	46.5	37.9	29.9
Seattle-Tacoma, Washington	35.2	37.4	38.5	41.2	46.3	51.9	55.2	55.7	51.9	45.8	40.1	35.8
Spokane, Washington	20.8	25.9	29.6	34.7	41.9	49.2	54.4	54.3	45.8	36.0	28.8	21.7
Charleston, West Virginia	23.0	25.7	35.0	42.8	51.5	59.8	64.4	63.4	56.5	44.2	36.3	28.0
Milwaukee, Wisconsin	11.6	15.9	26.2	35.8	44.8	55.0	62.0	60.8	52.8	41.8	30.7	17.5
Cheyenne, Wyoming	15.2	18.1	22.1	30.1	39.4	48.3	54.6	52.8	43.7	33.9	23.7	16.7
San Juan, Puerto Rico	70.8	70.6	71.6	72.9	74.5	76.1	76.8	76.7	76.2	75.5	74.0	72.4

Source: 1994 Statistical Abstract of the United States on CD-ROM [machine-readable datafiles]. CD-8A-94. Washington, DC: U.S. Department of Commerce, Economics and Statistics Administration, Bureau of the Census, Data User Services Division, January 1995. *Note:* 1. City office data.

Weather Conditions

★146★

Humidity in East North Central United States, by City

Table shows the average relative humidity in selected cities. Figures are airport data, except as noted. For period of record through 1991, except as noted.

[In percentages]

City and state	Length of record (years)	Annual		January		July	
		Morning	Afternoon	Morning	Afternoon	Morning	Afternoon
Cairo, Illinois	(NA)	(NA)	59	(NA)	67	(NA)	59
Chicago, Illinois	33	77	60	75	67	79	56
Moline, Illinois	31	77	59	73	65	82	56
Peoria, Illinois	32	79	62	78	68	82	59
Rockford, Illinois	28	80	61	78	70	83	56
Springfield, Illinois	32	78	61	77	68	81	57
Evansville, Indiana	30	79	59	75	66	83	57
Fort Wayne, Indiana	30	79	62	78	71	81	55
Indianapolis, Indiana	32	80	62	78	70	84	59
South Bend, Indiana	28	79	62	79	72	81	56
Alpena, Michigan	26	83	61	80	70	86	53
Detroit, Michigan	33	79	60	78	69	81	53
Flint, Michigan	28	79	62	78	71	82	55
Grand Rapids, Michigan	28	80	62	80	72	82	55
Houghton Lake, Michigan	14	83	63	83	72	84	54
Lansing, Michigan	28	83	64	82	75	85	56
Muskegon, Michigan	30	79	64	80	75	81	59
Sault Sainte Marie, Michigan	50	85	67	81	75	90	61
Akron, Ohio	28	77	61	76	69	82	56
Greater Cincinnati Airport	29	77	59	75	67	83	57
Cleveland, Ohio	31	77	62	75	69	81	57
Columbus, Ohio	32	77	59	74	67	82	56
Dayton, Ohio	28	77	60	75	69	79	55
Mansfield, Ohio	10	79	63	78	71	82	58
Toledo, Ohio	36	80	60	76	69	84	55
Youngstown, Ohio	43	81	62	79	72	85	55
Green Bay, Wisconsin	30	80	63	76	70	82	57
La Crosse, Wisconsin	31	79	61	76	67	81	57
Madison, Wisconsin	32	81	61	78	69	84	57
Milwaukee, Wisconsin	31	78	64	75	68	80	61

Source: 1994 Statistical Abstract of the United States on CD-ROM [machine-readable datafiles]. CD-8A-94. Washington, DC: U.S. Department of Commerce, Economics and Statistics Administration, Bureau of the Census, Data User Services Division, January 1995. Primary source: U.S. National Oceanic and Atmospheric Administration. *Comparative Climatic Data* (annual). *Note:* "NA" represents "not available."

★ 147 ★
Weather Conditions
Humidity in East South Central United States, by City

Table shows the average relative humidity in selected cities. Figures are airport data, except as noted. For period of record through 1991, except as noted.

[In percentages]

City and state	Length of record (years)	Annual		January		July	
		Morning	Afternoon	Morning	Afternoon	Morning	Afternoon
Birminghan, Alabama	28	80	57	76	61	86	60
Huntsville, Alabama	24	81	58	78	65	86	59
Mobile, Alabama	29	83	57	79	61	87	60
Montgomery, Alabama	28	81	56	77	60	87	60
Jackson, Kentucky	74	58	71	63	84	61	(NA)
Lexington, Kentucky	27	77	60	76	68	83	58
Louisville, Kentucky	31	76	58	72	64	81	58
Paducah, Kentucky	7	82	58	78	65	88	57
Jackson, Mississippi	28	87	58	84	65	90	59
Meridian, Mississippi	27	86	55	83	60	90	58
Tupelo, Mississippi	8	80	57	77	62	85	56
Bristol/Johnson City/Kingsport, Tennessee	30	81	57	77	62	88	61
Chattanooga, Tennessee	51	83	56	79	62	88	57
Knoxville, Tennessee	31	81	59	77	64	87	61
Memphis, Tennessee	52	76	57	75	63	79	57
Nashville, Tennessee	26	79	57	75	63	85	57

Source: 1994 Statistical Abstract of the United States on CD-ROM [machine-readable datafiles]. CD-8A-94. Washington, DC: U.S. Department of Commerce, Economics and Statistics Administration, Bureau of the Census, Data User Services Division, January 1995. Primary source: U.S. National Oceanic and Atmospheric Administration. *Comparative Climatic Data* (annual). *Note:* "NA" represents "not available."

★ 148 ★
Weather Conditions
Humidity in Middle Atlantic United States, by City

Table shows the average relative humidity in selected cities. Figures are airport data, except as noted. For period of record through 1991, except as noted.

[In percentages]

City and state	Length of record (years)	Annual		January		July	
		Morning	Afternoon	Morning	Afternoon	Morning	Afternoon
Atlantic City, New Jersey	27	82	56	76	58	87	57
Newark, New Jersey	26	72	53	70	58	73	52
Albany, New York	26	79	57	76	63	84	55
Binghamton, New York	40	79	63	78	70	81	57
Buffalo, New York	31	79	63	77	72	79	55

[Continued]

★ 148 ★

Humidity in Middle Atlantic United States, by City

[Continued]

City and state	Length of record (years)	Annual		January		July	
		Morning	Afternoon	Morning	Afternoon	Morning	Afternoon
Islip, New York	7	80	59	75	61	86	61
New York, New York (Central Park)	49	70	56	65	60	74	55
New York, New York (John F. Kennedy Airport)	30	74	58	68	59	79	59
New York, New York (La Guardia Airport)	29	68	55	63	57	72	53
Rochester, New York	28	80	61	76	69	83	54
Syracuse, New York	28	80	61	76	68	84	55
Allentown, Pennsylvania	41	78	56	74	62	82	53
Erie, Pennsylvania	36	76	59	72	65	81	56
Harrisburg, Pennsylvania	26	77	66	75	72	80	64
Middletown/Harrisburg International Airport	49	74	54	69	58	79	52
Philadelphia, Pennsylvania	49	74	54	69	58	79	52
Pittsburgh, Pennsylvania	32	76	55	71	59	81	54
Avoca, Pennsylvania	31	75	57	73	65	80	54
Williamsport, Pennsylvania	40	81	57	75	62	89	55

Source: 1994 Statistical Abstract of the United States on CD-ROM [machine-readable datafiles]. CD-8A-94. Washington, DC: U.S. Department of Commerce, Economics and Statistics Administration, Bureau of the Census, Data User Services Division, January 1995. Primary source: U.S. National Oceanic and Atmospheric Administration. *Comparative Climatic Data* (annual).

★ 149 ★

Weather Conditions

Humidity in New England, by City

Table shows the average relative humidity in selected cities. Figures are airport data, except as noted. For period of record through 1991, except as noted.

[In percentages]

City and state	Length of record (years)	Annual		January		July	
		Morning	Afternoon	Morning	Afternoon	Morning	Afternoon
Bridgeport, Connecticut	14	76	60	69	60	82	61
Hartford, Connecticut	32	76	52	69	56	82	51
Caribou, Maine	19	82	61	74	66	84	58
Portland, Maine	51	82	59	74	60	89	59
Blue Hill, Massachusetts	33	79	58	72	62	85	57
Boston, Massachusetts	27	72	58	65	57	77	56
Worcester, Massachusetts	32	75	57	69	58	79	57
Concord, New Hampshire	25	82	54	74	58	90	51
Mt. Washington, New Hampshire	33	87	84	82	83	93	87
Providence, Rhode Island	28	76	55	69	56	83	56
Burlington, Vermont	26	77	59	70	63	82	53

Source: 1994 Statistical Abstract of the United States on CD-ROM [machine-readable datafiles]. CD-8A-94. Washington, DC: U.S. Department of Commerce, Economics and Statistics Administration, Bureau of the Census, Data User Services Division, January 1995. Primary source: U.S. National Oceanic and Atmospheric Administration. *Comparative Climatic Data* (annual).

★ 150 ★

Weather Conditions

Humidity in Pacific United States, by City

Table shows the average relative humidity in selected cities. Figures are airport data, except as noted. For period of record through 1991, except as noted.

[In percentages]

City and state	Length of record (years)	Annual		January		July	
		Morning	Afternoon	Morning	Afternoon	Morning	Afternoon
Anchorage, Alaska	38	76	63	73	72	80	62
Annette, Alaska	26	84	73	80	75	89	70
Barrow, Alaska	42	81	78	69	69	94	84
Barter Island, Alaska	40	80	78	70	70	93	86
Bethel, Alaska	41	85	72	76	75	92	67
Bettles, Alaska	44	76	62	69	67	85	54
Big Delta, Alaska	16	72	57	66	65	77	52
Cold Bay, Alaska	22	87	80	85	82	92	82
Fairbanks, Alaska	41	73	57	69	69	82	50
Gulkana, Alaska	14	79	57	73	70	84	49
Homer, Alaska	41	83	70	79	76	90	71
Juneau, Alaska	25	86	73	81	77	87	70
King Salmon, Alaska	43	83	68	78	75	90	64
Kodiak, Alaska	44	81	73	79	75	88	77
Kotzebue, Alaska	29	80	75	72	72	87	76
McGrath, Alaska	40	78	60	72	71	85	55
Nome, Alaska	28	80	74	74	74	89	79
St. Paul Island, Alaska	14	89	84	84	83	96	89
Talkeetna, Alaska	29	83	63	73	68	92	61
Unalakleet, Alaska	9	78	72	69	69	87	75
Valdez, Alaska	16	83	70	79	75	92	71
Yakutat, Alaska	27	90	77	83	81	96	78
Bakersfield, California	19	65	38	83	62	48	21
Bishop, California	(NA)	(NA)	21	(NA)	35	(NA)	14
Blue Canyon, California	13	54	50	56	58	41	34
Fresno, California	28	78	40	91	67	61	22
Long Beach, California	25	79	53	75	51	82	52
Los Angeles, California	32	79	64	70	59	86	68
Los Angeles, California[1]	17	75	53	63	50	84	53
Mount Shasta, California	13	72	47	76	66	64	28
Redding, California	5	71	35	81	53	56	18
Sacramento, California	31	82	45	90	70	76	28
San Diego, California	31	76	62	70	56	82	66
San Francisco, California	32	84	62	86	66	86	59
San Francisco, California[1]	7	85	66	81	63	92	74
Santa Barbara, California	4	80	59	77	55	88	64
Santa Maria, California	19	86	60	81	59	88	60
Stockton, California	19	78	44	90	70	65	26
Hilo, Hawaii	42	86	68	83	67	88	68
Honolulu, Hawaii	22	76	56	81	61	73	51
Kahului, Hawaii	10	81	58	85	63	80	55

[Continued]

★ 150 ★

Humidity in Pacific United States, by City

[Continued]

City and state	Length of record (years)	Annual		January		July	
		Morning	Afternoon	Morning	Afternoon	Morning	Afternoon
Lihue, Hawaii	41	81	67	82	67	79	66
Astoria, Oregon	38	89	73	86	78	90	69
Burns, Oregon	1	80	(NA)	91	77	65	25
Eugene, Oregon	34	91	60	92	80	88	38
Medford, Oregon	30	84	47	90	71	73	26
Pendleton, Oregon	50	70	48	80	75	54	23
Portland, Oregon	51	86	60	86	75	82	45
Salem, Oregon	29	88	59	87	75	86	40
Sexton Summit, Oregon	7	75	59	80	72	65	40
Olympia, Washington	32	92	64	92	80	91	50
Quillayute, Washington	25	93	73	91	84	94	64
Seattle-Tacoma Airport, Washington	32	83	62	81	74	82	49
Spokane, Washington	32	78	52	85	78	64	27
Yakima, Washington	44	77	44	83	71	68	25

Source: 1994 Statistical Abstract of the United States on CD-ROM [machine-readable datafiles]. CD-8A-94. Washington, DC: U.S. Department of Commerce, Economics and Statistics Administration, Bureau of the Census, Data User Services Division, January 1995. Primary source: U.S. National Oceanic and Atmospheric Administration. *Comparative Climatic Data* (annual). *Notes:* "NA" represents "not available." 1. City office data.

★ 151 ★

Weather Conditions

Humidity in South Atlantic United States, by City

Table shows the average relative humidity in selected cities. Figures are airport data, except as noted. For period of record through 1991, except as noted.

[In percentages]

City and state	Length of record (years)	Annual		January		July	
		Morning	Afternoon	Morning	Afternoon	Morning	Afternoon
Wilmington, Delaware	44	78	55	73	60	83	54
Washington, District of Columbia (Dulles Airport)	(NA)	(NA)	55	(NA)	58	(NA)	55
Washington National Airport (District of Columbia)	31	72	53	67	55	77	53
Apalachicola, Florida	37	85	67	83	66	87	71
Daytona Beach, Florida	47	86	61	85	59	89	65
Fort Myers, Florida	30	87	56	86	57	89	60
Gainesville, Florida	8	91	60	88	63	94	64
Jacksonville, Florida	55	86	56	85	57	88	58
Key West, Florida	40	79	67	81	69	77	66
Miami, Florida	27	81	61	81	59	82	63
Orlando, Florida	27	87	55	85	56	90	59
Pensacola, Florida	26	82	60	80	62	86	64
Tallahassee, Florida	30	88	55	85	59	93	61
Tampa, Florida	28	85	58	85	59	86	63

[Continued]

★ 151 ★

Humidity in South Atlantic United States, by City
[Continued]

City and state	Length of record (years)	Annual		January		July	
		Morning	Afternoon	Morning	Afternoon	Morning	Afternoon
Vero Beach, Florida	8	85	60	86	59	89	65
West Palm Beach, Florida	27	81	60	81	58	85	64
Athens, Georgia	36	79	56	75	58	87	59
Atlanta, Georgia	31	77	56	74	59	85	60
Augusta, Georgia	26	84	51	79	54	87	55
Columbus, Georgia	26	82	54	79	59	86	58
Macon, Georgia	27	83	54	79	58	87	57
Savannah, Georgia	27	83	53	78	54	87	57
Baltimore, Maryland	38	75	54	69	57	81	53
Asheville, North Carolina	27	87	58	81	59	95	63
Cape Hatteras, North Carolina	34	83	66	78	68	89	70
Charlotte, North Carolina	31	76	54	72	56	83	57
Greensboro/Winston-Salem/High Point, North Carolina	28	79	55	74	56	87	59
Raleigh, North Carolina	27	80	54	73	55	88	58
Wilmington, North Carolina	28	84	56	78	56	89	63
Charleston Airport, South Carolina	85	56	80	56	90	62	
Columbia, South Carolina	25	83	51	78	54	87	54
Greenville-Spartanburg Airport, South Carolina	29	78	54	73	55	85	58
Lynchburg, Virginia	(NA)	(NA)	53	(NA)	53	(NA)	57
Norfolk, Virginia	43	78	57	72	59	84	59
Richmond, Virginia	57	82	53	77	57	88	56
Roanoke, Virginia	27	75	52	67	52	84	55
Wallops Island, Virginia	22	81	63	74	63	88	66
Beckley, West Virginia	28	81	61	78	67	90	62
Charleston, West Virginia	44	79	56	74	63	90	60
Elkins, West Virginia	6	88	59	81	65	97	61
Huntington, West Virginia	29	78	58	73	65	88	60

Source: 1994 Statistical Abstract of the United States on CD-ROM [machine-readable datafiles]. CD-8A-94. Washington, DC: U.S. Department of Commerce, Economics and Statistics Administration, Bureau of the Census, Data User Services Division, January 1995. Primary source: U.S. National Oceanic and Atmospheric Administration. Comparative Climatic Data (annual). Note: "NA" represents "not available."

★ 152 ★
Weather Conditions

Humidity in U.S. Territories and Administered Areas, by City

Table shows the average relative humidity in selected cities. Figures are airport data, except as noted. For period of record through 1991, except as noted.

[In percentages]

Location	Length of record (years)	Annual		January		July	
		Morning	Afternoon	Morning	Afternoon	Morning	Afternoon
Chuuk, East Caroline Islands	21	86	77	82	76	89	78
Guam	3	92	76	88	75	94	78
Johnston Island	23	79	70	76	68	79	69
Koror	21	91	77	90	76	91	78
Majuro, Marshall Islands	35	82	76	80	75	83	77
Pago Pago, American Samoa	23	87	76	89	76	83	75
Pohnpei, Caroline Islands	21	91	79	84	78	95	79
San Juan, Puerto Rico	36	83	65	82	64	84	67
Wake Island	44	80	68	76	66	81	70
Yap, West Caroline Islands	22	89	76	87	76	91	77

Source: 1994 Statistical Abstract of the United States on CD-ROM [machine-readable datafiles]. CD-8A-94. Washington, DC: U.S. Department of Commerce, Economics and Statistics Administration, Bureau of the Census, Data User Services Division, January 1995. Primary source: U.S. National Oceanic and Atmospheric Administration. *Comparative Climatic Data* (annual).

★ 153 ★
Weather Conditions

Humidity in West North Central United States, by City

Table shows the average relative humidity in selected cities. Figures are airport data, except as noted. For period of record through 1991, except as noted.

[In percentages]

City and state	Length of record (years)	Annual		January		July	
		Morning	Afternoon	Morning	Afternoon	Morning	Afternoon
Des Moines, Iowa	30	75	60	74	67	76	57
Dubuque, Iowa	(NA)	(NA)	62	(NA)	68	(NA)	59
Sioux City, Iowa	31	76	60	76	68	78	58
Waterloo, Iowa	32	80	62	76	69	84	58
Concordia, Kansas	29	73	57	75	64	70	50
Dodge City, Kansas	28	69	50	72	58	63	43
Goodland, Kansas	25	79	48	76	60	81	38
Topeka, Kansas	27	77	59	75	63	78	58
Wichita, Kansas	38	73	55	76	63	67	48
Duluth, Minnesota	30	77	63	74	70	82	59

[Continued]

★ 153 ★

Humidity in West North Central United States, by City
[Continued]

City and state	Length of record (years)	Annual		January		July	
		Morning	Afternoon	Morning	Afternoon	Morning	Afternoon
International Falls, Minnesota	49	78	62	73	68	84	57
Minneapolis-St.Paul, Minnesota	32	73	60	72	67	74	54
Rochester, Minnesota	31	80	65	78	74	83	60
Saint Cloud, Minnesota	19	80	60	76	69	85	55
Columbia, Missouri	22	77	60	75	65	80	55
Kansas City, Missouri	19	74	59	72	63	75	56
Springfield, Missouri	31	78	58	73	61	82	56
St. Louis, Missouri	31	76	59	77	66	77	56
Grand Island, Nebraska	30	74	55	74	62	74	52
Lincoln, Nebraska	19	77	57	76	63	75	52
Norfolk, Nebraska	15	75	56	72	63	76	53
North Platte, Nebraska	27	74	53	76	62	73	50
Omaha Eppley Airport, Nebraska	27	76	59	75	65	78	57
Omaha, Nebraska[1]	7	72	59	70	61	74	60
Scottsbluff, Nebraska	26	77	44	74	57	80	36
Valentine, Nebraska	24	70	51	72	62	66	46
Bismarck, North Dakota	32	74	56	75	68	74	46
Fargo, North Dakota	32	76	62	74	71	78	54
Williston, North Dakota	24	73	57	78	72	67	45
Aberdeen, South Dakota	13	76	60	73	70	75	52
Huron, South Dakota	32	77	59	74	67	78	52
Rapid City, South Dakota	41	71	50	68	63	73	40
Sioux Falls, South Dakota	28	76	60	75	68	75	53

Source: 1994 Statistical Abstract of the United States on CD-ROM [machine-readable datafiles]. CD-8A-94. Washington, DC: U.S. Department of Commerce, Economics and Statistics Administration, Bureau of the Census, Data User Services Division, January 1995. Primary source: U.S. National Oceanic and Atmospheric Administration. *Comparative Climatic Data* (annual). *Notes:* "NA" represents "not available." 1. City office data.

★ 154 ★

Weather Conditions

Humidity in West South Central United States, by City

Table shows the average relative humidity in selected cities. Figures are airport data, except as noted. For period of record through 1991, except as noted.

[In percentages]

City and state	Length of record (years)	Annual		January		July	
		Morning	Afternoon	Morning	Afternoon	Morning	Afternoon
Fort Smith, Arkansas	27	79	56	77	61	81	54
Little Rock, Arkansas	31	79	57	76	61	83	56
Baton Rouge, Louisiana	32	84	59	81	64	87	62
Lake Charles, Louisiana	27	89	63	86	68	91	64
New Orleans, Louisiana	43	85	63	82	66	89	66
Shreveport, Louisiana	39	80	58	78	63	83	57
Oklahoma City, Oklahoma	26	72	54	72	59	70	49
Tulsa, Oklahoma	31	73	56	72	59	71	53
Abilene, Texas	28	65	50	66	54	58	45
Amarillo, Texas	30	64	45	65	50	61	42
Austin, Texas	30	75	57	72	60	75	51
Brownsville, Texas	25	86	60	87	68	86	55
Corpus Christi, Texas	27	86	62	85	69	88	57
Dallas-Fort Worth, Texas	28	72	56	73	60	67	49
Del Rio, Texas	16	65	54	66	55	59	52
El Paso, Texas	31	57	28	66	35	63	30
Galveston, Texas	44	81	72	83	77	80	70
Houston, Texas	22	86	60	82	64	86	58
Lubbock, Texas	44	63	47	65	50	62	47
Midland-Odessa, Texas	28	62	43	64	47	57	42
Port Arthur, Texas	29	88	64	86	68	92	65
San Angelo, Texas	31	68	49	69	52	61	44
San Antonio, Texas	49	76	55	76	59	75	52
Victoria, Texas	27	85	59	84	65	87	56
Waco, Texas	28	75	57	77	63	68	48
Wichita Falls, Texas	31	73	51	73	56	65	43

Source: 1994 Statistical Abstract of the United States on CD-ROM [machine-readable datafiles]. CD-8A-94. Washington, DC: U.S. Department of Commerce, Economics and Statistics Administration, Bureau of the Census, Data User Services Division, January 1995. Primary source: U.S. National Oceanic and Atmospheric Administration. *Comparative Climatic Data* (annual).

★ 155 ★

Weather Conditions

Humidity in Western United States, by City

Table shows the average relative humidity in selected cities. Figures are airport data, except as noted. For period of record through 1991, except as noted.

[In percentages]

City and state	Length of record (years)	Annual		January		July	
		Morning	Afternoon	Morning	Afternoon	Morning	Afternoon
Flagstaff, Arizona	34	69	39	73	50	68	38
Phoenix, Arizona	31	51	23	66	32	45	20
Tucson, Arizona	51	52	25	63	32	57	28
Winslow, Arizona	18	62	30	79	50	58	27
Yuma, Arizona	14	53	23	57	28	50	22
Alamosa, Colorado	35	78	40	78	59	84	36
Colorado Springs, Colorado	31	62	40	56	46	68	39
Denver, Colorado	31	67	40	63	49	68	34
Grand Junction, Colorado	28	60	36	78	63	49	22
Pueblo, Colorado	13	68	37	66	50	72	32
Boise, Idaho	52	69	43	81	70	54	21
Lewiston, Idaho	37	75	48	81	70	61	24
Pocatello, Idaho	28	72	44	79	71	64	24
Billings, Montana	32	66	44	64	56	63	31
Glasgow, Montana	27	75	50	75	72	72	33
Great Falls, Montana	30	67	45	66	60	66	29
Helena, Montana	26	71	45	71	62	66	29
Kalispell, Montana	27	82	54	80	74	83	35
Missoula, Montana	31	83	52	85	76	77	31
Elko, Nevada	26	70	36	79	59	56	19
Ely, Nevada	39	66	36	72	55	52	22
Las Vegas, Nevada	31	40	21	55	31	29	15
Reno, Nevada	28	70	31	79	50	63	18
Winnemucca, Nevada	42	64	33	78	57	45	15
Albuquerque, New Mexico	31	60	29	70	40	60	27
Clayton, New Mexico	38	68	41	64	47	76	41
Roswell, New Mexico	19	66	33	71	41	69	32
Milford, Utah	(NA)	(NA)	35	(NA)	60	(NA)	20
Salt Lake City, Utah	32	67	43	79	69	52	22
Casper, Wyoming	27	71	43	69	61	69	26
Cheyenne, Wyoming	32	65	44	57	50	70	38
Lander, Wyoming	45	64	43	67	60	55	27
Sheridan, Wyoming	27	72	48	69	64	72	33

Source: 1994 Statistical Abstract of the United States on CD-ROM [machine-readable datafiles]. CD-8A-94. Washington, DC: U.S. Department of Commerce, Economics and Statistics Administration, Bureau of the Census, Data User Services Division, January 1995. Primary source: U.S. National Oceanic and Atmospheric Administration. *Comparative Climatic Data* (annual). *Note:* "NA" represents "not available."

★ 156 ★
Weather Conditions

Sunshine in East North Central United States, by City

Table shows the average percentage of possible sunshine in selected cities. Figures are airport data, except as noted. For period of record through 1991, except as noted.

City and state	Length of record (years)	Possible sunshine
Cairo, Illinois	45	61
Chicago, Illinois	11	54
Moline, Illinois	48	55
Peoria, Illinois	48	57
Springfield, Illinois	43	59
Evansville, Indiana	51	60
Fort Wayne, Indiana	45	59
Indianapolis, Indiana	47	55
Alpena, Michigan	32	49
Detroit, Michigan	26	53
Grand Rapids, Michigan	28	47
Lansing, Michigan	37	51
Marquette, Michigan	11	45
Sault Sainte Marie, Michigan	50	47
Greater Cincinnati Airport	8	52
Cleveland, Ohio	48	49
Columbus, Ohio	40	49
Dayton, Ohio	48	54
Toledo, Ohio	36	52
Green Bay, Wisconsin	42	54
Madison, Wisconsin	45	55
Milwaukee, Wisconsin	51	54

Source: 1994 Statistical Abstract of the United States on CD-ROM [machine-readable datafiles]. CD-8A-94. Washington, DC: U.S. Department of Commerce, Economics and Statistics Administration, Bureau of the Census, Data User Services Division, January 1995. Primary source: U.S. National Oceanic and Atmospheric Administration. *Comparative Climatic Data* (annual).

★ 157 ★

Weather Conditions

Sunshine in East South Central United States, by City

Table shows the average percentage of possible sunshine in selected cities. Figures are airport data, except as noted. For period of record through 1991, except as noted.

City and state	Length of record (years)	Possible sunshine
Birminghan, Alabama	34	58
Birmingham, Alabama[1]	10	57
Montgomery, Alabama	41	59
Jackson, Kentucky	(NA)	10
Louisville, Kentucky	44	56
Paducah, Kentucky	7	57
Jackson, Mississippi	27	60
Tupelo, Mississippi	8	64
Chattanooga, Tennessee	61	57
Knoxville, Tennessee	49	55
Memphis, Tennessee	35	64
Nashville, Tennessee	49	56

Source: 1994 Statistical Abstract of the United States on CD-ROM [machine-readable datafiles]. CD-8A-94. Washington, DC: U.S. Department of Commerce, Economics and Statistics Administration, Bureau of the Census, Data User Services Division, January 1995. Primary source: U.S. National Oceanic and Atmospheric Administration. *Comparative Climatic Data* (annual). *Notes:* "NA" represents "not available." 1. City office data.

★ 158 ★

Weather Conditions

Sunshine in Middle Atlantic United States, by City

Table shows the average percentage of possible sunshine in selected cities. Figures are airport data, except as noted. For period of record through 1991, except as noted.

City and state	Length of record (years)	Possible sunshine
Atlantic City, New Jersey	31	56
Albany, New York	53	52
Binghamton, New York	40	48
Buffalo, New York	48	49
New York, New York (Central Park)	105	58
Rochester, New York	51	51

[Continued]

★ 158 ★

Sunshine in Middle Atlantic United States, by City
[Continued]

City and state	Length of record (years)	Possible sunshine
Syracuse, New York	42	46
Allentown, Pennsylvania	7	55
Erie, Pennsylvania	36	50
Middletown/Harrisburg International Airport	53	58
Philadelphia, Pennsylvania	53	58
Pittsburgh, Pennsylvania	49	56
Avoca, Pennsylvania	39	46

Source: 1994 Statistical Abstract of the United States on CD-ROM [machine-readable datafiles]. CD-8A-94. Washington, DC: U.S. Department of Commerce, Economics and Statistics Administration, Bureau of the Census, Data User Services Division, January 1995. Primary source: U.S. National Oceanic and Atmospheric Administration. *Comparative Climatic Data* (annual).

★ 159 ★
Weather Conditions

Sunshine in New England, by City

Table shows the average percentage of possible sunshine in selected cities. Figures are airport data, except as noted. For period of record through 1991, except as noted.

City and state	Length of record (years)	Possible sunshine
Hartford, Connecticut	37	56
Portland, Maine	51	57
Blue Hill, Massachusetts	105	52
Boston, Massachusetts	56	58
Concord, New Hampshire	50	54
Mt. Washington, New Hampshire	53	33
Providence, Rhode Island	38	58
Burlington, Vermont	48	49

Source: 1994 Statistical Abstract of the United States on CD-ROM [machine-readable datafiles]. CD-8A-94. Washington, DC: U.S. Department of Commerce, Economics and Statistics Administration, Bureau of the Census, Data User Services Division, January 1995. Primary source: U.S. National Oceanic and Atmospheric Administration. *Comparative Climatic Data* (annual).

★ 160 ★

Weather Conditions

Sunshine in Pacific United States, by City

Table shows the average percentage of possible sunshine in selected cities. Figures are airport data, except as noted. For period of record through 1991, except as noted.

City and state	Length of record (years)	Possible sunshine
Anchorage, Alaska	36	43
Juneau, Alaska	33	30
Nome, Alaska	39	41
Eureka, California	81	50
Fresno, California	42	79
Los Angeles, California[1]	32	73
Redding, California	5	88
Sacramento, California	43	78
San Diego, California	51	68
Stockton, California	38	66
Hilo, Hawaii	41	41
Honolulu, Hawaii	39	69
Kahului, Hawaii	29	67
Lihue, Hawaii	41	57
Portland, Oregon	42	48
Quillayute, Washington	25	33
Seattle, Washington[1]	31	43
Seattle-Tacoma Airport, Washington	25	46
Spokane, Washington	43	54
Walla Walla, Washington	70	54

Source: 1994 Statistical Abstract of the United States on CD-ROM [machine-readable datafiles]. CD-8A-94. Washington, DC: U.S. Department of Commerce, Economics and Statistics Administration, Bureau of the Census, Data User Services Division, January 1995. Primary source: U.S. National Oceanic and Atmospheric Administration. *Comparative Climatic Data* (annual). *Note:* 1. City office data.

★ 161 ★

Weather Conditions

Sunshine in South Atlantic United States, by City

Table shows the average percentage of possible sunshine in selected cities. Figures are airport data, except as noted. For period of record through 1991, except as noted.

City and state	Length of record (years)	Possible sunshine
Washington National Airport (District of Columbia)	43	56
Apalachicola, Florida	56	67
Jacksonville, Florida	40	63
Key West, Florida	32	76
Miami, Florida	15	72
Tampa, Florida	44	66
Atlanta, Georgia	56	61
Macon, Georgia	43	66
Savannah, Georgia	41	62
Baltimore, Maryland	40	57
Asheville, North Carolina	27	59
Cape Hatteras, North Carolina	29	59
Charlotte, North Carolina	41	63
Greensboro/Winston-Salem/High Point, North Carolina	63	60
Raleigh, North Carolina	37	59
Wilmington, North Carolina	40	63
Charleston Airport, South Carolina	63	42
Columbia, South Carolina	38	64
Greenville-Spartanburg Airport, South Carolina	29	61
Lynchburg, Virginia	47	59
Norfolk, Virginia	27	61
Richmond, Virginia	41	62
Elkins, West Virginia	8	40

Source: 1994 Statistical Abstract of the United States on CD-ROM [machine-readable datafiles]. CD-8A-94. Washington, DC: U.S. Department of Commerce, Economics and Statistics Administration, Bureau of the Census, Data User Services Division, January 1995. Primary source: U.S. National Oceanic and Atmospheric Administration. *Comparative Climatic Data* (annual).

★ 162 ★

Weather Conditions

Sunshine in U.S. Territories and Administered Areas, by City

Table shows the average percentage of possible sunshine in selected cities. Figures are airport data, except as noted. For period of record through 1991, except as noted.

Location	Length of record (years)	Possible sunshine
Chuuk, East Caroline Islands	31	49
Guam	29	45
Johnston Island	22	71
Koror	31	53
Majuro, Marshall Islands	31	59
Pago Pago, American Samoa	24	41
Pohnpei, Caroline Islands	33	42
San Juan, Puerto Rico	36	66
Wake Island	22	70
Yap, West Caroline Islands	32	56

Source: 1994 Statistical Abstract of the United States on CD-ROM [machine-readable datafiles]. CD-8A-94. Washington, DC: U.S. Department of Commerce, Economics and Statistics Administration, Bureau of the Census, Data User Services Division, January 1995. Primary source: U.S. National Oceanic and Atmospheric Administration. *Comparative Climatic Data* (annual).

★ 163 ★

Weather Conditions

Sunshine in West North Central United States, by City

Table shows the average percentage of possible sunshine in selected cities. Figures are airport data, except as noted. For period of record through 1991, except as noted.

City and state	Length of record (years)	Possible sunshine
Des Moines, Iowa	41	59
Sioux City, Iowa	51	61
Concordia, Kansas	29	68
Dodge City, Kansas	49	70
Topeka, Kansas	42	60
Wichita, Kansas	38	65
Duluth, Minnesota	41	52

[Continued]

★ 163 ★

Sunshine in West North Central United States, by City
[Continued]

City and state	Length of record (years)	Possible sunshine
Minneapolis-St. Paul, Minnesota	53	58
Columbia, Missouri	22	56
Kansas City, Missouri	19	62
Springfield, Missouri	46	61
St. Louis, Missouri	32	57
Lincoln, Nebraska	35	62
North Platte, Nebraska	39	66
Omaha, Nebraska[1]	55	60
Valentine, Nebraska	29	66
Bismarck, North Dakota	52	59
Fargo, North Dakota	49	57
Williston, North Dakota	28	61
Huron, South Dakota	50	64
Rapid City, South Dakota	49	63

Source: 1994 Statistical Abstract of the United States on CD-ROM [machine-readable datafiles]. CD-8A-94. Washington, DC: U.S. Department of Commerce, Economics and Statistics Administration, Bureau of the Census, Data User Services Division, January 1995. Primary source: U.S. National Oceanic and Atmospheric Administration. *Comparative Climatic Data* (annual). *Note:* 1. City office data.

★ 164 ★

Weather Conditions

Sunshine in West South Central United States, by City

Table shows the average percentage of possible sunshine in selected cities. Figures are airport data, except as noted. For period of record through 1991, except as noted.

City and state	Length of record (years)	Possible sunshine
Fort Smith, Arkansas	46	61
Little Rock, Arkansas	32	62
North Little Rock, Arkansas	14	72
Lake Charles, Louisiana	10	69
New Orleans, Louisiana	18	59
Shreveport, Louisiana	39	63
Amarillo, Texas	50	73
Austin, Texas	50	60
Brownsville, Texas	49	60

[Continued]

★ 164 ★

Sunshine in West South Central United States, by City
[Continued]

City and state	Length of record (years)	Possible sunshine
Corpus Christi, Texas	49	61
Dallas-Fort Worth, Texas	13	63
El Paso, Texas	49	84
Galveston, Texas	100	62
Houston, Texas	22	56
Lubbock, Texas	19	71
Midland-Odessa, Texas	11	73
Port Arthur, Texas	26	58
San Antonio, Texas	49	60

Source: 1994 Statistical Abstract of the United States on CD-ROM [machine-readable datafiles]. CD-8A-94. Washington, DC: U.S. Department of Commerce, Economics and Statistics Administration, Bureau of the Census, Data User Services Division, January 1995. Primary source: U.S. National Oceanic and Atmospheric Administration. *Comparative Climatic Data* (annual).

★ 165 ★

Weather Conditions

Sunshine in Western United States, by City

Table shows the average percentage of possible sunshine in selected cities. Figures are airport data, except as noted. For period of record through 1991, except as noted.

City and state	Length of record (years)	Possible sunshine
Flagstaff, Arizona	12	78
Phoenix, Arizona	96	86
Tucson, Arizona	44	85
Yuma, Arizona	41	90
Denver, Colorado	42	70
Grand Junction, Colorado	45	70
Pueblo, Colorado	50	76
Boise, Idaho	49	64
Pocatello, Idaho	42	64
Billings, Montana	52	60
Great Falls, Montana	46	61
Helena, Montana	51	59
Missoula, Montana	46	54
Ely, Nevada	52	73
Las Vegas, Nevada	42	85

[Continued]

★ 165 ★

Sunshine in Western United States, by City

[Continued]

City and state	Length of record (years)	Possible sunshine
Reno, Nevada	43	79
Winnemucca, Nevada	41	68
Albuquerque, New Mexico	52	76
Roswell, New Mexico	7	74
Milford, Utah	16	70
Salt Lake City, Utah	53	66
Cheyenne, Wyoming	52	65
Lander, Wyoming	45	69
Sheridan, Wyoming	51	62

Source: *1994 Statistical Abstract of the United States on CD-ROM* [machine-readable datafiles]. CD-8A-94. Washington, DC: U.S. Department of Commerce, Economics and Statistics Administration, Bureau of the Census, Data User Services Division, January 1995. Primary source: U.S. National Oceanic and Atmospheric Administration. *Comparative Climatic Data* (annual).

★ 166 ★

Weather Conditions

Wind Speed in East North Central United States, by City

Table shows the average wind speed for period of record through 1991, except as noted, for selected cities. Figures are airport data, except as noted.

[In miles per hour]

City and state	Length of record (years)	Annual	January	July
Cairo, Illinois	22	8.5	9.8	6.5
Chicago, Illinois	33	10.4	11.7	8.2
Moline, Illinois	48	10.0	11.0	7.7
Peoria, Illinois	48	10.0	11.1	7.8
Rockford, Illinois	41	10.0	10.6	8.1
Springfield, Illinois	44	11.1	12.6	8.4
Evansville, Indiana	51	8.0	9.3	6.2
Fort Wayne, Indiana	45	10.0	11.5	8.0
Indianapolis, Indiana	43	9.6	10.9	7.4
South Bend, Indiana	43	10.3	11.9	8.2
Alpena, Michigan	31	8.1	8.9	7.0
Detroit, Michigan	33	10.4	12.0	8.5
Flint, Michigan	50	10.2	11.8	8.1
Grand Rapids, Michigan	28	9.8	11.5	8.2
Houghton Lake, Michigan	14	8.9	10.1	7.6

[Continued]

★ 166 ★

Wind Speed in East North Central United States, by City

[Continued]

City and state	Length of record (years)	Annual	January	July
Lansing, Michigan	32	10.0	11.9	8.0
Muskegon, Michigan	30	10.7	12.6	8.7
Sault Sainte Marie, Michigan	50	9.2	9.7	7.8
Akron, Ohio	43	9.8	11.6	7.6
Greater Cincinnati Airport	44	9.1	10.7	7.2
Cleveland, Ohio	50	10.6	12.3	8.6
Columbus, Ohio	42	8.4	10.0	6.6
Dayton, Ohio	48	9.9	11.5	7.9
Mansfield, Ohio	11	11.0	13.4	8.4
Toledo, Ohio	36	9.4	11.0	7.4
Youngstown, Ohio	42	9.9	11.7	7.7
Green Bay, Wisconsin	42	10.0	11.0	8.2
La Crosse, Wisconsin	39	8.8	8.6	7.6
Madison, Wisconsin	45	9.9	10.6	8.1
Milwaukee, Wisconsin	51	11.6	12.7	9.7

Source: 1994 Statistical Abstract of the United States on CD-ROM [machine-readable datafiles]. CD-8A-94. Washington, DC: U.S. Department of Commerce, Economics and Statistics Administration, Bureau of the Census, Data User Services Division, January 1995. Primary source: U.S. National Oceanic and Atmospheric Administration. *Comparative Climatic Data* (annual).

★ 167 ★

Weather Conditions

Wind Speed in East South Central United States, by City

Table shows the average wind speed for period of record through 1991, except as noted, for selected cities. Figures are airport data, except as noted.

[In miles per hour]

City and state	Length of record (years)	Annual	January	July
Birminghan, Alabama	48	7.2	8.1	5.7
Huntsville, Alabama	24	8.2	9.3	6.3
Mobile, Alabama	43	9.0	10.4	7.0
Montgomery, Alabama	47	6.6	7.7	5.7
Jackson, Kentucky	7.1	8.0	5.6	11
Lexington, Kentucky	44	9.3	10.9	7.2
Louisville, Kentucky	44	8.4	9.6	6.8
Paducah, Kentucky	7	7.8	9.2	6.1
Jackson, Mississippi	28	7.4	8.5	6.0

[Continued]

★ 167 ★

Wind Speed in East South Central United States, by City

[Continued]

City and state	Length of record (years)	Annual	January	July
Meridian, Mississippi	32	6.1	7.1	4.8
Tupelo, Mississippi	8	7.0	7.4	5.9
Bristol/Johnson City/Kingsport, Tennessee	37	5.5	6.5	4.2
Chattanooga, Tennessee	51	6.1	6.9	5.0
Knoxville, Tennessee	49	7.0	7.9	6.1
Memphis, Tennessee	43	8.9	10.1	7.4
Nashville, Tennessee	50	8.0	9.2	6.5
Oak Ridge, Tennessee	16	4.4	4.8	3.9

Source: 1994 Statistical Abstract of the United States on CD-ROM [machine-readable datafiles]. CD-8A-94. Washington, DC: U.S. Department of Commerce, Economics and Statistics Administration, Bureau of the Census, Data User Services Division, January 1995. Primary source: U.S. National Oceanic and Atmospheric Administration. *Comparative Climatic Data* (annual).

★ 168 ★

Weather Conditions

Wind Speed in Middle Atlantic States, by City

Table shows the average wind speed for period of record through 1991, except as noted, for selected cities. Figures are airport data, except as noted.

[In miles per hour]

City and state	Length of record (years)	Annual	January	July
Atlantic City, New Jersey	33	10.0	11.0	8.4
Atlantic City, New Jersey[1]	(NA)	(NA)	(NA)	30
Newark, New Jersey	47	10.2	11.2	8.8
Albany, New York	53	8.9	9.8	7.4
Binghamton, New York	40	10.3	11.6	8.4
Buffalo, New York	52	12.0	14.3	10.3
Islip, New York	8	8.9	9.3	7.2
New York, New York (Central Park)	58	9.4	10.7	7.6
New York, New York (John F. Kennedy Airport)	33	12.0	13.4	10.3
New York, New York (La Guardia Airport)	43	12.2	13.8	10.3
Rochester, New York	51	9.7	11.7	8.0
Syracuse, New York	42	9.5	10.8	8.0
Allentown, Pennsylvania	42	9.2	10.5	7.2
Erie, Pennsylvania	36	8.3	8.9	7.3
Harrisburg, Pennsylvania	37	11.2	13.4	9.0
Middletown/Harrisburg International Airport	49	7.6	8.2	6.2
Philadelphia, Pennsylvania	49	7.6	8.2	6.2

[Continued]

★ 168 ★

Wind Speed in Middle Atlantic States, by City

[Continued]

City and state	Length of record (years)	Annual	January	July
Pittsburgh, Pennsylvania	51	9.5	10.3	8.1
Avoca, Pennsylvania	39	9.1	10.6	7.2
Williamsport, Pennsylvania	30	7.8	9.0	6.3

Source: 1994 Statistical Abstract of the United States on CD-ROM [machine-readable datafiles]. CD-8A-94. Washington, DC: U.S. Department of Commerce, Economics and Statistics Administration, Bureau of the Census, Data User Services Division, January 1995. Primary source: U.S. National Oceanic and Atmospheric Administration. Comparative Climatic Data (annual). Notes: "NA" represents "not available." 1. City office data.

★ 169 ★

Weather Conditions

Wind Speed in New England, by City

Table shows the average wind speed for period of record through 1991, except as noted, for selected cities. Figures are airport data, except as noted.

[In miles per hour]

City and state	Length of record (years)	Annual	January	July
Bridgeport, Connecticut	23	12.0	13.2	10.0
Hartford, Connecticut	37	8.5	9.0	7.5
Caribou, Maine	15	11.2	12.4	9.8
Portland, Maine	51	8.8	9.2	7.6
Blue Hill, Massachusetts	56	15.4	17.4	13.0
Boston, Massachusetts	34	12.5	13.9	11.0
Worcester, Massachusetts	29	10.0	11.9	8.4
Concord, New Hampshire	49	6.7	7.2	5.7
Mt. Washington, New Hampshire	56	35.3	46.2	25.3
Providence, Rhode Island	38	10.6	11.2	9.5
Burlington, Vermont	48	9.0	9.7	7.9

Source: 1994 Statistical Abstract of the United States on CD-ROM [machine-readable datafiles]. CD-8A-94. Washington, DC: U.S. Department of Commerce, Economics and Statistics Administration, Bureau of the Census, Data User Services Division, January 1995. Primary source: U.S. National Oceanic and Atmospheric Administration. Comparative Climatic Data (annual).

★ 170 ★

Weather Conditions

Wind Speed in Pacific United States, by City

Table shows the average wind speed for period of record through 1991, except as noted, for selected cities. Figures are airport data, except as noted.

[In miles per hour]

City and state	Length of record (years)	Annual	January	July
Anchorage, Alaska	38	7.0	6.4	7.2
Annette, Alaska	31	10.6	12.0	8.0
Barrow, Alaska	58	11.9	11.5	11.6
Barter Island, Alaska	33	13.2	15.1	10.9
Bethel, Alaska	33	12.8	14.5	11.0
Bettles, Alaska	18	6.7	6.0	6.7
Big Delta, Alaska	20	8.2	10.8	6.0
Cold Bay, Alaska	36	17.0	17.8	15.7
Fairbanks, Alaska	40	5.4	3.1	6.6
Gulkana, Alaska	8	6.8	5.1	8.2
Homer, Alaska	17	7.6	8.2	7.2
Juneau, Alaska	46	8.3	8.2	7.5
King Salmon, Alaska	36	10.8	10.7	10.1
Kodiak, Alaska	38	10.8	12.8	7.6
Kotzebue, Alaska	45	13.0	14.5	12.9
McGrath, Alaska	41	5.2	3.0	6.0
Nome, Alaska	44	10.6	11.5	9.9
St. Paul Island, Alaska	17	17.6	20.5	12.3
Talkeetna, Alaska	10	4.8	6.4	4.0
Valdez, Alaska	11	6.0	7.4	4.9
Yakutat, Alaska	43	7.4	7.5	6.7
Bakersfield, California	43	6.4	5.2	7.2
Blue Canyon, California	15	6.8	7.9	5.8
Eureka, California	54	6.8	6.9	6.8
Fresno, California	42	6.3	5.2	7.3
Long Beach, California	26	6.3	5.6	6.8
Los Angeles, California	43	7.5	6.7	7.8
Los Angeles, California[1]	24	6.2	6.8	5.4
Mount Shasta, California	3	5.1	5.0	4.4
Redding, California	5	7.2	6.2	7.3
Sacramento, California	42	7.9	7.2	9.0
San Diego, California	51	6.9	5.9	7.4
San Francisco, California	64	10.6	7.2	13.6
San Francisco, California[1]	28	8.7	6.7	11.2
Santa Barbara, California	4	6.1	4.8	6.5
Santa Maria, California	15	7.0	6.7	6.5
Stockton, California	35	7.4	6.7	8.2
Hilo, Hawaii	42	7.2	7.5	6.9
Honolulu, Hawaii	42	11.4	9.6	13.2
Kahului, Hawaii	23	12.8	10.8	15.6
Lihue, Hawaii	41	12.3	10.9	13.6

[Continued]

★ 170 ★

Wind Speed in Pacific United States, by City
[Continued]

City and state	Length of record (years)	Annual	January	July
Astoria, Oregon	38	8.6	9.1	8.7
Eugene, Oregon	39	7.6	8.0	8.0
Medford, Oregon	42	4.8	4.0	5.8
Pendleton, Oregon	38	8.7	7.9	8.9
Portland, Oregon	43	7.9	9.9	7.6
Salem, Oregon	43	7.1	8.1	6.7
Sexton Summit, Oregon	6	11.8	12.8	11.8
Olympia, Washington	39	6.7	7.1	6.2
Quillayute, Washington	25	6.1	6.6	5.6
Seattle-Tacoma Airport, Washington	43	9.0	9.7	8.3
Spokane, Washington	44	8.9	8.8	8.6
Walla Walla, Washington	47	5.3	5.1	5.4
Yakima, Washington	39	7.1	5.7	7.8

Source: 1994 Statistical Abstract of the United States on CD-ROM [machine-readable datafiles]. CD-8A-94. Washington, DC: U.S. Department of Commerce, Economics and Statistics Administration, Bureau of the Census, Data User Services Division, January 1995. Primary source: U.S. National Oceanic and Atmospheric Administration. *Comparative Climatic Data* (annual). *Note:* 1. City office data.

★ 171 ★

Weather Conditions

Wind Speed in South Atlantic United States, by City

Table shows the average wind speed for period of record through 1991, except as noted, for selected cities. Figures are airport data, except as noted.

[In miles per hour]

City and state	Length of record (years)	Annual	January	July
Wilmington, Delaware	43	9.1	9.8	7.8
Washington, District of Columbia (Dulles Airport)	29	7.4	8.1	6.1
Washington National Airport (District of Columbia)	43	9.4	10.0	8.2
Apalachicola, Florida	43	7.8	8.3	6.4
Daytona Beach, Florida	46	8.7	8.9	7.4
Fort Myers, Florida	45	8.0	8.4	6.7
Gainesville, Florida	8	6.5	7.0	5.7
Jacksonville, Florida	42	8.0	8.2	7.1
Key West, Florida	38	11.2	12.0	9.6
Miami, Florida	42	9.3	9.5	7.9
Orlando, Florida	43	8.5	8.9	7.4
Pensacola, Florida	28	8.4	9.0	6.9

[Continued]

★ 171 ★

Wind Speed in South Atlantic United States, by City
[Continued]

City and state	Length of record (years)	Annual	January	July
Tallahassee, Florida	30	6.3	6.8	5.1
Tampa, Florida	45	8.4	8.6	7.2
Vero Beach, Florida	8	8.4	8.7	7.0
West Palm Beach, Florida	49	9.6	10.0	7.7
Athens, Georgia	36	7.4	8.4	6.3
Atlanta, Georgia	53	9.1	10.4	7.6
Augusta, Georgia	40	6.5	7.0	5.9
Columbus, Georgia	33	6.7	7.3	5.7
Macon, Georgia	43	7.5	8.0	6.8
Savannah, Georgia	41	7.9	8.5	7.1
Baltimore, Maryland	41	9.2	9.7	8.0
Asheville, North Carolina	27	7.6	9.6	5.9
Cape Hatteras, North Carolina	34	11.1	12.0	10.0
Charlotte, North Carolina	42	7.4	7.9	6.6
Greensboro/Winston-Salem/High Point, North Carolina	63	7.5	8.1	6.5
Raleigh, North Carolina	42	7.7	8.5	6.6
Wilmington, North Carolina	40	8.7	9.0	8.0
Charleston Airport, South Carolina	8.6	9.1	7.9	49
Charleston, South Carolina[1]	(NA)	(NA)	(NA)	18
Columbia, South Carolina	43	6.9	7.2	6.3
Greenville-Spartanburg Airport, South Carolina	29	6.9	7.4	5.9
Lynchburg, Virginia	28	7.7	8.6	6.5
Norfolk, Virginia	43	10.6	11.5	9.0
Richmond, Virginia	43	7.7	8.1	6.8
Roanoke, Virginia	43	8.0	9.5	6.5
Beckley, West Virginia	28	9.0	10.5	6.8
Charleston, West Virginia	44	6.3	7.5	5.0
Elkins, West Virginia	24	6.2	7.3	4.3
Huntington, West Virginia	29	6.6	7.6	5.2

Source: 1994 Statistical Abstract of the United States on CD-ROM [machine-readable datafiles]. CD-8A-94. Washington, DC: U.S. Department of Commerce, Economics and Statistics Administration, Bureau of the Census, Data User Services Division, January 1995. Primary source: U.S. National Oceanic and Atmospheric Administration. *Comparative Climatic Data* (annual). *Notes:* "NA" represents "not available." 1. City office data.

★ 172 ★

Weather Conditions

Wind Speed in U.S. Territories and Administered Areas, by City

Table shows the average wind speed for period of record through 1991, except as noted, for selected cities. Figures are airport data, except as noted.

[In miles per hour]

Location	Length of record (years)	Annual	January	July
Chuuk, East Caroline Islands	26	8.8	10.8	7.3
Guam	6	7.4	8.2	5.1
Johnston Island	23	15.8	14.4	16.0
Koror	26	7.2	8.4	6.5
Majuro, Marshall Islands	27	10.3	12.9	8.5
Pago Pago, American Samoa	24	10.6	9.0	12.9
Pohnpei, Caroline Islands	17	6.3	8.4	4.9
San Juan, Puerto Rico	36	8.4	8.5	9.6
Wake Island	39	13.8	13.6	12.6
Yap, West Caroline Islands	22	8.1	10.0	6.4

Source: 1994 Statistical Abstract of the United States on CD-ROM [machine-readable datafiles]. CD-8A-94. Washington, DC: U.S. Department of Commerce, Economics and Statistics Administration, Bureau of the Census, Data User Services Division, January 1995. Primary source: U.S. National Oceanic and Atmospheric Administration. *Comparative Climatic Data* (annual).

★ 173 ★

Weather Conditions

Wind Speed in West North Central United States, by City

Table shows the average wind speed for period of record through 1991, except as noted, for selected cities. Figures are airport data, except as noted.

[In miles per hour]

City and state	Length of record (years)	Annual	January	July
Des Moines, Iowa	42	10.9	11.7	(NA)
Sioux City, Iowa	50	11.0	11.3	9.2
Waterloo, Iowa	35	10.7	11.5	8.5
Concordia, Kansas	29	12.3	12.2	11.7
Dodge City, Kansas	49	14.0	13.6	13.1
Goodland, Kansas	43	12.6	12.4	12.0
Topeka, Kansas	42	10.0	10.0	8.6

[Continued]

★ 173 ★

Wind Speed in West North Central United States, by City
[Continued]

City and state	Length of record (years)	Annual	January	July
Wichita, Kansas	38	12.3	12.2	11.3
Duluth, Minnesota	42	11.1	11.6	9.4
International Falls, Minnesota	39	8.9	8.9	7.7
Minneapolis-St. Paul, Minnesota	53	10.6	10.5	9.4
Rochester, Minnesota	31	13.1	14.5	10.9
Saint Cloud, Minnesota	9	8.0	8.2	7.0
Columbia, Missouri	21	9.9	10.9	8.3
Kansas City, Missouri	19	10.8	11.5	9.4
Springfield, Missouri	46	10.6	11.6	8.5
St. Louis, Missouri	42	9.7	10.6	8.0
Grand Island, Nebraska	42	11.9	11.7	10.6
Lincoln, Nebraska	19	10.4	10.0	9.8
Norfolk, Nebraska	15	11.6	12.3	10.0
North Platte, Nebraska	39	10.2	9.3	9.6
Omaha Eppley Airport, Nebraska	55	10.6	10.9	8.9
Omaha, Nebraska[1]	7	9.2	10.2	7.6
Scottsbluff, Nebraska	40	10.6	10.7	9.3
Valentine, Nebraska	23	9.7	9.3	9.1
Bismarck, North Dakota	52	10.2	10.0	9.2
Fargo, North Dakota	49	12.3	12.7	10.6
Williston, North Dakota	27	10.1	9.9	9.4
Aberdeen, South Dakota	18	11.2	11.3	9.5
Huron, South Dakota	52	11.5	11.4	10.4
Rapid City, South Dakota	41	11.3	10.9	10.2
Sioux Falls, South Dakota	43	11.1	11.1	9.8

Source: 1994 Statistical Abstract of the United States on CD-ROM [machine-readable datafiles]. CD-8A-94. Washington, DC: U.S. Department of Commerce, Economics and Statistics Administration, Bureau of the Census, Data User Services Division, January 1995. Primary source: U.S. National Oceanic and Atmospheric Administration. *Comparative Climatic Data* (annual). *Notes:* "NA" represents "not available." 1. City office data.

★174★

Weather Conditions

Wind Speed in West South Central United States, by City

Table shows the average wind speed for period of record through 1991, except as noted, for selected cities. Figures are airport data, except as noted.

[In miles per hour]

City and state	Length of record (years)	Annual	January	July
Fort Smith, Arkansas	46	7.6	8.2	6.3
Little Rock, Arkansas	49	7.8	8.5	6.7
Baton Rouge, Louisiana	40	7.7	8.9	5.9
Lake Charles, Louisiana	30	8.7	10.0	6.5
New Orleans, Louisiana	43	8.2	9.4	6.1
Shreveport, Louisiana	39	8.4	9.3	7.1
Oklahoma City, Oklahoma	43	12.4	12.8	10.9
Tulsa, Oklahoma	43	10.3	10.4	9.3
Abilene, Texas	47	12.0	11.8	10.8
Amarillo, Texas	50	13.6	12.9	12.6
Austin, Texas	50	9.2	9.7	8.3
Brownsville, Texas	49	11.5	11.3	11.3
Corpus Christi, Texas	49	12.0	12.1	11.5
Dallas-Fort Worth, Texas	38	10.8	11.1	9.6
Del Rio, Texas	16	9.9	8.8	10.9
El Paso, Texas	49	8.9	8.3	8.3
Galveston, Texas	93	11.0	11.6	9.8
Houston, Texas	22	7.9	8.2	6.9
Lubbock, Texas	42	12.4	12.1	11.3
Midland-Odessa, Texas	38	11.1	10.3	10.7
Port Arthur, Texas	38	9.8	10.8	7.6
San Angelo, Texas	42	10.4	10.2	9.7
San Antonio, Texas	49	9.2	9.0	9.1
Victoria, Texas	30	10.0	10.5	8.9
Waco, Texas	42	11.3	11.6	10.7
Wichita Falls, Texas	43	11.6	11.3	10.9

Source: 1994 Statistical Abstract of the United States on CD-ROM [machine-readable datafiles]. CD-8A-94. Washington, DC: U.S. Department of Commerce, Economics and Statistics Administration, Bureau of the Census, Data User Services Division, January 1995. Primary source: U.S. National Oceanic and Atmospheric Administration. *Comparative Climatic Data* (annual).

★ 175 ★

Weather Conditions

Wind Speed in Western United States, by City

Table shows the average wind speed for period of record through 1991, except as noted, for selected cities. Figures are airport data, except as noted.

[In miles per hour]

City and state	Length of record (years)	Annual	January	July
Flagstaff, Arizona	24	6.7	6.9	5.6
Phoenix, Arizona	46	6.3	5.2	7.2
Tucson, Arizona	46	8.3	7.8	8.4
Winslow, Arizona	35	8.9	7.1	9.1
Yuma, Arizona	28	7.8	7.4	9.5
Alamosa, Colorado	1	8.5	6.3	8.6
Colorado Springs, Colorado	43	10.1	9.5	9.3
Denver, Colorado	43	8.7	8.6	8.3
Grand Junction, Colorado	45	8.1	5.6	9.3
Pueblo, Colorado	37	8.7	8.0	8.7
Boise, Idaho	52	8.7	8.0	8.4
Pocatello, Idaho	39	10.2	10.7	9.1
Billings, Montana	52	11.2	13.1	9.6
Glasgow, Montana	22	10.8	10.1	10.7
Great Falls, Montana	50	12.8	15.3	10.1
Helena, Montana	51	7.7	6.8	7.9
Kalispell, Montana	29	6.5	5.9	6.7
Missoula, Montana	47	6.2	5.2	6.9
Elko, Nevada	40	6.0	5.3	6.2
Ely, Nevada	53	10.4	10.1	10.3
Las Vegas, Nevada	43	9.3	7.5	10.3
Reno, Nevada	49	6.6	5.6	7.1
Winnemucca, Nevada	38	8.0	7.6	8.4
Albuquerque, New Mexico	52	9.0	8.1	9.1
Clayton, New Mexico	3	11.8	11.7	10.6
Roswell, New Mexico	19	8.6	7.7	8.6
Salt Lake City, Utah	62	8.8	7.6	9.6
Casper, Wyoming	41	12.9	16.5	10.1
Cheyenne, Wyoming	34	13.0	15.3	10.4
Lander, Wyoming	45	6.8	6.0	7.6
Sheridan, Wyoming	51	8.0	7.7	7.3

Source: 1994 Statistical Abstract of the United States on CD-ROM [machine-readable datafiles]. CD-8A-94. Washington, DC: U.S. Department of Commerce, Economics and Statistics Administration, Bureau of the Census, Data User Services Division, January 1995. Primary source: U.S. National Oceanic and Atmospheric Administration. *Comparative Climatic Data* (annual).

Chapter 4
LAND AND LAND USE

This chapter covers a variety of subjects on land area and use. Much of the material relates to land-based industries such as agriculture, forestry, and mineral and metal production. Major topics include Conservation Reserve Program, crops and cropland (with data for specific crops), erosion, forest fires, forest insects and disease, forests and trees, land area and ownership, land use, mineral and metal production, parks and recreation areas, population and population density, and wetlands.

Related topics—for example, habitat and conservation—are found elsewhere in *Statistical Record of the Environment.* Rivers and bodies of water are covered in the Air and Water chapter. Wildlife habitat and conservation, as well as wildlife-related recreation, are profiled in the Wildlife and Habitat chapter. Global warming and natural disasters are covered in the Climate and Weather Conditions chapter. Releases and transfers of toxic chemicals to land are reviewed in the Toxic and Hazardous substances chapter. A separate chapter—Wastes and Resource Recovery—is comprised of tables on solid waste management. Financial matters are covered in the Costs and Expenditures chapter; land-related business issues such as lumber consumption and production also are presented in the Markets and Companies chapter.

Conservation Reserve Program

★ 176 ★

Conservation Reserve Program, by Region

Table shows participation in the Conservation Reserve Program (CRP) by area of the country. Farmers participating in the CRP voluntarily remove cropland from production in exchange for annual per acre rent and payment of one-half the cost of establishing conserving land cover on the site. Contracts are between 10 and 15 years in duration. In the 12th sign up, a total of 36.5 million acres had been committed to the CRP.

Region	Accepted contracts	Accepted acres	Average rental rate ($/acre)[1]	Average erosion reduction (tons/acre)[1]
Northeast	268	9,808	55.06	7
Appalachian	1,254	47,332	57.83	20
Southeast	1,263	54,801	44.61	13
Delta	731	41,348	46.87	13
Corn Belt	8,525	415,612	84.89	15
Lake States	4,324	176,214	62.11	9
Northern Plains	1,329	95,302	47.60	17
Southern Plains	924	125,362	40.54	29
Mountain	547	95,701	36.38	17
Pacific	339	38,493	55.37	13
U.S.	19,504	1,099,976	63.09	16

Source: "CRP Enrollment Reaches 36.5 Million Acres." *Agricultural Outlook* (October 1992), p. 25.
Note: 1. Per year.

★ 177 ★
Conservation Reserve Program

Conservation Reserve Program Sign Up Periods

Table shows participation in the Conservation Reserve Program (CRP) for each sign up initiative. Farmers participating in the CRP voluntarily remove cropland from production in exchange for annual per acre rent and payment of one-half the cost of establishing conserving land cover on the site. Contracts are between 10 and 15 years in duration. In the 12th sign up, a total of 36.5 million acres had been committed to the CRP.

Region	Accepted contracts (thousand)	Accepted acres (million)	Average rental rate ($/acre)[1]	Average erosion reduction (tons/acre)[1]
1985 farm act				
#1 March 1986	9.4	0.75	42.06	26
#2 May 1986	21.5	2.77	44.05	27
#3 August 1986	34.0	4.70	46.96	25
#4 February 1987	88.0	9.48	51.19	19
#5 July 1987	43.7	4.44	48.03	17
#6 February 1988	42.7	3.38	47.90	18
#7 July-August 1988	30.4	2.60	49.71	17
#8 February 1989	28.8	2.46	51.04	14
#9 July-August 1989	34.8	3.33	50.99	14
1990 farm act				
#10 March 1991	8.6	.48	53.66	17
#11 July 1991	14.7	.99	59.37	15
#12 June 1992[1]	19.5	1.10	63.09	16
Total	376.2	36.50	49.70	19

Source: "CRP Enrollment Reaches 36.5 Million Acres." *Agricultural Outlook* (October 1992), p. 25.
Notes: Tentative results. 1. Per year.

★ 178 ★

Conservation Reserve Program

Conservation Reserve Program Status

The Conservation Reserve Program (CRP) asks participating farmers to retire highly erodible or environmentally sensitive land from production for 10 to 15 years in exchange for annual rent and a subsidy to assist in establishing a conserving land cover. In total, 377,000 CRP contracts have committed approximately 36.5 million acres of land to the program. The most recent sign up for farmers occurred in 1992. Contracts on 2 million acres expire in October of 1995. The table shows the status of CRP through sign ups 1 to 12.

Item	Status
Contracts	377,000
Enrollment (acres)	36,500,000
Total erosion reduction (tons/year)	700,000,000
Average erosion reduction (tons/acre/year)	19
Total rental cost ($/year)	1,800,000,000
Average rental cost ($/acre/year)	50
Acres planted in trees (%)	6
Base reduction (acres)	23,300,000

Source: Osborn, Tim. "The Conservation Reserve Program: Status, Future, and Policy Options." *Journal of Soil and Water Conservation* (July-August 1993), p. 273.

Crops and Cropland

★ 179 ★

Agricultural Productivity Indexes: 1951-1991

[Index (1982 = 100)]

Year	Farm input[1]				Farm output			Total produc-tivity[4]
	Labor	Mechanical	Chemical	Total	Crops[2]	Live-stock[3]	Total	
1951	228	58	42	96	39	63	49	51
1955	211	70	45	99	43	70	54	54
1960	163	69	58	97	48	75	59	60
1965	141	69	73	93	56	82	66	71
1970	119	78	76	93	58	90	71	77
1975	114	89	91	96	76	87	80	84
1980	108	102	131	106	78	99	87	82
1985	89	86	101	95	104	103	104	110

[Continued]

★ 179 ★

Agricultural Productivity Indexes: 1951-1991
[Continued]

Year	Farm input[1]				Farm output			Total produc-tivity[4]
	Labor	Mechanical	Chemical	Total	Crops[2]	Live-stock[3]	Total	
1990	87	64	90	89	111	112	112	126
1991	88	63	94	89	106	114	110	127

Source: Executive Office of the President of the United States. *Environmental Quality 24: The Twenty-fourth Annual Report of the Council on Environmental Quality.* Prepared by Ray Clark. Written by Carroll Curtis. Edited by Barry Walsh. Washington, DC: U.S. Government Printing Office, 1994, p. 456. Primary source: U.S. Department of Agriculture. Economic Research Service. *Agricultural Outlook.* Washington, DC: U.S. Department of Agriculture, Economic Research Service (monthly). *Notes:* 1. Inputs exclude farm real estate, feed, seed and livestock purchases, taxes and interest, and miscellaneous. 2. Crop outputs include feed grains, hay and forage, vegetables, fruit, nuts, sugar crops, cotton, tobacco, oil crops, and miscellaneous. 3. Livestock outputs, include meat animals, dairy products, poultry and eggs, wool, mohair, honey, and beeswax. 4. Output/input.

★ 180 ★

Crops and Cropland

Crop Acreage, by State: 1987-1993

Table shows the acreage harvested for crops in each state except Alaska.

[In thousand acres]

State	1987	1988	1989	1990	1991	1992	1993[1]
United States[2]	289,422	289,275	305,072	308,318	303,864[3]	307,171[3]	295,918[3]
Alabama	2,358	2,385	2,334	2,338	2,229	2,130	2,116
Arizona	723	784	830	802	770	736	695
Arkansas	7,132	7,538	7,603	8,080	7,863	8,110	8,165
California	4,950	5,100	4,892	4,789	4,396	4,459	4,403
Colorado	5,634	5,609	5,677	5,862	5,591	5,395	5,625
Connecticut	132	125	128	129	125	128	125
Delaware	514	504	537	496	556	515	499
Florida	1,108	1,115	1,128	1,076	1,048	1,071	1,046
Georgia	3,601	3,749	4,200	3,788	3,777	3,693	3,523
Hawaii	87	86	81	79	74	68	64
Idaho	4,141	3,925	4,226	4,175	4,079	4,006	4,322
Illinois	20,335	21,581	22,977	22,759	22,906	23,237	21,934
Indiana	10,781	11,082	11,631	11,485	11,527	11,709	11,767
Iowa	20,956	23,092	24,097	23,276	23,356	23,666	21,916
Kansas	19,924	19,191	18,794	20,978	20,712	20,266	20,454
Kentucky	4,975	4,968	5,487	5,505	5,495	5,419	5,419
Louisiana	3,905	4,291	4,075	4,346	3,665	4,029	3,729
Maine	356	346	364	361	351	375	373
Maryland	1,493	1,492	1,601	1,551	1,562	1,619	1,569
Massachusetts	158	143	136	135	136	135	134
Michigan	6,124	6,401	6,360	6,510	6,733	6,817	6,751
Minnesota	17,397	18,756	18,652	18,765	18,692	19,301	16,940
Mississippi	5,020	5,145	4,611	4,719	4,478	4,855	4,708
Missouri	12,436	12,684	13,249	12,685	12,900	12,904	11,542

[Continued]

★ 180 ★

Crop Acreage, by State: 1987-1993

[Continued]

State	1987	1988	1989	1990	1991	1992	1993[1]
Montana	9,242	7,118	9,475	8,926	8,687	8,369	8,891
Nebraska	15,932	16,765	17,450	18,044	18,366	18,330	17,917
Nevada	558	549	554	520	495	403	527
New Hampshire	102	99	93	91	92	103	106
New Jersey	381	365	378	361	380	391	413
New Mexico	953	936	968	880	1,042	1,051	995
New York	3,628	3,439	3,560	3,538	3,443	3,185	3,150
North Carolina	4,155	4,070	4,492	4,336	4,397	4,519	4,127
North Dakota	19,415	16,031	20,520	21,014	20,655	21,011	19,782
Ohio	9,698	9,731	10,259	10,132	9,972	10,087	10,037
Oklahoma	8,353	8,482	9,396	9,688	8,518	9,392	8,771
Oregon	2,257	2,165	2,337	2,290	2,260	2,147	2,260
Pennsylvania	4,257	4,199	4,198	4,094	4,067	4,065	4,035
Rhode Island	13	11	10	10	10	11	12
South Carolina	1,925	2,019	2,280	2,046	1,824	1,885	1,603
South Dakota	14,601	13,478	15,196	15,528	15,606	15,858	14,223
Tennessee	4,463	4,547	4,569	4,477	4,379	4,326	4,408
Texas	16,267	16,520	16,690	18,544	17,714	18,769	18,524
Utah	1,080	1,026	983	992	973	990	1,031
Vermont	465	453	442	441	434	463	434
Virginia	2,732	2,707	2,767	2,725	2,656	2,705	2,659
Washington	3,902	3,726	3,876	3,999	3,861	3,957	4,227
West Virginia	657	644	664	668	615	639	621
Wisconsin	8,351	8,430	8,615	8,550	8,449	8,096	7,498
Wyoming	1,796	1,674	1,628	1,735	1,899	1,723	1,804

Source: 1994 Statistical Abstract of the United States on CD-ROM [machine-readable datafiles]. CD-8A-94. Washington, DC: U.S. Department of Commerce, Economics and Statistics Administration, Bureau of the Census, Data User Services Division, January 1995. Primary sources: U.S. Department of Agriculture. National Agricultural Statistics Service, *Crop Production* (annual); and *Crop Values* (annual). *Notes:* 1. Preliminary. 2. Excludes Alaska. 3. Includes sunflower and sugarbeet acreage unallocated by state.

★ 181 ★

Crops and Cropland

Crop Loss

Table shows major threats to crop production.

[In percentages]

Cause	Loss
Drought	55.0
Excessive moisture	16.0
Frost/freeze	11.0
Hail	8.0
Wind	3.0
Disease	3.0
Flood	2.0

[Continued]

★ 181 ★

Crop Loss
[Continued]

Cause	Loss
Insects	1.0
Others	1.0

Source: "How Does Crop Loss Happen?" ABA Banking Journal (January 1994), p. 27.

★ 182 ★

Crops and Cropland

Cropland: 1970-1993

Table shows the cropland used for crops and acreage of crops harvested in selected years.

Year	Cropland used for crops					Acres of crops harvested[2] (million)
	Number (million acres)				Index (1977 = 100)	
	Total	Cropland harvested[1]	Crop failure	Cultivated summer fallow		
1970	332	289	5	38	88	293
1971	340	300	6	34	90	305
1972	334	289	7	38	88	294
1973	352	316	5	31	93	321
1974	361	322	8	31	96	328
1975	367	330	6	31	97	336
1976	369	330	8	31	98	337
1977	378	338	9	31	100	345
1978	369	330	7	32	97	338
1979	378	340	6	32	100	348
1980	382	342	10	30	101	352
1981	387	351	6	30	102	366
1982	383	347	5	31	101	362
1983	333	294	5	34	88	306
1984	373	337	6	30	99	348
1985	372	334	7	31	98	342
1986	357	316	9	32	94	325
1987	331	293	6	32	88	302
1988	327	287	10	30	87	298
1989	341	306	8	27	90	318
1990	341	310	6	25	90	322
1991	337	306	7	24	89	318

[Continued]

★ 182 ★

Cropland: 1970-1993
[Continued]

Year	Cropland used for crops					Acres of crops harvested[2] (million)
	Number (million acres)				Index (1977 = 100)	
	Total	Cropland harvested[1]	Crop failure	Cultivated summer fallow		
1992[3]	340	308	9	23	90	320
1993[3]	332	299	11	22	88	309

Source: 1994 Statistical Abstract of the United States on CD-ROM [machine-readable datafiles]. CD-8A-94. Washington, DC: U.S. Department of Commerce, Economics and Statistics Administration, Bureau of the Census, Data User Services Division, January 1995. Primary sources: U.S. Department of Agriculture. Economic Research Service. *Economic Indicators of the Farm Sector: Production and Efficiency Statistics* (annual); U.S. Department of Agriculture. *Agricultural Statistics* (annual); beginning 1991 data from *Agricultural Resources: Cropland, Water, and Conservation Situation and Outlook Report. Notes:* 1. Land supporting one or more harvested crops. 2. Area in principal crops harvested as reported by Crop Reporting Board plus acreages in fruits, vegetables for sale, tree nuts, and farm gardens. 3. Preliminary.

★ 183 ★

Crops and Cropland

Cropland Harvested: 1950-1990

Table shows cropland acreages harvested for export and domestic uses.

[In million acres, except as noted]

Year	Total cropland harvested	Cropland used to produce:			Crop acreage in exports (%)
		Exports	Domestic use goods	Domestic use per capita (acres)	
1950	345	50	295	1.82	14.49
1955	340	47	293	1.72	13.82
1960	324	64	260	1.41	19.75
1965	298	76	222	1.14	25.50
1970	293	72	221	1.08	24.57
1975	336	100	236	1.09	29.76
1980	352	137	215	0.94	38.92
1985	342	81	261	1.09	23.68
1990	322	83	239	0.95	25.78

Source: Executive Office of the President of the United States. *Environmental Quality 24: The Twenty-fourth Annual Report of the Council on Environmental Quality.* Prepared by Ray Clark. Written by Carroll Curtis. Edited by Barry Walsh. Washington, DC: U.S. Government Printing Office, 1994, p. 454. Primary source: U.S. Department of Agriculture. Economic Research Service. *Economic Indicators of the Farm Sector: Production and Efficiency Statistics.* ECIFS 10-3. Washington, DC: U.S. Department of Agriculture, Economic Research Service, May 1992.

★ 184 ★

Crops and Cropland

Cropland Use: 1945-1993

Table shows major uses of cropland. Acres of idle cropland, cropland pasture, and total cropland are estimated only for years coinciding with Census of Agriculture years. Data are for the conterminous United States. Cropland diversions occur under federal farm programs (annual commodity programs, Conservation Reserve Program, and Wetlands Reserve Program).

[In million acres]

Year	Cropland used for crops						Diverted from production
	Harvested	Failed	Cultivated summer fallow	Idle	Cropland pasture	Total	
1945	353	10	40	NA	47	454	NA
1949	352	9	26	22	67	478	NA
1954	339	13	28	19	66	465	NA
1959	317	10	31	33	66	457	22.5
1964	292	6	37	52	57	444	55.0
1969	286	6	41	51	88	472	57.5
1974	322	8	31	21	83	465	2.7
1978	330	7	32	26	76	471	18.3
1982	347	5	31	21	65	469	11.1
1987	293	6	32	68	65	464	76.2
1992	296	6	27	40	67	435	29.6
1993	299	11	23	NA	NA	NA	60.0

Source: Executive Office of the President of the United States. *Environmental Quality 24: The Twenty-fourth Annual Report of the Council on Environmental Quality.* Prepared by Ray Clark. Written by Carroll Curtis. Edited by Barry Walsh. Washington, DC: U.S. Government Printing Office, 1994, p. 453. Primary sources: U.S. Department of Agriculture. Economic Research Service. *Cropland, Water, and Conservation Situation and Outlook Report.* AR-30. Washington, DC: U.S. Department of Agriculture, Economic Research Service, May 1993; U.S. Department of Agriculture. Economic Research Service. *RTD Updates: 1994 Cropland Use.* Washington, DC: U.S. Department of Agriculture, Economic Research Service, September 1994; U.S. Department of Commerce. Bureau of the Census. *Census of Agriculture for 1992.* Washington, DC: U.S. Department of Commerce, Bureau of the Census, 1994; and earlier census reports. *Note:* "NA" stands for "not available."

★ 185 ★

Crops and Cropland

Farms and Farmland: 1900-1992

Table shows the number of farms and amount of land in farms.

Year	Farm size category in acres									
	1-49		50-499		500-999		1,000+		Total	
	Number (million)	Area (million acres)	Number (million)	Area (million acres)	Number (million)	Area (million acres)	Number (million)	Area (million acres)	Number (million)	Area (billion acres)
1900	1.93	49	3.37	520	0.10	68	0.05	200	5.74	0.84
1910	2.25	49	3.93	570	0.13	84	0.05	167	6.37	0.88
1920	2.31	59	3.93	580	0.15	100	0.07	221	6.45	0.96
1925	2.42	57	3.75	550	0.14	97	0.06	224	6.37	NA
1930	2.36	56	3.69	550	0.16	109	0.08	277	6.30	0.99
1935	2.69	59	3.86	540	0.17	114	0.09	310	6.81	NA
1940	2.29	50	3.55	540	0.16	112	0.10	366	6.10	1.07
1945	2.25	47	3.32	520	0.17	119	0.11	460	5.86	1.14
1950	1.97	39	3.12	500	0.18	126	0.12	495	5.39	1.16
1954	1.70	32	2.76	460	0.19	132	0.13	531	4.78	1.16
1959	1.06	22	2.32	410	0.20	137	0.14	555	3.71	1.12
1964	0.82	17	1.98	360	0.21	145	0.15	585	3.16	1.11
1969	0.64	14	1.73	320	0.22	148	0.15	578	2.73	1.06
1974	0.51	11	1.44	273	0.21	142	0.16	590	2.31	1.02
1978	0.54	12	1.34	256	0.21	147	0.16	600	2.26	1.02
1982	0.64	13	1.24	233	0.20	141	0.16	600	2.24	0.99
1987	0.60	12	1.12	212	0.20	139	0.17	602	2.09	0.96
1992	0.56	11	1.01	190	0.19	129	0.17	615	1.93	0.95

Source: Executive Office of the President of the United States. *Environmental Quality 24: The Twenty-fourth Annual Report of the Council on Environmental Quality.* Prepared by Ray Clark. Written by Carroll Curtis. Edited by Barry Walsh. Washington, DC: U.S. Government Printing Office, 1994, p. 452. Primary source: U.S. Department of Commerce. Bureau of the Census. *Historical Statistics of the United States Colonial Times to 1970.* Washington, DC: U.S. Department of Commerce, Bureau of the Census, 1976; U.S. Department of Commerce. Bureau of the Census. *Census of Agriculture for 1992*, Washington, DC: U.S. Department of Commerce, Bureau of the Census, 1994; and earlier census reports. *Note:* "NA" stands for "not available."

★ 186 ★

Crops and Cropland

Irrigated Farmland: 1900-1993

[In million acres]

Year	Western states[1]	Other states	Total
1900	7.5	0.3	7.8
1910	11.3	0.4	11.7
1920	13.9	0.6	14.5
1930	14.1	0.6	14.7
1940	17.2	0.7	18.0
1950	24.3	1.5	25.8

[Continued]

★ 186 ★

Irrigated Farmland: 1900-1993
[Continued]

Year	Western states[1]	Other states	Total
1959	30.7	2.4	33.2
1969	34.8	4.3	39.1
1978	43.2	7.2	50.4
1982	41.3	7.7	49.0
1983	36.3	7.5	43.8
1984	41.1	8.3	49.4
1985	40.9	8.8	49.7
1986	40.0	8.6	48.6
1987	37.5	8.9	46.4
1988	39.0	9.6	48.6
1989	40.9	9.9	50.8
1990	41.1	10.3	51.4
1991	41.2	10.9	52.2
1992	40.7	11.6	52.3
1993	40.1	11.2	51.3

Source: Executive Office of the President of the United States. *Environmental Quality 24: The Twenty-fourth Annual Report of the Council on Environmental Quality.* Prepared by Ray Clark. Written by Carroll Curtis. Edited by Barry Walsh. Washington, DC: U.S. Government Printing Office, 1994, p. 460. Primary sources: U.S. Department of Agriculture, Economic Research Service. *Cropland, Water, and Conservation Situation and Outlook Report.* AR-30. Washington, DC: U.S. Department of Agriculture, Economic Research Service, May 1993; U.S. Department of Agriculture, Economic Research Service. *RTD Updates: Irrigated Lands in Farms.* Washington, DC: U.S. Department of Agriculture, Economic Research Service, December 1993; U.S. Department of Commerce. Bureau of the Census. *Census of Agriculture for 1992.* Washington, DC: U.S. Department of Commerce, Bureau of the Census, 1994; and earlier census reports. *Notes:* Data for 1900-1982 and 1987 are from the Census of Agriculture. The 1992 Census of Agriculture was not available at the time this table was prepared. Estimates for other years are constructed from data provided by the U.S. Department of Agriculture (USDA), National Agricultural Statistics (NASS). 1. The Western states are: Arizona, California, Colorado, Idaho, Kansas, Montana, Nebraska, Nevada, New Mexico, North Dakota, Oklahoma, Oregon, South Dakota, Texas, Utah, Washington, and Wyoming.

Crops and Cropland: Specific Crops

★ 187 ★

Barley: 1984-1993

Table shows barley production, supply, and disappearance for 1984 through 1993. Acreage, production, and yield of crops periodically revised on basis of census data.

Year	Acreage			Yield per acre (bushels)	Pro-duction (million bushels)	Farm price[2] (dollars per bushel)	Farm value (million dollars)	Total supply[3] (million bushels)	Disappearance		Ending stocks (million bushels)
	Set aside[1] (million)	Planted (million)	Harvested (million)						Total[4] (million bushels)	Exports (million bushels)	
1984	0.5	12.0	11.2	53.4	598	2.29	1,372	795	547	72	247
1985	0.7	13.2	11.6	51.0	590	1.98	1,133	844	517	20	327
1986	2.0	13.0	12.0	50.8	609	1.61	994	942	606	134	336
1987	2.9	10.9	10.0	52.4	521	1.81	967	869	548	121	321
1988	2.8	9.8	7.6	38.0	290	2.80	775	622	425	79	196
1989	2.3	9.1	8.3	48.6	404	2.42	968	614	453	84	161
1990	2.9	8.2	7.5	56.1	422	2.14	912	596	461	81	135
1991	2.1	8.9	8.4	55.2	464	2.10	997	624	496	94	129
1992	2.3	7.8	7.3	62.5	458	2.04	954	598	447	80	151
1993	2.2	7.8	6.8	58.9	400	2.00	814	586	450	75	136

Source: 1994 Statistical Abstract of the United States on CD-ROM [machine-readable datafiles]. CD-8A-94. Washington, DC: U.S. Department of Commerce, Economics and Statistics Administration, Bureau of the Census, Data User Services Division, January 1995. Primary sources: For production—U.S. Department of Agriculture. National Agricultural Statistics Service. *Crop Production* (annual); and *Crop Values* (annual). For supply and disappearance—U.S. Department of Agriculture. Economic Research Service. *Feed Situation* (quarterly); *Fats and Oils Situation* (quarterly); *Wheat Situation* (quarterly); *Tobacco Situation* (quarterly); *Cotton and Wool Outlook Statistics* (periodic); and *Agricultural Supply and Demand Estimates* (periodic). All data are also in *Agricultural Statistics* (annual) and *Agricultural Outlook* (monthly). *Notes:* 1993 data are preliminary. 1. Acreage set aside under diversion, PIK (payment-in-kind) and acreage reduction programs. 2. Except as noted, marketing year average price. U.S. prices are computed by weighting U.S. monthly prices by estimated monthly marketings and do not include an allowance for outstanding loans and government purchases and payments. 3. Comprises production, imports, and beginning stocks. 4. Includes feed, residual, and other domestic uses not shown separately.

★ 188 ★

Crops and Cropland: Specific Crops

Corn: 1984-1993

Table shows production, supply, and disappearance of corn for grain during 1984 through 1993. Marketing year begins September 1 for corn. Acreage, production, and yield of crops periodically revised on basis of census data.

Year	Acreage			Yield per acre (bushels)	Pro-duction (million bushels)	Farm price[2] (dollars per bushel)	Farm value (million dollars)	Total supply[3] (million bushels)	Disappearance		Ending stocks (million bushels)
	Set aside[1] (million)	Planted (million)	Harvested (million)						Total[4] (million bushels)	Exports (million bushels)	
1984	3.9	80.5	71.9	106.7	7,672	2.63	20,085	8,680	7,032	1,850	1,648
1985	5.4	83.4	75.2	118.0	8,876	2.23	19,522	10,534	6,494	1,227	4,040
1986	14.3	76.6	68.9	119.4	8,226	1.50	12,541	12,267	7,385	1,492	4,882
1987	23.1	66.2	59.5	119.8	7,131	1.94	14,108	12,016	7,757	1,716	4,259
1988	20.5	67.7	58.3	84.6	4,929	2.54	12,661	9,191	7,260	2,026	1,930

[Continued]

★ 188 ★

Corn: 1984-1993

[Continued]

Year	Acreage			Yield per acre (bushels)	Pro-duction (million bushels)	Farm price[2] (dollars per bushel)	Farm value (million dollars)	Total supply[3] (million bushels)	Disappearance		Ending stocks (million bushels)
	Set aside[1] (million)	Planted (million)	Harvested (million)						Total[4] (million bushels)	Exports (million bushels)	
1989	10.8	72.2	64.7	116.3	7,525	2.36	17,897	9,458	8,113	2,368	1,344
1990	10.7	74.2	67.0	118.5	7,934	2.28	18,192	9,282	7,761	1,725	1,521
1991	7.4	76.0	68.8	108.6	7,475	2.37	17,864	9,016	7,916	1,584	1,100
1992	5.2	79.3	72.2	131.4	9,482	2.07	19,735	10,589	8,476	1,663	2,113
1993	10.4	73.3	63.0	100.7	6,344	2.60	16,597	8,477	7,675	1,300	802

Source: 1994 Statistical Abstract of the United States on CD-ROM [machine-readable datafiles]. CD-8A-94. Washington, DC: U.S. Department of Commerce, Economics and Statistics Administration, Bureau of the Census, Data User Services Division, January 1995. Primary sources: For production—U.S. Department of Agriculture. National Agricultural Statistics Service. *Crop Production* (annual); and *Crop Values* (annual). For supply and disappearance—U.S. Department of Agriculture. Economic Research Service. *Feed Situation* (quarterly); *Fats and Oils Situation* (quarterly); *Wheat Situation* (quarterly); *Tobacco Situation* (quarterly); *Cotton and Wool Outlook Statistics* (periodic); and *Agricultural Supply and Demand Estimates* (periodic). All data are also in *Agricultural Statistics* (annual) and *Agricultural Outlook* (monthly). *Notes:* 1993 data are preliminary. 1. Acreage set aside under diversion, PIK (payment-in-kind) and acreage reduction programs. 2. Except as noted, marketing year average price. U.S. prices are computed by weighting U.S. monthly prices by estimated monthly marketings and do not include an allowance for outstanding loans and government purchases and payments. 3. Comprises production, imports, and beginning stocks. 4. Includes feed, residual, and other domestic uses not shown separately.

★ 189 ★

Crops and Cropland: Specific Crops

Cotton: 1984-1993

Table shows cotton production, supply, and disappearance for 1984 through 1993. Marketing year begins August 1 for cotton. Acreage, production, and yield of crops periodically revised on basis of census data.

Year	Acreage			Yield per acre (pounds)	Pro-duction[2] (million bales)	Farm price[3] (cents per pound)	Farm value (million dollars)	Total supply[4] (million bushels)	Disappearance		Ending stocks (million bales)[2]
	Set aside[1] (million)	Planted (million)	Harvested (million)						Total[5] (million bales)[2]	Exports (million bales)[2]	
1984	2.5	11.1	10.4	600	13.0[6]	57.8	3,604	15.8	11.8	6.2	4.1[7]
1985	3.6	10.7	10.2	630	13.4[6]	56.3	3,628	17.6	8.4	2.0	9.3[7]
1986	4.2	10.0	8.5	552	9.7[6]	52.4	2,449	19.1	14.1	6.7	5.0[7]
1987	4.0	10.4	10.0	706	14.8[6]	64.3	4,555	19.8	14.2	6.6	5.8[7]
1988	2.2	12.5	11.9	619	15.4[6]	56.6	4,190	21.2	13.9	6.1	7.1[7]
1989	3.5	10.6	9.5	614	12.2[6]	66.2	3,877	19.3	16.5	7.7	3.0[7]
1990	2.0	12.3	11.7	634	15.5[6]	67.1	5,076	18.5	16.4	7.8	2.3[7]
1991	1.2	14.1	13.0	652	17.6[6]	58.1	4,913	20.0	16.3	6.7	3.7[7]

[Continued]

★ 189 ★

Cotton: 1984-1993

[Continued]

Year	Acreage			Yield per acre (pounds)	Pro- duction[2] (million bales)	Farm price[3] (cents per pound)	Farm value (million dollars)	Total supply[4] (million bushels)	Disappearance		Ending stocks (million bales)[2]
	Set aside[1] (million)	Planted (million)	Harvested (million)						Total[5] (million bales)[2]	Exports (million bales)[2]	
1992	1.7	13.2	11.1	699	16.2[6]	54.9	4,274	19.9	15.4	5.2	4.7[7]
1993	1.4	13.4	12.8	607	16.2[6]	54.3[8]	4,220	20.8	16.4	6.2	4.5[7]

Source: 1994 Statistical Abstract of the United States on CD-ROM [machine-readable datafiles]. CD-8A-94. Washington, DC: U.S. Department of Commerce, Economics and Statistics Administration, Bureau of the Census, Data User Services Division, January 1995. Primary sources: For production—U.S. Department of Agriculture. National Agricultural Statistics Service. *Crop Production* (annual); and *Crop Values* (annual). For supply and disappearance—U.S. Department of Agriculture. Economic Research Service. *Feed Situation* (quarterly); *Fats and Oils Situation* (quarterly); *Wheat Situation* (quarterly); *Tobacco Situation* (quarterly); *Cotton and Wool Outlook Statistics* (periodic); and *Agricultural Supply and Demand Estimates* (periodic). All data are also in *Agricultural Statistics* (annual) and *Agricultural Outlook* (monthly). *Notes:* 1993 data are preliminary. 1. Acreage set aside under diversion, PIK (payment-in-kind) and acreage reduction programs. 2. Bales of 480 pounds, net weight. 3. Except as noted, marketing year average price. U.S. prices are computed by weighting U.S. monthly prices by estimated monthly marketings and do not include an allowance for outstanding loans and government purchases and payments. 4. Comprises production, imports, and beginning stocks. 5. Includes feed, residual, and other domestic uses not shown separately. 6. State production figures, which conform with U.S. Bureau of the Census annual ginning enumeration with allowance for cross-state ginnings, rounded to thousands and added for U.S. totals. 7. Stock estimates based on Census Bureau data which results in an unaccounted difference between supply and use estimates and changes in ending stocks. 8. Weighted average for August 1-December 1.

★ 190 ★

Crops and Cropland: Specific Crops

Hay: 1984-1993

Table shows hay production, supply, and disappearance for 1984 through 1993. Marketing year begins May 1 for hay. Acreage, production, and yield of crops periodically revised on basis of census data.

Year	Acreage			Yield per acre (short tons)	Pro- duction (million short tons)	Farm price[2] (dollars per ton)	Farm value (million dollars)	Total supply[3] (million short tons)	Disappearance		Ending stocks (million short tons)
	Set aside[1] (million)	Planted (million)	Harvested (million)						Total[4] (million short tons)	Exports (million short tons)	
1984	0	(NA)	61.4	2.45	151	72.70[5]	10,204	171	144	(NA)	27
1985	0	(NA)	60.4	2.46	149	67.60[5]	9,437	176	149	(NA)	27
1986	0	(NA)	62.4	2.49	156	59.80[5]	8,611	182	150	(NA)	32
1987	0	(NA)	60.1	2.45	148	65.00[5]	8,845	180	153	(NA)	27
1988	0	(NA)	65.1	1.94	126	85.20[5]	10,457	153	136	(NA)	18
1989	0	(NA)	63.3	2.30	146	87.40[5]	11,514	163	136	(NA)	27
1990	0	(NA)	61.4	2.39	147	80.60[5]	10,462	174	147	(NA)	27
1991	0	(NA)	62.5	2.45	153	71.20[5]	10,006	180	152	(NA)	29
1992	0	(NA)	59.6	2.50	149	74.30[5]	10,573	178	157	(NA)	21
1993	0	(NA)	60.4	2.26	149	81.00[5]	10,909	175	(NA)	(NA)	(NA)

Source: 1994 Statistical Abstract of the United States on CD-ROM [machine-readable datafiles]. CD-8A-94. Washington, DC: U.S. Department of Commerce, Economics and Statistics Administration, Bureau of the Census, Data User Services Division, January 1995. Primary sources: For production—U.S. Department of Agriculture. National Agricultural Statistics Service. *Crop Production* (annual); and *Crop Values* (annual). For supply and disappearance—U.S. Department of Agriculture. Economic Research Service. *Feed Situation* (quarterly); *Fats and Oils Situation* (quarterly); *Wheat Situation* (quarterly); *Tobacco Situation* (quarterly); *Cotton and Wool Outlook Statistics* (periodic); and *Agricultural Supply and Demand Estimates* (periodic). All data are also in *Agricultural Statistics* (annual) and *Agricultural Outlook* (monthly). *Notes:* "NA" indicates "not available." 1993 data are preliminary. 1. Acreage set aside under diversion, PIK (payment-in-kind) and acreage reduction programs. 2. Except as noted, marketing year average price. U.S. prices are computed by weighting U.S. monthly marketings and do not include an allowance for outstanding loans and government purchases and payments. 3. Comprises production, imports, and beginning stocks. 4. Includes feed, residual, and other domestic uses not shown separately. 5. Prices are for hay sold baled. Season average prices received by farmers. U.S. prices are computed by weighting state prices by estimated sales and include an allowance for outstanding loans and government purchases, if any, for crops under government programs.

★ 191 ★

Crops and Cropland: Specific Crops

Potatoes: 1984-1993

Table shows potato production, supply, and disappearance for 1984 through 1993. Acreage, production, and yield of crops periodically revised on basis of census data.

Year	Acreage			Yield per acre (hundred-weight)	Pro-duction (million hundred-weight)	Farm price[2] (dollars per hundred-weight)	Farm value (million dollars)	Total supply[3] (million hundred-weight)	Disappearance		Ending stocks (million hundred-weight)
	Set aside[1] (million)	Planted (million)	Harvested (million)						Total[4] (million hundred-weight)	Exports (million hundred-weight)	
1985	(NA)	1.4	1.3	299	407	3.92	1,568	583	293[5]	9[6]	(NA)
1986	(NA)	1.2	1.2	296	362	5.03	1,808	567	309[5]	11[6]	(NA)
1987	(NA)	1.3	1.3	301	389	4.38	1,682	574	307[5]	13[6]	(NA)
1988	(NA)	1.3	1.3	283	356	6.02	2,144	558	300[5]	16[6]	(NA)
1989	(NA)	1.3	1.3	289	370	7.36	2,717	555	315[5]	16[6]	(NA)
1990	(NA)	1.4	1.4	293	402	6.08	2,431	582	319[5]	17[6]	(NA)
1991	(NA)	1.4	1.4	304	418	4.96	2,043	618	330[5]	17[6]	(NA)
1992	(NA)	1.3	1.3	323	425	5.52	2,336	640	339[5]	19[6]	(NA)
1993	(NA)	1.4	1.3	318	419	6.22	2,599	642	345[5]	23[6]	(NA)
										24[6]	

Source: 1994 Statistical Abstract of the United States on CD-ROM [machine-readable datafiles]. CD-8A-94. Washington, DC: U.S. Department of Commerce, Economics and Statistics Administration, Bureau of the Census, Data User Services Division, January 1995. Primary sources: For production—U.S. Department of Agriculture. National Agricultural Statistics Service. *Crop Production* (annual); and *Crop Values* (annual). For supply and disappearance—U.S. Department of Agriculture. Economic Research Service. *Feed Situation* (quarterly); *Fats and Oils Situation* (quarterly); *Wheat Situation* (quarterly); *Tobacco Situation* (quarterly); *Cotton and Wool Outlook Statistics* (periodic); and *Agricultural Supply and Demand Estimates* (periodic). All data are also in *Agricultural Statistics* (annual) and *Agricultural Outlook* (monthly). *Notes:* "NA" indicates "not available." 1993 data are preliminary. 1. Acreage set aside under diversion, PIK (payment-in-kind) and acreage reduction programs. 2. Except as noted, marketing year average price. U.S. prices are computed by weighting U.S. monthly prices by estimated monthly marketings and do not include an allowance for outstanding loans and government purchases and payments. 3. Comprises production, imports, and beginning stocks. 4. Includes feed, residual, and other domestic uses not shown separately. 5. Covers potatoes used for table use, frozen and canned products, chips, and dehydration. 6. Covers fresh potatoes, chips, frozen and dehydrated products.

★ 192 ★

Crops and Cropland: Specific Crops

Rice: 1984-1993

Table shows rough rice production, supply, and disappearance for 1984 through 1993. Marketing year begins August 1 for rice. Acreage, production, and yield of crops periodically revised on basis of census data.

Year	Acreage			Yield per acre (pounds)	Pro-duction (million hundred-weight)	Farm price[2] (dollars per hundred-weight)	Farm value (million dollars)	Total supply[3] (million hundred-weight)	Disappearance		Ending stocks (million hundred-weight)
	Set aside[1] (million)	Planted (million)	Harvested (million)						Total[4] (million hundred-weight)	Exports (million hundred-weight)	
1984	.8	2.8	2.8	4,954	139	8.04	1,118	187	123	62	65
1985	1.3	2.5	2.5	5,414	135	6.53	882	202	125	59	77
1986	1.5	2.4	2.4	5,651	133	3.75	499	213	162	84	51
1987	1.6	2.4	2.3	5,555	130	7.27	942	184	153	72	31
1988	1.1	2.9	2.9	5,514	160	6.83	1,092	195	168	86	27
1989	1.2	2.7	2.7	5,749	155	7.35	1,134	186	159	77	26
1990	1.0	2.9	2.8	5,529	156	6.70	1,047	187	163	71	25
1991	0.7	2.9	2.8	5,674	157	7.58	1,201	187	160	66	27

[Continued]

★ 192 ★

Rice: 1984-1993
[Continued]

Year	Acreage			Yield per acre (pounds)	Pro-duction (million hundred-weight)	Farm price[2] (dollars per hundred-weight)	Farm value (million dollars)	Total supply[3] (million hundred-weight)	Disappearance		Ending stocks (million hundred-weight)
	Set aside[1] (million)	Planted (million)	Harvested (million)						Total[4] (million hundred-weight)	Exports (million hundred-weight)	
1992	0.4	3.2	3.1	5,736	180	5.89	1,057	213	174	77	39
1993	0.7	2.9	2.8	5,510	156	9.00	1,429	202	182	83	21

Source: 1994 Statistical Abstract of the United States on CD-ROM [machine-readable datafiles]. CD-8A-94. Washington, DC: U.S. Department of Commerce, Economics and Statistics Administration, Bureau of the Census, Data User Services Division, January 1995. Primary sources: For production—U.S. Department of Agriculture. National Agricultural Statistics Service. *Crop Production* (annual); and *Crop Values* (annual). For supply and disappearance—U.S. Department of Agriculture. Economic Research Service. *Feed Situation* (quarterly); *Fats and Oils Situation* (quarterly); *Wheat Situation* (quarterly); *Tobacco Situation* (quarterly); *Cotton and Wool Outlook Statistics* (periodic); and *Agricultural Supply and Demand Estimates* (periodic). All data are also in *Agricultural Statistics* (annual) and *Agricultural Outlook* (monthly). *Notes:* 1993 data are preliminary. 1. Acreage set aside under diversion, PIK (payment-in-kind) and acreage reduction programs. 2. Except as noted, marketing year average price. U.S. prices are computed by weighting U.S. monthly prices by estimated monthly marketings and do not include an allowance for outstanding loans and government purchases and payments. 3. Comprises production, imports, and beginning stocks. 4. Includes feed, residual, and other domestic uses not shown separately.

★ 193 ★

Crops and Cropland: Specific Crops

Sorghum: 1984-1993

Table shows production, supply, and disappearance of sorghum for grain for 1984 through 1993. Marketing year begins September 1 for sorghum. Acreage, production, and yield of crops periodically revised on basis of census data.

Year	Acreage			Yield per acre (bushels)	Pro-duction (million bushels)	Farm price[2] (dollars per bushel)	Farm value (million dollars)	Total supply[3] (million bushels)	Disappearance		Ending stocks (million bushels)
	Set aside[1] (million)	Planted (million)	Harvested (million)						Total[4] (million bushels)	Exports (million bushels)	
1984	0.6	17.3	15.4	56.4	866	2.32	2,139	1,154	854	297	300
1985	0.9	18.3	16.8	66.8	1,120	1.93	2,243	1,421	870	178	551
1986	2.7	15.3	13.9	67.7	939	1.37	1,322	1,490	746	198	743
1987	4.1	11.8	10.5	69.4	731	1.70	1,179	1,474	811	232	663
1988	3.9	10.3	9.0	63.8	577	2.27	1,337	1,239	800	311	440
1989	3.3	12.6	11.1	55.4	615	2.10	1,288	1,055	835	303	220
1990	3.3	10.5	9.1	63.1	573	2.12	1,221	793	650	232	143
1991	2.4	11.1	9.9	59.3	585	2.25	1,331	727	674	292	53
1992	2.0	13.3	12.2	72.8	884	1.89	1,684	937	762	277	175
1993	2.2	10.5	9.5	59.9	568	2.40	1,316	743	658	175	85

Source: 1994 Statistical Abstract of the United States on CD-ROM [machine-readable datafiles]. CD-8A-94. Washington, DC: U.S. Department of Commerce, Economics and Statistics Administration, Bureau of the Census, Data User Services Division, January 1995. Primary sources: For production—U.S. Department of Agriculture. National Agricultural Statistics Service. *Crop Production* (annual); and *Crop Values* (annual). For supply and disappearance—U.S. Department of Agriculture. Economic Research Service. *Feed Situation* (quarterly); *Fats and Oils Situation* (quarterly); *Wheat Situation* (quarterly); *Tobacco Situation* (quarterly); *Cotton and Wool Outlook Statistics* (periodic); and *Agricultural Supply and Demand Estimates* (periodic). All data are also in *Agricultural Statistics* (annual) and *Agricultural Outlook* (monthly). *Notes:* 1993 data are preliminary. 1. Acreage set aside under diversion, PIK (payment-in-kind) and acreage reduction programs. 2. Except as noted, marketing year average price. U.S. prices are computed by weighting U.S. monthly prices by estimated monthly marketings and do not include an allowance for outstanding loans and government purchases and payments. 3. Comprises production, imports, and beginning stocks. 4. Includes feed, residual, and other domestic uses not shown separately.

★ 194 ★
Crops and Cropland: Specific Crops

Soybeans: 1984-1993

Table shows soybean production, supply, and disappearance for 1984 through 1993. Marketing year begins September 1 for soybeans. Acreage, production, and yield of crops periodically revised on basis of census data.

Year	Acreage			Yield per acre (bushels)	Pro-duction (million bushels)	Farm price[2] (dollars per bushel)	Farm value (million dollars)	Total supply[3] (million bushels)	Disappearance		Ending stocks (million bushels)
	Set aside[1] (million)	Planted (million)	Harvested (million)						Total[4] (million bushels)	Exports (million bushels)	
1984	0	67.8	66.1	28.1	1,861	5.84	10,748	2,037	1,721	598	316
1985	0	63.1	61.6	34.1	2,099	5.05	10,581	2,415	1,879	740	536
1986	0	60.4	58.3	33.3	1,943	4.78	9,263	2,479	2,042	757	436
1987	0	58.2	57.2	33.9	1,938	5.88	11,391	2,375	2,073	802	302
1988	0	58.8	57.4	27.0	1,549	7.42	11,488	1,855	1,673	527	182
1989	0	60.8	59.5	32.3	1,924	5.69	10,732	2,109	1,870	623	239
1990	0	57.8	56.5	34.1	1,926	5.74	11,042	2,168	1,839	557	329
1991	0	59.2	58.0	34.2	1,987	5.58	11,092	2,319	2,041	684	278
1992	0	59.1	58.2	37.6	2,188	5.56	12,154	2,468	2,176	770	292
1993	0	59.4	56.4	32.0	1,809	6.50	11,735	2,106	1,956	615	150

Source: 1994 Statistical Abstract of the United States on CD-ROM [machine-readable datafiles]. CD-8A-94. Washington, DC: U.S. Department of Commerce, Economics and Statistics Administration, Bureau of the Census, Data User Services Division, January 1995. Primary sources: For production—U.S. Department of Agriculture. National Agricultural Statistics Service. *Crop Production* (annual); and *Crop Values* (annual). For supply and disappearance— U.S. Department of Agriculture. Economic Research Service. *Feed Situation* (quarterly); *Fats and Oils Situation* (quarterly); *Wheat Situation* (quarterly); *Tobacco Situation* (quarterly); *Cotton and Wool Outlook Statistics* (periodic); and *Agricultural Supply and Demand Estimates* (periodic). All data are also in *Agricultural Statistics* (annual) and *Agricultural Outlook* (monthly). *Notes:* 1993 data are preliminary. 1. Acreage set aside under diversion, PIK (payment-in-kind) and acreage reduction programs. 2. Except as noted, marketing year average price. U.S. prices are computed by weighting U.S. monthly prices by estimated monthly marketings and do not include an allowance for outstanding loans and government purchases and payments. 3. Comprises production, imports, and beginning stocks. 4. Includes feed, residual, and other domestic uses not shown separately.

★ 195 ★
Crops and Cropland: Specific Crops

Tobacco: 1984-1993

Table shows tobacco production, supply, and disappearance for 1984 through 1993. Crop year for flue-cured and cigar wrapper tobacco is July through June; crop year for all other types is October through September. Data on farm-sales-weight basis. Acreage, production, and yield of crops periodically revised on basis of census data.

Year	Acreage			Yield per acre (pounds)	Pro-duction (million pounds)	Farm price[2] (dollars per pound)	Farm value (million dollars)	Total supply[3] (million pounds)	Disappearance		Ending stocks (million pounds)
	Set aside[1] (million)	Planted (million)	Harvested (million)						Total[4] (million pounds)	Exports (million pounds)	
1984	(NA)	(NA)	0.8	2,183	1,728	1.81[5]	3,121	5,545	1,621	666	3,924[6]
1985	(NA)	(NA)	0.7	2,197	1,511	1.65[5]	2,486	5,435	1,620	620	3,815[6]
1986	(NA)	(NA)	0.6	2,001	1,164	1.52[5]	1,772	4,978	1,572	591	3,406[6]
1987	(NA)	(NA)	0.6	2,028	1,189	1.57[5]	1,870	4,597	1,688	573	2,909[6]
1988	(NA)	(NA)	0.6	2,160	1,370	1.65[5]	2,261	4,279	1,565	555	2,714[6]
1989	(NA)	(NA)	0.7	2,016	1,367	1.71[5]	2,338	4,081	1,677	582	2,401[6]
1990	(NA)	(NA)	0.7	2,218	1,626	1.74[5]	2,827	4,026	1,794	631	2,232[6]
1991	(NA)	(NA)	0.8	2,179	1,664	1.77[5]	2,951	3,896	1,616	640	2,280[6]

[Continued]

★ 195 ★

Tobacco: 1984-1993

[Continued]

Year	Acreage			Yield per acre (pounds)	Pro-duction (million pounds)	Farm price[2] (dollars per pound)	Farm value (million dollars)	Total supply[3] (million pounds)	Disappearance		Ending stocks (million pounds)
	Set aside[1] (million)	Planted (million)	Harvested (million)						Total[4] (million pounds)	Exports (million pounds)	
1992	(NA)	(NA)	0.8	2,195	1,722	1.78[5]	3,059	4,001	1,565	629	2,436[6]
1993	(NA)	(NA)	0.7	2,162	1,615	1.76[5]	2,837	4,041	(NA)	(NA)	(NA)

Source: 1994 Statistical Abstract of the United States on CD-ROM [machine-readable datafiles]. CD-8A-94. Washington, DC: U.S. Department of Commerce, Economics and Statistics Administration, Bureau of the Census, Data User Services Division, January 1995. Primary sources: For production—U.S. Department of Agriculture. National Agricultural Statistics Service. *Crop Production* (annual); and *Crop Values* (annual). For supply and disappearance—U.S. Department of Agriculture. Economic Research Service. *Feed Situation* (quarterly); *Fats and Oils Situation* (quarterly); *Wheat Situation* (quarterly); *Tobacco Situation* (quarterly); *Cotton and Wool Outlook Statistics* (periodic); and *Agricultural Supply and Demand Estimates* (periodic). All data are also in *Agricultural Statistics* (annual) and *Agricultural Outlook* (monthly). *Notes:* "NA" indicates "not available." 1993 data are preliminary. 1. Acreage set aside under diversion, PIK (payment-in-kind) and acreage reduction programs. 2. Except as noted, marketing year average price. U.S. prices are computed by weighting U.S. monthly prices by estimated monthly marketings and do not include an allowance for outstanding loans and government purchases and payments. 3. Comprises production, imports, and beginning stocks. 4. Includes feed, residual, and other domestic uses not shown separately. 5. Season average prices received by farmers. U.S. prices are computed by weighting State prices by estimated sales and include an allowance for outstanding loans and government purchases, if any, for crops under government programs. 6. Includes tobacco carried over on farms.

★ 196 ★

Crops and Cropland: Specific Crops

Wheat: 1984-1993

Table shows wheat production, supply, and disappearance for 1984 through 1993. Marketing year begins June 1 for wheat. Acreage, production, and yield of crops periodically revised on basis of census data.

Year	Acreage			Yield per acre (bushels)	Pro-duction (million bushels)	Farm price[2] (dollars per bushel)	Farm value (million dollars)	Total supply[3] (million bushels)	Disappearance		Ending stocks (million bushels)
	Set aside[1] (million)	Planted (million)	Harvested (million)						Total[4] (million bushels)	Exports (million bushels)	
1984	18.3	79.2	66.9	38.8	2,595	3.39	8,797	4,003	2,578	1,421	1,425
1985	18.8	75.5	64.7	37.5	2,424	3.08	7,374	3,865	1,960	909	1,905
1986	21.0	72.0	60.7	34.4	2,091	2.42	5,044	4,017	2,196	999	1,821
1987	23.9	65.8	55.9	37.7	2,108	2.57	5,498	3,945	2,684	1,588	1,261
1988	22.4	65.5	53.2	34.1	1,812	3.72	6,684	3,096	2,394	1,415	702
1989	9.6	76.6	62.2	32.7	2,037	3.72	7,542	2,762	2,225	1,232	536
1990	7.5	77.2	69.3	39.5	2,736	2.61	7,184	3,309	2,443	1,068	866
1991	15.6	69.9	57.7	34.3	1,981	3.00	5,957	2,888	2,416	1,280	472
1992	7.3	72.3	62.4	39.4	2,459	3.24	7,984	3,001	2,472	1,354	529
1993	5.3	72.2	62.6	38.3	2,402	3.20	7,713	3,021	2,423	1,225	598

Source: 1994 Statistical Abstract of the United States on CD-ROM [machine-readable datafiles]. CD-8A-94. Washington, DC: U.S. Department of Commerce, Economics and Statistics Administration, Bureau of the Census, Data User Services Division, January 1995. Primary sources: For production—U.S. Department of Agriculture. National Agricultural Statistics Service. *Crop Production* (annual); and *Crop Values* (annual). For supply and disappearance—U.S. Department of Agriculture. Economic Research Service. *Feed Situation* (quarterly); *Fats and Oils Situation* (quarterly); *Wheat Situation* (quarterly); *Tobacco Situation* (quarterly); *Cotton and Wool Outlook Statistics* (periodic); and *Agricultural Supply and Demand Estimates* (periodic). All data are also in *Agricultural Statistics* (annual) and *Agricultural Outlook* (monthly). *Notes:* 1993 data are preliminary. 1. Acreage set aside under diversion, PIK (payment-in-kind) and acreage reduction programs. 2. Except as noted, marketing year average price. U.S. prices are computed by weighting U.S. monthly prices by estimated monthly marketings and do not include an allowance for outstanding loans and government purchases and payments. 3. Comprises production, imports, and beginning stocks. 4. Includes feed, residual, and other domestic uses not shown separately.

Erosion

★ 197 ★

Sheet and Rill Erosion: 1982-1992

Table shows sheet and rill soil erosion on nonfederal agricultural land.

| Year | Cropland | | | Pasture | | Range | |
	Cultivated (tons per acre per year)	Uncultivated (tons per acre per year)	Total (billion tons per year)	Tons per acre per year	Billion tons per year	Tons per acre per year	Billion tons per year
1982	4.70	1.10	1.73	1.10	0.15	1.20	0.49
1987	4.10	1.20	1.56	1.00	0.13	1.20	0.48
1992	3.50	0.90	1.19	1.00	0.13	1.20	0.47

Source: Executive Office of the President of the United States. *Environmental Quality 24: The Twenty-fourth Annual Report of the Council on Environmental Quality.* Prepared by Ray Clark. Written by Carroll Curtis. Edited by Barry Walsh. Washington, DC: U.S. Government Printing Office, 1994, p. 455. Primary source: U.S. Department of Agriculture. Soil Conservation Service. *Summary Report 1992 National Resources Inventory.* Washington, DC: U.S. Department of Agriculture, Soil Conservation Service, 1994.

★ 198 ★

Erosion

Wind Erosion: 1982-1992

Table shows wind erosion on nonfederal agricultural land.

| Year | Cropland | | | Pasture (million tons per year) | Range (billion tons per year) |
	Cultivated (tons per acre per year)	Uncultivated (tons per acre per year)	Total (billion tons per year)		
1982	3.70	0.50	1.38	13.19	1.92
1987	3.70	0.50	1.30	12.79	1.77
1992	2.90	0.40	0.96	12.59	1.76

Source: Executive Office of the President of the United States. *Environmental Quality 24: The Twenty-fourth Annual Report of the Council on Environmental Quality.* Prepared by Ray Clark. Written by Carroll Curtis. Edited by Barry Walsh. Washington, DC: U.S. Government Printing Office, 1994, p. 455. Primary source: U.S. Department of Agriculture. Soil Conservation Service. *Summary Report 1992 National Resources Inventory.* Washington, DC: U.S. Department of Agriculture, Soil Conservation Service, 1994.

Forest Fires

★ 199 ★

Forest Fire Damage: 1930-1993

Table shows forest fire damage and tree planting; that is, reforestation. Reforestation refers to acres planted in seedlings and direct seeded.

[In million acres]

Year	Forest fire damage	Reforest-ation
1930	52.3	0.14
1940	25.9	0.52
1950	15.5	0.50
1955	8.1	0.78
1960	4.5	2.14
1965	2.7	1.29
1970	3.3	1.60
1975	1.8	1.93
1980	5.3	2.27
1985	5.2	2.70
1990	4.6	2.86
1991	NA	2.56
1992	NA	2.55
1993	NA	2.42

Source: Executive Office of the President of the United States. *Environmental Quality 24: The Twenty-fourth Annual Report of the Council on Environmental Quality.* Prepared by Ray Clark. Written by Carroll Curtis. Edited by Barry Walsh. Washington, DC: U.S. Government Printing Office, 1994, p. 465. Primary sources: U.S. Department of Agriculture. Forest Service. *Wildfire Statistics.* Washington, DC: U.S. Department of Agriculture, annual; U.S. Department of Agriculture. Forest Service. *U.S. Forest Planting Report.* Washington, DC: U.S. Department of Agriculture, annual. *Note:* "NA" stands for "not available."

★ 200 ★

Forest Fires

Forest Fire Management: 1993

Table shows the forest fires of 1993 and the agencies responsible for their management.

Agency	Fires	Acres burned
Bureau of Indian Affairs	3,706	41,205
Bureau of Land Management	1,997	610,353
U.S. Fish and Wildlife Service	421	37,245
National Park Service	608	63,820
States	44,532	787,263
U.S. Forest Service	7,546	257,661
Total	58,810	1,797,547

Source: "Fires Managed by Agency—1993." *Emergency Medical Services* 24, no. 1 (January 1995), p. 46. Primary source: Intelligence reported to the National Interagency Coordination Center (Boise, Idaho).

★ 201 ★

Forest Fires

Wildfires: 1991

Table shows the cause, number, and acreage burned for wildfires in all regions during 1991.

Statistical cause	Number of wildfires	Acres burned
Lightning	5,739	41,173
Equipment	368	5,779
Smoking	401	4,138
Campfire	1,481	19,241
Debris burning	413	29,779
Railroad	48	1,973
Arson	1,281	27,682
Children	152	412
Miscellaneous	1,000	33,363
Total	10,883	163,540

Source: U.S. Department of Agriculture. Forest Service. *1991 National Forest Fire Report.* Prepared by the State and Private Forestry Fire and Aviation Management Staff. Washington, DC: U.S. Department of Agriculture, Forest Service, September 1993, p. 11.

Forest Insects and Disease

★ 202 ★

Forestland Damage, by Insect: 1968-1993

Table shows forestland damaged by insects.

[In million acres]

Year	Eastern spruce budworm	Western spruce budworm	Gypsy moth	Mountain pine beetle	Southern pine beetle
1968	1.3	5.3	0.1	NA	NA
1969	1.2	4.6	0.3	NA	NA
1970	2.0	4.0	1.0	NA	NA
1971	1.6	4.8	1.9	NA	NA
1972	2.8	5.5	1.4	NA	NA
1973	4.2	4.4	1.8	NA	NA
1974	10.8	5.5	0.8	NA	NA
1975	9.2	5.3	0.5	NA	NA
1976	9.1	5.8	0.9	NA	NA
1977	10.3	6.5	1.6	NA	NA
1978	7.7	5.2	1.3	4.0	NA
1979	6.6	5.0	0.6	4.4	15.0
1980	6.6	4.0	5.0	4.7	12.1
1981	4.5	5.5	12.9	4.7	0.9
1982	4.2	8.7	8.2	4.2	7.3
1983	6.5	11.0	2.4	3.6	11.4
1984	6.1	10.6	1.0	3.3	NA
1985	5.2	12.8	1.7	3.3	15.5
1986	1.0	13.2	2.4	3.5	26.4
1987	0.8	8.0	1.3	2.4	13.8
1988	0.3	6.1	0.7	2.2	7.9
1989	0.2	3.1	3.0	1.6	5.3
1990	0.2	4.6	7.3	0.9	4.2
1991	0.1	7.2	4.2	0.6	10.7
1992	0.1	4.6	3.1	15.8	14.3
1993	0.1	0.4	1.4	0.8	10.4

Source: Executive Office of the President of the United States. *Environmental Quality 24: The Twenty-fourth Annual Report of the Council on Environmental Quality.* Prepared by Ray Clark. Written by Carroll Curtis. Edited by Barry Walsh. Washington, DC: U.S. Government Printing Office, 1994, p. 466. Primary sources: U.S. Department of Agriculture. Forest Service. *Forest Insect and Disease Conditions in the United States, 1979-1983.* Washington, DC: U.S. Department of Agriculture, Forest Service, 1985; U.S. Department of Agriculture. Forest Service. *Forest Insect and Disease Conditions in the United States.* Washington, DC: U.S. Department of Agriculture, Forest Service, annual from 1986. *Notes:* "NA" stands for "not available." Acreage for mountain pine beetle in 1992 includes 15.2 million acres in California not previously reported.

★ 203 ★

Forest Insects and Disease

Gypsy Moth Defoliation: 1988-1992

According to the source: "Just over 3 million acres of forests and trees were defoliated by gypsy moth in 1992. This is the second year of decline following the 7.3 million acres that were defoliated in 1990" (p. 3). Table shows acres of aerially detected defoliation for selected states.

State	1992	1991	1990	1989	1988
Connecticut	31,637	50,154	176,576	78,430	1,600
Delaware	4,943	13,475	3,790	1,888	800
Maine	278,485	614,509	270,433	35,000	100
Maryland	38,704	75,197	133,062	97,911	58,500
Massachusetts	123,794	282,143	83,595	950	0
Michigan	712,227	626,689	358,338	294,344	70,400
New Hampshire	182,575	180,870	133,200	18,395	1,000
New Jersey	165,960	169,900	431,235	137,310	7,400
New York	60,022	175,960	354,162	421,138	5,700
Ohio	1,130	345	115	0	-
Pennsylvania	641,445	1,230,066	4,357,700	1,506,790	312,100
Rhode Island	0	0	0	0	700
Vermont	83	3,596	63,000	27,335	700
Virginia	748,000	616,200	594,000	289,332	191,000
Washington, DC	0	125	10	0	0
West Virginia	67,508	112,900	345,078	86,736	59,300
Total	3,056,513	4,152,129	7,304,294	2,995,559	709,300

Source: U.S. Department of Agriculture. Forest Service. Forest Pest Management. *Forest Insect and Disease Conditions in the United States, 1992.* Washington, DC: U.S. Department of Agriculture, Forest Service, Forest Pest Management, November 1993, p. 4. *Note:* "-" indicates data not reported in source.

★ 204 ★

Forest Insects and Disease

Mountain Pine Beetle Damage: 1988-1992

Mountain pine beetle-affected acreage increased in 1992 to 641,400 acres from 617,000 acres affected in 1991. Table below shows acreage affected by mountain pine beetles.

State	1992	1991	1990	1989	1988
Arizona	0	0	600	900	600
Colorado	0	1,500	9,800	12,000	13,000
Idaho	22,400	22,500	15,200	41,600	42,300
Montana	65,900	160,000	195,200	421,500	546,700
New Mexico	1,200	1,400	800	1,000	1,000
Oregon	303,000	249,600	245,100	887,926	1,311,400
South Dakota	13,600	10,000	6,800	2,400	2,600

[Continued]

★ 204 ★

Mountain Pine Beetle Damage: 1988-1992
[Continued]

State	1992	1991	1990	1989	1988
Utah	4,100	1,300	2,000	4,500	12,500
Washington	125,200	155,400	431,700	231,375	220,300
Wyoming	106,000	15,400	28,300	11,400	55,600
Total	641,400	617,100	935,500	1,614,601	2,206,000

Source: U.S. Department of Agriculture. Forest Service. Forest Pest Management. *Forest Insect and Disease Conditions in the United States, 1992.* Washington, DC: U.S. Department of Agriculture, Forest Service, Forest Pest Management, November 1993, p. 10.

★ 205 ★

Forest Insects and Disease

Southern Pine Beetle Outbreak: 1988-1992

Southern pine beetle-affected acreage increased 33 percent between 1991 and 1992 following a 150 percent increase between 1990 and 1991. The table shows the acres of outbreak; that is, acres of host type having one or more multiple-tree spots per 1,000 acres.

State	1992	1991	1990	1989	1988
Alabama	5,815,700	3,937,100	0	724,000	4,762,400
Arkansas	55,800	0	0	0	0
Georgia	870,985	346,500	0	850,000	1,057,400
Louisiana	3,112,400	1,197,600	0	17,000	17,000
Mississippi	406,100	1,278,400	0	319,000	715,100
North Carolina	334,251	40,067	111,358	342,000	497,000
South Carolina	469,188	2,413,632	2,320,664	753,000	609,100
Tennessee	45,900	0	0	427,000	278,100
Texas	2,663,300	1,495,900	1,800,000	1,901,000	0
Virginia	533,580	35,045	0	0	0
Total	14,307,204	10,744,244	4,232,022	5,333,000	7,936,100

Source: U.S. Department of Agriculture. Forest Service. Forest Pest Management. *Forest Insect and Disease Conditions in the United States, 1992.* Washington, DC: U.S. Department of Agriculture, Forest Service, Forest Pest Management, November 1993, p. 8.

★ 206 ★

Forest Insects and Disease

Spruce Budworm Defoliation: 1988-1992

Spruce budworm population remained low in 1992. Table shows acres of aerially detected defoliation.

State	1992	1991	1990	1989	1988
Maine	0	0	0	4,800	65,000
Michigan	0	0	2,500	0	0
Minnesota	126,000	108,000	198,000	140,000	200,000
Total	126,000	108,000	200,500	144,800	265,000

Source: U.S. Department of Agriculture. Forest Service. Forest Pest Management. *Forest Insect and Disease Conditions in the United States, 1992.* Washington, DC: U.S. Department of Agriculture, Forest Service, Forest Pest Management, November 1993, p. 9.

★ 207 ★

Forest Insects and Disease

Western Spruce Budworm Defoliation: 1988-1992

Western spruce budworm defoliation decreased to 4.6 million acres in 1992 from 7.2 million acres recorded in 1991. Table shows acres of aerially detected defoliation.

State	1992	1991	1990	1989	1988
Arizona	11,500	0	25,600	720	5,800
Colorado	272,200	509,000	52,100	52,000	427,000
Idaho	89,800	61,500	48,000	26,600	61,000
Montana	941,300	1,595,733	1,492,400	1,191,300	2,064,000
New Mexico	9,400	218,610	310,500	90,080	477,700
Oregon	1,937,700	3,724,900	2,344,300	1,416,681	2,740,400
Washington	1,329,500	1,027,700	351,000	362,251	231,600
Wyoming	2,500	33,500	8,100	0	55,800
Total	4,593,900	7,170,943	4,632,000	3,139,632	6,063,300

Source: U.S. Department of Agriculture. Forest Service. Forest Pest Management. *Forest Insect and Disease Conditions in the United States, 1992.* Washington, DC: U.S. Department of Agriculture, Forest Service, Forest Pest Management, November 1993, p. 13.

Forests and Trees

★ 208 ★

Forest and Timberland Area: 1952-1992

Table shows the acreage of total forest land, timberland ownership, and sawtimber and growing stock volumes as of January 1.

Year and division	Total forest land (million acres)	Timberland, ownership[1]					Sawtimber, net volume[3]		Growing stock, net volume[4]	
		All owner-ship (million acres)	Federally owned or managed (million acres)	State, county, and municipal (million acres)	Private		Total (billion board feet)	Softwood (billion board feet)	Total (billion cubic feet)	Softwood (billion cubic feet)
					Total (million acres)	Percent of total				
United States, 1952	664	509	118	27	363	71.4	2,563	2,095	616	432
North	(NA)	154	11	18	125	81.1	222	57	104	27
South	(NA)	205	15	3	187	91.5	453	204	148	60
Rocky Mountains	(NA)	67	44	2	20	30.2	394	381	93	88
Pacific Coast	(NA)	83	48	4	31	37.2	1,494	1,453	271	257
United States, 1962	759	515	119	27	369	71.6	2,581	2,069	666	450
North	(NA)	157	11	18	128	81.8	259	60	128	34
South	(NA)	209	15	3	191	91.5	517	257	174	75
Rocky Mountains	(NA)	67	45	2	20	29.7	403	390	99	93
Pacific Coast	(NA)	83	49	4	30	36.2	1,401	1,353	264	248
United States, 1970	754	504	116	29	360	71.4	2,587	2,035	694	458
North	(NA)	154	11	18	126	81.4	295	81	146	39
South	(NA)	203	15	3	185	91.0	569	302	191	87
Rocky Mountains	(NA)	65	42	2	20	30.6	398	384	101	95
Pacific Coast	(NA)	82	47	5	29	35.9	1,325	1,268	257	238
United States, 1977	737	492	107	31	354	71.9	2,665	2,029	733	467
North	162	153	10	18	125	81.4	340	95	163	44
South	219	200	15	3	181	90.8	678	354	223	101
Rocky Mountains	141	60	38	2	20	32.5	395	381	101	95
Pacific Coast	214	79	43	7	29	36.1	1,252	1,199	245	227
United States, 1987	731	485	97	34	354	73.0	2,853	2,040	766	453
North	165	154	11	19	124	80.6	459	126	190	48
South	203	197	16	4	177	89.9	781	388	245	106
Rocky Mountains	142	61	39	3	20	32.3	411	394	108	100
Pacific Coast	220	72	31	8	32	44.9	1,202	1,132	223	199
United States, 1992	737	490	97	35	358	73.1	2,992	2,047	786	450
North	168	158	11	19	127	80.8	540	137	207	51
South	212	199	16	4	179	89.7	842	389	251	103
Rocky Mountains	140	63	40	3	20	32.3	415	397	110	101
Pacific Coast	217	70	30	8	32	45.1	1,196	1,124	218	195

Source: 1994 Statistical Abstract of the United States on CD-ROM [machine-readable datafiles]. CD-8A-94. Washington, DC: U.S. Department of Commerce, Economics and Statistics Administration, Bureau of the Census, Data User Services Division, January 1995. Primary source: U.S. Forest Service. *Forest Resources of the United States, 1992. Notes:* "NA" represents "not available." 1. Timberland is forest land that is producing or is capable of crops of industrial wood and not withdrawn from timber utilization by statute or administrative regulation. Areas qualifying as timberland have the capability of producing in excess of 20 cubic feet per acre per year of industrial wood in natural stands. Currently inaccessible and inoperable areas are included. 2. Includes Indian lands. 3. Sawtimber is timber suitable for sawing into lumber. Live trees of commercial species contain at least one 12-foot sawlog or two noncontiguous 8-foot logs, and meet regional specifications for freedom from defect. Softwood trees must be at least 9.0-inches diameter, and hardwood trees must be at least 11.0-inches diameter at 4 1/2 feet above ground. International 1/4-inch rule. 4. Live trees of commercial species meeting specified standards of quality or vigor. Cull trees are excluded. Includes only trees 5.0-inches diameter or larger at 4 1/2 feet above ground.

★ 209 ★

Forests and Trees

National Forest System

For fiscal years ending in year shown.

Item	Unit	1970	1980	1985	1990	1991	1992
Timber cut, total value	Million dollars	309	737	725	1,191	1,012	938
Commercial and cost sales:[1]							
Volume	Million board feet	11,527	9,178	10,941	10,500	8,475	7,290
Value	Million dollars	308	730	721	1,188	1,009	935
Free use:							
Volume	Million board feet	179	2,070	399	151	121	80
Value[2]	Million dollars	0.3	5.7	2.2	1.0	1.0	0.8
Misc. forest products:							
Value	Million dollars	0.7	1.1	1.7	2.6	2.7	2.7
Livestock grazing:[3]							
Cattle and horses[4]	1,000	1,521	1,565	1,236	1,265	(NA)	1,607
Sheep and goats	1,000	1,328	1,183	958	1,029	(NA)	2,105
Roads and trails:							
Road construction[5]	Miles	925	1,903	857	910	853	942
Trail construction [6]	Miles	2,419	987	1,635	1,921	1,976	278
Receipts, total	Million dollars	300	703	636	971	772	614
Timber use	Million dollars	284	625	515	849	667	520
Grazing use	Million dollars	4	16	9	10	11	11
Special land use, etc	Million dollars	11	62	112	112	93	84
Payments to local govt.[7]	Million dollars	73	240	229	368	335	(NA)
25-percent fund[8]	Million dollars	72	234	212	358	327	(NA)
Other[9]	Million dollars	1	7	17	10	8	(NA)
Allotments to Forest Service, total[10]	Million dollars	30	73	60	106	88	(NA)
Roads and trails	Million dollars	29	65	55	91	73	(NA)
Other	Million dollars	1	8	5	14	16	(NA)

Source: 1994 Statistical Abstract of the United States on CD-ROM [machine-readable datafiles]. CD-8A-94. Washington, DC: U.S. Department of Commerce, Economics and Statistics Administration, Bureau of the Census, Data User Services Division, January 1995. Primary sources: U.S. Forest Service. In *Agricultural Statistics* (annual); and unpublished data. *Notes:* "NA" represents "not available." 1. Includes land exchanges. 2. Includes some free use timber not reducible to board feet. 3. For 1970, data for livestock permitted to graze; 1980-1990 for number actually grazed. Calendar-year data, prior to 1980. Excludes Puerto Rico. 4. Excludes animals under 6 months of age. 1970 includes swine. Includes burros beginning in 1980. 5. Includes reconstruction. 6. Beginning 1980, includes work accomplished by Human Resource Programs and volunteers. Also includes reconstruction. 7. Payments made in following year. 8. Includes Tongass Alaska suspense account. 9. Includes Arizona and New Mexico School Fund (through 1982), State of Minnesota, and receipts paid to counties under Bankhead-Jones Farm Tenant Act. 10. For use in following year.

★ 210 ★
Forests and Trees

National Forest System – Forests and Land: 1891- 1993

Year	Forests (number)	Land (million acres)
1891	1	1.24
1895	17	17.93
1900	38	46.52
1905	83	75.35
1910	149	168.03
1915	162	162.77
1920	152	156.03
1925	159	158.40
1930	149	160.09
1935	142	163.31
1940	160	174.77
1945	155	177.64
1950	151	179.69
1955	149	180.30
1960	151	180.84
1965	154	182.14
1970	154	182.57
1975	155	183.28
1980	155	183.06
1985	156	186.31
1990	156	187.08
1993	155	187.23

Source: Executive Office of the President of the United States. *Environmental Quality 24: The Twenty-fourth Annual Report of the Council on Environmental Quality.* Prepared by Ray Clark. Written by Carroll Curtis. Edited by Barry Walsh. Washington, DC: U.S. Government Printing Office, 1994, p. 473. Primary source: U.S. Department of Agriculture. Forest Service. *Land Areas of the National Forest System.* Washington, DC: U.S. Department of Agriculture, Forest Service, annual.

★ 211 ★
Forests and Trees

National Forest System Land, by State: 1990-1991

As of September 30.

[In thousand acres]

State	Gross area within unit boundaries[1]		National Forest System land[2]		Other lands within unit boundaries	
	1990	1991	1990	1991	1990	1991
United States	231,443	231,502	191,324	191,453	40,119	40,049
Alabama	1,280	1,288	658	659	622	629
Alaska	24,345	24,345	22,220	22,193	2,126	2,152
Arizona	11,880	11,887	11,239	11,247	642	641
Arkansas	3,490	3,490	2,509	2,529	981	961
California	24,401	24,401	20,619	20,616	3,782	3,785
Colorado	16,039	16,037	14,462	14,467	1,577	1,570
Connecticut	0	(Z)	0	(Z)	0	0
Delaware	0	0	0	0	0	0
Florida	1,246	1,254	1,128	1,135	118	119
Georgia	1,846	1,846	859	860	987	986
Hawaii	0	(Z)	0	(Z)	0	0
Idaho	21,674	21,674	20,438	20,441	1,236	1,233
Illinois	840	840	266	268	573	572
Indiana	644	644	188	189	456	455
Iowa	0	0	0	0	0	0
Kansas	116	116	108	108	8	8
Kentucky	2,102	2,102	670	673	1,431	1,428
Louisiana	1,022	1,022	601	601	422	421
Maine	93	93	53	53	40	40
Maryland	0	0	0	0	0	0
Massachusetts	0	0	0	0	0	0
Michigan	4,885	4,895	2,816	2,849	2,069	2,046
Minnesota	5,467	5,467	2,810	2,815	2,657	2,652
Mississippi	2,310	2,310	1,150	1,153	1,160	1,157
Missouri	3,082	3,082	1,475	1,478	1,606	1,603
Montana	19,101	19,102	16,806	16,806	2,295	2,296
Nebraska	442	442	352	352	90	90
Nevada	6,275	6,275	5,797	5,801	478	474
New Hampshire	825	825	720	721	105	104
New Jersey	0	0	0	0	0	0
New Mexico	10,367	10,367	9,321	9,321	1,046	1,045
New York	13	13	13	13	0	0
North Carolina	3,165	3,165	1,232	1,234	1,934	1,932
North Dakota	1,106	1,106	1,106	1,106	0	(Z)
Ohio	833	833	203	212	630	622
Oklahoma	461	465	297	301	165	164
Oregon	17,502	17,504	15,651	15,655	1,851	1,849
Pennsylvania	744	744	513	513	231	231
Rhode Island	0	0	0	0	0	0
South Carolina	1,376	1,376	607	609	768	767
South Dakota	2,344	2,352	1,996	2,013	349	339
Tennessee	1,212	1,212	628	628	585	585

[Continued]

★ 211 ★

National Forest System Land, by State: 1990-1991
[Continued]

State	Gross area within unit boundaries[1]		National Forest System land[2]		Other lands within unit boundaries	
	1990	1991	1990	1991	1990	1991
Texas	1,994	1,994	753	755	1,241	1,240
Utah	9,186	9,186	8,099	8,099	1,087	1,087
Vermont	815	816	340	345	475	471
Virginia	3,223	3,223	1,645	1,648	1,578	1,575
Washington	10,050	10,061	9,151	9,160	899	901
West Virginia	1,863	1,863	1,025	1,025	838	838
Wisconsin	2,023	2,023	1,517	1,518	506	505
Wyoming	9,704	9,704	9,255	9,255	449	449

Source: 1994 Statistical Abstract of the United States on CD-ROM [machine-readable datafiles]. CD-8A-94. Washington, DC: U.S. Department of Commerce, Economics and Statistics Administration, Bureau of the Census, Data User Services Division, January 1995. Primary source: U.S. Forest Service. *Land Areas of the National Forest System* (annual). *Notes:* "Z" indicates less than 500 acres. 1. Comprises all publicly and privately owned land within authorized boundaries of national forests, purchase units, national grasslands, land utilization projects, research and experimental areas, and other areas. 2. Federally owned land within the "gross area within unit boundaries."

★ 212 ★

Forests and Trees

Timberland, by Owner: 1952-1992

Table shows timberland ownership in the United States.

[In million acres]

Year	Farmer	Other private	Forest industry	National forests	Other public	Total
1952	172.8	124.3	59.0	94.7	50.7	508.9
1962	143.6	157.6	61.4	96.8	49.3	515.1
1977	114.5	163.5	68.9	88.7	49.5	491.1
1987	95.8	187.8	70.3	85.2	45.8	484.9
1992	82.5	205.1	70.5	84.7	46.8	489.6

Source: Executive Office of the President of the United States. *Environmental Quality 24: The Twenty-fourth Annual Report of the Council on Environmental Quality.* Prepared by Ray Clark. Written by Carroll Curtis. Edited by Barry Walsh. Washington, DC: U.S. Government Printing Office, 1994, p. 462. Primary source: U.S. Department of Agriculture. Forest Service. *Forest Statistics of the United States, 1992.* General Technical Report RM-234. Washington, DC: U.S. Department of Agriculture, Forest Service, 1993.

★ 213 ★
Forests and Trees

Tree Planting – Federal Land, by State: 1992-1993

Table shows the acreage of tree planting, including seeding, on federal land from October 1, 1992, through September 30, 1993.

State	National Forest System	Department of the Interior	Other federal	Total
Alabama	4,036	0	707	4,743
Alaska	879	0	0	879
Arizona	1,365	494	0	1,859
Arkansas	4,124	295	839	5,258
California	44,254	433	23	44,710
Colorado	701	186	20	907
Connecticut	0	0	17	17
Delaware	0	0	0	0
Florida	6,637	15	4,643	11,295
Georgia	2,240	100	531	2,871
Hawaii	0	0	0	0
Idaho	39,962	584	0	40,546
Illinois	0	30	110	140
Indiana	0	5	21	26
Iowa	0	0	128	128
Kansas	0	0	98	98
Kentucky	706	0	87	793
Louisiana	4,047	55	245	4,347
Maine	0	2	0	2
Maryland	0	0	0	0
Massachusetts	0	0	15	15
Michigan	3,843	180	42	4,065
Minnesota	2,200	789	2	2,991
Mississippi	10,818	90	848	11,756
Missouri	466	70	374	910
Montana	24,231	1,403	1	25,635
Nebraska	0	127	30	157
Nevada	5	91	0	96
New Hampshire	5	0	0	5
New Jersey	0	0	50	50
New Mexico	1,505	1,220	0	2,725
New York	10	0	82	92
North Carolina	2,416	200	499	3,115
North Dakota	0	155	49	204
Ohio	116	0	47	163
Oklahoma	692	171	83	946
Oregon	76,593	20,853	0	97,446
Pennsylvania	142	0	59	201
Rhode Island	0	0	0	0
South Carolina	5,211	0	2,679	7,890
South Dakota	0	80	308	388
Tennessee	1,194	10	301	1,505
Texas	1,751	90	670	2,511

[Continued]

★ 213 ★

Tree Planting – Federal Land, by State: 1992-1993
[Continued]

State	National Forest System	Department of the Interior	Other federal	Total
Utah	1,471	0	0	1,471
Vermont	98	0	0	98
Virginia	736	0	489	1,225
Washington	21,233	5,649	226	27,108
West Virginia	134	0	30	164
Wisconsin	1,212	1,504	56	2,772
Wyoming	1,667	58	0	1,725
Total	266,700	34,939	14,409	316,048

Source: U.S. Department of Agriculture. Forest Service. State and Private Forestry. *Tree Planting in the United States, 1993.* Washington, DC: U.S. Department of Agriculture, Forest Service, State and Private Forestry, 1993, p. 10.

★ 214 ★

Forests and Trees

Tree Planting – Non-Federal Land, by State: 1992-1993

Table shows the acreage of tree planting, including seeding, on non-federal land from October 1, 1992, through September 30, 1993.

State	State forest land	Other state land	Local government	Total
Alabama	193	-	-	193
Alaska	789	55	224	1,068
Arizona	-	-	5	5
Arkansas	0	1,344	80	1,424
California	200	120	12	332
Colorado	23	62	26	111
Connecticut	18	-	-	18
Delaware	-	-	-	-
Florida	1,365	1,208	0	2,573
Georgia	314	-	30	344
Hawaii	35	-	-	35
Idaho	2,844	0	400	3,244
Illinois	-	-	-	-
Indiana	-	40	-	40
Iowa	319	76	242	637
Kansas	-	2	-	2
Kentucky	0	19	0	19
Louisiana	20	850	-	870
Maine	-	-	-	-
Maryland	106	140	176	422
Massachusetts	-	-	-	-

[Continued]

★ 214 ★

Tree Planting – Non-Federal Land, by State: 1992-1993
[Continued]

State	State forest land	Other state land	Local government	Total
Michigan	4,505	10	1,000	5,515
Minnesota	7,410	-	3,600	11,010
Mississippi	-	6,893	1,362	8,255
Missouri	-	-	-	-
Montana	300	-	-	300
Nebraska	-	285	40	325
Nevada	-	37	30	67
New Hampshire	-	-	-	-
New Jersey	-	-	-	-
New Mexico	0	0	0	0
New York	-	-	-	-
North Carolina	30	207	-	237
North Dakota	5	201	-	206
Ohio	216	-	-	216
Oklahoma	0	0	0	0
Oregon	4,395	0	0	4,395
Pennsylvania	-	-	-	-
Rhode Island	-	-	-	-
South Carolina	674	466	19	1,159
South Dakota	0	0	0	0
Tennessee	46	158	-	204
Texas	0	8	0	8
Utah	5	-	-	5
Vermont	-	-	-	-
Virginia	350	450	-	800
Washington	11,721	-	1,222	12,943
West Virginia	-	-	-	-
Wisconsin	912	215	4,194	5,321
Wyoming	-	-	-	-
Total[1]	36,828	12,847	12,753	62,428

Source: U.S. Department of Agriculture. Forest Service. State and Private Forestry. *Tree Planting in the United States, 1993.* Washington, DC: U.S. Department of Agriculture, Forest Service, State and Private Forestry, 1993, p. 11. *Notes:* "-" indicates data not available. 1. Total includes figures for U.S. territories and holdings; for example, Guam, Puerto Rico, and Palau.

★ 215 ★

Forests and Trees

Tree Planting – Private Land, by State: 1992-1993

Table shows the acreage of tree planting, including seeding, on private land from October 1, 1992, through September 30, 1993.

State	Nonindustrial private	Forest industry	Other industry	Total
Alabama	94,972	116,367	-	211,339
Alaska	305	-	-	305
Arizona	374	236	-	610
Arkansas	50,290	45,328	0	95,618
California	9,650	16,550	385	26,585
Colorado	5,510	-	18	5,528
Connecticut	310	-	-	310
Delaware	2,848	1,100	-	3,948
Florida	66,167	124,733	0	190,900
Georgia	171,189	110,078	-	281,267
Hawaii	81	-	-	81
Idaho	1,281	7,952	0	9,233
Illinois	8,271	-	-	8,271
Indiana	4,069	34	1,271	5,374
Iowa	7,897	-	-	7,897
Kansas	2,019	5	-	2,024
Kentucky	8,780	1,235	2,062	12,077
Louisiana	29,800	115,000	-	144,800
Maine	1,120	7,000	-	8,120
Maryland	5,726	1,624	-	7,350
Massachusetts	265	-	-	265
Michigan	5,993	4,000	1,000	10,993
Minnesota	12,942	2,132	-	15,074
Mississippi	158,286	85,967	-	244,253
Missouri	11,258	-	-	11,258
Montana	117	9,405	-	9,522
Nebraska	6,300	-	-	6,300
Nevada	247	-	20	267
New Hampshire	168	-	-	168
New Jersey	568	-	-	568
New Mexico	169	0	0	169
New York	993	-	-	993
North Carolina	68,938	38,809	1,800	109,547
North Dakota	5,565	-	-	5,565
Ohio	2,291	1,714	-	4,005
Oklahoma	6,525	8,000	0	14,525
Oregon	19,039	73,827	0	92,866
Pennsylvania	671	-	-	671
Rhode Island	155	-	-	155
South Carolina	47,881	69,911	1,285	119,077
South Dakota	4,392	0	0	4,392
Tennessee	3,928	18,576	-	22,504
Texas	33,018	77,386	0	110,404
Utah	64	-	-	64

[Continued]

★ 215 ★

Tree Planting – Private Land, by State: 1992-1993
[Continued]

State	Nonindustrial private	Forest industry	Other industry	Total
Vermont	170	-	-	170
Virginia	57,427	30,782	-	88,209
Washington	61,124	62,267	-	123,391
West Virginia	1,843	1,450	-	3,293
Wisconsin	16,480	3,909	-	20,389
Wyoming	128	-	-	128
Total[1]	997,997	1,035,377	7,841	2,041,215

Source: U.S. Department of Agriculture. Forest Service. State and Private Forestry. *Tree Planting in the United States, 1993.* Washington, DC: U.S. Department of Agriculture, Forest Service, State and Private Forestry, 1993, p. 12. *Notes:* "-" indicates data not available. 1. Total includes figures for U.S. territories and holdings; for example, Guam, Puerto Rico, and Palau.

★ 216 ★

Forests and Trees

Tropical Rainforest's Medicinal Plants

According to the source: "Forty million acres of tropical rainforest ... are being cut and cleared every year.... Less than 1 percent of 250,000 known tropical rainforest plants have been screened for use in life-saving drugs" (p. 40).

Source: "Hold Your Own Earth Summit." *EPA Journal* 19, no. 2 (April-June 1993), p. 40.

Land Area

★ 217 ★

Elevations – Highest Points, by State

Table shows the highest points in each state. Territories and other areas are shown as well. Data are arranged alphabetically by state or area.

Elevation (state or area)	Feet	Meters
Cheaha Mountain (Alabama)	2,405	733
Mount McKinley (Alaska)[1]	20,320	6,198
Humphreys Peak (Arizona)	12,633	3,853
Magazine Mountain (Arkansas)	2,753	840

[Continued]

★217★

Elevations – Highest Points, by State
[Continued]

Elevation (state or area)	Feet	Meters
Mount Whitney (California)	14,494	4,419
Mt. Elbert (Colorado)	14,433	4,402
Mt. Frissell on South slope (Connecticut)	2,380	726
Ebright Road, New Castle County (Delaware)[2]	442	135
Tenleytown at Reno Reservoir (District of Columbia)	410	125
Sec. 30, T6N, R20W, Walton County (Florida)[3]	345	105
Brasstown Bald (Georgia)	4,784	1,459
Puu Wekiu (Hawaii)	13,796	4,208
Borah Peak (Idaho)	12,662	3,862
Charles Mound (Illinois)	1,235	377
Franklin Twp., Wayne County (Indiana)	1,257	383
Sec. 29, T100N, R41W, Osceola County (Iowa)[3]	1,670	509
Mount Sunflower (Kansas)	4,039	1,232
Black Mountain (Kentucky)	4,139	2,162
Driskill Mountain (Louisiana)	535	163
Mount Katahdin (Maine)	5,267	1,606
Backbone Mountain (Maryland)	3,360	1,025
Mount Greylock (Massachusetts)	3,487	1,064
Mount Arvon (Michigan)	1,979	604
Eagle Mountain, Cook County (Minnesota)	2,301	702
Woodall Mountain (Mississippi)	806	246
Taum Sauk Mountain (Missouri)	1,772	540
Granite Peak (Montana)	12,799	3,904
Johnson Twp., Kimball County (Nebraska)	5,424	1,654
Boundary Peak (Nevada)	13,140	4,007
Mount Washington (New Hampshire)	6,288	1,918
High Point (New Jersey)	1,803	550
Wheeler Peak (New Mexico)	13,161	4,014
Mount Marcy (New York)	5,344	1,630
Mount Mitchell (North Carolina)	6,684	2,039
White Butte, Slope County (North Dakota)	3,506	1,069
Campbell Hill (Ohio)	1,549	472
Black Mesa (Oklahoma)	4,973	1,517
Mount Hood (Oregon)	11,239	3,428
Mount Davis (Pennsylvania)	3,213	980
Jerimoth Hill (Rhode Island)	812	248
Sassafras Mountain (South Carolina)	3,560	1,086
Harney Peak (South Dakota)	7,242	2,209
Clingmans Dome (Tennessee)	6,643	2,026
Guadalupe Peak (Texas)	8,749	2,668
Kings Peak (Utah)	13,528	4,126
Mount Mansfield (Vermont)	4,393	1,340
Mount Rogers (Virginia)	5,729	1,747
Mount Rainier (Washington)	14,410	4,395
Spruce Knob (West Virginia)	4,861	1,483
Timms Hill (Wisconsin)	1,951	595
Gannett Peak (Wyoming)	13,804	4,210

[Continued]

★ 217 ★

Elevations – Highest Points, by State
[Continued]

Elevation (state or area)	Feet	Meters
Other areas:		
Lata Mountain (American Samoa)	3,160	964
Mount Lamlam (Guam)	1,332	406
Cerro de Punta (Puerto Rico)	4,390	1,339
Crown Mountain (Virgin Islands)	1,556	475

Source: 1994 Statistical Abstract of the United States on CD-ROM [machine-readable datafiles]. CD-8A-94. Washington, DC: U.S. Department of Commerce, Economics and Statistics Administration, Bureau of the Census, Data User Services Division, January 1995. Primary source: U.S. Geological Survey. *Elevations and Distances in the United States* (1989). *Notes:* One foot equals .305 meter. "Twp." stands for "township." 1. Highest point in the United States. 2. At Delaware-Pennsylvania state line. 3. "Sec." denotes section; "T," township; "R," range; "N," north; "W," west.

★ 218 ★

Land Area

Elevations – Lowest Points, by State

Table shows the lowest points in each state. Territories and other areas are shown as well. Data are arranged alphabetically by state or area.

Elevation (state or area)	Feet	Meters
Gulf of Mexico (Alabama)	[1]	[1]
Pacific Ocean (Alaska)	[1]	[1]
Colorado River (Arizona)	70	21
Ouachita River (Arkansas)	55	17
Death Valley (California)[2]	-282	-86
Arkansas River (Colorado)	3,350	1,022
Long Island Sound (Connecticut)	[1]	[1]
Atlantic Ocean (Delaware)	[1]	[1]
Potomac River (District of Columbia)	1	(Z)
Atlantic Ocean (Florida)	[1]	[1]
Atlantic Ocean (Georgia)	[1]	[1]
Pacific Ocean (Hawaii)	[1]	[1]
Snake River (Idaho)	710	217
Mississippi River (Illinois)	279	85
Ohio River (Indiana)	320	98
Mississippi River (Iowa)	480	146
Verdigris River (Kansas)	679	207
Mississippi River (Kentucky)	257	78
New Orleans (Louisiana)	-8	-2
Atlantic Ocean (Maine)	[1]	[1]
Atlantic Ocean (Maryland)	[1]	[1]
Atlantic Ocean (Massachusetts)	[1]	[1]
Lake Erie (Michigan)	571	174
Lake Superior (Minnesota)	600	183
Gulf of Mexico (Mississippi)	[1]	[1]
St. Francis River (Missouri)	230	70

[Continued]

★218★

Elevations – Lowest Points, by State

[Continued]

Elevation (state or area)	Feet	Meters
Kootenai River (Montana)	1,800	549
Missouri River (Nebraska)	840	256
Colorado River (Nevada)	479	146
Atlantic Ocean (New Hampshire)	1	1
Atlantic Ocean (New Jersey)	1	1
Red Bluff Reservoir (New Mexico)	2,842	867
Atlantic Ocean (New York)	1	1
Atlantic Ocean (North Carolina)	1	1
Red River (North Dakota)	750	229
Ohio River (Ohio)	455	139
Little River (Oklahoma)	289	88
Pacific Ocean (Oregon)	1	1
Delaware River (Pennsylvania)	1	1
Atlantic Ocean (Rhode Island)	1	1
Atlantic Ocean (South Carolina)	1	1
Big Stone Lake (South Dakota)	966	295
Mississippi River (Tennessee)	178	54
Gulf of Mexico (Texas)	1	1
Beaverdam Wash (Utah)	2,000	610
Lake Champlain (Vermont)	95	29
Atlantic Ocean (Virginia)	1	1
Pacific Ocean (Washington)	1	1
Potomac River (West Virginia)	240	73
Lake Michigan (Wisconsin)	579	177
Belle Fourche River (Wyoming)	3,099	945
Other areas:		
Pacific Ocean (American Samoa)	1	1
Pacific Ocean (Guam)	1	1
Atlantic Ocean (Puerto Rico)	1	1
Atlantic Ocean (Virgin Islands)	1	1

Source: *1994 Statistical Abstract of the United States on CD-ROM* [machine-readable datafiles]. CD-8A-94. Washington, DC: U.S. Department of Commerce, Economics and Statistics Administration, Bureau of the Census, Data User Services Division, January 1995. Primary source: U.S. Geological Survey. *Elevations and Distances in the United States* (1989). *Notes:* One foot equals .305 meter. "Z" represents less than .5 meter. 1. Sea level. 2. Lowest point in the United States.

★ 219 ★

Land Area

Elevations – Mean Elevations, by State

Table shows the mean elevations in each state. Territories and other areas are shown as well.

State or other area	Feet	Meters
United States	2,500	763
Alabama	500	153
Alaska	1,900	580
Arizona	4,100	1,251
Arkansas	650	198
California	2,900	885
Colorado	6,800	2,074
Connecticut	500	153
Delaware	60	18
District of Columbia	150	46
Florida	100	31
Georgia	600	183
Hawaii	3,030	924
Idaho	5,000	1,525
Illinois	600	183
Indiana	700	214
Iowa	1,100	336
Kansas	2,000	610
Kentucky	750	229
Louisiana	100	31
Maine	600	183
Maryland	350	107
Massachusetts	500	153
Michigan	900	275
Minnesota	1,200	366
Mississippi	300	92
Missouri	800	244
Montana	3,400	1,037
Nebraska	2,600	793
Nevada	5,500	1,678
New Hampshire	1,000	305
New Jersey	250	76
New Mexico	5,700	1,739
New York	1,000	305
North Carolina	700	214
North Dakota	1,900	580
Ohio	850	259
Oklahoma	1,300	397
Oregon	3,300	1,007
Pennsylvania	1,100	336
Rhode Island	200	61
South Carolina	350	107
South Dakota	2,200	671

[Continued]

★ 219 ★

Elevations – Mean Elevations, by State
[Continued]

State or other area	Feet	Meters
Tennessee	900	275
Texas	1,700	519
Utah	6,100	1,861
Vermont	1,000	305
Virginia	950	290
Washington	1,700	519
West Virginia	1,500	458
Wisconsin	1,050	320
Wyoming	6,700	2,044
Other areas:		
American Samoa	1,300	397
Guam	330	101
Puerto Rico	1,800	549
Virgin Islands	750	229

Source: 1994 Statistical Abstract of the United States on CD-ROM [machine-readable datafiles]. CD-8A-94. Washington, DC: U.S. Department of Commerce, Economics and Statistics Administration, Bureau of the Census, Data User Services Division, January 1995. Primary source: U.S. Geological Survey. *Elevations and Distances in the United States* (1983). *Note:* One foot equals .305 meter.

★ 220 ★
Land Area

Land Area: 1990

Table shows the total area and land area of U.S. regions, divisions, states, and territories.

Region, division, state, and other area	Total area		Land area	
	Square miles	Square kilometers	Square miles	Square kilometers
United States	3,717,522	9,628,382	3,536,338	9,159,115
Northeast	176,618	457,441	162,274	420,290
New England	68,655	177,816	62,811	162,680
Maine	33,741	87,389	30,865	79,940
New Hampshire	9,283	24,043	8,969	23,230
Vermont	9,615	24,903	9,249	23,955
Massachusetts	9,241	23,934	7,838	20,300
Rhode Island	1,231	3,188	1,045	2,707
Connecticut	5,544	14,359	4,845	12,549
Middle Atlantic	107,963	279,624	99,463	257,609
New York	53,989	139,832	47,224	122,310

[Continued]

★ 220 ★

Land Area: 1990

[Continued]

Region, division, state, and other area	Total area		Land area	
	Square miles	Square kilometers	Square miles	Square kilometers
New Jersey	8,215	21,277	7,419	19,215
Pennsylvania	45,759	118,516	44,820	116,084
Midwest	821,765	2,128,371	751,520	1,946,437
East North Central	301,371	780,551	243,539	630,766
Ohio	44,828	116,105	40,953	106,068
Indiana	36,420	94,328	35,870	92,903
Illinois	57,918	150,008	55,593	143,986
Michigan	96,705	250,466	56,809	147,135
Wisconsin	65,500	169,645	54,314	140,673
West North Central	520,394	1,347,820	507,981	1,315,671
Minnesota	86,943	225,182	79,617	206,208
Iowa	56,276	145,755	55,875	144,716
Missouri	69,709	180,546	68,898	178,446
North Dakota	70,704	183,123	68,994	178,694
South Dakota	77,121	199,743	75,896	196,571
Nebraska	77,359	200,360	76,878	199,114
Kansas	82,282	213,110	81,823	211,922
South	907,237	2,349,744	871,070	2,256,071
South Atlantic	284,146	735,938	266,221	689,512
Delaware	2,397	6,208	1,955	5,063
Maryland	12,297	31,849	9,775	25,317
District of Columbia	68	176	61	158
Virginia	42,326	109,624	39,598	102,559
West Virginia	24,232	62,761	24,087	62,385
North Carolina	52,672	136,420	48,718	126,180
South Carolina	31,189	80,780	30,111	77,987
Georgia	58,977	152,750	57,919	150,010
Florida	59,988	155,369	53,997	139,852
East South Central	183,079	474,175	178,615	462,613
Kentucky	40,411	104,664	39,732	102,906
Tennessee	42,145	109,156	41,219	106,757
Alabama	52,237	135,294	50,750	131,443
Mississippi	48,286	125,061	46,914	121,507
West South Central	440,012	1,139,631	426,234	1,103,946
Arkansas	53,182	137,741	52,075	134,874
Louisiana	49,650	128,594	43,566	112,836
Oklahoma	69,903	181,049	68,679	177,879
Texas	267,277	692,247	261,914	678,357
West	1,811,902	4,692,826	1,751,474	4,536,318
Mountain	863,614	2,236,760	856,121	2,217,353
Montana	147,046	380,849	145,556	376,990
Idaho	83,574	216,457	82,751	214,325

[Continued]

Land and Land Use

★ 220 ★

Land Area: 1990

[Continued]

Region, division, state, and other area	Total area		Land area	
	Square miles	Square kilometers	Square miles	Square kilometers
Wyoming	97,819	253,351	97,105	251,502
Colorado	104,100	269,619	103,729	268,658
New Mexico	121,598	314,939	121,364	314,333
Arizona	114,006	295,276	113,642	294,333
Utah	84,904	219,901	82,168	212,815
Nevada	110,567	286,369	109,806	284,398
Pacific	948,288	2,456,066	895,353	2,318,964
Washington	70,637	182,950	66,581	172,445
Oregon	97,093	251,471	96,002	248,645
California	158,869	411,471	155,973	403,970
Alaska	615,230	1,593,446	570,374	1,477,269
Hawaii	6,459	16,729	6,423	16,636
Other areas:				
Puerto Rico	3,508	9,085	3,427	8,875
American Samoa	90	233	77	200
Guam	217	561	210	543
Northern Mariana Islands	189	490	179	464
Palau	241	624	177	458
Virgin Islands of the United States	171	443	134	346

Source: 1994 Statistical Abstract of the United States on CD-ROM [machine-readable datafiles]. CD-8A-94. Washington, DC: U.S. Department of Commerce, Economics and Statistics Administration, Bureau of the Census, Data User Services Division, January 1995. Primary source: U.S. Bureau of the Census. 1990 Census of Population and Housing. Series CPH-1. Note: One square mile equals 2.59 square kilometers.

★ 221 ★

Land Area

Land Expansion of the United States

Table shows the territorial expansion of the United States, as well as acquisitions of other areas. Boundaries of all acquisitions listed were indefinite, at least in part, at time of acquisition.

Accession	Acquisi- tion date	Land area	
		Square miles	Square kilometers
Total	(X)	3,540,558	9,170,043
United States[1]	(X)	3,536,338	9,159,116
Territory in 1790[2]	(X)	895,415	2,319,125
Louisiana Purchase	1803	909,380	2,355,294

[Continued]

★ 221 ★

Land Expansion of the United States
[Continued]

Accession	Acquisi-tion date	Land area	
		Square miles	Square kilometers
Purchase of Florida	1819	58,666	151,945
Texas	1845	388,687	1,006,699
Oregon Territory	1846	286,541	742,141
Mexican Cession	1848	529,189	1,370,600
Gadsden Purchase	1853	29,670	76,845
Alaska	1867	570,374	1,477,266
Hawaii	1898	6,423	16,636
Other areas:[1]			
Puerto Rico	1898[3]	3,427	8,875
Guam	1898[4]	210	543
American Samoa	1899[5]	77	200
Virgin Islands of the U.S	1917	134	346
Palau[6]	1947	179	464
Northern Mariana Islands[5]	1947[7]	177	458
All other	(X)	16	41

Source: 1994 Statistical Abstract of the United States on CD-ROM [machine-readable datafiles]. CD-8A-94. Washington, DC: U.S. Department of Commerce, Economics and Statistics Administration, Bureau of the Census, Data User Services Division, January 1995. Primary sources: Unless otherwise noted—U.S. Geological Survey. *Boundaries of the United States and the Several States.* Paper 909 (1976). *Notes:* "X" indicates "not applicable." One square mile equals 2.59 square kilometers. 1. Source: U.S. Bureau of the Census. *1990 Census of Population and Housing.* Series CPH-1. Based on 1990 Census; sum of areas listed will not equal these figures. 2. Source: U.S. Bureau of the Census. *1990 Census of Population and Housing.* Series CPH-1. Based on 1990 Census; sum of areas listed will not equal these figures. Includes that part of drainage basin of Red River of the North, south of 49th parallel, sometimes considered part of Louisiana Purchase, but excludes the Great Lakes. 3. Ceded by Spain in 1898, ratified in 1899, and became Commonwealth of Puerto Rico by Act of Congress on July 25, 1952. 4. Acquired 1898; ratified 1899. 5. Acquired 1899; ratified 1900. 6. Remaining portion of the Trust Territory of the Pacific Islands (TTPI), under U.N. trusteeship since 1947. The Federated States of Micronesia and the Marshall Islands, also formerly part of the TTPI, became freely associated States in 1986 and are not included in the table. 7. Attained Commonwealth status in 1986, separate from the TTPI, of which it had been a part since 1947.

★ 222 ★

Land Area

Land Ownership: 1900-1991

Table shows land ownership in the United States.

[In percentages]

Year	Private land	Public domain
1900	52.7	47.3
1910	68.5	31.5
1920	73.8	26.2
1930	74.0	26.0

[Continued]

★ 222 ★

Land Ownership: 1900-1991
[Continued]

Year	Private land	Public domain
1945	73.7	26.3
1949	73.5	26.5
1954	73.5	26.5
1959	61.0	39.0
1964	60.4	39.6
1969	66.5	33.5
1974	66.5	33.5
1978	67.2	32.9
1982	67.9	32.2
1987	68.1	31.9
1991	71.4	28.6

Source: Executive Office of the President of the United States. *Environmental Quality 24: The Twenty-fourth Annual Report of the Council on Environmental Quality.* Prepared by Ray Clark. Written by Carroll Curtis. Edited by Barry Walsh. Washington, DC: U.S. Government Printing Office, 1994, p. 451. Primary sources: Daugherty, A.B. *Major Uses of Land in the United States: 1987.* AER 643. Washington, DC: U.S. Department of Agriculture, Economic Research Service, 1991, p. 20, appendix table 1; earlier reports in this series and unpublished revisions; U.S. Department of Commerce. Bureau of the Census. *Statistical Abstract of the United States.* Washington, DC: U.S. Department of Commerce, Bureau of the Census, annual. *Notes:* The total land area of the United States increased with the addition of Alaska and Hawaii as states. Other changes in the total land area result from refinements in measuring techniques. Public land includes original public-domain lands vested in the U.S. government by virtue of its sovereignty as well as lands acquired by the U.S. government by purchase, condemnation, and gift. Historical estimates are based on imperfect data.

Land Area: Federal

★ 223 ★

Federal Land and Buildings: 1970-1991

Table shows federal land and buildings owned and leased, as well as predominant land usage for fiscal years ending in years shown. Covers federal real property throughout the world, except as noted. Cost of land figures represent total cost of property owned in year shown.

Item	Unit	1970	1975	1980	1985	1990	1991
Federally owned: Land	Million acres	762	761	720	727	650	650
Buildings, number[1]	1,000	418	405	403	454	446	441
Buildings, floor area[1]	Million square feet	2,542	2,502	2,522	2,860	2,859	2,960
Cost of land, buildings, etc.[2]	Billion dollars	79	91	107	148	180	181
Federally leases: Land	Million acres	1.6	1.2	1.4	1.3	0.9	(NA)
Buildings, floor area[1]	Million square feet	182	210	214	237	234	242
Rental property, cost	Million dollars	451	664	1,054	1,681	2,125	(NA)
Predominant usage (U.S. only)	Million acres	761	760	720	727	650	650
Forest and wildlife	Million acres	503	502	422	431	368	(NA)

[Continued]

★ 223 ★

Federal Land and Buildings: 1970-1991

[Continued]

Item	Unit	1970	1975	1980	1985	1990	1991
Grazing	Million acres	164	164	162	155	154	(NA)
Parks and historic sites	Million acres	25	25	93	94	96	(NA)
Other	Million acres	70	69	43	48	33	(NA)

Source: 1994 Statistical Abstract of the United States on CD-ROM [machine-readable datafiles]. CD-8A-94. Washington, DC: U.S. Department of Commerce, Economics and Statistics Administration, Bureau of the Census, Data User Services Division, January 1995. Primary source: U.S. General Services Administration. *Inventory Report on Real Property Owned by the United States Throughout the World* (annual). *Notes:* "NA" represents "not available." 1. Excludes data for Department of Defense military functions outside 2. Includes other uses not shown separately.

★ 224 ★

Land Area: Federal

Federal Offshore Activities: 1975-1992

Table shows data related to federal offshore leasing, exploration, production, and revenue.

Item	Unit	1975	1980	1985	1990	1991	1992
Tracts offered	Number	1,374	483	15,754	10,459	16,800	9,618
Tracts leased	Number	321	218	667	825	676	204
Acres offered	1,000	7,247	2,563	87,029	56,788	80,288	52,380
Acres leased	1,000	1,680	1,134	3,512	4,263	3,416	1,021
Bonus paid for leased tracts	Billion dollars	1.1	4.2	1.5	0.6	0.4	0.1
New wells being drilled:							
Active	Number	97	191	195	120	64	104
Suspended	Number	292	739	348	266	249	180
Wells completed	Number	6,104	9,638	12,285	13,167	13,184	13,209
Wells plugged and abandoned	Number	5,617	8,057	10,487	14,677	15,430	16,348
Revenue, total[1]	Billion dollars	1.7	6.4	5.2	3.3	2.8	2.5
Bonuses	Billion dollars	1.1	4.2	1.5	0.6	0.4	0.1
Oil and gas royalties[1]	Billion dollars	0.6	2.1	3.6	2.6	2.3	2.3
Rentals	Billion dollars	(Z)	(Z)	0.1	0.1	0.1	0.1
Production, value[2]	Billion dollars	3.9	13.1	22.2	16.5	14.2	14.5
Crude oil	Billion dollars	2.2	4.8	9.6	5.9	5.2	5.3
Condensate	Billion dollars	0.2	0.4	1.0	1.1	1.1	1.0
Natural gas	Billion dollars	1.5	7.9	11.5	9.5	7.9	8.2
Production:[2]							
Crude oil	Million barrels	303	259	352	274	263	301

[Continued]

★ 224 ★

Federal Offshore Activities: 1975-1992
[Continued]

Item	Unit	1975	1980	1985	1990	1991	1992
Condensate	Million barrels	27	19	37	51	52	52
Natural gas	Billion cubic feet	3,459	4,641	4,000	5,093	4,516	4,685

Source: 1994 Statistical Abstract of the United States on CD-ROM [machine-readable datafiles]. CD-8A-94. Washington, DC: U.S. Department of Commerce, Economics and Statistics Administration, Bureau of the Census, Data User Services Division, January 1995. Primary source: U.S. Department of the Interior. Minerals Management Service. *Federal Offshore Statistics* (annual). *Notes:* "Z" denotes less than $50 million. 1. Includes condensate royalties. 2. Production value is value at time of production, not current value.

★ 225 ★

Land Area: Federal

Federal Public Domain Acquisitions

Areas of acquisitions are as computed in 1912 and do not necessarily agree with figures in square miles shown elsewhere, which include later adjustments and reflect subsequent remeasurement. Excludes outlying areas of the United States amounting to 645,949 acres in 1978.

[In million acres]

Year and acquisition	Acreage		
	Total	Land	Inland water
Aggregate	1,837.8	1,804.7	33.1
1781-1802 (State Cessions)	236.8	233.4	3.4
1803, Louisiana Purchase[1]	529.9	523.4	6.5
1819, Cession from Spain	46.1	43.3	2.8
Red River Basin[2]	29.6	29.1	0.5
1846, Oregon Compromise	183.4	180.6	2.7
1848, Mexican Cession[1]	338.7	334.5	4.2
1850, Purchase from Texas	78.9	78.8	.1
1853, Gadsden Purchase	19.0	19.0	(Z)
1867, Alaska Purchase	375.3	362.5	12.8

Source: 1994 Statistical Abstract of the United States on CD-ROM [machine-readable datafiles]. CD-8A-94. Washington, DC: U.S. Department of Commerce, Economics and Statistics Administration, Bureau of the Census, Data User Services Division, January 1995. Primary source: Except as noted—U.S. Department of the Interior. Bureau of Land Management. Estimated area; all other data—Office of the Secretary. *Areas of Acquisitions to the Territory of the U.S.* (1922). *Notes:* "Z" represents less than 50,000. 1. Data for Louisiana Purchase exclude areas eliminated by Treaty of 1819 with Spain. Such areas are included in figures for Mexican Cession. 2. Represents drainage basin of Red River of the North, south of 49th parallel. Authorities differ as to method and date of its acquisition. Some hold it as part of the Louisiana Purchase; others, as acquired from Great Britain.

★ 226 ★

Land Area: Federal

Federal Public Domain Area: 1978-1991

Areas of acquisitions are as computed in 1912 and do not necessarily agree with figures in square miles shown elsewhere, which include later adjustments and reflect subsequent remeasurement. Excludes outlying areas of the United States amounting to 645,949 acres in 1978.

[In million acres]

| Year | Land area[1] | | Acquired |
	Total	Public domain	
1978	775.2	712.0	63.3
1979	744.1	684.3	59.8
1980	719.5	648.0	71.5
1981	730.8	668.7	62.2
1982	729.8	670.0	59.8
1983	732.0	672.4	59.6
1984	726.6	658.9	67.7
1985	726.7	656.2	70.5
1986	727.1	662.7	64.4
1987	724.3	661.0	63.3
1988	688.2	623.2	65.0
1989	662.2	597.9	64.3
1990	649.8	587.4	62.4
1991	649.3	587.6	61.8

Source: 1994 Statistical Abstract of the United States on CD-ROM [machine-readable datafiles]. CD-8A-94. Washington, DC: U.S. Department of Commerce, Economics and Statistics Administration, Bureau of the Census, Data User Services Division, January 1995. Primary source: Except as noted—U.S. Department of the Interior. Bureau of Land Management. Estimated area; all other data—Office of the Secretary. *Areas of Acquisitions to the Territory of the U.S.* (1922). *Notes:* 1. Owned by federal government. Comprises original public domain plus acquired lands. Estimated from imperfect data available for indicated Prior to 1959, excludes Alaska, and 1960, Hawaii. Source: Beginning 1955, U.S. General Services Administration. *Inventory Report on Real Property Owned by the United States Throughout the World* (annual).

★ 227 ★

Land Area: Federal

Federally Owned Land, by State: 1960-1991

As of end of fiscal year. Public lands include any land and interest in land owned by the United States that are administered by the Secretary of Interior through the Bureau of Land Management (BLM), without regard to how the United States acquired ownership, except for (1) lands located on the Outer Continental Shelf, and (2) lands held for the benefit of Indians, Aleuts, and Eskimos. Includes public domain and acquired lands.

[In thousand acres, except percentage]

Year, region, division, and state	Total	Not owned by federal government	Owned by federal government[1]	
			Acres	Percent
1960	2,273,407	1,501,894	771,512	33.9
1965	2,271,343	1,505,546	765,797	33.7
1970	2,271,343	1,510,042	761,301	33.5
1975	2,271,343	1,510,929	760,414	33.5
1976	2,271,343	1,509,151	762,192	33.6
1977	2,271,343	1,529,834	741,509	32.6
1978	2,271,343	1,496,094	775,249	34.1
1979	2,271,343	1,501,479	769,863	33.9
1980	2,271,343	1,551,822	719,522	31.7
1981	2,271,343	1,540,528	730,815	32.2
1982	2,271,343	1,541,522	729,821	32.1
1983	2,271,343	1,539,301	732,042	32.2
1984	2,271,343	1,544,785	726,559	32.0
1985	2,271,343	1,544,658	726,686	32.0
1986	2,271,343	1,544,230	727,113	32.0
1987	2,271,343	1,547,277	724,066	31.9
1988	2,271,343	1,583,090	688,253	30.3
1989	2,271,343	1,609,185	662,158	29.2
1990	2,271,343	1,621,541	649,802	28.6
1991, total	2,271,343	1,621,998	649,346	28.6
Northeast	104,700	102,411	2,288	2.2
New England	40,401	39,079	1,322	3.3
Maine	19,848	19,692	155	0.8
New Hampshire	5,769	5,035	734	12.7
Vermont	5,937	5,579	358	6.0
Massachusetts	5,035	4,969	66	1.3
Rhode Island	677	675	2	0.3
Connecticut	3,135	3,129	6	0.2
Middle Atlantic	64,299	63,332	966	1.5
New York	30,681	30,472	209	0.7
New Jersey	4,813	4,664	149	3.1
Pennsylvania	28,804	28,196	608	2.1
Midwest	482,870	459,425	23,446	4.9
East North Central	156,679	146,849	9,830	6.3
Ohio	26,222	25,880	342	1.3
Indiana	23,158	22,757	401	1.7

[Continued]

★ 227 ★

Federally Owned Land, by State: 1960-1991
[Continued]

Year, region, division, and state	Total	Not owned by federal government	Owned by federal government[1]	
			Acres	Percent
Illinois	35,795	34,834	961	2.7
Michigan	36,492	31,903	4,589	12.6
Wisconsin	35,011	31,474	3,537	10.1
West North Central	326,191	312,576	13,616	4.2
Minnesota	51,206	45,839	5,367	10.5
Iowa	35,860	35,524	336	0.9
Missouri	44,248	42,152	2,096	4.7
North Dakota	44,452	42,574	1,879	4.2
South Dakota	48,882	46,076	2,806	5.7
Nebraska	49,032	48,322	710	1.4
Kansas	52,511	52,089	422	0.8
Southern	561,238	540,183	21,055	3.8
South Atlantic	171,325	161,181	10,144	5.9
Delaware	1,266	1,239	27	2.2
Maryland	6,319	6,133	187	3.0
District of Columbia	39	29	10	26.1
Virginia	25,496	23,900	1,597	6.3
West Virginia	15,411	14,382	1,028	6.7
North Carolina	31,403	29,432	1,970	6.3
South Carolina	19,374	18,652	722	3.7
Georgia	37,295	35,807	1,488	4.0
Florida	34,721	31,607	3,114	9.0
East South Central	115,141	110,686	4,455	3.9
Kentucky	25,512	24,433	1,080	4.2
Tennessee	26,728	25,734	994	3.7
Alabama	32,678	31,603	1,075	3.3
Mississippi	30,223	28,916	1,306	4.3
West South Central	274,772	268,316	6,456	2.3
Arkansas	33,599	30,837	2,762	8.2
Louisiana	28,868	28,123	745	2.6
Oklahoma	44,088	43,383	705	1.6
Texas	168,218	165,973	2,245	1.3
Western	1,122,535	519,978	602,557	53.7
Mountain	548,449	283,625	264,823	48.3
Montana	93,271	67,129	26,142	28.0
Idaho	52,933	20,319	32,614	61.6
Wyoming	62,343	31,866	30,477	48.9
Colorado	66,486	42,332	24,154	36.3
New Mexico	77,766	52,564	25,203	32.4
Arizona	72,688	38,380	34,308	47.2
Utah	52,697	19,036	33,661	63.9
Nevada	70,264	12,000	58,265	82.9
Pacific	574,086	236,353	337,733	58.8

[Continued]

★ 227 ★

Federally Owned Land, by State: 1960-1991
[Continued]

Year, region, division, and state	Total	Not owned by federal government	Owned by federal government[1]	
			Acres	Percent
Washington	42,694	30,614	12,080	28.3
Oregon	61,599	29,308	32,291	52.4
California	100,207	55,500	44,707	44.6
Alaska	365,482	117,461	248,021	67.9
Hawaii	4,106	3,471	634	15.5

Source: *1994 Statistical Abstract of the United States on CD-ROM* [machine-readable datafiles]. CD-8A-94. Washington, DC: U.S. Department of Commerce, Economics and Statistics Administration, Bureau of the Census, Data User Services Division, January 1995. Primary source: U.S. General Services Administration. *Inventory Report on Real Property Owned by the United States Throughout the World* (annual). *Note:* 1. Excludes trust properties.

Land Use

★ 228 ★

Land Cover and Use, by State

Table shows surface and—for nonfederal land—use of each state's land. Excludes Alaska and District of Columbia.

[In thousand acres]

Region, division, and state	Total surface area[1]	Federal land	Nonfederal land							
			Total	Developed[2]	Rural land					
					Total	Cropland	Pasture land	Rangeland	Forest land	Minor cover/uses
United States	1,937,726	404,069	1,484,156	77,305	1,406,851	422,416	129,021	401,685	393,904	59,826
Northeast	108,080	2,392	100,778	9,611	91,166	14,532	7,669	0	64,246	4,720
New England	42,670	1,332	38,609	3,005	35,604	2,311	1,248	0	30,307	1,739
Maine	21,290	161	19,517	508	19,009	943	419	0	16,933	714
New Hampshire	5,938	729	4,971	372	4,599	163	115	0	4,052	269
Vermont	6,153	335	5,556	208	5,348	653	388	0	4,184	122
Massachusetts	5,302	89	4,849	1,063	3,786	291	179	0	2,937	379
Rhode Island	776	4	661	161	500	22	37	0	404	37
Connecticut	3,212	14	3,056	693	2,362	239	110	0	1,797	218
Middle Atlantic	65,410	1,060	62,168	6,606	55,562	12,221	6,422	0	33,939	2,981
New York	31,429	234	29,782	2,485	27,297	5,774	3,686	0	16,650	1,187
New Jersey	4,984	148	4,563	1,325	3,239	673	229	0	1,890	447
Pennsylvania	28,997	677	27,823	2,796	25,027	5,774	2,507	0	15,398	1,348
Midwest	490,474	17,883	460,128	23,789	436,339	233,455	40,718	71,859	71,637	18,670
East North Central	159,066	6,269	148,602	12,368	136,233	72,743	12,982	0	42,482	8,027
Ohio	26,451	347	25,686	2,925	22,762	12,537	2,444	0	6,426	1,354
Indiana	23,159	487	22,302	1,780	20,522	13,930	2,073	0	3,698	821
Illinois	36,061	492	34,792	2,792	32,000	25,121	2,689	0	3,447	744

[Continued]

★ 228 ★

Land Cover and Use, by State
[Continued]

Region, division, and state	Total surface area[1]	Federal land	Nonfederal land Total	Developed[2]	Rural land Total	Cropland	Pasture land	Rangeland	Forest land	Minor cover/uses
Michigan	37,457	3,130	33,051	2,921	30,130	9,484	2,735	0	15,483	2,429
Wisconsin	35,938	1,813	32,770	1,951	30,820	11,671	3,041	0	13,428	2,680
West North Central	331,408	11,615	311,527	11,421	300,105	160,713	27,736	71,859	29,155	10,643
Minnesota	54,017	3,390	47,077	2,136	44,941	22,990	3,425	157	13,952	4,417
Iowa	36,016	172	35,387	1,688	33,699	27,031	3,866	0	1,841	961
Missouri	44,606	2,060	41,655	2,165	39,491	15,090	12,606	56	10,959	781
North Dakota	45,250	1,882	42,255	1,242	41,013	28,064	1,206	9,933	428	1,382
South Dakota	49,354	2,873	45,467	1,064	44,403	17,819	2,354	22,152	565	1,513
Nebraska	49,507	652	48,218	1,250	46,967	20,601	1,957	22,900	728	782
Kansas	52,658	587	51,467	1,876	49,592	29,119	2,324	16,660	681	808
Southern	575,044	26,391	527,041	30,657	496,384	107,532	67,937	113,837	189,507	17,571
South Atlantic	178,469	12,757	156,196	13,346	142,849	26,495	16,165	3,592	88,408	8,190
Delaware	1,309	33	1,213	165	1,048	521	30	0	357	141
Maryland	6,695	159	6,048	936	5,111	1,795	514	0	2,415	388
Virginia	26,091	2,368	22,812	1,663	21,150	3,309	3,315	0	13,622	904
West Virginia	15,508	1,116	14,227	532	13,695	1,053	1,892	0	10,466	284
North Carolina	33,708	2,309	28,622	2,487	26,135	6,548	1,992	0	16,528	1,067
South Carolina	19,912	1,340	17,785	1,422	16,363	3,371	1,177	0	11,073	742
Georgia	37,702	2,062	34,664	2,375	32,289	6,307	3,040	0	21,860	1,083
Florida	37,545	3,369	30,825	3,766	27,059	3,592	4,205	3,592	12,088	3,583
East South Central	116,446	5,116	108,068	5,705	102,363	22,870	18,493	96	58,115	2,789
Kentucky	25,862	1,169	24,023	1,224	22,799	5,818	5,955	0	10,054	972
Tennessee	26,972	1,369	24,759	1,669	23,090	5,765	5,019	0	11,601	706
Alabama	33,091	904	31,230	1,640	29,591	4,210	3,595	96	21,017	673
Mississippi	30,521	1,674	28,056	1,172	26,884	7,078	3,924	0	15,443	439
West South Central	280,129	8,518	262,778	11,606	251,172	58,167	33,279	110,149	42,984	6,593
Arkansas	34,040	3,129	29,904	1,232	28,672	8,182	5,678	164	14,268	380
Louisiana	30,561	1,174	26,472	1,455	25,016	6,484	2,276	234	12,736	3,286
Oklahoma	44,772	1,176	42,431	1,716	40,715	11,557	7,590	14,546	6,505	517
Texas	170,756	3,040	163,971	7,203	156,768	31,944	17,735	95,204	9,476	2,410
Western	764,128	357,403	396,209	13,247	382,962	66,896	12,697	215,989	68,514	18,865
Mountain	552,680	266,171	280,033	5,964	274,069	44,235	7,828	182,653	27,532	11,822
Montana	94,109	27,074	65,682	999	64,682	17,881	3,169	36,769	5,253	1,611
Idaho	53,481	33,190	19,628	477	19,152	6,532	1,354	6,596	4,071	600
Wyoming	62,598	29,457	32,576	501	32,075	2,362	928	26,784	984	1,017
Colorado	66,618	23,833	42,320	1,375	40,945	10,967	1,266	23,427	4,079	1,207
New Mexico	77,819	26,423	51,144	698	50,445	2,297	186	40,782	4,685	2,496
Arizona	72,960	30,647	41,994	1,116	40,878	1,306	81	31,867	4,912	2,712
Utah	54,336	35,476	16,440	465	15,975	2,002	563	8,507	3,194	1,711
Nevada	70,759	60,071	10,250	333	9,916	889	282	7,921	356	469
Pacific	211,448	91,232	116,176	7,283	108,893	22,662	4,869	33,337	40,982	7,043
Washington	43,608	12,471	29,947	1,564	28,383	7,758	1,421	5,574	12,634	997
Oregon	62,127	32,305	28,918	941	27,977	4,438	1,916	9,152	11,857	705
California	101,572	46,014	53,654	4,621	49,033	10,209	1,501	17,719	15,073	4,531
Hawaii	4,141	443	3,657	157	3,500	348	31	891	1,419	811

Source: 1994 Statistical Abstract of the United States on CD-ROM [machine-readable datafiles]. CD-8A-94. Washington, DC: U.S. Department of Commerce, Economics and Statistics Administration, Bureau of the Census, Data User Services Division, January 1995. Primary source: U.S. Department of Agriculture, Soil Conservation Service, and Iowa State University, Statistical Laboratory. *Summary Report, 1987 National Resources Inventory.* Statistical Bulletin No. 790 (December 1989). *Notes:* 1. Includes water area not shown separately. 2. Includes urban and built-up areas in units of 10 acres or greater, and rural transportation.

★ 229 ★

Land Use

Land Cover and Use – Percent Distribution, by State

Table shows surface and—for nonfederal land—use of each state's land. Excludes Alaska and District of Columbia.

[In percentages]

Region, division, and state	Total surface area[1]	Federal land	Nonfederal land							
			Total	Developed[2]	Rural land					
					Total	Cropland	Pasture land	Rangeland	Forest land	Minor cover/uses
United States	100.00	20.85	76.59	3.99	72.60	21.80	6.66	20.73	20.33	3.09
Northeast	5.58	0.12	5.20	0.50	4.70	0.75	0.40	0.00	3.32	0.24
New England	2.20	0.07	1.99	0.16	1.84	0.12	0.06	0.00	1.56	0.09
Maine	1.10	0.01	1.01	0.03	0.98	0.05	0.02	0.00	0.87	0.04
New Hampshire	0.31	0.04	0.26	0.02	0.24	0.01	0.01	0.00	0.21	0.01
Vermont	0.32	0.02	0.29	0.01	0.28	0.03	0.02	0.00	0.22	0.01
Massachusetts	0.27	0.00	0.25	0.05	0.20	0.02	0.01	0.00	0.15	0.02
Rhode Island	0.04	0.00	0.03	0.01	0.03	0.00	0.00	0.00	0.02	0.00
Connecticut	0.17	0.00	0.16	0.04	0.12	0.01	0.01	0.00	0.09	0.01
Middle Atlantic	3.38	0.05	3.21	0.34	2.87	0.63	0.33	0.00	1.75	0.15
New York	1.62	0.01	1.54	0.13	1.41	0.30	0.19	0.00	0.86	0.06
New Jersey	0.26	0.01	0.24	0.07	0.17	0.03	0.01	0.00	0.10	0.02
Pennsylvania	1.50	0.03	1.44	0.14	1.29	0.30	0.13	0.00	0.79	0.07
Midwest	25.31	0.92	23.75	1.23	22.52	12.05	2.10	3.71	3.70	0.96
East North Central	8.21	0.32	7.67	0.64	7.03	3.75	0.67	0.00	2.19	0.41
Ohio	1.37	0.02	1.33	0.15	1.17	0.65	0.13	0.00	0.33	0.07
Indiana	1.20	0.03	1.15	0.09	1.06	0.72	0.11	0.00	0.19	0.04
Illinois	1.86	0.03	1.80	0.14	1.65	1.30	0.14	0.00	0.18	0.04
Michigan	1.93	0.16	1.71	0.15	1.55	0.49	0.14	0.00	0.80	0.13
Wisconsin	1.85	0.09	1.69	0.10	1.59	0.60	0.16	0.00	0.69	0.14
West North Central	17.10	0.60	16.08	0.59	15.49	8.29	1.43	3.71	1.50	0.55
Minnesota	2.79	0.17	2.43	0.11	2.32	1.19	0.18	0.01	0.72	0.23
Iowa	1.86	0.01	1.83	0.09	1.74	1.39	0.20	0.00	0.10	0.05
Missouri	2.30	0.11	2.15	0.11	2.04	0.78	0.65	0.00	0.57	0.04
North Dakota	2.34	0.10	2.18	0.06	2.12	1.45	0.06	0.51	0.02	0.07
South Dakota	2.55	0.15	2.35	0.05	2.29	0.92	0.12	1.14	0.03	0.08
Nebraska	2.55	0.03	2.49	0.06	2.42	1.06	0.10	1.18	0.04	0.04
Kansas	2.72	0.03	2.66	0.10	2.56	1.50	0.12	0.86	0.04	0.04
Southern	29.68	1.36	27.20	1.58	25.62	5.55	3.51	5.87	9.78	0.91
South Atlantic	9.21	0.66	8.06	0.69	7.37	1.37	0.83	0.19	4.56	0.42
Delaware	0.07	0.00	0.06	0.01	0.05	0.03	0.00	0.00	0.02	0.01
Maryland	0.35	0.01	0.31	0.05	0.26	0.09	0.03	0.00	0.12	0.02
Virginia	1.35	0.12	1.18	0.09	1.09	0.17	0.17	0.00	0.70	0.05
West Virginia	0.80	0.06	0.73	0.03	0.71	0.05	0.10	0.00	0.54	0.01
North Carolina	1.74	0.12	1.48	0.13	1.35	0.34	0.10	0.00	0.85	0.06
South Carolina	1.03	0.07	0.92	0.07	0.84	0.17	0.06	0.00	0.57	0.04
Georgia	1.95	0.11	1.79	0.12	1.67	0.33	0.16	0.00	1.13	0.06
Florida	1.94	0.17	1.59	0.19	1.40	0.19	0.22	0.19	0.62	0.18
East South Central	6.01	0.26	5.58	0.29	5.28	1.18	0.95	0.00	3.00	0.14
Kentucky	1.33	0.06	1.24	0.06	1.18	0.30	0.31	0.00	0.52	0.05
Tennessee	1.39	0.07	1.28	0.09	1.19	0.30	0.26	0.00	0.60	0.04
Alabama	1.71	0.05	1.61	0.08	1.53	0.22	0.19	0.00	1.08	0.03
Mississippi	1.58	0.09	1.45	0.06	1.39	0.37	0.20	0.00	0.80	0.02
West South Central	14.46	0.44	13.56	0.60	12.96	3.00	1.72	5.68	2.22	0.34
Arkansas	1.76	0.16	1.54	0.06	1.48	0.42	0.29	0.01	0.74	0.02

[Continued]

★ 229 ★

Land Cover and Use – Percent Distribution, by State

[Continued]

Region, division, and state	Total surface area[1]	Federal land	Nonfederal land							
			Total	Developed[2]	Rural land					
					Total	Cropland	Pasture land	Rangeland	Forest land	Minor cover/uses
Louisiana	1.58	0.06	1.37	0.08	1.29	0.33	0.12	0.01	0.66	0.17
Oklahoma	2.31	0.06	2.19	0.09	2.10	0.60	0.39	0.75	0.34	0.03
Texas	8.81	0.16	8.46	0.37	8.09	1.65	0.92	4.91	0.49	0.12
Western	39.43	18.44	20.45	0.68	19.76	3.45	0.66	11.15	3.54	0.97
Mountain	28.52	13.74	14.45	0.31	14.14	2.28	0.40	9.43	1.42	0.61
Montana	4.86	1.40	3.39	0.05	3.34	0.92	0.16	1.90	0.27	0.08
Idaho	2.76	1.71	1.01	0.02	0.99	0.34	0.07	0.34	0.21	0.03
Wyoming	3.23	1.52	1.68	0.03	1.66	0.12	0.05	1.38	0.05	0.05
Colorado	3.44	1.23	2.18	0.07	2.11	0.57	0.07	1.21	0.21	0.06
New Mexico	4.02	1.36	2.64	0.04	2.60	0.12	0.01	2.10	0.24	0.13
Arizona	3.77	1.58	2.17	0.06	2.11	0.07	0.00	1.64	0.25	0.14
Utah	2.80	1.83	0.85	0.02	0.82	0.10	0.03	0.44	0.16	0.09
Nevada	3.65	3.10	0.53	0.02	0.51	0.05	0.01	0.41	0.02	0.02
Pacific	10.91	4.71	6.00	0.38	5.62	1.17	0.25	1.72	2.11	0.36
Washington	2.25	0.64	1.55	0.08	1.46	0.40	0.07	0.29	0.65	0.05
Oregon	3.21	1.67	1.49	0.05	1.44	0.22	0.10	0.47	0.61	0.04
California	5.24	2.37	2.77	0.24	2.53	0.53	0.08	0.91	0.78	0.23
Hawaii	0.21	0.02	0.19	0.01	0.18	0.02	0.00	0.05	0.07	0.04

Source: *1994 Statistical Abstract of the United States on CD-ROM* [machine-readable datafiles]. CD-8A-94. Washington, DC: U.S. Department of Commerce, Economics and Statistics Administration, Bureau of the Census, Data User Services Division, January 1995. Primary source: U.S. Department of Agriculture, Soil Conservation Service, and Iowa State University, Statistical Laboratory. *Summary Report, 1987 National Resources Inventory.* Statistical Bulletin No. 790 (December 1989). *Notes:* 1. Includes water area not shown separately. 2. Includes urban and built-up areas in units of 10 acres or greater, and rural transportation.

★ 230 ★

Land Use

Land Trusts

More than 2.5 million acres of land have been protected through the efforts of land trusts. There are 889 land trusts in the United States, including the Mountains to Sound Greenway Trust (Washington), Yakima Greenway Foundation (Washington), Trust for the Public Land (Texas), Iowa Natural Heritage Trust, Brandywine Conservancy (Pennsylvania), Vermont Land Trust, and Florida Keys Sea and Land Trust.

Source: "A Land Trust Sampler." *American City & County* (March 1992), p. 42.

★ 231 ★

Land Use

Land Use: 1900-1991

Table shows land use in the United States.

[In million acres]

Year	Crop-land	Grazing land	Forest-land	Other land[1]	Total
1900	319	1,044	366	175	1,904
1910	347	814	562	181	1,904
1920	402	750	567	185	1,904
1930	413	708	607	176	1,904
1945	451	660	602	562	2,275
1949	478	633	760	402	2,273
1954	466	634	615	558	2,273
1959	458	633	745	435	2,271
1964	444	641	732	449	2,266
1969	472	604	723	465	2,264
1974	465	598	718	483	2,264
1978	471	587	703	503	2,264
1982	469	597	655	544	2,265
1987	464	591	648	562	2,265
1991	NA	NA	NA	NA	NA

Source: Executive Office of the President of the United States. *Environmental Quality 24: The Twenty-fourth Annual Report of the Council on Environmental Quality.* Prepared by Ray Clark. Written by Carroll Curtis. Edited by Barry Walsh. Washington, DC: U.S. Government Printing Office, 1994, p. 451. Primary sources: Daugherty, A.B. *Major Uses of Land in the United States: 1987.* AER 643. Washington, DC: U.S. Department of Agriculture, Economic Research Service, 1991, p. 20, appendix table 1; earlier reports in this series and unpublished revisions; U.S. Department of Commerce. Bureau of the Census. *Statistical Abstract of the United States.* Washington, DC: U.S. Department of Commerce, Bureau of the Census, annual. *Notes:* "NA" stands for "not available." The total land area of the United States increased with the addition of Alaska and Hawaii as states. Other changes in the total land area result from refinements in measuring techniques. 1. Includes rural transportation areas, areas used primarily for recreation and wildlife purposes, various public installations and facilities, farmsteads and farm roads, urban areas, areas in miscellaneous uses not inventoried, marshes, open swamps, bare rock areas, desert, tundra, and other land generally having low value for agricultural purposes.

★ 232 ★
Land Use

Rangeland: 1936-1992

Table shows condition of nonfederal and Bureau of Land Management rangeland.

[In percentage of rangeland acreage]

Rangeland condition	Nonfederal				Bureau of Land Management				
	1963	1977	1982	1987	1936	1966	1975	1986	1992
Excellent	5	12	4	3	2	2	2	4	5
Good	15	28	30	30	14	17	15	30	34
Fair	40	42	45	47	48	52	50	41	38
Poor	40	18	16	14	36	30	33	18	13
Unclassified	NA	NA	5	6	NA	NA	NA	NA	11

Source: Executive Office of the President of the United States. *Environmental Quality 24: The Twenty-fourth Annual Report of the Council on Environmental Quality.* Prepared by Ray Clark. Written by Carroll Curtis. Edited by Barry Walsh. Washington, DC: U.S. Government Printing Office, 1994, p. 461. Primary sources: U.S. Department of Agriculture. Soil Conservation Service. *National Resources Inventory.* Washington, DC: U.S. Department of the Agriculture, Soil Conservation Service, 1977, 1982, and 1987: U.S. Department of the Interior. Bureau of Land Management. *Public Land Statistics* Washington, DC: U.S. Department of Labor, Bureau of Land Management (annual). *Notes:* "NA" represents "not available." Data are not strictly comparable because of different survey methods. Soil Conservation Service (SCS) data from the 1992 *National Resources Inventory* (NRI) on the condition of nonfederal rangeland are pending. Bureau of Land Management (BLM) data are expressed as the degree of similarity of present vegetation to potential natural, or climax, plant community: "Excellent" indicates 76-100 percent similarity; "Good" indicates 51-75 percent similarity; "Fair" indicates 26-50 percent similarity; and "Poor" indicates 0-25 percent similarity. "Unclassified" included rangeland for which data and estimates are not available. BLM data are based on information from ecological site inventories (49 percent of the public lands), from estimates based on earlier inventories (30 percent of the public lands), and from estimates based on professional judgment alone (21 percent of the public lands). Data are updated annually to reflect new information and changes in range condition classes.

Mineral and Metal Production

★ 233 ★

Industrial Mineral Production: 1980-1993

Table shows the production quantities of selected industrial minerals. Data represent production as measured by mine shipments, mine sales, or marketable production (including consumption by producers).

Mineral	Unit	Production quantity				
		1980	1990	1991	1992	1993
Total mineral production	(X)	(X)	(X)	(X)	(X)	(X)
Industrial minerals	(X)	(X)	(X)	(X)	(X)	(X)
Abrasive stone[1]	Metric tons	572	3,709	2,205	1,732	(NA)
Asbestos (sales)	1,000 metric tons	80	(D)	(D)	15.6	15.4
Asphalt; related bitumens (native)[2]	Million metric tons	1	25	26	25	(NA)
Barite, primary[3]	1,000 metric tons	2,037	430	448	326	303
Boron minerals[3]	1,000 metric tons	1,401	1,094	1,240	1,009	526

[Continued]

★ 233 ★

Industrial Mineral Production: 1980-1993
[Continued]

Mineral	Unit	Production quantity				
		1980	1990	1991	1992	1993
Bromine[3]	1,000 metric tons	172	177	170	171	168
Calcium chloride (natural)	1,000 short tons	581	(D)	(D)	(D)	-
Carbon dioxide, natural (estimate)	Million cubic feet	1,628	-	-	-	-
Cement: Portland	Million short tons	71.6	75.6	68.7	72.8	76.6
Masonry	Million short tons	3.0	3.3	2.6	2.9	3.0
Clays	1,000 metric tons	44,262	42,904	44,092	40,712	44,183
Diatomite	1,000 metric tons	625	631	610	595	622
Feldspar[4]	1,000 metric tons	644	630	580	726	760
Fluorspar, finished shipments	1,000 metric tons	84	64	58	51	50
Garnet (abrasive)	1,000 metric tons	24.4	47.0	50.9	54.1	46.1
Gemstones (estimate)	(X)	(NA)	(NA)	(NA)	(NA)	(NA)
Gypsum, crude	Million short tons	12.4	16.4	15.5	16.3	17.0
Helium[5]	Million cubic meters	41	87	88	94	93
Lime[3]	Million short tons	19.0	17.5	17.3	17.9	18.3
Mica, scrap and flake[3]	1,000 metric tons	105	109	103	85	89
Peat (sales by producers)	1,000 short tons	788	795	777	719	700
Perlite, processed[3]	1,000 metric tons	579	576	514	541	548
Phosphate rock (marketable)	Million metric tons	54.4	46.3	48.1	47.0	35.0
Potash (K equivalent)[6]	1,000 metric tons	2,217	1,716	1,709	1,767	1,500
Pumice and pumicite (sales by producers)	1,000 metric tons	492	443	401	481	492
Pyrites	1,000 metric tons	847	(D)	(D)	(D)	(D)
Salt (common)[3]	Million metric tons	36.6	36.9	35.9	34.8	41.6
Sand and gravel[3]	Million metric tons	719	852	852	858	884
Construction	Million metric tons	692	826	829	834	859
Industrial	Million metric tons	27	26	23	24	25
Sodium carbonate (natural) (soda ash)	1,000 metric tons	(D)	9,156	9,005	9,379	9,200
Sodium sulfate (natural)	1,000 metric tons	529	349	354	337	315
Stone:[7]	Million metric tons	893	1,110	1,002	1,055	1,110
Crushed and broken	Million metric tons	692	826	829	834	859
Dimension	1,000 metric tons	27	26	23	24	25
Sulfur: Frasch mines (shipments)	1,000 metric tons	7,400	3,676	3,119	2,600	2,200
Talc and pyrophyllite, crude[8]	1,000 metric tons	1,125	1,267	1,037	997	1,008
Tripoli	1,000 metric tons	110	94	89	85	(NA)
Vermiculite concentrate	1,000 metric tons	306	208	168	190	185
Undistributed[9]	(X)	(X)	(X)	(X)	(X)	(X)

Source: 1994 Statistical Abstract of the United States on CD-ROM [machine-readable datafiles]. CD-8A-94. Washington, DC: U.S. Department of Commerce, Economics and Statistics Administration, Bureau of the Census, Data User Services Division, January 1995. Primary sources: U.S. Bureau of Mines. Minerals Yearbook (through 1991); Annual Reports and Mineral Commodities Summaries (annual); U.S. Energy Information Administration. Annual Energy Review; Uranium Industry Annual; Petroleum Supply Annual. Volume 1; Natural Gas Annual; and Quarterly Coal Report. Notes: "-" represents zero. "D" indicates "withheld to avoid disclosing individual company data." "NA" represents "not available." "X" represents "not applicable." 1. Includes grindstones, oilstones, whetstones, and deburring media. Excludes grinding pebbles, and tubemill liners. 2. Contains bituminous limestone and sandstone, and gilsonite. Includes road oil, 1989-1992. Value excluded from industrial minerals, 1989-1992. 3. Sold or used by producers. 4. Includes aplite, 1992-1993. 5. 1980, crude and refined; thereafter, refined only. 6. Content of ore and concentrate. 7. Excludes abrasive stone, bituminous limestone and sandstone, and ground soapstone, all included elsewhere in table; 1993 excludes dimension stone. State ranks based on publishable data. Includes calcareous marl and slate. 8. For 1991-1992, production quantity, talc only; 1989-1992 dollar value is for talc only. 9. Comprises value of items that cannot be disclosed.

★ 234 ★
Mineral and Metal Production

Industrial Mineral Production Values: 1980-1993

Table shows production values for selected industrial minerals. Data represent production as measured by mine shipments, mine sales, or marketable production (including consumption by producers).

Mineral	Unit	Production value (million dollars)				
		1980	1990	1991	1992	1993
Total mineral production	(X)	146,750	141,741	(NA)	(NA)	(NA)
Industrial minerals	(X)	16,218	21,022	20,047	20,496	20,631
Abrasive stone[1]	Metric tons	2	(Z)	(Z)	(Z)	(NA)
Asbestos (sales)	1,000 metric tons	31	(3)	(3)	6	6
Asphalt; related bitumens (native)[2]	Million metric tons	25	3,480	2,979	2,794	(NA)
Barite, primary[4]	1,000 metric tons	66	16	21	20	18
Boron minerals[4]	1,000 metric tons	367	436	443	339	324
Bromine[4]	1,000 metric tons	96	173	167	170	110
Calcium chloride (natural)	1,000 short tons	48	(3)	(3)	(3)	(X)
Carbon dioxide, natural (estimate)	Million cubic feet	3	-	-	-	(X)
Cement: Portland	Million short tons	3,613	3,683	3,343	3,500	3,666
Masonry	Million short tons	188	225	188	195	200
Clays	1,000 metric tons	899	1,620	1,505	1,482	1,773
Diatomite	1,000 metric tons	101	138	140	120	115
Feldspar[5]	1,000 metric tons	23	28	26	29	30
Fluorspar, finished shipments	1,000 metric tons	13	(3)	(3)	(3)	(3)
Garnet (abrasive)	1,000 metric tons	2	7	8	5	5
Gemstones (estimate)	(X)	7	53	84	66	52
Gypsum, crude	Million short tons	103	100	94	101	105
Helium[6]	Million cubic meters	30	113	175	187	185
Lime[4]	Million short tons	843	902	890	950	971
Mica, scrap and flake[4]	1,000 metric tons	6	6	6	5	5
Peat (sales by producers)	1,000 short tons	16	19	18	17	17
Perlite, processed[4]	1,000 metric tons	17	17	15	16	17
Phosphate rock (marketable)	Million metric tons	1,257	1,075	1,031	1,058	753
Potash (K equivalent)[7]	1,000 metric tons	354	303	305	334	275
Pumice and pumicite (sales by producers)	1,000 metric tons	4	11	9	15	15
Pyrites	1,000 metric tons	14	(3)	(3)	(3)	(3)
Salt (common)[4]	Million metric tons	656	827	802	803	854
Sand and gravel[4]	Million metric tons	2,289	3,686	3,658	3,766	3,897
Construction	Million metric tons	1,996	3,249	3,268	3,341	3,495
Industrial	Million metric tons	293	436	390	425	402
Sodium carbonate (natural) (soda ash)	1,000 metric tons	(3)	836	836	836	718
Sodium sulfate (natural)	1,000 metric tons	36	34	31	26	26
Stone:[8]	Million metric tons	3,405	5,822	5,396	5,775	6,021
Crushed and broken	Million metric tons	3,255	5,591	5,187	5,594	6,021
Dimension	1,000 metric tons	139	231	210	181	(3)
Sulfur: Frasch mines (shipments)	1,000 metric tons	721	335	272	159	70
Talc and pyrophyllite, crude[9]	1,000 metric tons	19	31	32	31	27
Tripoli	1,000 metric tons	1	3	3	3	(NA)

[Continued]

★ 234 ★

Industrial Mineral Production Values: 1980-1993

[Continued]

Mineral	Unit	Production value (million dollars)				
		1980	1990	1991	1992	1993
Vermiculite concentrate	1,000 metric tons	24	19	13	15	(D)
Undistributed[10]	(X)	941	504	538	478	374

Source: 1994 Statistical Abstract of the United States on CD-ROM [machine-readable datafiles]. CD-8A-94. Washington, DC: U.S. Department of Commerce, Economics and Statistics Administration, Bureau of the Census, Data User Services Division, January 1995. Primary sources: U.S. Bureau of Mines. Minerals Yearbook (through 1991); Annual Reports and Mineral Commodities Summaries (annual); U.S. Energy Information Administration. Annual Energy Review; Uranium Industry Annual; Petroleum Supply Annual. Volume 1; Natural Gas Annual; and Quarterly Coal Report. Notes: "-" represents zero. "NA" represents "not available." "X" represents "not applicable." 1. Includes grindstones, oilstones, whetstones, and deburring media. Excludes grinding pebbles, and tubemill liners. 2. Contains bituminous limestone and sandstone, and gilsonite. Includes road oil, 1989-1992. Value excluded from industrial minerals, 1989-1992. 3. Value included in "Industrial minerals, undistributed." 4. Sold or used by producers. 5. Includes aplite, 1992-1993. 6. 1980, crude and refined; thereafter, refined only. 7. Content of ore and concentrate. 8. Excludes abrasive stone, bituminous limestone and sandstone, and ground soapstone, all included elsewhere in table; 1993 excludes dimension stone. State ranks based on publishable data. Includes calcareous marl and slate. 9. For 1991-1992, production quantity, talc only; 1989-1992 dollar value is for talc only. 10. Comprises value of items that cannot be disclosed.

★ 235 ★

Mineral and Metal Production

Metal Production: 1980-1993

Table shows the production quantities of selected metals. Data represent production as measured by mine shipments, mine sales, or marketable production (including consumption by producers).

Metal	Unit	Production quantity				
		1980	1990	1991	1992	1993
Metals	(X)	(X)	(X)	(X)	(X)	(X)
Antimony ore and concentrate[1]	Metric tons	311	(D)	(D)	(D)	(D)
Bauxite (dried)[2]	1,000 metric tons	1,559	(D)	(D)	(D)	(D)
Copper[3]	1,000 metric tons	1,181	1,588	1,631	1,765	1,773
Gold[3]	Metric tons	30	295	296	329	332
Iron ore[4]	Million metric tons	70.7	57.0	56.8	55.6	55.2
Lead[3]	1,000 metric tons	550	484	466	398	379
Magnesium metal[5]	1,000 metric tons	(NA)	139	131	137	145
Manganiferous ore[6]	1,000 metric tons	158	(D)	(D)	(D)	(D)
Mercury[7]	Metric tons	1,057	562	58	64	70
Molybdenum[8]	1,000 metric tons	68	62	54	50	39
Nickel[9]	1,000 metric tons	14.7	0.3	5.5	6.7	2.5
Palladium metal	Kilograms	(D)	5,930	6,050	6,470	6,500
Platinum metal	Kilograms	(D)	1,810	1,730	1,840	1,800
Silver[3]	Metric tons	1,006	2,125	1,855	1,804	1,750
Titanium concentrate: Ilmenite[10]	1,000 metric tons	539	(D)	(D)	(D)	(D)
Tungsten ore and concentrate[9]	Metric tons	2,738	(D)	(D)	(D)	(D)
Vanadium[3]	Metric tons	4,360	(D)	(D)	(D)	(D)

[Continued]

★ 235 ★

Metal Production: 1980-1993

[Continued]

Metal	Unit	Production quantity				
		1980	1990	1991	1992	1993
Zinc mine production[3]	1,000 metric tons	317	515	518	523	505
Undistributed	(X)	(X)	(X)	(X)	(X)	(X)

Source: 1994 Statistical Abstract of the United States on CD-ROM [machine-readable datafiles]. CD-8A-94. Washington, DC: U.S. Department of Commerce, Economics and Statistics Administration, Bureau of the Census, Data User Services Division, January 1995. Primary sources: U.S. Bureau of Mines. *Minerals Yearbook* (through 1991); *Annual Reports and Mineral Commodities Summaries* (annual); U.S. Energy Information Administration. *Annual Energy Review; Uranium Industry Annual; Petroleum Supply Annual.* Volume 1; *Natural Gas Annual;* and *Quarterly Coal Report. Notes:* "D" indicates "withheld to avoid disclosing individual company data." "NA" represents "not available." "X" represents "not applicable." 1. Antimony content. 2. Dried equivalent. 3. Recoverable content of ores, etc. 4. Represents shipments; includes byproduct ores. Gross weight. 5. For 1980-1985, magnesieum chroride for magnesium metal included in "Metals undistributed," canvass for magnesium chloride for magnesium metal discontinued in 1986. 6. 5 to 35 percent manganiferous ore. Gross weight. 7. 1986-1989, mercury produced as the primary product only; thereafter, mercury produced as a byproduct of gold ores only. 8. Content of concentrate. 9. Content of ore and concentrate. 10. Gross weight.

★ 236 ★

Mineral and Metal Production

Metal Production Values: 1980-1993

Table shows production values for selected metals. Data represent production as measured by mine shipments, mine sales, or marketable production (including consumption by producers).

Mineral	Unit	Production value (million dollars)				
		1980	1990	1991	1992	1993
Metals	(X)	8,922	12,442	11,022	11,537	11,876
Antimony ore and concentrate[1]	Metric tons	(2)	(2)	(2)	(2)	(2)
Bauxite (dried)[3]	1,000 metric tons	22	(2)	(2)	(2)	(2)
Copper[4]	1,000 metric tons	2,667	4,311	3,931	4,180	3,595
Gold[4]	Metric tons	594	3,650	3,457	3,650	3,793
Iron ore,[5]	Million metric tons	2,544	1,741	1,674	1,732	1,700
Lead[4]	1,000 metric tons	515	491	344	308	267
Magnesium metal[6]	1,000 metric tons	(NA)	433	337	360	406
Manganiferous ore[7]	1,000 metric tons	2	(2)	(2)	(2)	(2)
Mercury[8]	Metric tons	12	(2)	0.2	0.4	0.4
Molybdenum[9]	1,000 metric tons	1,344	348	250	209	165
Nickel[10]	1,000 metric tons	(2)	(NA)	(NA)	(2)	(2)
Palladium metal	Kilograms	(2)	22	17	18	26
Platinum metal	Kilograms	(2)	27	21	21	21
Silver[4]	Metric tons	667	329	241	229	236
Titanium concentrate: Ilmenite[11]	1,000 metric tons	32	(2)	(2)	(2)	(2)
Tungsten ore and concentrate[10]	Metric tons	51	(2)	(2)	(2)	(2)
Vanadium[4]	Metric tons	64	(2)	(2)	(2)	(2)

[Continued]

★ 236 ★

Metal Production Values: 1980-1993

[Continued]

Mineral	Unit	Production value (million dollars)				
		1980	1990	1991	1992	1993
Zinc mine production[4]	1,000 metric tons	262	847	602	674	512
Undistributed	(X)	145	242	148	156	179

Source: 1994 Statistical Abstract of the United States on CD-ROM [machine-readable datafiles]. CD-8A-94. Washington, DC: U.S. Department of Commerce, Economics and Statistics Administration, Bureau of the Census, Data User Services Division, January 1995. Primary sources: U.S. Bureau of Mines. *Minerals Yearbook* (through 1991); *Annual Reports and Mineral Commodities Summaries* (annual); U.S. Energy Information Administration. *Annual Energy Review; Uranium Industry Annual; Petroleum Supply Annual.* Volume 1; *Natural Gas Annual;* and *Quarterly Coal Report. Notes:* "NA" represents "not available." "X" represents "not applicable." 1. Antimony content. 2. Included with "Metals, undistributed." 3. Dried equivalent. 4. Recoverable content of ores, etc. 5. Represents shipments; includes byproduct ores. Gross weight. 6. For 1980-1985, magnesieum chroride for magnesium metal included in "Metals undistributed," canvass for magnesium chloride for magnesium metal discontinued in 1986. 7. 5 to 35 percent manganiferous ore. Gross weight. 8. 1986-1989, mercury produced as the primary product only; thereafter, mercury produced as a byproduct of gold ores only. 9. Content of concentrate. 10. Content of ore and concentrate. 11. Gross weight.

★ 237 ★

Mineral and Metal Production

Mineral and Metal Products: 1980-1992

Table shows the quantity and value of imports and exports for selected mineral and metal products. Imports represent imports for consumption. Exports include shipments under foreign aid programs. Beginning 1989, import and export data are not necessarily comparable to prior data due to change in tariff schedule to Harmonized System.

Product	Unit	Quantity					Value (million dollars)				
		1980	1985	1990	1991	1992	1980	1985	1990	1991	1992
Imports											
Petroleum (crude)[1]	Million barrels	1,317	2,128	2,222	2,124	(NA)	37,859	35,041	43,833	37,123	(NA)
Gem stones: Diamonds	Million carats	8.2	10.1	7.5	8.5	9.4	2,905	4,358	3,955	3,992	4,144
Ores and concentrates:											
Chromium (Cr_2O_3 content)	1,000 metric tons	122	237	134	94	99	15	44	22	15	15
Copper	1,000 metric tons	11.1	46.5	91.5	60.8	102.1	10	51	131	69	125
Iron	Million metric tons	17.5	19.6	18.1	13.3	12.5	529	522	560	437	396
Tungsten	1,000 metric tons	5.8	7.9	6.4	7.8	2.5	52	45	31	43	16
Metals:											
Aluminum	1,000 metric tons	882	923	960	1,025	1156	1,293	1,898	1,597	1,428	1,501
Cobalt[2]	1,000 metric tons	10.6	5.4	6.0	6.4	5.3	203	92	107	158	246
Copper refined ingots, etc	1,000 metric tons	445	300	262	289	289	633	854	675	685	660
Gold (refined bullion)	Metric tons	188	97	65	147	141	2,294	1,199	795	1,722	1,568
Iron and steel products (major)	Million metric tons	24.9	18.1	17.8	16.2	17.4	11,495	10,649	11,612	11,962	10,977
Platinum group[3]	Metric tons	139	113	125	126	132	1,118	1,382	1,906	1,743	1,484
Silver (refined bullion)	Metric tons	2,910	3,062	2,698	2,525	2,662	785	579	437	339	341
Zinc: Blocks, pigs, slabs	1,000 metric tons	639	712	632	549	(NA)	636	1,184	992	620	(NA)
Exports											
Fuels:[1]											
Bituminous coal	Million short tons	80.8	90.8	95.3	98.4	(NA)	4,090	4,243	4,464	4,588	(NA)
Petroleum (crude)	Million barrels	5.8	3.8	8.0	2.7	(NA)	185	62.1	198.6	54.1	(NA)
Nonmetallic minerals:											
Gem stones: Diamonds	Million carats	2.3	1.1	1.2	1.8	4	575	1,244	1,433	1,383	1,450
Nitrogen compounds (maj.)	Million metric tons	9.5	12.5	11.9	13.9	12.8	1,635	(NA)	(NA)	(NA)	(NA)
Phosphatic fertilizers[4]	Million metric tons	7.4	9.6	9.2	11.5	10.3	1,350	1,760	1,515	1,974	(NA)

[Continued]

★ 237 ★

Mineral and Metal Products: 1980-1992

[Continued]

Product	Unit	Quantity					Value (million dollars)				
		1980	1985	1990	1991	1992	1980	1985	1990	1991	1992
Metals:											
Aluminum: Ingots, slabs, crude	1,000 metric tons	260	593	684	793	604	397	1,260	1,169	1,274	843
Plates, sheets, bars, etc	1,000 metric tons	198	416	419	489	534	497	1,196	1,278	1,384	1,416
Gold (refined bullion)	Metric tons	108	124	141	174	257	1,285	1,490	1,719	2,039	2,877
Iron and steel products (major)	Million metric tons	1.3	4.7	4.7	6.6	4.7	1,627	2,582	4,665	5,753	5,374
Magnesium[5]	1,000 metric tons	43.9	56.6	51.8	55.2	52	137	170	164	150	132
Molybdenum[6]	Metric tons	139	253	180	88	74	1	3	2	1	1
Silver (refined bullion)	Metric tons	322	430	736	787	911	86	78	120	115	126
Scrap exports:											
Aluminum	1,000 metric tons	258	575	537	461	295	276	769	719	542	300
Iron and steel	Million metric tons	8.9	11.3	11.7	9.5	9.4	938	1,785	1,653	1,253	1,113

Source: 1994 Statistical Abstract of the United States on CD-ROM [machine-readable datafiles]. CD-8A-94. Washington, DC: U.S. Department of Commerce, Economics and Statistics Administration, Bureau of the Census, Data User Services Division, January 1995. Primary sources—except as noted: U.S. Bureau of Mines. *Minerals Yearbook* (1984 and 1988-1991) and *Annual Reports*, 1992. *Notes:* "NA" stands for "not available." 1. Source: U.S. Bureau of the Census. *U.S. Imports for Consumption and General Imports: TSUSA Commodity and Country.* FT 246 (annual); and *U.S. Exports, Schedule B Commodity and Country.* FT 446 (annual); 1989 and 1990, *U.S. Exports of Merchandise* and *U.S. Imports of Merchandise* compact discs (December issues). 2. Includes unwrought metal, waste and scrap. 3. Unwrought and semimanufactured. 4. Superphosphates and ammonium phosphates. 5. Metal and alloys, scrap, semimanufactured forms. 6. Metals and alloys, crude and scrap.

★ 238 ★

Mineral and Metal Production

Mineral Fuel Production: 1980-1993

Table shows the production quantities of selected mineral fuels. Data represent production as measured by mine shipments, mine sales, or marketable production (including consumption by producers).

Mineral	Unit	Production quantity				
		1980	1990	1991	1992	1993
Total mineral production	(X)	(X)	(X)	(X)	(X)	(X)
Mineral fuels	(X)	(X)	(X)	(X)	(X)	(X)
Coal: Bituminous and lignite	Million short tons	824	1,026	993	998	(NA)
Pennsylvania anthracite coal	Million short tons	6	4	3	3	(NA)
Natural gas (wet)	Trillion cubic feet	20.18	1,859	1,871	1,871	(NA)
Petroleum (crude)	Million barrels[1]	3,146	2,685	2,707	2,625	(NA)
Uranium[2]	Million pounds	43.7	8.9	8.0	5.6	(NA)

Source: 1994 Statistical Abstract of the United States on CD-ROM [machine-readable datafiles]. CD-8A-94. Washington, DC: U.S. Department of Commerce, Economics and Statistics Administration, Bureau of the Census, Data User Services Division, January 1995. Primary sources: U.S. Bureau of Mines. *Minerals Yearbook* (through 1991); *Annual Reports and Mineral Commodities Summaries* (annual); U.S. Energy Information Administration. *Annual Energy Review; Uranium Industry Annual; Petroleum Supply Annual.* Volume 1; *Natural Gas Annual;* and *Quarterly Coal Report. Notes:* "NA" represents "not available." "X" represents "not applicable." 1. 42 gallon barrels. 2. Recoverable content of ores, etc.

★ 239 ★

Mineral and Metal Production

Mineral Fuel Production Values: 1980-1993

Table shows production values for selected mineral fuels. Data represent production as measured by mine shipments, mine sales, or marketable production (including consumption by producers).

Mineral	Unit	Production value (million dollars)				
		1980	1990	1991	1992	1993
Total mineral production	(X)	146,750	141,741	(NA)	(NA)	(NA)
Mineral fuels	(X)	121,612	108,422	(NA)	(NA)	(NA)
Coal: Bituminous and lignite	Million short tons	20,197	22,274	21,598	(NA)	(NA)
Pennsylvania anthracite	Million short tons	259	133	(NA)	(NA)	(NA)
Natural gas (wet)	Trillion cubic feet	32,090	31,658	30,327	32,571	(NA)
Petroleum (crude)	Million barrels[1]	67,930	53,772	44,666	(NA)	(NA)
Uranium[2]	Million pounds	1,136	140	(NA)	(NA)	(NA)

Source: 1994 Statistical Abstract of the United States on CD-ROM [machine-readable datafiles]. CD-8A-94. Washington, DC: U.S. Department of Commerce, Economics and Statistics Administration, Bureau of the Census, Data User Services Division, January 1995. Primary sources: U.S. Bureau of Mines. *Minerals Yearbook* (through 1991); *Annual Reports and Mineral Commodities Summaries* (annual); U.S. Energy Information Administration. *Annual Energy Review; Uranium Industry Annual; Petroleum Supply Annual.* Volume 1; *Natural Gas Annual;* and *Quarterly Coal Report. Notes:* "NA" represents "not available." 1. 42 gallon barrels. 2. Recoverable content of ores, etc.

★ 240 ★

Mineral and Metal Production

Mining and Primary Metal Production Indexes: 1970-1993

[1987 = 100]

Industry group	1970	1975	1980	1990	1991	1992	1993
Mining	100.4	98.0	110.0	102.6	101.1	98.7	97.2
Coal	67.2	71.5	90.2	113.2	109.2	105.5	103.8
Anthracite	274.1	175.0	169.6	103.2	72.7	66.1	(NA)
Bituminous	66.0	71.0	89.7	113.3	109.4	105.8	(NA)
Oil and gas extraction	104.8	101.8	112.1	95.5	95.8	93.2	92.2
Crude oil and natural gas	122.3	107.5	108.4	93.7	95.5	94.0	(NA)
Oil and gas drilling	65.2	109.7	181.2	109.0	93.3	78.3	82.5
Metal mining	129.5	106.4	108.8	153.1	155.8	161.2	166.3
Iron ore	194.4	172.1	149.4	117.9	122.3	120.5	120.8
Nonferrous ores	111.5	88.7	95.0	160.5	156.9	(NA)	(NA)
Copper ore	123.2	101.5	93.1	126.8	130.9	146.3	142.7
Lead and zinc ores	192.2	189.9	166.7	196.6	199.0	187.5	176.2
Primary metals, manufacturing	115.2	107.2	110.8	106.5	98.3	101.1	106.4
Nonferrous metals	77.1	75.3	92.5	99.5	95.3	96.1	99.5
Copper	135.2	103.0	94.7	102.2	109.7	109.9	117.7

[Continued]

★ 240 ★

Mining and Primary Metal Production Indexes: 1970-1993

[Continued]

Industry group	1970	1975	1980	1990	1991	1992	1993
Aluminum	107.8	105.2	138.7	121.0	123.2	120.5	110.5
Iron and steel	148.2	133.5	126.0	111.5	100.5	104.7	111.5

Source: *1994 Statistical Abstract of the United States on CD-ROM* [machine-readable datafiles]. CD-8A-94. Washington, DC: U.S. Department of Commerce, Economics and Statistics Administration, Bureau of the Census, Data User Services Division, January 1995. Primary source: Board of Governors of the Federal Reserve System. *Federal Reserve Bulletin* (monthly). *Note:* "NA" represents "not available."

★ 241 ★

Mineral and Metal Production

Nonfuel Mineral Commodities: 1993

Table provides preliminary estimates of mineral disposition.

Mineral	Unit	Mineral disposition			
		Produc-tion	Ex-ports	Net import reli-ance[1] (per-cent)	Con-sumption, apparent
Aluminum	1,000 metric tons	5,300	1,200	16	6,300
Antimony (contained)	Metric tons	37,000[2]	5,000	57	44,600
Arsenic	Metric tons	-	230[3]	100	23,900
Asbestos	1,000 metric tons	15	32	95	33
Barite	1,000 metric tons	300	20	58	720
Bauxite and alumina	1,000 metric tons	(D)	1,305	100	4,500
Beryllium (contained)	Metric tons	159	16	4	165
Bismuth (contained)	Metric tons	(D)	70	(D)	1,450[4]
Boron (B_2O_3 content)	1,000 metric tons	526	580[5]	[6]	244
Bromine (contained)	1,000 metric tons	168	25	[6]	157
Cadmium (contained)	Metric tons	1,050[2]	16	66	3,110
Cement	1,000 short tons	79,600	710	7	84,708
Chromium	1,000 metric tons	88[7]	18	82	488
Clays	1,000 metric tons	44,183	4,045	[6]	40,184
Cobalt (contained)	Metric tons	1,600[7]	900	75	6,320
Columbium (contained)	Metric tons	-	100	100	3,400
Copper (contained)	1,000 metric tons	1,770	200	6	2,450
Diamond (industrial)	Million carats	116	100	15	136
Diatomite	1,000 metric tons	622	167	[6]	457
Feldspar	1,000 metric tons	760	19	[6]	749
Fluorspar	1,000 metric tons	152	13	89	438
Gallium (contained)	Kilograms	-	(NA)	(NA)	11,000[8]
Garnet (industrial)	Metric tons	52,400	12,100	[6]	52,100
Gemstones	Million dollars	72	1,612	98	3,644
Germanium (contained)	Kilograms	10,000[2]	(NA)	(NA)	25,000
Gold (contained)	Metric tons	390[2]	(NA)	(NA)	(NA)

[Continued]

★ 241 ★

Nonfuel Mineral Commodities: 1993
[Continued]

Mineral	Unit	Mineral disposition			
		Production	Exports	Net import reliance[1] (percent)	Consumption, apparent
Graphite (crude)	1,000 metric tons	-	18	100	34
Gypsum (crude)	1,000 short tons	17,000	50	29	25,000
Indium	Metric tons	(NA)	(NA)	(NA)	35[9]
Iodine	Metric tons	1,900	1,700	51	3,900
Iron ore (usable)	Million metric tons	55	4	12	63
Iron and steel scrap (metal)	Million metric tons	75	11	[6]	67
Iron and steel slag	1,000 metric tons	21,000	4	0.5	20,961[8]
Lead (contained)	1,000 metric tons	1,170	130	11	1,280
Lime	1,000 short tons	18,300	66	(NA)	18,431
Magnesium compounds	1,000 metric tons	420	50	26	570
Magnesium metal	1,000 metric tons	202	42	[6]	153
Manganese (gross weight)	1,000 metric tons	-	34	100	650[10]
Mercury	Metric tons	270	90	(NA)	(NA)
Mica, scrap and flake	1,000 metric tons	89	5	11	98
Molybdenum (contained)	Metric tons	45,400	34,000	[6]	16,300
Nickel (contained)	Metric tons	4,878	33,210	64	152,000
Nitrogen (fixed)-ammonia	1,000 metric tons	12,700	400	15	15,010
Nonrenewable organics	Million metric tons	117	8	4	122
Peat	1,000 short tons	600	10	56	1,370
Perlite	1,000 metric tons	548	30	3	563
Phosphate rock	1,000 metric tons	35,000	3,000	[6]	36,000
Platinum-group metals	Kilograms	64,400	86,000	88	112,300
Potash (K_2O equivalent)	1,000 metric tons	1,500	360	71	5,120
Pumice and pumicite	1,000 metric tons	492	20	25	652
Salt	1,000 metric tons	37,700	700	12	43,000
Silicon (contained)	1,000 metric tons	370	31	34	560
Silver (contained)	Metric tons	2,200	1,700	(NA)	4,000
Sodium carbonate (soda ash)	1,000 metric tons	9,200	2,900	[6]	6,496
Sodium sulfate	1,000 metric tons	615	100	9	677
Stone (crushed)	Million short tons	1,223	4	-	1,227
Sulfur (all forms)	1,000 metric tons	10,600	570	15	12,600
Talc	1,000 metric tons	928	168	[6]	839
Thallium (contained)	Kilograms	-	(NA)	100	800
Tin (contained)	Metric tons	8,500[7]	2,300	81	45,914
Titanium dioxide	1,000 metric tons	1,158	258	[6]	1,071
Tungsten (contained)	Metric tons	(D)	20	84	6,800[11]
Vermiculite	1,000 metric tons	185	5	16	220

[Continued]

★ 241 ★

Nonfuel Mineral Commodities: 1993
[Continued]

Mineral	Unit	Mineral disposition			
		Production	Exports	Net import reliance[1] (percent)	Consumption, apparent
Zinc (contained)	1,000 metric tons	380	510	26	1,360
Zirconium content (Z,02)	Metric tons	(D)	25,950	(D)	(D)

Source: 1994 Statistical Abstract of the United States on CD-ROM [machine-readable datafiles]. CD-8A-94. Washington, DC: U.S. Department of Commerce, Economics and Statistics Administration, Bureau of the Census, Data User Services Division, January 1995. Primary source: U.S. Bureau of Mines. *Mineral Commodity Summaries*, (annual). *Notes:* "-" represents or rounds to zero. "D" denotes data withheld to avoid disclosure. "NA" stands for "not available." 1. Calculated as a percent of apparent consumption. 2. Refinery production. 3. Metal price. 4. Reported consumption. 5. Gross weight. 6. Net exporter. 7. Secondary production. 8. Gross weight. 9. Cents per pound. 10. Estimated manganese content. 11. All forms.

★ 242 ★

Mineral and Metal Production

Nonfuel Mineral Production, by State or Area: 1980-1993

Table shows the value of domestic nonfuel mineral production in each state, by U.S. regions.

[In million dollars]

State	1980	1985	1990	1991	1992	1993	Principal minerals in order of value
United States	25,140	23,303	33,452	30,579	32,012	31,556	(X)
Northeast	1,581	1,964	2,479	2,095	2,308	2,411	(X)
New England	268	325	446	347	423	421	(X)
Maine	37	41	55	41	56	61	Cement (Portland), sand and gravel, and stone.
New Hampshire	25	33	36	30	42	36	Sand and gravel, stone, and gypsum.
Vermont	43	50	87	60	60[1]	45	Stone, sand and gravel, and talc.
Massachusetts	91	117	128	112	147	166	Stone, sand and gravel, and lime.
Rhode Island	6	12	18	13	21	27[1]	Sand and gravel (construction), stone, and sand and gravel (industrial).
Connecticut	66	72	122	91	97	86	Stone, sand and gravel (construction), and sand and gravel (industrial).
Middle Atlantic	1,313	1,639	2,033	1,748	1,885	1,990	(X)
New York	496	657	773	699	766	845	Stone, salt, and sand and gravel.
New Jersey	149	178	229	205	240	252	Stone, sand and gravel (construction), and sand and gravel (industrial).
Pennsylvania	668	804	1,031	844	879	893	Stone, cement (Portland), and lime.
Midwest	6,610	6,034	7,163	6,755	7,261	6,958	(X)
East North Central	2,930	2,869	3,483	3,479	3,762	3,655	(X)
Ohio	562	594	733	684	742	814	Stone, sand and gravel, and salt.
Indiana	288	303	428	403	477	501	Stone, cement (Portland), and sand and gravel.
Illinois	443	460	667	673	734	732	Stone, sand and gravel, and cement (Portland).
Michigan	1,485	1,387	1,440	1,503	1,587	1,408	Iron ore, cement (Portland), and sand and gravel.
Wisconsin	152	125	215	216	222	200	Stone, sand and gravel, and lime.
West North Central	3,680	3,165	3,680	3,276	3,499	3,303	(X)
Minnesota	1,782	1,548	1,482	1,289	1,364	1,323	Iron ore, sand and gravel, and stone.
Iowa	252	228	310	344	391	344	Stone, cement (Portland), and sand and gravel.
Missouri	1,054	735	1,105	880	897	785	Lead, cement (Portland), and stone.
North Dakota	22	24	25	17[1]	26	25[1]	Sand and gravel (construction), lime, and sand and gravel (industrial).
South Dakota	228	208	319	290	301	324	Gold, cement (Portland), and sand and gravel.
Nebraska	80	100	90	89	115	118	Sand and gravel (construction), cement (Portland), and stone.
Kansas	262	322	349	367	405	384	Salt, helium, and stone.
South	7,320	8,029	9,291	8,285	8,560	8,901	(X)
South Atlantic	3,454	3,998	5,132	4,497	4,651	4,941	(X)
Delaware	2	4	10	5	9	11[1]	Sand and gravel (construction).

[Continued]

★ 242 ★

Nonfuel Mineral Production, by State or Area: 1980-1993

[Continued]

State	1980	1985	1990	1991	1992	1993	Principal minerals in order of value
Maryland	186	258	368	348	339	361	Stone, cement (Portland), and sand and gravel.
Virginia	305	381	507	428	462	515	Stone, cement (Portland), and sand and gravel.
West Virginia	106	105	133	117	112	111	Stone, cement (Portland), and sand and gravel.
North Carolina	380	466	586	557	596	594	Stone, phosphate rock, and lithium minerals.
South Carolina	195	276	450	340	247	361	Cement (Portland), stone, and gold.
Georgia	771	946	1,504	1,306	1,346	1,691	Clays, stone, and cement (Portland).
Florida	1,509	1,562	1,574	1,396	1,440	1,297	Phosphate rock, stone, and cement (Portland).
East South Central	1,030	1,251	1,692	1,533	1,640	1,663	(X)
Kentucky	204	268	359	343	401	416	Stone, lime, and cement (Portland).
Tennessee	394	473	663	548	576	538	Stone, zinc, and cement (Portland).
Alabama	328	407	559	540	543	570	Stone, cement (Portland), and lime.
Mississippi	104	103	111	102	120	139	Sand and gravel, cement (Portland), and clays (Fuller's earth).
West South Central	2,836	2,780	2,467	2,255	2,269	2,297	(X)
Arkansas	293	270	381	361	404	365	Stone, bromine, and cement (Portland).
Louisiana	584	521	368	352	309	256	Salt, sand and gravel, and sulphur.
Oklahoma	224	252	259	276	253	282	Stone, cement (Portland), and sand and gravel.
Texas	1,735	1,737	1,459	1,266	1,303	1,394	Cement (Portland), stone, and magnesium metal.
West	9,629	7,276	14,512	13,435	13,858	13,235	(X)
Mountain	7,223	4,669	10,380	9,581	10,154	9,683	(X)
Montana	280	200	573	534	539	496	Gold, copper, and cement (Portland).
Idaho	522	359	375	298	306	283	Phosphate rock, gold, and sand and gravel.
Wyoming	761	551	911	929	951	858	Soda ash, clays, and helium.
Colorado	1,265	408	377	338	385	432	Sand and gravel, cement (Portland), and stone.
New Mexico	766	657	1,103	986	871	788	Copper, potash, and sand and gravel.
Arizona	2,471	1,550	3,085	2,877	3,166	2,742	Copper, sand and gravel, and cement (Portland).
Utah	764	313	1,335	1,190	1,348	1,350	Copper, gold, and magnesium.
Nevada	394	631	2,621	2,429	2,588	2,734	Gold, sand and gravel, and silver.
Pacific	2,406	2,607	4,132	3,854	3,704	3,552	(X)
Washington	207	222	483	483	469	480	Sand and gravel, magnesium metal, and gold.
Oregon	152	130	205	198	214	234	Stone, sand and gravel, and cement (Portland).
California	1,872	2,112	2,771	2,538	2,346	2,282	Sand and gravel, cement (Portland), and gold.
Alaska	115	90	577	494	526	421	Zinc, gold, and sand and gravel.
Hawaii	60	53	106	141	149	135[1]	Stone, cement (Portland) and (masonry), and gemstones.

Source: 1994 Statistical Abstract of the United States on CD-ROM [machine-readable datafiles]. CD-8A-94. Washington, DC: U.S. Department of Commerce, Economics and Statistics Administration, Bureau of the Census, Data User Services Division, January 1995. Primary sources: U.S. Bureau of Mines. Minerals Yearbook (annual) and Mineral Commodities Summary (annual). Notes: "X" represents "not applicable." 1. Partial data only.

★ 243 ★

Mineral and Metal Production

Principal Fuel, Nonmetal, and Metal Production: 1980-1993

Table shows U.S. production of principal fuels, nonmetals, and metals as a percent of world production.

Mineral	Unit	World Production				U.S. Production as percent of world production			
		1980	1985	1990	1993, estimated	1980	1985	1990	1993, estimated
Fuels:[1]									
Coal	Billion short tons	4.2	4.8	5.2	(NA)	20	18	20	(NA)
Petroleum (crude)	Billion barrels	21.7	19.6	22	(NA)	14	17	12	(NA)
Natural gas (dry, marketable)	Trillion cubic feet	53.1	62	74.3	(NA)	37	26	24	(NA)
Natural gas plant liquids	Billion barrels	1.4	1.5	1.8	(NA)	43	38	32	(NA)
Nonmetals:									
Asbestos	1,000 metric tons	4,699	4,249	4,003	3,110	2	1	(D)	(Z)
Barite	1,000 metric tons	7,495	6,067	5,633	5,200	27	11	8	8
Feldspar	1,000 metric tons	3,202	4,039	5,456	5,900	20	16	12	13
Fluorspar	1,000 metric tons	5,006	4,979	5,131	3,660	2	1	1	1
Gypsum	Million metric tons	78	87	100	98	14	15	15	16
Mica (including scrap)	1,000 metric tons	228	255	215	185	46	49	51	48
Nitrogen, (fixed) - ammonia	Million metric tons	74	91	97	93	20	14	13	14

[Continued]

★ 243 ★

Principal Fuel, Nonmetal, and Metal Production: 1980-1993

[Continued]

Mineral	Unit	World Production				U.S. Production as percent of world production			
		1980	1985	1990	1993, estimated	1980	1985	1990	1993, estimated
Phosphate rock (gross weight)	Million metric tons	144	149	162	131	38	34	29	27
Potash (K₂O equivalent)	Million metric tons	28	29	28	22	8	4	6	6
Sulfur, elemental	Million metric tons	55	54	58	53	22	22	20	20
Metals, mine basis:									
Bauxite	Million metric tons	89	84	109	101	2	1	(D)	(D)
Columbium concentrates (Columbium content)	1,000 metric tons	15	15	15	15	(NA)	-	(NA)	-
Copper	1,000 metric tons	7,405	7,988	9,017	9,300	16	14	18	19
Gold	Metric tons	1,219	1,532	2,133	2,290	2	5	14	14
Iron ore (gross weight)	Million metric tons	891	861	982	940	8	6	6	6
Lead[2]	1,000 metric tons	3,470	3,431	3,353	3,200	17	12	15	13
Mercury	Metric tons	6,806	6,136	4,523	2,900	16	9	12	2
Molybdenum	1,000 metric tons	111	98	128	108	62	50	48	42
Nickel[2]	1,000 metric tons	779	813	965	826	2	1	(Z)	(Z)
Silver	1,000 metric tons	11	13	16	15	9	9	13	11
Tantalum concentrates (tantalum content)	Metric tons	544	315	400	290	(NA)	-	(NA)	-
Titanium concentrates:									
Ilmenite	1,000 metric tons	3,726	3,457	4,072	3,300	14	(D)	(D)	(D)
Rutile	1,000 metric tons	436	373	481	430	(D)	(D)	(D)	(D)
Tungsten[2]	1,000 metric tons	52	47	43	26	5	2	14	(D)
Vanadium[2]	1,000 metric tons	37	30	31	28	12	(D)	(D)	(D)
Zinc[2]	1,000 metric tons	5,954	6,758	7,184	7,000	6	4	8	8
Metals, smelter basis:									
Aluminum	1,000 metric tons	15,383	15,398	19,292	(NA)	30	23	21	(NA)
Cadmium	1,000 metric tons	18	19	20	(NA)	9	8	8	(NA)
Copper	1,000 metric tons	7,649	8,630	9,472	(NA)	14	14	15	(NA)
Iron, pig	Million metric tons	514	499	532	(NA)	12	9	9	(NA)
Lead[3]	1,000 metric tons	5,430	5,641	5,763	(NA)	23	20	23	(NA)
Magnesium[4]	1,000 metric tons	316	325	354	(NA)	49	42	39	(NA)
Raw Steel	Million metric tons	717	718	771	(NA)	14	11	12	(NA)
Tin[5]	1,000 metric tons	251	193	223	(NA)	1	2	-	(NA)
Zinc	1,000 metric tons	6,049	6,786	7,060	(NA)	6	5	5	(NA)

Source: *1994 Statistical Abstract of the United States on CD-ROM* [machine-readable datafiles]. CD-8A-94. Washington, DC: U.S. Department of Commerce, Economics and Statistics Administration, Bureau of the Census, Data User Services Division, January 1995. Primary source, except as noted: U.S. Bureau of Mines. *Annual Reports,* and *Mineral Commodity Summaries* (annual). *Notes:* "-" represents or rounds to zero. "D" denotes data withheld to avoid disclosing company data. "NA" represents "not available." "Z" indicates less than half the unit of measure. 1. Source: Energy Information Administration. *International Energy Annual.* 2. Content of ore and concentrate. 3. Refinery production. 4. Primary production; no smelter processing necessary. 5. Production from primary sources only.

★ 244 ★

Mineral and Metal Production

World Mineral Production: 1985-1993

Table shows world production of major mineral commodities.

Commodity	Unit	1985	1990	1991	1992, estimated	1993, estimated	Leading producers, 1992
Mineral fuels[1]							
Coal	Million metric tons	4,349	4,745	4,506	4,527	(NA)	China, United States, Russia
Dry natural gas	Trillion cubic feet	61.8	73.7	74.8	75.0	(NA)	Russia, United States, Canada
Natural gas plant liquids[2]	Million barrels[3]	1,437	1,728	1,809	1,868	(NA)	United States, Saudi Arabia, Canada
Petroleum, crude	Million barrels[3]	19,703	22,072	21,938	21,993	(NA)	Saudi Arabia, Russia, United States
Petroleum, refined	Million barrels[3]	21,114	23,791	23,624	(NA)	(NA)	United States, Russia, Japan (for 1991)
Nonmetallic minerals							
Cement, hydraulic	Million metric tons	960	1,148	1,190	1,254	1,266	China, Japan, United States

[Continued]

★ 244 ★

World Mineral Production: 1985-1993
[Continued]

Commodity	Unit	1985	1990	1991	1992, estimated	1993, estimated	Leading producers, 1992
Diamond, gem and industrial	1,000 carats	66,018	110,919	105,855	107,771	(NA)	Australia, Russia, Botswana
Nitrogen in ammonia	Million metric tons	91.0	97.1	94.0	92.5	92.5	China, United States, Russia
Phosphate rock	Million metric tons	149	162	150	144	131	United States, China, Morocco
Potash, marketable	Million metric tons	29.2	27.8	26.1	24.3	22.4	Canada, Belarus, Russia
Salt	Million metric tons	173	184	192	185	185	United States, China, Germany
Sulfur, elemental basis	Million metric tons	53.8	58.1	55.0	52.4	53.0	United States, Russia, Canada
Metals							
Aluminum[4]	Million metric tons	15.4	19.3	19.5	19.2	19.0	United States, Russia, Canada
Bauxite, gross weight	Million metric tons	84.2	108.6	108.2	103.6	101.0	Australia, Guinea, Jamaica
Chromite, gross weight[2]	1,000 metric tons	10,945	12,968	13,445	10,896	10,000	Kazakhstan, South Africa, India
Copper, metal content[5]	1,000 metric tons	7,988	9,017	9,187	9,290	9,300	Chile, United States, Japan
Gold, metal content	Metric tons	1,532	2,133	2,149	2,248	2,290	South Africa, United States, Australia
Iron ore, gross weight[6]	Million metric tons	861	982	956	930	940	China, Brazil, Australia
Lead, metal content[5]	1,000 metric tons	3,431	3,353	3,276	3,242	3,200	Australia, United States, China
Manganese ore, gross weight	Million metric tons	25.4	25.3	21.2	19.9	20.4	Ukraine, China, South Africa
Nickel, metal content[5]	1,000 metric tons	813	965	949	922	826	Russia, Canada, New Caledonia
Steel, crude	Million metric tons	718	771	736	721	728	Japan, United States, China
Tin, metal content[5]	1,000 metric tons	181	222	203	179	175	China, Brazil, Indonesia
Zinc, metal content[5]	1,000 metric tons	6,758	7,184	7,170	7,137	7,000	Canada, Australia, China

Source: 1994 Statistical Abstract of the United States on CD-ROM [machine-readable datafiles]. CD-8A-94. Washington, DC: U.S. Department of Commerce, Economics and Statistics Administration, Bureau of the Census, Data User Services Division, January 1995. Primary sources—except as noted: U.S. Bureau of Mines. *Minerals Yearbook* (1989); *Annual Reports* (1992); and *Mineral Commodity Summaries* (1994). *Notes:* "NA" stand for "not available." 1. Source: Energy Information Administration. *International Energy Annual.* 1992 data preliminary. 2. Excludes mainland China. 3. 42-gallon barrels. 4. Unalloyed ingot metal. 5. Mine output. 6. Includes iron ore concentrates and iron ore agglomerates.

Parks and Recreation Areas

★ 245 ★

Federal Agency Administered Areas – Visits: 1977-1993

Year	National Park Service (million visits)	Fish and Wildlife Service wildlife refuges (million visitors)	Bureau of Reclamation (million visitors)	National Forest Service forest national lands (million visitor days)	Corps of Engineers reservoirs (million visitor days)	Bureau of Land Management (million visitor days)
1977	NA	27	55	205	424	NA
1978	NA	26	63	219	439	NA
1979	NA	25	59	220	449	NA
1980	198	23	60	234	457	NA
1981	211	26	69	236	469	64

[Continued]

★ 245 ★

Federal Agency Administered Areas – Visits: 1977-1993
[Continued]

Year	National Park Service (million visits)	Fish and Wildlife Service wildlife refuges (million visitors)	Bureau of Reclamation (million visitors)	National Forest Service forest national lands (million visitor days)	Corps of Engineers reservoirs (million visitor days)	Bureau of Land Management (million visitor days)
1982	214	24	63	233	480	40
1983	217	22	66	228	480	42
1984	218	23	76	228	482	34
1985	216	24	76	225	502	31
1986	237	25	80	237	506	36
1987	246	25	80	239	181	64
1988	250	26	82	242	191	57
1989	256	26	84	253	191	50
1990	263	27	80	263	190	70
1991	268	28	80	279	192	68
1992	275	28	83	287	203	65
1993	273	28	84	296	200	39

Source: Executive Office of the President of the United States. *Environmental Quality 24: The Twenty-fourth Annual Report of the Council on Environmental Quality.* Prepared by Ray Clark. Written by Carroll Curtis. Edited by Barry Walsh. Washington, DC: U.S. Government Printing Office, 1994, p. 477. Primary sources: U.S. Army Corps of Engineers. Directorate of Civil Works. Operations, Construction and Readiness Division. Natural Resources Management Branch. *Visitation to Corps Recreation Areas.* Washington, DC: Corps of Engineers, unpublished data; U.S. Department of Agriculture. Forest Service. Recreation Information Management System Database (Washington, DC). Unpublished data; U.S. Department of the Interior. Bureau of Land Management. *Public Land Statistics.* Washington, DC: U.S. Department of the Interior, Bureau of Land Management, annual; U.S. Department of the Interior. Bureau of Reclamation. *Utilization of Recreation Areas on Reclamation Projects.* Denver, CO: U.S. Department of the Interior, Bureau of Reclamation. Data from the Commissioner's annual reports; U.S. Department of the Interior. Fish and Wildlife Service. Refuge Division. Public use statistics database through 1987, with estimates for 1988-1993, and unpublished data; U.S. Department of the Interior. National Park Service. Statistical Office. *National Park Statistical Abstract.* Denver, CO: U.S. Department of the Interior, National Park Service, annual. *Notes:* "NA" stands for "not available." Bureau of Land Management visitation data from 1981 through 1992 not strictly comparable with 1993 data because of differences in collection methodology and estimation accuracy. Visitor days for Bureau of Land Management are reported as 8-hour visitor days; for National Forest Service and Corps of Engineers as 12-hour visitor days; and for Corps of Engineers as recreation days of use (1977-1986) and visitor days (after 1986). Bureau of Reclamation data for 1993 are preliminary.

★ 246 ★

Parks and Recreation Areas

Federal Recreation Area Visits: 1978-1992

Table shows visitation to federal recreation areas for years ending September 30. Covers persons entering and using a recreation area over a specified period of time.

[In million visitor hours]

Administrating federal agency	1978	1980	1985	1990	1991	1992
All areas	7,094	6,367	6,403	7,567	7,829	7,995
Fish and Wildlife Service	84	17	65	(NA)	(NA)	(NA)
Forest Service	2,622	2,819	2,705	3,157	3,346	3,452
U.S. Army Corps of Engineers[1]	2,071	1,926	1,721	2,280	2,306	2,306
National Park Service	1,154	1,042	1,298	1,322	1,344	1,390
Bureau of Land Management[2]	634	68	246	518	540	563
Bureau of Reclamation	431	407	289	280	280	269
Tennessee Valley Authority[3]	97	87	79	10	13	14

Source: 1994 Statistical Abstract of the United States on CD-ROM [machine-readable datafiles]. CD-8A-94. Washington, DC: U.S. Department of Commerce, Economics and Statistics Administration, Bureau of the Census, Data User Services Division, January 1995. Primary sources: 1978 through 1980, U.S. Heritage Conservation and Recreation Service. *Federal Recreation Fee Report* (annual); thereafter, U.S. National Park Service. *Notes:* "NA" represents "not available." One recreation visitor day is the recreation use of national forest land or water that aggregates 12 visitor hours. This may entail 1 person for 12 hours, 12 persons for 1 hour, or any equivalent combination of individual or group use, either continuous or intermittent. 1. Beginning 1986, not comparable with previous years. 2. Data not comparable for all years. 3. Beginning in 1989, the Tennessee Valley Authority (TVA) discontinued reporting visitation to nonfee charging areas. Data for 1987 and 1988 have been adjusted to reflect this policy.

★ 247 ★

Parks and Recreation Areas

National Forest Recreation Use: 1980-1992

Table shows the recreation visitor days and ways in which visitors use national forest areas. Represents recreational use of national forest land and water in states that have Forest Service recreation programs. For years ending September 30. Data are estimated.

Year and activity	Recrea-tion visitor-days[1] (1,000)
1980	233,549
1981	235,709
1982	233,438
1983	227,708
1984	227,554
1985	225,407
1986	226,533
1987	238,458
1988	242,316

[Continued]

★ 247 ★

National Forest Recreation Use: 1980-1992
[Continued]

Year and activity	Recrea-tion visitor-days[1] (1,000)
1989	252,495
1990	263,051
1991	278,849
1992, total	287,691
Mechanized travel and viewing scenery	100,916
Camping, picnicking and swimming	77,211
Hiking, horseback riding and water travel	24,239
Winter sports	18,045
Hunting	16,962
Resorts, cabins and organization camps	16,480
Fishing	16,268
Nature studies	2,497
Other[2]	15,073

Source: 1994 Statistical Abstract of the United States on CD-ROM [machine-readable datafiles]. CD-8A-94. Washington, DC: U.S. Department of Commerce, Economics and Statistics Administration, Bureau of the Census, Data User Services Division, January 1995. Primary source: U.S. Forest Service. Unpublished data. Notes: 1. One recreation visitor-day is the recreation use of National Forest land or water that aggregates 12 visitor-hours. This may entail 1 person for 12 hours, 12 persons for 1 hour, or any equivalent combination of individual or group use, either continuous or intermittent. 2. Includes team sports, gathering forest products, attending talks and programs, and other uses.

★ 248 ★

Parks and Recreation Areas

National Forest Recreation Use, by State: 1990-1992

Table shows the recreation visitor days for national forest areas. One recreation visitor day is the recreation use of national forest land or water that aggregates 12 visitor hours. This may entail 1 person for 12 hours, 12 persons for 1 hour, or any equivalent combination of individual or group use, either continuous or intermittent. Represents recreational use of national forest land and water in states that have a Forest Service recreation program. For years ending September 30. Data are estimated.

[In thousands]

State or area	1990	1991	1992
United States	263,051	278,849	287,691
Alabama	698	677	701
Alaska	5,414	5,718	5,888
Arizona	19,039	21,549	25,544
Arkansas	2,441	2,109	2,153

[Continued]

★ 248 ★

National Forest Recreation Use, by State: 1990-1992

[Continued]

State or area	1990	1991	1992
California	61,007	65,221	67,614
Colorado	25,204	25,998	29,053
Florida	2,961	3,081	3,104
Georgia	2,833	2,839	2,993
Idaho	11,819	12,909	13,087
Illinois	1,638	843	900
Indiana	569	594	552
Kansas	61	66	76
Kentucky	2,447	2,112	2,113
Louisiana	527	486	507
Massachusetts	58	61	61
Michigan	4,916	8,153	4,755
Minnesota	5,399	4,956	5,739
Mississippi	1,177	1,285	1,298
Missouri	1,713	1,742	1,803
Montana	9,704	10,595	11,046
Nebraska	149	147	200
Nevada	3,278	3,283	3,360
New Hampshire	2,676	4,014	3,037
New Mexico	7,704	8,065	8,603
New York	72	45	31
North Carolina	5,472	5,692	5,767
North Dakota	169	199	142
Ohio	504	522	672
Oklahoma	387	373	369
Oregon	21,036	21,037	19,898
Pennsylvania	2,631	2,977	2,942
South Carolina	816	943	950
South Dakota	2,966	3,095	3,244
Tennessee	2826	2,924	2,978
Texas	2,155	2,253	2,273
Utah	12,744	13,337	18,413
Vermont	1,369	1,571	1,565
Virginia	3,900	4,173	4,269
Washington	22,451	22,458	18,740
West Virginia	1,234	1,340	1,264
Wisconsin	2,095	2,215	2,185
Wyoming	6,609	6,914	7,516
Puerto Rico	186	280	289

Source: 1994 Statistical Abstract of the United States on CD-ROM [machine-readable datafiles]. CD-8A-94. Washington, DC: U.S. Department of Commerce, Economics and Statistics Administration, Bureau of the Census, Data User Services Division, January 1995. Primary source: U.S. Forest Service. Unpublished data.

★ 249 ★

Parks and Recreation Areas

National Park System: 1981-1992

Table shows finances, visits, and land area of national park system for fiscal years ending in year shown, except as noted. Includes data for five areas in Puerto Rico and Virgin Islands, one area in American Samoa, and one area in Guam.

Item	1981	1985	1990	1991	1992
Finances (million dollars):[1]					
Expenditures reported	715.3	848.1	986.1	1,104.4	1,268.7
Salaries and wages	297.0	369.4	459.1	495.3	518.1
Improvements, maintenance	82.3	127.4	160.0	179.6	212.1
Construction	123.2	84.7	108.5	134.1	193.3
Other	212.8	266.6	258.5	295.4	345.2
Funds available	945.9	1,248.2	1,505.5	1,988.4	2,274.8
Appropriations	546.8	821.6	1,052.5	1,284.7	1,392.8
Other[2]	399.1	426.6	453.0	703.7	882.0
Revenue from operations	22.9	50.6	78.6	78.1	88.3
Recreation visits (millions):[3]					
All areas	238.6	263.4	258.7	267.8	274.7
National parks[4]	50.4	50.0	57.7	57.4	58.7
National monuments	15.9	15.9	23.9	25.8	26.6
National historical, commemorative, archaeological[5]	58.4	61.9	57.5	61.0	63.3
National parkways	34.9	40.0	29.1	28.8	30.7
National recreation areas[4]	47.7	49.4	47.2	49.8	50.3
National seashores and lakeshores	17.8	25.3	23.3	24.4	23.9
National Capital Parks	6.7	8.3	7.5	7.5	8.1
Miscellaneous other areas	6.8	12.6	12.5	13.1	13.1
Recreation overnight stays (millions)[3]	16.4	15.8	17.6	17.7	18.3
In commercial lodgings	3.4	3.5	3.9	4.0	4.1
In Park Service campgrounds	8.9	7.3	7.9	7.8	8.1
In tents	4.2	3.6	4.1	4.2	4.4
In recreation vehicles	4.7	3.8	3.8	3.6	3.7
In backcountry	2.3	1.7	1.7	2.0	2.2
Other	1.8	3.2	4.2	3.9	3.9
Land (1,000 acres):[6]					
Total	73,665	75,749	76,362	76,607	76,492
Parks	44,470	45,739	46,089	46,135	46,208
Recreation areas	3,327	3,335	3,344	3,346	3,347
Other	25,868	26,675	26,929	27,126	26,937
Acquisition, gross	70	34	21	66	23
By purchase	60	29	18	15	21
By gift	6	2	2	43	1
By transfer or exchange	4	3	3	8	1

[Continued]

★ 249 ★

National Park System: 1981-1992
[Continued]

Item	1981	1985	1990	1991	1992
Exclusion	(Z)	(Z)	1	(Z)	(Z)
Acquisition, net	70	34	21	66	23

Source: 1994 Statistical Abstract of the United States on CD-ROM [machine-readable datafiles]. CD-8A-94. Washington, DC: U.S. Department of Commerce, Economics and Statistics Administration, Bureau of the Census, Data User Services Division, January 1995. Primary sources: U.S. National Park Service. Visits. *National Park Statistical Abstract* (annual); and unpublished data. *Notes:* "Z" represents less than 500 acres. 1. Financial data are those associated with the National Park System. Certain other functions of the National Park Service (principally the activities absorbed from the former Heritage Conservation and Recreation Service in 1981) are excluded. 2. Includes funds carried over from prior years. 3. For calendar year. 4. Combined data for North Cascades National Park and two adjacent National Recreation Areas are included in National Parks total. 5. Includes military areas. 6. Federal land only, as of December 31. Federal land acreages, in addition to National Park Service administered lands, also include lands within national park system area boundaries but under the administration of other agencies. Year-to-year changes in the federal lands figures include changes in the acreages of these other lands and hence often differ from "net acquisition."

★ 250 ★

Parks and Recreation Areas

National Park System – Units and Land: 1872-1993

Year	Units (number)	Land (million acres)
1872	1	2.2
1880	5	2.2
1890	12	3.8
1900	17	4.1
1910	45	7.9
1920	62	9.9
1930	98	10.8
1940	161	22.3
1950	182	24.6
1960	187	26.2
1970	282	29.6
1980	333	77.0
1990	358	80.1
1993	368	80.3

Source: Executive Office of the President of the United States. *Environmental Quality 24: The Twenty-fourth Annual Report of the Council on Environmental Quality.* Prepared by Ray Clark. Written by Carroll Curtis. Edited by Barry Walsh. Washington, DC: U.S. Government Printing Office, 1994, p. 473. Primary source: U.S. Department of the Interior. National Park Service. *Areas Administered by the National Park Service: Information.* Washington, DC: U.S. Department of the Interior, National Park Service, annual.

★ 251 ★

Parks and Recreation Areas

Recreational Use of Public Lands: 1982-1992

Table shows recreational use of public land administered by the Bureau of Land Management. For years ending September 30. Beginning 1987, increase due to an estimated longer length of stay per visit, especially in California.

[In thousands]

Year and state	Number of visits	Type of recreation use (visitor hours)										
		Total	Off-highway vehicle travel	Other motor-ized travel	Non motor-ized travel	Camping	Hunting	Miscellaneous site-based activities	Fishing	Boating	Miscellaneous water-based activities	Snow and ice-based recreational activity, winter sports
1982	58,135	316,959	19,471	32,646	11,237	63,928	108,996	44,587	19,287	10,101	1,043	5,663
1983	56,270	334,010	24,397	35,534	12,237	84,066	92,974	39,734	20,290	16,869	4,992	2,917
1984	59,228	271,373	21,348	25,433	9,579	73,032	73,898	37,650	14,263	11,184	2,092	2,894
1985	51,739	244,612	36,995	24,053	10,047	65,397	51,842	23,098	14,254	11,710	2,193	5,023
1986	54,253	284,142	49,688	25,866	14,397	95,196	35,570	19,331	18,227	15,891	3,951	6,025
1987	56,427	514,716	123,325	34,325	19,172	195,315	57,624	38,412	22,932	15,140	5,212	3,259
1988	57,460	492,756	122,014	35,748	19,761	178,703	55,285	38,340	21,617	13,294	4,979	3,015
1989	60,957	493,214	65,808	74,075	36,676	173,597	46,760	45,871	23,392	18,491	5,425	3,119
1990	71,820	523,753	63,016	83,445	41,316	165,366	47,053	57,958	28,664	20,806	8,313	7,816
1991	72,541	539,779	50,849	85,835	44,398	196,310	49,593	59,928	20,939	19,676	8,353	3,898
1992	69,418	519,429	46,411	93,477	43,845	181,536	44,557	59,857	19,768	18,735	7,586	3,657
Alaska	254	5,901	138	509	81	3,909	452	233	299	164	4	112
Arizona[1]	10,888	60,239	715	522	2,728	33,818	2,392	10,352	952	6,313	2,443	4
California	26,001	227,095	29,814	46,834	23,820	86,385	9,102	25,227	2,344	1,472	1,865	232
Colorado	3,860	24,223	1,436	6,311	945	5,902	5,058	1,627	761	1,774	65	344
Idaho	2,658	18,567	1,069	1,334	711	5,385	2,484	1,563	2,452	1,467	577	1,525
Montana[2]	2,290	13,184	2,523	1,169	494	3,175	2,862	433	1,720	439	55	314
Nevada	3,693	26,544	1,470	11,235	2,775	4,396	2,200	2,622	1,332	227	162	125
New Mexico	3,063	18,755	2,573	1,402	1,297	3,815	5,676	2,086	1,071	763	69	3
Oregon[3]	6,823	60,513	1,812	8,216	5,432	15,830	6,312	10,493	7,199	2,892	1,810	517
Utah	9,054	54,593	4,527	15,429	5,248	16,917	4,802	3,769	435	2,872	484	110
Wyoming	834	9,815	334	516	314	2,004	3,217	1,452	1,203	352	52	371

Source: 1994 Statistical Abstract of the United States on CD-ROM [machine-readable datafiles]. CD-8A-94. Washington, DC: U.S. Department of Commerce, Economics and Statistics Administration, Bureau of the Census, Data User Services Division, January 1995. Primary source: U.S. Bureau of Land Management. *Public Land Statistics* (annual). *Notes:* 1. Includes concession visitation data. 2. Includes North Dakota and South Dakota. 3. Includes Washington.

★ 252 ★

Parks and Recreation Areas

State Parks and Recreation Areas, by State: 1991

Table shows acreage, visitors, and revenue for parks and recreation areas in each state. For years ending June 30. Data are shown as reported by state park directors. In some states, park agencies have under their control forests, fish and wildlife areas, and/or other areas. In other states, agencies are responsible for state parks only.

State	Acreage (1,000)	Visitors (1,000)		Revenue	
				Total ($1,000)	Per-cent of oper-ating budget
		Total[1]	Day		
United States	11,148	736,897	680,398	454,248	41.5
Alabama	50	6,084	4,985	22,505	80.7
Alaska	3,169	6,815	6,110	853	16.5
Arizona	42	2,236	1,891	2,073	35.1
Arkansas	47	6,949	6,312	11,227	59.5
California	1,314	70,444	64,467	70,211	43.9
Colorado	307	8,653	8,148	10,854	108.0
Connecticut	172	6,743	6,392	3,327	32.2
Delaware	13	3,212	2,961	3,889	48.1
Florida	444	13,087	12,063	16,248	41.3
Georgia	57	16,262	15,595	14,811	39.7
Hawaii	25	19,112	19,023	1,231	17.7
Idaho	42	2,500	2,193	1,651	36.6
Illinois	405	34,594	33,819	3,058	9.7
Indiana	57	10,536	8,600	9,011	74.2
Iowa	82	12,111	11,736	1,571	21.0
Kansas	30	4,117	2,470	2,426	32.3
Kentucky	42	27,272	26,207	37,668	69.1
Louisiana	39	1,107	788	1,860	30.5
Maine	75	2,448	2,211	1,310	31.4
Maryland	226	7,828	7,293	6,320	27.4
Massachusetts	273	11,975	11,206	10,408	60.5
Michigan	264	25,260	19,868	21,383	79.3
Minnesota	231	7,981	7,124	7,117	40.2
Mississippi	23	3,912	3,168	4,796	44.3
Missouri	117	14,998	13,919	3,780	21.0
Montana	32	1,652	1,099	1,022	43.9
Nebraska	142	9,215	7,754	7,550	92.2
Nevada	142	2,563	2,402	756	16.4
New Hampshire	31	2,815	2,655	4,000	125.0
New Jersey	303	10,945	10,492	6,514	23.8
New Mexico	123	4,251	1,700	2,657	29.3
New York	260	60,744	58,208	32,914	30.1
North Carolina	134	9,463	9,221	1,700	16.0
North Dakota	19	954	809	813	50.7
Ohio	208	67,222	64,730	12,082	26.9
Oklahoma	77	16,031	14,221	15,320	47.4

[Continued]

★ 252 ★

State Parks and Recreation Areas, by State: 1991
[Continued]

State	Acreage (1,000)	Visitors (1,000)		Revenue	
		Total[1]	Day	Total ($1,000)	Per-cent of oper-ating budget
Oregon	90	39,479	37,288	7,682	30.5
Pennsylvania	277	36,311	34,585	7,150	13.2
Rhode Island	9	5,075	4,759	2,854	47.1
South Carolina	80	7,970	7,001	10,587	61.4
South Dakota	92	5,894	5,545	3,810	62.4
Tennessee	133	26,974	25,814	19,737	53.9
Texas	499	23,957	21,515	12,722	37.0
Utah	97	4,940	4,495	2,970	24.3
Vermont	90	982	586	4,402	95.0
Virginia	59	3,862	3,456	2,686	28.5
Washington	241	46,813	44,487	6,292	25.0
West Virginia	202	8,278	7,577	12,973	58.6
Wisconsin	139	12,252	10,787	5,221	40.8
Wyoming	120	2,018	662	247	7.9

Source: 1994 Statistical Abstract of the United States on CD-ROM [machine-readable datafiles]. CD-8A-94. Washington, DC: U.S. Department of Commerce, Economics and Statistics Administration, Bureau of the Census, Data User Services Division, January 1995. Primary source: National Association of State Park Directors (Tallahassee, Florida). *Annual Information Exchange. Note:* 1. Includes overnight visitors.

Population and Population Density

★ 253 ★

Population and Population Growth Rate: 1901-1993

Table shows U.S. total population and the population growth rate since 1901.

[In millions, except as noted]

Year	Population	Growth rate (%)
1901	77.58	2.0
1905	83.82	2.0
1910	92.41	2.1
1915	100.55	1.4
1920	106.46	1.3

[Continued]

★ 253 ★

Population and Population Growth Rate: 1901-1993
[Continued]

Year	Population	Growth rate (%)
1925	115.83	1.5
1930	123.19	0.9
1935	127.36	0.7
1940	132.59	0.9
1945	140.47	1.0
1950	152.27	1.7
1955	165.93	1.8
1960	180.67	1.6
1965	194.30	1.2
1970	205.05	1.3
1975	215.97	1.0
1980	227.73	1.2
1985	238.47	0.9
1990	249.90	1.0
1991	252.67	1.1
1992	255.46	1.1
1993	258.25	1.1

Source: Executive Office of the President of the United States. *Environmental Quality 24: The Twenty-fourth Annual Report of the Council on Environmental Quality.* Prepared by Ray Clark. Written by Carroll Curtis. Edited by Barry Walsh. Washington, DC: U.S. Government Printing Office, 1994, p. 383. Primary sources: U.S. Department of Commerce. Bureau of the Census. *Estimates of the Population of the United States to January 1, 1994.* In *Current Population Reports.* Series P-25, no. 1115. Washington, DC: U.S. Department of Commerce, Bureau of the Census, 1994, p. 2, table 1; earlier reports in this series. *Notes:* The population estimates shown here are based on the April 1, 1990, population as enumerated in the 1990 census. Estimates for dates prior to April 1, 1990, have been revised. Except for 1991, annual population estimates are as of July 1 for the given year. Total population for the years 1917-1919, 1930-1939, and 1940-1993 are resident population plus Armed Forces overseas. All years 1901-1939 exclude Alaska and Hawaii.

★ 254 ★

Population and Population Density

Population, by Age Structure: 1940-1991

Table shows the age structure of the population, including armed forces overseas. Annual population estimates for July 1 of each year.

[In years]

Year	Age classes							
	Less than 5	5-14	15-24	25-34	35-44	45-54	55-64	Older than 64
1940	10.6	22.3	24.0	21.5	18.4	15.6	10.7	9.0
1950	16.3	24.5	22.3	23.9	21.6	17.4	13.4	12.4
1960	20.3	35.7	24.6	22.9	24.2	20.6	15.6	16.7
1970	17.2	40.7	36.5	25.3	23.1	23.3	18.7	20.1

[Continued]

★ 254 ★

Population, by Age Structure: 1940-1991
[Continued]

Year	Age classes							
	Less than 5	5-14	15-24	25-34	35-44	45-54	55-64	Older than 64
1980	16.5	34.8	42.8	37.6	25.9	22.7	21.8	25.7
1985	17.8	33.7	40.2	41.9	31.8	22.5	22.1	28.4
1991	19.2	35.9	36.6	43.1	39.4	25.7	21.0	31.8

Source: Executive Office of the President of the United States. *Environmental Quality 24: The Twenty-fourth Annual Report of the Council on Environmental Quality.* Prepared by Ray Clark. Written by Carroll Curtis. Edited by Barry Walsh. Washington, DC: U.S. Government Printing Office, 1994, p. 384. Primary sources: U.S. Department of Commerce. Bureau of the Census. *Historical Statistics of the United States: Colonial Times to 1970.* Series A 30-37. Washington, DC: U.S. Department of Commerce, Bureau of the Census, 1976; U.S. Department of Commerce. Bureau of the Census. *U.S. Population Estimates, by Age, Sex, and Race, and Hispanic Origin.* In *Current Population Reports.* Series P-25, nos. 1045 and 1095. Washington, DC: U.S. Department of Commerce, Bureau of the Census, 1990 and 1993; and earlier reports in this series.

★ 255 ★

Population and Population Density

Population, by Type of Area: 1950-1990

Table shows the change in the population of urban, suburban, and rural areas from 1950 through 1990. Urban population refers to population living inside central cities of metropolitan areas (MAs). Suburban population refers to population living in MA suburbs outside central cities. Rural population refers to nonmetropolitan population. MAs are defined for each population census.

[In millions, except as noted]

Year	Urban population		Suburban population		Rural population	
	Number	%	Number	%	Number	%
1950	49.661	32.8	35.193	23.3	66.472	43.9
1960	58.004	32.3	54.881	30.6	66.438	37.0
1970	63.797	31.4	75.622	37.2	63.793	31.4
1980	67.949	30.0	101.481	44.8	57.115	25.2
1990	77.844	31.3	114.882	46.2	55.984	22.5

Source: Executive Office of the President of the United States. *Environmental Quality 24: The Twenty-fourth Annual Report of the Council on Environmental Quality.* Prepared by Ray Clark. Written by Carroll Curtis. Edited by Barry Walsh. Washington, DC: U.S. Government Printing Office, 1994, p. 385. Primary source: U.S. Department of Commerce. Bureau of the Census. *Population Censuses Number of Inhabitants: U.S. Summary, 1950 to 1990.* Washington, DC: U.S. Department of Commerce, Bureau of the Census, 1991.

★ 256 ★

Population and Population Density

Population Change Components: 1940-1991

Table shows components of total population change; for example, births and deaths.

[In millions]

Year	Births	Deaths	Net Civilian immigration	Net change
1940	2.570	1.432	0.077	1.221
1945	2.873	1.549	0.162	1.462
1950	3.645	1.468	0.299	2.486
1955	4.128	1.537	0.337	2.925
1960	4.307	1.708	0.328	2.901
1965	3.801	1.830	0.373	2.315
1970	3.739	1.927	0.438	2.617
1975	3.144	1.894	0.449	2.165
1980	3.612	1.990	0.845	2.510
1985	3.761	2.087	0.649	2.171
1991	4.094	2.157	0.866	2.803

Source: Executive Office of the President of the United States. *Environmental Quality 24: The Twenty-fourth Annual Report of the Council on Environmental Quality.* Prepared by Ray Clark. Written by Carroll Curtis. Edited by Barry Walsh. Washington, DC: U.S. Government Printing Office, 1994, p. 384. Primary sources: U.S. Department of Commerce. Bureau of the Census. *U.S. Population Estimates, by Age, Sex, and Race, and Hispanics Origin.* In *Current Population Reports.* Series P-25, nos. 1045 and 1095. Washington, DC: U.S. Department of Commerce, Bureau of the Census, 1990 and 1993; and earlier reports in the series.

★ 257 ★

Population and Population Density

Population Density: 1960-1991

Table shows the population density of the total United States, the interior United States, and counties in coastal regions. Coastal area includes 672 counties and independent cities with at least 15 percent of their land area either in a coastal watershed or in a coastal cataloging unit defined in 1992 by the National Oceanic and Atmospheric Administration.

Land area and year	Total United States	Counties in coastal regions				Interior of the United States
		Pacific	Gulf of Mexico	Atlantic	Great Lakes	
Land area (thousand square miles)	3,536.3	509.9	114.5	147.8	115.4	2,648.7
Population (millions)						
1960	179.3	18.0	8.4	44.5	23.7	84.8
1970	203.3	22.9	10.0	51.1	26.0	93.3
1980	226.5	27.0	13.1	53.7	26.0	106.7
1990	248.7	33.2	15.2	59.0	26.0	115.3
1991	252.2	33.9	15.6	59.5	26.1	117.1

[Continued]

★ 257 ★

Population Density: 1960-1991

[Continued]

Land area and year	Total United States	Counties in coastal regions				Interior of the United States
		Pacific	Gulf of Mexico	Atlantic	Great Lakes	
Population per square mile						
1960	50.7	35.3	73.2	301.0	205.2	32.0
1970	57.5	44.8	87.7	345.8	225.3	35.2
1980	64.1	52.9	114.4	363.6	225.6	40.3
1990	70.3	65.1	133.1	399.2	224.8	43.5
1991	71.3	66.4	136.0	402.6	226.4	44.2

Source: Executive Office of the President of the United States. *Environmental Quality 24: The Twenty-fourth Annual Report of the Council on Environmental Quality.* Prepared by Ray Clark. Written by Carroll Curtis. Edited by Barry Walsh. Washington, DC: U.S. Government Printing Office, 1994, p. 386. Primary sources: U.S. Department of Commerce. Bureau of the Census. *Statistical Abstract of the United States, 1993;* data from the 1990 Census of Population and Housing. Washington, DC: U.S. Department of Commerce, Bureau of the Census.

★ 258 ★

Population and Population Density

Population Migration, by Region: 1960-1992

Table shows gains and losses of net population migration for various regions of the country.

[In millions]

Region	Gains and losses			
	1960-1970	1970-1980	1980-1990	1990-1991
Midwest	-0.752	-2.703	-2.293	0.148
Northeast	0.324	-2.888	-0.592	-0.395
South	0.593	5.992	5.143	1.252
West	2.855	4.115	4.568	0.920

Source: Executive Office of the President of the United States. *Environmental Quality 24: The Twenty-fourth Annual Report of the Council on Environmental Quality.* Prepared by Ray Clark. Written by Carroll Curtis. Edited by Barry Walsh. Washington, DC: U.S. Government Printing Office, 1994, p. 385. Primary sources: U.S. Department of Commerce. Bureau of the Census. *Current Population Reports.* Series P-25, Nos. 460, 957,and 1106. Washington, DC: U.S. Department of Commerce, Bureau of the Census; and earlier reports in this series. *Notes:* Migration for 1980-1990 is from components of population change used in developing postcensal 1980-based state population estimates. Migration for 1990-1992 is derived from summing the international migration, the federal U.S. citizenship, and residual change components.

Wetlands

★ 259 ★

Constructed Wetlands

The North American Wetland Treatment System Database files contain information on sites, systems, permits, cells, operations, and other data. The table below reflects distribution of treatment wetlands in the database. Figures show number of constructed wetlands.

State	Constructed wetlands
South Dakota	42
Florida	29
Arizona	22
Louisiana	14
Mississippi	10
California	7
Kentucky	7
Michigan	7
South Carolina	7
North Dakota	6
Alabama	5
New York	5
Illinois	4
Oregon	4
Missouri	3
Tennessee	3
Texas	3
Arizona	2
Maryland	2
Minnesota	2
Nevada	2
Wisconsin	2
Iowa	1
Massachusetts	1
Maine	1
North Carolina	1
New Jersey	1
New Mexico	1
Pennsylvania	1
Virginia	1
Washington	1

Source: "Distribution of Treatment Wetlands in the North American Database." *Water Environment & Technology* (February 1994), p. 32.

★ 260 ★
Wetlands

Wetland Losses: 1780-1991

Table shows annual loss rates of wetlands from 1780 through 1991.

Period	Acres
1780s-1950s	624,000
1950s-1970s	458,000
1970s-1980s	290,000
1987-1991	108,000[1]

Source: "Wetlands: The Losses Are Slowing." *Builder* (June 1994), p. 40. Primary sources: U.S. Fish and Wildlife Service; U.S. Soil Conservation Service; Beveridge & Diamond. *Notes:* 1. Excludes wetlands lost on federal and nonrural lands and wetland gains.

Chapter 5
WILDLIFE AND HABITAT

Tables on wildlife and habitat cover animals (mammals), birds, endangered species, fish and fisheries (including commercial applications), marine mammals and sea turtles, wildlife habitat and conservation, and wildlife-related recreation such as hunting and sport fishing. Related data on parks and recreation areas, forests, and other aspects of habitat can be found in the Land and Land Use chapter. Spending is covered in the Costs and Expenditures chapter. Product and international trade information has been included in the Markets and Companies chapter.

Animals

★ 261 ★

Wild Horses and Burro Herds: 1991

Table shows the wild horse and burro population as of October 1, 1991, as well as appropriate management levels and excesses for each. Data are for herd areas administered by the Bureau of Land Management and by the Forest Service.

Herds	Population		Appropriate management level		Excess	
	Bureau of Land Management	Forest Service	Bureau of Land Management	Forest Service[1]	Bureau of Land Management	Forest Service
Horses	44,080	1,952	25,992	1,481	18,088	471
Burros	6,617	164	3,805	110	2,812	54

Source: U.S. Department of the Interior. Bureau of Land Management and U.S. Department of Agriculture. Forest Service. *Ninth Report to Congress on the Administration of the Wild Free-Roaming Horse and Burro Act.* Washington, DC: U.S. Department of the Interior, Bureau of Land Management, and U.S. Department of Agriculture, Forest Service, n.d., pp. 52, 57. *Note:* 1. Desired population levels.

★ 262 ★

Animals

Wolf Population Projections

```
┌─────────────────────────────────────────────────────┐
│  ┌──────────────────────────────────────────┐        │
│  │ 2003 - 129                               │        │
│  ├───────────────────────────────────┐      │        │
│  │ 2002 - 101                        │               │
│  ├──────────────────────────┐        │               │
│  │ 2001 - 83                │                         │
│  ├──────────────────┐       │                         │
│  │ 2000 - 68        │                                 │
│  ├─────────────┐    │                                 │
│  │ 1999 - 56   │                                      │
│  ├──────────┐  │                                      │
│  │ 1998 - 45│                                         │
│  ├──────┐   │                                         │
│  │1997-27│                                            │
│  ├──┐      1996 - 14                                  │
│  │  │                                                 │
│  ├─┐       1995 - 8                                   │
│  │ │                                                  │
└─────────────────────────────────────────────────────┘
```

A past program of the federal government awarded bounties in an effort to eliminate wolves that threatened livestock and game. In 1995, in order to save the species from extinction, Canadian wolves were transplanted from Alberta to sites in Idaho and Yellowstone National Park. In total, 30 wolves were expected to be released in 1995. The table below projects the population of surviving wolves in Idaho and Yellowstone locations.

Year	Number of wolves
1995	8
1996	14
1997	27
1998	45
1999	56
2000	68
2001	83
2002	101
2003	129

Source: Kanamine, Linda. "An Uneasy Welcome for Gray Wolves." *USA TODAY,* 13 January 1995, p. 5D. Primary sources: U.S. Department of the Interior; *USA TODAY* research.

Birds

★ 263 ★

Bald Eagles

In 1963 less than 420 pairs of adult bald eagles could be found in nesting areas in the 48 contiguous states. By 1994, the eagle was removed from the endangered species list owing to a resurgence in its population. The table below shows the pairs of adult bald eagles occupying nesting areas in the contiguous United States.

Year	Pairs of adults
1963	417
1974	791
1981	1,188
1984	1,757
1986	1,875
1988	2,475
1989	2,680
1990	3,020
1991	3,391
1992	3,747
1993	4,016

Source: Cushman, John H., Jr. "Eagles to Fly Free of the Endangered List." *New York Times,* 30 June 1994, p. A8. Primary source: Department of the Interior.

★ 264 ★
Birds

Birds Threatened by Braer Tanker Oil Spill: 1993

Shags		
	Long-tailed ducks - 300	
	Eider ducks - 200	
	Black guillemots - 150	
	Great northern divers	

In January 1993 the tanker *Braer* ran aground, spilling 25 million gallons of crude oil off the coast of the Shetland Islands. Although light crude oil, the spill nevertheless posed risks to area wildlife, notably suffocation and damage to nesting spots of local birds. The table below shows birds threatened by the oil spill.

Bird	Number
Shags (sea birds)	2,000
Long-tailed ducks	300
Eider ducks	200
Black guillemots	150
Great northern divers (loons)	50

Source: Luhan, Michael. "Weather Foils Oil Cleanup." *USA TODAY,* 6 January 1993, p. 8A. Primary sources: Associated Press; Royal Society for the Protection of Birds.

★ 265 ★
Birds

Ducks: 1955-1992

Table shows population estimates for selected duck species.

[In millions]

Year	Northern pintail	Mallard	Canvas back	Redhead	Gadwall	Green-winged teal	Blue-winged teal	Scaup	American widgeon	Northern shoveler	Total
1955	9.39	8.36	0.60	0.57	0.66	1.82	5.38	5.61	3.07	1.57	37.03
1956	9.90	9.84	0.70	0.76	0.78	1.48	4.76	5.73	3.12	1.63	38.70
1957	6.31	9.15	0.62	0.54	0.69	1.05	4.31	5.75	2.85	1.46	32.73
1958	5.55	10.99	0.74	0.44	0.45	1.33	5.16	5.29	2.42	1.19	33.57
1959	5.48	8.75	0.48	0.49	0.53	2.60	5.05	6.96	3.70	1.46	35.50
1960	5.41	7.16	0.60	0.49	0.72	1.39	4.18	4.83	2.94	1.74	29.47
1961	3.68	6.91	0.43	0.32	0.59	1.71	3.66	5.34	2.82	1.26	26.70
1962	3.40	5.14	0.35	0.50	0.85	0.70	2.94	5.24	1.88	1.18	22.18
1963	3.62	6.72	0.50	0.41	1.09	1.16	3.68	5.40	1.71	1.28	25.57
1964	3.01	5.74	0.65	0.53	0.83	1.51	3.96	5.06	2.49	1.61	25.38
1965	3.55	5.10	0.50	0.60	1.27	1.24	3.70	4.65	2.31	1.37	24.31

[Continued]

★ 265 ★

Ducks: 1955-1992
[Continued]

Year	Northern pintail	Mallard	Canvas back	Redhead	Gadwall	Green-winged teal	Blue-winged teal	Scaup	American widgeon	Northern shoveler	Total
1966	4.76	6.68	0.66	0.71	1.67	1.58	3.72	4.43	2.28	2.10	28.59
1967	5.27	7.47	0.50	0.73	1.38	1.59	4.51	4.93	2.32	2.29	31.00
1968	3.47	7.02	0.56	0.49	1.95	1.41	3.46	4.36	2.28	1.65	26.64
1969	5.90	7.54	0.50	0.63	1.57	1.47	4.13	5.13	2.92	2.15	31.94
1970	6.37	9.96	0.58	0.62	1.61	2.17	4.86	5.63	3.45	2.22	37.47
1971	5.87	9.31	0.44	0.53	1.60	1.88	4.61	5.06	3.28	2.01	34.60
1972	7.02	9.25	0.43	0.55	1.62	1.89	4.28	7.93	3.17	2.44	38.59
1973	4.35	8.06	0.62	0.50	1.25	1.94	3.33	6.22	2.86	1.62	30.75
1974	6.58	6.68	0.50	0.63	1.59	1.84	4.97	5.72	2.67	2.01	33.19
1975	5.88	7.49	0.59	0.83	1.64	1.67	5.83	6.43	2.69	1.96	35.01
1976	5.48	7.89	0.61	0.67	1.25	1.54	4.75	5.78	2.48	1.76	32.21
1977	3.94	7.40	0.67	0.64	1.31	1.29	4.59	6.25	2.56	1.48	30.11
1978	5.11	7.35	0.37	0.74	1.56	2.19	4.47	5.94	3.29	1.98	32.99
1979	5.38	7.82	0.57	0.70	1.75	2.02	4.86	7.54	3.09	2.39	36.12
1980	4.51	7.57	0.73	0.75	1.39	1.99	4.88	6.31	3.56	1.90	33.61
1981	3.47	6.37	0.61	0.60	1.40	1.85	3.73	5.92	2.92	2.32	29.19
1982	3.71	6.25	0.51	0.62	1.64	1.54	3.66	5.47	2.44	2.14	27.98
1983	3.51	6.31	0.52	0.71	1.52	1.84	3.37	7.14	2.61	1.87	29.38
1984	2.97	5.25	0.52	0.67	1.53	1.36	3.96	6.91	2.99	1.62	27.77
1985	2.51	4.75	0.37	0.58	1.30	1.44	3.46	5.04	2.04	1.70	23.19
1986	2.74	6.84	0.44	0.56	1.54	1.68	4.46	5.20	1.73	2.12	27.31
1987	2.63	5.61	0.45	0.50	1.31	2.00	3.52	4.84	1.98	1.95	24.80
1988	2.01	6.33	0.44	0.44	1.35	2.06	3.98	4.68	2.19	1.68	25.16
1989	2.11	5.65	0.48	0.51	1.42	1.84	3.13	4.34	1.97	1.54	23.00
1990	2.26	5.45	0.54	0.48	1.67	1.79	2.78	4.29	1.86	1.76	22.88
1991	1.80	5.44	0.49	0.45	1.58	1.56	3.76	5.26	2.25	1.72	24.31
1992	2.10	5.98	0.48	0.60	2.03	1.77	4.33	4.64	2.21	1.95	26.09
1993	2.05	5.71	0.47	0.49	1.76	1.70	3.19	4.08	2.05	2.05	23.10

Source: Executive Office of the President of the United States. *Environmental Quality 24: The Twenty-fourth Annual Report of the Council on Environmental Quality.* Prepared by Ray Clark. Written by Carroll Curtis. Edited by Barry Walsh. Washington, DC: U.S. Government Printing Office, 1994, p. 487. Primary source: U.S. Department of the Interior. Fish and Wildlife Service. Office of Migratory Bird Management. *Status of Waterfowl and Fall Flight Forecast.* Prepared in conjunction with the Canadian Wildlife Service. Washington, DC: Department of the Interior, annual.

★ 266 ★
Birds

Goose and Swan Population: 1970-1992

Table contains estimates of goose and swan population for selected species. Data for Canada goose aggregate population totals for 13 separate populations that nest in North America. Data for snow goose aggregate population totals for greater snow goose, lesser snow goose, and Ross' goose populations. Tundra swan estimates include the eastern population only. The 1993 survey of greater white-fronted geese was incomplete.

[In thousands]

Year	Canada goose	Snow goose	Greater white-fronted goose	Brant	Tundra swan Eastern	Tundra swan Western
1970	1,582	818	136	142	55	31
1971	1,628	1,116	168	300	58	99
1972	1,696	1,413	84	198	63	83
1973	1,804	1,084	174	166	57	34
1974	1,795	1,285	201	219	64	70
1975	1,804	1,167	174	212	67	54
1976	1,996	1,679	180	249	79	51
1977	2,318	1,311	255	221	76	47
1978	2,419	2,072	336	209	70	46
1979	2,158	1,415	300	173	79	54
1980	2,159	1,525	377	215	64	65
1981	2,458	1,524	232	291	93	84
1982	2,198	1,916	416	227	73	91
1983	2,490	1,914	355	233	87	67
1984	2,283	1,593	190	387	81	62
1985	2,555	2,223	254	291	94	49
1986	2,706	1,646	373	246	91	66
1987	2,707	2,080	323	220	95	53
1988	2,848	1,995	303	278	77	59
1989	3,097	2,222	377	273	91	79
1990	2,705	1,994	475	287	90	40
1991	3,880	2,440	492	279	97	49
1992	3,574	2,386	418	303	110	64
1993	3,045	1,971	330	225	76	62

Source: Executive Office of the President of the United States. *Environmental Quality 24: The Twenty-fourth Annual Report of the Council on Environmental Quality.* Prepared by Ray Clark. Written by Carroll Curtis. Edited by Barry Walsh. Washington, DC: U.S. Government Printing Office, 1994, p. 488. Primary source: U.S. Department of the Interior. Fish and Wildlife Service. Office of Migratory Bird Management. *Status of Waterfowl and Fall Flight Forecast.* Prepared in conjunction with the Canadian Wildlife Service. Washington, DC: Department of the Interior, annual.

★ 267 ★

Birds

Herring Gull Egg Contamination in Lake Erie: 1974–1991

[In parts per million in whole egg samples, wet weight]

Year	DDE	Dieldrin	Mirex	HCB	PCBs
1974	7.13	0.35	0.64	0.29	72.46
1975	7.41	0.33	0.32	0.19	62.30
1977	7.49	0.40	0.45	0.37	68.70
1978	4.29	0.24	0.20	0.09	44.43
1979	3.10	0.25	0.17	0.11	48.44
1980	2.98	0.21	0.18	0.09	46.38
1981	3.90	0.22	0.25	0.09	56.49
1982	3.07	0.25	0.13	0.08	58.89
1983	2.39	0.20	0.17	0.05	37.31
1984	3.23	0.33	0.22	0.06	46.20
1985	2.83	0.19	0.14	0.06	38.41
1986	2.77	0.23	0.14	0.06	33.35
1987	1.77	0.14	0.12	0.03	23.16
1988	2.07	0.17	0.10	0.05	27.50
1989	2.69	0.17	0.18	0.05	39.21
1990	2.01	0.10	0.11	0.03	30.09
1991	2.12	0.08	0.07	0.02	26.55

Source: Executive Office of the President of the United States. *Environmental Quality 24: The Twenty-fourth Annual Report of the Council on Environmental Quality.* Prepared by Ray Clark. Written by Carroll Curtis. Edited by Barry Walsh. Washington, DC: U.S. Government Printing Office, 1994, pp. 484-486. Primary source: Environment Canada. Canadian Wildlife Service. Canada Centre for Inland Waters. *Organochlorine Contaminant Concentrations in Herring Gull Eggs From Great Lakes Colonies.* Burlington, ON, Canada: Environment Canada, annual. *Notes:* "DDE" represents derivatives of dichloro-diphenyl-trichloro ethane (DDT). "HCB" represents "hexachloro-benzene." "PCBs" represent "polychlorinated biphenyls." Data are not available for 1976.

★ 268 ★

Birds

Herring Gull Egg Contamination in Lake Huron: 1974–1991

[In parts per million in whole egg samples, wet weight]

Year	DDE	Dieldrin	Mirex	HCB	PCBs
1974	17.40	0.50	1.34	0.38	71.01
1975	14.03	0.36	0.51	0.21	42.67
1977	16.17	0.54	0.44	0.36	70.28
1978	6.53	0.22	0.21	0.11	32.38
1979	2.30	0.30	0.19	0.10	28.66
1980	2.71	0.24	0.11	0.07	20.41
1981	3.82	0.24	0.26	0.07	25.39
1982	4.43	0.28	0.48	0.08	34.29
1983	2.74	0.22	0.15	0.05	18.28

[Continued]

★ 268 ★

Herring Gull Egg Contamination in Lake Huron: 1974-1991

[Continued]

Year	DDE	Dieldrin	Mirex	HCB	PCBs
1984	2.56	0.22	0.34	0.07	19.95
1985	2.77	0.30	0.22	0.06	16.90
1986	2.05	0.21	0.12	0.05	12.00
1987	1.32	0.22	0.08	0.02	8.33
1988	1.40	0.22	0.07	0.04	8.83
1989	1.57	0.20	0.09	0.03	10.19
1990	1.86	0.14	0.11	0.03	11.34
1991	1.97	0.16	0.11	0.03	10.01

Source: Executive Office of the President of the United States. *Environmental Quality 24: The Twenty-fourth Annual Report of the Council on Environmental Quality.* Prepared by Ray Clark. Written by Carroll Curtis. Edited by Barry Walsh. Washington, DC: U.S. Government Printing Office, 1994, pp. 484-486. Primary source: Environment Canada. Canadian Wildlife Service. Canada Centre for Inland Waters. *Organochlorine Contaminant Concentrations in Herring Gull Eggs From Great Lakes Colonies.* Burlington, ON, Canada: Environment Canada, annual. *Notes:* "DDE" represents derivatives of dichloro-diphenyl-trichloro ethane (DDT). "HCB" represents "hexachloro-benzene." "PCBs" represent "polychlorinated biphenyls." Data are not available for 1976.

★ 269 ★

Birds

Herring Gull Egg Contamination in Lake Michigan: 1974-1991

[In parts per million in whole egg samples, wet weight]

Year	DDE	Dieldrin	Mirex	HCB	PCBs
1976	33.40	0.82	0.36	0.14	118.42
1977	29.25	0.68	0.14	0.24	107.80
1978	22.36	0.87	0.21	0.12	90.74
1980	12.17	0.70	0.10	0.09	57.83
1982	15.86	0.81	0.09	0.09	65.41
1983	6.46	0.61	0.05	0.05	30.27
1984	7.85	0.53	0.09	0.06	31.47
1985	6.98	0.47	0.12	0.05	31.94
1986	7.48	0.38	0.07	0.07	27.25
1987	3.95	0.33	0.06	0.04	16.58
1988	5.04	0.55	0.03	0.04	19.14
1989	4.74	0.54	0.04	0.04	21.00
1990	8.12	0.54	0.06	0.05	32.19
1991	10.52	0.34	0.12	0.05	31.27

Source: Executive Office of the President of the United States. *Environmental Quality 24: The Twenty-fourth Annual Report of the Council on Environmental Quality.* Prepared by Ray Clark. Written by Carroll Curtis. Edited by Barry Walsh. Washington, DC: U.S. Government Printing Office, 1994, pp. 484-486. Primary source: Environment Canada. Canadian Wildlife Service. Canada Centre for Inland Waters. *Organochlorine Contaminant Concentrations in Herring Gull Eggs From Great Lakes Colonies.* Burlington, ON, Canada: Environment Canada, annual. *Notes:* "DDE" represents derivatives of dichloro-diphenyl-trichloro ethane (DDT). "HCB" represents "hexachloro-benzene." "PCBs" represent "polychlorinated biphenyls." Data are not available for 1979 and 1981.

★ 270 ★
Birds

Herring Gull Egg Contamination in Lake Ontario: 1974-1991

[In parts per million in whole egg samples, wet weight]

Year	DDE	Dieldrin	Mirex	HCB	PCBs
1974	22.30	0.47	6.99	0.58	152.37
1975	22.80	0.29	4.70	0.33	143.11
1977	14.88	0.39	2.48	0.80	102.50
1978	10.65	0.26	1.59	0.32	72.43
1979	8.94	0.21	1.89	0.21	69.60
1980	7.62	0.19	1.65	0.17	56.43
1981	11.00	0.28	2.67	0.24	78.90
1982	10.04	0.28	3.05	0.16	62.90
1983	4.78	0.18	1.43	0.08	42.59
1984	6.26	0.21	1.87	0.12	51.11
1985	6.02	0.15	1.47	0.07	35.58
1986	4.41	0.16	1.10	0.07	27.86
1987	2.60	0.13	0.68	0.04	16.48
1988	4.25	0.15	0.82	0.07	23.53
1989	5.28	0.22	1.15	0.07	32.45
1990	3.36	0.10	0.64	0.03	18.44
1991	3.53	0.14	0.58	0.03	17.06

Source: Executive Office of the President of the United States. *Environmental Quality 24: The Twenty-fourth Annual Report of the Council on Environmental Quality.* Prepared by Ray Clark. Written by Carroll Curtis. Edited by Barry Walsh. Washington, DC: U.S. Government Printing Office, 1994, pp. 484-486. Primary source: Environment Canada. Canadian Wildlife Service. Canada Centre for Inland Waters. *Organochlorine Contaminant Concentrations in Herring Gull Eggs From Great Lakes Colonies.* Burlington, ON, Canada: Environment Canada, annual. *Notes:* "DDE" represents derivatives of dichloro-diphenyl-trichloro ethane (DDT). "HCB" represents "hexachloro-benzene." "PCBs" represent "polychlorinated biphenyls." Data are not available for 1976.

★ 271 ★
Birds

Herring Gull Egg Contamination in Lake Superior: 1974-1991

[In parts per million in whole egg samples, wet weight]

Year	DDE	Dieldrin	Mirex	HCB	PCBs
1974	16.59	0.51	1.04	0.26	62.08
1975	23.10	0.38	0.96	0.18	76.24
1977	11.92	0.38	0.33	0.24	55.22
1978	9.64	0.39	0.28	0.12	41.57
1979	6.83	0.60	0.26	0.14	58.74
1980	3.67	0.34	0.13	0.08	25.58
1981	5.74	0.44	0.14	0.12	33.84
1982	6.29	0.39	0.37	0.08	34.74
1983	3.17	0.33	0.15	0.05	21.42

[Continued]

★ 271 ★

Herring Gull Egg Contamination in Lake Superior: 1974-1991

[Continued]

Year	DDE	Dieldrin	Mirex	HCB	PCBs
1984	2.94	0.36	0.12	0.05	16.91
1985	3.13	0.32	0.11	0.05	15.89
1986	3.22	0.34	0.11	0.05	14.10
1987	2.52	0.20	0.10	0.04	12.35
1988	2.94	0.34	0.06	0.05	13.43
1989	2.50	0.34	0.07	0.05	15.09
1990	2.64	0.30	0.06	0.03	11.62
1991	3.60	0.27	0.07	0.04	14.09

Source: Executive Office of the President of the United States. *Environmental Quality 24: The Twenty-fourth Annual Report of the Council on Environmental Quality.* Prepared by Ray Clark. Written by Carroll Curtis. Edited by Barry Walsh. Washington, DC: U.S. Government Printing Office, 1994, pp. 484-486. Primary source: Environment Canada. Canadian Wildlife Service. Canada Centre for Inland Waters. *Organochlorine Contaminant Concentrations in Herring Gull Eggs From Great Lakes Colonies.* Burlington, ON, Canada: Environment Canada, annual. *Notes:* "DDE" represents derivatives of dichloro-diphenyl-trichloro ethane (DDT). "HCB" represents "hexachloro-benzene." "PCBs" represent "polychlorinated biphenyls." Data are not available for 1976.

★ 272 ★

Birds

Neotropical Migrant Birds: 1966-1991

Table shows the long- and short-term trends in percent change per year for neotropical migrant birds.

Common name	Long-term trend (1966-1991)	Short-term trend (1982-1991)
American redstart	-0.6	-1.8
Baltimore oriole	0.4	-1.1
Blackpoll warbler	3.0	-8.9
Blue-winged warbler	-0.1	-1.9
Cape May warbler	3.2	-9.4
Cerulean warbler	-2.7	-0.3
Chestnut-sided warbler	-0.5	-0.5
Chuck-will's-widow	-0.9	-0.4
Common yellowthroat	-0.5	-2.5
Eastern wood pewee	-2.1	-1.4
Golden-cheeked warbler	-11.8	-11.8
Golden-winged warbler	-2.4	-1.4
Gray catbird	-0.5	-0.4
Great-crested flycatcher	0.0	-0.8
Indigo bunting	-1.6	-0.5
Kentucky warbler	-0.7	-1.2
Least flycatcher	-0.7	-0.4
Louisiana waterthrush	-1.4	0.1
Nashville warbler	1.7	-2.7

[Continued]

★ 272 ★

Neotropical Migrant Birds: 1966-1991
[Continued]

Common name	Long-term trend (1966-1991)	Short-term trend (1982-1991)
Northern parula	1.0	-1.0
Northern waterthrush	0.8	-0.7
Olive-sided flycatcher	-2.5	-2.6
Orchard oriole	-1.3	0.3
Ovenbird	0.7	-0.4
Prairie warbler	-2.4	-0.6
Prothonotary warbler	-0.5	-1.6
Red-eyed vireo	1.4	1.6
Rose-breasted grosbeak	0.0	-3.9
Ruby-throated hummingbird	1.4	1.7
Scarlet tanager	0.2	-0.1
Solitary vireo	3.3	5.8
Summer tanager	-0.2	-1.7
Tennessee warbler	4.5	-12.3
Veery	-1.0	-0.4
Whip-poor-will	-1.0	-3.6
White-eyed vireo	-0.2	0.0
Wilson's warbler	0.9	-4.4
Wood thrush	-2.0	-1.9
Yellow-bellied flycatcher	5.1	8.4
Yellow-billed cuckoo	-1.3	-4.0
Yellow-breasted chat	-0.5	-2.5

Source: Executive Office of the President of the United States. *Environmental Quality 24: The Twenty-fourth Annual Report of the Council on Environmental Quality.* Prepared by Ray Clark. Written by Carroll Curtis. Edited by Barry Walsh. Washington, DC: U.S. Government Printing Office, 1994, pp. 481-482. Primary source: U.S. Fish and Wildlife Service. Breeding Bird Survey (Laurel, MD). Unpublished data.

★ 273 ★

Birds

Resident Birds: 1966-1991

Table shows the long- and short-term trends for resident birds as percent changes each year.

Common name	Long-term trend (1966-1991)	Short-term trend (1982-1991)
Black-capped chickadee	1.9	1.9
Brown-headed nuthatch	-0.8	-1.6
Carolina chickadee	-0.4	-1.4
Carolina wren	0.9	2.8
Downy woodpecker	0.3	-0.1
Great horned owl	0.5	-2.5

[Continued]

★ 273 ★

Resident Birds: 1966-1991
[Continued]

Common name	Long-term trend (1966-1991)	Short-term trend (1982-1991)
Hairy woodpecker	1.1	1.2
House sparrow	-1.4	-3.1
Northern bobwhite	-2.4	-3.5
Northern cardinal	-0.3	0.4
Northern mockingbird	-1.0	1.1
Pileated woodpecker	·1.2	0.4
Red-cockaded woodpecker	-0.4	0.4
Spotted owl	-0.5	-0.6
Tufted titmouse	0.5	2.0

Source: Executive Office of the President of the United States. *Environmental Quality 24: The Twenty-fourth Annual Report of the Council on Environmental Quality.* Prepared by Ray Clark. Written by Carroll Curtis. Edited by Barry Walsh. Washington, DC: U.S. Government Printing Office, 1994, pp. 481. Primary source: U.S. Fish and Wildlife Service. Breeding Bird Survey (Laurel, MD). Unpublished data.

Endangered Species

★ 274 ★

Endangered Species, by Group

Table shows the groups with the most endangered species. Data are for the United States only.

Group	Number of species
Plants	274
Birds	57
Fishes	52
Clams	40
Mammals	37
Insects	13
All others	32

Source: "Plants Are Most Endangered." *USA TODAY,* 29 December 1993, p. 1A. Primary source: U.S. Fish and Wildlife Service.

★ 275 ★

Endangered Species

Endangered Species, by State

Habitat loss, wetlands drainage, natural enemies, and human interference have compromised the existence of many plants and animals. The Endangered Species Act, administered by the Fish and Wildlife Service, seeks to save 490 threatened or endangered plants and 422 animals from extinction. Since it became effective in 1973, 13 of the 912 species listed as in jeopardy have been reclassified: 6 species are reported saved; 7 species are now recorded as extinct. An additional 14 species are presumed extinct. As of December 1994, there were no formal plans to save 304 listed species; drafts of plans existed for 101 species, and 500 species had finalized recovery plans. According to the Fish and Wildlife Service, 40 percent of the species listed as endangered are stabilized or improving, despite new species being added to the endangered list monthly. The table below shows the states with the most endangered species.

State	Number of endangered species
Hawaii	215
California	138
Florida	97
Alabama	88
Tennessee	74

Source: Kanamine, Linda. "Support for Controversial Progam Slips." *USA TODAY*, 2 December 1994, pp. 1-2A. Primary sources: U.S. Fish and Wildlife Service; *USA TODAY* research.

★ 276 ★
Endangered Species

Endangered U.S. Wildlife and Plants: 1980-1993

```
┌──────────────────────────────────────────────────────┐
│ ┌────────────────────────────────────────────────┐   │
│ │ Total - 572                                      │   │
│ └────────────────────────────────────────────────┘   │
│ ┌──────────────────────────────┐                      │
│ │ Plants - 317                 │                      │
│ └──────────────────────────────┘                      │
│ ┌─────┐                                                │
│ │     │  Birds - 57                                    │
│ └─────┘                                                │
│ ┌─────┐                                                │
│ │     │  Fishes - 55                                   │
│ └─────┘                                                │
│ ┌─────┐                                                │
│ │     │  Clams - 51                                    │
│ └─────┘                                                │
│ ┌─────┐                                                │
│ │     │  Mammals - 37                                  │
│ └─────┘                                                │
│ ▯ Insects - 13                                         │
│ ▯ Snails - 12                                          │
│ ▯ Crustaceans - 11                                     │
│ ▯ Reptiles - 8                                         │
│ ▯ Amphibians - 6                                       │
│ ▯ Arachnids - 5                                        │
│                 Chart shows data from column 9.        │
└──────────────────────────────────────────────────────┘
```

Table shows the number of endangered wildlife and plant species in the United States. Endangered species are those in danger of becoming extinct throughout all or part of their natural ranges. See also related table on threatened wildlife and plants.

Group	1980	1981	1983	1985	1987	1989	1991	1992	1993
Amphibians	5	5	5	5	5	6	6	6	6
Arachnids	0	0	0	0	3	3	3	3	5
Birds	66	52	66	59	76	61	73	57	57
Clams	23	23	23	22	30	34	40	40	51
Crustaceans	1	1	2	3	7	8	8	8	11
Fishes	34	29	33	30	47	49	54	52	55
Insects	7	7	7	8	10	10	13	13	13
Mammals	32	15	33	20	50	32	55	37	37
Plants	51	48	55	67	158	163	229	274	317
Reptiles	13	7	14	8	15	9	16	8	8
Snails	2	2	3	3	3	3	7	8	12
Total	234	189	241	225	404	378	504	505	572

Source: Executive Office of the President of the United States. *Environmental Quality 24: The Twenty-fourth Annual Report of the Council on Environmental Quality.* Prepared by Ray Clark. Written by Carroll Curtis. Edited by Barry Walsh. Washington, DC: U.S. Government Printing Office, 1994, p. 497. Primary source: U.S. Department of the Interior. Fish and Wildlife Service. Division of Endangered Species and Habitat Conservation (Washington, DC). Unpublished data.

★ 277 ★

Endangered Species

Threatened and Endangered Wildlife and Plant Species: 1989 and 1994

Table shows the number of endangered species—those in danger of becoming extinct throughout all or a significant part of its natural range—and threatened species—those likely to become endangered in the foreseeable future.

Item	Mammals	Birds	Reptiles	Amphibians	Fishes	Snails	Clams	Crustaceans	Insects	Arachnids	Plants
					1989						
Endangered species[1]	290	221	74	13	58	4	34	8	10	(NA)	159
U.S. only	31	61	8	5	45	3	32	8	10	(NA)	152
U.S. and foreign	19	15	7	0	2	0	0	0	0	(NA)	6
Foreign only[2]	240	145	59	8	11	1	2	0	0	(NA)	1
Threatened species[1]	30	10	32	4	30	5	0	1	7	(NA)	48
U.S. only	5	7	14	4	24	5	0	1	7	(NA)	40
U.S. and foreign	2	3	4	0	6	0	0	0	0	(NA)	6
Foreign only[2]	23	0	14	0	0	0	0	0	0	(NA)	2
					1994						
Endangered species[1]	307	226	80	14	64	15	52	11	23	4	386
U.S. only	36	57	9	6	60	14	50	11	16	4	375
U.S. and foreign	20	16	8	0	3	0	0	0	3	0	10
Foreign only[2]	251	153	63	8	1	1	2	0	4	0	1
Threatened species[1]	31	17	32	5	38	7	6	2	9	0	85
U.S. only	5	8	14	4	32	7	6	2	9	0	74
U.S. and foreign	4	9	4	1	6	0	0	0	0	0	9
Foreign only[2]	22	0	14	0	0	0	0	0	0	0	2

Source: 1994 Statistical Abstract of the United States on CD-ROM [machine-readable datafiles]. CD-8A-94. Washington, DC: U.S. Department of Commerce, Economics and Statistics Administration, Bureau of the Census, Data User Services Division, January 1995. Primary source: U.S. Fish and Wildlife Service. *Endangered Species Technical Bulletin* (quarterly) *Notes:* "NA" represents "not available or applicable." 1. Total. 2. Species outside U.S. and outlying areas as determined by Fish and Wildlife Service.

★ 278 ★

Endangered Species

Threatened Wildlife and Plants: 1980-1993

```
Total - 142

Plants - 62

Fishes - 30

     Reptiles - 14

   Insects - 9

   Birds - 7

   Mammals - 6

   Snails - 6

  Amphibians - 4

 Crustaceans - 2

 Clams - 2

 Arachnids - 0
```
                    Chart shows data from column 8.

Table shows the number of threatened wildlife and plant species in the United States. Threatened species are those likely to become endangered in the foreseeable future; that is, in danger of becoming extinct throughout all or part of their natural ranges. See also related table on endangered wildlife and plants.

Group	1980	1981	1983	1985	1987	1989	1991	1992	1993
Amphibians	3	3	3	3	4	4	5	4	4
Arachnids	0	0	0	0	0	0	0	0	0
Birds	3	3	3	3	10	7	12	7	8
Clams	0	0	0	0	0	0	2	2	5
Crustaceans	0	0	1	1	1	1	2	2	2
Fishes	12	12	12	14	30	25	34	30	31
Insects	6	4	6	4	7	7	9	9	9
Mammals	3	3	3	4	7	6	8	6	6
Plants	7	7	10	10	44	42	61	62	69
Reptiles	10	8	12	8	18	14	18	14	14
Snails	5	5	5	5	5	6	6	6	7
Total	49	45	55	52	126	112	157	142	155

Source: Executive Office of the President of the United States. *Environmental Quality 24: The Twenty-fourth Annual Report of the Council on Environmental Quality.* Prepared by Ray Clark. Written by Carroll Curtis. Edited by Barry Walsh. Washington, DC: U.S. Government Printing Office, 1994, p. 497. Primary source: U.S. Department of the Interior. Fish and Wildlife Service. Division of Endangered Species and Habitat Conservation (Washington, DC). Unpublished data.

Fish and Fisheries

★ 279 ★

Aquacultured Species: 1993

Table shows output for 1993 for principal U.S. aquacultured species, excluding mollusks.

[In million pounds]

Species	Output
Catfish	459.0
Trout	54.6
Crawfish	54.0
Salmon	22.0
Tilapia	12.5
Shrimp	6.6

Source: "Principal U.S. Aquacultured Species." *Restaurant Business,* 20 May 1994, p. 65. Primary source: U.S. Department of Agriculture.

★ 280 ★
Fish and Fisheries

Catfish Production and Value: 1980-1992

Table shows U.S. private aquaculture production of catfish. Figures also show value.

Item	Unit	1980	1985	1986	1987	1988	1989	1990	1991	1992
Fish sold to processors	Million lb.	46.5	191.6	213.8	280.5	295.1	341.9	360.4	390.9	457.4
Avg. price paid by processors	Cents/lb.	67.6	72.5	66.8	61.8	76.4	71.7	75.8	63.1	59.8
Value	Million $	31.4	138.9	142.8	173.3	225.5	245.1	273.2	246.7	273.5
Processor sales	Million lb.	27.8	99.3	113.9	146.5	149.6	176.3	183.1	199.8	231.3
Avg. price received by processors	Cents/lb.	166.1	165.4	195.7	193.3	220.8	211.2	224.0	208.6	200.2
Value	Million $	46.2	164.2	222.9	283.2	330.3	372.3	410.1	416.8	463.1
Inventory[1]	Million lb.	1.0	4.7	5.0	4.2	5.3	8.8	8.1	9.4	9.6

Source: 1994 Statistical Abstract of the United States on CD-ROM [machine-readable datafiles]. CD-8A-94. Washington, DC: U.S. Department of Commerce, Economics and Statistics Administration, Bureau of the Census, Data User Services Division, January 1995. Primary source: U.S. Dept. of Agriculture. National Agricultural Statistics Service. *Notes:* "Avg." is the abbreviation for "average"; "lb." is the abbreviation for "pound." 1. January 1.

★ 281 ★

Fish and Fisheries

Commercial Harvest of Marine and Estuarine Fisheries, by Species: 1950-1993

Table shows the commercial harvest of selected species.

[In million pounds]

Year	Bay scallops	Sea scallops	Oysters	Shrimp	American lobster	Spiny lobster	King salmon	Striped bass
1950	1.60	19.98	76.41	191.70	23.20	2.49	37.36	7.70
1960	2.03	26.60	60.01	249.45	31.17	3.20	24.06	8.20
1970	1.70	5.85	53.60	367.46	34.15	10.34	31.69	11.19
1980	2.13	28.16	50.83	339.70	37.22	7.03	28.53	4.54
1981	1.42	25.96	52.61	354.47	39.13	6.30	31.07	3.86
1982	2.67	19.94	56.19	283.63	43.08	6.98	34.60	2.17
1983	1.48	19.23	54.05	249.67	44.80	4.80	24.42	1.68
1984	1.48	17.19	54.77	301.35	45.55	6.69	31.71	2.70
1985	1.59	14.96	50.88	333.64	46.95	6.18	27.19	1.20
1986	0.84	19.26	48.77	400.19	45.73	5.43	30.85	0.34
1987	0.50	31.40	39.81	363.14	45.85	6.53	39.93	0.43
1988	0.59	30.30	31.89	330.87	48.64	5.97	45.67	0.41
1989	0.31	33.33	29.25	351.51	52.93	6.85	31.47	0.29
1990	0.54	39.17	29.19	346.49	61.02	7.12	25.75	1.06
1991	0.44	39.30	31.86	320.09	63.34	7.10	20.14	0.73
1992	0.36	33.53	36.16	337.77	55.84	4.87	17.78	1.28
1993	0.52	18.12	33.58	292.89	56.51	6.08	18.64	1.68

Source: Executive Office of the President of the United States. *Environmental Quality 24: The Twenty-fourth Annual Report of the Council on Environmental Quality.* Prepared by Ray Clark. Written by Carroll Curtis. Edited by Barry Walsh. Washington, DC: U.S. Government Printing Office, 1994, p. 492. Primary source: U.S. Department of Commerce. National Oceanic and Atmospheric Administration. National Marine Fisheries Service. *Fisheries of the United States.* Washington, DC: U.S. Department of Commerce, National Oceanic and Atmospheric Administration, National Marine Fisheries Service, annual.

★ 282 ★

Fish and Fisheries

Domestic Catch Disposition: 1970-1992

| Total - 9,637 |
| Fresh and frozen - 7,288 |
| Reduced to meal, oil, etc. - 1,696 |
| Canned - 543 |
| Cured - 100 |

Chart shows data from column 7.

Table shows the disposition of U.S. domestic catch. In addition to whole fish, a large portion of waste (400-500 million pounds) derived from canning, filleting, and dressing fish and shellfish is utilized in production of fish meal and oil in each year shown. Data for 1980 through 1990 are preliminary.

[Live weight catch in million pounds]

Disposition	1970	1975	1980	1985	1990	1991	1992
Total	4,917	4,877	6,482	6,258	9,404	9,484	9,637
Fresh and frozen	1,595	1,744	2,621	2,242	6,501	6,541	7,288
Canned	1,150	907	1,161	1,232	751	674	543
Cured	71	55	96	70	126	119	100
Reduced to meal, oil, etc.	2,101	2,171	2,604	2,714	2,026	2,150	1,696

Source: 1994 Statistical Abstract of the United States on CD-ROM [machine-readable datafiles]. CD-8A-94. Washington, DC: U.S. Department of Commerce, Economics and Statistics Administration, Bureau of the Census, Data User Services Division, January 1995. Primary sources: U.S. National Oceanic and Atmospheric Administration. National Marine Fisheries Service. *Fishery Statistics of the United States* (annual); and *Fisheries of the United States* (annual).

★ 283 ★

Fish and Fisheries

Domestic Fish and Shellfish Catch and Value, by Species: 1985-1992

Table shows the domestic fish and shellfish catch since 1985, with 5-year averages.

Species	1985-1989 5-year average	1987-1991 5-year average	Quantity (1,000 pounds)				Value ($1,000)			
			1985	1990	1991	1992	1985	1990	1991	1992
Total	(X)	(X)	6,257,642	9,403,571	9,484,194	9,637,303	2326237	3,521,995	3,308,272	3,677,935
Fish, total[1]	(X)	(X)	5,214,363	8,091,068	7,993,274	8,174,183	1193427	1,900,097	1,679,911	2,012,605
Anchovies	13,335	14,221	14,566	13,189	19,245	13,679	2704	2,723	6,813	5,228
Bluefish	14,044	13,908	13,743	13,802	13,232	11,595	2363	3,239	2,731	2,694
Butterfish	8,605	7,109	10,338	6,532	6,181	7,608	3537	3,334	3,171	3,701
Cod, Atlantic	71,511	80,423	82,823	95,881	92,636	61,283	35140	61,329	74,093	52,013
Cod, Pacific	206,934	378,013	120,275	526,396	553,716	550,528	18556	91,384	122,934	132,480
Croaker	10,681	8,283	11,088	6,720	4,761	5,077	3658	3,390	2,146	1,893
Flounders	199,118	258,060	195,718	254,519	404,955	645,829	129121	112,921	144,789	143,511
Haddock	8,459	5,281	14,416	5,440	4,053	5,111	13545	5,967	4,581	5,582
Halibut	74,321	73,935	61,032	70,454	66,339	68,579	38376	96,700	99,532	53,773
Herring, Atlantic sea	80,221	96,950	57,133	113,095	107,067	122,993	2968	5,746	6,339	6,821
Herring, Pacific sea	129,243	120,927	142,074	108,120	123,141	159,054	47025	32,178	30,832	35,907

[Continued]

★ 283 ★

Domestic Fish and Shellfish Catch and Value, by Species: 1985-1992

[Continued]

Species	1985-1989 5-year average	1987-1991 5-year average	Quantity (1,000 pounds)				Value ($1,000)			
			1985	1990	1991	1992	1985	1990	1991	1992
Jack mackerel	24,433	18,043	20,852	8,959	3,618	2,624	1770	535	24,433	245
Mackerel, Pacific	88,732	85,964	75,453	83,721	63,336	41,879	6324	5,081	4,872	4,118
Menhaden	2,383,569	2,145,260	2,739,401	1,962,160	1,977,060	1,644,342	100680	93,896	77,694	82,973
Mullet	27,442	30,326	21,205	28,554	12,717	22,479	5720	12,738	10,569	9,730
Ocean perch, Atlantic	4,837	2,088	9,666	1,322	1,176	1,867	3179	703	543	790
Ocean perch, Pacific	15,770	29,040	9,034	60,972	29,994	45,484	1757	8,494	6,445	13,561
Pollock, Alaska	878,909	2,026,927	92,833	3,108,031	2,855,316	2,952,130	5409	268,344	241,551	324,735
Pollock, Atlantic	39,978	28,066	43,477	21,042	17,344	15,843	6978	10,516	9,901	10,543
Rockfish	109,934	120,908	82,109	131,545	97,466	125,069	23107	38,504	109,934	47,280
Sablefish	91,209	96,242	63,380	89,802	83,610	75,451	28692	58,865	78,166	79,634
Salmon	667,900	694,093	726,946	733,146	783,285	715,828	439795	612,367	359,720	582,850
Scup or porgy	14,082	13,166	15,996	11,452	16,145	14,014	9338	8,677	9,127	8,669
Sea trout, gray	17,930	14,239	16,400	9,880	8,668	7,467	7330	5,777	4,854	4,479
Shark, Dogfish	11,944	21,442	11,563	35,793	34,376	42,327	842	3,801	3,444	4,675
Snapper, red	4,303	3,462	5,181	3,101	2,358	3,471	10661	8,411	5,681	7,354
Swordfish	11,255	18,632	12,258	13,797	17,963	19,713	33191	40,851	50,155	60,320
Tuna	94,337	79,782	83,054	62,393	35,695	56,803	52515	105,040	75,053	90,822
Whiting	38,813	38,126	44,545	44,500	36,533	35,893	8274	11,281	11,219	10,990
Shellfish, total[1]	(X)	(X)	1,043,279	1,312,503	1,490,920	1,463,120	1132810	1,621,898	1,628,361	1,665,330
Clams	140,041	135,541	150,551	139,198	134,243	142,449	128349	130,194	125,266	127,329
Crabs	398,733	489,957	337,632	499,416	649,993	624,322	203044	483,837	414,835	471,323
Lobsters, American	47,866	54,296	46,152	61,017	63,337	55,841	114895	154,677	165,026	160,951
Oysters	37,268	32,535	44,173	29,193	31,859	36,156	70053	93,718	97,996	114,536
Scallops, Calico	8,146	5,605	12,513	1,135	286	25	12524	1,281	858	78
Scallops, sea	26,435	35,114	15,829	39,917	39,302	33,528	74562	153,696	158,932	162,229
Shrimp	355,881	342,422	333,691	346,494	320,087	337,765	472850	491,433	512,848	479,954
Squid, Atlantic	38,551	56,638	7,157	59,809	70,929	81,944	7256	21,178	30,346	33,925
Squid, Pacific	49,728	57,765	22,276	36,082	68,640	30,436	4047	2,636	5,288	2,698

Source: 1994 Statistical Abstract of the United States on CD-ROM [machine-readable datafiles]. CD-8A-94. Washington, DC: U.S. Department of Commerce, Economics and Statistics Administration, Bureau of the Census, Data User Services Division, January 1995. Primary source: U.S. National Oceanic and Atmospheric Administration. National Marine Fisheries Service. *Fisheries of the United States* (annual). *Notes:* "X" indicates "not applicable." 1. Includes other types of fish and shellfish, not shown separately.

★ 284 ★

Fish and Fisheries

Domestic Fisheries – Catch, by Selected Ports: 1985-1992

Table shows the catch of domestic fisheries in selected ports. See also related table on quantity and value of catch.

Port	Catch (million pounds)				Value (million dollars)			
	1985	1990	1991	1992	1985	1990	1991	1992
New Bedford, Massachusetts	90.6	114.8	106.4	103.3	103.2	160.4	157.7	151.8
Dutch Harbor-Unalaska, Alaska	106.3	509.9	731.7	736.0	21.3	126.2	130.6	194.0
Kodiak, Alaska	96.1	272.5	287.3	274.0	65.8	101.7	96.9	90.0
Dulac-Chauvin, Louisiana	398.6	164.4	166.8	65.0	59.9	52.7	50.1	52.1
Empire-Venice, Louisiana	224.5	244.2	309.4	269.1	34.3	46.3	50.2	50.1
Gloucester, Massachusetts	116.5	126.2	107.2	101.7	37.1	40.5	40.0	34.1
Petersburg, Alaska	(NA)	67.5	90.3	81.0	(NA)	39.4	34.6	33.0
Cordova, Alaska	(NA)	70.8	47.5	30.0	(NA)	36.8	19.5	17.0
Cape May-Wildwood, New Jersey	30.3	69.2	93.1	93.9	18.1	34.4	40.1	34.9

[Continued]

★ 284 ★

Domestic Fisheries – Catch, by Selected Ports: 1985-1992
[Continued]

Port	Catch (million pounds)				Value (million dollars)			
	1985	1990	1991	1992	1985	1990	1991	1992
Point Judith, Rhode Island	56.8	58.7	64.7	66.7	28.0	32.2	37.5	36.6
Portland, Maine	36.1	48.9	63.4	59.2	17.2	31.7	44.1	43.6
Ketchikan, Alaska	(NA)	52.6	68.5	70.0	(NA)	28.3	21.9	27.0
Beaufort-Morehead City, North Carolina	133.2	102.0	137.0	78.7	22.7	23.0	23.0	16.2
Morgan City-Berwick, Louisiana	7.7	146.5	112.3	130.8	(NA)	19.7	9.4	14.3
Pascagoula-Moss Point, Mississippi	423.2	303.9	227.3	177.0	18.4	18.8	15.1	12.4
Los Angeles, California	150.3	158.5	141.5	94.9	32.5	21.3	17.4	14.6
Astoria, Oregon	25.5	41.2	53.0	67.0	9.5	16.2	17.0	19.0
Port Hueneme-Oxnard-Ventura, California	19.9	39.4	52.0	18.7	5.4	12.5	14.0	10.7
Intercoastal City, Louisiana	(NA)	173.0	211.4	175.9	(NA)	7.6	12.0	10.4

Source: 1994 Statistical Abstract of the United States on CD-ROM [machine-readable datafiles]. CD-8A-94. Washington, DC: U.S. Department of Commerce, Economics and Statistics Administration, Bureau of the Census, Data User Services Division, January 1995. Primary source: U.S. National Oceanic and Atmospheric Administration. National Marine Fisheries Service. *Fisheries of the United States* (annual). *Note:* "NA" represents "not available."

★ 285 ★

Fish and Fisheries

Fish

Table shows the number of threatened native freshwater fish species in each state, as well as the total number of native species.

State	Imperiled native freshwater fish species	Total number of fish species
Alabama	30	257
Alaska	-	-
Arizona	22	26
Arkansas	18	189
California	42	58
Colorado	9	47
Connecticut	2	55
Delaware	2	70
District of Columbia	-	-
Florida	10	119
Georgia	20	219
Hawaii	-	-
Idaho	5	36
Illinois	12	188
Indiana	8	188
Iowa	7	134
Kansas	9	118
Kentucky	18	220

[Continued]

★ 285 ★

Fish
[Continued]

State	Imperiled native freshwater fish species	Total number of fish species
Louisiana	11	150
Maine	4	49
Maryland	4	99
Massachusetts	2	62
Michigan	7	131
Minnesota	7	135
Mississippi	14	200
Missouri	14	197
Montana	6	57
Nebraska	6	81
Nevada	39	43
New Hampshire	3	55
New Jersey	2	77
New Mexico	20	66
New York	10	155
North Carolina	21	182
North Dakota	5	76
Ohio	8	153
Oklahoma	10	151
Oregon	25	57
Pennsylvania	8	156
Rhode Island	2	43
South Carolina	8	119
South Dakota	5	87
Tennessee	40	257
Texas	23	143
Utah	11	26
Vermont	2	88
Virginia	21	201
Washington	4	47
West Virginia	9	148
Wisconsin	8	144
Wyoming	8	49

Source: Stevens, William K. "The 25th Anniversary of Earth Day: How Has the Environment Fared?" *New York Times,* 18 April 1995, p. B5. Primary source: National Biological Service. *Note:* "-" represents "not available."

★ 286 ★

Fish and Fisheries

Fish and Shellfish Catch and Value, by Distance Caught Off U.S. Shores and by Selected Species: 1992

Table shows the U.S. catch and value of selected species of fish and shellfish caught off the shores of the United States. Catch is shown in live weight, except as indicated. Includes landings by U.S. flag vessels at Puerto Rico and other ports outside the 50 states and joint venture catches. Data are preliminary.

Species	Total U.S. catch (million pounds)	By distance from U.S. shores						Value of U.S. catch[1] (million dollars)
		Catch (million pounds)			Percent of U.S. catch			
		3 miles or less[1]	3 to 200 miles	International waters[2]	3 miles or less[1]	3 to 200 miles	International waters[2]	
Total, 1992	10,235	3,505	6,176	554	34	60	6	3,883
Fish[3]	1,105	267	825	13	24	75	1	483
Cod	612	34	578	0	6	94	0	184
Flounder	646	46	600	0	7	93	0	144
Halibut	70	4	66	0	6	94	0	55
Herring, sea	291	203	88	0	70	30	0	43
Mackerel	78	41	37	0	53	47	0	15
Menhaden	1,705	1,370	335	0	80	20	0	84
Pollock	2,968	177	2,791	0	6	94	0	335
Salmon, Pacific	716	710	6	0	99	1	0	582
Tuna	577	1	35	541	(Z)	6	94	280
Shellfish[3]	153	145	8	(Z)	95	5	0	205
Clams (meats)	142	43	99	0	30	70	0	127
Crabs	624	242	382	0	39	61	0	471
Lobsters	61	48	13	(Z)	79	21	0	181
Scallops (meats)	34	3	31	0	9	91	0	164
Shrimp	341	140	201	0	41	59	0	493
Squid	112	31	81	0	28	72	0	37

Source: 1994 Statistical Abstract of the United States on CD-ROM [machine-readable datafiles]. CD-8A-94. Washington, DC: U.S. Department of Commerce, Economics and Statistics Administration, Bureau of the Census, Data User Services Division, January 1995. Primary sources: U.S. National Oceanic and Atmospheric Administration. National Marine Fisheries Service. *Fishery Statistics of the United States* (annual); and *Fisheries of the United States* (annual). *Notes:* "Z" represents less than 500,000 pounds or .05 percent. 1. Includes all landings in Great Lakes and other inland waters. 2. Greater than 200 nautical miles seaward from the U.S. shores except for two states. The boundaries for the Gulf Coast of Florida and Texas are 9 nautical miles. 3. Includes other species, not shown separately.

★ 287 ★

Fish and Fisheries

Fisheries: 1993

Table shows the utilization status of assessed fisheries in U.S. waters as of 1993. Determinations of fisheries utlization are based on traditional principles of fishery science. Overutilized status indicates more fishing effort is used than is necessary to achieve long-term average catch. Fully utilized status means amount of fishing is about equal to the effort needed to achieve long-term average catch. Underutilized is when more effort is required to achieve long-term average catch.

Fisheries	Utilization status of assessed fisheries				Total assessed
	Unknown	Over	Full	Under	
Alaska groundfish	1	0	17	5	23
Alaska salmon	-	-	5	-	5
Alaska shellfish	-	0	3	1	4
Atlantic anadromous	3	1	1	-	5
Atlantic coastal migratory pelagic	3	3	-	1	7
Atlantic/Gulf/Caribbean reef fish	17	10	1	-	28
Atlantic highly migratory pelagic	2	4	4	-	10
Atlantic shark	1	1	1	-	3
Northeast demersal	2	14	6	3	25
Northeast invertebrate	-	2	3	-	5
Northeast pelagic	-	-	1	5	6
Pacific coast and Alaska pelagic	-	-	5	1	6
Pacific coast groundfish	4	1	11	1	17
Pacific coast salmon	-	5	-	-	5
Pacific highly migratory pelagic	8	2	2	4	16
Southeast/Caribbean invertebrate	5	8	1	-	14
Southeast drum and croaker	4	3	-	-	7
Southeast menhaden and butterfish	-	-	3	-	3
Western Pacific bottomfish[1]	-	2	-	4	6
Western Pacific invertebrate	-	1	-	0	1
Nearshore resources	20	10	6	-	36
Total assessed species	70	67	70	25	232
Percent of total	30	29	30	11	100

Source: Executive Office of the President of the United States. *Environmental Quality 24: The Twenty-fourth Annual Report of the Council on Environmental Quality.* Prepared by Ray Clark. Written by Carroll Curtis. Edited by Barry Walsh. Washington, DC: U.S. Government Printing Office, 1994, p. 494. Primary sources: Department of Commerce. National Oceanic and Atmospheric Administration. National Marine Fisheries Service, *Our Living Oceans: Report on the Status of U.S. Living Marine Resources.* NOAA Tech. Memo. NMFS-F/SPO-2. Washington, DC: Department of Commerce, 1993; and unpublished data. *Notes:* "-" represents "data not available or applicable." Demersal fish include bottom-dwelling fish such as flounders, skates, and dogfish. Pelagic fish include mid-water fish such as blue fish, anchovies, sardines, and squids. Anadromous fish are those which ascend rivers to spawn, such as salmon, shad, and striped bass. Invertebrate fish are lobsters, clams, scallops, and shrimp. Highly migratory fish are high sea (oceanic) fish such as tuna, swordfish, and billfishes. Coastal migratory fish include fish that range from shore to the outer edge of the U.S. continental shelf; for instance, king and Spanish mackerel, dolphin fish, and cobia. Reef fish are those that prefer coral reefs, artificial structures, and other hard bottom areas, such as snappers, groupers, and amberjacks. Reef fish include tilefish that prefer sand bottom areas. 1. Also includes armorhead.

★ 288 ★

Fish and Fisheries

Fisheries – Catch of Principal Species, by Area: 1980-1992

Table shows the catch of principal species by area of the United States. Figures reflect catch in million pounds, live weight. See also related table on the quantity and value of catch for fisheries throughout the United States.

Catch for certain species, by area	1980	1985	1987	1988	1989	1990	1991	1992
New England:								
Clams	15	22	18	17	16	15	12	15
Cod	118	83	59	75	78	95	92	61
Crabs	7	8	6	13	11	9	9	7
Flounder	118	98	68	59	50	60	50	53
Haddock	55	14	7	6	4	5	4	5
Herring, sea	184	52	84	89	90	113	106	115
Lobster, American	36	44	43	45	49	55	56	52
Ocean perch, Atlantic	24	10	4	2	1	1	1	2
Pollock	40	43	45	33	23	21	17	16
Scallops, sea	17	10	18	18	21	25	24	21
Squid	6	15	18	44	47	36	42	46
Whiting	18	31	26	25	23	28	26	28
Middle Atlantic:								
Clams (meats)	40	73	68	62	80	93	97	110
Scup or porgy	8	2	6	4	4	4	7	6
Squid	3	8	20	17	17	6	26	35
Chesapeake Bay:								
Crabs	65	91	76	78	89	91	98	54
Clams	36	47	44	47	38	27	21	13
Scallops, sea	6	3	7	7	8	9	9	7
Flounder	10	6	6	8	4	2	4	6
Oysters	21	8	9	5	4	4	3	2
South Atlantic:								
Menhaden	218	105	57	75	68	74	113	60
Shrimp	33	28	23	24	34	28	37	25
Crabs	55	48	47	54	52	54	57	64
Scallops	1	13	10	14	5	2	1	(Z)
Gulf States:								
Crabs	45	53	71	83	61	51	65	71
Mullet	31	17	26	27	27	24	25	19
Oysters (meats)	17	25	18	16	15	11	13	18
Shrimp	208	263	257	226	228	247	229	222
Pacific Coast:								
Anchovies	107	15	13	12	13	13	19	14
Bonito	14	5	11	9	2	8	1	2
Cod	20	120	171	267	372	526	554	551
Crabs	347	129	174	217	199	281	409	418
Flounder	60	68	106	133	133	182	330	574
Hake	12	16	39	16	17	21	56	124
Halibut	19	61	76	81	75	70	66	69
Herring, sea	107	142	123	131	119	108	123	159
Jack mackerel	44	21	27	23	28	9	4	3
Mackerel	65	75	94	100	89	84	63	42

[Continued]

★ 288 ★

Fisheries – Catch of Principal Species, by Area: 1980-1992
[Continued]

Catch for certain species, by area	1980	1985	1987	1988	1989	1990	1991	1992
Oysters	7	8	10	10	8	11	10	7
Pollock	3	93	552	1,257	2,362	3,108	2,855	2,952
Rockfish	106	82	118	124	134	132	97	125
Sablefish	22	63	103	108	98	90	84	75
Salmon	614	727	552	562	785	733	783	716
Shrimp	98	35	72	74	81	59	47	84
Tuna	387	64	69	73	56	34	13	35
Hawaii:								
Tuna	7	11	10	11	14	14	9	(NA)

Source: *1994 Statistical Abstract of the United States on CD-ROM* [machine-readable datafiles]. CD-8A-94. Washington, DC: U.S. Department of Commerce, Economics and Statistics Administration, Bureau of the Census, Data User Services Division, January 1995. Primary sources: National Oceanic and Atmospheric Administration. National Marine Fisheries Service. *Fishery Statistics of the United States* (annual); and *Fisheries of the United States* (annual). *Note:* "NA" indicates "not available." "Z" represents less than 500,000.

★ 289 ★
Fish and Fisheries

Fisheries – Commercial Catch, by Country: 1985-1991

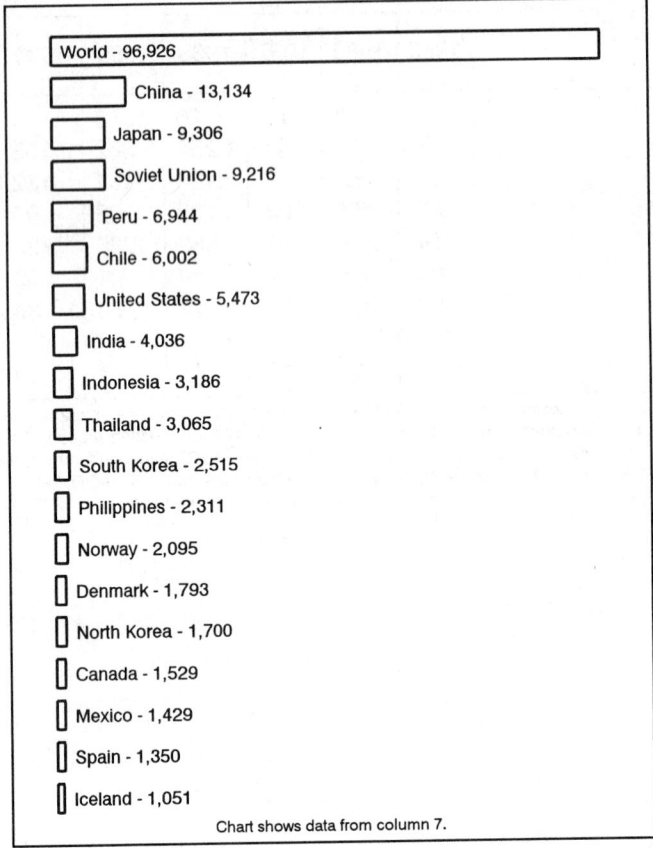

World - 96,926

China - 13,134

Japan - 9,306

Soviet Union - 9,216

Peru - 6,944

Chile - 6,002

United States - 5,473

India - 4,036

Indonesia - 3,186

Thailand - 3,065

South Korea - 2,515

Philippines - 2,311

Norway - 2,095

Denmark - 1,793

North Korea - 1,700

Canada - 1,529

Mexico - 1,429

Spain - 1,350

Iceland - 1,051

Chart shows data from column 7.

Table shows the commercial catch of fish, crustaceans, and mollusks (including weight of shells) for selected countries. Data do not include marine mammals and aquatic plants.

[In thousands of metric tons, live weight]

Country	1985	1986	1987	1988	1989	1990	1991
World	86,398	92,829	94,399	99,062	100,333	97,434	96,926
Canada	1,453	1,512	1,565	1,610	1,572	1,624	1,529
Chile	4,804	5,571	4,814	5,209	6,454	5,195	6,002
China[1]	6,779	8,000	9,346	10,358	11,219	12,095	13,134
Denmark	1,765	1,848	1,706	1,971	1,927	1,517	1,793
Iceland	1,680	1,658	1,632	1,759	1,504	1,508	1,051
India	2,826	2,923	2,906	3,125	3,640	3,794	4,036
Indonesia	2,333	2,456	2,583	2,789	2,948	3,043	3,186
Japan	11,409	11,976	11,857	11,966	11,173	10,350	9,306
Mexico	1,226	1,315	1,419	1,372	1,469	1,400	1,429
North Korea[2]	1,700	1,700	1,700	1,700	1,700	1,750	1,700
Norway	2,119	1,913	1,949	1,839	1,908	1,711	2,095
Peru	4,137	5,616	4,587	6,641	6,853	6,875	6,944
Philippines	1,865	1,916	1,988	2,010	2,098	2,208	2,311
South Korea	2,650	3,103	2,876	2,728	2,833	2,833	2,515
Soviet Union[3]	10,523	11,259	11,159	11,332	11,310	10,389	9,216

[Continued]

★ 289 ★

Fisheries – Commercial Catch, by Country: 1985-1991
[Continued]

Country	1985	1986	1987	1988	1989	1990	1991
Spain	1,483	1,488	1,524	1,592	1,559	1,450	1,350
Thailand	2,225	2,536	2,779	2,642	2,699	2,786	3,065
United States	4,949	5,166	5,986	5,937	5,763	5,858	5,473

Source: 1994 Statistical Abstract of the United States on CD-ROM [machine-readable datafiles]. CD-8A-94. Washington, DC: U.S. Department of Commerce, Economics and Statistics Administration, Bureau of the Census, Data User Services Division, January 1995. Primary source: U.S. National Oceanic and Atmospheric Administration. National Marine Fisheries Service. *Fisheries of the United States* (annual). Data from Food and Agricultural Organization of the United Nations (Rome, Italy). *Notes:* 1. Mainland. 2. Estimated. 3. Former.

★ 290 ★

Fish and Fisheries

Fisheries – Employment, Fishing Craft, and Establishments: 1970- 1991

Table shows an industry summary for fisheries as of December 31. Figures for 1979 through 1989 are preliminary. Data for employment and establishments exclude Alaska.

[In thousands]

Item	1970	1975	1980	1985	1990[1]	1991[1]
Persons employed in U.S	227	260	296	351	(NA)	(NA)
Fishermen	140	168	193	239	(NA)	(NA)
Shore workers[2]	87	92	103	112	72	73
Craft used	88	103	113	130	95	(NA)
Vessels, 5 net tons and over	14	16	19	24	32	(NA)
Motorboats	72	85	93	104	63	(NA)
Other boats	2	2	1	2	(NA)	(NA)
Fishery shore establishments	3.7	3.6	3.6	4.0	4.6	4.6

Source: 1994 Statistical Abstract of the United States on CD-ROM [machine-readable datafiles]. CD-8A-94. Washington, DC: U.S. Department of Commerce, Economics and Statistics Administration, Bureau of the Census, Data User Services Division, January 1995. Primary sources: U.S. National Oceanic and Atmospheric Administration. National Marine Fisheries Service. *Fishery Statistics of the United States* (annual); and *Fisheries of the United States* (annual). *Notes:* "NA" represents "not available." 1. Estimated and excludes Mississippi River. Maryland and Virginia represent only federal collected data. 2. Seasonal average for processors and wholesaling plants.

★ 291 ★

Fish and Fisheries

Fisheries – Quantity and Value of Catch, by Region and State: 1980-1992

Table shows the quantity and value of catch for fisheries in each region of the United States and in each state. Figures reflect catch in million pounds, live weight. Values are shown in million dollars. See also related table on catch of principal species by area.

Region, state, catch, and value	1980	1985	1987	1988	1989	1990	1991	1992
Total:								
Catch	6,482	6,258	6,896	7,193	8,463	9,403	9,484	9,637
Value	2,237	2,326	3,115	3,520	3,238	3,522	3,308	3,678
New England:								
Catch	788	590	545	570	565	649	646	647
Value	327	419	512	494	509	543	594	604
Maine:								
Catch	245	175	170	157	151	169	192	201
Value	93	101	132	124	133	130	155	163
New Hampshire:								
Catch	19	8	8	11	11	11	11	10
Value	5	5	8	9	10	10	13	12
Massachusetts:								
Catch	438	296	258	287	269	328	289	274
Value	178	232	279	274	273	303	296	280
Rhode Island:								
Catch	81	104	100	106	125	132	139	142
Value	46	70	77	69	75	73	85	86
Connecticut:								
Catch	5	7	9	9	9	9	15	20
Value	5	12	16	17	18	27	45	63
Middle Atlantic:								
Catch	244	151	163	156	172	207	234	261
Value	97	101	128	129	133	150	154	155
New York:								
Catch	39	39	41	38	37	49	51	50
Value	45	38	53	54	51	56	53	54
New Jersey:								
Catch	201	108	116	113	128	149	175	204
Value	50	61	73	72	79	89	97	97
Delaware:								
Catch	4	5	6	6	7	9	8	7
Value	2	2	2	3	3	4	4	4
Chesapeake Bay:								
Catch	717	815	791	730	778	867	770	688
Value	130	124	160	148	152	160	142	127
Maryland:								
Catch	80	92	81	80	85	81	89	57
Value	45	47	52	44	52	54	47	36
Virginia:								
Catch	637	723	710	651	693	787	681	631
Value	85	76	106	104	100	107	95	91

[Continued]

★ 291 ★

Fisheries – Quantity and Value of Catch, by Region and State: 1980-1992

[Continued]

Region, state, catch, and value	1980	1985	1987	1988	1989	1990	1991	1992
South Atlantic:								
Catch	473	311	235	280	256	262	293	238
Value	148	156	150	174	169	170	169	152
North Carolina:								
Catch	356	215	157	191	164	176	213	154
Value	69	65	63	76	71	72	67	57
South Carolina:								
Catch	21	13	15	16	20	14	19	19
Value	20	14	22	21	25	24	28	26
Georgia:								
Catch	19	17	15	17	16	13	16	18
Value	20	21	20	21	20	20	24	23
Florida (east coast):								
Catch	77	66	48	56	56	58	45	47
Value	39	57	45	55	53	54	50	46
Gulf States:								
Catch	1,979	2,412	2,501	1,938	1,790	1,625	1,679	1,426
Value	463	597	720	708	649	640	641	652
Florida (west coast):								
Catch	115	117	124	126	141	122	117	105
Value	86	114	111	114	132	116	112	109
Alabama:								
Catch	25	30	24	24	25	23	22	24
Value	25	41	45	40	38	36	37	36
Mississippi:								
Catch	334	471	436	336	298	320	239	188
Value	25	40	48	61	44	42	34	31
Louisiana:								
Catch	1,412	1,693	1,804	1,356	1,228	1,061	1,193	1,013
Value	174	225	316	317	265	263	244	295
Texas:								
Catch	94	103	111	96	96	99	108	96
Value	153	177	200	176	170	182	214	181
Great Lakes:[1]								
Catch	44	54	42	38	38	45	39	31
Value	14	15	17	19	20	20	21	22
Mississippi River and tributaries:								
Catch	85	92	110	(NA)	(NA)	(NA)	(NA)	(NA)
Value	21	29	39	(NA)	(NA)	(NA)	(NA)	(NA)
Pacific Coast:								
Catch	2,140	1,816	2,493	3,457	4,840	5,722	5,795	6,319
Value	1,025	863	1,360	1,808	1,560	1,775	1,529	1,895
Washington:								
Catch	156	167	205	174	163	137	152	122

[Continued]

★ 291 ★

Fisheries – Quantity and Value of Catch, by Region and State: 1980-1992
[Continued]

Region, state, catch, and value	1980	1985	1987	1988	1989	1990	1991	1992
Value	86	93	150	172	135	118	110	105
Oregon:								
Catch	126	101	139	149	170	139	150	257
Value	56	46	95	98	79	70	63	76
California:								
Catch	804	363	452	496	418	347	348	302
Value	323	133	173	199	123	127	140	136
Alaska:								
Catch	1,054	1,185	1,697	2,639	4,089	5,099	5,145	5,638
Value	560	591	942	1,339	1,223	1,459	1,216	1,578
Hawaii:								
Catch	11	17	16	21	24	26	28	28
Value	12	22	29	40	47	65	58	70

Source: 1994 Statistical Abstract of the United States on CD-ROM [machine-readable datafiles]. CD-8A-94. Washington, DC: U.S. Department of Commerce, Economics and Statistics Administration, Bureau of the Census, Data User Services Division, January 1995. Primary sources: National Oceanic and Atmospheric Administration. National Marine Fisheries Service. *Fishery Statistics of the United States* (annual); and *Fisheries of the United States* (annual). *Notes:* "NA" indicates "not available." 1. Collected largely by state fishery agencies and compiled by state fishery agencies and National Marine Fisheries Service. Includes, in addition to the Great Lakes, small amounts for Lake St. Clair, Lake of the Woods, Namakan Lake, and Rainy Lake.

★ 292 ★

Fish and Fisheries

Fisheries – Quantity and Value of Domestic Catch: 1960-1992

Table shows the quantity and value of domestic fish catch. Data for 1979 through 1992 are preliminary.

Year	Quantity (million pounds[1])			Value (million dollars)	Average price per pound (cents)
	Total	For human food	For indus- trial products[2]		
1960	4,942	2,498	2,444	354	7.2
1965	4,777	2,587	2,190	446	9.3
1970	4,917	2,537	2,380	613	12.5
1971	5,018	2,441	2,577	651	13.0
1972	4,806	2,435	2,371	748	15.6
1973	4,858	2,398	2,460	937	19.3
1974	4,967	2,496	2,471	932	18.7
1975	4,877	2,465	2,412	977	20.0
1976	5,388	2,775	2,613	1,349	25.0
1977	5,271	2,952	2,319	1,554	29.5

[Continued]

★ 292 ★

Fisheries – Quantity and Value of Domestic Catch: 1960-1992
[Continued]

Year	Quantity (million pounds[1])			Value (million dollars)	Average price per pound (cents)
	Total	For human food	For indus-trial products[2]		
1978	6,028	3,177	2,851	1,854	30.7
1979	6,267	3,318	2,949	2,234	35.6
1980	6,482	3,654	2,828	2,237	34.5
1981	5,977	3,547	2,430	2,388	40.0
1982	6,367	3,285	3,082	2,390	37.5
1983	6,439	3,238	3,201	2,355	36.6
1984	6,438	3,320	3,118	2,350	36.5
1985	6,258	3,294	2,964	2,326	37.2
1986	6,031	3,393	2,638	2,763	45.8
1987	6,896	3,946	2,950	3,115	45.2
1988	7,192	4,588	2,604	3,520	48.9
1989	8,463	6,204	2,259	3,238	38.30
1990	9,404	7,041	2,363	3,522	37.50
1991	9,484	7,031	2,453	3,308	34.90
1992	9,637	7,618	2,019	3,678	38.19

Source: 1994 Statistical Abstract of the United States on CD-ROM [machine-readable datafiles]. CD-8A-94. Washington, DC: U.S. Department of Commerce, Economics and Statistics Administration, Bureau of the Census, Data User Services Division, January 1995. Primary sources: U.S. National Oceanic and Atmospheric Administration. National Marine Fisheries Service. Fishery Statistics of the United States (annual); and Fisheries of the United States (annual). Notes: 1. Live weight. 2. Meal, oil, fish solubles, homogenized condensed fish, shell products, bait, and animal food.

★ 293 ★

Fish and Fisheries

Fishery Bycatch Discard Rates: 1990-1992

Table shows fisheries in terms of highest recorded bycatch discard rates. Figures presented by weight.

Fishery Description	Kg discard per Kg target	Year
Indonesian Shrimp Trawl[1]	11.750	1992
Australian Shrimp Trawl[1]	11.100	1990
Mexican Shrimp Trawl[1]	10.000	1990
U.S. Southeast Shrimp Trawl[1]	8.000	1991
U.S. Gulf of Mexico Shrimp Trawl[1]	6.259	1991
Brazil Shrimp Trawl[1]	5.856	1990
Bering Sea Sablefish Pot	3.514	1992

[Continued]

★ 293 ★

Fishery Bycatch Discard Rates: 1990-1992
[Continued]

Fishery Description	Kg discard per Kg target	Year
Bering Sea Rock Sole Trawl	2.606	1992
British Columbia Cod Trawl	2.510	1992
Gulf of Alaska Flatfish Trawl	2.076	1992

Source: "Reducing Bycatch." *National Fisherman* (May 1994), p. 17. *Notes:* "Kg" stands for "kilogram" 1. Total bycatch, not just discards.

★ 294 ★

Fish and Fisheries

Fishery Items: 1980-1992

Tuna, canned - 923

Shrimp - 820

Clams - 155

American lobster - 95

Snow crab - 88

Spiny lobster - 81

Salmon, canned - 75

Scallops - 69

Oysters - 50

Sardines, canned - 41

King crab - 15

Crab meat, canned - 9

Chart shows data from column 6.

Table shows the supply of selected fishery items from 1980 through 1992. Totals available for U.S. consumption are supply minus exports plus imports. Round weight is the complete or full weight as caught. Data are preliminary.

[In million pounds]

Item	Unit	1980	1985	1990	1991	1992
Tuna, canned	Canned weight	666	759	856	933	923
Shrimp	Heads-off weight	425	633	734	744	820
Clams	Meat weight	102	164	152	144	155
Salmon, canned	Canned weight	126	113	148	131	75
American lobster	Round weight	69	108	95	107	95
Spiny lobster	Round weight	127	154	89	85	81
Scallops	Meat weight	51	72	74	62	69

[Continued]

★ 294 ★

Fishery Items: 1980-1992
[Continued]

Item	Unit	1980	1985	1990	1991	1992
Sardines, canned	Canned weight	69	76	61	52	41
Oysters	Meat weight	71	90	56	47	50
Crab meat, canned	Canned weight	9	8	9	11	9
Snow crab	Round weight	54	45	37	60	88
King crab	Round weight	133	11	19	20	15

Source: *1994 Statistical Abstract of the United States on CD-ROM* [machine-readable datafiles]. CD-8A-94. Washington, DC: U.S. Department of Commerce, Economics and Statistics Administration, Bureau of the Census, Data User Services Division, January 1995. Primary source: U.S. National Oceanic and Atmospheric Administration. National Marine Fisheries Service. *Fisheries of the United States* (annual). *Note:* B6.

★ 295 ★

Fish and Fisheries

Fishery Products – Canned, Fresh, and Frozen: 1980-1992

Table shows production and value of fishery products. Fresh fishery product figures exclude Alaska and Hawaii. Canned fishery product data are for natural pack only.

Product	Production (million pounds)					Value (million $)				
	1980	1985	1990	1991	1992	1980	1985	1990	1991	1992
Canned[1]	1,516	1,161	1,178	1,386	1,343	1,928	1,360	1,562	1,644	1569
Tuna	602	545	581	593	609	1,144	821	902	877	888
Salmon	200	159	196	196	152	376	228	366	413	289
Clam products	77	117	110	129	126	66	109	76	84	84
Mackerel[2]	38	15	23	9	5	12	7	11	3	2
Sardines, Maine	20	20	13	14	17	32	38	17	19	25
Shrimp	16	4	1	1	1	80	19	3	4	4
Crabs	5	1	1	(Z)	(Z)	19	2	4	(Z)	1
Squid	4	4	(NA)	(NA)	(NA)	1	1	(NA)	(NA)	(NA)
Oysters[3]	(Z)	2	1	1	(NA)	(Z)	2	1	2	(NA)
Fish fillets and steaks[4]	202	246	441	473	404	261	440	843	1,021	918
Cod	31	57	65	71	62	43	89	132	180	157
Flounder	49	69	54	48	43	87	157	154	147	124
Haddock	17	8	7	8	5	29	19	24	30	19
Ocean perch, Atlantic	7	2	1	1	1	9	3	1	1	3
Rockfish	14	18	33	22	18	13	25	53	36	28
Pollack, Atlantic	9	15	12	8	9	9	17	21	18	19
Pollack, Alaska	(NA)	11	164	152	125	(NA)	24	174	206	161
Other	74	66	105	163	141	71	106	284	403	407

Source: *1994 Statistical Abstract of the United States on CD-ROM* [machine-readable datafiles]. CD-8A-94. Washington, DC: U.S. Department of Commerce, Economics and Statistics Administration, Bureau of the Census, Data User Services Division, January 1995. Primary source: U.S. National Oceanic and Atmospheric Administration. National Marine Fisheries Service. *Fisheries of the United States* (annual). *Notes:* "NA" represents "not available." "Z" indicates less than 500,000 pounds or $500,000. 1. Includes other products, not shown separately. 2. Includes Jack and a small amount of Pacific mackerel. 3. Includes oyster specialties. 4. Fresh and frozen.

★ 296 ★

Fish and Fisheries

Fishery Products – Domestic Catch and Import: 1970-1992

Table summarizes domestic catch and imports of fishery products. Data from 1979 through 1992 are preliminary. See also related table on commercial catch for selected countries.

[Live weight, in million pounds, except percentages]

Item	1970	1980	1985	1990	1991	1992
Total	11,474	11,357	15,150	16,349	16,364	16,106
For human food	6,213	8,006	9,337	12,662	13,020	13,242
Finfish	(NA)	6,139	6,991	10,120	10,186	10,297
Shellfish[1]	(NA)	1,867	2,346	2,542	2,834	2,945
For industrial use	5,261	3,351	5,813	3,687	3,344	2,864
Domestic catch	4,917	6,482	6,258	9,404	9,484	9,637
Percent of total	42.8	57.1	41.3	57.5	58.0	60.0
For human food	2,537	3,654	3,294	7,041	7,031	7,618
Finfish	(NA)	2,516	2,273	5,747	5,564	6,182
Shellfish[1]	(NA)	1,138	1,021	1,294	1,467	1,436
For industrial use	2,380	2,828	2,964	2,363	2,453	2,019
Imports[2]	6,557	4,875	8,892	6,945	6,879	6,469
Percent of total	57.2	42.9	58.7	42.5	42.0	40.0
For human food	3,676	4,352	6,043	5,621	5,989	5,624
Finfish	(NA)	3,623	4,718	4,373	4,622	4,115
Shellfish[1]	(NA)	729	1,325	1,248	1,367	1,509
For industrial use[3]	2,881	523	2,849	1,324	890	845

Source: 1994 Statistical Abstract of the United States on CD-ROM [machine-readable datafiles]. CD-8A-94. Washington, DC: U.S. Department of Commerce, Economics and Statistics Administration, Bureau of the Census, Data User Services Division, January 1995. Primary sources: U.S. National Oceanic and Atmospheric Administration. National Marine Fisheries Service. *Fishery Statistics of the United States* (annual); and *Fisheries of the United States* (annual). *Notes:* "NA" represents "not available." 1. For univalve and bivalve mollusks (conchs, clams, oysters, scallops, etc.), the weight of meats, excluding the shell, is reported. 2. Excludes imports of edible fishery products consumed in Puerto Rico; includes landings of tuna caught by foreign vessels in American Samoa. 3. Fish meal and sea herring.

★ 297 ★

Fish and Fisheries

Fishery Products – Processed: 1980-1992

Table shows the production and value of processed fishery products from 1980 through 1992. Includes Puerto Rico and American Samoa.

Product	Production (million pounds)					Value (million dollars)				
	1980	1985	1990	1991	1992	1980	1985	1990	1991	1992
Total[1]	(X)	(X)	(X)	(X)	(X)	4,456	4,936	(X)	(X)	(X)
Fresh and frozen[2]	(X)	(X)	(X)	(X)	(X)	2,110	3,242	(X)	(X)	(X)
Fillets	197	232	414	420	348	247	408	764	907	774
Steaks	5	13	26	53	56	14	32	80	114	144
Fish sticks	88	96	65	63	58	89	111	75	78	56
Fish portions	344	330	243	205	194	388	368	353	313	296
Breaded shrimp	83	95	111	116	122	254	355	353	335	349
Canned products[3]	1,516	1,161	1,178	1,386	1343	1,928	1,360	1,562	1,644	1,569
Fish and shellfish	1,009	913	957	981	936	1,782	1,269	1,415	1,439	1,322
Animal food	507	248	221	405	407	146	91	147	205	247
Industrial products	(X)	(X)	(X)	(X)	(X)	270	182	207	208	192
Meal and scrap	724	722	577	613	538	134	84	121	128	120
Oil (body and liver)	312	285	282	267	181	58	42	29	30	27
Solubles	267	323	186	170	93	14	19	14	12	8
Other	(X)	(X)	(X)	(X)	(X)	64	37	43	38	37

Source: 1994 Statistical Abstract of the United States on CD-ROM [machine-readable datafiles]. CD-8A-94. Washington, DC: U.S. Department of Commerce, Economics and Statistics Administration, Bureau of the Census, Data User Services Division, January 1995. Primary source: U.S. National Oceanic and Atmospheric Administration, National Marine Fisheries Service, *Fisheries of the United States*, annual. *Notes:* "X" indicated "not applicable." 1. Includes cured fish. 2. Includes items not shown (dressed fish, shellfish not breaded, specialties). 3. Includes salmon eggs for bait.

★ 298 ★

Fish and Fisheries

Frozen Seafood Products – Bait and Animal Food: February 1993-February 1994

According to the source: "The supply of fresh and frozen fish and shellfish held in warehouses across the United States decreased 11 percent from ... [January 1994 to February 1994] to 304.9 million pounds." Table below shows the freezings and holdings, including imported fish, from February 1993 and February 1994. Data are preliminary.

[In thousand pounds]

Fish	Freezings		Holdings[1]	
	February 1993	February 1994	February 1993	February 1994
Bait and animal food[2]	3,661	2,772	9,093	10,239
Surimi	0	0	24,227	19,174
Analog products	30	11	3,861	5,382

Source: U.S. Department of Commerce. National Oceanic and Atmospheric Administration. *Commerce News,* 22 March 1994, n.p. Data were collected from public and private refrigerated warehouses where fishery products normally are stored for 30 days or more. Prepared by Fisheries Statistics Division. *Notes:* 1. Includes imported frozen fish. 2. Saltwater and freshwater species.

★ 299 ★

Fish and Fisheries

Frozen Seafood Products – Cured Fish: February 1993-February 1994

According to the source: "The supply of fresh and frozen fish and shellfish held in warehouses across the United States decreased 11 percent from ... [January 1994 to February 1994] to 304.9 million pounds." Table below shows the freezings and holdings, including imported fish, from February 1993 and February 1994. Data are preliminary.

[In thousand pounds]

Fish	Freezings		Holdings[1]	
	February 1993	February 1994	February 1993	February 1994
Cured fish, total	0	0	689	279
Herring, salted	0	0	4	38
Salmon, mild cured	0	0	75	58
Smoked or kippered	0	0	89	152
Other salted	0	0	521	31

Source: U.S. Department of Commerce. National Oceanic and Atmospheric Administration. *Commerce News,* 22 March 1994, n.p. Data were collected from public and private refrigerated warehouses where fishery products normally are stored for 30 days or more. Prepared by Fisheries Statistics Division. *Note:* 1. Includes imported frozen fish.

★ 300 ★

Fish and Fisheries

Frozen Seafood Products – Freshwater Fish: February 1993-February 1994

According to the source: "The supply of fresh and frozen fish and shellfish held in warehouses across the United States decreased 11 percent from the ... [January 1994 to February 1994] to 304.9 million pounds." Table below shows the freezings and holdings, including imported fish, from February 1993 and February 1994. Data are preliminary.

[In thousand pounds]

Fish	Freezings		Holdings[1]	
	February 1993	February 1994	February 1993	February 1994
Freshwater, total	16	15	12,569	5,590
Fillets and steaks	0	0	942	774
Round, dressed, etc.				
Catfish	0	0	10,337	3,687
Chubs	0	0	10	0
Rainbow trout	16	14	1,089	542
Whitefish	0	0	4	10
Unclassified[2]	0	1	187	577

Source: U.S. Department of Commerce. National Oceanic and Atmospheric Administration. *Commerce News*, 22 March 1994, n.p. Data were collected from public and private refrigerated warehouses where fishery products normally are stored for 30 days or more. Prepared by Fisheries Statistics Division. *Notes:* 1. Includes imported frozen fish. 2. Except bait.

★ 301 ★

Fish and Fisheries

Frozen Seafood Products – Saltwater Fish: February 1993-February 1994

According to the source: "The supply of fresh and frozen fish and shellfish held in warehouses across the United States decreased 11 percent from ... [January 1994 to February 1994] to 304.9 million pounds." Table below shows the freezings and holdings, including imported fish, from February 1993 and February 1994. Data are preliminary.

[In thousand pounds]

Fish	Freezings		Holdings[1]	
	February 1993	February 1994	February 1993	February 1994
Saltwater, total	3,323	1,803	195,664	174,416
Blocks and slabs, total	43	0	47,220	29,292
Alaska pollack	0	0	11,738	10,145
Cod	12	0	9,709	4,029
Flounder and sole	0	0	1,169	764
Greenland turbot	0	0	30	51

[Continued]

★ 301 ★

Frozen Seafood Products – Saltwater Fish: February 1993- February 1994
[Continued]

Fish	Freezings		Holdings[1]	
	February 1993	February 1994	February 1993	February 1994
Haddock	0	0	938	926
Ocean perch	0	0	171	27
Saithe and other pollack	4	0	6,957	3,174
Whiting	0	0	3,396	746
Minced (grated), all species	7	0	9,590	5,661
Unclassified[2]	20	0	3,522	3,769
Fillets and steaks, total	401	242	68,116	77,812
Alaska pollack	54	0	15,986	23,980
Cod	13	2	15,273	26,198
Flounder	42	48	8,258	3,958
Greenland turbot	0	0	82	46
Haddock	6	0	1,812	1,145
Halibut	0	5	1,047	1,038
Ocean perch	1	4	2,867	1,450
Rockfish[3]	108	91	612	507
Saithe and other pollack	0	0	3,821	2,188
Salmon	87	92	1,101	983
Whiting	15	0	2,954	3,698
Wolf fish	0	0	79	36
Unclassified	75	0	14,224	12,585
Fish sticks and portions[4]	5	5	21,671	17,890
Round, dressed, etc.				
Halibut	0	0	7,191	4,272
Sablefish	65	67	862	148
Salmon	1	6	33,065	28,730
Chum or fall	0	0	10,453	12,493
King or chinook	1	2	1,794	2,114
Pink	0	0	5,861	4,916
Silver or coho	0	0	5,771	2,993
Sockeye	0	0	7,980	2,733
Unclassified	0	4	1,206	3,481
Whiting	0	0	2,746	893
Unclassified[6]	2,813	1,488	14,793	15,379

Source: U.S. Department of Commerce. National Oceanic and Atmospheric Administration. *Commerce News,* 22 March 1994, n.p. Data were collected from public and private refrigerated warehouses where fishery products normally are stored for 30 days or more. Prepared by Fisheries Statistics Division. *Notes:* 1. Includes imported frozen fish. 2. Cured fish category not applicable to freezings. "Unclassified" also may include blocks made from species listed separately and from minced (grated) blocks. 3. Except Pacific Ocean perch. 4. Cooked and uncooked, all species. 5. Included with unclassified saltwater fish. 6. Except bait.

★ 302 ★

Fish and Fisheries

Frozen Seafood Products – Shellfish: February 1993- February 1994

According to the source: "The supply of fresh and frozen fish and shellfish held in warehouses across the United States decreased 11 percent from ... [January 1994 to February 1994] to 304.9 million pounds." Table below shows the freezings and holdings, including imported fish, from February 1993 and February 1994. Data are preliminary.

[In thousand pounds]

Shellfish	Freezings		Holdings[1]	
	February 1993	February 1994	February 1993	February 1994
Shellfish	4,378	4,168	100,296	114,610
Clams and clam meats	704	438	3,010	5,408
Crabs	1,089	530	15,629	16,130
Dungeness	738	31	2,780	4,388
King				
Meat	0	0	77	37
Sections	1	1	1,802	2,110
Snow (tanner)				
Meat	0	0	834	620
Sections	319	473	9,367	7,259
Unclassified	31	25	769	1,716
Frog legs	0	0	46	23
Lobsters				
Spiny (tails)	0	0	2,214	2,234
Unclassified (whole and meat)	0	0	781	1,349
Oyster meats	33	25	172	131
Scallop meats	30	17	2,564	3,971
Shrimp	2,418	3,081	42,133	45,204
Breaded	579	731	6,166	3,250
Peeled, including deveined	522	793	12,109	15,328
Raw, headless	1,305	1,546	15,273	17,089
Unclassified	12	11	8,585	9,537
Squid	25	0	2,688	12,449
Unclassified shellfish	49	66	2,971	3,155

Source: U.S. Department of Commerce. National Oceanic and Atmospheric Administration. *Commerce News,* 22 March 1994, n.p. Data were collected from public and private refrigerated warehouses where fishery products normally are stored for 30 days or more. Prepared by Fisheries Statistics Division. *Note:* 1. Includes imported frozen fish.

★ 303 ★
Fish and Fisheries

Lake Trout Contaminant Levels: 1970-1990

Table shows contaminant levels in lake trout from the Great Lakes.

[In micrograms per gram wet weight]

Year	Lake Superior		Lake Huron		Lake Michigan		Lake Ontario	
	DDT	PCBs	DDT	PCBs	DDT	PCBs	DDT	PCBs
1970	NA	NA	NA	NA	19.19	NA	NA	NA
1971	NA	NA	NA	NA	13.00	NA	NA	NA
1972	NA	NA	NA	NA	11.31	12.86	NA	NA
1973	NA	NA	NA	NA	9.96	18.93	NA	NA
1974	NA	NA	NA	NA	8.42	22.91	NA	NA
1975	NA	NA	NA	NA	7.50	22.28	NA	NA
1976	NA	NA	NA	NA	5.65	18.68	NA	NA
1977	1.20	1.87	NA	NA	6.34	11.58	1.93	8.33
1978	1.00	0.93	2.19	2.92	4.58	8.18	1.58	6.15
1979	1.10	0.88	2.85	3.66	6.91	8.82	1.52	6.17
1980	0.62	1.89	1.53	3.44	4.74	9.93	1.38	5.67
1981	0.81	1.40	1.75	3.51	3.22	6.49	1.42	5.17
1982	0.29	0.48	1.31	2.10	2.74	5.63	1.88	6.33
1984	0.16	0.82	1.29	1.98	2.22	4.48	1.85	5.43
1986	0.18	0.33	0.80	1.39	1.10	2.59	1.09	2.89
1988	0.24	0.24	0.60	1.17	1.44	3.15	0.96	2.50
1990	0.18	0.45	0.54	1.50	1.39	2.72	0.99	2.18

Source: Executive Office of the President of the United States. *Environmental Quality 24: The Twenty-fourth Annual Report of the Council on Environmental Quality.* Prepared by Ray Clark. Written by Carroll Curtis. Edited by Barry Walsh. Washington, DC: U.S. Government Printing Office, 1994, pp. 491. Primary source: U.S. Environmental Protection Agency. Great Lakes Program Office (Chicago, Illinois; 1994). *Notes:* "DDT" represents dichloro-diphenyl-trichloro ethane and its derivatives. "PCBs" represent "polychlorinated biphenyls." "NA" stands for "not applicable."

★ 304 ★

Fish and Fisheries

Overfishing

Technological advancements now employed by the fishing industry have contributed to the depletion of fish stocks throughout the world. High-tech location devices find fish that otherwise would have been undetected by commercial fishing enterprises. According to the source, "the electronics make overfishing easier, ... and overfishing is a key in the depletion of fish stocks already subject to cycles governed by weather, slight changes in water temperature and other natural factors" (pp. 1E, 6E). The table shows the decline of selected fish species, comparing peak catch with that of 1992.

[Catch in million tons]

Species	Region	Peak year	Peak catch	1992 catch	Percent change
Polar cod	Newfoundland, Iceland, Greenland	1971	0.35	0.02	-94
South African pilchard	Coast of Africa	1968	1.7	0.1	-94
Silver hake	New England coast	1973	0.43	0.05	-88
Cape hake	New England coast	1972	1.1	0.2	-82
Greater yellow croaker	U.S. south Atlantic coast	1974	0.2	0.04	-80
Haddock	North Atlantic	1969	1.0	0.2	-80
North Pacific hake	Canada and North America	1987	0.3	0.06	-80
Peruvian anchovy[1]	Coast of Peru	1970	13.1	5.5	-80
Pacific herring	North Pacific	1964	0.7	0.2	-71
Chub mackerel	North Atlantic	1978	3.4	0.9	-74
Atlantic cod	North Atlantic	1968	3.9	1.2	-69
Atlantic herring	North Atlantic	1966	4.1	1.5	-63
Atlantic redfish	North Atlantic	1976	0.7	0.3	-57
Blue whiting	Atlantic coast of North America and Europe	1980	1.1	0.5	-55
Japanese pilchard	Coast of Japan	1988	5.4	2.5	-54
South American pilchard	Pacific coast of South America	1985	6.5	3.1	-52
Cape horse mackerel	North Atlantic	1977	0.7	0.4	-43
Alaska pollack	Alaska	1986	6.8	5.0	-26

Source: Heinlein, Gary. "Overfishing: A Big Net Loss." *Detroit News,* 5 June 1995, pp. 1E, 6E. Primary source: Weber, Peter. *Net Loss: Fish, Jobs, and the Marine Environment. Notes:* 1. The catch of the Peruvian anchovy hit a low of 94,000 tons in 1984, less than one percent of the 1970 level, before climbing to the 1992 level.

★ 305 ★

Fish and Fisheries

Trout Production and Value: 1988-1993

Table shows U.S. private aquaculture trout production and value. Periods are from September 1 of the previous year to August 31 of stated year. Data are for food-size fish; that is, those over 12-inches long.

Item	Unit	1988	1989	1990	1991	1992	1993
Number sold	Million	70.5	67.4	67.8	67.7	64.5	60.9
Total weight	Million lb.	56.0	55.5	56.8	58.9	55.2	54.6
Total value of sales	Million $	57.9	60.0	64.6	58.3	51.0	54.3
Average price received	$/lb.	1.03	1.08	1.14	0.99	0.92	0.99
Average weight	Lb.	0.79	0.82	0.84	0.87	0.86	0.90

Source: 1994 Statistical Abstract of the United States on CD-ROM [machine-readable datafiles]. CD-8A-94. Washington, DC: U.S. Department of Commerce, Economics and Statistics Administration, Bureau of the Census, Data User Services Division, January 1995. Primary source: U.S. Dept. of Agriculture. National Agricultural Statistics Service. *Note:* "lb." is the abbreviation for "pound(s)."

★ 306 ★

Fish and Fisheries

Wild Fish Population

Overfishing, development, and pollution threaten fish living in oceans and seas throughout the world. In both 1990 and 1991, world catch figures began to decline. According to the source, experts "now believe that the limit to sustainable landings of wild fish was exceeded decades earlier. In more and more waters, too few fish have been left in the sea to maintain spawning stocks" (p. 21). The table below shows the stocks of the 12 main wild fish species in 1991.

[In million tonnes]

Species	Amount
Alaska pollack	4.89
Atlantic cod	1.33
Atlantic herring	1.36
Capefin	1.25
Chilean jack mackerel	3.86
Club mackerel	1.17
European pilchard	1.97
Japanese pilchard	3.71
Peruvian anchovy	4.02
Skipjack tuna	1.66
South American pilchard	4.19
Yellowfin tuna	1.01

Source: "The Tragedy of the Oceans." *The Economist,* 19 March 1994, pp. 21-24. Primary sources: Renewable Resources Assessment Group, Imperial College.

Marine Mammals and Sea Turtles

★ 307 ★

Manatee Deaths

In 1992 the manatee population totaled over 1,850. By the beginning of 1995 when an aerial count of manatees was conducted, only 1,443 creatures were observed. According to the source, "the high mortality rate and low population estimate have alarmed scientists" (p. 2A). In 1990, for example, 206 manatees died—the highest single year mortality recorded. In 1992, numbers dwindled by an additional 192, and in the first three months of 1995, 47 more manatees died.

Source: Clary, Mike. "Manatees' Death Rate Alarms Scientists." *Detroit News,* 1 March 1995, p. 2A.

★ 308 ★

Marine Mammals and Sea Turtles

Marine Mammals: 1993

Table shows the status of marine mammals in U.S. waters. Data are provided by area. Figures reflect the abundance of and trends for selected species.

Marine mammal and area	Number of individuals	Trend
California/Washington		
California sea lion[1]	111,016	Increasing
Harbor seal	23,113	Increasing?
East Pacific		
Humpback whale (E)	2,000	Unknown
Eastern Tropical Pacific		
Coastal common dolphin	406,100	Stable
Coastal spotted dolphin	29,800	Stable
East spinner dolphin	631,800	Stable
North common dolphin	476,300	Stable
North spotted dolphin	738,100	Stable
North striped dolphin	172,000	Stable
South common dolphin	2,210,900	Stable
South spotted dolphin	1,298,400	Increasing
South striped dolphin	1,918,000	Stable
Whitebelly spotted dolphin	1,019,307	Stable
Gulf of Mexico		
Bottlenose dolphin	40,000	Stable
Mid-Atlantic coastal		
Bottlenose dolphin	600	Unknown

[Continued]

★ 308 ★

Marine Mammals: 1993
[Continued]

Marine mammal and area	Number of individuals	Trend
North Pacific		
Gray whale	23,859	Increasing
Stellar sea lion (T)	40,000	Declining
Northwest Atlantic		
Beaked whale	Unknown	Unknown
Bottlenose dolphin (offshore)	11,500	Unknown
Fin whale (E)	5,200	Unknown
Harbor porpoise	37,500	Unknown
Harbor seal	12,500	Increasing?
Humpback whale (E)	5,500	Unknown
Pilot whale	11,200	Unknown
Right whale (E)	350	Unknown
Spotted dolphin	200	Unknown
Whitesided dolphin	27,600	Unknown
Pribilof Islands		
Northern fur seal[2] (D)	1,016,000	Stable or increasing
Washington/Oregon		
Harbor porpoise	4,000	Unknown
West Arctic		
Bowhead whale (E)	7,500	Increasing

Source: Executive Office of the President of the United States. *Environmental Quality 24: The Twenty-fourth Annual Report of the Council on Environmental Quality.* Prepared by Ray Clark. Written by Carroll Curtis. Edited by Barry Walsh. Washington, DC: U.S. Government Printing Office, 1994, p. 495. Primary sources: Department of Commerce. National Oceanic and Atmospheric Administration. National Marine Fisheries Service, *Our Living Oceans: Report on the Status of U.S. Living Marine Resources.* NOAA Tech. Memo. NMFS-F/SPO-2. Washington, DC: Department of Commerce, 1993; and unpublished data. *Notes:* "E" indicates "endangered"; "T" indicates "threatened"; and "D" indicated "depleted." Abundance estimates range from 1,050-7,500 for offshore North Atlantic Bluenose dolphin, 17,254-37,946 for Whitesided dolphin, and 1,398-2,040 for East Pacific Humpback whale. 1. No significant trend for Northern fur seal on St. Paul; declining at 6 percent each year on St. George. 2. California sea lion status unknown, but believed to be at or above the level of maximum net production.

★ 309 ★

Marine Mammals and Sea Turtles

Sea Turtles: 1993

Table shows the number of nesting female sea turtles in U.S. waters. Data are provided by area. Figures reflect the abundance of and trends for selected species.

Marine mammal and area	Number of nesting females	Trend
Atlantic		
Green (T, E)[1]	600-800	Increasing
Hawksbill (E)	Unknown	Declining
Kemp's ridley (E)[2]	900	Stable
Leatherback (E)	Unknown	Unknown
Loggerhead (T)	18,000-21,000	Stable
Pacific		
Green (T)[3]	475	Increasing
Hawksbill (E)[4]	75	Unknown
Leatherback (E)	Unknown	Unknown
Loggerhead (T)	Unknown	Unknown

Source: Executive Office of the President of the United States. *Environmental Quality 24: The Twenty-fourth Annual Report of the Council on Environmental Quality.* Prepared by Ray Clark. Written by Carroll Curtis. Edited by Barry Walsh. Washington, DC: U.S. Government Printing Office, 1994, p. 496. Primary sources: Department of Commerce. National Oceanic and Atmospheric Administration. National Marine Fisheries Service, *Our Living Oceans: Report on the Status of U.S. Living Marine Resources.* NOAA Tech. Memo. NMFS-F/SPO-2. Washington, DC: Department of Commerce, 1993; and unpublished data. *Notes:* "E" indicates "endangered"; "T" indicates "threatened." 1. Endangered in Florida, threatened elsewhere. 2. Atlantic Kemp's ridley is declining at an average rate of 3 percent each year since 1978. 3. Historic level for Hawaii only. Current level is 2,000 in Hawaii and 100-300 in American Samoa. Current level in Guam is unknown. 4. Current abundance data are for Hawaii. Figures for Guam and American Samoa are unknown.

★ 310 ★
Marine Mammals and Sea Turtles

Whale Population

Sperm - 1,950,000	
Minke - 880,000	
Fin - 110,000	
Sei - 54,000	
Brydes - 43,000	
Gray - 18,000	
Blue - 11,700	
Humpback - 10,000	
Bowhead - 7,800	
Right - 3,200	

Chart shows data from column 2.

In 1986 a moratorium was declared on commercial whaling due to public concern regarding cruelty (for example, grenade-tipped harpoons) toward a dwindling species. The table below shows current whale populations and populations prior to commercial whaling activities.

Species	Population	
	Before commercial whaling	Current
Blue	228,000	11,700
Bowhead	30,000	7,800
Brydes	90,000	43,000
Fin	548,000	110,000
Gray	20,000	18,000
Humpback	115,000	10,000
Minke	490,000	880,000
Right	100,000	3,200
Sei	256,000	54,000
Sperm	2,400,000	1,950,000

Source: Kanamine, Linda. ''Whaling Panel Faces 30-Foot, 10-Ton Epic.'' *USA TODAY,* 23 May 1994, p. 6A. Primary source: World Wildlife Fund.

Wildlife Habitat and Conservation

★ 311 ★

Marine Sanctuaries: 1975-1993

Table shows the number and size of national marine sanctuaries from 1975 through 1993.

Year	Number	Square nautical miles
1975	2	101.0
1976	2	101.0
1977	2	101.0
1978	2	101.0
1979	2	101.0
1980	3	1,353.0
1981	6	2,323.3
1983	6	2,323.3
1984	6	2,323.3
1986	7	2,323.5
1987	7	2,323.5
1988	7	2,323.5
1989	8	2,720.5
1990	9	5,520.5
1991	9	5,520.5
1992	13	10,724.2
1993	13	10,724.2

Source: Executive Office of the President of the United States. *Environmental Quality 24: The Twenty-fourth Annual Report of the Council on Environmental Quality.* Prepared by Ray Clark. Written by Carroll Curtis. Edited by Barry Walsh. Washington, DC: U.S. Government Printing Office, 1994, p. 475. Primary source: U.S. Department of Commerce. National Oceanic and Atmospheric Administration. Sanctuaries and Reserves Division. Unpublished data.

★ 312 ★

Wildlife Habitat and Conservation

National Estuarine Research Reserves: 1975-1993

Table shows the number and acreage of national estuarine research reserves from 1975 through 1993.

Year	Number	Acres
1975	1	4,700
1976	3	14,205
1977	3	14,205
1978	4	22,605

[Continued]

★ 312 ★

National Estuarine Research Reserves: 1975-1993
[Continued]

Year	Number	Acres
1979	5	216,363
1980	9	223,426
1981	11	229,652
1983	14	240,571
1984	15	242,121
1986	16	245,149
1987	16	245,149
1988	17	247,348
1989	18	253,477
1990	18	259,945
1991	19	399,302
1992	21	400,559
1993	22	401,570

Source: Executive Office of the President of the United States. *Environmental Quality 24: The Twenty-fourth Annual Report of the Council on Environmental Quality.* Prepared by Ray Clark. Written by Carroll Curtis. Edited by Barry Walsh. Washington, DC: U.S. Government Printing Office, 1994, p. 475. Primary source: U.S. Department of Commerce. National Oceanic and Atmospheric Administration. Sanctuaries and Reserves Division. Unpublished data.

★ 313 ★

Wildlife Habitat and Conservation

National Wild and Scenic River System: 1968-1993
[In miles]

Year	Cumulative length
1968	773
1969	773
1970	868
1971	868
1972	895
1973	961
1974	1,018
1975	1,145
1976	1,610
1977	1,610
1978	2,299
1979	2,299
1980	5,662
1981	6,908
1982	6,908
1983	6,908
1984	7,217
1985	7,224
1986	7,363
1987	7,709

[Continued]

★ 313 ★

National Wild and Scenic River System: 1968-1993

[Continued]

Year	Cumulative length
1988	9,264
1989	9,281
1990	9,318
1991	9,463
1992	10,506
1993	10,516

Source: Executive Office of the President of the United States. *Environmental Quality 24: The Twenty-fourth Annual Report of the Council on Environmental Quality.* Prepared by Ray Clark. Written by Carroll Curtis. Edited by Barry Walsh. Washington, DC: U.S. Government Printing Office, 1994, p. 474. Primary source: U.S. Department of the Interior. National Park Service. River Mileage Classifications for Components of the National Wild and Scenic River System (Washington, DC). Unpublished data.

★ 314 ★

Wildlife Habitat and Conservation

National Wilderness Preservation System: 1964-1993

[In million acres]

Year	Land
1964	9.24
1965	9.24
1966	9.24
1967	9.24
1968	10.03
1969	10.19
1970	10.40
1971	10.40
1972	11.03
1973	11.03
1974	11.38
1975	12.72
1976	14.45
1977	14.49
1978	19.00
1979	19.00
1980	79.71
1981	79.84
1982	79.88
1983	80.21
1984	88.55
1985	88.70
1986	88.80
1987	88.99
1988	90.81

[Continued]

★ 314 ★

National Wilderness Preservation System: 1964-1993

[Continued]

Year	Land
1989	91.46
1990	94.97
1991	95.03
1992	95.39
1993	95.44

Source: Executive Office of the President of the United States. *Environmental Quality 24: The Twenty-fourth Annual Report of the Council on Environmental Quality.* Prepared by Ray Clark. Written by Carroll Curtis. Edited by Barry Walsh. Washington, DC: U.S. Government Printing Office, 1994, p. 474. Primary source: U.S. Department of Agriculture. Forest Service. *National Wilderness Preservation System Fact Sheet.* Washington, DC: U.S. Department of Agriculture, Forest Service, annual.

★ 315 ★

Wildlife Habitat and Conservation

National Wildlife Refuge System: 1920-1993

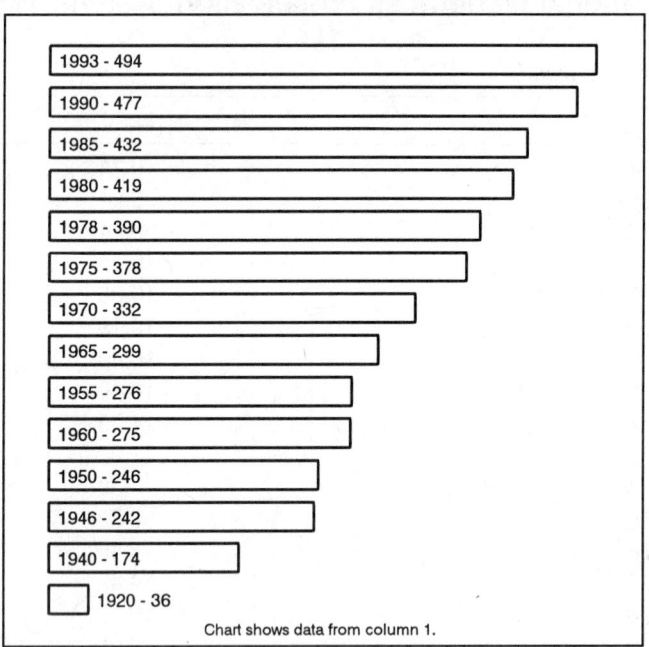

1993 - 494	
1990 - 477	
1985 - 432	
1980 - 419	
1978 - 390	
1975 - 378	
1970 - 332	
1965 - 299	
1955 - 276	
1960 - 275	
1950 - 246	
1946 - 242	
1940 - 174	
1920 - 36	

Chart shows data from column 1.

Table shows the number of units and land that comprise the National Wildlife Refuge System.

[Land in million acres]

Year	Units	Land
1920	36	NA
1940	174	NA
1946	242	17.5
1950	246	17.1

[Continued]

★ 315 ★

National Wildlife Refuge System: 1920-1993
[Continued]

Year	Units	Land
1955	276	17.3
1960	275	17.3
1965	299	28.4
1970	332	29.2
1975	378	32.3
1978	390	32.6
1980	419	69.9
1985	432	88.3
1990	477	89.1
1993	494	89.2

Source: Executive Office of the President of the United States. *Environmental Quality 24: The Twenty-fourth Annual Report of the Council on Environmental Quality.* Prepared by Ray Clark. Written by Carroll Curtis. Edited by Barry Walsh. Washington, DC: U.S. Government Printing Office, 1994, p. 473. Primary source: U.S. Department of the Interior. Fish and Wildlife Service. *Lands Under the Control of the Fish and Wildlife Service.* Washington, DC: U.S. Department of the Interior, Fish and Wildlife Service, annual. *Note:* "NA" indicates "not available."

★ 316 ★

Wildlife Habitat and Conservation

Shellfish Bed Closures, by Region: 1966-1990

Table shows prohibited acres for selected years since 1966.

[In thousands]

Year	Northeast	Southeast	Gulf of Mexico	Pacific
1966	443.1	790.0	523.7	3.4
1971	710.4	1,702.4	592.1	317.4
1974	710.8	1,896.6	829.1	316.8
1980	781.8	877.9	889.1	317.5
1985	709.1	612.0	1,649.0	157.0
1990	1,020.0	630.0	2,405.0	183.0

Source: Executive Office of the President of the United States. *Environmental Quality 24: The Twenty-fourth Annual Report of the Council on Environmental Quality.* Prepared by Ray Clark. Written by Carroll Curtis. Edited by Barry Walsh. Washington, DC: U.S. Government Printing Office, 1994, p. 431. Primary source: U.S. Department of Commerce. National Oceanic and Atmospheric Administration. National Ocean Survey. Ocean Assessments Division. Strategic Assessment Branch. *The 1990 National Shellfish Register of Classified Estuarine Waters.* Rockville, MD: U.S. Deparment of Commerce, National Oceanic and Atmospheric Administration, 1991. Data compiled from the National Estuarine Inventory database.

★ 317 ★
Wildlife Habitat and Conservation

Wildlife Charities

National Wildlife Federation - 86.2

World Wildlife Fund - 83.3

Ducks Unlimited - 80.4

Nature Conservancy - 78.9

National Audubon Society - 73.0

North Shore Animal League - 70.8

Chart shows data from column 2.

Money magazine reported donations to wildlife charities rising only 2 percent one year. Moreover, typical donations are small, thus increasing the need for fund raising. Money raised through contributions and fund raising support education and animal preservation, among other programs. The table below shows various wildlife charities' income and program spending as a percent of income. Data appear in order of program spending.

Charity	Income (million $)	Program spending as a percent of income
National Wildlife Federation	91.7	86.2
World Wildlife Fund	60.8	83.3
Ducks Unlimited	58.7	80.4
Nature Conservancy	278.5	78.9
National Audubon Society	36.6	73.0
North Shore Animal League	34.3	70.8

Source: "Dues and Popular Products Make National Wildlife Thrive." *Money* (December 1994), p. 163.

★318★

Wildlife Habitat and Conservation

Wildlife Habitat Loss and Population

Recent studies show a link between population density and the environment. For instance, the Food and Agricultural Organization reported an association between population density and deforestation, and the United Nations Population Fund identified a similar relationship between population density and loss of wildlife habitat. The table below demonstrates that countries with lower population densities lose far less original wildlife habitat. Data are from 50 countries divided into quintiles and ranked by habitat loss.

[In percentages]

Average population density	Original habitat remaining[1]
1,888 people per square kilometer	15
1,189 people per square kilometer	22
454 people per square kilometer	33
379 people per square kilometer	45
294 people per square kilometer	59

Source: Harrison, Paul. "Counting Heads, Taking Stock." *The Amicus Journal* (winter 1994), p. 22. Primary source: Harrison, Paul. *The Third Revolution* (1B Tauris, 1992). *Note:* 1. By population density.

Wildlife-Related Recreation

★319★

Anglers and Hunters: 1991

An angler or hunter is defined as anyone 16 years old or older who fished or hunted in 1991. Based on the 1991 National Survey of Fishing, Hunting, and Wildlife-Associated Recreation conducted for the U.S. Fish and Wildlife Service by the U.S. Bureau of the Census. Table shows the number of anglers and hunters, as well as the number of fishing and hunting days.

Type of fishing	Anglers		Days of fishing[1] (million)	Type of hunting	Hunters		Days of hunting[1] (million)
	Number (1,000)	Percent of population			Number (1,000)	Percent of population	
Total, all fishing	35,578[2]	19	511[2]	Total, all hunting	14,063[2]	7	236[2]
All freshwater fishing	31,041[2]	16	440[2]	Big game	10,745	6	128
Freshwater, except Great Lakes	30,186	16	431	Small game	7,642	4	77

[Continued]

★ 319 ★

Anglers and Hunters: 1991
[Continued]

Type of fishing	Anglers		Days of fishing[1] (million)	Type of hunting	Hunters		Days of hunting[1] (million)
	Number (1,000)	Percent of population			Number (1,000)	Percent of population	
Great Lakes	2,552	1	25	Migratory birds	3,009	2	22
Saltwater	8,885	5	75	Other animals	1,411	1	19

Source: 1994 Statistical Abstract of the United States on CD-ROM [machine-readable datafiles]. CD-8A-94. Washington, DC: U.S. Department of Commerce, Economics and Statistics Administration, Bureau of the Census, Data User Services Division, January 1995. Primary source: U.S. Fish and Wildlife Service. *1991 National Survey of Fishing, Hunting, and Wildlife-Associated Recreation. Notes:* 1. Any part of a day constitutes a day. 2. Includes duplication for persons who participate in more than one category.

★ 320 ★

Wildlife-Related Recreation

Marine Recreational Fisheries Catch: 1979-1993

Table shows recreational catch for marine fisheries. Data cover Atlantic, Gulf, and Pacific coasts.

[In millions]

Year	Atlantic and Gulf coasts		Pacific coast	
	Fish caught	Angler trips	Fish caught	Angler trips
1979	439	63	49	8
1980	463	74	84	15
1981	331	52	51	11
1982	371	61	53	11
1983	398	69	45	11
1984	356	62	47	10
1985	382	71	43	10
1986	411	62	55	11
1987	288	55	46	10
1988	324	66	51	12
1989	240	48	41	9
1990	231	40	NA	NA
1991	380	59	NA	NA
1992	285	52	NA	NA
1993	267	47	26	6

Source: Executive Office of the President of the United States. *Environmental Quality 24: The Twenty-fourth Annual Report of the Council on Environmental Quality.* Prepared by Ray Clark. Written by Carroll Curtis. Edited by Barry Walsh. Washington, DC: U.S. Government Printing Office, 1994, p. 493. Primary source: U.S. Department of Commerce. National Oceanic and Atmospheric Administration. National Marine Fisheries Service. *Fisheries of the United States: Current Fisheries Statisitcs.* Washington, DC: U.S. Department of Commerce, annual. *Notes:* "NA" represents "not available." 1993 data for Pacific coast does not include Washington. 1993 data are preliminary.

★ 321 ★

Wildlife-Related Recreation

Nonconsumptive Wildlife-Related Recreation:
1975-1991

1985 - 205.342	
1991 - 169.785	
1980 - 166.833	
1975 - 64.307	

Chart shows data from column 6.

Table shows participants in nonconsumptive wildlife-related recreation occurring within one mile of their homes.

Year	Visit public parks	Observe wildlife	Photograph wildlife	Feed wildlife	Maintain natural areas and/or planting	Total
1975	NA	49.314	14.993	NA	NA	64.307
1980	13.477	55.870	12.401	62.463	22.622	166.833
1985	16.480	63.641	18.047	85.800	21.374	205.342
1991	15.525	54.653	16.990	65.423	17.194	169.785

Source: Executive Office of the President of the United States. *Environmental Quality 24: The Twenty-fourth Annual Report of the Council on Environmental Quality.* Prepared by Ray Clark. Written by Carroll Curtis. Edited by Barry Walsh. Washington, DC: U.S. Government Printing Office, 1994, p. 476. Primary sources: U.S. Department of the Interior. Fish and Wildlife Service. *1991 National Survey of Fishing, Hunting, and Wildlife-Associated Recreation.* Washington, DC: U.S. Department of the Interior, Fish and Wildlife Service, 1993, p. 98, table 46; and earlier reports. *Note:* "NA" represents "not applicable or not available."

★ 322 ★

Wildlife-Related Recreation

Sport Fishing and Hunting Licenses: 1970-1992

For fiscal years ending in year shown. Table shows the number of sport fishing and hunting licenses sold to residents and nonresidents, as well as paid license holders. See also related table on cost of sport fishing and hunting licenses.

[In millions, except as indicated]

Item	1970	1975	1980	1985	1990	1991	1992
Fishing licenses							
Sales	31.1	34.7	35.2	35.7	37.0	37.0	37.4
Resident	26.8	30.0	30.1	30.5	31.0	31.1	31.4
Nonresident	4.3	4.7	5.1	5.2	6.0	5.9	6.0
Paid license holders[1]	24.4	27.5	28.0	29.7	30.7	30.7	30.6
Hunting licenses							
Sales	22.2	25.9	27.0	27.7	30.0	30.7	31.3

[Continued]

★ 322 ★

Sport Fishing and Hunting Licenses: 1970-1992
[Continued]

Item	1970	1975	1980	1985	1990	1991	1992
Resident	21.0	24.7	25.6	26.1	27.4	28.5	29.1
Nonresident	1.2	1.3	1.4	1.6	2.3	2.2	2.2
Paid license holders[1]	15.4	16.6	16.3	15.9	15.8	15.7	15.7
Federal duck stamps sold (1,000)	2,072	2,222	2,090	1,914	1,401	1,420	1,330

Source: 1994 Statistical Abstract of the United States on CD-ROM [machine-readable datafiles]. CD-8A-94. Washington, DC: U.S. Department of Commerce, Economics and Statistics Administration, Bureau of the Census, Data User Services Division, January 1995. Primary source: U.S. Fish and Wildlife Service. Federal Aid in Fish and Wildlife Restoration (annual). Notes: 1. Resident and nonresident. Includes multiple counting of license holders who brought nonresident licenses as well as a home state license. "Licenses" includes licenses, tags, permits, and stamps.

Chapter 6
ENERGY

Modern forms of energy consumption are responsible for a large portion of environmental concern. The combustion of fossil fuels and the production of petroleum-based chemicals cause much of the air pollution and toxic waste in the United States and elsewhere. Nuclear energy has its own distinct impact. At the same time, the use of alternative forms of energy (solar, wind, biomass, and the like) provide opportunities both to limit dependence on diminishing energy stocks and to reduce pollution.

This chapter presents information on energy consumption, electromagnetic fields, energy sources, nuclear power, energy production, and energy supply and reserves.

Energy recovery is covered in the Toxic and Hazardous Substances and Waste and Resource Recovery chapters. Tables on energy-related spending will be found in the Costs and Expenditures chapter, and tables pertinent to the energy industry are included in the Markets and Companies chapter.

Consumption

★ 323 ★

Energy Consumption, by Major Source: 1960-1993

Table shows total consumption and percent of consumption for major energy sources.

| Year | Total consumption (quadrillion Btu) | Percent of consumption | | | | Consumption/ production ratio |
		Coal	Petroleum[1]	Natural gas[2]	Other[3]	
1960	43.8	22.5	45.5	28.3	3.8	1.06
1965	52.7	22.0	44.1	29.9	4.0	1.07
1970	66.4	18.5	44.4	32.8	4.3	1.07
1975	70.5	17.9	46.4	28.3	7.4	1.18
1980	76.0	20.3	45.0	26.9	7.8	1.17

[Continued]

★ 323 ★

Energy Consumption, by Major Source: 1960-1993
[Continued]

Year	Total con-sumption (quadrillion Btu)	Percent of consumption				Consump-tion/ produc-tion ratio
		Coal	Petro-leum[1]	Natu-ral gas[2]	Other[3]	
1985	74.0	23.6	41.8	24.1	10.5	1.14
1990	81.3	23.5	41.3	23.8	11.5	1.20
1991	81.1	23.1	40.5	24.2	12.2	1.20
1992	82.4	22.9	40.7	24.4	11.9	1.23
1993	84.0[4]	23.4	40.2	24.8	11.6	1.28

Source: 1994 Statistical Abstract of the United States on CD-ROM [machine-readable datafiles]. CD-8A-94. Washington, DC: U.S. Department of Commerce, Economics and Statistics Administration, Bureau of the Census, Data User Services Division, January 1995. Primary source: U.S. Energy Information Administration. *Annual Energy Review. Notes:* Btu denotes British thermal units. 1. Consumption includes domestically produced crude oil, natural gas liquids, and lease condensate, plus imported crude oil and products. 2. Consumption excludes natural gas liquids. 3. Comprised of hydropower, nuclear power, geothermal energy, and other. 4. Represents peak year for U.S. energy consumption.

★ 324 ★

Consumption

Energy Consumption, by Sector: 1950-1993

Table shows U.S. end-use energy consumption by sector for 1950 through 1993.

[In quadrillion Btu]

Year	Residential and commercial	Industrial	Transportation	Total end-use	Electricity losses	Total
1950	7.11	13.85	8.41	29.46	3.62	33.08
1951	7.41	15.13	8.96	31.58	3.89	35.47
1952	7.52	14.71	8.93	31.23	4.07	35.30
1953	7.38	15.45	9.04	31.95	4.32	36.27
1954	7.63	14.44	8.85	30.98	4.29	35.27
1955	8.18	16.35	9.49	34.08	4.74	38.82
1956	8.57	16.87	9.82	35.31	5.07	40.38
1957	8.43	16.90	9.86	35.23	5.25	40.48
1958	9.01	16.16	9.96	35.17	5.18	40.35
1959	9.31	16.91	10.31	36.57	5.57	42.14
1960	9.98	17.40	10.58	37.98	5.82	43.80
1961	10.26	17.45	10.75	38.48	5.98	44.46
1962	10.87	18.09	11.19	40.18	6.35	46.53
1963	11.03	18.87	11.64	41.56	6.76	48.32
1964	11.27	19.98	11.97	43.25	7.25	50.50
1965	11.78	20.73	12.42	44.94	7.74	52.68
1966	12.41	21.71	13.08	47.22	8.44	55.66
1967	13.12	21.77	13.73	48.64	8.93	57.57
1968	13.71	22.66	14.85	51.24	9.76	61.00

[Continued]

★ 324 ★

Energy Consumption, by Sector: 1950-1993
[Continued]

Year	Residential and commercial	Industrial	Transportation	Total end-use	Electricity losses	Total
1969	14.47	23.54	15.48	53.51	10.68	64.19
1970	14.93	23.91	16.07	54.93	11.50	66.43
1971	15.34	23.70	16.71	55.77	12.12	67.89
1972	15.89	24.61	17.68	58.21	13.05	71.26
1973	15.77	25.92	18.58	60.29	13.99	74.28
1974	15.25	24.99	18.10	58.36	14.18	72.54
1975	15.20	22.74	18.22	56.19	14.36	70.55
1976	16.00	24.01	19.08	59.14	15.22	74.36
1977	15.82	24.59	19.79	60.25	16.04	76.29
1978	16.02	24.64	20.59	61.27	16.82	78.09
1979	15.71	25.68	20.45	61.50	17.04	78.90
1980	15.08	23.85	19.67	58.62	17.34	75.96
1981	14.54	22.53	19.48	56.59	17.40	73.99
1982	14.63	20.02	19.04	53.72	17.12	70.85
1983	14.40	19.40	19.11	52.92	17.60	70.52
1984	14.96	21.18	19.77	55.95	18.19	74.14
1985	14.84	20.52	20.04	55.42	18.56	73.98
1986	14.79	20.10	20.78	55.71	18.59	74.30
1987	15.15	21.12	21.42	57.70	19.19	76.89
1988	16.00	22.09	22.27	60.40	19.82	80.22
1989	16.26	22.27	22.53	61.11	20.22	81.33
1990	15.57	22.84	22.50	60.96	20.31	81.26
1991	15.98	22.57	21.17	60.75	20.46	81.12
1992	16.09	23.50	22.46	62.05	20.09	82.14
1993	16.80	23.68	22.83	63.31	20.65	83.96

Source: Executive Office of the President of the United States. *Environmental Quality 24: The Twenty-fourth Annual Report of the Council on Environmental Quality.* Prepared by Ray Clark. Written by Carroll Curtis. Edited by Barry Walsh. Washington, DC: U.S. Government Printing Office, 1994, p. 415. Primary source: U.S. Department of Energy. Energy Information Administration. *Annual Energy Review, 1993,* DOE/EIA-0384(93). Washington, DC: U.S. Department of Energy, Energy Information Administration, 1994, p. 39, table 2.1. *Note:* "Btu" represents British thermal units.

★ 325 ★

Consumption

Energy Consumption, by Selected Indicators: 1970-1993

Item	1970	1975	1980	1985	1990	1991	1992	1993
Average annual percent change[1]								
Gross domestic product[2]	3.0	-0.8	-0.5	3.1	1.2	-0.7	2.5	3.0
Energy consumption, total[3]	4.6	-2.8	-3.8	-0.2	-0.1	-0.2	1.3	2.2
Petroleum products	4.8	-2.2	-8.2	-0.4	-1.9	-2.1	2.1	0.7
Natural gas (dry)	6.5	-8.5	-1.3	-3.7	-0.5	1.6	2.6	3.2

[Continued]

★ 325 ★

Energy Consumption, by Selected Indicators: 1970-1993

[Continued]

Item	1970	1975	1980	1985	1990	1991	1992	1993
Coal	1.1	0.0	2.5	2.4	0.9	-1.7	0.5	4.0
Per capita (million Btu)								
Energy consumption	327	327	334	311	326	322	322	326
Energy consumption per dollar of GDP[2]	23.1	21.9	20.1	17.3	16.6	16.7	16.5	16.3
Amounts (1,000 Btu)								
Energy consumption[3]	66,430	70,546	75,955	73,981	81,265	81,116	82,144	83,957
Petroleum products	29,520	32,731	34,202	30,922	33,553	32,845	33,527	33,768
Natural gas (dry)	21,790	19,948	20,394	17,834	19,296	19,606	20,131	20,786
Coal	12,260	12,663	15,423	17,478	19,101	18,770	18,868	19,629
Resident population (1,000)	203,984	215,465	227,225	237,924	249,399	252,137	255,078	257,908
GDP in constant (1987) dollars (billion dollars)	2,873.9	3,221.7	3,776.3	4,279.8	4,897.3	4,861.4	4,986.3	5,136.0

Source: 1994 Statistical Abstract of the United States on CD-ROM [machine-readable datafiles]. CD-8A-94. Washington, DC: U.S. Department of Commerce, Economics and Statistics Administration, Bureau of the Census, Data User Services Division, January 1995. Primary sources: U.S. Energy Information Administration. Annual Energy Review and Monthly Energy Review. Notes: Btu represents British thermal units. "Z" indicates less than .05 percent. 1. Represents annual average for period of intervals shown; for 1970, change from 1969. Percent change derived from Btu values. Minus sign (-) indicates decrease. 2. Gross domestic product (GDP) in constant (1987) dollars. 3. Includes types of fuel or power, not shown separately.

★ 326 ★

Consumption

Energy Consumption, by State: 1991

Table shows consumption of selected energy sources by end-use sectors in each state, by U.S. region.

[In trillion Btu, except as indicated]

Region, division, and state	Resident population, July 1, 1991	Total[1]	Per capita[2] (million Btu)	End-use sector				Source				
				Residential	Commercial	Industrial	Transportation	Petroleum	Natural gas (dry)	Coal	Hydroelectric power	Nuclear electric power
United States	252,137	81,119	321.7	16,377	13,020	29,601[3]	22,121	32,846	19,625	18,754	3,116	6,579
Northeast	50,970	13,270	260.4	3,285	3,097	3,346	3,542	6,012	2,943	2,124	651	1,562
New England	13,201	3,920	296.9	1,030	1,071	812	1,007	1,898	905	353	349	373
Maine	1,236	362	292.9	79	58	119	106	229	5	9	52	67
New Hampshire	1,108	239	215.8	69	40	54	75	143	14	35	23	73
Vermont	568	132	232.5	39	25	26	42	75	7	(Z)	33	44
Massachusetts	5,995	1,313	219.0	376	342	213	382	759	261	117	23	47
Rhode Island	1,004	215	214.2	60	46	50	58	92	56	(Z)	2	0
Connecticut	3,290	732	222.5	221	172	135	204	419	105	23	6	132
Middle Atlantic	37,769	9,350	247.6	2,255	2,026	2,534	2,535	4,114	2,038	1,771	302	1,189
New York	18,047	3,558	197.2	951	1,013	693	901	1,669	900	344	297	306
New Jersey	7,773	2,300	295.9	485	481	539	795	1,202	476	62	(2)[4]	266
Pennsylvania	11,949	3,492	292.3	819	532	1,302	839	1,243	662	1,365	7	617
Midwest	60,180	19,687	327.1	4,581	3,192	7,197	4,718	6,652	4,814	6,696	172	1,769
East North Central	42,392	13,787	325.2	3,216	2,195	5,253	3,124	4,397	3,447	4,679	45	1,339

[Continued]

★ 326 ★

Energy Consumption, by State: 1991
[Continued]

Region, division, and state	Resident population, July 1, 1991	Total[1]	Per capita[2] (million Btu)	End-use sector				Source				
				Residential	Commercial	Industrial	Transportation	Petroleum	Natural gas (dry)	Coal	Hydroelectric power	Nuclear electric power
Ohio	10,940	3,687	337.0	828	582	1,490	787	1,090	799	1,413	2	159
Indiana	5,607	2,421	431.8	440	272	1,147	562	806	464	1,340	4	0
Illinois	11,525	3,513	304.8	889	658	1,219	747	1,110	1,006	758	1	772
Michigan	9,375	2,754	293.8	697	442	927	689	911	844	760	6	290
Wisconsin	4,947	1,412	285.4	362	241	470	339	480	334	408	32	118
West North Central	17,788	5,900	331.7	1,365	997	1,944	1,594	2,255	1,367	2,017	127	430
Minnesota	4,426	1,364	308.2	324	197	485	357	511	318	301	32	130
Iowa	2,790	937	335.9	220	146	347	225	309	235	346	9	44
Missouri	5,156	1,513	293.4	399	295	346	473	622	259	534	11	107
North Dakota	633	320	505.3	54	40	159	67	114	42	379	23	0
South Dakota	702	205	292.2	53	33	53	67	101	27	36	41	0
Nebraska	1,590	522	328.2	127	116	132	147	204	114	152	11	86
Kansas	2,491	1,039	417.2	188	170	422	258	394	372	269	(Z)	63
South	86,920	33,578	386.3	5,893	4,443	14,508	8,737	13,772	8,592	7,834	499	2,586
South Atlantic	44,436	12,508	281.5	2,916	2,290	3,567	3,736	5,185	1,553	3,593	166	1,641
Delaware	681	237	348.1	47	35	90	64	136	43	57	0	0
Maryland	4,863	1,215	249.8	322	178	379	336	495	178	275	15	97
District of Columbia	594	175	294.5	34	81	34	27	35	31	2	0	0
Virginia	6,288	1,848	293.9	421	384	466	578	744	182	357	(Z)	256
West Virginia	1,799	783	435.2	129	87	423	144	293	119	800	11	0
North Carolina	6,749	1,962	290.7	458	340	632	532	725	172	522	62	326
South Carolina	3,561	1,209	339.6	240	162	495	312	408	137	291	26	463
Georgia	6,628	2,057	310.3	441	323	630	663	791	332	646	49	279
Florida	13,273	3,022	227.7	824	700	418	1,080	1,558	359	643	3	220
East South Central	15,350	5,763	375.4	1,119	651	2,451	1,543	1,999	949	2,186	259	446
Kentucky	3,715	1,476	397.3	280	183	638	376	508	196	805	38	0
Tennessee	4,952	1,746	352.6	383	200	724	440	567	235	566	109	178
Alabama	4,090	1,591	389.0	287	164	731	409	526	261	720	112	170
Mississippi	2,592	950	366.5	169	104	358	318	398	257	95	0	98
West South Central	27,134	15,307	564.1	1,858	1,502	8,490	3,458	6,588	6,090	2,055	74	499
Arkansas	2,371	770	324.8	167	105	268	230	271	213	216	37	136
Louisiana	4,244	3,469	817.4	294	214	2,217	745	1,444	1,579	214	0	150
Oklahoma	3,168	1,283	405.0	241	183	515	344	432	582	292	19	0
Texas	17,352	9,785	563.9	1,156	1,000	5,490	2,139	4,441	3,716	1,333	18	213
West	54,066	15,503	286.7	2,803	2,677	4,757	5,265	6,590	3,735	2,271	2,004	670
Mountain	14,021	4,563	325.4	870	858	1,458	1,378	1,703	1,035	2,071	343	270
Montana	807	342	423.5	61	52	146	83	145	47	180	124	0
Idaho	1,038	388	373.9	81	71	146	90	127	53	12	87	0
Wyoming	458	391	853.8	36	40	236	78	116	103	450	8	0
Colorado	3,370	964	286.1	217	237	234	277	345	268	322	17	0
New Mexico	1,547	588	380.0	76	94	189	229	236	227	234	2	0
Arizona	3,746	924	246.7	205	204	184	331	353	128	348	75	270
Utah	1,767	566	320.4	108	89	217	153	207	142	345	6	0
Nevada	1,288	400	310.6	86	71	106	137	174	67	180	24	0
Pacific	40,046	10,940	273.2	1,933	1,819	3,299	3,887	4,887	2,700	200	1,661	400
Washington	5,016	1,965	391.7	390	294	700	581	776	178	89	908	45
Oregon	2,919	953	326.5	210	166	276	301	363	127	33	460	16
California	30,407	7,162	235.5	1,264	1,273	1,922	2,703	3,283	2,024	64	283	339

[Continued]

★ 326 ★

Energy Consumption, by State: 1991

[Continued]

Region, division, and state	Resident population, July 1, 1991	Total[1]	Per capita[2] (million Btu)	End-use sector				Source				
				Resi-dential	Com-mercial	Indus-trial	Trans-porta-tion	Petro-leum	Natu-ral gas (dry)	Coal	Hydro-electric power	Nu-clear electric power
Alaska	569	588	1033.9	46	58	334	149	198	368	13	9	0
Hawaii	1,135	272	239.7	23	28	67	153	267	3	1	1	0

Source: 1994 Statistical Abstract of the United States on CD-ROM [machine-readable datafiles]. CD-8A-94. Washington, DC: U.S. Department of Commerce, Economics and Statistics Administration, Bureau of the Census, Data User Services Division, January 1995. Primary source: U.S. Energy Information Administration. *State Energy Data Report, 1991. Notes:* Btu represents British thermal unites. "Z" indicates less than .05 trillion Btu. 1. Sources of energy include geothermal, wood and waste, and net interstate sales of electricity, including losses, not shown separately. 2. Based on estimated resident population as of July 1. 3. Includes 8.9 trillion Btu of net imports of coal coke not allocated by state. 4. A negative number occurs when more electricity is expended than is created during peak demand periods.

★ 327 ★

Consumption

Energy Consumption Per Dollar of Gross Domestic Product: 1950-1993

Table shows U.S. energy consumption per dollar of gross domestic product (GDP). GDP is expressed in constant 1987 dollars.

[In thousand Btu per 1987 dollar]

Year	Petroleum & natural gas	Other energy	Total
1950	13.49	9.72	23.32
1951	13.78	8.98	22.76
1952	13.85	7.88	21.73
1953	13.92	7.60	21.52
1954	14.44	6.63	21.07
1955	14.85	7.11	21.95
1956	15.28	7.11	22.39
1957	15.30	6.73	22.02
1958	15.96	6.10	22.06
1959	16.09	5.76	21.83
1960	16.39	5.83	22.23
1961	16.38	5.59	21.97
1962	16.34	5.52	21.87
1963	16.30	5.52	21.81
1964	16.06	5.51	21.57
1965	15.79	5.53	21.33
1966	15.82	5.45	21.27
1967	16.10	5.34	21.44
1968	16.51	5.30	21.81
1969	17.06	5.28	22.34
1970	17.86	5.26	23.12
1971	17.94	5.03	22.97
1972	17.91	5.03	22.93

[Continued]

★ 327 ★

Energy Consumption Per Dollar of Gross Domestic Product: 1950-1993
[Continued]

Year	Petroleum & natural gas	Other energy	Total
1973	17.55	5.18	22.73
1974	16.99	5.34	22.33
1975	16.35	5.55	21.90
1976	16.42	5.57	22.00
1977	16.15	5.44	21.59
1978	15.65	5.43	21.09
1979	15.22	5.56	20.76
1980	14.46	5.65	20.11
1981	13.49	5.76	19.25
1982	12.96	5.88	18.84
1983	12.14	5.92	18.05
1984	11.95	5.93	17.87
1985	11.39	5.89	17.29
1986	11.10	5.77	16.87
1987	11.15	5.79	16.94
1988	11.18	5.82	17.00
1989	11.08	5.73	16.81
1990	10.79	5.80	16.59
1991	10.79	5.90	16.69
1992	10.76	5.71	16.47
1993	10.62	5.72	16.34

Source: Executive Office of the President of the United States. *Environmental Quality 24: The Twenty-fourth Annual Report of the Council on Environmental Quality.* Prepared by Ray Clark. Written by Carroll Curtis. Edited by Barry Walsh. Washington, DC: U.S. Government Printing Office, 1994, p. 417. Primary source: U.S. Department of Energy. Energy Information Administration. *Annual Energy Review, 1993.* DOE/EIA-0384(93). Washington, DC: U.S. Department of Energy, Energy Information Administration, 1994, p. 17, table 1.7. *Notes:* Previous year data may have been revised. Current year data are preliminary and may be revised in the future.

★ 328 ★

Consumption

Liquefied Petroleum Gas Consumption: 1980-1992

Includes ethane, propane, normal butane, and isobutane. Reported consumption of ethane-propane mixtures have been allocated 70 percent ethane and 30 percent propane. Reported consumption of butane-propane mixtures have been allocated 60 percent butane and 40 percent propane.

[In millions of 42-gallon barrels]

Item	1980	1985	1986	1987	1988	1989	1990	1991	1992
Consumption	538	584	552	588	604	609	568	616	629
Ethane	164	210	181	178	190	170	186	208	209
Propane	298	322	303	337	338	361	335	358	378
Butane (including isobutane)	76	52	68	73	80	69	47	50	42
Stocks, December 31	116	74	103	97	97	80	98	92	98

Source: 1994 Statistical Abstract of the United States on CD-ROM [machine-readable datafiles]. CD-8A-94. Washington, DC: U.S. Department of Commerce, Economics and Statistics Administration, Bureau of the Census, Data User Services Division, January 1995. Primary source: U.S. Energy Information Administration. *Petroleum Supply Annual.*

★ 329 ★

Consumption

Manufacturing Energy Consumption, by End Use: 1991

Table shows manufacturing energy consumption for fuel purposes by type of fuel. The derived estimates presented in this table are for the primary consumption of energy for heat and power and as feedstocks or raw material inputs. Primary consumption is defined as the consumption of the energy that was originally produced offsite or was produced onsite from input materials not classified as energy. Examples of the latter are hydrogen produced from the electrolysis of brine; the output of captive (onsite) mines or wells; woodchips, bark, and woodwaste from wood purchased as a raw material input; and waste materials such as wastepaper and packing materials. Primary consumption excludes quantities of energy that are produced from other energy inputs and, therefore, avoids double counting. Based on the 1991 Manufacturing Energy Consumption Survey and subject to sampling variability.

[In trillion Btu]

End-use categories[1]	Total	Net electri-city[2]	Resi-dual fuel oil	Distil-late fuel oil and diesel fuel[3]	Natural gas[4]	Liquified petroleum gas	Coal (exclud-ing coal coke and breeze)	Other[5]
Total inputs	15,027	2,370	414	139	5,506	105	1,184	5,309
Boiler fuel	(X)	(D)	296	40	2,098	18	859	(X)
Direct process uses	(X)	1,864	109	34	2,578	64	314	(X)
Process heating	(X)	235	107	19	2,382	49	314	(X)
Process cooling and refrigeration	(X)	124	(Z)	(Z)	13	(Z)	0	(X)
Machine drive	(X)	1,187	2	14	127	15	0	(X)
Electro-chemical processes	(X)	304	(X)	(X)	(X)	(X)	(X)	(X)

[Continued]

★ 329 ★

Manufacturing Energy Consumption, by End Use: 1991

[Continued]

End-use categories[1]	Total	Net electri-city[2]	Resi-dual fuel oil	Distil-late fuel oil and diesel fuel[3]	Natural gas[4]	Liquified petroleum gas	Coal (exclud-ing coal coke and breeze)	Other[5]
Other process use	(X)	15	(Z)	1	56	(Z)	(Z)	(X)
Direct nonprocess uses	(X)	396	7	53	702	19	(D)	(X)
Facility heating, ventilation, and air conditioning[6]	(X)	192	4	8	283	3	(Z)	(X)
Facility lighting	(X)	161	(X)	(X)	(X)	(X)	(X)	(X)
Facility support	(X)	36	(D)	(Z)	23	(Z)	0	(X)
Onsite transportation	(X)	4	(X)	38	(Z)	16	(X)	(X)
Conventional electricity generation	(X)	(X)	2	4	347	(Z)	(D)	(X)
Other nonprocess use	(X)	4	(D)	2	49	(Z)	0	(X)
End-use not reported	5,547	(D)	2	12	128	4	(D)	5,309

Source: 1994 Statistical Abstract of the United States on CD-ROM [machine-readable datafiles]. CD-8A-94. Washington, DC: U.S. Department of Commerce, Economics and Statistics Administration, Bureau of the Census, Data User Services Division, January 1995. Primary source: U.S. Energy Information Administration. Manufacturing Energy Consumption, 1991 (forthcoming). Notes: Btu represents British thermal units. "X" denotes "not applicable"; "D" shows figures withheld to avoid disclosing data for individual establishments; "Z" indicates less than 0.5 trillion Btu. 1. Allocations to specific end-uses are made on the basis of reasonable approximations by respondents. 2. "Net electricity" is obtained by summing purchases, transfers in, and generation from noncombustible renewable resources, from resources, minus quantities sold and transferred out. It does not include electricity inputs from onsite cogeneration or generation from combustible fuels because that energy has already been included as generating fuel (for example, coal). 3. Includes numbers 1, 2, and 4 fuel oils and numbers 1, 2, and 4 diesel fuels. 4. Includes natural gas obtained form utilities, transmission pipelines, and any other suppliers such as brokers and producers. 5. Includes net steam (the sum of purchases, generation from renewables, and net transfers) and other energy that respondents indicated was used to produce heat and power. 6. Excludes steam and hot water.

★ 330 ★

Consumption

Manufacturing Primary Energy Consumption, by Industry: 1991

Table shows manufacturing primary energy consumption for all purposes by type of fuel. The derived estimates presented in this table are for the primary consumption of energy for heat and power and as feedstocks or raw material inputs. Primary consumption is defined as the consumption of the energy that was originally produced offsite or was produced onsite from input materials not classified as energy. Examples of the latter are hydrogen produced from the electrolysis of brine; the output of captive (onsite) mines or wells; woodchips, bark, and woodwaste from wood purchased as a raw material input; and waste materials such as wastepaper and packing materials. Primary consumption excludes quantities of energy that are produced from other energy inputs and, therefore, avoids double counting. Based on the 1991 Manufacturing Energy Consumption Survey and subject to sampling variability.

[In trillion Btu]

Industry	SIC[1] code	Total	Net electricity[2]	Residual fuel oil	Distillate fuel oil[3]	Natural gas[4]	Liquified petroleum gas	Coal	Coke and breeze	Other[5]
All industries	(X)	20,257	2,370	454	146	6,095	1,574	2,006	308	7,304
Food and kindred products	20	956	169	27	17	(D)	5	154	(D)	(D)
Tobacco products	21	24	3	1	(Z)	4	(Z)	15	0	(Z)
Textile mill products	22	274	101	12	6	108	2	31	0	13
Apparel and other textile products	23	44	19	(S)	1	19	1	2	0	1
Lumber and wood products	24	451	61	2	16	41	4	2	0	325
Furniture and fixtures	25	68	17	1	1	19	1	4	0	26
Paper and allied products	26	2,506	201	156	9	(D)	5	296	(D)	(D)
Printing and publishing	27	108	53	(Z)	2	48	1	0	0	4
Chemicals and allied products	28	5,051	440	(D)	14	2,227	(D)	(D)	10	526
Petroleum and coal products	29	5,967	105	65	21	838	(D)	(D)	(D)	4,864
Rubber and miscellaneous plastic products	30	238	116	8	3	96	3	7	0	6
Leather and leather products	31	12	3	1	1	5	(Z)	(S)	0	1
Stone, clay, and glass products	32	880	105	9	20	381	(D)	293	(D)	(D)
Primary metal industries	33	2,467	499	(D)	11	708	(D)	853	278	72
Fabricated metal products	34	307	102	3	6	175	4	5	(D)	(D)
Industrial machinery and equipment	35	237	101	3	4	109	2	11	1	5
Electric and electronic equipment	36	212	102	4	2	79	1	(D)	(D)	(D)
Transportation equipment	37	323	118	12	7	133	2	(D)	(D)	17
Instruments and related products	38	98	42	3	(D)	26	(S)	(D)	0	(D)
Miscellaneous manufacturing industries	39	32	12	1	(D)	15	(Z)	1	0	(S)

Source: 1994 Statistical Abstract of the United States on CD-ROM [machine-readable datafiles]. CD-8A-94. Washington, DC: U.S. Department of Commerce, Economics and Statistics Administration, Bureau of the Census, Data User Services Division, January 1995. Primary source: U.S. Energy Information Administration. *Manufacturing Energy Consumption, 1991* (forthcoming). *Notes:* Btu represents British thermal units. "X" denotes "not applicable"; "D" shows figures withheld to avoid disclosing data for individual establishments; "S" shows figures withheld because Relative Standard Error is greater than 50 percent. "Z" indicates less than 0.5 trillion Btu. 1. Standard Industrial Classification Code. 2. Net electricity is obtained by aggregating purchases, transfers in, and generation from noncombustible renewable resources minus quantities sold and transferred out. Excludes electricity inputs from onsite cogeneration or generation from combustible fuels because that energy has already been included as generating fuel (for example, coal). 3. Includes numbers 1, 2, and 4 fuel oils and numbers 1, 2, and 4 diesel fuels. 4. Includes natural gas obtained from utilities, transmission pipelines, and any other supplier such as brokers and producers. 5. Includes net steam, and other energy that respondents indicated was used to produce heat and power or as feedstock/raw material inputs.

★ 331 ★
Consumption

Natural Gas Consumption: 1980-1992

Item	Unit	1970	1975	1980	1985	1990	1991	1992
Consumption, total	Trillion cubic feet	21.1	19.5	19.9	17.3	18.7	19.1	19.7
Residential	Trillion cubic feet	4.8	4.9	4.8	4.4	4.4	4.6	4.7
Commercial[1]	Trillion cubic feet	2.4	2.5	2.6	2.4	2.6	2.7	2.8
Industrial	Trillion cubic feet	9.3	8.4	8.2	6.9	8.3	8.4	8.8
Lease and plant fuel	Trillion cubic feet	1.4	1.4	1.0	1.0	1.2	1.2	1.2
Other industrial	Trillion cubic feet	7.9	7.0	7.2	5.9	7.0	7.2	7.6
Electric utilities	Trillion cubic feet	3.9	3.2	3.7	3.0	2.8	2.8	2.8
Transportation[2]	Trillion cubic feet	0.7	0.6	0.6	0.5	0.7	0.6	0.7

Source: 1994 Statistical Abstract of the United States on CD-ROM [machine-readable datafiles]. CD-8A-94. Washington, DC: U.S. Department of Commerce, Economics and Statistics Administration, Bureau of the Census, Data User Services Division, January 1995. Primary sources: U.S. Energy Information Administration. *Annual Energy Review, International Energy Annual, Natural Gas Annual* (Volumes I and II) and *Monthly Energy Review. Notes:* "NA" indicates "not available." 1. Includes deliveries to municipalities and public authorities for institutional heating and other purposes. 2. Pipeline fuel and vehicle fuel.

★ 332 ★
Consumption

Per Capita Energy Consumption: 1950-1993

From the source: "End-use energy consumption is total energy consumption less losses incurred in the generation, transmission, and distribution of electricity, less powerplant electricity use and unaccounted for electrical system energy losses. Per capita data are based upon the resident population of 50 states and the District of Columbia, estimated for July 1 of each year, except for April decennial census years. Previous year data may have been revised. Current-year data are preliminary and may be revised in [the] future" (p. 416).

[In million Btu]

Year	Total energy consumption	End-use energy consumption
1950	219	194
1951	230	205
1952	226	199
1953	228	201
1954	218	191
1955	235	206
1956	240	210
1957	236	206
1958	232	202
1959	238	206
1960	244	212
1961	243	210
1962	250	216
1963	256	220

[Continued]

★ 332 ★

Per Capita Energy Consumption: 1950-1993
[Continued]

Year	Total energy consumption	End-use energy consumption
1964	264	226
1965	272	232
1966	285	241
1967	292	246
1968	306	257
1969	319	266
1970	327	270
1971	328	270
1972	340	278
1973	351	285
1974	340	273
1975	327	261
1976	342	272
1977	347	274
1978	352	276
1979	351	275
1980	335	259
1981	322	246
1982	305	231
1983	301	225
1984	314	236
1985	310	231
1986	308	229
1987	316	235
1988	326	243
1989	328	242
1990	327	240
1991	322	235
1992	322	236
1993	326	245

Source: Executive Office of the President of the United States. *Environmental Quality 24: The Twenty-fourth Annual Report of the Council on Environmental Quality.* Prepared by Ray Clark. Written by Carroll Curtis. Edited by Barry Walsh. Washington, DC: U.S. Government Printing Office, 1994, p. 416. Primary source: U.S. Department of Energy. Energy Information Administration. *Annual Energy Review, 1993.* DOE/EIA-0384(93). Washington, DC: U.S. Department of Energy, Energy Information Administration, 1994, p. 13, table 1.5. *Note:* "Btu" stands for British thermal units.

★ 333 ★

Consumption

Primary Energy Consumption, by End-Use Sector: 1960-1993

For residential and commercial, industrial, and transportation sectors, data represent only fossil fuels consumed directly.

[In quadrillion Btu, except percentages]

Year	Total consumption	Residential and commercial	Industrial and miscellaneous	Transportation	Electricity generation	Percent of total			
						Residential and commercial	Industrial and miscellaneous	Transportation	Electricity generation
1960	43.8	8.8	16.3	10.6	8.2	20.1	37.2	24.2	18.7
1970	66.4	12.1	21.9	16.1	16.3	18.2	33.0	24.2	24.5
1975	70.6	11.6	20.4	18.2	20.4	16.4	28.9	25.8	28.9
1980	76.0	10.7	21.1	19.7	24.5	14.1	27.8	25.9	32.2
1985	74.0	9.8	17.7	20.0	26.5	13.2	23.9	27.0	35.8
1990	81.3	9.6	19.6	22.5	29.6	11.8	24.1	27.7	36.4
1991	81.1	9.8	19.3	22.1	29.9	12.1	23.8	27.3	36.9
1992	82.1	10.0	20.2	22.4	29.5	12.2	24.6	27.3	36.0
1993	84.0	10.4	20.3	22.8	30.4	12.4	24.2	27.1	36.3

Source: 1994 Statistical Abstract of the United States on CD-ROM [machine-readable datafiles]. CD-8A-94. Washington, DC: U.S. Department of Commerce, Economics and Statistics Administration, Bureau of the Census, Data User Services Division, January 1995. Primary sources: U.S. Energy Information Administration. *Annual Energy Review* and *Monthly Energy Review* (March 1994). *Note:* Btu represents British thermal units.

★ 334 ★

Consumption

Renewable Energy Consumption Estimates, by Type: 1990-1992

Renewable energy is obtained from sources that are essentially inexhaustible unlike fossil fuels of which there is a finite supply.

[In quadrillion Btu, except as noted]

Source and sector	Quantity			Percent change	
	1990	1991	1992	1990 -1991	1991 -1992
Sources					
Total	6.01	6.20	6.04	3.2	-2.6
Consumption for electricity	3.77	4.01	3.77	6.4	-6.0
Electric utilities	3.13	3.09	2.70	-1.3	-12.6
Hydroelectric power	2.93	2.90	2.51	-1.0	-13.4

[Continued]

★ 334 ★

Renewable Energy Consumption Estimates, by Type: 1990-1992

[Continued]

Source and sector	Quantity			Percent change	
				1990	1991
	1990	1991	1992	-1991	-1992
Geothermal energy	0.18	0.17	0.17	-5.6	0.0
Biofuels[1]	0.02	0.02	0.02	0.0	0.0
Wind energy[2]	(Z)	(Z)	(Z)	(X)	(X)
Nonutility power generators	0.62	0.69	0.78	11.3	13.0
Hydroelectric power	0.08	0.08	0.10	1.2	19.0
Geothermal, solar, and wind energy	0.10	0.11	0.13	10.0	18.2
Biofuels[1]	0.44	0.49	0.55	13.0	11.3
Net imported electricity	0.02	0.23	0.29	1,050.0	26.1
Consumption for other uses[3]	2.23	2.19	2.27	-1.8	3.7
Biofuels[1]	2.17	2.13	2.21	-1.8	3.8
Solar and photovoltaic energy	0.06	0.06	0.06	0.0	0.0
Sectors					
Total	6.01	6.20	6.04	3.2	-2.6
Residential and commercial	0.64	0.67	0.71	4.7	6.0
Industrial	2.13	2.14	2.26	0.5	5.6
Transportation	0.08	0.07	0.08	-12.5	14.3
Electric utilities	3.15	3.32	3.00	5.4	-9.6

Source: *1994 Statistical Abstract of the United States on CD-ROM* [machine-readable datafiles]. CD-8A-94. Washington, DC: U.S. Department of Commerce, Economics and Statistics Administration, Bureau of the Census, Data User Services Division, January 1995. Primary source: U.S. Energy Information Administration. *Annual Energy Review. Notes:* Btu represents British thermal units. "Z" indicates less than 0.005 quadrillion Btu. "X" indicates "not applicable." 1. Biofuels are fuelwood, wood byproducts, waste wood, municipal solid waste, manufacturing process waste, and alcohol fuels. 2. Also includes photovoltaic and solar thermal energy. 3. Included are nonutility thermal energy uses, such as space heating and industrial process heat production. Excluded are estimates for mechanical energy, such as shaft power from dams, wind machines, and solar-powered motors and activators.

★ 335 ★

Consumption

Renewable Energy Resources Consumption: 1988-1992

Table shows U.S. consumption of renewable energy resources such as hydroelectric and geothermal power from 1988 through 1992.

[In quadrillion Btu]

Year	Hydro-electric power	Geo-thermal power	Biofuels	Solar energy	Wind energy
1988	2.34	0.22	3.17	0.09	0.04
1989	2.80	0.20	2.92	0.09	0.04
1990	3.03	0.25	2.63	0.07	0.02
1991	3.21	0.25	2.64	0.07	0.03
1992	2.90	0.26	2.79	0.07	0.03

Source: Executive Office of the President of the United States. *Environmental Quality 24: The Twenty-fourth Annual Report of the Council on Environmental Quality*. Prepared by Ray Clark. Written by Carroll Curtis. Edited by Barry Walsh. Washington, DC: U.S. Government Printing Office, 1994, p. 418. Primary sources: U.S. Department of Energy. Energy Information Administration. *Annual Energy Review, 1993*. DOE/EIA-0384(93). Washington, DC: U.S. Department of Energy, Energy Information Administration, 1994, p. 263, table 10.1; and earlier reports in the series.

★ 336 ★

Consumption

Residential Energy Consumption, by Region: 1980-1990

For period April to March for 1980-1985; January to December for 1987 and 1990. Excludes Alaska and Hawaii in 1980. Covers occupied units only. Excludes household usage of gasoline for transportation and the use of wood or coal. Based on Residential Energy Consumption Survey.

[In quadrillion Btu, except as noted]

Fuel	1980	1981	1982	1983	1985	1987	1990 Total	Northeast	Midwest	South	West
Total	9.74	9.32	9.51	8.62	9.04	9.13	9.22	2.30	2.81	2.60	1.51
Average per household (million Btu)	126	114	114	103	105	101	98	120	122	81	78
Natural gas	5.31	4.94	5.39	4.77	4.98	4.83	4.86	1.03	1.88	1.03	0.92
Electricity	2.42	2.46	2.48	2.42	2.48	2.76	3.03	0.47	0.66	1.36	0.54
Fuel oil, kerosene	1.71	1.55	1.33	1.14	1.26	1.22	1.04	0.78	0.13	0.11	0.02
Liquid petroleum gas	0.31	0.36	0.31	0.29	0.31	0.32	0.28	0.02	0.13	0.10	0.03

Source: *1994 Statistical Abstract of the United States on CD-ROM* [machine-readable datafiles]. CD-8A-94. Washington, DC: U.S. Department of Commerce, Economics and Statistics Administration, Bureau of the Census, Data User Services Division, January 1995. Primary sources: U.S. Energy Information Administration. *Household Energy Consumption and Expenditures, 1990*; and prior reports. *Note:* Btu represents British thermal units.

★ 337 ★
Consumption

Residential Energy Consumption, by Type of Fuel and Selected Household Characteristics: 1990

For period January through December 1990. Covers occupied units only. Excludes household usage of gasoline for transportation and the use of wood or coal. Based on Residential Energy Consumption Survey.

[In quadrillion Btu, except as noted]

Characteristic	Total[1]	Average per house- hold[1] (million Btu)	Natural gas	Electricity	Fuel oil[2]
Total households	9.22	98	4.86	3.03	1.05
Single family detached	6.61	113	3.45	2.20	0.74
Single family attached	0.52	87	0.28	0.19	0.06
2- to 4-unit building	0.94	95	0.62	0.20	0.11
5- or more unit building	0.73	51	0.36	0.28	0.08
Mobile home	0.41	78	0.15	0.16	0.04
Year house built:					
1939 or earlier	2.57	120	1.57	0.51	0.42
1940 to 1949	0.74	105	0.45	0.19	0.07
1950 to 1959	1.47	110	0.81	0.41	0.22
1960 to 1969	1.41	95	0.77	0.48	0.13
1970 to 1979	1.82	85	0.78	0.82	0.17
1980 to 1984	0.58	72	0.21	0.32	0.01
1985 to 1990	0.63	80	0.28	0.30	(B)
Heating and cooling degree day zones:[3]					
Less than 2,000 CDD and –					
More than 7,000 HDD	1.12	111	0.53	0.29	0.21
5,500 to 7,000 HDD	3.29	123	2.04	0.75	0.43
4,000 to 5,499 HDD	2.12	102	1.06	0.67	0.34
Less than 4,000 HDD	1.41	73	0.72	0.59	0.04
More than 2,000 CDD and less than 4,000 HDD	1.28	75	0.50	0.74	(B)
1990 family income:					
Less than $10,000	1.27	80	0.70	0.36	0.15
$10,000 to $19,999	1.66	84	0.88	0.53	0.17
$20,000 to $34,999	2.27	93	1.17	0.77	0.25
$35,000 to $49,999	1.75	105	0.90	0.62	0.19
$50,000 or more	2.27	132	1.21	0.75	0.27

Source: 1994 Statistical Abstract of the United States on CD-ROM [machine-readable datafiles]. CD-8A-94. Washington, DC: U.S. Department of Commerce, Economics and Statistics Administration, Bureau of the Census, Data User Services Division, January 1995. Primary source: U.S. Energy Information Administration. *Household Energy Consumption and Expenditures* (1990). *Notes:* Btu represents British thermal units. "B" indicates base figure too small to meet statistical standards for reliability of derived figure. 1. Includes liquid petroleum gas, not shown separately. 2. Includes kerosene. 3. "CDD" stands for "cooling degree day"; "HDD" stands for "heating degree day."

★ 338 ★

Consumption

Wood Energy Consumption, by Region and Sector: 1980-1990

[In trillion Btu, except percentages]

Year	Total energy con-sumption	Total wood con-sumption	Percent of total energy con-sumption	Region				Sector			
				North-east	Mid-west	South	West	Resi-dential	Indus-trial	Com-mer-cial	Elec-tric utili-ties
1980	75,960	2,483	3.3	386	329	1,380	388	859	1,600	21	4
1981	73,990	2,412	3.3	389	331	1,291	402	869	1,519	21	3
1982	70,850	2,395	3.4	351	339	1,334	372	937	1,434	22	2
1983	70,520	2,556	3.6	369	318	1,471	396	925	1,606	22	3
1984	74,100	2,633	3.6	349	341	1,482	461	923	1,679	22	9
1987	76,840	2,437	3.2	350	474	1,147	467	852	1,576	(1)	9
1989	81,350	2,604	3.2	432	552	1,161	459	918	1,673	(1)	13
1990	81,290	2,267	2.8	256	330	1,176	505	581	1,674	(1)	12

Source: 1994 Statistical Abstract of the United States on CD-ROM [machine-readable datafiles]. CD-8A-94. Washington, DC: U.S. Department of Commerce, Economics and Statistics Administration, Bureau of the Census, Data User Services Division, January 1995. Primary source: U.S. Energy Information Administration. *Annual Energy Review. Notes:* 1. Commercial wood energy is not included because there are no accurate data sources to provide reliable estimates.

★ 339 ★

Consumption

Wood Energy Consumption – Wood-Burning Households: 1980-1990

Based on Residential Energy Consumption Survey.

Item	Unit	Households that burn wood					Households that burn wood as main heating fuel				
		1980	1982	1984	1987	1990	1980	1982	1984	1987	1990
Number of households	Millions	21.6	21.4	22.9	22.5	22.9	4.7	5.6	6.4	5.0	3.9
Percent of all households	Percent	26.4	25.6	26.6	24.8	24.3	5.8	6.7	7.5	5.6	4.1
Number of cords burned	Millions	42.7	48.6	49.0	42.6	29.1	22.4	28.7	29.4	23.5	15.0
Average number per household	Number	2.0	2.3	2.1	1.9	1.3	4.7	5.1	4.6	4.7	3.9
Median number per household	Number	0.7	1.0	1.0	0.7	0.5	3.3	4.0	4.0	4.0	3.3
Wood energy consumption	Trillion Btu	854	971	981	853	582	448	574	589	470	300

Source: 1994 Statistical Abstract of the United States on CD-ROM [machine-readable datafiles]. CD-8A-94. Washington, DC: U.S. Department of Commerce, Economics and Statistics Administration, Bureau of the Census, Data User Services Division, January 1995. Primary source: U.S. Energy Information Administration. *Annual Energy Review. Note:* "Btu" represents British thermal units.

★ 340 ★

Consumption

World Petroleum Consumption: 1983-1992

Table shows world petroleum consumption of major consuming countries.

[In million barrels per day]

Country	1983	1984	1985	1986	1987	1988	1989	1990	1991	1992, preliminary
World, total	58.74	59.84	60.10	61.76	63.01	64.83	66.03	66.16	66.71	66.74
North America, total	18.03	18.66	18.70	19.28	19.74	20.53	20.73	20.41	20.14	20.53
Canada	1.45	1.47	1.50	1.51	1.55	1.69	1.73	1.69	1.62	1.64
Mexico	1.35	1.45	1.47	1.49	1.52	1.55	1.66	1.73	1.80	1.85
United States	15.23	15.73	15.73	16.28	16.67	17.28	17.33	16.99	16.71	17.03
Central & South America, total	3.19	3.22	3.19	3.41	3.52	3.57	3.58	3.60	3.65	3.68
Brazil	0.98	1.03	1.08	1.24	1.26	1.30	1.32	1.34	1.35	1.41
Venezuela	0.40	0.38	0.38	0.40	0.40	0.40	0.39	0.40	0.41	0.43
Western Europe, total	12.38	12.41	12.39	12.79	12.93	13.08	13.16	13.25	13.66	13.78
Belgium	0.41	0.39	0.40	0.46	0.45	0.47	0.46	0.46	0.50	0.51
France	1.84	1.75	1.78	1.77	1.79	1.80	1.86	1.82	1.94	1.93
Germany	2.66	2.66	2.70	2.86	2.77	2.74	2.58	2.66	2.83	2.84
Italy	1.75	1.65	1.72	1.74	1.86	1.84	1.93	1.87	1.86	1.94
Netherlands	0.61	0.61	0.62	0.68	0.69	0.72	0.71	0.74	0.76	0.77
Spain	1.01	0.91	0.85	0.88	0.90	0.98	1.03	1.01	1.07	1.11
United Kingdom	1.53	1.85	1.63	1.65	1.60	1.70	1.74	1.75	1.80	1.80
Eastern Europe, former U.S.S.R.	10.47	10.42	10.46	10.46	10.51	10.38	10.19	9.73	9.43	7.63
Middle East, total	2.61	2.67	2.85	2.98	3.06	3.15	3.36	3.47	3.40	3.71
Iran	0.79	0.77	0.79	0.83	0.87	0.87	0.97	1.00	1.08	1.12
Saudi Arabia	0.79	0.85	0.94	0.97	0.98	0.99	1.02	1.06	1.00	1.10
Africa, total	1.70	1.76	1.83	1.83	1.84	1.91	1.99	2.10	2.15	2.24
Egypt	0.38	0.41	0.43	0.43	0.44	0.44	0.44	0.47	0.46	0.49
South Africa	0.34	0.36	0.35	0.35	0.35	0.34	0.35	0.38	0.40	0.41
Far East & Oceania, total	10.36	10.70	10.69	11.03	11.42	12.21	13.03	13.61	14.28	15.18
Australia	0.59	0.61	0.63	0.63	0.64	0.65	0.69	0.71	0.71	0.71
China	1.73	1.74	1.89	2.00	2.12	2.28	2.38	2.30	2.50	2.63
India	0.77	0.82	0.90	0.95	0.99	1.08	1.15	1.17	1.19	1.25
Indonesia	0.47	0.47	0.47	0.47	0.49	0.52	0.58	0.65	0.70	0.77
Japan	4.40	4.58	4.38	4.44	4.48	4.75	4.98	5.14	5.28	5.45
Taiwan	0.34	0.38	0.38	0.41	0.42	0.48	0.52	0.54	0.55	0.58
Thailand	0.21	0.23	0.23	0.23	0.26	0.28	0.35	0.41	0.44	0.48
Percent change from prior year										
World, total	(NA)	1.9	0.4	2.8	2.0	2.9	1.9	0.2	0.8	0.0

[Continued]

★ 340 ★

World Petroleum Consumption: 1983-1992
[Continued]

Country	1983	1984	1985	1986	1987	1988	1989	1990	1991	1992, preliminary
North America, total	(NA)	3.5	0.2	3.1	2.4	4.0	1.0	-1.5	-1.3	1.9
Canada	(NA)	1.4	2.0	0.7	2.6	9.2	2.2	-2.3	-4.1	1.2
Mexico	(NA)	7.4	1.4	1.4	2.0	2.0	7.1	4.2	4.0	2.8
United States	(NA)	3.3	0.0	3.5	2.4	3.7	0.2	-1.9	-1.6	1.9
Central & South America, total	(NA)	0.9	-0.9	6.9	3.2	1.4	0.3	0.6	1.4	0.8
Brazil	(NA)	5.1	4.9	14.8	1.6	3.2	1.5	1.5	0.7	4.4
Venezuela	(NA)	-5.0	0.0	5.3	0.0	0.0	-2.5	2.6	2.5	4.9
Western Europe, total	(NA)	0.2	-0.2	3.2	1.1	1.2	0.6	0.7	3.1	0.9
Belgium	(NA)	-4.9	2.6	15.0	-2.2	4.4	-2.1	0.0	8.7	2.0
France	(NA)	-4.9	1.7	-0.6	1.1	0.4	3.3	-1.9	6.6	-0.5
Germany	(NA)	0.0	1.5	5.9	-3.1	-1.1	-5.8	3.1	6.4	0.4
Italy	(NA)	-5.7	4.2	1.2	6.9	-1.3	5.1	-3.1	-0.5	4.3
Netherlands	(NA)	0.0	1.6	9.7	1.5	4.3	-1.4	4.2	2.7	1.3
Spain	(NA)	-9.9	-6.6	3.5	2.3	8.9	5.1	-1.9	5.9	3.7
United Kingdom	(NA)	20.9	-11.9	1.2	-3.0	6.1	2.5	0.6	2.9	0.0
Eastern Europe and former U.S.S.R.	(NA)	-0.5	0.4	0.0	0.5	-1.2	-1.8	-4.5	-3.1	-19.1
Middle East, total	(NA)	2.3	6.7	4.6	2.7	2.9	6.7	3.3	-2.0	9.1
Iran	(NA)	-2.5	2.6	5.1	4.8	0.0	11.5	3.1	8.0	3.7
Saudi Arabia	(NA)	7.6	10.6	3.2	1.0	1.0	3.0	3.9	-5.7	10.0
Africa, total	(NA)	3.5	4.0	0.0	0.5	3.8	4.2	5.5	2.4	4.2
Egypt	(NA)	7.9	4.9	0.0	2.3	0.0	0.0	6.8	-2.1	6.5
South Africa	(NA)	5.9	-2.8	0.0	0.0	-2.9	2.9	8.6	5.3	2.5
Far East & Oceania, total	(NA)	3.3	-0.1	3.2	3.5	6.9	6.7	4.5	4.9	6.3
Australia	(NA)	3.4	3.3	0.0	1.6	1.6	6.2	2.9	0.0	0.0
China	(NA)	0.6	8.6	5.8	6.0	7.5	4.4	-3.4	8.7	5.2
India	(NA)	6.5	9.8	5.6	4.2	9.1	6.5	1.7	1.7	5.0
Indonesia	(NA)	0.0	0.0	0.0	4.3	6.1	11.5	12.1	7.7	10.0
Japan	(NA)	4.1	-4.4	1.4	0.9	6.1	4.8	3.2	2.7	3.2
Taiwan	(NA)	11.8	0.0	7.9	2.4	14.3	8.3	3.8	1.9	5.5
Thailand	(NA)	9.5	0.0	0.0	13.0	7.7	25.0	17.1	7.3	9.1

Source: 1994 Statistical Abstract of the United States on CD-ROM [machine-readable datafiles]. CD-8A-94. Washington, DC: U.S. Department of Commerce, Economics and Statistics Administration, Bureau of the Census, Data User Services Division, January 1995. Primary sources: Energy Information Administration, *Annual Energy Review* and *Monthly Energy Review. Note:* "NA" stands for "not available."

Electromagnetic Fields

★ 341 ★

Electromagnetic Fields Near Powerlines

Studies have linked exposure to electromagnetic fields to cancer in humans. Different studies have drawn conflicting results, so study conclusions are unclear. The table shows electromagnetic fields near powerlines.

[In milliGauss]

Transmission line	Distance			
	50 feet	100 feet	200 feet	300 feet
115 Kilovolts				
Average usage	7	2	.4	.2
Peak usage	14	4	.9	.4
230 Kilovolts				
Average usage	20	7	1.8	.8
Peak usage	40	15	3.6	1.6
500 Kilovolts				
Average usage	29	13	3.2	1.4
Peak usage	62	27	6.7	3

Source: Dana, Amy, and Tom Turner. "Currents of Controversy." *Amicus Journal* 15, no. 2 (summer 1993), p. 30. Primary source: Bonneville Power Administration.

★ 342 ★

Electromagnetic Fields

Magnetic Field Emissions of Household Appliances

Electromagnetic fields are created when electricity is transmitted through a wire. Exposure to electromagnetic fields is thought to affect human cell division and reproduction.

[In milliGauss]

Appliance	Magnetic field	Distance
Computer	7-20	6 inches
Dial-face clock	1-30	1 foot
Digital bedroom clock	1-8	1 foot
Electric blanket	20	1 yard[1]
Electric shaver	4-600	6 inches
Fluorescent desk lamp	6-30	1 foot
Hair dryer	1-700	6 inches
Microwave oven	100-300	6 inches
Toaster	3-7	1 foot

[Continued]

★ 342 ★

Magnetic Field Emissions of Household Appliances
[Continued]

Appliance	Magnetic field	Distance
Television set	1.5	1 yard[2]
Vacuum cleaner	4-50	1 yard

Source: "The Facts on Electromagnetic Fields." *ABA Journal* (January 1994), p. 43. Primary sources: U.S. Environmental Agency; *ABA Journal* research. *Notes:* Emission levels vary greatly depending on distance, brand, and high, medium or low setting. 1. Or as low as 2 mG in newer models. 2. Also varies by model age and screen size.

★ 343 ★

Electromagnetic Fields

Magnetic Field Emissions of Office Equipment

Electric pencil sharpeners - 300

Air cleaners - 250

Copy machines - 200

Fluorescent lights - 100

Video display terminals - 20

Fax machines - 9

According to the source: "Exposure to electromagnetic fields is certainly an important emerging issue. The research data are not conclusive but appear to point to some potential for biological effects in humans, especially in children. Already some power companies are taking preventive measures where possible" (p. 17). Table shows magnetic fields of items found in offices.

[In milliGauss]

Source	Magnetic field
Electric pencil sharpeners	300
Air cleaners	250
Copy machines	200
Fluorescent lights	100
Video display terminals	20
Fax machines	9

Source: "Electromagnetic Energy Spectrum." *International Insurance Monitor* (May 1994), p. 17. *Note:* Data show highest magnetic field at 6-feet distance.

Energy Sources

★ 344 ★

Firewood

Table shows heat generated by various types of firewood.

[In million British thermal units per cord]

Wood	Heat generation
Osage orange	30.7
Shagbark	29.1
Black locust	28.1
White oak	27.0
Red oak	25.3
Sugar maple	25.0
Ash	23.6
Black walnut	21.8
Hackberry	21.6
Red elm	21.4
Sycamore	20.7
American elm	20.1
Silver maple	20.1
Short leaf pine	19.0
Red cedar	18.9
Box elder	17.5
Cottonwood	16.1
Basswood	14.7

Source: Everly, Steve. "Looking at Firewood's Quality." *Kansas City Star*, 20 November 1994, p. 4. Primary source: University of Missouri Extension.

★ 345 ★

Energy Sources

Prime Movers: 1950-1992

Table shows the total horsepower of all prime movers as of January, except as noted. Prior to 1960, excludes Alaska and Hawaii, except as noted. Prime movers are mechanical engines and turbines and work animals that originally convert fuels or force (as wind or falling water) into work and power. Electric motors that obtain their power from prime movers are excluded to avoid duplication.

[In millions, except percentages]

| Year | Total horse-power | Automotive[1] | | Nonautomotive | | | | | | | |
		Total	Percent of total	Total	Facto-ries[2]	Mines[2]	Rail-roads[3]	Merchant ships and sailing vessels[4]	Farms	Electric central stations[5]	Air-craft[6]
1950	4,868	4,404	90.5	464	33	22	111	23[7]	165	88	22[7]
1955	7,158	6,632	92.7	526	36	31	60	24[7]	212	138	26[7]
1960	11,008	10,367	94.2	641	42	35	47	24	240	217	37
1965	15,096	14,306	94.8	790	48	40	44	24	272	307	55
1970	20,408	19,325	94.7	1,083	54	45	54	22	290	435	183
1975	25,100	23,752	94.6	1,348	60	47	62	22	318	654	185
1980	28,922	27,362	94.6	1,564	64	48	63	28	345	806	210
1985	32,529	30,792	94.7	1,737	65	47	58	29	358	942	270
1990	34,958	33,158	94.7	1,800	67	48	50	28	356	984	267
1991	33,905	32,100	94.7	1,805	68	48	50	27	355	991	266
1992	35,300	33,431	94.7	1,869	68	47	50	29	352	1,057[8]	266

Source: 1994 Statistical Abstract of the United States on CD-ROM [machine-readable datafiles]. CD-8A-94. Washington, DC: U.S. Department of Commerce, Economics and Statistics Administration, Bureau of the Census, Data User Services Division, January 1995. Primary source: John A. Waring (Arlington, Virginia). Unpublished estimates. *Notes:* 1. As of July 1, except beginning 1992, as of January 1. Includes passenger cars, trucks, buses, and motorcycles. 2. Beginning 1965, data are estimates. This is an extension of trends, since government agencies suspended compilation of these power capacity statistics. Beginning 1992, includes vessels on the Great Lakes. 3. Beginning 1965, not strictly comparable with earlier years. 4. This is an extension of trends, since government agencies suspended compilation of these power capacity statistics. Beginning 1992, includes vessels onthe Great Lakes. 5. As of July 1, except beginning 1992, as of January 1. 6. Beginning 1965, not strictly comparable with earlier years. Includes private planes and commercial airlines. 7. Includes Alaska and Hawaii. 8. Includes 57 million horsepower in cogenerating and industrial electric power capacity.

★ 346 ★

Energy Sources

Solar Collector Shipments, by Type, End Use, and Market Sector: 1974-1992

Solar collector is a device for intercepting sunlight, converting the light to heat, and carrying the heat to where it will be either used or stored. 1985 data are not available.

[In thousand square feet, except number of manufacturers]

| Year | Number of manu- fac- turers | Total ship- ments[1] | Collector type | | End use | | | Market sector | | |
			Low temper- ature	Medium temper- ature, special, other	Pool heat- ing	Hot water	Space heat- ing	Resi- dential	Com- mercial	Indus- trial
1974	45	1,274	1,137	137	(NA)	(NA)	(NA)	(NA)	(NA)	(NA)
1975	131	3,743	3,026	717	(NA)	(NA)	(NA)	(NA)	(NA)	(NA)
1976	186	5,801	3,876	1,925	(NA)	(NA)	(NA)	(NA)	(NA)	(NA)
1977	321	10,312	4,743	5,569	6,334	1,713	1,699	7,978	1,680	105
1978	340	10,860	5,872	4,988	5,970	2,513	1,736	8,095	1,848	263
1979	349	14,251	8,395	5,857	8,551	2,958	1,722	11,387	2,015	314
1980	233	19,398	12,233	7,165	12,029	4,790	1,688	16,077	2,417	488
1981	203	20,133	8,677	11,456	9,781	7,204	2,017	15,773	2,561	1,518
1982	265	18,621	7,476	11,145	7,035	7,444	2,367	13,729	3,789	560
1983	203	16,828	4,853	11,975	4,839	9,323	2,082	11,780	3,039	1,665
1984[2]	225	17,191	4,479	11,939	4,427	8,930	2,370	13,980	2,091	289
1986[2]	98	9,360	3,751	1,111	3,494	1,181	127	4,131	703	13
1987[2]	59	7,269	3,157	957	3,111	964	23	3,775	305	11
1988[2]	51	8,174	3,326	732	3,304	726	7	3,796	255	7
1989[2]	44	11,482	4,283	1,989	4,688	1,374	205	5,804	424	42
1990	48	11,378	3,621	2,519	5,016	1,091	2	5,835	294	22
1991	48	6,574	5,585	989	5,535	989	24	6,322	225	13
1992	45	7,086	6,187	897	6,210	801	35	6,832	204	27

Source: 1994 Statistical Abstract of the United States on CD-ROM [machine-readable datafiles]. CD-8A-94. Washington, DC: U.S. Department of Commerce, Economics and Statistics Administration, Bureau of the Census, Data User Services Division, January 1995. Primary source: U.S. Energy Information Administration. *Solar Collecting Manufacturing Activity* (annual). *Notes:* "NA" stands for "not available." 1. Includes other end uses and market sectors not shown separately. 2. Declines between 1984 and 1989 are primarily due to the expiration of the federal energy tax credit and industry consolidation.

★ 347 ★

Energy Sources

Water Power, by U.S. Division: 1950-1992

Table shows developed and undeveloped capacity of water power as of December 31. Excludes Alaska and Hawaii for 1950 and all capacity of reversible equipment at pumped storage projects. Also excludes capacity precluded from development due to wild and scenic river legislation.

[In million kilowatts]

Division	Developed installed capacity						Estimated undeveloped capacity					
	1950	1960	1970	1980	1990	1992	1950	1960	1970	1980	1990	1992
United States	18.7	33.2	52.0	64.4	73.0	74.1	87.6	114.2	128.0	129.9	73.9	73.67
New England	1.2	1.5	1.5	1.5	1.9	1.9	3.3	2.9	3.3	4.7	4.4	4.4
Middle Atlantic	1.7	2.5	4.3	4.3	4.9	4.9	6.6	7.6	4.5	5.1	5.1	4.9
East North Central	0.9	0.9	0.9	0.9	1.1	1.2	2.3	3.0	1.6	2.0	1.7	1.7
West North Central	0.6	1.6	2.7	2.8	3.1	3.1	5.8	6.4	4.4	3.4	3.1	3.1
South Atlantic	2.8	3.8	5.3	5.9	6.7	6.7	8.2	8.4	9.6	9.6	7.0	7.2
East South Central	2.7	3.8	5.2	5.6	5.9	5.9	4.7	4.6	3.8	3.3	2.4	2.4
West South Central	0.5	0.9	1.9	2.3	2.7	2.7	3.6	3.9	3.3	4.7	4.6	4.6
Mountain	2.3	4.6	6.2	7.4	9.2	9.5	23.4	23.6	26.7	34.2	19.4	19.1
Pacific	6.0	13.6	23.9	33.7	37.5	38.2	29.8	53.8	53.8	62.9	26.2	26.2

Source: 1994 Statistical Abstract of the United States on CD-ROM [machine-readable datafiles]. CD-8A-94. Washington, DC: U.S. Department of Commerce, Economics and Statistics Administration, Bureau of the Census, Data User Services Division, January 1995. Primary sources: U.S. Federal Energy Regulatory Commission (formerly U.S. Federal Power Commission). *Hydroelectric Power Resources of the United States, Developed and Undeveloped* (1 January 1988), and unpublished data.

Nuclear Power

★ 348 ★

Irradiated Fuel From Commercial Nuclear Plants:
1990 and 2000

Total - 193,065

United States - 40,000

Other - 36,715

Canada - 33,900

Soviet Union - 30,000

France - 20,000

Japan - 18,000

Germany - 8,950

Sweden - 5,100

Chart shows data from column 2.

Table shows the accumulated irradiated fuel from commercial nuclear plants throughout the world, excluding 16,500 tonnes in France and 25,000 tonnes in Britain produced by dual-use military-civilian reactors.

Country	Tonnes	
	1990	2000
United States	21,800	40,000
Canada	17,700	33,900
Soviet Union	9,000	30,000
France	7,300	20,000
Japan	7,500	18,000
Germany	3,800	8,950
Sweden	2,360	5,100
Other	14,540	36,715
Total	84,000	193,065

Source: "Indicators." *Far Eastern Economic Review*, 19 October 1992, p. 22. Primary source: Worldwatch Institute.

★ 349 ★

Nuclear Power

Nuclear Energy Production: 1958-1993

Table shows U.S. energy production for a 35-year span.

Year	Number of nuclear generating units	Net generation of electricity (billion kilowatthours)
1958	1	0.2
1959	1	0.2
1960	3	0.5
1961	3	1.7
1962	5	2.3
1963	6	3.2
1964	6	3.3
1965	6	3.7
1966	8	5.5
1967	10	7.7
1968	11	12.5
1969	14	13.9
1970	18	21.8
1971	21	38.1
1972	29	54.1
1973	39	83.5
1974	48	114.0
1975	54	172.5
1976	61	191.1
1977	65	250.9
1978	70	276.4
1979	68	255.2
1980	70	251.1
1981	74	272.7
1982	77	282.8
1983	80	293.7
1984	86	327.6
1985	95	383.7
1986	100	414.0
1987	107	455.3
1988	108	527.0
1989	110	529.4
1990	111	576.9
1991	111	612.6
1992	109	618.8
1993	109	610.3

Source: Executive Office of the President of the United States. *Environmental Quality 24: The Twenty-fourth Annual Report of the Council on Environmental Quality.* Prepared by Ray Clark. Written by Carroll Curtis. Edited by Barry Walsh. Washington, DC: U.S. Government Printing Office, 1994, p. 413. Primary source: U.S. Department of Energy. Energy Information Administration. *Annual Energy Review, 1993.* DOE/EIA-0384(93). Washington, DC: U.S. Department of Energy, Energy Information Administration, 1994, p. 257, table 9.2. *Notes:* Previous year data may have been revised. Current year data are preliminary and may be revised in future publications.

★ 350 ★
Nuclear Power

Nuclear Generating Capacity, by State: 1993

Capacity by energy source generally shows a geographical pattern such as significant petroleum-fired capacity in the northeastern United States, hydroelectric in the West, and gas-fired capacity in the coastal South. The table below shows nuclear generating capacity of each state as of December 31, 1993. Total nuclear capacity was 99,041 megawatts.

[In megawatts]

State	Nuclear capacity
Alabama	3,001-9,000
Alaska	0
Arizona	3,001-9,000
Arkansas	1-3,000
California	3,001-9,000
Colorado	0
Connecticut	3,001-9,000
Delaware	0
District of Columbia	1-3,000
Florida	3,001-9,000
Georgia	3,001-9,000
Hawaii	0
Idaho	0
Illinois	9,001-15,000
Indiana	0
Iowa	1-3,000
Kansas	1-3,000
Kentucky	0
Louisiana	1-3,000
Maine	1-3,000
Maryland	1-3,000
Massachusetts	1-3,000
Michigan	3,001-9,000
Minnesota	1-3,000
Mississippi	1-3,000
Missouri	1-3,000
Montana	0
Nebraska	1-3,000
Nevada	0
New Hampshire	1-3,000
New Jersey	3,001-9,000
New Mexico	0
New York	3,001-9,000
North Carolina	3,001-9,000
North Dakota	0
Ohio	1-3,000
Oklahoma	0
Oregon	0

[Continued]

★ 350 ★

Nuclear Generating Capacity, by State: 1993
[Continued]

State	Nuclear capacity
Pennsylvania	3,001-9,000
Rhode Island	0
South Carolina	3,001-9,000
South Dakota	0
Tennessee	1-3,000
Texas	3,001-9,000
Utah	0
Vermont	1-3,000
Virginia	3,001-9,000
Washington	1-3,000
West Virginia	0
Wisconsin	1-3,000
Wyoming	0

Source: U.S. Department of Energy. Energy Information Administration. Office of Coal, Nuclear, Electric, and Alternate Fuels. *Inventory of Power Plants in the United States. 1993.* Washington, DC: U.S. Department of Energy, Energy Information Administration, Office of Coal, Nuclear, Electric, and Alternate Fuels, December 1994, p. 10. Primary source: Energy Information Administration. *Annual Electric Generator Report.* Form EIA-860.

★ 351 ★

Nuclear Power

Nuclear Power Plants: 1957-1992

Table shows number, capacity, and generation of nuclear power plants.

Item	1957	1960	1965	1970	1975	1980	1985	1990	1991	1992
Operable generating units[1]	1	3	6	18	54	70	95	111	111	109
Net summer capability (million kW)[2]	0.1	0.4	0.8	7.0	37.3	51.8	79.4	99.6	99.6	99.0
Electricity generated (billion kWh)	(Z)	0.5	3.7	21.8	172.5	251.1	383.7	576.9	612.6	618.8
Percent of total electric utility generation	(Z)	0.1	0.3	1.4	9.0	11.0	15.5	20.5	21.7	22.1
Capacity factor[3]	(NA)	(NA)	(NA)	(NA)	55.9	56.3	58.0	66.0	70.2	70.9

Source: *1994 Statistical Abstract of the United States on CD-ROM* [machine-readable datafiles]. CD-8A-94. Washington, DC: U.S. Department of Commerce, Economics and Statistics Administration, Bureau of the Census, Data User Services Division, January 1995. Primary source: U.S. Energy Information Administration. *Notes:* "kW" represents kilowatts; "kWh" represents kilowatt hours. "NA" stands for "not available." "Z" indicates less than .05 billion kWh or 1. As of year end. 2. As of year end. Net summer capability is the peak steady hourly output that generating equipment is expected to supply to system load, exclusive of auxiliary and other powerplant, as demonstrated by test at the time of summer peak demand. 3. Weighted average of monthly capacity factors. Monthly factors are derived by dividing actual monthly generation by the maximum possible generation for the month (hours in month times net maximum dependable capacity).

★ 352 ★

Nuclear Power

Nuclear Power Plants, by State: 1992

Table shows the number of power plants, net generation, and net summer capability.

Region, division and state	Number of units	Net generation		Net summer capability	
		Total (mil. kWh)	Percent of total	Total (mil. kWh)	Percent of total
United States	109	618,776	22.1	99.0	14.2
Northeast	27	144,357	36.6	23.8	23.6
New England	8	38,474	45.5	6.4	28.2
Maine	1	5,358	64.3	0.9	28.2
New Hampshire	1	7,869	58.5	1.2	45.9
Vermont	1	3,735	79.5	0.5	45.3
Massachusetts	1	4,742	14.4	0.7	7.0
Connecticut	4	16,771	66.7	3.2	46.0
Middle Atlantic	19	105,883	34.2	17.4	22.2
New York	6	24,155	21.5	4.8	15.5
New Jersey	4	21,596	69.3	3.9	27.9
Pennsylvania	9	60,133	36.2	8.7	26.1
Midwest	31	158,499	22.6	25.7	15.3
East North Central	23	118,604	24.3	20.1	17.7
Ohio	2	14,805	10.9	2.0	7.5
Illinois	13	73,742	59.1	12.6	38.6
Michigan	5	18,849	22.8	3.9	17.6
Wisconsin	3	11,027	24.1	1.5	14.3
West North Central	8	39,895	18.7	5.6	10.2
Minnesota	3	11,166	29.6	1.5	17.4
Iowa	1	3,405	11.6	0.5	6.4
Missouri	1	8,084	14.3	1.1	7.3
Nebraska	2	8,748	39.1	1.3	23.0
Kansas	1	8,491	26.7	1.2	12.0
South	42	244,804	20.6	39.2	13.3
South Atlantic	27	155,401	28.4	23.5	17.7
Maryland	2	10,664	26.9	1.7	15.2
Virginia	4	23,334	47.7	3.3	24.1
North Carolina	5	22,754	27.4	4.6	23.0
South Carolina	7	45,537	63.7	6.4	39.0
Georgia	4	27,996	30.5	3.7	17.5
Florida	5	25,116	18.7	3.8	11.5
East South Central	8	43,225	16.4	8.3	14.1
Tennessee	2	15,654	20.8	2.3	14.1
Alabama	5	19,397	21.4	4.8	24.3
Mississippi	1	8,174	39.9	1.1	16.3
West South Central	7	46,178	12.2	7.3	7.2
Arkansas	2	11,326	30.3	1.7	17.6
Louisiana	2	10,356	18.8	2.0	12.0
Texas	3	24,496	10.2	3.6	5.8

[Continued]

★ 352 ★

Nuclear Power Plants, by State: 1992
[Continued]

Region, division and state	Number of units	Net generation		Net summer capability	
		Total (mil. kWh)	Percent of total	Total (mil. kWh)	Percent of total
West	9	71;118	13.9	10.3	7.8
Mountain	3	25,609	10.0	3.8	7.7
Arizona	3	25,609	36.5	3.8	25.4
Pacific	6	45,509	17.8	6.5	7.9
Washington	1	5,692	6.8	1.1	4.5
Oregon	1	4,573	11.1	1.1	9.8
California	4	35,244	29.5	4.3	9.8

Source: *1994 Statistical Abstract of the United States on CD-ROM* [machine-readable datafiles]. CD-8A-94. Washington, DC: U.S. Department of Commerce, Economics and Statistics Administration, Bureau of the Census, Data User Services Division, January 1995. Primary sources: U.S. Energy Information Administration. *Electric Power Annual* and *Electric Power Monthly* (December issues).

★ 353 ★

Nuclear Power

World Nuclear Energy

Pressurized water reactors - 195	
Boiling water reactors - 91	
VVER - 44	
	Graphite moderated - 38
	Heavy water - 32
	RBMK - 15
	Fast Breeders - 7
Others - 1	

Chart shows data from column 2.

Table shows world nuclear energy by reactor types. According to the source, "of the seven main nuclear power reactor types in the world about half are pressurized light water reactors (PLWRs).... There are more than 400 reactors operating today in the world, and they turn out about 18% of the electricity consumed worldwide. This electricity is produced from a series of different types of reactors.... The bulk of the 423 reactors are constituted by pressurized water reactors (PWR). Boiling water reactors (BWR) account for 91 reactors. The remainder are spread over different types of reactors. The much discussed RBMKs (Chernobyl-type reactors) number 15" (p. 5).

Type	Power (MWe)	Number of units	Percent of total units
Graphite moderated	13,974	38	9.0
Heavy water	18,054	32	7.6
Pressurized water reactors	182,964	195	46.1
Boiling water reactors	75,282	91	21.6
Fast Breeders	2,412	7	1.7
VVER	27,790	44	10.5
RBMK	14,829	15	3.5
Others	150	1	.002

Source: "France: A Nuclear Success Story." *Energy* (June 1994), p. 5. *Note:* "MWe" represents megawatts of electric power.

Production

★ 354 ★

Coal and Coke Production: 1970-1992

Includes coal consumed at mines. Demonstrated coal reserve base for United States on January 1, 1992, was an estimated 476 billion tons. Recoverability varies between 40 and 90 percent for individual deposits; 50 percent or more of overall U.S. coal reserve base is believed to be recoverable.

Item	Unit	1970	1975	1980	1985	1990	1991	1992
Coal production, total[1]	Mil. sh. tons	613	655	830	884	1,029	996	998
Value	Mil. dol.	3,882	12,670	20,453	22,277	(NA)	(NA)	(NA)
Anthracite production	Mil. sh. tons	9.7	6.2	6.1	4.7	3.5	3.4	(NA)
Bituminous coal and lignite:[2]								
Number of mines	Number	5,601	6,168	5,598	4,547	3,243	2,846	2,746
Production	Mil. sh. tons	603	648	824	879	1,026	993	995
Value, total	Mil. dol.	3,774	12,469	20,196	22,061	22,274	21,598	(NA)
Average per ton	Dollars	6.26	19.23	24.52	25.10	21.71	21.75	21.03
Exports	Mil. sh. tons	71	66	90	93	106	109	103
Value	Mil. dol.	961	3,259	4,627	4,465	4,510	4,619	(NA)
Imports	1,000 sh. tons	36	940	1,194	1,952	2,699	3,390	3,803
Method of mining:								
Underground	Mil. sh. tons	339	293	337	350	425	407	407
Surface	Mil. sh. tons	264	356	487	529	605	589	590
Percent of total production	Percent	43.8	54.8	59.1	60.2	58.7	59.1	59.1
Value	Mil. dol.	(Z)	22	30	70	(NA)	(NA)	(NA)
Consumption[3]	Mil. sh. tons	523	563	703	818	895	888	893
Electric power utilities	Mil. sh. tons	320	406	569	694	774	772	780
Industrial	Mil. sh. tons	184	146	126	116	116	109	107
Productivity average:[4]								
Daily employment	1,000	140	190	225	169	131	121	110
Days worked	Number	228	232	210	204	216	224	228
Tons per worker:								
Per day	Sh. tons	18.84	14.74	16.32	23.13	32.90	35.18	37.71
Per year	Sh. tons	4,296	3,420	3,427	4,719	7,106	7,880	(NA)
Production, by state:								
Alabama	Mil. sh. tons	21	23	26	28	29	27	26
Illinois	Mil. sh. tons	65	60	63	59	60	60	60
Indiana	Mil. sh. tons	22	25	31	33	36	32	31
Kentucky	Mil. sh. tons	125	144	150	152	173	159	161
Montana	Mil. sh. tons	3	22	30	33	38	38	39
Ohio	Mil. sh. tons	55	47	39	36	35	31	30
Pennsylvania	Mil. sh. tons	90	90	93	71	71	65	68
Virginia	Mil. sh. tons	35	36	41	41	47	42	43
West Virginia	Mil. sh. tons	144	109	122	128	169	167	162
Wyoming	Mil. sh. tons	7	24	95	141	184	194	190
Other states	Mil. sh. tons	44	76	140	161	187	181	189
World production	Mil. sh. tons	3,295	3,665	4,103	4,779	5,214	4,952	4,975

[Continued]

★ 354 ★

Coal and Coke Production: 1970-1992

[Continued]

Item	Unit	1970	1975	1980	1985	1990	1991	1992
Coke production[5]	Mil. sh. tons	66.5	57.2	46.1	28.7	27.6	24.0	23.0
Oven coke[6]	Mil. sh. tons	65.7	56.5	46.1	28.7	27.6	24.0	23.0
Value of product at plant	Mil. dol.	2,193	5,261	6,029	(NA)	(NA)	(NA)	(NA)
Coke and breeze	Mil. dol.	1,899	4,607	4,784	(NA)	(NA)	(NA)	(NA)
Avg. market value per ton	Dollars	28	84	103	103	(NA)	(NA)	(NA)
Coal carbonized	Mil. sh. tons	96.5	83.6	66.7	41.1	38.9	33.9	32.4
Average value per ton	Dollars	12.47	44.21	56.26	54.30	47.73	48.88	47.9
Yield of coke from coal	Percent	69.1	68.4	69.2	69.8	71.0	71.0	(NA)

Source: 1994 Statistical Abstract of the United States on CD-ROM [machine-readable datafiles]. CD-8A-94. Washington, DC: U.S. Department of Commerce, Economics and Statistics Administration, Bureau of the Census, Data User Services Division, January 1995. Primary sources:—1970 and 1975: U.S. Bureau of Mines. Minerals Yearbook; thereafter—U.S. Energy Information Administration. Coal Production, (annual); Annual Energy Review; Quarterly Coal Report; and unpublished data. Notes: "NA" reflects "not available;" "Z" denotes less than $500,000. 1. Includes bituminous coal, lignite, and anthracite. 2. All domestic production data for 1970 and 1975 are for mines producing 1,000 short tons or more per year; thereafter, data are for all mines. 3. Includes some categories not shown separately. 4. Data for 1970 and 1975 are for mines producing 1,000 short tons or more per year; thereafter, for mines producing 10,000 short tons more. Beginning 1984, includes anthracite. 5. Includes beehive coke. 6. Prior to 1980, excludes screenings or breeze; thereafter includes beehive and other nonrecoverable coke-oven operations.

★ 355 ★

Production

Coal Production, by Rank and Mining Method: 1950-1993

Table shows rank and mining methods for U.S. coal production.

[In million metric tons]

Year	Rank				Mining method	
	Bituminous	Sub-bituminous	Lignite	Anthracite	Under-ground	Surface
1950	468.38	[1]	[1]	40.01	381.92	126.46
1955	421.48	[1]	[1]	23.77	324.77	120.56
1960	376.94	[1]	[1]	17.06	265.44	128.55
1961	365.60	[1]	[1]	15.79	253.65	127.82
1962	382.92	[1]	[1]	15.33	261.18	137.08
1963	416.31	[1]	[1]	16.60	280.32	152.59
1964	441.80	[1]	[1]	15.60	297.28	160.12
1965	464.57	[1]	[1]	13.52	306.63	171.46
1966	484.35	[1]	[1]	11.70	310.80	185.25
1967	501.31	[1]	[1]	11.16	319.69	192.78
1968	494.60	[1]	[1]	10.43	314.43	190.60
1969	496.41	7.53	4.54	9.53	316.79	201.12
1970	524.81	14.88	7.26	8.80	308.89	246.85
1971	472.92	20.14	7.89	7.89	251.47	257.36
1972	505.12	24.95	9.98	6.44	276.69	269.80
1973	492.06	30.75	12.97	6.17	272.25	270.79
1974	494.05	38.28	14.06	5.99	252.20	301.28
1975	523.90	46.36	17.96	5.62	266.26	327.68

[Continued]

★ 355 ★

Coal Production, by Rank and Mining Method: 1950-1993
[Continued]

Year	Rank				Mining method	
	Bituminous	Sub-bituminous	Lignite	Anthracite	Under-ground	Surface
1976	533.79	58.79	23.13	5.62	268.07	353.26
1977	526.07	74.48	25.58	5.35	241.86	390.63
1978	484.44	87.82	31.21	4.54	220.26	387.73
1979	555.47	110.22	38.56	4.35	291.12	417.49
1980	570.44	133.99	42.82	5.53	306.17	446.52
1981	551.57	144.88	45.99	4.90	287.12	460.21
1982	562.64	145.97	47.54	4.17	307.72	452.69
1983	515.83	136.98	52.89	3.72	272.52	436.99
1984	589.22	162.57	57.24	3.81	319.42	493.42
1985	556.92	174.81	65.68	4.26	318.24	483.35
1986	562.55	172.00	69.31	3.90	326.95	480.72
1987	577.51	181.62	71.12	3.27	338.29	495.23
1988	578.87	202.76	77.20	3.27	359.73	524.37
1989	598.56	209.74	78.38	2.99	357.25	532.43
1990	628.86	221.63	79.92	3.18	385.10	548.39
1991	590.31	231.60	78.47	3.08	369.41	534.15
1992	591.39	228.70	81.74	3.18	369.41	533.97
1993	536.06	237.96	81.47	3.27	350.54	508.21

Source: Executive Office of the President of the United States. *Environmental Quality 24: The Twenty-fourth Annual Report of the Council on Environmental Quality.* Prepared by Ray Clark. Written by Carroll Curtis. Edited by Barry Walsh. Washington, DC: U.S. Government Printing Office, 1994, p. 409. Primary source: U.S. Department of Energy. Energy Information Administration. *Annual Energy Review, 1993.* DOE/EIA-0384(93). Washington, DC: U.S. Department of Energy, Energy Information Administration, 1994, p. 213, table 7.2. *Notes:* Previous year data may have been revised. Current year data are preliminary and may be revised in the future. 1. Included in bituminous coal.

★ 356 ★
Production

Crude Petroleum and Natural Gas Production, by State: 1985-1992

State	Crude petroleum						Natural gas marketed production[1]					
	Quantity (million barrels)			Value (million dollars)			Quantity (billion cubic feet)			Value (million dollars)		
	1985	1990	1992	1985	1990	1992	1985	1990	1992	1985	1990	1992
Total[2]	3,274	2,685	2,625	78,884	53,772	41,968	17,270	18,594	18,712	43,343	31,658	32,571
Alabama	22	18	19	579	387	347	107	135	355	398	373	814
Alaska	666	658	627	10,655	10,086	7,180	321	403	444	236	554	625
Arkansas	19	10	10	443	222	178	155	175	202	393	360	435
California	424	322	305	8,386	5,732	4,139	491	363	366	1,653	857	856
Colorado	30	31	30	758	722	567	178	243	323	517	377	443
Florida	11	6	5	(NA)	(NA)	(NA)	11	6	7	26	15	17
Illinois	30	20	19	795	467	372	1	1	(Z)	4	1	1
Indiana	5	3	3	134	73	58	(Z)	(Z)	(Z)	1	1	(Z)

[Continued]

★ 356 ★

Crude Petroleum and Natural Gas Production, by State: 1985-1992

[Continued]

State	Crude petroleum						Natural gas marketed production[1]					
	Quantity (million barrels)			Value (million dollars)			Quantity (billion cubic feet)			Value (million dollars)		
	1985	1990	1992	1985	1990	1992	1985	1990	1992	1985	1990	1992
Kansas	75	59	54	1,939	1,359	992	528	574	658	671	893	1,013
Kentucky	8	5	5	201	124	103	73	75	80	174	169	153
Louisiana	508	148	143	5,387	3,409	2,718	5,014	5,242	4,914	13,355	9,587	8,502
Michigan	27	20	16	726	458	296	132	140	195	475	420	528
Mississippi	31	30	25	796	630	421	144	95	92	456	167	150
Montana	30	20	18	734	429	316	52	50	54	125	90	87
Nebraska	7	5	5	163	119	96	2	1	1	6	2	2
New Mexico	79	66	70	2,028	1,472	1,298	905	965	1,269	2,370	1,629	2,030
New York	1	(Z)	(Z)	25	9	8	32	25	24	106	55	53
North Dakota	51	39	33	1,307	849	593	73	52	55	138	93	108
Ohio	15	8	9	361	196	174	182	155	145	560	393	340
Oklahoma	163	117	102	4,256	2,690	1,908	1,936	2,258	2,017	4,930	3,548	3,430
Pennsylvania	5	2	2	114	54	41	150	178	139	474	417	270
Texas	889	674	651	23	15,060	11,919	6,053	6,343	6,146	14,097	9,939	10,878
Utah	41	23	23	773	524	441	83	146	171	293	249	279
West Virginia	4	2	2	86	43	37	145	178	182	558	568	548
Wyoming	129	103	97	3,061	2,169	1,586	417	736	843	1,252	856	952

Source: 1994 Statistical Abstract of the United States on CD-ROM [machine-readable datafiles]. CD-8A-94. Washington, DC: U.S. Department of Commerce, Economics and Statistics Administration, Bureau of the Census, Data User Services Division, January 1995. Primary sources: U.S. Energy Information Administration. Energy Data Reports, Petroleum Supply Annual, Natural Gas Annual, and Natural Gas Monthly. Notes: "NA" stands for not available. "Z" denotes less than 500 million cubic feet or less than 500,000 dollars or barrels. 1. Excludes nonhydrocarbon gases. 2. Includes other states not shown separately. State production does not include state offshore production.

★ 357 ★

Production

Crude Petroleum and Natural Gas Wells: 1970-1992

Includes all costs incurred for drilling and equipping wells to point of completion as productive wells or abandonment after drilling becomes unproductive. Based on sample of operators of different size drilling establishments.

Item	Unit	1970	1975	1980	1985	1990	1991	1992
Wells drilled	Number	27,177	36,960	62,011	67,821	28,513	27,194	22,388
Offshore	Number	1,058	1,028	1,272	1,247	704	718	440
Footage drilled	Million feet	136.9	177.6	296.0	314.5	143.8	138.7	121.9
Drilling cost	Million dollars	2,579	6,571	22,800	23,697	10,937	11,461	8,566
Average depth per well	Feet	5,037	4,806	4,773	4,637	5,043	5,100	5,445
Average cost per well	$1,000	95	178	368	349	384	421	383
Offshore	$1,000	566	1,142	3,024	4,073	3,112	3,550	3,223
Average cost per foot	Dollars	18.84	36.99	77.02	75.35	76.07	82.64	70.27

Source: 1994 Statistical Abstract of the United States on CD-ROM [machine-readable datafiles]. CD-8A-94. Washington, DC: U.S. Department of Commerce, Economics and Statistics Administration, Bureau of the Census, Data User Services Division, January 1995. Primary source: American Petroleum Institute. Joint Association Survey on Drilling Costs, (annual).

★ 358 ★

Production

Electric Energy, by State: 1990-1992

Table shows net generation and net summer capability. Covers utilities for public use. Capacity as of December 31.

Division and state	Net generation (billion kilowatt hours)				Net summer capability (million kilowatts)	
	1990	1991	Total	Percent from coal	1990	1992
United States	2,808.2	2,825.0	2,797.2	56.3	690.5	695.1
Northeast	94.1	87.0	84.6	19.3	23.4	22.6
Maine	9.1	9.5	8.3	-	2.4	2.4
New Hampshire	10.8	12.7	13.5	23.7	2.6	2.5
Vermont	5.0	5.3	4.7	-	1.1	1.1
Massachusetts	36.5	35.8	32.8	33.3	9.9	9.5
Rhode Island	0.6	0.2	0.1	-	0.3	0.2
Connecticut	32.2	23.6	25.2	8.5	7.1	7.0
Middle Atlantic	330.8	325.5	309.4	42.8	78.4	78.4
New York	128.7	126.1	112.2	22.2	31.2	31.1
New Jersey	36.5	37.0	31.2	17.4	13.7	13.8
Pennsylvania	165.7	162.4	166.0	61.6	33.4	33.4
East North Central	485.8	500.5	487.6	73.9	113.1	113.5
Ohio	126.5	132.7	136.3	88.4	27.0	27.1
Indiana	97.7	98.2	97.3	98.4	20.6	20.8
Illinois	127.0	127.9	124.8	39.9	32.6	32.6
Michigan	89.1	94.6	82.7	74.3	22.3	22.4
Wisconsin	45.6	47.1	46.5	70.5	10.6	10.5
West North Central	218.4	221.2	212.8	75.3	54.2	54.7
Minnesota	41.6	40.4	37.8	64.7	8.8	8.9
Iowa	29.0	31.2	29.4	84.4	8.0	8.1
Missouri	59.0	60.1	56.6	82.7	15.2	15.4
North Dakota	26.8	27.5	28.6	94.0	4.5	4.5
South Dakota	6.4	6.6	6.2	42.0	2.7	2.7
Nebraska	21.6	23.0	22.4	55.4	5.5	5.5
Kansas	33.9	32.3	31.8	69.7	9.6	9.7
South Atlantic	533.8	541.1	547.5	58.2	129.2	133.2
Delaware	7.1	7.6	6.3	60.9	2.0	2.1
Maryland	31.5	38.2	39.6	59.7	9.8	10.9
District of Columbia	0.4	0.2	0.1	-	0.8	0.8
Virginia	47.2	48.9	49.0	46.3	13.7	13.8
West Virginia	77.4	71.3	72.3	99.1	14.4	14.4
North Carolina	79.8	83.5	83.0	65.1	20.2	20.1
South Carolina	69.3	69.8	71.5	32.2	14.9	16.3
Georgia	97.6	90.8	91.8	63.5	20.7	21.4
Florida	123.6	130.7	134.0	46.0	32.7	33.4
East South Central	246.9	257.8	264.0	72.7	59.5	58.6
Kentucky	73.8	75.5	77.4	95.0	15.5	15.3
Tennessee	73.9	73.9	75.4	66.3	17.0	16.3
Alabama	76.2	85.1	90.8	66.8	20.0	19.9
Mississippi	22.9	23.3	20.5	38.1	7.0	7.0

[Continued]

★ 358 ★

Electric Energy, by State: 1990-1992
[Continued]

Division and state	Net generation (billion kilowatt hours)				Net summer capability (million kilowatts)	
	1990	1991	Total	Percent from coal	1990	1992
West South Central	374.3	378.7	378.5	49.2	101.2	101.9
Arkansas	37.1	38.4	37.4	53.6	9.6	9.6
Louisiana	58.2	57.2	55.2	35.9	16.8	16.7
Oklahoma	45.1	44.9	45.9	60.2	12.8	12.9
Texas	234.0	238.3	240.0	49.5	62.0	62.7
Mountain	247.4	249.1	257.2	76.3	49.3	49.7
Montana	25.7	28.2	25.5	67.2	4.9	4.9
Idaho	8.6	8.3	6.3	-	2.3	2.4
Wyoming	39.4	38.7	41.9	98.3	5.8	5.8
Colorado	31.3	31.0	31.9	94.1	6.6	6.6
New Mexico	28.5	25.1	27.7	91.5	5.0	5.1
Arizona	62.3	66.8	70.1	49.4	14.9	15.0
Utah	32.3	30.2	32.9	95.8	4.8	4.8
Nevada	19.3	20.9	21.0	78.4	4.9	5.1
Pacific	276.7	264.2	255.7	5.3	82.1	82.5
Washington	100.5	101.4	84.1	11.4	24.2	24.2
Oregon	49.2	46.3	41.2	8.9	11.2	11.2
California	114.5	105.0	119.3	-	43.7	43.8
Alaska	4.5	4.3	4.2	7.0	1.5	1.7
Hawaii	8.0	7.3	6.9	-	1.5	1.6

Source: 1994 Statistical Abstract of the United States on CD-ROM [machine-readable datafiles]. CD-8A-94. Washington, DC: U.S. Department of Commerce, Economics and Statistics Administration, Bureau of the Census, Data User Services Division, January 1995. Primary sources—1980: U.S. Energy Information Administration. *Power Production, Fuel Consumption, and Installed Capacity Data* (annual); thereafter: *Electric Power Annual, Electric Power Monthly* (December issues), and *Inventory of Power Plants in the United States* (annual). *Note:* "-" represents zero.

★ 359 ★
Production

Electricity Production, by Energy Source: 1950-1993

Table shows the U.S. production of electricity for various energy sources during a 43 year-span. Production refers to electric utility net generation of electricity for distribution.

[Billion kilowatthours]

Year	Fossil-fired steam			Internal combustion and gas turbine	Nuclear power	Hydroelectric	Geothermal & other[1]	Total
	Coal	Natural gas	Petroleum					
1950	155	45	34	4	0	96	<1	329
1955	301	95	37	4	0	113	<1	547
1960	403	158	48	4	1	146	<1	756
1961	422	169	49	5	2	152	<1	794
1962	450	184	49	5	2	169	<1	855

[Continued]

★ 359 ★

Electricity Production, by Energy Source: 1950-1993
[Continued]

Year	Fossil-fired steam			Internal combustion and gas turbine	Nuclear power	Hydroelectric	Geothermal & other[1]	Total
	Coal	Natural gas	Petroleum					
1963	494	202	52	5	3	166	<1	917
1964	526	220	57	5	3	177	<1	984
1965	571	222	65	5	4	194	<1	1,055
1966	613	251	79	5	6	195	1	1,144
1967	630	265	89	5	8	222	1	1,214
1968	685	304	104	9	13	222	1	1,329
1969	706	333	138	14	14	250	1	1,442
1970	704	361	174	22	22	248	1	1,532
1971	713	360	206	28	38	266	1	1,613
1972	771	361	253	36	54	273	2	1,750
1973	848	323	296	36	83	272	2	1,861
1974	828	304	279	38	114	301	3	1,867
1975	853	288	273	28	173	300	3	1,918
1976	944	284	302	29	191	284	4	2,038
1977	985	292	338	34	251	220	4	2,124
1978	976	290	345	36	276	280	3	2,206
1979	1,075	311	290	32	255	280	4	2,247
1980	1,162	326	238	28	251	276	6	2,286
1981	1,203	325	202	25	273	261	6	2,295
1982	1,192	291	144	16	283	309	5	2,241
1983	1,259	261	141	17	294	332	6	2,310
1984	1,342	284	117	17	328	321	9	2,416
1985	1,402	279	97	16	384	281	11	2,470
1986	1,386	236	133	15	414	291	12	2,487
1987	1,464	258	115	18	455	250	12	2,572
1988	1,541	236	144	22	527	223	12	2,704
1989	1,554	245	151	29	529	265	11	2,784
1990	1,560	246	113	22	577	280	11	2,808
1991	1,551	246	108	22	613	276	10	2,825
1992	1,576	246	86	21	619	240	10	2,797
1993	1,639	238	96	25	610	269	10	2,882

Source: Executive Office of the President of the United States. *Environmental Quality 24: The Twenty-fourth Annual Report of the Council on Environmental Quality.* Prepared by Ray Clark. Written by Carroll Curtis. Edited by Barry Walsh. Washington, DC: U.S. Government Printing Office, 1994, p. 412. Primary source: U.S. Department of Energy. Energy Information Administration. *Annual Energy Review, 1993.* DOE/EIA-0384(93). Washington, DC: U.S. Department of Energy, Energy Information Administration, 1994, p. 235, table 8.3. *Notes:* Previous year data may have been revised. Current year data are preliminary and may be revised in the future. 1. Includes wood, waste, photovoltaic, and solar thermal energy.

★ 360 ★

Production

Energy Production, by Major Source: 1960-1993

Table shows total production and percent of production for major energy sources.

Year	Total production (quadrillion Btu)	Percent of production				Consumption/ production ratio
		Coal	Petro-leum[1]	Natu-ral gas[2]	Other[3]	
1960	41.5	26.1	36.0	34.0	3.9	1.06
1965	49.3	26.5	33.5	35.8	4.3	1.07
1970	62.1	23.5	32.9	38.9	4.7	1.07
1975	59.9	25.0	29.6	36.8	8.6	1.18
1980	64.8	28.7	28.2	34.2	8.9	1.17
1985	64.9	29.8	29.3	29.6	11.3	1.14
1990	67.9[4]	33.1	22.9	30.3	13.7	1.20
1991	67.5	32.0	23.3	30.4	14.3	1.20
1992	66.9	32.3	22.8	31.0	13.9	1.23
1993	65.8	31.1	22.0	32.5	14.4	1.28

Source: 1994 Statistical Abstract of the United States on CD-ROM [machine-readable datafiles]. CD-8A-94. Washington, DC: U.S. Department of Commerce, Economics and Statistics Administration, Bureau of the Census, Data User Services Division, January 1995. Primary source: U.S. Energy Information Administration. *Annual Energy Review. Notes:* Btu denotes British thermal units. 1. Production includes crude oil and lease condensate. 2. Production includes natural gas liquids. 3. Comprised of hydropower, nuclear power, geothermal energy, and other. 4. Represents peak year for U.S. energy production.

★ 361 ★

Production

Energy Production, by Selected Indicators: 1970-1993

Item	1970	1975	1980	1985	1990	1991	1992	1993
Average annual percent change[1]								
Gross domestic product[2]	3.0	-0.8	-0.5	3.1	1.2	-0.7	2.5	3.0
Energy production, total[3]	4.6	-1.6	1.5	-1.7	2.6	-0.5	-0.9	-1.6
Crude oil[4]	4.2	-4.7	0.8	0.8	-3.4	0.8	-3.1	-5.0
Natural gas	6.4	-7.7	-0.8	-5.9	2.8	-0.7	0.8	3.3
Coal	2.2	6.3	5.9	-2.0	5.1	-3.9	(-Z)	-5.2
Per capita (million Btu)								
Energy production	304	278	285	273	272	268	262	255
Amounts (1,000 Btu)								
Energy production[3]	62,070	59,860	64,761	64,871	67,853	67,484	66,853	65,809
Crude oil[4]	20,400	17,729	18,249	18,992	15,571	15,701	15,223	14,476
Natural gas	21,670	19,640	19,908	16,980	18,362	18,229	18,375	18,983

[Continued]

★ 361 ★

Energy Production, by Selected Indicators: 1970-1993

[Continued]

Item	1970	1975	1980	1985	1990	1991	1992	1993
Coal	14,610	14,990	18,597	19,325	22,456	21,594	21,593	20,491
Resident population (1,000)	203,984	215,465	227,225	237,924	249,399	252,137	255,078	257,908
GDP in constant (1987) dollars (billion dollars)	2,873.9	3,221.7	3,776.3	4,279.8	4,897.3	4,861.4	4,986.3	5,136.0

Source: 1994 Statistical Abstract of the United States on CD-ROM [machine-readable datafiles]. CD-8A-94. Washington, DC: U.S. Department of Commerce, Economics and Statistics Administration, Bureau of the Census, Data User Services Division, January 1995. Primary sources: U.S. Energy Information Administration. *Annual Energy Review* and *Monthly Energy Review. Notes:* Btu represents British thermal units. "Z" indicates less than .05 percent. 1. Represents annual average for period of intervals shown; for 1970, change from 1969. Percent change derived from Btu values. Minus sign (-) indicates decrease. 2. Gross domestic product (GDP) in constant (1987) dollars. 3. Includes types of fuel or power, not shown separately. 4. Includes lease condensate.

★ 362 ★

Production

Energy Production, by Source: 1950-1993

The table shows U.S. energy production over a 43-year span.

[In quadrillion Btu]

Year	Coal	Crude oil & NGPL	Natural gas	Hydro-electric	Nuclear	Geothermal and other[1]	Total
1950	14.06	12.27	6.23	1.42	0.00	0.01	33.98
1955	12.37	15.65	9.34	1.36	0.00	<0.005	38.73
1960	10.82	16.39	12.66	1.61	0.01	<0.01	41.49
1961	10.45	16.76	13.10	1.66	0.02	<0.01	41.99
1962	10.90	17.11	13.72	1.82	0.03	<0.01	43.58
1963	11.85	17.68	14.51	1.77	0.04	<0.01	45.85
1964	12.52	17.96	15.30	1.89	0.04	<0.01	47.72
1965	13.06	18.40	15.78	2.06	0.04	<0.01	49.34
1966	13.47	19.56	17.01	2.06	0.06	<0.01	52.17
1967	13.83	20.83	17.94	2.35	0.09	0.01	55.04
1968	13.61	21.63	19.07	2.35	0.14	0.01	56.81
1969	13.86	21.98	20.45	2.65	0.15	0.01	59.10
1970	14.61	22.91	21.67	2.63	0.24	0.01	62.07
1971	13.19	22.57	22.28	2.82	0.41	0.01	61.29
1972	14.09	22.64	22.21	2.86	0.58	0.03	62.42
1973	13.99	22.06	22.19	2.86	0.91	0.04	62.06
1974	14.07	21.04	21.21	3.18	1.27	0.05	60.84
1975	14.99	20.10	19.64	3.15	1.90	0.07	59.86
1976	15.65	19.59	19.48	2.98	2.11	0.08	59.89
1977	15.76	19.78	19.57	2.33	2.70	0.09	60.22
1978	14.91	20.68	19.49	2.94	3.02	0.06	61.10
1979	17.54	20.39	20.08	2.93	2.78	0.09	63.80
1980	18.60	20.50	19.91	2.90	2.74	0.11	64.76
1981	18.38	20.46	19.70	2.76	3.01	0.12	64.42
1982	18.64	20.50	18.32	3.27	3.13	0.10	63.96

[Continued]

★ 362 ★

Energy Production, by Source: 1950-1993
[Continued]

Year	Coal	Crude oil & NGPL	Natural gas	Hydro-electric	Nuclear	Geothermal and other[1]	Total
1983	17.25	20.57	16.59	3.53	3.20	0.13	61.28
1984	19.72	21.12	18.01	3.39	3.55	0.17	65.96
1985	19.33	21.23	16.98	2.97	4.15	0.21	64.87
1986	19.51	20.53	16.54	3.07	4.47	0.23	64.35
1987	20.14	19.89	17.14	2.63	4.91	0.25	64.95
1988	20.74	19.54	17.60	2.33	5.66	0.24	66.10
1989	21.35	18.28	17.85	2.77	5.68	0.22	66.13
1990	22.46	17.74	18.36	2.93	6.16	0.20	67.85
1991	21.59	18.01	18.23	2.88	6.58	0.19	67.48
1992	21.59	17.58	18.38	2.50	6.61	0.19	66.85
1993	20.49	16.88	19.98	2.76	6.52	0.18	65.81

Source: Executive Office of the President of the United States. *Environmental Quality 24: The Twenty-fourth Annual Report of the Council on Environmental Quality.* Prepared by Ray Clark. Written by Carroll Curtis. Edited by Barry Walsh. Washington, DC: U.S. Government Printing Office, 1994, p. 408. Primary source: U.S. Department of Energy. Energy Information Administration. *Annual Energy Review, 1993.* DOE/EIA-0384(93). Washington, DC: U.S. Department of Energy, Energy Information Administration, 1994, p. 7, table 1.2. *Notes:* "Btu" represents British thermal units. "NGPL" stands for natural gas plant liquids. Previous year data may have been revised. Current year data are preliminary and may be revised in the future. 1. Includes electricity produced from wood, waste, wind, photovoltaic, and solar thermal sources.

★ 363 ★
Production

Liquefied Petroleum Gas Production: 1980-1992

Includes ethane, propane, normal butane, and isobutane.

[In millions of 42-gallon barrels]

Item	1980	1985	1986	1987	1988	1989	1990	1991	1992
Production	561	622	619	638	663	654	638	683	720
At natural gas plants	441	479	466	474	481	452	456	488	500
At refineries	121	143	152	164	182	202	182	196	222
Imports	79	68	88	69	76	66	68	54	57
Refinery input	85	111	110	111	117	115	107	111	172
Exports	9	23	15	14	18	13	14	15	18

Source: 1994 Statistical Abstract of the United States on CD-ROM [machine-readable datafiles]. CD-8A-94. Washington, DC: U.S. Department of Commerce, Economics and Statistics Administration, Bureau of the Census, Data User Services Division, January 1995. Primary source: U.S. Energy Information Administration. *Petroleum Supply Annual.*

★ 364 ★

Production

Natural Gas Plant Liquid Production and Value: 1970-1992

[In barrels of 42 gallons]

Item	Unit	1970	1975	1980	1985	1990	1991	1992
Field production[1]	Million barrels	606	596	576	587	566	606	621
Pentanes plus	Million barrels	197	149	126	103	112	118	121
Liquefied petroleum gases	Million barrels	400	444	441	479	454	488	500
Natural gas processed	Trillion cubic feet	19	18	15	13	15	16	16

Source: 1994 Statistical Abstract of the United States on CD-ROM [machine-readable datafiles]. CD-8A-94. Washington, DC: U.S. Department of Commerce, Economics and Statistics Administration, Bureau of the Census, Data User Services Division, January 1995. Primary sources: Through 1975—U.S. Bureau of Mines. *Minerals Yearbook;* thereafter—U.S. Energy Information Administration. *Energy Data Reports, Petroleum Statement Annual, Petroleum Supply Annual,* and *Natural Gas Annual. Note:* 1. Includes other finished petroleum products, not shown separately.

★ 365 ★

Production

Natural Gas Production: 1980-1992

Table compares world and U.S. production of natural gas.

Item	Unit	1970	1975	1980	1985	1990	1991	1992
World production (dry)	Trillion cubic feet	(NA)	44.1	53.1	62.0	74.3	74.8	(NA)
U.S. production (dry)	Trillion cubic feet	21.0	19.2	19.4	16.4	17.8	17.8	17.7
Percent U.S. of world	Percent	56.0	43.6	36.5	26.4	24.0	23.7	(NA)

Source: 1994 Statistical Abstract of the United States on CD-ROM [machine-readable datafiles]. CD-8A-94. Washington, DC: U.S. Department of Commerce, Economics and Statistics Administration, Bureau of the Census, Data User Services Division, January 1995. Primary sources: U.S. Energy Information Administration. *Annual Energy Review, International Energy Annual, Natural Gas Annual* (Volumes I and II) and *Monthly Energy Review. Note:* "NA" indicates "not available."

★ 366 ★

Production

Natural Gas Well Production: 1901-1993

Table shows well production of U.S. natural gas since 1901. Production data are for marketed production, including extraction loss and transfers to natural gas plant liquids.

[In trillion cubic feet]

Year	Well production
1901	0.18
1910	0.51
1920	0.81
1930	1.98
1940	2.73
1950	6.28
1960	12.77
1970	21.92
1980	20.18
1981	19.96
1982	18.58
1983	16.88
1984	18.30
1985	17.27
1986	16.86
1987	17.43
1988	17.92
1989	18.10
1990	18.59
1991	18.53
1992	18.71
1993	19.33

Source: Executive Office of the President of the United States. *Environmental Quality 24: The Twenty-fourth Annual Report of the Council on Environmental Quality.* Prepared by Ray Clark. Written by Carroll Curtis. Edited by Barry Walsh. Washington, DC: U.S. Government Printing Office, 1994, p. 411. Primary sources: Bureau of the Census. *Historical Statistics of the United States: Colonial Times to 1970.* Series M 143, 138. Washington, DC: U.S. Department of Commerce, Bureau of the Census, 1976; U.S. Department of Energy. Energy Information Administration. *Annual Energy Review, 1993.* DOE/EIA-0384(93). Washington, DC: U.S. Department of Energy, Energy Information Administration, 1994, p. 191, table 6.2. *Notes:* Previous year data may have been revised. Current year data are preliminary and may be revised in the future.

★ 367 ★

Production

World Crude Oil Production, by Country: 1973-1992

[In thousand barrels]

Country	1973	1975	1980	1985	1990	1991	1992
Total	55,679	52,828	59,599	53,981	60,471	60,105	60,255
Algeria	1,097	983	1,106	1,037	1,175	1,230	1,217
Iraq	2,018	2,262	2,514	1,433	2,040	305	450
Kuwait	3,020	2,084	1,656	1,023	1,175	190	1,029
Libya	2,175	1,480	1,787	1,059	1,375	1,483	1,483
Qatar	570	438	472	301	406	395	396
Saudi Arabia	7,596	7,075	9,900	3,388	6,410	8,115	8,438
United Arab Emirates	1,533	1,664	1,709	1,193	2,117	2,386	2,325
Indonesia	1,339	1,307	1,577	1,325	1,462	1,592	1,566
Iran	5,861	5,350	1,662	2,250	3,088	3,312	3,429
Nigeria	2,054	1,783	2,055	1,495	1,810	1,892	1,982
Venezuela	3,366	2,346	2,168	1,677	2,137	2,375	2,334
Canada	1,798	1,430	1,435	1,471	1,553	1,548	1,598
Mexico	465	705	1,936	2,745	2,553	2,680	2,668
United Kingdom	2	12	1,622	2,530	1,820	1,797	1,825
United States	9,208	8,375	8,597	8,971	7,355	7,417	7,171
China	1,090	1,490	2,114	2,505	2,774	2,835	2,838
U.S.S.R (former)	8,324	9,523	11,706	11,585	10,880	9,887	8,388
Other	3,804	4,139	5,408	7,821	10,070	10,373	10,820
Arab OPEC	18,009	15,985	19,144	9,434	14,698	14,104	15,338
Total OPEC	30,988	27,154	26,781	16,353	23,465	23,569	24,947

Source: 1994 Statistical Abstract of the United States on CD-ROM [machine-readable datafiles]. CD-8A-94. Washington, DC: U.S. Department of Commerce, Economics and Statistics Administration, Bureau of the Census, Data User Services Division, January 1995. Primary source: U. S. Energy Information Administration. *Monthly Energy Review. Note:* "OPEC" denotes Organization of Petroleum Exporting Countries.

★ 368 ★

Production

World Natural Gas Production: 1980-1992

[In quadrillion Btu]

Region and country	1980	1985	1990	1991	1992[1]
World total	52.79	60.62	72.00	73.96	74.27
North America	23.53	20.80	22.99	23.37	23.76
Canada	2.64	2.98	3.72	4.18	4.56
Mexico	0.97	0.92	0.91	0.90	0.89
United States	19.91	16.91	18.36	18.28	18.31
Central and South America[2]	1.39	1.84	2.22	2.22	2.21
Argentina	0.26	0.47	0.59	0.60	0.57
Colombia	0.11	0.16	0.17	0.18	0.17
Trinidad and Tobago	0.08	0.23	0.19	0.21	0.20
Venezuela	0.56	0.70	0.98	0.94	0.96

[Continued]

★ 368 ★

World Natural Gas Production: 1980-1992
[Continued]

Region and country	1980	1985	1990	1991	1992[1]
Other	(NA)	0.28	0.29	0.29	0.31
Western Europe[2]	7.02	6.25	6.47	7.56	7.60
France	0.24	0.17	0.09	0.12	0.13
Germany	(NA)	(NA)	(NA)	0.60	0.60
Italy	0.43	0.52	0.62	0.62	0.65
Netherlands	3.21	2.59	2.41	2.72	2.73
Norway	1.01	1.07	1.09	1.05	1.07
United Kingdom	1.31	1.61	1.86	2.01	1.98
Yugoslavia (former)	0.07	0.09	0.10	0.10	0.10
Other	(NA)	0.20	0.30	0.35	0.35
Eastern Europe and former U.S.S.R.	16.24	23.11	28.34	28.04	26.85
Hungary	0.23	0.29	0.18	0.20	0.19
Poland	0.23	0.23	0.14	0.15	0.15
Romania	1.35	1.43	1.16	0.98	0.88
U.S.S.R. (former)	14.28	21.12	26.82	26.68	(X)
Russia	(X)	(X)	(X)	(X)	21.08
Turkmenistan	(X)	(X)	(X)	(X)	1.98
Ukraine	(X)	(X)	(X)	(X)	0.69
Uzbekistan	(X)	(X)	(X)	(X)	1.32
Other	(X)	0.04	0.03	0.03	0.58
Middle East	1.40	2.50	3.89	3.89	4.31
Bahrain	0.10	0.17	0.21	0.24	0.26
Iran	0.26	0.63	0.88	0.97	0.93
Kuwait	0.15	0.15	0.19	0.02	0.23
Qatar	0.19	0.20	0.29	0.22	0.22
Saudi Arabia	0.39	0.75	1.13	1.18	1.26
United Arab Emirates	0.21	0.51	0.82	0.96	1.03
Other		0.09	0.37	0.30	0.38
Africa	0.73	1.97	2.60	2.82	2.92
Algeria	0.44	1.44	1.90	2.05	2.09
Egypt	0.03	0.18	0.30	0.34	0.36
Libya	0.19	0.19	0.23	0.25	0.26
Nigeria	0.04	0.11	0.14	0.18	0.20
Other		0.04	0.04	0.01	0.01
Far East and Oceania	2.49	4.16	5.48	6.06	6.62
Australia	0.33	0.47	0.68	0.80	0.88
Bangladesh	0.05	0.10	0.16	0.17	0.19
Brunei	0.35	0.33	0.35	0.31	0.31
China	0.53	0.48	0.53	0.55	0.52
India	0.05	0.14	0.41	0.46	0.48
Indonesia	0.66	1.29	1.60	1.81	2.00
Japan	0.04	0.10	0.08	0.08	0.08
Malaysia	0.04	0.45	0.68	0.77	0.95
New Zealand	0.05	0.13	0.14	0.19	0.20
Pakistan	0.28	0.36	0.40	0.52	0.56

[Continued]

★ 368 ★

World Natural Gas Production: 1980-1992
[Continued]

Region and country	1980	1985	1990	1991	1992[1]
Thailand	-	0.13	0.22	0.25	0.27
Other	(NA)	0.19	0.23	0.16	0.17

Source: 1994 Statistical Abstract of the United States on CD-ROM [machine-readable datafiles]. CD-8A-94. Washington, DC: U.S. Department of Commerce, Economics and Statistics Administration, Bureau of the Census, Data User Services Division, January 1995. Primary source: U. S. Energy Information Administration. *International Energy Annual* (1992). *Notes:* "NA" represents "not available." "X" represents "not applicable." 1. Preliminary. 2. Includes countries not shown separately.

★ 369 ★
Production

World Primary Energy Production, by Region and Type of Fuel: 1975-1992
[In quadrillion Btu]

Region and type of fuel	1975	1980	1985	1990	1991	1992
World total	245.0	286.6	302.1	344.0	340.8	343.1
Region						
North America	71.1	80.5	84.1	88.2	89.1	88.8
United States	59.8	64.7	64.6	67.7	67.4	66.7
Central and South America	10.6	12.1	13.5	16.6	17.4	17.6
Western Europe	21.4	28.7	36.4	37.8	39.0	39.3
Eastern Europe and Soviet Union	55.9	69.3	74.5	79.1	70.8	67.0
Middle East	43.5	42.2	25.7	41.0	40.2	43.9
Africa	13.3	17.3	18.4	21.5	23.4	23.7
Far East and Oceania	29.3	36.5	49.5	59.9	60.9	62.8
Type of fuel						
Crude oil	111.6	127.6	115.4	129.3	128.6	129.2
Natural gas	43.9	52.8	60.6	72.0	74.0	74.3
Natural gas liquids	4.4	5.5	5.7	7.0	7.3	7.6
Coal	66.3	75.0	84.2	92.8	86.7	87.6
Hydroelectric power	15.0	18.2	20.7	22.5	22.9	22.9
Nuclear	3.9	7.6	15.4	20.3	21.3	21.5

Source: 1994 Statistical Abstract of the United States on CD-ROM [machine-readable datafiles]. CD-8A-94. Washington, DC: U.S. Department of Commerce, Economics and Statistics Administration, Bureau of the Census, Data User Services Division, January 1995. Primary source: U.S. Energy Information Administration. *International Energy Annual. Note:* Btu represents British thermal units.

Supply and Reserves

★ 370 ★

Crude Oil, Natural Gas, and Natural Gas Plant Liquids Reserves: 1977-1992

Table shows the U.S. proved reserves of crude oil, dry natural gas, and natural gas plant liquids for the 15 year-span covering 1977 through 1992.

Year	Billion barrels of crude oil	Trillion cubic feet of natural gas	Billion barrels of natural gas plant liquids
1977	31.8	207.4	NA
1978	31.4	208.0	6.8
1979	29.8	201.0	6.6
1980	29.8	199.0	6.7
1981	29.4	201.7	7.1
1982	27.9	201.5	7.2
1983	27.7	200.5	7.9
1984	28.4	197.5	7.6
1985	28.4	193.4	7.9
1986	26.9	191.6	8.2
1987	27.3	187.2	8.1
1988	26.8	168.0	8.2
1989	26.5	167.1	7.8
1990	26.3	169.3	7.6
1991	24.7	167.1	7.5
1992	23.7	165.0	7.5

Source: Executive Office of the President of the United States. *Environmental Quality 24: The Twenty-fourth Annual Report of the Council on Environmental Quality.* Prepared by Ray Clark. Written by Carroll Curtis. Edited by Barry Walsh. Washington, DC: U.S. Government Printing Office, 1994, p. 407. Primary sources: U.S. Department of Energy. Energy Information Administration. *Annual Energy Review, 1993.* DOE/EIA-0384(93). Washington, DC: U.S. Department of Energy, Energy Information Administration, 1994, p. 129, table 4.9; U.S. Department of Energy. Energy Information Administration. *U.S. Crude Oil, Natural Gas, Natural Gas Plant Liquids Reserves 1992 Annual Report.* DOE/EIA-0216(92). Washington, DC: U.S. Department of Energy, Energy Information Administration, 1993, p. 8, table 1. *Note:* "NA" stands for "not available or applicable."

★ 371 ★

Supply and Reserves

Domestic Motor Gasoline Supply: 1975-1993

[In 1,000 barrels per day, except as noted]

Item	1975	1980	1985	1990	1991	1992	1993
Supply[1]	6,675	6,579	6,831	7,235	7,188	7,268	7,483
Unleaded	(NA)	3,067	4,406	6,850	6,935	7,162	(NA)
Production	6,520	6,506	6,419	6,959	6,975	7,058	7,351
Net imports	182	140	381	342	297	294	249
Stocks (million barrels)[2]	235	261	223	220	219	216	226

Source: 1994 Statistical Abstract of the United States on CD-ROM [machine-readable datafiles]. CD-8A-94. Washington, DC: U.S. Department of Commerce, Economics and Statistics Administration, Bureau of the Census, Data User Services Division, January 1995. Primary source: U.S. Energy Information Administration. *Monthly Energy Review. Notes:* 1. Production plus net imports less net increase in primary stocks. 2. End of year, includes motor gasoline blending components.

★ 372 ★

Supply and Reserves

Energy Supply and Disposition, by Type of Fuel: 1960-1993

[In quadrillion Btu]

Type of fuel	1960	1965	1970	1975	1980	1985	1990	1991	1992	1993
Production	41.49	49.34	62.07	59.86	64.76	64.87	67.85[1]	67.48	66.85	65.81
Crude oil[2]	14.93	16.52	20.40	17.73	18.25	18.99	15.57	15.70	15.19	14.48
Natural gas liquids	1.46	1.88	2.51	2.37	2.25	2.24	2.17	2.31	2.36	2.40
Natural gas[3]	12.66	15.78	21.67	19.64	19.91	16.98	18.36	18.28	18.27	18.98
Coal	10.82	13.06	14.61	14.99	18.60	19.33	22.46	21.59	21.56	20.49
Nuclear power	(Z)	(Z)	0.24	1.90	2.74	4.15	6.16	6.58	6.65	6.52
Hydropower	1.61	2.06	2.63	3.15	2.90	2.97	2.93	2.88	2.51	2.76
Geothermal and other	(Z)	(Z)	(Z)	0.07	0.11	0.21	0.20	0.19	0.19	0.21
Net trade[4]	-2.70	-4.07	-5.70	-11.70	-12.30	-7.90	-14.07	-13.36	-14.63	-16.88
Exports	1.48	1.85	2.66	2.36	3.72	4.23	4.91	5.22	5.02	4.31
Coal	1.02	1.38	1.94	1.76	2.42	2.44	2.77	2.85	2.68	(NA)
Imports	4.23	5.92	8.39	14.11	15.97	12.10	18.99	18.58	19.65	21.19
Crude oil	2.20	2.65	2.81	8.72	11.19	6.81	12.77	12.55	13.19	(NA)
Consumption	43.80	52.68	66.43	70.55	75.96	73.98	81.26	81.14	82.36	83.96[5]
Petroleum products	19.92	23.25	29.52	32.73	34.20	30.92	33.55	32.85	33.47	33.77
Natural gas[3]	12.39	15.77	21.79	19.95	20.40	17.83	19.30	19.63	20.32	20.79
Coal	9.84	11.58	12.26	12.66	15.42	17.48	19.10	18.77	18.92	19.63
Nuclear power	(Z)	(Z)	0.24	1.90	2.74	4.15	6.16	6.58	6.65	6.52

[Continued]

★ 372 ★

Energy Supply and Disposition, by Type of Fuel: 1960-1993

[Continued]

Type of fuel	1960	1965	1970	1975	1980	1985	1990	1991	1992	1993
Hydropower[6]	1.66	2.06	2.65	3.22	3.12	3.40	2.95	3.12	2.79	3.06
Geothermal and other	(Z)	(Z)	(Z)	0.09	0.08	0.20	0.21	0.20	0.22	0.20

Source: 1994 Statistical Abstract of the United States on CD-ROM [machine-readable datafiles]. CD-8A-94. Washington, DC: U.S. Department of Commerce, Economics and Statistics Administration, Bureau of the Census, Data User Services Division, January 1995. Primary sources: U.S. Energy Information Administration. Annual Energy Review and Monthly Energy Review (March 1994). Notes: "Btu" represents British thermal units. "Z" indicates less than 50 trillion. "NA" stands for "not available." 1. Represents peak year for U.S. energy production. 2. Includes lease condensate. 3. Dry marketed gas. 4. Exports minus imports. 5. Represents peak year for U.S. energy consumption. 6. Includes industrial generation of hydropower and net electricity imports.

★ 373 ★

Supply and Reserves

Natural Gas Supply and Reserves: 1980-1992

Item	Unit	1970	1975	1980	1985	1990	1991	1992
Producing wells (year end)	1,000	117	130	182	243	270	277	076
Production value at wells	Billion dollars	3.7	8.9	32.1	43.2	31.8	30.3	32.6
Average per 1,000 cu. ft	Dollars	0.17	0.44	1.59	2.51	1.71	1.64	1.74
Proved reserves[1]	Trillion cubic feet	291	228	199	193	169	167	165
Marketed production[2]	Trillion cubic feet	21.9	20.1	20.2	17.3	18.6	18.6	(NA)
Drawn from storage	Trillion cubic feet	1.5	1.8	2.0	2.4	2.0	2.8	2.7
Imports[3]	Trillion cubic feet	0.8	1.0	1.0	1.0	1.5	1.8	2.1
Extraction losses[4]	Trillion cubic feet	0.9	0.9	0.8	0.8	0.8	0.8	(NA)
Exports	Trillion cubic feet	0.1	0.1	0.1	0.1	0.1	0.1	0.2
Additions to storage[5]	Trillion cubic feet	1.9	2.1	2.0	2.2	2.5	2.7	2.5

Source: 1994 Statistical Abstract of the United States on CD-ROM [machine-readable datafiles]. CD-8A-94. Washington, DC: U.S. Department of Commerce, Economics and Statistics Administration, Bureau of the Census, Data User Services Division, January 1995. Primary sources—except as noted: U.S. Energy Information Administration. Annual Energy Review, International Energy Annual, Natural Gas Annual (Volume I and II) and Monthly Energy Review. Notes: "NA" indicates "not available." 1. Estimated, end of year. Source: U.S. Energy Information Administration. U.S. Crude Oil, Natural Gas, and Natural Gas Liquids Reserves, (annual). 2. Marketed production includes gross withdrawals from reservoirs less quantities used for reservoir repressuring and quantities vented or flared. For 1980 and thereafter, it excludes the nonhydrocarbon gases subsequently removed. 3. Includes imports of liquefied natural gas. 4. Volumetric reduction in natural gas resulting from the extraction of natural gas constitutents at natural gas processing plants. 5. Beginning with 1980, includes liquefied natural gas (LNG) storage in above ground tanks.

★ 374 ★

Supply and Reserves

Strategic Petroleum Reserve: 1977-1993

The Strategic Petroleum Reserve is a stock of petroleum maintained by the federal government for use during periods of major supply interruption.

[In million barrels, except as noted]

Year	Crude oil imports	Domestic crude oil deliveries	Stocks at year-end			Days of net petroleum imports[3] visitor
			Quantity[1]	Percent of crude oil stocks[2]	Percent of total petroleum stocks	
1977	7.54	0.37[4]	7.46	2.1	0.6	1
1978	58.80	0.00	66.86	17.8	5.2	8
1979	24.43	(Z)	91.19	21.2	6.8	11
1980	16.07	1.30	107.80	23.1	7.7	17
1981	93.30	28.79	230.34	38.8	15.5	43
1982	60.19	3.79	293.83	45.7	20.5	68
1983	85.29	0.42	379.09	52.4	26.1	88
1984	72.04	0.05	450.51	56.6	28.9	96
1985	43.12	0.17	493.32	60.6	32.5	115
1986	17.56	1.21	511.57	60.7	32.1	94
1987	26.52	2.69	540.65	60.9	33.6	91
1988	18.76	(Z)	559.52	63.0	35.0	85
1989	20.35	0	579.86	63.0	36.8	81
1990	9.77	0	585.69	64.5	36.1	82
1991	0	0	568.51	63.7	35.2	86
1992	3.59	2.60	574.72	64.4	36.1	83
1993	5.37	6.96	587.08	63.6	35.7	78

Source: *1994 Statistical Abstract of the United States on CD-ROM* [machine-readable datafiles]. CD-8A-94. Washington, DC: U.S. Department of Commerce, Economics and Statistics Administration, Bureau of the Census, Data User Services Division, January 1995. Primary source: U.S. Energy Information Administration. *Annual Energy Review.* Notes: "Z" indicates less than .005 million barrels. 1. Stocks do not include imported quantities in transit to Strategic Petroleum Reserve terminals, pipeline fill, and above ground storage. 2. Including lease condensate stocks. 3. Derived by dividing end-of-year strategic petroleum reserve stocks by annual average daily net imports of all petroleum. Calculated prior to rounding. 4. The quantity of domestic fuel oil that was in storage prior to injection of foreign crude oil.

★ 375 ★

Supply and Reserves

Uranium Supply: 1970-1991

Table shows uranium supply, enrichment, and discharged commercial reactor fuel. Years ending Dec. 31, except as noted.

Item	Unit	1970	1975	1980	1985	1990	1991
Uranium concentrate							
Production	Million pounds	25.81	23.20	43.70	11.31	8.89	7.95
Exports	Million pounds	4.20	1.00	5.80	5.30	2.00	2.00
Imports	Million pounds	0	1.40	3.60	11.70	23.70	14.00
Delivered price	Dollars/pound	(NA)	10.50	26.00	31.43	15.70	13.66
Enrichment[1]							
Enriched product[2]	Million Swu[3]	5.10	9.92	10.69	10.2	10.2	10.3
For domestic customers	Million Swu[3]	3.74	4.36	6.89	6.0	6.8	6.7
For foreign customers	Million Swu[3]	1.36	5.56	3.80	4.2	3.4	3.6
Sales	Million dollars	(NA)	376	1,379	1,403	1,148	1,156
Discharged commercial reactor fuel[5]							
Annual discharge	Metric tons	82	499	1,193	1,330	(NA)	(NA)
Inventory, year end[6]	Metric tons	118	1,538	6,434	12,481	(NA)	(NA)
Onsite storage	Metric tons	(NA)	(NA)	(NA)	11,953	(NA)	(NA)
Offsite storage	Metric tons	(NA)	(NA)	(NA)	528	(NA)	(NA)

Source: 1994 Statistical Abstract of the United States on CD-ROM [machine-readable datafiles]. CD-8A-94. Washington, DC: U.S. Department of Commerce, Economics and Statistics Administration, Bureau of the Census, Data User Services Division, January 1995. Primary sources—except as noted: U.S. Energy Information Administration. *Annual Energy Review* and *Uranium Industry Annual*; unpublished data. *Notes:* "NA" stands for "not available." 1. Beginning 1984, represents fiscal years. 2. Based on sales. 3. Separative work units. The standard measure of enrichment services is based on operating tails assay in effect at the time the enriched product was placed in inventory. 4. January-September only. 5. Uranium content. Source: Nuclear Assurance Corporation (Atlanta, Georgia). 6. Reprocessed fuel not included as inventory.

★ 376 ★

Supply and Reserves

U.S. Petroleum Balance: 1980-1992

[In million barrels]

Item	1980	1985	1990	1991	1992
Petroleum products supplied	6,242	5,740	6,201	6,101	6,234
New supply of products	6,249	5,676	6,259	6,110	6,206
Production of products	5,765	5,363	5,934	5,933	6,050
	17	94	(27)	5	(30)
Crude input to refineries	4,934	4,381	4,894	4,855	4,909
Oil, field production	3,146	3,275	2,685	2,707	2,624
Alaska	592	666	647	656	627
Lower 48 States	2,555	2,608	2,037	2,050	1,997
Net imports	1,821	1,094	2,112	2,068	2,194

[Continued]

★ 376 ★

U.S. Petroleum Balance: 1980-1992
[Continued]

Item	1980	1985	1990	1991	1992
Imports (gross excluding SPR)[1]	1,910	1,125	2,142	2,111	2,223
SPR imports[1]	16	43	10	0	4
Exports	-105	75	40	42	32
Other sources	33	12	98	80	90
Natural gas plant liquids (NGPL), supply	577	604	574	613	628
Other liquids	253	378	465	466	513
Net imports of refined products	484	313	326	177	156
Imports	578	523	598	500	471
Exports	94	210	272	323	315
Stock withdrawal, refined products	-7	64	-59	(10)	28
Ending stocks, all oils	1,392	1,519	1,621	1,617	1,592
Crude oil and lease condensate	358	321	323	325	318
Srategic petroleum reserve (SPR)[1]	108	493	586	569	575
Unfinished oils	124	107	(NA)	(NA)	(NA)
Gasoline blending components	17	33	(NA)	(NA)	(NA)
Pentanes plus	(NA)	8	(NA)	(NA)	(NA)
Finished refined products	785	557	712	724	(NA)
Product type supplied					
Total products	6,242	5,740	5,942	6,083	6,326
Finished motor gasoline	2,407	2,493	2,567	2,630	2,678
Distillate fuel oil	1,049	1,047	1,064	1,086	1,140
Residual fuel oil	918	439	518	462	5,030
Liquified petroleum gases[2]	414	584	552	588	604
Pentanes plus, other liquids, etc	1,454	1,155	1,223	1,304	1,369
Crude oil	(NA)	22	18	12	15

Source: *1994 Statistical Abstract of the United States on CD-ROM* [machine-readable datafiles]. CD-8A-94. Washington, DC: U.S. Department of Commerce, Economics and Statistics Administration, Bureau of the Census, Data User Services Division, January 1995. Primary source: U.S. Energy Information Administration. *Petroleum Supply Annual. Notes:* "NA" represents "not available." 1. "SPR" denotes Strategic Petroleum Reserve. 2. Includes ethane.

Chapter 7
TOXIC AND HAZARDOUS SUBSTANCES

This chapter covers agricultural chemicals; toxic chemicals (including accidents, spills, and emissions); hazardous material such as bioaccumulators, carcinogens, and ozone depleters; Superfund; and the Toxic Release Inventory. Radioactive substances are included as well.

The Toxic Release Inventory is compiled annually by the U.S. Environmental Protection Agency. These data are presented in detail in this chapter to facilitate the review of toxic chemicals as a whole rather than in segments such as air, water, or land. Complimentary information on air and water pollution has been included in the Air and Water chapter. The Costs and Expenditures chapter includes related tables on pollution control and abatement expenditures for Toxic Release Inventory industries. The Wastes and Resource Recovery chapter also features several tables on chemical transfers.

Superfund and hazardous waste sites primarily are a solid waste disposal problem that impact land and, through land, ground water. The slow seepage of wastes from old and forgotten sites into aquifers also is a great danger: Wastes buried decades ago might suddenly emerge as an immediate health problem in the form of contaminated drinking water. Additional information on hazardous waste sites will be found in the Wastes and Resource Recovery chapter. Tables profiling health risks and issues have been included in the Costs and Expenditures chapter.

Agricultural Chemicals

★ 377 ★

Agricultural Chemicals Used in Lettuce Production

Active ingredient	Purpose	Acreage treated				
		Arizona	Florida	Michigan	Texas	Total[1]
		Percent of planted area				
Acephate	Insecticide	40.7	0	0	10.5	34.2
Chlorpyrifos	Insecticide	.2	1.1	16.8	31.3	1.6
DCPA	Herbicide	0	0	0	10.5	.4
Diazinon	Insecticide	50.1	3.5	3.4	22.6	42.9

[Continued]

★ 377 ★

Agricultural Chemicals Used in Lettuce Production
[Continued]

Active ingredient	Purpose	Acreage treated				
		Arizona	Florida	Michigan	Texas	Total[1]
DCNA	Fungicide	0	0	0	0	0
Endosulfan	Insecticide	58.9	0	0	7.9	49.2
Methamidophos	Insecticide	.8	87.3	0	0	11.1
Permethrin	Insecticide	74.6	89.8	93.2	78.6	76.8

		Acres				
Total planted area	NA	50,500	8,000	1,000	2,300	66,800

Source: "Addressing Pesticide Residues." *Food Review* (October-December 1992), p. 5. *Notes:* "NA" stands for "not applicable." 1. Total of four survey states.

★ 378 ★

Agricultural Chemicals

Farm Fertilizer Use: 1940-1993

Table shows quantity of farm fertilizer use. Quantity refers to tonnages of primary nutrients, nitrogen, phosphorus, and potash applied to farm fields and excludes fertilizer use on lawns, golf courses, home gardens, and other nonfarm lands.

[In million tons]

Year	Quantity
1940	1.8
1945	2.7
1950	4.1
1955	6.1
1960	7.5
1965	11.0
1970	16.1
1975	17.6
1980	23.1
1985	21.7
1990	20.6
1991	20.5
1992	20.7
1993	20.9

Source: Executive Office of the President of the United States. *Environmental Quality 24: The Twenty-fourth Annual Report of the Council on Environmental Quality.* Prepared by Ray Clark. Written by Carroll Curtis. Edited by Barry Walsh. Washington, DC: U.S. Government Printing Office, 1994, p. 458. Primary sources: U.S. Department of Agriculture. Economic Research Service. *Agricultural Research: Inputs Situation and Outlook Report.* AR-32. Washington, DC: U.S. Department of Agriculture, Economic Research Service, October 1993; U.S. Department of Agriculture. Economic Research Service. *RTD Updates: Fertilizer.* Washington, DC: U.S. Department of Agriculture, Economic Research Service, March 1994.

★ 379 ★

Agricultural Chemicals

Farm Pesticide Use: 1964-1993

[In million pounds of active ingredients]

Year	Herbicides	Insecticides	Fungicides	Total
1964	76	143	72	291
1966	112	138	79	328
1971	207	127	130	464
1976	374	130	146	650
1982	451	71	30	552
1986	410	59	6	475
1987	365	57	7	429
1988	372	60	8	440
1989	394	61	8	463
1990	392	63	8	463
1991	403	66	9	478
1992	412	67	8	487
1993	398	66	8	472

Source: Executive Office of the President of the United States. *Environmental Quality 24: The Twenty-fourth Annual Report of the Council on Environmental Quality.* Prepared by Ray Clark. Written by Carroll Curtis. Edited by Barry Walsh. Washington, DC: U.S. Government Printing Office, 1994, p. 459. Primary source: U.S. Department of Agriculture. Economic Research Service. *Agricultural Resources: Inputs Situation and Outlook Report.* AR-32. Washington, DC: U.S. Department of Agriculture, Economic Research Service, October 1993. *Notes:* For the years 1964, 1966, 1972, and 1976, estimates of pesticides use are for total use on all crops in the United States. The 1982 estimates are for major field and forage crops only and represent 33 major producing states, excluding California. The 1986-1993 estimates are for major U.S. field crops. Detail may not agree with totals because of independent rounding.

★ 380 ★

Agricultural Chemicals

Pesticide Consumption: 1983-1998

Total pesticide consumption - 27,500
North America - 7,377
Western Europe - 7,173
Asia/Oceania - 6,814
Eastern Europe - 2,571
Latin America - 2,307
Africa/Mideast - 1,258

Chart shows data from column 2.

According to the source, "the worldwide demand for active ingredients used in pesticides/insecticides will grow 4.4 percent annually to more than $34 billion in 1998" (p. 26).

[In million U.S. dollars except percentages]

Item	1983	1993	1998	Annual growth (%)	
				1993/1983	1998\1993
Total pesticide consumption[1]	20,507	27,500	34,150	3.0	4.4
North America	3,991	7,377	8,980	6.3	4.0
Latin America	1,258	2,307	3,000	6.3	5.4
Western Europe	5,847	7,173	9,000	2.1	4.6
Eastern Europe	2,898	2,571	3,190	-1.2	4.4
Africa/Mideast	942	1,258	1,610	2.9	5.1
Asia/Oceania	5,571	6,814	8,370	2.0	4.2

Source: "Demand for Pesticides Rising to $34B by '98." *InTech* (March 1995), p. 26. Primary source: The Fredonia Group. *Note:* 1. Active ingredients.

★ 381 ★

Agricultural Chemicals

Pesticides Used in Mexico

Table shows insecticides, herbicides, and fungicides commonly used in Mexico. Approximately 1 percent of produce imported from Mexico by the United States is randomly tested by the Food and Drug Administration (FDA). Four percent of tested produce contain excessive traces of agricultural chemicals.

Pesticides	Tons[1]
Insecticides	
Parathion-methyl	2,040
Methamidophos	1,103
Endosulfan	505
Carbaryl	328
Methomyl	268
Chlorphyriphos	266

[Continued]

★ 381 ★

Pesticides Used in Mexico
[Continued]

Pesticides	Tons[1]
Carbofuran	238
Herbicides	
2,4-D	2,177
Paraquat	764
Atrazine	666
Glyphosate	471
Diuron	394
Fungicides	
Mancozeb	2,468
Copper products	1,806
Chlorothalonil	635
Quintozene, or PCNB	573
Captan	313

Source: "Commonly Used Pesticides in Mexico." *Business Mexico* (1993), p. 22. Primary source: Mexican Association for the Pesticide and Fertilizer Industry (AMIPFAC), 1990. *Note:* 1. Active ingredients.

Chemicals

★ 382 ★

Chemical Releases: 1992

Table shows the releases of all Toxic Release Inventory (TRI) chemicals.

[In pounds]

Chemical	Rank by total releases	Fugitive or nonpoint air emissions	Stack or point air emissions	Surface water discharges	Underground injection	Releases to land	Total releases
Acetaldehyde	45	1,963,416	4,452,705	77,188	1,905,859	289	8,399,457
Acetamide	143	3	17	1	100,800	0	100,821
Acetone	7	62,963,625	70,989,876	999,584	3,180,700	559,265	138,693,050
Acetonitrile	27	733,502	394,331	48,976	20,111,640	29	21,288,478
Acrolein	136	12,775	12,830	0	113,680	0	139,285
Acrylamide	54	24,374	4,180	10,324	4,188,680	963	4,228,521
Acrylic acid	52	284,227	264,012	19,147	4,484,000	407	5,051,793
Acrylonitrile	51	335,086	1,264,985	1,483	3,861,550	8,071	5,471,175
Allyl alcohol	132	48,016	48,088	9,839	73,060	0	179,003
Allyl chloride	138	96,328	25,306	5	833	0	122,472
Aluminum (fume or dust)	59	494,503	1,959,744	82,140	250	1,192,193	3,728,830
Aluminum oxide	130	5,843	14,007	265	0	195,538	215,653

[Continued]

★ 382 ★

Chemical Releases: 1992

[Continued]

Chemical	Rank by total releases	Fugitive or nonpoint air emissions	Stack or point air emissions	Surface water discharges	Underground injection	Releases to land	Total releases
(fibrous forms)							
4-Aminoazobenzene	252	0	1	0	250	0	251
4-Aminobiphenyl	270	0	0	0	3	0	3
Ammonia	1	38,878,070	123,206,765	40,824,196	251,783,103	9,165,277	463,857,411
Ammonium nitrate (solution)	16	57,029	1,273,889	6,762,487	37,531,805	2,624,432	48,249,642
Ammonium sulfate (solution)	34	123,880	111,020	4,429,219	5,705,957	4,069,490	14,439,566
Aniline	76	181,632	227,372	16,261	1,195,676	1,173	1,622,114
o-Anisidine	218	405	16	107	0	2,167	2,695
p-Anisidine	263	5	6	5	0	0	16
Anthracene	153	20,386	33,648	1,030	0	3,070	58,134
Antimony	160	4,994	16,779	7,879	0	10,246	39,898
Antimony compounds	75	48,363	348,106	45,835	3,773	1,260,253	1,706,330
Arsenic	73	1,217	4,439	1,236	0	1,814,303	1,821,195
Arsenic compounds	68	10,578	127,046	6,597	33,000	2,452,391	2,629,612
Asbestos (friable)	128	5,291	5,973	250	0	235,900	247,414
Barium	120	61,459	31,787	5,514	0	232,547	331,307
Barium compounds	50	235,555	404,462	120,428	1,251	4,825,948	5,587,644
Benzal chloride	232	956	17	0	0	0	973
Benzene	39	7,640,101	4,744,478	24,918	355,683	340,636	13,105,816
Benzoic trichloride	205	5,851	228	0	0	0	6,079
Benzoyl chloride	189	11,738	1,900	5	0	0	13,643
Benzoyl peroxide	196	837	1,827	5	0	6,200	8,869
Benzyl chloride	165	25,003	10,099	15	50	43	35,210
Beryllium	176	1	1,867	39	0	21,358	23,265
Beryllium compounds	155	0	511	5	0	48,000	48,516
Biphenyl	94	676,939	145,397	9,483	49,127	4,622	885,568
Bis(2-chloroethyl) ether	216	2,673	514	5	0	0	3,192
Bis(chloromethyl) ether	246	3	306	0	0	0	309
Bis(2-chloro-1-methyl-ethyl)ether	193	8,000	1,430	1,900	0	0	11,330
Bis(2-ethylhexyl) adipate	121	75,921	154,947	1,628	0	95,291	327,787
Bromochlorodifluoromethane (Halon 1211)	183	7,923	8,824	0	0	0	16,747
Bromoform	186	11,120	5	0	4,500	0	15,625
Bromomethane	64	528,321	2,472,829	390	1,000	0	3,002,540
Bromotrifluoromethane (Halon 1301)	141	105,490	4,661	0	0	0	110,151
1,3-Butadiene	57	2,229,847	1,613,853	1,364	1,000	372	3,846,436
Butyl acrylate	116	184,349	158,966	2,261	0	834	346,410
n-Butyl alcohol	21	7,134,970	22,588,357	35,369	2,324,731	57,220	32,140,647
sec-Butyl alcohol	97	208,247	460,823	15,706	25,450	762	710,988
tert-Butyl alcohol	70	1,245,810	426,219	147,629	640,123	14	2,459,795
Butyl benzyl phthalate	117	151,715	186,523	957	0	6,109	345,304
1,2-Butylene oxide	148	59,828	15,024	5,773	0	0	80,625
Butyraldehyde	100	214,563	281,946	470	128,051	256	625,286
C.I. basic green 4	261	5	5	40	0	0	50
C.I. basic red 1	273	0	0	0	0	0	0
C.I. disperse yellow 3	228	428	0	23	0	780	1,231
C.I. food red 15	271	0	2	0	0	0	2
C.I. solvent yellow 14	273	0	0	0	0	0	0
Cadmium	184	2,295	6,461	638	0	7,036	16,430

[Continued]

★ 382 ★

Chemical Releases: 1992
[Continued]

Chemical	Rank by total releases	Fugitive or nonpoint air emissions	Stack or point air emissions	Surface water discharges	Underground injection	Releases to land	Total releases
Cadmium compounds	137	11,347	49,037	780	1,211	65,407	127,782
Calcium cyanamide	163	8,000	405	0	0	30,005	38,410
Captan	192	1,647	5,189	10	5,000	10	11,856
Carbaryl	195	2,525	7,172	15	0	265	9,977
Carbon disulfide	10	2,636,114	90,240,923	45,087	2,704	21	92,924,849
Carbon tetrachloride	80	416,994	973,268	2,441	45,984	333	1,439,020
Carbonyl sulfide	32	4,222	16,198,944	0	0	0	16,203,166
Catechol	122	9,925	917	223,299	3,507	59,154	296,802
Chlordane	222	1,713	0	1	0	0	1,714
Chlorine	14	1,634,189	68,278,693	1,217,091	48,252	46,171	71,224,396
Chlorine dioxide	63	60,490	3,035,936	761	0	6	3,097,193
Chloroacetic acid	187	10,778	1,024	3,199	0	0	15,001
Chlorobenzene	71	1,026,324	1,201,951	20,799	72,000	817	2,321,891
Chloroethane	67	1,533,378	1,224,260	1,957	210	0	2,759,805
Chloroform	29	6,017,425	11,017,501	654,452	50,240	28,582	17,768,200
Chloromethane	49	1,325,645	4,317,830	30,961	86,709	0	5,761,145
Chloromethyl methyl ether	227	35	1,186	10	0	0	1,231
Chlorophenols	134	3,226	6,057	290	133,204	0	142,777
Chloroprene	78	152,543	1,344,852	47	54,000	1,811	1,553,253
Chlorothalonil	181	3,185	2,695	6	0	12,250	18,136
Chromium	79	411,832	112,207	19,104	333	961,167	1,504,643
Chromium compounds	26	128,783	334,902	269,667	32,137	23,165,988	23,931,477
Cobalt	162	16,478	13,084	2,156	500	6,931	39,149
Cobalt compounds	124	7,840	23,471	99,289	18,420	126,946	275,966
Copper	35	476,395	1,018,974	41,474	16,736	12,647,313	14,200,892
Copper compounds	18	3,563,732	2,766,265	72,413	201,431	34,489,362	41,093,203
Creosote	84	565,353	728,211	11,835	5	2,634	1,308,038
p-Cresidine	237	240	100	5	0	255	600
Cresol (mixed isomers)	87	193,663	298,657	2,747	614,578	1,097	1,110,742
m-Cresol	106	51,679	5,100	220	450,000	0	506,999
o-Cresol	105	20,426	3,061	14	490,000	3	513,504
p-Cresol	125	36,611	3,777	943	232,900	1,513	275,744
Cumene	58	1,245,131	2,479,290	2,250	15,100	783	3,742,554
Cumene hydroperoxide	119	66,077	12,009	217	259,000	21	337,324
Cupferron	267	0	10	0	0	0	10
Cyanide compounds	55	80,916	974,494	81,369	2,963,579	12,936	4,113,294
Cyclohexane	36	5,004,598	8,596,357	21,039	230,985	107,748	13,960,727
2,4-D (acetic acid)	175	3,292	3,493	262	1,200	15,302	23,549
Decabromodiphenyl oxide	101	11,940	25,027	3,878	285	531,040	572,170
4,4'-Diaminodiphenyl ether	238	5	264	312	0	0	581
Diaminotoluene (mixed isomers)	170	13,913	4,570	695	10,000	85	29,263
2,4-Diaminotoluene	220	1,150	755	5	0	0	1,910
Dibenzofuran	169	16,474	13,282	260	0	211	30,227
1,2-Dibromo-3-chloropropane	247	294	0	0	0	0	294
1,2-Dibromoethane	167	10,921	21,931	106	1,823	6	34,787
Dibromotetrafluoroethane (Halon 2402)	234	154	614	0	0	0	768
Dibutyl phthalate	123	104,628	65,671	5,991	110,000	764	287,054
Dichlorobenzene (mixed isomers)	212	725	3,796	0	4	0	4,525

[Continued]

★ 382 ★

Chemical Releases: 1992
[Continued]

Chemical	Rank by total releases	Fugitive or nonpoint air emissions	Stack or point air emissions	Surface water discharges	Underground injection	Releases to land	Total releases
1,2-Dichlorobenzene	113	182,216	166,843	2,395	3,700	6,469	361,623
1,3-Dichlorobenzene	210	1,102	3,033	877	0	0	5,012
1,4-Dichlorobenzene	118	74,313	263,633	2,021	2,000	622	342,589
3,3'-Dichlorobenzidine	265	5	5	0	0	0	10
Dichlorobromomethane	254	194	0	0	0	0	194
Dichlorodifluoromethane (CFC-12)	41	6,871,649	4,391,045	2,235	1,722	23	11,266,674
1,2-Dichloroethane	60	650,901	2,514,306	12,296	6,927	1,858	3,186,288
1,2-Dichloroethylene	177	15,623	7,604	5	24	1	23,257
Dichloromethane	13	27,495,557	46,467,648	221,192	1,183,867	79,313	75,447,577
2,4-Dichlorophenol	194	274	303	0	9,735	0	10,312
1,2-Dichloropropane	99	205,467	414,450	6,089	0	1,206	627,212
2,3-Dichloropropene	133	160,000	326	1,600	745	0	162,671
1,3-Dichloropropylene	159	32,315	10,292	67	0	0	42,674
Dichlorotetrafluoroethane (CFC-114)	89	934,198	146,026	255	1	0	1,080,480
Dichlorvos	229	541	558	5	0	0	1,104
Dicofol	240	255	256	0	0	0	511
Diethanolamine	93	170,229	86,577	403,692	55,526	178,766	894,790
Di-(2-ethylhexyl) phthalate	91	149,292	724,491	947	35	101,712	976,477
Diethyl phthalate	145	10,824	82,934	470	0	505	94,733
Diethyl sulfate	191	3,284	9,952	5	0	5	13,246
3,3'-Dimethoxybenzidine	268	0	0	8	0	0	8
1,1-Dimethyl hydrazine	243	83	286	0	0	5	374
2,4-Dimethylphenol	146	19,320	8,390	4	66,000	10	93,724
Dimethyl phthalate	149	11,352	67,335	662	855	5	80,209
Dimethyl sulfate	201	6,050	973	161	0	0	7,184
m-Dinitrobenzene	226	502	749	0	0	0	1,251
o-Dinitrobenzene	255	51	106	0	0	0	157
p-Dinitrobenzene	256	50	80	0	0	0	130
4,6-Dinitro-o-cresol	260	2	31	20	0	0	53
2,4-Dinitrophenol	161	14,680	5,632	128	18,925	6	39,371
2,4-Dinitrotoluene	221	1,707	57	105	0	0	1,869
2,6-Dinitrotoluene	239	422	3	126	0	0	551
Dinitrotoluene (mixed isomers)	150	5,928	10,816	291	50,000	0	67,035
1,4-Dioxane	86	410,648	273,837	447,066	0	3,297	1,134,848
Epichlorohydrin	103	402,097	120,556	3,165	0	1,655	527,473
2-Ethoxyethanol	112	117,490	279,496	18	0	35	397,039
Ethyl acrylate	131	107,913	97,399	734	3,200	1,114	210,360
Ethylbenzene	42	3,236,753	6,766,461	15,778	193,882	289,108	10,501,982
Ethyl chloroformate	214	2,231	1,138	26	0	5	3,400
Ethylene	19	16,595,902	20,010,924	13,413	0	0	36,620,239
Ethylene glycol	30	3,180,308	7,070,854	1,326,208	4,923,321	684,588	17,185,279
Ethyleneimine	273	0	0	0	0	0	0
Ethylene oxide	81	662,386	638,649	1,991	120,000	837	1,423,863
Ethylene thiourea	248	5	280	0	0	0	285
Fluometuron	236	301	303	5	0	0	609
Formaldehyde	31	1,847,451	9,055,776	441,244	4,916,248	174,429	16,435,148
Freon 113	25	17,610,197	6,954,728	1,916	214	9,028	24,576,083
Glycol ethers	17	10,590,821	34,937,784	350,489	194,386	140,595	46,214,075

[Continued]

★ 382 ★

Chemical Releases: 1992
[Continued]

Chemical	Rank by total releases	Fugitive or nonpoint air emissions	Stack or point air emissions	Surface water discharges	Underground injection	Releases to land	Total releases
Heptachlor	235	460	250	1	0	0	711
Hexachlorobenzene	207	4,138	333	227	794	0	5,492
Hexachloro-1,3-butadiene	202	1,916	2,218	1,911	738	0	6,783
Hexachlorocyclopentadiene	197	7,112	1,268	0	5	0	8,385
Hexachloroethane	178	1,738	19,284	3	1,670	0	22,695
Hydrazine	179	13,033	6,238	842	0	10	20,123
Hydrazine sulfate	139	0	2	0	120,000	0	120,002
Hydrochloric acid	2	4,393,471	72,715,559	1,927,193	207,817,749	432,770	287,286,742
Hydrogen cyanide	62	65,822	2,275,468	3,947	801,646	17	3,146,900
Hydrogen fluoride	43	4,158,141	5,599,637	4,205	1	27,887	9,789,871
Hydroquinone	126	4,533	8,985	3,967	250,750	0	268,235
Isobutyraldehyde	111	114,601	289,005	351	3,840	1	407,798
Isopropyl alcohol (manufacturing)[1]	82	381,879	998,990	15	0	330	1,381,214
4,4'-Isopropylidenediphenol	104	109,282	76,427	7,463	41,000	287,138	521,310
Lead	69	167,966	244,838	11,641	1	2,045,059	2,469,505
Lead compounds	38	447,167	986,955	60,934	2,880	11,913,242	13,411,178
Lindane	231	507	531	0	0	0	1,038
Maleic anhydride	108	100,959	355,296	405	5	2,327	458,992
Maneb	224	510	535	0	0	250	1,295
Manganese	46	570,920	299,310	234,925	304	6,521,605	7,627,064
Manganese compounds	15	501,113	1,297,031	733,225	22,569	61,485,334	64,039,272
Mercury	185	8,416	4,055	266	0	3,117	15,854
Mercury compounds	213	2,488	761	297	9	17	3,572
Methanol	3	33,921,970	160,868,717	16,422,600	27,084,182	3,328,541	241,626,010
Methoxychlor	233	261	557	5	0	5	828
2-Methoxyethanol	77	891,829	527,586	165,535	0	4	1,584,954
Methyl acrylate	127	129,009	136,816	1,279	77	705	267,886
Methyl tert-butyl ether	65	829,786	1,990,920	102,851	68,445	288	2,992,290
4,4'-Methylenebis (2-chloroaniline)	262	12	5	0	0	2	19
Methylenebis(phenyl-isocyanate)	107	274,052	146,080	30	0	77,201	497,363
Methylene bromide	164	23,361	14,790	0	250	0	38,401
4,4'-Methylenedianiline	180	6,487	3,889	420	8,865	55	19,716
Methyl ethyl ketone	11	31,107,484	59,397,157	153,249	365,395	241,794	91,265,079
Methyl hydrazine	273	0	0	0	0	0	0
Methyl iodide	166	21,980	3,405	11	9,500	0	34,896
Methyl isobutyl ketone	23	7,814,570	18,079,207	96,387	129,100	194,986	26,314,250
Methyl isocyanate	198	6,851	803	0	0	0	7,654
Methyl methacrylate	66	734,794	1,820,951	34,595	220,000	4,003	2,814,343
Molybdenum trioxide	115	50,338	59,606	59,441	162,705	14,651	346,741
Monochloropenta-fluoroethane (CFC-115)	109	296,585	125,102	5	0	0	421,692
Naphthalene	53	1,368,999	1,233,810	28,936	78,227	1,667,141	4,377,113
alpha-Naphthylamine	266	5	5	0	0	0	10
Nickel	61	516,037	198,687	44,910	5,309	2,395,966	3,160,909
Nickel compounds	74	59,632	89,950	66,305	292,453	1,305,284	1,813,624
Nitric acid	24	720,461	2,310,467	53,725	22,081,766	664,849	25,831,268
Nitrilotriacetic acid	203	4	0	4,069	2,700	0	6,773
5-Nitro-o-anisidine	264	5	10	0	0	0	15

[Continued]

★ 382 ★

Chemical Releases: 1992
[Continued]

Chemical	Rank by total releases	Fugitive or nonpoint air emissions	Stack or point air emissions	Surface water discharges	Underground injection	Releases to land	Total releases
Nitrobenzene	92	38,744	12,909	442	864,949	0	917,044
Nitroglycerin	152	2,059	27,073	12,906	0	16,150	58,188
2-Nitrophenol	258	5	7	48	0	0	60
4-Nitrophenol	219	715	105	1,700	0	0	2,520
2-Nitropropane	140	36,262	9,380	900	65,581	0	112,123
p-Nitrosodiphenylamine	211	24	0	0	4,900	0	4,924
N,N-Dimethylaniline	158	19,366	24,012	2,039	0	0	45,417
N-Nitrosodiphenylamine	273	0	0	0	0	0	0
Parathion	249	10	255	5	0	0	270
Pentachlorophenol	182	7,470	6,224	3,127	0	270	17,091
Peracetic acid	204	2,589	3,379	14	5	520	6,507
Phenol	37	2,990,363	4,749,651	165,074	5,552,077	190,230	13,647,395
p-Phenylenediamine	208	2,737	2,710	0	0	3	5,450
2-Phenylphenol	172	6,957	17,865	97	0	5	24,924
Phosgene	209	3,596	1,684	5	5	0	5,290
Phosphoric acid	4	326,636	868,973	158,674,836	35,230	46,725,635	206,631,310
Phosphorus (yellow or white)	114	25,507	2,397	2,861	5	327,970	358,740
Phthalic anhydride	95	116,352	633,112	5,240	0	1,079	755,783
Picric acid	90	2	1	2	1,068,674	2	1,068,681
Polybrominated biphenyls	251	0	250	0	0	5	255
Polychlorinated biphenyls (PCBs)	272	0	0	0	0	1	1
Propane sultone	253	250	0	0	0	0	250
Propionaldehyde							

Source: U.S. Environmental Protection Agency. "Toxic Release Inventory, 1992." In *National Economic, Social, and Environmental Data Bank* [CD-ROM]. Prepared by U.S. Department of Commerce, Economics and Statistics Administration. Washington, DC: U.S. Department of Commerce, National Economic, Social, and Environmental Data Bank, Economics and Statistics Administration, Office of Business Analysis, February 1995. *Notes:* 1. Only facilities that manufacture isopropyl alcohol by the "strong acid process" are required to report for TRI. Because no U.S. manufacturers use this process, no reports should have been filed for this chemical.

★ 383 ★
Chemicals

Chemical Releases – Top 25 Chemicals: 1992

Table shows the top 25 chemicals reported as released. Includes offsite disposal.

[In pounds]

Chemical	Quantity released or disposed of
Ammonia	455,599,635
Hydrochloric acid	298,900,276
Methanol	259,001,005
Phosphoric acid	196,807,410
Sulfuric acid	187,976,508
Toluene	186,681,857

[Continued]

★ 383 ★

Chemical Releases – Top 25 Chemicals: 1992
[Continued]

Chemical	Quantity released or disposed of
Acetone	139,039,676
Zinc compounds	120,490,959
1,1,1-Trichloroethane	112,587,880
Xylene (mixed isomers)	108,789,871
Carbon disulfide	93,554,822
Methyl ethyl ketone	88,491,478
Dichloromethane	75,729,079
Manganese compounds	75,565,406
Chlorine	71,168,030
Glycol ethers	49,847,660
Ammonium nitrate (solution)	49,700,242
Copper compounds	46,462,501
Ethylene	35,854,137
Chromium compounds	35,745,584
Styrene	33,687,236
n-Butyl alcohol	32,300,656
Nitric acid	29,559,498
Copper	29,512,497
Ammonium sulfate (solution)	29,261,313
Subtotal	2,842,315,216
Total for all TRI chemicals	3,401,386,170

Source: U.S. Environmental Protection Agency. "Toxic Release Inventory, 1992." In *National Economic, Social, and Environmental Data Bank* [CD-ROM]. Prepared by U.S. Department of Commerce, Economics and Statistics Administration. Washington, DC: U.S. Department of Commerce, National Economic, Social, and Environmental Data Bank, Economics and Statistics Administration, Office of Business Analysis, February 1995. *Note:* "TRI" represents Toxic Release Inventory.

★ 384 ★

Chemicals

Chemicals With Largest Discharges to Surface Water: 1992

Table shows the 15 Toxic Release Inventory (TRI) chemicals with the largest discharges to surface water.

[In pounds]

Chemical	Amount not in stormwater	Amount in stormwater	Total surface water discharges
Phosphoric acid	86,162,576	72,512,260	158,674,836
Ammonia	40,529,007	295,189	40,824,196
Sulfuric acid	32,646,906	72,620	32,719,526
Methanol	16,419,684	2,916	16,422,600
Ammonium nitrate (solution)	6,585,021	177,466	6,762,487
Ammonium sulfate (solution)	4,429,218	1	4,429,219
Hydrochloric acid	1,925,638	1,555	1,927,193
Ethylene glycol	1,303,082	23,126	1,326,208
Chlorine	1,217,051	40	1,217,091
Zinc compounds	988,022	21,717	1,009,739
Acetone	997,814	1,770	999,584
Manganese compounds	725,717	7,508	733,225
Chloroform	653,843	609	654,452
1,4-Dioxane	447,065	1	447,066
Formaldehyde	437,491	3,753	441,244
Subtotal	195,468,135	73,120,531	268,588,666
Total for all TRI chemicals	199,708,213	73,224,740	272,932,953

Source: U.S. Environmental Protection Agency. "Toxic Release Inventory, 1992." In *National Economic, Social, and Environmental Data Bank* [CD-ROM]. Prepared by U.S. Department of Commerce, Economics and Statistics Administration. Washington, DC: U.S. Department of Commerce, National Economic, Social, and Environmental Data Bank, Economics and Statistics Administration, Office of Business Analysis, February 1995.

★ 385 ★

Chemicals

Chemicals With Largest Emissions to Air: 1992

Table shows the 15 Toxic Release Inventory (TRI) chemicals with the largest emissions to air.

[In pounds]

Chemical	Fugitive or nonpoint air emissions	Stack or point air emissions	Total air emissions
Methanol	33,921,970	160,868,717	194,790,687
Toluene	64,986,449	126,010,712	190,997,161
Ammonia	38,878,070	123,206,765	162,084,835
Acetone	62,963,625	70,989,876	133,953,501
1,1,1-Trichloroethane	56,479,078	58,465,308	114,944,386
Xylene (mixed isomers)	26,080,470	83,631,841	109,712,311
Carbon disulfide	2,636,114	90,240,923	92,877,037
Methyl ethyl ketone	31,107,484	59,397,157	90,504,641
Hydrochloric acid	4,393,471	72,715,559	77,109,030
Dichloromethane	27,495,557	46,467,648	73,963,205
Chlorine	1,634,189	68,278,693	69,912,882
Glycol ethers	10,590,821	34,937,784	45,528,605
Ethylene	16,595,902	20,010,924	36,606,826
Styrene	13,149,414	19,185,202	32,334,616
n-Butyl alcohol	7,134,970	22,588,357	29,723,327
Subtotal	398,047,584	1,056,995,466	1,455,043,050
Total for all TRI chemicals	549,351,729	1,295,606,607	1,844,958,336

Source: U.S. Environmental Protection Agency. "Toxic Release Inventory, 1992." In *National Economic, Social, and Environmental Data Bank* [CD-ROM]. Prepared by U.S. Department of Commerce, Economics and Statistics Administration. Washington, DC: U.S. Department of Commerce, National Economic, Social, and Environmental Data Bank, Economics and Statistics Administration, Office of Business Analysis, February 1995.

★ 386 ★
Chemicals

Chemicals With Largest Releases to Air, Water, and Land: 1992

Table shows the 50 Toxic Release Inventory (TRI) chemicals with the largest air, water, and land releases.

[In pounds]

Chemical	Fugitive or nonpoint air emissions	Stack or point air emissions	Surface water discharges	Releases to land	Total air/ water/land releases
Methanol	33,921,970	160,868,717	16,422,600	3,328,541	214,541,828
Ammonia	38,878,070	123,206,765	40,824,196	9,165,277	212,074,308
Phosphoric acid	326,636	868,973	158,674,836	46,725,635	206,596,080
Toluene	64,986,449	126,010,712	84,024	708,278	191,789,463
Acetone	62,963,625	70,989,876	999,584	559,265	135,512,350
1,1,1-Trichloroethane	56,479,078	58,465,308	13,132	76,381	115,033,899
Xylene (mixed isomers)	26,080,470	83,631,841	41,504	1,434,430	111,188,245
Carbon disulfide	2,636,114	90,240,923	45,087	21	92,922,145
Methyl ethyl ketone	31,107,484	59,397,157	153,249	241,794	90,899,684
Zinc compounds	1,506,116	2,678,676	1,009,739	76,540,392	81,734,923
Hydrochloric acid	4,393,471	72,715,559	1,927,193	432,770	79,468,993
Dichloromethane	27,495,557	46,467,648	221,192	79,313	74,263,710
Chlorine	1,634,189	68,278,693	1,217,091	46,171	71,176,144
Manganese compounds	501,113	1,297,031	733,225	61,485,334	64,016,703
Sulfuric acid	1,570,940	22,150,513	32,719,526	1,737,032	58,178,011
Glycol ethers	10,590,821	34,937,784	350,489	140,595	46,019,689
Copper compounds	3,563,732	2,766,265	72,413	34,489,362	40,891,772
Ethylene	16,595,902	20,010,924	13,413	0	36,620,239
Styrene	13,149,414	19,185,202	23,502	304,179	32,662,297
n-Butyl alcohol	7,134,970	22,588,357	35,369	57,220	29,815,916
Trichloroethylene	15,269,203	14,305,372	8,153	20,726	29,603,454
Methyl isobutyl ketone	7,814,570	18,079,207	96,387	194,986	26,185,150
Freon 113	17,610,197	6,954,728	1,916	9,028	24,575,869
Chromium compounds	128,783	334,902	269,667	23,165,988	23,899,340
Propylene	12,981,892	8,235,849	989	0	21,218,730
Chloroform	6,017,425	11,017,501	654,452	28,582	17,717,960
Carbonyl sulfide	4,222	16,198,944	0	0	16,203,166
Zinc (fume or dust)	634,722	905,990	46,975	13,041,123	14,628,810
Copper	476,395	1,018,974	41,474	12,647,313	14,184,156
Cyclohexane	5,004,598	8,596,357	21,039	107,748	13,729,742
Lead compounds	447,167	986,955	60,934	11,913,242	13,408,298
Benzene	7,640,101	4,744,478	24,918	340,636	12,750,133
Tetrachloroethylene	5,198,796	7,112,439	10,207	9,354	12,330,796
Ethylene glycol	3,180,308	7,070,854	1,326,208	684,588	12,261,958
Formaldehyde	1,847,451	9,055,776	441,244	174,429	11,518,900
Dichlorodifluoromethane (CFC-12)	6,871,649	4,391,045	2,235	23	11,264,952
Ammonium nitrate (solution)	57,029	1,273,889	6,762,487	2,624,432	10,717,837
Ethylbenzene	3,236,753	6,766,461	15,778	289,108	10,308,100
Hydrogen fluoride	4,158,141	5,599,637	4,205	27,887	9,789,870
Trichlorofluoromethane (CFC-11)	3,655,417	5,809,097	1,448	19,761	9,485,723
Ammonium sulfate (solution)	123,880	111,020	4,429,219	4,069,490	8,733,609
Phenol	2,990,363	4,749,651	165,074	190,230	8,095,318
Manganese	570,920	299,310	234,925	6,521,605	7,626,760

[Continued]

355

★ 386 ★

Chemicals With Largest Releases to Air, Water, and Land: 1992

[Continued]

Chemical	Fugitive or nonpoint air emissions	Stack or point air emissions	Surface water discharges	Releases to land	Total air/ water/land releases
Acetaldehyde	1,963,416	4,452,705	77,188	289	6,493,598
1,2,4-Trimethylbenzene	2,229,766	3,028,445	8,481	511,202	5,777,894
Chloromethane	1,325,645	4,317,830	30,961	0	5,674,436
Barium compounds	235,555	404,462	120,428	4,825,948	5,586,393
Naphthalene	1,368,999	1,233,810	28,936	1,667,141	4,298,886
Vinyl acetate	1,079,209	3,073,769	7,208	5,249	4,165,435
p-Xylene	1,035,834	2,985,051	1,868	4,101	4,026,854
Subtotal	520,674,527	1,249,871,432	270,476,368	320,646,199	2,361,668,526
Total for all TRI chemicals	549,351,729	1,295,606,607	272,932,953	337,809,053	2,455,700,342

Source: U.S. Environmental Protection Agency. "Toxic Release Inventory, 1992." In *National Economic, Social, and Environmental Data Bank* [CD-ROM]. Prepared by U.S. Department of Commerce, Economics and Statistics Administration. Washington, DC: U.S. Department of Commerce, National Economic, Social, and Environmental Data Bank, Economics and Statistics Administration, Office of Business Analysis, February 1995.

★ 387 ★

Chemicals

Chemicals With Largest Releases to Land: 1992

Table shows the 15 Toxic Release Inventory (TRI) chemicals with the largest releases to land.

[In pounds]

Chemical	Total releases to land	Releases to onsite landfills	Releases to onsite land treatment	Releases to onsite surface impoundments	Other onsite land disposal
Zinc compounds	76,540,392	20,357,694	255,532	10,360,696	45,566,470
Manganese compounds	61,485,334	45,028,568	105,113	13,562,669	2,788,984
Phosphoric acid	46,725,635	9,354,622	307,850	13,038,209	24,024,954
Copper compounds	34,489,362	8,650,729	605,659	4,337,377	20,895,597
Chromium compounds	23,165,988	3,106,881	243,576	19,727,213	88,318
Zinc (fume or dust)	13,041,123	7,019,005	850	98,439	5,922,829
Copper	12,647,313	724,703	246	11,657,180	265,184
Lead compounds	11,913,242	2,564,930	22,676	1,180,564	8,145,072
Ammonia	9,165,277	1,471,936	4,474,688	3,037,199	181,454
Manganese	6,521,605	4,994,530	605	268,075	1,258,395
Barium compounds	4,825,948	1,907,488	45,310	1,723,736	1,149,414
Ammonium sulfate (solution)	4,069,490	0	3,618,487	450,753	250
Methanol	3,328,541	1,477,773	129,709	1,586,094	134,965
Ammonium nitrate (solution)	2,624,432	28,850	1,528,008	1,025,157	42,417
Arsenic compounds	2,452,391	77,943	27,010	1,700,706	646,732

[Continued]

★ 387 ★

Chemicals With Largest Releases to Land: 1992
[Continued]

Chemical	Total releases to land	Releases to onsite landfills	Releases to onsite land treatment	Releases to onsite surface impoundments	Other onsite land disposal
Subtotal	312,996,073	106,765,652	11,365,319	83,754,067	111,111,035
Total for all TRI chemicals	337,809,053	112,526,010	12,649,589	90,429,416	122,204,038

Source: U.S. Environmental Protection Agency. "Toxic Release Inventory, 1992." In *National Economic, Social, and Environmental Data Bank* [CD-ROM]. Prepared by U.S. Department of Commerce, Economics and Statistics Administration. Washington, DC: U.S. Department of Commerce, National Economic, Social, and Environmental Data Bank, Economics and Statistics Administration, Office of Business Analysis, February 1995.

★ 388 ★
Chemicals

Chemicals With Largest Total Releases: 1992

Table shows the 50 Toxic Release Inventory (TRI) chemicals with the largest total releases.

[In pounds]

Chemical	Fugitive or nonpoint air emissions	Stack or point air emissions	Surface water discharges	Underground injection	Releases to land	Total releases
Ammonia	38,878,070	123,206,765	40,824,196	251,783,103	9,165,277	463,857,411
Hydrochloric acid	4,393,471	72,715,559	1,927,193	207,817,749	432,770	287,286,742
Methanol	33,921,970	160,868,717	16,422,600	27,084,182	3,328,541	241,626,010
Phosphoric acid	326,636	868,973	158,674,836	35,230	46,725,635	206,631,310
Toluene	64,986,449	126,010,712	84,024	1,573,901	708,278	193,363,364
Sulfuric acid	1,570,940	22,150,513	32,719,526	98,631,395	1,737,032	156,809,406
Acetone	62,963,625	70,989,876	999,584	3,180,700	559,265	138,693,050
1,1,1-Trichloroethane	56,479,078	58,465,308	13,132	561	76,381	115,034,460
Xylene (mixed isomers)	26,080,470	83,631,841	41,504	219,270	1,434,430	111,407,515
Carbon disulfide	2,636,114	90,240,923	45,087	2,704	21	92,924,849
Methyl ethyl ketone	31,107,484	59,397,157	153,249	365,395	241,794	91,265,079
Zinc compounds	1,506,116	2,678,676	1,009,739	126,947	76,540,392	81,861,870
Dichloromethane	27,495,557	46,467,648	221,192	1,183,867	79,313	75,447,577
Chlorine	1,634,189	68,278,693	1,217,091	48,252	46,171	71,224,396
Manganese compounds	501,113	1,297,031	733,225	22,569	61,485,334	64,039,272
Ammonium nitrate (solution)	57,029	1,273,889	6,762,487	37,531,805	2,624,432	48,249,642
Glycol ethers	10,590,821	34,937,784	350,489	194,386	140,595	46,214,075
Copper compounds	3,563,732	2,766,265	72,413	201,431	34,489,362	41,093,203
Ethylene	16,595,902	20,010,924	13,413	0	0	36,620,239
Styrene	13,149,414	19,185,202	23,502	83,170	304,179	32,745,467
n-Butyl alcohol	7,134,970	22,588,357	35,369	2,324,731	57,220	32,140,647
Trichloroethylene	15,269,203	14,305,372	8,153	466	20,726	29,603,920
Methyl isobutyl ketone	7,814,570	18,079,207	96,387	129,100	194,986	26,314,250
Nitric acid	720,461	2,310,467	53,725	22,081,766	664,849	25,831,268
Freon 113	17,610,197	6,954,728	1,916	214	9,028	24,576,083
Chromium compounds	128,783	334,902	269,667	32,137	23,165,988	23,931,477
Acetonitrile	733,502	394,331	48,976	20,111,640	29	21,288,478
Propylene	12,981,892	8,235,849	989	5	0	21,218,735

[Continued]

★ 388 ★

Chemicals With Largest Total Releases: 1992
[Continued]

Chemical	Fugitive or nonpoint air emissions	Stack or point air emissions	Surface water discharges	Underground injection	Releases to land	Total releases
Chloroform	6,017,425	11,017,501	654,452	50,240	28,582	17,768,200
Ethylene glycol	3,180,308	7,070,854	1,326,208	4,923,321	684,588	17,185,279
Formaldehyde	1,847,451	9,055,776	441,244	4,916,248	174,429	16,435,148
Carbonyl sulfide	4,222	16,198,944	0	0	0	16,203,166
Zinc (fume or dust)	634,722	905,990	46,975	120,000	13,041,123	14,748,810
Ammonium sulfate (solution)	123,880	111,020	4,429,219	5,705,957	4,069,490	14,439,566
Copper	476,395	1,018,974	41,474	16,736	12,647,313	14,200,892
Cyclohexane	5,004,598	8,596,357	21,039	230,985	107,748	13,960,727
Phenol	2,990,363	4,749,651	165,074	5,552,077	190,230	13,647,395
Lead compounds	447,167	986,955	60,934	2,880	11,913,242	13,411,178
Benzene	7,640,101	4,744,478	24,918	355,683	340,636	13,105,816
Tetrachloroethylene	5,198,796	7,112,439	10,207	12,780	9,354	12,343,576
Dichlorodifluoromethane (CFC-12)	6,871,649	4,391,045	2,235	1,722	23	11,266,674
Ethylbenzene	3,236,753	6,766,461	15,778	193,882	289,108	10,501,982
Hydrogen fluoride	4,158,141	5,599,637	4,205	1	27,887	9,789,871
Trichlorofluoromethane (CFC-11)	3,655,417	5,809,097	1,448	8	19,761	9,485,731
Acetaldehyde	1,963,416	4,452,705	77,188	1,905,859	289	8,399,457
Manganese	570,920	299,310	234,925	304	6,521,605	7,627,064
1,2,4-Trimethylbenzene	2,229,766	3,028,445	8,481	14,409	511,202	5,792,303
Vinyl acetate	1,079,209	3,073,769	7,208	1,616,385	5,249	5,781,820
Chloromethane	1,325,645	4,317,830	30,961	86,709	0	5,761,145
Barium compounds	235,555	404,462	120,428	1,251	4,825,948	5,587,644
Subtotal	519,723,657	1,248,357,369	270,548,265	700,474,113	319,639,835	3,058,743,239
Total for all TRI chemicals	549,351,729	1,295,606,607	272,932,953	725,946,415	337,809,053	3,181,646,757

Source: U.S. Environmental Protection Agency. "Toxic Release Inventory, 1992." In *National Economic, Social, and Environmental Data Bank* [CD-ROM]. Prepared by U.S. Department of Commerce, Economics and Statistics Administration. Washington, DC: U.S. Department of Commerce, National Economic, Social, and Environmental Data Bank, Economics and Statistics Administration, Office of Business Analysis, February 1995.

★ 389 ★

Chemicals

Chemicals With Largest Underground Injection: 1992

Table shows the 15 Toxic Release Inventory (TRI) chemicals with the largest underground injection.

[In pounds]

Chemical	Underground injection
Ammonia	251,783,103
Hydrochloric acid	207,817,749
Sulfuric acid	98,631,395
Ammonium nitrate (solution)	37,531,805
Methanol	27,084,182
Nitric acid	22,081,766

[Continued]

★ 389 ★

Chemicals With Largest Underground Injection:
1992
[Continued]

Chemical	Underground injection
Acetonitrile	20,111,640
Ammonium sulfate (solution)	5,705,957
Phenol	5,552,077
Ethylene glycol	4,923,321
Formaldehyde	4,916,248
Acrylic acid	4,484,000
Acrylamide	4,188,680
Acrylonitrile	3,861,550
Acetone	3,180,700
Subtotal	701,854,173
Total for all TRI chemicals	725,946,415

Source: U.S. Environmental Protection Agency. "Toxic Release Inventory, 1992." In *National Economic, Social, and Environmental Data Bank* [CD-ROM]. Prepared by U.S. Department of Commerce, Economics and Statistics Administration. Washington, DC: U.S. Department of Commerce, National Economic, Social, and Environmental Data Bank, Economics and Statistics Administration, Office of Business Analysis, February 1995.

★ 390 ★

Chemicals

Toxic Chemical Accidents, by Chemical Released: 1988-1992

```
┌─────────────────────────────────────────────────────┐
│  ┌──────────────────────────────────────────────┐   │
│  │ Total - 18,749                               │   │
│  └──────────────────────────────────────────────┘   │
│  ┌──────────┐                                        │
│  │          │ Polychlorinated biphenyls - 3,586      │
│  └──────────┘                                        │
│  ┌────────┐                                          │
│  │        │ Ammonia, anhydrous - 3,333               │
│  └────────┘                                          │
│  ┌──────┐                                            │
│  │      │ Sulfuric acid - 2,387                      │
│  └──────┘                                            │
│  ┌─────┐                                             │
│  │     │ Chlorine - 2,099                            │
│  └─────┘                                             │
│  ┌────┐                                              │
│  │    │ Hydrochloric acid - 1,504                    │
│  └────┘                                              │
│  ┌────┐                                              │
│  │    │ Ethylene glycol - 1,470                      │
│  └────┘                                              │
│  ┌───┐                                               │
│  │   │ Sulfur dioxide - 1,310                        │
│  └───┘                                               │
│  ┌───┐                                               │
│  │   │ Radioactive materials - 1,073                 │
│  └───┘                                               │
│  ┌──┐                                                │
│  │  │ Benzene - 1,048                                │
│  └──┘                                                │
│  ┌──┐                                                │
│  │  │ Hydrogen sulfide - 939                         │
│  └──┘                                                │
│              Chart shows data from column 1.         │
└─────────────────────────────────────────────────────┘
```

Polychlorinated biphenyls accounted for nearly 3,600 chemical accidents from 1988 through 1992. According to one study, 15 chemicals account for two-thirds of all chemical accidents.

Chemical	Accidents	
	Total	With injuries[1]
Polychlorinated biphenyls	3,586	34
Ammonia, anhydrous	3,333	389
Sulfuric acid	2,387	130
Chlorine	2,099	409
Hydrochloric acid	1,504	143
Ethylene glycol	1,470	18
Sulfur dioxide	1,310	86
Radioactive materials	1,073	30
Benzene	1,048	14
Hydrogen sulfide	939	49
Total[2]	18,749	1,302

Source: Seltzer, Richard. "New Actions to Prevent Chemical Accidents Urged." *C&EN*, 5 September 1994, p. 20. Primary source: Emergency Response Notification System database (1988-1992). Compiled by the National Environmental Law Center and U.S. Public Interest Research Group. *Notes:* 1. Accidents resulting in immediately reported deaths, injuries, or evacuations but excluding chronic health and environmental effects. 2. For top 10 chemicals releases (but many accident notification forms do not properly identify all chemicals released).

★ 391 ★
Chemicals

Toxic Chemical Accidents, by State: 1988-1992

```
Total - 34,575
Others - 15,172
        California - 4,820
        Texas - 4,532
      Louisiana - 2,505
    Pennsylvania - 1,395
   Ohio - 1,269
   Kentucky - 1,166
   Illinois - 1,085
   Florida - 905
   Michigan - 869
   New Jersey - 857
                    Chart shows data from column 1.
```

Table shows states with most toxic chemical accidents. According to the source, "more than half the accidents occurred in 10 states, led by California and Texas, with Louisiana third. Just 63 of the U.S.'s 3,181 counties account for more than 40 percent of the incidents" (p. 20).

State	Accidents	
	Total	With injuries[1]
California	4,820	409
Texas	4,532	176
Louisiana	2,505	60
Pennsylvania	1,395	78
Ohio	1,269	84
Kentucky	1,166	36
Illinois	1,085	64
Florida	905	84
Michigan	869	50
New Jersey	857	64
Others	15,172	1,081
Total[2]	34,575	2,186

Source: Seltzer, Richard. "New Actions to Prevent Chemical Accidents Urged." *C&EN*, 5 September 1994, p. 20. Primary source: Emergency Response Notification System database (1988-1992). Compiled by the National Environmental Law Center and U.S. Public Interest Research Group. *Notes:* 1. Accidents resulting in immediately reported deaths, injuries, or evacuations but excluding chronic health and environmental effects. 2. For all 50 states, Puerto Rico, District of Columbia, Virgin Islands, and Guam.

★ 392 ★

Chemicals

Toxic Chemical Emissions: 1988-1992

Table shows changes in each state's toxic chemical emissions from 1988 through 1992.

[In percentages]

State	Change
Alabama	-9.79
Alaska	-46.02
Arizona	-34.21
Arkansas	-36.87
California	-39.52
Colorado	-64.33
Connecticut	-52.06
Delaware	-36.24
Florida	-36.89
Georgia	-43.52
Hawaii	-59.19
Idaho	-52.93
Illinois	-18.21
Indiana	-43.11
Iowa	-24.69
Kansas	-30.35
Kentucky	-20.70
Louisiana	-36.41
Maine	-20.37
Maryland	-48.10
Massachusetts	-51.36
Michigan	-26.23
Minnesota	-48.64
Mississippi	-00.87
Missouri	-43.24
Montana	+23.89
Nebraska	-31.18
Nevada	+41.43
New Hampshire	-54.64
New Jersey	-52.40
New Mexico	-34.57
New York	-45.41
North Carolina	-13.34
North Dakota	+45.01
Ohio	-39.62
Oklahoma	-36.48
Oregon	-14.52
Pennsylvania	-40.90
Rhode Island	-59.31
South Carolina	-4.59
South Dakota	+14.68
Tennessee	-10.91
Texas	-45.29
Utah	-41.73

[Continued]

★ 392 ★

Toxic Chemical Emissions: 1988-1992
[Continued]

State	Change
Vermont	-49.22
Virginia	-55.51
Washington	-40.33
West Virginia	-43.39
Wisconsin	-29.27
Wyoming	-66.98
Total	-34.94

Source: "Nationline: Correction." *USA TODAY,* 21 April 1994, p. 3A.

★ 393 ★

Chemicals

Toxic Chemical Releases in Alabama, by Chemical: 1990

Figures indicate pounds released by chemical and by type of emission per year.

Chemical	Fugitive air	Stack air	Water	Injection	Land	Public treatment	Other offsite	Total releases
1,1,1-trichloroethane	1,662,062	1,033,374	1,030	0	0	510	189,949	2,886,925
1,1-dimethyl hydrazine	8	2	0	0	0	0	78	88
1,2,4-trichlorobenzene	3,006	13,751	0	0	0	250	48,648	65,655
1,2,4-trimethylbenzene	93,115	499,038	0	0	0	250	250	592,653
1,2-dichlorobenzene	262	5,513	0	0	0	20,213	0	25,988
1,2-dichloroethane	2	0	0	0	0	0	1,556	1,558
1,3-butadiene	3,367	18,050	0	0	0	0	928	22,345
1,4-dioxane	1,700	10	0	0	0	0	37,640	39,350
2,4-d	250	0	0	0	0	0	250	500
2,4-dimethylphenol	55	0	5	0	0	1,977	0	2,037
2-ethoxyethanol	1,701	10	0	0	0	141	0	1,852
2-methoxyethanol	250	250	0	0	0	750	0	1,250
4,4'-isopropylidenediphenol	250	5,905	0	0	0	0	0	6,155
4,4'-methylenedianiline	5	5	0	0	0	0	0	10
Acetaldehyde	248,500	69,007	0	0	0	0	0	317,507
Acetone	590,882	987,899	65,379	0	30,396	255	103,221	1,778,032
Acetonitrile	250	750	0	0	0	750	0	1,750
Acrylamide	250	250	250	0	250	0	0	1,000
Acrylic acid	500	1,000	0	0	0	250	250	2,000
Acrylonitrile	20,510	150,380	0	0	0	40	93	171,023
Aluminum (fume or dust)	655	250	0	0	250	250	77,459	78,864
Aluminum oxide (fibrous forms)	250	0	0	0	20,000	0	3,168	23,418
Ammonia	1,774,114	556,305	1,874,263	4,907,609	165,293	133,900	31,324	9,442,808
Ammonium nitrate (solution)	1,000	250	268,510	0	228,340	19,344	0	517,444
Ammonium sulfate (solution)	2	0	250	0	0	107,130	0	107,382
Aniline	2,400	250	250	0	750	0	15	3,665
Anthracene	3,184	1,548	11	0	0	0	480,250	484,993
Antimony	41	100	5	0	7	124	57,250	57,527
Antimony compounds	67	256	5,600	0	0	0	7,093	13,016
Arsenic	65	85	0	5	26	4	53,810	53,995
Arsenic compounds	81	811	23	0	96	0	6,240	7,251

[Continued]

Toxic Chemical Releases in Alabama, by Chemical: 1990

[Continued]

Chemical	Fugitive air	Stack air	Water	Injection	Land	Public treatment	Other offsite	Total releases
Asbestos (friable)	260	7	0	0	2,750	0	765,294	768,311
Barium	34,012	265	1,069	0	5,753	0	34,000	75,099
Barium compounds	85,155	587	500	0	178,000	230	63,307	327,779
Benzene	202,267	631,484	725	7,729	15	257	193,888	1,036,365
Biphenyl	11,403	22,890	7	0	0	155,009	1,150	190,459
Bis(2-ethylhexyl) adipate	5	2,205	0	0	900	0	7,400	10,510
Bromomethane	970	210,000	0	0	0	0	0	210,970
Butyl acrylate	1,657	16,703	0	0	0	0	6	18,366
Butyl benzyl phthalate	750	0	0	0	0	0	250	1,000
Butyraldehyde	330	2,200	2,800	0	21	0	0	5,351
Cadmium	0	0	0	0	0	0	8,601	8,601
Cadmium compounds	0	102	62	0	13	0	25,915	26,092
Carbon disulfide	529,202	46,048,069	4,861	0	0	0	0	46,582,132
Carbon tetrachloride	83,607	390,384	755	0	0	0	51,556	526,302
Carbonyl sulfide	0	78,483	0	0	0	0	0	78,483
Catechol	365	5	30,600	0	19,143	0	4,050	54,163
Chlorine	60,298	962,239	21,368	0	255	13,900	0	1,058,060
Chlorine dioxide	290	1,003,938	5	0	0	0	0	1,004,233
Chloroacetic acid	337	250	0	0	0	0	0	587
Chlorobenzene	3,908	360	5	0	0	0	1,150,000	1,154,273
Chloroethane	250	1,116	0	0	0	0	0	1,366
Chloroform	1,019,384	1,732,535	121,796	0	4,426	0	1,000	2,879,141
Chloromethane	253	17,228	0	0	0	0	0	17,481
Chromium	8,586	1,640	4,093	5	35,578	804	216,844	267,550
Chromium compounds	36,997	3,520	1,670	5	5,955	1,300	516,692	566,139
Cobalt	255	0	0	0	0	256	2,105	2,616
Cobalt compounds	5	20	33,000	0	250	0	120,039	153,314
Copper	2,882	7,894	5,340	5	33,885	13,762	73,185	136,953
Copper compounds	2,841	15,339	129	0	61	9,831	197,593	225,794
Creosote	101,031	148,167	3	0	39	319	322,760	572,319
Cresol (mixed isomers)	1,038	1,827	39	0	0	12,267	0	15,171
Cumene	4,457	35,254	0	0	16,307	0	16,307	72,325
Cyanide compounds	765	9,368	7,114	0	563	625	223,509	241,944
Cyclohexane	160,704	207,214	5	913	0	260	2,112	371,208
Di(2-ethylhexyl) phthalate	4,380	38,064	0	0	0	0	0	42,444
Dibenzofuran	2,861	1,101	12	0	0	0	48,250	52,224
Dichloromethane	1,119,335	68,607	154	0	5	5	144,488	1,332,594
Diethanolamine	1,825	500	750	0	0	15,051	10,700	28,826
Diethyl sulfate	230	0	0	0	0	0	0	230
Dimethyl phthalate	0	250	0	0	0	0	0	250
Epichlorohydrin	11,755	3,250	10,250	0	7,450	0	750	33,455
Ethyl acrylate	784	1,008	0	0	0	0	6	1,798
Ethylbenzene	39,671	67,798	265	616	265	267	23,963	132,845
Ethylene	47,477	6,072	0	0	0	0	0	53,549
Ethylene glycol	189,698	38,064	15,051	0	250	23,752	18,650	285,465
Formaldehyde	30,103	250,056	1,499	0	750	10,997	39,772	333,177
Freon 113	433,637	223,988	5	0	0	5	60,204	717,839
Glycol ethers	116,869	1,246,150	755	0	0	49,500	39,002	1,452,276
Hexachloroethane	250	5,100	0	0	0	0	0	5,350
Hydrazine	577	251	1,050	0	0	0	2,901	4,779
Hydrochloric acid	38,327	4,465,368	15	0	5	1,398	175,093	4,680,206
Hydrogen cyanide	6,964	2,343	0	0	0	250	256	9,813

[Continued]

★ 393 ★

Toxic Chemical Releases in Alabama, by Chemical: 1990
[Continued]

Chemical	Fugitive air	Stack air	Water	Injection	Land	Public treatment	Other offsite	Total releases
Hydrogen fluoride	2,400	83,594	5	0	0	0	1,450	87,449
Isobutyraldehyde	15,940	269,860	60	0	0	0	0	285,860
Isopropyl alcohol (manufacturing)	31	0	0	0	0	250	0	281
Lead	7,874	17,191	372	0	11,172	579	1,216,816	1,254,004
Lead compounds	2,552	8,421	500	0	52,000	0	260,147	323,620
M-xylene	8,098	102,036	5	0	5	5	0	110,149
Maleic anhydride	5	5	0	0	0	0	0	10
Manganese	27,561	13,757	12,995	0	408,787	511	81,062	544,673
Manganese compounds	35,206	13,013	52,575	0	650,250	755	2,802,821	3,554,620
Mercury	1,261	899	69	0	250	0	29,000	31,479
Methanol	1,719,046	6,333,608	100,835	1,385,873	71,116	35,254	1,191,844	10,837,576
Methyl acrylate	12,000	23,000	0	0	0	0	0	35,000
Methyl ethyl ketone	1,467,906	4,896,567	8,218	39	14,255	680	406,270	6,793,935
Methyl isobutyl ketone	201,765	530,342	4,005	0	3,600	1,661	204,951	946,324
Methyl methacrylate	5,245	44,855	0	0	0	0	6	50,106
Methyl tert-butyl ether	4,068	26,097	0	0	0	0	0	30,165
Methylenebis(phenylisocyanate)	32,377	38,841	5	0	161,258	5	222,358	454,844
Molybdenum trioxide	500	250	500	0	0	0	250	1,500
N,N-dimethylaniline	1,560	4,300	10	0	0	0	0	5,870
N-butyl alcohol	72,302	184,623	10	0	0	255	86,843	344,033
N-dioctyl phthalate	0	250	0	0	0	0	0	250
Naphthalene	58,329	40,109	173	0	0	61,475	148,750	308,836
Nickel	6,811	1,588	10,910	0	11,717	1,131	29,332	61,489
Nickel compounds	33,023	797	1,600	0	30	1,163	12,507	49,120
Nitric acid	4,663	4,431	10	0	255	10,340	0	19,699
Nitrilotriacetic acid	5	0	7,700	0	0	0	0	7,705
Nitrobenzene	1,000	500	750	0	750	250	11,600	14,850
O-cresol	750	0	0	0	0	0	0	750
O-xylene	4,164	46,812	10	0	5	5	0	50,996
P-cresol	250	0	1,600	0	2,500	0	4,220	8,570
P-nitrosodiphenylamine	24	0	0	0	0	0	1,300	1,324
P-xylene	36,298	830,036	5	0	15	5	0	866,359
Pentachlorophenol	11,472	5,310	251	0	0	35	10,541	27,609
Phenol	37,252	57,078	9,137	0	52,663	3,023	91,648	250,801
Phosgene	43	8	0	0	0	0	0	51
Phosphoric acid	14,010	3,046	285	5	6,669	39,541	58,347	121,903
Phosphorus (yellow or white)	333	0	0	0	0	5	1,577	1,915
Phthalic anhydride	5	384	0	0	0	0	4,443	4,832
Polychlorinated biphenyls (PCBs)	0	0	0	0	0	0	38,204	38,204
Propylene	2,340	939	0	0	0	0	0	3,279
Quinoline	15,512	395	7	0	0	0	400	16,314
Sec-butyl alcohol	2,499	6	0	0	0	0	2,252	4,757
Selenium	250	250	250	0	0	250	750	1,750
Silver	1	0	0	0	0	0	0	1
Styrene	274,843	40,600	20	5	20	5	315,672	631,165
Sulfuric acid	13,561	890,457	535	0	50,965	52,494	231,712	1,239,724
Tert-butyl alcohol	250	0	0	0	0	0	0	250
Tetrachloroethylene	63,671	20,344	0	0	0	109,026	2,856	195,897
Tetrachlorvinphos	0	0	0	0	0	0	86,000	86,000
Thiourea	250	250	5	0	5	0	0	510
Titanium tetrachloride	0	0	0	0	0	0	1,508,100	1,508,100
Toluene	1,787,826	3,613,810	167	8,728	10,044	556	976,587	6,397,718

[Continued]

★ 393 ★

Toxic Chemical Releases in Alabama, by Chemical: 1990
[Continued]

Chemical	Fugitive air	Stack air	Water	Injection	Land	Public treatment	Other offsite	Total releases
Toluene-2,4-diisocyanate	5	1,238	0	0	0	0	14,706	15,949
Toluene-2,6-diisocyanate	0	305	0	0	0	0	3,864	4,169
Trichloroethylene	714,273	325,150	0	0	0	250	31,504	1,071,177
Vanadium (fume or dust)	5	5	5	0	0	5	750	770
Vinyl acetate	6,459	16,744	0	0	0	0	0	23,203
Vinyl bromide	290	910	270	0	0	0	0	1,470
Vinylidene chloride	200	2,730	100	0	0	0	0	3,030
Xylene (mixed isomers)	1,442,392	3,336,575	659	5,700	510	45,941	720,193	5,551,970
Zinc (fume or dust)	48,563	41,650	505	0	49,750	1,010	30,955	172,433
Zinc compounds	19,142	38,759	100,722	0	875,882	34,196	1,338,962	2,407,663

Source: U.S. Environmental Protection Agency. "Toxic Chemical Releases, 1990." In *National Economic, Social, and Environmental Data Bank* [CD-ROM]. Prepared by U.S. Department of Commerce, Economics and Statistics Administration. Washington, DC: U.S. Department of Commerce, National Economic, Social, and Environmental Data Bank, Economics and Statistics Administration, Office of Business Analysis, February 1995.

★ 394 ★
Chemicals

Toxic Chemical Releases in Alaska, by Chemical: 1990

Figures indicate pounds released by chemical and by type of emission per year.

Chemical	Fugitive air	Stack air	Water	Injection	Land	Public treatment	Other offsite	Total releases
1,2,4-trimethylbenzene	3,595	1,522	250	0	280	0	10	5,657
2-methoxyethanol	5	0	0	0	0	0	0	5
Acetone	250	22,260	2,506	0	0	0	0	25,016
Ammonia	157,104	13,326,700	363,231	0	4,500	0	0	13,851,535
Benzene	69,003	12,920	54	5	171	1	15	82,169
Chlorine	750	3,975	255	0	5	0	0	4,985
Chloroform	70,088	136,903	78,400	0	0	0	0	285,391
Copper compounds	0	0	250	0	250	0	0	500
Cumene	132	116	0	0	0	0	0	248
Cyclohexane	16,599	5,051	5	0	200	0	10	21,865
Ethylbenzene	14,272	701	13	5	320	1	15	15,327
Ethylene glycol	0	250	8,000	0	250	0	0	8,500
Formaldehyde	250	5	0	0	0	0	0	255
Glycol ethers	5	70	0	0	0	0	0	75
Hydrochloric acid	250	548,250	2,142,000	0	0	0	0	2,690,500
Methanol	1,500	327,505	2,952,070	0	250	0	0	3,281,325
Molybdenum trioxide	0	0	0	0	5	0	0	5
Naphthalene	374	571	250	0	250	0	10	1,455
Nickel compounds	0	0	250	0	255	0	0	505
Nitric acid	1	10	5	0	0	0	0	16
Phenol	250	0	62	0	0	0	0	312
Phosphoric acid	0	0	5	0	0	0	0	5
Sulfuric acid	5	182,005	21,905	0	21,150	0	0	225,065
Toluene	28,039	4,973	42	5	400	1	15	33,475

[Continued]

★ 394 ★

Toxic Chemical Releases in Alaska, by Chemical: 1990

[Continued]

Chemical	Fugitive air	Stack air	Water	Injection	Land	Public treatment	Other offsite	Total releases
Xylene (mixed isomers)	33,875	3,943	36	5	540	1	15	38,415
Zinc compounds	0	0	250	0	250	0	0	500

Source: U.S. Environmental Protection Agency. "Toxic Chemical Releases, 1990." In *National Economic, Social, and Environmental Data Bank* [CD-ROM]. Prepared by U.S. Department of Commerce, Economics and Statistics Administration. Washington, DC: U.S. Department of Commerce, National Economic, Social, and Environmental Data Bank, Economics and Statistics Administration, Office of Business Analysis, February 1995.

★ 395 ★

Chemicals

Toxic Chemical Releases in Arizona, by Chemical: 1990

Figures indicate pounds released by chemical and by type of emission per year.

Chemical	Fugitive air	Stack air	Water	Injection	Land	Public treatment	Other offsite	Total releases
1,1,1-trichloroethane	0	1,939,676	5	0	5	589	116,241	2,056,516
1,2,4-trimethylbenzene	0	133	0	0	0	0	0	133
Acetone	0	2,334,192	0	0	49,621	71,752	202,626	2,658,191
Aluminum (fume or dust)	0	33,173	0	0	0	0	0	33,173
Aluminum oxide (fibrous forms)	0	391,777	0	0	501,042	0	0	892,819
Ammonia	0	129,420	20	15	460	145,955	1,685	277,555
Ammonium nitrate (solution)	0	0	0	0	2,600	120,592	0	123,192
Ammonium sulfate (solution)	0	0	0	0	0	478,659	0	478,659
Antimony	0	5	0	0	0	0	0	5
Antimony compounds	0	1,760	5	0	1,326,430	250	0	1,328,445
Arsenic compounds	0	15,786	5	0	977,997	250	7,820	1,001,858
Barium compounds	0	255	0	0	2,346,100	0	250	2,346,605
Benzene	0	9,273	0	0	0	5	0	9,278
Beryllium compounds	0	1	0	0	0	1	470	472
Bromomethane	0	44,100	0	0	0	0	0	44,100
C.I. solvent yellow 3	0	0	5	0	0	5	0	10
Cadmium compounds	0	2,652	3	0	104,219	250	0	107,124
Captan	0	6	0	0	0	0	0	6
Carbon disulfide	0	5	0	0	0	0	0	5
Catechol	0	25,000	0	0	19,352	500	6,800	51,652
Chlorine	0	34,731	0	0	0	510	0	35,241
Chlorine dioxide	0	5	5	5	5	0	0	20
Chloroform	0	0	0	0	31,015	0	0	31,015
Chromium	0	7	0	0	0	5	880	892
Chromium compounds	0	780	0	0	2,223,607	333	153,035	2,377,755
Cobalt	0	10	0	0	0	0	1,300	1,310
Cobalt compounds	0	0	0	0	153,200	0	0	153,200
Copper	0	1,402	0	0	10,145,815	881	23,624	10,171,722
Copper compounds	0	256,035	31	0	11,771,656	2,420	67,216	12,097,358
Creosote	0	2,400	0	0	0	0	0	2,400

[Continued]

★ 395 ★

Toxic Chemical Releases in Arizona, by Chemical: 1990

[Continued]

Chemical	Fugitive air	Stack air	Water	Injection	Land	Public treatment	Other offsite	Total releases
Cyanide compounds	0	6	0	0	0	23	30	59
Cyclohexane	0	250	0	0	0	5	0	255
Dibutyl phthalate	0	0	0	0	0	5	0	5
Dichloromethane	0	155,694	0	0	0	0	66,654	222,348
Ethylbenzene	0	11,034	0	0	0	5	510	11,549
Ethylene glycol	0	255	0	0	0	32,400	0	32,655
Ethylene oxide	0	15,400	0	0	0	0	0	15,400
Formaldehyde	0	250	0	0	0	26,000	5	26,255
Freon 113	0	281,925	0	0	0	260	53,397	335,582
Glycol ethers	0	193,307	0	0	5	165,830	3,156	362,298
Hydrochloric acid	0	173,910	20	10	47	2,340	4,460	180,787
Hydrogen fluoride	0	12,201	0	0	0	255	3,101	15,557
Isopropyl alcohol (manufacturing)	0	1,000	0	0	0	0	0	1,000
Lead	0	1,940	0	0	374,960	283	1,500	378,683
Lead compounds	0	61,466	21	0	2,794,950	300	3,533	2,860,270
Manganese	0	0	0	0	0	250	250	500
Manganese compounds	0	0	0	0	0	10	10	20
Methanol	0	1,184,296	0	0	2,242,905	12,719	30,187	3,470,107
Methyl ethyl ketone	0	293,914	0	0	0	0	196,023	489,937
Methyl isobutyl ketone	0	750	0	0	0	500	49,750	51,000
Methylenebis(phenylisocyanate)	0	5	0	0	0	0	0	5
N-butyl alcohol	0	72,913	0	0	0	0	0	72,913
Naphthalene	0	520	0	0	0	0	0	520
Nickel	0	2	0	0	0	250	270	522
Nickel compounds	0	168	17	0	1,114,775	500	500	1,115,960
Nitric acid	0	48,027	0	0	300	150,740	650	199,717
O-xylene	0	26	0	0	0	0	0	26
Parathion	0	21	0	0	0	0	0	21
Phenol	0	27,110	0	0	0	500	37,800	65,410
Phosphoric acid	0	3,406	0	0	5	27,260	250	30,921
Polychlorinated biphenyls (PCBs)	0	0	0	0	0	0	7,763	7,763
Selenium	0	250	0	0	171,033	0	0	171,283
Selenium compounds	0	0	0	0	28,800	0	0	28,800
Silver	0	250	0	0	250	0	0	500
Silver compounds	0	253	2	0	4,421	250	0	4,926
Styrene	0	162,377	0	0	0	0	0	162,377
Sulfuric acid	0	241,924	0	0	44,110	91,543	20,753	398,330
Tetrachloroethylene	0	19,250	0	0	0	5	2,241	21,496
Thiourea	0	0	0	0	0	750	0	750
Toluene	0	283,241	0	0	0	5	67,134	350,380
Trichloroethylene	0	37,800	0	0	0	0	16,700	54,500
Trifluralin	0	37	0	0	0	0	0	37
Xylene (mixed isomers)	0	229,168	0	0	0	530	14,457	244,155

[Continued]

★ 395 ★

Toxic Chemical Releases in Arizona, by Chemical: 1990
[Continued]

Chemical	Fugitive air	Stack air	Water	Injection	Land	Public treatment	Other offsite	Total releases
Zinc (fume or dust)	0	16,003	0	0	20,588	0	14,718	51,309
Zinc compounds	0	41,525	19	0	22,573,050	255	255	22,615,104

Source: U.S. Environmental Protection Agency. "Toxic Chemical Releases, 1990." In *National Economic, Social, and Environmental Data Bank* [CD-ROM]. Prepared by U.S. Department of Commerce, Economics and Statistics Administration. Washington, DC: U.S. Department of Commerce, National Economic, Social, and Environmental Data Bank, Economics and Statistics Administration, Office of Business Analysis, February 1995.

★ 396 ★

Chemicals

Toxic Chemical Releases in Arkansas, by Chemical: 1990

Figures indicate pounds released by chemical and by type of emission per year.

Chemical	Fugitive air	Stack air	Water	Injection	Land	Public treatment	Other offsite	Total releases
1,1,1-trichloroethane	0	1,458,571	61	0	0	250	155,835	1,614,717
1,2,4-trimethylbenzene	0	17,839	5	0	0	0	385	18,229
1,2-dibromoethane	0	14,204	0	255	0	0	13,980	28,439
1,2-dichlorobenzene	0	36,000	0	0	10	0	155,110	191,120
1,2-dichloroethane	0	38,000	0	4,800	0	0	2,100	44,900
2,4-dichlorophenol	0	250	0	0	0	0	0	250
2-nitropropane	0	5	0	0	0	0	5,600	5,605
4,4'-methylenedianiline	0	251	0	0	0	0	2,400	2,651
Acetone	0	1,896,628	32,606	0	1,049	5	135,388	2,065,676
Acetonitrile	0	240	81	0	0	0	0	321
Acrylamide	0	250	0	0	0	0	0	250
Acrylic acid	0	250	750	0	0	0	0	1,000
Allyl alcohol	0	250	750	0	0	0	0	1,000
Allyl chloride	0	500	10	0	0	0	0	510
Aluminum (fume or dust)	0	73,703	250	0	1,586	0	6,847	82,386
Aluminum oxide (fibrous forms)	0	969	15	5	20	0	0	1,009
Ammonia	0	3,206,355	1,999,248	7,240,000	7,005	856,370	8,264	13,317,242
Ammonium nitrate (solution)	0	0	90,250	0	437	552,160	0	642,847
Ammonium sulfate (solution)	0	0	348,000	0	0	0	0	348,000
Anthracene	0	200	0	0	0	0	0	200
Antimony	0	38	3	0	0	5	316	362
Antimony compounds	0	255	5	0	250	5	10,296	10,811
Arsenic	0	8	1	0	5	0	10	24
Arsenic compounds	0	785	0	0	5	0	1,218	2,008
Asbestos (friable)	0	250	250	0	111,000	250	0	111,750
Barium	0	250	0	0	0	0	2,382	2,632
Barium compounds	0	8,518	15	0	1,502	0	93	10,128
Benzene	0	12,152	24	0	2	0	0	12,178
Biphenyl	0	0	0	0	0	9,426	0	9,426
Bromoform	0	0	0	0	72,000	0	0	72,000
Bromomethane	0	137,283	0	28,000	0	552,160	172	717,615
Butyl benzyl phthalate	0	5	0	0	0	0	0	5
Cadmium	0	5	0	0	0	5	5	15
Captan	0	0	0	0	0	0	500	500

[Continued]

★ 396 ★

Toxic Chemical Releases in Arkansas, by Chemical: 1990

[Continued]

Chemical	Fugitive air	Stack air	Water	Injection	Land	Public treatment	Other offsite	Total releases
Carbon disulfide	0	1,675,945	1,305	0	0	0	0	1,677,250
Carbon tetrachloride	0	30,200	0	120	0	0	2,700	33,020
Carbonyl sulfide	0	109,780	0	0	0	0	0	109,780
Catechol	0	5	5,315	0	1,132	0	0	6,452
Chlorine	0	160,921	2,200	0	24,000	17,155	1,005	205,281
Chlorine dioxide	0	114,100	0	0	0	0	0	114,100
Chlorobenzene	0	585	20	0	20	0	3,600	4,225
Chloroethane	0	250	0	0	0	0	0	250
Chloroform	0	139,400	6,955	10	1,305	0	0	147,670
Chloromethane	0	33,700	0	0	0	0	0	33,700
Chlorothalonil	0	14	0	0	0	40	88	142
Chromium	0	1,760	257	0	6,212	671	82,862	91,762
Chromium compounds	0	1,806	1,900	0	1,690,612	358	42,693	1,737,369
Cobalt	0	0	0	0	0	0	10,338	10,338
Copper	0	11,881	1,212	0	152,908	2,051	99,256	267,308
Copper compounds	0	1,934	754	0	5	273	1,412	4,378
Creosote	0	4,979	20	0	472	3	4,914	10,388
Cumene	0	755	0	0	0	0	0	755
Cyanide compounds	0	1,117	0	0	0	250	1,430	2,797
Cyclohexane	0	6,056	18,358	0	0	0	0	24,414
Decabromodiphenyl oxide	0	21,010	5	0	750	5	229,602	251,372
Di(2-ethylhexyl) phthalate	0	27,158	0	0	0	0	63,241	90,399
Dibutyl phthalate	0	266	0	0	0	0	250	516
Dichloromethane	0	1,212,658	1,635	372,528	20	10	73,885	1,660,736
Diethanolamine	0	250	750	0	0	0	0	1,000
Dimethyl phthalate	0	2,723	0	0	0	0	1,597	4,320
Epichlorohydrin	0	431	250	0	0	0	0	681
Ethylbenzene	0	82,996	10	0	250	0	6,753	90,009
Ethylene	0	76,809	0	0	0	0	0	76,809
Ethylene glycol	0	10,113	41,134	5	473	22,649	50,688	125,062
Ethylene oxide	0	110,000	0	0	0	0	0	110,000
Fluometuron	0	9	0	0	0	33	92	134
Formaldehyde	0	206,743	3,405	0	5	1,850	34,173	246,176
Freon 113	0	212,199	15	5	20	5	5,118	217,362
Glycol ethers	0	242,073	5	0	0	10	118,712	360,800
Hydrochloric acid	0	492,647	15	9,939,019	385	7,800	201,920	10,641,786
Hydrogen fluoride	0	300	0	0	0	0	160	460
Hydroquinone	0	0	60	0	0	0	0	60
Isobutyraldehyde	0	320	5	0	0	0	0	325
Isopropyl alcohol (manufacturing)	0	29,015	0	0	0	0	26,241	55,256
Lead	0	6,009	0	0	167,729	0	77,762	251,500
Lead compounds	0	2,090	1,288	0	268	267	343,458	347,371
M-xylene	0	61	5	0	0	0	183	249
Maleic anhydride	0	0	0	0	0	0	1,243	1,243
Manganese	0	2,970	0	0	250	250	13,051	16,521
Manganese compounds	0	2,943	2,033	0	1,092	301	380,005	386,374
Methanol	0	1,921,052	1,210	0	24,385	255	1,100,912	3,047,814
Methyl acrylate	0	2,150	5	0	0	0	0	2,155
Methyl ethyl ketone	0	1,928,383	255	0	250	5	411,946	2,340,839
Methyl isobutyl ketone	0	513,039	5	0	0	10	48,926	561,980
Methyl methacrylate	0	13,784	5	0	0	0	3	13,792
Methylene bromide	0	750	0	0	0	0	0	750

[Continued]

★ 396 ★

Toxic Chemical Releases in Arkansas, by Chemical: 1990

[Continued]

Chemical	Fugitive air	Stack air	Water	Injection	Land	Public treatment	Other offsite	Total releases
Methylenebis(phenylisocyanate)	0	14,255	0	0	0	0	7,350	21,605
N-butyl alcohol	0	144,225	10	0	0	5	19,544	163,784
Naphthalene	0	255	0	0	0	0	0	255
Nickel	0	756	5	0	0	1,000	10,812	12,573
Nickel compounds	0	8	950	0	1,054,001	256	29,250	1,084,465
Nitric acid	0	24,500	10	0	0	0	250	24,760
O-xylene	0	37	5	0	0	0	88	130
Pentachlorophenol	0	0	610	0	250	0	3,886	4,746
Phenol	0	4,633	1,937	7,250	0	0	4,541	18,361
Phosphoric acid	0	14,610	274	0	45	117,698	733	133,360
Phosphorus (yellow or white)	0	5	5	0	0	5	0	15
Phthalic anhydride	0	16,505	0	0	0	0	8,239	24,744
Propylene	0	6,533	0	0	0	0	0	6,533
Propylene oxide	0	3,650	0	0	0	0	0	3,650
Quintozene	0	0	0	0	0	0	255	255
Styrene	0	97,490	0	0	500	255	730,621	828,866
Sulfuric acid	0	160,765	15	2,956,792	17,083	8,380	164,425	3,307,460
Tert-butyl alcohol	0	9,900	0	0	0	0	0	9,900
Tetrachloroethylene	0	54,016	0	0	0	0	64,943	118,959
Titanium tetrachloride	0	75	0	0	0	0	0	75
Toluene	0	2,559,772	45	4,970	520	10	567,385	3,132,702
Toluenediisocyanate (mixed isomers)	0	291	0	0	0	0	0	291
Toluene-2,4-diisocyanate	0	250	0	0	0	0	0	250
Toluene-2,6-diisocyanate	0	250	0	0	0	0	0	250
Trichloroethylene	0	327,374	0	0	0	0	58,294	385,668
Trifluralin	0	61	0	0	0	50	45	156
Vinyl bromide	0	5	0	0	0	0	0	5
Xylene (mixed isomers)	0	2,186,877	520	0	315	255	154,508	2,342,475
Zinc (fume or dust)	0	2,487	490	0	114,994	470	6,276	124,717
Zinc compounds	0	38,779	40,029	250	4,839	3,179	1,975,374	2,062,450

Source: U.S. Environmental Protection Agency. "Toxic Chemical Releases, 1990." In *National Economic, Social, and Environmental Data Bank* [CD-ROM]. Prepared by U.S. Department of Commerce, Economics and Statistics Administration. Washington, DC: U.S. Department of Commerce, National Economic, Social, and Environmental Data Bank, Economics and Statistics Administration, Office of Business Analysis, February 1995.

★ 397 ★

Chemicals

Toxic Chemical Releases in California, by Chemical: 1990

Figures indicate pounds released by chemical and by type of emission per year.

Chemical	Fugitive air	Stack air	Water	Injection	Land	Public treatment	Other offsite	Total releases
1,1,1-trichloroethane	9,989,808	12,973,297	127	15	17,294	19,176	1,002,403	24,002,120
1,1-dimethyl hydrazine	5	306	0	0	0	0	8,400	8,711
1,2,4-trichlorobenzene	86	4,984	0	0	0	1,153	67	6,290
1,2,4-trimethylbenzene	116,208	26,064	206	76	678	720	55,610	199,562
1,2-butylene oxide	750	1,675	0	0	0	0	7,930	10,355
1,2-dibromoethane	1,022	505	0	0	0	250	5	1,782
1,2-dichlorobenzene	500	5,800	0	0	0	0	41,900	48,200
1,2-dichloroethane	1,901	1,550	87	0	0	251	1,000	4,789

[Continued]

★ 397 ★

Toxic Chemical Releases in California, by Chemical: 1990
[Continued]

Chemical	Fugitive air	Stack air	Water	Injection	Land	Public treatment	Other offsite	Total releases
1,2-dichloropropane	10	42	190	0	0	2	0	244
1,3-butadiene	6,790	1,287	0	0	0	0	348	8,425
1,3-dichloropropylene	311	550	0	0	0	0	513	1,374
1,4-dichlorobenzene	5	5	0	0	0	0	0	10
1,4-dioxane	2,613	16,793	0	0	0	145,862	483	165,751
2,4-d	250	0	0	0	0	0	0	250
2-ethoxyethanol	12,017	10,560	0	0	0	9	100,364	122,950
2-methoxyethanol	25,936	99,231	5	0	0	2,341	6,300	133,813
2-phenylphenol	260	10	5	5	510	255	500	1,545
4,4'-isopropylidenediphenol	310	500	0	0	0	15	2,786	3,611
4,4'-methylenebis(2-chloro aniline)	0	0	0	0	0	0	5	5
4,4'-methylenedianiline	3	250	0	0	0	150	4,377	4,780
4,6-dinitro-o-cresol	1	0	0	0	0	0	0	1
Acetaldehyde	1,000	15,970	0	0	0	43,180	0	60,150
Acetone	2,085,775	1,326,090	89,214	15	40	161,267	576,816	4,239,217
Acetonitrile	255	255	0	0	0	5	4,812	5,327
Acrylamide	276	277	0	0	0	1	22,583	23,137
Acrylic acid	15	21	0	0	0	251	460	747
Acrylonitrile	2,115	64	0	0	0	6	2,282	4,467
Allyl alcohol	110	0	0	0	0	0	395	505
Aluminum (fume or dust)	4,877	14,711	5	0	55,790	5	30,669	106,057
Aluminum oxide (fibrous forms)	14,756	131,500	0	0	0	1,285	766,018	913,559
Ammonia	2,190,994	7,161,938	1,508,822	1,738,327	426,653	13,705,501	695,558	27,427,793
Ammonium nitrate (solution)	580	6,770	420	5	2,305,585	1,670,766	0	3,984,126
Ammonium sulfate (solution)	1,260	7,545	0	0	1,301,042	1,454,802	194,950	2,959,599
Anthracene	0	1,000	0	0	0	250	0	1,250
Antimony	427	1,765	5	0	0	8,354	59,819	70,370
Antimony compounds	4,185	308	5	0	25	479	21,192	26,194
Arsenic	96	515	13	0	0	734	18,535	19,893
Arsenic compounds	277	796	18	0	1,052	70	5,053	7,266
Asbestos (friable)	1,010	1,020	0	0	0	0	1,611,211	1,613,241
Barium	4,281	0	0	0	4,281	10	11,572	20,144
Barium compounds	8,195	3,485	6	0	55,453	1,818	183,584	252,541
Benzene	170,859	146,129	318	4,158	403	59,094	19,564	400,525
Benzoyl chloride	5	5	0	0	0	5	0	15
Benzoyl peroxide	15	5	0	0	0	43,200	189	43,409
Benzyl chloride	5	5	0	0	0	5	250	265
Bis(2-ethylhexyl) adipate	505	8,945	0	0	0	500	8,262	18,212
Bromomethane	20,322	17,877	0	0	0	0	0	38,199
Butyl acrylate	7,438	23,740	0	0	0	979	826	32,983
Butyl benzyl phthalate	4,883	1,010	0	0	250	11,755	20	17,918
Cadmium	15	5	260	5	265	617	9	1,176
Cadmium compounds	5	56	0	0	0	306	5,950	6,317
Captan	0	0	0	0	0	0	250	250
Carbaryl	1	47	0	0	0	0	948	996
Carbon disulfide	2,305	1,550	0	0	0	0	0	3,855
Carbon tetrachloride	26,183	28,824	0	0	0	0	13,505	68,512
Carbonyl sulfide	0	305,000	0	0	0	0	0	305,000
Catechol	15	15	39,460	0	0	0	260	39,750
Chlorine	58,836	529,848	8,398	20	42,788	57,231	43,450	740,571
Chlorine dioxide	3,551	220,753	755	5	5	500	0	225,569
Chloroacetic acid	250	0	0	0	0	250	5	505
Chlorobenzene	130	3,610	0	0	0	0	2	3,742
Chloroethane	90,000	95,000	0	0	0	0	0	185,000
Chloroform	104,964	242,024	90,720	0	0	9	830	438,547
Chloromethane	20,291	885	0	0	0	0	28,740	49,916
Chromium	5,757	5,246	7,045	5	8,821	14,599	199,415	240,888
Chromium compounds	7,129	3,963	30,358	0	88,509	11,455	628,211	769,625
Cobalt	148	20	1	0	250	48	2,207	2,674

[Continued]

★ 397 ★

Toxic Chemical Releases in California, by Chemical: 1990

[Continued]

Chemical	Fugitive air	Stack air	Water	Injection	Land	Public treatment	Other offsite	Total releases
Cobalt compounds	916	6	0	0	0	945	7,626	9,493
Copper	12,186	9,936	1,499	30	850	13,044	644,481	682,026
Copper compounds	4,320	4,222	838	0	1,593	16,614	636,489	664,076
Creosote	6,787	21,074	25	0	0	2,800	13,030	43,716
Cresol (mixed isomers)	8,350	1,022	630	0	268	13,312	29,198	52,780
Cumene	4,140	1,275	0	0	86	250	5,649	11,400
Cumene hydroperoxide	12	507	0	0	0	0	0	519
Cyanide compounds	270	311	0	0	5	2,336	6,905	9,827
Cyclohexane	235,563	58,531	55	231	62	1,358	39,727	335,527
Decabromodiphenyl oxide	750	95	0	0	0	0	1,500	2,345
Di(2-ethylhexyl) phthalate	6,921	3,306	0	0	0	256	114,916	125,399
Diaminotoluene (mixed isomers)	2	0	0	0	0	80	5	87
Dibutyl phthalate	260	10	0	0	0	0	0	270
Dichlorobenzene (mixed isomers)	16,000	0	0	0	0	0	5	16,005
Dichloromethane	2,296,822	3,531,617	5	10	3,819	4,029	679,401	6,515,703
Dichlorvos	5	0	0	0	0	5	20	30
Dicofol	0	0	0	0	0	0	36	36
Diethanolamine	1,091	286	5	5	1,760	1,954,692	1,277	1,959,116
Diethyl phthalate	1,200	0	0	0	0	520	0	1,720
Dimethyl phthalate	3,735	4,432	0	0	0	170	2,122	10,459
Dimethyl sulfate	2,564	0	0	0	0	0	0	2,564
Epichlorohydrin	15	129	0	0	0	5	0	149
Ethyl acrylate	540	397	0	5	20	257	511	1,730
Ethylbenzene	101,848	41,886	293	325	267	5,399	46,447	196,465
Ethylene	113,531	42,681	0	0	0	0	1	156,213
Ethylene glycol	109,734	53,751	255	0	255	563,809	238,492	966,296
Ethylene oxide	30,276	8,453	0	0	0	0	0	38,729
Formaldehyde	60,287	328,716	25	5	2,270	75,470	20,066	486,839
Freon 113	3,328,191	1,684,089	302	0	750	2,357	169,965	5,185,654
Glycol ethers	908,978	1,430,906	15	10	1,829	510,008	136,966	2,988,712
Hexachlorobenzene	0	2	0	0	0	0	13,330	13,332
Hexachloroethane	8	79	0	0	0	0	0	87
Hydrazine	255	250	0	0	0	5	8,400	8,910
Hydrochloric acid	475,359	740,606	430,884	13,869	268	33,615	1,293,234	2,987,835
Hydrogen cyanide	250	72,200	0	0	0	0	0	72,450
Hydrogen fluoride	7,215	21,360	5	0	5,172	17,507	108,077	159,336
Hydroquinone	261	95	515	5	285	753	312	2,226
Isopropyl alcohol (manufacturing)	103,835	131,590	5	0	0	863	57,080	293,373
Lead	13,098	57,056	405	0	0	2,520	1,253,253	1,326,332
Lead compounds	8,114	15,387	488	0	63,107	5,974	1,045,261	1,138,331
M-cresol	34	27	0	0	0	0	0	61
M-xylene	33,886	9,456	289	0	44	3	43,243	86,921
Maleic anhydride	1,394	1,188	0	0	0	270	6,200	9,052
Manganese	4,159	2,446	13,704	10	54	4,181	39,320	63,874
Manganese compounds	4,517	2,577	4,406	0	226,528	1,945	672,502	912,475
Mercury compounds	5	5	0	0	0	8	500	518
Methanol	876,770	5,471,623	8,614,713	5	15,856	8,606,711	419,180	24,004,858
Methyl acrylate	57	250	0	0	0	65	0	372
Methyl ethyl ketone	796,157	1,733,259	6	5	1,363	4,213	436,186	2,971,189
Methyl hydrazine	1	0	0	0	0	0	0	1
Methyl isobutyl ketone	339,877	357,862	5	5	928	359,715	113,189	1,171,581
Methyl methacrylate	24,992	9,428	251	5	20	268	22,706	57,670
Methyl tert-butyl ether	22,813	18,301	8,194	0	0	51,237	363	100,908
Methylenebis(phenylisocyanate)	47,366	1,354	0	0	0	1	7,569	56,290
Molybdenum trioxide	585	265	0	0	250	10,900	48,613	60,613
N-butyl alcohol	706,581	1,039,531	0	0	0	1,361	44,303	1,791,776
N-dioctyl phthalate	15	5	0	0	0	0	0	20
Naphthalene	39,070	7,369	57	0	216	1,139	38,863	86,714
Nickel	7,607	5,031	1,159	5	23,857	6,878	104,755	149,292

[Continued]

★ 397 ★

Toxic Chemical Releases in California, by Chemical: 1990
[Continued]

Chemical	Fugitive air	Stack air	Water	Injection	Land	Public treatment	Other offsite	Total releases
Nickel compounds	2,751	3,790	2,437	0	470	8,991	243,320	261,759
Nitric acid	29,069	65,544	85	20	2,955	108,169	653,555	859,397
Nitrilotriacetic acid	5	250	0	0	0	250	0	505
Nitroglycerin	0	5	0	0	0	0	0	5
O-cresol	1,003	1,000	0	0	250	8,115	14,510	24,878
O-xylene	24,000	5,240	156	0	26	2	29,981	59,405
P-cresol	1,039	750	0	0	250	13,911	0	15,950
P-xylene	14,693	4,645	135	0	21	1	20,762	40,257
Parathion	9	4	0	0	0	0	40	53
Pentachlorophenol	7	24	0	0	0	3,400	268	3,699
Phenol	65,397	419,003	3,594	5	810	911,306	70,289	1,470,404
Phosphoric acid	6,589	12,408	265	10	35,484	437,437	159,814	652,007
Phthalic anhydride	1,519	2,384	0	0	0	16	5,932	9,851
Polychlorinated biphenyls (PCBs)	0	0	0	0	58,178	0	58,178	116,356
Propylene	462,650	56,572	0	0	250	1,340	500	521,312
Propylene oxide	12,623	86,247	0	0	0	2,200	0	101,070
Sec-butyl alcohol	6,355	1,055	0	0	0	5	845	8,260
Selenium compounds	0	0	0	0	0	0	250	250
Silver	1,331	5	0	0	0	1	0	1,337
Silver compounds	35	48	0	0	0	4	18,000	18,087
Styrene	917,798	1,415,165	5	0	1,470	2,162	338,358	2,674,958
Sulfuric acid	81,160	133,021	220,660	300	220,326	597,489	1,232,629	2,485,585
Tert-butyl alcohol	750	1,000	0	0	0	0	0	1,750
Tetrachloroethylene	1,449,882	2,268,134	0	0	960	1,921	76,289	3,797,186
Thiourea	1,010	10	0	0	0	4,705	100	5,825
Titanium tetrachloride	1,250	100	0	0	0	0	0	1,350
Toluene	1,416,654	1,278,646	329	11,458	1,433	66,109	1,000,517	3,775,146
Toluenediisocyanate (mixed isomers)	2,780	1,484	0	0	5	0	500	4,769
Toluene-2,4-diisocyanate	1,053	4,347	0	0	0	0	3,130	8,530
Toluene-2,6-diisocyanate	262	1,372	0	0	0	0	500	2,134
Trichloroethylene	22,245	41,650	15	0	0	230	17,665	81,805
Urethane	250	0	0	0	250	0	500	1,000
Vanadium (fume or dust)	0	250	0	0	0	0	8,082	8,332
Vinyl acetate	19,690	23,413	0	0	0	11,698	736	55,537
Vinyl chloride	50	770	0	0	0	5	0	825
Xylene (mixed isomers)	843,224	1,405,018	394	317	60,663	46,074	679,912	3,035,602
Zinc (fume or dust)	6,634	12,521	35	10	30	1,929	81,501	102,660
Zinc compounds	7,450	23,468	2,656	0	62,042	24,054	6,327,122	6,446,792

Source: U.S. Environmental Protection Agency. "Toxic Chemical Releases, 1990." In *National Economic, Social, and Environmental Data Bank* [CD-ROM]. Prepared by U.S. Department of Commerce, Economics and Statistics Administration. Washington, DC: U.S. Department of Commerce, National Economic, Social, and Environmental Data Bank, Economics and Statistics Administration, Office of Business Analysis, February 1995.

★ 398 ★
Chemicals

Toxic Chemical Releases in Colorado, by Chemical: 1990

Figures indicate pounds released by chemical and by type of emission per year.

Chemical	Fugitive air	Stack air	Water	Injection	Land	Public treatment	Other offsite	Total releases
1,1,1-trichloroethane	811,748	205,262	5	0	0	27	114,532	1,131,574
1,1,2,2-tetrachloroethane	10,000	0	0	0	0	0	0	10,000
1,2,4-trimethylbenzene	33,210	1,966	3	0	260	77	2,550	38,066
1,2-dichlorobenzene	250	250	0	0	0	0	0	500
1,2-dichloroethane	360	22,000	2	0	0	0	860,260	882,622
1,3-butadiene	200	300	0	0	0	0	0	500
2-methoxyethanol	2,900	0	0	0	0	0	0	2,900
Acetone	123,784	325,993	0	0	0	21,473	142,450	613,700
Aluminum (fume or dust)	250	1,999	0	0	0	0	250	2,499
Ammonia	42,661	125,455	120,034	0	12,466	102,756	20,040	423,412
Ammonium sulfate (solution)	0	0	0	0	0	0	1,000	1,000
Antimony	500	250	0	0	0	250	20,288	21,288
Arsenic	0	0	0	0	0	1	57,130	57,131
Arsenic compounds	0	0	0	0	0	0	250	250
Barium compounds	252	13	0	0	0	0	40,844	41,109
Benzene	7,561	25,646	3	0	1,776	46	235	35,267
Benzoyl peroxide	8	0	0	0	0	0	810	818
Butyl benzyl phthalate	0	0	0	0	0	250	750	1,000
Cadmium	0	250	0	0	0	5	500	755
Cadmium compounds	5	391	0	0	250	2	0	648
Captan	250	5	0	0	0	0	10,134	10,389
Carbaryl	5	5	0	0	0	0	500	510
Carbon tetrachloride	5	250	0	0	0	250	3,205	3,710
Chlorine	3,394	355	26	0	0	250	0	4,025
Chlorobenzene	0	50	0	0	0	0	0	50
Chloroform	250	250	0	0	0	250	12,043	12,793
Chloromethane	250	750	0	0	0	0	0	1,000
Chromium	3,850	425	5	0	110,561	10	1,258	116,109
Chromium compounds	577	795	82	0	0	79	48,676	50,209
Cobalt	250	0	0	0	0	0	250	500
Copper	801	606	0	5	2,910	811	76,482	81,615
Copper compounds	12	755	850	0	0	610	21,800	24,027
Creosote	2,342	2,668	0	0	335	58	224,106	229,509
Cumene	1,900	14	3	0	0	0	410	2,327
Cyanide compounds	5	5	0	5	5	251	2,450	2,721
Cyclohexane	5,851	14,766	3	0	1,051	0	196	21,867
Dibutyl phthalate	0	0	40	0	0	0	0	40
Dichloromethane	84,523	115,529	6	0	0	251	111,566	311,875
Ethylbenzene	3,540	2,271	3	0	505	47	410	6,776
Ethylene	10,140	0	0	0	0	0	0	10,140
Ethylene glycol	183,981	28	52,319	0	119,188	131,250	412,809	899,575
Ethylene oxide	10	9,449	0	0	0	15,743	0	25,202
Formaldehyde	0	183,314	0	0	0	200	0	183,514
Freon 113	552,254	410,765	0	0	0	751	97,089	1,060,859
Glycol ethers	228,916	396,610	0	0	1,195	17,255	22,159	666,135

[Continued]

★ 398 ★

Toxic Chemical Releases in Colorado, by Chemical: 1990
[Continued]

Chemical	Fugitive air	Stack air	Water	Injection	Land	Public treatment	Other offsite	Total releases
Hydrochloric acid	5,362	13,164	250	5	41,355	58,263	80,153	198,552
Hydrogen fluoride	501	2,063	0	0	0	5	1	2,570
Isopropyl alcohol (manufacturing)	0	0	0	0	0	0	1,000	1,000
Lead	968	1,627	0	0	19,119	289	5,935	27,938
Lead compounds	1	326	110	0	250	0	440	1,127
Lindane	250	5	0	0	0	0	2,291	2,546
M-xylene	1,300	2,300	0	0	0	0	0	3,600
Maleic anhydride	5	0	0	0	0	0	0	5
Manganese	2,075	7,039	5	255	10,961	73	44,999	65,407
Manganese compounds	1,039	256	24	0	2,150	0	85	3,554
Methanol	99,858	578,049	40	0	0	48,400	155,084	881,431
Methoxychlor	250	250	0	0	0	0	1,005	1,505
Methyl acrylate	0	80	0	0	0	0	0	80
Methyl ethyl ketone	45,683	234,514	250	0	0	0	44,162	324,609
Methyl isobutyl ketone	250	14,288	0	0	0	0	0	14,538
Methyl tert-butyl ether	700	16,200	1,043	0	0	0	0	17,943
Methylenebis(phenylisocyanate)	322	418	10	0	0	0	34,674	35,424
N-butyl alcohol	251,005	404,713	0	0	0	0	3,362	659,080
Naphthalene	1,100	72	5	0	0	0	2,700	3,877
Nickel	1,041	280	5	5	6,108	366	60,603	68,408
Nickel compounds	24	0	740	0	0	0	850	1,614
Nitric acid	817	11,750	45	0	850	33,601	0	47,063
O-xylene	560	1,100	0	0	0	0	0	1,660
P-xylene	500	920	0	0	0	0	0	1,420
Parathion	250	250	0	0	0	0	18,866	19,366
Phosphoric acid	1,625	2,357	0	0	72,519	120,081	77,830	274,412
Phosphorus (yellow or white)	500	0	0	0	0	0	250	750
Propylene	24,332	655	0	0	0	0	0	24,987
Propylene oxide	0	36	0	0	0	0	0	36
Selenium compounds	16	0	0	0	0	0	58	74
Silver compounds	0	0	30	0	200	0	0	230
Styrene	33,436	6,270	0	0	0	0	13,150	52,856
Sulfuric acid	4,349	6,782	0	5	485	120,097	59,440	191,158
Tetrachloroethylene	191,943	79,655	0	0	0	44	27,135	298,777
Toluene	171,419	389,944	8	0	2,681	3,040	61,639	628,731
Toluenediisocyanate (mixed isomers)	255	250	0	0	0	0	1,570	2,075
Trichloroethylene	14,327	500	0	0	0	18	43,223	58,068
Vanadium (fume or dust)	250	0	0	0	0	0	250	500
Vinylidene chloride	0	670	20	0	0	0	0	690
Xylene (mixed isomers)	41,304	64,763	3	0	2,296	250	26,453	135,069
Zinc (fume or dust)	250	0	0	0	0	0	60,250	60,500
Zinc compounds	4,266	16,563	0	0	68,535	504	230,563	320,431

Source: U.S. Environmental Protection Agency. "Toxic Chemical Releases, 1990." In National Economic, Social, and Environmental Data Bank [CD-ROM]. Prepared by U.S. Department of Commerce, Economics and Statistics Administration. Washington, DC: U.S. Department of Commerce, National Economic, Social, and Environmental Data Bank, Economics and Statistics Administration, Office of Business Analysis, February 1995.

★ 399 ★
Chemicals

Toxic Chemical Releases in Connecticut, by Chemical: 1990

Figures indicate pounds released by chemical and by type of emission per year.

Chemical	Fugitive air	Stack air	Water	Injection	Land	Public treatment	Other offsite	Total releases
1,1,1-trichloroethane	4,121,299	3,083,015	1,647	0	0	1,636	558,774	7,766,371
1,2,4-trimethylbenzene	3,402	3	0	0	0	0	10,780	14,185
1,3-butadiene	1,300	57,000	0	0	0	0	20,000	78,300
1,4-dioxane	5	120	0	0	0	0	0	125
2-ethoxyethanol	500	8,650	0	0	0	0	3,750	12,900
2-methoxyethanol	0	0	0	0	0	0	2,000	2,000
4,4'-isopropylidenediphenol	5	250	0	0	0	0	1,000	1,255
4,4'-methylenedianiline	250	250	0	0	0	1,409	1,140	3,049
Acetaldehyde	590	9	0	0	0	671	0	1,270
Acetone	184,340	222,820	400,000	0	5	379,319	612,244	1,798,728
Acetonitrile	421	190	0	0	0	6,541	1,665	8,817
Acrylamide	255	255	796	0	0	0	1,621	2,927
Acrylic acid	764	5,597	250	0	0	0	9,437	16,048
Acrylonitrile	5,001	1,705	217	0	0	0	30,190	37,113
Aluminum (fume or dust)	480	190	0	0	0	0	58	728
Aluminum oxide (fibrous forms)	1,000	250	5	0	0	0	107,553	108,808
Ammonia	102,417	265,836	427,405	0	0	67,097	12,913	875,668
Ammonium nitrate (solution)	0	0	250	0	0	0	0	250
Ammonium sulfate (solution)	0	0	1,000	0	0	42,015	250	43,265
Aniline	10,271	250	0	0	0	97,791	996	109,308
Anthracene	5	250	0	0	0	0	250	505
Antimony compounds	257	505	0	0	0	8	29,855	30,625
Asbestos (friable)	0	750	0	0	0	0	250	1,000
Barium compounds	256	501	32	0	41	11	167,516	168,357
Benzene	4,600	5,400	110	0	0	0	5,803	15,913
Benzoyl chloride	150	4	0	0	0	0	46	200
Benzoyl peroxide	0	0	0	0	0	0	250	250
Bis(2-ethylhexyl) adipate	0	0	0	0	0	0	400	400
Butyl acrylate	255	255	0	0	5	750	750	2,015
Cadmium	110	636	7	0	0	0	2	755
Cadmium compounds	8	263	0	0	0	252	6,423	6,946
Captan	1	29	0	0	0	0	2,202	2,232
Carbon disulfide	4,336	182,989	250	0	250	3,878	384	192,087
Chlorine	2,116	1,500	1,370	0	0	1,624	5	6,615
Chloroacetic acid	0	5	250	0	0	0	0	255
Chloroethane	64,755	99,255	250	0	0	5	0	164,265
Chloroform	3,200	10,000	750	0	0	0	35,000	48,950
Chloromethane	71,000	33,700	140,000	0	0	0	250	244,950
Chromium	2,207	1,626	482	0	0	40,672	109,015	154,002
Chromium compounds	1,581	2,412	1,330	0	27,551	950	123,909	157,733
Cobalt	131	252	65	0	0	5	1,611	2,064
Cobalt compounds	500	250	0	0	0	0	250	1,000
Copper	5,148	14,537	4,527	0	39,400	1,944	157,470	223,026
Copper compounds	5,140	1,351	949	0	407	1,960	122,760	132,567
Creosote	750	750	0	0	0	0	0	1,500
Cumene	170	330	0	0	0	0	114,014	114,514
Cyanide compounds	1,218	5,167	355	0	0	943	147,476	155,159
Decabromodiphenyl oxide	0	250	0	0	0	0	4,252	4,502
Di(2-ethylhexyl) phthalate	250	799	14	0	0	0	51,820	52,883
Dibutyl phthalate	0	0	0	0	0	5	2,244	2,249
Dichloromethane	761,200	1,419,445	120,052	0	11	250	345,227	2,646,185

[Continued]

★ 399 ★

Toxic Chemical Releases in Connecticut, by Chemical: 1990

[Continued]

Chemical	Fugitive air	Stack air	Water	Injection	Land	Public treatment	Other offsite	Total releases
Diethanolamine	410	325	0	0	0	34,102	327	35,164
Diethyl phthalate	0	1,737	0	0	0	0	6,500	8,237
Dimethyl phthalate	250	750	0	0	0	0	0	1,000
Ethyl acrylate	1,450	550	98	0	5	750	210	3,063
Ethylbenzene	5,660	13,677	15	0	0	15,800	124,077	159,229
Ethylene glycol	1,916	501	6,489	0	0	250	25,617	34,773
Ethylene oxide	2,760	34,440	0	0	0	12,072	0	49,272
Ethylene thiourea	5	5	0	0	0	0	500	510
Formaldehyde	63,861	126,477	310,913	0	0	61,593	22,960	585,804
Freon 113	1,041,354	404,244	0	0	0	0	132,050	1,577,648
Glycol ethers	89,282	228,289	5,010	0	5	203,169	165,916	691,671
Hydrazine	5	0	0	0	0	0	0	5
Hydrochloric acid	41,073	37,843	19,380	0	73	85,419	319,989	503,777
Hydrogen fluoride	808	6,510	5	0	0	0	30,540	37,863
Hydroquinone	0	0	0	0	0	27,823	6,911	34,734
Isopropyl alcohol (manufacturing)	505	7,300	0	0	0	0	0	7,805
Lead	1,296	2,567	1,262	0	770	505	34,687	41,087
Lead compounds	555	1,292	33	0	0	6	243,015	244,901
M-xylene	0	0	250	0	0	0	0	250
Maleic anhydride	291	1,021	0	0	0	0	1,000	2,312
Manganese	520	282	11	0	0	1,550	8,295	10,658
Manganese compounds	1,147	59	0	0	1,489	44	1,116	3,855
Methanol	327,253	460,772	2,082,517	0	5	32,771	797,526	3,700,844
Methyl acrylate	150	10	160	0	0	0	4	324
Methyl ethyl ketone	159,387	522,161	39	0	255	250	550,876	1,232,968
Methyl isobutyl ketone	11,681	69,441	11,000	0	5	5	24,593	116,725
Methyl methacrylate	31,652	38,203	104	0	5	33,500	8,562	112,026
Methylenebis(phenylisocyanate)	1,005	1,030	0	0	0	0	9,395	11,430
N,N-dimethylaniline	250	250	0	0	0	124,790	42,711	168,001
N-butyl alcohol	56,365	79,852	256,623	0	10	5	41,173	434,028
N-dioctyl phthalate	10	505	0	0	0	0	500	1,015
Naphthalene	785	364	37	0	0	0	6,044	7,230
Nickel	2,991	3,647	12,636	0	1,600	12,696	95,263	128,833
Nickel compounds	1,687	1,485	887	0	0	1,366	150,134	155,559
Nitric acid	12,143	69,578	265	0	5	21,642	1,547,793	1,651,426
Nitrobenzene	250	80	5	0	0	0	5,675	6,010
O-xylene	14,277	1,958	0	0	0	50,839	54,399	121,473
P-cresol	750	750	0	0	0	1,975	0	3,475
P-phenylenediamine	0	0	0	0	0	23,199	250	23,449
Phenol	2,096	5,613	0	0	0	53,098	82,768	143,575
Phosphoric acid	18,390	15,798	255	0	0	22,155	19,129	75,727
Phthalic anhydride	0	25	7	0	0	250	4,377	4,659
Propylene oxide	7,654	10,077	0	0	0	231,043	0	248,774
Sec-butyl alcohol	100	13,000	0	0	0	0	2,250	15,350
Silver	4	258	0	0	0	1	0	263
Silver compounds	11	256	0	0	5	0	250	522
Styrene	54,972	106,419	28	0	0	10	399,267	560,696
Sulfuric acid	21,532	53,455	65,514	0	47	32,601	643,535	816,684
Tetrachloroethylene	401,523	345,811	45	0	2	0	471,580	1,218,961
Toluene	212,393	676,616	120,139	0	5	304,707	1,471,031	2,784,891
Toluenediisocyanate (mixed isomers)	250	250	0	0	0	0	0	500
Trichloroethylene	130,879	59,188	148	0	0	0	15,075	205,290

[Continued]

★ 399 ★

Toxic Chemical Releases in Connecticut, by Chemical: 1990

[Continued]

Chemical	Fugitive air	Stack air	Water	Injection	Land	Public treatment	Other offsite	Total releases
Vinyl acetate	250	250	0	0	5	250	0	755
Xylene (mixed isomers)	72,006	143,105	294	0	255	74,755	186,799	477,214
Zinc (fume or dust)	10,077	10	254	0	28,500	0	141,338	180,179
Zinc compounds	3,380	16,956	15,341	0	65,026	2,907	431,737	535,347

Source: U.S. Environmental Protection Agency. "Toxic Chemical Releases, 1990." In *National Economic, Social, and Environmental Data Bank* [CD-ROM]. Prepared by U.S. Department of Commerce, Economics and Statistics Administration. Washington, DC: U.S. Department of Commerce, National Economic, Social, and Environmental Data Bank, Economics and Statistics Administration, Office of Business Analysis, February 1995.

★ 400 ★

Chemicals

Toxic Chemical Releases in Delaware, by Chemical: 1990

Figures indicate pounds released by chemical and by type of emission per year.

Chemical	Fugitive air	Stack air	Water	Injection	Land	Public treatment	Other offsite	Total releases
1,1,1-trichloroethane	45,250	3,727	0	0	0	0	7,373	56,350
1,2,4-trichlorobenzene	13,711	1,710	139	0	0	0	0	15,560
1,2,4-trimethylbenzene	3,602	4,177	567	0	9	7,985	36,889	53,229
1,2-dichlorobenzene	51,617	3,485	485	0	0	250	29,670	85,507
1,2-dichloroethane	0	0	8	0	0	0	0	8
1,2-dichloropropane	1,100	0	0	0	0	0	0	1,100
1,3-butadiene	21,657	28,098	0	0	0	0	0	49,755
1,3-dichlorobenzene	2,814	2,498	35	0	0	0	0	5,347
1,3-dichloropropylene	250	2,880	0	0	0	0	755	3,885
1,4-dichlorobenzene	46,144	22,785	362	0	0	0	5	69,296
2-methoxyethanol	4	120	70	0	0	0	0	194
4,4'-isopropylidenediphenol	5	1,831	3	0	42	3,848	0	5,729
Acetone	136,589	94,522	0	0	0	40,730	73,672	345,513
Acrylic acid	125	3	0	0	0	0	0	128
Acrylonitrile	1,345	9,327	0	0	0	1,603	5	12,280
Aluminum (fume or dust)	250	250	0	0	0	750	0	1,250
Ammonia	51,178	20,122	129,163	0	45	184,502	34,720	419,730
Ammonium sulfate (solution)	6	0	0	0	0	0	0	6
Aniline	505	20	5	0	0	51,550	0	52,080
Anthracene	250	250	0	0	0	0	250	750
Antimony	5	3	0	0	0	0	51	59
Antimony compounds	5	250	0	0	0	0	2,165	2,420
Benzene	38,767	34,825	556	0	340	0	111	74,599
Biphenyl	18,246	7,870	5	0	0	202,720	2,335	231,176
Bis(2-chloroethyl) ether	5	250	5	0	0	550	100	910
Butyl acrylate	321	190	0	0	0	42	1	554
Cadmium compounds	0	250	0	0	0	0	0	250
Carbon disulfide	17,000	19,400	0	0	0	0	0	36,400
Carbon tetrachloride	3,686	114,093	0	0	0	0	6,696	124,475

[Continued]

★ 400 ★

Toxic Chemical Releases in Delaware, by Chemical: 1990

[Continued]

Chemical	Fugitive air	Stack air	Water	Injection	Land	Public treatment	Other offsite	Total releases
Carbonyl sulfide	0	582,000	0	0	0	0	0	582,000
Chlorine	9,208	9,551	8,976	0	57,900	22,500	68	108,203
Chlorobenzene	63,390	15,771	126	0	0	0	0	79,287
Chromium	250	0	0	0	0	250	11	511
Chromium compounds	1,856	1,026	0	0	0	15,246	26,062	44,190
Copper	5	0	0	0	5	0	5	15
Copper compounds	250	4	0	0	0	0	0	254
Cumene	19	1,850	7	0	0	7,972	8,783	18,631
Cyclohexane	1,600	21	510	0	41	0	0	2,172
Decabromodiphenyl oxide	5	250	0	0	0	0	7,208	7,463
Di(2-ethylhexyl) phthalate	250	250	5	0	0	0	250	755
Dibenzofuran	250	250	0	0	0	0	250	750
Dichloromethane	41,523	135,290	5	0	0	143,096	2,961	322,875
Diethanolamine	1,700	0	170,000	0	9	0	0	171,709
Diethyl sulfate	5	112	5	0	0	134	2,470	2,726
Epichlorohydrin	3,700	3,400	0	0	0	46,000	0	53,100
Ethyl acrylate	367	899	0	0	0	208	0	1,474
Ethylbenzene	1,829	872	503	0	530	4,023	2,635	10,392
Ethylene	1,900	0	0	0	0	0	0	1,900
Ethylene glycol	111	1,245	1,094	0	9	22,402	1,522	26,383
Ethylene oxide	18,783	2,758	17	0	0	816	0	22,374
Formaldehyde	5,007	27	0	0	0	5	0	5,039
Freon 113	250	14,718	0	0	0	0	84	15,052
Glycol ethers	3,502	95,546	10	0	0	85,312	17	184,387
Hydrochloric acid	9,240	728,448	5	0	0	390	925,476	1,663,559
Hydrogen fluoride	1,500	590	0	0	0	0	0	2,090
Lead compounds	158	2,418	100	0	0	14	24	2,714
M-xylene	909	250	0	0	0	0	0	1,159
Manganese compounds	752	1,047	0	0	63,250	0	0	65,049
Mercury	312	45	16	0	0	0	8,112	8,485
Methanol	647,440	651,449	524	0	9	2,914,674	38,845	4,252,941
Methyl ethyl ketone	105,917	182,736	5	0	0	2,980	111,423	403,061
Methyl isobutyl ketone	8,800	35,570	0	0	0	160	0	44,530
Methyl methacrylate	1,544	4,434	0	0	0	285	9,988	16,251
Methyl tert-butyl ether	5,546	1,380	520	0	440	0	0	7,886
Methylenebis(phenylisocyanate)	5	5	0	0	0	0	760	770
N-butyl alcohol	18,021	126,570	0	0	0	0	16,043	160,634
Naphthalene	26,000	3,700	510	0	80	0	0	30,290
Nickel	500	3,280	18	0	0	21,097	29,658	54,553
Nickel compounds	250	5	0	0	5	18	7,800	8,078
Nitric acid	10	10	0	0	0	0	0	20
O-cresol	160	100	0	0	0	0	0	260
O-xylene	680	42	0	0	0	230	0	952
P-xylene	424	250	0	0	0	0	0	674
Phenol	253	10	335	0	0	396	30	1,024
Phosphoric acid	5	37,275	0	0	0	750	0	38,030

[Continued]

★ 400 ★

Toxic Chemical Releases in Delaware, by Chemical: 1990

[Continued]

Chemical	Fugitive air	Stack air	Water	Injection	Land	Public treatment	Other offsite	Total releases
Phosphorus (yellow or white)	1,037	0	0	0	0	0	0	1,037
Propylene	20,000	0	0	0	0	0	0	20,000
Propylene oxide	33	150	1	0	0	700	0	884
Selenium compounds	250	0	0	0	0	0	0	250
Styrene	6,959	29,676	0	0	0	177	1,357	38,169
Sulfuric acid	2,659	54,020	14,005	0	0	45,344	10,530	126,558
Tetrachloroethylene	545	25,980	5	0	0	290	31,202	58,022
Titanium tetrachloride	540	0	0	0	0	0	0	540
Toluene	89,972	140,655	648	0	974	145,805	119,024	497,078
Toluenediisocyanate (mixed isomers)	16	0	0	0	0	0	0	16
Trichloroethylene	82,000	330,000	0	0	0	0	1,600	413,600
Vinyl acetate	10,569	2,695	0	0	0	536	309	14,109
Vinyl chloride	28,583	129,508	42	0	2,211	0	3,130	163,474
Xylene (mixed isomers)	71,496	519,864	538	0	4,200	3,401	72,921	672,420
Zinc compounds	9,702	3,944	101,573	0	250	24,019	62,500	201,988

Source: U.S. Environmental Protection Agency. "Toxic Chemical Releases, 1990." In *National Economic, Social, and Environmental Data Bank* [CD-ROM]. Prepared by U.S. Department of Commerce, Economics and Statistics Administration. Washington, DC: U.S. Department of Commerce, National Economic, Social, and Environmental Data Bank, Economics and Statistics Administration, Office of Business Analysis, February 1995.

★ 401 ★

Chemicals

Toxic Chemical Releases in Florida, by Chemical: 1990

Figures indicate pounds released by chemical and by type of emission per year.

Chemical	Fugitive air	Stack air	Water	Injection	Land	Public treatment	Other offsite	Total releases
1,1,1-trichloroethane	1,255,022	667,706	0	366	0	260	90,007	2,013,361
1,1,2,2-tetrachloroethane	2	209	0	0	0	0	0	211
1,1,2-trichloroethane	3	313	0	0	0	0	0	316
1,2,4-trichlorobenzene	29	7,011	0	779	0	0	19,789	27,608
1,2,4-trimethylbenzene	37,510	339	0	0	0	250	938	39,037
1,2-dichlorobenzene	12	2,820	0	313	0	0	19,802	22,947
1,4-dichlorobenzene	5	5	0	5	20	0	0	35
2,4-d	0	0	0	0	10,412	0	0	10,412
2,4-dinitrotoluene	0	0	0	0	0	0	50	50
2-ethoxyethanol	250	0	0	0	0	0	0	250
2-phenylphenol	0	0	0	0	0	750	0	750
4,4'-isopropylidenediphenol	19	0	0	0	0	0	1,626	1,645
4,4'-methylenebis(2-chloro aniline)	750	0	0	0	0	0	0	750
Acetaldehyde	0	45,000	0	7,200	0	0	0	52,200
Acetone	4,572,976	852,922	22,385	68,789	280	683,709	529,946	6,731,007
Acrylamide	0	6	0	0	0	74	169	249
Acrylic acid	2	5,806	0	0	0	0	0	5,808
Acrylonitrile	25,769	41,909	0	43,070	0	0	50	110,798
Aluminum (fume or dust)	5	0	0	0	0	0	250	255
Aluminum oxide (fibrous forms)	250	0	0	0	0	0	5,500	5,750
Ammonia	7,706,427	5,228,695	2,216,803	119,625	3,237,812	106,313	188,558	18,804,233
Ammonium nitrate (solution)	750	201,850	238,935	14,000,000	398,235	0	475,053	15,314,823

[Continued]

★ 401 ★

Toxic Chemical Releases in Florida, by Chemical: 1990

[Continued]

Chemical	Fugitive air	Stack air	Water	Injection	Land	Public treatment	Other offsite	Total releases
Ammonium sulfate (solution)	0	0	228,560	0	500	0	750	229,810
Antimony	1	2	9	0	0	6	5	23
Antimony compounds	5	256	0	8	0	0	1,850	2,119
Arsenic	1	1	0	0	31,034	2	1,854	32,892
Arsenic compounds	45	1,280	0	0	11	0	8,851	10,187
Asbestos (friable)	255	255	0	0	0	0	61,121	61,631
Barium compounds	116	241	0	0	11,498	0	49,032	60,887
Biphenyl	39,328	902	0	10,000	0	36,802	20	87,052
Bromomethane	500	5,462	0	0	0	0	0	5,962
Cadmium	0	0	0	0	250	0	40,061	40,311
Cadmium compounds	2	33	13	0	0	0	130,011	130,059
Catechol	10	5	10,010	0	266	34,848	5,361	50,500
Chlorine	247,220	340,177	1,257	0	267	11,560	0	600,481
Chlorine dioxide	203,412	147,800	0	0	0	5	0	351,217
Chloroacetic acid	250	0	0	0	0	0	250	500
Chloroform	333,562	599,000	18,300	0	11	53,983	100	1,004,956
Chloroprene	250	250	0	0	0	0	0	500
Chlorothalonil	5	12	0	0	0	2	145	164
Chromium	37,604	5	0	0	67	1	10,767	48,444
Chromium compounds	869	5,172	0	0	76,680	255	56,823	139,799
Cobalt	5	0	0	0	0	0	500	505
Cobalt compounds	0	10	0	0	0	0	5,707	5,717
Copper	1,786	515	770	22,000	490	781	600,542	626,884
Copper compounds	3,466	2,254	500	22	28,570	3,065	190,575	228,452
Creosote	2,841	1,684	0	0	0	4	0	4,529
Cumene	250	250	0	0	0	250	51,337	52,087
Cyclohexane	62,009	1,201,243	0	95,000	0	4	0	1,358,256
Decabromodiphenyl oxide	0	254	0	38	0	0	5,950	6,242
Di(2-ethylhexyl) phthalate	10	0	0	0	0	250	0	260
Dibenzofuran	250	250	0	0	0	0	250	750
Dibutyl phthalate	0	1,100	3	110,000	0	0	30,503	141,606
Dichloromethane	355,272	893,038	250	0	0	765	47,278	1,296,603
Diethanolamine	128	0	0	0	0	0	0	128
Dimethyl phthalate	31,675	0	0	500	0	150	1,813	34,138
Ethylbenzene	14,869	8,890	0	0	0	16,513	3,831	44,103
Ethylene glycol	37,225	130,382	1,778	6,996	2,007	75,927	258,847	513,162
Ethylene oxide	255	47,420	0	0	0	13,424	0	61,099
Formaldehyde	2,104	39,900	0	0	0	18,359	1,000	61,363
Freon 113	1,145,980	783,538	0	1,597	0	15	47,142	1,978,272
Glycol ethers	307,044	400,027	15	4,405	20	300,421	107,839	1,119,771
Hydrazine	5	5	0	0	0	0	0	10
Hydrochloric acid	9,910	1,651,943	10	4,189,141	2,510	21,196	145,891	6,020,601
Hydrogen fluoride	251	40,978	0	0	0	1	28,947	70,177
Hydroquinone	250	0	0	0	0	0	250	500
Isobutyraldehyde	3,600	1,300	0	0	0	0	0	4,900
Isopropyl alcohol (manufacturing)	13,193	22,077	0	0	0	260	0	35,530
Lead	321	1,164	294	0	0	226	298,437	300,442
Lead compounds	9,307	5,674	0	0	1,492	6	29,755	46,234
M-xylene	250	0	0	0	0	0	0	250
Maleic anhydride	1,166	10,662	0	0	250	0	597,373	609,451
Manganese	1,607	5	0	0	1,604	875	2,545	6,636
Manganese compounds	10,333	3,372	508	53	1,092,938	0	527	1,107,731
Mercury compounds	0	5	0	0	0	0	250	255
Methanol	2,369,921	2,572,295	10,825	125,042	7,746	15,700,060	888,126	21,674,015
Methyl ethyl ketone	545,471	554,814	0	53,000	0	126	279,897	1,433,308
Methyl isobutyl ketone	29,497	49,072	0	0	0	0	50,570	129,139
Methyl methacrylate	5,646	7,787	0	0	0	0	1,025	14,458
Methyl tert-butyl ether	250	250	0	0	0	0	0	500
Methylenebis(phenylisocyanate)	5,779	341	0	0	0	0	2,800	8,920

[Continued]

★ 401 ★

Toxic Chemical Releases in Florida, by Chemical: 1990

[Continued]

Chemical	Fugitive air	Stack air	Water	Injection	Land	Public treatment	Other offsite	Total releases
N,N-dimethylaniline	0	0	0	0	0	0	17	17
N-butyl alcohol	238,880	335,847	0	2,400,000	0	0	24,849	2,999,576
Naphthalene	250	0	0	0	0	5	0	255
Nickel	558	5	260	6,100	755	0	65,521	73,199
Nickel compounds	788	376	36	0	45,803	0	196,690	243,693
Nitric acid	1,982	8,494	0	53,005	520	35,005	137,324	236,330
Nitrobenzene	27	2,920	0	0	0	0	0	2,947
Nitroglycerin	1	250	1,019	0	0	0	22,094	23,364
Phenol	53,657	25,668	11,200	389	470	877	19,113	111,374
Phosphoric acid	3,791	13,032	20	15	31,539,557	67,124	70,191	31,693,730
Phthalic anhydride	954	4,345	0	0	250	0	22,130	27,679
Picric acid	0	0	0	15,000	0	0	0	15,000
Propionaldehyde	0	0	0	32,000	0	0	0	32,000
Propylene	755	750	0	0	0	0	0	1,505
Propylene oxide	754	250	0	0	0	0	0	1,004
Sec-butyl alcohol	2,221	10	0	170,000	0	0	921	173,152
Styrene	1,398,689	708,013	0	0	1,015	6	144,274	2,251,997
Sulfuric acid	11,841	2,001,429	15	255	518,770	24,425	483,872	3,040,607
Tert-butyl alcohol	0	0	0	500	0	0	100	600
Tetrachloroethylene	128,126	53,963	0	0	0	755	32,226	215,070
Toluene	1,408,475	1,280,364	0	0	0	8,160	257,671	2,954,670
Toluenediisocyanate (mixed isomers)	51	4,923	0	0	0	0	0	4,974
Toluene-2,4-diisocyanate	260	301	0	0	0	0	250	811
Toluene-2,6-diisocyanate	250	262	0	0	0	0	0	512
Trichloroethylene	207,586	250,848	0	0	0	0	41,339	499,773
Vinyl chloride	2,000	11,000	0	0	0	0	250	13,250
Xylene (mixed isomers)	471,325	388,391	0	792	0	73,760	63,529	997,797
Zinc (fume or dust)	2,697	5	0	5	400	0	911	4,018
Zinc compounds	71,125	34,358	17,847	51	9,960	969	109,004	243,314

Source: U.S. Environmental Protection Agency. "Toxic Chemical Releases, 1990." In *National Economic, Social, and Environmental Data Bank* [CD-ROM]. Prepared by U.S. Department of Commerce, Economics and Statistics Administration. Washington, DC: U.S. Department of Commerce, National Economic, Social, and Environmental Data Bank, Economics and Statistics Administration, Office of Business Analysis, February 1995.

★ 402 ★

Chemicals

Toxic Chemical Releases in Georgia, by Chemical: 1990

Figures indicate pounds released by chemical and by type of emission per year.

Chemical	Fugitive air	Stack air	Water	Injection	Land	Public treatment	Other offsite	Total releases
1,1,1-trichloroethane	1,860,855	1,956,392	526	5	20	4,902	276,657	4,099,357
1,1,2-trichloroethane	250	22,500	0	0	0	0	20,670	43,420
1,2,4-trichlorobenzene	3,814	2,957	1,242	0	710	0	0	8,723
1,2,4-trimethylbenzene	129,465	44,671	5	0	610	0	7,542	182,293
1,2-dichlorobenzene	56	0	0	0	0	76	0	132
1,2-dichloroethane	117	382	0	0	0	0	0	499
1,3-butadiene	29,294	20,976	5	0	0	0	44,800	95,075
1,4-dichlorobenzene	1,160	0	0	0	0	209	0	1,369
2,4-d	0	0	0	0	0	0	75	75
2-ethoxyethanol	255	35,981	0	0	0	3,511	0	39,747
4,4'-isopropylidenediphenol	176	128	0	0	0	191	2,877	3,372

[Continued]

★ 402 ★

Toxic Chemical Releases in Georgia, by Chemical: 1990

[Continued]

Chemical	Fugitive air	Stack air	Water	Injection	Land	Public treatment	Other offsite	Total releases
Acetone	1,086,261	5,480,645	68,349	0	2,640	412,627	473,932	7,524,454
Acrylamide	690	1,000	0	0	0	1,000	0	2,690
Acrylic acid	1,392	842	0	0	0	510	675	3,419
Acrylonitrile	71	0	0	0	0	0	417	488
Allyl chloride	57,240	0	0	0	0	5,908	0	63,148
Aluminum (fume or dust)	750	4,009	250	0	0	250	52,566	57,825
Aluminum oxide (fibrous forms)	259	593	4,531	0	19	0	152,608	158,010
Ammonia	1,018,290	3,675,009	1,333,549	0	327,024	740,866	78,692	7,173,430
Ammonium nitrate (solution)	755	12,400	1,828,394	0	1,780	0	750	1,844,079
Ammonium sulfate (solution)	750	117,208	306,987	5	19,270	1,853,028	436,393	2,733,641
Anthracene	10	5	0	0	5	0	0	20
Antimony	71	303	0	0	0	255	21,499	22,128
Antimony compounds	1,005	1,200	0	0	0	507	35,323	38,035
Arsenic	42	21	0	0	0	0	4,200	4,263
Arsenic compounds	1,863	785	0	0	280	0	109,080	112,008
Asbestos (friable)	0	0	0	0	0	0	34,121	34,121
Barium compounds	4,254	12,078	17,000	0	2,200	3,471	5,994,884	6,033,887
Benzene	148,641	622,931	25	0	0	5	1,790	773,392
Benzoyl chloride	113	0	0	0	0	0	0	113
Benzoyl peroxide	5	5	0	0	0	180	51	241
Beryllium	0	5	0	0	0	0	0	5
Biphenyl	6,505	19,005	14,375	5	4,270	367,607	0	411,767
Bis(2-ethylhexyl) adipate	282	6,650	0	0	0	0	5	6,937
Bromomethane	24,250	5,320	0	0	0	0	0	29,570
Butyl acrylate	306	199	0	0	0	820	385	1,710
Butyl benzyl phthalate	4,855	5,506	0	0	0	6,132	22,002	38,495
C.I. disperse yellow 3	0	0	0	0	0	250	0	250
Cadmium	0	5	1	0	0	1	0	7
Cadmium compounds	250	221	1	0	0	10	255	737
Captan	260	285	255	0	255	0	2,255	3,310
Carbaryl	255	360	255	0	255	0	505	1,630
Carbon disulfide	1,650	385	0	0	0	250	0	2,285
Carbon tetrachloride	0	5	0	0	0	0	0	5
Carbonyl sulfide	0	247,000	0	0	0	0	0	247,000
Catechol	645	5	24,160	0	1,102	18,000	602	44,514
Chlorine	74,094	343,430	123,627	0	75	1,005	750	542,981
Chlorine dioxide	355	248,500	0	0	0	0	0	248,855
Chloroethane	266,000	94,000	0	0	0	0	0	360,000
Chloroform	782,000	1,270,000	24,960	0	1,310	0	433	2,078,703
Chloromethane	2,310	22,500	0	0	0	220	0	25,030
Chlorothalonil	53	9	0	0	0	8	1,642	1,712
Chromium	550	1,059	261	0	1,130	267	8,716	11,983
Chromium compounds	1,395	3,031	117,711	0	241,035	889	418,581	782,642
Cobalt	250	250	0	0	0	250	250	1,000
Cobalt compounds	799	457	0	0	28	31	5,157	6,472
Copper	11,509	19,603	383	250	4,772	2,226	74,990	113,733
Copper compounds	3,639	871	93	0	25	206	65,591	70,425
Creosote	11,250	56,250	0	0	0	0	26,135	93,635
Cresol (mixed isomers)	1,200	7,900	0	0	0	32	0	9,132
Cumene	286,881	23,597	0	0	0	55,435	1	365,914
Cyanide compounds	1,010	896	509	0	0	313	13,108	15,836
Cyclohexane	53,162	280,420	5	0	0	5	5,850	339,442

[Continued]

★ 402 ★

Toxic Chemical Releases in Georgia, by Chemical: 1990

[Continued]

Chemical	Fugitive air	Stack air	Water	Injection	Land	Public treatment	Other offsite	Total releases
Decabromodiphenyl oxide	0	0	0	0	0	0	24,000	24,000
Di(2-ethylhexyl) phthalate	992	408	0	0	0	250	20,099	21,749
Dibenzofuran	10	5	5	0	5	0	0	25
Dibutyl phthalate	285	527	0	0	0	3,403	725	4,940
Dichloromethane	893,688	2,505,505	27,721	5	787	3,726	143,821	3,575,253
Dichlorvos	0	5	0	0	0	0	0	5
Dicofol	13	5	0	0	0	0	250	268
Diethanolamine	385	515	1,100	0	0	2,419	929	5,348
Diethyl phthalate	2,650	3,400	0	0	5	255	9,800	16,110
Diethyl sulfate	5	0	0	0	5	0	0	10
Dimethyl phthalate	750	0	0	0	0	0	0	750
Dimethyl sulfate	0	10	0	0	0	0	0	10
Epichlorohydrin	6,089	2,451	0	0	0	708	1	9,249
Ethyl acrylate	261	427	0	0	0	755	333	1,776
Ethylbenzene	85,833	63,346	5	0	400	1,180	235,227	385,991
Ethylene glycol	5,593	8,161	39,155	5	8,021	417,526	442,861	921,322
Ethylene oxide	34,956	159,167	0	0	0	20,959	0	215,082
Fluometuron	10	10	0	0	0	0	1,500	1,520
Formaldehyde	85,075	396,095	789	0	5	868	5,060	487,892
Freon 113	274,296	119,213	0	0	0	312	22,855	416,676
Glycol ethers	317,836	1,270,947	40,956	5	31,943	90,705	185,313	1,937,705
Hydrochloric acid	19,022	5,221,154	290	5	3,620	1,280	31,340	5,276,711
Hydrogen fluoride	782	1,495	5	5	20	334	5	2,646
Hydroquinone	1	1	0	0	0	1,200	314	1,516
Isopropyl alcohol (manufacturing)	10,614	75,010	0	0	0	250	67,703	153,577
Lead	5,838	10,478	257	0	38,400	634	314,207	369,814
Lead compounds	4,636	9,987	277	0	250	544	114,040	129,734
Lindane	5	11	0	0	0	0	192	208
Maleic anhydride	14,329	540	5	0	0	454	1,907	17,235
Maneb	5	5	0	0	0	0	1,250	1,260
Manganese	4,307	2,914	5	250	3,745	774	65,812	77,807
Manganese compounds	1,818	520	0	0	0	2,645	56,952	61,935
Mercury	2,092	521	27	0	0	0	4,980	7,620
Methanol	1,762,381	18,967,078	263,570	0	89,905	3,599,616	513,807	25,196,357
Methoxychlor	250	250	250	0	250	0	250	1,250
Methyl acrylate	391	1,150	0	0	0	25	0	1,566
Methyl ethyl ketone	702,572	1,770,022	0	0	902	3,555	365,942	2,842,993
Methyl isobutyl ketone	1,445,729	442,710	0	0	255	28,574	49,858	1,967,126
Methyl methacrylate	2,761	3,931	0	0	0	1,670	913	9,275
Methylenebis(phenylisocyanate)	4,482	15,896	0	0	1,500	750	3,200	25,828
Molybdenum trioxide	250	250	0	0	0	0	1,500	2,000
N,N-dimethylaniline	250	0	0	0	0	0	0	250
N-butyl alcohol	127,953	917,622	0	0	0	2,719	14,779	1,063,073
N-dioctyl phthalate	3,971	680	0	0	0	250	352	5,253
Naphthalene	51,892	13,823	2,981	0	6,356	0	10,406	85,458
Nickel	1,011	1,955	548	0	416	1,219	20,231	25,380
Nickel compounds	751	1,581	9,616	0	528	1,007	16,286	29,769
Nitric acid	24,432	61,256	5	0	170	1,130	33,141	120,134
Nitrilotriacetic acid	5	250	0	0	0	1,000	0	1,255
O-xylene	3,600	4,429	0	0	0	36	0	8,065
Parathion	17	32	5	0	5	0	7,655	7,714
Pentachlorophenol	6	255	250	0	250	0	2,877	3,638

[Continued]

★ 402 ★

Toxic Chemical Releases in Georgia, by Chemical: 1990

[Continued]

Chemical	Fugitive air	Stack air	Water	Injection	Land	Public treatment	Other offsite	Total releases
Phenol	7,982	182,950	1,828	0	3,700	7	192,787	389,254
Phosphoric acid	28,032	18,896	47	0	755	69,484	80,894	198,108
Phthalic anhydride	1,983	71	0	0	0	250	360	2,664
Propoxur	5	5	0	0	0	250	250	510
Propylene	16,108	1,050	0	0	0	0	0	17,158
Propylene oxide	290	3,857	0	0	0	0	0	4,147
Propyleneimine	4	0	0	0	0	0	0	4
Sec-butyl alcohol	8,581	2,850	0	0	0	0	0	11,431
Selenium compounds	500	5	0	0	0	0	250	755
Silver	0	0	1	0	0	1	0	2
Silver compounds	0	12	0	0	0	1	0	13
Sodium sulfate (solution)	0	0	0	0	0	800,000	0	800,000
Styrene	331,422	635,635	10	0	2,750	758	1,001,448	1,972,023
Sulfuric acid	25,246	1,206,391	4,548	5	51,828	95,053	259,287	1,642,358
Tert-butyl alcohol	17,000	5,700	0	0	0	0	12,000	34,700
Tetrachloroethylene	340,233	178,531	0	0	0	339	21,912	541,015
Thiourea	5	5	0	0	0	750	0	760
Titanium tetrachloride	7,700	0	0	0	0	0	0	7,700
Toluene	2,229,027	2,987,436	2,354	5	72	1,685	355,330	5,575,909
Toluenediisocyanate (mixed isomers)	641	786	0	0	0	0	3,917	5,344
Toluene-2,4-diisocyanate	254	385	0	0	0	0	0	639
Toluene-2,6-diisocyanate	252	283	0	0	0	0	0	535
Trichloroethylene	961,158	1,005,124	174	0	0	5	65,550	2,032,011
Trifluralin	5	5	0	0	0	0	1,250	1,260
Vinyl acetate	2,260	32,975	0	0	0	1,035	3,043	39,313
Vinyl chloride	11	1	0	0	0	0	1,000	1,012
Vinylidene chloride	3,700	30	0	0	200	0	130,800	134,730
Xylene (mixed isomers)	997,041	2,702,730	519	0	4,505	7,259	1,201,952	4,914,006
Zinc (fume or dust)	2,930	12,524	750	250	72,000	19	42,336	130,809
Zinc compounds	22,084	32,310	12,180	10	131,259	23,035	434,677	655,555

Source: U.S. Environmental Protection Agency. "Toxic Chemical Releases, 1990." In *National Economic, Social, and Environmental Data Bank* [CD-ROM]. Prepared by U.S. Department of Commerce, Economics and Statistics Administration. Washington, DC: U.S. Department of Commerce, National Economic, Social, and Environmental Data Bank, Economics and Statistics Administration, Office of Business Analysis, February 1995.

★ 403 ★

Chemicals

Toxic Chemical Releases in Hawaii, by Chemical: 1990

Figures indicate pounds released by chemical and by type of emission per year.

Chemical	Fugitive air	Stack air	Water	Injection	Land	Public treatment	Other offsite	Total releases
1,2,4-trimethylbenzene	25,700	1,500	5	0	500	0	500	28,205
1,2-dibromoethane	250	250	0	0	0	0	0	500
1,2-dichloroethylene	250	5	0	0	0	0	0	255
1,3-butadiene	250	5	0	0	0	0	0	255
2-methoxyethanol	755	250	5	0	5	0	0	1,015
Acetone	9,672	0	0	0	0	0	0	9,672

[Continued]

★ 403 ★

Toxic Chemical Releases in Hawaii, by Chemical: 1990
[Continued]

Chemical	Fugitive air	Stack air	Water	Injection	Land	Public treatment	Other offsite	Total releases
Ammonia	9,555	6,105	15,700	90,000	250	5	0	121,615
Ammonium nitrate (solution)	0	0	0	0	9,174	0	0	9,174
Ammonium sulfate (solution)	0	0	0	0	0	340,000	0	340,000
Arsenic compounds	15	15	0	0	250	0	1,133	1,413
Benzene	54,400	18,000	0	0	5	0	250	72,655
Chlorine	10	10	250	250	21,300	47,800	0	69,620
Chromium compounds	15	15	0	0	250	0	1,027	1,307
Copper compounds	15	15	0	0	250	0	794	1,074
Cyclohexane	17,800	18,000	5	0	250	0	250	36,305
Dichloromethane	11,570	17,354	0	0	0	0	0	28,924
Ethylbenzene	11,300	1,600	0	0	250	0	250	13,400
Ethylene	5,900	250	0	0	5	0	0	6,155
Glycol ethers	61,740	20,580	0	0	0	0	750	83,070
Hydrochloric acid	0	0	0	0	250	0	0	250
Lead	5	250	0	0	5	0	5	265
M-xylene	45,900	4,400	5	0	250	0	750	51,305
Manganese	0	0	0	250	0	0	500	750
Methanol	250	5	0	0	0	0	0	255
Methyl tert-butyl ether	1,200	0	0	0	0	0	0	1,200
N-butyl alcohol	54,300	18,100	0	0	0	0	750	73,150
Naphthalene	6,650	1,100	5	0	250	0	750	8,755
Nickel	5	0	5	0	5	0	0	15
O-xylene	21,800	2,200	5	0	250	0	250	24,505
P-xylene	15,300	1,000	5	0	250	0	250	16,805
Phosphoric acid	0	0	0	0	0	250	0	250
Propylene	113,800	5,300	0	0	0	0	0	119,100
Styrene	390	2,462	0	0	0	0	0	2,852
Sulfuric acid	20	5,755	0	21,000	10	5	0	26,790
Toluene	81,300	14,200	0	0	250	0	250	96,000
Toluene-2,4-diisocyanate	250	14	0	0	0	0	0	264
Toluene-2,6-diisocyanate	250	4	0	0	0	0	0	254

Source: U.S. Environmental Protection Agency. "Toxic Chemical Releases, 1990." In National Economic, Social, and Environmental Data Bank [CD-ROM]. Prepared by U.S. Department of Commerce, Economics and Statistics Administration. Washington, DC: U.S. Department of Commerce, National Economic, Social, and Environmental Data Bank, Economics and Statistics Administration, Office of Business Analysis, February 1995.

★ 404 ★
Chemicals

Toxic Chemical Releases in Idaho, by Chemical: 1990

Figures indicate pounds released by chemical and by type of emission per year.

Chemical	Fugitive air	Stack air	Water	Injection	Land	Public treatment	Other offsite	Total releases
1,1,1-trichloroethane	4,321	102,077	0	0	0	2	29,085	135,485
Acetaldehyde	0	66,966	0	0	0	0	0	66,966
Acetone	80,399	150,697	7,100	0	5,700	381	70,335	314,612
Ammonia	889,382	1,815,827	359,198	0	2,769,005	331,820	0	6,165,232
Ammonium nitrate (solution)	5	5	0	0	210,000	16,000	0	226,010
Ammonium sulfate (solution)	5	5	0	0	0	1,087,000	0	1,087,010
Antimony	0	2	0	0	0	9	155	166
Barium	0	0	25,100	0	0	0	0	25,100
Barium compounds	0	0	0	0	0	500	250	750
Cadmium compounds	195	8,549	0	0	10,045	0	9	18,798
Captan	2	0	0	0	0	0	317	319
Chlorine	1,280	22,255	0	0	0	20,465	0	44,000
Chlorine dioxide	250	114,000	0	0	0	250	0	114,500
Chloroform	344,000	560,000	17,000	0	0	0	0	921,000
Chromium	10	0	0	0	0	0	0	10
Chromium compounds	2,006	1,481	26,000	0	12,090	0	4	41,581
Copper	0	0	0	0	0	3,418	13,608	17,026
Copper compounds	253	5	0	0	0	150	4,139	4,547
Cyanide compounds	6	644	0	0	0	255	12	917
Ethylene glycol	251	145	0	0	250	38,960	0	39,606
Ethylene oxide	250	250	0	0	0	0	0	500
Formaldehyde	4,942	82,521	0	0	0	90	0	87,553
Freon 113	221,036	47,586	0	0	12,000	16	17,341	297,979
Glycol ethers	1,250	1,000	0	0	97,000	614	54,931	154,795
Hydrochloric acid	750	1,723	0	0	5	0	0	2,478
Hydrogen fluoride	63,500	24,256	0	0	0	250	0	88,006
Lead	252	424	0	0	0	1,100	10,114	11,890
Lindane	1	0	0	0	0	0	54	55
Manganese	0	0	40,000	0	0	0	0	40,000
Manganese compounds	5	5	0	0	0	0	0	10
Methanol	274,686	510,970	0	0	1,000	2,000	0	788,656
Methyl ethyl ketone	250	3,900	0	0	0	0	1,200	5,350
Methylenebis(phenylisocyanate)	0	130	0	0	0	0	0	130
Nickel compounds	2	0	0	0	0	510	110	622
Nitric acid	757	7,878	0	0	0	48,000	905	57,540
Pentachlorophenol	252	15	0	0	146	0	24	437
Phosphoric acid	255	36,114	0	0	12	89,972	0	126,353
Phosphorus (yellow or white)	14	17	0	0	2,189,313	0	0	2,189,344
Styrene	33,064	36,797	0	0	0	0	250	70,111
Sulfuric acid	13,250	140,043	0	0	500	1,221,963	0	1,375,756
Tetrachloroethylene	750	7,632	0	0	0	0	0	8,382
Toluene	500	0	0	0	0	0	0	500

[Continued]

★ 404 ★

Toxic Chemical Releases in Idaho, by Chemical: 1990

[Continued]

Chemical	Fugitive air	Stack air	Water	Injection	Land	Public treatment	Other offsite	Total releases
Xylene (mixed isomers)	250	0	0	0	0	0	6,900	7,150
Zinc compounds	2,485	0	0	0	127,604	322	154	130,565

Source: U.S. Environmental Protection Agency. "Toxic Chemical Releases, 1990." In *National Economic, Social, and Environmental Data Bank* [CD-ROM]. Prepared by U.S. Department of Commerce, Economics and Statistics Administration. Washington, DC: U.S. Department of Commerce, National Economic, Social, and Environmental Data Bank, Economics and Statistics Administration, Office of Business Analysis, February 1995.

★ 405 ★

Chemicals

Toxic Chemical Releases in Illinois, by Chemical: 1990

Figures indicate pounds released by chemical and by type of emission per year.

Chemical	Fugitive air	Stack air	Water	Injection	Land	Public treatment	Other offsite	Total releases
1,1,1-trichloroethane	5,385,714	3,664,032	399	10	45	6,555	617,596	9,674,351
1,1,2-trichloroethane	330	6,320	0	0	0	0	3,904	10,554
1,2,4-trichlorobenzene	0	0	0	0	0	0	94,630	94,630
1,2,4-trimethylbenzene	65,810	43,297	230	0	1,113	1,151	26,607	138,208
1,2-dichlorobenzene	1,700	3,800	0	0	0	7,300	95,700	108,500
1,2-dichloroethane	18,427	38,576	0	0	0	8,112	10,686	75,801
1,3-butadiene	24,847	16,706	46	0	0	0	0	41,599
1,3-dichlorobenzene	40	180	0	0	0	30	1,213	1,463
1,3-dichloropropylene	5	250	0	0	0	0	0	255
1,4-dichlorobenzene	8,100	14,300	0	0	0	4,000	160,600	187,000
1,4-dioxane	15,755	11,018	75	0	13	250	235	27,346
2,4-d	5	5	0	0	0	5	1,045	1,060
2-ethoxyethanol	274	13,120	0	0	0	4	1,434	14,832
2-nitrophenol	0	0	0	0	0	4,600	34,900	39,500
2-nitropropane	3,500	3,300	0	0	0	0	0	6,800
2-phenylphenol	0	0	0	0	0	677	0	677
3,3'-dichlorobenzidine	0	5	0	0	0	255	0	260
4,4'-isopropylidenediphenol	1,267	751	0	0	0	0	41,912	43,930
4,4'-methylenebis(2-chloro aniline)	0	250	0	0	0	0	0	250
4,4'-methylenedianiline	0	11	0	0	0	125	44	180
4-nitrophenol	7,300	0	0	0	0	270,000	56,000	333,300
Acetaldehyde	213	12	0	0	0	0	0	225
Acetone	1,109,656	2,273,767	11,125	10	295	523,289	661,071	4,579,213
Acetonitrile	1,720	1,160	0	0	0	910	0	3,790
Acrylamide	42	14	0	5	20	730	297	1,108
Acrylic acid	8,133	53,441	804	0	94,040	10	22,333	178,761
Acrylonitrile	16,034	270,454	16	0	15	0	6,524	293,043
Aluminum (fume or dust)	35,625	34,788	9,300	0	315,082	1,519	496,581	892,895
Aluminum oxide (fibrous forms)	504	4,033	3,500	0	31,040	880	185,373	225,330
Ammonia	2,925,145	3,228,586	4,743,337	5	758,948	4,476,879	195,891	16,328,791
Ammonium nitrate (solution)	255	19,914	4,000	0	27,816	250	0	52,235
Ammonium sulfate (solution)	15	5	898,223	5	5	17,450,610	61,739	18,410,602
Aniline	101,220	35,555	0	0	0	776,847	283,792	1,197,414
Anthracene	1,990	1,040	0	0	0	625	6,471	10,126
Antimony	260	1,007	0	0	0	5	2,380	3,652
Antimony compounds	520	522	257	176	0	272	8,761	10,508
Arsenic	250	1,700	0	0	0	250	1,175	3,375
Arsenic compounds	261	261	2	1,250	5	8	4,594	6,381
Asbestos (friable)	260	5	0	0	0	0	353	618

[Continued]

★ 405 ★

Toxic Chemical Releases in Illinois, by Chemical: 1990
[Continued]

Chemical	Fugitive air	Stack air	Water	Injection	Land	Public treatment	Other offsite	Total releases
Barium	30	484	4,119	0	42,300	0	2,995	49,928
Barium compounds	37,885	8,336	255	0	231,310	54,793	3,414,113	3,746,692
Benzene	547,087	778,337	654	0	641	217,933	421,756	1,966,408
Benzoyl peroxide	10	0	0	0	0	0	140	150
Benzyl chloride	155	125	0	0	0	254	18	552
Biphenyl	3,075	552	0	0	0	5	5,656	9,288
Bis(2-ethylhexyl) adipate	11,409	368	0	0	0	500	7,727	20,004
Bromomethane	71,400	0	0	0	0	0	0	71,400
Butyl acrylate	3,487	22,301	115	0	57	250	4,533	30,743
Butyl benzyl phthalate	603	9,721	139	5	1,083	975	282,050	294,576
Butyraldehyde	5	0	0	0	0	0	0	5
Cadmium	510	1,901	0	0	0	1,005	17,732	21,148
Cadmium compounds	1,255	877	0	0	0	1,013	17,530	20,675
Captan	250	97	0	0	0	5	0	352
Carbon disulfide	8,850	4,101,900	0	0	0	25,750	500	4,137,000
Carbon tetrachloride	8,308	3,070	20	182	0	10	14,666	26,256
Chloramben	5	5	0	0	0	0	15,591	15,601
Chlorine	51,891	4,064,148	20,458	1,329	45,475	98,162	232,016	4,513,479
Chlorobenzene	40,000	10,000	0	0	0	57,000	167,740	274,740
Chloroethane	190,250	84,000	0	0	0	0	0	274,250
Chloroform	1,070	4,190	0	0	0	255	49,100	54,615
Chloromethane	313,271	677,755	0	0	0	250	7	991,283
Chlorophenols	5	5	0	0	0	250	250	510
Chlorothalonil	10	4	0	0	0	250	1,157	1,421
Chromium	10,871	6,986	1,212	0	256,227	3,704	583,995	862,995
Chromium compounds	17,124	10,786	10,320	0	296,672	26,303	722,257	1,083,462
Cobalt	260	255	106	0	4,000	255	2,211	7,087
Cobalt compounds	10	1,828	2,180	0	0	7,934	11,939	23,891
Copper	28,587	26,558	9,186	10	29,510	12,799	879,466	986,116
Copper compounds	18,827	57,968	8,276	5	590	13,293	2,516,646	2,615,605
Creosote	13,355	51,245	0	0	4,793	3,623	806,098	879,114
Cresol (mixed isomers)	26,975	39,254	37	0	3	13	32,188	98,470
Cumene	12,460	140,958	0	0	0	0	8,072	161,490
Cumene hydroperoxide	217	383	0	0	5	0	1,600	2,205
Cyanide compounds	7,364	298,506	893	0	0	9,093	34,825	350,681
Cyclohexane	168,014	831,389	63	0	762	2,400	85,864	1,088,492
Decabromodiphenyl oxide	250	500	0	0	5,800	0	0	6,550
Di(2-ethylhexyl) phthalate	991	47,276	0	0	0	757	80,686	129,710
Dibenzofuran	1,500	710	0	0	0	0	250	2,460
Dibutyl phthalate	1,315	3,584	0	0	0	980	7,211	13,090
Dichloromethane	1,348,617	1,932,881	5	0	0	17,544	250,517	3,549,564
Diethanolamine	4,063	20,169	11,350	0	0	371,236	35,772	442,590
Diethyl phthalate	750	0	0	0	0	0	500	1,250
Diethyl sulfate	3	0	0	0	0	0	0	3
Dimethyl phthalate	0	0	0	0	0	0	500	500
Dimethyl sulfate	550	0	0	0	0	0	0	550
Epichlorohydrin	10,131	12,198	0	0	0	250	0	22,579
Ethyl acrylate	3,607	2,801	47	0	24	500	4,033	11,012
Ethylbenzene	139,837	96,013	450	0	1,383	19,170	82,473	339,326
Ethylene	898,379	2,035,838	0	0	0	0	0	2,934,217
Ethylene glycol	154,419	127,832	173,335	5	23,911	664,286	281,416	1,425,204
Ethylene oxide	22,767	98,796	5	0	0	5,305	0	126,873
Ethylene thiourea	0	19	0	0	0	0	5,624	5,643
Formaldehyde	63,017	82,617	10	5	54,020	39,325	25,848	264,842
Freon 113	1,574,196	402,412	36	5	20	40,960	86,471	2,104,100
Glycol ethers	687,518	2,456,465	700	5	322	966,967	764,812	4,876,789
Hydrazine	260	250	80	0	0	2,700	0	3,290
Hydrochloric acid	557,421	2,843,804	5,423	9,285,794	3,065	17,602,266	1,410,639	31,708,412
Hydrogen cyanide	632	26	0	0	0	0	0	658

[Continued]

★ 405 ★

Toxic Chemical Releases in Illinois, by Chemical: 1990
[Continued]

Chemical	Fugitive air	Stack air	Water	Injection	Land	Public treatment	Other offsite	Total releases
Hydrogen fluoride	89,181	45,526	0	5	250	2,310	54	137,326
Hydroquinone	5	29	0	0	0	2,167	0	2,201
Isopropyl alcohol (manufacturing)	37,025	108,076	15	5	25	24	391,519	536,689
Lead	10,497	20,428	1,445	5	89,520	1,930	350,172	473,997
Lead compounds	52,757	45,775	8,297	0	431,830	4,060	1,758,860	2,301,579
Lindane	5	18	0	0	0	5	0	28
M-cresol	10	1,767	0	0	0	6,786	0	8,563
M-xylene	10,594	125,471	0	0	0	0	0	136,065
Maleic anhydride	3,443	238,773	58	0	58	640,005	4,349	886,686
Manganese	93,790	18,936	11,459	0	803,951	4,894	492,691	1,425,721
Manganese compounds	37,376	30,057	3,576	0	3,607,623	5,404	3,578,823	7,262,859
Mercury	5	4	0	0	0	0	0	9
Methanol	1,131,871	1,020,103	81,827	10	881	3,713,991	3,681,417	9,630,100
Methyl acrylate	471	2,402	0	0	0	0	0	2,873
Methyl ethyl ketone	2,236,643	3,231,528	29	15	107	80,887	1,280,131	6,829,340
Methyl isobutyl ketone	239,260	715,242	0	0	260	160,132	518,886	1,633,780
Methyl methacrylate	6,415	43,940	92	0	46	505	4,332	55,330
Methyl tert-butyl ether	5	9,715	0	0	0	0	0	9,720
Methylenebis(phenylisocyanate)	7,291	5,517	0	0	54,000	0	45,641	112,449
Molybdenum trioxide	26	406	1,285	0	0	455	16,196	18,368
N-butyl alcohol	212,092	912,949	0	0	0	1,743	108,517	1,235,301
N-dioctyl phthalate	50	103	0	0	0	4,350	28,250	32,753
Naphthalene	339,743	103,083	15	0	0	20,756	74,402	537,999
Nickel	26,438	11,532	2,560	5	12,471	5,654	499,091	557,751
Nickel compounds	3,651	6,215	2,003	0	41	6,237	254,037	272,184
Nitric acid	42,443	33,878	10	5	102,987	889,966	294,394	1,363,683
Nitroglycerin	0	0	0	0	0	0	439	439
O-cresol	900	11,316	0	0	0	43,422	80	55,718
O-xylene	13,727	52,374	0	0	0	0	0	66,101
P-cresidine	2,437	13	0	0	0	0	0	2,450
P-cresol	1,220	224,772	0	0	0	863,246	0	1,089,238
Peracetic acid	0	250	0	0	0	0	0	250
Phenol	66,635	494,830	2,395	0	501	1,374,788	718,675	2,657,824
Phosphoric acid	72,068	247,972	196,955	24	305,355	1,694,209	320,069	2,836,652
Phosphorus (yellow or white)	260	250	2,073	0	0	501	6,700	9,784
Phthalic anhydride	21,963	84,420	0	0	0	5	918,731	1,025,119
Polychlorinated biphenyls (PCBs)	0	0	0	0	0	0	1,850	1,850
Propionaldehyde	1,700	3,900	0	0	0	0	0	5,600
Propylene	373,154	68,133	15	0	0	0	0	441,302
Propylene oxide	9,434	2,182	0	0	0	410	1,145	13,171
Pyridine	150	26	0	0	0	0	0	176
Quinoline	978	1,938	0	0	0	0	0	2,916
Quintozene	5	16	0	0	0	5	0	26
Sec-butyl alcohol	29,441	49,378	0	0	0	70	7,794	86,683
Selenium compounds	500	329	0	0	0	61	3,880	4,770
Silver	5	5	0	0	0	10	0	20
Silver compounds	255	255	0	0	0	260	3,775	4,545
Styrene	281,222	911,214	536	0	551	291	623,551	1,817,365
Sulfuric acid	112,213	421,466	1,238	160,015	4,598	8,808,286	2,888,214	12,396,030
Tert-butyl alcohol	11,903	31,607	0	0	0	130,000	4,410	177,920
Tetrachloroethylene	246,493	739,125	0	0	12	3,811	235,176	1,224,617
Thiourea	255	5	0	0	0	1,250	255	1,765
Toluene	5,865,668	6,831,351	1,096	10	5,936	30,920	1,933,246	14,668,227
Toluenediisocyanate (mixed isomers)	250	255	0	0	0	0	500	1,005
Toluene-2,4-diisocyanate	775	1,267	0	0	0	0	26,330	28,372
Toluene-2,6-diisocyanate	275	513	0	0	0	0	6,670	7,458
Trichloroethylene	1,188,040	2,369,220	314	0	0	536	405,726	3,963,836
Trifluralin	474	255	0	0	5	0	3,421	4,155
Vanadium (fume or dust)	902	815	150	0	35,600	250	0	37,717

[Continued]

★ 405 ★

Toxic Chemical Releases in Illinois, by Chemical: 1990

[Continued]

Chemical	Fugitive air	Stack air	Water	Injection	Land	Public treatment	Other offsite	Total releases
Vinyl acetate	38,492	196,462	1,176	0	1,101	0	333,473	570,704
Vinyl chloride	14,890	61,340	24	15	60	0	2,552	78,881
Vinylidene chloride	7,005	6,450	0	5	20	0	255	13,735
Xylene (mixed isomers)	2,010,484	4,562,698	614	5	8,656	301,359	994,330	7,878,146
Zinc (fume or dust)	149,163	183,757	4,852	0	2,632,367	4,541	766,863	3,741,543
Zinc compounds	267,501	310,709	15,928	750	5,035,314	63,476	10,158,396	15,852,074

Source: U.S. Environmental Protection Agency. "Toxic Chemical Releases, 1990." In *National Economic, Social, and Environmental Data Bank* [CD-ROM]. Prepared by U.S. Department of Commerce, Economics and Statistics Administration. Washington, DC: U.S. Department of Commerce, National Economic, Social, and Environmental Data Bank, Economics and Statistics Administration, Office of Business Analysis, February 1995.

★ 406 ★

Chemicals

Toxic Chemical Releases in Indiana, by Chemical: 1990

Figures indicate pounds released by chemical and by type of emission per year.

Chemical	Fugitive air	Stack air	Water	Injection	Land	Public treatment	Other offsite	Total releases
1,1,1-trichloroethane	7,057,684	4,156,937	3,800	0	0	784	508,969	11,728,174
1,2,4-trichlorobenzene	250	3,700	0	0	0	0	0	3,950
1,2,4-trimethylbenzene	85,352	60,886	250	0	46	22,040	115,355	283,929
1,2-butylene oxide	250	750	5	0	5	0	0	1,010
1,2-dichlorobenzene	53,976	16,346	10	0	0	0	203,025	273,357
1,2-dichloroethane	81,027	1,805,373	255	0	5	250	1,805	1,888,715
1,3-butadiene	2,239	1,363	0	5	15	0	0	3,622
1,4-dichlorobenzene	90	36,000	0	0	0	0	0	36,090
1,4-dioxane	22,105	5	0	0	0	0	500	22,610
2,3-dichloropropene	720	0	0	0	0	0	0	720
2,4-dimethylphenol	0	0	0	26,600	0	0	0	26,600
2,4-dinitrotoluene	1	0	0	0	0	0	0	1
2-ethoxyethanol	32,549	1,651	0	0	0	0	0	34,200
2-methoxyethanol	2,200	41	0	0	0	0	0	2,241
2-phenylphenol	5	5	0	0	0	250	0	260
4,4'-isopropylidenediphenol	950	263	435	0	0	750	133,413	135,811
Acetaldehyde	2,942	81,665	0	0	0	5	0	84,612
Acetone	4,735,508	9,893,901	1,355	0	272	205,370	5,312,720	20,149,126
Acetonitrile	241,292	499,347	255	0	5	210,800	910,400	1,862,099
Acrylic acid	58	20	0	0	0	0	0	78
Acrylonitrile	354	178	0	5	15	3	3	558
Allyl alcohol	250	250	5	0	0	0	0	505
Aluminum (fume or dust)	14,976	35,425	0	0	37,690	205	1,020,089	1,108,385
Aluminum oxide (fibrous forms)	980	8,016	500	0	24,000	571	779,155	813,222
Ammonia	1,822,911	1,161,710	1,428,987	1,121,005	313,615	1,469,442	534,101	7,851,771
Ammonium nitrate (solution)	1,550	250	88	0	1,560	660	65,407	69,515
Ammonium sulfate (solution)	500	5	10	0	0	0	83,750	84,265
Anthracene	1,742	17,250	0	0	0	327	250	19,569
Antimony	80	355	0	0	3,800	65	26,560	30,860
Antimony compounds	2,023	1,073	0	0	1,800	13,328	764,661	782,885
Arsenic	40	24	0	0	0	3	7,700	7,767
Arsenic compounds	191	431	0	0	0	261	26,384	27,267
Asbestos (friable)	0	250	0	0	0	0	154,797	155,047
Barium	0	0	0	0	0	0	3,048	3,048
Barium compounds	3,096	50,655	5	250	500	26,965	295,800	377,271
Benzene	1,374,431	1,370,707	261	10,000	18	9,857	38,110	2,803,384

[Continued]

★ 406 ★

Toxic Chemical Releases in Indiana, by Chemical: 1990
[Continued]

Chemical	Fugitive air	Stack air	Water	Injection	Land	Public treatment	Other offsite	Total releases
Benzoyl peroxide	5	0	0	0	0	0	0	5
Benzyl chloride	5	5	0	0	0	250	0	260
Biphenyl	682	974	0	0	0	250	3,750	5,656
Bis(2-ethylhexyl) adipate	3,200	1,570	5,500	0	0	750	40,250	51,270
Butyl acrylate	59	92	0	0	0	12	10	173
Butyl benzyl phthalate	5,133	38,165	0	0	0	5	5	43,308
Butyraldehyde	7	5	0	0	0	0	0	12
Cadmium	5	5	9	0	5	265	9,570	9,859
Cadmium compounds	5	250	0	0	0	0	1,093	1,348
Carbon disulfide	89,577	1,723,497	0	0	0	0	249	1,813,323
Carbon tetrachloride	250	0	20	0	0	0	52,326	52,596
Carbonyl sulfide	0	6,673	0	0	0	0	0	6,673
Chlorine	33,673	494,208	17,532	18,905	25	5,505	41,115	610,963
Chloroacetic acid	5	0	0	0	0	0	0	5
Chloroform	4,500	7,100	362	0	0	0	4,639	16,601
Chloromethane	505	19,692	0	0	0	250	5	20,452
Chromium	25,802	181,847	457	30	240,054	2,264	1,255,359	1,705,813
Chromium compounds	8,293	16,964	11,376	6,162	2,034,573	7,664	1,687,757	3,772,789
Cobalt	284	845	0	0	1,785	277	1,061	4,252
Cobalt compounds	750	576	3	1,201	251	265	9,264	12,310
Copper	12,038	21,216	1,351	0	61,760	9,661	1,765,383	1,871,409
Copper compounds	5,100	4,050	1,052	0	71,000	3,016	151,568	235,786
Creosote	58	32,229	0	0	0	607	137,519	170,413
Cresol (mixed isomers)	98,237	128,144	5	0	0	381	260,021	486,788
Cumene	10,391	220,104	0	0	0	3,200	4,255	237,950
Cumene hydroperoxide	2,530	0	0	0	0	0	0	2,530
Cyanide compounds	80,901	2,705	37,169	31,800	34	2,013	4,982	159,604
Cyclohexane	62,568	155,357	251	0	0	250	24,605	243,031
Decabromodiphenyl oxide	3,733	5	0	0	0	0	3,985	7,723
Di(2-ethylhexyl) phthalate	3,020	164,502	755	0	0	827	42,603	211,707
Dibenzofuran	1,330	250	0	0	0	250	250	2,080
Dibutyl phthalate	5	5	0	0	0	0	1,461	1,471
Dichloromethane	6,042,848	5,952,974	9,721	0	255	3,717	477,890	12,487,405
Diethanolamine	157,660	1,965	0	0	0	318,126	52,096	529,847
Diethyl phthalate	8	0	0	0	0	0	4,800	4,808
Dimethyl phthalate	5	540	0	0	110	0	897	1,552
Ethyl acrylate	57	23	0	0	0	0	0	80
Ethylbenzene	93,062	238,737	255	0	21	1,305	64,362	397,742
Ethylene	243,859	71,086	0	0	0	0	0	314,945
Ethylene glycol	19,444	25,099	1,011,555	0	35,154	183,712	189,508	1,464,472
Ethylene oxide	304	65,993	0	0	0	0	0	66,297
Formaldehyde	29,991	220,507	2,860	0	0	93,076	39,674	386,108
Freon 113	901,628	590,743	0	0	0	260	53,165	1,545,796
Glycol ethers	328,809	1,486,620	43,747	0	659	99,596	288,058	2,247,489
Hydrochloric acid	84,374	1,571,151	525	7,827,910	525	688,216	554,589	10,727,290
Hydrogen cyanide	45	0	0	0	0	0	0	45
Hydrogen fluoride	452,440	555,670	5	0	0	3,900	44,060	1,056,075
Isopropyl alcohol (manufacturing)	69,255	97,683	0	0	0	5	14,839	181,782
Lead	7,954	13,664	278	0	11,006	5,248	717,430	755,580
Lead compounds	9,548	16,247	15,138	750	297,979	3,396	1,592,079	1,935,137
M-cresol	250	250	0	0	0	0	0	500
M-xylene	0	18,177	0	0	0	0	11,694	29,871
Maleic anhydride	555	4,145	0	0	0	5	380	5,085
Manganese	115,741	364,069	557	0	1,867,385	1,290	2,107,392	4,456,434
Manganese compounds	100,043	362,474	250	0	39,752,250	1,520	987,831	41,204,368
Mercury	10	0	0	0	0	0	44,121	44,131
Methanol	1,067,580	2,822,613	510	0	641,155	156,177	1,540,918	6,228,953
Methyl ethyl ketone	1,297,015	4,367,065	5	0	5	1,265	981,212	6,646,567
Methyl isobutyl ketone	277,639	1,695,203	10	0	0	2,099	105,714	2,080,665

[Continued]

★ 406 ★

Toxic Chemical Releases in Indiana, by Chemical: 1990
[Continued]

Chemical	Fugitive air	Stack air	Water	Injection	Land	Public treatment	Other offsite	Total releases
Methyl methacrylate	809	264	0	0	0	11	759	1,843
Methyl tert-butyl ether	2,717	24,605	5	0	0	0	17,000	44,327
Methylenebis(phenylisocyanate)	42,327	5,198	5	0	0	3,255	404,350	455,135
Molybdenum trioxide	260	767	0	5	317	0	229,832	231,181
N,N-dimethylaniline	5	0	0	0	0	0	1,331	1,336
N-butyl alcohol	204,361	895,680	5	0	0	1,700,307	249,996	3,050,349
Naphthalene	186,156	104,134	0	14,000	27	338	74,390	379,045
Nickel	6,924	91,008	423	1,630	6,138	3,816	224,445	334,384
Nickel compounds	12,961	11,968	3,360	9,105	96,113	23,825	275,252	432,584
Nitric acid	84,391	79,381	275	5	0	78,983	433,859	676,894
Nitroglycerin	2	0	0	0	0	0	0	2
O-cresol	0	0	0	0	0	0	462	462
O-xylene	5	5	0	0	0	5	0	15
P-phenylenediamine	130	0	0	0	0	0	136	266
Peracetic acid	250	250	5	0	5	0	0	510
Phenol	490,752	394,088	23,140	115,700	784	638	234,245	1,259,347
Phosphoric acid	6,780	58,730	13,920	10	83,248	99,132	279,264	541,084
Phosphorus (yellow or white)	135	0	0	0	0	0	840	975
Phthalic anhydride	1,811	1,125	50	0	0	5,242	2,184	10,412
Polychlorinated biphenyls (PCBs)	5	0	0	0	0	0	12,039	12,044
Propionaldehyde	59	4,158	0	0	0	0	0	4,217
Propylene	161,067	15,072	0	0	0	0	0	176,139
Propylene oxide	580	74,166	0	0	0	5,131	886	80,763
Pyridine	6,238	22,389	5	0	5	45,935	4,780	79,352
Quinoline	860	500	0	0	0	250	2,450	4,060
Sec-butyl alcohol	1,005	11,505	0	0	0	0	1,750	14,260
Selenium compounds	0	0	0	0	0	0	250	250
Styrene	962,314	1,195,675	0	0	3,001	277	527,070	2,688,337
Sulfuric acid	41,443	162,862	111,063	6,865	5,019	1,490,243	572,212	2,389,707
Tert-butyl alcohol	1,660	600	0	0	0	0	5	2,265
Tetrachloroethylene	1,977,404	465,507	920	0	0	255	230,932	2,675,018
Toluene	5,316,807	10,765,478	731	0	384	44,736	1,818,471	17,946,607
Toluenediisocyanate (mixed isomers)	263	1,382	0	0	0	5	0	1,650
Toluene-2,4-diisocyanate	250	406	0	0	0	0	1,080	1,736
Toluene-2,6-diisocyanate	265	290	0	0	0	0	270	825
Trichloroethylene	1,752,185	1,926,045	500	0	0	1,425	238,844	3,918,999
Trifluralin	9,900	750	5	0	0	0	33,000	43,655
Urethane	0	2,800	0	0	0	0	0	2,800
Vanadium (fume or dust)	5	5	0	0	0	0	0	10
Vinyl acetate	1,053	0	0	0	0	0	0	1,053
Vinyl chloride	250	250	0	0	0	250	11,388	12,138
Vinylidene chloride	250	250	0	0	0	0	1,700	2,200
Xylene (mixed isomers)	1,889,725	7,747,204	1,024	0	101	22,267	995,749	10,656,070
Zinc (fume or dust)	24,028	15,815	422	0	54,297	3,198	186,169	283,929
Zinc compounds	55,286	66,731	95,681	250	2,949,306	10,661	2,215,173	5,393,088

Source: U.S. Environmental Protection Agency. "Toxic Chemical Releases, 1990." In *National Economic, Social, and Environmental Data Bank* [CD-ROM]. Prepared by U.S. Department of Commerce, Economics and Statistics Administration. Washington, DC: U.S. Department of Commerce, National Economic, Social, and Environmental Data Bank, Economics and Statistics Administration, Office of Business Analysis, February 1995.

★ 407 ★

Chemicals

Toxic Chemical Releases in Iowa, by Chemical: 1990

Figures indicate pounds released by chemical and by type of emission per year.

Chemical	Fugitive air	Stack air	Water	Injection	Land	Public treatment	Other offsite	Total releases
1,1,1-trichloroethane	815,365	1,738,743	263	0	7,755	284	90,726	2,653,136
1,1,2-trichloroethane	3,800	95,000	5	0	0	0	450	99,255
1,2,4-trimethylbenzene	13,885	118,225	57	0	0	0	800	132,967
1,2-dichloroethane	5,000	38,000	740	0	0	0	0	43,740
1,3-butadiene	22,350	150,250	0	0	0	0	0	172,600
1,4-dioxane	0	17,019	0	0	0	0	0	17,019
2,4-d	250	0	0	0	0	0	750	1,000
2-nitropropane	0	750	0	0	0	0	0	750
Acetaldehyde	0	80,000	0	0	0	0	0	80,000
Acetone	368,206	1,674,181	258	0	194	1,251	35,823	2,079,913
Acrylic acid	5	19,000	0	0	0	0	32,000	51,005
Acrylonitrile	7,500	490,000	22	0	0	0	3,700	501,222
Aluminum (fume or dust)	1,750	13,059	0	0	0	250	15,379	30,438
Ammonia	1,233,815	7,133,929	2,102,240	0	8,752	915,420	1,039,476	12,433,632
Ammonium nitrate (solution)	6,585	26,850	115,937	0	250	0	0	149,622
Ammonium sulfate (solution)	500	500	0	0	0	0	250	1,250
Aniline	270	150	5	0	0	1	0	426
Anthracene	0	0	0	0	10	0	1,000	1,010
Arsenic compounds	5	5	380	0	0	40	106,270	106,700
Barium	5	5	15	5	14,983	0	250	15,263
Barium compounds	258	538	20	0	6,250	314	10,626	18,006
Benzene	11,010	13,605	1	0	0	0	1,200	25,816
Bromomethane	1,600	0	0	0	0	0	0	1,600
Butyl acrylate	91	258	0	0	0	0	750	1,099
Butyl benzyl phthalate	1	5	0	0	0	0	0	6
Cadmium	5	6	1	0	5	0	323	340
Cadmium compounds	5	5	0	0	0	10	505	525
Chlorine	18,778	416,317	17,371	0	5	1,000	0	453,471
Chlorobenzene	8,500	5,500	7	0	0	0	8,800	22,807
Chromium	3,999	6,030	2	0	5,451	1,041	151,649	168,172
Chromium compounds	1,261	1,585	391	0	9,615	1,814	286,350	301,016
Cobalt	500	0	0	0	250	0	250	1,000
Copper	4,977	44,269	760	0	255	2,104	12,043	64,408
Copper compounds	1,328	7,838	0	0	250	1,582	6,621	17,619
Cumene	1,110	12,720	14	0	0	0	72	13,916
Cyclohexane	6,955	793,210	0	0	0	0	14,000	814,165
Di(2-ethylhexyl) phthalate	5	0	0	0	0	0	1,000	1,005
Dichloromethane	320,182	542,419	0	0	0	325	2,596	865,522
Dichlorvos	280	5	0	0	0	0	5	290
Diethanolamine	500	250	5,500	0	250	30,000	0	36,500
Dimethyl phthalate	0	250	0	0	0	0	0	250
Epichlorohydrin	250	250	0	0	0	0	0	500
Ethylbenzene	11,476	37,790	109	0	5	10	689	50,079
Ethylene	620,000	372,000	0	0	0	0	0	992,000
Ethylene glycol	27,046	20,914	16,972	0	255	4,159,073	18,416	4,242,676
Ethylene oxide	1,255	755	0	0	0	250	0	2,260
Formaldehyde	40,534	7,851	345	0	0	0	110	48,840
Freon 113	396,759	21,100	0	0	0	0	127	417,986
Glycol ethers	192,769	683,115	475	0	80	409,312	526,673	1,812,424
Hydrochloric acid	12,081	54,984	40	5	780	53,595	37,739	159,224
Hydrogen fluoride	255	755	0	0	0	10	0	1,020

[Continued]

★ 407 ★

Toxic Chemical Releases in Iowa, by Chemical: 1990

[Continued]

Chemical	Fugitive air	Stack air	Water	Injection	Land	Public treatment	Other offsite	Total releases
Isopropyl alcohol (manufacturing)	6,152	0	0	0	0	0	10,000	16,152
Lead	520	1,233	514	0	5	321	37,935	40,528
Lead compounds	1,762	10,096	74	0	30,005	1,033	43,123	86,093
M-xylene	108	612	0	0	0	0	0	720
Maleic anhydride	5	5	0	0	0	0	35,000	35,010
Manganese	7,701	16,316	1,645	5	10,120	769	125,031	161,587
Manganese compounds	5,435	3,185	3,933	0	32,100	111,284	149,746	305,683
Mercury compounds	0	0	0	0	0	0	5	5
Methanol	312,356	2,386,544	22,620	0	8	784,440	78,546	3,584,514
Methyl ethyl ketone	232,486	2,303,974	250	0	289	25	201,549	2,738,573
Methyl isobutyl ketone	20,447	354,062	250	0	37	15	31,757	406,568
Methyl methacrylate	92	2,141	0	0	0	0	0	2,233
Methylenebis(phenylisocyanate)	1,085	30,435	0	0	7,750	0	10,505	49,775
Molybdenum trioxide	3,050	10,450	12,800	0	750	0	0	27,050
N-butyl alcohol	46,648	221,331	143	0	22	250	1,758	270,152
N-dioctyl phthalate	6	0	0	0	0	0	0	6
Naphthalene	2,375	99,653	10	0	0	0	1,200	103,238
Nickel	3,330	3,376	0	0	2,000	776	37,388	46,870
Nickel compounds	1,010	755	128	0	755	344	9,972	12,964
Nitric acid	1,265	7,600	10	0	34,040	78,927	15	121,857
Peracetic acid	5	250	0	0	0	250	0	505
Phenol	129,057	105,773	47	0	2,170	4	94,261	331,312
Phosphoric acid	2,736	4,446	4,315	0	43,248	196,802	5	251,552
Phthalic anhydride	98	4	0	0	0	0	0	102
Propylene	18,380	24,427	0	0	0	0	0	42,807
Propylene oxide	0	250	0	0	0	0	0	250
Selenium	250	0	10	0	0	0	500	760
Selenium compounds	251	250	0	0	0	0	560	1,061
Silver	250	250	0	0	0	250	250	1,000
Styrene	73,133	732,676	16	0	5	750	64,032	870,612
Sulfuric acid	15,567	30,016	20	5	25	467,063	16,545	529,241
Tetrachloroethylene	226,570	997,001	1,052	0	0	5	7,413	1,232,041
Toluene	773,329	6,123,538	250	0	63,257	264	283,590	7,244,228
Toluenediisocyanate (mixed isomers)	250	250	0	0	0	0	0	500
Trichloroethylene	31,292	69,955	5	0	0	0	7,641	108,893
Trifluralin	252	8	2	0	0	4	20,777	21,043
Vinyl acetate	34,000	20,000	0	0	0	0	0	54,000
Xylene (mixed isomers)	813,630	2,863,495	1,203	0	1,098	269	112,560	3,792,255
Zinc (fume or dust)	35,236	46,255	1,700	0	0	0	13,502	96,693
Zinc compounds	7,037	11,607	875	0	0	4,136	281,717	305,372

Source: U.S. Environmental Protection Agency. "Toxic Chemical Releases, 1990." In *National Economic, Social, and Environmental Data Bank* [CD-ROM]. Prepared by U.S. Department of Commerce, Economics and Statistics Administration. Washington, DC: U.S. Department of Commerce, National Economic, Social, and Environmental Data Bank, Economics and Statistics Administration, Office of Business Analysis, February 1995.

★ 408 ★
Chemicals

Toxic Chemical Releases in Kansas, by Chemical: 1990

Figures indicate pounds released by chemical and by type of emission per year.

Chemical	Fugitive air	Stack air	Water	Injection	Land	Public treatment	Other offsite	Total releases
1,1,1-trichloroethane	1,125,187	309,497	255	580	500	1,900	189,889	1,627,808
1,1,2,2-tetrachloroethane	0	0	0	0	0	0	27	27
1,2,4-trimethylbenzene	169,599	10,640	225	0	0	13,500	0	193,964
1,2-dichloroethane	4,005	14,200	10	5,000	0	0	0	23,215
1,2-dichloroethylene	12	7,600	0	360	0	0	0	7,972
1,2-dichloropropane	850	2	0	0	0	0	0	852
1,3-butadiene	50	0	0	0	0	0	0	50
2,4-d	260	255	0	0	0	5	750	1,270
2,4-dimethylphenol	0	0	0	0	0	0	2	2
2-ethoxyethanol	48,002	48,001	10	0	0	0	5	96,018
2-methoxyethanol	0	250	250	0	250	0	0	750
2-phenylphenol	5	5	15	5	20	250	500	800
4,4'-methylenedianiline	250	250	0	250	0	0	0	750
Acetaldehyde	5,750	750	0	0	0	0	0	6,500
Acetone	854,291	509,962	7,015	0	0	94,206	133,147	1,598,621
Acrylic acid	10	0	0	0	0	10	0	20
Acrylonitrile	2,800	250	0	250	0	0	0	3,300
Allyl chloride	5,900	5	0	250	0	0	0	6,155
Aluminum (fume or dust)	0	34,109	0	0	3,004	0	37,706	74,819
Aluminum oxide (fibrous forms)	250	250	0	0	0	0	0	500
Ammonia	1,404,629	3,917,931	62,870	4,417	1,039,851	102,885	949,734	7,482,317
Ammonium nitrate (solution)	0	1,750	956,300	0	82,760	1,525,003	0	2,565,813
Ammonium sulfate (solution)	0	0	0	0	0	288,000	741,062	1,029,062
Antimony	15	505	0	0	0	260	510	1,290
Antimony compounds	250	0	0	0	0	0	20,656	20,906
Arsenic compounds	250	250	199	0	0	5	27,680	28,384
Asbestos (friable)	250	5	0	0	0	0	3,350	3,605
Barium	0	101	0	0	0	0	250	351
Barium compounds	505	350	660	0	1,598	255	8,583	11,951
Benzene	136,968	199,987	326	0	90	0	55	337,426
Benzoyl chloride	250	250	0	0	0	5	0	505
Benzoyl peroxide	250	4	0	0	0	1,300	240	1,794
Bis(2-ethylhexyl) adipate	0	0	0	0	0	0	1,942	1,942
Butyl acrylate	1,691	290	0	0	0	10	0	1,991
Butyl benzyl phthalate	750	0	0	0	0	0	0	750
Cadmium	0	0	0	0	0	0	250	250
Cadmium compounds	5	5	0	0	0	250	252	512
Calcium cyanamide	12,000	620	0	0	40,000	0	0	52,620
Carbon disulfide	340,000	1,298,076	0	0	0	0	250	1,638,326
Carbon tetrachloride	6,865	89,205	5	31,000	0	0	5,437	132,512
Carbonyl sulfide	0	157,679	0	0	0	0	0	157,679
Chlorine	15,714	18,305	280	8,605	10,520	17,750	5	71,179
Chloroethane	7	0	0	110	0	0	0	117
Chloroform	8,400	243,800	0	77,000	0	0	13,471	342,671
Chloromethane	9,362	80,095	0	46,000	0	0	0	135,457
Chlorophenols	1,600	0	0	51,000	0	0	0	52,600
Chromium	1,005	325	0	0	7,700	1,593	36,284	46,907
Chromium compounds	32,154	24,190	265	250	6,368	1,442	583,144	647,813
Cobalt compounds	19	25	0	0	0	0	479	523
Copper	32	415	4	0	3	63	118,645	119,162
Copper compounds	17,262	520	1,256	0	0	550	275,575	295,163

[Continued]

★ 408 ★

Toxic Chemical Releases in Kansas, by Chemical: 1990

[Continued]

Chemical	Fugitive air	Stack air	Water	Injection	Land	Public treatment	Other offsite	Total releases
Cresol (mixed isomers)	1,100	0	0	0	0	0	0	1,100
Cumene	160,410	220,650	535	0	250	2,951	260	385,056
Cumene hydroperoxide	28,000	4,000	0	0	0	0	0	32,000
Cyanide compounds	0	0	0	0	0	5	256	261
Cyclohexane	105,620	37,100	105	0	0	0	9,700	152,525
Di(2-ethylhexyl) phthalate	0	0	0	0	0	0	750	750
Dichloromethane	164,276	253,763	10	33,000	0	250	15,550	466,849
Dichlorvos	5	250	0	0	0	0	2,920	3,175
Diethanolamine	4,950	3,300	5,805	0	0	1,000	0	15,055
Epichlorohydrin	33,120	33,160	0	0	0	5	0	66,285
Ethyl acrylate	1,480	47	0	0	0	10	0	1,537
Ethylbenzene	125,712	82,769	380	0	500	255	7,050	216,666
Ethylene	146,744	923,700	0	0	0	0	0	1,070,444
Ethylene glycol	6,955	761	17	0	250	8,575	17,800	34,358
Ethylene oxide	2,500	20,964	5	0	0	32,617	0	56,086
Formaldehyde	15,360	221,623	0	250	0	7,678	7,872	252,783
Freon 113	137,676	161,734	10	0	0	250	376	300,046
Glycol ethers	12,117	150,156	10	0	5	68,785	15,763	246,836
Hexachloro-1,3-butadiene	26	23	0	330	0	0	8	387
Hexachlorobenzene	27	2	0	220	0	0	22	271
Hexachloroethane	28	26	0	1,500	0	0	96	1,650
Hydrochloric acid	5,266	39,018	765	45,090,005	20	18,360	376,715	45,530,149
Hydrogen fluoride	105,159	3,550	10	0	0	5	71,100	179,824
Hydroquinone	0	0	0	0	0	5	0	5
Isopropyl alcohol (manufacturing)	11,460	0	0	0	0	0	5,460	16,920
Lead	260	2,637	27	0	120,000	70	3,872	126,866
Lead compounds	2,038	6,970	13	0	750	1,052	236,810	247,633
M-xylene	50,617	4,401	0	0	0	0	0	55,018
Manganese	8,763	5	0	0	0	2,452	11,528	22,748
Manganese compounds	3,077	4,448	1,200	0	375	12,280	1,325,722	1,347,102
Mercury compounds	0	0	0	0	0	0	2	2
Methanol	54,655	958,683	785	250,250	590	201,520	27,688	1,494,171
Methyl ethyl ketone	810,797	1,171,318	10	0	0	250	430,000	2,412,375
Methyl isobutyl ketone	26,831	52,098	10	0	0	0	55,405	134,344
Methyl methacrylate	1,851	558	0	0	0	10	0	2,419
Methyl tert-butyl ether	3,400	570	0	0	0	0	0	3,970
Methylenebis(phenylisocyanate)	310	270	0	5	20	0	5,200	5,805
N-butyl alcohol	29,355	370,913	5	0	0	24,526	33,367	458,166
N-dioctyl phthalate	1,500	0	0	0	0	0	6,600	8,100
Naphthalene	74,478	757	10	0	0	0	375	75,620
Nickel	500	1,460	0	0	5	5	10,055	12,025
Nickel compounds	23,012	480	51	0	0	250	4,961	28,754
Nitric acid	3,010	4,470	25	0	1,250	15,853	43,675	68,283
O-toluidine	250	5	0	250	0	0	0	505
O-xylene	2,830	167	0	0	0	0	20,931	23,928
P-cresol	607	4	0	0	0	0	24,402	25,013
Parathion	5	0	0	0	0	0	0	5
Phenol	78,251	307,452	437	0	0	194,765	25,279	606,184
Phosgene	48	20	0	0	0	0	0	68
Phosphoric acid	2,649	98,943	20	5	1,015	1,985	42,162	146,779
Phosphorus (yellow or white)	1,800	0	0	0	0	0	0	1,800
Propylene	222,755	1,601,520	0	0	0	0	0	1,824,275

[Continued]

★ 408 ★

Toxic Chemical Releases in Kansas, by Chemical: 1990
[Continued]

Chemical	Fugitive air	Stack air	Water	Injection	Land	Public treatment	Other offsite	Total releases
Propylene oxide	500	500	255	0	0	1,081	0	2,336
Pyridine	750	250	0	250	0	0	0	1,250
Styrene	153,162	278,202	0	0	750	1,010	250	433,374
Sulfuric acid	25,675	23,873	25	13,000,000	2,197	51,660	1,317,380	14,420,810
Tetrachloroethylene	55,161	561,937	260	11,000	0	750	71,770	700,878
Tetrachlorvinphos	0	0	0	0	0	0	6,228	6,228
Toluene	1,035,907	1,827,186	706	2,800	540	1,265	529,958	3,398,362
Toluenediisocyanate (mixed isomers)	250	250	0	0	0	0	250	750
Toluene-2,4-diisocyanate	250	0	0	0	0	0	0	250
Toluene-2,6-diisocyanate	250	0	0	0	0	0	0	250
Trichlorfon	250	250	0	0	0	125	995	1,620
Trichloroethylene	201,523	2,183,767	255	800	0	337	111,358	2,498,040
Urethane	10	10	0	0	0	0	0	20
Vinyl acetate	4,351	4,801	0	0	0	694	0	9,846
Vinyl chloride	10	1	0	170	0	0	0	181
Vinylidene chloride	10	9	0	150	0	0	0	169
Xylene (mixed isomers)	496,051	1,547,199	1,535	0	1,060	770	212,725	2,259,340
Zinc compounds	13,832	8,056	1,650	90,000	1,255	425	114,445	229,663

Source: U.S. Environmental Protection Agency. "Toxic Chemical Releases, 1990." In *National Economic, Social, and Environmental Data Bank* [CD-ROM]. Prepared by U.S. Department of Commerce, Economics and Statistics Administration. Washington, DC: U.S. Department of Commerce, National Economic, Social, and Environmental Data Bank, Economics and Statistics Administration, Office of Business Analysis, February 1995.

★ 409 ★

Chemicals

Toxic Chemical Releases in Kentucky, by Chemical: 1990

Figures indicate pounds released by chemical and by type of emission per year.

Chemical	Fugitive air	Stack air	Water	Injection	Land	Public treatment	Other offsite	Total releases
1,1,1-trichloroethane	1,364,207	850,835	590	0	0	835	92,066	2,308,533
1,1,2,2-tetrachloroethane	115	12	0	0	0	0	1,180	1,307
1,1,2-trichloroethane	700	90	0	0	0	0	165,017	165,807
1,2,4-trichlorobenzene	251	2	0	0	0	0	157,660	157,913
1,2,4-trimethylbenzene	18,503	20,750	50	0	0	0	12,307	51,610
1,2-dichloroethane	173,000	270,002	0	0	0	0	255,999	699,001
1,2-dichloroethylene	390	0	0	0	0	0	4,000	4,390
1,3-butadiene	121,958	190,084	511	0	1	5	1,633	314,192
2-ethoxyethanol	4,836	66	0	0	0	82,196	8,383	95,481
2-methoxyethanol	35	19	0	0	0	28	40	122
4,4'-isopropylidenediphenol	469	482	0	0	0	190	3,075	4,216
Acetaldehyde	96,011	2,562	250	0	0	0	0	98,823
Acetone	609,409	2,024,449	8,010	0	360	562	439,650	3,082,440
Acetonitrile	36	202	0	0	0	10	0	248
Acrylamide	4	5	0	0	0	148	5,975	6,132
Acrylic acid	1,453	1,142	251	0	250	294	28,441	31,831
Acrylonitrile	32,490	132,499	9	0	2	70,577	4,221	239,798
Allyl alcohol	4,400	1	540	0	0	0	540	5,481
Allyl chloride	4,000	48	120	0	0	0	6,231	10,399

[Continued]

★ 409 ★

Toxic Chemical Releases in Kentucky, by Chemical: 1990
[Continued]

Chemical	Fugitive air	Stack air	Water	Injection	Land	Public treatment	Other offsite	Total releases
Aluminum (fume or dust)	108,608	281,150	26,778	0	106,100	13,001	8,249,707	8,785,344
Aluminum oxide (fibrous forms)	250	0	0	0	0	0	0	250
Ammonia	266,819	570,164	379,200	10	847,275	423,984	68,132	2,555,584
Ammonium nitrate (solution)	5	10	0	0	281	83,225	0	83,521
Ammonium sulfate (solution)	6,035	0	0	0	1,433	5,731	660	13,859
Anthracene	607	511	253	0	1,472	0	2,313	5,156
Antimony	6	17	0	0	0	5	5	33
Antimony compounds	1,876	14,683	1,291	0	0	2,187	50,538	70,575
Arsenic	0	0	0	0	0	0	3,300	3,300
Arsenic compounds	20	5,220	5	5	5	250	12,458	17,963
Asbestos (friable)	5	250	0	0	0	0	141,776	142,031
Barium	250	253	0	0	0	250	6,477	7,230
Barium compounds	2,155	5,414	15	5	260	50,950	543,514	602,313
Benzene	264,641	186,445	432	0	260	22,100	231,436	705,314
Benzoyl peroxide	32	5	0	0	0	0	1,300	1,337
Benzyl chloride	43	741	0	0	0	0	0	784
Biphenyl	646	79	50	0	39	0	2,873	3,687
Butyl acrylate	19,435	24,396	0	0	0	2,742	2,290	48,863
Butyl benzyl phthalate	3,479	3,210	0	0	0	250	345	7,284
Butyraldehyde	1,699	0	0	0	0	0	0	1,699
Cadmium	5	0	0	0	0	0	0	5
Cadmium compounds	520	1,315	0	0	0	780	49,134	51,749
Captan	5	0	0	0	0	0	250	255
Carbaryl	250	0	0	0	0	0	250	500
Carbon disulfide	350	60	0	0	0	120	0	530
Carbon tetrachloride	6,405	6,525	131	0	0	10	1,353	14,424
Catechol	0	0	2,440	0	53	0	0	2,493
Chlorine	10,894	40,530	6,024	0	0	75,722	755	133,925
Chlorine dioxide	250	40,300	0	0	0	0	0	40,550
Chlorobenzene	1,855	1,703	0	0	0	8	1,582	5,148
Chloroethane	690	0	0	0	0	0	2,300	2,990
Chloroform	66,296	127,080	9,050	0	1,505	3,149	27,005	234,085
Chloromethane	44,001	400,004	1,400	0	1	0	0	445,406
Chloroprene	94,305	371,602	0	0	0	60,194	730	526,831
Chlorothalonil	22	39	0	0	0	0	313	374
Chromium	2,751	2,390	865	0	2,872	1,460	25,478	35,816
Chromium compounds	2,491	26,129	3,612	0	3,525	2,686	118,871	157,314
Cobalt	750	521	109	0	0	5	7,323	8,708
Cobalt compounds	10	260	5	0	0	78	285	638
Copper	21,173	4,212	1,281	0	27,441	4,782	104,461	163,350
Copper compounds	1,337	1,839	540	0	350	5,327	178,614	188,007
Creosote	9,002	15,685	0	0	5,439	5	1,126,900	1,157,031
Cresol (mixed isomers)	507	75,758	0	0	0	0	44,535	120,800
Cumene	44,220	20,230	50	0	0	0	5,319	69,819
Cumene hydroperoxide	20	262	0	0	0	5	20	307
Cyanide compounds	765	4,482	1,600	0	250	27,959	11,080	46,136
Cyclohexane	17,408	31,400	99	0	0	750	131,363	181,020
Decabromodiphenyl oxide	98	10	32	0	0	9	1,331	1,480
Di(2-ethylhexyl) phthalate	10	14,619	0	0	0	21	3,964	18,614
Dibenzofuran	206	206	0	0	103	0	91	606
Dibutyl phthalate	2,524	3,520	0	0	0	0	10	6,054
Dichloromethane	868,068	650,083	252	0	0	17,937	72,170	1,608,510

[Continued]

★ 409 ★

Toxic Chemical Releases in Kentucky, by Chemical: 1990
[Continued]

Chemical	Fugitive air	Stack air	Water	Injection	Land	Public treatment	Other offsite	Total releases
Diethanolamine	17,295	6	16,116	0	0	3,228	250	36,895
Diethyl sulfate	4	0	0	0	0	0	0	4
Dimethyl phthalate	10	5	0	0	0	371	15	401
Epichlorohydrin	1,153	4,373	0	0	0	962	0	6,488
Ethyl acrylate	8,090	14,686	8	0	9	5,187	4,416	32,396
Ethylbenzene	33,300	72,021	68	0	10	731	195,393	301,523
Ethylene	205,939	1,818,231	550	0	0	0	110	2,024,830
Ethylene glycol	65,193	87,586	8,785	0	1,506	153,940	150,680	467,690
Ethylene oxide	18,836	903	0	0	0	35,956	0	55,695
Formaldehyde	23,325	29,976	19,767	0	4	3,033	2,799	78,904
Freon 113	155,454	191,917	0	0	0	255	11,538	359,164
Glycol ethers	208,332	1,452,644	0	0	2,620	250,029	366,931	2,280,556
Hydrazine	1	0	0	0	0	0	0	1
Hydrochloric acid	62,084	1,585,187	335	9,447,819	15	280	1,995,273	13,090,993
Hydrogen cyanide	450	55	0	0	0	0	0	505
Hydrogen fluoride	3,963	814,906	0	0	0	5	86,310	905,184
Hydroquinone	250	0	0	0	0	0	0	250
Isopropyl alcohol (manufacturing)	24,720	96,670	250	5	5	5	500	122,155
Lead	3,055	822	2,960	5	29,237	286	7,159	43,524
Lead compounds	3,440	29,583	750	0	150	3,965	503,580	541,468
Lindane	250	0	0	0	0	0	500	750
M-cresol	5	5	0	0	0	0	0	10
M-xylene	2,341	123,479	0	0	0	0	23,589	149,409
Maleic anhydride	501	258	0	0	0	5	346	1,110
Maneb	5	0	0	0	0	0	250	255
Manganese	10,237	5,630	260	0	8,103	515	14,910	39,655
Manganese compounds	44,157	6,926	14,870	0	10,800	1,311	978,366	1,056,430
Mercury	0	1,200	17	0	0	0	12,000	13,217
Methanol	2,233,093	2,161,848	117,111	0	15,255	16,545	1,037,528	5,581,380
Methyl acrylate	9,300	3,028	0	0	0	1,558	507	14,393
Methyl ethyl ketone	338,702	1,066,145	0	0	0	9,531	360,245	1,774,623
Methyl isobutyl ketone	144,802	370,554	5	0	0	147,821	274,410	937,592
Methyl methacrylate	62,713	172,641	1	0	0	49,530	10,418	295,303
Methyl tert-butyl ether	4,450	50,900	0	0	0	0	0	55,350
Methylenebis(phenylisocyanate)	8,625	786	0	5	20	615	28,231	38,282
Molybdenum trioxide	270	28	750	0	0	2,215	23,793	27,056
N-butyl alcohol	79,262	646,237	0	0	0	30,862	239,291	995,652
N-dioctyl phthalate	301	0	0	0	0	0	0	301
Naphthalene	34,346	21,994	316	5	836	656	47,107	105,260
Nickel	3,497	4,379	1,010	0	12,550	1,457	72,519	95,412
Nickel compounds	3,744	18,090	1,061	0	150	9,498	182,131	214,674
Nitric acid	4,781	48,825	0	0	0	3,960	108,683	166,249
O-cresol	260	265	0	0	0	0	0	525
P-cresol	250	250	0	0	0	0	0	500
Pentachlorophenol	5	5	250	0	0	250	9,700	10,210
Phenol	2,795	86,647	2,725	0	586	23,969	67,357	184,079
Phosphoric acid	1,706	6,935	0	0	0	364,055	75,845	448,541
Phosphorus (yellow or white)	1,490	1,490	0	0	0	0	0	2,980
Phthalic anhydride	47,124	943	0	0	0	30	992	49,089
Polychlorinated biphenyls (PCBs)	0	0	0	0	0	0	400,597	400,597
Propylene	80,342	25,000	500	0	0	0	50,854	156,696
Propylene oxide	5,482	5,167	0	0	0	3	0	10,652

[Continued]

★ 409 ★

Toxic Chemical Releases in Kentucky, by Chemical: 1990

[Continued]

Chemical	Fugitive air	Stack air	Water	Injection	Land	Public treatment	Other offsite	Total releases
Quinoline	49	49	0	0	24	0	22	144
Sec-butyl alcohol	506	37,118	0	0	0	0	0	37,624
Selenium	250	5	0	0	0	0	1,500	1,755
Selenium compounds	255	255	5	0	0	99	525	1,139
Styrene	237,513	455,793	102	0	7	2,862	101,721	797,998
Sulfuric acid	31,354	130,258	38,779	5	327	230,536	388,380	819,639
Tert-butyl alcohol	250	4,570	0	0	0	0	750	5,570
Tetrachloroethylene	174,198	338,645	0	0	0	265	72,077	585,185
Titanium tetrachloride	5	0	0	0	0	0	0	5
Toluene	1,481,998	7,082,402	719	5	1,530	36,075	949,801	9,552,530
Toluenediisocyanate (mixed isomers)	12	261	0	0	0	1	7	281
Toluene-2,4-diisocyanate	24	260	0	0	0	0	19,493	19,777
Toluene-2,6-diisocyanate	5	255	0	0	0	0	4,855	5,115
Trichloroethylene	110,323	310,839	0	0	600	15	117,647	539,424
Vinyl acetate	471,014	175,856	1,086	0	8	250	30,016	678,230
Vinyl chloride	42,250	37,350	0	0	0	0	12,630	92,230
Vinylidene chloride	14,270	22,000	7	0	4	0	0	36,281
Xylene (mixed isomers)	689,771	3,907,316	550	0	760	4,904	1,234,915	5,838,216
Zinc (fume or dust)	56,712	6,368	6,588	0	2,800	441	548,838	621,747
Zinc compounds	10,269	8,968	1,139	0	12,267	10,949	413,973	457,565

Source: U.S. Environmental Protection Agency. "Toxic Chemical Releases, 1990." In National Economic, Social, and Environmental Data Bank [CD-ROM]. Prepared by U.S. Department of Commerce, Economics and Statistics Administration. Washington, DC: U.S. Department of Commerce, National Economic, Social, and Environmental Data Bank, Economics and Statistics Administration, Office of Business Analysis, February 1995.

★ 410 ★

Chemicals

Toxic Chemical Releases in Louisiana, by Chemical: 1990

Figures indicate pounds released by chemical and by type of emission per year.

Chemical	Fugitive air	Stack air	Water	Injection	Land	Public treatment	Other offsite	Total releases
1,1,1-trichloroethane	551,806	252,421	386	0	0	10	13,539	818,162
1,1,2,2-tetrachloroethane	16,823	4,754	1,679	80	245	0	58,340	81,921
1,1,2-trichloroethane	50,220	31,419	1,008	1,086	245	0	141,516	225,494
1,1-dimethyl hydrazine	91	56	250	0	0	0	68	465
1,2,4-trichlorobenzene	5	250	0	0	0	0	257	512
1,2,4-trimethylbenzene	84,055	79,239	229	5,500	69	0	3,543	172,635
1,2-butylene oxide	10,664	3,824	0	0	0	0	0	14,488
1,2-dibromoethane	173	0	0	0	0	0	64	237
1,2-dichlorobenzene	20	9,200	39	15,000	0	0	8,201	32,460
1,2-dichloroethane	383,186	419,084	14,863	771,840	98	0	786,826	2,375,897
1,2-dichloroethylene	9,901	34,363	53	0	118	0	1	44,436
1,2-dichloropropane	27,300	30,800	2,003	0	0	0	3,680	63,783
1,3-butadiene	300,767	47,940	0	1,600	0	0	549	350,856
1,3-dichlorobenzene	0	0	0	0	0	0	1	1
1,3-dichloropropylene	6,800	2,700	0	0	0	0	0	9,500
1,4-dichlorobenzene	0	0	0	0	0	0	1	1
1,4-dioxane	25,617	20,694	29,902	0	0	0	29,000	105,213
2,4-dimethylphenol	0	0	5	0	0	0	0	5
2,4-dinitrotoluene	1,332	51,000	40	74,000	0	0	108,200	234,572

[Continued]

★ 410 ★

Toxic Chemical Releases in Louisiana, by Chemical: 1990

[Continued]

Chemical	Fugitive air	Stack air	Water	Injection	Land	Public treatment	Other offsite	Total releases
2,6-dinitrotoluene	308	16,000	40	19,000	0	0	27,100	62,448
2-ethoxyethanol	0	270	0	0	0	0	0	270
2-methoxyethanol	295	3,254	136	0	0	0	0	3,685
2-nitrophenol	0	4	29	0	0	0	994	1,027
2-nitropropane	51,000	17,000	1,100	0	0	0	0	69,100
4,4'-isopropylidenediphenol	0	250	254	0	0	0	250	754
4,4'-methylenedianiline	10	26	300	57,000	0	0	31,400	88,736
4,6-dinitro-o-cresol	0	7	131	0	0	0	413	551
4-nitrophenol	260	82	0	1,200	0	0	1,217	2,759
Acetaldehyde	23,436	312,407	41,258	0	0	0	8,372	385,473
Acetone	432,474	649,980	84,002	1,743,775	2,196	0	88,720	3,001,147
Acetonitrile	96,523	40,279	3,505	12,102,954	4	0	10,743	12,254,008
Acrolein	5,122	9,307	0	0	0	0	0	14,429
Acrylamide	91	347	261	1,400,000	0	0	10,052	1,410,751
Acrylic acid	3,606	4,490	19,744	9,100,000	0	0	2,160	9,130,000
Acrylonitrile	9,380	37,750	32	460,000	0	0	1,262	508,424
Allyl alcohol	82	3	910	0	0	0	190,876	191,871
Allyl chloride	81,100	11,036	0	0	0	0	45,505	137,641
Aluminum (fume or dust)	1,913	0	0	0	0	0	3,100	5,013
Aluminum oxide (fibrous forms)	0	2	0	0	0	3	817	822
Ammonia	2,336,663	46,591,060	4,516,023	85,953,957	90,999	0	52,689	139,541,391
Ammonium nitrate (solution)	0	65	999,547	1,000,000	0	0	1,100	2,000,712
Ammonium sulfate (solution)	0	250	2,275,322	346,425	0	0	42,250	2,664,247
Aniline	1,586	15,036	2,000	2,299,002	0	0	95,996	2,413,620
Anthracene	21	23	72	0	0	1	943	1,060
Antimony	500	252	0	160	0	5	625	1,542
Antimony compounds	250	825	1,280	0	68,109	3	1,320	71,787
Arsenic	250	0	0	0	0	0	0	250
Arsenic compounds	270	270	260	0	27,194	1	7,633	35,628
Asbestos (friable)	1	268	255	0	165,003	0	16,457	181,984
Barium compounds	19,125	61,612	1,506	0	0	752	13,335	96,330
Benzene	979,480	523,615	2,263	134,977	1,202	0	73,161	1,714,698
Biphenyl	7,700	2,620	300	0	12	0	0	10,632
Bis(2-chloro-1-methylethyl) ether	2,400	2,000	12,000	0	0	0	0	16,400
Bis(2-chloroethyl) ether	9	0	73	0	0	0	3,235	3,317
Butyl acrylate	11,799	12,489	1,354	0	0	0	0	25,642
Butyl benzyl phthalate	317	26	1	0	0	0	1,773	2,117
Carbon disulfide	12,956	6,379,473	0	2,800	0	0	0	6,395,229
Carbon tetrachloride	44,363	164,472	1,444	5	5	0	78,664	288,953
Carbonyl sulfide	2,501	1,829,127	0	0	0	0	0	1,831,628
Catechol	5	5	14,663	0	906	0	0	15,579
Chlorine	107,649	500,964	51,453	43,010	50	17,100	616	720,842
Chlorine dioxide	761	55,500	0	0	0	0	0	56,261
Chloroacetic acid	255	299	0	0	0	0	12	566
Chlorobenzene	23,376	255,400	413	43,010	15	0	152,771	474,985
Chloroethane	37,486	298,820	1	0	39	0	189,020	525,366
Chloroform	384,343	795,291	18,534	12,475	1,513	0	157,946	1,370,102
Chloromethane	658,390	248,757	279	0	0	0	36	907,462
Chromium	501	30	62	0	0	0	64,168	64,761
Chromium compounds	30,957	297	4,453	690	30,858	311	23,552	91,118
Cobalt compounds	255	500	2,120	18,000	400	0	9,541	30,816
Copper	1,005	383	84	5	5	266	33,901	35,649
Copper compounds	6,375	296	5,497	1,600	501	23,911	274,086	312,266
Creosote	124,826	252,828	0	0	0	4,217	14,247	396,118
Cresol (mixed isomers)	39,800	38	202	0	402	0	7,886	48,328
Cumene	28,437	350,755	129	0	0	0	10,553	389,874
Cumene hydroperoxide	480	0	16	0	0	0	0	496
Cyanide compounds	0	201,000	0	0	0	0	0	201,000
Cyclohexane	86,445	326,830	486	2,300	167	0	4,993	421,221

[Continued]

★ 410 ★

Toxic Chemical Releases in Louisiana, by Chemical: 1990

[Continued]

Chemical	Fugitive air	Stack air	Water	Injection	Land	Public treatment	Other offsite	Total releases
Di(2-ethylhexyl) phthalate	0	0	0	0	0	0	250	250
Diaminotoluene (mixed isomers)	4,644	404	192	89,000	0	0	599,256	693,496
Dibenzofuran	1	1	0	0	0	1	0	3
Dibutyl phthalate	1,729	149	6	0	13	0	0	1,897
Dichlorobenzene (mixed isomers)	0	250	0	0	0	0	11,608	11,858
Dichlorobromomethane	632	0	0	0	0	0	0	632
Dichloromethane	63,039	826,578	764	0	5	252	4,794	895,432
Diethanolamine	250	5,592	13,221	100,000	9	5	750	119,827
Diethyl phthalate	0	0	0	0	0	32	0	32
Dinitrotoluene (mixed isomers)	1,464	6	31	0	0	0	11,284	12,785
Epichlorohydrin	20,164	34,540	95	0	160	0	19	54,978
Ethyl acrylate	3,945	17,314	463	0	0	0	0	21,722
Ethylbenzene	231,015	338,590	1,013	7,000	879	0	66,988	645,485
Ethylene	1,802,869	4,300,620	0	0	0	0	0	6,103,489
Ethylene glycol	349,686	812,031	87,952	31,000	250	3,798	116,887	1,401,604
Ethylene oxide	55,701	150,886	2,345	0	0	0	57	208,989
Formaldehyde	145,333	63,687	26,913	4,600,000	510	0	21,335	4,857,778
Freon 113	203,689	193,165	387	0	0	0	5	397,246
Glycol ethers	272,469	106,634	6,180	0	0	1,322	78,046	464,651
Hexachloro-1,3-butadiene	2,732	1,506	715	0	0	0	73,317	78,270
Hexachlorobenzene	2	200	101	0	0	0	982	1,285
Hexachloroethane	1,201	644	1	0	334	0	54,948	57,128
Hydrazine	464	1,853	1	0	0	0	87	2,405
Hydrazine sulfate	0	0	0	138,941	0	0	0	138,941
Hydrochloric acid	72,769	1,917,036	6,461	610,800	696	5	2,110,549	4,718,316
Hydrogen cyanide	1,616	8,074	479	0	0	0	974	11,143
Hydrogen fluoride	17,820	64,514	0	0	0	0	356	82,690
Hydroquinone	51	1	0	82,000	0	0	15	82,067
Isopropyl alcohol (manufacturing)	304,611	0	36	0	0	0	43,696	348,343
Lead	3,484	402	0	0	0	401	23,329	27,616
Lead compounds	27,109	11,262	599	0	134,970	288	45,533	219,761
M-xylene	38,700	111,900	0	0	0	0	0	150,600
Maleic anhydride	1,744	62,947	250	0	0	0	1,002	65,943
Manganese	4,437	553	0	0	250	0	37,556	42,796
Manganese compounds	835	10	0	0	0	0	15	860
Mercury	1,055	1,443	29	0	0	0	49,939	52,466
Mercury compounds	0	0	12	21	0	0	4	37
Methanol	2,152,618	4,866,294	1,796,866	8,275,579	50,294	10	141,125	17,282,786
Methyl acrylate	813	2,316	0	99	0	0	0	3,228
Methyl ethyl ketone	830,694	417,593	430	0	3	0	186,344	1,435,064
Methyl isobutyl ketone	233,093	72,617	330	50,901	0	0	103,304	460,245
Methyl methacrylate	6,800	134,250	250	210,000	0	0	3,000	354,300
Methyl tert-butyl ether	54,795	124,630	6,304	8,600	120	0	0	194,449
Methylenebis(phenylisocyanate)	35	643	0	0	250	0	298,220	299,148
Molybdenum trioxide	375	2,050	6,505	170,000	4,929	0	5,929	189,788
N-butyl alcohol	155,995	374,176	4,823	0	2	0	60,045	595,041
N-nitrosodiphenylamine	0	0	0	0	0	0	1,853,445	1,853,445
Naphthalene	42,836	17,595	755	9,400	46	1	38,799	109,432
Nickel	260	34	6,693	0	0	0	31,091	38,078
Nickel compounds	255	502	5,811	8,615	2,810	32	188,512	206,537
Nitric acid	806	525,383	10	3,300,000	0	0	62	3,826,261
Nitrobenzene	27	8	0	554,000	0	0	14,130	568,165
O-toluidine	103	605	2	0	0	0	7,061	7,771
O-xylene	26,900	100,694	0	0	0	0	19,831	147,425
P-cresol	8	22	0	1,997	0	0	0	2,027
P-xylene	14,300	106,100	0	0	0	0	0	120,400
Pentachlorophenol	0	5	0	0	0	500	1,680	2,185
Peracetic acid	0	419	105	0	0	0	0	524
Phenol	63,015	48,852	2,501	624,600	5,022	0	65,107	809,097

[Continued]

★ 410 ★

Toxic Chemical Releases in Louisiana, by Chemical: 1990

[Continued]

Chemical	Fugitive air	Stack air	Water	Injection	Land	Public treatment	Other offsite	Total releases
Phosgene	103	4	0	0	0	0	738	845
Phosphoric acid	563	29,347	74,437,761	1,500,005	635,636	10	295,827	76,899,149
Phthalic anhydride	230	280,001	0	0	0	0	52,000	332,231
Polychlorinated biphenyls (PCBs)	0	0	0	0	0	0	15	15
Propionaldehyde	2,500	390	0	0	0	0	0	2,890
Propylene	2,390,539	696,442	0	0	0	0	0	3,086,981
Propylene oxide	36,000	39,191	1	0	0	0	57	75,249
Pyridine	972	5	0	0	0	0	1,009	1,986
Sec-butyl alcohol	96,454	66,570	955	0	0	0	172	164,151
Selenium	250	0	0	0	0	0	0	250
Selenium compounds	250	0	1	0	0	0	40,950	41,201
Silver	0	0	34	0	0	0	730	764
Silver compounds	0	0	0	0	0	5	0	5
Styrene	1,752,962	409,001	371	0	0	0	2,136,730	4,299,064
Styrene oxide	1,275	878	0	0	0	0	0	2,153
Sulfuric acid	36,761	1,165,704	16,303,261	80,000,000	148,642	255	26,272	97,680,895
Tert-butyl alcohol	2,232	55	100	0	0	0	0	2,387
Tetrachloroethylene	133,993	203,174	3,049	7	23	250	718,638	1,059,134
Tetrachlorvinphos	250	0	0	0	0	0	250	500
Titanium tetrachloride	0	100	0	0	0	0	0	100
Toluene	2,564,747	1,491,195	6,191	1,317,540	10,296	10	1,126,277	6,516,256
Toluenediisocyanate (mixed isomers)	1	285	0	0	0	0	97,702	97,988
Toluene-2,4-diisocyanate	3,106	50	0	0	0	0	4,305	7,461
Toluene-2,6-diisocyanate	802	12	0	0	0	0	1,073	1,887
Trichloroethylene	287,661	216,125	1,662	0	3	0	135,850	641,301
Vinyl acetate	113,274	316,168	110	0	0	0	216	429,768
Vinyl chloride	93,998	84,082	6,641	408	0	0	28	185,157
Vinylidene chloride	21,645	177,891	49	0	2	0	25	199,612
Xylene (mixed isomers)	1,437,347	755,580	2,929	47,700	4,678	10	285,308	2,533,552
Zinc (fume or dust)	30,179	4,021	0	0	50	0	147,313	181,563
Zinc compounds	154,832	1,182	144,785	4,390	128,136	9	436,552	869,886

Source: U.S. Environmental Protection Agency. "Toxic Chemical Releases, 1990." In *National Economic, Social, and Environmental Data Bank* [CD-ROM]. Prepared by U.S. Department of Commerce, Economics and Statistics Administration. Washington, DC: U.S. Department of Commerce, National Economic, Social, and Environmental Data Bank, Economics and Statistics Administration, Office of Business Analysis, February 1995.

★ 411 ★

Chemicals

Toxic Chemical Releases in Maine, by Chemical: 1990

Figures indicate pounds released by chemical and by type of emission per year.

Chemical	Fugitive air	Stack air	Water	Injection	Land	Public treatment	Other offsite	Total releases
1,1,1-trichloroethane	391,261	932,441	0	0	0	267	76,229	1,400,198
1,4-dioxane	1,313	17,448	0	0	0	0	0	18,761
2-ethoxyethanol	647	27,921	0	0	0	0	4,296	32,864
4,4'-methylenebis(2-chloro aniline)	0	0	0	0	0	0	1,200	1,200
Acetaldehyde	0	2,600	13,000	0	0	0	250	15,850
Acetone	352,593	444,028	33,978	0	5,350	1,528	60,566	898,043
Aluminum (fume or dust)	250	0	0	0	0	0	0	250
Ammonia	90,000	151,361	139,464	0	0	5	10	380,840

[Continued]

★ 411 ★

Toxic Chemical Releases in Maine, by Chemical: 1990
[Continued]

Chemical	Fugitive air	Stack air	Water	Injection	Land	Public treatment	Other offsite	Total releases
Ammonium nitrate (solution)	0	0	136,948	0	0	0	1,500	138,448
Ammonium sulfate (solution)	0	1,750	62,138	0	0	123,600	500	187,988
Arsenic compounds	5	5	0	0	5	0	250	265
Asbestos (friable)	5	0	0	0	0	0	0	5
Barium compounds	1	1	0	0	0	0	19,597	19,599
Biphenyl	0	17,876	0	0	0	365	0	18,241
Catechol	0	0	9,916	0	250	0	10,042	20,208
Chlorine	9,802	1,317,026	44,623	0	0	0	0	1,371,451
Chlorine dioxide	7,472	558,732	0	0	0	0	0	566,204
Chloroform	369,707	712,780	40,376	0	250	0	240	1,123,353
Chromium	46	100	2	0	0	5	2,359	2,512
Chromium compounds	315	266	37	0	3,845	124,670	25,053	154,186
Copper	521	69	9	0	5	287	2,192	3,083
Copper compounds	505	505	250	0	255	500	26,724	28,739
Cyanide compounds	500	500	0	0	0	6	368	1,374
Dichlorobenzene (mixed isomers)	0	53,033	0	0	0	6,250	0	59,283
Dichloromethane	28,252	750	0	0	0	0	37,461	66,463
Diethanolamine	0	0	24,000	0	0	14,100	0	38,100
Dimethyl sulfate	5	0	0	0	0	0	0	5
Epichlorohydrin	250	250	0	0	0	250	0	750
Ethylene glycol	3,700	9,100	35,400	0	123,500	27,748	5	199,453
Formaldehyde	1,888	148,335	0	0	0	250	250	150,723
Freon 113	21,726	23,500	0	0	0	5	4,500	49,731
Glycol ethers	24,069	1,381,233	17,406	0	0	1,550	2,682	1,426,940
Hydrochloric acid	4,426	507,202	160	0	53,539	2,075	250	567,652
Hydrogen fluoride	250	270	0	0	0	0	36,600	37,120
Isopropyl alcohol (manufacturing)	750	5,500	0	0	0	0	0	6,250
Lead compounds	428	25	0	0	0	0	5,408	5,861
Maleic anhydride	250	250	0	0	0	250	5	755
Manganese	260	8,650	0	0	3,400	0	15,377	27,687
Mercury	1,000	15	6	0	1	0	543	1,565
Methanol	460,152	1,532,961	2,950	0	291,250	250	404,852	2,692,415
Methyl acrylate	580	3,000	0	0	0	0	250	3,830
Methyl ethyl ketone	67,558	124,869	0	0	0	0	19,427	211,854
Methyl isobutyl ketone	480	13,270	0	0	0	0	0	13,750
Methyl methacrylate	15,450	228,600	0	0	250	0	10,037	254,337
Methylenebis(phenylisocyanate)	0	350	0	0	0	0	4,200	4,550
Molybdenum trioxide	250	250	0	0	0	10,819	3,546	14,865
N-butyl alcohol	33,082	70,160	250	0	0	0	11,235	114,727
Naphthalene	11,631	17,153	0	0	0	0	26,983	55,767
Nickel	15	0	0	0	0	255	766	1,036
Nickel compounds	900	460	96	0	0	250	12,803	14,509
Nitric acid	3,048	11,170	0	0	0	250	33,186	47,654
Phenol	9,248	13,403	5	0	0	250	250	23,156
Phosphoric acid	250	2,707	5	0	0	12,500	17,273	32,735
Propylene	505	0	0	0	0	0	0	505

[Continued]

★ 411 ★

Toxic Chemical Releases in Maine, by Chemical: 1990

[Continued]

Chemical	Fugitive air	Stack air	Water	Injection	Land	Public treatment	Other offsite	Total releases
Propylene oxide	252	2,525	0	0	0	0	250	3,027
Styrene	38,385	33,547	0	0	0	500	250	72,682
Sulfuric acid	1,511	2,461,987	4,981	0	826	443,498	51,388	2,964,191
Tetrachloroethylene	750	50,000	0	0	0	0	17,777	68,527
Toluene	225,535	242,825	0	0	0	0	210,574	678,934
Trichloroethylene	3,908	35,172	0	0	0	0	23,524	62,604
Xylene (mixed isomers)	90,970	247,705	0	0	0	5	66,878	405,558
Zinc (fume or dust)	597	2,321	0	0	0	0	28,900	31,818
Zinc compounds	505	755	1,550	0	0	255	74,226	77,291

Source: U.S. Environmental Protection Agency. "Toxic Chemical Releases, 1990." In National Economic, Social, and Environmental Data Bank [CD-ROM]. Prepared by U.S. Department of Commerce, Economics and Statistics Administration. Washington, DC: U.S. Department of Commerce, National Economic, Social, and Environmental Data Bank, Economics and Statistics Administration, Office of Business Analysis, February 1995.

★ 412 ★

Chemicals

Toxic Chemical Releases in Maryland, by Chemical: 1990

Figures indicate pounds released by chemical and by type of emission per year.

Chemical	Fugitive air	Stack air	Water	Injection	Land	Public treatment	Other offsite	Total releases
1,1,1-trichloroethane	1,037,783	298,460	0	0	250	285	101,659	1,438,437
1,2,4-trimethylbenzene	298	1,138	5	0	18	3	28	1,490
1,2-dichloroethane	21,471	15,190	0	0	0	0	0	36,661
2-ethoxyethanol	3,031	0	0	0	0	0	148	3,179
4,4'-isopropylidenediphenol	12,038	3,405	0	0	0	5	250	15,698
4,4'-methylenebis(2-chloro aniline)	5	5	0	0	0	0	150	160
Acetaldehyde	0	135,603	0	0	0	0	0	135,603
Acetone	77,456	138,335	0	0	0	30,766	131,072	377,629
Acetonitrile	2,967	494	5	5	5	9,108	1,113	13,697
Acrylamide	250	250	0	0	0	0	8,600	9,100
Acrylic acid	80	4	0	0	0	0	88	172
Aluminum (fume or dust)	5,437	1,956	10	0	255	260	104,657	112,575
Ammonia	249,820	378,215	391,749	10	304	1,651,010	16,060	2,687,168
Ammonium nitrate (solution)	0	0	71,000	0	250	0	1,102	72,352
Ammonium sulfate (solution)	3	0	312,482	0	0	1,000	0	313,485
Anthracene	12	140	0	0	440	0	0	592
Antimony compounds	3	6,193	0	0	1	535	164	6,896
Arsenic compounds	25	25	0	0	5	0	4,125	4,180
Asbestos (friable)	0	0	0	0	11,100	0	11,100	22,200
Barium compounds	8,094	1,095	3,014	0	274	408	73,716	86,601
Benzene	25,350	68,170	3,421	0	510	2,000	9,010	108,461
Biphenyl	2	68	0	0	86	0	0	156
Bis(2-ethylhexyl) adipate	2,135	1	1	0	0	0	8,061	10,198
Butyl acrylate	2,736	253	0	0	0	0	866	3,855
Cadmium compounds	0	175	394	0	0	72	184	825
Captan	5	250	0	0	0	0	250	505

[Continued]

★ 412 ★

Toxic Chemical Releases in Maryland, by Chemical: 1990

[Continued]

Chemical	Fugitive air	Stack air	Water	Injection	Land	Public treatment	Other offsite	Total releases
Carbaryl	250	3,027	0	0	0	0	1,258	4,535
Carbon tetrachloride	1,969	295	0	0	0	5	203,457	205,726
Carbonyl sulfide	0	750	0	0	0	0	0	750
Catechol	507	155	0	0	0	34,247	7,466	42,375
Chlorine	4,830	93,955	200	0	5	54,997	0	153,987
Chlorine dioxide	35	160,000	0	0	0	0	0	160,035
Chloroform	0	240,000	0	0	0	48,000	0	288,000
Chlorothalonil	82	7	0	0	0	18	361	468
Chromium	510	260	773	0	596	528	28,002	30,669
Chromium compounds	3,347	2,394	13,357	0	97,523	920	162,723	280,264
Cobalt compounds	273	524	265	0	5	5	5,187	6,259
Copper	1,005	3,314	250	0	0	832	68,333	73,734
Copper compounds	702	727	12,828	0	39,005	415	20,450	74,127
Cresol (mixed isomers)	8	870	0	0	280	0	0	1,158
Cumene	218	93	0	0	0	0	0	311
Cyanide compounds	222	190,040	32,400	0	6,400	2,973	304	232,339
Cyclohexane	2,110	1,072	320	0	0	250	250	4,002
Di(2-ethylhexyl) phthalate	550	6	1	5	20	0	300	882
Dibenzofuran	7	0	0	0	260	0	0	267
Dibutyl phthalate	116	0	1	0	0	0	145	262
Dichloromethane	409,237	217,780	5	5	5	5	58,175	685,212
Diethanolamine	5	5	0	0	0	0	0	10
Ethyl acrylate	1,200	750	0	0	0	0	0	1,950
Ethylbenzene	10,971	26,777	3	0	32	566	8,598	46,947
Ethylene	3,600	0	0	0	0	0	0	3,600
Ethylene glycol	66,215	3,631	104	0	5	81,803	223,224	374,982
Ethylene oxide	1,280	300	0	0	0	25	0	1,605
Formaldehyde	1,842	1,616	0	0	5	50	2,700	6,213
Freon 113	152,888	29,777	0	0	0	5	5,200	187,870
Glycol ethers	249,082	303,215	251	0	252	103,961	51,566	708,327
Hydrochloric acid	16,422	1,745,202	5	5	270	159,364	36,170	1,957,438
Hydrogen fluoride	26,900	42,255	5	0	0	0	22,786	91,946
Hydroquinone	251	0	0	0	0	0	0	251
Lead	8,410	285	6	0	0	528	44,684	53,913
Lead compounds	1,179	1,238	7,344	0	120,004	286	21,362	151,413
Maleic anhydride	878	1	0	0	0	0	34	913
Maneb	5	250	0	0	0	0	750	1,005
Manganese	255	850	0	0	0	507	72,746	74,358
Manganese compounds	49,573	37,023	83,811	0	1,003,037	255	5,155	1,178,854
Methanol	94,227	507,483	6,098	5	261	2,083,835	245,548	2,937,457
Methyl ethyl ketone	272,599	539,042	0	0	0	5,107	100,653	917,401
Methyl isobutyl ketone	62,825	135,748	0	5	5	2,001	25,676	226,260
Methyl methacrylate	5,202	1,169	0	0	0	0	4,166	10,537
Methylene bromide	76	328	0	0	0	4,349	0	4,753
Methylenebis(phenylisocyanate)	2,005	0	0	0	0	0	444	2,449
Molybdenum trioxide	250	3,200	1,800	0	250	0	19,053	24,553
N-butyl alcohol	87,308	123,877	0	0	0	1,100	7,413	219,698
N-dioctyl phthalate	0	0	0	0	0	0	54,130	54,130
Naphthalene	277	2,909	8,000	0	4,600	4	0	15,790
Nickel	265	265	250	0	250	513	11,556	13,099
Nickel compounds	1,203	1,041	30,804	0	38,005	574	14,793	86,420
Nitric acid	809	11,675	5	0	40,486	255	158,311	211,541

[Continued]

★412★

Toxic Chemical Releases in Maryland, by Chemical: 1990

[Continued]

Chemical	Fugitive air	Stack air	Water	Injection	Land	Public treatment	Other offsite	Total releases
Phenol	3,801	5,150	5,000	0	2,100	2,360	40,550	58,961
Phosphoric acid	910	760	0	5	52,002	25,926	255	79,858
Phthalic anhydride	1,345	1,207	20	0	5,700	14	32,000	40,286
Propylene	753	0	0	0	0	0	0	753
Pyridine	86	1	0	0	0	4	49,783	49,874
Quinoline	5	86	0	0	74	0	0	165
Sec-butyl alcohol	218	6,074	0	0	0	0	0	6,292
Selenium compounds	0	23	4	0	0	0	62	89
Styrene	82,418	149,985	1	0	20	0	6,486	238,910
Sulfuric acid	49,967	466,129	163,091	5	3,110	112,939	71,660	866,901
Tetrachloroethylene	14,671	87,500	0	0	0	0	250	102,421
Titanium tetrachloride	250	0	0	0	0	0	0	250
Toluene	2,116,380	533,346	96	0	206	1,813	337,218	2,989,059
Toluenediisocyanate (mixed isomers)	318	256	0	0	0	0	510	1,084
Toluene-2,4-diisocyanate	65	6	0	0	0	0	5	76
Toluene-2,6-diisocyanate	5	5	0	0	0	0	5	15
Trichloroethylene	140,730	47,005	0	0	0	0	3,300	191,035
Vanadium (fume or dust)	250	5	10	0	0	0	250	515
Xylene (mixed isomers)	297,553	415,714	137	0	684	2,063	96,600	812,751
Zinc (fume or dust)	1,009	255	0	0	0	361	17,074	18,699
Zinc compounds	1,592	4,226	129,730	5	440,038	5,661	115,670	696,922
Zineb	5	250	0	0	0	0	750	1,005

Source: U.S. Environmental Protection Agency. "Toxic Chemical Releases, 1990." In *National Economic, Social, and Environmental Data Bank* [CD-ROM]. Prepared by U.S. Department of Commerce, Economics and Statistics Administration. Washington, DC: U.S. Department of Commerce, National Economic, Social, and Environmental Data Bank, Economics and Statistics Administration, Office of Business Analysis, February 1995.

★413★

Chemicals

Toxic Chemical Releases in Massachusetts, by Chemical: 1990

Figures indicate pounds released by chemical and by type of emission per year.

Chemical	Fugitive air	Stack air	Water	Injection	Land	Public treatment	Other offsite	Total releases
1,1,1-trichloroethane	2,348,685	1,504,878	255	5	20	3,728	572,122	4,429,693
1,1,2-trichloroethane	16,610	0	0	0	0	0	0	16,610
1,2,4-trimethylbenzene	19	648	0	0	0	0	5,437	6,104
1,2-dichlorobenzene	2,488	4,369	0	0	0	1,668	203,076	211,601
1,4-dichlorobenzene	21,942	267,869	0	0	0	550	1,050	291,411
1,4-dioxane	4,668	5,684	0	0	0	0	773	11,125
2-ethoxyethanol	251	434	0	0	0	6	54	745
2-methoxyethanol	97,088	78,705	0	0	0	585	147,404	323,782
4,4'-isopropylidenediphenol	42	0	0	0	0	20,000	0	20,042
Acetaldehyde	7,300	21,000	0	0	0	30,000	0	58,300
Acetone	316,737	753,027	21,955	0	4,300	28,864	762,899	1,887,782
Acetonitrile	608	1,755	0	0	0	1	42,262	44,626
Acrylamide	250	250	0	0	0	250	334	1,084
Acrylic acid	527	784	0	0	0	5,650	0	6,961
Acrylonitrile	1,022	836	0	0	0	1,100	20,108	23,066

[Continued]

★413★

Toxic Chemical Releases in Massachusetts, by Chemical: 1990
[Continued]

Chemical	Fugitive air	Stack air	Water	Injection	Land	Public treatment	Other offsite	Total releases
Allyl chloride	0	250	0	0	0	250	0	500
Aluminum (fume or dust)	255	755	0	0	0	0	24,000	25,010
Aluminum oxide (fibrous forms)	293	0	0	0	15,313	17,405	57,200	90,211
Ammonia	123,130	237,198	29,156	0	10	838,306	75,175	1,302,975
Ammonium sulfate (solution)	0	0	187,600	0	0	230,439	0	418,039
Antimony compounds	1,929	1,695	45	0	0	611	44,794	49,074
Arsenic	0	0	0	0	0	0	250	250
Arsenic compounds	10	260	5	0	5	0	570	850
Barium compounds	1,156	5,961	45	0	250	2,029	196,213	205,654
Benzoyl peroxide	6	6	0	0	0	0	30	42
Biphenyl	0	0	0	0	0	63,701	0	63,701
Bis(2-ethylhexyl) adipate	655	2,276	0	0	0	8,491	18,230	29,652
Bromomethane	18,566	6,960	0	0	0	0	2,649	28,175
Butyl acrylate	1,147	1,669	0	0	0	100,500	2,915	106,231
Butyl benzyl phthalate	262	25	10	5	20	1,485	1,520	3,327
Butyraldehyde	1,900	56,000	0	0	0	350,000	1,430	409,330
Cadmium	255	255	0	0	0	24	16,964	17,498
Cadmium compounds	104	5	36	0	0	250	3,400	3,795
Chlorine	766	680	0	0	0	19,583	0	21,029
Chlorobenzene	795	1,207	0	0	0	0	0	2,002
Chloroform	2,154	0	0	0	0	0	1,260	3,414
Chloromethane	0	33,258	0	0	0	0	1,254	34,512
Chromium	2,023	1,310	339	0	255	26,933	310,864	341,724
Chromium compounds	1,086	1,294	353	0	2,887	1,677	43,672	50,969
Cobalt	500	502	10	0	0	20	11,712	12,744
Cobalt compounds	500	500	0	0	0	0	1,000	2,000
Copper	1,961	4,588	615	0	1,157	5,313	607,560	621,194
Copper compounds	832	4,729	2,078	0	10,827	2,103	212,257	232,826
Creosote	0	750	0	0	0	0	1,262	2,012
Cyanide compounds	20	531	47	0	0	289	6,220	7,107
Cyclohexane	282,954	14,453	0	0	0	17	30,680	328,104
Decabromodiphenyl oxide	72	44	0	0	0	1,250	8,409	9,775
Di(2-ethylhexyl) phthalate	1,601	8,379	0	0	0	4,384	146,201	160,565
Dibutyl phthalate	250	250	0	0	0	48	11,245	11,793
Dichloromethane	292,008	1,047,287	250	0	0	3,518	248,869	1,591,932
Diethanolamine	1,378	250	0	0	0	250	11,000	12,878
Diethyl sulfate	1	0	0	0	0	0	0	1
Dimethyl phthalate	250	0	0	0	0	0	3,709	3,959
Epichlorohydrin	120	17,250	0	0	0	690	0	18,060
Ethyl acrylate	921	2,002	0	0	0	1,060	2,387	6,370
Ethylbenzene	10,513	4,132	5	0	0	1,538	155,104	171,292
Ethylene glycol	14,399	74,324	0	0	0	116,605	11,055	216,383
Ethylene oxide	4,450	10,180	0	0	0	0	0	14,630
Formaldehyde	5,868	168,200	3,070	0	26	811,171	30,290	1,018,625
Freon 113	1,381,983	620,030	5	0	0	10	111,633	2,113,661
Glycol ethers	59,081	306,927	755	5	20	166,320	258,016	791,124
Hydrazine	38	0	0	0	0	0	0	38
Hydrochloric acid	26,268	59,852	910	5	30	131,428	237,094	455,587
Hydrogen fluoride	1,150	11,787	0	0	0	2,000	321,554	336,491
Hydroquinone	0	0	0	0	0	113	0	113
Isopropyl alcohol (manufacturing)	20,587	132,576	0	0	0	0	64,414	217,577
Lead	272	260	0	0	0	9	28,433	28,974

[Continued]

★ 413 ★

Toxic Chemical Releases in Massachusetts, by Chemical: 1990
[Continued]

Chemical	Fugitive air	Stack air	Water	Injection	Land	Public treatment	Other offsite	Total releases
Lead compounds	3,772	1,251	373	0	0	2,035	101,766	109,197
M-xylene	750	750	0	0	0	0	10,280	11,780
Maleic anhydride	0	340	0	0	0	0	0	340
Manganese	587	285	750	0	7,674	527	78,554	88,377
Manganese compounds	10	15	250	0	0	462	188,562	189,299
Methanol	165,802	653,561	255	5	2,060	1,147,110	1,057,755	3,026,548
Methyl acrylate	150	2,100	0	0	0	4,100	15,000	21,350
Methyl ethyl ketone	591,366	1,358,801	5	0	0	175,408	1,251,238	3,376,818
Methyl isobutyl ketone	39,762	67,013	0	0	0	1	76,964	183,740
Methyl methacrylate	7,123	44,368	0	0	0	26,500	11,953	89,944
Methylenebis(phenylisocyanate)	776	2,757	0	0	0	0	5,385	8,918
N-butyl alcohol	34,520	118,743	0	0	0	900,987	96,869	1,151,119
N-dioctyl phthalate	762	1,513	5	0	0	0	24,277	26,557
Naphthalene	433	418	0	0	0	0	0	851
Nickel	2,498	3,289	563	0	250	2,313	267,419	276,332
Nickel compounds	789	1,068	256	0	0	1,467	21,190	24,770
Nitric acid	11,848	54,639	0	0	5,800	41,027	591,979	705,293
P-phenylenediamine	40	0	0	0	0	0	400	440
P-xylene	0	250	0	0	0	0	1,000	1,250
Pentachlorophenol	5	5	5	0	0	0	780	795
Phenol	8,311	27,882	0	0	0	2,971	141,601	180,765
Phosphoric acid	1,620	7,192	5	0	24,150	115,563	255	148,785
Phthalic anhydride	473	744	0	0	0	5	0	1,222
Polychlorinated biphenyls (PCBs)	0	0	0	0	0	0	91,123	91,123
Propylene oxide	5	250	0	0	0	0	500	755
Propyleneimine	73	8	0	0	0	0	0	81
Sec-butyl alcohol	1	330	0	0	0	0	0	331
Selenium	0	0	0	0	0	250	250	500
Selenium compounds	5	0	0	0	0	250	500	755
Silver	10	755	0	0	0	518	255	1,538
Silver compounds	250	255	24	0	0	469	1,132	2,130
Styrene	39,958	78,739	10	5	5	541	524,740	643,998
Sulfuric acid	55,351	98,809	11,960	10	90	1,576,371	768,857	2,511,448
Tert-butyl alcohol	250	0	0	0	0	0	750	1,000
Tetrachloroethylene	83,057	199,503	0	0	0	678	26,891	310,129
Thiourea	5	10	0	0	0	250	200	465
Toluene	1,330,457	2,711,143	525	5	2,101	4,583	1,705,150	5,753,964
Toluenediisocyanate (mixed isomers)	10	2,794	0	0	0	0	0	2,804
Toluene-2,4-diisocyanate	258	1,265	0	0	0	0	114	1,637
Toluene-2,6-diisocyanate	1	2	0	0	0	0	3	6
Trichloroethylene	912,958	668,664	251	0	84	571	209,567	1,792,095
Vinyl acetate	2,450	66,059	0	0	0	80,000	17,990	166,499
Xylene (mixed isomers)	92,249	354,099	5	0	250	22,482	413,915	883,000
Zinc (fume or dust)	750	1,261	261	0	0	501	4,200	6,973
Zinc compounds	2,832	7,966	1,128	5	154	54,216	388,202	454,503

Source: U.S. Environmental Protection Agency. "Toxic Chemical Releases, 1990." In *National Economic, Social, and Environmental Data Bank* [CD-ROM]. Prepared by U.S. Department of Commerce, Economics and Statistics Administration. Washington, DC: U.S. Department of Commerce, National Economic, Social, and Environmental Data Bank, Economics and Statistics Administration, Office of Business Analysis, February 1995.

★ 414 ★

Chemicals

Toxic Chemical Releases in Michigan, by Chemical: 1990

Figures indicate pounds released by chemical and by type of emission per year.

Chemical	Fugitive air	Stack air	Water	Injection	Land	Public treatment	Other offsite	Total releases
1,1,1-trichloroethane	2,171,463	2,887,564	484	10	45	3,067	382,649	5,445,282
1,2,4-trimethylbenzene	31,352	89,742	255	0	0	12,290	52,374	186,013
1,2-butylene oxide	27,604	11,552	4,620	0	0	0	0	43,776
1,2-dichloroethane	24,899	73,474	250	44,061	0	2,250	89,450	234,384
1,3-butadiene	29,832	541	2	0	0	0	0	30,375
1,3-dichloropropylene	204	23	0	0	0	0	0	227
1,4-dioxane	250	250	0	0	0	5	0	505
2,4,6-trichlorophenol	0	78	79	0	0	0	0	157
2,4-d	0	132	4	0	0	0	0	136
2,4-dichlorophenol	0	310	90	0	0	0	0	400
2-ethoxyethanol	33,480	101,286	9	0	0	4,000	0	138,775
2-methoxyethanol	15,750	3,899	0	4,540	0	750	0	24,939
2-nitropropane	5	0	0	0	0	0	0	5
2-phenylphenol	10	358	112	0	0	0	0	480
3,3'-dichlorobenzidine	5	5	1	0	0	250	16,751	17,012
4,4'-isopropylidenediphenol	42	161	0	0	0	0	6,085	6,288
Acetone	2,448,490	7,026,047	10,724	1,523,597	1,645	1,420,885	623,766	13,055,154
Acetonitrile	10,747	38,200	5	288,662	0	115,255	7,560	460,429
Acrylamide	2,732	2,390	1,752	5	20	1,500	0	8,399
Acrylic acid	2,326	6,387	97	0	0	5	1,297	10,112
Acrylonitrile	12,992	3,946	401	0	5	5	85	17,434
Allyl alcohol	40	37	0	0	0	160	185,001	185,238
Allyl chloride	1,099	2,030	5	0	0	5	783	3,922
Aluminum (fume or dust)	1,770	16,607	5,757	0	35,700	6,004	190,772	256,610
Aluminum oxide (fibrous forms)	755	2,800	0	0	0	0	26,000	29,555
Ammonia	927,557	2,064,661	273,115	1,079,693	215	1,602,750	314,090	6,262,081
Ammonium nitrate (solution)	505	255	6,310	0	386	1,452	1,505	10,413
Ammonium sulfate (solution)	5	250	0	0	0	865,976	750	866,981
Aniline	5	250	0	0	0	5	14,400	14,660
Anthracene	4,760	313	0	0	0	13,266	167	18,506
Antimony	6	6	5	0	0	0	12,082	12,099
Antimony compounds	2,758	10,581	98	0	119	5	180,803	194,364
Arsenic	12	0	0	0	2,050	5	5	2,072
Arsenic compounds	30	25	5	5	25	0	3,297	3,387
Barium	1,633	15,750	255	0	93,510	520	13,686	125,354
Barium compounds	3,567	9,064	6,223	35	8,020	29,689	486,926	543,524
Benzene	228,978	299,722	1,682	11,609	0	5,612	242,690	790,293
Benzoyl peroxide	12,230	0	0	0	0	5	10	12,245
Benzyl chloride	4,700	250	0	0	0	0	250	5,200
Beryllium	0	250	5	0	0	0	1,250	1,505
Biphenyl	1,129	801	7	0	0	0	112,421	114,358
Bis(2-ethylhexyl) adipate	1,250	3,350	250	0	0	0	7,038	11,888
Bromomethane	0	14,233	0	0	0	0	0	14,233
Butyl acrylate	422	921	0	0	0	250	887	2,480
Butyl benzyl phthalate	845	19	250	0	0	251	85,253	86,618
Butyraldehyde	1,000	35,000	0	0	0	450	1,108	37,558
Cadmium	953	2,082	0	0	6,350	155	42,291	51,831
Cadmium compounds	1,005	500	0	0	0	1,500	68,950	71,955
Carbon disulfide	956	483	0	0	0	0	0	1,439
Carbon tetrachloride	1,189	36,395	31	0	0	0	10,862	48,477
Catechol	0	0	3,181	0	8,900	9,400	352	21,833
Chlorine	35,640	35,670	3,549	250	5	44,280	300	119,694
Chlorine dioxide	14	12,010	0	0	0	0	0	12,024
Chloroacetic acid	0	10	1,441	0	0	0	5	1,451
Chlorobenzene	20,373	18,039	20	0	0	5	98,382	136,819
Chloroethane	27,636	117,521	0	0	0	0	841	145,998
Chloroform	78,960	152,586	2,146	0	150	21,850	27,608	283,300

[Continued]

★ 414 ★

Toxic Chemical Releases in Michigan, by Chemical: 1990
[Continued]

Chemical	Fugitive air	Stack air	Water	Injection	Land	Public treatment	Other offsite	Total releases
Chloromethane	48,583	545,543	452	0	0	10	87,876	682,464
Chlorophenols	0	330	17	0	0	0	0	347
Chromium	7,807	5,052	54	7	90,760	39,259	705,484	848,423
Chromium compounds	6,280	5,320	4,395	72,869	5	34,108	599,887	722,864
Cobalt	3,730	2,371	510	0	0	1,515	42,845	50,971
Cobalt compounds	250	10	0	0	5	260	260	785
Copper	30,555	15,077	2,968	11	35,026	6,496	243,627	333,760
Copper compounds	1,206,640	826,839	1,563	18,120	16,412,426	7,841	166,944	18,640,373
Cresol (mixed isomers)	2,507	275	0	0	0	9,419	4,324	16,525
Cumene	6,642	2,008	0	0	0	3,600	1,125	13,375
Cumene hydroperoxide	16,185	1,205	0	0	0	3,000	3,411	23,801
Cyanide compounds	384	1,033	10	31,438	0	2,974	109,676	145,515
Cyclohexane	5,603	11,547	0	0	0	250	45,028	62,428
Decabromodiphenyl oxide	2,887	11,297	0	0	0	0	4,255	18,439
Di(2-ethylhexyl) phthalate	525	381,004	0	0	0	0	31,366	412,895
Diaminotoluene (mixed isomers)	5	5	110	0	5	0	600	725
Dibenzofuran	6,140	449	0	0	0	39,798	0	46,387
Dibutyl phthalate	5	25,001	0	0	0	0	2,828	27,834
Dichloromethane	1,267,475	4,081,618	833	174,418	0	454,172	734,456	6,712,972
Diethanolamine	1,466	3,862	57,354	57,000	8,750	154,837	90,885	374,154
Dimethyl phthalate	5	5	0	0	0	0	6	16
Epichlorohydrin	2,047	1,038	5	0	0	755	5	3,850
Ethyl acrylate	369	10	0	0	0	0	0	379
Ethylbenzene	204,785	623,289	355	5	20	2,872	111,822	943,148
Ethylene	31,293	95,307	10,659	0	0	0	194,000	331,259
Ethylene glycol	164,507	41,983	50,283	110	17,023	293,412	189,589	756,907
Ethylene oxide	6,406	37,249	251	0	5	12	351	44,274
Formaldehyde	134,781	349,210	8,744	5	6,325	1,184,460	184,020	1,867,545
Freon 113	1,215,288	555,340	1,396	5	20	250	70,791	1,843,090
Glycol ethers	563,599	2,947,896	73,946	11,000	2,116	1,668,441	218,883	5,485,881
Hexachloroethane	0	0	0	0	0	0	32,695	32,695
Hydrazine	5	5	0	0	0	5	0	15
Hydrochloric acid	123,365	1,715,081	280	175,023	225,945	1,192,032	5,270,982	8,702,708
Hydrogen fluoride	8,987	4,272	0	0	0	750	104,844	118,853
Isopropyl alcohol (manufacturing)	8,660	90,529	5	0	0	114	21,765	121,073
Lead	8,447	18,865	5,028	0	221,200	1,895	490,265	745,700
Lead compounds	5,279	1,635	277	0	0	3,318	231,708	242,217
M-cresol	5	5	0	0	0	398	0	408
M-xylene	820	291	1	0	0	0	0	1,112
Maleic anhydride	10	10	8	5	0	0	333	366
Manganese	39,997	119,587	3,190	5	2,363,516	3,077	1,826,700	4,356,072
Manganese compounds	6,724	2,955	10,611	0	5,850	31,251	1,408,779	1,466,170
Mercury	5	0	0	0	0	5	5	15
Methanol	1,277,951	3,301,036	167,068	4,554,860	30,600	3,745,232	1,109,234	14,185,981
Methyl acrylate	12	3	45	0	0	0	4	64
Methyl ethyl ketone	824,738	5,132,685	5	5	5	20,975	656,510	6,634,923
Methyl isobutyl ketone	689,390	2,286,546	290	0	0	13,909	262,833	3,252,968
Methyl methacrylate	2,221	15,682	0	0	0	3,350	908	22,161
Methyl tert-butyl ether	6,818	6,535	272	0	0	250	6,485	20,360
Methylenebis(phenylisocyanate)	5,476	46,735	0	0	250	5	166,473	218,939
Molybdenum trioxide	6,781	5	0	0	0	755	0	7,541
N-butyl alcohol	212,036	1,797,800	107	0	0	49,590	139,842	2,199,375
N-dioctyl phthalate	250	5	0	0	0	250	0	505
Naphthalene	17,381	264,666	2	1,545	0	24,146	71	307,811
Nickel	8,128	6,285	1,368	31	9,455	12,515	641,701	679,483
Nickel compounds	2,875	3,754	989	3,005	1,274	57,982	2,112,647	2,182,526
Nitric acid	19,302	75,276	250	5	41,224	84,776	1,194,105	1,414,938
Nitrilotriacetic acid	5	250	0	0	0	1,300	0	1,555
O-cresol	250	250	0	0	0	0	0	500

[Continued]

★ 414 ★

Toxic Chemical Releases in Michigan, by Chemical: 1990

[Continued]

Chemical	Fugitive air	Stack air	Water	Injection	Land	Public treatment	Other offsite	Total releases
Peracetic acid	1,305	0	0	0	1,821	0	1,821	4,947
Phenol	28,885	169,262	2,860	49,878	22,550	110,282	58,469	442,186
Phosgene	250	63	5	5	0	0	5	328
Phosphoric acid	22,995	37,292	255	5	25	235,457	517,974	814,003
Phosphorus (yellow or white)	0	0	0	0	0	0	835	835
Phthalic anhydride	760	10,740	0	0	0	0	2,300	13,800
Polychlorinated biphenyls (PCBs)	0	0	0	0	0	0	1,381,074	1,381,074
Propylene	120,789	23,601	0	0	0	0	3,926,000	4,070,390
Propylene oxide	12,863	61,058	66,000	0	250	2,230	250	142,651
Pyridine	7,950	1,005	5	5,100	0	0	5	14,065
Quinoline	683	77	0	0	0	4,642	0	5,402
Sec-butyl alcohol	17,777	45,906	0	0	0	1,079	750	65,512
Selenium	5	0	0	0	0	5	5	15
Silver	235	346	0	0	0	5	5	591
Styrene	265,037	1,158,280	340	0	5	793	229,037	1,653,492
Sulfuric acid	106,170	554,366	880	32	29,602	140,402	4,955,519	5,786,971
Tert-butyl alcohol	6,000	9,200	0	85,821	0	0	5	101,026
Tetrachloroethylene	73,022	31,117	55	5	20	2,150	275,775	382,144
Thiourea	255	255	0	0	0	250	505	1,265
Titanium tetrachloride	5	19	0	0	0	0	0	24
Toluene	4,667,782	9,986,605	1,342	2,445	25	113,276	3,182,957	17,954,432
Toluenediisocyanate (mixed isomers)	546	6,882	0	0	250	0	780	8,458
Toluene-2,4-diisocyanate	505	272	0	0	0	0	37	814
Toluene-2,6-diisocyanate	505	13,266	0	0	0	2,000	9	15,780
Trichloroethylene	1,349,459	940,810	263	0	2,432	1,076	111,913	2,405,953
Vinyl acetate	1,100	42,400	0	0	0	2,300	3,084	48,884
Vinyl chloride	672	251	10	0	0	0	14	947
Vinylidene chloride	2,582	19,687	46	0	0	0	258	22,573
Xylene (mixed isomers)	1,893,059	9,912,896	441	10,517	85	19,244	1,749,346	13,585,588
Zinc (fume or dust)	7,025	255,461	15	0	5,880,000	2,264	132,372	6,277,137
Zinc compounds	133,471	121,934	18,658	184,520	270	38,887	22,235,812	22,733,552

Source: U.S. Environmental Protection Agency. "Toxic Chemical Releases, 1990." In *National Economic, Social, and Environmental Data Bank* [CD-ROM]. Prepared by U.S. Department of Commerce, Economics and Statistics Administration. Washington, DC: U.S. Department of Commerce, National Economic, Social, and Environmental Data Bank, Economics and Statistics Administration, Office of Business Analysis, February 1995.

★ 415 ★

Chemicals

Toxic Chemical Releases in Minnesota, by Chemical: 1990

Figures indicate pounds released by chemical and by type of emission per year.

Chemical	Fugitive air	Stack air	Water	Injection	Land	Public treatment	Other offsite	Total releases
1,1,1-trichloroethane	0	2,101,683	51	0	0	1,372	233,294	2,336,400
1,1,2-trichloroethane	0	30,000	4	0	0	0	0	30,004
1,2,4-trimethylbenzene	0	47,932	16	0	6	0	378	48,332
1,2-dibromoethane	0	4	0	0	0	0	0	4
1,2-dichloroethane	0	4,302	14	0	0	0	0	4,316
1,3-butadiene	0	15,000	26	0	1	0	0	15,027
1,4-dioxane	0	35,908	0	0	0	42,903	1,120	79,931
2,4-d	0	0	0	0	0	0	1,804	1,804
2,4-dimethylphenol	0	0	0	0	56	0	2	58

[Continued]

★ 415 ★

Toxic Chemical Releases in Minnesota, by Chemical: 1990
[Continued]

Chemical	Fugitive air	Stack air	Water	Injection	Land	Public treatment	Other offsite	Total releases
2-ethoxyethanol	0	168,056	5	0	0	1,550	52,018	221,629
2-methoxyethanol	0	21,410	0	0	0	0	0	21,410
4,4'-isopropylidenediphenol	0	0	0	0	0	0	42	42
4,4'-methylenedianiline	0	0	0	0	0	0	7,106	7,106
Acetone	0	870,839	19,000	0	93	34,908	188,682	1,113,522
Acrylic acid	0	120	2	0	0	0	0	122
Acrylonitrile	0	0	0	0	0	0	2,116	2,116
Aluminum (fume or dust)	0	38,378	0	0	0	251	80,500	119,129
Aluminum oxide (fibrous forms)	0	255	5	0	0	250	108,800	109,310
Ammonia	0	337,906	636,257	5	99,945	384,767	9,871	1,468,751
Ammonium sulfate (solution)	0	2,591	53,946	0	0	1,488,980	0	1,545,517
Antimony	0	140	0	0	0	60	19,000	19,200
Antimony compounds	0	251	5	0	36	25	1,049	1,366
Arsenic	0	70	0	0	0	8	5,800	5,878
Arsenic compounds	0	254	150	0	440	0	1,379	2,223
Barium	0	255	0	0	50,000	0	20,566	70,821
Barium compounds	0	1,570	980	0	1,600	926	54,695	59,771
Benzene	0	201,210	22	0	340	0	3	201,575
Beryllium compounds	0	0	65	0	0	0	0	65
Biphenyl	0	0	16	0	0	0	2	18
Butyl benzyl phthalate	0	0	0	0	0	0	882	882
C.I. basic green 4	0	0	250	0	0	5	250	505
Cadmium	0	0	0	0	0	0	1,362	1,362
Cadmium compounds	0	46	52	0	8	1	444	551
Carbon disulfide	0	19	0	0	0	0	0	19
Carbon tetrachloride	0	250	0	0	0	0	0	250
Catechol	0	0	1,601	0	4,600	15,246	60	21,507
Chlorine	0	391,865	14,060	0	0	47,500	131,389	584,814
Chlorine dioxide	0	41,350	0	0	0	0	0	41,350
Chloroform	0	151,456	70,000	0	12	17,784	0	239,252
Chromium	0	410	1,337	0	500	1,612	15,623	19,482
Chromium compounds	0	2,381	615	0	12,649	46,408	95,040	157,093
Cobalt	0	0	33	0	0	0	3	36
Cobalt compounds	0	921	130	0	560	0	28,555	30,166
Copper	0	4,910	10	0	250	4,616	47,584	57,370
Copper compounds	0	1,343	15	5	238	4,750	10,211	16,562
Cresol (mixed isomers)	0	0	0	0	1	0	0	1
Cumene	0	500	16	0	0	0	252	768
Cyanide compounds	0	550	0	0	0	4,904	30,383	35,837
Cyclohexane	0	634,681	38	0	9	37	126,276	761,041
Decabromodiphenyl oxide	0	0	0	0	250	0	1,404	1,654
Di(2-ethylhexyl) phthalate	0	460	0	0	2,990	0	3,225	6,675
Dichloromethane	0	1,091,973	125	0	0	4,061	80,442	1,176,601
Diethanolamine	0	255	0	0	0	16,734	250	17,239
Diethyl phthalate	0	39,368	0	0	0	385,566	3,596	428,530
Ethyl acrylate	0	930	0	0	0	0	0	930
Ethylbenzene	0	529,812	31	0	134	522	9,903	540,402
Ethylene	0	400	250	0	0	0	0	650
Ethylene glycol	0	3,789	16,379	0	0	259,419	11,250	290,837
Ethylene oxide	0	347	0	0	0	250	0	597
Formaldehyde	0	647,001	1,100	0	0	13,209	4,685	665,995
Freon 113	0	506,024	0	0	0	301	7,599	513,924

[Continued]

★ 415 ★

Toxic Chemical Releases in Minnesota, by Chemical: 1990
[Continued]

Chemical	Fugitive air	Stack air	Water	Injection	Land	Public treatment	Other offsite	Total releases
Glycol ethers	0	456,556	16	0	0	239,434	18,621	714,627
Hydrochloric acid	0	537,749	12	0	670	61,291	387,140	986,862
Hydrogen cyanide	0	110	810	0	0	0	0	920
Hydrogen fluoride	0	4,450	0	0	0	0	23	4,473
Isopropyl alcohol (manufacturing)	0	17,149	0	0	0	1,010	0	18,159
Lead	0	7,155	330	0	0	230	191,168	198,883
Lead compounds	0	5,293	525	0	200,740	943	55,592	263,093
Maleic anhydride	0	151	0	0	0	5	58	214
Manganese	0	443	57	0	155	755	10,207	11,617
Manganese compounds	0	3,625	105	0	81,900	4,510	3,864	94,004
Mercury compounds	0	81	0	0	7	0	0	88
Methanol	0	1,548,935	20,000	0	930	2,336,378	127,460	4,033,703
Methyl acrylate	0	2,500	0	0	0	0	0	2,500
Methyl ethyl ketone	0	12,299,665	1,910	0	0	3,663	572,804	12,878,042
Methyl isobutyl ketone	0	550,731	0	0	0	250	32,903	583,884
Methyl methacrylate	0	1,490	2,100	0	0	0	255	3,845
Methylenebis(phenylisocyanate)	0	960	0	0	0	0	2,191	3,151
N-butyl alcohol	0	629,355	5	0	0	505	11,606	641,471
Naphthalene	0	2,243	16	0	550	0	1,275	4,084
Nickel	0	785	101	0	0	1,990	41,874	44,750
Nickel compounds	0	573	405	0	53,830	2,230	3,826	60,864
Nitric acid	0	22,333	5	0	0	1,131,840	246,031	1,400,209
Pentachlorophenol	0	250	1	0	0	1	1,540	1,792
Peracetic acid	0	66	0	0	0	500	0	566
Phenol	0	136,313	1,680	0	84	505	15,415	153,997
Phosphoric acid	0	1,800	5	0	20	202,414	8,100	212,339
Phosphorus (yellow or white)	0	5	0	0	0	250	0	255
Phthalic anhydride	0	1,447	0	0	0	0	225	1,672
Propylene	0	77,000	250	0	41	0	0	77,291
Propylene oxide	0	750	0	0	0	0	0	750
Selenium compounds	0	15	630	0	46	0	0	691
Silver compounds	0	0	65	0	0	0	181	246
Styrene	0	159,701	16	5	8,943	0	30,954	199,619
Sulfuric acid	0	108,381	20	5	10,720	82,039	231,909	433,074
Tert-butyl alcohol	0	30,404	0	0	0	0	0	30,404
Tetrachloroethylene	0	211,883	0	0	0	368	0	212,251
Toluene	0	12,037,917	79	0	8,094	6,979	658,839	12,711,908
Toluenediisocyanate (mixed isomers)	0	250	0	0	0	0	0	250
Toluene-2,4-diisocyanate	0	92	0	0	0	0	1,720	1,812
Toluene-2,6-diisocyanate	0	5	5	0	0	5	250	265
Trichloroethylene	0	400,269	55	0	0	765	17,242	418,331
Xylene (mixed isomers)	0	4,186,466	55	0	800	1,032	238,254	4,426,607
Zinc (fume or dust)	0	27,957	0	0	0	3,107	29,244	60,308
Zinc compounds	0	22,188	6,635	0	1,001,930	2,074	115,619	1,148,446

Source: U.S. Environmental Protection Agency. "Toxic Chemical Releases, 1990." In *National Economic, Social, and Environmental Data Bank* [CD-ROM]. Prepared by U.S. Department of Commerce, Economics and Statistics Administration. Washington, DC: U.S. Department of Commerce, National Economic, Social, and Environmental Data Bank, Economics and Statistics Administration, Office of Business Analysis, February 1995.

★ 416 ★
Chemicals

Toxic Chemical Releases in Mississippi, by Chemical: 1990

Figures indicate pounds released by chemical and by type of emission per year.

Chemical	Fugitive air	Stack air	Water	Injection	Land	Public treatment	Other offsite	Total releases
1,1,1-trichloroethane	1,208,643	992,414	2	0	0	730	85,234	2,287,023
1,2,4-trichlorobenzene	5	0	0	0	0	0	0	5
1,2,4-trimethylbenzene	107,203	102,612	250	5	0	0	19,071	229,141
1,2-dichloroethane	755	250	0	750	0	0	0	1,755
1,3-butadiene	920	250	0	0	0	0	0	1,170
1,4-dioxane	250	0	0	0	0	0	0	250
2,4-d	10	5	0	0	0	0	250	265
2,4-diaminoanisole	21	5	0	0	0	0	0	26
2,4-dinitrophenol	2	2	0	0	0	6	0	10
2,4-dinitrotoluene	5	2	0	0	0	12	0	19
2-ethoxyethanol	27,296	0	0	0	0	0	0	27,296
2-methoxyethanol	250	0	0	0	0	0	0	250
4,6-dinitro-o-cresol	2	2	0	0	0	1	0	5
Acetone	323,460	1,170,181	33,862	0	76	1	9,414	1,536,994
Acetonitrile	5	0	0	0	0	0	0	5
Acrylic acid	505	1,250	0	0	0	0	0	1,755
Acrylonitrile	3,905	2,939	0	0	0	0	288,885	295,729
Aluminum (fume or dust)	750	750	526	0	3,635	1,015	9,687	16,363
Aluminum oxide (fibrous forms)	250	0	0	0	0	0	17,126	17,376
Ammonia	1,555,077	12,475,484	575,581	0	601,537	176,241	1,013	15,384,933
Ammonium nitrate (solution)	0	0	923,868	0	0	0	0	923,868
Ammonium sulfate (solution)	96	0	5	0	0	10	671	782
Aniline	2,003	1,788	0	0	0	5	5,339	9,135
Anthracene	26	10	0	0	5	6	0	47
Antimony	5	5	0	0	0	5	14,639	14,654
Antimony compounds	5	500	0	0	0	5	2,101	2,611
Arsenic	5	250	0	0	0	0	15,130	15,385
Arsenic compounds	270	520	255	0	250	0	11,180	12,475
Barium	50	150	100	0	2,500	0	3,357	6,157
Barium compounds	760	755	0	5	270	0	10,322	12,112
Benzene	109,428	168,737	505	0	1,505	6	1,548	281,729
Biphenyl	16,000	0	0	0	0	0	0	16,000
Bis(2-ethylhexyl) adipate	0	250	0	0	0	0	0	250
Bromoform	5	0	0	0	0	0	0	5
Bromomethane	0	9,850	0	0	0	0	0	9,850
Butyl acrylate	250	250	0	0	0	0	0	500
Butyl benzyl phthalate	274	293	0	0	0	250	0	817
Cadmium	0	0	0	0	0	0	1,925	1,925
Cadmium compounds	255	302	15	5	270	5	260	1,112
Captan	255	250	250	0	250	0	250	1,255
Carbaryl	255	255	250	0	250	0	250	1,260
Carbon tetrachloride	2,550	0	0	0	0	0	250	2,800
Carbonyl sulfide	0	5,821,000	0	0	0	0	0	5,821,000
Catechol	0	0	6,634	0	18	0	0	6,652
Chlordane	5	0	0	0	0	0	0	5
Chlorine	108,134	204,308	507,963	0	600	80,250	5	901,260
Chlorine dioxide	20	65,213	5	0	0	0	5	65,243
Chloroform	116,113	138,512	12,558	0	16	0	312	267,511
Chloromethane	250	250	0	0	0	0	0	500
Chromium	1,035	1,754	106	5	15,809	11	608,357	627,077
Chromium compounds	1,530	2,057	15,191	0	11,406	5	24,562	54,751

[Continued]

417

★ 416 ★

Toxic Chemical Releases in Mississippi, by Chemical: 1990

[Continued]

Chemical	Fugitive air	Stack air	Water	Injection	Land	Public treatment	Other offsite	Total releases
Cobalt compounds	250	0	250	0	0	0	0	500
Copper	770	4,565	5	5	20	782	13,793	19,940
Copper compounds	8,079	785	798	0	300	268	31,449	41,679
Creosote	14,595	285,319	0	0	497	3,802	90,461	394,674
Cresol (mixed isomers)	5,635	1,700	0	0	0	0	500	7,835
Cumene	39,000	11,250	250	0	0	0	250	50,750
Cumene hydroperoxide	250	750	0	0	6,415	0	0	7,415
Cupferron	5	0	0	0	0	0	0	5
Cyanide compounds	250	500	8	0	0	500	11,827	13,085
Cyclohexane	40,020	17,250	255	0	250	0	0	57,775
Di(2-ethylhexyl) phthalate	2,391	9,463	3	0	0	0	22,891	34,748
Dibenzofuran	9	27	0	0	0	3	0	39
Dibutyl phthalate	5	0	0	0	0	0	250	255
Dichloromethane	1,400,405	3,397,475	0	0	0	250	63,373	4,861,503
Dichlorvos	250	0	0	0	0	0	0	250
Dicofol	0	250	5	0	0	0	0	255
Diethanolamine	250	0	250	0	0	0	0	500
Epichlorohydrin	6,969	10,525	0	0	0	0	248	17,742
Ethyl acrylate	11,250	1,000	0	0	0	0	8,150	20,400
Ethylbenzene	69,823	199,126	510	0	250	0	10,441	280,150
Ethylene	70,250	0	0	0	0	0	0	70,250
Ethylene glycol	1,756	109,147	1,000	0	5	2,600	5,243	119,751
Ethylene oxide	26,801	94,051	0	0	0	0	0	120,852
Formaldehyde	13,373	164,983	250	0	250	801	6,048	185,705
Freon 113	420,329	18,451	0	0	0	0	82,969	521,749
Glycol ethers	125,709	551,315	0	0	0	51	1,923	678,998
Hexachloroethane	5	5	0	0	0	0	0	10
Hydrazine sulfate	0	0	0	0	0	0	250	250
Hydrochloric acid	183,782	1,267,758	770	33,000,000	2,005	1,255	24,765	34,480,335
Hydrogen fluoride	750	250	0	0	0	0	0	1,000
Hydroquinone	5	0	0	0	5	0	250	260
Isopropyl alcohol (manufacturing)	15,462	51,643	0	0	0	0	1,000	68,105
Lead	2,265	1,275	0	0	41,000	13	81,499	126,052
Lead compounds	1,011	3,566	80	0	250	258	3,668	8,833
Lindane	250	250	250	0	5	0	5	760
M-cresol	250	250	0	0	0	0	0	500
M-dinitrobenzene	5	1	0	0	0	0	0	6
M-xylene	170,250	23,935	250	0	250	0	0	194,685
Maleic anhydride	780	370	250	0	0	0	0	1,400
Manganese	1,341	1,247	0	0	0	250	13,220	16,058
Manganese compounds	9,360	7,641	16,000	0	4,500,505	250	33,460	4,567,216
Mercury	250	0	0	0	0	0	250	500
Mercury compounds	250	0	0	0	5	0	250	505
Methanol	463,578	1,961,921	89,083	0	4,090	265,795	424,287	3,208,754
Methoxychlor	250	250	250	0	5	0	5	760
Methyl acrylate	250	250	0	0	0	0	0	500
Methyl ethyl ketone	712,793	3,947,894	11	0	250	645	122,219	4,783,812
Methyl isobutyl ketone	136,309	654,076	2	0	0	5	30,471	820,863
Methyl methacrylate	40,828	9,998	0	0	0	0	51,500	102,326
Methyl tert-butyl ether	71,000	160,000	250	0	0	0	0	231,250
Methylenebis(phenylisocyanate)	814	350	0	0	0	0	1,891	3,055
Molybdenum trioxide	255	250	1,700	0	0	0	2,607	4,812

[Continued]

★ 416 ★

Toxic Chemical Releases in Mississippi, by Chemical: 1990

[Continued]

Chemical	Fugitive air	Stack air	Water	Injection	Land	Public treatment	Other offsite	Total releases
N-butyl alcohol	430,916	241,100	5	0	0	0	2,289	674,310
N-dioctyl phthalate	5	250	39	0	0	0	7,999	8,293
Naphthalene	101,458	38,189	500	0	0	3	2,400	142,550
Nickel	1,026	255	5	0	0	5	20,286	21,577
Nickel compounds	755	255	2,055	0	255	5	16,324	19,649
Nitric acid	37,598	57,774	37,153	0	0	500	250	133,275
Nitrobenzene	3,244	7,124	0	0	0	12	1,044	11,424
O-dinitrobenzene	1	1	0	0	0	0	0	2
O-toluidine	551	288	0	0	0	1	417	1,257
O-xylene	87,000	14,250	250	0	250	0	0	101,750
P-xylene	160,000	23,000	250	0	250	0	0	183,500
Parathion	10	10	5	0	5	0	5	35
Pentachlorophenol	21	389	0	0	0	53	3,717	4,180
Phenol	49,072	70,872	619	0	2,103	12	6,956	129,634
Phosphoric acid	1,265	303	270	0	250	299	13,016	15,403
Phosphorus (yellow or white)	11,400	0	0	0	0	0	0	11,400
Phthalic anhydride	0	0	0	0	0	0	2,024	2,024
Picric acid	1	1	0	0	0	1	1,044	1,047
Polychlorinated biphenyls (PCBs)	0	0	0	0	0	0	505	505
Propoxur	250	0	0	0	0	0	0	250
Propylene	184,605	255	0	0	0	0	0	184,860
Propylene oxide	9,852	7,922	0	0	0	0	0	17,774
Quinoline	3	49	0	0	0	1	0	53
Selenium	0	0	6	0	0	0	0	6
Selenium compounds	0	3,300	250	0	0	0	0	3,550
Styrene	36,249	38,396	250	5	20	0	295,312	370,232
Sulfuric acid	27,738	164,574	1,242	7,395,000	18,365	98,015	173,735	7,878,669
Tert-butyl alcohol	250	0	0	0	0	0	250	500
Tetrachloroethylene	1,250	10,650	0	0	0	0	0	11,900
Titanium tetrachloride	13,800	0	0	0	0	0	0	13,800
Toluene	3,299,804	2,873,366	2,622	255	1,531	2,315	297,684	6,477,577
Toluenediisocyanate (mixed isomers)	753	1,220	0	0	0	0	0	1,973
Toluene-2,4-diisocyanate	1,955	3,400	0	0	0	0	250	5,605
Toluene-2,6-diisocyanate	255	500	0	0	0	0	0	755
Toxaphene	0	0	0	0	0	0	2,200	2,200
Trichloroethylene	1,149,139	279,007	5	0	0	0	8,983	1,437,134
Trifluralin	0	250	5	0	0	0	18,000	18,255
Vinyl chloride	3,017	60,976	12	0	0	0	0	64,005
Xylene (mixed isomers)	1,111,251	3,320,937	760	0	289	627,835	270,174	5,331,246
Zinc (fume or dust)	5	5	15	5	10,023	80	750	10,883
Zinc compounds	2,830	23,184	12,850	0	12,920	1,155	419,124	472,063
Zineb	5	0	0	0	0	0	0	5

Source: U.S. Environmental Protection Agency. "Toxic Chemical Releases, 1990." In *National Economic, Social, and Environmental Data Bank* [CD-ROM]. Prepared by U.S. Department of Commerce, Economics and Statistics Administration. Washington, DC: U.S. Department of Commerce, National Economic, Social, and Environmental Data Bank, Economics and Statistics Administration, Office of Business Analysis, February 1995.

★417★

Chemicals

Toxic Chemical Releases in Missouri, by Chemical: 1990

Figures indicate pounds released by chemical and by type of emission per year.

Chemical	Fugitive air	Stack air	Water	Injection	Land	Public treatment	Other offsite	Total releases
1,1,1-trichloroethane	1,702,857	2,507,066	0	0	1	795	433,981	4,644,700
1,1,2,2-tetrachloroethane	1	1	0	0	0	0	0	2
1,1,2-trichloroethane	13,000	29,001	0	0	0	850	1,200,000	1,242,851
1,2,4-trimethylbenzene	36,764	49,311	39	0	0	1,305	15,568	102,987
1,2-dichlorobenzene	783	1,082	0	0	0	0	0	1,865
1,2-dichloroethane	11,386	101,153	2,501	0	250	0	20,670	135,960
1,4-dichlorobenzene	11	29	0	0	0	0	0	40
1,4-dioxane	1,295	2,297	0	0	0	5	4,696	8,293
2,4-d	1,500	1,500	5	0	0	5,321	41,032	49,358
2,4-dimethylphenol	430	250	0	0	0	81	880	1,641
2-ethoxyethanol	3,924	3,513	0	0	0	0	0	7,437
2-methoxyethanol	1,914	6,812	0	0	0	0	22,334	31,060
2-nitropropane	83	37	0	0	0	0	0	120
2-phenylphenol	250	0	0	0	0	250	0	500
4,4'-isopropylidenediphenol	250	500	0	0	0	5	1,140	1,895
4,4'-methylenedianiline	5	0	0	0	0	0	326	331
4-nitrophenol	0	0	0	0	0	130,000	5,400	135,400
Acetaldehyde	57,000	0	0	0	0	0	0	57,000
Acetone	779,632	1,396,188	5	0	250	102,527	265,171	2,543,773
Acetonitrile	0	2	0	0	0	0	0	2
Acrylamide	250	1	0	0	0	1,000	0	1,251
Acrylic acid	2	0	0	0	0	0	0	2
Allyl alcohol	49	0	0	0	0	0	0	49
Aluminum (fume or dust)	35,046	160,741	255	0	5	250	206,417	402,714
Aluminum oxide (fibrous forms)	67,250	0	0	0	180,940	0	0	248,190
Ammonia	695,776	1,300,804	401,135	5	28,632	25,158,198	28,010	27,612,560
Ammonium nitrate (solution)	5	95,250	1,062,843	0	29,710	340,000	0	1,527,808
Ammonium sulfate (solution)	684	5	5	0	5	330,000	0	330,699
Aniline	1,100	50	0	0	0	3,500	0	4,650
Antimony	5	9	250	0	750	5	1,500	2,519
Antimony compounds	505	261	104	0	35,865	260	11,539	48,534
Arsenic compounds	42	172	30	0	25,962	14	36,425	62,645
Barium	5	5	15	5	20	0	0	50
Barium compounds	2,844	9,156	5	0	755	2,705	104,660	120,125
Benzene	20,362	2,855	250	0	250	5	0	23,722
Benzoyl peroxide	0	0	0	0	0	0	68	68
Benzyl chloride	0	0	0	0	0	1,000	0	1,000
Biphenyl	550	0	0	0	0	0	561	1,111
Bis(2-chloroethyl) ether	307	250	5	0	0	0	14,844	15,406
Bis(2-ethylhexyl) adipate	0	0	0	0	0	0	1,480	1,480
Bromomethane	13,210	8,806	0	0	0	0	0	22,016
Butyl acrylate	1,580	14,500	0	0	0	0	0	16,080
Butyl benzyl phthalate	1,956	734	5	0	5	555	12,860	16,115
Cadmium	0	4,080	0	0	2,316	0	2,316	8,712
Cadmium compounds	604	13,597	161	0	10,246	299	4,711	29,618
Captan	0	43	0	0	0	0	8,517	8,560
Carbaryl	18	1,558	0	0	0	0	1,621	3,197
Carbon disulfide	796	6	0	0	0	170	0	972
Carbon tetrachloride	227	33	0	0	0	0	0	260
Chlorine	31,402	9,602	13,484	5	25	186,007	38,180	278,705
Chloroacetic acid	800	1,900	0	0	0	0	0	2,700
Chlorobenzene	2,692	12,206	5	0	5	12,000	97,000	123,908
Chloroethane	440,000	430,000	0	0	0	0	0	870,000
Chloroform	13,250	251,219	0	0	0	3,550	246,421	514,440
Chloromethane	553	340,270	0	0	9	28	0	340,860
Chlorophenols	119	4	24	0	2	0	6	155
Chlorothalonil	2	0	0	0	0	12	1,178	1,192

[Continued]

★ 417 ★

Toxic Chemical Releases in Missouri, by Chemical: 1990
[Continued]

Chemical	Fugitive air	Stack air	Water	Injection	Land	Public treatment	Other offsite	Total releases
Chromium	4,133	1,592	140	0	2,754	1,342	139,046	149,007
Chromium compounds	3,585	6,347	5	0	91,374	1,790	117,465	220,566
Cobalt	255	255	0	0	0	10	8,501	9,021
Cobalt compounds	250	279	2	0	59	10	505	1,105
Copper	2,799	3,938	735	0	23,585	3,000	265,370	299,427
Copper compounds	7,747	25,450	106	0	341,398	2,617	117,574	494,892
Creosote	144	7,201	0	0	0	1,619	22,868	31,832
Cresol (mixed isomers)	4,805	4,906	0	0	0	315	13,285	23,311
Cumene	11,405	749	0	0	0	1,011	2,541	15,706
Cumene hydroperoxide	490	0	0	0	0	0	0	490
Cupferron	0	480	0	0	0	530	0	1,010
Cyanide compounds	250	262	5	0	5	42	15,846	16,410
Cyclohexane	39,898	196,884	0	0	0	140	24,393	261,315
Decabromodiphenyl oxide	250	0	0	0	0	250	1,049	1,549
Di(2-ethylhexyl) phthalate	26,878	520	0	0	0	288	128,254	155,940
Dibutyl phthalate	57	289	0	0	0	250	660	1,256
Dichloromethane	836,279	1,779,118	510	0	5	13,569	275,597	2,905,078
Dichlorvos	10	0	0	0	0	0	796	806
Diethanolamine	1,010	8,484	0	0	0	10,168	5	19,667
Dimethyl phthalate	4,100	9,600	0	0	0	0	0	13,700
Dimethyl sulfate	65	9	0	0	0	0	0	74
Epichlorohydrin	251	1	0	0	0	0	0	252
Ethylbenzene	116,986	625,102	1	0	0	647	28,403	771,139
Ethylene glycol	141,478	13,401	1,115	5	2,325	245,603	25,631	429,558
Ethylene oxide	12,551	1,005	0	0	0	0	0	13,556
Fluometuron	0	0	0	0	0	52	1,801	1,853
Formaldehyde	72,041	337,420	902	0	5	470,249	9,988	890,605
Freon 113	369,253	464,211	11	0	0	26	42,735	876,236
Glycol ethers	514,925	1,595,883	350	0	1,681	330,380	59,646	2,502,865
Hexachloro-1,3-butadiene	550	0	0	0	0	940	7,000	8,490
Hexachloroethane	250	250	0	0	0	0	0	500
Hydrazine	526	13	0	0	0	0	0	539
Hydrochloric acid	44,888	44,897	795	0	31,056	49,060	11,273	181,969
Hydrogen fluoride	173,802	120,271	0	0	0	292	19,800	314,165
Isopropyl alcohol (manufacturing)	51,311	140,318	0	0	0	10,005	17,951	219,585
Lead	926	4,702	255	0	36,673	327	91,673	134,556
Lead compounds	60,912	364,334	1,179	0	5,122,155	1,481	430,518	5,980,579
M-xylene	15	56	0	0	0	0	5	76
Maleic anhydride	5,258	20,005	0	0	0	250	16,023	41,536
Manganese	2,828	1,766	265	5	1,035	1,126	88,525	95,550
Manganese compounds	9,135	16,433	0	0	0	38,985	187,346	251,899
Mercury	0	30	0	0	0	0	80	110
Methanol	480,219	2,711,584	6,681	0	139,005	1,867,619	310,611	5,515,719
Methoxychlor	1	91	0	0	0	0	227	319
Methyl ethyl ketone	738,893	2,263,951	0	0	0	17,890	579,721	3,600,455
Methyl isobutyl ketone	164,326	1,105,030	20	0	5	5,290	42,527	1,317,198
Methyl methacrylate	1,865	40,005	0	0	0	5	250	42,125
Methyl tert-butyl ether	0	250	0	0	0	0	0	250
Methylenebis(phenylisocyanate)	24,111	14,043	0	0	505	0	70,210	108,869
N-butyl alcohol	388,567	1,870,469	250	0	0	311,586	26,596	2,597,468
N-dioctyl phthalate	500	501	0	0	0	5	1,333	2,339
Naphthalene	1,524	44,043	6	0	5	2,301	1,519	49,398
Nickel	4,142	1,290	320	0	1,705	3,915	198,440	209,812
Nickel compounds	2,154	1,336	10	0	35,631	2,352	75,162	116,645
Nitric acid	31,027	48,619	1,585	0	4,555	86,945	517,310	690,041
Nitrobenzene	690	46	0	0	0	110	0	846
Nitroglycerin	500	255	10,311	0	250	0	0	11,316
O-xylene	3,677	34,234	5	0	5	0	3	37,924
Pentachlorophenol	9	11	0	0	0	5	1,095	1,120

[Continued]

★417★

Toxic Chemical Releases in Missouri, by Chemical: 1990

[Continued]

Chemical	Fugitive air	Stack air	Water	Injection	Land	Public treatment	Other offsite	Total releases
Phenol	9,539	33,547	0	0	0	4,385	68,032	115,503
Phosphoric acid	3,111	6,688	730	5	61,648	279,813	192,226	544,221
Phosphorus (yellow or white)	0	0	0	0	0	0	3,474	3,474
Phthalic anhydride	38	1,334	250	0	0	34,400	4,303	40,325
Polychlorinated biphenyls (PCBs)	0	0	0	0	0	0	121,000	121,000
Propoxur	0	0	0	0	0	0	31	31
Propylene oxide	2,705	7,219	0	0	0	0	0	9,924
Sec-butyl alcohol	3,080	1,105	0	0	0	6,405	31	10,621
Selenium compounds	250	5	0	0	0	0	250	505
Silver compounds	5	250	250	0	0	5	0	510
Sodium hydroxide (solution)	0	0	0	0	0	17,650	0	17,650
Styrene	92,046	487,860	1,065	0	0	400	16,111	597,482
Sulfuric acid	40,243	66,436	7,809	0	24,947	89,662	456,195	685,292
Tert-butyl alcohol	22,334	5,465	0	0	0	0	0	27,799
Tetrachloroethylene	70,329	404,325	0	0	0	95,100	53,209	622,963
Tetrachlorvinphos	0	4	0	0	0	28	850	882
Toluene	1,101,381	3,754,423	107	0	5	9,737	1,013,784	5,879,437
Toluenediisocyanate (mixed isomers)	1,000	503	0	0	0	0	250	1,753
Toluene-2,4-diisocyanate	255	260	0	0	5	0	500	1,020
Toluene-2,6-diisocyanate	10	260	0	0	5	0	500	775
Trichlorfon	0	1	6	0	0	0	12	19
Trichloroethylene	687,995	586,442	0	0	0	93	70,217	1,344,747
Trifluralin	0	0	0	0	0	34	5,556	5,590
Vanadium (fume or dust)	0	0	0	0	0	0	3,474	3,474
Vinyl acetate	278	61	0	0	0	0	0	339
Vinyl chloride	629	684	0	0	0	0	0	1,313
Xylene (mixed isomers)	1,047,267	6,642,232	255	0	250	13,282	488,093	8,191,379
Zinc (fume or dust)	2,755	6,135	0	0	250	1,688	114,110	124,938
Zinc compounds	54,195	126,176	1,750	0	16,648,658	56,412	219,297	17,106,488

Source: U.S. Environmental Protection Agency. "Toxic Chemical Releases, 1990." In *National Economic, Social, and Environmental Data Bank* [CD-ROM]. Prepared by U.S. Department of Commerce, Economics and Statistics Administration. Washington, DC: U.S. Department of Commerce, National Economic, Social, and Environmental Data Bank, Economics and Statistics Administration, Office of Business Analysis, February 1995.

★418★

Chemicals

Toxic Chemical Releases in Montana, by Chemical: 1990

Figures indicate pounds released by chemical and by type of emission per year.

Chemical	Fugitive air	Stack air	Water	Injection	Land	Public treatment	Other offsite	Total releases
1,2,4-trimethylbenzene	47,150	6,661	9	0	1,800	250	1,222	57,092
1,3-butadiene	880	60	0	0	0	0	0	940
2,4-d	250	250	0	0	250	250	11,955	12,955
Acetone	2,400	3,500	6,800	0	0	0	0	12,700
Ammonia	43,100	254,020	87,805	0	13,900	0	5	398,830
Antimony compounds	70	2,400	0	0	282,000	12	0	284,482
Arsenic compounds	37,010	4,410	0	0	306,000	26	500	347,946
Benzene	47,650	6,670	9	0	703	250	5,970	61,252
Cadmium compounds	7,000	11,000	0	0	118,000	9	0	136,009
Carbon tetrachloride	960	0	0	0	0	0	0	960

[Continued]

★ 418 ★

Toxic Chemical Releases in Montana, by Chemical: 1990

[Continued]

Chemical	Fugitive air	Stack air	Water	Injection	Land	Public treatment	Other offsite	Total releases
Catechol	0	0	9,000	0	8,800	0	0	17,800
Chlorine	65,330	0	0	0	0	0	0	65,330
Chlorine dioxide	27,400	0	0	0	0	0	0	27,400
Chloroform	80,500	0	800	0	0	0	0	81,300
Chromium compounds	260	260	0	0	0	0	500	1,020
Copper	0	250	0	0	0	0	0	250
Copper compounds	4,260	16,446	0	0	1,300,000	280	860	1,321,846
Cumene	9,700	22	4	0	0	0	222	9,948
Cyclohexane	31,500	1,300	9	0	400	0	487	33,696
Diethanolamine	5,600	5	890	0	0	0	500	6,995
Ethylbenzene	42,750	2,273	9	0	850	250	684	46,816
Ethylene	71,000	4,200	0	0	0	0	0	75,200
Ethylene glycol	500	255	0	0	0	250	5	1,010
Formaldehyde	6,609	190,583	0	0	750	0	94,374	292,316
Hydrochloric acid	500	2,400	0	0	5	0	0	2,905
Hydrogen fluoride	447,800	88,400	0	0	0	0	0	536,200
Lead compounds	59,470	51,505	5	0	3,000,008	122	260	3,111,370
Manganese compounds	60	970	0	0	3,012,000	13	0	3,013,043
Methanol	128,850	12,700	0	0	0	0	0	141,550
Methyl isobutyl ketone	8,199	9,732	0	0	0	0	94,124	112,055
Methyl isocyanate	0	500	0	0	500	0	0	1,000
Methyl tert-butyl ether	6,100	660	0	0	0	0	0	6,760
N-butyl alcohol	250	7,200	0	0	250	5	5	7,710
Naphthalene	9,100	113	8	0	23	0	194	9,438
Nickel	0	250	0	0	0	0	0	250
Nickel compounds	50	86	0	0	4,000	3	0	4,139
Pentachlorophenol	5	5	0	0	0	0	0	10
Phenol	250	250	0	0	0	0	0	500
Phosphoric acid	0	0	0	0	0	27,000	16,250	43,250
Phosphorus (yellow or white)	250	2,800	0	0	0	0	0	3,050
Propylene	110,000	9,490	0	0	0	0	0	119,490
Silver compounds	340	770	0	0	9,800	2	0	10,912
Styrene	747	0	0	0	0	0	94,124	94,871
Sulfuric acid	1,255	46,710	0	0	8,105	0	0	56,070
Toluene	141,646	11,230	9	0	3,003	750	6,900	163,538
Trichloroethylene	7,516	5	0	0	0	0	7,421	14,942
Xylene (mixed isomers)	223,250	9,850	5	0	4,221	250	6,600	244,176
Zinc compounds	17,250	21,401	0	0	32,020,000	320	0	32,058,971

Source: U.S. Environmental Protection Agency. "Toxic Chemical Releases, 1990." In *National Economic, Social, and Environmental Data Bank* [CD-ROM]. Prepared by U.S. Department of Commerce, Economics and Statistics Administration. Washington, DC: U.S. Department of Commerce, National Economic, Social, and Environmental Data Bank, Economics and Statistics Administration, Office of Business Analysis, February 1995.

★ 419 ★

Chemicals

Toxic Chemical Releases in Nebraska, by Chemical: 1990

Figures indicate pounds released by chemical and by type of emission per year.

Chemical	Fugitive air	Stack air	Water	Injection	Land	Public treatment	Other offsite	Total releases
1,1,1-trichloroethane	653,578	464,042	0	0	0	15	55,368	1,173,003
1,2,4-trimethylbenzene	360	16	0	0	0	0	1	377
Acetone	181,783	194,273	10	0	0	38	18,943	395,047
Acrylic acid	250	250	5	0	0	0	3,000	3,505
Ammonia	1,027,540	2,993,754	347,346	0	18,229	441,959	1,338,457	6,167,285
Ammonium nitrate (solution)	3,200	322,000	142,900	0	250	0	0	468,350
Ammonium sulfate (solution)	0	5	0	0	0	443,122	1,226,604	1,669,731
Antimony	255	1,500	0	0	0	0	250	2,005
Antimony compounds	8,450	32,350	2,500	0	750	1,600	538,619	584,269
Arsenic compounds	250	3,760	1,230	0	750	250	41,900	48,140
Barium	30	5	5	5	20	0	0	65
Barium compounds	250	5	0	0	250	70	80,086	80,661
Benzoyl peroxide	5	0	0	0	0	0	0	5
Bis(2-ethylhexyl) adipate	0	0	0	0	0	0	3,840	3,840
Bromomethane	5	0	0	0	0	0	0	5
Cadmium	1	4	0	0	0	0	0	5
Captan	250	250	0	0	0	0	500	1,000
Carbaryl	250	250	0	0	0	0	500	1,000
Chlorine	3,780	15,730	6,361	0	0	13,005	0	38,876
Chromium	514	17	7	0	0	3,941	23,788	28,267
Chromium compounds	260	773	358	0	250	38,852	189,529	230,022
Cobalt	5	0	5	0	0	0	1,500	1,510
Cobalt compounds	5	0	0	0	0	0	12,800	12,805
Copper	821	2,905	257	0	2	70	9,971	14,026
Copper compounds	8,546	8,844	372	0	250	20	17,898	35,930
Di(2-ethylhexyl) phthalate	2,410	0	0	0	0	10	4,476	6,896
Dichloromethane	101,904	1,131,258	5	0	0	0	250	1,233,417
Dimethyl phthalate	2,090	0	0	0	0	0	839	2,929
Ethylbenzene	3,200	2,100	0	0	0	0	0	5,300
Ethylene glycol	505	900	0	0	0	3,550	7,050	12,005
Freon 113	369,251	43,400	0	0	0	0	36,275	448,926
Glycol ethers	52,621	162,402	5	0	0	9,321	1,150	225,499
Hydrochloric acid	4,238	6,180	0	0	250	17	250	10,935
Hydrogen fluoride	250	0	0	0	5	0	0	255
Lead	1,255	18,304	5	0	710	23	20,147	40,444
Lead compounds	2,843	35,112	4,415	0	36,489	280	624,437	703,576
Lindane	250	250	0	0	0	0	0	500
Maneb	250	250	0	0	0	0	0	500
Manganese	3,075	510	505	5	20	276	14,731	19,122
Manganese compounds	1,352	3,755	0	0	0	0	1,005	6,112
Methanol	16,069	283,066	2,800	0	0	119	755	302,809
Methyl ethyl ketone	268,413	942,853	15	0	250	0	40,259	1,251,790
Methyl isobutyl ketone	19,197	70,268	0	0	0	0	5	89,470
Methyl methacrylate	2,388	0	0	0	0	0	750	3,138
Methylenebis(phenylisocyanate)	28,500	501	0	0	0	0	3,250	32,251

[Continued]

★419★

Toxic Chemical Releases in Nebraska, by Chemical: 1990
[Continued]

Chemical	Fugitive air	Stack air	Water	Injection	Land	Public treatment	Other offsite	Total releases
N-butyl alcohol	11,840	133,531	0	0	0	0	74	145,445
Naphthalene	750	110,000	0	0	0	21,125	750	132,625
Nickel	772	505	550	0	0	2,341	14,589	18,757
Nickel compounds	0	0	0	0	0	170	38,300	38,470
Nitric acid	1,785	3,348	10,500	0	1,000	253	5,600	22,486
Pentachlorophenol	5	5	0	0	0	0	5	15
Phenol	11,000	0	0	0	0	0	1,300	12,300
Phosphoric acid	1,748	936	5	0	155	195,256	0	198,100
Silver compounds	5	250	250	0	250	250	250	1,255
Styrene	73,700	24,866	0	0	0	0	62,238	160,804
Sulfuric acid	5,395	6,909	38,805	0	255	610	564,954	616,928
Tetrachloroethylene	34,779	94,923	0	0	0	0	750	130,452
Tetrachlorvinphos	250	250	0	0	0	0	500	1,000
Toluene	1,341,653	3,692,156	5	0	0	5,905	72,221	5,111,940
Toluene-2,4-diisocyanate	250	250	0	0	0	0	5,400	5,900
Trichloroethylene	6,000	36,000	0	0	0	5	40,617	82,622
Trifluralin	500	250	0	0	0	0	0	750
Xylene (mixed isomers)	324,404	1,231,559	15	0	255	5	34,042	1,590,280
Zinc (fume or dust)	403	6,871	0	0	0	0	255	7,529
Zinc compounds	28,255	60,901	3,230	0	500	6,672	2,078,682	2,178,240

Source: U.S. Environmental Protection Agency. "Toxic Chemical Releases, 1990." In *National Economic, Social, and Environmental Data Bank* [CD-ROM]. Prepared by U.S. Department of Commerce, Economics and Statistics Administration. Washington, DC: U.S. Department of Commerce, National Economic, Social, and Environmental Data Bank, Economics and Statistics Administration, Office of Business Analysis, February 1995.

★ 420 ★

Chemicals

Toxic Chemical Releases in Nevada, by Chemical: 1990

Figures indicate pounds released by chemical and by type of emission per year.

Chemical	Fugitive air	Stack air	Water	Injection	Land	Public treatment	Other offsite	Total releases
1,1,1-trichloroethane	5,010	24,098	0	0	0	0	500	29,608
Acetone	82,650	2,060	0	0	0	0	1,500	86,210
Ammonia	14,345	6,800	1	0	0	0	0	21,146
Asbestos (friable)	0	0	0	0	0	0	37,739	37,739
Barium compounds	255	755	250	0	0	0	0	1,260
Benzene	221	8	0	0	0	0	0	229
Cadmium compounds	5	5	0	0	0	0	0	10
Chlorine	11,058	8,925	0	0	0	0	0	19,983
Chromium	986	0	0	0	740	526	10,209	12,461
Chromium compounds	0	0	0	0	172,862	0	1,700	174,562
Cobalt	421	250	0	0	0	122	2,205	2,998
Copper	250	250	0	0	0	6	1,221	1,727

[Continued]

★ 420 ★

Toxic Chemical Releases in Nevada, by Chemical: 1990
[Continued]

Chemical	Fugitive air	Stack air	Water	Injection	Land	Public treatment	Other offsite	Total releases
Copper compounds	5	250	0	0	0	5	182	442
Cyanide compounds	250	0	0	0	0	0	0	250
Di(2-ethylhexyl) phthalate	500	250	0	0	0	0	250	1,000
Ethylene glycol	250	250	0	0	0	187	0	687
Freon 113	5,520	0	0	0	0	0	0	5,520
Glycol ethers	2,966	1,239	0	0	250	2	36,418	40,875
Hydrochloric acid	1,409	1,455	0	0	6,440	13,600	0	22,904
Hydrogen fluoride	250	250	0	0	750	0	0	1,250
Lead compounds	5	0	0	0	0	0	0	5
Manganese	250	750	0	0	84,000	0	0	85,000
Manganese compounds	8,800	4,100	0	0	2,151,400	0	0	2,164,300
Methanol	37,314	0	0	0	0	0	0	37,314
Methyl ethyl ketone	750	28,470	0	0	0	0	0	29,220
Methylenebis(phenylisocyanate)	5	0	0	0	0	250	0	255
Nickel	931	250	0	0	0	313	5,802	7,296
Nickel compounds	0	250	0	0	0	0	0	250
Nitric acid	10	2,045	0	0	0	0	19,555	21,610
Pentachlorophenol	0	0	0	0	750	0	0	750
Styrene	10,243	0	0	0	0	0	0	10,243
Sulfuric acid	526	761	0	0	130,000	250	2,950	134,487
Tetrachloroethylene	10	0	0	0	0	0	0	10
Toluene	170,905	206,760	0	0	0	11	1,500	379,176
Xylene (mixed isomers)	28,460	47,489	0	0	0	0	1,250	77,199
Zinc compounds	0	0	0	0	0	5	18,500	18,505

Source: U.S. Environmental Protection Agency. "Toxic Chemical Releases, 1990." In *National Economic, Social, and Environmental Data Bank* [CD-ROM]. Prepared by U.S. Department of Commerce, Economics and Statistics Administration. Washington, DC: U.S. Department of Commerce, National Economic, Social, and Environmental Data Bank, Economics and Statistics Administration, Office of Business Analysis, February 1995.

★ 421 ★
Chemicals

Toxic Chemical Releases in New Hampshire, by Chemical: 1990

Figures indicate pounds released by chemical and by type of emission per year.

Chemical	Fugitive air	Stack air	Water	Injection	Land	Public treatment	Other offsite	Total releases
1,1,1-trichloroethane	578,752	482,505	16	5	20	37	90,555	1,151,890
1,1,2-trichloroethane	5	0	0	0	0	0	0	5
1,2,4-trimethylbenzene	5,001	2,170	0	0	0	5	517	7,693
2-ethoxyethanol	0	250	0	0	0	0	0	250
2-methoxyethanol	89,735	31,603	0	0	0	0	13,340	134,678
4,4'-isopropylidenediphenol	0	0	0	0	0	250	750	1,000
Acetone	173,706	164,591	4,200	5	8,520	0	42,480	393,502
Ammonia	53,284	82,106	146,451	0	0	32,327	111,970	426,138

[Continued]

★ 421 ★

Toxic Chemical Releases in New Hampshire, by Chemical: 1990
[Continued]

Chemical	Fugitive air	Stack air	Water	Injection	Land	Public treatment	Other offsite	Total releases
Ammonium nitrate (solution)	0	0	0	0	0	62,000	0	62,000
Ammonium sulfate (solution)	0	0	0	0	0	114,065	0	114,065
Antimony	0	0	0	0	0	0	250	250
Antimony compounds	0	0	0	0	0	250	1,263	1,513
Arsenic compounds	5	5	5	0	0	0	181	196
Benzene	250	250	0	0	0	0	10	510
Butyl acrylate	403	140	0	0	0	118	0	661
Catechol	0	0	1,055	0	2,980	0	0	4,035
Chlorine	500	690,250	0	0	0	0	0	690,750
Chlorine dioxide	250	640,000	0	0	0	0	0	640,250
Chloroform	35,797	55,974	5,634	0	20	0	13,000	110,425
Chromium	430	129	5	0	0	6	16,310	16,880
Chromium compounds	5	5	5	0	0	0	6,602	6,617
Cobalt	7	1	0	0	0	0	16	24
Copper	586	511	0	0	0	1,496	171,208	173,801
Copper compounds	19	309	5	0	0	837	29,240	30,410
Cresol (mixed isomers)	171	9,382	0	0	0	0	1,410	10,963
Cumene	5	5	0	0	0	5	0	15
Cumene hydroperoxide	0	0	0	0	0	0	250	250
Cyanide compounds	2	8	254	0	0	6	368	638
Di(2-ethylhexyl) phthalate	500	500	250	0	250	0	250	1,750
Dibutyl phthalate	0	0	0	0	0	5	0	5
Dichloromethane	105,217	398,680	0	5	15	532	14,186	518,635
Diethanolamine	0	0	3	0	0	0	0	3
Diethyl phthalate	5	5	0	0	0	5	0	15
Ethylbenzene	0	0	0	0	0	5	0	5
Ethylene glycol	5	5	0	0	0	5	400	415
Ethylene oxide	0	3,400	0	0	0	0	0	3,400
Formaldehyde	944	3,224	10,009	0	0	0	302	14,479
Freon 113	483,286	415,264	5	0	0	15	41,926	940,496
Glycol ethers	4,400	61,947	0	0	6,533	130,713	2,825	206,418
Hydrochloric acid	1,217	1,827	0	0	0	80,315	144,274	227,633
Hydrogen cyanide	1,741	521	0	0	0	0	990	3,252
Hydrogen fluoride	0	250	0	0	0	5	0	255
Hydroquinone	0	135	0	0	0	500	250	885
Isopropyl alcohol (manufacturing)	3,855	0	0	0	0	0	19,175	23,030
Lead	755	250	0	0	0	18	4,052	5,075
Lead compounds	29	32	9	0	0	2	518	590
Manganese	377	123	1	0	0	1	4,528	5,030
Methanol	78,555	88,273	0	5	20	5,277	17,293	189,423
Methyl ethyl ketone	131,340	715,920	5	5	20	0	129,535	976,825
Methyl isobutyl ketone	787	288,874	0	0	0	5	49,398	339,064
Methyl methacrylate	7,125	0	0	0	0	0	250	7,375
Methylenebis(phenylisocyanate)	260	260	0	0	0	0	5,173	5,693
N-butyl alcohol	499	19,650	0	0	0	0	423	20,572
Nickel	1,357	459	5	0	0	6	39,732	41,559

[Continued]

★ 421 ★

Toxic Chemical Releases in New Hampshire, by Chemical: 1990

[Continued]

Chemical	Fugitive air	Stack air	Water	Injection	Land	Public treatment	Other offsite	Total releases
Nickel compounds	3	6	0	0	0	1	652	662
Nitric acid	882	772	0	0	0	325	5	1,984
Phenol	1,326	8,103	0	0	0	0	26,332	35,761
Phosphoric acid	5	255	5	0	0	3,176	22	3,463
Phthalic anhydride	5	0	0	0	0	0	0	5
Propylene	0	1,250	0	0	0	0	0	1,250
Selenium	0	0	0	0	0	0	750	750
Styrene	53,709	3,711	1	0	0	244	3,479	61,144
Sulfuric acid	1,710	68,073	86,320	0	87,790	17,331	19,603	280,827
Tetrachloroethylene	112,625	11,137	0	0	0	259	8,100	132,121
Toluene	114,227	1,009,991	0	5	20	5	103,946	1,228,194
Toluenediisocyanate (mixed isomers)	0	1	0	0	0	0	130	131
Toluene-2,4-diisocyanate	255	5	0	0	0	0	250	510
Trichloroethylene	142,762	135,000	0	0	0	5	4,722	282,489
Vinyl acetate	41	271	0	0	0	0	0	312
Xylene (mixed isomers)	68,199	282,010	0	0	2	5	17,654	367,870
Zinc (fume or dust)	250	250	0	0	0	0	0	500
Zinc compounds	59	260	0	5	20	113	102,278	102,735

Source: U.S. Environmental Protection Agency. "Toxic Chemical Releases, 1990." In *National Economic, Social, and Environmental Data Bank* [CD-ROM]. Prepared by U.S. Department of Commerce, Economics and Statistics Administration. Washington, DC: U.S. Department of Commerce, National Economic, Social, and Environmental Data Bank, Economics and Statistics Administration, Office of Business Analysis, February 1995.

★ 422 ★

Chemicals

Toxic Chemical Releases in New Jersey, by Chemical: 1990

Figures indicate pounds released by chemical and by type of emission per year.

Chemical	Fugitive air	Stack air	Water	Injection	Land	Public treatment	Other offsite	Total releases
1,1,1-trichloroethane	917,522	472,742	311	10	2,425	17,544	762,717	2,173,271
1,1,2,2-tetrachloroethane	17	30	0	0	0	119	22,000	22,166
1,2,4-trichlorobenzene	250	0	0	0	0	11,500	27,786	39,536
1,2,4-trimethylbenzene	18,144	7,580	239	0	255	365	1,503	28,086
1,2-dibromoethane	241	20,072	0	0	0	0	0	20,313
1,2-dichlorobenzene	2,135	3,231	3,915	0	32,578	23,219	2,827	67,905
1,2-dichloroethane	278	44,812	22,772	0	3	2,254	1,500	71,619
1,2-dichloropropane	1,860	6,439	587	0	0	0	1,139	10,025
1,3-butadiene	324	27	0	0	0	0	0	351
1,4-dichlorobenzene	250	0	0	0	0	0	0	250
1,4-dioxane	5	0	0	0	0	0	0	5
2,4-diaminotoluene	1	1	0	0	0	501	0	503
2,4-dimethylphenol	288	251	0	0	0	237	12	788
2,4-dinitrotoluene	11	16	2,253	0	2,148	0	0	4,428
2,6-xylidine	0	17	1,906	0	0	0	0	1,923
2-ethoxyethanol	880	4,280	0	0	0	7,800	930	13,890

[Continued]

★ 422 ★

Toxic Chemical Releases in New Jersey, by Chemical: 1990
[Continued]

Chemical	Fugitive air	Stack air	Water	Injection	Land	Public treatment	Other offsite	Total releases
2-methoxyethanol	2,361	8,990	0	0	0	4,339	17,830	33,520
2-nitropropane	2,943	250	0	0	0	0	500	3,693
2-phenylphenol	250	5	0	0	0	2,322	0	2,577
3,3'-dichlorobenzidine	5	5	0	0	0	0	0	10
3,3'-dimethoxybenzidine	3	1	0	0	0	37	0	41
3,3'-dimethylbenzidine	0	0	0	0	0	5	0	5
4,4'-diaminodiphenyl ether	0	150	163	0	0	0	0	313
4,4'-isopropylidenediphenol	260	255	10	0	5	0	22,127	22,657
4,4'-methylenedianiline	160	450	18	0	5	0	3,416	4,049
4-nitrophenol	0	0	0	0	0	750	0	750
5-nitro-o-anisidine	5	5	0	0	0	5	0	15
Acetaldehyde	5	0	0	0	0	0	0	5
Acetone	1,603,488	1,702,994	1,631	5	55,506	1,345,226	2,175,093	6,883,943
Acetonitrile	10,335	12,152	0	0	0	341,450	79,900	443,837
Acrylamide	127	8	0	0	0	21	295	451
Acrylic acid	4,981	4,943	0	0	0	2,717	7,823	20,464
Acrylonitrile	1,083	2,302	3	0	0	0	1,983	5,371
Allyl alcohol	255	395	0	0	0	750	5,344	6,744
Allyl chloride	1,036	1,000	0	0	0	46	10,131	12,213
Aluminum (fume or dust)	2,455	10,750	0	0	0	0	1,477,949	1,491,154
Aluminum oxide (fibrous forms)	1,000	250	0	0	0	0	1,404,650	1,405,900
Ammonia	226,821	372,088	245,983	0	266	3,557,257	27,077	4,429,492
Ammonium nitrate (solution)	0	0	0	0	0	320,000	0	320,000
Ammonium sulfate (solution)	121	260	0	0	0	12,101,738	200,158	12,302,277
Aniline	1,695	1,733	2	0	0	21,000	1	24,431
Anthracene	250	253	47	0	241	0	264	1,055
Antimony	505	510	255	0	250	255	500	2,275
Antimony compounds	1,583	1,324	792	0	0	30	59,278	63,007
Arsenic	5	5	0	0	0	0	255	265
Arsenic compounds	5	6	0	0	0	10	1,280	1,301
Asbestos (friable)	250	10	0	0	0	250	1,460,225	1,460,735
Barium	250	0	0	0	0	0	500	750
Barium compounds	5,341	8,151	8,698	5	201,750	99,461	155,110	478,516
Benzal chloride	0	6	0	0	0	0	37,000	37,006
Benzene	82,354	45,890	799	0	83	120,186	22,024	271,336
Benzoyl chloride	0	3	0	0	0	0	0	3
Benzoyl peroxide	78	0	0	0	0	0	252	330
Benzyl chloride	2,765	3,855	0	0	0	6,358	231,500	244,478
Biphenyl	2,882	0	5	0	0	25,787	0	28,674
Bis(2-chloroethyl) ether	250	5	0	0	0	250	0	505
Bis(2-ethylhexyl) adipate	6,230	6,611	0	0	0	4,503	11,798	29,142
Bis(chloromethyl) ether	0	3	0	0	0	0	0	3
Bromomethane	15,500	0	0	0	0	0	0	15,500
Butyl acrylate	4,084	548	3	0	0	613	1,377	6,625
Butyl benzyl phthalate	1,775	9,850	252	0	1,900	215	107,968	121,960
Butyraldehyde	250	250	0	0	0	250	0	750
C.I. basic green 4	6	1	0	0	0	641	0	648
Cadmium	510	255	5	0	0	255	1,506	2,531
Cadmium compounds	1,002	1,056	0	0	0	350	6,442	8,850
Carbaryl	250	0	0	0	0	0	250	500
Carbon disulfide	9,300	15,275	0	0	0	1,102	8,300	33,977
Carbon tetrachloride	2,841	1,832	322	0	0	0	0	4,995

[Continued]

★ 422 ★

Toxic Chemical Releases in New Jersey, by Chemical: 1990
[Continued]

Chemical	Fugitive air	Stack air	Water	Injection	Land	Public treatment	Other offsite	Total releases
Catechol	0	0	0	0	0	46,000	0	46,000
Chlorine	27,875	45,791	17,899	0	0	18,285	45,810	155,660
Chloroacetic acid	22	2,192	0	0	0	748	3,650	6,612
Chlorobenzene	360	497	3,229	0	3,222	1,123	44,711	53,142
Chloroethane	3,090	64,054	35,728	0	54	0	0	102,926
Chloroform	118,420	2,840	586	0	0	21,986	118,351	262,183
Chloromethane	7,450	750	0	0	0	250	0	8,450
Chloromethyl methyl ether	0	91	0	0	0	0	0	91
Chlorophenols	250	250	0	0	0	750	0	1,250
Chloroprene	250	250	0	0	0	0	1,778	2,278
Chromium	1,775	2,390	287	10	290	1,202	66,283	72,237
Chromium compounds	3,597	4,712	6,578	0	69,595	70,481	179,352	334,315
Cobalt	505	1,006	250	0	0	3,321	22,038	27,120
Cobalt compounds	760	1,010	362	0	5	642	9,473	12,252
Copper	28,662	60,747	1,388	0	5	1,954	751,692	844,448
Copper compounds	4,079	9,242	1,165	5	750	12,513	96,191	123,945
Creosote	6,279	5,166	0	0	5	707	55,331	67,488
Cresol (mixed isomers)	8,953	1,167	0	0	700	1,015	1,037	12,872
Cumene	22,583	79,957	259	0	750	13	2,313	105,875
Cumene hydroperoxide	0	0	0	0	250	0	250	500
Cyanide compounds	600	1,255	250	0	250	651	575	3,581
Cyclohexane	22,768	34,827	128	0	5	260	13,690	71,678
Decabromodiphenyl oxide	238	6	250	0	0	0	26,831	27,325
Di(2-ethylhexyl) phthalate	3,376	9,290	724	0	11,835	72,531	115,931	213,687
Dibenzofuran	250	250	0	0	0	0	250	750
Dibutyl phthalate	1,291	1,039	260	0	135	1,529	5,055	9,309
Dichlorobenzene (mixed isomers)	2,300	2,300	0	0	0	20,000	157,100	181,700
Dichloromethane	292,720	575,808	17,344	5	2,920	300,341	745,461	1,934,599
Diethanolamine	1,614	1,335	5	0	0	211,119	639	214,712
Diethyl phthalate	3,046	4,475	250	0	5	46,105	30,545	84,426
Diethyl sulfate	261	261	0	0	0	266	0	788
Dimethyl sulfate	295	290	375	0	0	0	0	960
Dinitrotoluene (mixed isomers)	75	114	7,081	0	363	0	0	7,633
Epichlorohydrin	5,521	10,341	10	0	4	6,525	45,375	67,776
Ethyl acrylate	2,562	604	4	0	0	1,605	2,581	7,356
Ethylbenzene	23,736	38,414	225	0	226	9,120	85,556	157,277
Ethylene	25,197	130,051	0	0	0	11	0	155,259
Ethylene glycol	69,995	46,350	328	5	25	2,921,234	77,268	3,115,205
Ethylene oxide	21,940	11,958	3,480	0	7	10	15	37,410
Ethylene thiourea	0	1	0	0	0	0	8,235	8,236
Formaldehyde	15,362	72,615	4,078	0	4	44,865	94,920	231,844
Freon 113	482,494	231,616	9,348	5	9,495	36,885	44,759	814,602
Glycol ethers	166,790	824,791	5,522	5	340	1,769,146	56,130	2,822,724
Hexachloroethane	5	5	0	0	0	0	0	10
Hydrazine	1,005	1,005	18	0	5	500	747	3,280
Hydrazine sulfate	5	252	0	0	0	250	0	507
Hydrochloric acid	64,896	158,644	426	0	0	176,172	41,678	441,816
Hydrogen cyanide	0	750	0	0	0	0	0	750
Hydrogen fluoride	5,888	1,983	49	0	0	0	88,236	96,156
Hydroquinone	34	255	0	0	0	1,124	6,943	8,356
Isobutyraldehyde	0	250	0	0	0	35,649	13,987	49,886
Isopropyl alcohol (manufacturing)	3,966	4,247	20	5	20	31,208	24,254	63,720

[Continued]

★ 422 ★

Toxic Chemical Releases in New Jersey, by Chemical: 1990

[Continued]

Chemical	Fugitive air	Stack air	Water	Injection	Land	Public treatment	Other offsite	Total releases
Lead	2,520	4,306	11	0	4	260	35,340	42,441
Lead compounds	4,577	56,128	19,387	0	154,653	104,961	970,837	1,310,543
Lindane	0	0	0	0	0	0	5	5
M-dinitrobenzene	500	7,360	0	0	358	0	0	8,218
M-xylene	644	117	5	0	5	250	25	1,046
Maleic anhydride	1,516	1,966	10	0	2,500	1,244	8,128	15,364
Manganese	5,270	756	264	0	33	518	357,469	364,310
Manganese compounds	5,077	3,305	819	5	45,880	6,064,597	4,487	6,124,170
Mercury	38	1	1	0	0	5	11	56
Mercury compounds	5	6	0	0	0	261	14,848	15,120
Methanol	458,144	1,853,621	14,166	0	2,223	22,728,422	4,558,542	29,615,118
Methyl acrylate	3,428	2,330	0	0	0	2,522	375	8,655
Methyl ethyl ketone	564,217	1,163,174	1,062	0	44,992	72,055	1,102,786	2,948,286
Methyl isobutyl ketone	213,127	496,830	1,180	0	22,449	248,994	199,748	1,182,328
Methyl methacrylate	2,366	6,375	1,135	0	0	642	7,882	18,400
Methyl tert-butyl ether	10,625	150,611	3,209	0	0	663	1,790	166,898
Methylenebis(phenylisocyanate)	7,453	2,374	0	0	0	0	63,339	73,166
Michler's ketone	0	0	0	0	0	0	27,591	27,591
Molybdenum trioxide	5	5	250	0	0	0	750	1,010
N,N-dimethylaniline	416	358	0	0	0	12,172	4,657	17,603
N-butyl alcohol	161,788	956,734	7,136	0	60,520	462,079	1,785,108	3,433,365
N-dioctyl phthalate	510	2,250	0	0	0	5	3,062	5,827
Naphthalene	10,699	4,165	245	0	7,209	280	2,669	25,267
Nickel	770	956	505	5	0	5,012	4,205	11,453
Nickel compounds	1,521	5,609	817	10	5,920	1,929	131,430	147,236
Nitric acid	28,994	134,386	0	5	25	126,691	1,033,664	1,323,765
Nitrobenzene	750	250	0	0	0	0	0	1,000
Nitroglycerin	250	13,621	0	0	0	0	10,400	24,271
O-cresol	5	67	31	0	5	0	11,506	11,614
O-dinitrobenzene	50	1,039	0	0	49	0	0	1,138
O-toluidine	424	6	0	0	0	8,411	0	8,841
O-xylene	3,414	1,218	5	0	40	271	69,505	74,453
P-cresol	250	750	0	0	0	0	1,043	2,043
P-dinitrobenzene	50	759	0	0	14	0	0	823
P-phenylenediamine	58	0	0	0	0	0	0	58
P-xylene	347	50	5	0	5	0	5	412
Peracetic acid	1	1	0	0	0	0	0	2
Phenol	21,317	13,179	2,267	0	19,337	1,022,250	135,357	1,213,707
Phosgene	2	725	0	0	0	0	0	727
Phosphoric acid	5,944	16,251	2,078	0	767	216,869	200,596	442,505
Phthalic anhydride	3,989	17,342	27	0	3,405	1,473	364,621	390,857
Polychlorinated biphenyls (PCBs)	0	0	0	0	13,188	0	22,183	35,371
Propionaldehyde	505	2,190	0	0	0	0	0	2,695
Propylene	115,590	41,958	0	0	0	0	0	157,548
Propylene oxide	9,757	115,341	0	0	5	4,255	15	129,373
Propyleneimine	250	313	0	0	0	250	0	813
Saccharin (manufacturing)	6	5	0	0	0	421	243	675
Sec-butyl alcohol	3,306	4,625	380	0	0	929	9,483	18,723
Selenium	5	5	0	0	0	5	0	15
Selenium compounds	505	505	0	0	0	5	1,012	2,027
Silver	1,010	2,690	10	0	0	15	1,755	5,480
Silver compounds	0	0	0	0	0	752	4,447	5,199

[Continued]

★ 422 ★

Toxic Chemical Releases in New Jersey, by Chemical: 1990
[Continued]

Chemical	Fugitive air	Stack air	Water	Injection	Land	Public treatment	Other offsite	Total releases
Styrene	23,296	67,323	260	0	5	696	18,052	109,632
Styrene oxide	260	5	0	0	0	0	0	265
Sulfuric acid	68,686	137,698	1,567	10	28,795	143,785	1,682,212	2,062,753
Tert-butyl alcohol	19,685	779	0	0	0	80,659	1,201	102,324
Tetrachloroethylene	140,805	129,936	113	0	0	63	34,170	305,087
Tetrachlorvinphos	0	0	0	0	0	0	4,300	4,300
Thiourea	5	5	1	0	0	750	945	1,706
Titanium tetrachloride	1,225	250	0	0	0	0	13,361	14,836
Toluene	1,344,792	2,817,062	2,822	5	3,993	471,176	3,121,499	7,761,349
Toluenediisocyanate (mixed isomers)	69	1,033	0	0	0	5	68	1,175
Toluene-2,4-diisocyanate	1,851	829	0	0	0	0	5	2,685
Toluene-2,6-diisocyanate	1	17	0	0	0	0	0	18
Trichloroethylene	456,612	422,326	59	0	0	1,760	84,698	965,455
Trifluralin	750	0	0	0	0	5	0	755
Urethane	250	250	0	0	0	0	2,528	3,028
Vanadium (fume or dust)	250	250	0	0	0	0	0	500
Vinyl acetate	13,894	118,139	13	0	0	52,932	21,777	206,755
Vinyl chloride	25,300	117,400	39	0	0	0	264	143,003
Xylene (mixed isomers)	596,073	1,479,818	1,876	5	154,699	87,768	1,408,825	3,729,064
Zinc (fume or dust)	2,555	6,492	5	0	250	1,019	2,849,018	2,859,339
Zinc compounds	17,679	12,283	4,771	10	131,900	556,086	650,573	1,373,302

Source: U.S. Environmental Protection Agency. "Toxic Chemical Releases, 1990." In *National Economic, Social, and Environmental Data Bank* [CD-ROM]. Prepared by U.S. Department of Commerce, Economics and Statistics Administration. Washington, DC: U.S. Department of Commerce, National Economic, Social, and Environmental Data Bank, Economics and Statistics Administration, Office of Business Analysis, February 1995.

★ 423 ★

Chemicals

Toxic Chemical Releases in New Mexico, by Chemical: 1990

Figures indicate pounds released by chemical and by type of emission per year.

Chemical	Fugitive air	Stack air	Water	Injection	Land	Public treatment	Other offsite	Total releases
1,1,1-trichloroethane	88,866	145,495	0	0	0	5	31,449	265,815
1,2,4-trimethylbenzene	4,817	10,928	0	0	500	0	250	16,495
1,3-butadiene	9	97	0	0	0	0	0	106
2-methoxyethanol	5	250	0	0	0	0	0	255
Acetone	54,192	97,541	0	0	250	15	9,309	161,307
Ammonia	4,800	260	5	5	20	255	515	5,860
Ammonium sulfate (solution)	250	0	0	0	0	0	0	250
Antimony compounds	5	0	0	0	0	0	0	5
Arsenic compounds	5	5	0	0	0	0	250	260
Barium	0	5	0	0	0	520	23,080	23,605
Barium compounds	0	0	0	0	1,558,000	0	0	1,558,000
Benzene	31,841	27,278	0	0	7,196	0	500	66,815
Chlorine	1,005	255	0	5	5	5	0	1,275
Chromium	500	500	0	0	250	10	255	1,515
Chromium compounds	10	255	0	0	20,298	0	4,250	24,813
Cobalt	255	810	5	0	250	250	250	1,820

[Continued]

★ 423 ★

Toxic Chemical Releases in New Mexico, by Chemical: 1990

[Continued]

Chemical	Fugitive air	Stack air	Water	Injection	Land	Public treatment	Other offsite	Total releases
Copper	500	750	0	0	0	5	255	1,510
Copper compounds	7,505	336,005	0	0	20,638,255	0	500	20,982,265
Cumene	250	250	0	0	0	250	500	1,250
Cyclohexane	10,057	15,344	0	0	1,304	0	500	27,205
Ethylbenzene	4,393	19,163	0	0	4,860	0	500	28,916
Ethylene	16,358	550	0	0	0	0	0	16,908
Ethylene glycol	759	510	0	5	255	505	500	2,534
Ethylene oxide	250	250	0	0	0	0	0	500
Formaldehyde	0	87,172	0	0	0	0	250	87,422
Freon 113	217,211	20,970	0	0	0	5	106,160	344,346
Glycol ethers	250	24,079	0	0	0	25,255	500	50,084
Hydrochloric acid	1,457	136,500	0	0	4,551	2,350	750	145,608
Hydrogen fluoride	1,971	7,726	0	0	697	750	250	11,394
Lead	0	30	0	0	0	5,300	49,000	54,330
Lead compounds	255	753	0	0	1,000	0	250	2,258
Manganese	250	250	0	0	0	5	10	515
Manganese compounds	5	250	0	0	1,000	0	250	1,505
Methanol	3,355	2,238	0	0	250	255	1,750	7,848
Methyl ethyl ketone	250	4,560	0	0	250	5	250	5,315
Methyl tert-butyl ether	2,701	3,918	0	0	255	0	5	6,879
Methylenebis(phenylisocyanate)	8	0	0	0	0	0	5	13
Naphthalene	255	10	0	0	1,005	250	750	2,270
Nickel	505	1,330	4	0	250	330	10	2,429
Nitric acid	505	1,286	0	0	0	250	250	2,291
Phenol	5	5	0	0	3,527	0	750	4,287
Phosphoric acid	505	250	0	0	250	250	1,000	2,255
Propylene	13,671	4,407	0	0	0	0	0	18,078
Silver	5	5	0	0	0	250	0	260
Styrene	4,938	0	0	0	0	0	0	4,938
Sulfuric acid	2,812	678,575	0	5	255	20,850	15,250	717,747
Toluene	47,118	165,599	0	0	16,045	255	18,583	247,600
Toluenediisocyanate (mixed isomers)	5	84	0	0	0	0	0	89
Vinyl acetate	5	5	0	0	15	0	5	30
Xylene (mixed isomers)	25,949	94,063	0	0	15,290	250	2,500	138,052
Zinc (fume or dust)	0	0	0	0	0	11,000	0	11,000
Zinc compounds	0	24,020	0	0	7,907,500	0	0	7,931,520

Source: U.S. Environmental Protection Agency. "Toxic Chemical Releases, 1990." In *National Economic, Social, and Environmental Data Bank* [CD-ROM]. Prepared by U.S. Department of Commerce, Economics and Statistics Administration. Washington, DC: U.S. Department of Commerce, National Economic, Social, and Environmental Data Bank, Economics and Statistics Administration, Office of Business Analysis, February 1995.

★ 424 ★

Chemicals

Toxic Chemical Releases in New York, by Chemical: 1990

Figures indicate pounds released by chemical and by type of emission per year.

Chemical	Fugitive air	Stack air	Water	Injection	Land	Public treatment	Other offsite	Total releases
1,1,1-trichloroethane	1,916,791	4,418,318	127	15	504	1,954	577,627	6,915,336
1,1,2-trichloroethane	430	5,600	0	0	0	0	31	6,061
1,2,4-trimethylbenzene	20,242	118,353	0	0	0	5	47,083	185,683
1,2-butylene oxide	165	790	0	0	0	0	5	960
1,2-dibromoethane	250	250	0	0	0	5	69,390	69,895
1,2-dichlorobenzene	265	3,615	180	0	0	240	484,560	488,860
1,2-dichloroethane	6,390	8,633	0	0	0	2,955	158,125	176,103
1,2-dichloropropane	20,000	370,000	0	0	300	0	195	390,495
1,3-butadiene	69,593	2,224	0	0	0	0	0	71,817
1,4-dioxane	3,810	37,991	0	0	0	0	251	42,052
2,4-diaminoanisole sulfate	0	0	0	0	0	250	0	250
2,4-diaminotoluene	0	6	0	0	0	1,000	0	1,006
2,4-dichlorophenol	9	0	0	0	0	0	0	9
2,4-dimethylphenol	89	110	0	0	0	0	165	364
2,4-dinitrophenol	7	250	0	0	0	5	35	297
2-ethoxyethanol	903	11,064	0	0	0	0	4,537	16,504
2-methoxyethanol	27,154	250,121	0	0	0	442,700	415,354	1,135,329
4,4'-isopropylidenediphenol	760	276	14	0	0	1,452	788	3,290
4,4'-methylenebis(2-chloro aniline)	250	250	0	0	0	0	750	1,250
4,4'-methylenedianiline	250	0	0	0	0	0	0	250
Acetaldehyde	3,285	20,000	0	0	0	0	23	23,308
Acetone	3,690,722	3,359,106	31,820	0	1,475	424,646	1,343,564	8,851,333
Acetonitrile	22,978	67,150	0	0	0	33,105	24,668	147,901
Acrylamide	0	0	0	0	0	0	13	13
Acrylic acid	250	250	0	0	0	0	10,660	11,160
Acrylonitrile	750	580	13	0	0	0	0	1,343
Allyl chloride	1,505	250	0	0	0	250	750	2,755
Aluminum (fume or dust)	57,056	54,471	0	0	0	0	1,710,079	1,821,606
Aluminum oxide (fibrous forms)	250	1,726	0	0	0	500	191,668	194,144
Ammonia	517,972	605,401	489,463	5	1,840	1,639,712	81,675	3,336,068
Ammonium nitrate (solution)	5	26,005	5	0	100,306	250	33,990	160,561
Ammonium sulfate (solution)	6,505	255	5	0	0	1,910,110	389,900	2,306,775
Aniline	2,543	16,338	22,941	0	0	300,072	3,820	345,714
Anthracene	440	0	0	0	0	0	0	440
Antimony	250	5	5	0	0	0	0	260
Antimony compounds	266	1,571	15	0	1,000	1,814	114,899	119,565
Arsenic compounds	13	1,925	0	0	0	5	6,442	8,385
Asbestos (friable)	0	431	0	0	0	0	355,699	356,130
Barium	10	25	0	0	0	0	1,927	1,962
Barium compounds	15,177	43,971	9,323	0	52,150	677,369	994,277	1,792,267
Benzal chloride	240	0	0	0	0	0	0	240
Benzene	356,684	14,355	255	0	0	250	915	372,459
Benzoic trichloride	2,590	10	0	0	0	0	90	2,690
Benzoyl chloride	3,032	1,128	0	0	260	225	3	4,648
Benzoyl peroxide	0	1,668	0	0	0	2,755	6,284	10,707
Benzyl chloride	62	0	0	0	0	0	0	62
Biphenyl	87	3	0	0	0	0	0	90
Bis(2-ethylhexyl) adipate	2,193	3	0	0	0	0	500	2,696
Bromomethane	39,000	0	0	0	0	0	0	39,000
Butyl acrylate	254	360	0	0	0	0	0	614
Butyl benzyl phthalate	257	1,500	3	0	27	20,797	19,023	41,607

[Continued]

★ 424 ★

Toxic Chemical Releases in New York, by Chemical: 1990

[Continued]

Chemical	Fugitive air	Stack air	Water	Injection	Land	Public treatment	Other offsite	Total releases
C.I. food red 15	0	2	0	0	0	270	0	272
Cadmium	255	5	0	0	0	5	0	265
Cadmium compounds	4,800	767	69	0	0	755	67,648	74,039
Captan	0	4	0	0	0	0	50	54
Carbon disulfide	52,827	1,084,730	0	0	0	11,769	0	1,149,326
Carbon tetrachloride	6,673	1,878	0	0	0	514	2,354	11,419
Catechol	0	45	5	0	5	250	0	305
Chlorine	18,834	93,831	11,750	10	47,090	15,744	82	187,341
Chlorine dioxide	380	60,134	0	0	0	831	0	61,345
Chloroacetic acid	750	8	0	0	0	0	0	758
Chlorobenzene	270	277	95	0	0	147	6,265	7,054
Chloroform	42,253	26,114	3,040	0	0	187	221,426	293,020
Chloromethane	17,000	3,600	2,100	0	0	0	0	22,700
Chromium	2,044	4,009	50	0	26,239	5,789	125,185	163,316
Chromium compounds	2,708	6,718	1,392	0	255	44,777	490,299	546,149
Cobalt	0	1,709	5	0	0	5	91	1,810
Cobalt compounds	17	41	69	0	0	938	3,963	5,028
Copper	11,483	9,954	2,638	10	1,860	4,710	637,744	668,399
Copper compounds	2,776	26,203	10,014	5	1,306,171	7,729	165,354	1,518,252
Creosote	90	250	0	0	0	5	3,610	3,955
Cresol (mixed isomers)	6,618	2,780	5	0	0	5	82,357	91,765
Cumene	1,271	14,933	31	0	0	0	15,953	32,188
Cumene hydroperoxide	370	6	410	0	0	0	0	786
Cyanide compounds	765	2,933	2,792	0	0	7,037	7,125	20,652
Cyclohexane	78,380	190,380	0	0	270	0	256	269,286
Decabromodiphenyl oxide	5	0	0	0	2,000	3,496	51,255	56,756
Di(2-ethylhexyl) phthalate	1,260	1,370	3	0	0	544	82,496	85,673
Dibenzofuran	270	0	0	0	0	0	0	270
Dibutyl phthalate	1,295	9,255	0	0	9	250	6,861	17,670
Dichloromethane	3,466,602	6,417,452	45	15	9,273	33,796	398,757	10,325,940
Diethanolamine	867	1,609	8,900	0	1,000	21,762	24,001	58,139
Diethyl phthalate	5	5	0	0	0	5	282	297
Dimethyl phthalate	1,336	1,650	3	0	0	28,348	0	31,337
Dimethyl sulfate	750	8	0	0	0	5	33	796
Epichlorohydrin	230	58	26	0	0	0	1	315
Ethylbenzene	15,045	80,245	295	0	10	258	205,416	301,269
Ethylene	26,000	0	0	0	0	0	0	26,000
Ethylene glycol	27,030	67,630	174,331	0	16	270,980	56,745	596,732
Ethylene oxide	5,290	21,190	0	0	0	11,703	0	38,183
Formaldehyde	40,088	161,978	133,187	5	305	62,888	93,337	491,788
Freon 113	1,928,247	478,827	255	0	0	15	259,939	2,667,283
Glycol ethers	520,611	1,303,864	15,050	5	30	269,004	259,472	2,368,036
Hexachloro-1,3-butadiene	25	0	0	0	0	18	20	63
Hexachlorocyclopentadiene	960	42	5	0	0	0	20,150	21,157
Hydrazine	153	8	0	0	0	2	2,176	2,339
Hydrochloric acid	107,201	7,011,618	5,697	10	1,470	290,064	716,272	8,132,332
Hydrogen fluoride	112,748	105,820	255	0	17	1,009	136,967	356,816
Hydroquinone	360	4,648	0	0	0	115,251	2,201	122,460
Isopropyl alcohol (manufacturing)	18,055	145,770	10,800	0	5	1,900	18,107	194,637
Lead	8,741	6,498	1,085	5	738	800	184,689	202,556
Lead compounds	2,188	18,373	5,817	5	3,537	580	1,774,965	1,805,465
M-cresol	41	500	0	0	0	0	25	566

[Continued]

★ 424 ★

Toxic Chemical Releases in New York, by Chemical: 1990
[Continued]

Chemical	Fugitive air	Stack air	Water	Injection	Land	Public treatment	Other offsite	Total releases
M-xylene	1,300	16,000	0	0	0	5	9,577	26,882
Maleic anhydride	940	4,478	0	0	0	250	4,659	10,327
Manganese	11,005	6,288	196	0	65,653	14,937	23,667	121,746
Manganese compounds	3,454	11,592	55,021	0	500	15,475	123,329	209,371
Mercury	1,336	617	3	0	0	20	9,799	11,775
Mercury compounds	0	0	0	0	0	0	14	14
Methanol	2,460,327	5,489,077	242,691	10	10,182	4,342,311	1,954,129	14,498,727
Methyl acrylate	0	210	0	0	0	0	0	210
Methyl ethyl ketone	561,766	1,526,394	58	0	64	50,813	580,260	2,719,355
Methyl iodide	250	250	0	0	0	0	0	500
Methyl isobutyl ketone	1,423,042	555,342	19,255	0	0	221,555	356,901	2,576,095
Methyl methacrylate	833	82,620	0	0	0	0	0	83,453
Methyl tert-butyl ether	250	0	0	0	0	0	0	250
Methylenebis(phenylisocyanate)	1,005	505	0	0	0	0	11,052	12,562
Molybdenum trioxide	500	250	0	0	0	0	0	750
N,N-dimethylaniline	1,064	17,605	13,522	0	0	31,490	19,854	83,535
N-butyl alcohol	421,677	760,850	22	0	680	226,211	170,835	1,580,275
N-dioctyl phthalate	250	0	3	0	1	0	750	1,004
Naphthalene	15,262	7,070	0	0	0	0	580	22,912
Nickel	2,767	10,775	467	5	12,886	2,855	97,202	126,957
Nickel compounds	1,564	3,189	1,792	5	270	7,971	96,178	110,969
Nitric acid	11,682	118,757	2,515	5	40	110,198	361,914	605,111
Nitrobenzene	720	13	0	0	0	750	0	1,483
O-cresol	15,753	3,494	5	0	0	5	11,061	30,318
O-toluidine	2,031	164	0	0	0	9,900	300	12,395
O-xylene	540	11,000	0	0	0	0	0	11,540
P-anisidine	0	5	0	0	0	0	0	5
P-cresol	250	2,063	250	0	0	0	21,546	24,109
P-phenylenediamine	0	0	0	0	0	250	0	250
P-xylene	3,250	387	0	0	8	0	750	4,395
Peracetic acid	0	2,530	3	0	0	0	0	2,533
Phenol	78,151	109,848	2,217	0	500	168,967	780,491	1,140,174
Phosgene	368	498	10	5	20	0	0	901
Phosphoric acid	21,159	7,552	1,015	0	13,185	372,082	62,797	477,790
Phosphorus (yellow or white)	0	0	5	0	0	5	3	13
Phthalic anhydride	506	10,147	0	0	0	250	7,441	18,344
Polychlorinated biphenyls (PCBs)	0	0	0	0	0	0	17,406	17,406
Propylene	4,674	4	0	0	0	0	0	4,678
Propylene oxide	24,750	18,450	0	0	13	803	1,293	45,309
Pyridine	20,439	8,494	0	0	0	4,426	1,009	34,368
Quinoline	76	7	0	0	0	0	0	83
Sec-butyl alcohol	6,794	55,685	1,970	0	51	738	2,650	67,888
Selenium	0	38	0	0	0	5	15,033	15,076
Silver	30	345	0	0	250	970	25	1,620
Silver compounds	10	9,911	87	0	0	1,452	371	11,831
Styrene	66,467	31,714	0	0	0	10	60,894	159,085
Sulfuric acid	40,280	439,203	8,837	5	9,407	484,818	483,856	1,466,406
Tert-butyl alcohol	9,440	12,688	271,115	0	24,000	16,931	27,911	362,085
Tetrachloroethylene	570,049	1,344,368	562	0	0	423	505,342	2,420,744
Thiourea	0	0	0	0	0	0	1,800	1,800
Titanium tetrachloride	28	0	0	0	0	0	0	28
Toluene	2,877,591	5,131,297	2,580	10	627	14,880	1,165,180	9,192,165

[Continued]

★ 424 ★

Toxic Chemical Releases in New York, by Chemical: 1990

[Continued]

Chemical	Fugitive air	Stack air	Water	Injection	Land	Public treatment	Other offsite	Total releases
Toluenediisocyanate (mixed isomers)	918	262	0	0	0	0	4,151	5,331
Toluene-2,4-diisocyanate	250	250	0	0	0	0	250	750
Trichloroethylene	1,222,226	1,483,916	469	0	9,005	503	379,172	3,095,291
Trifluralin	42	0	0	0	0	0	152	194
Vanadium (fume or dust)	20	230	5	0	0	0	0	255
Vinyl acetate	1,250	3,500	0	0	0	250	750	5,750
Vinyl chloride	19,011	52,771	0	0	0	306	858	72,946
Vinylidene chloride	941	87	0	0	0	0	0	1,028
Xylene (mixed isomers)	469,383	2,248,830	920	5	310	1,970	1,913,555	4,634,973
Zinc (fume or dust)	9,054	31,987	5	5	20	1,138	164,972	207,181
Zinc compounds	14,281	58,431	43,746	0	146,962	17,409	1,210,956	1,491,785

Source: U.S. Environmental Protection Agency. "Toxic Chemical Releases, 1990." In National Economic, Social, and Environmental Data Bank [CD-ROM]. Prepared by U.S. Department of Commerce, Economics and Statistics Administration. Washington, DC: U.S. Department of Commerce, National Economic, Social, and Environmental Data Bank, Economics and Statistics Administration, Office of Business Analysis, February 1995.

★ 425 ★

Chemicals

Toxic Chemical Releases in North Carolina, by Chemical: 1990

Figures indicate pounds released by chemical and by type of emission per year.

Chemical	Fugitive air	Stack air	Water	Injection	Land	Public treatment	Other offsite	Total releases
1,1,1-trichloroethane	3,710,481	1,668,543	10	0	0	23,200	216,622	5,618,856
1,2,4-trichlorobenzene	38,050	102,139	1,936	0	15	83,425	9,337	234,902
1,2,4-trimethylbenzene	8,978	2,701	170	0	470	16,951	10,184	39,454
1,2-dichlorobenzene	250	250	0	0	0	20,500	0	21,000
1,2-dichloroethane	225,861	170,043	0	0	0	6	16,910	412,820
1,2-dichloroethylene	68,800	0	0	0	0	0	0	68,800
1,3-butadiene	4,400	1,790	0	0	0	0	10	6,200
1,4-dioxane	72,837	35,078	42,666	0	2	0	3,856	154,439
2,4-d	250	0	0	0	0	0	0	250
2,4-dimethylphenol	750	4,000	0	0	0	0	500	5,250
2,4-dinitrophenol	0	0	1,600	0	7	0	0	1,607
2-ethoxyethanol	0	250	0	0	0	0	750	1,000
2-methoxyethanol	11,622	267	4,755	0	188	43	18,419	35,294
4,4'-methylenedianiline	250	0	0	0	0	0	250	500
Acetaldehyde	689,304	768,669	6,041	0	5	0	463	1,464,482
Acetone	1,969,679	4,631,200	23,005	0	315	142,104	223,414	6,989,717
Acetonitrile	248	15,637	25	0	0	2,226	2,602	20,738
Acrylamide	1,124	459	0	0	0	250	594	2,427
Acrylic acid	7,158	14,614	0	0	0	59	11,631	33,462
Acrylonitrile	1,298	11,668	0	0	0	500	260	13,726
Allyl alcohol	2,906	592	0	0	0	0	0	3,498
Allyl chloride	3,924	20,078	0	0	0	0	0	24,002
Alpha-naphthylamine	250	250	0	0	0	0	0	500
Aluminum (fume or dust)	320	6,688	0	0	0	505	139,817	147,330
Aluminum oxide (fibrous forms)	255	255	250	0	250	0	66,038	67,048
Ammonia	1,294,498	2,244,097	614,107	5	163,380	784,673	3,907	5,104,667

[Continued]

★ 425 ★

Toxic Chemical Releases in North Carolina, by Chemical: 1990

[Continued]

Chemical	Fugitive air	Stack air	Water	Injection	Land	Public treatment	Other offsite	Total releases
Ammonium nitrate (solution)	30,250	580	71,075	5	1,636	0	0	103,546
Ammonium sulfate (solution)	25	5	27,705	0	250	356,200	152,025	536,210
Aniline	7,250	23,255	2	0	250	250	11,500	42,507
Anthracene	265	1,864	0	0	0	0	250	2,379
Antimony	0	4,513	0	0	0	287	1,748	6,548
Antimony compounds	779	563	529	0	2,645	759	59,840	65,115
Arsenic	255	250	250	0	250	0	172,908	173,913
Arsenic compounds	37	315	0	0	1	1	50,773	51,127
Asbestos (friable)	250	882	0	0	12,409	0	246,659	260,200
Barium	255	252	0	0	0	840	4,500	5,847
Barium compounds	11,940	11,499	0	0	4,950	1,900,706	464,477	2,393,572
Benzene	340	275,040	0	0	0	0	0	275,380
Benzyl chloride	255	250	0	0	0	250	0	755
Biphenyl	128,639	59,873	505	5	295	55,794	6,709	251,820
Bis(2-ethylhexyl) adipate	257	277	0	0	0	332	1,300	2,166
Bromomethane	500	795,391	0	0	0	0	0	795,891
Butyl acrylate	2,265	745	0	0	0	250	1,255	4,515
Butyl benzyl phthalate	287	22	0	0	0	10,811	2,781	13,901
Butyraldehyde	1,700	1,100	612	0	0	0	0	3,412
C.I. disperse yellow 3	364	0	26	0	843	0	219	1,452
Cadmium compounds	500	501	0	0	0	1	1,854	2,856
Catechol	5	5	9,560	0	268	0	13,000	22,838
Chlorine	106,369	319,320	71,076	0	10	120,812	5	617,592
Chlorine dioxide	6,265	378,400	5	0	0	0	0	384,670
Chloroacetic acid	250	0	0	0	0	0	1,046	1,296
Chlorobenzene	300	10,600	65	0	0	0	0	10,965
Chloroform	1,129,000	1,105,250	33,440	0	258	75,000	1,101	2,344,049
Chlorophenols	250	250	250	0	0	0	0	750
Chlorothalonil	8	0	0	0	0	420	260	688
Chromium	1,367	846	252	0	627	316	59,856	63,264
Chromium compounds	2,311	39,855	5,705	0	7,436,356	4,867	80,281	7,569,375
Cobalt	250	5,452	2,313	0	3,100	7	1,900	13,022
Cobalt compounds	502	6,282	37,765	0	79	823	64,177	109,628
Copper	3,805	7,112	1,072	0	250	2,113	78,931	93,283
Copper compounds	2,892	19,796	1,273	5	51,030	2,941	120,241	198,178
Creosote	186	10,469	0	0	0	0	257,271	267,926
Cresol (mixed isomers)	42,022	31,010	0	0	0	5	18,235	91,272
Cumene	1,161	328	0	0	0	0	0	1,489
Cyanide compounds	255	255	0	0	0	6	5	521
Cyclohexane	122,122	147,933	0	0	0	250	6,914	277,219
Decabromodiphenyl oxide	44	2,267	10	0	480	20,765	34,763	58,329
Di(2-ethylhexyl) phthalate	2,578	230,407	0	0	0	1,280	5,215	239,480
Dibenzofuran	283	264	0	0	0	0	250	797
Dibutyl phthalate	255	5	30	0	0	1,205	40,642	42,137
Dichlorobenzene (mixed isomers)	9	1,800	1	0	2	0	9,300	11,112
Dichloromethane	2,186,609	5,022,148	20	0	5	23,235	179,383	7,411,400
Diethanolamine	724	7,419	805	5	20	15,666	4,114	28,753
Diethyl phthalate	130	10	0	0	0	1,500	0	1,640
Diethyl sulfate	504	10	5	5	20	5	0	549
Dimethyl phthalate	1,836	2,614	6	0	5	58,815	0	63,276
Dimethyl sulfate	72	1	0	0	0	5	0	78
Epichlorohydrin	3,004	1,293	0	0	0	250	0	4,547

[Continued]

Toxic Chemical Releases in North Carolina, by Chemical: 1990

[Continued]

Chemical	Fugitive air	Stack air	Water	Injection	Land	Public treatment	Other offsite	Total releases
Ethyl acrylate	1,260	513	5	0	0	500	265	2,543
Ethylbenzene	58,034	24,577	0	0	0	250	6,499	89,360
Ethylene	50	38,260	0	0	0	0	0	38,310
Ethylene glycol	440,847	535,015	79,511	0	7,380	157,501	297,467	1,517,721
Ethylene oxide	4,950	26,330	10	0	0	14	0	31,304
Fluometuron	0	0	0	0	0	81,000	0	81,000
Formaldehyde	274,470	939,372	3,464	0	4,691	261,016	2,545	1,485,558
Freon 113	1,081,982	368,259	5	0	0	250	258,969	1,709,465
Glycol ethers	152,364	1,226,447	13,897	0	9,270	233,679	81,279	1,716,936
Hydrochloric acid	72,437	3,288,275	260	0	21	30,695	186,377	3,578,065
Hydrogen fluoride	87,210	102,135	0	0	0	0	250	189,595
Isopropyl alcohol (manufacturing)	18,070	311,944	0	0	0	1,505	10,750	342,269
Lead	1,022	3,200	255	0	0	320	5,232	10,029
Lead compounds	2,859	6,819	0	0	6,016	41	97,956	113,691
M-xylene	4,691	18,764	0	0	0	0	1,250	24,705
Maleic anhydride	300	4	0	0	250	0	100	654
Manganese	1,442	1,048	255	0	1,027	480	95,112	99,364
Manganese compounds	10,773	9,295	26,929	0	819,214	453	284,472	1,151,136
Mercury	1,055	52	4	0	0	2	695	1,808
Methanol	1,724,111	14,023,381	240,647	5	14,571	395,569	184,599	16,582,883
Methyl acrylate	430	256	0	0	0	250	255	1,191
Methyl ethyl ketone	2,509,414	5,485,213	0	0	0	1,515	730,654	8,726,796
Methyl isobutyl ketone	6,087	250,766	0	0	0	5	24,404	281,262
Methyl methacrylate	2,110	1,619	0	0	0	250	1,115	5,094
Methylenebis(phenylisocyanate)	1,345	260	0	5	20	0	421	2,051
Molybdenum trioxide	150	0	0	0	0	150	150	450
N-butyl alcohol	181,143	2,141,350	8,150	5	2,460	39,995	49,462	2,422,565
N-dioctyl phthalate	255	647	0	0	0	250	11,250	12,402
Naphthalene	25,713	7,583	5	5	20	588	1,160	35,074
Nickel	800	1,146	37	5	111	978	107,621	110,698
Nickel compounds	417	312	60	0	85,195	1,627	25,090	112,701
Nitric acid	6,109	8,169	5	0	11,685	27,405	116,615	169,988
Nitrobenzene	35,000	2,800	0	0	5	0	6,850	44,655
O-anisidine	0	1,076	29	0	0	0	0	1,105
O-toluidine	3	3	0	0	0	0	0	6
O-xylene	666,310	52,110	0	0	0	0	29	718,449
P-cresol	40	5	28	0	0	77	11,945	12,095
P-xylene	473,790	2,624,070	2	0	2	0	24	3,097,888
Pentachlorophenol	5	0	0	0	0	0	31,825	31,830
Phenol	267,914	89,559	15,378	0	15	49,970	165,890	588,726
Phosphoric acid	6,511	4,196	15,525	10	24,329,318	99,239	255,207	24,710,006
Phosphorus (yellow or white)	0	5	0	0	0	0	0	5
Phthalic anhydride	256	2,218	0	0	0	5	254	2,733
Picric acid	0	0	2	0	2	0	0	4
Propylene oxide	5	24,929	0	0	0	5	10	24,949
Pyridine	1,700	8,300	0	0	0	100	10	10,110
Sec-butyl alcohol	5	0	0	0	0	5	0	10
Selenium compounds	500	5	0	0	0	0	250	755
Silver compounds	0	5	344	0	5	255	5	614
Styrene	375,978	195,507	15	0	0	885	34,765	607,150
Sulfuric acid	12,813	1,142,438	19,870	15	26,573	193,458	156,488	1,551,655
Tert-butyl alcohol	0	0	0	0	0	0	9	9

[Continued]

★ 425 ★

Toxic Chemical Releases in North Carolina, by Chemical: 1990

[Continued]

Chemical	Fugitive air	Stack air	Water	Injection	Land	Public treatment	Other offsite	Total releases
Tetrachloroethylene	257,876	496,903	1	0	0	99,765	109,048	963,593
Thiourea	0	5	0	0	0	90	0	95
Toluene	3,277,999	11,012,581	20	5	357	73,009	1,565,012	15,928,983
Toluenediisocyanate (mixed isomers)	1,201	2,135	0	0	0	0	250	3,586
Toluene-2,4-diisocyanate	258	799	0	0	0	0	0	1,057
Toluene-2,6-diisocyanate	6	512	0	0	0	0	0	518
Trichloroethylene	308,125	257,503	10	0	0	768	16,922	583,328
Vinyl acetate	1,984	6,893	0	0	0	250	2,000	11,127
Vinyl chloride	0	0	0	0	0	250	0	250
Vinylidene chloride	1,000	6	0	0	0	0	0	1,006
Xylene (mixed isomers)	310,958	1,890,127	5	0	0	216,453	129,476	2,547,019
Zinc (fume or dust)	786	6,359	250	0	250	2,517	75,462	85,624
Zinc compounds	32,880	50,379	277	0	22,758	5,453	784,777	896,524

Source: U.S. Environmental Protection Agency. "Toxic Chemical Releases, 1990." In *National Economic, Social, and Environmental Data Bank* [CD-ROM]. Prepared by U.S. Department of Commerce, Economics and Statistics Administration. Washington, DC: U.S. Department of Commerce, National Economic, Social, and Environmental Data Bank, Economics and Statistics Administration, Office of Business Analysis, February 1995.

★ 426 ★

Chemicals

Toxic Chemical Releases in North Dakota, by Chemical: 1990

Figures indicate pounds released by chemical and by type of emission per year.

Chemical	Fugitive air	Stack air	Water	Injection	Land	Public treatment	Other offsite	Total releases
1,1,1-trichloroethane	69,761	18,064	0	0	0	0	8,364	96,189
1,2,4-trimethylbenzene	19,828	107,623	0	0	0	0	5,846	133,297
1,3-butadiene	385	0	0	0	0	0	0	385
2-methoxyethanol	4	44	0	0	0	0	0	48
Acetone	10,108	16,518	0	0	0	0	0	26,626
Aluminum (fume or dust)	0	5	0	0	0	0	5	10
Ammonia	13,680	102,818	250	0	5	10,500	0	127,253
Arsenic compounds	5	250	0	0	0	0	0	255
Barium compounds	0	250	0	0	250	0	0	500
Benzene	24,136	92,404	0	0	0	0	2,598	119,138
Bromomethane	10,800	0	0	0	0	0	0	10,800
Carbon tetrachloride	3,506	0	0	0	0	0	0	3,506
Chlorine	13,807	0	0	0	0	0	0	13,807
Chromium	0	3,665	84	0	29,343	5	402	33,499
Chromium compounds	5	255	0	0	250	35	0	545
Copper	0	5	0	0	0	250	250	505
Copper compounds	5	250	0	0	0	0	0	255
Cumene	44	666	0	0	0	0	0	710
Cyclohexane	15,153	27,715	0	0	0	0	872	43,740
Diethanolamine	307	0	0	0	0	0	0	307
Ethylbenzene	5,740	26,862	0	0	0	0	2,320	34,922

[Continued]

★ 426 ★

Toxic Chemical Releases in North Dakota, by Chemical: 1990

[Continued]

Chemical	Fugitive air	Stack air	Water	Injection	Land	Public treatment	Other offsite	Total releases
Ethylene	7,579	0	0	0	0	0	0	7,579
Ethylene glycol	1,007	0	0	0	0	1,130	0	2,137
Formaldehyde	10	255	0	0	0	0	0	265
Freon 113	1,609	62,066	0	0	0	0	0	63,675
Hydrochloric acid	500	500	0	0	0	103,760	0	104,760
Hydrogen fluoride	3,978	0	0	0	0	0	0	3,978
Lead	0	5	0	0	0	5	250	260
Lead compounds	53	0	0	0	38,543	0	3,745	42,341
Lindane	0	4	0	0	0	0	0	4
Maneb	0	11	0	0	0	0	0	11
Manganese	250	250	0	0	0	0	250	750
Manganese compounds	0	17,250	0	0	250	0	0	17,500
Methanol	261	24,305	0	0	0	0	0	24,566
Methyl ethyl ketone	2,950	316,844	0	0	0	0	13,399	333,193
Methyl isobutyl ketone	750	14,675	0	0	0	0	6,351	21,776
Naphthalene	962	5,285	0	0	0	0	3,898	10,145
Nickel	0	250	0	0	0	5	250	505
Nitric acid	0	15	0	0	0	15,446	0	15,461
Phosphoric acid	0	20	0	0	32,760	61,787	0	94,567
Propylene	54,704	0	0	0	0	0	0	54,704
Styrene	29,396	26,865	0	0	0	0	1,860	58,121
Sulfuric acid	631	0	0	0	0	29,932	0	30,563
Toluene	91,547	388,898	0	0	0	0	6,261	486,706
Xylene (mixed isomers)	96,760	271,239	0	0	0	0	18,244	386,243

Source: U.S. Environmental Protection Agency. "Toxic Chemical Releases, 1990." In *National Economic, Social, and Environmental Data Bank* [CD-ROM]. Prepared by U.S. Department of Commerce, Economics and Statistics Administration. Washington, DC: U.S. Department of Commerce, National Economic, Social, and Environmental Data Bank, Economics and Statistics Administration, Office of Business Analysis, February 1995.

★ 427 ★

Chemicals

Toxic Chemical Releases in Ohio, by Chemical: 1990

Figures indicate pounds released by chemical and by type of emission per year.

Chemical	Fugitive air	Stack air	Water	Injection	Land	Public treatment	Other offsite	Total releases
1,1,1-trichloroethane	6,029,966	5,829,246	1,446	15	15,936	7,162	1,110,414	12,994,185
1,2,4-trichlorobenzene	32,900	43,900	0	0	0	41,740	5,105	123,645
1,2,4-trimethylbenzene	32,613	90,230	1	0	0	267	19,152	142,263
1,2-dibromoethane	7,300	2	0	0	0	0	3,400	10,702
1,2-dichlorobenzene	83	9	0	0	0	0	1,096	1,188
1,2-dichloroethane	251	645	0	0	0	0	0	896
1,3-butadiene	80,174	179,677	41	5	25	13,371	23,647	296,940
1,4-dichlorobenzene	6,375	40,200	0	0	0	8,136	0	54,711
1,4-dioxane	46,832	3,377	4,406	0	0	27	972	55,614
2,4-d	255	1,810	0	0	0	0	1,043	3,108

[Continued]

★ 427 ★

Toxic Chemical Releases in Ohio, by Chemical: 1990

[Continued]

Chemical	Fugitive air	Stack air	Water	Injection	Land	Public treatment	Other offsite	Total releases
2-ethoxyethanol	7,603	35,295	0	0	0	0	4,041	46,939
2-methoxyethanol	145	2,105	0	0	0	5	782	3,037
2-phenylphenol	45	12	0	0	0	443	0	500
4,4'-diaminodiphenyl ether	5	750	250	0	0	0	5,607	6,612
4,4'-isopropylidenediphenol	37,010	30,012	250	23,000	0	5	155,701	245,978
4,4'-methylenebis(2-chloro aniline)	500	750	0	0	0	0	0	1,250
Acetaldehyde	2,250	219,971	250	0	0	1,032	250	223,753
Acetamide	0	0	5	0	0	0	0	5
Acetone	2,111,374	5,122,925	4,467	630,000	3,914	83,232	1,636,594	9,592,506
Acetonitrile	12,442	81,968	250	3,300,000	0	0	5,200	3,399,860
Acrylamide	343	250	5	0	5	250	590	1,443
Acrylic acid	1,579	2,364	5	4,100,000	5	501	4,532	4,108,986
Acrylonitrile	63,581	144,637	285	1,300,000	0	146,615	57,940	1,713,058
Allyl alcohol	30	2,300	0	0	0	110,000	58,000	170,330
Aluminum (fume or dust)	85,852	161,917	12,031	5	540,287	556	256,455	1,057,103
Aluminum oxide (fibrous forms)	4,102	36,609	0	0	0	755	935,627	977,093
Ammonia	3,747,904	7,436,043	5,206,018	11,657,010	16,640	8,983,578	177,586	37,224,779
Ammonium nitrate (solution)	2,016	5,371	65,200	0	750	10,788	8,768	92,893
Ammonium sulfate (solution)	10	16,626	34,000	0	11,283	1,999,991	2,083	2,063,993
Aniline	18,805	115,050	0	79,000	0	41,250	17,200	271,305
Anthracene	3,977	6,301	500	0	536	1,591	23,099	36,004
Antimony	1,304	11,267	180	0	0	301	8,471	21,523
Antimony compounds	4,825	10,362	30	5	25	1,393	169,646	186,286
Arsenic	255	5	0	0	0	0	1,505	1,765
Arsenic compounds	275	270	5	0	0	0	2,543	3,093
Asbestos (friable)	766	1,498	0	0	0	0	300,407	302,671
Barium	3,289	9,967	262	0	4,655	10,380	227,064	255,617
Barium compounds	29,405	48,070	4,138	5	26,084	84,170	974,230	1,166,102
Benzene	1,322,700	1,048,442	524	35,250	550	72	4,421	2,411,959
Benzoic trichloride	750	5	0	0	0	0	0	755
Benzoyl chloride	495	75	0	0	0	0	0	570
Benzoyl peroxide	5	0	0	0	5	250	54	314
Benzyl chloride	5	250	0	0	0	5	0	260
Beryllium	5	1,105	29	0	6,517	0	114	7,770
Biphenyl	9,616	5,844	501	0	143	6,617	7,186	29,907
Bis(2-ethylhexyl) adipate	17,392	10,756	30	0	0	5,305	22,721	56,204
Butyl acrylate	14,291	12,096	11	0	0	1,421	1,279	29,098
Butyl benzyl phthalate	2,089	10,413	250	0	0	9,003	72,684	94,439
Butyraldehyde	1,500	250	0	0	0	0	0	1,750
Cadmium	515	257	0	5	20	1,584	56,167	58,548
Cadmium compounds	2,771	2,644	38	5	25	1,142	66,750	73,375
Captan	250	16,000	0	5,500	0	0	5	21,755
Carbaryl	250	0	0	0	0	0	0	250
Carbon disulfide	1,009	1,124,251	0	1,100	0	0	250	1,126,610
Carbon tetrachloride	3,169	32,560	5	250	250	40,440	500	77,174
Carbonyl sulfide	0	237,550	0	0	0	0	0	237,550
Catechol	0	0	100	0	0	0	1,300	1,400
Chlorine	79,259	265,179	39,975	0	501	125,793	100,522	611,229
Chlorine dioxide	5	2,500	0	0	0	0	0	2,505
Chloroacetic acid	0	0	0	0	0	0	1,800	1,800
Chlorobenzene	1,476,986	602,811	0	0	0	77,012	614,689	2,771,498
Chloroethane	265,000	200,000	0	0	0	0	0	465,000
Chloroform	102,024	39,185	3,500	0	0	2,943	20,285	167,937
Chloromethane	101,905	371,827	0	0	0	5,278	0	479,010
Chlorophenols	1	50	0	0	0	128	0	179
Chloroprene	0	0	0	0	0	0	1,738	1,738
Chlorothalonil	0	490	0	0	0	0	1,300	1,790
Chromium	100,216	83,643	1,419	5	26,236	10,142	1,123,745	1,345,406
Chromium compounds	21,192	43,959	37,608	5	1,672,054	26,920	3,151,610	4,953,348

[Continued]

★ 427 ★

Toxic Chemical Releases in Ohio, by Chemical: 1990

[Continued]

Chemical	Fugitive air	Stack air	Water	Injection	Land	Public treatment	Other offsite	Total releases
Cobalt	1,762	2,807	35	0	750	237	6,452	12,043
Cobalt compounds	2,284	2,159	248	5	940	1,209	57,240	64,085
Copper	108,028	38,347	3,670	0	5,616	9,948	369,936	535,545
Copper compounds	8,280	12,581	3,027	0	36,271	38,073	456,798	555,030
Creosote	75,948	103,402	5	0	0	0	5,000	184,355
Cresol (mixed isomers)	1,159	9,984	250	0	200	7,405	8,077	27,075
Cumene	18,527	252,607	14	5,400	0	0	99,730	376,278
Cumene hydroperoxide	14,005	5	0	20,000	0	0	180,255	214,265
Cyanide compounds	2,913	57,394	8,638	680,005	270	6,212	26,837	782,269
Cyclohexane	420,071	1,150,379	979	0	0	15	621,169	2,192,613
Decabromodiphenyl oxide	1,000	2,437	0	0	0	5	41,948	45,390
Di(2-ethylhexyl) phthalate	23,689	10,386	3	0	0	900	125,205	160,183
Diaminotoluene (mixed isomers)	570	26	0	0	0	270	710	1,576
Dibenzofuran	5,563	4,490	500	0	529	0	12,954	24,036
Dibutyl phthalate	512	18	8	0	0	521	1,910	2,969
Dichlorobenzene (mixed isomers)	9,590	248	0	0	0	19	33,187	43,044
Dichloromethane	1,064,560	2,158,829	255	0	250	2,622	306,844	3,533,360
Diethanolamine	8,718	33,201	260	0	0	113,919	11,752	167,850
Diethyl phthalate	0	0	0	0	0	49	750	799
Diethyl sulfate	5	5	0	0	0	5	0	15
Dimethyl phthalate	530	6,408	10	0	255	0	2,222	9,425
Dimethyl sulfate	104	37	0	0	0	0	0	141
Epichlorohydrin	214	668	0	0	0	0	0	882
Ethyl acrylate	3,500	9,818	0	0	0	114	4,980	18,412
Ethylbenzene	137,484	879,989	22	1,100	0	3,115	142,824	1,164,534
Ethylene	87,928	39,611	14	0	11,000	0	14	138,567
Ethylene glycol	75,540	500,365	54,125	5	38,545	288,580	469,297	1,426,457
Ethylene oxide	779	32,898	0	0	0	3,316	0	36,993
Ethylene thiourea	0	5	0	0	0	250	2,250	2,505
Formaldehyde	100,176	816,966	38,750	5	99,486	144,915	877,674	2,077,972
Freon 113	1,006,703	396,103	5	0	150	510	126,977	1,530,448
Glycol ethers	758,228	3,759,735	3,699	0	19,950	731,917	1,099,493	6,373,022
Hexachlorocyclopentadiene	750	0	0	0	0	0	0	750
Hexachloroethane	8	4	0	0	0	0	38,536	38,548
Hydrazine	300	0	0	0	0	0	0	300
Hydrochloric acid	167,354	2,792,852	36,385	2,600,020	7,080	862,247	14,135,895	20,601,833
Hydrogen cyanide	2,300	12,000	250	0	0	0	250	14,800
Hydrogen fluoride	126,061	211,461	7,200	5	29	29,153	1,161,582	1,535,491
Hydroquinone	250	95	3,600	5	0	0	2,300	6,250
Isopropyl alcohol (manufacturing)	73,755	127,323	0	0	0	21,750	63,305	286,133
Lead	19,582	44,622	1,602	5	530,747	2,170	1,712,393	2,311,121
Lead compounds	14,676	30,780	10,113	10	670,877	11,904	1,201,512	1,939,872
Maleic anhydride	2,506	2,266	6	0	5	5	8,970	13,758
Manganese	101,122	119,074	3,585	0	496,151	10,019	2,128,291	2,858,242
Manganese compounds	743,924	157,347	174,908	15	14,694,524	226,899	6,111,742	22,109,359
Mercury	1,296	2,250	6	0	2	0	2,772	6,326
Mercury compounds	255	7	1	0	0	0	8,312	8,575
Methanol	1,708,920	5,155,228	8,717	775,015	810	7,226,814	439,943	15,315,447
Methyl acrylate	608	21,959	0	0	0	0	10,140	32,707
Methyl ethyl ketone	3,772,727	4,903,387	151	5	39	8,587	1,635,239	10,320,135
Methyl isobutyl ketone	385,438	1,226,369	115	0	1	7,494	530,324	2,149,741
Methyl methacrylate	53,866	62,790	5	0	0	2,441	3,339	122,441
Methyl tert-butyl ether	505	6,692	0	0	0	5	0	7,202
Methylenebis(phenylisocyanate)	46,892	11,858	0	0	255	30	45,194	104,229
Molybdenum trioxide	877	2,312	0	5	0	323	11,259	14,776
N,N-dimethylaniline	250	5	0	0	0	29,833	0	30,088
N-butyl alcohol	460,240	2,550,489	1,905	0	10	131,203	258,033	3,401,880
N-dioctyl phthalate	2,510	4,760	505	0	0	483	9,563	17,821
Naphthalene	58,428	82,083	764	0	3,089	5,743	123,817	273,924

[Continued]

★ 427 ★

Toxic Chemical Releases in Ohio, by Chemical: 1990

[Continued]

Chemical	Fugitive air	Stack air	Water	Injection	Land	Public treatment	Other offsite	Total releases
Nickel	126,090	91,977	1,304	5	19,563	6,326	588,148	833,413
Nickel compounds	7,291	5,571	5,152	0	46,460	30,389	653,124	747,987
Nitric acid	41,543	347,746	28,533	5	29	950,975	4,868,266	6,237,097
O-cresol	828	9	0	0	0	250	343	1,430
O-toluidine	250	0	0	0	0	0	250	500
O-xylene	0	0	0	0	0	0	11,325	11,325
P-anisidine	5	5	0	0	0	5	0	15
P-cresidine	165	70	0	0	0	18,750	0	18,985
P-cresol	0	0	0	0	0	0	185	185
P-phenylenediamine	0	0	0	0	0	60	0	60
Peracetic acid	0	0	0	0	0	1,250	0	1,250
Phenol	338,009	669,277	15,171	0	23,638	581,326	704,168	2,331,589
Phosgene	1	15	0	0	0	0	0	16
Phosphoric acid	33,646	94,879	18,515	5	41,390	392,456	729,152	1,310,043
Phosphorus (yellow or white)	270	15	5	0	0	0	250	540
Phthalic anhydride	6,071	5,591	0	0	0	10	20,613	32,285
Polychlorinated biphenyls (PCBs)	0	0	0	0	0	0	22,808	22,808
Propylene	144,324	165,200	14	0	0	0	12	309,550
Propylene oxide	373	9,086	0	0	0	0	0	9,459
Pyridine	3,348	6,299	5	210,000	0	0	80,695	300,347
Quinoline	1,549	2,000	5	0	100	0	3,800	7,454
Quintozene	0	0	0	0	0	0	832	832
Saccharin (manufacturing)	62	3	0	0	0	10	1,100	1,175
Sec-butyl alcohol	6,110	69,957	250	0	0	0	6,142	82,459
Selenium compounds	500	20	0	0	0	58	2,590	3,168
Silver	255	505	0	0	0	5	15	780
Styrene	1,289,995	908,472	321	10	23,495	39,018	1,041,242	3,302,553
Sulfuric acid	148,678	1,376,041	59,406	20	30,605	820,032	5,171,740	7,606,522
Tert-butyl alcohol	635	380	0	0	0	0	0	1,015
Tetrachloroethylene	325,418	1,748,967	250	0	0	1,280	199,524	2,275,439
Thiourea	5	5	0	0	0	750	0	760
Thorium dioxide	0	0	0	0	0	0	128	128
Titanium tetrachloride	890	413	0	0	0	0	0	1,303
Toluene	3,671,067	8,274,040	1,473	3,305	2,525	68,551	1,628,825	13,649,786
Toluenediisocyanate (mixed isomers)	1,029	546	0	0	0	0	750	2,325
Toluene-2,4-diisocyanate	250	20,302	0	0	0	0	47	20,599
Toluene-2,6-diisocyanate	250	501	0	0	0	0	12	763
Trichloroethylene	733,336	394,473	290	5	20	521	150,866	1,279,511
Trifluralin	755	750	0	0	0	0	0	1,505
Vanadium (fume or dust)	510	9,788	250	0	25,807	0	0	36,355
Vinyl acetate	25,668	150,621	2,046	0	11,000	8,230	5,938	203,503
Vinyl chloride	38,895	306	250	0	0	0	5,551	45,002
Vinylidene chloride	750	250	0	0	0	54	5	1,059
Xylene (mixed isomers)	1,994,134	10,857,640	858	0	765	40,837	2,195,856	15,090,090
Zinc (fume or dust)	35,141	108,172	1,227	5	4,112	3,557	2,363,396	2,515,610
Zinc compounds	92,828	189,353	56,755	20	4,039,257	74,084	11,773,920	16,226,217

Source: U.S. Environmental Protection Agency. "Toxic Chemical Releases, 1990." In *National Economic, Social, and Environmental Data Bank* [CD-ROM]. Prepared by U.S. Department of Commerce, Economics and Statistics Administration. Washington, DC: U.S. Department of Commerce, National Economic, Social, and Environmental Data Bank, Economics and Statistics Administration, Office of Business Analysis, February 1995.

★ 428 ★
Chemicals

Toxic Chemical Releases in Oklahoma, by Chemical: 1990

Figures indicate pounds released by chemical and by type of emission per year.

Chemical	Fugitive air	Stack air	Water	Injection	Land	Public treatment	Other offsite	Total releases
1,1,1-trichloroethane	629,254	316,883	35	0	0	510	117,690	1,064,372
1,1,2-trichloroethane	6,000	262,000	5	5	5	5	4,891	272,911
1,2,4-trichlorobenzene	0	0	0	0	0	0	29,300	29,300
1,2,4-trimethylbenzene	63,747	51,240	50	0	890	0	0	115,927
1,3-butadiene	3,446	457	0	0	0	0	0	3,903
1,4-dichlorobenzene	156	102	0	0	18	26	0	302
1,4-dioxane	5	0	0	0	0	0	5	10
2-ethoxyethanol	0	27,828	0	0	0	0	0	27,828
2-methoxyethanol	3,000	0	0	0	0	0	0	3,000
4,4'-isopropylidenediphenol	36	55	0	0	0	0	0	91
4,4'-methylenedianiline	0	729	0	0	0	0	0	729
Acetone	395,311	13,022	0	0	11	1,831	47,544	457,719
Aluminum (fume or dust)	4,137	260,005	0	5	160,270	5	203,181	627,603
Aluminum oxide (fibrous forms)	1,255	255	0	5	270	5	87,060	88,850
Ammonia	783,521	9,705,526	120,215	825,300	1,234	1,600	53,050	11,490,446
Ammonium nitrate (solution)	755	579,000	345,000	3,165,000	1,020	0	554,520	4,645,295
Anthracene	5	5	0	0	0	0	0	10
Antimony	0	0	0	0	5	0	0	5
Antimony compounds	0	3	0	15	0	0	5	23
Arsenic	0	0	250	0	5	0	0	255
Arsenic compounds	1	5	0	11	0	0	0	17
Asbestos (friable)	5	0	0	0	0	0	16,850	16,855
Barium	0	0	0	0	5	0	78,334	78,339
Barium compounds	250	0	5	0	255	0	500	1,010
Benzene	47,698	35,460	50	0	61	0	2	83,271
Butyl benzyl phthalate	0	0	0	0	0	250	250	500
Cadmium	0	0	0	0	5	0	0	5
Cadmium compounds	9	6,468	0	1,560	250	0	250	8,537
Carbon disulfide	0	588,965	0	0	0	0	0	588,965
Carbon tetrachloride	2,115	0	0	0	0	0	0	2,115
Carbonyl sulfide	0	120,027	0	0	0	0	0	120,027
Catechol	5	5	250	0	250	0	0	510
Chlorine	21,012	16,195	5	0	0	1,229	35,000	73,441
Chloroform	15,000	150,000	580	0	260	0	0	165,840
Chromium	3,644	535	1,375	5	9,070	263	79,637	94,529
Chromium compounds	324	411	310	0	4,150	95	563,811	569,101
Cobalt	505	0	0	0	250	0	0	755
Cobalt compounds	18	3,155	0	32	0	5	1,785	4,995
Copper	9,152	1,121	5	10	24,840	565	234,283	269,976
Copper compounds	631	723	255	84	750	331	56,449	59,223
Cresol (mixed isomers)	630	41	66	0	0	0	0	737
Cumene	23,000	741	35	0	720	0	0	24,496
Cyanide compounds	144	14	0	0	0	250	250	658
Cyclohexane	175,980	45,598	43	0	16	4	0	221,641
Di(2-ethylhexyl) phthalate	255	8,933	0	0	0	0	4,600	13,788
Dibenzofuran	5	5	0	0	0	0	0	10
Dibutyl phthalate	0	970	0	0	0	0	2,507	3,477
Dichloromethane	364,732	1,164,715	0	0	7	8	250	1,529,712
Diethanolamine	10,657	751	0	0	4,500	0	9,100	25,008
Diethyl sulfate	5	5	0	0	0	0	0	10
Dimethyl sulfate	5	5	0	0	0	0	0	10

[Continued]

★ 428 ★

Toxic Chemical Releases in Oklahoma, by Chemical: 1990
[Continued]

Chemical	Fugitive air	Stack air	Water	Injection	Land	Public treatment	Other offsite	Total releases
Ethylbenzene	9,807	38,853	50	0	220	6	16	48,952
Ethylene	68,995	160,133	0	0	0	0	0	229,128
Ethylene glycol	22,807	13,480	64,055	753	5	18,500	83,578	203,178
Ethylene oxide	2,200	7,700	0	0	0	0	0	9,900
Formaldehyde	4,701	1,864	250	0	250	0	7,060	14,125
Freon 113	200,480	221,758	0	0	0	0	2,449	424,687
Glycol ethers	56,568	333,254	0	0	0	9,711	9,692	409,225
Hydrochloric acid	5,063	287,067	5	0	8,352	15,345	2,216,404	2,532,236
Hydrogen fluoride	35,836	17,252	0	0	0	0	38,000	91,088
Isopropyl alcohol (manufacturing)	2,200	16,502	0	0	0	0	0	18,702
Lead	307	599	253	0	505	293	32,559	34,516
Lead compounds	824	8,064	14	298	10,950	270	11,096	31,516
M-cresol	250	5	0	0	0	5	1,027	1,287
Maleic anhydride	0	500	0	0	0	0	0	500
Manganese	3,025	1,005	15	5	770	290	27,761	32,871
Manganese compounds	2,612	1,155	5	1,758	14,310	5	1,815	21,660
Methanol	134,415	3,331,564	3,310	5	6,705	10	54,081	3,530,090
Methyl ethyl ketone	221,073	883,957	430	5	5	5	222,190	1,327,665
Methyl isobutyl ketone	20,431	159,374	0	0	0	5	8,501	188,311
Methyl methacrylate	5	0	0	0	0	0	0	5
Methyl tert-butyl ether	7,029	31,000	35	0	0	0	0	38,064
Methylenebis(phenylisocyanate)	301	1,995	15	5	20	5	49,978	52,319
Molybdenum trioxide	69	1	0	0	0	0	0	70
N-butyl alcohol	17,890	269,221	0	0	0	567	1,386	289,064
Naphthalene	20,114	1,815	63	0	3,574	0	48	25,614
Nickel	3,277	560	0	5	1,270	512	76,756	82,380
Nickel compounds	602	655	250	0	750	350	3,285	5,892
Nitric acid	2,755	210,488	0	0	2,938	16,050	663,650	895,881
Pentachlorophenol	1	0	0	0	40	0	0	41
Phenol	3,955	11,420	814	0	5	0	62,090	78,284
Phosphoric acid	1,250	1,011	100	0	755	24,010	66,147	93,273
Phthalic anhydride	250	1,335	0	0	0	5	250	1,840
Polychlorinated biphenyls (PCBs)	0	0	0	0	0	0	11,600	11,600
Propylene	138,088	64,633	0	0	0	0	0	202,721
Propylene oxide	1,000	2,920	0	0	0	0	0	3,920
Quinoline	5	5	0	0	0	0	0	10
Selenium	0	0	0	0	250	0	0	250
Selenium compounds	5	5	5	0	0	5	0	20
Silver compounds	0	16	0	15	0	0	0	31
Sodium hydroxide (solution)	250	250	0	5	20	5	255	785
Styrene	289,468	290,487	0	0	0	0	5,753	585,708
Sulfuric acid	23,862	42,732	5	0	53,253	47,621	6,136,452	6,303,925
Tert-butyl alcohol	500	0	0	0	0	0	0	500
Tetrachloroethylene	569,632	218,050	0	0	0	5	8,002	795,689
Toluene	1,272,302	835,510	55	1,005	521	29	144,507	2,253,929
Trichloroethylene	147,223	30,000	0	0	0	0	23,276	200,499
Vanadium (fume or dust)	0	5	0	0	0	0	0	5
Vinyl chloride	1,400	64,300	0	0	0	12	0	65,712
Xylene (mixed isomers)	163,956	972,717	65	5	2,256	116	33,017	1,172,132

[Continued]

★ 428 ★

Toxic Chemical Releases in Oklahoma, by Chemical: 1990

[Continued]

Chemical	Fugitive air	Stack air	Water	Injection	Land	Public treatment	Other offsite	Total releases
Zinc (fume or dust)	8,072	4,158	0	0	250	399	1,339,326	1,352,205
Zinc compounds	6,579	19,351	950	25,811	5,907	762	522,180	581,540

Source: U.S. Environmental Protection Agency. "Toxic Chemical Releases, 1990." In *National Economic, Social, and Environmental Data Bank* [CD-ROM]. Prepared by U.S. Department of Commerce, Economics and Statistics Administration. Washington, DC: U.S. Department of Commerce, National Economic, Social, and Environmental Data Bank, Economics and Statistics Administration, Office of Business Analysis, February 1995.

★ 429 ★

Chemicals

Toxic Chemical Releases in Oregon, by Chemical: 1990

Figures indicate pounds released by chemical and by type of emission per year.

Chemical	Fugitive air	Stack air	Water	Injection	Land	Public treatment	Other offsite	Total releases
1,1,1-trichloroethane	331,362	355,323	250	0	0	9	122,812	809,756
1,2,4-trimethylbenzene	16,971	2,178	0	0	0	5	1,810	20,964
2,4-d	250	0	0	0	0	0	260	510
2-ethoxyethanol	1,600	9,342	0	0	0	0	750	11,692
Acetone	564,179	1,876,297	23,016	0	429	103,465	155,480	2,722,866
Acrylic acid	5	5	0	0	0	0	250	260
Acrylonitrile	250	0	0	0	0	0	0	250
Aluminum (fume or dust)	750	0	0	0	0	0	0	750
Aluminum oxide (fibrous forms)	0	250	0	0	0	0	77,000	77,250
Ammonia	273,353	784,225	415,256	0	458,750	375,425	388,520	2,695,529
Ammonium nitrate (solution)	1,505	8,900	6,800	0	0	0	0	17,205
Ammonium sulfate (solution)	0	0	0	0	250	250	0	500
Anthracene	4	23	5	0	0	0	2	34
Antimony	6	7	0	0	0	5	10	28
Antimony compounds	250	0	0	0	0	0	4,000	4,250
Arsenic	0	0	292	0	250	0	1,040	1,582
Arsenic compounds	10	10	24	0	5	0	841	890
Asbestos (friable)	0	0	0	0	0	0	44	44
Barium	10	255	0	0	0	5	10	280
Barium compounds	296	269	750	0	0	5	92,255	93,575
Benzene	1,129	162	0	0	0	226	0	1,517
Butyl acrylate	500	500	0	0	0	0	0	1,000
Butyl benzyl phthalate	5	332	0	0	0	12	4,160	4,509
Cadmium compounds	250	0	5	0	0	0	0	255
Carbaryl	5	0	0	0	0	0	5	10
Catechol	10	5	6,407	0	9,039	35,305	154,191	204,957
Chlorine	10,230	550,253	2,490	0	5	273	255	563,506
Chlorine dioxide	10	229,168	0	0	0	0	0	229,178
Chloroform	147,983	458,143	13,740	0	2,700	102,253	14,500	739,319
Chloromethane	67,200	33,600	0	0	0	0	0	100,800
Chlorophenols	250	0	0	0	0	0	250	500
Chromium	2,396	3,027	5	0	260	29,195	32,331	67,214
Chromium compounds	361	2,933	8,663	5	2,425	2,189	38,983	55,559
Cobalt compounds	21	532	0	0	0	29	9,418	10,000
Copper	2,121	273	346	0	250	846	21,557	25,393

[Continued]

★ 429 ★

Toxic Chemical Releases in Oregon, by Chemical: 1990

[Continued]

Chemical	Fugitive air	Stack air	Water	Injection	Land	Public treatment	Other offsite	Total releases
Copper compounds	270	286	283	0	5	1,783	50,155	52,782
Creosote	5,198	98,831	3	0	1,700	0	1,575	107,307
Cumene	56	1	0	0	0	0	0	57
Cyanide compounds	250	0	229	0	2,500	261	160,526	163,766
Cyclohexane	1,318	279	0	0	0	226	0	1,823
Decabromodiphenyl oxide	250	0	0	0	0	0	6,400	6,650
Di(2-ethylhexyl) phthalate	240	4,600	27	0	0	0	110	4,977
Dibutyl phthalate	0	0	0	0	0	0	250	250
Dichloromethane	42,666	503,651	0	0	0	5	12,323	558,645
Epichlorohydrin	1,357	853	0	0	0	298	0	2,508
Ethyl acrylate	5	5	0	0	0	0	1,600	1,610
Ethylbenzene	1,421	916	0	0	0	255	1,435	4,027
Ethylene glycol	1,007	380	12,255	0	84,000	35,143	4,022	136,807
Formaldehyde	223,276	560,427	9,405	0	5,000	23,237	45,728	867,073
Freon 113	197,657	500,915	0	0	0	1,654	15,751	715,977
Glycol ethers	52,330	155,427	22,000	0	0	176,223	73,705	479,685
Hydrochloric acid	11,812	356,752	945	0	5	165,248	14,010	548,772
Hydrogen fluoride	57,789	156,970	3,000	0	250	2,517	500	221,026
Isopropyl alcohol (manufacturing)	0	25,335	0	0	0	0	0	25,335
Lead	4,152	255	0	0	0	250	1,000	5,657
Lead compounds	1,807	1,582	600	0	0	255	23,500	27,744
Maleic anhydride	10	10	0	0	0	0	750	770
Manganese	5,975	761	5	0	1,950	10	2,283	10,984
Manganese compounds	18	518	5	5	20	273	47,249	48,088
Methanol	638,650	2,892,016	3,288	0	657,661	6,422,246	87,083	10,700,944
Methyl acrylate	250	250	0	0	0	0	0	500
Methyl ethyl ketone	192,884	944,347	0	0	0	170	161,435	1,298,836
Methyl isobutyl ketone	198,950	154,830	6,700	0	0	5	3,120	363,605
Methyl methacrylate	900	2,098	0	0	0	0	0	2,998
Methylenebis(phenylisocyanate)	1,268	264	15	5	20	0	1	1,573
Molybdenum trioxide	5	250	5	0	0	5	250	515
N-butyl alcohol	6,746	70,276	5	0	0	19,800	8,080	104,907
Naphthalene	0	35,391	15	5	20	0	0	35,431
Nickel	1,270	31,704	25	0	2,438,850	260	2,450	2,474,559
Nickel compounds	647	970	1,005	0	0	1,562	30,264	34,448
Nitric acid	10,790	11,874	5	0	34,200	286	17,455	74,610
Pentachlorophenol	264	279	566	0	250	0	2,655	4,014
Phenol	43,954	32,714	280	0	3,827	510	13,603	94,888
Phosphoric acid	260	2,932	10	0	5	15,738	105,000	123,945
Phthalic anhydride	5	5	0	0	0	0	8,600	8,610
Polychlorinated biphenyls (PCBs)	0	0	0	0	0	0	22,600	22,600
Propylene	250	0	0	0	0	0	0	250
Styrene	215,818	227,513	5	0	0	5	750	444,091
Sulfuric acid	60,236	141,074	10	0	7,016	28,687	123,050	360,073
Tetrachloroethylene	250	37,950	0	0	0	0	7,680	45,880
Thorium dioxide	0	250	0	0	0	0	0	250
Titanium tetrachloride	250	250	0	0	0	0	0	500
Toluene	862,890	1,289,670	0	0	0	1,070	177,921	2,331,551
Toluenediisocyanate (mixed isomers)	0	118	0	0	0	0	0	118
Toluene-2,4-diisocyanate	10	255	0	0	0	0	250	515
Trichloroethylene	331,141	418,616	0	0	0	12	57,820	807,589
Vinyl acetate	1,000	1,500	0	0	0	0	0	2,500

[Continued]

★ 429 ★

Toxic Chemical Releases in Oregon, by Chemical: 1990

[Continued]

Chemical	Fugitive air	Stack air	Water	Injection	Land	Public treatment	Other offsite	Total releases
Xylene (mixed isomers)	185,800	543,377	15	5	20	339	24,588	754,144
Zinc (fume or dust)	43,994	2,002	54	0	250	5	1,045	47,350
Zinc compounds	8,698	51,005	22,750	0	6,383	750	32,054	121,640

Source: U.S. Environmental Protection Agency. "Toxic Chemical Releases, 1990." In *National Economic, Social, and Environmental Data Bank* [CD-ROM]. Prepared by U.S. Department of Commerce, Economics and Statistics Administration. Washington, DC: U.S. Department of Commerce, National Economic, Social, and Environmental Data Bank, Economics and Statistics Administration, Office of Business Analysis, February 1995.

★ 430 ★

Chemicals

Toxic Chemical Releases in Pennsylvania, by Chemical: 1990

Figures indicate pounds released by chemical and by type of emission per year.

Chemical	Fugitive air	Stack air	Water	Injection	Land	Public treatment	Other offsite	Total releases
1,1,1-trichloroethane	4,903,896	2,754,745	282	0	1,610	3,381	598,685	8,262,599
1,1,2,2-tetrachloroethane	250	250	250	0	250	0	3,600	4,600
1,2,4-trichlorobenzene	0	250	0	0	0	44,800	0	45,050
1,2,4-trimethylbenzene	32,538	19,809	750	0	1,783	22,000	29,156	106,036
1,2-dichlorobenzene	9,800	36,900	1	0	0	15	112,930	159,646
1,2-dichloroethane	20,251	47,895	370	0	0	16,388	76,335	161,239
1,3-butadiene	135	69,000	0	0	1,595	0	17	70,747
1,4-dioxane	23,458	0	0	0	0	0	374	23,832
2,4-dimethylphenol	5	91	0	0	0	0	106	202
2,4-dinitrophenol	16,977	7,235	14	0	0	0	0	24,226
2-ethoxyethanol	250	10,210	0	0	0	0	780	11,240
2-methoxyethanol	656,951	301,301	0	0	0	73,000	1,656	1,032,908
3,3'-dimethoxybenzidine	0	0	4	0	0	0	0	4
4,4'-isopropylidenediphenol	261	1,095	0	0	0	0	14,926	16,282
4-nitrophenol	8	0	0	0	0	24	0	32
Acetaldehyde	0	167	0	0	14	53,062	5	53,248
Acetone	1,546,851	1,631,718	6,041	0	2,500	1,959,671	943,161	6,089,942
Acetonitrile	3,400	9,950	15	0	0	1,300	199,500	214,165
Acrylamide	545	279	250	5	20	0	6,607	7,706
Acrylic acid	6,711	3,348	250	0	0	10	8,261	18,580
Acrylonitrile	901	3,290	250	0	5	32,340	765	37,551
Alpha-naphthylamine	0	0	0	0	0	0	534	534
Aluminum (fume or dust)	14,307	62,162	750	0	500	506	7,531	85,756
Aluminum oxide (fibrous forms)	0	0	0	0	0	0	737,100	737,100
Ammonia	1,176,474	2,983,952	770,640	0	2,444	372,202	164,336	5,470,048
Ammonium nitrate (solution)	329,956	316,621	131	0	53,200	846,476	64,682	1,611,066
Ammonium sulfate (solution)	447	102	142,215	0	0	706,516	409,168	1,258,448
Aniline	340	249	181	0	0	5	0	775
Anthracene	1,796	112	5	0	0	0	25,382	27,295
Antimony	26	76	5	5	5	34	92	243
Antimony compounds	1,510	2,477	29	5	5	3,305	237,960	245,291
Arsenic	0	10	5	0	0	5	6,607	6,627
Arsenic compounds	535	1,790	108	0	0	10	16,576	19,019
Asbestos (friable)	3,000	2,120	0	0	0	4,150	352,050	361,320

[Continued]

★ 430 ★

Toxic Chemical Releases in Pennsylvania, by Chemical: 1990
[Continued]

Chemical	Fugitive air	Stack air	Water	Injection	Land	Public treatment	Other offsite	Total releases
Barium	268	7	250	0	0	250	26,755	27,530
Barium compounds	3,088	26,946	2,614	0	214,006	37,362	1,455,849	1,739,865
Benzene	1,663,583	958,920	616	0	94	47,830	531,973	3,203,016
Benzoyl chloride	250	0	0	0	0	0	0	250
Benzoyl peroxide	255	5	0	0	0	83	3,512	3,855
Benzyl chloride	434	37	0	0	0	8,845	0	9,316
Beryllium	4	1	8	0	0	0	7	20
Beryllium compounds	1	210	23	0	40,000	0	651	40,885
Biphenyl	25,595	15,772	2,502	0	0	46,638	15,678	106,185
Bis(2-ethylhexyl) adipate	1,975	267	5	0	0	1,300	615	4,162
Bis(chloromethyl) ether	2	0	0	0	0	0	0	2
Bromomethane	73,208	0	0	0	0	0	0	73,208
Butyl acrylate	17,695	6,378	26,465	0	0	16,792	37,298	104,628
Butyl benzyl phthalate	10,200	86,900	5	0	0	11,810	52,110	161,025
Butyraldehyde	120	107	0	0	0	0	23	250
Cadmium	539	950	572	0	6,900	36	6,745	15,742
Cadmium compounds	2,043	4,017	298	0	0	416	21,066	27,840
Carbaryl	0	5	0	0	0	0	0	5
Carbon disulfide	23,100	247,700	5	0	0	0	755	271,560
Carbon tetrachloride	10	41,000	0	0	0	250	2	41,262
Catechol	0	0	110	0	0	33,300	90	33,500
Chlorine	19,320	213,512	2,871	0	4	3,385	1,750	240,842
Chlorine dioxide	17	70,000	0	0	0	0	0	70,017
Chloroacetic acid	21	0	0	0	0	37	0	58
Chlorobenzene	1,232	481	250	0	0	1,083	160,660	163,706
Chloroethane	5,000	85,200	0	0	0	0	1,630	91,830
Chloroform	312,757	626,042	10,061	0	17	116,550	1,120	1,066,547
Chloromethane	3,199	79,550	84	0	0	10,886	9,400	103,119
Chloromethyl methyl ether	33	0	0	0	0	0	0	33
Chlorophenols	1,184	128	10	0	0	0	0	1,322
Chlorothalonil	0	4	0	0	0	0	79	83
Chromium	14,506	13,816	8,973	0	1,314,479	3,690	748,530	2,103,994
Chromium compounds	22,847	33,217	15,902	0	213,077	8,300	1,519,039	1,812,382
Cobalt	1,648	373	4,631	0	1,496	255	4,104	12,507
Cobalt compounds	202	1,138	1,448	0	1,853	514	21,162	26,317
Copper	28,513	106,392	8,622	5	11,541	7,050	3,306,109	3,468,232
Copper compounds	5,511	16,104	4,427	0	293,035	10,778	212,212	542,067
Creosote	46,229	10,633	0	0	0	677	99,974	157,513
Cresol (mixed isomers)	83,539	8,391	5	0	0	2,879	6,696	101,510
Cumene	204,712	939,153	5	0	7	175,250	65,174	1,384,301
Cumene hydroperoxide	250	750	0	0	0	0	3,300	4,300
Cyanide compounds	17,828	123,176	9,752	0	0	6,897	61,487	219,140
Cyclohexane	27,859	427,029	2	0	0	15,000	500	470,390
Decabromodiphenyl oxide	515	1,347	5	0	0	215	104,656	106,738
Di(2-ethylhexyl) phthalate	5,850	73,754	318	5	10	3,435	94,164	177,536
Dibenzofuran	451	5	0	0	0	0	22,055	22,511
Dibutyl phthalate	835	750	0	0	0	1,000	1,994	4,579
Dichloromethane	2,104,591	1,564,876	653	10	40	1,890	1,409,303	5,081,363
Diethanolamine	2,692	777	505	0	95,275	3,781	24,697	127,727
Diethyl phthalate	518	3,600	0	0	0	270	1,980	6,368
Diethyl sulfate	1,357	2	0	0	0	500	0	1,859
Dimethyl phthalate	5	500	0	0	2	610	22,050	23,167

[Continued]

★ 430 ★

Toxic Chemical Releases in Pennsylvania, by Chemical: 1990
[Continued]

Chemical	Fugitive air	Stack air	Water	Injection	Land	Public treatment	Other offsite	Total releases
Dimethyl sulfate	1,166	1	0	0	0	0	0	1,167
Epichlorohydrin	5	13	0	0	0	0	7,421	7,439
Ethyl acrylate	21,163	9,538	250	0	0	0	36,219	67,170
Ethylbenzene	40,051	107,766	304	0	83	8,007	173,449	329,660
Ethylene	245,048	19,596	0	0	0	0	0	264,644
Ethylene glycol	64,502	173,887	95,850	0	1,528	74,244	146,218	556,229
Ethylene oxide	130,740	41,134	0	0	0	38,103	0	209,977
Formaldehyde	89,949	145,397	1,290	5	1,420	2,483,702	25,779	2,747,542
Freon 113	1,509,576	554,412	5	0	0	10	134,934	2,198,937
Glycol ethers	352,049	946,658	866	0	4,655	162,609	922,840	2,389,677
Hydrazine	0	0	0	0	0	5	750	755
Hydrochloric acid	395,058	3,703,115	2,055	5	1,499	63,190	1,680,248	5,845,170
Hydrogen cyanide	3	63	0	0	0	3	0	69
Hydrogen fluoride	57,567	300,682	595	5	1,109	280	1,096,741	1,456,979
Hydroquinone	1	1	0	0	0	0	62	64
Isobutyraldehyde	0	8	0	0	0	74	0	82
Isopropyl alcohol (manufacturing)	49,996	12,007	0	0	0	0	37,588	99,591
Lead	321,885	25,708	4,494	5	2,005	770	1,533,020	1,887,887
Lead compounds	52,866	90,076	8,235	5	320,168	2,474	1,909,873	2,383,697
M-cresol	3,328	788	0	0	0	0	12,690	16,806
M-xylene	2,707	4,886	0	0	0	0	66,891	74,484
Maleic anhydride	9,639	5,819	0	0	0	74	39,069	54,601
Manganese	101,064	17,173	20,315	0	1,279,017	1,762	1,263,539	2,682,870
Manganese compounds	55,187	39,002	30,515	0	8,701,703	774	3,368,725	12,195,906
Mercury	5	0	0	0	5	5	5	20
Mercury compounds	255	255	0	0	0	5	1,175	1,690
Methanol	1,078,512	1,755,721	5,118	0	215,795	8,299,908	3,104,167	14,459,221
Methyl acrylate	832	449	250	0	0	188	1,848	3,567
Methyl ethyl ketone	1,901,939	2,656,457	33,045	0	250	34,516	1,732,930	6,359,137
Methyl isobutyl ketone	1,283,957	699,992	3,616	5	20	21,793	610,165	2,619,548
Methyl methacrylate	168,693	151,197	250	0	250	18,070	223,185	561,645
Methyl tert-butyl ether	13,336	21,040	250	0	0	68,000	0	102,626
Methylenebis(phenylisocyanate)	33,668	275	0	0	255	250	9,590	44,038
Molybdenum trioxide	5,203	9,869	63,150	0	32,864	0	18,928	130,014
N,N-dimethylaniline	7	0	0	0	0	0	0	7
N-butyl alcohol	122,820	487,373	0	0	0	7,079	1,265,323	1,882,595
N-dioctyl phthalate	643	39	0	5	5	595	2,578	3,865
Naphthalene	274,618	98,203	415	0	250	1,795	365,486	740,767
Nickel	12,146	9,376	11,042	0	376,816	1,742	405,609	816,731
Nickel compounds	13,288	16,100	5,201	0	175,970	6,465	515,319	732,343
Nitric acid	162,360	470,307	26,390	5	26,300	15,450	6,060,395	6,761,207
Nitrilotriacetic acid	5	250	0	0	0	750	0	1,005
Nitroglycerin	250	250	250	0	0	0	0	750
O-anisidine	0	0	0	0	0	5,610	0	5,610
O-cresol	8	253	0	0	0	0	14,363	14,624
O-toluidine	250	250	0	0	8,486	0	250	9,236
O-xylene	4,153	12,370	0	0	0	0	32,394	48,917
P-cresol	1,858	625	0	0	0	0	16,396	18,879
P-xylene	1,450	3,857	0	0	0	0	32,500	37,807
Phenol	142,265	229,696	8,387	0	1,538	194,072	403,783	979,741
Phosphoric acid	26,022	23,339	1,160	0	44,001	488,894	273,391	856,807
Phosphorus (yellow or white)	256	11	250	0	0	5	510	1,032

[Continued]

★ 430 ★

Toxic Chemical Releases in Pennsylvania, by Chemical: 1990

[Continued]

Chemical	Fugitive air	Stack air	Water	Injection	Land	Public treatment	Other offsite	Total releases
Phthalic anhydride	2,663	19,759	5	0	0	749	89,732	112,908
Polychlorinated biphenyls (PCBs)	0	0	0	0	0	0	5,958	5,958
Propionaldehyde	10,448	861	0	0	0	0	0	11,309
Propylene	103,661	19,484	0	0	0	0	0	123,145
Propylene oxide	3,544	118	0	0	0	1,834	0	5,496
Pyridine	783	198	6,800	0	0	0	5	7,786
Quinoline	216	1,566	0	0	0	0	9,861	11,643
Sec-butyl alcohol	3,055	21,505	0	0	0	0	5,555	30,115
Selenium	0	1	0	0	0	5	4,108	4,114
Selenium compounds	0	3	0	0	0	0	265	268
Silver	6	7	250	0	0	2	250	515
Silver compounds	0	0	0	0	0	5	0	5
Styrene	342,897	787,090	674	0	2,605	14,374	251,898	1,399,538
Sulfuric acid	96,806	655,620	134,593	10	41,174	219,738	20,629,822	21,777,763
Tert-butyl alcohol	255	3,773	0	0	0	0	5	4,033
Tetrachloroethylene	97,924	339,480	31	0	0	4,738	387,691	829,864
Toluene	4,350,180	7,691,882	7,128	20	383	72,606	4,110,346	16,232,545
Toluenediisocyanate (mixed isomers)	946	1,456	0	0	0	0	1,760	4,162
Toluene-2,4-diisocyanate	15	15	0	0	0	0	3,200	3,230
Toluene-2,6-diisocyanate	10	5	0	0	0	0	250	265
Trichlorfon	0	3	0	0	0	0	0	3
Trichloroethylene	1,300,780	1,291,022	849	0	10	1,248	335,127	2,929,036
Trifluralin	5	0	0	0	0	0	0	5
Vanadium (fume or dust)	256	6	250	0	1,400	5	0	1,917
Vinyl acetate	20,885	99,599	250	0	250	210	3,682	124,876
Vinyl chloride	21,299	116,976	0	0	250	1,074	250	139,849
Xylene (mixed isomers)	866,350	3,553,452	854	10	700	50,448	1,827,173	6,298,987
Zinc (fume or dust)	88,507	70,795	3,406	0	7,631	518	372,098	542,955
Zinc compounds	391,991	1,053,596	81,231	0	1,610,509	16,312	3,225,288	6,378,927

Source: U.S. Environmental Protection Agency. "Toxic Chemical Releases, 1990." In *National Economic, Social, and Environmental Data Bank* [CD-ROM]. Prepared by U.S. Department of Commerce, Economics and Statistics Administration. Washington, DC: U.S. Department of Commerce, National Economic, Social, and Environmental Data Bank, Economics and Statistics Administration, Office of Business Analysis, February 1995.

★ 431 ★

Chemicals

Toxic Chemical Releases in Puerto Rico, by Chemical: 1990

Figures indicate pounds released by chemical and by type of emission per year.

Chemical	Fugitive air	Stack air	Water	Injection	Land	Public treatment	Other offsite	Total releases
1,1,1-trichloroethane	348,520	98,288	0	0	0	256	77,040	524,104
1,2,4-trimethylbenzene	21,807	1,188	10	0	0	0	0	23,005
1,2-dichloroethane	884	16,926	0	0	0	81	5,348	23,239
1,4-dioxane	1,170	260	0	0	0	18,471	583	20,484
2-methoxyethanol	230,882	750	0	0	2,537	1,766	225,576	461,511
Acetone	1,904,216	963,612	5	5	120	568,375	334,304	3,770,637
Acetonitrile	7,800	1,950	0	0	100	3,105	3,502	16,457

[Continued]

★ 431 ★

Toxic Chemical Releases in Puerto Rico, by Chemical: 1990

[Continued]

Chemical	Fugitive air	Stack air	Water	Injection	Land	Public treatment	Other offsite	Total releases
Aluminum oxide (fibrous forms)	45,075	0	0	0	0	0	0	45,075
Ammonia	26,531	81,376	117,310	5	120	603,803	750	829,895
Ammonium sulfate (solution)	250	0	0	0	0	4,632,830	10	4,633,090
Aniline	250	250	0	0	5	56,000	0	56,505
Antimony compounds	5	250	15	5	20	5	250	550
Arsenic compounds	5	250	0	0	0	0	5	260
Benzene	232,302	93,700	21	0	0	0	17	326,040
Benzyl chloride	40	0	0	0	0	0	0	40
Biphenyl	19	0	10	0	0	0	0	29
Bromomethane	0	7,140	0	0	0	0	0	7,140
Butyl acrylate	354	1	0	0	0	0	0	355
Carbon disulfide	1,100	840,000	0	0	0	15,000	0	856,100
Chlorine	3,682	808	0	5	11,200	5	0	15,700
Chlorobenzene	930	60	0	0	0	100	0	1,090
Chloroform	8,032	41,570	0	0	0	132,796	1,049	183,447
Chloromethane	5,500	2,700	0	0	0	0	0	8,200
Chromium	250	0	0	0	0	1	2,612	2,863
Chromium compounds	10	255	750	0	0	0	5	1,020
Cobalt	250	0	0	0	0	0	250	500
Copper	1,012	200	278	0	5	1,031	4,500	7,026
Copper compounds	20	773	15	5	20	519	36,382	37,734
Cumene hydroperoxide	5	0	0	0	0	0	750	755
Cyanide compounds	1,750	1,000	0	0	0	1,302	0	4,052
Cyclohexane	169,399	70,432	12	0	0	0	55,180	295,023
Di(2-ethylhexyl) phthalate	0	250	0	0	0	0	0	250
Dibutyl phthalate	137	230	0	0	0	380	380	1,127
Dichloromethane	1,298,217	2,657,456	0	0	0	185,729	321,487	4,462,889
Dichlorvos	250	0	0	0	0	0	0	250
Diethanolamine	250	250	0	0	0	250	129,536	130,286
Epichlorohydrin	4,170	40	0	0	0	0	0	4,210
Ethylbenzene	37,892	12,448	11	0	0	0	10	50,361
Ethylene glycol	58,723	10	0	0	2,986	16,949	5,609	84,277
Ethylene oxide	28,470	242,448	0	0	0	2,783	0	273,701
Formaldehyde	255	1,366	0	0	0	33,819	0	35,440
Freon 113	449,219	982,804	0	0	0	25	125,336	1,557,384
Glycol ethers	35,332	132,854	0	458	0	9,161	2,390	180,195
Hydrochloric acid	41,240	36,034	10	0	221	2,015	2,720	82,240
Hydrogen fluoride	505	505	0	0	0	0	0	1,010
Isopropyl alcohol (manufacturing)	505	500	0	0	0	3,500	0	4,505
Lead	257	206	0	0	0	2	22	487
M-xylene	95,089	26,836	10	0	0	0	10	121,945
Manganese	0	0	0	0	0	361	250	611
Manganese compounds	0	251	0	0	0	273	0	524
Mercury	0	0	0	0	0	0	250	250
Methanol	588,038	307,695	0	250	60	1,443,015	2,801,196	5,140,254
Methyl ethyl ketone	272,687	20,299	0	0	0	250	17,233	310,469

[Continued]

★ 431 ★

Toxic Chemical Releases in Puerto Rico, by Chemical: 1990

[Continued]

Chemical	Fugitive air	Stack air	Water	Injection	Land	Public treatment	Other offsite	Total releases
Methyl isobutyl ketone	32,216	18,531	0	0	0	510	37,675	88,932
Methyl methacrylate	2,004	2,002	0	0	0	0	73,500	77,506
Methyl tert-butyl ether	102,304	55,027	10	0	0	0	0	157,341
N-butyl alcohol	33,868	742,273	0	0	0	171,554	24,961	972,656
Nickel	250	250	0	0	0	250	250	1,000
Nickel compounds	10	264	0	0	0	272	11,122	11,668
Nitric acid	760	502	5	0	0	5	7,035	8,307
O-xylene	91,699	33,937	10	0	0	0	10	125,656
P-xylene	111,431	115,051	10	0	0	0	10	226,502
Phenol	1,646	0	64	0	0	0	0	1,710
Phosphoric acid	31,893	815	10	0	0	30	15	32,763
Propylene	3,139	554	0	0	0	0	0	3,693
Pyridine	500	1,000	0	0	0	203,428	0	204,928
Silver	505	505	3	0	0	256	268	1,537
Styrene	1,759	1,200	0	0	0	7	0	2,966
Sulfuric acid	8,447	2,933	255	5	8,025	18,270	91,025	128,960
Tetrachloroethylene	17,333	77,304	0	0	0	0	10,009	104,646
Toluene	908,776	324,876	12	0	38	71,228	175,481	1,480,411
Toluene-2,4-diisocyanate	5	0	0	0	0	0	0	5
Trichloroethylene	560	10,000	0	0	0	0	0	10,560
Vinyl acetate	2,217	76	0	0	0	29	0	2,322
Xylene (mixed isomers)	64,366	22,848	13	0	0	2,780	16,074	106,081
Zinc (fume or dust)	250	0	0	0	0	2,255	8,710	11,215
Zinc compounds	260	255	0	0	0	250	0	765

Source: U.S. Environmental Protection Agency. "Toxic Chemical Releases, 1990." In *National Economic, Social, and Environmental Data Bank* [CD-ROM]. Prepared by U.S. Department of Commerce, Economics and Statistics Administration. Washington, DC: U.S. Department of Commerce, National Economic, Social, and Environmental Data Bank, Economics and Statistics Administration, Office of Business Analysis, February 1995.

★ 432 ★

Chemicals

Toxic Chemical Releases in Rhode Island, by Chemical: 1990

Figures indicate pounds released by chemical and by type of emission per year.

Chemical	Fugitive air	Stack air	Water	Injection	Land	Public treatment	Other offsite	Total releases
1,1,1-trichloroethane	937,784	260,442	1	0	0	2	106,024	1,304,253
1,2,4-trichlorobenzene	0	15,500	0	0	0	2,736	0	18,236
1,2-dichlorobenzene	250	1,156	0	0	0	1,156	0	2,562
1,2-dichloroethane	117	1,463	0	0	0	0	44,195	45,775
2-methoxyethanol	250	4,000	0	0	0	0	22,100	26,350
4,4'-isopropylidenediphenol	78	0	0	0	0	40	80	198
Acetone	206,052	318,830	6,142	0	0	5	361,446	892,475
Allyl alcohol	669	23	0	0	0	150	0	842

[Continued]

★ 432 ★

Toxic Chemical Releases in Rhode Island, by Chemical: 1990

[Continued]

Chemical	Fugitive air	Stack air	Water	Injection	Land	Public treatment	Other offsite	Total releases
Ammonia	156,883	2,165	28,295	0	0	74,869	250	262,462
Ammonium sulfate (solution)	0	0	0	0	0	2,900	0	2,900
Aniline	5	251	1	0	0	2,387	43,924	46,568
Antimony compounds	260	10	0	0	1,262	9	1,776	3,317
Arsenic compounds	255	255	5	0	0	5	5,776	6,296
Barium compounds	5	5	134	0	0	9	14,268	14,421
Benzoyl chloride	0	1	0	0	0	0	0	1
Benzyl chloride	162	0	0	0	0	15,912	162	16,236
Biphenyl	830	0	0	0	0	57,119	830	58,779
Bis(2-ethylhexyl) adipate	5	5	0	0	0	5	20	35
Butyl benzyl phthalate	5	5	0	0	0	5	20	35
Cadmium compounds	5	5	0	0	0	9	265	284
Chlorine	527	785	0	0	0	0	19	1,331
Chromium	5	250	0	0	0	250	3,850	4,355
Chromium compounds	255	5	0	0	0	14	1,015	1,289
Copper	522	2,276	18	0	0	771	40,282	43,869
Copper compounds	598	52	845	0	0	4,848	71,524	77,867
Cyanide compounds	258	84	0	0	0	626	9,115	10,083
Cyclohexane	250	930	0	0	0	0	5,190	6,370
Decabromodiphenyl oxide	5	5	0	0	0	5	20	35
Di(2-ethylhexyl) phthalate	500	1,005	0	0	0	5	2,665	4,175
Dibutyl phthalate	250	750	0	0	0	0	0	1,000
Dichloromethane	45,297	98,497	652	0	0	5	50,548	194,999
Diethanolamine	500	250	0	0	0	250	0	1,000
Epichlorohydrin	9,340	153	0	0	0	250	3,306	13,049
Ethylbenzene	46	65	0	0	0	5	0	116
Ethylene glycol	2,601	13,104	25,090	0	0	1,929	85,595	128,319
Ethylene oxide	185	41,920	0	0	0	0	0	42,105
Formaldehyde	2,655	700	0	0	5	2,210	0	5,570
Freon 113	226,267	78,786	1	0	0	10	24,110	329,174
Glycol ethers	8,332	60,977	0	0	5	755	44,730	114,799
Hydrochloric acid	7,648	20,926	5	0	0	68,487	65,339	162,405
Hydrogen fluoride	13,300	3,050	0	0	0	0	0	16,350
Lead	263	343	253	0	0	75	8	942
Lead compounds	515	260	5	0	0	46	25,584	26,410
M-cresol	5	250	0	0	0	250	1,000	1,505
Maleic anhydride	3	0	0	0	0	5	5	13
Manganese	250	250	0	0	0	250	16,539	17,289
Manganese compounds	543	0	0	0	0	0	0	543
Methanol	19,845	270,581	0	0	0	911,137	177,025	1,378,588
Methyl ethyl ketone	56,068	189,351	0	0	0	0	199,029	444,448
Methyl isobutyl ketone	250	3,000	0	0	0	0	880	4,130
Methyl methacrylate	250	0	0	0	0	0	0	250
Methylenebis(phenylisocyanate)	755	516	0	0	0	0	2,614	3,885
N-butyl alcohol	28,354	5,273	0	0	0	250	11,257	45,134
Nickel	9	3	1	0	0	722	15,517	16,252

[Continued]

★ 432 ★

Toxic Chemical Releases in Rhode Island, by Chemical: 1990
[Continued]

Chemical	Fugitive air	Stack air	Water	Injection	Land	Public treatment	Other offsite	Total releases
Nickel compounds	285	1	0	0	0	500	1,752	2,538
Nitric acid	4,370	2,352	0	0	0	10,559	18,800	36,081
O-anisidine	0	10	112	0	0	0	99	221
O-cresol	5	1,020	0	0	0	1,020	0	2,045
P-cresol	5	750	0	0	0	750	1,000	2,505
Phenol	255	250	0	0	0	20	750	1,275
Phosphoric acid	1,005	1,009	0	0	0	255	13,860	16,129
Phosphorus (yellow or white)	4	63	0	0	0	0	0	67
Polychlorinated biphenyls (PCBs)	0	0	0	0	0	0	250	250
Propylene	12,300	0	0	0	0	0	0	12,300
Propylene oxide	5	250	0	0	0	0	0	255
Sec-butyl alcohol	750	0	0	0	0	0	0	750
Silver	250	259	0	0	0	507	0	1,016
Silver compounds	0	1	0	0	0	0	0	1
Styrene	33,716	496	0	0	0	140	3,432	37,784
Sulfuric acid	18,488	10,686	5	0	0	56,075	12,007	97,261
Tetrachloroethylene	5,695	90,244	0	0	0	5	22,886	118,830
Toluene	917,413	593,107	115	0	0	63	68,983	1,579,681
Toluenediisocyanate (mixed isomers)	750	750	0	0	0	0	0	1,500
Trichloroethylene	158,599	55,195	0	0	0	5	35,515	249,314
Xylene (mixed isomers)	61,734	97,503	0	0	0	410	91,423	251,070
Zinc (fume or dust)	505	431	3	0	0	322	2,467	3,728
Zinc compounds	515	460	0	0	0	1,625	91,189	93,789

Source: U.S. Environmental Protection Agency. "Toxic Chemical Releases, 1990." In *National Economic, Social, and Environmental Data Bank* [CD-ROM]. Prepared by U.S. Department of Commerce, Economics and Statistics Administration. Washington, DC: U.S. Department of Commerce, National Economic, Social, and Environmental Data Bank, Economics and Statistics Administration, Office of Business Analysis, February 1995.

★ 433 ★
Chemicals

Toxic Chemical Releases in South Carolina, by Chemical: 1990

Figures indicate pounds released by chemical and by type of emission per year.

Chemical	Fugitive air	Stack air	Water	Injection	Land	Public treatment	Other offsite	Total releases
1,1,1-trichloroethane	1,559,034	2,901,775	17	0	580	2,171	137,548	4,601,125
1,1,2,2-tetrachloroethane	5	5	0	0	0	5	750	765
1,2,4-trichlorobenzene	1,592	11,250	0	0	0	43,504	81	56,427
1,2,4-trimethylbenzene	26,685	212,969	250	0	0	505	6,615	247,024
1,2-butylene oxide	40	1,170	0	0	0	0	0	1,210
1,2-dichlorobenzene	2,714	1,765	745	0	0	0	0	5,224
1,2-dichloroethane	501	39,104	0	0	0	48,689	913,472	1,001,766
1,3-butadiene	750	4,100	0	0	0	0	0	4,850
1,4-dioxane	30,664	43,005	102,917	0	12,280	3,415	15,430	207,711
2,4-diaminotoluene	3,800	120	250	0	0	0	0	4,170
2-ethoxyethanol	356	750	0	0	0	0	500	1,606

[Continued]

★ 433 ★

Toxic Chemical Releases in South Carolina, by Chemical: 1990
[Continued]

Chemical	Fugitive air	Stack air	Water	Injection	Land	Public treatment	Other offsite	Total releases
2-methoxyethanol	0	340,000	1,400	0	0	0	3,590	344,990
4,4'-diaminodiphenyl ether	0	0	0	0	0	250	250	500
4,4'-isopropylidenediphenol	0	0	19	0	0	0	18,000	18,019
4,4'-methylenedianiline	250	250	0	0	0	0	0	500
Acetaldehyde	795,392	460,405	17,249	0	29,646	0	565	1,303,257
Acetone	2,576,990	6,398,209	50,044	5	1,895	3,256	737,609	9,768,008
Acetonitrile	0	3,423	1,012	0	0	0	0	4,435
Acrylamide	259	256	250	0	250	180	2	1,197
Acrylic acid	2,379	1,181	514	0	38	1,455	1,526	7,093
Acrylonitrile	88,442	203,617	378	0	37	550	266	293,290
Allyl alcohol	862	150	0	0	0	0	3,683	4,695
Aluminum (fume or dust)	269	13,960	0	0	0	0	0	14,229
Aluminum oxide (fibrous forms)	250	5	15	5	20	0	0	295
Ammonia	1,719,672	1,059,304	386,325	5	129,244	228,646	51,617	3,574,813
Ammonium nitrate (solution)	250	0	750	0	0	0	0	1,000
Ammonium sulfate (solution)	255	250	30,636	0	320,750	28,150	122,419	502,460
Aniline	11,786	8,145	1,016	0	250	0	14,290	35,487
Anthracene	0	0	0	0	0	2,055	0	2,055
Antimony	0	0	0	0	0	5	1,610	1,615
Antimony compounds	791	760	3,480	0	13,008	8,503	110,429	136,971
Arsenic	0	0	13	0	0	0	2,690	2,703
Arsenic compounds	275	35	5	0	5	0	68,518	68,838
Asbestos (friable)	0	276	0	0	0	0	500	776
Barium	73	39	0	0	730	0	0	842
Barium compounds	1,267	5,602	205	0	5	2,296	419,361	428,736
Benzene	500,456	196,878	288	0	0	15,250	5,616	718,488
Benzoyl peroxide	5	5	5	0	0	0	0	15
Benzyl chloride	4,510	1,135	250	0	0	12,250	47,732	65,877
Biphenyl	290,684	69,252	1,518	0	27,069	10,600	4,134	403,257
Bis(2-ethylhexyl) adipate	250	1,730	0	0	0	22	2,880	4,882
Bromomethane	0	341,000	0	0	0	0	0	341,000
Butyl acrylate	3,856	1,912	268	0	6	1,022	1,649	8,713
Butyl benzyl phthalate	1	1	5	0	739	0	0	746
C.I. basic green 4	3	1	0	0	0	360	0	364
Cadmium compounds	260	255	250	0	5	500	395	1,665
Carbon disulfide	250	0	0	0	0	0	0	250
Catechol	500	0	25,767	0	250	0	5	26,522
Chlorine	51,488	119,822	22,542	0	15	7,100	0	200,967
Chlorine dioxide	1,260	282,946	0	0	0	0	0	284,206
Chlorobenzene	3,398	15,276	250	0	5	250	78,348	97,527
Chloroethane	160	2,700	0	0	0	0	242,600	245,460
Chloroform	177,468	321,224	13,154	0	250	0	0	512,096
Chloromethane	4,487	176,982	0	0	0	26,301	0	207,770
Chromium	3,522	4,096	337	0	20,493	825	192,146	221,419
Chromium compounds	1,097	2,366	235	5	902	8,184	185,893	198,682
Cobalt	15	10	5	0	5	2	14,403	14,440
Cobalt compounds	0	125	9,445	0	25,420	0	5,810	40,800
Copper	2,472	1,046	807	0	2,812	1,266	181,943	190,346
Copper compounds	954	2,321	1,217	0	2,225	2,218	1,494,678	1,503,613
Creosote	5,721	6,600	122	0	761	7	425,692	438,903
Cresol (mixed isomers)	100	900	0	0	0	0	1,480	2,480
Cumene	6,664	50,825	5	0	0	5	0	57,499

[Continued]

★ 433 ★

Toxic Chemical Releases in South Carolina, by Chemical: 1990

[Continued]

Chemical	Fugitive air	Stack air	Water	Injection	Land	Public treatment	Other offsite	Total releases
Cyanide compounds	255	251	248	0	0	256	16,019	17,029
Cyclohexane	4,826	208,806	274	0	0	0	250	214,156
Decabromodiphenyl oxide	68	250	1,785	5	20	10,850	31,776	44,754
Di(2-ethylhexyl) phthalate	260	797	5	0	0	1,900	9,900	12,862
Diaminotoluene (mixed isomers)	1,200	0	250	0	250	0	4,989	6,689
Dibutyl phthalate	250	240	0	0	0	250	970	1,710
Dichlorobenzene (mixed isomers)	250	250	0	0	0	250	0	750
Dichloromethane	776,323	909,641	2,626	0	2,000	7	297,268	1,987,865
Diethanolamine	1,550	515	251	0	5,800	2,005	22,590	32,711
Diethyl phthalate	10	20,150	0	0	5	125	12,855	33,145
Diethyl sulfate	5	5	0	0	5	5	0	20
Dimethyl phthalate	755	2,940	0	0	5	5	8,666	12,371
Dimethyl sulfate	255	5	0	0	0	0	0	260
Epichlorohydrin	255	250	0	0	0	0	0	505
Ethyl acrylate	3,262	2,508	261	0	0	1,005	703	7,739
Ethylbenzene	21,269	22,935	0	0	0	15	5,450	49,669
Ethylene	30,399	352,317	5	0	0	0	0	382,721
Ethylene glycol	558,446	317,086	54,390	0	313,856	536,264	191,540	1,971,582
Ethylene oxide	10,594	48,586	89	0	0	78	0	59,347
Formaldehyde	97,770	377,156	3,891	0	1,301	68,216	74,729	623,063
Freon 113	577,547	90,342	5	0	260	260	75,136	743,550
Glycol ethers	165,872	1,123,294	5,577	0	3,555	81,917	56,010	1,436,225
Hydrazine	5	0	0	0	0	7,900	0	7,905
Hydrochloric acid	45,704	2,677,722	10	0	5	24,530	67,860	2,815,831
Hydrogen cyanide	12,750	82,023	0	0	0	37	0	94,810
Hydrogen fluoride	72,466	11,317	11	0	0	0	317	84,111
Isopropyl alcohol (manufacturing)	7,412	131,674	0	0	0	255	7,283	146,624
Lead	437	7,181	3	0	14,370	525	18,407	40,923
Lead compounds	1,265	3,983	505	0	250	792	124,196	130,991
M-cresol	15	68	0	0	0	0	0	83
Maleic anhydride	4,410	507	5	0	0	5	623	5,550
Manganese	3,823	421	0	0	3,765	515	23,560	32,084
Manganese compounds	4,235	5,530	49,500	2	359,867	3,634	122,195	544,963
Mercury compounds	5	15	0	0	0	0	2,133	2,153
Methanol	1,213,992	13,563,031	74,970	0	171,020	1,458,030	1,195,824	17,676,867
Methyl acrylate	2,444	5,003	5	0	0	251	345	8,048
Methyl ethyl ketone	2,900,862	1,606,193	2,361	5	20	1,605	312,911	4,823,957
Methyl isobutyl ketone	201,587	220,268	254	0	5	990	35,823	458,927
Methyl methacrylate	2,531	1,183	255	0	2	546	263	4,780
Methylene bromide	6,685	302	0	0	0	0	49,085	56,072
Methylenebis(phenylisocyanate)	1,265	65,510	0	0	5	0	8,663	75,443
N,N-dimethylaniline	0	250	0	0	0	250	0	500
N-butyl alcohol	116,024	706,007	252	0	0	58,313	98,664	979,260
N-dioctyl phthalate	0	250	0	0	0	0	500	750
Naphthalene	3,293	7,350	0	0	0	255	5	10,903
Nickel	1,526	426	19	0	33	1,330	28,290	31,624
Nickel compounds	760	510	2,239	0	5	823	13,843	18,180
Nitric acid	7,932	17,827	28,765	5	270	20,950	114,924	190,673
Nitrobenzene	250	0	0	0	0	250	0	500
O-anisidine	250	250	0	0	250	0	0	750
O-xylene	19,071	4,571	35	0	0	0	0	23,677
P-anisidine	0	0	5	0	0	0	0	5

[Continued]

★ 433 ★

Toxic Chemical Releases in South Carolina, by Chemical: 1990

[Continued]

Chemical	Fugitive air	Stack air	Water	Injection	Land	Public treatment	Other offsite	Total releases
P-cresidine	5	0	0	0	250	0	0	255
P-xylene	37,700	588,000	0	0	0	0	0	625,700
Pentachlorophenol	103	37	143	0	0	89	2,233	2,605
Phenol	37,010	150,570	10,001	0	11,255	406	7,033	216,275
Phosgene	5	5	0	0	0	0	0	10
Phosphoric acid	24,734	2,225	1,130	10	285	47,606	72,697	148,687
Phthalic anhydride	5	253	0	0	0	0	1,500	1,758
Polychlorinated biphenyls (PCBs)	0	0	0	0	0	0	34,000	34,000
Propionaldehyde	160	290	0	0	0	69	0	519
Propylene	18,758	36,318	0	0	0	0	0	55,076
Propylene oxide	7,063	9,368	450	0	0	22	0	16,903
Sec-butyl alcohol	3,846	917	0	0	0	0	1,964	6,727
Silver	10	262	0	0	0	264	269	805
Silver compounds	0	0	0	0	0	0	415	415
Styrene	202,766	454,146	2,015	5	260	761	38,697	698,650
Sulfuric acid	12,363	686,279	27,950	5	3,851	3,833	157,047	891,328
Tert-butyl alcohol	1	1	0	0	0	0	0	2
Tetrachloroethylene	240,847	213,999	14,767	0	0	110,611	78,748	658,972
Titanium tetrachloride	250	0	0	0	0	0	0	250
Toluene	2,696,378	5,546,704	2,643	5	5,133	1,915	489,306	8,742,084
Toluenediisocyanate (mixed isomers)	1	5	0	0	0	0	0	6
Toluene-2,4-diisocyanate	5	347	0	0	0	0	0	352
Toluene-2,6-diisocyanate	1	25	0	0	0	0	0	26
Trichloroethylene	271,951	254,251	0	0	0	334	95,254	621,790
Vinyl acetate	8,528	16,650	311	0	738	611	250	27,088
Xylene (mixed isomers)	421,002	2,021,362	4,481	5	296	119,536	381,118	2,947,800
Zinc (fume or dust)	23,939	93,475	10	0	250	555	124,833	243,062
Zinc compounds	3,079	8,668	5,493	0	3,816	12,461	496,507	530,024

Source: U.S. Environmental Protection Agency. "Toxic Chemical Releases, 1990." In *National Economic, Social, and Environmental Data Bank* [CD-ROM]. Prepared by U.S. Department of Commerce, Economics and Statistics Administration. Washington, DC: U.S. Department of Commerce, National Economic, Social, and Environmental Data Bank, Economics and Statistics Administration, Office of Business Analysis, February 1995.

★ 434 ★

Chemicals

Toxic Chemical Releases in South Dakota, by Chemical: 1990

Figures indicate pounds released by chemical and by type of emission per year.

Chemical	Fugitive air	Stack air	Water	Injection	Land	Public treatment	Other offsite	Total releases
1,1,1-trichloroethane	44,119	168,515	0	0	0	0	18,205	230,839
1,2,4-trichlorobenzene	5	0	0	0	0	0	19,826	19,831
Acetone	57,500	750	0	0	0	0	9,900	68,150
Ammonia	106,501	1,000	2,400	0	0	125,992	34,248	270,141
Ammonium nitrate (solution)	5	0	5,467	0	0	5	0	5,477
Arsenic compounds	0	250	0	0	0	0	1,600	1,850
Barium compounds	0	0	0	0	0	5	10	15
Chlorine	260	5,233	0	0	0	750	0	6,243

[Continued]

★ 434 ★

Toxic Chemical Releases in South Dakota, by Chemical: 1990

[Continued]

Chemical	Fugitive air	Stack air	Water	Injection	Land	Public treatment	Other offsite	Total releases
Chromium	255	250	0	0	0	250	0	755
Chromium compounds	0	250	0	0	0	0	2,100	2,350
Creosote	750	6,850	0	0	0	0	0	7,600
Cyclohexane	1,665	439,207	0	0	0	0	19,704	460,576
Ethylene glycol	0	0	0	0	0	5	10	15
Formaldehyde	13,000	76,000	0	0	1	0	0	89,001
Freon 113	18,955	205,540	0	0	0	0	18,736	243,231
Hydrochloric acid	0	0	0	0	0	5	0	5
Lead	5	755	0	0	0	0	19,890	20,650
Lead compounds	1,817	181,689	0	0	0	0	0	183,506
Manganese	739	0	0	0	0	0	0	739
Manganese compounds	0	250	0	0	0	0	250	500
Methanol	4,575	137,332	0	0	0	0	19,371	161,278
Methyl ethyl ketone	2,005	153,606	0	0	0	0	46,608	202,219
Methyl isobutyl ketone	0	43,000	0	0	0	0	0	43,000
Nickel	250	0	0	0	0	0	0	250
Nitric acid	0	3,000	0	0	0	28,006	0	31,006
Phosphoric acid	0	200	37,000	0	0	55,780	23,518	116,498
Propylene	250	0	0	0	0	0	0	250
Silver	5	5	0	0	0	0	0	10
Styrene	4,749	41,800	0	0	0	0	336	46,885
Sulfuric acid	255	5	0	0	0	755	5	1,020
Tetrachloroethylene	250	1,250	0	0	0	0	0	1,500
Toluene	70,456	396,091	0	0	0	0	83,574	550,121
Xylene (mixed isomers)	139,376	561,070	0	0	0	0	19,595	720,041
Zinc (fume or dust)	250	0	0	0	0	0	0	250
Zinc compounds	5	255	0	0	0	250	64,660	65,170

Source: U.S. Environmental Protection Agency. "Toxic Chemical Releases, 1990." In *National Economic, Social, and Environmental Data Bank* [CD-ROM]. Prepared by U.S. Department of Commerce, Economics and Statistics Administration. Washington, DC: U.S. Department of Commerce, National Economic, Social, and Environmental Data Bank, Economics and Statistics Administration, Office of Business Analysis, February 1995.

★ 435 ★

Chemicals

Toxic Chemical Releases in Tennessee, by Chemical: 1990

Figures indicate pounds released by chemical and by type of emission per year.

Chemical	Fugitive air	Stack air	Water	Injection	Land	Public treatment	Other offsite	Total releases
1,1,1-trichloroethane	2,671,819	3,518,677	74	0	255	1,336	472,058	6,664,219
1,1,2,2-tetrachloroethane	28	42	0	0	0	0	0	70
1,2,4-trimethylbenzene	42,303	144,318	0	0	0	0	0	186,621
1,2-butylene oxide	11,638	250	0	0	0	250	250	12,388
1,2-dichlorobenzene	66	32	0	0	0	0	270,000	270,098
1,3-butadiene	4,900	223,000	0	0	0	257	5	228,162

[Continued]

★ 435 ★

Toxic Chemical Releases in Tennessee, by Chemical: 1990
[Continued]

Chemical	Fugitive air	Stack air	Water	Injection	Land	Public treatment	Other offsite	Total releases
1,4-dioxane	7,496	14,978	12,001	0	0	0	46	34,521
2,4-dimethylphenol	0	0	3	0	0	1,735	0	1,738
2,4-dinitrophenol	120	1	87,000	0	0	0	0	87,121
2-ethoxyethanol	90,675	8,348	41,000	0	0	655	14,960	155,638
2-methoxyethanol	32,000	1	24,000	0	0	0	0	56,001
2-phenylphenol	8,100	590	3	0	0	0	0	8,693
4,4'-isopropylidenediphenol	0	0	0	0	0	750	0	750
4,4'-methylenebis(2-chloro aniline)	5	0	0	0	0	0	0	5
4-nitrophenol	2	1	31	0	0	0	0	34
Acetaldehyde	126,044	706,568	3	0	0	0	346	832,961
Acetone	30,647,854	6,223,475	78,791	0	8,892	50,117	377,589	37,386,718
Acetonitrile	1,200	2,777	1	0	0	0	26,500	30,478
Acrylamide	195	276	0	0	0	309	543	1,323
Acrylic acid	869	23,748	0	0	0	99,545	1,020	125,182
Acrylonitrile	1,847	2,565	0	0	0	5,975	60	10,447
Allyl chloride	27	0	0	0	0	0	0	27
Aluminum (fume or dust)	108,295	34,674	255	0	260	510	217,977	361,971
Ammonia	1,218,688	3,971,638	231,442	7,616,857	13,393	1,124,523	576,489	14,753,030
Ammonium nitrate (solution)	933	0	5	0	0	0	0	938
Ammonium sulfate (solution)	0	23,000	3,740,000	4,875,546	1,800	10,149,051	250	18,789,647
Aniline	520	89	3	0	0	0	0	612
Antimony	128	417	0	0	24,000	120	105	24,770
Antimony compounds	500	30	250	0	150	772	87,149	88,851
Arsenic	59	81	0	0	7,200	9	310	7,659
Arsenic compounds	25	335	0	0	0	0	19,242	19,602
Asbestos (friable)	2	1,862	0	0	0	2	1,011,000	1,012,866
Barium	50	250	5	0	0	0	270	575
Barium compounds	4,078	9,692	505	0	812,335	19,186	985,114	1,830,910
Benzal chloride	1,504	5	0	0	0	5	0	1,514
Benzene	18,158	181,679	0	75	0	2,414	3	202,329
Benzoic trichloride	4,970	10	0	0	0	5	0	4,985
Benzoyl chloride	10,202	441	0	0	0	1,118	640,694	652,455
Benzyl chloride	6,380	62	0	0	0	253	250	6,945
Biphenyl	104,247	40,130	1	0	0	2,525	6,823	153,726
Bis(2-chloroethyl) ether	1,751	38	0	0	0	18,991	0	20,780
Bis(2-ethylhexyl) adipate	3,250	9,600	1,128	0	2,924	855	35,463	53,220
Bromomethane	36,800	171,000	0	0	0	0	0	207,800
Butyl acrylate	5,241	678	0	0	0	322	5,280	11,521
Butyl benzyl phthalate	250	500	5	0	0	1,600	38,850	41,205
Butyraldehyde	11,000	120,000	0	0	0	0	0	131,000
Cadmium	250	250	250	0	75,676	5	5	76,436
Cadmium compounds	250	0	0	0	0	1	278	529
Captan	5	250	0	0	0	250	250	755
Carbon disulfide	2,138,416	27,541,000	32,650	0	250	63,843	0	29,776,159
Carbon tetrachloride	13,707	10,700	0	0	0	570	82,996	107,973
Carbonyl sulfide	0	8,500,000	0	0	0	0	0	8,500,000
Catechol	0	0	1,531	0	7	0	28	1,566
Chlordane	4,239	178	1	0	0	99	523	5,040
Chlorine	237,609	266,858	45,333	0	234	44,235	610	594,879
Chlorine dioxide	10	9,556	0	0	0	0	0	9,566
Chloroacetic acid	0	0	0	0	0	750	0	750
Chlorobenzene	5,139	753	0	2,196	0	0	0	8,088
Chloroethane	274	0	0	0	0	0	0	274
Chloroform	279,374	18,611	21,855	0	61	0	3	319,904
Chloromethane	14,288	100,020	0	0	0	3,605	2,200	120,113
Chromium	17,156	50,527	295	5	20	1,447	203,357	272,807
Chromium compounds	1,658	3,165	335	0	187,516	4,208	81,294	278,176
Cobalt	279	1,320	250	0	621	240	0	2,710
Cobalt compounds	323	13,888	2,200	0	3,400	255	5,410	25,476

[Continued]

★ 435 ★

Toxic Chemical Releases in Tennessee, by Chemical: 1990

[Continued]

Chemical	Fugitive air	Stack air	Water	Injection	Land	Public treatment	Other offsite	Total releases
Copper	11,592	15,786	2,600	0	225,204	3,615	419,257	678,054
Copper compounds	5,285	5,982	1,077	200	47,088	2,884	34,909	97,425
Creosote	5	5	0	0	0	0	52,000	52,010
Cresol (mixed isomers)	15,707	11,001	16	0	0	9,020	4,805	40,549
Cumene	1,220	1,316	0	0	0	0	0	2,536
Cumene hydroperoxide	291	0	0	0	0	0	0	291
Cyanide compounds	5	6,909	504	0	0	10	4,973	12,401
Cyclohexane	39,266	154,102	0	0	0	0	0	193,368
Decabromodiphenyl oxide	250	0	250	0	0	250	206,000	206,750
Di(2-ethylhexyl) phthalate	26,179	46,766	265	0	3,900	2,827	142,507	222,444
Dibutyl phthalate	31,065	1,327	1	0	1	0	17,931	50,325
Dichlorobenzene (mixed isomers)	207	37	0	6	0	0	0	250
Dichloromethane	1,682,483	1,441,836	3,320	0	0	10,079	38,444	3,176,162
Diethanolamine	260	253	4,400	0	0	58,163	500	63,576
Diethyl phthalate	1,300	8,100	2,436	0	22	0	63	11,921
Diethyl sulfate	6	6	0	0	0	0	255	267
Dimethyl phthalate	1,445	6,591	83	0	1	250	2,591	10,961
Dimethyl sulfate	6	8	0	0	0	0	0	14
Epichlorohydrin	1,122	42	0	0	0	250	0	1,414
Ethyl acrylate	5,046	1,824	0	0	0	520	5,704	13,094
Ethylbenzene	97,825	229,213	0	0	0	114	300	327,452
Ethylene	2,480	124,200	0	0	0	0	0	126,680
Ethylene glycol	84,556	171,099	220,000	0	94,000	178,949	58,617	807,221
Ethylene oxide	7,271	63,802	0	0	0	0	0	71,073
Ethylene thiourea	0	0	0	0	0	5	0	5
Formaldehyde	9,486	339,391	505	0	0	19,112	30	368,524
Freon 113	302,434	165,699	74	0	0	268	46,643	515,118
Glycol ethers	264,248	1,440,092	1,900	0	1,501	70,339	92,860	1,870,940
Heptachlor	3,797	0	1	0	0	58	85,306	89,162
Hexachlorobenzene	829	1	0	0	0	23	2,695	3,548
Hexachlorocyclopentadiene	82,097	726	0	0	0	904	22,259	105,986
Hydrazine	4,563	72	5	0	0	250	0	4,890
Hydrochloric acid	146,910	1,490,303	302	41,000,000	21,123	1,346	596,278	43,256,262
Hydrogen cyanide	250	4,040	0	0	0	0	0	4,290
Hydrogen fluoride	1,706	597,254	0	0	0	6,705	8,200	613,865
Hydroquinone	307	460	95	0	0	0	0	862
Isobutyraldehyde	24	9,600	0	0	0	0	0	9,624
Isopropyl alcohol (manufacturing)	13,826	129,459	0	0	0	0	6,129	149,414
Lead	7,205	12,104	505	5	601,762	679	106,541	728,801
Lead compounds	17,991	12,377	250	0	783	585	28,662	60,648
M-cresol	0	0	0	0	0	0	4	4
Maleic anhydride	7,998	1,235	250	0	250	255	1,034	11,022
Manganese	5,441	10,928	18,895	5	235,943	346	67,018	338,576
Manganese compounds	117,346	88,985	110,546	0	1,710,432	16,453	2,439,490	4,483,252
Mercury	1,045	240	25	0	3,926	0	5	5,241
Methanol	2,006,719	9,871,186	14,400	571,294	2,829	3,843,689	501,961	16,812,078
Methyl acrylate	2,044	905	0	0	0	168	3,774	6,891
Methyl ethyl ketone	408,161	1,834,560	1,464	5	20	260	250,549	2,495,019
Methyl iodide	25	10	1	0	0	0	0	36
Methyl isobutyl ketone	533,015	852,539	18	0	0	6,988	88,155	1,480,715
Methyl methacrylate	10,098	14,636	0	0	0	2,075	42,108	68,917
Methyl tert-butyl ether	0	5,985	0	0	0	0	0	5,985
Methylene bromide	1,603	12,250	0	0	0	4,230	0	18,083
Methylenebis(phenylisocyanate)	844	6,821	10	0	0	0	3,160	10,835
Molybdenum trioxide	0	5	0	0	0	0	0	5
N,N-dimethylaniline	13,250	3,212	2,437	0	0	0	39,600	58,499
N-butyl alcohol	37,304	378,815	252	0	5	0	78,291	494,667
N-dioctyl phthalate	250	250	250	0	0	0	1,123	1,873
Naphthalene	2,411	4,595	0	0	0	5	0	7,011

[Continued]

★ 435 ★

Toxic Chemical Releases in Tennessee, by Chemical: 1990

[Continued]

Chemical	Fugitive air	Stack air	Water	Injection	Land	Public treatment	Other offsite	Total releases
Nickel	11,722	31,632	604	5	25	7,277	444,321	495,586
Nickel compounds	2,520	1,263	756	0	34,896	6,210	104,056	149,701
Nitric acid	13,038	132,580	0	0	160	81,224	39,895	266,897
O-xylene	227,750	79,250	1,800	0	0	0	82	308,882
P-cresol	0	0	0	0	0	0	4	4
P-xylene	122,020	125,000	0	0	0	0	0	247,020
Pentachlorophenol	250	750	0	0	0	5	0	1,005
Phenol	24,447	61,755	271	0	6,090	24,822	8,028	125,413
Phosgene	590	0	0	0	0	0	0	590
Phosphoric acid	26,120	15,059	15	0	0	211,220	315,105	567,519
Phosphorus (yellow or white)	250	252	5	0	340	0	0	847
Phthalic anhydride	103	3,453	0	0	0	0	13	3,569
Polychlorinated biphenyls (PCBs)	0	0	0	0	0	0	14,444	14,444
Propionaldehyde	78,000	580,000	4	0	0	0	0	658,004
Propylene	2,075	3,079	0	0	0	0	0	5,154
Pyridine	7,405	110	450	0	0	0	3	7,968
Quinone	710	890	2	0	0	0	0	1,602
Saccharin (manufacturing)	0	250	0	0	0	250	2,700	3,200
Sec-butyl alcohol	459	52,805	0	1,484	0	0	0	54,748
Silver	250	250	0	0	0	0	0	500
Styrene	245,249	1,067,928	0	0	0	2,821	8,992	1,324,990
Sulfuric acid	26,637	454,413	140,184	0	13,431	188,297	929,859	1,752,821
Tert-butyl alcohol	14,613	1,201	0	0	0	250	5,934	21,998
Tetrachloroethylene	123,100	312,076	74	0	0	22	15,205	450,477
Thorium dioxide	250	360	0	0	0	660	410,000	411,270
Titanium tetrachloride	8,000	10,000	0	0	0	0	0	18,000
Toluene	4,364,154	8,995,259	1,265	5	20	50,473	857,184	14,268,360
Toluenediisocyanate (mixed isomers)	1,514	1,726	0	0	0	0	0	3,240
Toluene-2,4-diisocyanate	10	90	0	0	0	0	5	105
Toluene-2,6-diisocyanate	7	26	0	0	0	0	5	38
Trichloroethylene	449,993	650,376	0	0	0	318	122,643	1,223,330
Vinyl acetate	675	80	0	0	0	64	310	1,129
Xylene (mixed isomers)	1,109,364	3,942,828	510	803	264	8,969	818,744	5,881,482
Zinc (fume or dust)	41,564	171,710	2,790	5	2,369,040	260	20,941	2,606,310
Zinc compounds	140,464	46,308	17,172	0	2,617,788	49,344	965,111	3,836,187

Source: U.S. Environmental Protection Agency. "Toxic Chemical Releases, 1990." In *National Economic, Social, and Environmental Data Bank* [CD-ROM]. Prepared by U.S. Department of Commerce, Economics and Statistics Administration. Washington, DC: U.S. Department of Commerce, National Economic, Social, and Environmental Data Bank, Economics and Statistics Administration, Office of Business Analysis, February 1995.

★ 436 ★

Chemicals

Toxic Chemical Releases in Texas, by Chemical: 1990

Figures indicate pounds released by chemical and by type of emission per year.

Chemical	Fugitive air	Stack air	Water	Injection	Land	Public treatment	Other offsite	Total releases
1,1,1-trichloroethane	3,181,135	2,304,375	922	540	9,993	23,235	406,753	5,926,953
1,1,2,2-tetrachloroethane	11,082	970	1,600	0	0	0	64,630	78,282
1,1,2-trichloroethane	13,905	15,154	329	0	15	0	483,313	512,716
1,2,4-trichlorobenzene	1,257	3,050	250	2,700	0	255	238,720	246,232
1,2,4-trimethylbenzene	251,275	147,953	695	23,001	1,875	10,553	47,415	482,767
1,2-butylene oxide	3,519	4,758	0	0	0	0	0	8,277
1,2-dibromoethane	751	250	0	240	125	0	25	1,391

[Continued]

★ 436 ★

Toxic Chemical Releases in Texas, by Chemical: 1990
[Continued]

Chemical	Fugitive air	Stack air	Water	Injection	Land	Public treatment	Other offsite	Total releases
1,2-dichlorobenzene	6,115	2,969	250	0	0	1,876	1,085,988	1,097,198
1,2-dichloroethane	158,120	167,680	6,891	221	6,995	278	285,125	625,310
1,2-dichloroethylene	1,958	1,220	1	0	0	0	0	3,179
1,2-dichloropropane	58,230	92,000	1,400	0	0	0	0	151,630
1,3-butadiene	2,180,072	790,732	110,603	0	4,788	750	58,192	3,145,137
1,3-dichloropropylene	39,000	6,500	310	0	0	0	0	45,810
1,4-dichlorobenzene	1,000	5,600	250	250	0	0	9,200	16,300
1,4-dioxane	8,155	1,700	12,000	0	250	0	478	22,583
2,3-dichloropropene	89,020	870	590	37,170	0	0	164,340	291,990
2,4-d	250	5	250	2,100	0	0	0	2,605
2,4-dichlorophenol	250	5	5	20,400	0	0	60,800	81,460
2,4-dimethylphenol	251	251	0	30,300	0	0	12,225	43,027
2,4-dinitrophenol	5	98	460	111,500	3,300	250	3,888	119,501
2,4-dinitrotoluene	3,253	250	250	0	5	0	12,521	16,279
2,6-dinitrotoluene	750	250	250	0	0	0	3,130	4,380
2-ethoxyethanol	16,960	26,929	5	0	0	4,900	261	49,055
2-methoxyethanol	32,683	4,383	0	0	253	4,005	960	42,284
2-nitropropane	5,300	80	0	87,000	0	0	0	92,380
4,4'-isopropylidenediphenol	37,375	43,755	1,422	0	555,870	250	61,490	700,162
4,4'-methylenedianiline	2,439	2,546	850	0	0	0	34,832	40,667
4,6-dinitro-o-cresol	5	30	0	0	0	44,755	204,160	248,950
Acetaldehyde	324,313	1,113,666	5	1,956,298	0	21,856	25,140	3,441,278
Acetamide	12	23	0	0	0	0	0	35
Acetone	6,678,379	5,483,005	40,071	696,165	10,159	617,621	862,135	14,387,535
Acetonitrile	318,725	91,367	5,261	3,753,639	134	6,742	384,878	4,560,746
Acrolein	694	6,906	5	103,059	5	5	108	110,782
Acrylamide	680	262	250	2,814,300	0	4	6,280	2,821,776
Acrylic acid	118,164	22,273	21,010	8,325,000	0	0	122,163	8,608,610
Acrylonitrile	83,748	182,962	260	3,121,951	4	1,504	429,109	3,819,538
Allyl alcohol	3,117	603	0	0	0	6,300	0	10,020
Allyl chloride	11,296	1,165	0	950	0	0	170,600	184,011
Aluminum (fume or dust)	20,036	66,800	615	0	45,080	5	81,001	213,537
Aluminum oxide (fibrous forms)	260	5	15	5	20	0	50,000	50,305
Ammonia	8,128,713	3,555,879	2,311,392	135,729,291	1,958,001	2,173,467	2,881,394	156,738,137
Ammonium nitrate (solution)	500	4,578	120	15,000,000	0	757,000	5,800	15,767,998
Ammonium sulfate (solution)	848	184,600	210,000	0	818,022	2,243,450	250	3,457,170
Aniline	7,061	22,266	310	57,750	5	9	195,275	282,676
Anthracene	798	1,392	19	0	895	250	313,554	316,908
Antimony	1,335	14,905	3,987	0	80,455	145	34,931	135,758
Antimony compounds	3,365	5,648	5	5,850	72,410	206	39,317	126,801
Arsenic	298	596	765	0	9,705	7	4,221	15,592
Arsenic compounds	1,762	46,333	240	22,000	510	750	111,512	183,107
Asbestos (friable)	10	255	5	0	0	0	1,341,145	1,341,415
Barium	250	3,309	22,773	0	27,673	48	32,125	86,178
Barium compounds	22,180	499,658	9,410	4	33,209	0	154,775	719,236
Benzene	2,701,410	1,667,183	6,893	450,265	699,324	113,471	412,193	6,050,739
Benzoyl chloride	3,170	3,750	0	67,501	0	0	0	74,421
Benzoyl peroxide	10	5	0	5	20	255	0	295
Benzyl chloride	6,498	801	15	315	270	168	50	8,117
Biphenyl	23,657	77,792	250	53,209	1,703	750	225,094	382,455
Bis(2-chloro-1-methylethyl) ether	1,400	430	0	0	0	0	0	1,830
Bis(2-chloroethyl) ether	883	30	0	0	0	12,000	2,518	15,431
Bis(2-ethylhexyl) adipate	0	0	0	0	0	1,069	0	1,069
Butyl acrylate	32,322	22,117	5	0	0	250	59,424	114,118
Butyl benzyl phthalate	1,015	3,910	0	250	0	8,055	122,411	135,641
Butyraldehyde	185,338	91,245	5	1,937	350	0	522	279,397
Cadmium compounds	1,950	6,805	0	0	1,000	512	21,437	31,704
Carbaryl	505	1,000	0	0	250	0	255	2,010
Carbon disulfide	15,371	1,253,042	144	0	0	0	231,331	1,499,888

[Continued]

★ 436 ★

Toxic Chemical Releases in Texas, by Chemical: 1990
[Continued]

Chemical	Fugitive air	Stack air	Water	Injection	Land	Public treatment	Other offsite	Total releases
Carbon tetrachloride	101,801	267,375	1,729	0	750	0	525,379	897,034
Carbonyl sulfide	9,720	408,198	0	0	0	0	0	417,918
Catechol	5	0	7,690	0	2,355	88,000	0	98,050
Chlorine	400,079	1,024,466	62,763	765	1,570	9,436	1,371	1,500,450
Chlorine dioxide	1,510	244,900	0	0	0	0	0	246,410
Chloroacetic acid	10	10	0	0	0	0	5	25
Chlorobenzene	110,123	833,267	1,014	4,200	1,000	0	102,121	1,051,725
Chloroethane	65,145	571,419	18	0	0	0	0	636,582
Chloroform	313,986	726,016	14,236	75	771	190,000	56,000	1,301,084
Chloromethane	493,362	1,541,804	46	153,605	250	29	0	2,189,096
Chlorophenols	250	5	250	123,100	0	0	805,900	929,505
Chloroprene	52,592	119,600	750	0	750	0	173,500	347,192
Chlorothalonil	2,585	9,089	9	0	0	5	197,604	209,292
Chromium	16,688	14,790	3,373	5	205,090	2,308	354,687	596,941
Chromium compounds	25,331	146,813	16,179	3,145	1,232,371	22,439	784,816	2,231,094
Cobalt	548	163	250	0	22,001	315	13,005	36,282
Cobalt compounds	676	7,116	1,050	75	6,870	2,450	23,909	42,146
Copper	33,496	307,525	1,407	5	561,828	4,954	170,880	1,080,095
Copper compounds	177,802	86,601	6,239	168,575	30,007	2,384	222,757	694,365
Creosote	38,755	159,647	275	5	20	428	269,805	468,935
Cresol (mixed isomers)	26,529	10,706	543	1,634,529	260	1,000	105,720	1,779,287
Cumene	480,168	239,758	496	8,002	1,546	3,865	2,562	736,397
Cumene hydroperoxide	33,680	5,518	1	25,518	0	750	0	65,467
Cupferron	0	0	34	0	0	0	0	34
Cyanide compounds	3,968	43,556	9,728	2,640,412	8,780	35,539	623,187	3,365,170
Cyclohexane	3,517,109	3,290,615	2,903	228,815	29,904	6,705	35,407	7,111,458
Decabromodiphenyl oxide	2,605	8,650	250	0	10,000	0	6,500	28,005
Di(2-ethylhexyl) phthalate	11,629	4,395	0	250	276	2,315	65,686	84,551
Diaminotoluene (mixed isomers)	10,019	5,420	250	0	0	80,000	562,365	658,054
Dibenzofuran	500	500	10	0	0	0	5	1,015
Dibutyl phthalate	5,371	1,876	0	0	0	9,270	1,900	18,417
Dichlorobenzene (mixed isomers)	1,250	1,250	0	5	20	250	1,500	4,275
Dichloromethane	1,555,294	1,078,536	2,325	270,017	443	4,980	230,498	3,142,093
Dichlorvos	0	250	0	0	0	0	250	500
Diethanolamine	44,298	3,384	37,880	5	3,478	64,742	138,041	291,828
Diethyl phthalate	2,952	2,723	0	0	0	750	250	6,675
Diethyl sulfate	2,417	29	0	0	250	5	101	2,802
Dimethyl phthalate	750	510	1,426	250	55	0	10,119	13,110
Dinitrotoluene (mixed isomers)	2,300	200	0	0	0	690,000	4,800	697,300
Epichlorohydrin	131,892	33,541	0	79,220	30	0	612,590	857,273
Ethyl acrylate	41,444	17,410	20	5	440	2	27,374	86,695
Ethyl chloroformate	1,300	470	0	0	0	0	0	1,770
Ethylbenzene	645,040	1,029,120	5,135	204,574	17,413	28,354	319,526	2,249,162
Ethylene	10,664,352	11,647,913	10	27,500	0	0	287	22,340,062
Ethylene glycol	245,719	334,492	73,965	68,989	290,633	428,218	1,980,426	3,422,442
Ethylene oxide	149,690	153,603	2,615	49,280	24,030	3,368	2,300	384,886
Formaldehyde	290,871	927,357	6,779	3,584,544	7,500	57,004	65,736	4,939,791
Freon 113	1,873,634	641,154	5	198	8,171	5,300	51,333	2,579,795
Glycol ethers	530,524	1,529,682	12,592	1,144	374	305,588	556,093	2,935,997
Hexachloro-1,3-butadiene	31	13	0	0	0	0	4,000	4,044
Hexachlorobenzene	400	5	23	0	0	0	35,981	36,409
Hexachlorocyclopentadiene	5	5	5	5	0	0	1,700	1,720
Hexachloroethane	130	43	0	0	0	0	1,966	2,139
Hydrazine	13,104	758	260	423	0	0	10,413	24,958
Hydrochloric acid	348,138	3,458,482	100,311	366,505	487	1,650,331	7,962,439	13,886,693
Hydrogen cyanide	28,730	271,785	37	1,597,552	48	0	1,657	1,899,809
Hydrogen fluoride	657,943	769,900	260	0	0	2,104	266,025	1,696,232
Hydroquinone	3,607	16	5	202,010	5	125,554	426	331,623
Isobutyraldehyde	117,267	59,904	15	864	1	0	28,000	206,051

[Continued]

★ 436 ★

Toxic Chemical Releases in Texas, by Chemical: 1990
[Continued]

Chemical	Fugitive air	Stack air	Water	Injection	Land	Public treatment	Other offsite	Total releases
Isopropyl alcohol (manufacturing)	53,168	11,754	0	0	0	0	27,387	92,309
Lead	10,221	27,286	2,465	10	2,756,214	1,048	329,970	3,127,214
Lead compounds	18,224	69,028	9,256	551	17,817	2,286	614,757	731,919
Lindane	0	0	0	0	0	0	5	5
M-xylene	77,255	66,343	266	0	576	0	6,518	150,958
Maleic anhydride	30,619	40,600	271	5	265	250	9,218	81,228
Maneb	5	5	5	0	0	0	3,600	3,615
Manganese	11,671	23,207	6,227	5	25,434	1,350	202,371	270,265
Manganese compounds	32,421	14,137	7,030	1,014	151,402	6,814	1,173,429	1,386,247
Mercury	0	0	0	0	0	0	2	2
Methanol	3,250,786	5,422,550	760,491	9,432,604	546,580	10,589,468	4,597,891	34,600,370
Methyl acrylate	37,907	88,434	5	0	0	0	710,911	837,257
Methyl ethyl ketone	3,414,324	2,204,422	13,842	64,115	17,841	2,392	712,318	6,429,254
Methyl iodide	29,168	113	0	5,085	0	0	228	34,594
Methyl isobutyl ketone	275,233	654,660	6,365	1,300	230	270	69,119	1,007,177
Methyl isocyanate	5	0	0	0	0	0	0	5
Methyl methacrylate	25,658	282,479	0	5	20	4,726	602,168	915,056
Methyl tert-butyl ether	338,748	1,358,698	22,575	103,800	686	3,131	381	1,828,019
Methylene bromide	15,900	0	0	0	0	0	0	15,900
Methylenebis(phenylisocyanate)	38,357	1,889	15	5	270	0	190,893	231,429
Molybdenum trioxide	1,150	9,193	13,590	640	2,020	5,300	169,494	201,387
N-butyl alcohol	784,232	2,313,283	2,820	1,129,431	5,306	77,835	686,313	4,999,220
N-dioctyl phthalate	10	0	1,040	0	255	0	0	1,305
Naphthalene	231,715	471,973	19,562	3,192	106,606	26,522	752,378	1,611,948
Nickel	20,804	36,337	2,108	1,305	48,208	6,733	95,852	211,347
Nickel compounds	5,003	2,842	3,040	239,087	234,531	7,728	848,104	1,340,335
Nitric acid	42,706	148,931	25	28,558,842	4,785	8,339,915	1,069,629	38,164,833
Nitrobenzene	5,605	640	583	54,000	0	0	69,053	129,881
O-anisidine	250	5	0	0	0	0	0	255
O-cresol	895	544	0	0	0	0	13,900	15,339
O-toluidine	1,505	754	250	0	0	10,000	4,113	16,622
O-xylene	122,337	78,761	260	0	1,266	3,326	22,282	228,232
P-cresol	1,735	1	77	0	123	0	0	1,936
P-phenylenediamine	540	0	0	0	0	0	0	540
P-xylene	76,347	193,764	265	0	826	0	140	271,342
Pentachlorophenol	251	254	0	0	0	5	0	510
Phenol	801,892	95,711	137,954	3,623,617	19,093	311,181	1,193,279	6,182,727
Phosgene	553	684	0	0	0	0	970	2,207
Phosphoric acid	13,695	38,906	1,495	30	113,100	231,812	399,464	798,502
Phosphorus (yellow or white)	6	0	0	0	0	0	41	47
Phthalic anhydride	54,169	68,929	0	0	250	5	752,907	876,260
Picric acid	0	0	0	1,234,930	0	0	0	1,234,930
Polychlorinated biphenyls (PCBs)	0	0	0	0	0	0	300,030	300,030
Propionaldehyde	247,259	56,566	487	2,394	0	0	1,457	308,163
Propoxur	0	0	0	0	0	0	250	250
Propylene	5,985,348	5,993,682	10	5	25	0	930,000	12,909,070
Propylene oxide	246,140	223,159	4,015	120,005	3,625	570	7,850	605,364
Propyleneimine	2	0	0	0	0	0	0	2
Pyridine	11,120	7,365	15	299,605	20	11,000	1,780	330,905
Quinoline	250	250	0	0	0	0	0	500
Quinone	1	1	3	0	0	0	0	5
Sec-butyl alcohol	11,934	31,569	750	0	0	5	28,103	72,361
Selenium	0	0	186	0	0	0	0	186
Selenium compounds	750	14,205	0	5,000	10	0	2,150	22,115
Silver	250	0	0	5	5	3	14	277
Silver compounds	1,000	250	490	250	630	1	181	2,802
Sodium hydroxide (solution)	0	0	0	0	0	5	5	10
Styrene	951,646	2,718,088	30,625	29,010	30,675	99,153	778,242	4,637,439
Styrene oxide	0	5	0	0	0	0	0	5

[Continued]

★ 436 ★

Toxic Chemical Releases in Texas, by Chemical: 1990

[Continued]

Chemical	Fugitive air	Stack air	Water	Injection	Land	Public treatment	Other offsite	Total releases
Sulfuric acid	187,933	472,615	142,123	8,575,553	9,372	7,129,800	18,752,001	35,269,397
Tert-butyl alcohol	1,085,260	215,842	40	909,061	842	1,397,000	391,674	3,999,719
Tetrachloroethylene	213,235	108,057	321	0	0	500	365,292	687,405
Thallium	0	250	5	0	0	0	916	1,171
Thallium compounds	5	250	0	0	255	5	0	515
Thiourea	255	10	0	4,800	5	750	150	5,970
Titanium tetrachloride	7,904	755	0	0	0	5	454,432	463,096
Toluene	4,522,923	4,601,612	5,040	48,053	111,321	54,710	4,002,101	13,345,760
Toluenediisocyanate (mixed isomers)	1,964	1,684	20	5	20	0	19,205	22,898
Toluene-2,4-diisocyanate	505	1,000	0	0	0	0	9,625	11,130
Toluene-2,6-diisocyanate	500	500	0	0	0	0	250	1,250
Trade secret	0	0	530	0	0	0	9,500	10,030
Trichloroethylene	1,152,247	420,395	8,788	0	750	281	118,216	1,700,677
Trifluralin	250	250	0	0	0	0	0	500
Urethane	250	250	0	5	20	750	0	1,275
Vanadium (fume or dust)	5	750	0	0	0	0	28,076	28,831
Vinyl acetate	406,538	3,029,133	553	1,360,901	1,034	2,389	1,638,009	6,438,557
Vinyl chloride	21,570	84,008	273	0	0	0	92,958	198,809
Vinylidene chloride	16,050	2,400	29	0	0	0	0	18,479
Xylene (mixed isomers)	2,331,678	5,727,443	4,308	39,536	148,390	48,734	1,146,064	9,446,153
Zinc (fume or dust)	51,262	911	11,376	0	4,024	31	89,084	156,688
Zinc compounds	96,881	208,951	52,238	2,394	132,250	14,894	5,068,121	5,575,729

Source: U.S. Environmental Protection Agency. "Toxic Chemical Releases, 1990." In *National Economic, Social, and Environmental Data Bank* [CD-ROM]. Prepared by U.S. Department of Commerce, Economics and Statistics Administration. Washington, DC: U.S. Department of Commerce, National Economic, Social, and Environmental Data Bank, Economics and Statistics Administration, Office of Business Analysis, February 1995.

★ 437 ★

Chemicals

Toxic Chemical Releases in Utah, by Chemical: 1990

Figures indicate pounds released by chemical and by type of emission per year.

Chemical	Fugitive air	Stack air	Water	Injection	Land	Public treatment	Other offsite	Total releases
1,1,1-trichloroethane	1,487,593	2,039,901	3	0	4,556	5	86,379	3,618,437
1,2,4-trimethylbenzene	52,242	5,471	0	0	0	91	1,342	59,146
1,2-dibromoethane	250	0	0	0	0	0	0	250
1,2-dichloroethane	1,100	0	0	0	0	0	0	1,100
1,4-dioxane	19,850	39,009	0	0	0	0	597	59,456
Acetone	178,024	72,219	5	5	20	7,280	22,269	279,822
Aluminum (fume or dust)	250	5	0	0	755	0	1,200	2,210
Ammonia	8,372	74,180	271,464	0	44,572	132,452	360	531,400
Ammonium nitrate (solution)	0	0	250	0	722,718	530,473	370,000	1,623,441
Ammonium sulfate (solution)	0	0	0	0	56,728	250	42,008	98,986
Anthracene	225	4	0	0	0	56	48	333
Arsenic compounds	3,205	17,005	750	0	1,300,005	0	16,000,250	17,321,215
Asbestos (friable)	0	0	0	0	0	0	47,768	47,768
Barium	0	0	0	0	58,869	0	0	58,869
Barium compounds	15	5,284	250	0	950,000	5	5,055	960,609
Benzene	143,248	51,856	0	0	0	12,308	771	208,183
Biphenyl	36	27	0	0	0	0	15	78

[Continued]

★ 437 ★

Toxic Chemical Releases in Utah, by Chemical: 1990

[Continued]

Chemical	Fugitive air	Stack air	Water	Injection	Land	Public treatment	Other offsite	Total releases
Cadmium	0	181	0	0	0	0	592	773
Cadmium compounds	250	750	250	0	67,000	0	500,000	568,250
Chlorine	152,423	88,067,770	0	0	0	3,100	0	88,223,293
Chromium	505	459	0	0	238,546	1	8,465	247,976
Chromium compounds	50,438	1,069	250	0	87,378	0	6,150	145,285
Cobalt compounds	11	77	0	0	400	0	2	490
Copper	581	706	30	0	2,685	505	24,261	28,768
Copper compounds	11,266	57,300	1,400	0	3,300,703	255	36,053,807	39,424,731
Creosote	296	1,480	0	0	0	0	0	1,776
Cresol (mixed isomers)	816	2,221	250	0	5	0	35	3,327
Cumene	100	164	0	0	0	0	0	264
Cyclohexane	45,444	40,343	0	0	0	3,500	1,981	91,268
Di(2-ethylhexyl) phthalate	0	8,307	0	0	0	0	14,000	22,307
Dibenzofuran	26	0	0	0	0	0	0	26
Dichloromethane	41,183	1,419,192	0	0	139	0	22,589	1,483,103
Diethanolamine	0	0	0	0	0	13,610	0	13,610
Ethylbenzene	19,281	3,537	0	0	0	521	347	23,686
Ethylene	35,651	750	0	0	0	0	0	36,401
Ethylene glycol	1,480	10	0	0	4,392	21,285	0	27,167
Ethylene oxide	2,698	3,966	0	0	0	16,029	0	22,693
Formaldehyde	250	250	0	5	20	0	0	525
Freon 113	322,972	435,762	3	0	4,571	3	13,132	776,443
Glycol ethers	8,912	13,904	0	0	250	18,115	9,644	50,825
Hydrochloric acid	1,708,372	6,856,907	0	5	505	20,859	260	8,586,908
Hydrogen cyanide	0	68,464	0	0	0	0	0	68,464
Hydrogen fluoride	8,573	24,115	0	0	0	64	21,942	54,694
Hydroquinone	0	0	0	0	0	250	0	250
Lead	0	8,612	0	0	73	250	43,312	52,247
Lead compounds	9,354	32,760	255	0	1,200,743	755	29,000,270	30,244,137
M-xylene	3,973	750	0	0	0	750	5	5,478
Manganese	4,196	5	0	0	2,426,125	0	38	2,430,364
Manganese compounds	450	500	755	0	200	2	254	2,161
Methanol	104,400	98,787	70	5	20	2,527	3,565	209,374
Methyl ethyl ketone	44,386	39,306	0	0	0	0	13,855	97,547
Methyl isobutyl ketone	29,500	82,102	0	5	275	0	1,015	112,897
Methylenebis(phenylisocyanate)	250	0	0	0	0	0	0	250
Molybdenum trioxide	291	1,254	0	0	7,735	12	114	9,406
N-butyl alcohol	250	250	0	5	20	0	0	525
Naphthalene	49,442	7,606	0	0	0	50	1,824	58,922
Nickel	255	5	0	0	750	9	10	1,029
Nickel compounds	3,299	211	0	0	1,245	2	10	4,767
Nitric acid	3,242	126,487	0	0	7,790	13,589	73,052	224,160
Nitroglycerin	50	0	0	0	0	84	3	137
O-xylene	2,410	573	0	0	0	250	5	3,238
P-xylene	1,491	250	0	0	0	250	5	1,996
Phenol	4,412	20,049	146	0	0	0	19	24,626
Phosphoric acid	1,317	869	0	0	20	25,654	49,000	76,860
Propylene	50,223	1,400	0	0	0	0	0	51,623
Quinoline	72	0	0	0	0	0	0	72
Selenium compounds	750	6,400	250	0	120,005	0	5,400	132,805
Silver	5	85	0	0	0	0	0	90
Silver compounds	250	1,000	250	0	6,100	0	50,500	58,100

[Continued]

★ 437 ★

Toxic Chemical Releases in Utah, by Chemical: 1990
[Continued]

Chemical	Fugitive air	Stack air	Water	Injection	Land	Public treatment	Other offsite	Total releases
Styrene	49,650	0	0	0	0	0	0	49,650
Sulfuric acid	24,562	531,943	15	5	100,035	43,068	64,407	764,035
Tetrachloroethylene	10,235	0	0	0	0	0	0	10,235
Thiourea	0	0	0	0	250	0	0	250
Toluene	303,791	241,744	0	5	20	9,111	6,788	561,459
Xylene (mixed isomers)	6,675,630	187,198	0	5	20	18,095	15,525	6,896,473
Zinc (fume or dust)	0	36,653	0	0	0	0	119,718	156,371
Zinc compounds	2,577	11,545	2,089	0	2,000,458	257	5,395,656	7,412,582

Source: U.S. Environmental Protection Agency. "Toxic Chemical Releases, 1990." In *National Economic, Social, and Environmental Data Bank* [CD-ROM]. Prepared by U.S. Department of Commerce, Economics and Statistics Administration. Washington, DC: U.S. Department of Commerce, National Economic, Social, and Environmental Data Bank, Economics and Statistics Administration, Office of Business Analysis, February 1995.

★ 438 ★

Chemicals

Toxic Chemical Releases in Vermont, by Chemical: 1990

Figures indicate pounds released by chemical and by type of emission per year.

Chemical	Fugitive air	Stack air	Water	Injection	Land	Public treatment	Other offsite	Total releases
1,1,1-trichloroethane	85,898	241,343	0	0	0	5	42,320	369,566
Acetone	31,950	41,875	15	5	20	5	12,600	86,470
Aluminum (fume or dust)	5	250	0	0	0	250	5	510
Ammonia	0	3,900	70,000	0	0	0	187	74,087
Antimony	3	12	0	0	0	12	31	58
Barium	0	250	0	0	0	250	4,934	5,434
Barium compounds	425	1,280	0	0	0	5	8,567	10,277
Chlorine	280	0	0	0	0	0	0	280
Chromium	0	315	0	0	50	58	1,913	2,336
Chromium compounds	5	250	0	0	0	250	752	1,257
Copper	0	250	0	0	5	0	1,208	1,463
Copper compounds	0	0	0	0	0	250	4,400	4,650
Di(2-ethylhexyl) phthalate	250	0	0	0	0	250	1,000	1,500
Ethylene glycol	5	2,025	20	0	0	5	0	2,055
Formaldehyde	0	1,135	0	0	0	0	0	1,135
Freon 113	9,200	21,501	0	0	0	12	370	31,083
Glycol ethers	750	2,500	0	0	0	250	250	3,750
Hydrochloric acid	785	5,426	0	0	0	0	4,284	10,495
Hydrogen fluoride	254	2,508	0	0	0	0	8,100	10,862
Lead	16	186	0	0	0	99	188	489
Lead compounds	182	1,503	0	0	0	2	1,896	3,583
Manganese compounds	1	1	0	0	0	0	10,001	10,003
Mercury compounds	1	1	0	0	0	0	13	15
Methanol	13,511	33,775	0	0	0	1,305	1,528	50,119
Methyl ethyl ketone	8,450	17,900	0	0	0	250	27,116	53,716
Methyl isobutyl ketone	26,225	61,357	0	0	0	0	1,428	89,010

[Continued]

★ 438 ★

Toxic Chemical Releases in Vermont, by Chemical: 1990
[Continued]

Chemical	Fugitive air	Stack air	Water	Injection	Land	Public treatment	Other offsite	Total releases
N-butyl alcohol	990	3,259	0	0	43,418	250	250	48,167
Nickel	0	0	0	0	0	65	38	103
Nitric acid	761	3,011	21,123	0	0	10	19,882	44,787
Phenol	5	5	0	0	0	0	0	10
Phosphoric acid	5	518	0	0	0	36,510	7,886	44,919
Silver compounds	1	0	0	0	0	0	2	3
Styrene	5,400	0	0	0	0	0	0	5,400
Sulfuric acid	544	34,668	0	0	545	2,610	17,616	55,983
Tetrachloroethylene	0	4,600	0	0	0	0	0	4,600
Toluene	51,688	122,532	0	0	0	255	16,890	191,365
Trichloroethylene	10	3,350	0	0	0	0	2,802	6,162
Xylene (mixed isomers)	12,880	19,186	0	0	0	250	2,633	34,949
Zinc (fume or dust)	0	250	0	0	0	0	327	577
Zinc compounds	0	0	0	0	0	0	750	750

Source: U.S. Environmental Protection Agency. "Toxic Chemical Releases, 1990." In *National Economic, Social, and Environmental Data Bank* [CD-ROM]. Prepared by U.S. Department of Commerce, Economics and Statistics Administration. Washington, DC: U.S. Department of Commerce, National Economic, Social, and Environmental Data Bank, Economics and Statistics Administration, Office of Business Analysis, February 1995.

★ 439 ★

Chemicals

Toxic Chemical Releases in Virgin Islands, by Chemical: 1990

Figures indicate pounds released by chemical and by type of emission per year.

Chemical	Fugitive air	Stack air	Water	Injection	Land	Public treatment	Other offsite	Total releases
1,1,1-trichloroethane	8,750	0	181	0	0	0	0	8,931
1,2,4-trimethylbenzene	13,700	432	250	0	250	0	0	14,632
1,3-butadiene	7,250	0	0	0	0	0	0	7,250
Ammonia	4,680	0	193,000	0	19,300	0	0	216,980
Anthracene	2,520	4	181	0	2	0	0	2,707
Benzene	60,500	100,000	472	0	5,680	0	0	166,652
Carbon tetrachloride	2,700	0	181	0	0	0	0	2,881
Cobalt compounds	5	0	0	0	1,180	0	0	1,185
Cumene	166	0	0	0	0	0	0	166
Cyclohexane	8,420	22,700	250	0	250	0	0	31,620
Ethylbenzene	57,100	20,900	181	0	19,000	0	0	97,181
Ethylene	58,000	0	0	0	0	0	0	58,000
Hydrochloric acid	250	0	0	0	0	0	0	250
Lead compounds	0	0	282	0	4,680	0	13,200	18,162
Methanol	0	694	0	0	0	0	0	694
Molybdenum trioxide	238	0	0	0	0	0	0	238
Naphthalene	2,580	622	181	0	992	0	0	4,375
Nickel compounds	54	0	86	0	9,900	0	0	10,040

[Continued]

★ 439 ★

Toxic Chemical Releases in Virgin Islands, by Chemical: 1990
[Continued]

Chemical	Fugitive air	Stack air	Water	Injection	Land	Public treatment	Other offsite	Total releases
P-xylene	165,000	88,500	0	0	0	0	0	253,500
Propylene	116,000	0	0	0	0	0	0	116,000
Toluene	172,000	71,900	256	0	9,870	0	0	254,026
Xylene (mixed isomers)	152,000	74,800	250	0	4,120	0	0	231,170

Source: U.S. Environmental Protection Agency. "Toxic Chemical Releases, 1990." In *National Economic, Social, and Environmental Data Bank* [CD-ROM]. Prepared by U.S. Department of Commerce, Economics and Statistics Administration. Washington, DC: U.S. Department of Commerce, National Economic, Social, and Environmental Data Bank, Economics and Statistics Administration, Office of Business Analysis, February 1995.

★ 440 ★

Chemicals

Toxic Chemical Releases in Virginia, by Chemical: 1990

Figures indicate pounds released by chemical and by type of emission per year.

Chemical	Fugitive air	Stack air	Water	Injection	Land	Public treatment	Other offsite	Total releases
1,1,1-trichloroethane	941,271	882,240	5	0	0	72	484,229	2,307,817
1,2,4-trichlorobenzene	9,145	59,506	250	0	0	0	516	69,417
1,2,4-trimethylbenzene	66,753	44,184	0	0	0	0	5,404	116,341
1,2-dichloropropane	71,000	62,000	73	0	0	0	0	133,073
1,3-butadiene	68	0	0	0	0	0	0	68
2,4-dinitrotoluene	0	0	1,030	0	0	0	49	1,079
2-ethoxyethanol	3,590	29,073	0	0	0	0	0	32,663
Acetaldehyde	10,300	90,185	0	0	0	5	0	100,490
Acetone	7,101,629	8,415,611	8,730	0	14,640	2,122,862	144,333	17,807,805
Acetonitrile	61,000	0	204	0	0	0	0	61,204
Acrylamide	34,239	250	0	0	0	750	2,421	37,660
Acrylic acid	59,124	21,949	191	0	0	5,880	1,910	89,054
Acrylonitrile	32,668	78,990	0	0	5	0	591	112,254
Allyl chloride	378	0	0	0	0	0	0	378
Aluminum (fume or dust)	3,695	242	23	0	0	0	0	3,960
Aluminum oxide (fibrous forms)	250	0	0	0	0	0	0	250
Ammonia	391,900	1,457,253	1,688,972	0	4,905	3,520,671	21,596	7,085,297
Ammonium nitrate (solution)	0	190	280,821	0	0	861,233	0	1,142,244
Ammonium sulfate (solution)	18	0	0	0	0	0	0	18
Antimony compounds	707	5,815	0	809	0	0	22,180	29,511
Arsenic	0	0	50	0	0	0	9,600	9,650
Arsenic compounds	41	41	42	5	20	0	9,440	9,589
Asbestos (friable)	31	0	0	0	0	0	11,970	12,001
Barium	250	0	0	0	0	5	0	255
Barium compounds	6,549	7,919	250	0	1,400,250	8,357	64,197	1,487,522
Benzene	295,523	300,024	242	0	0	1,236	157	597,182
Benzoyl peroxide	0	0	0	0	0	0	1,637	1,637
Biphenyl	50,422	17,152	1,355	0	0	43,478	2,150	114,557
Bis(2-ethylhexyl) adipate	1	0	0	0	0	0	0	1
Butyl acrylate	203	2	0	0	0	0	44	249
Butyl benzyl phthalate	2,506	12,033	0	0	0	5	3,866	18,410

[Continued]

★ 440 ★

Toxic Chemical Releases in Virginia, by Chemical: 1990
[Continued]

Chemical	Fugitive air	Stack air	Water	Injection	Land	Public treatment	Other offsite	Total releases
Butyraldehyde	204	14	5	0	0	5	20	248
C.I. basic green 4	0	5	0	0	0	0	250	255
Cadmium	672	35	1	0	0	10	760	1,478
Cadmium compounds	5	15	0	0	0	0	250	270
Carbaryl	5	250	0	0	0	0	750	1,005
Carbon disulfide	11,000	57,000	0	0	0	0	751	68,751
Carbon tetrachloride	0	9,000	0	0	0	0	18,000	27,000
Catechol	0	0	5,800	0	250	21,000	480	27,530
Chlorine	56,352	97,227	44,779	5	5	14,874	250	213,492
Chlorine dioxide	865	127,900	0	0	0	0	0	128,765
Chloroacetic acid	17,700	80	0	0	0	0	0	17,780
Chlorobenzene	413	0	0	0	0	0	1,460	1,873
Chloroethane	342,500	250	0	0	0	5	0	342,755
Chloroform	250,750	448,000	11,280	0	380	0	250	710,660
Chloromethane	16,940	228,300	0	0	0	20	0	245,260
Chromium	2,080	625	213	0	1,758	144	136,699	141,519
Chromium compounds	587	606	837	5	83	260	14,070	16,448
Cobalt	5	5	0	0	0	5	103,000	103,015
Cobalt compounds	7	202	143	0	18	10	486	866
Copper	11,538	1,848	246	0	8,791	15,368	60,272	98,063
Copper compounds	15,249	16,278	1,034	10	290	5,560	74,797	113,218
Creosote	14,355	27,695	2,400	0	712	4	121,703	166,869
Cresol (mixed isomers)	250	3,200	0	0	0	0	7,600	11,050
Cumene	750	0	0	0	0	0	0	750
Cyanide compounds	250	147	4	0	0	13	1,721	2,135
Cyclohexane	21,800	93,020	50	0	0	0	500	115,370
Decabromodiphenyl oxide	628	10	0	5	1,398	0	8,222	10,263
Di(2-ethylhexyl) phthalate	17,050	98,474	0	0	0	251	2,269	118,044
Dibutyl phthalate	10	1	204	0	9	0	7,579	7,803
Dichloromethane	709,346	988,313	1	0	0	245	166,566	1,864,471
Diethanolamine	5	0	0	0	0	0	0	5
Diethyl phthalate	250	0	11	0	0	250	250	761
Dimethyl phthalate	27,000	217,000	0	0	0	0	0	244,000
Dimethyl sulfate	2,060	7	0	0	0	0	0	2,067
Ethyl acrylate	1,651	306	0	0	0	250	309	2,516
Ethylbenzene	31,876	74,891	877	0	0	155	69,698	177,497
Ethylene	18,900	99,200	0	0	0	0	0	118,100
Ethylene glycol	117,280	625,644	7,928	0	831	2,429,935	522,810	3,704,428
Ethylene oxide	76,200	9,011	0	0	0	49,480	0	134,691
Formaldehyde	105,122	497,581	5,000	0	3,200	17,300	773	628,976
Freon 113	508,954	564,130	0	0	0	180	37,946	1,111,210
Glycol ethers	209,724	761,827	5	0	250	52,954	66,969	1,091,729
Hydrazine	1,040	220	0	0	0	0	0	1,260
Hydrochloric acid	299,087	3,373,429	5	0	5	2,365	73,346	3,748,237
Hydrogen fluoride	10	1,225	0	0	0	5	4,800	6,040
Isobutyraldehyde	12,200	5	0	0	0	5	0	12,210
Isopropyl alcohol (manufacturing)	2,883	138,634	0	0	0	0	4,280	145,797
Lead	18,696	2,019	4	0	0	1,099	9,148	30,966
Lead compounds	1,054	1,740	592	0	2	360	160,853	164,601
Maleic anhydride	400	251	5	0	0	5	5	666
Manganese	16,149	4,037	20	0	152,159	2,078	135,955	310,398
Manganese compounds	1,477	900	764	0	19	10	1,553	4,723

[Continued]

★ 440 ★

Toxic Chemical Releases in Virginia, by Chemical: 1990
[Continued]

Chemical	Fugitive air	Stack air	Water	Injection	Land	Public treatment	Other offsite	Total releases
Methanol	1,485,364	13,925,136	72,110	0	9,000	7,332,223	251,316	23,075,149
Methyl acrylate	3,772	8,342	0	0	0	250	294	12,658
Methyl ethyl ketone	3,191,389	4,025,146	77	0	0	1,765	185,455	7,403,832
Methyl isobutyl ketone	170,247	1,228,779	0	0	0	250	22,131	1,421,407
Methyl methacrylate	9,234	3,396	0	0	0	290	22,487	35,407
Methyl tert-butyl ether	6,700	15,000	0	0	0	0	0	21,700
Methylenebis(phenylisocyanate)	30,692	250	0	0	0	0	11,946	42,888
N-butyl alcohol	358,057	921,151	0	0	0	6,620	38,617	1,324,445
N-dioctyl phthalate	255	250	0	0	0	0	15,150	15,655
Naphthalene	11,769	24,718	0	0	0	0	14,438	50,925
Nickel	953	299	10	0	1,184	1,028	187,849	191,323
Nickel compounds	832	277	325	0	44	799	1,474	3,751
Nitric acid	5,054	12,608	1,445	0	690	20,998	75,699	116,494
Nitroglycerin	0	15,169	0	0	0	0	0	15,169
P-phenylenediamine	0	0	0	0	0	0	40,800	40,800
Phenol	126,787	50,847	242	0	64,824	4,504	53,152	300,356
Phosphoric acid	14,249	237,996	20	5	60	187,371	300	440,001
Phthalic anhydride	681	1,596	5	0	0	5	2,667	4,954
Propoxur	0	0	0	0	0	5	250	255
Propylene	58,670	251,305	0	0	0	0	0	309,975
Propylene oxide	630	5	0	0	0	0	0	635
Propyleneimine	1	1	0	0	0	0	0	2
Pyridine	790	70	0	0	0	50	2,000	2,910
Silver	0	0	0	0	0	7	14	21
Styrene	182,121	200,209	95	0	1	5	1,354,477	1,736,908
Sulfuric acid	7,754	844,889	2,652	10	540	162,380	2,201,445	3,219,670
Tert-butyl alcohol	47,000	0	0	0	120	167,000	25,000	239,120
Tetrachloroethylene	32,533	74,618	0	0	0	0	32,243	139,394
Toluene	1,594,692	7,590,026	329	5	86,275	28,049	384,150	9,683,526
Toluenediisocyanate (mixed isomers)	505	250	0	0	0	0	17,252	18,007
Toluene-2,4-diisocyanate	0	1	0	0	0	0	0	1
Trichloroethylene	81,297	384,466	0	0	0	0	190,724	656,487
Vanadium (fume or dust)	5	5	0	0	0	0	250	260
Vinyl acetate	4,747	260	0	0	0	20	0	5,027
Vinylidene chloride	67	1,645	0	0	0	0	0	1,712
Xylene (mixed isomers)	1,607,531	4,225,272	855	0	0	7,942	433,411	6,275,011
Zinc (fume or dust)	95,332	8,907	4,331	0	18,000	581	174,828	301,979
Zinc compounds	3,843	6,296	10,029	0	141,732	3,958	497,627	663,485

Source: U.S. Environmental Protection Agency. "Toxic Chemical Releases, 1990." In *National Economic, Social, and Environmental Data Bank* [CD-ROM]. Prepared by U.S. Department of Commerce, Economics and Statistics Administration. Washington, DC: U.S. Department of Commerce, National Economic, Social, and Environmental Data Bank, Economics and Statistics Administration, Office of Business Analysis, February 1995.

★ 441 ★

Chemicals

Toxic Chemical Releases in Washington, by Chemical: 1990

Figures indicate pounds released by chemical and by type of emission per year.

Chemical	Fugitive air	Stack air	Water	Injection	Land	Public treatment	Other offsite	Total releases
1,1,1-trichloroethane	812,582	588,508	265	0	0	765	136,890	1,539,010
1,2,4-trichlorobenzene	0	0	0	0	0	0	21,650	21,650
1,2,4-trimethylbenzene	26,982	2,030	271	0	510	5	10	29,808
1,2-dichloroethane	2,700	11,000	0	0	0	0	1,700	15,400
1,3-butadiene	11,930	52,027	0	0	0	0	0	63,957
1,4-dioxane	6,000	1,500	0	0	0	0	4,010	11,510
2,4-dimethylphenol	250	250	0	0	0	0	750	1,250
2-ethoxyethanol	1,600	40,000	0	0	0	0	250	41,850
2-methoxyethanol	2,075	7,965	0	0	0	5	260	10,305
Acetaldehyde	1,800	250	250	0	0	0	10	2,310
Acetone	1,174,551	1,095,128	57,859	5	3,220	3,887	249,769	2,584,419
Acrylamide	23	1	0	0	0	105	70	199
Acrylic acid	13	254	250	0	0	0	0	517
Aluminum (fume or dust)	66	30	0	0	32	0	3,600	3,728
Aluminum oxide (fibrous forms)	3	264	0	0	0	0	24,623	24,890
Ammonia	1,230,892	1,742,349	3,310,730	0	86,709	170,504	147,310	6,688,494
Ammonium nitrate (solution)	5	250	7,302	0	88,636	8,440	0	104,633
Ammonium sulfate (solution)	0	0	0	0	0	332,980	40	333,020
Anthracene	14	5,600	261	0	1,200	0	250	7,325
Antimony compounds	10	35	11,045	0	5,120	5	250	16,465
Arsenic	251	251	1	0	5	1	350	859
Arsenic compounds	10	255	303	0	5	0	4,486	5,059
Asbestos (friable)	260	64	5	5	20	0	20,078	20,432
Barium	250	250	0	0	0	0	0	500
Barium compounds	2	48,009	190	0	9,850	0	99,450	157,501
Benzene	79,356	208,331	516	0	900	5	455	289,563
Biphenyl	7,300	7,500	0	0	0	0	180	14,980
Cadmium	250	250	0	0	0	0	0	500
Cadmium compounds	255	302	250	0	0	5	23,939	24,751
Carbon disulfide	5	5	0	0	0	0	0	10
Catechol	10	10	8,868	0	9,150	0	3,950	21,988
Chlorine	38,692	661,012	47,323	5	44,315	40,663	250	832,260
Chlorine dioxide	6,025	268,144	10	5	10	5	0	274,199
Chloroform	1,016,553	1,005,949	347,276	0	11,655	0	260	2,381,693
Chromium	5,042	1,837	3,730	0	22,000	290	53,225	86,124
Chromium compounds	2,945	5,425	42,577	0	17,810	1,015	146,262	216,034
Cobalt compounds	0	8	180	0	0	0	1,900	2,088
Copper	782	2,089	25	0	23	538	89,289	92,746
Copper compounds	521	725	595	5	275	722	374,911	377,754
Creosote	28,052	90,466	252	0	759	44	44,126	163,699
Cresol (mixed isomers)	529	269	261	0	0	0	2,400	3,459
Cumene	500	3,605	21	0	5	5	5	4,141
Cyclohexane	28,000	5,275	516	0	15	5	5	33,816
Di(2-ethylhexyl) phthalate	605	406	0	0	0	0	580	1,591
Dichloromethane	686,070	384,200	2,150	0	750	43	25,346	1,098,559
Diethanolamine	13,900	0	0	0	0	20	0	13,920
Dimethyl phthalate	5	0	0	0	0	0	0	5
Ethylbenzene	21,203	12,350	271	0	500	5	240	34,569
Ethylene	26,836	27,850	0	0	0	0	0	54,686
Ethylene glycol	18,375	5,470	850	0	0	109,657	24,268	158,620
Formaldehyde	12,324	97,223	145,632	0	505	2,530	328	258,542

[Continued]

★ 441 ★

Toxic Chemical Releases in Washington, by Chemical: 1990
[Continued]

Chemical	Fugitive air	Stack air	Water	Injection	Land	Public treatment	Other offsite	Total releases
Freon 113	976,965	170,786	270	0	0	20	28,288	1,176,329
Glycol ethers	198,462	779,864	20	0	129	7,338	85,593	1,071,406
Hydrochloric acid	17,940	554,438	2,362	0	911	13,100	35,935	624,686
Hydrogen fluoride	523,659	991,838	5	0	0	230	65,150	1,580,882
Isopropyl alcohol (manufacturing)	13,604	65	0	0	32,900	0	8,500	55,069
Lead	1,811	1,838	30	5	20	5	280	3,989
Lead compounds	2,378	2,943	397	0	7,180	88	90,392	103,378
Manganese	6,534	3,924	511	0	0	793	182,645	194,407
Manganese compounds	4,719	7,278	4,165	0	13,505	5	7,164	36,836
Mercury	1,250	500	250	0	0	0	4,050	6,050
Methanol	767,640	1,276,728	363,220	0	130,755	18,575	108,885	2,665,803
Methyl ethyl ketone	1,187,611	1,322,814	1,020	0	5	2,661	442,663	2,956,774
Methyl isobutyl ketone	47,326	140,523	15	0	5	260	22,867	210,996
Methyl tert-butyl ether	750	250	0	0	0	0	0	1,000
Methylenebis(phenylisocyanate)	2,646	260	0	0	250	0	7,587	10,743
Molybdenum trioxide	10	10	255	0	0	0	6,392	6,667
N-butyl alcohol	157,865	537,538	2,015	0	5	10	21,269	718,702
Naphthalene	2,320	755	511	0	250	5	1,010	4,851
Nickel	3,726	1,265	5	0	0	294	14,464	19,754
Nickel compounds	250	0	540	0	3,200	0	755	4,745
Nitric acid	7,677	58,202	15	0	12	68,050	387,567	521,523
Pentachlorophenol	91	95	501	0	255	6	2,333	3,281
Phenol	23,560	11,535	2,285	0	7,000	2,036	6,120	52,536
Phosphoric acid	1,275	2,470	30	0	1,705	128,774	9,130	143,384
Polychlorinated biphenyls (PCBs)	0	0	0	0	0	0	22,417	22,417
Propylene	163,230	95,010	0	0	0	0	0	258,240
Selenium	250	250	0	0	0	0	0	500
Silver	250	250	0	0	0	0	0	500
Styrene	381,482	556,783	500	0	250	0	5,774	944,789
Sulfuric acid	6,366	540,481	8,138,320	0	130,350	376,756	221,210	9,413,483
Tetrachloroethylene	9,205	25,300	0	0	0	0	11,866	46,371
Thallium	250	250	0	0	0	0	0	500
Thiourea	5	5	0	0	0	750	0	760
Toluene	976,827	1,743,277	826	0	4,645	1,416	201,820	2,928,811
Toluenediisocyanate (mixed isomers)	10	216	0	0	0	0	0	226
Trichloroethylene	308,822	536,927	15	0	0	5	83,114	928,883
Xylene (mixed isomers)	606,586	799,749	546	5	10,145	1,807	90,216	1,509,054
Zinc (fume or dust)	12,106	12,376	1	0	6	41	1,915	26,445
Zinc compounds	7,904	15,029	5,774	0	5	1,550	54,169	84,431

Source: U.S. Environmental Protection Agency. "Toxic Chemical Releases, 1990." In *National Economic, Social, and Environmental Data Bank* [CD-ROM]. Prepared by U.S. Department of Commerce, Economics and Statistics Administration. Washington, DC: U.S. Department of Commerce, National Economic, Social, and Environmental Data Bank, Economics and Statistics Administration, Office of Business Analysis, February 1995.

★ 442 ★

Chemicals

Toxic Chemical Releases in West Virginia, by Chemical: 1990

Figures indicate pounds released by chemical and by type of emission per year.

Chemical	Fugitive air	Stack air	Water	Injection	Land	Public treatment	Other offsite	Total releases
1,1,1-trichloroethane	528,553	44,200	2,467	0	0	10	750	575,980
1,2,4-trichlorobenzene	2,300	250	3,600	0	0	0	9,800	15,950
1,2,4-trimethylbenzene	2,304	4,080	250	0	250	0	0	6,884
1,2-dichlorobenzene	16,603	29,511	6,765	0	0	0	13,503	66,382
1,2-dichloroethane	24,303	1,080,608	0	0	0	0	35,362	1,140,273
1,3-butadiene	158,897	77,270	0	0	23	0	16	236,206
1,3-dichlorobenzene	250	2,900	750	0	0	0	250	4,150
1,4-dichlorobenzene	11,000	335,000	3,300	0	0	0	9,900	359,200
1,4-dioxane	172	10,620	0	0	0	0	0	10,792
2,4-dinitrotoluene	1,710	3	162	0	0	0	0	1,875
2,6-dinitrotoluene	428	1	126	0	0	0	0	555
2-ethoxyethanol	10,020	802	986	0	0	0	0	11,808
2-methoxyethanol	18,515	646	9,719	0	0	48	0	28,928
4,4'-methylenedianiline	9,628	255	33	0	1	750	15	10,682
Acetaldehyde	109,588	78,003	39	0	0	24	0	187,654
Acetone	2,588,246	1,259,610	15,633	0	18,706	483,709	128,690	4,494,594
Acetonitrile	1,794	168	107	0	0	0	0	2,069
Acrylamide	0	0	0	0	0	30,528	0	30,528
Acrylic acid	6,098	1,055	0	0	0	10,730	0	17,883
Acrylonitrile	225,104	732,591	1,991	0	180	80,784	11,000	1,051,650
Allyl alcohol	368	2,874	0	0	0	645	0	3,887
Allyl chloride	1,363	294	0	0	0	0	0	1,657
Aluminum (fume or dust)	750	0	0	0	21,900	0	33	22,683
Aluminum oxide (fibrous forms)	0	0	250	0	0	750	13,999	14,999
Ammonia	594,235	597,901	868,631	0	1,200	196,943	2,194	2,261,104
Ammonium sulfate (solution)	250	250	310,000	0	0	250	0	310,750
Aniline	41,133	22,933	9,292	0	1,839	356,000	6,138	437,335
Anthracene	4,011	275	5	0	0	0	340	4,631
Antimony compounds	507	7	4,858	0	1,180	0	24,567	31,119
Arsenic	0	0	0	0	0	0	2,770	2,770
Arsenic compounds	255	9,334	43	0	0	0	20,005	29,637
Barium	133	0	233	0	54,405	0	0	54,771
Barium compounds	425	260	1,225	0	0	50	7,193	9,153
Benzene	1,415,129	225,685	2,626	0	255	0	250	1,643,945
Benzoyl peroxide	8	0	0	0	16,000	0	1,700	17,708
Biphenyl	2,140	1,333	2	0	1,960	0	0	5,435
Butyl benzyl phthalate	0	0	0	0	5,500	0	300	5,800
Butyraldehyde	9,931	4,521	1	0	0	188	979	15,620
Cadmium compounds	1	0	61	0	1,300	0	2,300	3,662
Carbaryl	0	114	0	0	4,800	0	0	4,914
Carbon disulfide	18,010	662,983	1,350	0	0	0	261	682,604
Carbon tetrachloride	74,561	39,420	1	0	0	0	5,570	119,552
Carbonyl sulfide	5	219,275	0	0	0	0	0	219,280
Chlorine	19,841	28,708	31,850	0	0	755	0	81,154
Chlorobenzene	63,055	413,126	67,394	0	0	0	1,059,180	1,602,755
Chloroform	88,647	248,932	1,021	0	12	0	22,300	360,912
Chloromethane	86,506	566,392	72	0	92,000	0	900	745,870
Chromium	1,734	17	30	0	44,334	0	8,064	54,179
Chromium compounds	3,484	3,598	24,248	0	4,303	5,866	1,237,064	1,278,563
Cobalt	3	1	0	0	0	0	1,500	1,504
Cobalt compounds	250	0	0	0	250	0	250	750

[Continued]

★ 442 ★

Toxic Chemical Releases in West Virginia, by Chemical: 1990
[Continued]

Chemical	Fugitive air	Stack air	Water	Injection	Land	Public treatment	Other offsite	Total releases
Copper	2,000	40,957	0	0	0	255	207,135	250,347
Copper compounds	656	840	81	0	49	1,900	26,265	29,791
Creosote	44,115	22,336	0	0	0	0	506,534	572,985
Cresol (mixed isomers)	1,363	800	27	0	1	0	18,046	20,237
Cumene	430	63,000	0	0	0	0	0	63,430
Cyanide compounds	56,000	540	9,900	0	610	0	0	67,050
Cyclohexane	11,699	105	250	0	5	0	0	12,059
Diaminotoluene (mixed isomers)	3,155	264	153	0	10	0	0	3,582
Dibenzofuran	1,295	255	5	0	0	0	370	1,925
Dichlorobenzene (mixed isomers)	0	750	0	0	0	0	0	750
Dichloromethane	90,186	1,090,008	870	0	250	0	146,370	1,327,684
Diethanolamine	131	10	32	0	5	1,148	255	1,581
Dimethyl sulfate	1,156	50	0	0	0	0	0	1,206
Epichlorohydrin	25	1,000	0	0	4	0	0	1,029
Ethyl acrylate	0	1,200	0	0	0	0	0	1,200
Ethyl chloroformate	2	50	0	0	0	0	0	52
Ethylbenzene	37,995	16,015	962	0	3,905	5	2,707	61,589
Ethylene	97,404	415,374	0	0	0	0	0	512,778
Ethylene glycol	484,725	856,997	264,888	0	3,385	84,487	3,853,318	5,547,800
Ethylene oxide	94,745	58,285	94	0	0	901	6	154,031
Formaldehyde	36,198	107,443	6,134	0	0	387	2,118	152,280
Freon 113	125,995	3,500	0	0	0	0	0	129,495
Glycol ethers	116,394	590,751	28,741	0	84	17,729	71,860	825,559
Hydrazine	761	103	0	0	0	0	0	864
Hydrochloric acid	165,442	1,515,956	11,265	0	41	750	75,569	1,769,023
Hydrogen cyanide	94	4,264	2,248	0	0	0	0	6,606
Hydrogen fluoride	70,188	13,442	5	0	0	0	0	83,635
Hydroquinone	565	5	250	0	0	250	856	1,926
Lead	505	6,167	1	0	0	250	2,914	9,837
Lead compounds	251	500	8,488	0	170	25	35,269	44,703
M-xylene	842	7,013	0	0	0	0	0	7,855
Maleic anhydride	1,154	3,898	250	0	117,238	0	0	122,540
Manganese	2,295	537	617	0	119,949	250	70,159	193,807
Manganese compounds	5,016	8,707	51,660	0	736,300	1,428	1,322,393	2,125,504
Mercury	2,000	562	298	0	0	0	1,210	4,070
Mercury compounds	1	0	45	0	3	0	8,500	8,549
Methanol	517,756	1,145,940	27,723	0	0	1,097,154	1,043,150	3,831,723
Methoxychlor	5	5	5	0	0	0	0	15
Methyl ethyl ketone	423,197	213,013	250	0	250	176	16,288	653,174
Methyl isobutyl ketone	130,690	246,042	343	0	23	242	204,524	581,864
Methyl isocyanate	12,978	890	0	0	0	0	0	13,868
Methyl methacrylate	20,001	110,601	2,523	0	0	0	10,720	143,845
Methylenebis(phenylisocyanate)	475	897	0	0	50	0	0	1,422
Molybdenum trioxide	240	310	0	0	0	650	14,003	15,203
N,N-dimethylaniline	750	7,520	61	0	0	0	700	9,031
N-butyl alcohol	91,280	222,416	38,752	0	29	2,919	102,052	457,448
Naphthalene	228,176	45,900	413	0	5,866	0	63,577	343,932
Nickel	1,425	500	0	0	0	255	56,356	58,536
Nickel compounds	8,419	8,618	2,606	0	4,463	8,959	78,449	111,514
Nitric acid	15,720	32,843	0	0	3,000	13,076	0	64,639
Nitrobenzene	3,688	628	81	0	0	0	0	4,397
Nitroglycerin	0	0	0	0	16,900	0	0	16,900

[Continued]

★ 442 ★

Toxic Chemical Releases in West Virginia, by Chemical: 1990

[Continued]

Chemical	Fugitive air	Stack air	Water	Injection	Land	Public treatment	Other offsite	Total releases
O-xylene	592	11,092	0	0	0	0	176,642	188,326
P-xylene	404	2,057	0	0	0	0	0	2,461
Phenol	26,670	3,345	5,645	0	469	0	612,377	648,506
Phosgene	458	408	0	0	0	0	0	866
Phosphoric acid	7,389	43	15	0	0	29,747	256	37,450
Phosphorus (yellow or white)	0	0	0	0	0	0	49	49
Phthalic anhydride	251	510	0	0	0	0	960	1,721
Propylene	582,094	92,145	78	0	0	0	177	674,494
Propylene oxide	98,737	173,657	58	0	0	507	0	272,959
Pyridine	4,291	641	56	0	0	0	0	4,988
Quinoline	255	255	5	0	0	0	0	515
Silver	0	0	0	0	3,220	0	0	3,220
Silver compounds	4,665	0	0	0	0	0	0	4,665
Sodium hydroxide (solution)	0	0	0	0	0	750	0	750
Styrene	223,422	849,402	80	0	90,393	84,898	24,100	1,272,295
Sulfuric acid	9,119	24,451	82,632	0	800	479,329	207,600	803,931
Tetrachloroethylene	32,000	0	0	0	0	0	0	32,000
Thiourea	250	0	566	0	0	0	0	816
Titanium tetrachloride	0	1	0	0	0	0	0	1
Toluene	1,143,594	1,079,789	35,226	0	479	0	612,526	2,871,614
Toluene-2,4-diisocyanate	5,369	299	0	0	0	0	0	5,668
Toluene-2,6-diisocyanate	1,342	15	0	0	0	0	0	1,357
Trichloroethylene	42,116	71,100	82	0	250	0	10,910	124,458
Vinyl acetate	11,571	20,955	13	0	0	59,931	2,832	95,302
Vinylidene chloride	1,101	22	0	0	0	932	0	2,055
Xylene (mixed isomers)	311,519	745,261	13,298	0	250	680	106,289	1,177,297
Zinc (fume or dust)	7,046	21,321	0	0	0	0	10,795	39,162
Zinc compounds	575	2,460	42,183	5	6,500,462	0	99,732	6,645,417

Source: U.S. Environmental Protection Agency. "Toxic Chemical Releases, 1990." In National Economic, Social, and Environmental Data Bank [CD-ROM]. Prepared by U.S. Department of Commerce, Economics and Statistics Administration. Washington, DC: U.S. Department of Commerce, National Economic, Social, and Environmental Data Bank, Economics and Statistics Administration, Office of Business Analysis, February 1995.

★ 443 ★

Chemicals

Toxic Chemical Releases in Wisconsin, by Chemical: 1990

Figures indicate pounds released by chemical and by type of emission per year.

Chemical	Fugitive air	Stack air	Water	Injection	Land	Public treatment	Other offsite	Total releases
1,1,1-trichloroethane	1,955,811	3,728,378	15	5	20	40,327	427,724	6,152,280
1,1,2-trichloroethane	2,070	0	0	0	0	0	0	2,070
1,2,4-trimethylbenzene	103,816	216,486	25	0	0	5	14,370	334,702
1,2-dichlorobenzene	1,300	0	0	0	0	250	120,250	121,800
1,2-dichloropropane	11,512	267,368	0	0	0	8,594	1,195	288,669
2-methoxyethanol	28,100	121,700	0	0	0	0	0	149,800
2-phenylphenol	0	0	0	0	0	250	0	250
4,4'-isopropylidenediphenol	851	571	5	0	0	14,583	8,954	24,964
4,4'-methylenedianiline	0	0	0	0	0	0	21,000	21,000

[Continued]

★ 443 ★

Toxic Chemical Releases in Wisconsin, by Chemical: 1990
[Continued]

Chemical	Fugitive air	Stack air	Water	Injection	Land	Public treatment	Other offsite	Total releases
Acetaldehyde	0	104,250	0	0	0	17,590	0	121,840
Acetone	939,657	1,069,907	3,750	0	0	104,577	808,550	2,926,441
Acetonitrile	5	250	0	0	0	5	15,560	15,820
Acrylamide	2	0	0	0	0	0	250	252
Acrylic acid	1,019	2,191	10	0	0	295	755	4,270
Acrylonitrile	350	1,300	0	0	0	500	200	2,350
Aluminum (fume or dust)	27,293	73,599	0	0	0	2,434	93,844	197,170
Aluminum oxide (fibrous forms)	17,200	17,200	0	0	0	0	585,400	619,800
Ammonia	296,510	843,219	367,692	0	113,080	1,904,876	41,454	3,566,831
Ammonium nitrate (solution)	5	750	274	0	0	0	3	1,032
Ammonium sulfate (solution)	5	250	2,705	0	0	1,871,900	0	1,874,860
Aniline	226	3	0	0	0	91	41	361
Antimony	65	7,408	5	0	73,000	0	15,750	96,228
Antimony compounds	0	250	0	0	0	0	4,350	4,600
Arsenic	0	0	0	0	0	0	250	250
Arsenic compounds	15	16	5	0	0	5	3,819	3,860
Barium	420	25	0	0	0	0	288	733
Barium compounds	6,164	3,853	250	0	25,100	4,155	465,690	505,212
Benzene	6,239	6,313	0	0	0	250	10	12,812
Benzyl chloride	5	5	0	0	0	0	0	10
Bis(2-ethylhexyl) adipate	10	260	5	0	250	5	250	780
Butyl acrylate	569	3,163	10	0	0	255	764	4,761
Butyl benzyl phthalate	250	755	0	0	250	1,261	42,602	45,118
Cadmium	260	505	0	0	0	510	42,382	43,657
Cadmium compounds	0	0	0	0	0	252	3,263	3,515
Carbon disulfide	250	84,000	0	0	0	0	1,200	85,450
Catechol	0	0	780	0	0	0	38,500	39,280
Chlorine	26,019	135,363	8,858	0	0	25,290	5	195,535
Chlorine dioxide	760	54,000	0	0	0	250	0	55,010
Chloroform	136,651	734,678	9,336	0	0	11,714	106,841	999,220
Chloromethane	4,640	89,100	0	0	0	74	0	93,814
Chromium	8,188	7,426	1,819	0	132	3,647	1,579,809	1,601,021
Chromium compounds	4,638	4,424	478	0	500	416,999	489,813	916,852
Cobalt	1,485	1,370	270	0	0	517	1,839	5,481
Cobalt compounds	11	3	0	0	0	0	39	53
Copper	21,319	28,439	1,611	0	13,329	7,528	324,349	396,575
Copper compounds	2,913	3,166	33	0	0	3,782	174,210	184,104
Creosote	15,692	11,977	0	0	50	0	4,380	32,099
Cresol (mixed isomers)	250	250	0	0	0	5	0	505
Cumene	7,861	12,239	2	0	0	0	738	20,840
Cumene hydroperoxide	500	0	0	0	0	0	250	750
Cyanide compounds	520	1,069	5	0	0	1,962	52,071	55,627
Cyclohexane	250	67,859	0	0	0	1,455	22,620	92,184
Decabromodiphenyl oxide	750	0	0	0	0	0	0	750
Di(2-ethylhexyl) phthalate	255	760	5	0	250	255	93,900	95,425
Dibutyl phthalate	13,385	279	5	0	0	255	488	14,412
Dichloromethane	575,386	870,530	170	0	5	1,977	250,628	1,698,696
Diethanolamine	505	778	5	0	0	28,189	39,500	68,977
Diethyl phthalate	0	0	0	0	0	750	13,350	14,100
Diethyl sulfate	250	0	0	0	0	250	0	500
Dimethyl sulfate	250	5	0	0	0	20	0	275
Epichlorohydrin	318	108	3	0	0	733	0	1,162

[Continued]

★ 443 ★

Toxic Chemical Releases in Wisconsin, by Chemical: 1990

[Continued]

Chemical	Fugitive air	Stack air	Water	Injection	Land	Public treatment	Other offsite	Total releases
Ethyl acrylate	277	763	5	0	0	250	502	1,797
Ethylbenzene	5,721	70,510	5	0	0	5	16,521	92,762
Ethylene	179	1,229	0	0	0	0	0	1,408
Ethylene glycol	11,001	303,857	10	0	10,550	97,910	128,560	551,888
Ethylene oxide	7,394	27,159	0	0	0	3,250	0	37,803
Formaldehyde	9,658	583,087	10,601	0	0	230,564	38,078	871,988
Freon 113	403,521	368,759	0	0	0	255	14,237	786,772
Glycol ethers	522,030	2,485,875	9,187	0	250	98,784	258,346	3,374,472
Hydrochloric acid	16,264	2,722,638	577	0	5	514,586	41,974	3,296,044
Hydrogen cyanide	0	87,960	0	0	0	0	0	87,960
Hydrogen fluoride	785	21,496	255	0	5	510	1,763	24,814
Hydroquinone	63	0	0	0	0	750	120,000	120,813
Isopropyl alcohol (manufacturing)	101,113	48,973	0	0	0	25,250	22,930	198,266
Isosafrole	5	0	0	0	0	250	0	255
Lead	4,900	23,676	260	0	270,550	1,568	58,661	359,615
Lead compounds	1,349	5,338	518	0	0	2,496	189,081	198,782
Maleic anhydride	274	260	5	0	0	5	128	672
Manganese	22,314	186,052	3,367	0	457,021	3,266	1,739,219	2,411,239
Manganese compounds	6,646	27,098	15,902	0	250	375	2,091,770	2,142,041
Mercury	5	5	0	0	0	5	250	265
Mercury compounds	0	0	0	0	0	0	250	250
Methanol	406,743	1,612,376	5	0	98,277	1,814,504	6,926,059	10,857,964
Methyl ethyl ketone	1,031,704	2,256,515	5	0	250	283,337	513,630	4,085,441
Methyl isobutyl ketone	86,519	468,854	5	0	0	27,395	17,241	600,014
Methyl methacrylate	20,370	20,143	10	5	0	1,167	1,014	42,709
Methyl tert-butyl ether	500	750	0	0	0	5	29,556	30,811
Methylenebis(phenylisocyanate)	4,573	4,623	5	0	5	5	19,947	29,158
Molybdenum trioxide	251	291	250	0	0	250	5,805	6,847
N-butyl alcohol	170,403	1,084,121	10	0	5	6,790	25,141	1,286,470
N-dioctyl phthalate	5,001	545	0	0	0	0	26,950	32,496
Naphthalene	1,630	10,775	250	0	0	0	318	12,973
Nickel	7,161	7,546	1,288	0	634	3,495	451,609	471,733
Nickel compounds	741	520	198	0	0	2,461	36,811	40,731
Nitric acid	11,189	268,169	20	5	66,437	536,972	5,332	888,124
O-cresol	7	4	0	0	0	254	22	287
O-xylene	15,900	9,900	0	0	0	190	15,910	41,900
Phenol	106,476	281,051	938	0	0	15,404	42,514	446,383
Phosphoric acid	4,633	8,343	40	5	41,109	765,961	263,455	1,083,546
Phosphorus (yellow or white)	0	0	0	0	0	781	0	781
Phthalic anhydride	316	2,907	5	0	0	5	5	3,238
Polychlorinated biphenyls (PCBs)	0	0	0	0	0	0	6,000	6,000
Propoxur	5	5	5	0	0	5	15	35
Propylene	5,950	2,890	0	0	0	0	0	8,840
Propylene oxide	2,590	3,876	0	0	0	620	0	7,086
Pyridine	5	10	0	0	0	5	34,400	34,420
Safrole	5	0	0	0	0	12	0	17
Sec-butyl alcohol	1,258	3,454	10	0	0	755	2,443	7,920
Selenium compounds	0	0	0	0	0	0	8	8
Silver	240	402	0	0	0	7	42	691
Sodium hydroxide (solution)	5	0	0	0	0	0	0	5
Styrene	813,957	424,128	10	0	0	1,065	163,088	1,402,248
Sulfuric acid	18,026	933,750	767	0	15	4,111,841	545,641	5,610,040

[Continued]

★ 443 ★

Toxic Chemical Releases in Wisconsin, by Chemical: 1990
[Continued]

Chemical	Fugitive air	Stack air	Water	Injection	Land	Public treatment	Other offsite	Total releases
Tert-butyl alcohol	750	2,300	5	0	0	750	2,250	6,055
Tetrachloroethylene	6,974	171,671	0	0	0	16,850	29,410	224,905
Toluene	1,015,911	3,484,446	260	0	5	2,371	429,228	4,932,221
Toluenediisocyanate (mixed isomers)	260	260	5	0	0	5	0	530
Toluene-2,4-diisocyanate	250	255	0	0	0	0	0	505
Toluene-2,6-diisocyanate	250	252	0	0	0	0	0	502
Trichloroethylene	279,044	526,290	0	0	0	255	107,045	912,634
Vinyl acetate	250	6,700	0	0	0	0	0	6,950
Xylene (mixed isomers)	629,457	3,837,648	1,032	0	0	2,870	364,886	4,835,893
Zinc (fume or dust)	9,364	93,384	1,300	0	27,700	1,255	189,394	322,397
Zinc compounds	5,777	65,171	15,682	0	2,203,970	26,805	467,714	2,785,119

Source: U.S. Environmental Protection Agency. "Toxic Chemical Releases, 1990." In *National Economic, Social, and Environmental Data Bank* [CD-ROM]. Prepared by U.S. Department of Commerce, Economics and Statistics Administration. Washington, DC: U.S. Department of Commerce, National Economic, Social, and Environmental Data Bank, Economics and Statistics Administration, Office of Business Analysis, February 1995.

★ 444 ★

Chemicals

Toxic Chemical Releases in Wyoming, by Chemical: 1990

Figures indicate pounds released by chemical and by type of emission per year.

Chemical	Fugitive air	Stack air	Water	Injection	Land	Public treatment	Other offsite	Total releases
1,1,1-trichloroethane	518	0	0	0	1,075	0	0	1,593
1,2,4-trimethylbenzene	32,978	9,747	0	0	10	0	0	42,735
2,4-dimethylphenol	5	0	0	0	246	0	0	251
2-methoxyethanol	250	2,200	0	0	0	0	0	2,450
Ammonia	215,821	476,360	120,060	988,000	6,000	0	0	1,806,241
Ammonium nitrate (solution)	0	721,890	0	5,747,200	700	0	0	6,469,790
Arsenic compounds	5	5	0	0	0	0	0	10
Benzene	29,164	26,805	0	0	2,055	0	271	58,295
Carbonyl sulfide	23	73	0	0	0	0	0	96
Chlorine	1,428	2,080	0	750	0	0	0	4,258
Chromium	250	0	0	0	0	0	0	250
Chromium compounds	10	3,507	0	0	84,575	0	0	88,092
Copper compounds	10	10	0	0	5	0	5	30
Cresol (mixed isomers)	5	5	0	0	1,735	0	0	1,745
Cumene	5	5	0	0	0	0	15	25
Cyclohexane	43,895	20,889	0	0	10	0	250	65,044
Diethanolamine	5	0	0	0	10	0	0	15
Ethylbenzene	26,404	11,988	0	0	9,538	0	105	48,035
Ethylene	17,989	3,039	0	0	0	0	0	21,028
Ethylene glycol	34	31	0	79,777	10	0	10	79,862
Formaldehyde	6,000	0	0	0	0	0	0	6,000
Glycol ethers	15,744	62,066	1	0	87,687	0	2,300	167,798
Hydrochloric acid	1,279	505	0	750	94,720	0	0	97,254

[Continued]

★ 444 ★

Toxic Chemical Releases in Wyoming, by Chemical: 1990

[Continued]

Chemical	Fugitive air	Stack air	Water	Injection	Land	Public treatment	Other offsite	Total releases
Hydrogen cyanide	0	72	0	0	0	0	0	72
Hydrogen fluoride	3,800	3,900	0	0	0	0	0	7,700
Lead compounds	5	134	0	0	745	0	0	884
Manganese	250	0	0	0	0	0	0	250
Methanol	4,753	844	0	0	11,428	0	1,504	18,529
Methyl ethyl ketone	211	1,899	0	0	0	0	8,663	10,773
Methyl tert-butyl ether	250	28,000	0	0	0	0	0	28,250
N-butyl alcohol	27,149	111,340	0	0	0	0	9,053	147,542
Naphthalene	21,683	6,831	0	0	10	0	134	28,658
Nitric acid	32,788	0	0	750	0	0	0	33,538
Pentachlorophenol	5	5	0	0	0	0	0	10
Phenol	255	0	18	0	1,382	0	0	1,655
Phosphoric acid	18	80,050	0	250	10	0	0	80,328
Propylene	45,100	6,700	0	0	0	0	0	51,800
Sulfuric acid	941	1,761,532	18	750	0	0	0	1,763,241
Thiourea	0	0	0	0	5	0	0	5
Toluene	143,954	74,423	0	0	11,985	0	176	230,538
Vanadium (fume or dust)	5	569	0	0	1,145	0	0	1,719
Xylene (mixed isomers)	161,702	65,583	0	0	10,677	250	1,116	239,328
Zinc compounds	0	0	0	0	0	0	2,620	2,620

Source: U.S. Environmental Protection Agency. "Toxic Chemical Releases, 1990." In *National Economic, Social, and Environmental Data Bank* [CD-ROM]. Prepared by U.S. Department of Commerce, Economics and Statistics Administration. Washington, DC: U.S. Department of Commerce, National Economic, Social, and Environmental Data Bank, Economics and Statistics Administration, Office of Business Analysis, February 1995.

★ 445 ★

Chemicals

Toxic Chemical Spills

According to the source, "toxic chemical accidents that threaten public health and the environment are occurring at the alarming rate of 19 per day" (p. 3A).

[In percentages]

Location	Spills
Factories, buildings	75.3
Roads	8.3
Railroads	5.4
Pipelines	3.1
Other	7.9

Source: Hoversten, Paul. "Toxic Alarm in 10 States." *USA TODAY*, 19 August 1994, p. 3A. Primary sources: Public Interest Research Group; National Environmental Law Center.

Hazardous Material

★ 446 ★

Bioaccumulator Releases: 1992

Table shows Toxic Release Inventory (TRI) releases of known or suspected bioaccumulators to air, surface water, and land.

[In pounds]

Chemical	Total air emissions	Surface water discharges	Releases to land	Total air, water, land releases
Aldrin	0	0	0	0
Anthracene	54,034	1,030	3,070	58,134
Benzoic trichloride	6,079	0	0	6,079
Chlordane	1,713	1	0	1,714
Decabromodiphenyl oxide	36,967	3,878	531,040	571,885
1,2-Dichlorobenzene	349,059	2,395	6,469	357,923
1,4-Dichlorobenzene	337,946	2,021	622	340,589
Di-(2-ethylhexyl) phthalate	873,783	947	101,712	976,442
Heptachlor	710	1	0	711
Hexachlorobenzene	4,471	227	0	4,698
Hexachloro-1,3-butadiene	4,134	1,911	0	6,045
Hexachlorocyclopentadiene	8,380	0	0	8,380
Hexachloroethane	21,022	3	0	21,025
Mercury	12,471	266	3,117	15,854
Mercury compounds	3,249	297	17	3,563
Methoxychlor	818	5	5	828
4,4'-Methylenebis(2-chloroaniline)	17	0	2	19
Pentachlorophenol	13,694	3,127	270	17,091
Polychlorinated biphenyls (PCBs)	0	0	1	1
Toxaphene	0	0	0	0
1,2,4-Trichlorobenzene	415,297	995	2,680	418,972
Total	2,143,844	17,104	649,005	2,809,953

Source: U.S. Environmental Protection Agency. "Toxic Release Inventory, 1992." In *National Economic, Social, and Environmental Data Bank* [CD-ROM]. Prepared by U.S. Department of Commerce, Economics and Statistics Administration. Washington, DC: U.S. Department of Commerce, National Economic, Social, and Environmental Data Bank, Economics and Statistics Administration, Office of Business Analysis, February 1995.

★ 447 ★

Hazardous Material

Carcinogen Releases – Top 25 Chemicals: 1988-1992

Table shows Toxic Release Inventory (TRI) releases for carcinogens with the largest air, water, and land releases in 1992.

[In pounds, except percentages]

Chemical	Total air/water/land releases				Percent change		
	1988	1990	1991	1992	1990-1991	1991-1992	1988-1992
Dichloromethane	129,245,570	100,832,043	80,342,239	74,263,710	-20.3	-7.6	-42.5
Styrene	33,660,878	31,457,700	29,534,636	32,662,297	-6.1	10.6	-3.0
Chloroform	27,062,294	24,100,379	20,036,804	17,717,960	-16.9	-11.6	-34.5
Benzene	31,963,557	26,011,365	17,463,639	12,750,133	-32.9	-27.0	-60.1
Tetrachloroethylene	36,112,904	22,663,065	16,800,115	12,330,796	-25.9	-26.6	-65.9
Formaldehyde	13,518,262	13,563,753	11,329,957	11,518,900	-16.5	1.7	-14.8
Acetaldehyde	6,929,055	7,303,810	7,237,135	6,493,598	-0.9	-10.3	-6.3
1,3-Butadiene	7,518,475	5,280,296	3,961,024	3,845,436	-25.0	-2.9	-48.9
1,2-Dichloroethane	4,578,872	5,660,948	4,117,838	3,179,361	-27.3	-22.8	-30.6
Nickel	1,766,717	3,522,808	952,811	3,155,600	-73.0	231.2	78.6
Lead	7,839,835	5,717,317	3,778,525	2,469,504	-33.9	-34.6	-68.5
Arsenic	190,236	58,016	1,743,023	1,821,195	2904.4	4.5	857.3
Acrylonitrile	4,217,126	3,153,912	2,203,837	1,609,625	-30.1	-27.0	-61.8
Nickel compounds	2,786,469	2,388,670	1,601,533	1,521,171	-33.0	-5.0	-45.4
Chromium	9,944,842	3,199,868	1,611,537	1,504,310	-49.6	-6.7	-84.9
Carbon tetrachloride	3,807,039	1,744,949	1,552,870	1,393,036	-11.0	-10.3	-63.4
Propylene oxide	3,398,316	1,479,897	1,485,630	1,350,853	0.4	-9.1	-60.2
Creosote	NA	2,036,151	1,767,001	1,308,033	-13.2	-26.0	-
Ethylene oxide	4,731,085	2,351,719	1,863,548	1,303,863	-20.8	-30.0	-72.4
1,4-Dioxane	827,655	970,021	1,064,667	1,134,848	9.8	6.6	37.1
Vinyl chloride	1,445,029	1,145,416	1,052,560	1,105,164	-8.1	5.0	-23.5
Di-(2-ethylhexyl) phthalate	1,165,141	1,342,608	1,325,102	976,442	-1.3	-26.3	-16.2
Epichlorohydrin	504,548	445,337	468,281	527,473	5.2	12.6	4.5
1,4-Dichlorobenzene	1,898,872	822,083	346,820	340,589	-57.8	-1.8	-82.1
Asbestos (friable)	2,171,075	456,323	559,470	247,414	22.6	-55.8	-88.6

Source: U.S. Environmental Protection Agency. "Toxic Release Inventory, 1992." In *National Economic, Social, and Environmental Data Bank* [CD-ROM]. Prepared by U.S. Department of Commerce, Economics and Statistics Administration. Washington, DC: U.S. Department of Commerce, National Economic, Social, and Environmental Data Bank, Economics and Statistics Administration, Office of Business Analysis, February 1995. *Notes:* "NA" refers to chemicals that were not reportable; for example, creosote was not reportable until 1990. "-" represents data omitted from source material.

★ 448 ★
Hazardous Material

Carcinogens: 1992

Table shows Toxic Release Inventory (TRI) releases of known or suspected carcinogens to air, surface water, and land.

[In pounds]

Chemical	Total air emissions	Surface water discharges	Releases to land	Total air, water, land releases
Acetaldehyde	6,416,121	77,188	289	6,493,598
Acetamide	20	1	0	21
Acrylamide	28,554	10,324	963	39,841
Acrylonitrile	1,600,071	1,483	8,071	1,609,625
4-Aminoazobenzene	1	0	0	1
4-Aminobiphenyl	0	0	0	0
o-Anisidine	421	107	2,167	2,695
Arsenic	5,656	1,236	1,814,303	1,821,195
Asbestos (friable)	11,264	250	235,900	247,414
Benzene	12,384,579	24,918	340,636	12,750,133
Benzoic trichloride	6,079	0	0	6,079
Beryllium	1,868	39	21,358	23,265
Bis(chloromethyl) ether	309	0	0	309
1,3-Butadiene	3,843,700	1,364	372	3,845,436
Cadmium	8,756	638	7,036	16,430
Carbon tetrachloride	1,390,262	2,441	333	1,393,036
Chloroform	17,034,926	654,452	28,582	17,717,960
Chloromethyl methyl ether	1,221	10	0	1,231
Chlorophenols	9,283	290	0	9,573
Chromium	524,039	19,104	961,167	1,504,310
Creosote	1,293,564	11,835	2,634	1,308,033
p-Cresidine	340	5	255	600
Cupferron	10	0	0	10
4,4'-Diaminodiphenyl ether	269	312	0	581
Diaminotoluene (mixed isomers)	18,483	695	85	19,263
2,4-Diaminotoluene	1,905	5	0	1,910
1,2-Dibromo-3-chloropropane	294	0	0	294
1,2-Dibromoethane	32,852	106	6	32,964
Dichlorobenzene (mixed isomers)	4,521	0	0	4,521
1,4-Dichlorobenzene	337,946	2,021	622	340,589
3,3'-Dichlorobenzidine	10	0	0	10
1,2-Dichloroethane	3,165,207	12,296	1,858	3,179,361
Dichloromethane	73,963,205	221,192	79,313	74,263,710
1,3-Dichloropropylene	42,607	67	0	42,674
Di-(2-ethylhexyl) phthalate	873,783	947	101,712	976,442
Diethyl sulfate	13,236	5	5	13,246
3,3'-Dimethoxybenzidine	0	8	0	8
1,1-Dimethyl hydrazine	369	0	5	374
Dimethyl sulfate	7,023	161	0	7,184
1,4-Dioxane	684,485	447,066	3,297	1,134,848

[Continued]

★ 448 ★

Carcinogens: 1992

[Continued]

Chemical	Total air emissions	Surface water discharges	Releases to land	Total air, water, land releases
Epichlorohydrin	522,653	3,165	1,655	527,473
Ethyl acrylate	205,312	734	1,114	207,160
Ethyleneimine	0	0	0	0
Ethylene oxide	1,301,035	1,991	837	1,303,863
Ethylene thiourea	285	0	0	285
Formaldehyde	10,903,227	441,244	174,429	11,518,900
Hexachlorobenzene	4,471	227	0	4,698
Hydrazine	19,271	842	10	20,123
Hydrazine sulfate	2	0	0	2
Lead	412,804	11,641	2,045,059	2,469,504
Lindane	1,038	0	0	1,038
4,4'-Methylenebis (2-chloroaniline)	17	0	2	19
4,4'-Methylenedianiline	10,376	420	55	10,851
alpha-Naphthylamine	10	0	0	10
Nickel	714,724	44,910	2,395,966	3,155,600
Nickel compounds	149,582	66,305	1,305,284	1,521,171
Nitrilotriacetic acid	4	4,069	0	4,073
2-Nitropropane	45,642	900	0	46,542
Poly brominated biphenyls	250	0	5	255
Polychlorinated biphenyls (PCBs)	0	0	1	1
Propane sultone	250	0	0	250
Propyleneimine	403	0	0	403
Propylene oxide	1,341,342	7,260	2,251	1,350,853
Saccharin (manufacturing)	323	0	0	323
Styrene	32,334,616	23,502	304,179	32,662,297
Styrene oxide	368	0	0	368
Tetrachloroethylene	12,311,235	10,207	9,354	12,330,796
Thiourea	952	727	256	1,935
Toluene-2,4-diisocyanate	14,032	0	250	14,282
Toluene-2,6-diisocyanate	5,319	0	250	5,569
Toluenediisocyanate (mixed isomers)	48,209	0	275	48,484
o-Toluidine	7,492	310	6,823	14,625
2,4,6-Trichlorophenol	86	1	0	87
Urethane	3,200	0	0	3,200
Vinyl bromide	32,900	0	0	32,900
Vinyl chloride	1,101,156	902	3,106	1,105,164

[Continued]

★ 448 ★

Carcinogens: 1992

[Continued]

Chemical	Total air emissions	Surface water discharges	Releases to land	Total air, water, land releases
Subtotal	185,199,825	2,109,923	9,862,130	197,171,878
Total for all TRI chemicals	1,844,958,336	272,932,953	337,809,053	3,181,646,757

Source: U.S. Environmental Protection Agency. "Toxic Release Inventory, 1992." In *National Economic, Social, and Environmental Data Bank* [CD-ROM]. Prepared by U.S. Department of Commerce, Economics and Statistics Administration. Washington, DC: U.S. Department of Commerce, National Economic, Social, and Environmental Data Bank, Economics and Statistics Administration, Office of Business Analysis, February 1995.

★ 449 ★

Hazardous Material

Hazardous Material, by State

Table shows the states that store the most hazardous substances per person.

[In pounds]

State	Amount
Louisiana	523
Alaska	187
Tennessee	173
Wyoming	125
Delaware	113
Texas	111
Maine	104
Iowa	89
Nebraska	79
West Virginia	78

Source: "Hazardous Material: The Top 10 States." *USA TODAY*, 2 December 1994, p. 3A. Primary source: National Environmental Law Center.

★ 450 ★

Hazardous Material

Metals and Metal Compound Releases: 1992

Table shows releases of Toxic Release Inventory (TRI) metals and metal compounds.

[In pounds]

Chemical	Fugitive or nonpoint air emissions	Stack or point air emissions	Surface water discharges	Underground injection	Releases to land	Total releases
Antimony and antimony compounds	53,357	364,885	53,714	3,773	1,270,499	1,746,228
Arsenic and arsenic compounds	11,795	131,485	7,833	33,000	4,266,694	4,450,807
Barium and barium compounds	297,014	436,249	125,942	1,251	5,058,495	5,918,951
Beryllium and beryllium compounds	1	2,378	44	0	69,358	71,781
Cadmium and cadmium compounds	13,642	55,498	1,418	1,211	72,443	144,212
Chromium and chromium compounds	540,615	447,109	288,771	32,470	24,127,155	25,436,120
Cobalt and cobalt compounds	24,318	36,555	101,445	18,920	133,877	315,115
Copper and copper compounds	4,040,127	3,785,239	113,887	218,167	47,136,675	55,294,095
Lead and lead compounds	615,133	1,231,793	72,575	2,881	13,958,301	15,880,683
Manganese and manganese compounds	1,072,033	1,596,341	968,150	22,873	68,006,939	71,666,336
Mercury and mercury compounds	10,904	4,816	563	9	3,134	19,426
Nickel and nickel compounds	575,669	288,637	111,215	297,762	3,701,250	4,974,533
Selenium and selenium compounds	4,528	29,418	5,963	3,700	99,121	142,730
Silver and silver compounds	10,181	26,185	9,779	24	20,818	66,987
Thallium and thallium compounds	255	500	0	0	505	1,260
Zinc and zinc compounds[1]	2,140,838	3,584,666	1,056,714	246,947	89,581,515	96,610,680
Total	9,410,410	12,021,754	2,918,013	882,988	257,506,779	282,739,944

Source: U.S. Environmental Protection Agency. "Toxic Release Inventory, 1992." In *National Economic, Social, and Environmental Data Bank* [CD-ROM]. Prepared by U.S. Department of Commerce, Economics and Statistics Administration. Washington, DC: U.S. Department of Commerce, National Economic, Social, and Environmental Data Bank, Economics and Statistics Administration, Office of Business Analysis, February 1995. *Note:* 1. Only fume or dust forms of zinc metal are reportable.

★ 451 ★

Hazardous Material

Metals and Metal Compound Transfers: 1992

Table shows Toxic Release Inventory (TRI) transfers of metals and metal compounds.

[In pounds]

Chemical	Transfers to recycling	Transfers to energy recovery	Transfers to treatment	Transfers to POTWs	Transfers to disposal	Other[1] offsite transfers	Total transfers
Antimony and antimony compounds	7,699,815	12,834	20,798,731	96,719	2,628,596	2,685	31,239,380
Arsenic and arsenic compounds	2,622,213	5	4,130,296	1,351	1,683,645	28,376	8,465,886
Barium and barium compounds	837,560	163,041	1,721,059	503,241	16,475,187	1,014,069	20,714,157
Beryllium and beryllium compounds	25,767	0	1,181	250	18,144	0	45,342
Cadmium and cadmium compounds	2,047,074	3,302	511,550	45,815	381,113	11,634	3,000,488
Chromium and chromium compounds	96,077,807	90,847	3,805,307	942,267	14,245,627	559,583	115,721,438
Cobalt and cobalt compounds	6,341,969	15,400	103,090	26,567	453,182	326	6,940,534
Copper and copper compounds	453,064,916	121,563	4,839,273	388,454	19,566,845	2,379,040	480,360,091
Lead and lead compounds	402,632,887	60,061	20,860,591	357,956	16,202,271	521,792	440,635,558
Manganese and manganese compounds	66,095,542	29,769	3,859,177	1,076,650	23,570,626	665,556	95,297,320

[Continued]

★ 451 ★

Metals and Metal Compound Transfers: 1992
[Continued]

Chemical	Transfers to recycling	Transfers to energy recovery	Transfers to treatment	Transfers to POTWs	Transfers to disposal	Other[1] offsite transfers	Total transfers
Mercury and mercury compounds	51,455	1	73,978	22	164,984	22	290,462
Nickel and nickel compounds	79,236,323	34,628	2,622,249	249,629	9,236,772	441,979	91,821,580
Selenium and selenium compounds	309,814	1,270	27,444	267	45,334	5	384,134
Silver and silver compounds	1,956,334	0	6,709	6,082	17,992	4,400	1,991,517
Thallium and thallium compounds	75,905	0	3,900	5	250	0	80,060
Zinc and zinc compounds[2]	289,732,321	450,378	38,260,235	723,960	47,906,132	3,389,470	380,462,496
Total	1,408,807,702	983,099	101,624,770	4,419,235	152,596,700	9,018,937	1,677,450,443

Source: U.S. Environmental Protection Agency. "Toxic Release Inventory, 1992." In National Economic, Social, and Environmental Data Bank [CD-ROM]. Prepared by U.S. Department of Commerce, Economics and Statistics Administration. Washington, DC: U.S. Department of Commerce, National Economic, Social, and Environmental Data Bank, Economics and Statistics Administration, Office of Business Analysis, February 1995. Notes: "POTWs" are publicly owned treatment works. 1. Other transfers are transfers reported with missing or invalid waste management codes. 2. Only fume or dust forms of zinc metal are reportable.

★ 452 ★

Hazardous Material

Ozone Depleter Releases: 1988, 1990-1992

Table shows Toxic Release Inventory (TRI) releases of ozone depleters to air, water, and land.

[In pounds, except percentages]

Chemical	Total air/water/land releases				Percent change		
	1988	1990	1991	1992	1990-1991	1991-1992	1988-1992
Bromochlorodifluoromethane (Halon 1211)	NA	NA	11,958	16,747	-	40.0	-
Bromomethane	2,772,795	2,988,363	3,038,283	3,001,540	1.7	-1.2	8.2
Bromotrifluoromethane (Halon 1301)	NA	NA	180,107	110,151	-	-38.8	-
Carbon tetrachloride	3,807,039	1,744,949	1,552,870	1,393,036	-11.0	-10.3	-63.4
Dibromotetrafluoroethane (Halon 2402)	NA	NA	6,550	768	-	-88.3	-
Dichlorodifluoromethane (CFC-12)	NA	NA	15,388,443	11,264,952	-	-26.8	-
Dichlorotetrafluoroethane (CFC-114)	NA	NA	1,900,333	1,080,479	-	-43.1	-
Freon 113	70,247,248	47,626,222	36,457,952	24,575,869	-23.4	-32.6	-65.0
Monochloropentafluoroethane (CFC-115)	NA	NA	375,168	421,692	-	12.4	-
1,1,1-Trichloroethane	178,596,202	166,284,259	141,150,514	115,033,899	-15.1	-18.5	-35.6
Trichlorofluoromethane (CFC-11)	NA	NA	11,811,520	9,485,723	-	-19.7	-

Source: U.S. Environmental Protection Agency. "Toxic Release Inventory, 1992." In National Economic, Social, and Environmental Data Bank [CD-ROM]. Prepared by U.S. Department of Commerce, Economics and Statistics Administration. Washington, DC: U.S. Department of Commerce, National Economic, Social, and Environmental Data Bank, Economics and Statistics Administration, Office of Business Analysis, February 1995. Notes: "NA" indicates chemicals (halons and CFCs) that were not reportable until 1991. "-" shows data not reported in original source.

★ 453 ★

Hazardous Material

Ozone Depleter Releases, by Source: 1992

Table shows the Toxic Release Inventory (TRI) releases of ozone depleters in 1992.

[In pounds]

Chemical	Fugitive or nonpoint air emissions	Stack or point air emissions	Surface water discharges	Underground injection	Releases to land	Total releases
Bromochlorodifluoromethane (Halon 1211)	7,923	8,824	0	0	0	16,747
Bromomethane	528,321	2,472,829	390	1,000	0	3,002,540
Bromotrifluoromethane (Halon 1301)	105,490	4,661	0	0	0	110,151
Carbon tetrachloride	416,994	973,268	2,441	45,984	333	1,439,020
Dibromotetrafluoroethane (Halon 2402)	154	614	0	0	0	768
Dichlorodifluoromethane (CFC-12)	6,871,649	4,391,045	2,235	1,722	23	11,266,674
Dichlorotetrafluoroethane (CFC-114)	934,198	146,026	255	1	0	1,080,480
Freon 113	17,610,197	6,954,728	1,916	214	9,028	24,576,083
Monochloropentafluoroethane (CFC-115)	296,585	125,102	5	0	0	421,692
1,1,1-Trichloroethane	56,479,078	58,465,308	13,132	561	76,381	115,034,460
Trichlorofluoromethane (CFC-11)	3,655,417	5,809,097	1,448	8	19,761	9,485,731
Total	86,906,006	79,351,502	21,822	49,490	105,526	166,434,346

Source: U.S. Environmental Protection Agency. "Toxic Release Inventory, 1992." In *National Economic, Social, and Environmental Data Bank* [CD-ROM]. Prepared by U.S. Department of Commerce, Economics and Statistics Administration. Washington, DC: U.S. Department of Commerce, National Economic, Social, and Environmental Data Bank, Economics and Statistics Administration, Office of Business Analysis, February 1995.

★ 454 ★

Hazardous Material

Ozone Depleter Transfers: 1992

Table shows Toxic Release Inventory (TRI) transfers of ozone depleters.

[In pounds]

Chemical	Transfers to recycling	Transfers to energy recovery	Transfers to treatment	Transfers to POTWs	Transfers to disposal	Other[1] offsite transfers	Total transfers
Bromochlorodifluoromethane (Halon 1211)	0	0	0	0	0	0	0
Bromomethane	0	3,500	255	0	250	0	4,005
Bromotrifluoromethane (Halon 1301)	0	0	0	0	0	0	0
Carbon tetrachloride	345,452	24,455	839,388	1,054	11,955	0	1,222,304
Dibromotetrafluoroethane (Halon 2402)	0	0	0	0	0	0	0
Dichlorodifluoromethane (CFC-12)	343,086	2,095	84,976	102,473	1,975	0	534,605
Dichlorotetrafluoroethane (CFC-114)	521	0	8,188	0	37	0	8,746
Freon 113	5,637,865	385,048	777,851	22,961	94,831	5,116	6,923,672
Monochloropentafluoroethane (CFC-115)	0	0	128	0	0	0	128
1,1,1-Trichloroethane	23,082,207	3,639,456	4,247,899	118,253	611,054	173,815	31,872,684

[Continued]

★ 454 ★

Ozone Depleter Transfers: 1992

[Continued]

Chemical	Transfers to recycling	Transfers to energy recovery	Transfers to treatment	Transfers to POTWs	Transfers to disposal	Other[1] offsite transfers	Total transfers
Trichlorofluoromethane (CFC-11)	212,631	39,404	208,369	5,925	137,674	0	604,003
Total	29,621,762	4,093,958	6,167,054	250,666	857,776	178,931	41,170,147

Source: U.S. Environmental Protection Agency. "Toxic Release Inventory, 1992." In *National Economic, Social, and Environmental Data Bank* [CD-ROM]. Prepared by U.S. Department of Commerce, Economics and Statistics Administration. Washington, DC: U.S. Department of Commerce, National Economic, Social, and Environmental Data Bank, Economics and Statistics Administration, Office of Business Analysis, February 1995. *Notes:* "POTWs" are publicly owned treatment works. 1. Other transfers are transfers reported with missing or invalid waste management codes.

Superfund

★ 455 ★

CERCLIS and NPL Sites: 1980-1993

The Superfund Law - officially the Comprehensive Environmental Response, Compensation and Liability Act - requires officials to identify hazardous waste sites, to determine which sites expose humans to the greatest risks, and to arrange for the clean up of such sites. Places identified as possible threats are listed as Comprehensive Environmental Response, Compensation and Liability Inventory Sites (CERCLIS). The very worst sites are classified as National Priority List (NPL) sites. Federal agencies responsible for determining the status of sites include the Environmental Protection Agency (EPA) and the Agency for Toxic Substances and Disease Registry (ATSDR). The table below shows the cumulative number of CERCLIS and NPL sites.

Year	CERCLIS	NPL
1980	8,000	NA
1981	10,500	115
1982	13,934	115
1983	16,307	545
1984	18,836	541
1985	22,455	857
1986	25,161	887
1987	27,507	950
1988	29,613	1,174
1989	31,522	1,224
1990	34,000	1,200
1991	35,798	1,185

[Continued]

★ 455 ★

CERCLIS and NPL Sites: 1980-1993
[Continued]

Year	CERCLIS	NPL
1992	37,598	1,252
1993	37,921	1,320

Source: Executive Office of the President of the United States. *Environmental Quality 24: The Twenty-fourth Annual Report of the Council on Environmental Quality.* Prepared by Ray Clark. Written by Carroll Curtis. Edited by Barry Walsh. Washington, DC: U.S. Government Printing Office, 1994, p. 507. Primary source: U.S. Environmental Protection Agency. Unpublished data. *Note:* "NA" stands for "not available."

★ 456 ★
Superfund

National Priority List Hazardous Waste Sites, by State or Area: 1990 and 1993

Table shows hazardous waste sites on the National Priority List in each state. Includes both proposed and final sites listed on the National Priority List for the Superfund program as authorized by the Comprehensive Environmental Response, Compensation and Liability Act of 1980 and the Superfund Amendments and Reauthorization Act of 1986.

State or area	1990			1993				
	Total sites	Rank	Percent distri-bution	Total sites	Rank	Percent distri-bution	Fed-eral	Non-Fed-eral
Total	1,207	(X)	(X)	1,270	(X)	(X)	143	1,127
United States	1,197	(X)	100.0	1,258	(X)	100.0	141	1,117
Alabama	12	27	1.0	14	26	1.1	3	11
Alaska	6	43	0.5	8	41	0.6	6	2
Arizona	11	29	0.9	10	36	0.8	3	7
Arkansas	10	34	0.8	12	29	1.0	0	12
California	88	3	7.4	95	3	7.6	22	73
Colorado	16	22	1.3	18	22	1.4	3	15
Connecticut	15	24	1.3	15	24	1.2	1	14
Delaware	20	19	1.7	19	21	1.5	1	18
District of Columbia	0	(X)	0.0	0	(X)	0.0	0	0
Florida	51	6	4.3	55	7	4.4	4	51
Georgia	13	26	1.1	13	27	1.0	2	11
Hawaii	7	42	0.6	3	47	0.2	2	1
Idaho	9	38	0.8	10	36	0.8	2	8
Illinois	37	10	3.1	37	10	2.9	4	33
Indiana	35	11	2.9	33	12	2.6	0	33
Iowa	21	18	1.8	20	19	1.6	1	19
Kansas	11	29	0.9	10	36	0.8	1	9
Kentucky	17	21	1.4	20	19	1.6	1	19
Louisiana	11	29	0.9	12	29	1.0	1	11
Maine	9	38	0.8	10	36	0.8	3	7

[Continued]

★ 456 ★

National Priority List Hazardous Waste Sites, by State or Area: 1990 and 1993
[Continued]

State or area	1990			1993				
	Total sites	Rank	Percent distribution	Total sites	Rank	Percent distribution	Federal	Non-Federal
Maryland	10	34	0.8	12	29	1.0	3	9
Massachusetts	25	14	2.1	31	13	2.5	8	23
Michigan	78	5	6.5	76	5	6.0	0	76
Minnesota	42	8	3.5	41	8	3.3	2	39
Mississippi	2	48	0.2	4	45	0.3	0	4
Missouri	24	15	2.0	23	17	1.8	3	20
Montana	10	34	0.8	8	41	0.6	0	8
Nebraska	6	43	0.5	10	36	0.8	1	9
Nevada	1	50	0.1	1	50	0.1	0	1
New Hampshire	16	22	1.3	17	23	1.4	1	16
New Jersey	109	1	9.1	109	1	8.7	6	103
New Mexico	10	34	0.8	11	34	0.9	2	9
New York	83	4	6.9	85	4	6.8	4	81
North Carolina	22	17	1.8	22	18	1.7	1	21
North Dakota	2	48	0.2	2	49	0.2	0	2
Ohio	33	12	2.8	36	11	2.9	3	33
Oklahoma	11	29	0.9	11	34	0.9	1	10
Oregon	8	40	0.7	12	29	1.0	2	10
Pennsylvania	95	2	7.9	99	2	7.9	4	95
Rhode Island	11	29	0.9	12	29	1.0	2	10
South Carolina	23	16	1.9	24	15	1.9	1	23
South Dakota	3	46	0.3	4	45	0.3	1	3
Tennessee	14	25	1.2	15	24	1.2	3	12
Texas	28	13	2.3	30	14	2.4	4	26
Utah	12	27	1.0	13	27	1.0	4	9
Vermont	8	40	0.7	8	41	0.6	0	8
Virginia	20	19	1.7	24	15	1.9	5	19
Washington	45	7	3.8	55	6	4.4	18	37
West Virginia	5	45	0.4	6	44	0.5	1	5
Wisconsin	39	9	3.3	40	9	3.2	0	40
Wyoming	3	46	0.3	3	47	0.2	1	2
Guam	1	(X)	(X)	2	(X)	(X)	1	1
Puerto Rico	9	(X)	(X)	9	(X)	(X)	1	8
Virgin Islands	0	(X)	(X)	1	(X)	(X)	0	1

Source: 1994 Statistical Abstract of the United States on CD-ROM [machine-readable datafiles]. CD-8A-94. Washington, DC: U.S. Department of Commerce, Economics and Statistics Administration, Bureau of the Census, Data User Services Division, January 1995. Primary source: U.S. Environmental Protection Agency. *Supplementary Materials: National Priorities List, Proposed Rule.* Vol. 3, no. 2 (June 1993). *Note:* "X" represents "not applicable."

★ 457 ★

Superfund

National Priority List Sites, by Setting

According to the source: "The Environmental Protection Agency estimates that between 20 and 40 million Americans live within four miles of the country's worst hazardous waste sites.... Approximately 36,000 sites are included in an EPA database of possible hazardous waste sites.... The worst of the sites known by EPA and evaluated by the agency are listed on the National Priorities List (NPL) of sites designated for cleanup under the Comprehensive Environmental Response, Compensation and Liability Act (the Superfund law). About 100 sites are added to the list each year" (p. 484). The table below shows NPL site settings and land uses.

[In percentages]

Setting/vicinity	Sites
Site setting	
Rural areas	42.0
Suburban areas	39.3
Urban areas	18.4
Land use in site vicinity	
Residential areas	81.8
Industrial areas	47.4
Commercial districts	41.6
Agricultural areas	34.5
Forests/fields	26.7
Military & other federal facilities	10.6
Mining	8.5
Other & unspecified	24.1

Source: Breslin, Karen. "In Our Own Backyards: The Continuing Threat of Hazardous Waste." *Environmental Health Perspectives* 101, no. 6 (November 1993), p. 484. Primary source: U.S. Environmental Protection Agency. *NPL Characterization Report* (1990).

★ 458 ★

Superfund

National Priority List Sites, by State or Territory: 1993

Table shows the distribution of National Priority List (NPL) sites as of June 1993. Number of sites totaled 1,270 at that time.

State or territory	Number of NPL sites
Alabama	14
Alaska	8
Arizona	10
Arkansas	12
California	95
Colorado	18

[Continued]

★ 458 ★

National Priority List Sites, by State or Territory:
1993
[Continued]

State or territory	Number of NPL sites
Connecticut	15
Delaware	19
Florida	55
Georgia	13
Hawaii	3
Idaho	10
Illinois	37
Indiana	33
Iowa	20
Kansas	10
Kentucky	20
Louisiana	12
Maine	10
Maryland	12
Massachusetts	31
Michigan	76
Minnesota	41
Mississippi	4
Missouri	23
Montana	8
Nebraska	10
Nevada	1
New Hampshire	17
New Jersey	109
New Mexico	11
New York	85
North Carolina	22
North Dakota	2
Ohio	36
Oklahoma	11
Oregon	12
Pennsylvania	99
Rhode Island	12
South Carolina	24
South Dakota	4
Tennessee	15
Texas	30
Utah	13
Vermont	8
Virginia	24
Washington	55
West Virginia	6
Wisconsin	40
Wyoming	3

[Continued]

★ 458 ★

National Priority List Sites, by State or Territory: 1993

[Continued]

State or territory	Number of NPL sites
Guam	2
Puerto Rico	9
Virgin Islands	1

Source: "Distribution of National Priority List Sites by States and Territories." *Best's Review-P/C* (May 1994), p. 34. Primary source: U.S. Environmental Protection Agency.

★ 459 ★

Superfund

Superfund Liability

Clean Sites Inc., a nonpartisan organization, has identified about 1,000 cities, villages, boroughs, towns, and townships with Superfund liabilities for the clean up of municipal landfills. As "potentially responsible parties," these communities likely will assume costs for the clean up of Superfund sites. The table below shows the population sizes of potentially responsible parties.

Population	Cities
Under 5,000	178
5,000 to 49,999	106
50,000 to 500,000	31
Over 500,000	17

Source: O'Reilly, James. "PCMI Option May Help Cities Deal With Superfund Liability." *American City & County* (January 1993), p. 33. Primary source: Clean Sites Inc. *Main Street Meets Superfund: Local Government Involvement At Superfund Hazardous Waste Sites, January 1992* (Alexandria, Virginia; 1992).

★ 460 ★
Superfund

Superfund Sites, by Metropolitan Area

New York - 56	
Philadelphia - 44	
San Francisco - 29	
Chicago - 22	
Minneapolis - 22	
Los Angeles - 21	
Seattle - 18	
Boston - 16	
Miami - 16	
Detroit - 11	

Table shows the metropolitan areas with the most Superfund sites.

Metropolitan area	Number of sites
New York	56
Philadelphia	44
San Francisco	29
Chicago	22
Minneapolis	22
Los Angeles	21
Seattle	18
Boston	16
Miami	16
Detroit	11

Source: "Superfund and the City." *Water Environment & Technology* (August 1994), p. 16. Primary sources: Environmental Protection Agency Superfund Program; *1994 Environmental Almanac.*

Toxic Release Inventory

★ 461 ★

Toxic Release Inventory Releases and Transfers: 1991-1992

Table provides a comparison of Toxic Release Inventory (TRI) releases and transfers between 1991 and 1992.

[In pounds, except as noted]

Releases and transfers	1991	1992	Change in amount	Percent change
Total facilities (number)	24,294	23,630	(664)	-2.7
Total forms (number)	83,815	81,016	(2,799)	-3.3
Total air emissions	2,036,678,204	1,844,958,336	(191,719,868)	-9.4
Fugitive air	633,586,799	549,351,729	(84,235,070)	-13.3
Point source air	1,403,091,405	1,295,606,607	(107,484,798)	-7.7
Surface water discharges	243,351,148	272,932,953	29,581,805	12.2
Underground injection	710,366,770	725,946,415	15,579,645	2.2
Releases to land	414,844,420	337,809,053	(77,035,367)	-18.6
Total releases	3,405,240,542	3,181,646,757	(223,593,785)	-6.6
Transfers to recycling	2,266,829,164	2,839,825,919	572,996,755	25.3
Transfers to energy recovery	443,311,526	477,639,264	34,327,738	7.7
Transfers to treatment	353,150,798	393,466,540	40,315,742	11.4
Transfers to POTWs	395,560,966	381,096,823	(14,464,143)	-3.7
Transfers to disposal	267,586,409	258,642,577	(8,943,832)	-3.3
Other off-site transfers[1]	10,316,150	16,933,490	6,617,340	64.1
Total transfers	3,736,755,013	4,367,604,613	630,849,600	16.9
Total releases and transfers	7,141,995,555	7,549,251,370	407,255,815	5.7

Source: U.S. Environmental Protection Agency. "Toxic Release Inventory, 1992." In *National Economic, Social, and Environmental Data Bank* [CD-ROM]. Prepared by U.S. Department of Commerce, Economics and Statistics Administration. Washington, DC: U.S. Department of Commerce, National Economic, Social, and Environmental Data Bank, Economics and Statistics Administration, Office of Business Analysis, February 1995. *Notes:* "POTWs" are publicly owned treatment works. 1. Other transfers are transfers reported with missing or invalid waste management codes.

★ 462 ★
Toxic Release Inventory

Toxic Release Inventory Releases, by State or Territory: 1992

Table shows the releases of all Toxic Release Inventory (TRI) chemicals. See also related table on transfers.

[In pounds]

State or territory	Fugitive or nonpoint air emissions	Stack or point air emissions	Surface water discharges	Underground injection	Releases to land	Total releases	Rank
Alabama	14,766,447	80,155,915	5,078,042	6,269,431	6,144,897	112,414,732	8
Alaska	946,556	9,999,390	3,907,576	192	457	14,854,171	37
American Samoa	11,240	0	0	0	0	11,240	53
Arizona	3,990,312	4,402,548	5	0	37,721,228	46,114,093	22
Arkansas	8,533,559	19,557,542	1,434,309	11,995,448	2,247,087	43,767,945	24
California	25,704,187	30,160,539	10,212,654	884,806	3,589,861	70,552,047	14
Colorado	2,234,375	2,856,197	139,955	500	277,861	5,508,888	44
Connecticut	5,939,914	7,569,385	3,067,723	0	3,902	16,580,924	34
Delaware	1,270,271	3,738,222	236,887	0	138,518	5,383,898	45
Florida	11,825,436	21,707,703	3,283,487	11,772,909	33,863,305	82,452,840	12
Georgia	12,320,452	38,149,707	3,679,910	15	1,265,341	55,415,425	20
Hawaii	449,878	146,108	7,210	269,261	1,510	873,967	51
Idaho	587,695	4,620,389	160,405	0	2,875,528	8,244,017	42
Illinois	23,293,102	49,905,112	5,744,242	20,942,184	18,293,118	118,177,758	7
Indiana	28,060,916	57,870,503	1,057,170	3,777,831	33,534,069	124,300,489	5
Iowa	5,800,992	26,812,863	1,276,714	0	1,528,882	35,419,451	26
Kansas	9,810,879	15,723,162	733,170	59,642,195	1,300,740	87,210,146	10
Kentucky	11,666,067	26,852,533	576,039	29,040,503	1,593,133	69,728,275	15
Louisiana	21,540,139	67,511,483	186,329,129	186,673,578	2,497,703	464,552,032	1
Maine	2,200,855	11,017,818	591,203	405	1,461,538	15,271,819	35
Maryland	3,813,351	6,758,618	838,672	0	1,592,309	13,002,950	41
Massachusetts	5,078,578	9,274,729	74,809	0	102,601	14,530,717	38
Michigan	16,745,464	49,633,661	750,074	6,083,782	10,313,476	83,526,457	11
Minnesota	5,729,081	23,881,866	502,921	0	1,505,226	31,619,094	27
Mississippi	13,160,820	41,190,276	1,545,410	57,994,938	5,803,832	119,695,276	6
Missouri	11,366,604	25,014,770	1,119,222	250	14,896,038	52,396,884	21
Montana	1,104,641	1,683,973	139,875	0	40,959,484	43,887,973	23
Nebraska	3,359,723	9,220,859	444,578	0	105,502	13,130,662	40
Nevada	366,694	510,501	370	0	2,768,641	3,646,206	46
New Hampshire	1,666,080	4,305,279	74,669	0	7,859	6,053,887	43
New Jersey	7,939,632	12,466,348	415,684	750	619,823	21,442,237	31
New Mexico	478,650	1,495,040	6	0	18,395,674	20,369,370	32
New York	16,323,183	38,965,922	1,779,412	0	1,575,410	58,643,927	19
North Carolina	17,818,822	64,264,845	750,668	0	20,749,490	103,583,825	9
North Dakota	492,407	1,262,958	118,022	0	30,759	1,904,146	49
Ohio	28,189,163	62,512,460	4,774,674	25,090,607	23,243,306	143,810,210	4
Oklahoma	7,901,256	16,301,942	1,075,537	2,029,508	864,194	28,172,437	28
Oregon	4,374,968	12,011,100	507,540	0	2,759,377	19,652,985	33
Pennsylvania	25,625,394	35,859,024	1,351,030	250	4,795,555	67,631,253	18
Puerto Rico	7,084,573	7,257,922	45,961	250	14,296	14,403,002	39
Rhode Island	2,024,624	1,294,828	115,849	0	16,830	3,452,131	47
South Carolina	16,899,203	45,038,227	1,053,027	0	4,934,161	67,924,618	17
South Dakota	491,448	2,418,172	57,005	0	5	2,966,630	48

[Continued]

★ 462 ★

Toxic Release Inventory Releases, by State or Territory: 1992

[Continued]

State or territory	Fugitive or nonpoint air emissions	Stack or point air emissions	Surface water discharges	Underground injection	Releases to land	Total releases	Rank
Tennessee	35,842,871	91,531,459	2,625,582	63,508,375	678,950	194,187,237	3
Texas	76,125,814	81,325,796	16,754,975	227,453,795	17,901,649	419,562,029	2
Utah	3,723,298	65,291,333	103,845	0	10,087,907	79,206,383	13
Vermont	343,399	486,575	32,363	0	7,753	870,090	52
Virgin Islands	1,192,682	362,207	111,274	0	614	1,666,777	50
Virginia	19,147,340	44,879,730	1,896,631	1	2,442,147	68,365,849	16
Washington	7,115,719	14,892,830	4,037,428	0	476,174	26,522,151	29
West Virginia	8,406,928	14,614,371	1,523,102	0	261,463	24,805,864	30
Wisconsin	7,612,029	29,402,986	676,379	300	1,523,745	39,215,439	25
Wyoming	854,018	1,438,881	120,529	12,514,351	36,125	14,963,904	36
Total	549,351,729	1,295,606,607	272,932,953	725,946,415	337,809,053	3,181,646,757	

Source: U.S. Environmental Protection Agency. "Toxic Release Inventory, 1992." In *National Economic, Social, and Environmental Data Bank* [CD-ROM]. Prepared by U.S. Department of Commerce, Economics and Statistics Administration. Washington, DC: U.S. Department of Commerce, National Economic, Social, and Environmental Data Bank, Economics and Statistics Administration, Office of Business Analysis, February 1995.

★ 463 ★

Toxic Release Inventory

Toxic Release Inventory Releases in the United States: 1988, 1990-1992

[In pounds]

Year	Fugitive or nonpoint air emissions	Stack or point air emissions	Surface water discharges	Underground injection	Releases to land	Total releases
1992	536,680,299	1,284,284,917	272,905,180	725,820,874	337,590,822	3,157,282,092
1991	616,663,149	1,388,425,487	243,331,324	710,237,637	414,576,639	3,373,234,236
1990	713,869,291	1,590,610,816	198,131,625	754,523,494	436,018,244	3,693,153,470
1988	829,601,355	1,853,850,246	311,236,419	1,343,657,667	514,592,116	4,852,937,803

Source: U.S. Environmental Protection Agency. "Toxic Release Inventory, 1992." In *National Economic, Social, and Environmental Data Bank* [CD-ROM]. Prepared by U.S. Department of Commerce, Economics and Statistics Administration. Washington, DC: U.S. Department of Commerce, National Economic, Social, and Environmental Data Bank, Economics and Statistics Administration, Office of Business Analysis, February 1995. *Notes:* Does not include data for aluminum oxide, delisted chemicals, or chemicals added in 1990 and 1991. Does not include Guam and Northern Mariana Islands.

★ 464 ★

Toxic Release Inventory

Toxic Release Inventory Releases to Air, Water, and Land, by State or Territory: 1992

Data are arranged in order of total air, water, and land releases.

[In pounds]

State or territory	Air emissions	Surface water discharges	Releases to land	Total air, water, land releases
Louisiana	89,051,622	186,329,129	2,497,703	277,878,454
Texas	157,451,610	16,754,975	17,901,649	192,108,234
Tennessee	127,374,330	2,625,582	678,950	130,678,862
Indiana	85,931,419	1,057,170	33,534,069	120,522,658
Ohio	90,701,623	4,774,674	23,243,306	118,719,603
Alabama	94,922,362	5,078,042	6,144,897	106,145,301
North Carolina	82,083,667	750,668	20,749,490	103,583,825
Illinois	73,198,214	5,744,242	18,293,118	97,235,574
Utah	69,014,631	103,845	10,087,907	79,206,383
Michigan	66,379,125	750,074	10,313,476	77,442,675
Florida	33,533,139	3,283,487	33,863,305	70,679,931
California	55,864,726	10,212,654	3,589,861	69,667,241
Virginia	64,027,070	1,896,631	2,442,147	68,365,848
South Carolina	61,937,430	1,053,027	4,934,161	67,924,618
Pennsylvania	61,484,418	1,351,030	4,795,555	67,631,003
Mississippi	54,351,096	1,545,410	5,803,832	61,700,338
New York	55,289,105	1,779,412	1,575,410	58,643,927
Georgia	50,470,159	3,679,910	1,265,341	55,415,410
Missouri	36,381,374	1,119,222	14,896,038	52,396,634
Arizona	8,392,860	5	37,721,228	46,114,093
Montana	2,788,614	139,875	40,959,484	43,887,973
Kentucky	38,518,600	576,039	1,593,133	40,687,772
Wisconsin	37,015,015	676,379	1,523,745	39,215,139
Iowa	32,613,855	1,276,714	1,528,882	35,419,451
Arkansas	28,091,101	1,434,309	2,247,087	31,772,497
Minnesota	29,610,947	502,921	1,505,226	31,619,094
Kansas	25,534,041	733,170	1,300,740	27,567,951
Washington	22,008,549	4,037,428	476,174	26,522,151
Oklahoma	24,203,198	1,075,537	864,194	26,142,929
West Virginia	23,021,299	1,523,102	261,463	24,805,864
New Jersey	20,405,980	415,684	619,823	21,441,487
New Mexico	1,973,690	6	18,395,674	20,369,370
Oregon	16,386,068	507,540	2,759,377	19,652,985
Connecticut	13,509,299	3,067,723	3,902	16,580,924
Maine	13,218,673	591,203	1,461,538	15,271,414
Alaska	10,945,946	3,907,576	457	14,853,979
Massachusetts	14,353,307	74,809	102,601	14,530,717
Puerto Rico	14,342,495	45,961	14,296	14,402,752
Nebraska	12,580,582	444,578	105,502	13,130,662
Maryland	10,571,969	838,672	1,592,309	13,002,950
Idaho	5,208,084	160,405	2,875,528	8,244,017
New Hampshire	5,971,359	74,669	7,859	6,053,887

[Continued]

★ 464 ★

Toxic Release Inventory Releases to Air, Water, and Land, by State or Territory: 1992

[Continued]

State or territory	Air emissions	Surface water discharges	Releases to land	Total air, water, land releases
Colorado	5,090,572	139,955	277,861	5,508,388
Delaware	5,008,493	236,887	138,518	5,383,898
Nevada	877,195	370	2,768,641	3,646,206
Rhode Island	3,319,452	115,849	16,830	3,452,131
South Dakota	2,909,620	57,005	5	2,966,630
Wyoming	2,292,899	120,529	36,125	2,449,553
North Dakota	1,755,365	118,022	30,759	1,904,146
Virgin Islands	1,554,889	111,274	614	1,666,777
Vermont	829,974	32,363	7,753	870,090
Hawaii	595,986	7,210	1,510	604,706
American Samoa	11,240	0	0	11,240
Total	1,844,958,336	272,932,953	337,809,053	2,455,700,342

Source: U.S. Environmental Protection Agency. "Toxic Release Inventory, 1992." In *National Economic, Social, and Environmental Data Bank* [CD-ROM]. Prepared by U.S. Department of Commerce, Economics and Statistics Administration. Washington, DC: U.S. Department of Commerce, National Economic, Social, and Environmental Data Bank, Economics and Statistics Administration, Office of Business Analysis, February 1995.

★ 465 ★

Toxic Release Inventory

Toxic Release Inventory Transfers: 1992

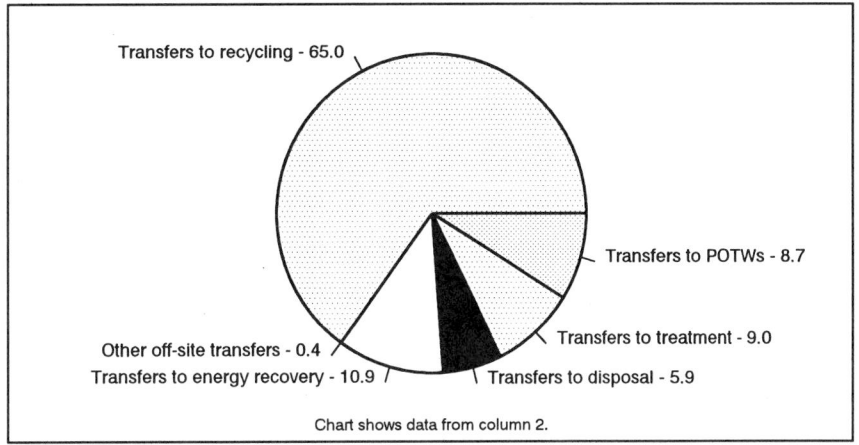

Chart shows data from column 2.

Table shows Toxic Release Inventory (TRI) transfers. Transfers for 1992 totaled 4,367,604,613 pounds.

1992 transfers	Pounds	Percent
Transfers to recycling	2,839,825,919	65.0
Transfers to energy recovery	477,639,264	10.9
Transfers to treatment	393,466,540	9.0
Transfers to POTWs	381,096,823	8.7
Transfers to disposal	258,642,577	5.9
Other off-site transfers	16,933,490	0.4

Source: U.S. Environmental Protection Agency. "Toxic Release Inventory, 1992." In *National Economic, Social, and Environmental Data Bank* [CD-ROM]. Prepared by U.S. Department of Commerce, Economics and Statistics Administration. Washington, DC: U.S. Department of Commerce, National Economic, Social, and Environmental Data Bank, Economics and Statistics Administration, Office of Business Analysis, February 1995. *Note:* "POTWs" are publicly owned treatment works.

★ 466 ★

Toxic Release Inventory

Toxic Release Inventory Transfers, by State or Territory: 1992

Table shows the transfers of all Toxic Release Inventory (TRI) chemicals. See also related table on releases.

[In pounds]

State or territory	Transfers to recycling	Transfers to energy recovery	Transfers to treatment	Transfers to POTWs	Transfers to disposal	Other[1] offsite transfers	Total transfers
Alabama	37,395,734	11,317,763	10,002,833	1,097,314	6,269,626	3,523,948	69,607,218
Alaska	242,373	0	3,088	20	40	0	245,521
American Samoa	0	0	0	0	0	0	0
Arizona	25,568,056	958,400	2,217,865	488,744	132,571	14,362	29,379,998

[Continued]

★ 466 ★

Toxic Release Inventory Transfers, by State or Territory: 1992
[Continued]

State or territory	Transfers to recycling	Transfers to energy recovery	Transfers to treatment	Transfers to POTWs	Transfers to disposal	Other[1] offsite transfers	Total transfers
Arkansas	52,662,167	5,068,940	1,403,473	507,607	5,172,469	57,677	64,872,333
California	123,936,368	12,450,501	6,854,269	21,250,793	5,848,678	114,136	170,454,745
Colorado	9,183,768	2,012,002	3,074,583	513,901	172,496	250	14,957,000
Connecticut	21,284,285	4,485,697	6,007,190	1,830,985	953,588	237,527	34,799,272
Delaware	7,768,213	1,388,720	767,827	2,461,868	42,934	0	12,429,562
Florida	20,008,993	4,939,383	5,962,703	12,513,210	1,990,984	1,500	45,416,773
Georgia	54,805,619	6,731,845	3,028,572	4,887,889	7,857,111	18,334	77,329,370
Hawaii	26,749	0	15	30,000	163,500	0	220,264
Idaho	346,467	302,663	70,395	2,063,990	35,465	0	2,818,980
Illinois	161,297,773	32,605,832	18,100,845	72,221,011	12,955,462	777,646	297,958,569
Indiana	341,282,661	18,015,870	41,190,745	4,402,399	14,430,737	820,996	420,143,408
Iowa	16,871,054	3,640,877	2,275,573	8,722,686	1,852,550	46,050	33,408,790
Kansas	44,222,880	2,316,495	4,021,017	3,608,102	9,162,353	104,452	63,435,299
Kentucky	62,743,147	11,127,746	9,551,771	2,414,318	3,243,462	676,902	89,757,346
Louisiana	231,989,078	6,882,645	5,135,902	65,044	3,834,727	250	247,907,646
Maine	2,539,404	430,462	262,611	662,867	902,685	4,320	4,802,349
Maryland	24,123,689	1,139,762	1,766,794	4,603,586	419,248	1,830	32,054,909
Massachusetts	19,512,246	8,908,572	5,583,501	5,086,842	1,699,677	246,583	41,037,421
Michigan	122,096,833	73,946,823	21,542,900	14,603,830	19,999,289	596,888	252,786,563
Minnesota	18,426,894	4,952,100	2,883,377	5,077,928	635,538	23,295	31,999,132
Mississippi	62,900,235	3,304,435	631,323	834,427	1,158,442	16,035	68,844,897
Missouri	183,300,509	11,583,162	74,159,677	22,893,750	2,849,323	83,784	294,870,205
Montana	2,481,824	117,064	10,142	27,798	154,333	0	2,791,161
Nebraska	14,210,583	1,133,219	1,909,910	1,458,203	3,918,367	1,264,675	23,894,957
Nevada	419,922	12,816	25,647	9,832	104,198	0	572,415
New Hampshire	6,993,658	428,063	580,617	500,121	348,950	1,000	8,852,409
New Jersey	103,116,529	28,817,117	18,778,453	37,871,671	2,602,616	262,619	191,449,005
New Mexico	313,771	227,060	75,712	213,548	23,729	350	854,170
New York	54,187,040	10,281,862	8,704,889	9,168,633	5,486,109	256,771	88,085,304
North Carolina	109,655,255	10,527,347	6,195,335	4,237,959	4,630,110	778,514	136,024,520
North Dakota	114,470	60,934	83,096	191,497	40,768	0	490,765
Ohio	187,635,645	37,352,001	31,058,073	20,745,800	28,139,365	1,690,674	306,621,558
Oklahoma	13,546,881	1,241,820	1,404,342	183,932	7,162,410	6,825	23,546,210
Oregon	12,604,632	589,211	764,380	4,275,478	3,118,674	4,800	21,357,175
Pennsylvania	119,900,060	18,172,115	29,273,713	13,205,484	23,937,935	3,164,684	207,653,991
Puerto Rico	11,836,770	9,262,409	4,178,882	4,744,380	425,286	45,188	30,492,915
Rhode Island	10,687,202	424,267	614,488	446,844	1,972,923	11,628	14,157,352
South Carolina	73,904,607	8,477,487	6,291,077	4,376,717	5,500,977	422,353	98,973,218
South Dakota	232,301	277,083	76,739	146,802	49,626	25,344	807,895
Tennessee	51,788,406	11,918,428	2,969,850	21,157,009	16,704,049	45,619	104,583,361
Texas	210,676,070	82,367,924	36,734,826	32,343,665	31,562,033	1,036,725	394,721,243
Utah	32,283,024	329,018	397,556	613,392	4,247,283	0	37,870,273
Vermont	4,317,515	531,800	155,838	69,162	37,273	0	5,111,588
Virgin Islands	703	0	176	0	57,180	0	58,059
Virginia	24,383,922	8,142,682	2,664,560	18,950,994	1,605,751	16,074	55,763,983

[Continued]

★ 466 ★

Toxic Release Inventory Transfers, by State or Territory: 1992

[Continued]

State or territory	Transfers to recycling	Transfers to energy recovery	Transfers to treatment	Transfers to POTWs	Transfers to disposal	Other[1] offsite transfers	Total transfers
Washington	73,415,105	874,582	987,801	479,968	1,150,347	16,173	76,923,976
West Virginia	36,690,521	9,950,309	2,676,802	1,912,254	2,591,662	21,812	53,843,360
Wisconsin	39,886,693	7,611,813	10,349,625	10,894,409	11,220,687	494,897	80,458,124
Wyoming	7,615	138	5,162	28,160	66,981	0	108,056
Total	2,839,825,919	477,639,264	393,466,540	381,096,823	258,642,577	16,933,490	4,367,604,613

Source: U.S. Environmental Protection Agency. "Toxic Release Inventory, 1992." In *National Economic, Social, and Environmental Data Bank* [CD-ROM]. Prepared by U.S. Department of Commerce, Economics and Statistics Administration. Washington, DC: U.S. Department of Commerce, National Economic, Social, and Environmental Data Bank, Economics and Statistics Administration, Office of Business Analysis, February 1995. *Notes:* "POTWs" are publicly owned treatment works. 1. Other transfers are transfers reported with missing or invalid waste management codes.

★ 467 ★

Toxic Release Inventory

Toxic Release Inventory Transfers in the United States: 1988, 1990-1992

[In pounds]

Year	Transfers to recycling[1]	Transfers to energy recovery[1]	Transfers to treatment	Transfers to POTWs	Transfers to disposal	Other offsite transfers[2]	Total transfers[3]
1992	2,838,465,419	477,307,370	389,675,327	380,708,363	256,005,214	16,876,490	4,359,038,183
1991	2,264,903,256	442,199,308	351,112,534	394,421,377	262,810,417	10,288,734	3,725,735,626
1990	NA	NA	374,810,144	469,486,355	433,105,439	55,963,051	1,333,364,989
1988	NA	NA	492,538,569	581,038,548	484,882,422	56,911,929	1,615,371,468

Source: U.S. Environmental Protection Agency. "Toxic Release Inventory, 1992." In *National Economic, Social, and Environmental Data Bank* [CD-ROM]. Prepared by U.S. Department of Commerce, Economics and Statistics Administration. Washington, DC: U.S. Department of Commerce, National Economic, Social, and Environmental Data Bank, Economics and Statistics Administration, Office of Business Analysis, February 1995. *Notes:* Does not include data for aluminum oxide, delisted chemicals, or chemicals added in 1990 and 1991. "POTWs" are publicly owned treatment works. Does not include Guam and Northern Mariana Islands. 1. "NA" indicates that transfers for recycling and energy recovery were not required to be reported for 1988 and 1990. 2. For 1991 and 1992, transfers reported with no waste management codes or invalid codes. For 1988 and 1990, transfers reported with no waste managment codes, invalid codes, or codes not required to be reported in 1988 and 1990. 3. Because transfers for recycling or energy recovery were not required to be reported in 1988 and 1990, total transfers in those years are not comparable total transfers reported in 1991 and 1992.

Toxic Release Inventory: Facilities and Sites

★ 468 ★

Chemical Company Toxic Releases and Transfers, by Media: 1993

The 1993 annual Chemical Manufacturers Association (CMA) survey indicated that chemical companies' toxic releases declined 16 percent that year. Transfers decreased by 21 percent, injections by 14 percent. The table below show releases by media and transfers.

[In million pounds]

	1990	1991	1992	1993[1]
Air	408	378	340	286
Water	9	9	7	7
Land	32	30	31	26
Total releases	449	417	378	319
Treatment	148	157	106	99
Land disposal	38	32	31	19
POTWs[2]	134	113	109	77
Total transfers[3]	320	302	246	195
Underground injection	426	421	425	365

Source: Lucas, Allison. "CMA Companies Report Reduction in Toxic Releases." *ChemicalWeek*, 22 March 1995, p. 20. *Notes:* 1. Projection based on a survey of 55 companies that account for 90 percent of Toxic Release Inventory (TRI) releases and transfers reported by CMA member companies. 2. Publicly owned treatment works. 3. Excludes transfers for recycling and energy recovery.

★ 469 ★

Toxic Release Inventory: Facilities and Sites

Facilities With Greatest Decrease in Air, Water, and Land Releases: 1991-1992

Table shows the 50 Toxic Release Inventory (TRI) facilities with the greatest decrease in air, water, and land releases from 1991 to 1992. Data reflect total decreases. Table does include facilities who reported in 1991, but not in 1992, or nonmanufacturing facilities who voluntarily reported. Numbers in parenthesis are negative.

[In pounds]

Facility (City, State)	Net change, 1991-1992				Water/land releases		
	Fugitive nonpoint air emissions	Stack point air emissions	Surface water discharges	Releases to land	1991	1992	Change, 1991-1992
BASF Corp. (Lowland, Tennessee)	(1,502,500)	(18,024,245)	(30,960)	(1,393,400)	21,190,120	239,015	(20,951,105)
Asarco Inc. (Hayden, Arizona)	36,377	(58,601)	0	(13,476,180)	26,483,591	12,985,187	(13,498,404)
Phelps Dodge Mining Co. (Playas, New Mexico)	0	(43,317)	0	(12,011,975)	23,847,647	11,792,355	(12,055,292)
Doe Run Co. (Herculaneum, Missouri)	(48)	(121,923)	253	(9,873,707)	16,473,112	6,477,687	(9,995,425)
Eastman Kodak Co. (Kingsport, Tennessee)	(15,658,333)	7,464,942	(81,052)	114,330	40,582,580	32,422,467	(8,160,113)

[Continued]

★ 469 ★

Facilities With Greatest Decrease in Air, Water, and Land Releases: 1991-1992

[Continued]

Facility (City, State)	Net change, 1991-1992				Water/land releases		
	Fugitive nonpoint air emissions	Stack point air emissions	Surface water discharges	Releases to land	1991	1992	Change, 1991-1992
3M Co. (Hutchinson, Minnesota)	(538,704)	(7,192,925)	0	0	13,384,468	5,652,839	(7,731,629)
Molycorp. Inc. (Mountain Pass, California)	(151,727)	(253,993)	0	(4,963,011)	6,388,368	1,019,637	(5,368,731)
Wheeling-Pittsburgh Steel Corp. (Mingo Junction, Ohio)	(130)	2	(46,314)	(4,277,000)	7,770,134	3,446,692	(4,323,442)
Westinghouse Electric Corp. (Ogden, Utah)	(245)	(28,800)	0	(4,276,100)	4,376,865	71,720	(4,305,145)
Du Pont (Memphis, Tennessee)	(61,586)	(4,044,534)	2,970	0	6,205,055	2,101,905	(4,103,150)
Magnesium Corporation of America (Rowley, Utah)	(125,492)	(3,903,400)	0	(250)	64,937,205	60,908,063	(4,029,142)
Kennecott Utah Copper (Magna, Utah)	1,900	(61,700)	(1,900)	(3,949,455)	14,234,230	10,223,075	(4,011,155)
Baxter Healthcare Corp. (Johnson City, Tennessee)	(76,335)	(3,821,812)	0	0	3,902,357	4,210	(3,898,147)
General Motors Corp. (Defiance, Ohio)	34,417	33,667	(43,532)	(3,919,726)	7,364,915	3,469,741	(3,895,174)
General Motors Corp. (Saginaw, Michigan)	(4,823)	(103,077)	0	(3,080,961)	9,008,413	5,819,552	(3,188,861)
Agrico Chemical Co. (Saint James, Louisiana)	(240)	(5,209,900)	2,150,600	16,000	93,843,660	90,800,120	(3,043,540)
General Electric Co. Plastics (Mount Vernon, Indiana)	(1,198,679)	(1,658,157)	6,531	0	4,965,224	2,114,919	(2,850,305)
Miles Inc. (Orange, Texas)	(2,173,000)	(454,945)	(132)	49	4,928,554	2,300,526	(2,628,028)
Armco Steel Co. L.P. (Middletown, Ohio)	(450,580)	(162,350)	(160,974)	(1,845,608)	5,019,633	2,400,121	(2,619,512)
Unocal Petroleum Products (Kenai, Alaska)	358,087	(2,941,800)	43,961	(4,615)	11,455,765	8,911,398	(2,544,367)
Texas Eastman Co. (Longview, Texas)	(827,267)	(1,402,703)	(30,074)	(3,002)	6,651,161	4,388,115	(2,263,046)
Upjohn Co. (Portage, Michigan)	(4,000)	(2,056,660)	(164,490)	0	5,147,475	2,922,325	(2,225,150)
Du Pont Delisle (Pass Christian, Mississippi)	(14,703)	(2,200,400)	0	(100)	6,158,833	3,943,630	(2,215,203)
Du Pont Johnsonville Plant (New Johnsonville, Tennessee)	(950)	(2,180,100)	0	(1,250)	7,217,900	5,035,600	(2,182,300)
Sabh Water Heater Group (Johnson City, Tennessee)	(312,272)	(1,860,223)	0	0	2,521,685	349,190	(2,172,495)
Phillips 66 Co. (Borger, Texas)	32,647	(2,118,412)	(112)	(2,211)	4,095,699	2,007,611	(2,088,088)
International Paper Co. (Binghamton, New York)	(917,195)	(1,136,195)	0	0	2,380,355	326,965	(2,053,390)
Reynolds Metals Co. (Muscle Shoals, Alabama)	(185,742)	(1,799,738)	26	0	2,830,297	844,843	(1,985,454)
Mulberry Phosphates Inc. (Mulberry, Florida)	(1,999,000)	41,037	(4,164)	0	2,059,899	97,772	(1,962,127)
Westvaco Corp. (Covington, Virginia)	(150)	(1,897,280)	3,940	808	6,849,620	4,956,938	(1,892,682)
Boeing Wichita (Wichita, Kansas)	1,241,186	(2,998,428)	11,890	0	6,227,418	4,482,066	(1,745,352)
Packaging Corporation of America (Clyattville, Georgia)	7,850	(1,304,000)	(285,400)	4,950	2,360,710	784,110	(1,576,600)
Georgia-Pacific Corp. (Brunswick, Georgia)	(5,890)	(1,502,768)	(9,700)	(28,095)	4,495,896	2,949,443	(1,546,453)
Triad Chemical (Donaldsonville, Louisiana)	(2,345)	(1,507,839)	(21,269)	0	5,658,778	4,127,325	(1,531,453)
Magma Copper Co. (San Manuel, Arizona)	(20,513)	41,750	0	(1,536,636)	24,077,899	22,562,500	(1,515,399)
Wheeling-Pittsburgh Steel Corp. (Follansbee, West Virginia)	(121,733)	(1,425,280)	81,238	0	2,704,874	1,239,099	(1,465,775)
Cominco Fertilizers (Beatrice, Nebraska)	(14,400)	(1,501,300)	78,900	500	1,925,710	489,410	(1,436,300)
Geneva Steel (Orem, Utah)	20,897	(11,045)	(27,023)	(1,412,210)	1,811,253	381,872	(1,429,381)
Agricultural Minerals Ltd. (Verdigris, Oklahoma)	0	(1,412,000)	(10,212)	(250)	2,954,598	1,532,136	(1,422,462)
Texasgulf Inc. (Aurora, North Carolina)	109,700	419,550	(16,650)	(1,913,400)	15,841,460	14,440,660	(1,400,800)
Occidental Chemical Corp. (White Springs, Florida)	(60,000)	(14,000)	(980)	(1,300,000)	8,973,510	7,598,530	(1,374,980)
Inland Steel Co. (East Chicago, Indiana)	(241,246)	32,080	(81,409)	(1,075,273)	32,549,405	31,183,557	(1,365,848)
Champion International Corp. (Courtland, Alabama)	(273,636)	(1,068,220)	(5,760)	(2,844)	2,110,361	759,901	(1,350,460)
Farmland Ind. Inc. (Lawrence, Kansas)	(9,914)	(1,152,075)	(175,290)	(70)	3,794,029	2,456,680	(1,337,349)
Arcadian Fertilizer L.P. (Lake Charles, Louisiana)	(180,136)	(1,070,000)	(63,000)	(11)	4,023,162	2,710,015	(1,313,147)
3M Co. (Brownwood, Texas)	(296)	(1,287,955)	0	(347)	2,520,455	1,231,857	(1,288,598)
Kohler Co. (Kohler, Wisconsin)	(351,969)	(210,136)	(51,296)	(651,675)	1,359,374	94,298	(1,265,076)
Du Pont Cape Fear Plant (Leland, North Carolina)	(101,466)	(1,165,793)	1,576	27,297	5,661,502	4,423,116	(1,238,386)
Marine Shale Processors Inc. (Amelia, Louisiana)	483	(1,224,435)	48	0	3,569,059	2,345,155	(1,223,904)
Aristech Chemical Corp. (Haverhill, Ohio)	230	(1,219,551)	57	0	2,651,831	1,432,567	(1,219,264)
Total	(25,743,471)	(76,778,987)	1,070,297	(70,835,428)	567,546,104	395,258,515	(172,287,589)

Source: U.S. Environmental Protection Agency. "Toxic Release Inventory, 1992." In *National Economic, Social, and Environmental Data Bank* [CD-ROM]. Prepared by U.S. Department of Commerce, Economics and Statistics Administration. Washington, DC: U.S. Department of Commerce, National Economic, Social, and Environmental Data Bank, Economics and Statistics Administration, Office of Business Analysis, February 1995.

★ 470 ★

Toxic Release Inventory: Facilities and Sites

Facilities With Greatest Decrease in Underground Injection: 1991-1992

Table shows the 50 Toxic Release Inventory (TRI) facilities with the greatest decrease in underground injection from 1991 to 1992. Data reflect total decreases. Table does include facilities who reported in 1991, but not in 1992, or nonmanufacturing facilities who voluntarily reported. Numbers in parenthesis are negative.

[In pounds]

Facility (City, State)	Underground injection		Change,
	1991	1992	1991-1992
BASF Corp. (Geismar, Louisiana)	12,000,036	0	(12,000,036)
Citgo Petroleum Corp. (Lake Charles, Louisiana)	9,284,726	3,930,990	(5,353,736)
Du Pont Johnsonville Plant (New Johnsonville, Tennessee)	52,000,000	47,000,000	(5,000,000)
BP Chemicals Inc. (Lima, Ohio)	24,508,895	20,363,250	(4,145,645)
Du Pont (La Porte, Texas)	7,681,000	3,710,700	(3,970,300)
Du Pont (Victoria, Texas)	25,602,557	22,060,820	(3,541,737)
Mobil Oil Corp. (Chalmette, Louisiana)	3,269,610	55,885	(3,213,725)
Monsanto Co. (Cantonment, Florida)	8,644,827	6,028,556	(2,616,271)
BP Chemicals Inc. (Port Lavaca, Texas)	28,963,776	26,767,584	(2,196,192)
Great Lakes Chemical Corp. (El Dorado, Arkansas)	4,052,730	1,935,400	(2,117,330)
Zeneca Inc. (Bucks, Alabama)	7,982,277	6,269,383	(1,712,894)
Engelhard Corp. (Jackson, Mississippi)	7,368,299	5,992,194	(1,376,105)
Zeneca Specialties (Mount Pleasant, Tennessee)	17,528,207	16,508,125	(1,020,082)
Texaco Refining & Marketing (Bakersfield, California)	1,692,592	738,005	(954,587)
Celanese Engineering Resins (Bishop, Texas)	1,941,082	1,134,480	(806,602)
Witco Corp. (Harvey, Louisiana)	1,023,000	290,000	(733,000)
Borden Chemicals & Plastics (Geismar, Louisiana)	1,418,488	949,028	(469,460)
Hoechst-Celanese Chemical (Bay City, Texas)	2,756,699	2,346,305	(410,394)
Wil-Gro Fertilizer Inc. (Pryor, Oklahoma)	1,223,200	823,270	(399,930)
Merichem Co. (Houston, Texas)	3,719,400	3,327,300	(392,100)
Ethyl Corp. (Magnolia, Arkansas)	1,837,800	1,500,000	(337,800)
W. R. Grace & Co. (Deer Park, Texas)	575,686	238,771	(336,915)
Aristech Chemical Corp. (Haverhill, Ohio)	2,270,220	1,984,103	(286,117)
Witco Corp. (Taft, Louisiana)	2,393,371	2,142,937	(250,434)
Du Pont (La Place, Louisiana)	1,020,610	810,188	(210,422)
Great Lakes Chemical Corp. (Marysville, Arkansas)	590,000	380,000	(210,000)
Upjohn Co. (Portage, Michigan)	2,635,900	2,465,990	(169,910)
Great Lakes Chemical Corp. (El Dorado, Arkansas)	800,344	632,015	(168,329)
Uniroyal Chemical Co. Inc. (Geismar, Louisiana)	9,769,920	9,617,920	(152,000)
Agricultural Minerals Ltd. (Verdigris, Oklahoma)	1,288,000	1,138,000	(150,000)
Sandoz Agro Inc. (Beaumont, Texas)	756,660	653,440	(103,220)
Texaco Refining & Marketing (Bakersfield, California)	242,128	143,276	(98,852)
BHP Petroleum Americas (Kapolei, Hawaii)	140,030	45,030	(95,000)
American Cyanamid Co. (Milton, Florida)	305,585	220,038	(85,547)
Western Sugar Co. (Lovell, Wyoming)	81,450	0	(81,450)
Plymouth Tube Co. (Streator, Illinois)	77,791	0	(77,791)
Asarco Inc. (Amarillo, Texas)	5,881,195	5,808,239	(72,956)
Total Petroleum Inc. (Alma, Michigan)	342,977	271,994	(70,983)
Arco Chemical Co. (Channelview, Texas)	998,083	928,895	(69,188)
Zeneca Inc. (Saint Gabriel, Louisiana)	83,278	23,866	(59,412)
Chevron Chemical Co. (Belle Chasse, Louisiana)	357,053	299,810	(57,243)
Cominco Fertilizers Inc. (Borger, Texas)	418,821	372,217	(46,604)

[Continued]

★ 470 ★

Facilities With Greatest Decrease in Underground Injection: 1991-1992
[Continued]

Facility (City, State)	Underground injection		Change, 1991-1992
	1991	1992	
Bit Mfg. Inc. (Copperhill, Tennessee)	34,000	250	(33,750)
Du Pont (Orange, Texas)	4,376,529	4,347,083	(29,446)
Imco Recycling Inc. (Sapulpa, Oklahoma)	58,000	43,900	(14,100)
BASF Corp. (Freeport, Texas)	13,000	520	(12,480)
Martin Marietta Magnesia (Manistee, Michigan)	96,000	85,000	(11,000)
Gelman Sciences Inc. (Ann Arbor, Michigan)	9,096	0	(9,096)
Diamond Shamrock Inc. (Sunray, Texas)	614,620	606,448	(8,172)
Oxy Petrochemical Inc. (Corpus Christi, Texas)	9,050	2,100	(6,950)
Total	260,738,598	204,993,305	(55,745,293)

Source: U.S. Environmental Protection Agency. "Toxic Release Inventory, 1992." In *National Economic, Social, and Environmental Data Bank* [CD-ROM]. Prepared by U.S. Department of Commerce, Economics and Statistics Administration. Washington, DC: U.S. Department of Commerce, National Economic, Social, and Environmental Data Bank, Economics and Statistics Administration, Office of Business Analysis, February 1995.

★ 471 ★
Toxic Release Inventory: Facilities and Sites

Facilities With Greatest Increase in Air, Water, and Land Releases: 1991-1992

Table shows the 50 Toxic Release Inventory (TRI) facilities with the greatest increase in air, water, and land releases from 1991 to 1992. Data reflect total increases. Table does include facilities who reported in 1992, but not in 1991, or nonmanufacturing facilities who voluntarily reported.

[In pounds]

Facility (City, State)	Net change, 1991-1992				Total air, water, and land releases		
	Fugitive nonpoint air emissions	Stack point air emissions	Surface water discharges	Releases to land	1991	1992	Change, 1991-1992
Lenzing Fibers Corp. (Lowland, Tennessee)	1,600,510	18,800,255	27,500	0	0	20,428,265	20,428,265
Arcadian Fertilizer L.P. (Geismar, Louisiana)	272,370	94,040	16,078,550	479,860	23,563,341	40,488,161	16,924,820
Mobil Mining & Minerals Co. (Pasadena, Texas)	12,980	(307,300)	13,864,810	(17,105)	969,191	14,522,576	13,553,385
Agrico Chemical Co. (Uncle Sam, Louisiana)	(6,164)	(405,660)	9,664,523	2,604	49,187,528	58,442,831	9,255,303
Amoco Oil Co. (Texas City, Texas)	(58,979)	(35,641)	151,130	4,437,496	1,137,130	5,631,136	4,494,006
IMC Fertilizer Inc. (Mulberry, Florida)	147,000	(84,100)	0	3,633,000	10,074,105	13,770,005	3,695,900
Arcadian Fertilizer L.P. (Memphis, Tennessee)	(41,703)	3,652,400	9,701	0	4,220,148	7,840,546	3,620,398
Cabot Corp. (Ville Platte, Louisiana)	1,000	2,881,900	0	0	793,200	3,676,100	2,882,900
Asarco Inc. (East Helena, Montana)	(9,068)	8,777	0	2,451,422	38,623,430	41,074,561	2,451,131
Nicca USA Inc. (Fountain Inn, South Carolina)	(5)	750	0	2,235,040	5	2,235,790	2,235,785
Cabot Corp. (Franklin, Louisiana)	1,000	1,872,464	0	0	2,453,900	4,327,364	1,873,464
CPI (Wisconsin Rapids, Wisconsin)	0	1,833,500	(350)	0	1,362,205	3,195,355	1,833,150
Aqualon Co. (Hopewell, Virginia)	1,499,037	239,794	(11)	(2,075)	1,261,700	2,998,445	1,736,745
Asarco Inc. (Annapolis, Missouri)	104,020	43,252	(239)	1,426,263	6,690,831	8,264,127	1,573,296
Grain Processing Corp. (Muscatine, Iowa)	(22,033)	1,555,745	0	0	820,166	2,353,878	1,533,712
Bowater Inc. (Catawba, South Carolina)	(5,915)	290,297	96,053	1,106,674	2,461,883	3,948,992	1,487,109
Missouri Chemical Works (Louisiana, Missouri)	1,487,740	(67,000)	(813)	12,000	385,015	1,816,942	1,431,927
Northway Cabinetry Div. (Rensselaer, Indiana)	1,382,650	19,900	0	0	318,950	1,721,500	1,402,550
ITT Rayonier Inc. (Port Angeles, Washington)	(365)	487,670	868,140	0	2,506,835	3,862,280	1,355,445
SCM Chemicals Americas (Ashtabula, Ohio)	640	1,331,102	0	0	49,961	1,381,703	1,331,742
Arco Chemical Co. (Pasadena, Texas)	980,416	130,605	0	0	1,493,394	2,604,415	1,111,021
Chevron USA Products Co. (Port Arthur, Texas)	1,006,464	112,545	(1,892)	(16,803)	1,883,910	2,984,224	1,100,314
Du Pont Repauno Plant (Gibbstown, New Jersey)	2,512	1,071,139	155	0	79,319	1,153,125	1,073,806
Georgia-Pacific Corp. (New Augusta, Mississippi)	(4,277)	1,149,403	(100,729)	(23,594)	491,514	1,512,317	1,020,803
Degussa Carbon Black Ivanhoe (Louisa, Louisiana)	0	1,017,000	0	0	1,400,000	2,417,000	1,017,000

[Continued]

★ 471 ★

Facilities With Greatest Increase in Air, Water, and Land Releases: 1991-1992
[Continued]

Facility (City, State)	Net change, 1991-1992				Total air, water, and land releases		
	Fugitive nonpoint air emissions	Stack point air emissions	Surface water discharges	Releases to land	1991	1992	Change, 1991-1992
Union Camp Corp. (Eastover, South Carolina)	10,845	978,200	(100)	(1,295)	337,075	1,324,725	987,650
SCM Chemicals (Ashtabula, Ohio)	635	973,570	(35)	0	18,679	992,849	974,170
Mobil Chemical Co. (Beaumont, Texas)	238,421	728,589	(1,203)	299	613,472	1,579,578	966,106
Northwestern Steel & Wire Co. (Sterling, Illinois)	(8,020)	(18,510)	980	990,000	11,975,640	12,940,090	964,450
Mead Coated Board Inc. (Cottonton, Alabama)	(2,915)	930,000	6,161	(1,245)	1,245,211	2,177,212	932,001
Hickory Springs Mfg. Co. (Conover, North Carolina)	(25,232)	935,002	0	0	451,837	1,361,607	909,770
Holliston Mills Inc. (Church Hill, Tennessee)	4,319	859,125	(300)	0	3,780,619	4,643,763	863,144
Ford Motor Co. (Claycomo, Missouri)	99,721	736,990	0	0	1,726,251	2,562,962	836,711
SCM Chemicals (Baltimore, Maryland)	141	809,286	275	0	86,200	895,902	809,702
Mobil Chemical Co. (Beaumont, Texas)	699,877	93,451	294	(4)	751,382	1,545,000	793,618
Eli Lilly & Co. (Clinton, Indiana)	(1,006,255)	1,900,753	19,945	(122,375)	3,209,685	4,001,753	792,068
Garden State Tanning (Fleetwood, Pennsylvania)	(37,019)	814,341	0	0	975,601	1,752,923	777,322
Mt. Joy Wire Corp. (Mount Joy, Pennsylvania)	744,844	5,378	0	0	293,360	1,043,582	750,222
Chrysler Corp. (Detroit, Michigan)	156,321	556,199	0	0	5,188	717,708	712,520
Sun Graphic Inc. (Pompano Beach, Florida)	96,700	589,844	0	0	14,612	701,156	686,544
Anchor Continental Inc. (Columbia, South Carolina)	20,118	649,001	0	0	2,279,583	2,948,702	669,119
Zexel USA Corp. (Grand Prairie, Texas)	663,202	375	0	0	66,440	730,017	663,577
Chino Mines Co. (Hurley, New Mexico)	0	(31,326)	0	683,500	6,826,658	7,478,832	652,174
Griffin Wheel Co. (Bessemer, Alabama)	0	0	0	647,800	92,760	740,560	647,800
Federal Paper Board Co. Inc. (Riegelwood, North Carolina)	(56,160)	689,440	(6,648)	9,500	3,044,860	3,680,992	636,132
James River U.S. Holdings Inc. (Berlin, New Hampshire)	(33,898)	677,874	14,145	(23,626)	582,773	1,217,268	634,495
Rhone-Poulenc Ag Co. (Institute, West Virginia)	52,707	576,406	2,405	2,160	890,453	1,524,131	633,678
Lubrizol Petroleum Chemicals (Pasadena, Texas)	82,428	537,470	0	0	204,662	824,560	619,898
American Tape Co. (Marysville, Michigan)	(1,930,150)	2,544,272	0	0	3,296,894	3,911,016	614,122
Lubrizol Corp. (Deer Park, Texas)	48,200	545,764	783	0	266,959	861,706	594,747
Total	8,168,660	52,774,331	40,693,230	17,909,496	195,264,515	314,810,232	119,545,717

Source: U.S. Environmental Protection Agency. "Toxic Release Inventory, 1992." In *National Economic, Social, and Environmental Data Bank* [CD-ROM]. Prepared by U.S. Department of Commerce, Economics and Statistics Administration. Washington, DC: U.S. Department of Commerce, National Economic, Social, and Environmental Data Bank, Economics and Statistics Administration, Office of Business Analysis, February 1995. *Notes:* Lenzing Fibers reporting first time in 1992 for operations bought in 1992 from BASF Corp. in Lowland, Tennessee.

★ 472 ★

Toxic Release Inventory: Facilities and Sites

Facilities With Greatest Increase in Underground Injection: 1991-1992

Table shows the 50 Toxic Release Inventory (TRI) facilities with the greatest increase in underground injection from 1991 to 1992. Data reflect total increases. Table does include facilities who reported in 1992, but not in 1991, or nonmanufacturing facilities who voluntarily reported.

[In pounds]

Facility (City, State)	Underground injection		Change, 1991-1992
	1991	1992	
Vulcan Chemicals (Wichita, Kansas)	44,860,820	59,536,672	14,675,852
Du Pont Delisle (Pass Christian, Mississippi)	41,000,000	52,000,000	11,000,000
Du Pont Louisville Plant (Louisville, Kentucky))	22,000,000	29,039,810	7,039,810
American Cyanamid Co. (Westwego, Louisiana)	141,330,450	146,355,805	5,025,355
Cabot Corp. (Tuscola, Illinois)	14,217,020	18,915,780	4,698,760
Angus Chemical Co. (Sterlington, Louisiana)	1,834,000	6,023,000	4,189,000
Du Pont Beaumont Plant (Beaumont, Texas)	33,187,515	37,368,768	4,181,253
Coastal Chem Inc. (Cheyenne, Wyoming)	8,570,642	12,514,351	3,943,709
Amoco Oil Co. (Texas City, Texas)	7,937,000	11,203,000	3,266,000

[Continued]

★ 472 ★

Facilities With Greatest Increase in Underground Injection: 1991-1992
[Continued]

Facility (City, State)	Underground injection		Change,
	1991	1992	1991-1992
Shell Oil Co. (Deer Park, Texas)	306,283	3,320,646	3,014,363
Rubicon Inc. (Geismar, Louisiana)	5,020,700	6,881,500	1,860,800
Hoechst-Celanese Chemical (Pasadena, Texas)	3,850,893	5,363,400	1,512,507
Monsanto Co. (Alvin, Texas)	54,019,610	55,343,664	1,324,054
National Steel Corp. (Portage, Indiana)	606,100	1,918,535	1,312,435
Monsanto Co. (Luling, Louisiana)	3,485,800	4,734,960	1,249,160
Kaiser Aluminum & Chemical (Mulberry, Florida)	4,736,000	5,483,168	747,168
Ethyl Corp. (Magnolia, Arkansas)	5,834,300	6,468,971	634,671
Sterling Chemicals Inc. (Texas City, Texas)	35,383,465	35,929,070	545,605
ISP Tech. Inc. (Texas City, Texas)	2,426,638	2,843,330	416,692
Warner-Lambert Co. (Holland, Michigan)	2,979,835	3,259,405	279,570
UOP (Blanchard, Louisiana)	4,301,039	4,550,163	249,124
Arkansas Chemicals Inc. (El Dorado, Arkansas)	916,325	1,079,062	162,737
Maui Pineapple Co. Ltd. (Kahului, Hawaii)	94,902	223,927	129,025
Bethlehem Steel Corp. (Burns Harbor, Indiana)	1,750,300	1,857,100	106,800
Armco Steel Co. L.P. (Middletown, Ohio)	2,600,000	2,700,000	100,000
LTV Steel Co. (Hennepin, Illinois)	1,900,250	2,000,250	100,000
Jetco Chemicals (Corsicana, Texas)	2,921,048	3,017,733	96,685
Rexene Corp. (Odessa, Texas)	120,470	156,245	35,775
Elf Atochem N.A. Inc. (Crosby, Texas)	472,554	497,644	25,090
Fermi National Accelerator (Batavia, Illinois)	0	24,000	24,000
Air Products & Chemicals Inc. (Wichita, Kansas)	54,289	68,273	13,984
IBP Inc. (Holcomb, Kansas)	19,650	33,250	13,600
Calumet Lubricants Co. (Princeton, Louisiana)	0	7,526	7,526
Phillips 66 Co. (Borger, Texas)	12,260	17,840	5,580
Zeneca Inc. (Perry, Ohio)	38,625	43,004	4,379
IBP Inc. (Amarillo, Texas)	29,240	33,120	3,880
Louisiana-Pacific Corp. (Samoa, California)	0	3,500	3,500
Macklanburg-Duncan Co. (Oklahoma City, Oklahoma)	0	3,062	3,062
Witco Oleo/Surfactant (Houston, Texas)	19,473	21,962	2,489
Morton International Inc. (Moss Point, Mississippi)	1,807	2,737	930
General Motors Corp. (Trenton, New Jersey)	0	750	750
Imco Recycling Inc. (Morgantown, Kentucky)	0	693	693
McCain Foods Inc. (Presque Isle, Maine)	0	400	400
BASF Corp. (Holland, Michigan)	702	1,101	399
Shieldalloy Metallurgical (Cambridge, Ohio)	0	250	250
Fansteel Hydro Carbide Corp. (Latrobe, Pennsylvania)	0	250	250
Carboloy Inc. (Warren, Michigan)	0	250	250
Vulcan-Brunswick (Antigo, Wisconsin)	0	250	250
Cabot Corp. (Pampa, Texas)	0	250	250

[Continued]

★ 472 ★

Facilities With Greatest Increase in Underground Injection: 1991-1992

[Continued]

Facility (City, State)	Underground injection		Change, 1991-1992
	1991	1992	
Flor-Quim Inc. (Patillas, Puerto Rico)	0	250	250
Total	448,840,005	520,848,677	72,008,672

Source: U.S. Environmental Protection Agency. "Toxic Release Inventory, 1992." In *National Economic, Social, and Environmental Data Bank* [CD-ROM]. Prepared by U.S. Department of Commerce, Economics and Statistics Administration. Washington, DC: U.S. Department of Commerce, National Economic, Social, and Environmental Data Bank, Economics and Statistics Administration, Office of Business Analysis, February 1995.

★ 473 ★

Toxic Release Inventory: Facilities and Sites

Facilities With Largest Air, Water, and Land Releases: 1992

Table shows the 50 Toxic Release Inventory (TRI) facilities with the largest air, water, and land releases.

[In pounds]

Facility name (City, State)	Fugitive or nonpoint air emissions	Stack or point air emissions	Surface water discharges	Releases to land	Total air/ water/land releases
Agrico Chemical Co. (Saint James, Louisiana)	245,020	6,578,450	83,615,400	361,250	90,800,120
Magnesium Corp. of America (Rowley, Utah)	208,063	60,700,000	0	0	60,908,063
Agrico Chemical Co. (Uncle Sam, Louisiana)	31,835	332,650	57,825,523	252,823	58,442,831
Courtaulds Fibers Inc. (Axis, Alabama)	294,365	42,002,750	57,005	450,000	42,804,120
Asarco Inc. (East Helena, Montana)	27,702	93,337	0	40,953,522	41,074,561
Arcadian Fertilizer L.P. (Geismar, Louisiana)	399,626	1,596,005	37,671,015	821,515	40,488,161
Eastman Kodak Co. (Kingsport, Tennessee)	16,610,411	15,314,059	301,554	196,443	32,422,467
Inland Steel Co. (East Chicago, Indiana)	312,234	290,450	576,691	30,004,182	31,183,557
Magma Copper Co. (San Manuel, Arizona)	12,050	209,950	0	22,340,500	22,562,500
Lenzing Fibers Corp. (Lowland, Tennessee)	1,600,510	18,800,255	27,500	0	20,428,265
Elkem Metals Co. (Marietta, Ohio)	3,510,582	519,050	3,033,700	9,449,000	16,512,332
Mobil Mining & Minerals Co. (Pasadena, Texas)	205,061	311,700	13,970,810	35,005	14,522,576
Texasgulf Inc. (Aurora, North Carolina)	310,010	2,043,500	46,900	12,040,250	14,440,660
Eastman Kodak Co. (Rochester, New York)	1,588,070	11,476,893	739,782	1,588	13,806,333
IMC Fertilizer Inc. (Mulberry, Florida)	156,105	880,900	0	12,733,000	13,770,005
Asarco Inc. (Hayden, Arizona)	627,917	87,405	0	12,269,865	12,985,187
Northwestern Steel & Wire Co. (Sterling, Illinois)	65,650	290,840	3,600	12,580,000	12,940,090
Phelps Dodge Mining Co. (Playas, New Mexico)	750	633,326	0	11,158,279	11,792,355
Mississippi Chemical Corp. (Yazoo City, Mississippi)	707,800	9,710,502	628,728	0	11,047,030
Kennecott Utah Copper (Magna, Utah)	44,255	332,600	3,500	9,842,720	10,223,075
American Chrome & Chemicals (Corpus Christi, Texas)	1,260	137,050	21,550	10,000,000	10,159,860
Unocal Petroleum Products (Kenai, Alaska)	506,697	8,125,260	279,056	385	8,911,398
Dow Chemical Co. (Freeport, Texas)	4,203,872	4,065,045	457,265	111,977	8,838,159
Occidental Chemical Corp. (Castle Hayne, North Carolina)	377	10,752	37	8,400,762	8,411,928
Hoechst-Celanese Corp. (Narrows, Virginia)	5,966,597	2,403,909	418	14,239	8,385,163
Asarco Inc. (Annapolis, Missouri)	143,686	74,582	34	8,045,825	8,264,127
Arcadian Fertilizer L.P. (Memphis, Tennessee)	93,556	7,510,525	236,465	0	7,840,546
Occidental Chemical Corp. (White Springs, Florida)	200,020	296,000	2,510	7,100,000	7,598,530
Chino Mines Co. (Hurley, New Mexico)	0	253,332	0	7,225,500	7,478,832
CF Ind. Inc. (Donaldsonville, Louisiana)	275,850	5,368,475	934,905	0	6,579,230

[Continued]

★ 473 ★

Facilities With Largest Air, Water, and Land Releases: 1992
[Continued]

Facility name (City, State)	Fugitive or nonpoint air emissions	Stack or point air emissions	Surface water discharges	Releases to land	Total air/ water/land releases
Doe Run Co. (Herculaneum, Missouri)	29,542	244,669	778	6,202,698	6,477,687
General Motors Corp. (Saginaw, Michigan)	82,742	285,165	0	5,451,645	5,819,552
Kerr-Mcgee Chemical Corp. (Hamilton, Mississippi)	35,655	233,210	51,450	5,469,000	5,789,315
Louisiana-Pacific Corp. (Samoa, California)	29,610	302,548	5,435,900	0	5,768,058
3M Co. (Hutchinson, Minnesota)	205,540	5,447,299	0	0	5,652,839
Amoco Oil Co. (Texas City, Texas)	559,691	93,448	296,030	4,681,967	5,631,136
Agrico Chemical Co. (Mulberry, Florida)	93,500	70,600	0	5,290,000	5,454,100
Westvaco Corp. (North Charleston, South Carolina)	1,125,079	4,217,200	10,901	0	5,353,180
Du Pont Johnsonville Plant (New Johnsonville, Tennessee)	45,300	4,990,300	0	0	5,035,600
Westvaco Corp. (Covington, Virginia)	6,560	4,858,100	84,600	7,678	4,956,938
Simpson Paper Co. (Eureka, California)	2,515	903,005	4,015,850	0	4,921,370
Mobil Oil Beaumont Refinery (Beaumont, Texas)	4,599,857	237,041	0	4,636	4,841,534
Shell Oil Co. (Deer Park, Texas)	3,395,327	1,075,360	24,712	295,667	4,791,066
Westinghouse Electric Corp. (Hampton, South Carolina)	11,992	4,744,090	38	0	4,756,120
Occidental Chemical Corp. (Niagara Falls, New York)	43	4,705,600	0	0	4,705,643
Holliston Mills Inc. (Church Hill, Tennessee)	23,212	4,619,070	1,247	234	4,643,763
American Synthetic Rubber (Louisville, Kentucky)	1,120,360	3,500,235	0	0	4,620,595
Farmland Ind. Inc. (Enid, Oklahoma)	180,910	4,402,350	23,960	755	4,607,975
Granite City Steel (Granite City, Illinois)	320,565	298,966	59,843	3,826,012	4,505,386
Boeing Wichita (Wichita, Kansas)	3,007,259	1,460,047	14,760	0	4,482,066
Subtotal	53,225,190	247,137,855	210,454,017	247,618,922	758,435,984
Total for all TRI facilities	549,351,729	1,295,606,607	272,932,953	337,809,053	2,455,700,342

Source: U.S. Environmental Protection Agency. "Toxic Release Inventory, 1992." In *National Economic, Social, and Environmental Data Bank* [CD-ROM]. Prepared by U.S. Department of Commerce, Economics and Statistics Administration. Washington, DC: U.S. Department of Commerce, National Economic, Social, and Environmental Data Bank, Economics and Statistics Administration, Office of Business Analysis, February 1995.

★ 474 ★

Toxic Release Inventory: Facilities and Sites

Facilities With Largest Total Releases: 1992

Table shows the 50 Toxic Release Inventory (TRI) facilities with the largest total releases.

[In pounds]

Facility (City, State)	Fugitive or nonpoint air emissions	Stack or point air emissions	Surface water discharges	Underground injection	Releases to land	Total releases
American Cyanamid Co. (Westwego, Louisiana)	73,059	362,055	297,671	146,355,805	0	147,088,590
Agrico Chemical Co. (Saint James, Louisiana)	245,020	6,578,450	83,615,400	0	361,250	90,800,120
Magnesium Corp. of America (Rowley, Utah)	208,063	60,700,000	0	0	0	60,908,063
Vulcan Chemicals (Wichita, Kansas)	92,238	345,210	0	59,536,672	0	59,974,120
Agrico Chemical Co. (Uncle Sam, Louisiana)	31,835	332,650	57,825,523	0	252,823	58,442,831
Du Pont Delisle (Pass Christian, Mississippi)	183,510	3,759,700	0	52,000,000	420	55,943,630
Monsanto Co. (Alvin, Texas)	38,894	253,234	400	55,343,664	252,000	55,888,192
Du Pont Johnsonville Plant (New Johnsonville, Tennessee)	45,300	4,990,300	0	47,000,000	0	52,035,600
Courtaulds Fibers Inc. (Axis, Alabama)	294,365	42,002,750	57,005	0	450,000	42,804,120
Asarco Inc. (East Helena, Montana)	27,702	93,337	0	0	40,953,522	41,074,561
Arcadian Fertilizer L.P. (Geismar, Louisiana)	399,626	1,596,005	37,671,015	0	821,515	40,488,161
Du Pont Beaumont Plant (Beaumont, Texas)	290,307	2,491,347	43,938	37,368,768	86	40,194,446
Sterling Chemicals Inc. (Texas City, Texas)	329,175	913,695	18,005	35,929,070	0	37,189,945
Eastman Kodak Co. (Kingsport, Tennessee)	16,610,411	15,314,059	301,554	0	196,443	32,422,467

[Continued]

★ 474 ★

Facilities With Largest Total Releases: 1992

[Continued]

Facility (City, State)	Fugitive or nonpoint air emissions	Stack or point air emissions	Surface water discharges	Underground injection	Releases to land	Total releases
Inland Steel Co. (East Chicago, Indiana)	312,234	290,450	576,691	0	30,004,182	31,183,557
Du Pont Louisville Plant (Louisville, Kentucky)	262,701	902,289	0	29,039,810	0	30,204,800
BP Chemicals Inc. (Port Lavaca, Texas)	19,624	49,986	21,590	26,767,584	299	26,859,083
BP Chemicals Inc. (Lima, Ohio)	369,950	2,496,355	62,860	20,363,250	0	23,292,415
Cabot Corp. (Tuscola, Illinois)	750	4,318,764	0	18,915,780	0	23,235,294
Du Pont (Victoria, Texas)	41,032	1,091,247	1,198	22,060,820	21,084	23,215,381
Magma Copper Co. (San Manuel, Arizona)	12,050	209,950	0	0	22,340,500	22,562,500
Lenzing Fibers Corp. (Lowland, Tennessee)	1,600,510	18,800,255	27,500	0	0	20,428,265
Amoco Oil Co. (Texas City, Texas)	559,691	93,448	296,030	11,203,000	4,681,967	16,834,136
Zeneca Specialties (Mount Pleasant, Tennessee)	98,989	83,122	0	16,508,125	0	16,690,236
Elkem Metals Co. (Marietta, Ohio)	3,510,582	519,050	3,033,700	0	9,449,000	16,512,332
Mobil Mining & Minerals Co. (Pasadena, Texas)	205,061	311,700	13,970,810	0	35,005	14,522,576
Texasgulf Inc. (Aurora, North Carolina)	310,010	2,043,500	46,900	0	12,040,250	14,440,660
Eastman Kodak Co. (Rochester, New York)	1,588,070	11,476,893	739,782	0	1,588	13,806,333
IMC Fertilizer Inc. (Mulberry, Florida)	156,105	880,900	0	0	12,733,000	13,770,005
Coastal Chem Inc. (Cheyenne, Wyoming)	188,955	659,635	0	12,514,351	0	13,362,941
Asarco Inc. (Hayden, Arizona)	627,917	87,405	0	0	12,269,865	12,985,187
Northwestern Steel & Wire Co. (Sterling, Illinois)	65,650	290,840	3,600	0	12,580,000	12,940,090
Phelps Dodge Mining Co. (Playas, New Mexico)	750	633,326	0	0	11,158,279	11,792,355
Mississippi Chemical Corp. (Yazoo City, Mississippi)	707,800	9,710,502	628,728	0	0	11,047,030
Uniroyal Chemical Co. Inc. (Geismar, Louisiana)	506,490	389,878	350	9,617,920	0	10,514,638
Kennecott Utah Copper (Magna, Utah)	44,255	332,600	3,500	0	9,842,720	10,223,075
American Chrome & Chemicals (Corpus Christi, Texas)	1,260	137,050	21,550	0	10,000,000	10,159,860
Unocal Petroleum Products (Kenai, Alaska)	506,697	8,125,260	279,056	192	385	8,911,590
Dow Chemical Co. (Freeport, Texas)	4,203,872	4,065,045	457,265	0	111,977	8,838,159
Hoechst-Celanese Chemical (Pasadena, Texas)	523,405	2,620,455	0	5,363,400	0	8,507,260
Occidental Chemical Corp. (Castle Hayne, North Carolina)	377	10,752	37	0	8,400,762	8,411,928
Hoechst-Celanese Corp. (Narrows, Virginia)	5,966,597	2,403,909	418	0	14,239	8,385,163
Asarco Inc. (Annapolis, Missouri)	143,686	74,582	34	0	8,045,825	8,264,127
Shell Oil Co. (Deer Park, Texas)	3,395,327	1,075,360	24,712	3,320,646	295,667	8,111,712
Arcadian Fertilizer L.P. (Memphis, Tennessee)	93,556	7,510,525	236,465	0	0	7,840,546
Occidental Chemical Corp. (White Springs, Florida)	200,020	296,000	2,510	0	7,100,000	7,598,530
Ethyl Corp. (Magnolia, Arkansas)	184,428	357,521	510	6,468,971	520,250	7,531,680
Chino Mines Co. (Hurley, New Mexico)	0	253,332	0	0	7,225,500	7,478,832
Rubicon Inc. (Geismar, Louisiana)	120,717	353,999	210	6,881,500	0	7,356,426
Du Pont (Orange, Texas)	514,805	1,951,235	41,503	4,347,083	0	6,854,626
Subtotal	45,913,428	224,639,912	200,308,020	626,906,411	222,160,403	1,319,928,174
Total for all TRI facilities	549,351,729	1,295,606,607	272,932,953	725,946,415	337,809,053	3,181,646,757

Source: U.S. Environmental Protection Agency. "Toxic Release Inventory, 1992." In National Economic, Social, and Environmental Data Bank [CD-ROM]. Prepared by U.S. Department of Commerce, Economics and Statistics Administration. Washington, DC: U.S. Department of Commerce, National Economic, Social, and Environmental Data Bank, Economics and Statistics Administration, Office of Business Analysis, February 1995.

★ 475 ★

Toxic Release Inventory: Facilities and Sites

Parent Companies With Largest Air, Water, and Land Releases: 1992

Table shows the 10 Toxic Release Inventory (TRI) parent companies with the largest air, water, and land releases.

[In pounds]

Company Name	Fugitive or nonpoint air emissions	Stack or point air emissions	Surface water discharges	Releases to land	Total air/ water/land releases
Freeport-McMoran	438,365	7,287,700	141,726,923	5,943,073	155,396,061
Asarco Inc.	865,694	886,387	15,767	61,339,387	63,107,235
Renco Group Inc.	287,643	60,897,054	10,756	1,038,630	62,234,083
Arcadian Fertilizer L.P.	1,410,591	14,314,308	40,170,999	828,931	56,724,829
Eastman Kodak Company	23,594,685	30,019,187	1,208,666	252,685	55,075,223
Courtaulds Coatings Inc.	352,500	42,479,197	58,415	450,000	43,340,112
DuPont	7,962,319	33,979,081	1,152,377	183,128	43,276,905
General Motors Corp.	6,387,677	25,045,585	122,934	8,822,700	40,378,896
3M Co.	2,157,170	27,877,803	3,933,702	82,445	34,051,120
Inland Steel Co.	325,139	379,280	576,691	30,004,182	31,285,292
Subtotal	43,781,783	243,165,582	188,977,230	108,945,161	584,869,756
Total	549,351,729	1,295,606,607	272,932,953	337,809,053	2,455,700,342

Source: U.S. Environmental Protection Agency. "Toxic Release Inventory, 1992." In *National Economic, Social, and Environmental Data Bank* [CD-ROM]. Prepared by U.S. Department of Commerce, Economics and Statistics Administration. Washington, DC: U.S. Department of Commerce, National Economic, Social, and Environmental Data Bank, Economics and Statistics Administration, Office of Business Analysis, February 1995.

★ 476 ★

Toxic Release Inventory: Facilities and Sites

Parent Companies With Largest Total Releases: 1992

Table shows the 10 Toxic Release Inventory (TRI) parent companies with the largest total releases.

[In pounds]

Parent company	Fugitive or nonpoint air emissions	Stack or point air emissions	Surface water discharges	Underground injection	Releases to land	Total releases
DuPont	7,962,319	33,979,081	1,152,377	196,337,387	183,128	239,614,292
Freeport-McMoran Inc.	438,365	7,287,700	141,726,923	0	5,943,073	155,396,061
American Cyanamid	1,003,125	2,818,067	748,694	146,575,843	13,895	151,159,624
Monsanto Company	1,040,597	6,323,243	2,490,316	66,107,180	286,006	76,247,342
Asarco Inc.	865,694	886,387	15,767	5,808,239	61,339,387	68,915,474
Renco Group Inc.	287,643	60,897,054	10,756	0	1,038,630	62,234,083
Vulcan Materials Company	190,004	852,599	29,030	59,536,672	5	60,608,310
Arcadian Fertilizer L.P.	1,410,591	14,314,308	40,170,999	0	828,931	56,724,829
Eastman Kodak Company	23,594,685	30,019,187	1,208,666	0	252,685	55,075,223
BP America	2,453,760	4,428,650	408,010	47,130,834	8,077	54,429,331

[Continued]

★ 476 ★

Parent Companies With Largest Total Releases: 1992

[Continued]

Parent company	Fugitive or nonpoint air emissions	Stack or point air emissions	Surface water discharges	Underground injection	Releases to land	Total releases
Subtotal	39,246,783	161,806,276	187,961,538	521,496,155	69,893,817	980,404,569
Total for all TRI facilities	549,351,729	1,295,606,607	272,932,953	725,946,415	337,809,053	3,181,646,757

Source: U.S. Environmental Protection Agency. "Toxic Release Inventory, 1992." In *National Economic, Social, and Environmental Data Bank* [CD-ROM]. Prepared by U.S. Department of Commerce, Economics and Statistics Administration. Washington, DC: U.S. Department of Commerce, National Economic, Social, and Environmental Data Bank, Economics and Statistics Administration, Office of Business Analysis, February 1995.

Toxic Release Inventory: Industry Statistics

★ 477 ★

Industries With Most Toxic Release Inventory Releases

Table shows industries with most Toxic Release Inventory (TRI) releases. Includes air, water, land, and underground injection.

[In million pounds]

Industry	Total release
Chemicals	1,550
Primary metals	433
Paper	242
Plastics	152
Transportation equipment	149

Source: "Top Industries for Total Release." *Ward's Auto World* 29, no. 7 (July 1993), p. 55. Primary sources: U.S. Environmental Protection Agency; Toxic Release Inventory.

★ 478 ★
Toxic Release Inventory: Industry Statistics

Toxic Release Inventory, by Industry and Source: 1988-1992

Based on reports from almost 23,000 manufacturing facilities that have 10 or more full-time employees and meet established thresholds for manufacturing, processing, or otherwise using the list of more than 300 chemicals covered. Only chemicals that were reportable in all years shown are compared so that data do not include any chemicals added or deleted to the list. The inventory was established under the Emergency Planning and Community Right-to-Know Act of 1986 (EPCRA).

[In pounds]

Industry	SIC[1] codes	1988	1989	1990	1991	1992
Total	(X)	4,852,937,803	4,377,396,313	3,693,153,470	3,373,234,236	3,157,282,092
Food and kindred products	20	28,197,500	36,960,315	38,932,898	39,469,019	38,568,497
Tobacco products	21	1,831,154	1,753,151	2,482,331	2,289,357	1,991,033
Textile mill products	22	38,234,887	32,188,662	27,130,717	24,991,973	21,467,273
Apparel and other textile products	23	1,063,597	1,397,561	1,318,381	1,387,419	1,576,282
Lumber and wood products	24	32,869,791	37,762,918	35,584,688	32,553,570	32,373,513
Furniture and fixtures	25	66,790,165	65,283,123	61,722,622	55,856,765	55,053,507
Paper and allied products	26	271,778,290	257,055,270	253,314,527	245,782,989	233,048,527
Printing and publishing	27	60,971,335	58,210,960	51,410,968	46,598,727	40,479,331
Chemical and allied products	28	2,324,425,060	2,083,432,858	1,619,534,304	1,541,464,274	1,527,344,618
Petroleum and coal products	29	92,777,209	94,681,573	85,789,682	78,166,045	82,733,063
Rubber and miscellaneous plastic products	30	170,356,398	184,010,450	177,453,661	149,751,724	134,412,512
Leather and leather products	31	15,806,499	13,467,549	12,745,990	9,855,927	10,495,995
Stone, clay, glass products	32	39,237,562	37,069,091	31,228,021	29,420,142	25,654,866
Primary metal industries	33	565,850,483	522,253,049	476,277,191	424,141,581	345,229,090
Fabricated metals products	34	136,899,670	137,299,491	128,220,910	110,990,161	101,202,243
Industrial machinery and equipment	35	60,578,676	57,804,936	48,833,857	38,622,092	33,670,024
Electronic and other electric equipment	36	125,705,476	100,383,459	82,327,303	65,987,104	52,216,161
Transportation equipment	37	216,578,872	205,320,094	175,274,491	149,517,702	135,987,336
Instruments and related products	38	57,075,215	52,473,236	44,259,199	39,618,487	32,984,291
Miscellaneous manufacturing industries	39	31,302,399	28,958,962	25,808,397	20,299,522	18,249,532
Multiple codes	20-39	498,383,769	358,857,440	299,724,027	239,833,159	217,833,016
No codes	20-39	16,223,796	10,772,165	13,779,305	26,636,497	14,711,382

Source: 1994 Statistical Abstract of the United States on CD-ROM [machine-readable datafiles]. CD-8A-94. Washington, DC: U.S. Department of Commerce, Economics and Statistics Administration, Bureau of the Census, Data User Services Division, January 1995. Primary source: U.S. Environmental Protection Agency. *1992 Toxic Release Inventory Public Data Release. Notes:* "X" stands for "not applicable." 1. Standard Industrial Classification.

★ 479 ★

Toxic Release Inventory: Industry Statistics

Toxic Release Inventory Releases and Transfers in All Industries: 1988-1991

Table shows environmental distribution of Toxic Release Inventory (TRI) releases and transfers.

[In million pounds]

Year	Releases					Transfers		Total releases and transfers
	Fugitive emissions	Stack emissions	Surface water discharge	Land disposal	Under-ground injection	To public sewage	To offsite location	
1988	823.74	1,842.37	311.07	527.55	1,343.63	574.05	1,028.11	6,450.52
1989	793.60	1,768.60	188.03	455.03	1,175.58	558.58	890.36	5,829.76
1990	706.75	1,575.96	196.83	462.68	745.41	466.12	842.45	4,996.21
1991	609.77	1,369.58	243.50	421.16	710.25	410.60	654.31	4,419.16

Source: Executive Office of the President of the United States. *Environmental Quality 24: The Twenty-fourth Annual Report of the Council on Environmental Quality.* Prepared by Ray Clark. Written by Carroll Curtis. Edited by Barry Walsh. Washington, DC: U.S. Government Printing Office, 1994, pp. 509-511. Primary source: U.S. Environmental Protection Agency. Office of Toxic Substances. *1991 Toxic Release Inventory.* Washington, DC: U.S. Environmental Protection Agency, 1993, pp. 234-237, table 3-9.

★ 480 ★

Toxic Release Inventory: Industry Statistics

Toxic Release Inventory Releases and Transfers in Apparel Industry: 1988-1991

Table shows environmental distribution of Toxic Release Inventory (TRI) releases and transfers.

[In million pounds]

Year	Releases					Transfers		Total releases and transfers
	Fugitive emissions	Stack emissions	Surface water discharge	Land disposal	Under-ground injection	To public sewage	To offsite location	
1988	0.28	0.74	(¹)	0.04	0.00	0.47	0.18	1.71
1989	0.52	0.83	(²)	(²)	0.00	0.44	0.26	2.06
1990	0.34	0.94	(²)	(²)	0.00	0.15	0.17	1.65
1991	0.42	0.95	(²)	0.02	0.00	0.19	0.27	1.84

Source: Executive Office of the President of the United States. *Environmental Quality 24: The Twenty-fourth Annual Report of the Council on Environmental Quality.* Prepared by Ray Clark. Written by Carroll Curtis. Edited by Barry Walsh. Washington, DC: U.S. Government Printing Office, 1994, pp. 509-511. Primary source: U.S. Environmental Protection Agency. Office of Toxic Substances. *1991 Toxic Release Inventory.* Washington, DC: U.S. Environmental Protection Agency, 1993, pp. 234-237, table 3-9. *Notes:* 1. Less than 5,000 pounds. 2. Less than 1,000 pounds.

★ 481 ★

Toxic Release Inventory: Industry Statistics

Toxic Release Inventory Releases and Transfers in Chemicals Industry: 1988-1991

Table shows environmental distribution of Toxic Release Inventory (TRI) releases and transfers.

[In million pounds]

| Year | Releases | | | | | Transfers | | Total |
	Fugitive emissions	Stack emissions	Surface water discharge	Land disposal	Under-ground injection	To public sewage	To offsite location	releases and transfers
1988	235.70	614.91	231.70	135.94	1,100.60	333.65	355.57	3,008.07
1989	226.88	551.19	110.20	106.57	1,085.48	351.58	295.44	2,729.34
1990	203.28	487.21	132.00	101.92	678.79	283.10	254.95	2,141.23
1991	181.85	422.31	187.98	89.87	656.04	236.34	277.06	2,051.44

Source: Executive Office of the President of the United States. *Environmental Quality 24: The Twenty-fourth Annual Report of the Council on Environmental Quality.* Prepared by Ray Clark. Written by Carroll Curtis. Edited by Barry Walsh. Washington, DC: U.S. Government Printing Office, 1994, pp. 509-511. Primary source: U.S. Environmental Protection Agency. Office of Toxic Substances. *1991 Toxic Release Inventory.* Washington, DC: U.S. Environmental Protection Agency, 1993, pp. 234-237, table 3-9.

★ 482 ★

Toxic Release Inventory: Industry Statistics

Toxic Release Inventory Releases and Transfers in Electrical Industry: 1988-1991

Table shows environmental distribution of Toxic Release Inventory (TRI) releases and transfers.

[In million pounds]

| Year | Releases | | | | | Transfers | | Total |
	Fugitive emissions	Stack emissions	Surface water discharge	Land disposal	Under-ground injection	To public sewage	To offsite location	releases and transfers
1988	36.73	86.21	0.69	1.44	0.04	18.80	44.16	188.09
1989	31.99	65.90	0.47	1.39	0.05	14.62	36.91	151.32
1990	25.64	52.74	0.41	2.73	0.02	11.97	34.15	127.67
1991	21.22	41.93	0.39	1.55	(1)	7.44	33.39	105.92

Source: Executive Office of the President of the United States. *Environmental Quality 24: The Twenty-fourth Annual Report of the Council on Environmental Quality.* Prepared by Ray Clark. Written by Carroll Curtis. Edited by Barry Walsh. Washington, DC: U.S. Government Printing Office, 1994, pp. 509-511. Primary source: U.S. Environmental Protection Agency. Office of Toxic Substances. *1991 Toxic Release Inventory.* Washington, DC: U.S. Environmental Protection Agency, 1993, pp. 234-237, table 3-9. *Note:* 1. Less than 5,000 pounds.

★ 483 ★

Toxic Release Inventory: Industry Statistics

Toxic Release Inventory Releases and Transfers in Fabricated Metals Industry: 1988-1991

Table shows environmental distribution of Toxic Release Inventory (TRI) releases and transfers.

[In million pounds]

Year	Releases					Transfers		Total releases and transfers
	Fugitive emissions	Stack emissions	Surface water discharge	Land disposal	Under-ground injection	To public sewage	To offsite location	
1988	50.90	79.37	1.52	4.20	0.39	17.14	77.15	230.67
1989	54.94	79.24	0.31	1.05	0.34	8.43	74.64	218.95
1990	48.04	77.27	0.51	0.83	(¹)	6.34	63.88	196.87
1991	43.32	64.27	0.28	1.34	(¹)	6.45	42.40	158.06

Source: Executive Office of the President of the United States. *Environmental Quality 24: The Twenty-fourth Annual Report of the Council on Environmental Quality.* Prepared by Ray Clark. Written by Carroll Curtis. Edited by Barry Walsh. Washington, DC: U.S. Government Printing Office, 1994, pp. 509-511. Primary source: U.S. Environmental Protection Agency. Office of Toxic Substances. *1991 Toxic Release Inventory.* Washington, DC: U.S. Environmental Protection Agency, 1993, pp. 234-237, table 3-9. *Note:* 1. Less than 1,000 pounds.

★ 484 ★

Toxic Release Inventory: Industry Statistics

Toxic Release Inventory Releases and Transfers in Food Industry: 1988-1991

Table shows environmental distribution of Toxic Release Inventory (TRI) releases and transfers.

[In million pounds]

Year	Releases					Transfers		Total releases and transfers
	Fugitive emissions	Stack emissions	Surface water discharge	Land disposal	Under-ground injection	To public sewage	To offsite location	
1988	13.52	4.39	3.65	5.51	1.03	38.34	3.16	69.58
1989	16.99	7.65	3.02	7.99	1.11	37.73	3.46	77.96
1990	15.01	11.13	3.84	8.49	0.04	40.44	4.50	83.54
1991	13.21	14.50	2.40	8.93	0.21	38.23	5.06	39.26

Source: Executive Office of the President of the United States. *Environmental Quality 24: The Twenty-fourth Annual Report of the Council on Environmental Quality.* Prepared by Ray Clark. Written by Carroll Curtis. Edited by Barry Walsh. Washington, DC: U.S. Government Printing Office, 1994, pp. 509-511. Primary source: U.S. Environmental Protection Agency. Office of Toxic Substances. *1991 Toxic Release Inventory.* Washington, DC: U.S. Environmental Protection Agency, 1993, pp. 234-237, table 3-9.

★ 485 ★

Toxic Release Inventory: Industry Statistics

Toxic Release Inventory Releases and Transfers in Furniture Industry: 1988-1991

Table shows environmental distribution of Toxic Release Inventory (TRI) releases and transfers.

[In million pounds]

Year	Releases					Transfers		Total
	Fugitive emissions	Stack emissions	Surface water discharge	Land disposal	Under-ground injection	To public sewage	To offsite location	releases and transfers
1988	9.15	56.96	(¹)	0.08	0.00	0.44	6.27	72.89
1989	10.65	54.04	(¹)	0.02	0.00	0.55	4.84	70.11
1990	8.67	52.46	0.01	0.08	(²)	0.33	4.30	65.84
1991	7.86	46.93	(²)	0.26	0.00	0.14	2.80	58.00

Source: Executive Office of the President of the United States. *Environmental Quality 24: The Twenty-fourth Annual Report of the Council on Environmental Quality.* Prepared by Ray Clark. Written by Carroll Curtis. Edited by Barry Walsh. Washington, DC: U.S. Government Printing Office, 1994, pp. 509-511. Primary source: U.S. Environmental Protection Agency. Office of Toxic Substances. *1991 Toxic Release Inventory.* Washington, DC: U.S. Environmental Protection Agency, 1993, pp. 234-237, table 3-9. *Notes:* 1. Less than 5,000 pounds. 2. Less than 1,000 pounds.

★ 486 ★

Toxic Release Inventory: Industry Statistics

Toxic Release Inventory Releases and Transfers in Leather Industry: 1988-1991

Table shows environmental distribution of Toxic Release Inventory (TRI) releases and transfers.

[In million pounds]

Year	Releases					Transfers		Total
	Fugitive emissions	Stack emissions	Surface water discharge	Land disposal	Under-ground injection	To public sewage	To offsite location	releases and transfers
1988	3.89	10.88	0.68	0.35	0.00	10.02	2.50	28.12
1989	3.41	9.49	0.23	0.26	0.00	9.55	2.84	25.78
1990	3.63	8.56	0.41	0.02	0.00	8.28	2.32	23.22
1991	3.58	5.99	0.12	0.08	0.00	5.69	1.86	17.32

Source: Executive Office of the President of the United States. *Environmental Quality 24: The Twenty-fourth Annual Report of the Council on Environmental Quality.* Prepared by Ray Clark. Written by Carroll Curtis. Edited by Barry Walsh. Washington, DC: U.S. Government Printing Office, 1994, pp. 509-511. Primary source: U.S. Environmental Protection Agency. Office of Toxic Substances. *1991 Toxic Release Inventory.* Washington, DC: U.S. Environmental Protection Agency, 1993, pp. 234-237, table 3-9.

★ 487 ★

Toxic Release Inventory: Industry Statistics

Toxic Release Inventory Releases and Transfers in Lumber Industry: 1988-1991

Table shows environmental distribution of Toxic Release Inventory (TRI) releases and transfers.

[In million pounds]

Year	Releases					Transfers		Total releases and transfers
	Fugitive emissions	Stack emissions	Surface water discharge	Land disposal	Under-ground injection	To public sewage	To offsite location	
1988	5.61	25.63	0.23	0.06	0.00	0.21	4.70	37.43
1989	6.04	29.17	0.19	0.11	(¹)	0.11	3.03	38.21
1990	6.12	27.42	0.09	0.11	(¹)	0.08	2.55	36.29
1991	6.21	24.08	0.11	0.08	0.00	0.13	1.19	31.81

Source: Executive Office of the President of the United States. *Environmental Quality 24: The Twenty-fourth Annual Report of the Council on Environmental Quality.* Prepared by Ray Clark. Written by Carroll Curtis. Edited by Barry Walsh. Washington, DC: U.S. Government Printing Office, 1994, pp. 509-511. Primary source: U.S. Environmental Protection Agency. Office of Toxic Substances. *1991 Toxic Release Inventory.* Washington, DC: U.S. Environmental Protection Agency, 1993, pp. 234-237, table 3-9. *Note:* 1. Less than 1,000 pounds.

★ 488 ★

Toxic Release Inventory: Industry Statistics

Toxic Release Inventory Releases and Transfers in Machinery Industry: 1988-1991

Table shows environmental distribution of Toxic Release Inventory (TRI) releases and transfers.

[In million pounds]

Year	Releases					Transfers		Total releases and transfers
	Fugitive emissions	Stack emissions	Surface water discharge	Land disposal	Under-ground injection	To public sewage	To offsite location	
1988	25.29	34.39	0.38	0.22	0.00	2.71	20.35	83.34
1989	26.06	30.59	0.41	0.31	(¹)	2.88	18.30	78.54
1990	20.01	28.63	0.21	0.01	(¹)	2.58	12.50	64.03
1991	14.54	23.50	0.05	0.44	(¹)	2.43	8.60	49.57

Source: Executive Office of the President of the United States. *Environmental Quality 24: The Twenty-fourth Annual Report of the Council on Environmental Quality.* Prepared by Ray Clark. Written by Carroll Curtis. Edited by Barry Walsh. Washington, DC: U.S. Government Printing Office, 1994, pp. 509-511. Primary source: U.S. Environmental Protection Agency. Office of Toxic Substances. *1991 Toxic Release Inventory.* Washington, DC: U.S. Environmental Protection Agency, 1993, pp. 234-237, table 3-9. *Note:* 1. Less than 1,000 pounds.

★ 489 ★
Toxic Release Inventory: Industry Statistics

Toxic Release Inventory Releases and Transfers in Measurement and Photography Industry: 1988-1991

Table shows environmental distribution of Toxic Release Inventory (TRI) releases and transfers.

[In million pounds]

Year	Releases					Transfers		Total
	Fugitive emissions	Stack emissions	Surface water discharge	Land disposal	Under-ground injection	To public sewage	To offsite location	releases and transfers
1988	17.21	38.84	0.69	0.37	(¹)	3.74	19.61	80.46
1989	16.73	35.03	0.43	0.05	(¹)	2.41	12.25	66.89
1990	13.61	30.14	0.07	0.03	(¹)	1.89	9.20	54.94
1991	11.77	26.66	0.74	0.06	(¹)	1.59	5.87	46.67

Source: Executive Office of the President of the United States. *Environmental Quality 24: The Twenty-fourth Annual Report of the Council on Environmental Quality.* Prepared by Ray Clark. Written by Carroll Curtis. Edited by Barry Walsh. Washington, DC: U.S. Government Printing Office, 1994, pp. 509-511. Primary source: U.S. Environmental Protection Agency. Office of Toxic Substances. *1991 Toxic Release Inventory.* Washington, DC: U.S. Environmental Protection Agency, 1993, pp. 234-237, table 3-9. *Note:* 1. Less than 1,000 pounds.

★ 490 ★
Toxic Release Inventory: Industry Statistics

Toxic Release Inventory Releases and Transfers in Miscellaneous Industries: 1988-1991

Table shows environmental distribution of Toxic Release Inventory (TRI) releases and transfers.

[In million pounds]

Year	Releases					Transfers		Total
	Fugitive emissions	Stack emissions	Surface water discharge	Land disposal	Under-ground injection	To public sewage	To offsite location	releases and transfers
1988	9.39	21.24	0.05	0.27	(¹)	0.45	9.21	40.52
1989	9.39	19.14	0.03	0.06	(¹)	0.73	13.46	42.82
1990	7.92	16.78	0.1	(²)	(¹)	0.63	6.34	31.69
1991	6.19	12.11	0.01	0.05	(¹)	0.80	3.18	22.33

Source: Executive Office of the President of the United States. *Environmental Quality 24: The Twenty-fourth Annual Report of the Council on Environmental Quality.* Prepared by Ray Clark. Written by Carroll Curtis. Edited by Barry Walsh. Washington, DC: U.S. Government Printing Office, 1994, pp. 509-511. Primary source: U.S. Environmental Protection Agency. Office of Toxic Substances. *1991 Toxic Release Inventory.* Washington, DC: U.S. Environmental Protection Agency, 1993, pp. 234-237, table 3-9. *Notes:* 1. Less than 1,000 pounds. 2. Less than 5,000 pounds.

★ 491 ★

Toxic Release Inventory: Industry Statistics

Toxic Release Inventory Releases and Transfers in Paper Industry: 1988-1991

Table shows environmental distribution of Toxic Release Inventory (TRI) releases and transfers.

[In million pounds]

| Year | Releases | | | | | Transfers | | Total |
	Fugitive emissions	Stack emissions	Surface water discharge	Land disposal	Under-ground injection	To public sewage	To offsite location	releases and transfers
1988	40.75	180.18	38.15	10.53	0.00	47.00	21.34	337.91
1989	37.24	168.12	41.10	10.01	(¹)	48.06	25.20	329.72
1990	35.51	169.28	35.66	7.48	(¹)	54.00	12.95	314.88
1991	28.93	179.32	29.66	4.09	(¹)	44.90	11.41	298.31

Source: Executive Office of the President of the United States. *Environmental Quality 24: The Twenty-fourth Annual Report of the Council on Environmental Quality.* Prepared by Ray Clark. Written by Carroll Curtis. Edited by Barry Walsh. Washington, DC: U.S. Government Printing Office, 1994, pp. 509-511. Primary source: U.S. Environmental Protection Agency. Office of Toxic Substances. *1991 Toxic Release Inventory.* Washington, DC: U.S. Environmental Protection Agency, 1993, pp. 234-237, table 3-9. *Note:* 1. Less than 1,000 pounds.

★ 492 ★

Toxic Release Inventory: Industry Statistics

Toxic Release Inventory Releases and Transfers in Petroleum Industry: 1988-1991

Table shows environmental distribution of Toxic Release Inventory (TRI) releases and transfers.

[In million pounds]

| Year | Releases | | | | | Transfers | | Total |
	Fugitive emissions	Stack emissions	Surface water discharge	Land disposal	Under-ground injection	To public sewage	To offsite location	releases and transfers
1988	45.18	19.60	3.27	2.66	20.49	10.83	8.79	110.82
1989	38.41	25.94	3.82	2.55	25.12	10.59	6.90	113.34
1990	35.79	23.19	3.88	2.53	16.45	6.95	6.45	95.23
1991	34.36	21.95	3.33	0.98	14.27	7.22	3.56	85.66

Source: Executive Office of the President of the United States. *Environmental Quality 24: The Twenty-fourth Annual Report of the Council on Environmental Quality.* Prepared by Ray Clark. Written by Carroll Curtis. Edited by Barry Walsh. Washington, DC: U.S. Government Printing Office, 1994, pp. 509-511. Primary source: U.S. Environmental Protection Agency. Office of Toxic Substances. *1991 Toxic Release Inventory.* Washington, DC: U.S. Environmental Protection Agency, 1993, pp. 234-237, table 3-9.

★ 493 ★

Toxic Release Inventory: Industry Statistics

Toxic Release Inventory Releases and Transfers in Plastics Industry: 1988-1991

Table shows environmental distribution of Toxic Release Inventory (TRI) releases and transfers.

[In million pounds]

Year	Releases					Transfers		Total
	Fugitive emissions	Stack emissions	Surface water discharge	Land disposal	Under-ground injection	To public sewage	To offsite location	releases and transfers
1988	50.06	118.86	0.63	0.17	(^{1})	4.84	24.08	198.64
1989	51.81	130.78	0.70	0.24	0.01	5.36	22.68	211.58
1990	57.58	119.51	0.45	0.19	0.01	4.54	20.57	202.85
1991	45.90	99.93	0.58	0.50	0.02	5.05	14.32	166.20

Source: Executive Office of the President of the United States. *Environmental Quality 24: The Twenty-fourth Annual Report of the Council on Environmental Quality.* Prepared by Ray Clark. Written by Carroll Curtis. Edited by Barry Walsh. Washington, DC: U.S. Government Printing Office, 1994, pp. 509-511. Primary source: U.S. Environmental Protection Agency. Office of Toxic Substances. *1991 Toxic Release Inventory.* Washington, DC: U.S. Environmental Protection Agency, 1993, pp. 234-237, table 3-9. *Note:* 1. Less than 5,000 pounds.

★ 494 ★

Toxic Release Inventory: Industry Statistics

Toxic Release Inventory Releases and Transfers in Primary Metals Industry: 1988-1991

Table shows environmental distribution of Toxic Release Inventory (TRI) releases and transfers.

[In million pounds]

Year	Releases					Transfers		Total
	Fugitive emissions	Stack emissions	Surface water discharge	Land disposal	Under-ground injection	To public sewage	To offsite location	releases and transfers
1988	65.91	174.28	17.68	279.73	41.61	22.91	275.14	877.27
1989	58.83	183.42	15.92	242.96	37.68	17.12	228.48	784.42
1990	55.67	154.19	10.76	272.28	15.64	9.53	288.51	806.59
1991	41.78	114.25	8.50	254.92	13.54	21.56	139.43	593.96

Source: Executive Office of the President of the United States. *Environmental Quality 24: The Twenty-fourth Annual Report of the Council on Environmental Quality.* Prepared by Ray Clark. Written by Carroll Curtis. Edited by Barry Walsh. Washington, DC: U.S. Government Printing Office, 1994, pp. 509-511. Primary source: U.S. Environmental Protection Agency. Office of Toxic Substances. *1991 Toxic Release Inventory.* Washington, DC: U.S. Environmental Protection Agency, 1993, pp. 234-237, table 3-9.

★ 495 ★

Toxic Release Inventory: Industry Statistics

Toxic Release Inventory Releases and Transfers in Printing Industry: 1988-1991

Table shows environmental distribution of Toxic Release Inventory (TRI) releases and transfers.

[In million pounds]

Year	Releases					Transfers		Total
	Fugitive emissions	Stack emissions	Surface water discharge	Land disposal	Under-ground injection	To public sewage	To offsite location	releases and transfers
1988	33.06	27.34	0.03	0.04	0.04	3.51	5.45	69.48
1989	31.24	25.77	(¹)	(¹)	0.00	0.83	4.56	62.40
1990	27.77	22.33	(²)	(¹)	(²)	0.35	4.23	54.68
1991	26.02	18.79	(²)	0.02	(²)	0.33	1.99	47.16

Source: Executive Office of the President of the United States. *Environmental Quality 24: The Twenty-fourth Annual Report of the Council on Environmental Quality.* Prepared by Ray Clark. Written by Carroll Curtis. Edited by Barry Walsh. Washington, DC: U.S. Government Printing Office, 1994, pp. 509-511. Primary source: U.S. Environmental Protection Agency. Office of Toxic Substances. *1991 Toxic Release Inventory.* Washington, DC: U.S. Environmental Protection Agency, 1993, pp. 234-237, table 3-9. *Notes:* 1. Less than 5,000 pounds. 2. Less than 1,000 pounds.

★ 496 ★

Toxic Release Inventory: Industry Statistics

Toxic Release Inventory Releases and Transfers in Stone and Clay Industry: 1988-1991

Table shows environmental distribution of Toxic Release Inventory (TRI) releases and transfers.

[In million pounds]

Year	Releases					Transfers		Total
	Fugitive emissions	Stack emissions	Surface water discharge	Land disposal	Under-ground injection	To public sewage	To offsite location	releases and transfers
1988	8.37	18.96	1.18	4.05	6.58	1.35	19.99	60.51
1989	8.54	17.92	0.22	3.39	6.57	1.12	14.73	52.48
1990	6.50	14.40	0.17	2.59	7.49	0.97	9.70	41.82
1991	3.93	16.96	0.16	2.34	7.47	1.69	12.81	45.34

Source: Executive Office of the President of the United States. *Environmental Quality 24: The Twenty-fourth Annual Report of the Council on Environmental Quality.* Prepared by Ray Clark. Written by Carroll Curtis. Edited by Barry Walsh. Washington, DC: U.S. Government Printing Office, 1994, pp. 509-511. Primary source: U.S. Environmental Protection Agency. Office of Toxic Substances. *1991 Toxic Release Inventory.* Washington, DC: U.S. Environmental Protection Agency, 1993, pp. 234-237, table 3-9.

★ 497 ★

Toxic Release Inventory: Industry Statistics

Toxic Release Inventory Releases and Transfers in Textiles Industry: 1988-1991

Table shows environmental distribution of Toxic Release Inventory (TRI) releases and transfers.

[In million pounds]

| Year | Releases | | | | | Transfers | | Total |
	Fugitive emissions	Stack emissions	Surface water discharge	Land disposal	Under-ground injection	To public sewage	To offsite location	releases and transfers
1988	10.80	26.13	1.01	0.15	0.00	14.63	3.71	56.44
1989	10.02	20.83	1.00	0.05	0.00	11.15	3.82	46.87
1990	7.33	19.00	0.48	0.04	(¹)	7.86	4.04	38.75
1991	6.08	18.35	0.26	0.07	0.00	6.77	2.68	34.20

Source: Executive Office of the President of the United States. *Environmental Quality 24: The Twenty-fourth Annual Report of the Council on Environmental Quality.* Prepared by Ray Clark. Written by Carroll Curtis. Edited by Barry Walsh. Washington, DC: U.S. Government Printing Office, 1994, pp. 509-511. Primary source: U.S. Environmental Protection Agency. Office of Toxic Substances. *1991 Toxic Release Inventory.* Washington, DC: U.S. Environmental Protection Agency, 1993, pp. 234-237, table 3-9. *Note:* 1. Less than 1,000 pounds.

★ 498 ★

Toxic Release Inventory: Industry Statistics

Toxic Release Inventory Releases and Transfers in Tobacco Industry: 1988-1991

Table shows environmental distribution of Toxic Release Inventory (TRI) releases and transfers.

[In million pounds]

| Year | Releases | | | | | Transfers | | Total |
	Fugitive emissions	Stack emissions	Surface water discharge	Land disposal	Under-ground injection	To public sewage	To offsite location	releases and transfers
1988	0.10	1.72	0.01	(¹)	0.00	0.79	0.31	2.94
1989	0.05	1.66	0.45	(²)	0.00	0.02	0.04	1.81
1990	0.18	2.28	0.02	(²)	0.00	0.01	0.04	2.53
1991	0.07	2.20	0.02	0.00	0.00	0.01	0.02	2.32

Source: Executive Office of the President of the United States. *Environmental Quality 24: The Twenty-fourth Annual Report of the Council on Environmental Quality.* Prepared by Ray Clark. Written by Carroll Curtis. Edited by Barry Walsh. Washington, DC: U.S. Government Printing Office, 1994, p. 509-511. Primary source: U.S. Environmental Protection Agency. Office of Toxic Substances. *1991 Toxic Release Inventory.* Washington, DC: U.S. Environmental Protection Agency, 1993, pp. 234-237, table 3-9. *Notes:* 1. Less than 1,000 pounds. 2. Less than 5,000 pounds.

★ 499 ★

Toxic Release Inventory: Industry Statistics

Toxic Release Inventory Releases and Transfers in Transportation Industry: 1988-1991

Table shows environmental distribution of Toxic Release Inventory (TRI) releases and transfers.

[In million pounds]

| Year | Releases | | | | | Transfers | | Total |
	Fugitive emissions	Stack emissions	Surface water discharge	Land disposal	Under-ground injection	To public sewage	To offsite location	releases and transfers
1988	76.25	135.21	0.37	2.46	81.85	7.41	54.94	276.72
1989	73.36	129.97	0.14	1.49	(¹)	7.98	42.13	255.06
1990	63.12	109.53	0.19	1.70	(¹)	8.90	37.48	220.92
1991	48.05	97.50	0.14	1.92	(¹)	7.42	25.77	180.80

Source: Executive Office of the President of the United States. *Environmental Quality 24: The Twenty-fourth Annual Report of the Council on Environmental Quality.* Prepared by Ray Clark. Written by Carroll Curtis. Edited by Barry Walsh. Washington, DC: U.S. Government Printing Office, 1994, pp. 509-511. Primary source: U.S. Environmental Protection Agency. Office of Toxic Substances. *1991 Toxic Release Inventory.* Washington, DC: U.S. Environmental Protection Agency, 1993, pp. 234-237, table 3-9. *Note:* 1. Less than 1,000 pounds.

Chapter 8
WASTES AND RESOURCE RECOVERY

Waste management has multiple aspects—municipal waste, hazardous waste, industrial waste, nuclear waste, and resource recovery, among others. This chapter covers chemical transfers, chemicals in waste, composting, hazardous waste, municipal solid waste (including specific materials), nuclear waste, recycling (including the recovery of specific materials and specific programs and facilities), waste generation and disposal, and waste minimization.

Waste generation refers to the production of waste by individuals and institutions. Solid waste is generated as an object becomes obsolete or unusable. The amount of waste generated does not always equal the amount of waste discarded. Discards are generated wastes that are thrown away. Other portions of waste may be recycled or reprocessed for future use, thus never becoming discards.

Studies of waste generation are based on examination of economic activity—how many refrigerators were purchased in a given year—and the life cycle of products—how many years does a refrigerator last before it becomes useless. Some products (facial tissue, for example) have very short life cycles. Others (clothing and appliances) can spend a long time in storage even after their usefulness has passed. Studies of discards and of waste compositions are based on the sampling of actual wastes as they are delivered to disposal or recycling facilities by the waste collecting industry.

Municipal waste is typically a combination of residential wastes (including yard wastes) and commercial wastes (discards from stores or offices). The term excludes industrial waste, building rubble ("C&D"—construction and demolition wastes), and old automobiles.

The Toxic and Hazardous Substances chapter also contains a great deal of data on chemical transfers—recycling and energy recovery—from the Toxic Release Inventory. Related legal issues are covered in the Politics, Opinion, Law chapter.

Chemical Transfers

★ 500 ★

Chemical Transfers Received, by State or Territory: 1992

Table shows total transfers of Toxic Release Inventory (TRI) chemicals received, including intrastate transfers and transfers into the state. Data are ordered by transfers received.

[In pounds]

Receiving state or territory	Transfers to recycling	Transfers to energy recovery	Transfers to treatment	Transfers to disposal	Other[1] offsite transfers	Total transfers received
Indiana	427,247,100	39,343,554	47,846,602	20,680,632	978,930	536,096,818
Texas	275,402,916	76,405,230	38,607,919	37,011,588	1,066,520	428,494,173
Pennsylvania	274,317,192	2,505,257	20,442,857	11,328,737	3,310,415	311,904,458
Ohio	149,000,052	66,327,282	46,526,751	43,555,191	1,672,991	307,082,267
Illinois	108,736,591	23,302,069	87,325,565	14,818,878	1,224,560	235,407,663
Michigan	139,285,021	49,909,303	18,797,146	18,984,417	662,797	227,638,684
Missouri	210,040,711	9,900,072	2,297,001	2,182,683	66,220	224,486,687
Louisiana	191,641,071	12,011,327	20,180,506	4,660,006	10,338	228,503,248
California	163,035,311	11,439,982	5,458,937	4,942,622	276,546	185,153,398
South Carolina	93,836,010	17,178,359	8,594,288	7,735,034	615,700	127,959,391
New Jersey	48,372,612	33,173,888	22,384,155	1,991,819	334,175	106,256,649
Alabama	47,191,090	35,072,721	4,752,530	8,351,728	65,067	95,433,136
Tennessee	68,090,063	10,574,977	4,608,310	9,218,653	44,407	92,536,410
Washington	66,303,524	642,731	1,077,627	2,920,059	825	70,944,766
Wisconsin	38,243,560	5,204,954	10,184,358	9,291,717	116,783	63,041,372
West Virginia	60,002,715	20,000	387,790	2,162,793	7,600	62,580,898
New York	49,438,781	2,921,609	3,411,654	4,581,509	128,167	60,481,720
Kentucky	16,061,547	24,889,462	6,127,330	2,784,909	559,278	50,422,526
North Carolina	39,096,444	3,034,005	2,599,952	4,171,112	564,904	49,466,417
Georgia	37,380,493	3,773,448	1,123,125	6,555,552	75,971	48,908,589
Connecticut	32,177,903	157,132	1,749,448	953,150	23,730	35,661,363
Florida	26,697,739	3,499,405	2,897,232	943,334	1,037	34,038,747
Kansas	14,872,027	5,461,941	2,847,834	8,994,377	4,598	32,180,777
Arkansas	11,112,985	8,089,545	6,908,029	4,200,891	17,201	30,328,651
Delaware	25,799,256	14,729	63,105	32,081	0	25,909,171
Massachusetts	15,579,311	4,492,603	3,279,057	1,610,052	339,160	25,300,183
Minnesota	16,463,571	4,528,645	3,548,983	240,095	5,405	24,786,699
Virginia	9,671,200	8,871,959	1,885,362	3,156,250	41,803	23,626,574
Wyoming	23,102,183	0	0	37,548	0	23,139,731
Puerto Rico	10,603,530	7,393,341	1,725,781	374,342	41,288	20,138,282
Montana	13,649,244	0	0	2,102,375	0	15,751,619
Arizona	12,708,225	500,008	1,875,156	94,073	1,822	15,179,284
Maryland	12,124,707	497,239	1,831,047	541,947	250	14,995,190
Oklahoma	8,137,543	1,146,380	916,442	2,531,026	3,164	12,734,555
District of Columbia	9,444,201	0	750	245	0	9,445,196
Utah	1,685,837	1,409	857,399	5,016,403	0	7,561,048
Iowa	4,136,272	82,045	1,259,933	1,511,950	750	6,990,950
Colorado	2,897,979	2,584,100	1,263,328	139,875	46,204	6,931,486

[Continued]

★ 500 ★

Chemical Transfers Received, by State or Territory: 1992
[Continued]

Receiving state or territory	Transfers to recycling	Transfers to energy recovery	Transfers to treatment	Transfers to disposal	Other[1] offsite transfers	Total transfers received
Nebraska	1,394,056	101,202	1,693,473	1,478,168	1,025,885	5,692,784
Oregon	3,448,112	38,571	527,299	1,225,272	0	5,239,254
Rhode Island	2,381,637	38,044	276,992	1,618,162	4,700	4,319,535
Mississippi	2,813,340	49,163	23,079	632,437	57,982	3,576,001
Idaho	2,289,647	285	259,604	223,971	0	2,773,507
Maine	1,278,527	295	7,550	791,942	0	2,078,314
Nevada	972,186	47	55,011	1,037,107	192	2,064,543
New Hampshire	1,127,143	0	48,634	176,512	0	1,352,289
North Dakota	103,517	750	49,000	95,483	0	248,750
South Dakota	3,705	0	32,967	43,456	0	80,128
New Mexico	26,600	0	30,000	18,885	0	75,485
Vermont	28,230	0	34,591	12,276	0	75,097
Alaska	0	0	30,462	407	0	30,869
Hawaii	0	0	0	3,803	0	3,803
Virgin Islands	0	0	0	0	0	0
American Samoa	0	0	0	0	0	0
Other[2]	69,772,702	2,460,196	4,754,589	875,043	3,536,125	81,398,655
Total	2,839,225,919	477,639,264	393,466,540	258,642,577	16,933,490	3,986,507,790

Source: U.S. Environmental Protection Agency. "Toxic Release Inventory, 1992." In *National Economic, Social, and Environmental Data Bank* [CD-ROM]. Prepared by U.S. Department of Commerce, Economics and Statistics Administration. Washington, DC: U.S. Department of Commerce, National Economic, Social, and Environmental Data Bank, Economics and Statistics Administration, Office of Business Analysis, February 1995. *Notes:* "POTWs" are publicly owned treatment works. 1. Other transfers are transfers reported with missing or invalid waste management codes. 2. Other locations includes other countries and sites not identified by state.

★ 501 ★

Chemical Transfers

Chemicals With Largest Offsite Transfers for Disposal: 1992

Table shows the 15 Toxic Release Inventory (TRI) chemicals with the largest offsite transfers for disposal.

[In pounds]

Chemical	Storage only	Underground injection	Landfill/ surface impoundment	Land treatment	Other land disposal	Other offsite management	Transfers to waste broker-disposal	Unknown	Total transfers to disposal
Zinc compounds	40,252	647,563	38,844,975	379,412	1,625,081	55,305	492,681	421,180	42,506,449
Sulfuric acid	307,166	29,768,760	3,101,227	86,816	27,720	79,023	527,707	304,214	34,202,633
Barium compounds	52,715	1,683	10,666,566	290	4,838,656	5,596	219,206	20,482	15,805,194
Lead compounds	3,524	1,570	12,523,511	65,005	398,315	39	148,766	59,321	13,200,051
Copper	6,688,646	6,609	4,765,325	37,656	294,819	2,276	1,263,787	80,460	13,139,578
Hydrochloric acid	5,703	11,624,725	888,446	0	35,696	25,400	378,338	22,825	12,981,133
Manganese compounds	128	56,074	12,389,456	75,126	79,760	130	260,324	36,079	12,897,077
Manganese	293	15,046	8,829,701	260,942	1,498,014	5	47,556	21,992	10,673,549
Chromium compounds	49,727	229,075	8,940,028	51,318	81,955	0	70,995	456,943	9,880,041
Ammonium sulfate (solution)	0	5,300,000	50,301	2,236,409	3,938	0	0	0	7,590,648
Asbestos (friable)	0	0	7,108,171	0	0	0	2,298	0	7,110,469
Copper compounds	83,541	29,876	6,152,504	5,914	76,112	26,677	26,883	25,760	6,427,267
Zinc (fume or dust)	2,100	22	1,952,109	1,620,395	16,263	1,800,000	2,432	6,362	5,399,683
Nickel compounds	19,048	43,034	4,892,376	3,751	7,055	770	13,540	38,792	5,018,366

[Continued]

531

★ 501 ★

Chemicals With Largest Offsite Transfers for Disposal: 1992

[Continued]

Chemical	Storage only	Underground injection	Landfill/ surface impoundment	Land treatment	Other land disposal	Other offsite management	Transfers to waste broker-disposal	Unknown	Total transfers to disposal
Chromium	10,340	122,270	3,872,086	25,156	208,973	6	89,801	36,954	4,365,586
Subtotal	7,263,183	47,846,307	124,976,782	4,848,190	9,192,357	1,995,227	3,544,314	1,531,364	201,197,724
Total for all TRI chemicals	8,696,804	57,100,146	162,489,061	8,506,916	10,796,542	2,538,009	6,003,166	2,511,933	258,642,577

Source: U.S. Environmental Protection Agency. "Toxic Release Inventory, 1992." In *National Economic, Social, and Environmental Data Bank* [CD-ROM]. Prepared by U.S. Department of Commerce, Economics and Statistics Administration. Washington, DC: U.S. Department of Commerce, National Economic, Social, and Environmental Data Bank, Economics and Statistics Administration, Office of Business Analysis, February 1995.

★ 502 ★

Chemical Transfers

Chemicals With Largest Offsite Transfers for Energy Recovery: 1992

Table shows the 15 Toxic Release Inventory (TRI) chemicals with the largest offsite transfers for energy recovery.

[In pounds]

Chemical	Energy recovery	Transfer to waste broker-energy recovery	Total offsite transfers to energy recovery
Toluene	54,294,172	24,582,255	78,876,427
Methanol	58,703,949	10,566,899	69,270,848
Xylene (mixed isomers)	44,907,229	19,344,823	64,252,052
Acetone	33,822,378	8,407,136	42,229,514
Methyl ethyl ketone	29,749,389	9,451,511	39,200,900
tert-Butyl alcohol	28,353,709	121,816	28,475,525
Methyl isobutyl ketone	6,686,291	10,657,238	17,343,529
Ethylene	14,003,679	3,738	14,007,417
Glycol ethers	8,762,733	2,877,456	11,640,189
Ethylbenzene	6,727,969	2,055,053	8,783,022
Styrene	6,966,175	1,611,561	8,577,736
n-Butyl alcohol	6,423,828	1,672,611	8,096,439
Ethylene glycol	4,621,017	2,845,091	7,466,108
Vinyl acetate	5,293,395	604,309	5,897,704
Hydrochloric acid	4,110	5,104,891	5,109,001
Subtotal	309,320,023	99,906,388	409,226,411
Total for all TRI chemicals	368,111,613	109,527,651	477,639,264

Source: U.S. Environmental Protection Agency. "Toxic Release Inventory, 1992." In *National Economic, Social, and Environmental Data Bank* [CD-ROM]. Prepared by U.S. Department of Commerce, Economics and Statistics Administration. Washington, DC: U.S. Department of Commerce, National Economic, Social, and Environmental Data Bank, Economics and Statistics Administration, Office of Business Analysis, February 1995.

★ 503 ★

Chemical Transfers

Chemicals With Largest Offsite Transfers for Recycling: 1992

Table shows the 15 Toxic Release Inventory (TRI) chemicals with the largest offsite transfers for recycling.

[In pounds]

Chemical	Solvents/ organics recovery	Metals recovery	Other reuse or recovery	Acid regeneration	Transfer to waste broker- recycling	Total offsite transfers to recycling
Sulfuric acid	599,989	714,858	49,155,955	869,730,583	1,177,146	921,378,531
Lead compounds	2,020	368,679,473	2,491,389	5	848,938	372,021,825
Copper	8,610	274,835,443	18,386,100	2,867	53,567,350	346,800,370
Zinc compounds	77,764	189,972,847	33,321,861	994	3,774,726	227,148,192
Copper compounds	591	88,236,793	1,234,260	19,450	16,773,452	106,264,546
Ethylene glycol	68,986,951	0	32,382,860	0	1,003,484	102,373,295
Chromium	545	45,161,425	8,596,182	50,000	14,129,965	67,938,117
Zinc (fume or dust)	16,980	60,081,581	575,394	0	1,910,174	62,584,129
Hydrochloric acid	7,207	2,410,440	47,232,394	7,711,629	2,087,136	59,448,806
Nickel	13,568	33,181,631	5,782,896	0	13,477,294	52,455,389
Xylene (mixed isomers)	36,491,565	13,410	1,531,691	0	1,051,791	39,088,457
Manganese compounds	174	20,521,353	12,388,746	0	3,158,526	36,068,799
Lead	8,666	27,199,620	1,031,901	0	2,370,875	30,611,062
Manganese	542	19,089,429	4,965,872	0	5,970,900	30,026,743
Toluene	27,529,926	3,569	1,492,213	0	923,517	29,949,225
Subtotal	133,745,098	1,130,101,872	220,569,714	877,515,528	122,225,274	2,484,157,486
Total for all TRI chemicals	337,103,432	1,216,073,083	257,875,423	880,950,772	147,823,209	2,839,825,919

Source: U.S. Environmental Protection Agency. "Toxic Release Inventory, 1992." In *National Economic, Social, and Environmental Data Bank* [CD-ROM]. Prepared by U.S. Department of Commerce, Economics and Statistics Administration. Washington, DC: U.S. Department of Commerce, National Economic, Social, and Environmental Data Bank, Economics and Statistics Administration, Office of Business Analysis, February 1995.

★ 504 ★

Chemical Transfers

Chemicals With Largest Offsite Transfers for Treatment: 1992

Table shows the 15 Toxic Release Inventory (TRI) chemicals with the largest offsite transfers for treatment.

[In pounds]

Chemical	Solidification/ stabilization	Incineration/ thermal treatment	Incineration/ insignificant fuel value	Wastewater treatment, excluding POTWs	Other waste treatment	Transfer to waste broker-waste treatment	Total transfers to treatment
Hydrochloric acid	1,280,013	79,763	132,919	8,160,970	14,437,517	18,472,102	42,563,284
Sulfuric acid	9,108,696	1,718,023	28,486	20,703,751	9,360,925	538,152	41,458,033
Methanol	8,906	22,696,354	4,344,395	11,708,875	816,392	323,783	39,898,705
Zinc compounds	32,985,556	193,385	835,725	1,231,782	1,436,515	209,569	36,892,532
Antimony compounds	20,375,154	249,825	39,115	20,261	28,266	33,517	20,746,138

[Continued]

★ 504 ★

Chemicals With Largest Offsite Transfers for Treatment: 1992

[Continued]

Chemical	Solidification/ stabilization	Incineration/ thermal treatment	Incineration/ insignificant fuel value	Wastewater treatment, excluding POTWs	Other waste treatment	Transfer to waste broker-waste treatment	Total transfers to treatment
Lead compounds	18,746,516	327,684	77,900	732,724	70,578	126,617	20,082,019
Toluene	59,008	17,025,436	1,700,080	348,772	476,562	167,314	19,777,172
Acetone	13,589	12,283,744	3,709,723	2,226,666	1,076,530	132,334	19,442,586
Dichloromethane	5,067	4,007,331	7,123,880	250,976	106,515	137,458	11,631,227
Nitric acid	501,456	7,034	14,885	3,794,629	5,998,019	301,875	10,617,898
Ethylene glycol	1,003,041	1,034,601	386,637	4,179,433	183,082	207,555	6,994,349
Ammonia	62,637	657,204	45,616	5,224,093	583,216	18,287	6,591,053
Xylene (mixed isomers)	49,434	5,208,638	636,416	222,056	239,489	58,067	6,414,100
Methyl ethyl ketone	8,830	5,052,105	562,228	92,384	256,615	254,028	6,226,190
1,1,1-Trichloroethane	31,346	1,564,812	1,940,585	82,989	440,748	187,419	4,247,899
Subtotal	84,239,249	72,105,939	21,578,590	58,980,361	35,510,969	21,168,077	293,583,185
Total for all TRI chemicals	100,521,880	122,409,549	31,602,579	70,577,964	41,483,326	26,871,242	393,466,540

Source: U.S. Environmental Protection Agency. "Toxic Release Inventory, 1992." In *National Economic, Social, and Environmental Data Bank* [CD-ROM]. Prepared by U.S. Department of Commerce, Economics and Statistics Administration. Washington, DC: U.S. Department of Commerce, National Economic, Social, and Environmental Data Bank, Economics and Statistics Administration, Office of Business Analysis, February 1995. *Note:* "POTWs" are publicly owned treatment works.

★ 505 ★

Chemical Transfers

Chemicals With Largest Offsite Transfers to Publicly Owned Treatment Works: 1992

Table shows the 15 Toxic Release Inventory (TRI) chemicals with the largest offsite transfers to publicly owned treatment works (POTWs).

[In pounds]

Chemical	Transfers to POTWs
Methanol	113,917,241
Ammonia	71,885,270
Ammonium sulfate (solution)	37,330,411
Sulfuric acid	35,866,416
Hydrochloric acid	29,390,927
Ethylene glycol	19,775,302
Glycol ethers	10,354,678
Acetone	9,431,457
Ammonium nitrate (solution)	6,856,667
Formaldehyde	5,635,857
Phosphoric acid	4,889,570
Phenol	4,547,598
Nitric acid	3,739,898
tert-Butyl alcohol	2,104,895
n-Butyl alcohol	2,070,978

[Continued]

★ 505 ★

Chemicals With Largest Offsite Transfers to Publicly Owned Treatment Works: 1992

[Continued]

Chemical	Transfers to POTWs
Subtotal	357,797,165
Total for all TRI chemicals	381,096,823

Source: U.S. Environmental Protection Agency. "Toxic Release Inventory, 1992." In *National Economic, Social, and Environmental Data Bank* [CD-ROM]. Prepared by U.S. Department of Commerce, Economics and Statistics Administration. Washington, DC: U.S. Department of Commerce, National Economic, Social, and Environmental Data Bank, Economics and Statistics Administration, Office of Business Analysis, February 1995.

Chemicals in Waste

★ 506 ★

Chemicals in Waste – Quantities: 1991-1992

Table shows the quantities of Toxic Release Inventory (TRI) chemicals in waste.

[In billion pounds, except percentages]

Management Activity	1991 quantity	1992 quantity	Percent change
Recycled on-site	16.171	15.884	-1.8
Recycled off-site	2.983	3.474	16.5
Used for energy recovery on-site	3.260	2.941	-9.8
Used for energy recovery off-site	0.500	0.628	25.6
Treated on-site	9.895	10.327	4.4
Treated off-site	0.710	0.678	-4.5
Released and disposed of on-site and off-site	3.644	3.401	-6.7
Total	37.162	37.334	0.5

Source: U.S. Environmental Protection Agency. "Toxic Release Inventory, 1992." In *National Economic, Social, and Environmental Data Bank* [CD-ROM]. Prepared by U.S. Department of Commerce, Economics and Statistics Administration. Washington, DC: U.S. Department of Commerce, National Economic, Social, and Environmental Data Bank, Economics and Statistics Administration, Office of Business Analysis, February 1995. *Notes:* 1991 amounts are as reported on the 1991 Form R and 1992 amounts are as reported on the 1992 Form R.

★ 507 ★

Chemicals in Waste

Chemicals in Waste – Quantities (Actual and Projected): 1991-1994

Table shows quantities of Toxic Release Inventory (TRI) chemicals in waste. All data are as reported on the 1991 Form R. Data for 1993 and 1994 are projections reported by facilities. As projections, those quantities do not represent estimates of actual quantities for 1993 or 1994.

Management activity	1991		1992		1993		1994	
	Pounds	Percent	Pounds	Percent	Pounds	Percent	Pounds	Percent
Recycled onsite	15,852,682,387	43.7	15,884,194,888	42.5	16,777,659,985	44.8	16,911,850,011	45.1
Recycled offsite	2,976,812,329	8.2	3,473,894,509	9.3	3,172,827,577	8.5	3,454,654,976	9.2
Energy recovery onsite	2,842,457,939	7.8	2,941,222,113	7.9	2,909,306,636	7.8	3,091,684,371	8.3
Energy recovery offsite	580,710,271	1.6	627,954,600	1.7	597,471,908	1.6	589,834,167	1.6
Treated onsite	9,868,146,903	27.2	10,326,749,494	27.7	10,184,180,233	27.2	10,097,658,804	27.0
Treated offsite	680,368,098	1.9	678,373,850	1.8	627,265,273	1.7	598,615,840	1.6
Quantity released	3,515,785,150	9.7	3,401,386,170	9.1	3,177,194,783	8.5	2,716,113,363	7.3
Total	36,316,963,077	100.0	37,333,775,624	100.0	37,445,906,395	100.0	37,460,411,532	100.0

Source: U.S. Environmental Protection Agency. "Toxic Release Inventory, 1992." In *National Economic, Social, and Environmental Data Bank* [CD-ROM]. Prepared by U.S. Department of Commerce, Economics and Statistics Administration. Washington, DC: U.S. Department of Commerce, National Economic, Social, and Environmental Data Bank, Economics and Statistics Administration, Office of Business Analysis, February 1995.

★ 508 ★

Chemicals in Waste

Chemicals in Waste – Receipt From Out of State: 1992

Table shows the receipt of Toxic Release Inventory (TRI) chemicals in waste from out of state for each state. Data are ordered by total received.

[In pounds]

Receiving state or territory	Transfers to recycling	Transfers to energy recovery	Transfers to treatment	Transfers to disposal	Other[1] offsite transfers	Total transfers received
Pennsylvania	186,980,818	1,650,866	5,151,736	1,037,884	211,007	195,032,311
Indiana	138,225,045	29,475,675	9,143,466	8,994,139	194,141	186,032,466
Texas	165,296,026	2,526,966	6,592,824	8,603,387	35,875	183,055,078
Illinois	80,791,172	14,206,162	74,771,971	4,836,778	595,209	175,201,292
Ohio	83,352,328	39,479,666	21,365,088	18,689,570	70,267	162,956,919
Louisiana	94,749,913	8,069,040	16,342,274	3,031,305	10,338	122,202,870
Michigan	60,425,014	12,088,268	5,871,137	3,987,610	89,414	82,461,443
South Carolina	58,669,499	13,618,245	5,186,743	2,940,239	235,938	80,650,664
Alabama	39,175,801	26,990,047	3,432,132	2,403,102	62,652	72,063,734
Missouri	52,227,096	6,550,120	1,332,393	248,947	45,219	60,403,775
New Jersey	30,496,336	12,724,825	14,421,814	429,701	95,456	58,168,132
California	54,983,566	598,587	488,459	81,408	167,102	56,319,122
Tennessee	38,814,673	8,068,349	3,532,780	731,820	2,150	51,149,772
West Virginia	35,856,149	2,060	387,718	468,888	7,600	36,722,415
New York	30,933,247	1,341,796	2,439,258	1,010,346	55,123	35,779,770

[Continued]

★ 508 ★

Chemicals in Waste – Receipt From Out of State: 1992

[Continued]

Receiving state or territory	Transfers to recycling	Transfers to energy recovery	Transfers to treatment	Transfers to disposal	Other[1] offsite transfers	Total transfers received
Kentucky	8,397,195	18,944,435	4,005,796	455,042	15,014	31,817,482
Georgia	21,561,809	3,228,999	639,857	208,842	75,758	25,715,265
Connecticut	22,833,083	60,921	692,422	387,056	23,730	23,997,212
Delaware	23,922,011	14,719	27,903	1,559	0	23,966,192
Wyoming	23,101,551	0	0	0	0	23,101,551
Wisconsin	17,414,774	4,091,295	976,420	235,944	60,002	22,778,435
Florida	17,960,599	2,788,307	928,013	66,206	1,037	21,744,162
Virginia	7,102,325	7,023,682	1,664,550	1,814,881	39,783	17,645,221
Arkansas	2,730,673	7,302,257	6,579,502	437,033	16,951	17,066,416
North Carolina	13,691,051	1,630,004	431,761	436,125	39,744	16,228,685
Montana	13,644,344	0	0	2,097,000	0	15,741,344
Minnesota	8,299,813	3,460,317	1,839,507	5,574	4,581	13,609,792
Massachusetts	7,784,577	985,769	1,315,891	554,046	219,059	10,859,342
District of Columbia	9,444,201	0	750	245	0	9,445,196
Maryland	5,791,618	488,925	1,723,413	298,877	250	8,303,083
Kansas	142,652	4,730,651	569,533	105,429	3,698	5,551,963
Washington	2,061,228	333,770	319,216	2,196,473	0	4,910,687
Oklahoma	1,587,769	931,489	871,876	1,223,433	2,914	4,617,481
Arizona	3,849,053	10,679	188,388	14,575	1,822	4,064,517
Idaho	2,289,647	35	197,355	191,052	0	2,678,089
Iowa	2,199,763	22,343	10,864	71,092	0	2,304,062
Nevada	972,186	0	52,489	963,838	192	1,988,705
Rhode Island	1,730,224	37,558	201,943	6,541	4,700	1,980,966
Utah	214,800	220	579,109	774,870	0	1,568,999
Colorado	800,395	640,693	30,544	26,683	45,954	1,544,269
Oregon	612,197	29,428	49,041	350,182	0	1,040,848
Mississippi	331,115	48,163	1,270	205,969	57,427	643,944
Nebraska	90,194	88,947	2,760	33,024	0	214,925
New Hampshire	38,107	0	69	100,272	0	138,448
North Dakota	9,917	0	0	95,034	0	104,951
New Mexico	24,350	0	0	13,200	0	37,550
South Dakota	3,700	0	31,967	0	0	35,667
Alaska	0	0	30,462	407	0	30,869
Maine	23,205	45	0	299	0	23,549
Vermont	4,130	0	14,167	266	0	18,563
Virgin Islands	0	0	0	0	0	0
Hawaii	0	0	0	0	0	0
American Samoa	0	0	0	0	0	0
Puerto Rico	0	0	0	0	0	0

[Continued]

★ 508 ★

Chemicals in Waste – Receipt From Out of State: 1992
[Continued]

Receiving state or territory	Transfers to recycling	Transfers to energy recovery	Transfers to treatment	Transfers to disposal	Other[1] offsite transfers	Total transfers received
Other[2]	69,772,702	2,460,196	4,754,589	875,043	3,536,125	81,398,655
Total	1,441,413,641	236,744,519	199,191,220	71,741,236	6,026,232	1,955,116,848

Source: U.S. Environmental Protection Agency. "Toxic Release Inventory, 1992." In *National Economic, Social, and Environmental Data Bank* [CD-ROM]. Prepared by U.S. Department of Commerce, Economics and Statistics Administration. Washington, DC: U.S. Department of Commerce, National Economic, Social, and Environmental Data Bank, Economics and Statistics Administration, Office of Business Analysis, February 1995. *Notes:* 1. Other transfers are transfers reported with missing or invalid waste management codes. 2. Other locations includes other countries and sites not identified by state.

★ 509 ★

Chemicals in Waste

Chemicals in Waste – Recycled or Energy Recovery, by Chemical: 1992

Table shows the quantities of Toxic Release Inventory (TRI) chemicals in waste that are recycled or used for energy recovery.

[In pounds]

Chemical	Recycled onsite	Recycled offsite	Energy recovery onsite	Energy recovery offsite
Acetaldehyde	120,001	251	10,253,924	167,669
Acetamide	0	0	42,896	0
Acetone	213,067,646	18,005,963	133,281,260	40,177,385
Acetonitrile	2,508,586,088	2,880,190	29,839,722	4,346,283
Acrolein	7,100	0	1,669,496	38,566
Acrylamide	3,290	0	0	123,134
Acrylic acid	1,437,450	70,909	13,986,624	4,189,944
Acrylonitrile	21,231,972	700	2,137,971	1,510,170
Allyl alcohol	204,087	0	540,065	111,950
Allyl chloride	917,000	0	3,065,000	31,000
Aluminum (fume or dust)	40,606,848	66,815,379	0	171,602
Aluminum oxide (fibrous forms)	58,608	724,431	0	11,628
4-Aminoazobenzene	0	0	0	0
4-Aminobiphenyl	0	0	0	0
Ammonia	211,456,668	18,117,158	53,293,518	262,578
Ammonium nitrate (solution)	61,022,341	8,693,580	0	0
Ammonium sulfate (solution)	879,902	976,312	0	0
Aniline	8,959,535	0	4,955,284	921,433
o-Anisidine	0	0	320	0
p-Anisidine	0	0	0	0
Anthracene	547,216	0	3,063,528	394,880
Antimony	2,122,109	1,597,207	0	1,300
Antimony compounds	16,376,518	1,698,663	0	11,767
Arsenic	327,411	13,876	0	4

[Continued]

★ 509 ★

Chemicals in Waste – Recycled or Energy Recovery, by Chemical: 1992

[Continued]

Chemical	Recycled onsite	Recycled offsite	Energy recovery onsite	Energy recovery offsite
Arsenic compounds	5,644,011	591,489	0	2
Asbestos (friable)	717,992	0	0	0
Barium	32,567	59,453	0	328
Barium compounds	20,463,906	736,044	0	187,676
Benzal chloride	0	0	0	34,000
Benzene	59,012,822	487,209	36,703,579	4,347,690
Benzoic trichloride	0	0	0	0
Benzoyl chloride	0	0	0	0
Benzoyl peroxide	4,800	6,400	0	2,246
Benzyl chloride	2,110	0	0	274,730
Beryllium	18,500	7,058	0	0
Beryllium compounds	12,000	10,540	0	0
Biphenyl	425,076	321,608	1,588,305	388,745
Bis(2-chloroethyl) ether	31	0	889,000	140
Bis(chloromethyl) ether	0	0	0	0
Bis(2-chloro-1-methylethyl)ether	2,400,000	0	5,590,000	0
Bis(2-ethylhexyl) adipate	1,716,068	143,555	52,350	222,515
Bromochlorodifluoromethane (Halon 1211)	45,000	0	0	0
Bromoform	0	0	0	0
Bromomethane	458,200	0	26,000	3,900
Bromotrifluoromethane (Halon 1301)	58,000	0	0	0
1,3-Butadiene	293,902,741	28,850,854	77,191,067	65,839
Butyl acrylate	143,267	80,026	1,230,659	44,990
n-Butyl alcohol	55,630,402	2,492,961	25,590,867	8,935,952
sec-Butyl alcohol	336,057	4,915	9,580,483	4,800,805
tert-Butyl alcohol	29,200	7,743	42,924,000	27,760,077
Butyl benzyl phthalate	1,895,154	55,920	14,031	98,679
1,2-Butylene oxide	8,200	0	51,000	350,012
Butyraldehyde	120,020	400	1,030,189	9,969
C.I. basic green 4	723	0	0	0
C.I. basic red 1	0	0	0	309
C.I. disperse yellow 3	0	0	0	0
C.I. food red 15	0	0	0	0
C.I. solvent yellow 14	0	0	0	0
Cadmium	1,009,617	313,649	0	0
Cadmium compounds	10,801,005	1,700,327	0	3,193
Calcium cyanamide	0	0	0	0
Captan	1,335	0	0	0
Carbaryl	45,445	0	0	0
Carbon disulfide	18,175,987	1	5,594,160	139,047
Carbon tetrachloride	16,629,476	344,453	4,889,374	6,451
Carbonyl sulfide	0	0	1,985,780	0
Catechol	303,851	60	38,971,978	361,770
Chlordane	170	0	0	0
Chlorine	108,182,213	633,929	77,480	23

[Continued]

★ 509 ★

Chemicals in Waste – Recycled or Energy Recovery, by Chemical: 1992

[Continued]

Chemical	Recycled onsite	Recycled offsite	Energy recovery onsite	Energy recovery offsite
Chlorine dioxide	2,013,000	0	0	0
Chloroacetic acid	15,342	0	0	22
Chlorobenzene	5,167,071	849,499	1,060,070	831,098
Chloroethane	2,544,300	221,446	16,339,568	15,655
Chloroform	6,353,787	1,417,917	6,471,447	565,883
Chloromethane	445,437	7,000	4,521,171	31,993
Chloromethyl methyl ether	0	0	0	0
Chlorophenols	2,016,087	0	0	0
Chloroprene	85,380	1,384,120	53,826	19,200
Chlorothalonil	2,516	1,750	0	0
Chromium	19,957,024	76,535,146	0	335
Chromium compounds	43,448,554	34,129,168	9,410	101,881
Cobalt	2,787,589	4,974,870	0	4,111
Cobalt compounds	741,749	1,703,799	0	10,908
Copper	251,127,564	388,377,676	20,000	819
Copper compounds	185,313,401	126,262,362	0	52,758
Creosote	14,440,400	6,100	2,000	114,746
p-Cresidine	0	0	6	0
Cresol (mixed isomers)	1,009,054	102,197	2,993,404	355,670
m-Cresol	1,800,243	320,890	541,520	44,717
o-Cresol	64,520	0	441,000	29,959
p-Cresol	55,890	200,000	492,000	163,193
Cumene	308,360,195	64,499	4,925,583	706,018
Cumene hydroperoxide	25,000	0	0	125
Cupferron	0	0	0	0
Cyanide compounds	588,869	73,104	344,000	600
Cyclohexane	39,491,269	542,496	10,347,228	3,018,871
2,4-D (acetic acid)	88,061	0	0	0
Decabromodiphenyl oxide	1,388,379	29,377	0	8,141
4,4'-Diaminodiphenyl ether	0	0	0	0
Diaminotoluene (mixed isomers)	0	0	4,270,555	367,800
2,4-Diaminotoluene	0	0	0	0
Dibenzofuran	114,295	0	1,400	800
1,2-Dibromo-3-chloropropane	0	0	0	0
1,2-Dibromoethane	61	0	750	3,362
Dibromotetrafluoroethane (Halon 2402)	0	0	0	0
Dibutyl phthalate	81,080	445	234,702	143,982
Dichlorobenzene (mixed isomers)	0	0	236,220	88
1,2-Dichlorobenzene	3,290,581	820,977	165,232	659,100
1,3-Dichlorobenzene	8,613	950	68,000	0
1,4-Dichlorobenzene	757,285	3	85,520	0
3,3'-Dichlorobenzidine	0	0	0	430
Dichlorobromomethane	0	0	0	0
Dichlorodifluoromethane (CFC-12)	882,277	368,177	114	2,007
1,2-Dichloroethane	126,527,252	19,128,820	33,659,857	68,802

[Continued]

★ 509 ★

Chemicals in Waste – Recycled or Energy Recovery, by Chemical: 1992

[Continued]

Chemical	Recycled onsite	Recycled offsite	Energy recovery onsite	Energy recovery offsite
1,2-Dichloroethylene	2,568,000	2,330	1,378,993	0
Dichloromethane	121,863,677	26,109,091	11,832,816	3,247,710
2,4-Dichlorophenol	1,008	0	0	0
1,2-Dichloropropane	46,537,442	0	16,800,000	0
2,3-Dichloropropene	2,700,000	0	900,000	0
1,3-Dichloropropylene	3,871,000	0	13,340,000	0
Dichlorotetrafluoroethane (CFC-114)	823,600	521	0	0
Dichlorvos	0	0	92	0
Dicofol	34	0	0	0
Diethanolamine	62,427	227,653	53,864	29,284
Di-(2-ethylhexyl) phthalate	3,718,731	3,393,958	431,445	278,527
Diethyl phthalate	590,320	297,764	191,500	57,626
Diethyl sulfate	0	5,000,000	0	2,731
3,3'-Dimethoxybenzidine	0	0	0	0
1,1-Dimethyl hydrazine	0	20	0	0
2,4-Dimethylphenol	220,361	13,455	293,474	72,190
Dimethyl phthalate	12,712	0	361,940	67,702
Dimethyl sulfate	0	48,266	0	0
m-Dinitrobenzene	0	0	3,000	0
o-Dinitrobenzene	0	0	0	0
p-Dinitrobenzene	0	0	0	0
4,6-Dinitro-o-cresol	0	0	395,000	210
2,4-Dinitrophenol	0	0	660,002	0
2,4-Dinitrotoluene	0	0	18,000	0
2,6-Dinitrotoluene	0	0	0	0
Dinitrotoluene (mixed isomers)	0	0	0	300
1,4-Dioxane	1,467,085	37,442	915,763	531,129
Epichlorohydrin	4,383,879	0	3,551,833	40,961
2-Ethoxyethanol	334,101	3,731	688,981	216,633
Ethyl acrylate	820	42,720	5,891,017	1,226,419
Ethylbenzene	20,982,288	3,340,218	40,936,634	9,084,334
Ethyl chloroformate	0	0	0	0
Ethylene	197,286,622	0	431,313,198	66,480,431
Ethylene glycol	345,926,377	102,553,538	6,337,919	7,264,756
Ethyleneimine	0	0	0	0
Ethylene oxide	286,701	0	86,000	0
Ethylene thiourea	0	0	0	1,764
Fluometuron	0	0	0	0
Formaldehyde	169,263,509	99,101	10,551,830	242,614
Freon 113	28,660,893	5,177,481	4,776	333,448
Glycol ethers	15,419,302	3,395,663	17,950,349	12,018,285
Heptachlor	0	0	0	0
Hexachlorobenzene	316,600	1	162,000	0
Hexachloro-1,3-butadiene	1,124,000	0	0	0
Hexachlorocyclopentadiene	0	0	0	900

[Continued]

★ 509 ★

Chemicals in Waste – Recycled or Energy Recovery, by Chemical: 1992

[Continued]

Chemical	Recycled onsite	Recycled offsite	Energy recovery onsite	Energy recovery offsite
Hexachloroethane	517,000	0	0	21,000
Hydrazine	0	0	0	250
Hydrazine sulfate	0	0	0	0
Hydrochloric acid	125,740,840	64,204,456	55,932	2,041
Hydrogen cyanide	184,712	0	23,305,069	168,014
Hydrogen fluoride	121,808,742	354,804	730,121	0
Hydroquinone	374	17	354,640	5,135
Isobutyraldehyde	9,245	400	4,392,846	1,074,876
Isopropyl alcohol (manufacturing)	58,161	224,011	2,957,230	203,307
4,4'-Isopropylidenediphenol	62,272	45,865	6,425,818	48,281
Lead	214,479,454	34,138,441	250	3,012,923
Lead compounds	624,622,931	417,515,419	4,000	37,842
Lindane	572	0	0	0
Maleic anhydride	1,970	888	2,375,712	91,708
Maneb	378	0	0	0
Manganese	14,233,601	56,052,224	0	309,200
Manganese compounds	119,240,927	37,333,722	0	28,180
Mercury	1,602,398	12,963	0	0
Mercury compounds	82,000	58,448	0	0
Methanol	476,357,827	14,418,924	329,376,147	70,312,950
Methoxychlor	0	0	0	0
2-Methoxyethanol	5,968,209	6,174	1,142,570	716,367
Methyl acrylate	0	12,000	392,792	400,488
Methyl tert-butyl ether	450,747	72,740	55,000	538,639
4,4'-Methylenebis(2-chloroaniline)	0	0	0	2,664
Methylenebis(phenylisocyanate)	30,548	368,060	214,963	75,539
Methylene bromide	2,600,000	0	0	0
4,4'-Methylenedianiline	940	0	55,630	29,100
Methyl ethyl ketone	169,763,949	26,505,126	84,226,588	39,688,668
Methyl hydrazine	0	0	0	0
Methyl iodide	0	0	1,200	0
Methyl isobutyl ketone	223,939,338	19,724,864	51,018,601	17,643,369
Methyl isocyanate	0	0	0	0
Methyl methacrylate	4,100,099	289,032	1,545,184	970,289
Molybdenum trioxide	4,384,291	3,924,831	0	28
Monochloropentafluoroethane (CFC-115)	53,300	0	0	0
Naphthalene	13,466,872	154,972	10,287,998	2,400,198
alpha-Naphthylamine	0	0	0	0
Nickel	20,917,707	57,484,501	0	14,343
Nickel compounds	24,512,812	32,089,843	0	5,883
Nitric acid	41,066,956	3,046,183	0	538
Nitrilotriacetic acid	0	0	0	0
5-Nitro-o-anisidine	0	0	0	0
Nitrobenzene	1,900,000	0	1,569,274	27,790
Nitroglycerin	20,058	0	0	25

[Continued]

★ 509 ★

Chemicals in Waste – Recycled or Energy Recovery, by Chemical: 1992
[Continued]

Chemical	Recycled onsite	Recycled offsite	Energy recovery onsite	Energy recovery offsite
2-Nitrophenol	100	0	13,227	0
4-Nitrophenol	0	0	580	0
2-Nitropropane	0	6,350	868,000	0
p-Nitrosodiphenylamine	0	0	8;500	15,000
N,N-Dimethylaniline	40,000	0	2,200	954,179
N-Nitrosodiphenylamine	0	0	0	0
Parathion	0	0	0	0
Pentachlorophenol	65,588	0	0	92,125
Peracetic acid	21,060	0	0	0
Phenol	30,576,995	770,875	18,210,523	2,631,184
p-Phenylenediamine	0	0	0	0
2-Phenylphenol	99	0	85	171
Phosgene	0	0	615,410	0
Phosphoric acid	81,547,444	9,375,372	7,000	1,898
Phosphorus (yellow or white)	661,058	214,794	0	0
Phthalic anhydride	726,821	1,080	1,581,851	3,650,357
Picric acid	0	0	579,002	35
Polybrominated biphenyls	0	0	0	0
Polychlorinated biphenyls (PCBs)	0	18,920	0	0
Propane sultone	0	0	0	0
Propionaldehyde	0	0	3,099,998	14,248
Propoxur	0	0	0	0
Propylene	343,447,371	0	642,776,137	101,936,982
Propyleneimine	0	0	0	0
Propylene oxide	13,854	880	5,309,500	567,596
Pyridine	4,738,597	0	797,701	522,737
Quinoline	3,390	0	250,300	210
Quinone	0	0	10,908	0
Quintozene	795	170,000	0	373
Saccharin (manufacturing)	0	0	0	0
Selenium	20	38,463	0	0
Selenium compounds	172,795	300,238	0	1,300
Silver	423,587	998,942	0	0
Silver compounds	267,784	1,364,917	0	0
Styrene	172,963,215	1,201,190	25,365,085	8,436,379
Styrene oxide	2,210	0	60,000	0
Sulfuric acid	5,747,645,488	1,320,807,382	62,612	40,816
1,1,2,2-Tetrachloroethane	13,081,938	1,446,254	53,600	0
Tetrachloroethylene	81,782,280	10,259,945	9,655,330	560,816
Tetrachlorvinphos	73,000	0	110	0
Thallium compounds	2,200	76,000	0	0
Thiourea	0	0	0	0
Thorium dioxide	0	0	0	0
Titanium tetrachloride	0	0	0	0
Toluene	627,080,929	27,395,427	255,986,447	82,041,437

[Continued]

★509★

Chemicals in Waste – Recycled or Energy Recovery, by Chemical: 1992
[Continued]

Chemical	Recycled onsite	Recycled offsite	Energy recovery onsite	Energy recovery offsite
Toluene-2,4-diisocyanate	724	9,060	37,941	720
Toluene-2,6-diisocyanate	57	1,800	13,435	48
Toluenediisocyanate (mixed isomers)	18,584	9,400	6,100,000	24,788
o-Toluidine	1,568,201	0	148,720	232,750
Trichlorfon	80	0	0	0
1,2,4-Trichlorobenzene	65,263	153,070	47,000	72,654
1,1,1-Trichloroethane	171,223,961	23,721,150	6,457,400	3,060,231
1,1,2-Trichloroethane	22,481,495	8,905,724	16,481,220	0
Trichloroethylene	225,757,972	8,109,967	1,421,546	884,498
Trichlorofluoromethane (CFC-11)	55,415,768	365,441	210,000	363,340
2,4,5-Trichlorophenol	0	0	0	0
2,4,6-Trichlorophenol	0	0	0	0
Trifluralin	1,270	0	11,000	5
1,2,4-Trimethylbenzene	9,274,818	464,335	3,312,356	2,242,051
Urethane	0	0	0	0
Vanadium (fume or dust)	268,000	92	0	0
Vinyl acetate	199,260	1,194,298	12,485,776	5,893,355
Vinyl bromide	0	0	0	0
Vinyl chloride	176,010,819	157,091	17,762,336	3,821
Vinylidene chloride	430,056	0	280,250	0
Xylene (mixed isomers)	113,109,364	36,346,209	174,899,155	63,988,345
m-Xylene	1,749,357	23,148	364,366	84,074
o-Xylene	2,760,363	135,412	47,328,889	2,332,979
p-Xylene	1,389,350	485	167,563	53,417
2,6-Xylidine	0	0	0	0
Zinc (fume or dust)	15,173,904	68,698,262	0	77,054
Zinc compounds	94,205,877	218,896,007	16,501	256,398
Mixtures and other trade names	0	440,667	4,979,069	32,185
Trade secret chemicals	1,147	68,000	451,000	23,000
Total	15,884,194,888	3,473,894,509	2,941,222,113	627,954,600

Source: U.S. Environmental Protection Agency. "Toxic Release Inventory, 1992." In *National Economic, Social, and Environmental Data Bank* [CD-ROM]. Prepared by U.S. Department of Commerce, Economics and Statistics Administration. Washington, DC: U.S. Department of Commerce, National Economic, Social, and Environmental Data Bank, Economics and Statistics Administration, Office of Business Analysis, February 1995.

★ 510 ★
Chemicals in Waste

Chemicals in Waste – Recycled or Energy Recovery, by Industry: 1992

Table shows the quantities of Toxic Release Inventory (TRI) chemicals in waste that are recycled or used for energy recovery.

[In pounds]

Industry	Recycled onsite	Recycled offsite	Energy recovery onsite	Energy recovery offsite
Food	31,701,726	1,330,241	156,082	124,261
Tobacco	55,317,334	1,914	0	6,882
Textiles	10,947,742	1,568,450	4,661,146	1,417,504
Apparel	197,228	285,177	0	404,996
Lumber	18,605,724	1,028,315	1,712,454	2,721,058
Furniture	2,281,916	3,118,595	40,450	7,095,848
Paper	169,536,888	3,249,614	250,582,639	7,629,470
Printing	190,153,960	4,417,365	664,580	4,812,175
Chemicals	11,293,387,355	504,361,461	1,111,234,613	342,662,500
Petroleum	385,462,126	917,389,170	682,916,702	149,862,827
Plastics	301,681,888	17,712,603	14,682,484	11,957,894
Leather	917,006	2,054,893	0	966,667
Stone/clay	96,428,221	3,101,227	604,968,544	3,364,555
Primary metals	1,800,647,752	866,344,562	48,372,554	18,778,573
Fabricated metals	258,886,428	250,090,237	82,177,521	14,071,001
Machinery	98,341,170	44,237,595	256,042	3,443,282
Electrical	290,545,346	351,234,470	6,781,882	11,198,118
Transportation	64,405,030	163,632,927	2,068,304	22,707,040
Measurement and photographic instruments	9,426,297	17,216,803	1,067,100	4,916,648
Miscellaneous	10,861,472	13,023,942	666,634	2,012,644
Multiple codes[1]	788,635,334	302,142,026	127,546,268	17,087,344
No codes[2]	5,826,945	6,352,922	666,114	713,313
Total	15,884,194,888	3,473,894,509	2,941,222,113	627,954,600

Source: U.S. Environmental Protection Agency. "Toxic Release Inventory, 1992." In *National Economic, Social, and Environmental Data Bank* [CD-ROM]. Prepared by U.S. Department of Commerce, Economics and Statistics Administration. Washington, DC: U.S. Department of Commerce, National Economic, Social, and Environmental Data Bank, Economics and Statistics Administration, Office of Business Analysis, February 1995. *Notes:* 1. Data from facilities that reported more than one 2-digit Standard Industrial Classification (SIC) code within range 20-39. 2. Data from facilities reporting no Standard Industrial Classifiaction (SIC) codes or reporting codes outside range 20-39.

★ 511 ★

Chemicals in Waste

Chemicals in Waste – Recycled or Energy Recovery, by State or Territory: 1992

Table shows the quantities of Toxic Release Inventory (TRI) chemicals in waste that are recycled or used for energy recovery. Data are arranged alphabetically by state or territory.

[In pounds]

State	Recycled onsite	Recycled offsite	Energy recovery onsite	Energy recovery offsite
Alabama	294,852,601	39,283,708	85,075,299	11,774,575
Alaska	8,739	242,373	1,522,000	0
American Samoa	0	0	0	0
Arizona	454,733,859	25,518,406	345,090	971,026
Arkansas	99,308,237	58,196,890	35,618,722	5,092,639
California	85,554,586	129,197,216	75,959,399	135,705,370
Colorado	22,494,840	9,503,098	8,653,400	2,048,948
Connecticut	201,523,913	24,564,766	5,918,299	4,409,037
Delaware	26,381,562	7,768,233	164,768	1,390,569
Florida	70,536,819	22,573,298	23,121,462	4,974,102
Georgia	371,278,014	60,974,809	49,823,661	6,979,833
Hawaii	3,766	26,749	1,600,000	0
Idaho	186,163	351,301	7	305,551
Illinois	177,903,370	157,513,868	164,946,248	64,625,696
Indiana	258,093,769	378,159,201	63,929,416	19,041,245
Iowa	21,625,258	19,360,970	1,579,358	3,599,343
Kansas	578,325,025	47,549,203	468,497,192	2,723,573
Kentucky	168,844,991	69,465,095	60,517,148	10,921,713
Louisiana	296,015,677	251,465,398	364,662,565	6,782,268
Maine	7,618,344	5,230,171	16,040,838	767,349
Maryland	44,500,808	23,082,530	9,280,033	1,221,418
Massachusetts	61,708,975	21,540,326	9,573,268	9,462,461
Michigan	330,817,210	196,800,836	66,761,085	68,930,729
Minnesota	100,741,120	18,163,842	8,261,143	4,950,943
Mississippi	4,211,725,514	67,777,089	21,934,282	3,409,032
Missouri	242,980,417	164,619,595	143,980,460	9,570,540
Montana	54,235,813	2,477,668	7,733,900	106,321
Nebraska	32,601,209	13,949,613	2,906,965	1,170,636
Nevada	2,998,665	3,600,722	0	12,769
New Hampshire	22,392,478	6,671,548	2,507,317	421,548
New Jersey	153,567,438	124,245,597	18,183,395	31,154,161
New Mexico	41,579,949	281,458	18,898,350	237,055
New York	537,230,073	59,100,681	18,387,095	10,563,804
North Carolina	186,728,290	119,247,339	23,379,714	10,450,740
North Dakota	35,769	139,690	0	70,727
Ohio	678,446,128	189,784,986	111,295,502	32,364,107
Oklahoma	25,753,108	17,963,266	21,108,693	1,262,554
Oregon	45,085,399	13,171,111	16,094,968	599,383
Pennsylvania	512,010,749	200,882,170	76,621,701	19,560,792
Puerto Rico	67,088,981	9,171,117	54,507	7,506,696
Rhode Island	9,516,459	12,372,023	281,411	405,737

[Continued]

★ 511 ★

Chemicals in Waste – Recycled or Energy Recovery, by State or Territory: 1992

[Continued]

State	Recycled onsite	Recycled offsite	Energy recovery onsite	Energy recovery offsite
South Carolina	301,485,103	87,092,555	65,011,780	8,633,429
South Dakota	512,567	268,633	0	276,635
Tennessee	177,683,665	58,427,129	57,177,550	12,130,349
Texas	4,268,140,060	492,513,094	634,996,412	82,144,973
Utah	55,718,999	35,114,437	24,221	311,725
Vermont	6,518,171	4,321,565	0	550,216
Virgin Islands	1,018,150	900,194	0	0
Virginia	109,310,974	25,192,289	55,581,490	8,969,976
Washington	98,572,475	69,177,522	100,896,066	851,285
West Virginia	314,508,554	37,419,363	10,098,004	10,009,900
Wisconsin	51,105,427	46,265,457	11,947,915	8,530,900
Wyoming	2,586,658	45,214,311	270,014	222
Total	15,884,194,888	3,473,894,509	2,941,222,113	627,954,600

Source: U.S. Environmental Protection Agency. "Toxic Release Inventory, 1992." In *National Economic, Social, and Environmental Data Bank* [CD-ROM]. Prepared by U.S. Department of Commerce, Economics and Statistics Administration. Washington, DC: U.S. Department of Commerce, National Economic, Social, and Environmental Data Bank, Economics and Statistics Administration, Office of Business Analysis, February 1995.

★ 512 ★

Chemicals in Waste

Chemicals in Waste – Transfers Within a State: 1992

Table shows transfers of Toxic Release Inventory (TRI) chemicals in waste in each state. Data are ordered by total transferred.

[In pounds]

State or territory	Transfers to recycling	Transfers to energy recovery	Transfers to treatment	Transfers to disposal	Other[1] offsite transfers	Total transfers within state
Indiana	289,022,055	9,867,879	38,703,136	11,686,493	784,789	350,064,352
Texas	110,106,890	73,878,264	32,015,095	28,408,201	1,030,645	245,439,095
Missouri	157,813,615	3,349,952	964,608	1,933,736	21,001	164,082,912
Michigan	78,860,007	37,821,035	12,926,009	14,996,807	573,383	145,177,241
Ohio	65,647,724	26,847,616	25,161,663	24,865,621	1,602,724	144,125,348
California	108,051,745	10,841,395	4,970,478	4,861,214	109,444	128,834,276
Pennsylvania	87,336,374	854,391	15,291,121	10,290,853	3,099,408	116,872,147
Louisiana	98,891,158	3,942,287	3,838,232	1,628,701	0	106,300,378
Washington	64,242,296	308,961	758,411	723,586	825	66,034,079
Illinois	27,945,419	9,095,907	12,553,594	9,982,100	629,351	60,206,371
New Jersey	17,876,276	20,449,063	7,962,341	1,562,118	238,719	48,088,517
South Carolina	35,166,511	3,560,114	3,407,545	4,794,795	379,762	47,308,727

[Continued]

★512★

Chemicals in Waste – Transfers Within a State: 1992

[Continued]

State or territory	Transfers to recycling	Transfers to energy recovery	Transfers to treatment	Transfers to disposal	Other[1] offsite transfers	Total transfers within state
Tennessee	29,275,390	2,506,628	1,075,530	8,486,833	42,257	41,386,638
Wisconsin	20,828,786	1,113,659	9,207,938	9,055,773	56,781	40,262,937
North Carolina	25,405,393	1,404,001	2,168,191	3,734,987	525,160	33,237,732
Kansas	14,729,375	731,290	2,278,301	8,888,948	900	26,628,814
West Virginia	24,146,566	17,940	72	1,693,905	0	25,858,483
New York	18,505,534	1,579,813	972,396	3,571,163	73,044	24,701,950
Alabama	8,015,289	8,082,674	1,320,398	5,948,626	2,415	23,369,402
Georgia	15,818,684	544,449	483,268	6,346,710	213	23,193,324
Puerto Rico	10,603,530	7,393,341	1,725,781	374,342	41,288	20,138,282
Kentucky	7,664,352	5,945,027	2,121,534	2,329,867	544,264	18,605,044
Massachusetts	7,794,734	3,506,834	1,963,166	1,056,006	120,101	14,440,841
Arkansas	8,382,312	787,288	328,527	3,763,858	250	13,262,235
Florida	8,737,140	711,098	1,969,219	877,128	0	12,294,585
Connecticut	9,944,820	96,211	1,057,026	566,094	0	11,664,151
Minnesota	8,163,758	1,068,328	1,709,476	234,521	824	11,176,907
Arizona	8,859,172	489,329	1,686,768	79,498	0	11,114,767
Oklahoma	6,549,774	214,891	44,566	1,307,593	250	8,117,074
Maryland	6,333,089	8,314	107,634	243,070	0	6,692,107
Utah	1,471,037	1,189	278,290	4,241,533	0	5,992,049
Virginia	2,568,875	1,848,277	220,812	1,341,369	2,020	5,981,353
Nebraska	1,303,862	12,255	1,690,713	1,445,144	1,025,885	5,477,859
Colorado	2,097,584	1,943,407	1,232,784	113,192	250	5,387,217
Iowa	1,936,509	59,702	1,249,069	1,440,858	750	4,686,888
Oregon	2,835,915	9,143	478,258	875,090	0	4,198,406
Mississippi	2,482,225	1,000	21,809	426,468	555	2,932,057
Rhode Island	651,413	486	75,049	1,611,621	0	2,338,569
Maine	1,255,322	250	7,550	791,643	0	2,054,765
Delaware	1,877,245	10	35,202	30,522	0	1,942,979
New Hampshire	1,089,036	0	48,565	76,240	0	1,213,841
North Dakota	93,600	750	49,000	449	0	143,799
Idaho	0	250	62,249	32,919	0	95,418
Nevada	0	47	2,522	73,269	0	75,838
Vermont	24,100	0	20,424	12,010	0	56,534
South Dakota	5	0	1,000	43,456	0	44,461
Wyoming	632	0	0	37,548	0	38,180
New Mexico	2,250	0	30,000	5,685	0	37,935
Montana	4,900	0	0	5,375	0	10,275
Hawaii	0	0	0	3,803	0	3,803
Virgin Islands	0	0	0	0	0	0
American Samoa	0	0	0	0	0	0

[Continued]

★512★

Chemicals in Waste – Transfers Within a State: 1992

[Continued]

State or territory	Transfers to recycling	Transfers to energy recovery	Transfers to treatment	Transfers to disposal	Other[1] offsite transfers	Total transfers within state
Alaska	0	0	0	0	0	0
Total	1,398,412,278	240,894,745	194,275,320	186,901,341	10,907,258	2,031,390,942

Source: U.S. Environmental Protection Agency. "Toxic Release Inventory, 1992." In *National Economic, Social, and Environmental Data Bank* [CD-ROM]. Prepared by U.S. Department of Commerce, Economics and Statistics Administration. Washington, DC: U.S. Department of Commerce, National Economic, Social, and Environmental Data Bank, Economics and Statistics Administration, Office of Business Analysis, February 1995. *Notes:* "POTWs" are publicly owned treatment works. 1. Other transfers are transfers reported with missing or invalid waste management codes.

★513★

Chemicals in Waste

Chemicals in Waste – Treated or Released, by Chemical: 1992

Table shows the quantities of Toxic Release Inventory (TRI) chemicals in waste undergoing onsite and/or offsite treatment or release. Table also shows totals released for production- and nonproduction-related wastes.

[In pounds]

Chemical	Treated onsite	Treated offsite	Quantity released or disposed of	Total Production-related wastes	Nonproduction-related wastes
Acetaldehyde	12,426,429	434,360	8,431,379	31,834,013	153
Acetamide	1	421	101,001	144,319	0
Acetone	105,711,876	22,784,463	139,039,676	672,068,269	257,235
Acetonitrile	11,122,888	3,118,155	21,429,372	2,581,322,698	12,758
Acrolein	1,455,260	255	135,163	3,305,840	1
Acrylamide	313,324	125,254	4,275,321	4,840,323	6,082
Acrylic acid	36,821,655	209,644	5,074,341	61,790,567	6,884
Acrylonitrile	15,182,383	1,032,266	5,442,217	46,537,679	4,477
Allyl alcohol	606,816	390,407	229,952	2,083,277	0
Allyl chloride	676,918	384,400	122,224	5,196,542	85
Aluminum (fume or dust)	16,406,505	1,856,716	5,967,550	131,824,600	1,546
Aluminum oxide (fibrous forms)	156,688	1,400,828	1,308,827	3,661,010	1
4-Aminoazobenzene	0	0	250	250	0
4-Aminobiphenyl	73,000	0	3	73,003	0
Ammonia	575,131,175	69,993,051	455,599,635	1,383,853,783	1,366,277
Ammonium nitrate (solution)	25,118,480	6,322,756	49,700,242	150,857,399	218,130
Ammonium sulfate (solution)	7,896,056	38,203,505	29,261,313	77,217,088	3,100
Aniline	2,844,826	2,164,070	1,783,054	21,628,202	40,844
o-Anisidine	3,858	6,818	2,637	13,633	0
p-Anisidine	1,040	33	55	1,128	0
Anthracene	7,561,977	135,950	569,044	12,272,595	12,578
Antimony	1,099,683	286,772	161,643	5,268,714	32
Antimony compounds	147,403	401,772	4,054,705	22,690,828	18,937
Arsenic	11,006	138,425	1,857,786	2,348,508	0
Arsenic compounds	338,342	655,364	4,106,260	11,335,468	40,407
Asbestos (friable)	776,955	1,951,539	4,949,097	8,395,583	374,618

[Continued]

★513★

Chemicals in Waste – Treated or Released, by Chemical: 1992

[Continued]

Chemical	Treated onsite	Treated offsite	Quantity released or disposed of	Total Production-related wastes	Total Nonproduction-related wastes
Barium	66,039	12,779	966,414	1,137,580	552
Barium compounds	2,827,675	3,944,761	18,462,353	46,622,415	39,866
Benzal chloride	2,600	4,343	973	41,916	0
Benzene	29,725,777	1,434,236	13,390,673	145,101,986	122,584
Benzoic trichloride	290,001	0	6,070	296,071	0
Benzoyl chloride	856,743	386,002	14,308	1,257,053	0
Benzoyl peroxide	132,668	54,562	19,671	220,347	0
Benzyl chloride	349,757	36,033	45,254	707,884	9
Beryllium	631	0	37,213	63,402	0
Beryllium compounds	0	440	52,126	75,106	0
Biphenyl	2,103,926	890,790	1,258,180	6,976,630	34,165
Bis(2-chloroethyl) ether	239,288	57,333	13,798	1,199,590	400
Bis(chloromethyl) ether	21	0	310	331	0
Bis(2-chloro-1-methylethyl)ether	4,858,000	0	11,300	12,859,300	0
Bis(2-ethylhexyl) adipate	236,678	21,819	611,877	3,004,862	312
Bromochlorodifluoromethane (Halon 1211)	0	0	16,749	61,749	0
Bromoform	0	6,400	14,100	20,500	0
Bromomethane	89,045	0	3,005,194	3,582,339	0
Bromotrifluoromethane (Halon 1301)	100	0	110,445	168,545	0
1,3-Butadiene	49,305,988	264,217	4,046,531	453,627,237	137,163
Butyl acrylate	2,634,025	241,213	351,856	4,726,036	8,355
n-Butyl alcohol	24,190,929	3,754,351	32,300,656	152,896,118	116,654
sec-Butyl alcohol	1,443,516	94,302	710,251	16,970,329	313
tert-Butyl alcohol	1,165,448	2,414,214	2,606,556	76,907,238	670
Butyl benzyl phthalate	1,896,638	281,276	734,483	4,976,181	494
1,2-Butylene oxide	295,394	0	87,072	791,678	426
Butyraldehyde	1,201,586	251,961	624,770	3,238,895	60
C.I. basic green 4	1,297	3,006	23,327	28,353	0
C.I. basic red 1	0	0	382	691	0
C.I. disperse yellow 3	1,088	1,041	1,231	3,360	0
C.I. food red 15	0	1,700	2	1,702	0
C.I. solvent yellow 14	0	0	0	0	0
Cadmium	131,868	48,199	153,619	1,656,952	985
Cadmium compounds	514,057	438,115	468,220	13,924,917	1,450
Calcium cyanamide	50,000	0	38,405	88,405	0
Captan	13,000	3,007	17,097	34,439	0
Carbaryl	432,942	9,916	37,436	525,739	0
Carbon disulfide	9,569,370	101,974	93,554,822	127,135,361	10,587
Carbon tetrachloride	15,007,086	833,039	1,426,570	39,136,449	83,930
Carbonyl sulfide	7,358,141	0	16,163,428	25,507,349	0
Catechol	29,836,026	204,568	363,130	70,041,383	245
Chlordane	10,000	720	1,700	12,590	0
Chlorine	249,878,302	908,902	71,168,030	430,848,879	35,581
Chlorine dioxide	31,908,704	84	3,112,849	37,034,637	966
Chloroacetic acid	979,519	657	16,746	1,012,286	1,566
Chlorobenzene	2,763,441	3,832,367	2,475,509	16,979,055	22,720
Chloroethane	22,750,982	172,186	2,758,993	44,803,130	126
Chloroform	21,854,747	1,612,837	17,802,805	56,079,423	46,723
Chloromethane	3,422,956	298,093	5,779,134	14,505,784	21,547
Chloromethyl methyl ether	34,858	0	1,301	36,159	0

[Continued]

★ 513 ★

Chemicals in Waste – Treated or Released, by Chemical: 1992
[Continued]

Chemical	Treated onsite	Treated offsite	Quantity released or disposed of	Total Production-related wastes	Nonproduction-related wastes
Chlorophenols	162,557	4,843	146,232	2,329,719	150
Chloroprene	9,101,830	208,210	1,559,346	12,411,912	10,177
Chlorothalonil	16,600	2,925	181,152	204,943	6
Chromium	1,551,068	1,394,122	5,395,166	104,832,861	188,015
Chromium compounds	54,314,995	3,322,787	35,745,584	171,072,379	1,272,980
Cobalt	118,685	24,190	128,158	8,037,603	1
Cobalt compounds	725,114	84,755	557,487	3,823,812	186
Copper	3,865,763	2,234,533	29,512,497	675,138,852	491,213
Copper compounds	141,946,469	2,419,471	46,462,501	502,456,962	930,700
Creosote	327,654	510,461	2,153,138	17,554,499	77,840
p-Cresidine	1,009	23,780	6,725	31,520	2
Cresol (mixed isomers)	7,784,616	177,280	960,567	13,382,788	16,504
m-Cresol	21,580	26,196	566,861	3,322,007	260
o-Cresol	15,456	37,540	541,166	1,129,641	6,400
p-Cresol	35,348	693,382	305,048	1,944,861	420
Cumene	2,535,561	83,887	3,715,939	320,391,682	12,065
Cumene hydroperoxide	544,937	2,092	360,020	932,174	180
Cupferron	0	69	10	79	0
Cyanide compounds	9,197,904	464,501	4,241,284	14,910,262	366
Cyclohexane	26,288,355	966,582	14,061,768	94,716,569	23,347
2,4-D (acetic acid)	28,935	26,466	57,207	200,669	4,353
Decabromodiphenyl oxide	16,102	250,077	1,157,192	2,849,268	584
4,4'-Diaminodiphenyl ether	1,200	21,115	1,768	24,083	0
Diaminotoluene (mixed isomers)	564,736	464,052	29,760	5,696,903	82
2,4-Diaminotoluene	0	10,388	1,941	12,329	0
Dibenzofuran	5,000,652	3,700	96,995	5,217,842	348
1,2-Dibromo-3-chloropropane	0	0	294	294	0
1,2-Dibromoethane	34,972	65,218	36,874	141,237	0
Dibromotetrafluoroethane (Halon 2402)	0	0	0	0	0
Dibutyl phthalate	174,762	126,309	342,347	1,103,627	36
Dichlorobenzene (mixed isomers)	396,826	224	3,842	637,200	0
1,2-Dichlorobenzene	2,976,118	3,084,228	482,566	11,478,802	130,708
1,3-Dichlorobenzene	10	4,718	5,022	87,313	0
1,4-Dichlorobenzene	1,698	134,374	351,236	1,330,116	1,118
3,3'-Dichlorobenzidine	5,722	16,035	5,700	27,887	0
Dichlorobromomethane	1	0	194	195	0
Dichlorodifluoromethane (CFC-12)	389,728	166,675	11,359,695	13,168,673	211,980
1,2-Dichloroethane	37,493,307	1,808,161	3,127,466	221,813,665	47,278
1,2-Dichloroethylene	4,697,043	410	23,222	8,669,998	33
Dichloromethane	35,365,596	12,445,135	75,729,079	286,593,104	56,850
2,4-Dichlorophenol	96,641	0	10,312	107,961	2,765
1,2-Dichloropropane	4,383,358	1,294	620,279	68,342,373	0
2,3-Dichloropropene	438,000	530,000	160,756	4,728,756	0
1,3-Dichloropropylene	440,267	2,810	41,720	17,695,797	0
Dichlorotetrafluoroethane (CFC-114)	240,000	8,277	1,080,021	2,152,419	6,633
Dichlorvos	940	2,135	1,455	4,622	0
Dicofol	0	370	209	613	0
Diethanolamine	2,011,464	890,307	1,561,157	4,836,156	3,301
Di-(2-ethylhexyl) phthalate	516,795	194,289	2,131,979	10,665,724	5,776
Diethyl phthalate	183,280	478,194	161,598	1,960,282	0

[Continued]

★513★

Chemicals in Waste – Treated or Released, by Chemical: 1992

[Continued]

Chemical	Treated onsite	Treated offsite	Quantity released or disposed of	Total Production-related wastes	Nonproduction-related wastes
Diethyl sulfate	5,353	1,134	3,706	5,012,924	0
3,3'-Dimethoxybenzidine	79	0	8	87	0
1,1-Dimethyl hydrazine	9,806	7,000	251	17,077	2
2,4-Dimethylphenol	106,359	10,415	135,578	851,832	0
Dimethyl phthalate	283,970	120,114	85,416	931,854	0
Dimethyl sulfate	1,067,258	10	6,026	1,121,560	4
m-Dinitrobenzene	850,000	0	1,241	854,241	0
o-Dinitrobenzene	224,243	0	157	224,400	0
p-Dinitrobenzene	30,000	0	130	30,130	0
4,6-Dinitro-o-cresol	65,080	6,825	5,648	472,763	1
2,4-Dinitrophenol	81,700	10	45,964	787,676	0
2,4-Dinitrotoluene	87,987	0	1,863	107,850	6
2,6-Dinitrotoluene	62,874	0	549	63,423	2
Dinitrotoluene (mixed isomers)	181,404	698,410	66,431	946,545	8,490
1,4-Dioxane	1,017,103	681,073	1,134,027	5,783,622	35,274
Epichlorohydrin	9,191,403	887,636	525,985	18,581,697	1,866
2-Ethoxyethanol	518,498	463,098	377,400	2,602,442	34,810
Ethyl acrylate	915,187	125,782	221,369	8,423,314	3,726
Ethylbenzene	9,987,555	1,350,020	10,857,715	96,538,764	204,372
Ethyl chloroformate	127,424	0	1,953	129,377	1
Ethylene	449,198,814	92,714	35,854,137	1,180,225,916	687,169
Ethylene glycol	54,514,498	24,438,011	20,109,179	561,144,278	198,170
Ethyleneimine	0	0	0	0	0
Ethylene oxide	6,345,506	48,147	1,435,389	8,201,743	19,237
Ethylene thiourea	18	282	12,919	14,983	0
Fluometuron	0	8,220	2,808	11,028	0
Formaldehyde	95,456,352	6,143,347	16,913,837	298,670,590	29,434
Freon 113	230,231,075	1,348,284	23,906,231	289,662,188	20,170
Glycol ethers	21,160,629	11,587,825	49,847,660	131,379,713	204,006
Heptachlor	14,000	94,000	210	108,210	0
Hexachlorobenzene	3,541,588	46,342	50,210	4,116,741	1,905
Hexachloro-1,3-butadiene	7,761,458	14,186	6,534	8,906,178	540,364
Hexachlorocyclopentadiene	250,000	34,392	10,915	296,207	230
Hexachloroethane	2,652,495	10,002	32,183	3,232,680	120,205
Hydrazine	10,264	132,698	25,608	168,820	290
Hydrazine sulfate	0	0	120,002	120,002	0
Hydrochloric acid	1,911,186,194	75,462,680	298,900,276	2,475,552,419	221,897
Hydrogen cyanide	10,791,230	309	3,123,903	37,573,237	1,152
Hydrogen fluoride	106,911,337	2,442,231	10,860,641	243,107,876	11,428
Hydroquinone	342,279	181,552	285,943	1,169,940	62
Isobutyraldehyde	246,311	38,274	406,607	6,168,559	0
Isopropyl alcohol (manufacturing)	15,733	141,341	1,222,666	4,822,449	0
4,4'-Isopropylidenediphenol	2,803,693	87,028	817,736	10,290,693	325
Lead	1,848,061	1,418,757	5,880,827	260,778,713	61,729
Lead compounds	34,392,942	3,788,206	26,999,354	1,107,360,694	1,287,095
Lindane	1,250	191	427	2,440	0
Maleic anhydride	33,328,347	621,104	460,619	36,880,348	87,141
Maneb	0	6	13,980	14,364	0
Manganese	851,050	946,165	20,320,149	92,712,389	48,056
Manganese compounds	376,756	5,337,587	75,565,406	237,882,578	11,393

[Continued]

★ 513 ★

Chemicals in Waste – Treated or Released, by Chemical: 1992

[Continued]

Chemical	Treated onsite	Treated offsite	Quantity released or disposed of	Total	
				Production-related wastes	Nonproduction-related wastes
Mercury	30,994	13,759	45,054	1,705,168	0
Mercury compounds	48	9,406	188,996	338,898	344
Methanol	953,847,754	135,191,045	259,001,005	2,238,505,652	639,753
Methoxychlor	0	253	178	431	0
2-Methoxyethanol	7,203,001	1,087,880	1,817,780	17,941,981	168
Methyl acrylate	1,961,993	42,433	270,844	3,080,550	824
Methyl tert-butyl ether	2,932,191	153,761	2,903,712	7,106,790	1,887
4,4'-Methylenebis(2-chloroaniline)	10	2,439	33,233	38,346	0
Methylenebis(phenylisocyanate)	239,022	664,888	2,040,760	3,633,780	24,923
Methylene bromide	96,754	3,831	37,612	2,738,197	0
4,4'-Methylenedianiline	35,943	86,221	26,608	234,442	55
Methyl ethyl ketone	50,463,297	6,274,738	88,491,478	465,413,844	121,088
Methyl hydrazine	0	0	1	1	0
Methyl iodide	43,873	0	34,230	79,303	0
Methyl isobutyl ketone	10,747,535	2,049,489	25,840,592	350,963,788	27,958
Methyl isocyanate	159,584	0	7,654	167,238	1
Methyl methacrylate	2,927,962	1,048,973	2,823,047	13,704,586	11,016
Molybdenum trioxide	1,165,373	119,935	720,580	10,315,038	174
Monochloropentafluoroethane (CFC-115)	19,000	130	419,169	491,599	900
Naphthalene	29,294,847	518,154	3,922,572	60,045,613	163,227
alpha-Naphthylamine	0	0	2	2	0
Nickel	1,925,038	1,102,546	6,051,436	87,495,571	6,611
Nickel compounds	1,044,151	1,513,795	4,293,605	63,460,089	2,173,457
Nitric acid	221,787,298	15,390,236	29,559,498	310,850,709	56,138
Nitrilotriacetic acid	791,761	8,556	6,773	807,090	0
5-Nitro-o-anisidine	43	2	39	84	0
Nitrobenzene	401,120	447,834	916,765	5,262,783	338
Nitroglycerin	375,208	70,314	41,802	507,407	0
2-Nitrophenol	10,367	429	47	24,170	0
4-Nitrophenol	119,475	620,133	2,530	742,718	99,000
2-Nitropropane	23,679	962	173,791	1,072,782	0
p-Nitrosodiphenylamine	0	0	4,924	28,424	0
N,N-Dimethylaniline	2,288	294,811	86,805	1,380,283	10
N-Nitrosodiphenylamine	0	500,000	0	500,000	0
Parathion	301	0	482	783	0
Pentachlorophenol	45,470	26,195	101,020	330,398	3,706
Peracetic acid	27,220	6,949	7,840	63,069	0
Phenol	102,456,730	6,065,012	15,654,693	176,366,012	39,447
p-Phenylenediamine	214,593	9,258	9,426	233,277	0
2-Phenylphenol	236,486	2,952	25,913	265,706	0
Phosgene	8,959,191	1,005	5,219	9,580,825	46
Phosphoric acid	389,135,391	5,248,000	196,807,410	682,122,515	12,122,137
Phosphorus (yellow or white)	40,545	2,106	359,033	1,277,536	34,382
Phthalic anhydride	25,672,226	353,698	927,214	32,913,247	30,702
Picric acid	2,200	0	1,068,681	1,649,918	0
Polybrominated biphenyls	0	0	500	500	0
Polychlorinated biphenyls (PCBs)	0	776,473	48,499	843,892	38,668
Propane sultone	0	0	120	120	0
Propionaldehyde	376,686	12,902	752,998	4,256,832	0
Propoxur	1	860	100	961	0

[Continued]

★ 513 ★

Chemicals in Waste – Treated or Released, by Chemical: 1992

[Continued]

Chemical	Treated onsite	Treated offsite	Quantity released or disposed of	Total Production-related wastes	Nonproduction-related wastes
Propylene	505,338,217	580,279	21,295,605	1,615,374,591	183,465
Propyleneimine	0	0	398	398	0
Propylene oxide	9,025,126	30,818	1,425,929	16,373,703	989
Pyridine	1,209,072	399,206	665,418	8,332,731	2,307
Quinoline	133,226	5,057	98,177	490,360	91
Quinone	310	0	24,029	35,247	0
Quintozene	0	2,523	1,742	175,433	1,800
Saccharin (manufacturing)	9,000	9,559	1,429	19,988	0
Selenium	500	504	4,477	43,964	0
Selenium compounds	93,700	24,517	166,384	758,934	10,003
Silver	229,148	996	16,745	1,669,418	0
Silver compounds	2,652,109	6,154	63,392	4,354,356	185
Styrene	11,447,521	3,479,761	33,687,236	256,580,387	106,470
Styrene oxide	28,481	0	329	91,020	3
Sulfuric acid	2,938,612,362	74,779,970	187,976,508	10,269,925,138	3,522,137
1,1,2,2-Tetrachloroethane	10,509,865	65,260	56,561	25,213,478	0
Tetrachloroethylene	15,421,358	1,963,634	12,552,614	132,195,977	237,639
Tetrachlorvinphos	0	134,675	105,320	313,105	0
Thallium compounds	0	4,205	1,170	83,575	0
Thiourea	12,136	5,689	23,491	41,316	0
Thorium dioxide	0	10	64,000	64,010	0
Titanium tetrachloride	36,394,611	3,267,833	153,747	39,816,191	1,798
Toluene	125,358,145	18,618,495	186,681,857	1,323,162,737	479,129
Toluene-2,4-diisocyanate	12,819	42,222	13,189	116,675	391
Toluene-2,6-diisocyanate	2,985	6,934	2,874	28,133	25
Toluenediisocyanate (mixed isomers)	59,790	189,148	51,305	6,453,015	44,240
o-Toluidine	145,271	13,558	45,829	2,154,329	0
Trichlorfon	214	3,251	116	3,661	5
1,2,4-Trichlorobenzene	301,462	1,675,809	513,864	2,829,122	50
1,1,1-Trichloroethane	1,653,692	4,310,414	112,587,880	323,014,728	103,973
1,1,2-Trichloroethane	20,994,148	3,305,959	567,677	72,736,223	40
Trichloroethylene	5,675,129	1,881,112	28,162,324	271,892,548	71,831
Trichlorofluoromethane (CFC-11)	272,158	421,115	9,647,521	66,695,343	18,832
2,4,5-Trichlorophenol	0	0	0	0	0
2,4,6-Trichlorophenol	800,103	0	86	800,189	0
Trifluralin	1,530	45,318	36,718	95,841	0
1,2,4-Trimethylbenzene	23,550,500	306,682	6,042,898	45,193,640	180,165
Urethane	0	11,100	6,486	17,586	0
Vanadium (fume or dust)	426,236	830	45,379	740,537	2
Vinyl acetate	11,653,496	962,567	7,155,692	39,544,444	8,047
Vinyl bromide	96,000	0	33,300	129,300	0
Vinyl chloride	27,389,458	22,397	1,086,384	222,432,306	54,340
Vinylidene chloride	5,815,247	104,552	242,823	6,872,928	1,067
Xylene (mixed isomers)	43,449,368	9,310,790	108,789,871	549,893,102	661,016
m-Xylene	203,017	124,991	1,348,989	3,897,942	9,450
o-Xylene	845,934	92,671	2,068,548	55,564,796	981
p-Xylene	138,867	71,672	3,985,990	5,807,344	16,956
2,6-Xylidine	1,458	0	50	1,508	0
Zinc (fume or dust)	1,194,724	2,632,606	15,854,563	103,631,113	777,619
Zinc compounds	15,196,176	21,109,269	120,490,959	470,171,187	1,374,675

[Continued]

★ 513 ★

Chemicals in Waste – Treated or Released, by Chemical: 1992

[Continued]

Chemical	Treated onsite	Treated offsite	Quantity released or disposed of	Total Production-related wastes	Total Nonproduction-related wastes
Mixtures and other trade names	72,894	1,762,733	1,694,943	8,982,491	87,879
Trade secret chemicals	131,064	14,000	4,110	692,321	20,000
Total	10,326,749,494	678,373,850	3,401,386,170	37,333,775,624	33,969,823

Source: U.S. Environmental Protection Agency. "Toxic Release Inventory, 1992." In *National Economic, Social, and Environmental Data Bank* [CD-ROM]. Prepared by U.S. Department of Commerce, Economics and Statistics Administration. Washington, DC: U.S. Department of Commerce, National Economic, Social, and Environmental Data Bank, Economics and Statistics Administration, Office of Business Analysis, February 1995.

★ 514 ★

Chemicals in Waste

Chemicals in Waste – Treated or Released, by Industry: 1992

Table shows the quantities of Toxic Release Inventory (TRI) chemicals in waste undergoing onsite and/or offsite treatment or release. Table also shows totals released for production- and nonproduction-related wastes.

[In pounds]

Industry	Treated onsite	Treated offsite	Quantity released or disposed of	Total Production-related wastes	Total Nonproduction-related wastes
Food	275,210,688	36,824,046	44,290,101	389,637,145	521,920
Tobacco	1,260,317	4,972	3,594,021	60,185,440	517
Textiles	49,652,644	7,290,569	24,685,875	100,223,930	44,464
Apparel	397,844	188,425	1,673,244	3,146,914	0
Lumber	4,488,763	912,590	33,622,710	63,091,614	102,048
Furniture	2,156,683	1,035,704	50,498,712	66,227,908	3,214,785
Paper	1,814,215,166	55,047,998	237,260,037	2,537,521,812	121,422
Printing	38,201,717	893,317	35,669,572	274,812,686	7,673
Chemicals	4,723,610,014	346,920,639	1,575,150,751	19,897,327,333	22,071,529
Petroleum	733,504,678	4,994,845	71,248,980	2,945,379,328	455,339
Plastics	67,890,609	4,715,631	148,653,273	567,294,382	212,285
Leather	25,541,620	4,703,821	18,296,212	52,480,219	5,627
Stone/clay	196,493,241	5,076,399	26,144,430	935,576,617	701,214
Primary metals	761,617,578	95,652,074	452,589,883	4,044,002,976	2,622,478
Fabricated metals	211,593,558	26,881,626	118,956,136	962,656,507	964,492
Machinery	19,682,541	4,572,128	36,467,293	207,000,051	999,508
Electrical	216,438,100	17,689,982	69,688,465	963,576,363	91,425
Transportation	62,042,259	13,421,456	143,682,705	471,959,721	82,903
Measurement and photographic instruments	51,609,272	5,995,031	35,508,526	125,739,677	513,576
Miscellaneous	7,148,715	1,517,754	19,783,346	55,014,507	246
Multiple codes[1]	897,395,152	40,937,548	238,433,670	2,412,177,342	1,177,914

[Continued]

★ 514 ★

Chemicals in Waste – Treated or Released, by Industry: 1992

[Continued]

| Industry | Treated onsite | Treated offsite | Quantity released or disposed of | Total | |
				Production-related wastes	Nonproduction-related wastes
No codes[2]	166,598,335	3,097,295	15,488,228	198,743,152	58,458
Total	10,326,749,494	678,373,850	3,401,386,170	37,333,775,624	33,969,823

Source: U.S. Environmental Protection Agency. "Toxic Release Inventory, 1992." In *National Economic, Social, and Environmental Data Bank* [CD-ROM]. Prepared by U.S. Department of Commerce, Economics and Statistics Administration. Washington, DC: U.S. Department of Commerce, National Economic, Social, and Environmental Data Bank, Economics and Statistics Administration, Office of Business Analysis, February 1995. *Notes:* 1. Data from facilities that reported more than one 2-digit Standard Industrial Classification (SIC) code within range 20-39. 2. Data from facilities reporting no Standard Industrial Classifiaction (SIC) codes or reporting codes outside range 20-39.

★ 515 ★

Chemicals in Waste

Chemicals in Waste – Treated or Released, by State or Territory: 1992

Table shows the quantities of Toxic Release Inventory (TRI) chemicals in waste undergoing onsite and/or offsite treatment or release. Table also shows totals released for production- and nonproduction-related wastes. Data are arranged alphabetically by state or territory.

[In pounds]

| State | Treated onsite | Treated offsite | Quantity released or disposed of | Total | |
				Production-related wastes	Nonproduction-related wastes
Alabama	619,858,050	12,902,168	117,448,738	1,181,195,139	53,966
Alaska	3,320,827	20	14,876,809	19,970,768	60,805
American Samoa	0	0	22,000	22,000	0
Arizona	48,007,235	5,966,099	45,985,272	581,526,987	69,305
Arkansas	143,137,066	1,853,004	40,370,640	383,577,198	3,620,136
California	245,578,903	27,080,667	83,550,909	782,627,050	2,065,950
Colorado	20,451,873	3,509,733	5,885,771	72,547,663	2,255
Connecticut	32,469,675	7,542,618	18,766,210	295,194,518	160,382
Delaware	64,122,308	3,222,664	5,347,535	108,397,639	55,949
Florida	167,233,550	16,993,899	84,530,878	389,964,008	124,224
Georgia	328,302,455	7,058,289	65,795,128	890,212,189	259,817
Hawaii	5,646,951	5,004	1,063,921	8,346,391	115
Idaho	24,931,723	489,498	9,750,864	36,015,107	80,727
Illinois	742,791,769	86,935,542	147,902,784	1,542,619,277	852,447
Indiana	259,966,320	37,562,387	139,135,032	1,155,887,370	231,830
Iowa	130,557,978	8,728,703	37,808,714	223,260,324	143,470
Kansas	61,071,028	6,463,744	95,831,891	1,260,461,656	219,118
Kentucky	134,916,074	11,893,887	72,600,159	529,159,067	357,317
Louisiana	1,207,650,066	5,961,985	468,351,402	2,600,889,361	1,513,369
Maine	78,717,656	726,719	16,122,259	125,223,336	117,264
Maryland	339,107,811	6,534,614	13,314,879	437,042,093	21,788
Massachusetts	43,630,313	10,479,869	16,225,883	172,621,095	38,622

[Continued]

★ 515 ★

Chemicals in Waste – Treated or Released, by State or Territory: 1992
[Continued]

State	Treated onsite	Treated offsite	Quantity released or disposed of	Total Production-related wastes	Nonproduction-related wastes
Michigan	336,521,622	31,192,534	102,066,219	1,133,090,235	248,237
Minnesota	56,946,869	7,901,803	32,041,235	229,006,955	27,050
Mississippi	173,749,487	2,905,379	111,756,199	4,593,256,982	579,503
Missouri	101,701,386	28,622,427	55,202,559	746,677,384	76,354
Montana	27,944,968	113,948	43,894,813	136,507,431	78,798
Nebraska	15,438,234	1,508,537	19,346,187	86,921,381	22,741
Nevada	20,675,905	26,846	3,804,218	31,119,125	1,599
New Hampshire	16,406,393	987,515	6,465,912	55,852,711	9,172
New Jersey	237,190,240	49,152,948	34,227,007	647,720,786	595,442
New Mexico	2,709,806	213,914	20,403,898	84,324,430	802
New York	233,092,526	16,719,391	64,324,120	939,417,690	338,054
North Carolina	456,541,092	11,217,054	105,778,442	913,342,671	112,638
North Dakota	2,244,829	192,756	1,942,968	4,626,739	1
Ohio	496,207,939	48,927,242	181,185,116	1,738,211,020	675,052
Oklahoma	60,581,292	3,130,389	29,535,173	159,334,475	72,314
Oregon	79,614,150	6,448,965	19,877,248	180,891,224	13,247
Pennsylvania	292,074,249	39,656,053	89,101,018	1,229,906,732	948,077
Puerto Rico	29,221,815	11,941,351	15,973,576	140,958,043	37,343
Rhode Island	18,628,986	843,872	5,932,205	47,980,693	103,289
South Carolina	172,197,342	11,641,796	66,102,726	712,164,731	1,216,478
South Dakota	36,656,570	197,148	3,001,585	40,913,138	300
Tennessee	211,025,714	23,390,920	203,242,913	743,078,240	974,554
Texas	1,553,154,669	66,444,091	406,646,461	7,504,039,760	16,385,392
Utah	130,489,559	1,202,177	82,210,618	305,071,736	969,224
Vermont	7,574,919	147,743	976,010	20,088,624	251
Virgin Islands	218,978	1,491	4,410,326	6,549,139	349
Virginia	318,960,295	21,479,870	68,846,360	608,341,254	58,439
Washington	202,834,587	7,182,973	27,265,961	506,780,869	58,940
West Virginia	192,838,736	4,050,416	27,635,912	596,560,885	139,714
Wisconsin	140,349,865	19,016,878	52,571,587	329,788,029	156,147
Wyoming	1,486,841	4,310	14,929,920	64,492,276	21,466
Total	10,326,749,494	678,373,850	3,401,386,170	37,333,775,624	33,969,823

Source: U.S. Environmental Protection Agency. "Toxic Release Inventory, 1992." In *National Economic, Social, and Environmental Data Bank* [CD-ROM]. Prepared by U.S. Department of Commerce, Economics and Statistics Administration. Washington, DC: U.S. Department of Commerce, National Economic, Social, and Environmental Data Bank, Economics and Statistics Administration, Office of Business Analysis, February 1995.

Composting

★516★

Composting Systems at Disney World

Table compares selected systems considered during an upgrade of Walt Disney World Resort Complex's composting facility.

[In dollars, except capacity figures]

System type	In-vessel system No. 1	In-vessel system No. 2	In-vessel system No. 3	Expanded outdoor aerated static-pile system
Capacity, dry kg/d				
Existing[1]	9,979	11,340	9,979	20,412
New	18,144	18,144	18,144	13,154
Total	28,123	29,484	28,123	33,566
Capital costs				
Supplier equipment	9,646,000	7,932,580	1,600,000	912,000
Nonsupplier equipment	10,742,860	9,216,720	6,590,000	9,473,000
Total	20,388,860	17,149,300	8,190,000	10,655,000
Debt service[2], per day/Mg	510.70	399.65	203.79	272.52
O&M costs, per dry Mg				
Amendment	107.70	117.76	117.65	7.93
Electricity & fuel	84.38	57.83	34.70	9.14
Labor	24.23	28.42	34.70	84.05
Maintenance	4.30	5.73	8.04	7.71
Replacement equipment[3]	10.13	13.22	11.02	12.78
Miscellaneous	NA	NA	5.40	NA
Total[4], per dry Mg	230.74	222.96	211.51	121.61
Unit costs[4], per dry Mg	740.81	622.61	415.30	394.13

Source: Harkness, Gregg E., Charles C. Reed, Charles J. Voss, and Curtis I. Kunihiro. "Composting in the Magic Kingdom." *Water Environment & Technology* (August 1994), p. 66. *Notes:* "NA" stands for "not available." 1. Existing capacity indicated is for existing in-vessel system except for outdoor composting expansion. 2. Based on amortization of 10 years at 11% interest. 3. Based on replacement of heavy equipment every 5 years and conveying equipment as is currently being experienced by Reedy Creek Improvement District/Reedy Creek Energy Services, Inc. 4. Some operations and administrative costs common to all alternatives are not included.

★ 517 ★

Composting

Municipal Solid Waste Composting Facilities: 1989-1993

```
┌─────────────────────────────────────────────┐
│  ┌──────────────────────────────────────┐    │
│  │ 1993 - 21                            │    │
│  └──────────────────────────────────────┘    │
│  ┌──────────────────────────────────────┐    │
│  │ 1992 - 21                            │    │
│  └──────────────────────────────────────┘    │
│  ┌────────────────────────────────┐          │
│  │ 1991 - 18                      │          │
│  └────────────────────────────────┘          │
│  ┌───────────────────────┐                   │
│  │ 1990 - 13             │                   │
│  └───────────────────────┘                   │
│  ┌───────────────┐                           │
│  │ 1989 - 7      │                           │
│  └───────────────┘                           │
└─────────────────────────────────────────────┘
```

Table shows the municipal solid waste (MSW) composting facilities in operation at the end of selected years.

Year	Operating facilities
1993	21
1992	21
1991	18
1990	13
1989	7

Source: "MSW Composting." *World Wastes* (April 1994), p. CS5. Primary source: The Composting Council.

★ 518 ★
Composting

Sludge Composting Facilities: 1985-1993

1993 - 182	
1992 - 159	
1991 - 149	
1990 - 133	
1989 - 119	
1985 - 79	

Table shows the sludge composting facilities in operation at the end of the selected years.

Year	Operating facilities
1993	182
1992	159
1991	149
1990	133
1989	119
1985	79

Source: "Sludge Composting." *World Wastes* (April 1994), p. CS8. Primary source: The Composting Council.

★ 519 ★
Composting

Source-Separated Composting Facilities: 1992

Source-separated composting includes food, paper, and other organics. At the end of 1992, there were 12 source-separated composting operating facilities.

Source: "Source-Separated Composting." *World Wastes* (April 1994), p. CS8. Primary source: The Composting Council.

★ 520 ★

Composting

Yard Waste Composting Facilities: 1988-1992

Table shows the yard waste composting facilities in operations at the end of each year.

Year	Operating facilities
1992	2,981
1991	2,201
1990	1,407
1989	986
1988	651

Source: "Yard Waste Composting." *World Waste* (April 1994), p. CS8. Primary source: The Composting Council.

Hazardous Waste

★ 521 ★

Hazardous Waste, by Country

Table shows hazardous waste generated by selected nations.

[In thousand metric tons]

Country	Year	Surface treatment of metals and plastics	Biocide products	Waste oil	Waste containing PCBs	Clinical and pharmaceutical	Photographic materials	Organic solvents	Paints and pigments	Resins and latex
Austria	1990	14,731	450	60,300	81	8,254	1,400	27,253	15,000	-
Canada[1]	1985	186,200	4,500	367,000	120,000	-	-	262,000	72,700	74,000
Czech Republic	1987	1,327,968	168	543,300	-	-	-	20,723	11,481	88,328
East Germany	1987	2,561,174	183	565,764	-	-	-	20,723	13,875	131,519
Finland	1987	1,813	361	35,684	1,789	97	547	7,384	5,787	2,123
France[2]	1990	-	-	409,000	17,000	-	-	285,000	-	-
Greece	1990	-	-	25,000	1,800	1,500	-	21,000	6,000	150
Hungary	1989	12,000	10,300	455,000	134	-	-	49,000	11,000	-
Ireland	1991	7,000	5	1,000	-	-	-	12,500	-	45,000
Japan[3]	1985	8,877,000	-	3,672,000	-	-	-	-	-	2,894,000
Luxembourg	1990	22,200	5	3,900	480	356	29	284	540	-
Netherlands	1990	22,000	1,800	279,000	400	1,000	21,000	69,000	25,000	20,000
New Zealand	1990	3,030	1,100	18,151	4	2770	451	3,690	29,381	12,892
Norway	1988	8,000	400	55,000	2,000	-	6,000	9,000	16,000	-
Poland	1990	-	-	41,400	-	-	-	-	175,900	-
Portugal	1989	-	-	16,473	703	-	-	-	-	-
Slovak Republic	1987	1,233,206	15	22,464	3,100	-	-	2,061	2,394	43,191
Spain	1990	-	-	320,000	2,200	-	-	5,400	-	-

[Continued]

★ 521 ★

Hazardous Waste, by Country
[Continued]

Country	Year	Surface treatment of metals and plastics	Biocide products	Waste oil	Waste containing PCBs	Clinical and pharmaceutical	Photographic materials	Organic solvents	Paints and pigments	Resins and latex
United States[4]	1990	1,962,379	13,216	4,960,000	5,015,050	2,800,000	-	70,000,000	693,833	41,000,000
West Germany	1987	219,527	-	859,456	10,537	-	-	454,489	225,525	867,015

Source: "Hazardous Waste: Who Generates How Much of What?" *Chemical Engineering* (May 1994), p. 41. Primary source: Organization for Economic Cooperation and Development. Latest available. data. *Notes:* Categories based on classification in the Basel Convention, Annex 4. "-" indicates data not reported in source. 1. Canada's totals for resins and latex refer to 1987; its PCB total includes 6,500 m.t. of high-level PCBs now in storage. 2. France's data for PCBs, solvents, paints and pigments and resins and latex, are from 1989. 3. Japan's waste oil total includes waste solvent. 4. U.S. data refer to 1989, 1990 and 1991; PCB data are based on a survey of hazardous waste generators in 1985 and do not reflect total volume; resins and latex includes plastics and rubber.

★ 522 ★

Hazardous Waste

Hazardous Waste Treatment

According to the source: "Although 95 percent (by weight) of hazardous waste produced by the 20,233 large quantity generators in the United States is handled on-site, 95 percent of these generators must ship all of their wastes to off-site facilities.... Most states do not have all the treatment options necessary to adequately handle waste produced within their borders, and.... Most states argue against restrictions on interstate shipments of hazardous waste and requirements for self-sufficiency" (p. 6). The table shows offsite hazardous waste treatment options.

[In percentages]

Option	Use
Landfill	26.3
Other treatment	16.3
Metals recovery	9.3
Aqueous inorganic treatment	8.3
Underground injection	7.3
Fuel blending	6.5
Energy recovery	5.6
Solvent recovery	4.7
Incineration	4.5
Stabilization	4.1
Aqueous organic and inorganic treatment	2.7
Other recovery	2.0
Invalid system type	1.3
Aqueous organic treatment	0.5
Land treatment	0.4
Sludge treatment	0.3

Source: "Analysis Supports Access to Off-Site Treatment Centers." *World Wastes* (October 1993), p. 6. Primary source: Environmental Information Ltd. *Interdependence in the Management of Hazardous Waste.*

★ 523 ★

Hazardous Waste

Industrial Hazardous Waste

In 1991, 38 billion pounds of toxic waste was created in the United States. The table shows waste generation by industry.

[In percentages]

Industry	Waste
Chemicals and allied products	33.8
Fabricated metal products	19.5
Electronic and electrical industry	13.2
Electroplating	11.8
Lumber and wood products	9.9
Primary metal products	8.6
Petroleum refining and related industries	8.5
Rubber and plastics products	7.4
Textile mill products	2.4
Construction	2.2
Paper and allied products	2.2
Electric power production and distribution	2.0
Food and kindred products	1.3
Agriculture	0.6

Source: "Industry Responsible for Generating Waste: Manufacturing Category Details." *Ward's Auto World* 29, no. 7 (July 1993), p. 55.

★ 524 ★

Hazardous Waste

Toxic Waste From Chemical Companies, by Method of Handling: 1992

The table shows methods used by chemical companies for handling toxic wastes in 1992.

[In million pounds]

Method	On-site	Off-site	Total
Energy	813.3	198.5	1,011.8
Recycled	6,466.5	352.8	6,819.3
Treated	3,706.6	224.6	3,931.2
Released (TRI)[1]	-	-	826.0
Total	10,986.4	775.9	12,588.3

Source: Begley, Ronald. "TRI Releases Down Sixth Year in a Row." *ChemicalWeek*, 20 April 1994, p. 7. Primary source: Chemical Manufacturers Association (CMA). *Notes:* "-" indicates data not reported in source. "TRI" represents Toxic Release Inventory. 1. Includes off-site land disposal.

Municipal Solid Waste

★ 525 ★

Mercury in Municipal Solid Waste: 1989-2000

According to the source: "Mercury emissions, a pollutant associated with incineration of municipal solid waste, could be reduced dramatically if batteries and fluorescent lamps are removed from the waste stream and wet scrubbers and carbon adsorption emissions controls are employed at resource recovery facilities" (p. 10). Table shows the discards of mercury in products in the municipal solid waste stream.

[In short tons]

Products	1989	1995	2000
Household batteries			
Alkaline batteries	419.4	41.6	0.0
Mercury-zinc batteries	196.6	131.5	98.5
Others	5.2	3.5	0.0
Subtotal	621.2	176.6	98.5
Electric lighting			
Fluorescent lamps	26.0	32.6	39.7
High intensity lamps	0.8	1.0	1.2
Subtotal	26.7	33.6	40.9
Paint residues	18.2	2.3	0.5
Fever thermometers	16.3	16.9	16.8
Thermometers	11.2	8.1	10.3
Pigments	10.0	3.0	1.5
Dental uses	4.0	2.9	2.3
Special paper coating	1.0	0.0	0.0
Mercury light switches	0.4	1.9	1.9
Total discards	709.0	245.3	172.7

Source: "NREL Identifies Means of Reducing Mercury Emissions." *World Wastes* (September 1993), p. 10. Primary source: Franklin Associates, Ltd.

★ 526 ★

Municipal Solid Waste

Municipal Solid Waste: 2000

Table shows projections for the generation, recovery, combustion, and disposal of municipal solid waste in the year 2000. Data based on 30 percent overall recovery scenario.

[In million tons]

Material	Generation	Recovery	Discards[1]
Paper and paperboard	84.7	33.8	50.9
Plastics	24.8	2.5	22.3
Yard waste	32.9	15.8	17.1
Wood	16.0	1.6	14.4
Food waste	13.2	0.0	13.2
Metals	17.1	6.4	10.8
Glass	13.5	4.7	8.8
Textiles	6.7	0.6	6.1
Rubber and leather	6.5	0.4	6.1
Other	6.7	1.0	5.7
Total	222.1	66.8	155.4

Source: "Generation, Recovery, Combustion and Disposal of Municipal Solid Waste, Year 2000." Nation's Cities Weekly, *16 November 1992, p. 8. Primary source: U.S. Environmental Protection Agency.* Characterization of Municipal Solid Waste in the United States: 1992 Update. Notes: *1. Combustion anticipated to be 42.6 million tons; landfills and other disposal expected to be 109.2 million tons.*

★ 527 ★

Municipal Solid Waste

Municipal Solid Waste Disposal: 1960-1990

Covers post-consumer residential and commercial solid wastes that comprise the major portion of typical municipal collections. Excludes mining, agricultural and industrial processing, demolition and construction wastes, sewage sludge, and junked autos and obsolete equipment wastes. Based on material-flows estimating procedure and wet weight as generated.

Item and material	1960	1965	1970	1975	1980	1985	1986	1987	1988	1989	1990
Landfill, other disposal (million tons)	54.9	69.6	88.2	99.7	123.3	136.4	139.8	140.0	135.1	132.4	130.4
Per person per day (pounds)	1.67	2.05	2.37	2.54	2.97	3.13	3.18	3.15	3.02	2.9	2.9

Percent change from prior year

Landfill, other disposal	(NA)	21.1	21.1	11.5	19.1	9.6	2.4	0.1	-3.6	-2.0	-1.5
Per person per day (pounds)	(NA)	18.5	13.5	6.7	14.5	5.1	1.6	-1.0	-4.3	-3.1	-2.4

Source: 1994 Statistical Abstract of the United States on CD-ROM [machine-readable datafiles]. CD-8A-94. Washington, DC: U.S. Department of Commerce, Economics and Statistics Administration, Bureau of the Census, Data User Services Division, January 1995. Primary source: Franklin Associates, Ltd. Characterization of Municipal Solid Waste in the Characterization of Municipal Solid Waste in the United States: 1992 Update *(Prairie Village, Kansas). Prepared for the U.S. Environmental Protection Agency. Note: "NA" stands for "not available."*

★ 528 ★

Municipal Solid Waste

Municipal Solid Waste Generation: 1960-1990

Covers post-consumer residential and commercial solid wastes that comprise the major portion of typical municipal collections. Excludes mining, agricultural and industrial processing, demolition and construction wastes, sewage sludge, and junked autos and obsolete equipment wastes. Based on material-flows estimating procedure and wet weight as generated.

Item and material	1960	1965	1970	1975	1980	1985	1986	1987	1988	1989	1990
Waste generated (million tons)	87.8	103.4	121.9	128.0	151.5	164.4	170.7	178.1	184.2	191.4	195.7
Per person per day (pounds)	2.66	3.00	3.27	3.26	3.65	3.77	3.88	4.01	4.12	4.2	4.3

Percent change from prior year

Waste generated	(NA)	15.1	15.2	4.8	15.5	7.8	3.7	4.2	3.3	3.8	2.2
Per person per day (pounds)	(NA)	11.3	8.3	-0.3	10.7	3.2	2.8	3.2	2.7	2.8	1.2

Percent distribution of generation

Paper and paperboard	34.1	36.8	36.3	33.6	36.1	37.4	38.4	39.1	38.9	37.6	37.5
Glass	7.6	8.4	10.4	10.5	9.9	8.0	7.6	6.9	6.8	6.7	6.7
Metals	12.0	10.7	11.6	11.2	9.6	8.6	8.5	8.3	8.3	8.2	8.3
Plastics	0.5	1.4	2.5	3.5	5.2	7.1	7.2	7.5	7.8	8.0	8.3
Rubber and leather	2.3	2.5	2.6	3.0	2.8	2.3	2.5	2.5	2.5	2.4	2.4
Textiles	1.9	1.8	1.6	1.7	1.7	1.7	1.6	2.1	2.1	2.9	2.9
Wood	3.4	3.4	3.3	3.4	4.4	5.0	5.3	5.5	6.1	6.1	6.3
Food wastes	13.9	12.3	10.5	10.5	8.7	8.0	7.7	7.4	7.2	6.9	6.7
Yard wastes	22.8	20.9	19.0	19.7	18.2	18.2	17.7	17.4	17.2	18.1	17.9
Other wastes	1.6	1.8	2.2	2.9	3.4	3.6	3.4	3.3	3.1	3.1	3.1

Source: 1994 Statistical Abstract of the United States on CD-ROM [machine-readable datafiles]. CD-8A-94. Washington, DC: U.S. Department of Commerce, Economics and Statistics Administration, Bureau of the Census, Data User Services Division, January 1995. Primary source: Franklin Associates, Ltd. *Characterization of Municipal Solid Waste in the Characterization of Municipal Solid Waste in the United States: 1992 Update* (Prairie Village, Kansas). Prepared for the U.S. Environmental Protection Agency. *Note:* "NA" stands for "not available."

★ 529 ★

Municipal Solid Waste

Municipal Solid Waste Generation, by Material: 1960-1990

Table shows the generation and recovery of selected materials in municipal solid waste. Covers post-consumer residential and commercial solid wastes which comprise the major portion of typical municipal collections. Excludes mining, agricultural and industrial processing, demolition and construction wastes, sewage sludge, and junked autos and obsolete equipment wastes. Based on material-flows estimating procedure and wet weight as generated.

[in million tons, except as indicated]

Item and material	1960	1965	1970	1975	1980	1985	1986	1987	1988	1989	1990
Waste generated, total	87.8	103.4	121.9	128.1	151.5	164.4	170.7	178.1	184.2	191.4	195.7
Paper and paperboard	29.9	38.0	44.2	43.0	54.7	61.5	65.6	69.6	71.7	71.9	73.3
Ferrous metals	9.9	10.1	12.6	12.3	11.6	10.9	11.1	11.3	11.6	12.0	12.3
Aluminum	0.4	0.5	0.8	1.1	1.8	2.3	2.4	2.4	2.5	2.5	2.7

[Continued]

★ 529 ★

Municipal Solid Waste Generation, by Material: 1960-1990

[Continued]

Item and material	1960	1965	1970	1975	1980	1985	1986	1987	1988	1989	1990
Other nonferrous metals	0.2	0.5	0.7	0.9	1.1	1.0	1.0	1.1	1.1	1.2	1.2
Glass	6.7	8.7	12.7	13.5	15.0	13.2	13.0	12.3	12.5	12.9	13.2
Plastics	0.4	1.4	3.1	4.5	7.9	11.6	12.2	13.4	14.4	15.4	16.2
Yard waste	20.0	21.6	23.2	25.2	27.5	30.0	30.2	31.0	31.6	34.7	35.0
Other wastes	20.3	22.6	24.6	27.6	31.9	33.9	35.2	37.0	38.8	40.8	41.8

Percent change from prior year

	1960	1965	1970	1975	1980	1985	1986	1987	1988	1989	1990
Waste generated, total	(NA)	15.1	15.2	4.8	15.4	7.8	3.7	4.2	3.3	3.8	2.2
Paper and paperboard	(NA)	21.3	14.0	-2.8	21.4	11.1	6.2	5.7	2.9	0.3	1.9
Ferrous metals	(NA)	2.0	19.8	-2.4	-6.0	-6.4	1.8	1.8	2.6	3.3	2.4
Aluminum	(NA)	20.0	37.5	27.3	38.9	21.7	4.2	0.0	4.0	0.0	7.4
Other nonferrous metals	(NA)	60.0	28.6	22.2	18.2	-10.0	0.0	9.1	0.0	8.3	0.0
Glass	(NA)	23.0	31.5	5.9	10.0	-13.6	-1.5	-5.7	1.6	3.1	2.3
Plastics	(NA)	71.4	54.8	31.1	43.0	31.9	4.9	9.0	6.9	6.5	4.9
Yard waste	(NA)	7.4	6.9	7.9	8.4	8.3	0.7	2.6	1.9	8.9	0.9
Other wastes	(NA)	10.2	8.1	10.9	13.5	5.9	3.7	4.9	4.6	4.9	2.4

Source: 1994 Statistical Abstract of the United States on CD-ROM [machine-readable datafiles]. CD-8A-94. Washington, DC: U.S. Department of Commerce, Economics and Statistics Administration, Bureau of the Census, Data User Services Division, January 1995. Primary source: Franklin Associates, Ltd. *Characterization of Municipal Solid Waste in the Characterization of Municipal Solid Waste in the United States: 1992 Update* (Prairie Village, Kansas). Prepared for the U.S. Environmental Protection Agency. *Note:* "NA" represents "not available."

★ 530 ★

Municipal Solid Waste

Municipal Solid Waste Management: 1960-1990

[In million tons]

Year	Gross discards	Recovery for recycling	Net discards	Combustion		Discards to landfills
				With energy recovery	Without energy recovery	
1960	87.8	5.9	81.9	0.0	27.0	54.9
1965	103.4	6.8	96.6	0.2	26.8	69.6
1970	121.9	8.6	113.3	0.4	24.7	88.2
1975	128.1	9.9	118.2	0.7	17.8	99.7
1980	151.4	14.5	136.9	2.7	11.0	123.3
1985	164.4	16.4	148.0	7.6	4.1	136.4
1990	195.7	33.4	162.3	29.7	2.2	130.4

Source: Executive Office of the President of the United States. *Environmental Quality 24: The Twenty-fourth Annual Report of the Council on Environmental Quality.* Prepared by Ray Clark. Written by Carroll Curtis. Edited by Barry Walsh. Washington, DC: U.S. Government Printing Office, 1994, p. 505. Primary source: U.S. Environmental Protection Agency. Office of Solid Waste and Emergency Response. *Characterization of Municipal Solid Waste in the United States: 1992 Update.* Washington, DC: U.S. Environmental Protection Agency, 1992.

★ 531 ★

Municipal Solid Waste

Municipal Solid Waste Recovery: 1960-1990

Covers post-consumer residential and commercial solid wastes which comprise the major portion of typical municipal collections. Excludes mining, agricultural and industrial processing, demolition and construction wastes, sewage sludge, and junked autos and obsolete equipment wastes. Based on material-flows estimating procedure and wet weight as generated.

[In million tons, except as indicated]

Item and material	1960	1965	1970	1975	1980	1985	1986	1987	1988	1989	1990
Waste generated, total	87.8	103.4	121.9	128.0	151.5	164.4	170.7	178.1	184.2	191.4	195.7
Materials recovered	5.9	6.8	8.6	9.9	14.5	16.4	18.3	20.1	23.5	29.9	33.4
Per person per day (pounds)	0.18	0.19	0.23	0.25	0.35	0.38	0.42	0.45	0.52	0.7	0.7
Combustion for energy recovery	(NA)	0.2	0.4	0.7	2.7	7.6	9.6	16.0	24.5	27.1	29.7
Per person per day (pounds)	(NA)	0.01	0.02	0.02	0.06	0.17	0.22	0.36	0.59	0.6	0.7
Combustion without energy recovery	27.0	26.8	24.7	17.8	11.0	4.1	3.0	2.0	1.0	2.0	2.2
Per person per day (pounds)	0.82	0.75	0.66	0.45	0.27	0.10	0.07	0.05	0.02	0.4	0.5

Percent change from prior year

Item and material	1960	1965	1970	1975	1980	1985	1986	1987	1988	1989	1990
Materials recovered	(NA)	13.2	20.9	13.1	31.7	11.6	10.4	9.0	14.5	21.4	10.5
Per person per day (pounds)	(NA)	5.3	17.4	8.0	28.6	7.9	9.5	6.7	13.5	21.2	9.6
Combustion for energy recovery	(NA)	(NA)	50.0	42.9	74.1	64.5	20.8	40.0	34.7	9.6	8.8
Per person per day (pounds)	(NA)	(NA)	50.0	0.0	66.7	64.7	22.7	38.9	39.0	1.7	7.7
Combustion without energy recovery	(NA)	-0.7	-8.5	-38.8	-61.8	-168.3	-36.7	-50.0	-100.0	50.0	9.1
Per person per day (pounds)	(NA)	-9.3	-13.6	-46.7	-66.7	-170.0	-42.9	-40.0	-150.0	95.0	20.0

Source: 1994 Statistical Abstract of the United States on CD-ROM [machine-readable datafiles]. CD-8A-94. Washington, DC: U.S. Department of Commerce, Economics and Statistics Administration, Bureau of the Census, Data User Services Division, January 1995. Primary source: Franklin Associates, Ltd. *Characterization of Municipal Solid Waste in the Characterization of Municipal Solid Waste in the United States: 1992 Update* (Prairie Village, Kansas). Prepared for the U.S. Environmental Protection Agency. *Note:* "NA" stands for "not available."

★ 532 ★

Municipal Solid Waste

Municipal Solid Waste Recovery, by Material: 1960-1990

Table shows recovery of selected materials in municipal solid waste. Covers post-consumer residential and commercial solid wastes which comprise the major portion of typical municipal collections. Excludes mining, agricultural and industrial processing, demolition and construction wastes, sewage sludge, and junked autos and obsolete equipment wastes. Based on material-flows estimating procedure and wet weight as generated.

Item and material	1960	1965	1970	1975	1980	1985	1986	1987	1988	1989	1990
Waste generated, total (million tons)	87.8	103.4	121.9	128.1	151.5	164.4	170.7	178.1	184.2	191.4	195.7
Percent change from prior year											
Materials recovered, total	5.9	6.8	8.6	9.9	14.5	16.4	18.3	20.1	23.5	29.9	33.4
Paper and paperboard	5.4	5.7	7.4	8.2	11.9	13.1	14.8	16.3	18.4	19.1	20.9
Ferrous metals	0.1	0.1	0.1	0.2	0.4	0.4	0.4	0.4	0.7	1.5	1.9
Aluminum	0.0	0.0	0.0	0.1	0.3	0.6	0.6	0.7	0.8	0.9	1.0

[Continued]

★ 532 ★

Municipal Solid Waste Recovery, by Material: 1960-1990
[Continued]

Item and material	1960	1965	1970	1975	1980	1985	1986	1987	1988	1989	1990
Other nonferrous metals	0.0	0.3	0.3	0.4	0.5	0.5	0.6	0.6	0.7	0.8	0.8
Glass	0.1	0.1	0.2	0.4	0.8	1.0	1.1	1.3	1.5	2.5	2.6
Plastics	0.0	0.0	0.0	0.0	0.0	0.1	0.1	0.1	0.2	0.3	0.4
Yard waste	0.0	0.0	0.0	0.0	0.0	0.0	0.0	0.0	0.5	3.5	4.2
Other wastes	0.3	0.6	0.6	0.6	0.6	0.7	0.7	0.7	0.7	1.3	1.6
Percent of generation recovered, total	6.7	6.6	7.1	7.7	9.6	10.0	10.7	11.2	12.8	15.6	17.1
Paper and paperboard	18.1	15.0	16.7	19.1	21.8	21.3	22.6	23.4	25.6	26.6	28.6
Ferrous metals	1.0	1.0	0.8	1.6	3.4	3.7	3.6	3.5	5.8	12.6	15.4
Aluminum	0.0	0.0	0.0	9.1	16.7	26.1	25.0	29.2	31.7	35.5	38.1
Other nonferrous metals	0.0	60.0	42.9	44.4	45.5	50.0	60.0	54.5	65.1	68.3	67.7
Glass	1.5	1.1	1.6	3.0	5.3	7.6	8.5	10.6	12.0	19.5	19.9
Plastics	0.0	0.0	0.0	0.0	0.0	0.9	0.8	0.7	1.1	1.7	2.2
Yard waste	0.0	0.0	0.0	0.0	0.0	0.0	0.0	0.0	1.6	10.0	12.0
Other wastes	1.5	2.7	2.4	2.2	1.9	2.1	2.0	1.9	1.8	3.2	3.8

Source: 1994 Statistical Abstract of the United States on CD-ROM [machine-readable datafiles]. CD-8A-94. Washington, DC: U.S. Department of Commerce, Economics and Statistics Administration, Bureau of the Census, Data User Services Division, January 1995. Primary source: Franklin Associates, Ltd. Characterization of Municipal Solid Waste in the United States: 1992 Update (Prairie Village, Kansas). Prepared for the U.S. Environmental Protection Agency.

Municipal Solid Waste: Specific Types

★ 533 ★

Municipal Solid Waste – Aluminum: 1960-1990
[In million tons]

Year	Aluminum	
	Generation	Recovery
1960	0.4	[1]
1965	0.5	[1]
1970	0.8	[1]
1975	1.1	0.1
1980	1.8	0.3
1985	2.3	0.6
1990	2.7	1.0

Source: Executive Office of the President of the United States. Environmental Quality 24: The Twenty-fourth Annual Report of the Council on Environmental Quality. Prepared by Ray Clark. Written by Carroll Curtis. Edited by Barry Walsh. Washington, DC: U.S. Government Printing Office, 1994, p. 505. Primary source: U.S. Environmental Protection Agency. Office of Solid Waste and Emergency Response. Characterization of Municipal Solid Waste in the United States: 1992 Update. Washington, DC: U.S. Environmental Protection Agency, 1992. Note: 1. Negligible (less than 50,000 tons or 0.05 percent).

★ 534 ★

Municipal Solid Waste: Specific Types

Municipal Solid Waste – Food: 1960-1990

[In million tons]

Year	Food	
	Generation	Recovery
1960	12.2	(¹)
1965	12.7	(¹)
1970	12.8	(¹)
1975	13.4	(¹)
1980	13.2	(¹)
1985	13.2	(¹)
1990	13.2	(¹)

Source: Executive Office of the President of the United States. *Environmental Quality 24: The Twenty-fourth Annual Report of the Council on Environmental Quality.* Prepared by Ray Clark. Written by Carroll Curtis. Edited by Barry Walsh. Washington, DC: U.S. Government Printing Office, 1994, p. 505. Primary source: U.S. Environmental Protection Agency. Office of Solid Waste and Emergency Response. *Characterization of Municipal Solid Waste in the United States: 1992 Update.* Washington, DC: U.S. Environmental Protection Agency, 1992. *Note:* 1. Negligible (less than 50,000 tons or 0.05 percent).

★ 535 ★

Municipal Solid Waste: Specific Types

Municipal Solid Waste – Glass: 1960-1990

[In million tons]

Year	Glass	
	Generation	Recovery
1960	6.7	0.1
1965	8.7	0.1
1970	12.7	0.2
1975	13.5	0.4
1980	15.0	0.8
1985	13.2	1.0
1990	13.2	2.6

Source: Executive Office of the President of the United States. *Environmental Quality 24: The Twenty-fourth Annual Report of the Council on Environmental Quality.* Prepared by Ray Clark. Written by Carroll Curtis. Edited by Barry Walsh. Washington, DC: U.S. Government Printing Office, 1994, p. 505. Primary source: U.S. Environmental Protection Agency. Office of Solid Waste and Emergency Response. *Characterization of Municipal Solid Waste in the United States: 1992 Update.* Washington, DC: U.S. Environmental Protection Agency, 1992.

★ 536 ★

Municipal Solid Waste: Specific Types

Municipal Solid Waste – Metal: 1960-1990

[In million tons]

Year	Metal	
	Generation	Recovery
1960	10.1	0.1
1965	10.6	0.4
1970	13.3	0.4
1975	13.2	0.6
1980	12.7	0.9
1985	11.9	0.6
1990	13.5	2.7

Source: Executive Office of the President of the United States. *Environmental Quality 24: The Twenty-fourth Annual Report of the Council on Environmental Quality.* Prepared by Ray Clark. Written by Carroll Curtis. Edited by Barry Walsh. Washington, DC: U.S. Government Printing Office, 1994, p. 505. Primary source: U.S. Environmental Protection Agency. Office of Solid Waste and Emergency Response. *Characterization of Municipal Solid Waste in the United States: 1992 Update.* Washington, DC: U.S. Environmental Protection Agency, 1992.

★ 537 ★

Municipal Solid Waste: Specific Types

Municipal Solid Waste – Paper: 1960-1990

[In million tons]

Year	Paper	
	Generation	Recovery
1960	29.9	5.4
1965	38.0	5.7
1970	44.2	7.4
1975	43.0	8.2
1980	54.7	11.9
1985	61.5	13.1
1990	73.3	20.9

Source: Executive Office of the President of the United States. *Environmental Quality 24: The Twenty-fourth Annual Report of the Council on Environmental Quality.* Prepared by Ray Clark. Written by Carroll Curtis. Edited by Barry Walsh. Washington, DC: U.S. Government Printing Office, 1994, p. 505. Primary source: U.S. Environmental Protection Agency. Office of Solid Waste and Emergency Response. *Characterization of Municipal Solid Waste in the United States: 1992 Update.* Washington, DC: U.S. Environmental Protection Agency, 1992.

★ 538 ★

Municipal Solid Waste: Specific Types

Municipal Solid Waste – Plastics: 1960-1990

[In million tons]

Year	Plastics	
	Generation	Recovery
1960	0.4	1
1965	1.4	1
1970	3.1	1
1975	4.5	1
1980	7.8	1
1985	11.6	0.1
1990	16.2	0.4

Source: Executive Office of the President of the United States. *Environmental Quality 24: The Twenty-fourth Annual Report of the Council on Environmental Quality.* Prepared by Ray Clark. Written by Carroll Curtis. Edited by Barry Walsh. Washington, DC: U.S. Government Printing Office, 1994, p. 505. Primary source: U.S. Environmental Protection Agency. Office of Solid Waste and Emergency Response. *Characterization of Municipal Solid Waste in the United States: 1992 Update.* Washington, DC: U.S. Environmental Protection Agency, 1992. *Note:* 1. Negligible (less than 50,000 tons or 0.05 percent).

★ 539 ★

Municipal Solid Waste: Specific Types

Municipal Solid Waste – Rubber and Leather: 1960-1990

[In million tons]

Year	Rubber and leather	
	Generation	Recovery
1960	2.0	0.3
1965	2.6	0.3
1970	3.2	0.3
1975	3.9	0.2
1980	4.3	0.1
1985	3.8	0.2
1990	4.6	0.2

Source: Executive Office of the President of the United States. *Environmental Quality 24: The Twenty-fourth Annual Report of the Council on Environmental Quality.* Prepared by Ray Clark. Written by Carroll Curtis. Edited by Barry Walsh. Washington, DC: U.S. Government Printing Office, 1994, p. 505. Primary source: U.S. Environmental Protection Agency. Office of Solid Waste and Emergency Response. *Characterization of Municipal Solid Waste in the United States: 1992 Update.* Washington, DC: U.S. Environmental Protection Agency, 1992.

★ 540 ★

Municipal Solid Waste: Specific Types

Municipal Solid Waste – Textiles: 1960-1990

[In million tons]

Year	Textiles	
	Generation	Recovery
1960	1.7	[1]
1965	1.9	[1]
1970	2.0	[1]
1975	2.2	[1]
1980	2.6	[1]
1985	2.8	[1]
1990	5.6	0.2

Source: Executive Office of the President of the United States. *Environmental Quality 24: The Twenty-fourth Annual Report of the Council on Environmental Quality.* Prepared by Ray Clark. Written by Carroll Curtis. Edited by Barry Walsh. Washington, DC: U.S. Government Printing Office, 1994, p. 505. Primary source: U.S. Environmental Protection Agency. Office of Solid Waste and Emergency Response. *Characterization of Municipal Solid Waste in the United States: 1992 Update.* Washington, DC: U.S. Environmental Protection Agency, 1992. *Note:* 1. Negligible (less than 50,000 tons or 0.05 percent).

★ 541 ★

Municipal Solid Waste: Specific Types

Municipal Solid Waste – Wood: 1960-1990

[In million tons]

Year	Wood	
	Generation	Recovery
1960	3.0	[1]
1965	3.5	[1]
1970	4.0	[1]
1975	4.4	[1]
1980	6.7	[1]
1985	8.2	[1]
1990	12.3	0.4

Source: Executive Office of the President of the United States. *Environmental Quality 24: The Twenty-fourth Annual Report of the Council on Environmental Quality.* Prepared by Ray Clark. Written by Carroll Curtis. Edited by Barry Walsh. Washington, DC: U.S. Government Printing Office, 1994, p. 505. Primary source: U.S. Environmental Protection Agency. Office of Solid Waste and Emergency Response. *Characterization of Municipal Solid Waste in the United States: 1992 Update.* Washington, DC: U.S. Environmental Protection Agency, 1992. *Note:* 1. Negligible (less than 50,000 tons or 0.05 percent).

★ 542 ★

Municipal Solid Waste: Specific Types

Municipal Solid Waste – Yard: 1960-1990

[In million tons]

| Year | Yard | |
	Generation	Recovery
1960	20.0	1
1965	21.6	1
1970	23.2	1
1975	25.2	1
1980	27.5	1
1985	30.0	1
1990	35.0	4.2

Source: Executive Office of the President of the United States. *Environmental Quality 24: The Twenty-fourth Annual Report of the Council on Environmental Quality.* Prepared by Ray Clark. Written by Carroll Curtis. Edited by Barry Walsh. Washington, DC: U.S. Government Printing Office, 1994, p. 505. Primary source: U.S. Environmental Protection Agency. Office of Solid Waste and Emergency Response. *Characterization of Municipal Solid Waste in the United States: 1992 Update.* Washington, DC: U.S. Environmental Protection Agency, 1992. *Note:* 1. Negligible (less than 50,000 tons or 0.05 percent).

Nuclear Waste

★ 543 ★

High-Level Nuclear Waste: 1980-1993

Table shows accumulated volume and radioactivity of high-level nuclear waste at U.S. Department of Energy/defense sites and at commercial sites.

| Year | Department of Energy/ defense sites | | Commercial sites | |
	Cumulative volume (thousand m^3)	Cumulative radioactivity (million curies)	Cumulative volume (thousand m^3)	Cumulative radioactivity (million curies)
1980	295	1,310	2.2	33.4
1981	305	1,577	2.2	32.7
1982	340	1,317	2.2	31.9
1983	351	1,248	2.2	31.2
1984	361	1,397	2.2	30.5
1985	355	1,465	2.2	29.8
1986	364	1,417	2.2	29.1
1987	379	1,277	2.2	28.4
1988	383	1,174	2.1	27.9
1989	379	1,081	2.4	27.3

[Continued]

★ 543 ★

High-Level Nuclear Waste: 1980-1993
[Continued]

Year	Department of Energy/defense sites		Commercial sites	
	Cumulative volume (thousand m³)	Cumulative radioactivity (million curies)	Cumulative volume (thousand m³)	Cumulative radioactivity (million curies)
1990	397	1,015	1.2	26.7
1991	395	971	1.7	26.2
1992	397	1,038	1.6	25.9
1993	417	1,004	2.5	25.3

Source: Executive Office of the President of the United States. *Environmental Quality 24: The Twenty-fourth Annual Report of the Council on Environmental Quality.* Prepared by Ray Clark. Written by Carroll Curtis. Edited by Barry Walsh. Washington, DC: U.S. Government Printing Office, 1994, p. 506. Primary source: U.S. Department of Energy. *Integrated Data Base for 1993: Spent Fuel and Radioactive Waste Inventories, Projections, and Characteristics.* Washington, DC: U.S. Department of of Energy, 1994. *Note:* Radioactivity added each year is decayed.

★ 544 ★

Nuclear Waste

Low-Level Nuclear Waste: 1962-1993

Table shows accumulated volume and radioactivity of low-level nuclear waste at commercial disposal sites.

Year	Cumulative volume (million m³)	Cumulative radioactivity (million curies)
1962	0.002	NA
1965	0.034	0.273
1970	0.138	0.855
1975	0.367	3.040
1980	0.768	4.547
1985	1.160	5.282
1990	1.384	4.979
1991	1.423	5.272
1992	1.472	5.708
1993	1.489	5.333

Source: Executive Office of the President of the United States. *Environmental Quality 24: The Twenty-fourth Annual Report of the Council on Environmental Quality.* Prepared by Ray Clark. Written by Carroll Curtis. Edited by Barry Walsh. Washington, DC: U.S. Government Printing Office, 1994, p. 506. Primary source: U.S. Department of Energy. *Integrated Data Base for 1993: Spent Fuel and Radioactive Waste Inventories, Projections, and Characteristics.* Washington, DC: U.S. Department of of Energy, 1994. *Notes:* "NA" stands for "not available." Radioactivity added each year is decayed.

Recycling

★ 545 ★

Recycling: 1993

According to the source: "Recycling growth now outpaces the growth of municipal solid waste (MSW). While the total volume of MSW generated in the U.S. rose to 207 million tons in 1993, according to a report issued by the U.S. Environmental Protection Agency (EPA; Washington, D.C.), the volume of reclaimed material rose faster, reaching 21.7 percent of the total waste stream" (p. 31). Table show the municipal solid waste material recycled in 1993.

Waste stream	Percent recycled	Percent of all municipal solid waste
Aluminum cans	63	0.5
Corrugated boxes	55	7.1
Newspapers	46	2.9
Steel cans	48	0.6
Plastic soda bottles	41	-
Plastics packaging	-	0.2
Office paper	36	1.3
Other paper	-	1.6
Glass containers	25	1.5
Wood packaging	-	0.6

Source: "Prime Time for Postconsumer Recycling." *Chemical Engineering* (February 1995), p. 31. Primary source: U.S. Environmental Protection Agency. *Note:* "-" indicates data not reported in source.

★ 546 ★
Recycling

Recycling Goals, by Selected States

According to the source: "At least 40 states have laws that are pushing municipalities to recycle large portions of trash—goals that in many cases are viewed by critics as both unrealistic and uneconomical" (p. B1). The table below shows recycling goals for selected states.

[In percentages]

State	Goal	Date
California	50	2000
Florida	30	1994
Illinois	25	2000
Massachusetts	56	2000
New Jersey	60	1995
New York	50	1997
Ohio	25	1994
Texas	25	1994

Source: Bailey, Jeff. "Recycling Mania Crashes and Burns in California." *Wall Street Journal,* 26 April 1994, p. B1. Primary source: National Solid Waste Management Association. *Note:* Definitions, methods and requirements vary.

★ 547 ★
Recycling

Recycling Knowledge

Data are from a survey of 2,600 apartment residents in 406 Virginia complexes. Responses show their attitudes, knowledge, and behavior regarding recycling. Figures reflect respondents providing the correct answer.

[In percentages]

Question	Correct answer	Respondents					
		Recyclers	Non-recyclers	Families	Elderly	High-rise apartment dwellers	Garden apartment dwellers
Aluminum is one of the most frequently recycled materials.	True	82	81	81	81	79	82
Polypropylene is a commonly recycled plastic.	False	8	7	8	0	6	8
Recycling is a good way for my community to earn money.	False	9	12	12	2	7	12
"Closed-loop recycling" is used	True	42	45	40	34	39	44

[Continued]

★547★

Recycling Knowledge
[Continued]

Question	Correct answer	Respondents					
		Recyclers	Non-recyclers	Families	Elderly	High-rise apartment dwellers	Garden apartment dwellers
to describe recycling a product back into the same product; for example, recycling a glass bottle into another glass bottle.							
It is often cheaper to bury trash in a landfill than to recycle it.	False	45	37	40	51	42	40
Transportation cost to take recycled materials to a processor can be a major barrier to a community recycling program.	True	47	45	44	56	44	46
Mixing colored and clear glass in a recycling container lowers the value of the glass when it is sold to a recycled glass processor.	True	48	33	41	36	35	43

Source: Johnson, Michael, and Kathleen Parrott. "Recycling: Before You Start." *Journal of Property Management* (July-August 1994), p. 46.

Recycling and Recovery of Specific Material

★548★

Aluminum Can Recycling: 1974-1994

Table shows recycled aluminum cans. Recycling reduces energy required to manufacture aluminum. In fact, recycling uses 95 percent less energy than making aluminum from ore.

[In percentages]

Year	Aluminum cans
1974	17
1978	27
1982	56
1986	49

[Continued]

★ 548 ★

Aluminum Can Recycling: 1974-1994
[Continued]

Year	Aluminum cans
1990	64
1994	65

Source: "Recycling: Earth Day Legacy." *USA TODAY*, 21 April 1995, p. 1B. Primary source: The Aluminum Association.

★ 549 ★

Recycling and Recovery of Specific Material

Chemicals Reported as Treated: 1992

Table shows the top 25 chemicals reported as treated.

[In pounds]

Chemical	Treated onsite	Treated offsite	Total treated
Sulfuric acid	2,938,612,362	74,779,970	3,013,392,332
Hydrochloric acid	1,911,186,194	75,462,680	1,986,648,874
Methanol	953,847,754	135,191,045	1,089,038,799
Ammonia	575,131,175	69,993,051	645,124,226
Propylene	505,338,217	580,279	505,918,496
Ethylene	449,198,814	92,714	449,291,528
Phosphoric acid	389,135,391	5,248,000	394,383,391
Chlorine	249,878,302	908,902	250,787,204
Freon 113	230,231,075	1,348,284	231,579,359
Nitric acid	221,787,298	15,390,236	237,177,534
Copper compounds	141,946,469	2,419,471	144,365,940
Toluene	125,358,145	18,618,495	143,976,640
Hydrogen fluoride	106,911,337	2,442,231	109,353,568
Acetone	105,711,876	22,784,463	128,496,339
Phenol	102,456,730	6,065,012	108,521,742
Formaldehyde	95,456,352	6,143,347	101,599,699
Ethylene glycol	54,514,498	24,438,011	78,952,509
Chromium compounds	54,314,995	3,322,787	57,637,782
Methyl ethyl ketone	50,463,297	6,274,738	56,738,035
1,3-Butadiene	49,305,988	264,217	49,570,205
Xylene (mixed isomers)	43,449,368	9,310,790	52,760,158
1,2-Dichloroethane	37,493,307	1,808,161	39,301,468
Acrylic acid	36,821,655	209,644	37,031,299
Titanium tetrachloride	36,394,611	3,267,833	39,662,444
Dichloromethane	35,365,596	12,445,135	47,810,731

[Continued]

★ 549 ★

Chemicals Reported as Treated: 1992
[Continued]

Chemical	Treated onsite	Treated offsite	Total treated
Subtotal	9,500,310,806	498,809,496	9,999,120,302
Total for all TRI chemicals	10,326,749,494	678,373,850	11,005,123,344

Source: U.S. Environmental Protection Agency. "Toxic Release Inventory, 1992." In *National Economic, Social, and Environmental Data Bank* [CD-ROM]. Prepared by U.S. Department of Commerce, Economics and Statistics Administration. Washington, DC: U.S. Department of Commerce, National Economic, Social, and Environmental Data Bank, Economics and Statistics Administration, Office of Business Analysis, February 1995. *Note:* "TRI" stands for Toxic Release Inventory.

★ 550 ★
Recycling and Recovery of Specific Material

Highway Use of Recycled Material

Recycled material has been used for highway asphalt pavement, concrete pavement, base course, and embankment, among other applications. The table shows waste material produced and recycled or reused for highways.

[In million metric tons, except as noted]

Waste material	Annual rates	
	Produced	Recycled reused
Blast furnace slag	NA	14.1
Carpet fiber wastes	2	NA
Coal combustion byproducts		
Coal fly ash	45	11
Coal bottom ash or bottom slag	16	5
Fuel gas desulfurization waste	18	NA
Glass	12	2.4
Mill tailings	432	[1]
Municipal waste combustion ash	7.3	[2]
Plastic	14.7	0.3
Reclaimed concrete pavement	3	NA
Reclaimed asphalt pavement	91	73
Roofing shingle waste		
Industry-produced	0.4	[1]
Re-roofing waste	7.7	NA
Scrap tires	2.3	0.4

[Continued]

★ 550 ★

Highway Use of Recycled Material
[Continued]

Waste material	Annual rates	
	Produced	Recycled reused
Steel slag	7.5	6.9
Waste rock	954	1

Source: Schroeder, Robin L. "The Use of Recycled Materials in Highway Construction." *Public Roads* 58, no. 2 (autumn 1994), p. 35. *Notes:* "NA" stands for "not available." 1. Less than 1 percent. 2. Less than 10 percent.

★ 551 ★

Recycling and Recovery of Specific Material

Newspaper Recycling: 1988-1991

Table shows discarded newspaper recycled into new paper or other products.

[In percentages]

Year	Recycled newspapers
1988	36
1989	41
1990	45
1991	52

Source: "Recycling Speeds Up Across the Nation." *Editor & Publisher*, 10 April 1993, p. 7E. Primary source: American Paper Institute.

★ 552 ★

Recycling and Recovery of Specific Material

Packaging Material Recycling in Germany: 1993

Paper, paperboard, corrugated - 80	
Bi-metal cans - 53	
Glass - 46	
Plastics - 27	
	Multi-material milk and juice cartons - 26
Aluminum - 25	

Chart shows data from column 2.

According to the source: "The 1991 Packaging Law phased in recycling for all packaging materials, from cardboard boxes to yogurt cups. The producer was to shoulder the burden. In response, German industry and commerce created the 'Duales System Deutschland' (DSD), which uses a Green Dot symbol on packaging to indicate that collection and recycling costs are included in the cost of the product" (p. 16). Table shows generation and recycling capacity for packaging material in Germany.

Packaging material	1992 generation (1,000 metric tons/year)	1993 recycling capacity (%)
Glass	4,300	46
Paper, paperboard, corrugated	1,500	80
Plastics	900	27
Bi-metal cans	650	53
Multi-material milk and juice cartons	170	26
Aluminum	120	25

Source: "German Waste Disposal Evolves Under New Laws." *World Wastes* (September 1993), p. 16. Primary source: *Der Spiegel.* Based on data from the Federal Environmental Agency and prognosis of the DSD.

★ 553 ★

Recycling and Recovery of Specific Material

Recovered Paper Utilization and Recovery Rates: 1960-1993

Recovery rate is ratio of total recovered paper to new supply. Recovered paper utilization is the ratio of recovered paper consumption at paper and board mills to paper and board production.

[In million short tons, except percentages]

Item	1960	1970	1975	1980	1985	1990	1991	1992	1993
Paper and board, production[1]	33.9	51.7	51.0	63.6	68.7	80.3	81.1	84.5	85.9
Wastepaper consumption	9.0	11.8	11.7	14.9	16.4	21.7	23.7	26.2	28.9
Wastepaper utilization rate (percent)	26.5	22.8	23.0	23.5	23.8	27.1	29.2	29.7	31.8
Other wastepaper uses[2]	0.20	0.42	0.54	0.47	0.53	1.00	1.08	1.10	1.15

[Continued]

★ 553 ★

Recovered Paper Utilization and Recovery Rates: 1960-1993

[Continued]

Item	1960	1970	1975	1980	1985	1990	1991	1992	1993
Wastepaper exports	0.15	0.41	0.86	2.64	3.56	6.51	6.60	6.40	5.90
Total wastepaper recovered	9.3	12.6	13.1	17.9	20.4	29.1	31.2	33.6	35.7
Paper and board, new supply[3]	38.5	56.0	54.1	67.2	76.1	86.7	84.9	88.1	90.9
Recovery rate (percent)	24.2	22.4	24.2	26.7	26.8	33.6	36.8	38.1	39.3

Source: 1994 Statistical Abstract of the United States on CD-ROM [machine-readable datafiles]. CD-8A-94. Washington, DC: U.S. Department of Commerce, Economics and Statistics Administration, Bureau of the Census, Data User Services Division, January 1995. Primary sources: American Forest and Paper Association. Statistics of Paper, Paperboard, and Woodpulp (annual); and unpublished data. Notes: 1. Excludes hard pressed board; includes construction paper and board, and wet machine board. 2. Estimated. 3. Excludes production of hard pressed board.

★ 554 ★

Recycling and Recovery of Specific Material

Recycled Chemicals: 1992

Table shows the top 25 chemicals reported as recycled.

[In pounds]

Chemical	Recycled onsite	Recycled offsite	Total recycled
Sulfuric acid	5,747,645,488	1,320,807,382	7,068,452,870
Acetonitrile	2,508,586,088	2,880,190	2,511,466,278
Lead compounds	624,622,931	417,515,419	1,042,138,350
Toluene	627,080,929	27,395,427	654,476,356
Copper	251,127,564	388,377,676	639,505,240
Methanol	476,357,827	14,418,924	490,776,751
Ethylene glycol	345,926,377	102,553,538	448,479,915
Propylene	343,447,371	0	343,447,371
1,3-Butadiene	293,902,741	28,850,854	322,753,595
Zinc compounds	94,205,877	218,896,007	313,101,884
Copper compounds	185,313,401	126,262,362	311,575,763
Cumene	308,360,195	64,499	308,424,694
Lead	214,479,454	34,138,441	248,617,895
Methyl isobutyl ketone	223,939,338	19,724,864	243,664,202
Trichloroethylene	225,757,972	8,109,967	233,867,939
Acetone	213,067,646	18,005,963	231,073,609
Ammonia	211,456,668	18,117,158	229,573,826
Ethylene	197,286,622	0	197,286,622
Methyl ethyl ketone	169,763,949	26,505,126	196,269,075
1,1,1-Trichloroethane	171,223,961	23,721,150	194,945,111
Hydrochloric acid	125,740,840	64,204,456	189,945,296
Vinyl chloride	176,010,819	157,091	176,167,910
Styrene	172,963,215	1,201,190	174,164,405
Formaldehyde	169,263,509	99,101	169,362,610
Manganese compounds	119,240,927	37,333,722	156,574,649

[Continued]

★ 554 ★

Recycled Chemicals: 1992
[Continued]

Chemical	Recycled onsite	Recycled offsite	Total recycled
Subtotal	14,196,771,709	2,899,340,507	17,096,112,216
Total for all TRI chemicals	15,884,194,888	3,473,894,509	19,358,089,397

Source: U.S. Environmental Protection Agency. "Toxic Release Inventory, 1992." In *National Economic, Social, and Environmental Data Bank* [CD-ROM]. Prepared by U.S. Department of Commerce, Economics and Statistics Administration. Washington, DC: U.S. Department of Commerce, National Economic, Social, and Environmental Data Bank, Economics and Statistics Administration, Office of Business Analysis, February 1995. *Note:* "TRI" stands for Toxic Release Inventory.

★ 555 ★

Recycling and Recovery of Specific Material

Scrap Tire Disposal

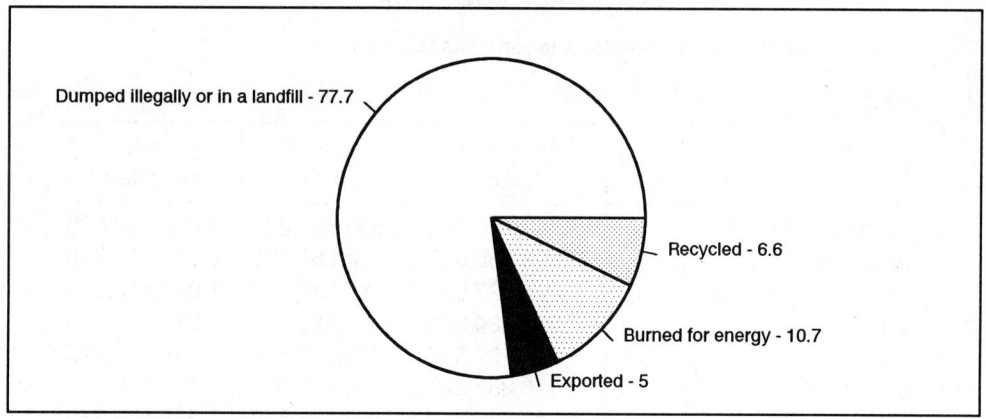

Table shows methods through which tires are disposed.

[In percentages]

Disposal method	Scrap tires
Exported	5
Recycled	6.6
Burned for energy	10.7
Dumped illegally or in a landfill	77.7

Source: "Where Tires Are Retired." *USA TODAY,* 4 October 1993, p. 1A. Primary source: National Solid Waste Management Associates (1990).

★ 556 ★

Recycling and Recovery of Specific Material

Scrap Tire Utilization: 1993

Section 1038 of the Intermodel Surface Transportation Efficiency Act (ISTEA, or "Ice Tea Bill") provides for the use of crumb rubber (shredded tires) in highway construction. Table shows passenger tire equivalents recovered in 1993.

[In millions]

Method	Tire equivalents recovered
Landfill/stockpile	220
Energy recovery	82
Fabricated products	14
Reclaim rubber[1]	14
Tire export	10
Civil engineering	7
Agricultural vehicles	3

Source: Freeman, Del. "The Section 1038 Debate on Recycled Roadways." *World Wastes* (March 1994), p. 40. Primary source: Goodyear. *Note:* 1. Includes asphalt addition.

Recycling and Recovery Programs and Facilities

★ 557 ★

Curbside Recycling Programs in Selected Cities

Philadelphia, Pennsylvania - 565,000

Jacksonville, Florida - 230,000

Milwaukee, Wisconsin - 135,000

Phoenix, Arizona - 80,000

Madison, Wisconsin - 58,000

Allentown, Pennsylvania - 36,000

Vancouver, Washington - 16,378

Loveland, Colorado - 13,700

Durham County, North Carolina - 13,400

Westerville, Ohio - 9,156

North August, Georgia - 7,400

Hartford, Vermont - 2,217

Chart shows data from column 1.

Biocycle surveyed 12 municipalities regarding their curbside recycling programs. The table below profiles each city's program.

Municipality	Households served	Collection frequency	Financing	Mandatory/ voluntary
Allentown, Pennsylvania	36,000	Weekly	Set fee	Mandatory
Durham County, North Carolina[1]	13,400	Biweekly	Tax base	Voluntary
Hartford, Vermont	2,217	Biweekly	Tax base	Mandatory
Jacksonville, Florida	230,000	Weekly	Tax base	Mandatory
Loveland, Colorado	13,700	Weekly	Variable fees	Voluntary
Madison, Wisconsin	58,000	Weekly	Tax base	Mandatory
Milwaukee, Wisconsin	135,000[2]	[3]	Tax base	Voluntary
North August, Georgia	7,400	Weekly	Set fee	Voluntary
Philadelphia, Pennsylvania	565,000	Biweekly	Tax base	Mandatory
Phoenix, Arizona	80,000[2]	Weekly	Set fee	Voluntary
Vancouver, Washington	16,378	Weekly	Variable fees	Mandatory
Westerville, Ohio	9,156	Weekly	Tax base	Voluntary

Source: Steuteville, Robert, Jay Freeborne, and Fulton Rockwell. "Trends in Curbside Recycling." *BioCycle* (July 1994), p. 33. *Notes:* 1. Unicorporated. 2. Represents a portion of the city. 3. 63,000 weekly; 72,000 monthly.

★ 558 ★

Recycling and Recovery Programs and Facilities

Materials Recovery Facilities

In 1992, Governmental Advisory Associates Inc. identified 222 material recovery facilities (MRFs). MRFs separate residential, commercial, and industrial recycled materials into marketable recyclable streams. The table below shows segments of the MRF universe.

[In percentages]

Segment	Facilities
Operational	74.7
Conceptual planning	12.6
Advanced planning	7.7
Shakedown	2.7
Construction	2.3

Source: "Recycling Market Recovers." *ENR*, 6 April 1992, p. 36C16. Primary source: Government Advisory Associates, Inc.

★ 559 ★

Recycling and Recovery Programs and Facilities

Publicly Owned Treatment Works Using Clarifiers

Greater than 19.9 mgd - 88
5.0 to 19.9 mgd - 80
0.1 to 4.9 mgd - 57

Table shows publicly owned treatment works (POTWs) in the United States that use clarifiers for primary treatment.

[In percentages]

POTW size	Clarifier use
Greater than 19.9 mgd	88
5.0 to 19.9 mgd	80
0.1 to 4.9 mgd	57

Source: "Percentage of U.S. Publicly Owned Treatment Works (POTWs) Using Clarifiers for Primary Treatment." *Water Environment & Technology* (March 1994), p. 13. Primary source: 1994-1995 WEF POTW Spending Survey. *Note:* "mgd" represents "million gallons per day."

★ 560 ★

Recycling and Recovery Programs and Facilities

Publicly Owned Treatment Works Using Land Spreading, Spraying, or Injection

| 5.0 to 19.9 mgd - 49 |
| 0.1 to 4.9 mgd - 42 |
| Greater than 19.9 mgd - 36 |

Table shows publicly owned treatment works (POTWs) in the United States that use land spreading, spraying, or injection for biosolids.

[In percentages]

POTW size	Land spreading, spraying, or injection use
Greater than 19.9 mgd	36
5.0 to 19.9 mgd	49
0.1 to 4.9 mgd	42

Source: "Percentage of U.S. Publicly Owned Treatment Works (POTWs) Using Land Spreading, Spraying, or Injection for Biosolids." *Water Environment & Technology* (January 1994), p. 15. Primary source: 1994-1995 WEF POTW Spending Survey. *Note:* "mgd" stands for million gallons per day.

★ 561 ★

Recycling and Recovery Programs and Facilities

Rural Recycling Programs: 1990

According to the source: "Volunteer-driven recycling programs are achieving success with central collection centers and collective marketing strategies" (p. 34). Table shows data on recycling programs in selected rural communities.

[In tons]

Item	Monroe, Wisconsin	Peterborough, New Hampshire	Sonoma County, California	La Crescent, Minnesota
Community statistics				
Population	10,220	5,239	388,222	4,305
Households	4,271	1,800	160,000	1,568
Businesses and institutions	437	267	15,000	205
Waste generation				
Municipal solid waste[1]	12,660	5,001	465,142	1,792
Residential waste[1]	3,802	2,003	124,845	1,109
Material recovery				
Municipal solid waste				
Recycled (%)	25	19	21	11

[Continued]

★ 561 ★

Rural Recycling Programs: 1990
[Continued]

Item	Monroe, Wisconsin	Peterborough, New Hampshire	Sonoma County, California	La Crescent, Minnesota
Composed (%)	3	0	<1	8
Residential waste Recycled (%)	21	42	15	28
Composed (%)	11	0	<1	13
Commercial waste Total Recovered (%)	27	4	10	9

Source: Burgert, Phil. "Recycling Programs Evolve in Rural Settings." *World Wastes* (November 1993), p. 34. Primary source: Institute for Local Self-Reliance.

★ 562 ★

Recycling and Recovery Programs and Facilities

School District Recycling

Paper - 87

Aluminum and aluminum cans - 63

Cardboard and corrugated boxes - 33

Plastic containers - 20

Glass - 17

Polystyrene - 5

Paperboard milk cartons - 4

Drink boxes - 2

The National School Public Relations Association found that nearly 4 out of 5 of 406 school districts surveyed participate in recycling programs. The table below shows the types of material recycled by school districts.

[In percentages]

Material	School districts recycling
Paper[1]	87
Aluminum and aluminum cans	63
Cardboard and corrugated boxes	33
Plastic containers	20
Glass	17
Polystyrene	5

[Continued]

★ 562 ★

School District Recycling

[Continued]

Material	School districts recycling
Paperboard milk cartons	4
Drink boxes	2

Source: "Recycling Gaining Momentum." *AS&U* (September 1994), p. 18. *Note:* 1. Includes computer, writing, copier, and/or colored paper.

Waste Disposal

★ 563 ★

Waste Disposal Methods

Table shows selected methods of waste disposal and amount of waste disposed through each.

[In percentages]

Method	Waste disposal
Landfill[1]	62
Recycling[2]	18
Waste-to-energy incineration[3]	16
Composting[4]	3
Incineration[5]	1

Source: "Where Does Your Garbage Go?" *Science World*, 9 December 1994, p. 15. Primary source: Franklin Associates, Ltd. (1994). *Notes:* 1. A dump piled high with paper, plastics, glass, metals, rubber, wood, leather, textiles, and yard and food wastes; covered with earth. 2. Process of sorting and reusing materials such as paper, glass, metals, textiles, rubber, and wood. 3. Burning paper, plastics, rubber, wood, yard and food wastes, and textiles as fuel to generate electricity. 4. Mixing organic materials (yard trimmings, paper, and food waste) with oxygen to promote decay. Bacteria break down the waste, releasing store nutrients. Composting facilities sell the leftovers as plant fertilizer. 5. Without energy recovery; burning solid wastes in a giant furnace.

★ 564 ★

Waste Disposal

Waste Handling: 1960-2000

```
┌─────────────────────────────────────────────────────┐
│  ┌─────────────────────────────────────────────────┐ │
│  │ Landfills - 49.3                                │ │
│  └─────────────────────────────────────────────────┘ │
│  ┌──────────────────────────────┐                    │
│  │ Burning for energy - 25.5    │                    │
│  └──────────────────────────────┘                    │
│  ┌─────────────────────────────┐                     │
│  │ Recycling - 25.2            │                     │
│  └─────────────────────────────┘                     │
│  │ Incineration - 0.1                                │
│                    Chart shows data from column 3.    │
└─────────────────────────────────────────────────────┘
```

According to the source, "almost a fifth of America's municipal garbage is now burned in a new generation of incinerators that also generate steam and electricity, according to the National Solid Wastes Management Association in Washington.... The 125 cities and counties with the incinerators had interpreted the Resource Conservation and Recovery Act as allowing them to dispose of the ash as ordinary waste even though tests periodically showed that some had levels of lead and cadmium exceeding Federal safety standards" (p. A12). The table below shows methods used to deal with wastes.

[In percentages]

Method	1960	1988	2000[1]
Incineration[2]	30.8	0.6	0.1[3]
Recycling	6.7	13.1	25.2
Burning for energy	0	13.5	25.5
Landfills	62.5	72.7	49.3

Source: Schneider, Keith. "Incinerators' Users Say Ruling Will Be Costly." *New York Times*, 3 May 1994, p. A12. Primary source: Solid Waste Management Association. *Notes:* 1. Estimated. 2. Excluding burning for energy. 3. Less than 0.1 percent.

★ 565 ★

Waste Disposal

Waste-by-Rail Transportation: 1993

As landfills move farther from large cities where most trash is produced, transporting trash becomes a business opportunity for railroads. "Railcycle"—moving solid waste from cities to landfills—is part of every major railroad's services. The table below shows waste-by-rail services.

Customer	Allied	Chambers	ECDC	ECO East	Epic/ Longo	Gallatin	Merco	OCON/ EST	Rabanco	Seamass	Various	WMX
Product	MSW	Ash/MSW	MSW/Soil	MSW	Sludge	Ash	Sludge	Sludge	MSW/C&D/Ash	MSW	Soil/Autofluff	MSW
Tons/day	1,000	900/450	1,000	450	850	250	600	400	1500/800/200	550	500/150/2500	1500
Origin	New York	New Jersey	California	New York	New Jersey	Minnesota	New York	New York	Washington, Oregon	Massachusetts	Utah, Minnesota, Alabama, California	Washington
Destination	Illinois	Virginia	Utah	Georgia	Texas, Illinois	Illinois	Texas	Arizona	Washington	Massachusetts	Oklahoma, Michigan, California	Oregon

Source: Cohan, Paul. "Waste-by-Rail: A System That's Been Working on American Railroads." *World Wastes* (December 1993), p. 36. Primary source: Fraser Group Inc. *Notes:* "MSW" stands for "municipal solid waste." "C&D" stands for "construction and demolition."

Waste Generation

★ 566 ★

Beach Litter: 1994

The 1994 coastal clean up, conducted by the Center for Marine Conservation, yielded 2.8 million pounds of trash. Volunteers cleaned 3,000 beaches and shorelines. Among the debris workers found more than 7,000 condoms, a Rolex watch, a bag of undelivered mail, Christmas trees, television sets, and a Bugs Bunny suit. The table below show the top 10 items retrieved from the shore.

[In percentages]

Item	Amount collected
Cigarette butts	22.8
Plastic pieces	6.3
Foam plastic pieces	5.4
Plastic bags, wrap	4.6
Paper pieces	4.3
Glass pieces	4.3
Plastic caps, lids	3.8
Glass bottles	3.5
Metal cans	3.3
Plastic straws	3.2

Source: Miller, Ken. "Beach Cleanup Finds Litter's Mounting." *USA TODAY*, 22 June 1995, p. 2A. Primary source: Center for Marine Conservation.

★ 567 ★

Waste Generation

Coastline Debris

Volunteers cleaned litter from beaches and shorelines—4,500 miles—across 32 states. More than 150,000 volunteers collected 7.3 million articles of debris in 3 hours. The table below shows the litter collected.

Item	Number
Cigarette butts	1,700,000
Glass[1]	344,502
Straws	203,330
Bottles	333,996
Cans	210,553
Cups	134,547
Balloons	40,508

[Continued]

★ 567 ★

Coastline Debris
[Continued]

Item	Number
Light bulbs and fluorescent tubes	30,326
Syringes	10,166

Source: "Waterways Filled With Trash, Survey Shows." *St. Louis Post-Dispatch*, 8 September 1994, p. 6A. Primary source: Center for Marine Conservation. *Note:* 1. Pieces of glass.

★ 568 ★

Waste Generation

Construction Waste: 1994

Data are based on a study by a solid waste management consulting firm (July 1994). The study showed concrete comprised the largest portion of construction waste in the survey area. Table below shows waste material from new commercial construction projects.

[In percentages]

Material	Volume
Concrete	32.9
Dimension wood	15.1
Roofing	9.6
Metal	8.8
Other	8.1
Cardboard	7.5
Brick	6.7
Drywall	6.6
Pallets	2.6
Asphalt	0.6

[Continued]

★ 568 ★

Construction Waste: 1994
[Continued]

Material	Volume
Plastic	0.5
Plywood	0.5

Source: "Survey of Construction Waste." *Building Design & Construction* (February 1995), p. 10. Primary source: GBB, solid waste management consultant (Falls Church, Virginia).

★ 569 ★

Waste Generation

Garbage, by City: 1994

Fourteen cities were surveyed regarding trash discarded per person. The table below shows pounds of garbage generated annually per person in survey cites.

City	Garbage
Philadelphia	974
Milwaukee	968
New York	940
St. Louis	893
Phoenix	862
Chicago	815
Dallas	784
Los Angeles	776
Boston	724
Jacksonville	571
Atlanta	556
San Diego	539
Seattle	522
Houston	475

Source: "Inundated by Garbage." *Consumers Digest* (May/June 1995), p. 11. Primary source: Carlisle Plastics Inc. (Minneapolis, Minnesota).

★ 570 ★

Waste Generation

Trash: 1994

Table shows the solid wastes produced annually as commercial and consumer trash. According to the source: "Consumer trash is really a tiny sliver of the big waste pie" (p. A6).

[In million tons]

Solid waste	Annual production
Commercial trash	87
Consumer trash	116

Source: "Trash Talk: Debunking the Mythology." *Wall Street Journal*, 19 January 1995, p. A6. Primary source: U.S. Environmental Protection Agency.

★ 571 ★

Waste Generation

Waste Generation: 1992

According to the source: "Industrial nonhazardous waste accounts for over one-eighth of all landfill waste, second only to waste from the mining industry" (p. 99). Table shows amounts of various wastes generated.

[In million tons]

Type of waste	Waste generated
Industrial nonhazardous waste	262
Municipal solid waste	131.3
Electrical utility waste	85
Cement kiln dust	4-12
Mining waste	1,500

Source: Berne, Steve. "In-plant Recycling—Responsible Manufacturing." *Prepared Foods* (February 1994), p. 99. Primary source: U.S. Environmental Protection Agency.

★ 572 ★

Waste Generation

Waste Generation by Americans

Americans generate more trash than any other nation—in excess of 234 million metric tons annually, or 2 kilograms per person daily.

Source: "War on Wastes." *Science World*, 9 December 1994, p. 14.

★ 573 ★
Waste Generation

Waste Generation, by Country

New York - 1.80

Delaware - 1.49

Japan - 1.38

France - 1.10

Singapore - 0.87

Pakistan - 0.60

Philippines - 0.50

Nigeria - 0.46

Table shows solid waste generation per person in selected nations. Data for United States represented by two states.

[In kilograms/day]

Location	Solid waste generation
New York	1.80
Delaware	1.49
Japan	1.38
France	1.10
Singapore	0.87
Pakistan	0.60
Philippines	0.50
Nigeria	0.46

Source: "Solid Waste Generation." *Wastes Management* (January 1994), p. 49.

Waste Minimization

★ 574 ★

Waste Minimization Assessment – Aerial Lift Manufacturing

"The U.S. Environmental Protection Agency (EPA) has funded a pilot project to assist small and medium-size manufacturers who want to minimize their generation of waste but who lack the expertise to do so. In an effort to assist these manufacturers, Waste Minimization Assessment Centers (WMACs) were established at selected universities and procedures were adapted from the EPA *Waste Minimization Opportunity Assessment Manual*.... The WMAC at Colorado State University performed an assessment at a plant that manufacturers aerial manlifts, ventilating driers, and air driers.... The team's report, detailing findings and recommendations, indicated that the waste streams generated in the greatest quantity are spent rinse waters from plating and and paint preparation, and the greatest cost savings could be achieved by replacing the currently used parts washer with a system that uses a less hazardous solvent" (p. 1).

[In pounds, except as noted]

Waste generated	Annual quantity generated	Annual waste management cost[1] ($)
Cooling fluid	21,870	5,680
Cutting fluid	36,440	6,530
Wastewater treatment sludge	41,690	6,890
Rinse water[2]	6,122,550	1,980
Waste alkaline solutions	29,990	10
Waste acidic solutions	59,980	20
Alkaline cleaner	8,330	0
Overflow rinse water	26,660	0
Phosphating solution	8,330	0
Rinse water[3]	992,940	320
Body wash	612,260	200
Paint solvent still bottoms	2,020	8,910
Evaporated paint solvent	2,270	1,570
Expired paint	10,120	19,650
Paint cleaning solvent	410	1,310
Waste oil	3,670	20
Absorbent clay	5,640	570
Cardboard	91,160	6,990

[Continued]

★574★

Waste Minimization Assessment – Aerial Lift Manufacturing

[Continued]

Waste generated	Annual quantity generated	Annual waste management cost[1] ($)
Nonreusable pallets	72,000	3,880
Petroleum naphtha	6,730	8,450

Source: U.S. Environmental Protection Agency. Risk Reduction Engineering Laboratory. Research and Development. *Waste Minimization Assessment for a Manufacturer of Aerial Lifts.* Prepared by Harry W. Edwards, Michael F. Kostrezewa, and Gwen P. Looby. Environmental Research Brief. EPA/600/S-94/011. Cincinnati, OH: U.S. Environmental Protection Agency, Risk Reduction Engineering Laboratory, Research and Development, September 1994, p. 4. *Notes:* 1. Includes waste treatment, disposal, and handling costs and applicable raw material costs. 2. Metal plating. Treated on-site; sewered. 3. Preparation of metal for painting. Treated on-site; sewered.

★575★

Waste Minimization

Waste Minimization Assessment – Caulk Manufacturing

"The U.S. Environmental Protection Agency (EPA) has funded a pilot project to assist small and medium-size manufacturers who want to minimize their generation of waste but who lack the expertise to do so. In an effort to assist these manufacturers, Waste Minimization Assessment Centers (WMACs) were established at selected universities and procedures were adapted from the EPA *Waste Minimization Opportunity Assessment Manual....* The WMAC at Colorado State University performed an assessment at a plant that manufactures latex and acrylic caulk.... The assessment team's report, detailing findings and recommendations, indicated that the greatest quantity of waste was generated by cleaning of equipment. The greatest cost saving opportunity recommended to the plant involved using a solvent recovery unit to recover water from waste cleaning water/caulk. The recovered water can be reused" (p. 1).

[In pounds, except as noted]

Waste generated	Annual quantity generated	Annual waste management cost[1] ($)
Cleaning water	59,500	NA
Mixed solvent wastes	10,700	6,800
Evaporated solvents	130	0
Waste Stoddard solvent[2]	1,160	460
Spent activated charcoal	1,050	1,575

[Continued]

★ 575 ★

Waste Minimization Assessment – Caulk Manufacturing

[Continued]

Waste generated	Annual quantity generated	Annual waste management cost[1] ($)
Waste Stoddard solvent[3]	1,160	460
Waste soybean oil	6,109[4]	970[5]

Source: U.S. Environmental Protection Agency. Risk Reduction Engineering Laboratory. Research and Development. *Waste Minimization Assessment for a Manufacturer of Caulk.* Prepared by Harry W. Edwards, Michael F. Kostrzewa, and Gwen P. Looby. Environmental Research Brief. EPA/600/S-94/017. Cincinnati, OH: U.S. Environmental Protection Agency, Risk Reduction Engineering Laboratory, Research and Development, September 1994, p. 3. *Notes:* "NA" stands for "not available." 1. Includes waste treatment and disposal costs. 2. Cleaning of tools and filling equipment in acrylic production line. Shipped off-site for recovery by distillation; reused. 3. Cleaning in maintenance area. Shipped off-site for recovery by distillation; reused. 4. Not a recurring stream. 5. Estimated cost to dispose of waste.

★ 576 ★

Waste Minimization

Waste Minimization Assessment – Coated Parts Manufacturing

"The U.S. Environmental Protection Agency (EPA) has funded a pilot project to assist small and medium-size manufacturers who want to minimize their generation of waste but who lack the expertise to do so. In an effort to assist these manufacturers, Waste Minimization Assessment Centers (WMACs) were established at selected universities and procedures were adapted from the EPA *Waste Minimization Opportunity Assessment Manual....* The WMAC at Colorado State University performed an assessment at a plant that produces specialty coated parts—approximately one million per year.... The team's report, detailing findings and recommendations, indicated that rinse water is the waste stream generated in the greatest quantity and that significant waste reduction could be achieved by redirecting the effluent from one rinse to another" (p. 1).

[In pounds, except as noted]

Waste stream generated	Annual quantity generated	Annual waste management cost[1] ($)
Cleaning, desmut, and coating solutions	7,500	1,030
Cleaning, coating, and sealing solutions	8,500	2,890
Rinse water	24,800,000	5,780
Spent methyl ethyl ketone	1,700	1,300
Spent xylene	1,380	900
Spent toluene	1,850	1,240
Spent isopropyl alcohol	420	830

[Continued]

★ 576 ★

Waste Minimization Assessment – Coated Parts Manufacturing
[Continued]

Waste stream generated	Annual quantity generated	Annual waste management cost[1] ($)
Spent methyl isobutyl ketone	1,700	1,640
Spent lacquer thinner	840	640
Paint sludge	2,200	2,440
Evaporated methyl ethyl ketone	2,330	870
Evaporated ethyl alcohol	70	110
Evaporated 1,1,1-trichloroethane	170	130

Source: U.S. Environmental Protection Agency. Risk Reduction Engineering Laboratory. Research and Development. *Waste Minimization Assessment for a Manufacturer of Coated Parts.* Prepared by Harry W. Edwards, Michael F. Kostrzewa, and Gwen P. Looby. Environmental Research Brief. EPA/600/S-94/014. Cincinnati, OH: U.S. Environmental Protection Agency, Risk Reduction Engineering Laboratory, Research and Development, September 1994, p. 4. *Notes:* 1. Includes waste treatment, disposal, and handling costs and applicable raw material costs.

★ 577 ★

Waste Minimization

Waste Minimization Assessment – Electrical Rotating Device Manufacturing

"The U.S. Environmental Protection Agency (EPA) has funded a pilot project to assist small and medium-size manufacturers who want to minimize their generation of waste but who lack the expertise to do so. In an effort to assist these manufacturers, Waste Minimization Assessment Centers (WMACs) were established at selected universities and procedures were adapted from the EPA *Waste Minimization Opportunity Assessment Manual....* The WMAC team at the University of Tennessee performed an assessment at a plant that manufactures several varieties of electrical rotating devices.... The team's report, detailing findings and recommendations, indicated that spent solutions from the four-stage aqueous cleaner are the waste streams generated in the greatest quantity and that significant cost savings could be achieved by discontinuing the use of Freon™ vapor degreasing for precision parts cleaning" (p. 1).

[In pounds, except as noted]

Waste generated	Annual quantity generated	Annual waste management cost[1] ($)
Oil-based lubricant	45,190	3,350
Water-based lubricant	36,530	4,900
Metal scrap	40,000	(57,370)[2]
Aqueous cleaner and rinse water	1,195,200	5,250
Rust-inhibitor solution	250	220
Spent passivating solution	660	940
Passivating rinse water	102,960	920
Spent Stoddard solvent	920	1,400
Evaporated Stoddard solvent	2,830	0
Spent TF-Freon™	23,760	1,820
Evaporated TF-Freon™	39,510	103,520
Spent chromic acid solution	1,650	1,200
Anodizing rinse water	597,600	4,100
Plastic flashing	40	140
Evaporated cooling water	796,800	160
Paint waste	27,500	30,200
Evaporated solvent	2,180	1,440
Stripper waste	1,450	2,800
Waste solder	200	(250)[2]
Epoxy waste	18,000	20,180
Waste powder coating	4,400	3,200
Acetone-wetted rags	6,340	5,360

[Continued]

★ 577 ★

Waste Minimization Assessment – Electrical Rotating Device Manufacturing
[Continued]

Waste generated	Annual quantity generated	Annual waste management cost[1] ($)
Wastewater treatment sludge	24,750	21,890
Still bottoms	2,640	9,940

Source: U.S. Environmental Protection Agency. Risk Reduction Engineering Laboratory. Research and Development. *Waste Minimization Assessment for a Manufacturer of Electrical Rotating Devices.* Prepared by Richard J. Jendrucko, Thomas N. Coleman, and Gwen P. Looby. Environmental Research Brief. EPA/600/S-94/018. Cincinnati, OH: U.S. Environmental Protection Agency, Risk Reduction Engineering Laboratory, Research and Development, September 1994, p. 6. *Notes:* 1. Includes waste treatment, disposal, and handling costs and applicable raw material costs. 2. Net credit received.

★ 578 ★
Waste Minimization

Waste Minimization Assessment – Felt Tip Marker, Stamp Pad, and Rubber Cement Manufacturing

"The U.S. Environmental Protection Agency (EPA) has funded a pilot project to assist small and medium-size manufacturers who want to minimize their generation of waste but who lack the expertise to do so. In an effort to assist these manufacturers, Waste Minimization Assessment Centers (WMACs) were established at selected universities and procedures were adapted from the EPA *Waste Minimization Opportunity Assessment Manual*.... The WMAC at the University of Tennessee performed an assessment at a plant that manufactures felt tip markers, stamp pads, and rubber cement.... The team's report, detailing findings and recommendations, indicated that a large quantity of scrap plastic is generated by the injection molding of markers and stamp pad cases, and that significant cost savings could be achieved by segregating scrap plastic and reusing it in subsequent production runs" (p. 1).

[In pounds, except as noted]

Waste stream generated	Annual quantity generated	Annual waste management cost[1] ($)
Off-specification filler overwrap	4,730	500
Empty dye containers	3,600	500
Evaporated n-propyl alcohol	41,470	16,170
Excess plastic runners	16,600	1,980
Unusable filler pieces	2,020	1,000
Hydraulic oil filters	170	2,280
Contaminated ink filters	2,360	1,640
Hydraulic oil/detergent solution	3,400	10,530

[Continued]

★ 578 ★

Waste Minimization Assessment – Felt Tip Marker, Stamp Pad, and Rubber Cement Manufacturing
[Continued]

Waste stream generated	Annual quantity generated	Annual waste management cost[1] ($)
Synthetic oil	2,410	8,620
Off-specification markers[2]	56,250	90
Off-specification markers[3]	506,250	830
Scrap packaging material	560	500
Plastic scrap	5,500	660
Color-streaked marker components	165,140	19,690
Plastic pellets/hydraulic oil	8,830	1,640
Ink system wash solvent	210	0
Scrap self-inking stamp pads	21,830	55,540
Wash water[4]	11,950	5,700
n-propyl alcohol wash-out	1,530	2,010
Evaporated n-propyl alcohol	380	150
Unused inking mixture	1,100	5,540
Empty solvent containers	900	500
Scrap cellophane overwrap	790	420
Off-specification plastic cases	2,030	240
Off-specification felt stamp pads	10,160	500
Contaminated plastic floor covering	50	630
Resins and powder dyes	50	560
Wash water[5]	27,890	13,290
Waste felt inserts	3,750	500
Waste foam inserts	4,500	500
Rubber cement residue	380	500
Evaporated rubber solvent	15,600	0
Wastewater treatment sludge	NA	0[6]

Source: U.S. Environmental Protection Agency. Risk Reduction Engineering Laboratory. Research and Development. *Waste Minimization Assessment for a Manufacturer of Felt Tip Markers, Stamp Pads, and Rubber Cement*. Prepared by Richard J. Jendrucko, Todd M. Thomas, and Gwen P. Looby. Environmental Research Brief. EPA/600/S-94/013. Cincinnati, OH: U.S. Environmental Protection Agency, Risk Reduction Engineering Laboratory, Research and Development, September 1994, p. 5. *Notes:* "NA" stands for "not available." 1. Includes waste treatment, disposal, and handling costs and applicable raw material costs. 2. Felt tip marker production. Donated to charitable organizations. 3. Felt tip marker production. Shipped to municipal landfill. 4. Stamp pad production. Treated on-site; sewered. 5. Ink mixer in stamp pad production. Treated on-site; sewered. 6. Waste is accumulating on-site; no waste was shipped off-site during the past year.

★ 579 ★

Waste Minimization

Waste Minimization Assessment – Finished Metal and Plastic Part Manufacturing

"The U.S. Environmental Protection Agency (EPA) has funded a pilot project to assist small and medium-size manufacturers who want to minimize their generation of waste but who lack the expertise to do so. In an effort to assist these manufacturers, Waste Minimization Assessment Centers (WMACs) were established at selected universities and procedures were adapted from the EPA *Waste Minimization Opportunity Assessment Manual....* The WMAC team at Colorado State University performed an assessment at a plant that applies coatings to metal and plastic components supplied by its customers.... The team's report, detailing findings and recommendations, indicated that large quantities of spent rinse water and process solutions, and spent solvent and still bottoms are generated by the plant and that the life of the black dye bath could be extended to yield significant cost savings" (p. 1).

[In pounds, except as noted]

Waste generated	Annual quantity generated	Annual waste management cost[1] ($)
Spent process solutions	3,140,810	37,920
Spent black dye solution	21,660	13,640
Spent rinse water	17,840,700	5,600
Caustic sludge	7,330	2,100
Spent solvent and still bottoms	13,580	11,970
Paint sludge	1,440	1,640
Evaporated solvent	2,940	870
Aluminum oxide sludge	NA	NA

Source: U.S. Environmental Protection Agency. Risk Reduction Engineering Laboratory. Research and Development. *Waste Minimization Assessment for a Manufacturer of Finished Metal and Plastic Parts.* Prepared by Harry W. Edwards, Michael F. Kostrzewa, and Gwen P. Looby. Environmental Research Brief. EPA/600/S-94/005. Cincinnati, OH: U.S. Environmental Protection Agency, Risk Reduction Engineering Laboratory, Research and Development, September 1994, p. 4. *Notes:* "NA" stands for "not available." 1. Includes waste treatment, disposal, and handling costs and applicable raw material costs.

★ 580 ★
Waste Minimization

Waste Minimization Assessment – Gravure-Coated Metalized Paper and Metalized Film Manufacturing

"The U.S. Environmental Protection Agency (EPA) has funded a pilot project to assist small and medium-size manufacturers who want to minimize their generation of waste but who lack the expertise to do so. In an effort to assist these manufacturers, Waste Minimization Assessment Centers (WMACs) were established at selected universities and procedures were adapted from the EPA *Waste Minimization Opportunity Assessment Manual*.... The WMAC at the University of Tennessee performed an assessment for a plant that manufactures gravure-coated metalized paper and film.... The team's report, detailing findings and recommendations, indicated that a large quantity of solvent evaporates from the plant's processes and that a large quantity of unused coating mixture is wasted. The greatest cost savings can be achieved by the plant through the installation of an automated system for mixing and diluting coating mixtures" (p. 1).

[In pounds, except as noted]

Waste generated	Annual quantity generated	Annual waste management cost[1] ($)
Isopropanol spills and leaks	440	420
Organic solvent evaporation[2]	24,750	9,650
Water-based coating mixture spills and leaks	680	720
Off-specification water-based coating mixture	6,250	6,760
Waste paper	960,000	621,180[3]
Organic solvent evaporation[4]	1,740,000	940
Isopropanol evaporation[5]	489,000	260
Isopropanol evaporation[6]	489,000	0
Isopropanol evaporation[7]	3,560	1,070
Unused water-based coating mixture	5,360	5,790
Solvent-soaked cleaning rags	11,680	26,640
Spent isopropanol cleaning solvent	17,460	18,440
Scrap aluminum	45,000	64,030
Nitrogen gas	9,631,320	402,240
Polypropylene and polyester film scrap	150,000	289,210
Cardboard cores	98,280	840
Organic solvent evaporation[8]	15,180	6,550
Spent organic solvent	3,560	2,570
Recoverable solvent	12,900	1,500
Still bottoms	30,110	35,790
Dry coating residue	1,760	4,420

Source: U.S. Environmental Protection Agency. Risk Reduction Engineering Laboratory. Research and Development. *Waste Minimization Assessment for a Manufacturer of Gravure-Coated Metalized Paper and Metalized Film.* Prepared by Richard J. Jendrucko, Thomas N. Coleman, and Gwen P. Looby. Environmental Research Brief. EPA/600/S-94/008. Cincinnati, OH: U.S. Environmental Protection Agency, Risk Reduction Engineering Laboratory, Research and Development, September 1994, p. 3. *Notes:* 1. Includes waste treatment, disposal, and handling costs and applicable raw material costs. 2. Mixing and supply drums in pre-coating. 3. Net cost of waste stream. Includes cost of handling waste plus raw material cost less revenue received. 4. Drying during pre-coating. Ducted to on-site incinerator; vented. 5. Drying during top-coating. Ducted to on-site incinerator; vented. 6. Drying during top-coating. Evaporates to plant air. 7. Supply drums in pre-coating and top coating evaporates to plant air. 8. Cleaning of pre-coater and top-coater. Evaporates to plant air.

★ 581 ★
Waste Minimization

Waste Minimization Assessment – Microelectronic Component Manufacturing

"The U.S. Environmental Protection Agency (EPA) has funded a pilot project to assist small and medium-size manufacturers who want to minimize their generation of waste but who lack the expertise to do so. In an effort to assist these manufacturers, Waste Minimization Assessment Centers (WMACs) were established at selected universities and procedures were adapted from the EPA *Waste Minimization Opportunity Assessment Manual*.... The WMAC at Colorado State University performed an assessment at a plant that manufactures microelectric components.... The team's report, detailing findings and recommendations, indicated that the waste streams generated in the greatest quantities are rinse water and waste developer and that significant cost savings could be realized by installing flow meters and flow reducers in certain production areas" (p. 1).

[In pounds, except as noted]

Waste stream generated	Annual quantity generated	Annual waste management cost[1] ($)
Waste acetone[2]	740	720
Evaporated acetone[3]	100	80
Waste isopropanol	380	460
Evaporated isopropanol	330	260
Waste developer (aquenous sodium hydroxide)	2,180	1,360
Waste photoresist	0[4]	0[4]
Waste acetone[5]	370	420
Evaporated acetone[6]	470	370
Waste hydrogen peroxide	0[7]	0[7]
Tri-iodide stripper/gold	1,830	650
Rinse water	37,800,000	7,660

Source: U.S. Environmental Protection Agency. Risk Reduction Engineering Laboratory. Research and Development. *Waste Minimization Assessment for a Manufacturer of Microelectronic Components.* Prepared by Harry W. Edwards, Michael F. Kostrzewa, and Gwen P. Looby. Environmental Research Brief. EPA/600/S-94/015. Cincinnati, OH: U.S. Environmental Protection Agency, Risk Reduction Engineering Laboratory, Research and Development, September 1994, p. 3. *Notes:* 1. Includes waste treatment, disposal, and handling costs and applicable raw material costs. 2. Initial cleaning of thin-film substrate. Shipped off-site for incineration. 3. Initial cleaning of thin-film substrate. Evaporates to plant air. 4. No waste was shipped off-site during the previous year; waste is accumulating on-site. No estimate of the quantity of accumulated waste was available. 5. Stripping following photolithography. Shipped off-site for incineration 6. Stripping following photolithography. Evaporates to plant air. 7. No waste was shipped off-site during the previous year; waste is accumulating on-site. Fifty-five pounds of waste had accumulated at the time of the assessment.

★ 582 ★

Waste Minimization

Waste Minimization Assessment – Mountings for Electronic Circuit Components Manufacturing

"The U.S. Environmental Protection Agency (EPA) has funded a pilot project to assist small and medium-size manufacturers who want to minimize their generation of waste but who lack the expertise to do so. In an effort to assist these manufacturers, Waste Minimization Assessment Centers (WMACs) were established at selected universities and procedures were adapted from the EPA *Waste Minimization Opportunity Assessment Manual*.... The WMAC at the University of Tennessee performed an assessment at a plant that manufactures ceramic mountings for electronic circuit components.... The team's report, detailing findings and recommendations, indicated that the waste stream generated in the greatest quantity is wastewater from the plating lines and that significant cost savings could be achieved by purifying and reusing the effluent from the on-site wastewater treatment plant" (p. 1).

[In pounds, except as noted]

Waste stream generated	Annual quantity generated	Annual waste management cost[1] ($)
Solvent-soaked clean-up rags	11,690	37,010
Evaporated organic solvents[2]	19,610	37,080
Evaporated organic solvents[3]	500	190
Contaminated toluene	1,090	2,770
Evaporated organic solvents[4]	4,260	1,800
Evaporated organic solvents[5]	4,760	16,620
Jars containing dried tungsten paste	2,140	2,460
Evaporated citric cleaner	980	2,140
Contaminated 1,1,1-trichloroethane	2,410	8,420
Evaporated 1,1,1-trichloroethane	3,340	1,940
Cleaning rags	3,180	0
Waste adhesive/solvent	1,000	2,730
Rinse water	19,469,030	68,400
Spent acid solution	777,100	2,730
Spent plating solution	5,910	20
Evaporated Freon	33,740	97,040
Contaminated Freon	4,930	34,330
Alkaline solution	74,950	260
Spent gold solution	26,700	(152,740)[6]
Spent gold filters	110	140
Rinse water and photochemicals	374,950	1,320

[Continued]

★ 582 ★

Waste Minimization Assessment – Mountings for Electronic Circuit Components Manufacturing
[Continued]

Waste stream generated	Annual quantity generated	Annual waste management cost[1] ($)
Wastewater treatment sludge	35,610	18,010
Miscellaneous solid waste	8,790	6,050

Source: U.S. Environmental Protection Agency. Risk Reduction Engineering Laboratory. Research and Development. *Waste Minimization Assessment for a Manufacturer of Mountings for Electronic Circuit Components.* Prepared by Richard J. Jendrucko, Kelly L. Binkley, and Gwen P. Looby. Environmental Research Brief. EPA/600/S-94/012. Cincinnati, OH: U.S. Environmental Protection Agency, Risk Reduction Engineering Laboratory, Research and Development, September 1994, p. 5. *Notes:* 1. Includes waste treatment, disposal, and handling costs and applicable raw material costs. 2. Ceramic tape production. Ducted to incinerator. 3. Equipment cleaning. Evaporates to plant air. 4. Tungsten paste production. Evaporates to plant air. 5. Laminating. Evaporates to plant air. 6. Net credit received.

★ 583 ★
Waste Minimization

Waste Minimization Assessment – Paint and Lacquer Manufacturing

"The U.S. Environmental Protection Agency (EPA) has funded a pilot project to assist small and medium-size manufacturers who want to minimize their generation of waste but who lack the expertise to do so. In an effort to assist these manufacturers, Waste Minimization Assessment Centers (WMACs) were established at selected universities and procedures were adapted from the EPA *Waste Minimization Opportunity Assessment Manual*.... The WMAC at the University of Tennessee performed an assessment for a plant that manufactures lacquers and paints.... The team's report, detailing findings and recommendations, indicated that waste solvent is the waste stream generated in the greatest quantity and that significant cost savings could be achieved by implementing a computer-based system for batch scheduling, inventory, and waste documentation" (p. 1).

[In pounds, except as noted]

Waste generated	Annual quantity generated	Annual waste management cost[1] ($)
Spills and leaks	6,320	3,160
Evaporated solvents	25,300	12,130
Off-specification paint	2,200	4,215
Latex sludge	208,330	22,780
Solvent-based paint sludge	17,520	4,200
Reclaimed solvents	180,000	2,150

[Continued]

★ 583 ★

Waste Minimization Assessment – Paint and Lacquer Manufacturing
[Continued]

Waste generated	Annual quantity generated	Annual waste management cost[1] ($)
Raw material storage bags	49,000	430
Spent filter cartridges	18,000	320
Raw material drums	12,000	320

Source: U.S. Environmental Protection Agency. Risk Reduction Engineering Laboratory. Research and Development. *Waste Minimization Assessment for a Manufacturer of Paints and Lacquers.* Prepared by Richard J. Jendrucko, Rebecca A. Bachschmidt, and Gwen P. Looby. Environmental Research Brief. EPA/600/S-94/007. Cincinnati, OH: U.S. Environmental Protection Agency, Risk Reduction Engineering Laboratory, Research and Development, September 1994, p. 3. *Notes:* 1. Includes waste treatment, disposal, and handling costs and applicable raw material costs.

★ 584 ★
Waste Minimization

Waste Minimization Assessment – Plier and Wrench Manufacturing

"The U.S. Environmental Protection Agency (EPA) has funded a pilot project to assist small and medium-size manufacturers who want to minimize their generation of waste but who lack the expertise to do so. In an effort to assist these manufacturers, Waste Minimization Assessment Centers (WMACs) were established at selected universities and procedures were adapted from the EPA *Waste Minimization Opportunity Assessment Manual....* The WMAC team at Colorado State University performed an assessment at a plant that manufactures pliers and wrenches.... The team's report, detailing findings and recommendations, indicated that the greatest quantity of waste in this plant came from the machining and plating operations. The greatest cost-saving opportunity recommended to the plant involved the replacement of 1,1,1-trichloroethane vapor degreasing with nonhazardous aqueous cleaning" (p. 1).

[In pounds, except as noted]

Waste generated	Annual quantity generated	Annual waste management cost[1] ($)
Spent cutting fluid	1,053,410	88,540
Waste oil	103,970	5,630
Reusable cutting fluid	2,041,690	2,100
Spent 1,1,1-trichloroethane	520	900
Still bottoms	520	900
Evaporated		

[Continued]

★ 584 ★

Waste Minimization Assessment – Plier and Wrench Manufacturing
[Continued]

Waste generated	Annual quantity generated	Annual waste management cost[1] ($)
1,1,1-trichloroethane	44,360	21,370
Spent perchloroethylene (no longer in use)	13,000	3,440
Waste methyl ethyl ketone	3,730	6,460
Evaporated methyl ethyl ketone	700	450
Evaporated xylene	10,080	2,600
Waste primer	4,100	9,250
Paint filters and rags	59,480	60,170
Waste plastic coating	7,500	14,700
Spent plastic stripper	420	260
Spent rinse water	22,178,950	54,280
Metal hydroxide sludge	164,330	32,450
Waste metal stripper	75,230	31,540
Waste buffing compound	3,330	1,530
Miscellaneous waste	5,550	3,280

Source: U.S. Environmental Protection Agency. Risk Reduction Engineering Laboratory. Research and Development. *Waste Minimization Assessment for a Manufacturer of Pliers and Wrenches.* Prepared by Harry W. Edwards, Michael F. Kostrzewa, and Gwen P. Looby. Environmental Research Brief. EPA/600/S-94/004. Cincinnati, OH: U.S. Environmental Protection Agency, Risk Reduction Engineering Laboratory, Research and Development, September 1994, p. 5. *Notes:* 1. Includes waste treatment, disposal, and handling costs and applicable raw material costs.

★ 585 ★

Waste Minimization

Waste Minimization Assessment – Prewashed Jean Manufacturing

"The U.S. Environmental Protection Agency (EPA) has funded a pilot project to assist small and medium-size manufacturers who want to minimize their generation of waste but who lack the expertise to do so. In an effort to assist these manufacturers, Waste Minimization Assessment Centers (WMACs) were established at selected universities and procedures were adapted from the EPA *Waste Minimization Opportunity Assessment Manual*.... The WMAC team at the University of Tennessee performed an assessment at a plant that prewashes denim jeans prior to retail sale.... The assessment team's report, detailing findings and recommendations, indicated that the waste generated in the greatest quantity is wastewater from the washers and tumblers and that the greatest cost savings could be realized by installing an onsite wastewater treatment plant" (p. 1).

[In pounds, except as noted]

Waste stream generated	Annual quantity generated	Annual waste management cost[1] ($)
Wastewater from washers	533,869,230	210,170
Wastewater from tumblers	53,387,090	20,980
Evaporated water	39,425,000	13,110
Pumice and lint	1,137,500	105,440
Pumice grit	349,500	37,580
General plant waste	1,650,000	73,760

Source: U.S. Environmental Protection Agency. Risk Reduction Engineering Laboratory. Research and Development. *Waste Minimization Assessment for a Manufacturer of Prewashed Jeans.* Prepared by Richard J. Jendrucko, Thomas N. Coleman, and Gwen P. Looby. Environmental Research Brief. EPA/600/S-94/006. Cincinnati, OH: U.S. Environmental Protection Agency, Risk Reduction Engineering Laboratory, Research and Development, September 1994, p. 3. *Notes:* 1. Includes waste treatment, disposal, and handling costs and applicable raw material costs.

★ 586 ★

Waste Minimization

Waste Minimization Assessment – Screwdriver Manufacturing

"The U.S. Environmental Protection Agency (EPA) has funded a pilot project to assist small and medium-size manufacturers who want to minimize their generation of waste but who lack the expertise to do so. In an effort to assist these manufacturers, Waste Minimization Assessment Centers (WMACs) were established at selected universities and procedures were adapted from the EPA *Waste Minimization Opportunity Assessment Manual*.... The WMAC team at Colorado State University performed an assessment at a plant that manufactures screwdrivers—over 30 million/ year.... The team's report, detailing findings and recommendations, indicated that the waste stream generated in the greatest quantity is waste plastic and that significant cost savings could be realized by pelletizing the plastic scrap before its sale to a recycler" (p. 1).

[In pounds, except as noted]

Waste generated	Annual quantity generated	Annual waste management cost[1] ($)
Waste plastic[2]	500,640	545,800
Waste plastic[3]	24,960	39,990
Waste plastic/metal	10,960	17,590
Waste oil	19,100	10,130
Spent cleaner	21,660	490
Rinse water	21,660	490
Spent acetone	11,870	13,020
Evaporated acetone	90,850	29,980
Spent isobutyl acetate	1,300	2,250
Evaporated isobutyl acetate	32,920	18,730
Solvent-based paint	26,380	51,980
Evaporated solvent	19,270	6,360
Cooling water	5,392,240	12,900
Petroleum naphtha	8,850	4,550

Source: U.S. Environmental Protection Agency. Risk Reduction Engineering Laboratory. Research and Development. *Waste Minimization Assessment for a Manufacturer of Screwdrivers.* Prepared by Harry W. Edwards, Michael F. Kostrzewa, and Gwen P. Looby. Environmental Research Brief. EPA/600/S-94/003. Cincinnati, OH: U.S. Environmental Protection Agency, Risk Reduction Engineering Laboratory, Research and Development, September 1994, p. 4. *Notes:* 1. Includes waste treatment, disposal, and handling costs and applicable raw material costs. 2. Cutting and machining of extruded plastic. 3. Spilled from bales of waste plastic.

★ 587 ★
Waste Minimization

Waste Minimization Assessment – Surgical Implant Manufacturing

"The U.S. Environmental Protection Agency (EPA) has funded a pilot project to assist small and medium-size manufacturers who want to minimize their generation of waste but who lack the expertise to do so. In an effort to assist these manufacturers, Waste Minimization Assessment Centers (WMACs) were established at selected universities and procedures were adapted from the EPA *Waste Minimization Opportunity Assessment Manual*.... The WMAC at Colorado State University performed an assessment at a plant that manufactures surgical implants from stainless steel and titanium stock.... The team's report, detailing findings and recommendations, indicated that wastewater and waste cutting fluid are the wastes generated in the greatest quantities and that significant cost savings would result from implementing a formal cutting fluid management plan" (p. 1).

[In pounds, except as noted]

Waste generated	Annual quantity generated	Annual waste management cost[1] ($)
Oil-based cutting fluid	85,900	88,100
Scrap metal[2]	80,600	(16,000)[3]
Water-based cutting fluid	76,000	58,530
Scrap metal[4]	27,400	(5,500)[3]
Rinse water	995,000	1,920
Spent electropolishing solution	18,300	8,060
Spent passivating solution	3,720	140
Wastewater[5]	6,350,000	12,250
Wastewater[6]	2,870,000	5,530
Wastewater treatment sludge	16,900	0[7]

Source: U.S. Environmental Protection Agency. Risk Reduction Engineering Laboratory. Research and Development. *Waste Minimization Assessment for a Manufacturer of Surgical Implants*. Prepared by Harry W. Edwards, Michael F. Kostrezewa, and Gwen P. Looby. Environmental Research Brief. EPA/600/S-94/009. Cincinnati, OH: U.S. Environmental Protection Agency, Risk Reduction Engineering Laboratory, Research and Development, September 1994, p. 3. *Notes:* 1. Includes waste treatment, disposal, and handling costs and applicable raw material costs. 2. Machining of fasteners. Sold to recyclers. 3. Credit received. 4. Machining of plates. Shipped off-site for disposal; recycled or incinerated. 5. Vibratory polishing of fasteners and plates. Treated on-site; sewered. 6. Sparge ring around clarifier in on-site wastewater treatment plant. Treated on-site wastewater treatment plant. Treated on-site; sewered. 7. Plant pays a flat monthly rate for trash hauling.

★ 588 ★
Waste Minimization

Waste Minimization Assessment – Truck Engine Part Manufacturing

"The U.S. Environmental Protection Agency (EPA) has funded a pilot project to assist small and medium-size manufacturers who want to minimize their generation of waste but who lack the expertise to do so. In an effort to assist these manufacturers, Waste Minimization Assessment Centers (WMACs) were established at selected universities and procedures were adapted from the EPA *Waste Minimization Opportunity Assessment Manual*.... The WMAC team at the University of Tennessee performed an assessment at a plant that manufactures turbochargers, fan drives, and vibration dampers for truck engines.... The team's report, detailing findings and recommendations, indicated that the plant could achieve significant cost savings by replacing its solvent-based painting system with an electrostatic powder coating system, thereby reducing paint overspray" (p. 1).

[In pounds, except as noted]

Waste generated	Annual quantity generated	Annual waste management cost[1] ($)
Rejected metal castings	102,800	0
Metal chips	398,772	-15,450
Wastewater (contains coolant, alkaline cleaner, iron phosphate cleaner)	3,046,080	118,820
Evaporated perchloroethylene	12,580	4,780
Perchloroethylene still bottoms	740	1,380
Spent hydraulic oil	23,080	1,660
Metal grindings and spent grinding wheels	12,000	1,610
Steam-washer sludge	6,000	16,450
Spent powder abrasive	8,000	810
Evaporated "Genesolv"	13,400	22,520
"Genesolv" still bottoms	590	2,170
Unusable Teflon™ dust	880	2,180
Evaporated mineral spirits	1,470	560
Spent mineral spirits	4,400	5,130
Residual primer mixture	6,600	16,450
Residual adhesive	550	1,660
Evaporated toluene	13,725	0
Evaporated methyl ethyl ketone	1,100	0
Paint overspray	1,000	7,530
Paint containers	1,440	1,310
Paint filters	30	2,980
Evaporated thinner	7,130	0
Cardboard	24,000	1,390

[Continued]

★ 588 ★

Waste Minimization Assessment – Truck Engine Part Manufacturing

[Continued]

Waste generated	Annual quantity generated	Annual waste management cost[1] ($)
Filters	180	6,080
Waste oil	27,950	2,020

Source: U.S. Environmental Protection Agency. Risk Reduction Engineering Laboratory. Research and Development. *Waste Minimization Assessment for a Manufacturer of Parts for Truck Engines.* Prepared by Richard J. Jendrucko, Kelly Binkley, Todd Thomas, Stephanie Wilson, Eric W. Daley, and Gwen P. Looby. Environmental Research Brief. EPA/600/S-94/019. Cincinnati, OH: U.S. Environmental Protection Agency, Risk Reduction Engineering Laboratory, Research and Development, September 1994, p. 4. *Notes:* 1. Includes waste treatment, disposal and handling costs and applicable raw material costs.

Chapter 9
COSTS AND EXPENDITURES

Tables that primarily present data on expenditures, budgets, prices, and costs—and in some cases projections of these—are featured in this chapter. Coverage includes costs and expenditures associated with chemical companies, energy industry, environmental compliance, government, health risks and issues, mineral and metal industries, municipal and public service, natural disasters, pollution abatement and control, taxes, timber and logging products, and wildlife and habitat. In some cases, specifically health-related tables, data show costs in terms of lives lost or affected.

Related economic data of a punitive nature (fines, for example) will be found in the Politics, Opinion, Law chapter. Sales, revenue, and other financial data also are included in the Markets and Companies chapter.

Chemical Companies

★ 589 ★

Chemical Company Environmental Spending

Table shows costs, sales, and environmental spending as a percentage of sales for selected chemical companies.

[In million dollars, except as noted]

Company	Operating costs	Capital costs	Total costs	Sales (in billion dollars)	Spending as a percentage of sales
Hoechst	943.17	307.74	1,250.91	27.84	4.49
BASF	635.43	88.27	723.70	10.53	6.87
Bayer Group	81.62	285.97	367.59	24.79	1.48
ICI	120.12	120.12	240.23	12.66	1.90
Dow	400.00	157.00	557.00	18.06	3.08
Rhone-Poulenc	188.20	135.94	324.15	14.23	2.28

[Continued]

★ 589 ★

Chemical Company Environmental Spending
[Continued]

Company	Operating costs	Capital costs	Total costs	Sales (in billion dollars)	Spending as a percentage of sales
Du Pont	1,000.00	500.00	1,500.00	37.84	3.96
Ciba	201.07	512.49	713.56	15.33	4.65
Akzo (HSE)	NA	NA	266.62	8.89	3.00
Sandoz	236.95	85.30	322.25	10.22	3.15
Roche	204.45	162.48	366.94	9.69	3.79
HULS	210.52	35.19	245.71	6.14	4.00
DSM	80.75	53.83	134.58	4.33	3.11
Exxon	NA	NA	156.00	10.06	1.55
Monsanto	233.00	53.00	286.00	7.90	3.62
Union Carbide	149.00	51.00	200.00	4.64	4.31
Elf Atochem	NA	NA	389.65	8.00	4.87

Source: "Touchstone of an Industrial Revolution." Financial Times, 30 June 1994, p. II. Primary sources: Company reports. Note: "NA" stands for "not available or applicable."

★ 590 ★

Chemical Companies

Chemical Company Spending on Environmental Projects: 1992-1994

Table shows the capital spending of selected chemical companies for environmental projects.

[In percentages]

	1992	1993	1994
Air Products and Chemicals	5.0	4.0	NA
Allied Signal	9	11	9
Arco Chemical	16	26	21
Ashland Chemical	21	18	17
Betz Laboratories	4	4	4
Dow Chemical	13	14	15
Dow Corning	4	7	5
Du Pont	11	21	22
Elf Atochem North America	16	34	25
Englehard	7	7	7
Ethyl	12	8	NA
FMC Corp.	33	26	23
H.B. Fuller	15	15	NA
W.R. Grace	7	9	10
Great Lakes Chemical	40	30	30
Hercules	10	NA	NA
Hoechst Celanese	30	30	30

[Continued]

★ 590 ★

Chemical Company Spending on Environmental Projects: 1992-1994

[Continued]

	1992	1993	1994
Lubrizol	10	15	NA
Lyondell Petrochemical	60	50	NA
Monsanto	15	15	15
Morton International	10	10	10
Nalco Chemical	19	19	13
OxyChem	27	40	NA
Olin	18	NA	NA
PPG Industries	14	17	20
Quantum Chemical	10	14	NA
Union Carbide	15	15	NA
Uniroyal Chemical	15	20	20
Vista Chemical	64	16	NA
Average increase	18	18	16

Source: "Capital Spending Going Toward Environmental Projects." *ChemicalWeek,* 3 February 1993, p. 42. Primary source: Responses to *ChemicalWeek* survey. *Note:* "NA" stands for "not available."

Energy

★ 591 ★

Electric Utility Prices, by End-Use Sector: 1970-1993

Table shows the average price of electricity sold. Prior to 1980, covers Class A and B privately owned electric utilities; thereafter, Class A utilities whose electric operating revenues were $100 million or more during the previous year.

[In cents per kilowatt hour]

Year	Current dollars				Constant (1987) dollars[2]			
	Total[1]	Resi-dential	Com-mercial	Indus-trial	Total[1]	Resi-dential	Com-mercial	Indus-trial
1970	1.7	2.2	2.1	1.0	4.8	6.3	6.0	2.8
1971	1.8	2.3	2.2	1.1	4.9	6.2	5.9	3.0
1972	1.9	2.4	2.3	1.2	4.9	6.2	5.9	3.1
1973	2.0	2.5	2.4	1.3	4.8	6.1	5.8	3.1
1974	2.5	3.1	3.0	1.7	5.6	6.9	6.7	3.8
1975	2.9	3.5	3.5	2.1	5.9	7.1	7.1	4.3
1976	3.1	3.7	3.7	2.2	5.9	7.1	7.1	4.2
1977	3.4	4.1	4.1	2.5	6.1	7.3	7.3	4.5
1978	3.7	4.3	4.4	2.8	6.1	7.1	7.3	4.6
1979	4.0	4.6	4.7	3.1	6.1	7.0	7.2	4.7
1980	4.7	5.4	5.5	3.7	6.6	7.5	7.7	5.2

[Continued]

★ 591 ★

Electric Utility Prices, by End-Use Sector: 1970-1993
[Continued]

Year	Current dollars				Constant (1987) dollars[2]			
	Total[1]	Resi-dential	Com-mercial	Indus-trial	Total[1]	Resi-dential	Com-mercial	Indus-trial
1981	5.5	6.2	6.3	4.3	7.0	7.9	8.0	5.4
1982	6.1	6.9	6.9	5.0	7.3	8.2	8.2	6.0
1983	6.3	7.2	7.0	5.0	7.2	8.3	8.0	5.7
1984	6.3	7.2	7.1	4.8	6.9	7.9	7.8	5.3
1985	6.4	7.4	7.3	5.0	6.8	7.8	7.7	5.3
1986	6.4	7.4	7.2	4.9	6.6	7.6	7.4	5.1
1987	6.4	7.5	7.1	4.8	6.4	7.4	7.1	4.8
1988	6.4	7.5	7.0	4.7	6.2	7.2	6.7	4.5
1989	6.5	7.6	7.2	4.7	6.0	7.0	6.6	4.3
1990	6.6	7.8	7.3	4.7	5.8	6.9	6.4	4.1
1991	6.7	8.0	7.5	4.8	5.7	6.8	6.4	4.1
1992	6.8	8.2	7.7	4.8	5.6	6.8	6.4	4.0
1993[3]	6.9	8.3	7.7	4.9	5.6	6.7	6.2	3.9

Source: *1994 Statistical Abstract of the United States on CD-ROM* [machine-readable datafiles]. CD-8A-94. Washington, DC: U.S. Department of Commerce, Economics and Statistics Administration, Bureau of the Census, Data User Services Division, January 1995. Primary source: U.S. Energy Information Administration. *Annual Energy Review. Notes:* 1. Includes other sectors not shown separately. 2. Based on the gross national product implicit price deflator. 3. Preliminary.

★ 592 ★

Energy

Energy Expenditures, by Sector: 1970-1992

Table reflects estimated energy expenditures for various sectors. According to the source, "there are no direct fuel costs for hydroelectric, geothermal, centralized solar, or wind energy. Wood and other biomass fuels are not included, except those consumed at electric utilities" (p. 419).

[In dollars per million Btu]

Year	Residential	Commercial	Industry	Transportation	Electric utility
1970	2.12	1.97	0.83	2.31	0.32
1973	2.73	2.60	1.08	2.59	0.49
1974	3.40	3.45	1.77	3.72	1.03
1975	3.83	4.09	2.20	4.02	0.96
1976	4.17	4.46	2.39	4.21	1.03
1977	4.82	5.21	2.75	4.49	1.19
1978	5.19	5.65	2.98	4.62	1.29
1979	6.01	6.24	3.58	6.21	1.48
1980	7.55	7.88	4.71	8.61	1.75
1981	8.93	9.55	5.58	9.84	2.00
1982	9.92	10.44	6.14	9.43	2.01
1983	10.85	11.05	6.30	8.44	1.98
1984	10.86	11.29	6.21	8.24	1.97

[Continued]

★ 592 ★

Energy Expenditures, by Sector: 1970-1992
[Continued]

Year	Residential	Commercial	Industry	Transportation	Electric utility
1985	11.14	11.71	6.09	8.26	1.85
1986	10.99	11.35	5.40	6.22	1.55
1987	10.95	11.06	5.19	6.57	1.51
1988	10.90	10.91	5.03	6.56	1.45
1989	11.26	11.40	5.11	7.16	1.48
1990	12.14	12.03	4.21	8.26	1.46
1991	12.35	12.21	4.41	7.75	1.37
1992	12.27	12.32	4.34	7.72	1.21

Source: Executive Office of the President of the United States. *Environmental Quality 24: The Twenty-fourth Annual Report of the Council on Environmental Quality.* Prepared by Ray Clark. Written by Carroll Curtis. Edited by Barry Walsh. Washington, DC: U.S. Government Printing Office, 1994, p. 419. Primary source: U.S. Department of Energy. Energy Information Administration. *State Energy Price and Expenditure Report, 1992.* DOE/EIA-0376(92). Washington, DC: U.S. Department of Energy, Energy Information Administration, 1994, p. 23. *Notes:* "Btu" represents British thermal units. Data for 1971 and 1972 are not available.

★ 593 ★

Energy

Energy Expenditures, by Source and Sector: 1970-1991

End-use sector and electric utilities exclude expenditures and prices on energy sources such as hydropower, solar, wind, and geothermal. Also excludes expenditures for reported amounts of energy consumed by the energy industry for production, transportation, and processing operations.

[In million dollars]

Source and sector	1970	1975	1980	1985	1990	1991
Total[1]	82,579	171,782	373,900	435,444	469,468	467,132
Natural gas	10,892	20,061	51,062	72,938	64,104	64,701
Petroleum products[2]	48,088	103,859	238,408	223,197	234,510	222,017
Motor gasoline	31,596	59,446	124,408	118,044	126,471	123,051
Coal	4,593	13,048	22,648	29,719	28,381	27,869
Electricity sales	23,351	50,680	98,098	149,242	176,742	184,822
Residential sector	20,083	36,844	68,825	98,307	109,265	114,740
Commercial sector	10,668	22,835	46,881	70,263	78,922	81,488
Industrial sector	16,458	41,169	94,520	105,723	100,951	99,701
Transportation sector[2]	35,370	70,934	163,674	161,150	180,330	171,203
Motor gasoline	30,525	57,992	121,809	115,201	123,775	120,555
Electric utilities	4,316	16,396	37,435	42,558	38,443	36,501

Source: 1994 Statistical Abstract of the United States on CD-ROM [machine-readable datafiles]. CD-8A-94. Washington, DC: U.S. Department of Commerce, Economics and Statistics Administration, Bureau of the Census, Data User Services Division, January 1995. Primary source: U.S. Energy Information Administration. *State Energy Price and Expenditure Report* (annual). *Notes:* 1. Includes electricity sales and sources or fuel types, not shown separately; excludes electricity generation. 2. Includes sources or fuel types, not shown separately.

★ 594 ★

Energy

Energy Expenditures, by State: 1991

Table shows energy expenditures by end-use sectors and by selected sources. End-use sector and electric utilities exclude expenditures on energy sources such as hydropower, solar, wind, and geothermal. Also excludes expenditures for reported amounts of energy consumed by the energy industry for production, transportation, and processing operations.

[In million dollars, except as indicated]

Region, division, and state	Total[1]	Per capita[2] (dollars)	Percent change, 1990-1991	Sector				Source				
				Residential	Commercial	Industrial	Transportation	Petroleum products Total	Gasoline	Natural gas	Coal	Electricity sales
United States	467,132	1,853	-0.5	114,740	81,488	99,701[3]	171,203	222,016	123,051	64,700	27,869	184,822
Northeast	90,251	1,771	1.3	26,855	20,208	14,402	28,786	41,168	22,348	12,837	3,182	37,703
New England	24,093	1,826	1.3	7,477	5,130	3,395	8,092	12,431	6,665	2,625	343	9,714
Maine	2,538	2,057	-0.1	708	379	504	947	1,538	715	27	25	979
New Hampshire	1,906	1,727	-3.0	597	301	318	691	1,045	609	87	25	979
Vermont	1,094	1,930	3.9	353	188	156	397	658	337	32	1	406
Massachusetts	10,598	1,767	0.8	3,264	2,498	1,301	3,535	5,284	2,864	1,471	205	4,271
Rhode Island	1,756	1,747	9.3	531	358	310	558	781	460	331	0	650
Connecticut	6,201	1,885	1.5	2,024	1,405	806	1,965	3,126	1,681	678	50	2,608
Middle Atlantic	66,159	1,752	1.3	19,378	15,079	11,007	20,695	28,737	15,683	10,212	2,839	27,988
New York	28,006	1,551	2.1	8,786	7,825	3,296	8,098	11,822	6,644	4,630	567	12,665
New Jersey	15,874	2,047	-0.0	4,115	3,558	2,562	5,639	7,671	3,728	2,296	109	6,088
Pennsylvania	22,279	1,863	1.2	6,478	3,695	5,149	6,957	9,244	5,311	3,286	2,163	9,235
Midwest	112,712	1,871	-0.3	28,861	18,298	26,502	39,051	49,448	29,707	19,328	9,598	42,353
East North Central	79,414	1,872	-0.6	20,660	13,157	19,556	26,041	32,897	19,962	14,679	7,159	30,549
Ohio	21,089	1,928	1.0	5,421	3,559	5,285	6,823	8,421	5,326	3,509	2,110	8,827
Indiana	11,920	2,125	-1.6	2,645	1,423	3,530	4,322	5,387	2,770	1,903	1,958	4,063
Illinois	21,500	1,863	-3.4	6,018	4,140	4,880	6,463	8,155	5,005	4,308	1,286	8,857
Michigan	16,754	1,786	1.1	4,340	2,789	4,201	5,425	7,034	4,456	3,538	1,232	6,042
Wisconsin	8,152	1,645	1.4	2,237	1,247	1,660	3,008	3,900	2,406	1,421	574	2,761
West North Central	33,298	1,869	0.2	8,201	5,140	6,946	13,011	16,551	9,745	4,648	2,439	11,805
Minnesota	7,597	1,714	1.9	1,869	949	1,741	3,039	3,832	2,398	1,111	390	2,639
Iowa	5,212	1,865	1.7	1,356	750	1,161	1,946	2,476	1,553	833	398	1,829
Missouri	9,393	1,821	0.1	2,539	1,634	1,509	3,711	4,562	2,786	1,157	718	3,654
North Dakota	1,589	2,502	1.1	303	202	505	579	831	415	110	442	416
South Dakota	1,270	1,804	-5.2	314	170	216	569	744	427	109	44	409
Nebraska	3,093	1,942	-0.4	681	562	556	1,295	1,634	882	438	118	1,019
Kansas	5,143	2,061	-2.3	1,139	875	1,258	1,872	2,473	1,284	890	330	1,839
South	173,973	2,002	-1.3	39,590	25,633	43,323	65,428	87,420	45,942	20,020	12,315	69,652
South Atlantic	77,618	1,748	-1.2	20,804	13,594	13,415	29,806	36,834	22,822	6,073	6,073	35,361
Delaware	1,388	2,040	-2.1	369	218	286	514	750	389	146	99	568
Maryland	8,049	1,657	2.3	2,310	1,093	1,658	2,988	3,809	2,433	822	445	3,483
District of Columbia	1,130	1,899	4.5	222	470	170	267	308	214	189	3	638
Virginia	11,038	1,758	-1.9	2,921	2,042	1,508	4,567	5,501	3,340	818	558	4,558
West Virginia	3,751	2,081	-3.4	742	457	1,271	1,282	2,012	1,007	455	1,209	1,133
North Carolina	12,601	1,871	0.6	3,391	1,988	2,579	4,643	5,849	3,735	676	926	5,973
South Carolina	6,840	1,921	-0.4	1,641	927	1,752	2,520	3,057	1,912	493	478	3,212
Georgia	12,479	1,884	-2.7	3,063	2,133	2,457	4,826	5,605	3,494	1,471	1,161	5,317
Florida	20,343	1,533	-2.6	6,145	4,267	1,732	8,200	9,943	6,297	1,004	1,195	10,479
East South Central	29,644	1,931	-1.8	6,423	3,570	7,862	11,789	14,212	8,366	2,886	3,175	12,139
Kentucky	7,188	1,936	-1.1	1,474	852	1,924	2,938	3,592	2,054	659	998	2,800
Tennessee	9,274	1,872	-3.9	2,024	1,074	2,548	3,628	4,271	2,655	830	725	4,041
Alabama	8,301	2,029	-0.4	1,858	1,001	2,309	3,133	3,832	2,260	872	1,292	3,357
Mississippi	4,881	1,882	-0.9	1,068	642	1,081	2,090	2,517	1,396	524	159	1,941
West South Central	66,711	2,457	-1.1	12,362	8,469	22,046	23,833	36,374	14,754	11,062	3,067	22,152
Arkansas	4,687	1,975	-0.2	1,169	621	1,032	1,866	2,223	1,342	636	347	1,860
Louisiana	13,168	3,095	-2.8	1,950	1,318	5,410	4,490	7,595	2,149	2,209	354	3,755
Oklahoma	5,996	1,888	-3.2	1,442	945	1,089	2,520	2,944	1,778	1,263	384	2,267
Texas	42,861	2,471	-0.4	7,802	5,586	14,515	14,958	23,613	9,485	6,954	1,981	14,271
West	90,154	1,668	-0.9	19,434	17,349	15,433	37,938	43,981	25,053	12,515	2,774	35,114
Mountain	25,204	1,796	1.4	5,476	4,728	4,628	10,372	12,604	7,347	2,957	2,408	9,594
Montana	1,695	2,096	1.4	322	232	419	723	972	493	169	127	546
Idaho	1,910	1,837	5.4	392	298	470	750	1,019	556	174	23	694
Wyoming	1,493	3,245	-1.8	194	184	539	575	777	318	180	388	488
Colorado	5,415	1,603	3.9	1,215	1,173	739	2,289	2,693	1,730	854	355	1,858
New Mexico	2,985	1,927	0.8	545	578	569	1,292	1,694	915	353	322	987
Arizona	6,432	1,716	-1.4	1,694	1,448	837	2,454	2,739	1,827	469	498	3,249
Utah	2,868	1,621	4.7	621	438	596	1,214	1,420	795	513	441	857
Nevada	2,405	1,875	-0.5	493	378	459	1,075	1,289	712	245	254	914

[Continued]

★ 594 ★

Energy Expenditures, by State: 1991
[Continued]

Region, division, and state	Total[1]	Per capita[2] (dollars)	Percent change, 1990-1991	Sector				Source				
				Residential	Commercial	Industrial	Transportation	Petroleum products		Natural gas	Coal	Electricity sales
								Total	Gasoline			
Pacific	64,950	1,623	-1.8	13,958	12,620	10,805	27,566	31,376	17,706	9,559	366	25,521
Washington	8,591	1,714	0.8	1,680	1,122	1,433	4,356	4,914	2,604	590	147	3,069
Oregon	5,008	1,714	0.6	1,014	756	904	2,334	2,693	1,542	472	39	1,855
California	47,460	1,562	-1.9	10,643	10,114	7,941	18,762	21,023	12,830	8,243	127	19,413
Alaska	1,852	3,249	-12.8	349	329	185	988	1,247	241	212	51	415
Hawaii	2,039	1,793	-4.8	273	298	341	1,127	1,499	490	41	2	769

Source: 1994 Statistical Abstract of the United States on CD-ROM [machine-readable datafiles]. CD-8A-94. Washington, DC: U.S. Department of Commerce, Economics and Statistics Administration, Bureau of the Census, Data User Services Division, January 1995. Primary source: U.S. Energy Information Administration. *State Energy Price and Expenditure Report* (annual). *Notes:* 1. Includes sources not shown separately. Total expenditures are the sum of purchases for each source (including electricity sales) less electric utility purchases of fuel. 2. Based on estimated population as of July 1. 3. Includes net imports of coal coke not shown separately by state.

★ 595 ★

Energy

Fossil Fuel Prices: 1960-1992

Table shows fossil fuel prices in current and constant (1987) dollars. All fuel prices taken as close to the point of production as possible.

[In cents per million Btu, except as indicated]

Fuel	1960	1965	1970	1975	1980	1985	1990	1991	1992
Current dollars									
Composite[1]	28.3	27.7	31.7	82.1	204.2	251.2	184.3	167.0	170.1
Crude oil	49.7	49.3	54.8	132.2	372.2	415.3	345.3	285.2	275.5
Natural gas	12.6	14.5	15.4	40.2	144.8	225.7	154.6	148.0	167.9
Bituminous coal[2]	18.8	17.9	26.2	83.9	109.4	114.8	99.5	98.9	97.7
Anthracite coal	33.8	36.3	48.8	149.5	185.9	204.2	174.5	161.0	175.2
Constant (1987) dollars									
Composite[1]	108.8	97.5	90.1	166.9	284.8	266.1	162.8	141.8	140.7
Crude oil	191.2	173.6	155.7	268.7	519.1	439.9	305.0	242.1	227.9
Natural gas	48.5	51.1	43.8	81.7	202.0	239.1	136.6	125.6	138.9
Bituminous coal[2]	72.3	63.0	74.4	170.5	152.6	121.6	88.1	84.0	80.8
Anthracite coal	130.0	127.8	138.6	303.9	259.3	216.3	154.2	136.7	144.9
GDP implicit price deflator (1987=100)[3]	26.0	28.4	35.2	49.2	71.7	94.4	113.2	117.8	120.9

Source: 1994 Statistical Abstract of the United States on CD-ROM [machine-readable datafiles]. CD-8A-94. Washington, DC: U.S. Department of Commerce, Economics and Statistics Administration, Bureau of the Census, Data User Services Division, January 1995. Primary source: U.S. Department of Energy. *Annual Energy Review. Notes:* "Btu" represents British thermal units. 1. Weighted by relative importance of individual fuels in total fuels production. 2. Includes lignite. 3. "GDP" stands for gross domestic product.

★ 596 ★

Energy

Fuel Prices, by Source and Sector: 1970-1991

Table shows average fuel prices. End-use sector and electric utilities exclude expenditures and prices on energy sources such as hydropower, solar, wind, and geothermal. Also excludes expenditures for reported amounts of energy consumed by the energy industry for production, transportation, and processing operations.

[In dollars per million Btu]

Sector	1970	1975	1980	1985	1990	1991
All sectors	1.65	3.33	6.91	8.42	8.37	8.33
Residential sector	2.12	3.83	7.55	11.14	12.14	12.34
Commercial sector	1.97	4.09	7.88	11.71	12.03	12.21
Industrial sector	0.83	2.20	4.71	6.09	5.40	5.34
Transportation sector	2.31	4.02	8.61	8.26	8.26	7.97
Electric utilities	0.32	0.96	1.75	1.85	1.46	1.37

Source: 1994 Statistical Abstract of the United States on CD-ROM [machine-readable datafiles]. CD-8A-94. Washington, DC: U.S. Department of Commerce, Economics and Statistics Administration, Bureau of the Census, Data User Services Division, January 1995. Primary source: U.S. Energy Information Administration. *State Energy Price and Expenditure Report* (annual). *Note:* Btu stands for British thermal units.

★ 597 ★

Energy

Petroleum Product Prices, by Country: 1993

Tables shows prices of selected petroleum products in various countries. As of January 1. Includes taxes.

[In U.S. dollars per gallon, except as noted]

Country	Automotive fuels		Residential			Industrial (U.S. dollars per barrel)	
	Premium gasoline	Diesel fuel	Light fuel oil	Kerosene	Liquified petroleum gases	Light fuel oil	Heavy fuel oil
Argentina	2.60	(NA)	0.92	0.92	(NA)	(NA)	(NA)
Australia[1]	1.83	1.72	(NA)	(NA)	(NA)	(NA)	(NA)
Austria	3.23	2.67	1.47	(NA)	1.82	44.76	45.08
Belgium[1]	3.32	2.34	0.91	(NA)	(NA)	32.04	16.53
Bolivia	2.49	1.42	0.83	0.88	(NA)	(NA)	(NA)
Brazil	2.01	1.27	(NA)	1.15	0.46	12.79	6.95
Burma	2.19	1.44	1.17	1.85	1.17	60.49	48.96
Canada[1]	1.85	1.55	1.12	(NA)	(NA)	26.34	15.72
Chile	1.59	1.26	(NA)	1.01	(NA)	(NA)	22.46
Denmark[1]	3.38	1.92	2.49	(NA)	(NA)	39.96	18.16
Dominican Republic	1.92	1.10	1.10	1.44	0.65	46.04	24.53
Ecuador	1.29[2]	0.78	0.37	0.03	(NA)	32.77	15.54
El Salvador	1.70	0.89	(NA)	0.87	0.62	40.16	17.67
Ethiopia	1.40[2]	1.07	(NA)	0.73	0.82	(NA)	17.57

[Continued]

★ 597 ★

Petroleum Product Prices, by Country: 1993
[Continued]

Country	Automotive fuels		Residential			Industrial (U.S. dollars per barrel)	
	Premium gasoline	Diesel fuel	Light fuel oil	Kerosene	Liquified petroleum gases	Light fuel oil	Heavy fuel oil
Finland[1]	3.28	2.26	1.17	(NA)	(NA)	40.18	20.31
France[1]	3.41	2.05	1.44	(NA)	(NA)	42.85	16.29
Germany[1]	3.25	2.20	1.09	(NA)	(NA)	39.75	18.34
Ghana	0.64	0.63	(NA)	0.63	(NA)	(NA)	15.23
Greece[1]	3.27	1.97	1.71	(NA)	(NA)	97.76	20.19
India	2.34	0.80	(NA)	0.33	0.41	26.25	21.14
Indonesia	1.01	0.55	0.40	0.55	(NA)	21.85	21.85
Ireland[1]	3.55	2.70	1.52	(NA)	(NA)	44.48	22.06
Israel	0.68	0.70	(NA)	0.69	(NA)	(NA)	16.29
Italy[1]	3.77	2.52	2.98	(NA)	(NA)	105.19	23.06
Jamaica	1.22	1.12	(NA)	0.94	(NA)	44.11	17.22
Japan	4.55	2.45	2.45	1.62	7.77	78.48	33.47
Luxembourg[1]	2.48	1.85	0.97	(NA)	(NA)	36.42	17.68
Mexico[1]	1.51[2]	0.89	(NA)	(NA)	(NA)	35.14	11.97
Morocco	2.91[2]	1.73	0.88	(NA)	(NA)	32.77	32.35
Netherlands[1]	3.86	2.28	1.43	(NA)	(NA)	(NA)	25.08
Norway[1]	4.34	1.52	1.65	(NA)	(NA)	56.67	52.55
Pakistan	1.25	0.65	0.52	0.77	(NA)	21.85	27.31
Panama	1.57	1.08	(NA)	1.06	4.37	47.89	26.68
Paraguay	1.80	1.14	1.01	0.98	(NA)	47.89	26.05
Peru	2.28	1.27	(NA)	1.09	(NA)	45.79	29.41
Philippines	1.37	0.94	0.94	0.94	(NA)	39.49	16.38
Portugal[1]	3.54	2.48	2.60	(NA)	(NA)	104.07	26.18
Saudi Arabia	(NA)	(NA)	(NA)	(NA)	(NA)	(NA)	(NA)
South Africa	0.67	0.69	(NA)	0.68	(NA)	(NA)	15.71
Spain[1]	3.21	2.24	1.54	(NA)	(NA)	56.20	18.35
Sweden[1]	4.20	2.05	2.03	(NA)	(NA)	35.43	27.29
Switzerland[1]	2.52[2]	2.65	0.83	(NA)	(NA)	31.98	18.85
Taiwan[1]	2.57	1.82	(NA)	(NA)	(NA)	37.24	21.88
Tunisia	2.11	1.24	1.18	0.72	0.63	9.62	(NA)
Turkey[1]	2.60	1.89	2.01	(NA)	(NA)	(NA)	24.56
United Kingdom[1]	2.77	2.36	0.80	(NA)	(NA)	(NA)	15.29
United States[1]	1.31	0.98	0.94	0.82	0.75	26.34	14.83
Uruguay	2.72	1.29	1.32	1.32	(NA)	(NA)	27.52
Venezuela	0.29	0.22	(NA)	0.14	(NA)	(NA)	7.04

Source: 1994 Statistical Abstract of the United States on CD-ROM [machine-readable datafiles]. CD-8A-94. Washington, DC: U.S. Department of Commerce, Economics and Statistics Administration, Bureau of the Census, Data User Services Division, January 1995. Primary source: Energy Information Administration. *International Energy Annual. Notes:* "NA" represents "not available." 1. Average for January. 2. Unleaded regular gasoline.

★ 598 ★

Energy

Residential Energy Expenditures, by Region: 1980-1990

For period April to March for 1980-1985; January to December for 1987 and 1990. Excludes Alaska and Hawaii in 1980. Covers occupied units only. Excludes household usage of gasoline for transportation and the use of wood or coal. Based on Residential Energy Consumption Survey.

[In billion dollars, except as noted]

Fuel	1980	1981	1982	1983	1985	1987	1990				
							Total	Northeast	Midwest	South	West
Total	63.2	74.8	85.0	87.8	97.0	97.7	110.2	28.3	26.9	37.2	17.9
Average per household (dollars)	815	917	1,022	1,048	1,123	1,080	1,172	1,471	1,166	1,151	920
Natural gas	17.8	19.3	24.5	27.1	29.8	26.1	27.3	7.3	9.2	5.9	4.8
Electricity	32.6	40.1	45.9	48.4	54.5	61.6	71.5	14.6	15.4	29.1	12.5
Fuel oil, kerosene	10.7	12.5	11.8	9.6	9.6	7.2	8.3	6.1	1.0	1.0	0.2
Liquid petroleum gas	2.1	2.9	2.7	2.7	3.1	2.8	3.1	0.3	1.3	1.2	0.4

Source: *1994 Statistical Abstract of the United States on CD-ROM* [machine-readable datafiles]. CD-8A-94. Washington, DC: U.S. Department of Commerce, Economics and Statistics Administration, Bureau of the Census, Data User Services Division, January 1995. Primary sources: U.S. Energy Information Administration. *Household Energy Consumption and Expenditures, 1990;* and prior reports.

★ 599 ★

Energy

Residential Energy Expenditures, by Type of Fuel and Selected Household Characteristics: 1990

For period January through December 1990. Covers occupied units only. Excludes household usage of gasoline for transportation and the use of wood or coal. Based on Residential Energy Consumption Survey.

[In billion dollars, except as noted]

Characteristic	Total[1]	Average per house-hold[1] (dollars)	Natural gas	Elec-tricity	Fuel oil[2]
Total households	110.2	1,172	27.3	71.5	8.3
Single family detached	78.2	1,340	18.8	51.0	5.9
Single family attached	6.8	1,129	1.7	4.6	0.5
2- to 4-unit building	10.2	1,015	3.8	5.3	0.9
5- or more unit building	9.8	677	2.2	7.1	0.5
Mobile home	5.3	1,011	0.8	3.5	0.4
Year house built:					
1939 or earlier	26.1	1,216	9.0	13.0	3.3
1940 to 1949	7.9	1,130	2.5	4.5	0.6
1950 to 1959	16.8	1,254	4.6	10.2	1.7
1960 to 1969	17.1	1,155	4.4	11.4	1.0

[Continued]

★ 599 ★

Residential Energy Expenditures, by Type of Fuel and Selected Household Characteristics: 1990

[Continued]

Characteristic	Total[1]	Average per house- hold[1] (dollars)	Natural gas	Elec- tricity	Fuel oil[2]
1970 to 1979	24.5	1,143	4.2	18.3	1.3
1980 to 1984	9.0	1,120	1.2	7.4	0.1
1985 to 1990	8.8	1,117	1.4	6.8	(B)
Heating and cooling degree day zones:[3]					
Less than 2,000 CDD and –					
More than 7,000 HDD	11.5	1,132	2.7	6.3	1.6
5,500 to 7,000 HDD	33.4	1,251	10.8	18.4	3.5
4,000 to 5,499 HDD	25.6	1,222	6.6	15.6	2.7
Less than 4,000 HDD	19.4	1,008	4.2	14.3	0.3
More than 2,000 CDD and less than					
4,000 HDD	20.4	1,197	3.0	16.9	(B)
1990 family income:					
Less than $10,000	14.1	888	4.0	8.2	1.2
$10,000 to $19,999	19.4	978	5.0	12.3	1.4
$20,000 to $34,999	27.1	1,115	6.4	17.9	2.1
$35,000 to $49,999	21.7	1,296	5.1	14.6	1.5
$50,000 or more	27.9	1,618	6.8	18.6	2.2

Source: *1994 Statistical Abstract of the United States on CD-ROM* [machine-readable datafiles]. CD-8A-94. Washington, DC: U.S. Department of Commerce, Economics and Statistics Administration, Bureau of the Census, Data User Services Division, January 1995. Primary source: U.S. Energy Information Administration. *Household Energy Consumption and Expenditures* (1990). *Notes:* "B" indicates base figure too small to meet statistical standards for reliability of derived figure. 1. Includes liquid petroleum gas, not shown separately. 2. Includes kerosene. 3. "CDD" stands for "cooling degree day"; "HDD" stands for "heating degree day."

★ 600 ★

Energy

Residential Energy Prices, by Region: 1980-1990

Table shows average prices for period April to March for 1980-1985; January to December for 1987 and 1990. Excludes Alaska and Hawaii in 1980. Covers occupied units only. Excludes household usage of gasoline for transportation and the use of wood or coal. Based on Residential Energy Consumption Survey.

[In dollars per million Btu]

| Fuel | 1980 | 1981 | 1982 | 1983 | 1985 | 1987 | 1990 | | | | |
							Total	Northeast	Midwest	South	West
Total	6.49	8.03	8.93	10.18	10.73	10.71	12.0	12.3	9.6	14.3	11.8
Natural gas	3.36	3.90	4.55	5.67	5.97	5.41	5.6	7.1	4.9	5.7	5.2
Electricity	13.46	16.32	18.51	19.98	21.94	22.34	23.6	31.2	23.2	21.4	23.2
Fuel oil, kerosene	6.29	8.04	8.89	8.42	7.64	5.89	7.9	7.9	7.8	8.4	7.9
Liquid petroleum gas	6.71	7.92	8.74	9.42	9.91	8.91	11.2	14.3	9.7	12.2	12.2

Source: 1994 Statistical Abstract of the United States on CD-ROM [machine-readable datafiles]. CD-8A-94. Washington, DC: U.S. Department of Commerce, Economics and Statistics Administration, Bureau of the Census, Data User Services Division, January 1995. Primary sources: U.S. Energy Information Administration. *Household Energy Consumption and Expenditures, 1990;* and prior reports. *Note:* Btu represents British thermal units.

Environmental Compliance

★ 601 ★

Automotive Safety and Emissions Equipment Costs

Basic car - 8,000
Accessories - 8,000
Safety & emissions equipment - 4,000

Table compares costs of special features such as power accessories with costs associated with government-required safety and emissions equipment. Data are for a $20,000 car.

[In dollars]

Component	Cost
Basic car	8,000
Accessories	8,000
Safety & emissions equipment	4,000

Source: "Car Boom Ending?" USA TODAY, 1 February 1995, p.1B.

★ 602 ★

Environmental Compliance

Automotive Safety and Pollution Regulation-Induced Costs: 1999 Models

Government regulations require the addition of certain features to make automobiles safer and more environmentally sound. Table shows the cost that these new features will add to sticker prices. Data are for 1999 car models.

[In dollars]

Features	Cost
Dual air bags	600
Preheated catalytic converter[1]	500
Anti-lock braking system	400
Upgraded diagnostic computer	300
Pup converter[1]	200
Upgraded vapor-trap system	100
Enhanced side-impact protection	50
Fuel tank vapor canister	50
Head injury padding	50

Source: "Safety Has a High Price Tag." *USA TODAY,* 6 December 1993, p. 1B. *Notes:* 1. Large engines would need a "pup" converter; smaller engines could use preheated catalytic converters.

★ 603 ★

Environmental Compliance

Environmental Compliance Costs of Builders

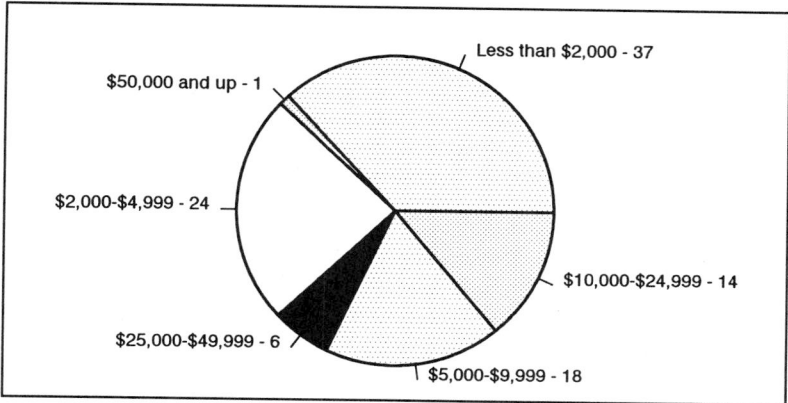

Table shows the cost per lot to builders for compliance with various federal, state, and local environmental regulations. On an average, environmental compliance adds $3,000 to the price of each lot. More than 20 percent of the builders surveyed reported spending $10,000 or more per lot in compliance costs.

[In percentages]

Cost	Builders
Less than $2,000	37
$2,000-$4,999	24
$5,000-$9,999	18
$10,000-$24,999	14
$25,000-$49,999	6
$50,000 and up	1

Source: "Environmental Compliance Costs (Per Lot)." *Builder* (February 1995), p. 27. Primary source: National Association of Home Builders of the United States.

★ 604 ★
Environmental Compliance

Environmental Compliance Costs of Corporations

According to the source, "the growing body of government regulation underscores the public desire for constraints on the misuse of corporate power. But regulation is not an optimal solution. As proponents of pollution trading are quick to point out, conventional regulation often fails to gain the best protection for each dollar spent, and in an ideal system corporations would act in the public interest because it is also in their self-interest" (p. 27). The table below shows annual environmental costs of corporations.

[In billion dollars]

Item	Cost
Stationary source air pollution	
Health costs	190.0
Household soiling	17.3
Architectural damage	13.3
Vegetation damage from acid rain	5.9
Mobile source air pollution	
Crop losses	3.1
Additional impairment in property value	2.6
Health costs	1.7
Water pollution	
Impairment of recreational activities	10.9
Loss to commercial fisheries	2.4
Aesthetic cost	2.2
Damage to health	1.1
Damage to fixtures and appliances	0.3
Hazardous waste	
Cleaning up existing sites	20.0
Total	272.2[1]

Source: Estes, Ralph. "A Free-Market Model." *Environmental Action* 25, no. 4 (winter 1994), p. 28. *Notes:* 1. Does not include noise pollution, aesthetic pollution, and hazardous waste currently generated.

Government

★ 605 ★

Environment-Related Federal Aid to State and Local Governments: 1970-1994

For fiscal year ending in year shown. Includes trust funds.

[In million dollars]

Program	1970	1975	1980	1985	1990	1991	1992	1993	1994
Natural resources and environment	411	2,437	5,363	4,069	3,745	4,040	3,929	3,796	4,192
Environmental Protection Agency	194	2,025	4,603	3,197	2,874	3,071	3,038	2,852	3,126
Energy	25	43	499	529	461	457	448	460	464
Agriculture	604	404	569	2,420	1,285	1,220	1,142	1,117	1,041

Source: *1994 Statistical Abstract of the United States on CD-ROM* [machine-readable datafiles]. CD-8A-94. Washington, DC: U.S. Department of Commerce, Economics and Statistics Administration, Bureau of the Census, Data User Services Division, January 1995. Primary source: U.S. Office of Management and Budget. *Historical Tables, Budget of the United States Government* (annual).

★ 606 ★

Government

Environment-Related Federal Aid to State and Local Governments, by State: 1993

Table compares total, per capita, and Environmental Protection Agency federal aid to state and local governments for fiscal year ending September 30.

[In million dollars, except per capita]

State or area	Federal aid[1]		EPA[3] waste treatment facilities con- struction
	Total	Per capita[2] (dollars)	
United States	195,201	746	2,126
Alabama	3,081	736	23
Alaska	948	1,583	6
Arizona	2,640	671	17
Arkansas	1,855	765	16
California	21,635	693	137
Colorado	2,109	592	14
Connecticut	2,691	821	29
Delaware	455	650	6
District of Columbia	1,961	3,392	11

[Continued]

★ 606 ★

Environment-Related Federal Aid to State and Local Governments, by State: 1993

[Continued]

State or area	Federal aid[1]		EPA[3] waste treatment facilities con- struction
	Total	Per capita[2] (dollars)	
Florida	7,579	554	77
Georgia	4,408	637	24
Hawaii	984	840	22
Idaho	712	648	4
Illinois	7,845	671	127
Indiana	3,732	653	33
Iowa	1,737	617	21
Kansas	1,608	635	20
Kentucky	3,041	802	33
Louisiana	4,817	1,122	23
Maine	1,166	941	19
Maryland	3,310	667	53
Massachusetts	5,520	918	166
Michigan	6,654	702	89
Minnesota	3,297	730	33
Mississippi	2,285	864	16
Missouri	3,566	681	52
Montana	831	990	11
Nebraska	1,108	690	8
Nevada	767	552	22
New Hampshire	652	579	20
New Jersey	6,189	786	60
New Mexico	1,534	949	9
New York	21,166	1,163	245
North Carolina	4,498	648	43
North Dakota	640	1,008	7
Ohio	7,716	696	124
Oklahoma	2,111	653	14
Oregon	2,099	692	29
Pennsylvania	8,517	707	71
Rhode Island	1,107	1,107	7
South Carolina	2,521	692	15
South Dakota	654	915	14
Tennessee	3,925	770	30
Texas	11,035	612	98
Utah	1,173	631	7
Vermont	557	967	8
Virginia	2,945	454	35
Washington	3,722	708	56
West Virginia	1,884	1,035	16
Wisconsin	3,397	674	86

[Continued]

★ 606 ★

Environment-Related Federal Aid to State and Local Governments, by State: 1993

[Continued]

State or area	Federal aid[1]		EPA[3] waste treatment facilities con- struction
	Total	Per capita[2] (dollars)	
Wyoming	645	1,372	4
Outlying areas	3,579	923	20
American Samoa	59	1,265	0
Guam	161	1,207	1
Northern Marianas	47	1,085	1
Puerto Rico	3,132	882	17
Virgin Islands	181	1,775	1
Undistributed amounts	592	(X)	0

Source: 1994 Statistical Abstract of the United States on CD-ROM [machine-readable datafiles]. CD-8A-94. Washington, DC: U.S. Department of Commerce, Economics and Statistics Administration, Bureau of the Census, Data User Services Division, January 1995. Primary source: U.S. Bureau of the Census. *Federal Expenditures by State for Fiscal Year 1993. Notes:* "X" represents "not applicable." 1. Includes amounts not shown separately. 2. Based on estimated resident population as of July 1. 3. Environmental Protection Agency.

★ 607 ★

Government

Federal Agency Spending on Environmental and Natural Resources: 1993

Table shows proportionate spending of federal agencies on the environment and natural resources. In total, agencies spent $22.7 billion during the 1993 fiscal year.

[In percentages]

Department or agency	Spending
Defense[1]	32
Interior	32
Agriculture[2]	27
Commerce[3]	9
State	0.25
Independent agencies	0.03

Source: Barr, Stephen. "Budget and Bureaucracy." *Washington Post,* 8 February 1995, p. A17. Primary source: General Accounting office. *Budget Function Classification: Relating Agency Spending and Personnel Levels to Budget Functions. Notes:* 1. Primarily Army Corps of Engineers. 2. Primarily U.S. Forest Service. 3. Primarily National Oceanic and Atmospheric Administration.

★ 608 ★

Government

Federal Outlays for Environment-Related Items: 1980-1994

Outlays stated in terms of checks issued or cash payments for fiscal years ending in year shown.

[In million dollars]

Agency and function	1980	1985	1990	1991	1992	1993	1994
Total outlays	590,947	946,391	1,252,705	1,323,793	1,380,856	1,408,205	1,483,829
Natural resources and environment	13,858	13,357	17,080	18,559	20,025	20,239	22,285
Water resources	4,223	4,122	4,401	4,366	4,559	4,258	5,596
Conservation and land management	1,043	1,481	3,553	4,047	4,581	4,777	4,772
Recreational resources	1,677	1,621	1,876	2,137	2,378	2,620	2,655
Pollution control and abatement	5,510	4,465	5,170	5,861	6,075	6,061	6,667
Other natural resources	1,405	1,668	2,080	2,148	2,432	2,522	2,595
Energy	10,156	5,685	3,341	2,436	4,500	4,319	4,988
Supply	8,367	2,615	1,976	1,945	3,226	3,286	3,743
Conservation	569	491	365	386	468	521	586
Emergency preparedness	342	1,838	442	(235)	319	336	279
Information, policy, and regulation	878	740	559	340	486	176	380
Agriculture	8,839	25,565	11,958	15,183	15,205	20,443	16,868
Farm income stabilization	7,441	23,751	9,761	12,924	12,666	17,799	14,162
Research and services	1,398	1,813	2,197	2,259	2,539	2,643	2,705
General science, space, and technology	5,832	8,627	14,444	16,111	16,409	17,030	17,279
General science and basic research	1,381	2,019	2,835	3,154	3,571	3,938	4,445

Source: 1994 Statistical Abstract of the United States on CD-ROM [machine-readable datafiles]. CD-8A-94. Washington, DC: U.S. Department of Commerce, Economics and Statistics Administration, Bureau of the Census, Data User Services Division, January 1995. Primary source: U.S. Office of Management and Budget. *Budget of the United States Government* (annual).

★ 609 ★

Government

Government Capital Investment in Water Treatment, Supply, and Resources: 1993-1995

Table shows infrastructure investment for water treatment and supply, rural water and wastewater programs, and water resources development. Discretionary budget authority.

[In billion dollars]

Investment	1993 actual	1994 enacted	1995 proposed	Percent change 1993-1994	Percent change 1994-1995
Water treatment and supply[1]:					
Clean water state revolving funds	1.9	1.2	1.6	-36.8	33.3
Drinking water state revolving funds	-	0.6	0.7	(X)	16.7
Targeted whitewater assistance	0.6	0.6	0.3	0	-50.0
Rural water/wastewater programs[2]:					
Grants and loans	0.5	0.6	0.7	20.0	16.7
Loan level	-0.8	-0.8	-1.0	0.0	25.0
Water resources development:					
Army Corps of Engineers	1.7	1.6	1.2	-5.9	-25.0
Bureau of Reclamation[3]	0.5	0.4	0.4	-20.0	0

Source: *1994 Statistical Abstract of the United States on CD-ROM* [machine-readable datafiles]. CD-8A-94. Washington, DC: U.S. Department of Commerce, Economics and Statistics Administration, Bureau of the Census, Data User Services Division, January 1995. Primary source: U.S. Office of Management and Budget. *Budget of the United States Government* (annual). *Notes:* "-" represents or rounds to zero. "X" stands for "not applicable." 1. Environmental Protection Agency. 2. Department of Agriculture. 3. Department of the Interior.

★ 610 ★

Government

State and Local Government Expenditures on Environment: 1956-1991

The table shows the expenditures for environment-related items such as natural resources and solid waste management. Data are shown in current as well as in inflation-adjusted 1987 dollars.

[In billion dollars]

Year	Natural resources Current dollars	Natural resources 1987 dollars	Parks and recreation Current dollars	Parks and recreation 1987 dollars	Sewerage Current dollars	Sewerage 1987 dollars	Solid waste management Current dollars	Solid waste management 1987 dollars	Total Current dollars	Total 1987 dollars
1959	1.08	4.20	0.73	2.85	1.01	3.95	0.60	2.34	3.53	13.78
1960	1.19	4.57	0.77	2.96	1.10	4.24	0.62	2.40	3.82	14.71
1961	1.33	5.05	0.86	3.26	1.10	4.19	0.67	2.56	4.00	15.22
1962	1.37	5.12	0.89	3.31	1.27	4.75	0.69	2.56	4.43	16.54
1963	1.59	5.84	0.98	3.60	1.46	5.38	0.72	2.66	5.00	18.38
1964	1.84	6.62	1.02	3.69	1.52	5.47	0.75	2.71	5.15	18.59
1965	1.86	6.55	1.10	3.89	1.57	5.52	0.79	2.79	5.50	19.38
1966	2.04	6.94	1.19	4.04	1.71	5.81	0.86	2.94	6.10	20.76

[Continued]

★ 610 ★

State and Local Government Expenditures on Environment: 1956-1991
[Continued]

Year	Natural resources Current dollars	Natural resources 1987 dollars	Parks and recreation Current dollars	Parks and recreation 1987 dollars	Sewerage Current dollars	Sewerage 1987 dollars	Solid waste management Current dollars	Solid waste management 1987 dollars	Total Current dollars	Total 1987 dollars
1967	2.34	7.74	1.29	4.26	1.64	5.40	0.89	2.93	6.29	20.74
1968	2.47	7.79	1.41	4.45	1.73	5.46	0.98	3.08	6.67	21.04
1969	2.55	7.66	1.65	4.94	1.90	5.69	1.07	3.23	7.17	21.52
1970	2.73	7.78	1.89	5.38	2.17	6.17	1.25	3.55	8.03	22.89
1971	3.08	8.33	2.11	5.70	2.65	7.15	1.44	3.89	9.28	25.08
1972	3.12	8.05	2.32	5.97	3.26	8.40	1.59	4.09	10.29	26.51
1973	3.28	7.94	2.56	6.20	3.60	8.73	1.72	4.16	11.16	27.02
1974	3.66	8.15	2.95	6.57	4.08	9.09	1.92	4.27	12.61	28.08
1975	4.22	8.58	3.46	7.04	5.26	10.70	2.18	4.42	15.12	30.74
1976	4.66	8.91	3.86	7.39	5.94	11.35	2.30	4.40	16.77	32.06
1977	4.05	6.13	4.92	8.80	7.05	12.62	2.37	4.25	18.39	32.91
1978	4.23	7.01	5.27	8.74	7.14	11.84	2.73	4.52	19.36	32.11
1979	4.71	7.18	5.90	9.00	8.80	13.43	2.99	4.57	22.39	34.18
1980	5.51	7.68	6.52	9.09	9.89	13.80	3.32	4.63	25.24	35.21
1981	6.18	7.83	7.06	8.95	11.12	14.10	3.78	4.79	28.14	35.66
1982	6.57	7.84	7.50	8.95	10.81	12.89	4.13	4.93	29.01	34.62
1983	7.08	8.12	8.05	9.23	11.24	12.89	4.36	5.00	30.74	35.25
1984	7.42	8.15	8.34	9.17	11.52	12.66	4.71	5.18	31.99	35.16
1985	8.36	8.85	9.16	9.70	12.19	12.91	5.21	5.52	34.92	36.99
1986	9.07	9.36	10.16	10.49	13.31	13.73	5.84	6.02	38.38	39.61
1987	9.94	9.94	11.02	11.02	15.15	15.15	6.50	6.05	42.61	42.61
1988	10.24	9.85	12.07	11.62	16.33	15.72	7.35	7.07	45.99	44.26
1989	11.09	10.22	12.93	11.92	17.04	15.71	8.73	8.05	49.79	45.89
1990	12.33	10.88	14.33	12.65	18.31	16.16	10.14	8.95	54.99	48.53
1991	12.58	10.69	15.93	13.53	19.68	16.72	11.34	9.63	59.53	50.58

Source: Executive Office of the President of the United States. *Environmental Quality 24: The Twenty-fourth Annual Report of the Council on Environmental Quality.* Prepared by Ray Clark. Written by Carroll Curtis. Edited by Barry Walsh. Washington, DC: U.S. Government Printing Office, 1994, p. 403. Primary sources: U.S. Department of Commerce. Bureau of the Census. *Historical Statistics on Governmental Finances and Employment.* GC82(6)- 4. Washington, DC: U.S. Department of Commerce, Bureau of the Census, 1982; U.S. Department of Commerce. Bureau of the Census. *Governmental Finances.* Series GF, no. 5. Washington, DC: U.S. Department of Commerce, Bureau of the Census, annual. *Notes:* Data for 1991 are preliminary. Gross domestic product deflators are used to calculate constant dollars.

★ 611 ★

Government

State Environmental Budgets

Table shows the percent of each state's budget spent on the environment.

State	Budget
Alabama	1.02
Alaska	4.00
Arizona	0.96
Arkansas	1.15
California	2.60

[Continued]

★ 611 ★

State Environmental Budgets
[Continued]

State	Budget
Colorado	1.65
Connecticut	0.77
Delaware	1.80
Florida	2.51
Georgia	1.07
Hawaii	0.85
Idaho	4.22
Illinois	2.26
Indiana	0.68
Iowa	1.44
Kansas	1.23
Kentucky	1.64
Louisiana	2.64
Maine	1.88
Maryland	1.60
Massachusetts	1.56
Michigan	1.42
Minnesota	1.46
Mississippi	1.40
Missouri	1.73
Montana	4.29
Nebraska	1.29
Nevada	2.57
New Hampshire	2.41
New Jersey	3.61
New Mexico	1.48
New York	0.59
North Carolina	1.00
North Dakota	2.32
Ohio	0.65
Oklahoma	0.79
Oregon	3.03
Pennsylvania	1.49
Rhode Island	1.86
South Carolina	1.21
South Dakota	1.85
Tennessee	1.34
Texas	0.60
Utah	1.80
Vermont	1.94
Virginia	1.47
Washington	2.63
West Virginia	1.68
Wisconsin	1.70
Wyoming	7.73

Source: "Rate Your State." *Science World,* 9 December 1994, pp. 18-19. Primary source: *The 1994 Information Please Environmental Almanac* (World Resources Institute, 1993).

★ 612 ★

Government

U.S. Department of Energy Environmental Management Program Budget: 1994

According to the source: "The Office of Environmental Restoration and Waste Management [EM] is divided into several functional programs. They include Environmental Restoration, Waste Management, Technology Development, Facility Transition and Management, Transportation Management, and Program Direction. The program most closely associated with environmental cleanup is Environmental Restoration, whose 1994 budget is $1.8 billion, accounting for 30.3 percent of the EM total" (p. 8).

[In percentages]

Program	Budget
Waste Management	50.2
Environmental restoration	30.3
Facility transition	11.1
Technology development	6.6
Other[1]	1.8

Source: U.S. Congress. Congressional Budget Office (CBO). *Cleaning Up the Department of Energy's Nuclear Weapons Complex.* A CBO Study. Washington, DC: U.S. Congress, Congressional Budget Office, May 1994, p. 8. Primary source: Congressional Budget Office. *Note:* 1. Includes Transportation Management and Program Direction.

★ 613 ★

Government

U.S. Environmental Protection Agency's Budget Requests and Appropriations: 1993

Table compares the 1993 budget requests of the U.S. Environmental Protection Agency with final appropriations.

[In thousand dollars, except as noted]

Budget area	National program managers' requests	Final appropriation	Difference (%)
Radiation	53,923	32,970	-39
Pesticides	203,548	133,074	-35
Hazardous waste	438,370	309,948	-29
Air	671,582	521,128	-22
Drinking water	185,934	144,710	-22
Water quality	514,509	412,173	-20
Toxics	185,757	155,891	-16

Source: Munson, Dick. "Follow the Money." *Amicus Journal* 15, no. 3 (fall 1993), p. 14. Primary source: Environmental Working Group.

★ 614 ★

Government

U.S. Environmental Protection Agency's Research Budget: 1996

Total - 629.4

Multimedia - 357.2

Air - 106.7

Superfund - 59.8

Hazardous waste - 22.8

Drinking water - 21.7

Water quality - 21.2

Toxic substances - 15.5

Pesticides - 13.6

Management and support - 8.0

Oil spills - 2.1

Leaking underground storage tanks - 0.8

Chart shows data from column 1.

The proposed 1996 research budget for the U.S. Environmental Protection Agency totaled $629.4 million, an increase of 88.8 percent from 1995. Table below shows funds allocated to various programs in 1996 budget.

[In million dollars]

Program	Amount budgeted	Percent change from 1995
Multimedia	357.2	96.5
Air	106.7	2.5
Superfund	59.8	-7.3
Hazardous waste	22.8	-3.9
Drinking water	21.7	-0.5
Water quality	21.2	-1.7
Toxic substances	15.5	-2.7
Pesticides	13.6	-0.2
Management and support	8.0	0.8
Oil spills	2.1	0.3
Leaking underground storage tanks	0.8	0.0
Total	629.4	88.8

Source: Lucas, Allison. "Clinton Proposes Federal R&D Boost, Despite Congressional Opposition." *ChemicalWeek,* 8 March 1995, p. 28. Primary source: U.S. Environmental Protection Agency.

★ 615 ★

Government

U.S. Government Outlays, by Superfunction: 1962-1993

Tables shows expenditures by the federal government on superfuntions such as national defense. Pollution control, for example, falls under the physical resources category. Data are for fiscal years from 1962 through 1993. See also related table for physical resources function.

[In billion current dollars, except total]

Year	National defense	Human resources	Physical resources	Net interest	Other	Undistrib- uted	Total (trillion current dollars)
1962	52	32	9	7	12	-5	0.11
1963	53	34	8	8	14	-6	0.11
1964	55	35	10	8	16	-6	0.12
1965	51	37	11	9	17	-6	0.12
1966	58	42	13	9	17	-7	0.13
1967	71	51	15	10	17	-7	0.16
1968	82	59	16	11	18	-8	0.18
1969	82	66	12	13	18	-8	0.18
1970	82	75	16	14	17	-9	0.20
1971	79	92	18	15	16	-10	0.21
1972	79	107	20	15	19	-10	0.23
1973	77	120	21	17	25	-13	0.25
1974	79	136	25	21	24	-17	0.27
1975	87	173	35	23	27	-14	0.33
1976	90	204	39	27	27	-14	0.37
1977	97	222	41	30	34	-15	0.41
1978	104	242	53	35	40	-16	0.46
1979	116	268	54	43	40	-17	0.50
1980	134	313	66	53	45	-20	0.59
1981	158	362	71	69	47	-28	0.68
1982	185	389	62	85	51	-26	0.75
1983	210	426	58	90	59	-34	0.81
1984	227	432	58	111	55	-32	0.85
1985	253	472	57	129	68	-33	0.95
1986	273	482	59	136	74	-33	0.99
1987	282	502	55	139	63	-36	1.00
1988	290	533	68	152	57	-37	1.06
1989	304	569	82	169	58	-37	1.14
1990	299	619	125	184	61	-37	1.25
1991	273	690	134	195	71	-39	1.32
1992	300	683	75	199	75	-39	1.29
1993	279	828	46	199	92	-37	1.41

Source: Executive Office of the President of the United States. *Environmental Quality 24: The Twenty-fourth Annual Report of the Council on Environmental Quality.* Prepared by Ray Clark. Written by Carroll Curtis. Edited by Barry Walsh. Washington, DC: U.S. Government Printing Office, 1994, pp. 400-402. Primary source: Office of Management and Budget. *The Budget for Fiscal Year, 1994.* Washington, DC: Office of Management and Budget, 1994, appendix 20-32.

★ 616 ★

Government

U.S. Government Outlays for Natural Resources and Environment: 1962-1993

Table shows U.S. government outlays for the natural resources and environment function, including conservation and land management and pollution control and abatement. Data are for fiscal years from 1962 through 1993.

[In billions]

Year	Water resources		Conservation and land management		Recreational resources		Pollution control and abatement		Other natural resources		Total	
	Current dollars	Constant 1987 dollars	Current dollars	Constant 1987 dollars	Current dollars	Constant 1987 dollars	Current dollars	Constant 1987 dollars	Current dollars	Constant 1987 dollars	Current dollars	Constant 1987 dollars
1962	1.3	4.8	0.3	1.3	0.2	0.6	0.1	0.3	0.2	0.7	2.0	7.6
1963	1.4	5.3	0.3	1.2	0.2	0.7	0.1	0.3	0.2	0.8	2.3	8.3
1964	1.5	5.3	0.3	1.2	0.2	0.7	0.1	0.4	0.3	0.9	2.4	8.6
1965	1.5	5.5	0.3	1.2	0.2	0.8	0.1	0.5	0.3	1.0	2.5	9.0
1966	1.7	5.9	0.3	1.1	0.2	0.8	0.2	0.5	0.3	1.1	2.7	9.4
1967	1.7	5.6	0.4	1.2	0.3	0.9	0.2	0.6	0.4	1.2	2.9	9.5
1968	1.6	5.3	0.4	1.3	0.3	1.0	0.2	0.8	0.4	1.2	3.0	9.6
1969	1.6	4.9	0.3	0.8	0.4	1.1	0.3	0.9	0.4	1.1	2.9	8.8
1970	1.5	4.4	0.4	1.1	0.4	1.1	0.4	1.1	0.4	0.2	3.1	8.9
1971	1.8	4.9	0.5	1.3	0.5	1.3	0.7	1.9	0.5	1.4	3.9	10.8
1972	1.9	5.1	0.4	1.2	0.5	0.4	0.8	2.0	0.6	0.5	4.2	11.1
1973	2.2	5.5	0.3	0.8	0.5	0.4	1.1	2.8	0.6	0.4	4.8	11.9
1974	2.2	5.1	0.1	0.3	0.6	0.5	2.0	4.7	0.7	0.5	5.7	13.2
1975	2.6	5.5	0.7	1.4	0.8	0.7	2.5	5.3	0.8	0.6	7.3	15.4
1976	2.7	5.4	0.6	1.2	0.9	0.7	3.1	6.0	0.9	0.7	8.2	16.0
1977	3.2	5.8	0.6	1.1	1.0	0.8	4.3	7.7	1.0	0.7	10.0	18.1
1978	3.4	5.8	1.0	1.7	1.4	2.4	4.0	6.7	1.2	1.9	11.0	18.4
1979	3.9	6.0	0.8	1.3	1.5	2.3	4.7	7.3	1.3	2.0	12.1	18.7
1980	4.2	6.0	1.0	1.5	1.7	2.4	5.5	7.8	1.4	2.0	13.9	19.6
1981	4.1	5.3	1.2	1.5	1.6	2.1	5.2	6.7	1.5	1.9	13.6	17.5
1982	3.9	4.7	1.1	1.3	1.4	1.7	5.0	6.0	1.5	0.8	13.0	15.6
1983	3.9	4.5	1.5	1.7	1.5	1.7	4.3	4.9	1.5	0.8	12.7	14.6
1984	4.1	4.5	1.3	1.4	1.6	1.7	4.0	4.5	1.6	1.8	12.6	13.9
1985	4.1	4.4	1.5	1.6	1.6	1.7	4.5	4.7	1.7	0.8	13.4	14.2
1986	4.0	4.2	1.4	1.4	1.5	1.6	4.8	5.0	1.9	0.9	13.6	14.0
1987	3.8	3.8	1.5	1.5	1.6	1.6	4.9	4.9	1.7	0.7	13.4	13.4
1988	4.0	3.9	2.2	2.1	1.7	1.6	4.8	4.6	1.9	1.8	14.6	14.1
1989	4.3	4.0	3.3	3.0	1.8	1.7	4.9	4.5	1.9	1.8	16.2	15.0
1990	4.4	3.9	3.6	3.2	1.9	1.7	5.1	4.6	2.1	1.9	17.1	15.4
1991	4.4	3.8	4.0	3.2	2.1	1.8	5.9	5.0	2.1	1.8	18.6	15.9
1992	4.6	3.8	4.6	3.8	2.4	2.0	6.1	5.0	2.4	2.0	20.0	16.5
1993	5.1	4.1	4.7	3.8	2.9	2.3	6.7	5.4	2.6	2.1	21.9	17.7

Source: Executive Office of the President of the United States. *Environmental Quality 24: The Twenty-fourth Annual Report of the Council on Environmental Quality.* Prepared by Ray Clark. Written by Carroll Curtis. Edited by Barry Walsh. Washington, DC: U.S. Government Printing Office, 1994, p. 402. Primary source: Office of Management and Budget. *The Budget for Fiscal Year 1994.* Washington, DC: Office of Management and Budget, 1994, appendix 20-32. *Note:* Gross domestic product deflators are used to calculate constant dollars.

★617★
Government

U.S. Government Outlays for Physical Resources Function: 1962-1993

This table shows the components of the major budgetary category for physical resources. Functions specifically related to environmental issues include those for natural resources and environment or energy. Pollution control, for example, is considered under the natural resources and environment heading.

[In billion current dollars]

Year	Physical resources function					
	Energy	Natural resources & environment	Commerce & housing credit	Trans-portation	Community & regional development	Total physical resources
1962	0.6	2.0	1.4	4.3	0.5	8.8
1963	0.5	2.3	0.1	4.6	0.6	8.0
1964	0.6	2.4	0.4	5.2	0.9	9.5
1965	0.7	2.5	1.2	5.8	1.1	11.3
1966	0.6	2.7	3.2	5.7	1.1	13.4
1967	0.8	2.9	4.0	5.9	1.1	14.7
1968	1.0	3.0	4.3	6.3	1.4	16.0
1969	1.0	2.9	-0.1	6.5	1.6	11.9
1970	1.0	3.1	2.1	7.0	2.4	15.6
1971	1.0	3.9	2.4	8.1	2.9	18.3
1972	1.3	4.2	2.2	8.4	3.4	19.6
1973	1.2	4.8	0.9	9.1	4.6	20.6
1974	1.3	5.7	4.7	9.2	4.2	25.1
1975	2.9	7.3	9.9	10.9	4.3	35.4
1976	4.2	8.2	7.6	13.7	5.4	39.2
1977	5.8	10.0	3.1	14.8	7.0	40.7
1978	8.0	11.0	6.3	15.5	11.8	52.6
1979	9.2	12.1	4.7	17.5	10.5	54.0
1980	10.2	13.9	9.4	21.3	11.3	66.0
1981	15.2	13.6	8.2	23.4	10.6	70.9
1982	13.5	13.0	6.3	20.6	8.3	61.8
1983	9.4	12.7	6.7	21.3	7.6	57.6
1984	7.1	12.6	6.9	23.7	7.7	57.9
1985	5.7	13.4	4.2	25.8	7.7	56.8
1986	4.7	13.6	4.9	28.1	7.2	58.6
1987	4.1	13.4	6.2	26.2	5.1	54.9
1988	2.3	14.6	18.8	27.3	5.3	68.3
1989	3.7	16.2	29.2	27.6	5.4	82.1
1990	2.4	17.1	67.1	29.5	8.5	124.6
1991	1.7	18.6	75.6	31.1	6.8	133.8
1992	4.5	20.0	10.1	33.3	6.8	54.7
1993	4.3	20.2	-22.7	35.0	9.1	45.9

Source: Executive Office of the President of the United States. *Environmental Quality 24: The Twenty-fourth Annual Report of the Council on Environmental Quality.* Prepared by Ray Clark. Written by Carroll Curtis. Edited by Barry Walsh. Washington, DC: U.S. Government Printing Office, 1994, pp. 401-402. Primary source: Office of Management and Budget. *The Budget for Fiscal Year, 1994.* Washington, DC: Office of Management and Budget, 1994, appendix 20-32.

Health

★ 618 ★

Environmental Causes of Premature Death

Table shows the lifetime probability of premature death per 100,000.

Cause	Probability
Motor vehicle/pedestrian	290
Environmental tobacco smoke	200
Diagnostic X-rays	75
Bicycling	75
Miami/New Orleans drinking water	7
Lightning	3
Hurricanes	3
Asbestos in schools	1

Source: "End the Phony 'Asbestos Panic.'" *USA TODAY,* 13 September 1993, p. 11A. Primary source: Symposium organized by the Energy and Environmental Policy Center of Harvard University in 1988.

★ 619 ★
Health

Migrant Worker Pesticide Exposure

The National Advisory Council on Migrant Health reported that "basic worker protection standards which were enacted in the early part of this century exempt agricultural workers" (p. 65). Pesticides in particular threaten the well being of migrant farm workers. The Environmental Protection Agency attributes the illnesses and injuries of 300,000 farm workers annually to pesticides.

Source: National Advisory Council on Migrant Health. *1993 Recommendations of the National Advisory Council on Migrant Health.* Rockville, MD: National Advisory Council on Migrant Health, May 1993, pp. 65-66.

★ 620 ★

Health

Occupational Disease-Related Deaths: 1980-1990

Table shows the number of deaths from selected occupational diseases for males by underlying and nonunderlying causes. Data are for 1978 through 1990.

	By underlying cause				By nonunderlying cause			
Year	Malignant neoplasm of perioneum and pleura (mesothelioma)	Coal workers pneumoconiosis	Asbestosis	Silicosis	Malignant neoplasm of perioneum and pleura (mesothelioma)	Coal workers pneumoconiosis	Asbestosis	Silicosis
1980	552	977	96	202	135	1,587	228	232
1983	584	926	128	149	115	1,758	321	205
1984	584	923	131	160	124	1,742	298	210
1985	571	947	130	138	102	1,652	382	187
1986	564	884	180	135	106	1,536	494	175
1987	575	823	195	153	111	1,419	488	173
1988	556	757	206	128	104	1,445	536	162
1989	565	725	261	130	83	1,402	588	156
1990	629	727	282	146	105	1,248	619	152

Source: Executive Office of the President of the United States. *Environmental Quality 24: The Twenty-fourth Annual Report of the Council on Environmental Quality.* Prepared by Ray Clark. Written by Carroll Curtis. Edited by Barry Walsh. Washington, DC: U.S. Government Printing Office, 1994, p. 516. Primary source: U.S. Department of Health and Human Services. National Center for Health Statistics. *Health United States, 1992.* Hyattsville, MD: Public Health Service, 1993, table 46, p. 82.

★ 621 ★

Health

Pesticide Residues in Domestic Foods, by Commodity Group: 1978-1993

Table shows percent of samples with residues found for each commodity group. Although a percentage of samples contain pesticide residues, the percent of samples with over-tolerance residues (as set by Environmental Protection Agency) is low. Between 1973 and 1986, 3 percent of samples were classed as violative; since 1987, less than 1 percent were violative.

Year	Grains & grain products	Milk, dairy products & eggs	Fish, shellfish & meats	Fruits	Vegetables	Other	Total
1978	54	43	80	48	34	42	47
1979	54	47	81	58	35	47	49
1980	52	36	71	53	40	36	46
1981	43	32	77	56	37	34	44
1982	42	34	72	49	36	32	41
1983	42	32	61	52	41	31	43
1984	54	31	75	38	33	31	37
1985	52	22	65	36	34	22	35
1986	60	21	68	57	39	48	44

[Continued]

★ 621 ★

Pesticide Residues in Domestic Foods, by Commodity Group: 1978-1993

[Continued]

Year	Grains & grain products	Milk, dairy products & eggs	Fish, shellfish & meats	Fruits	Vegetables	Other	Total
1987	57	24	73	50	37	37	42
1988	49	19	72	51	35	28	40
1989	44	13	65	44	32	20	35
1990	46	9	68	49	38	21	40
1991	42	22	42	51	32	19	36
1992	39	6	52	49	31	19	35
1993	34	6	47	30	61	17	36

Source: Executive Office of the President of the United States. *Environmental Quality 24: The Twenty-fourth Annual Report of the Council on Environmental Quality.* Prepared by Ray Clark. Written by Carroll Curtis. Edited by Barry Walsh. Washington, DC: U.S. Government Printing Office, 1994, p. 514. Primary source: U.S. Food and Drug Administration. "Food and Drug Administration Pesticide Program Residues in Foods." *Journal of the Association of Official Analytical Chemists.* Vols. 71-77 (1988, 1989, 1990, 1991, 1993, 1994). *Notes:* Domestic samples are collected as close as possible to the point of production. Fresh produce is analyzed as the unwashed whole, raw commodity. .

★ 622 ★

Health

Pesticide Residues in Human Diets: 1991-1993

Table shows the frequency of occurrence of pesticide residues in human diets.

Pesticide	Findings (number)	Occurrence (%)
Malathion	332	21
DDE, p,p'	298	19
Chloropyrifos-methyl	251	16
Endosulfan	162	10
Chloropyrifos	155	10
Dieldrin	142	9
Chlorpropham	90	6
Methamidophos	83	5
Diazinon	72	5
Carbaryl	66	4
Dicloran	61	4
Dimethoate	57	4
Thiabendazole	50	3
Acephate	48	3
Omethoate	40	3
Lindane	36	2
Permethrin	35	2

[Continued]

★ 622 ★

Pesticide Residues in Human Diets: 1991-1993

[Continued]

Pesticide	Findings (number)	Occurrence (%)
Propargite	33	2
Ethion	115	2

Source: Executive Office of the President of the United States. *Environmental Quality 24: The Twenty-fourth Annual Report of the Council on Environmental Quality.* Prepared by Ray Clark. Written by Carroll Curtis. Edited by Barry Walsh. Washington, DC: U.S. Government Printing Office, 1994, p. 515. Primary source: U.S. Food and Drug Administration. "Food and Drug Administration Pesticide Program Residues in Foods." *Journal of the Association of Official Analytical Chemists.* Vol. 77 (1994). *Notes:* Total number of findings is based on 1,566 food items in the Total Diet Study (1991-1993).

★ 623 ★

Health

Waterborne Disease Outbreaks: 1971-1992

Table shows the number of waterborne disease outbreaks by type of water supply system. The number of waterborne disease outbreaks reported to the Centers for Disease Control and the Environmental Protection Agency represents a fraction of the total number that occur. Therefore, these data should not be used to draw firm conclusions about the true incidence of waterborne disease outbreaks.

Year	Community	Non-community	Individual	Total	Total cases
1971	8	8	4	20	5,184
1972	9	19	2	30	1,650
1973	6	16	3	25	1,762
1974	11	9	5	25	8,356
1975	6	16	2	24	10,879
1976	9	23	3	35	5,068
1977	14	18	2	34	3,860
1978	10	19	3	32	11,435
1979	24	13	8	45	9,841
1980	26	20	7	53	20,045
1981	14	18	4	36	4,537
1982	26	15	3	44	3,588
1983	30	9	4	43	21,036
1984	12	5	10	27	1,800
1985	7	14	1	22	1,946
1986	10	10	2	22	1,569
1987	8	6	1	15	22,149
1988	6	10	1	16	2,169
1989	6	6	1	13	2,670
1990	6	7	2	15	1,748

[Continued]

★ 623 ★

Waterborne Disease Outbreaks: 1971-1992

[Continued]

Year	Community	Non-community	Individual	Total	Total cases
1991	2	13	0	15	12,960
1992	6	10	3	19	4,504

Source: Executive Office of the President of the United States. *Environmental Quality 24: The Twenty-fourth Annual Report of the Council on Environmental Quality.* Prepared by Ray Clark. Written by Carroll Curtis. Edited by Barry Walsh. Washington, DC: U.S. Government Printing Office, 1994, p. 512. Primary sources: U.S. Department of Health and Human Services. Public Health Service. Centers for Disease Control. "Waterborne Disease Outbreaks, 1991-1992." *Morbidity and Mortality Weekly Report,* 429(SS-5): 1-22. Atlanta, GA: U.S. Department of Health and Human Services, November 1993; and earlier reports.

Minerals and Metals

★ 624 ★

Mineral Prices: 1970-1993

Table shows the average prices of selected mineral products. Excludes Alaska and Hawaii, except as noted.

Year	Tantalum (dollar per pound)[1]	Copper, cathode[2] (cents per pound	Platinum[3] (dollar per troy ounce)	Gold (dollar per fine ounce)	Silver (dollar per fine ounce)	Lead[4] (cents per pound)	Tin [New York][5] (cents per pound)	Zinc[6] (cents per pound)	Sulfur, crude[7] (dollars per metric ton)	Bituminous coal[8] (dollars per short ton)	Crude petroleum[8] (dollars per barrel)	Natural gas[8] (dollars per 1,000 cubic feet)
1970	9.15	58	133	36	1.77	15.7	174.1	15.3	22.41[9]	6.26	3.18	0.17
1975	18.32	64	164	161	4.42	21.5	339.8	39.0	44.20[9]	19.23	7.67	0.44
1976	20.31	70	162	125	4.35	23.1	379.8	37.0	45.00[9]	19.43	8.19	0.58
1977	25.64	67	157	148	4.62	30.7	534.6	34.4	43.68[9]	19.82	8.57	0.79
1978	34.19	66	261	194	5.40	33.7	629.6	31.0	45.17	21.78	9.00	0.91
1979	80.00	92	445	308	11.09	52.6	753.9	37.3	55.75	23.65	12.64	1.18
1980	126.37	101	677	613	20.63	42.5	846.0	37.4	89.06	24.52	21.59	1.59
1981	99.51	84	446	460	10.52	36.5	733.1	44.6	111.48	26.29	31.77	1.98
1982	49.95	73	327	376	7.95	25.5	653.9	38.5	108.27	27.14	28.52	2.46
1983	30.60	77	424	424	11.44	21.7	654.8	41.4	87.24	25.85	26.19	2.59
1984	37.44	67	357	361	8.14	25.6	623.8	48.6	94.31	25.51	25.88	2.66
1985	33.68	67	291	318	6.14	19.1	596.0	40.4	106.46	25.10	24.09	2.51
1986	23.74	66	461	368	5.47	22.1	383.2	38.0	105.22	23.70	12.51	1.94
1987	27.08	83	553	478	7.01	35.9	418.8	41.9	89.78	23.00	15.40	1.67
1988	47.37	121	523	438	6.53	37.1	441.4	60.2	85.95	22.00	12.58	1.69
1989	44.93	131	507	383	5.50	39.4	520.2	82.0	86.62	21.76	15.86	1.69
1990	38.06	123	467	385	4.82	46.0	386.3	74.6	80.14	21.71	20.03	1.71
1991	36.70	109	371	363	4.04	33.5	362.9	52.8	71.45	21.45	16.54	1.64

[Continued]

★ 624 ★

Mineral Prices: 1970-1993
[Continued]

Year	Tan-talum (dollar per pound)[1]	Copper, cathode[2] (cents per pound)	Plati-num[3] (dollar per troy ounce)	Gold (dollar per fine ounce)	Silver (dollar per fine ounce)	Lead[4] (cents per pound)	Tin [New York][5] (cents per pound)	Zinc[6] (cents per pound)	Sulfur, crude[7] (dollars per metric ton)	Bitumi-nous coal[8] (dollars per short ton)	Crude petro-leum[8] (dollars per barrel)	Natural gas[8] (dollars per 1,000 cubic feet)
1992	34.42	107	356	345	3.94	35.1	402.4	58.4	48.14	21.17	15.99	1.74
1993[9]	(NA)	92	370	355	4.20	32.0	385.0	46.0	32.00	(NA)	14.23	2.01

Source: *1994 Statistical Abstract of the United States on CD-ROM* [machine-readable datafiles]. CD-8A-94. Washington, DC: U.S. Department of Commerce, Economics and Statistics Administration, Bureau of the Census, Data User Services Division, January 1995. Primary sources, except as noted: U.S. Bureau of Mines. *Mineral Facts and Problems* (1980); and *Mineral Commodity Summaries* (annual). Notes: "NA" represents "not available." 1. Dollars per pound of tantalum content. 2. Domestic market prices for wirebar, 1970, 1975-1977; prices for cathode thereafter. 3. Average annual dealer prices. 4. 1970, New York prices; beginning 1975, nationwide delivered basis. 5. Straits tin through 1975; thereafter, composite price. 6. Prime western. Beginning 1975, delivered price. 7. Free on board works. 8. Average value at the point of production. Source: U.S. Energy Information Administration. *Annual Energy Review.* 9. Preliminary.

★ 625 ★

Minerals and Metals

Nonfuel Mineral Commodity Prices: 1993

Table shows preliminary estimates of average prices for nonfuel mineral commodities.

[In dollars per metric ton, except as noted]

Mineral	Price
Aluminum	53[1]
Antimony (contained)	80[1]
Arsenic	54[2]
Asbestos	(D)
Barite	59.8
Bauxite and alumina	15-18
Beryllium (contained)	295[3]
Bismuth (contained)	2.5
Boron (B_2O_3 content)	276[4]
Bromine (contained)	656
Cadmium (contained)	0.45
Cement	49[5]
Chromium	110[6]
Clays	(NA)
Cobalt (contained)	13.8[7]
Columbium (contained)	2.67[8]
Copper (contained)	92
Diamond (industrial)	2.12[9]
Diatomite	185
Feldspar	39.08
Fluorspar	(NA)
Gallium (contained)	425[10]
Garnet (industrial)	100-2,000
Gemstones	[11]

[Continued]

★ 625 ★

Nonfuel Mineral Commodity Prices: 1993
[Continued]

Mineral	Price
Germanium (contained)	1,060
Gold (contained)	355
Graphite (crude)	767[12]
Gypsum (crude)	6[13]
Indium	180
Iodine	8
Iron ore (usable)	73-74[14]
Iron and steel scrap (metal)	106[15]
Iron and steel slag	6
Lead (contained)	32[1]
Lime	53[5]
Magnesium compounds	(NA)
Magnesium metal	1
Manganese (gross weight)	3[16]
Mercury	190[17]
Mica, scrap and flake	54
Molybdenum (contained)	5[10]
Nickel (contained)	5,130[18]
Nitrogen (fixed)-ammonia	110
Nonrenewable organics	107
Peat	24
Perlite	30[13]
Phosphate rock	22[13]
Platinum-group metals	370
Potash (K_2O equivalent)	124[13]
Pumice and pumicite	30[13]
Salt	111[19]
Silicon (contained)	42
Silver (contained)	5
Sodium carbonate (soda ash)	98
Sodium sulfate	114
Stone (crushed)	5[5]
Sulfur (all forms)	32[20]
Talc	13-400
Thallium (contained)	230[10]
Tin (contained)	244[1]
Titanium dioxide	1
Tungsten (contained)	44[21]
Vermiculite	(D)

[Continued]

★ 625 ★

Nonfuel Mineral Commodity Prices: 1993
[Continued]

Mineral	Price
Zinc (contained)	46
Zirconium content (Z,02)	200[22]

Source: 1994 Statistical Abstract of the United States on CD-ROM [machine-readable datafiles]. CD-8A-94. Washington, DC: U.S. Department of Commerce, Economics and Statistics Administration, Bureau of the Census, Data User Services Division, January 1995. Primary source: U.S. Bureau of Mines. *Mineral Commodity Summaries,* (annual). *Notes:* "D" denotes data withheld to avoid disclosure. "NA" stands for "not available." 1. Cents per pound. 2. Cents per pound. Metal price. 3. Metal, vacuum-cast ingot. Dollars per pound. 4. Granulated pentahydrate borax in bulk, f.o.b. mine. 5. Dollars per short ton. 6. Turkish. 7. Dollars per pound. 8. Columbite price. 9. Value of imports, dollars per carat. 10. Dollars per kilogram. 11. Variable, depending on size, type, and quality. 12. Price of flake imports. 13. F.o.b. mine (or mill). 14. Lake Superior pellets. Cents per long ton unit of iron, delivered rail of vessel at lower lake ports. 15. Delivered, No. 1 Heavy Melting composite price. 16. 46%- 48% Mn metallurgical ore, per unit contained Mn, c.i.f. U.S. ports. 17. Price per 76-pound flask. 18. London Metal Exchange cash price. 19. Vacuum and open pan, bulk, pellets and packaged, f.o.b. mine and plant. 20. Elemental sulfur, f.o.b. mine and/or plant. 21. Concentrate, unit WO_3 (7.93 kilograms of contained tungsten per unit). 22. Price for imported zircon, f.o.b. U.S. east coast.

Municipal and Public Service

★ 626 ★

Municipal Long-Term Funding

Table shows the answers of 300 recycling decision makers in curbside-active states to the question: "Which of the following resources should municipalities pursue for long-term funding?"

[In percentages]

Resource	Recycling decision makers
Revenue from sale of recyclables	80.0
Garbage fees	68.0
State grants	45.0
Federal grants	41.0
Packaging industry grants	40.0
Local taxes	40.0
Taxes on packaging manufacturers	28.0
Taxes on product manufacturers	27.0
State taxes	25.0

Source: "Which of the Following Resources Should Municipalities Pursue for Long-Term Funding?" *American City & County* (April 1992), p. 14. Primary source: ALCOA.

★ 627 ★

Municipal and Public Service

Public Service Costs

Table shows the estimated public service cost increases to local governments for 3 years, starting in 1993. Data are for services whose costs are expected to grow most rapidly.

[In percentages]

Service	Cost increase
Solid waste disposal	29
Recycling	26
Criminal justice	21
Education	18
Child care	18
Infrastructure improvements	17
Welfare	17

Source: "Innovative Strategies Needed to Cut Costs, Maintain Services." *Nation's Cities Weekly,* 19 July 1993, p. 5.

★ 628 ★

Municipal and Public Service

Wastewater Treatment Project Funding: 1995

Boston, Massachusetts - 250	
Rouge River	
Texas - 100	
	New York, New York - 70
	Cleveland, Ohio - 60
	Los Angeles, California - 50
	Los Angeles County, California - 50
	Mexico - 47.5
	San Diego, California - 45.5
	Newark, New Jersey - 44.3

Table shows the areas scheduled to receive the most funding for construction of wastewater treatment projects during the 1995 fiscal year.

[In million dollars]

Place	Amount
Boston, Massachusetts	250
Rouge River (Detroit, Michigan)	160
Texas[1]	100
New York, New York	70
Cleveland, Ohio	60
Los Angeles, California	50
Los Angeles County, California	50
Mexico[2]	47.5
San Diego, California	45.5
Newark, New Jersey	44.3

Source: "Congress Earmarks Grants for Wastewater Projects." *Water Environment & Technology* (January 1995), p. 24. *Notes:* 1. Colonias. 2. Border region.

Natural Disasters

★ 629 ★

Natural Disaster Projected Costs

Table shows the projected costs of future natural disasters in the United States.

[Cost in billion dollars]

Place	Disaster	Cost
San Francisco, California	8.2 earthquake	84.4
Memphis, Tennessee	8.6 earthquake	69.7
Los Angeles, California	7.0 earthquake	57.7
Miami, Florida	Class 5 hurricane	53.0
Asbury Park, New Jersey	Class 4 hurricane	52.0
New York, New York	Class 4 hurricane	45.0
Galveston, Texas	Class 5 hurricane	42.5
Hampton, Virginia	Class 5 hurricane	33.5
Seattle, Washington	7.5 earthquake	33.3
Honolulu, Hawaii	Class 4 hurricane	30.0
New Orleans, Louisiana	Class 5 hurricane	25.6

Source: "Natural Disasters More Frequent, Costly." *National Consumers League Bulletin* 55, no.5 (September/October 1993), n.p.

★ 630 ★

Natural Disasters

Severe Weather Costs, by Lives Lost: 1940-1993

```
Floods - 82

Lightning - 39

Tornadoes - 30

Hurricanes - 1
                        Chart shows data from column 7.
```

Table shows the deaths associated with severe weather. Excessive heat, according to the source, is one of the more lethal weather conditions. A heat wave in July 1995, for example, claimed more than 700 lives, 466 in Chicago alone. Similarly, storms and other dangerous weather are just as deadly. In total, more than 22,225 Americans have died due to lightning, tornadoes, floods, and hurricanes in the United States since 1940. The table below shows deaths associated with severe weather conditions, excluding heat.

Severe weather	Deaths						
	1940s	1950s	1960s	1970s	1980s	1990	1993
Floods	619	791	1,297	1,819	1,097	142	82
Lightning	3,293	1,841	1,332	978	726	74	39
Tornadoes	1,788	1,409	935	986	521	53	30
Hurricanes	216	877	587	217	118	0	1

Source: Sharn, Lori. "Heat Wave's Lethal Accomplice: Human Nature." *USA TODAY,* 24 July 1995, p. 5A. Primary source: National Weather Service.

Pollution Abatement and Control

★ 631 ★

Air Pollution Abatement Expenditures: 1972-1991

Table shows air pollution expenditures in constant 1987 dollars. Excludes agricultural production of crops and livestock, except feedlots.

[In million dollars]

Year	Total	Mobile sources[1]			Total[3]	Industrial	
		Total	Cars[2]	Trucks[2]		Facilities	Operations[4]
1972	16,682	5,091	4,262	830	11,591	6,006	5,110
1973	18,652	6,828	5,586	1,242	11,825	6,305	5,045
1974	25,598	14,028	6,222	1,551	11,570	6,702	4,390
1975	27,958	16,097	7,806	1,877	11,861	6,750	4,642
1976	28,821	17,112	8,291	2,182	11,709	5,982	5,136
1977	22,765	11,003	8,821	2,448	11,762	5,631	5,518

[Continued]

★ 631 ★

Air Pollution Abatement Expenditures: 1972-1991
[Continued]

| Year | Total | Mobile sources[1] | | | Total[3] | Industrial | |
		Total	Cars[2]	Trucks[2]		Facilities	Operations[4]
1978	23,513	11,497	9,049	2,851	12,016	5,594	5,841
1979	24,447	11,452	8,601	3,264	12,996	5,966	6,322
1980	25,661	12,367	9,103	2,840	13,294	6,011	6,443
1981	27,012	13,932	11,092	2,700	13,080	5,951	6,295
1982	25,719	13,754	10,914	2,777	11,965	5,501	5,601
1983	26,085	15,456	12,756	3,177	10,629	3,893	5,911
1984	27,659	16,896	14,119	4,090	10,763	3,820	6,151
1985	29,041	18,073	14,896	4,463	10,968	3,539	6,320
1987	28,548	17,629	13,166	4,433	10,919	3,728	6,575
1988	29,531	19,190	14,727	4,607	10,341	3,342	6,436
1989	26,010	16,222	(NA)	(NA)	9,788	3,270	6,069
1990	24,728	13,994	(NA)	(NA)	10,734	3,969	6,371
1991	22,995	11,902	(NA)	(NA)	11,093	4,932	5,784

Source: 1994 Statistical Abstract of the United States on CD-ROM [machine-readable datafiles]. CD-8A-94. Washington, DC: U.S. Department of Commerce, Economics and Statistics Administration, Bureau of the Census, Data User Services Division, January 1995. 1993). Primary source: U. S. Bureau of Economic Analysis. *Survey of Current Business* (May 1993). *Notes:* "NA" represents "not available." 1. Excludes expenditures to reduce emissions from sources other than cars and trucks. 2. Includes expenditures for devices such as catalytic convertors, and expenditures for devices. 3. Includes other expenditures not shown separately for fixed capital of government enterprises such as Tennessee Valley Authority. 4. Operation of facilities.

★ 632 ★

Pollution Abatement and Control

Pollution Abatement and Control Expenditures: 1972-1992

From the source: "Expenditures are for goods and services that U.S. residents use to produce cleaner air and water and to manage solid waste. Pollution abatement directly reduces emissions by preventing the generation of pollutants, by recycling the pollutants, or by treating the pollutants prior to discharge. Regulation and monitoring are government activities that stimulate and guide action to reduce pollutant emissions. Research and development by business and government not only support abatement but also help increase the efficiency of regulation and monitoring" (p. 390).

[In billion dollars]

| Year | Pollution abatement | | Regulation & monitoring | | Research & development | | Total | |
	Current	Constant[1]	Current	Constant[1]	Current	Constant[1]	Current	Constant[1]
1972	15.40	42.81	0.37	0.96	0.82	2.26	16.59	46.03
1973	18.01	46.17	0.49	1.19	0.90	2.33	19.40	49.68
1974	21.97	48.46	0.60	1.34	0.99	2.30	23.55	52.10
1975	26.69	53.59	0.65	1.35	1.10	2.31	28.44	57.25
1976	29.86	56.23	0.73	1.40	1.28	2.51	31.86	60.14
1977	32.74	57.49	0.83	1.51	1.48	2.71	35.05	61.70
1978	36.94	60.28	0.95	1.62	1.65	2.78	39.54	64.68
1979	42.27	61.42	1.07	1.71	1.78	2.75	45.12	65.88
1980	47.35	61.31	1.30	1.87	1.75	2.41	50.40	65.59
1981	51.15	59.68	1.38	1.81	1.71	2.12	54.24	63.61
1982	52.32	58.12	1.40	1.71	1.64	1.89	55.36	61.71

[Continued]

★ 632 ★

Pollution Abatement and Control Expenditures: 1972-1992
[Continued]

Year	Pollution abatement Current	Pollution abatement Constant[1]	Regulation & monitoring Current	Regulation & monitoring Constant[1]	Research & development Current	Research & development Constant[1]	Total Current	Total Constant[1]
1983	55.89	60.47	1.39	1.61	1.60	1.76	58.87	62.84
1984	62.56	65.81	1.36	1.51	1.50	1.60	65.42	68.91
1985	68.27	69.77	1.28	1.36	1.62	1.68	71.17	72.81
1986	72.11	74.11	1.53	1.59	1.75	1.79	75.39	77.49
1987	74.35	74.35	1.52	1.52	1.78	1.78	77.65	77.65
1988	80.24	78.03	1.70	1.64	1.87	1.79	83.81	81.47
1989	83.54	78.13	1.80	1.66	2.04	1.88	87.39	81.66
1990	89.32	80.71	1.78	1.64	1.77	1.56	92.87	83.90
1991	90.92	80.00	1.87	1.65	2.01	1.69	94.79	83.35
1992	98.14	84.33	1.85	1.62	1.97	1.65	101.95	87.59

Source: Executive Office of the President of the United States. *Environmental Quality 24: The Twenty-fourth Annual Report of the Council on Environmental Quality.* Prepared by Ray Clark. Written by Carroll Curtis. Edited by Barry Walsh. Washington, DC: U.S. Government Printing Office, 1994, p. 390. Primary sources: Rutledge, G. L. "Real Spending for Pollution Abatement and Control Increased in 1992; Largest Increase Since 1986." *U.S. Commerce Department News.* BEA-94-21. Washington, DC: U.S. Department of Commerce, Bureau of Economic Analysis, May 1994; Rutledge, G. L., and C. R. Vogan. "Pollution Abatement and Control Expenditures, 1972-1992." *Survey of Current Business.* Washington, DC: U.S. Department of Commerce, Bureau of Economic Analysis, May 1994, pp. 45-47, table 7. *Notes:* Data for 1992 are preliminary. Estimates do not include interest costs. Totals may not agree with detail because of independent rounding. 1. 1987 dollars.

★ 633 ★

Pollution Abatement and Control

Pollution Abatement and Control Expenditures, by Media: 1972-1991

Table shows pollution abatement and control expenditures in current and constant (1987) dollars.

[In million dollars]

Year	Total expenditures	Pollution abatement Total	Pollution abatement Personal consumption	Pollution abatement Business	Government Total	Government Federal	Government State and local	Government enterprises[1]	Regulation and monitoring	Research and development
Current dollars										
1972	17,037	15,848	1,349	11,090	3,409	139	1,311	1,959	367	823
1973	19,401	18,008	1,867	12,219	3,923	203	1,433	2,286	490	903
1974	23,614	22,031	2,330	14,689	5,012	294	1,592	3,126	595	988
1975	28,424	26,668	3,231	16,531	6,906	432	1,752	4,722	653	1,104
1976	31,917	29,913	3,777	18,457	7,679	469	1,834	5,376	725	1,279
1977	35,123	32,812	4,286	21,101	7,426	490	1,965	4,971	833	1,478
1978	39,457	36,860	4,772	23,266	8,822	472	2,212	6,139	949	1,647
1979	45,593	42,750	5,423	27,285	10,042	548	2,461	7,033	1,067	1,777
1980	51,478	48,432	6,568	30,618	11,246	494	2,778	7,973	1,296	1,751
1981	56,472	53,346	8,140	34,453	10,752	506	3,053	7,194	1,378	1,749
1982	56,576	53,395	8,309	34,151	10,935	550	3,274	7,111	1,397	1,783
1983	60,002	56,283	9,758	35,357	11,167	795	3,547	6,825	1,385	2,335
1984	66,445	62,746	10,771	39,467	12,508	944	3,886	7,679	1,362	2,337
1985	70,941	67,250	11,839	41,559	13,852	1,225	4,324	8,304	1,279	2,412
1986	74,178	70,074	12,244	42,636	15,195	1,346	4,793	9,056	1,532	2,573
1987	76,672	72,506	10,875	44,501	17,130	1,237	5,356	10,538	1,519	2,648
1988	81,081	76,605	12,044	46,928	17,633	1,402	6,149	10,082	1,695	2,781
1989	85,407	80,630	10,636	50,817	19,177	1,381	7,076	10,720	1,803	2,974
1990[2]	89,996	85,116	9,088	55,059	20,969	1,391	8,089	11,489	1,784	3,097
Air	29,167	26,638	9,088	17,279	271	71	13	187	476	2,053
Water	36,909	35,851	0	23,293	12,558	734	521	11,303	649	409
Solid Waste	28,405	24,200	0	16,409	7,791	304	7,487	0	408	197
1991[2]	91,456	86,419	7,285	57,135	21,998	1,417	8,980	11,601	1,818	3,220

[Continued]

★ 633 ★

Pollution Abatement and Control Expenditures, by Media: 1972-1991

[Continued]

Year	Total expenditures	Pollution abatement							Regulation and monitoring	Research and development
		Total	Personal consumption	Business	Government					
					Total	Federal	State and local	Government enterprises[1]		
Air	28,060	25,423	7,285	17,881	258	73	16	168	483	2,153
Water	37,310	36,205	0	23,486	12,719	753	533	11,433	677	427
Solid Waste	26,640	26,026	0	17,338	8,688	341	8,348	0	427	187
Constant (1987) dollars										
1972	46,298	43,080	3,449	30,533	9,098	402	3,669	5,028	959.00	2,259
1973	49,764	46,246	4,541	32,136	9,569	539	3,689	5,341	1,190	2,327
1974	52,324	48,687	4,948	32,627	11,113	688	3,617	6,807	1,340	2,297
1975	57,333	53,673	6,165	33,113	14,395	937	3,737	9,720	1,346	2,313
1976	60,504	56,595	6,725	34,877	14,993	953	3,707	10,333	1,403	2,507
1977	62,011	57,792	7,147	37,101	13,545	917	3,726	8,902	1,514	2,705
1978	64,863	60,296	7,412	38,151	14,734	809	3,892	10,032	1,788	2,779
1979	66,796	62,424	7,156	40,224	15,044	840	3,931	10,273	1,624	2,747
1980	67,291	63,005	7,311	40,148	15,546	679	4,051	10,816	1,873	2,414
1981	66,536	62,556	8,494	40,470	13,592	627	3,984	8,981	1,810	2,170
1982	63,219	59,457	8,518	37,790	13,150	649	4,068	8,434	1,709	2,053
1983	65,052	60,870	10,016	38,042	12,813	911	4,203	7,698	1,608	2,574
1984	69,981	65,996	10,967	41,178	13,851	1,048	4,381	8,422	1,507	2,478
1985	72,656	68,802	11,780	42,408	14,615	1,300	4,646	8,668	1,361	2,493
1986	76,384	72,163	12,685	43,797	15,681	1,402	4,990	9,289	1,589	2,633
1987	76,672	72,506	10,875	44,501	17,130	1,237	5,356	10,538	1,519	2,648
1988	79,086	74,785	11,831	45,963	16,991	1,340	5,875	9,777	1,643	2,658
1989	80,106	75,720	10,147	47,755	17,818	1,273	6,502	10,043	1,657	2,730
1990[2]	81,703	77,337	8,512	49,949	18,875	1,228	7,074	10,573	1,636	2,370
Air	26,988	24,728	8,512	15,974	242	62	11	168	446	1,814
Water	34,022	33,066	0	21,473	11,593	656	531	10,405	597	359
Solid Waste	21,484	20,938	0	14,197	6,741	269	6,472	0	372	173
1991[2]	80,597	76,270	6,654	50,728	18,888	1,220	7,621	10,047	1,611	2,716
Air	25,264	22,995	6,654	16,115	226	63	14	150	446	1,824
Water	33,554	32,589	0	21,481	11,108	652	558	9,897	607	359
Solid Waste	22,329	21,810	0	14,535	7,276	296	6,980	0	363	156

Source: 1994 Statistical Abstract of the United States on CD-ROM [machine-readable datafiles]. CD-8A-94. Washington, DC: U.S. Department of Commerce, Economics and Statistics Administration, Bureau of the Census, Data User Services Division, January 1995. Primary source: U. S. Bureau of Economic Analysis. *Survey of Current Business* (May 1993). *Notes:* 1. Fixed capital. 2. Includes "other and unallocated" expenditures (such as for noise, radiation, and pesticide pollution and business expenditures not assigned to media) which may be either positive or negative; therefore, data may not add.

★ 634 ★

Pollution Abatement and Control

Pollution Abatement and Control Expenditures, by Sector: 1972-1992

Expenditures are attributed to the sector that performs the air or water pollution abatement or solid waste collection and disposal.

[In billions of 1987 dollars]

Year	Pollution abatement					Regulation and monitoring		Research and development		
	Private		Government			Federal government	State government[2]	Private[4]	Federal government	State government[2]
	Personal[1]	Business	Federal	State[2]	Other[3]					
1972	3.45	30.24	0.40	3.69	5.03	0.48	0.48	1.44	0.55	0.27
1973	4.54	32.00	0.54	3.72	5.36	0.63	0.56	1.49	0.68	0.17
1974	4.95	32.46	0.69	3.66	6.71	0.74	0.61	1.42	0.78	0.09
1975	6.17	32.99	0.94	3.78	9.72	0.74	0.61	1.28	0.93	0.10
1976	6.74	34.60	0.95	3.70	10.24	0.74	0.67	1.39	1.02	0.09
1977	7.16	36.86	0.92	3.72	8.83	0.74	0.78	1.56	1.04	0.10
1978	7.43	38.31	0.81	3.88	9.85	0.83	0.80	1.69	0.99	0.10

[Continued]

★ 634 ★

Pollution Abatement and Control Expenditures, by Sector: 1972-1992
[Continued]

Year	Pollution abatement					Regulation and monitoring		Research and development		
	Private		Government			Federal	State		Federal	State
	Personal[1]	Business	Federal	State[2]	Other[3]	government	government[2]	Private[4]	government	government[2]
1979	7.17	39.39	0.84	3.92	10.11	0.91	0.80	1.76	0.87	0.12
1980	7.30	38.67	0.68	4.02	10.64	1.11	0.76	1.50	0.82	0.10
1981	8.47	37.73	0.63	4.07	8.78	1.04	0.77	1.28	0.81	0.04
1982	8.49	36.46	0.65	4.29	8.22	0.98	0.73	1.15	0.70	0.04
1983	9.99	37.45	0.91	4.53	7.58	0.92	0.69	1.01	0.71	0.04
1984	11.04	40.71	1.05	4.80	8.21	0.81	0.69	0.93	0.63	0.04
1985	11.94	42.83	1.30	5.20	8.51	0.61	0.75	1.04	0.62	0.02
1986	12.83	45.00	1.40	5.73	9.15	0.74	0.85	1.09	0.67	0.03
1987	11.08	44.43	1.24	6.27	10.34	0.70	0.82	1.12	0.63	0.03
1988	12.07	47.81	1.34	6.95	9.87	0.81	0.83	1.12	0.64	0.03
1989	10.44	48.78	1.27	7.98	9.66	0.78	0.88	1.14	0.72	0.03
1990	8.66	51.88	1.23	8.86	10.08	0.77	0.87	0.84	0.68	0.04
1991	6.76	52.66	1.22	9.77	9.60	0.76	0.89	1.00	0.65	0.04
1992	7.02	55.99	1.04	10.73	9.54	0.71	0.91	0.95	0.66	0.03

Source: Executive Office of the President of the United States. *Environmental Quality 24: The Twenty-fourth Annual Report of the Council on Environmental Quality.* Prepared by Ray Clark. Written by Carroll Curtis. Edited by Barry Walsh. Washington, DC: U.S. Government Printing Office, 1994, p. 392. Primary sources: Rutledge, G. L. "Real Spending for Pollution Abatement and Control Increased in 1992; Largest Increase Since 1986." *U.S. Commerce Department News.* BEA-94-21. Washington, DC: U.S. Department of Commerce, Bureau of Economic Analysis, May 1994; Rutledge, G. L., and C. R. Vogan. "Pollution Abatement and Control Expenditures, 1972-1992." *Survey of Current Business.* Washington, DC: U.S. Department of Commerce, Bureau of Economic Analysis, May 1994, pp. 45-47, table 7. *Notes:* Data do not include interest costs. Totals may not agree with detail on related tables because of independent rounding. Data for 1992 are preliminary. 1. Personal consumption, all of which is to purchase and operate motor vehicle emission abatement devices. 2. Includes expenditures by local authorities but excludes agricultural production except feedlot operations. 3. Refers to government enterprise fixed capital for publicly owned electric utilities and public sewer systems. 4. Private business spending.

★ 635 ★
Pollution Abatement and Control

Pollution Abatement and Control Expenditures, by Type of Pollution: 1981-1992

From the source: "Expenditures cover most, but not all, pollution abatement and control activities, which are defined as those resulting from rules, policies and conventions, and formal regulations restricting the release of pollutants into common-property media such as the air and water. Solid waste management includes the collection and disposal of solid waste and the alteration of processes that generate less solid waste" (p. 391).

[In billion dollars]

Year	Air		Water		Solid waste	
	Current	Constant[1]	Current	Constant[1]	Current	Constant[1]
1981	26.3	28.5	20.8	25.2	10.2	13.4
1982	26.1	27.2	21.1	24.2	9.9	12.1
1983	27.6	28.5	22.5	24.7	10.3	12.0
1984	30.4	31.0	24.7	26.2	11.8	13.2
1985	30.1	32.0	26.7	27.4	12.7	13.7
1986	32.1	33.3	28.2	28.7	14.3	14.8
1987	28.9	28.9	30.3	30.3	19.1	19.1
1988	31.2	30.5	30.9	30.1	22.1	21.8

[Continued]

★ 635 ★

Pollution Abatement and Control Expenditures, by Type of Pollution: 1981-1992
[Continued]

Year	Air		Water		Solid waste	
	Current	Constant[1]	Current	Constant[1]	Current	Constant[1]
1989	29.1	27.6	33.1	31.0	26.1	23.8
1990	28.1	26.0	36.4	33.4	29.4	25.4
1991	27.0	24.4	36.6	32.9	31.8	26.7
1992	28.6	25.3	38.2	33.9	36.1	29.2

Source: Executive Office of the President of the United States. *Environmental Quality 24: The Twenty-fourth Annual Report of the Council on Environmental Quality.* Prepared by Ray Clark. Written by Carroll Curtis. Edited by Barry Walsh. Washington, DC: U.S. Government Printing Office, 1994, p. 391. Primary sources: Rutledge, G. L. "Real Spending for Pollution Abatement and Control Increased in 1992; Largest Increase Since 1986." *U.S. Commerce Department News.* BEA-94-21. Washington, DC: U.S. Department of Commerce, Bureau of Economic Analysis, May 1994; Rutledge, G. L., and C. R. Vogan. "Pollution Abatement and Control Expenditures, 1972-1992." *Survey of Current Business.* Washington, DC: U.S. Department of Commerce, Bureau of Economic Analysis, May 1994, pp. 45-47, table 7. *Notes:* Data for 1992 are revised estimates. Estimates do not include interest costs. 1. 1987 dollars.

★ 636 ★

Pollution Abatement and Control

Pollution Abatement Capital Expenditures in the United States: 1988-1992

Pollution abatement expenditures are those with the primary purpose of protecting the environment by reducing or eliminating unwanted emissions or wastes that are created by the production process. Pollution abatement capital expenditures (PACE) by manufacturing establishments with 20 employees or more amounted to $8,393 million in 1992. Of this total, $7,867 million was attributable to a particular media: $4,403 million for air; $2,510 million for water; and $954 million for solid/contained waste. Spending for nonmedia and other was $526 million. Approximately 79 percent of the $8,383 million new capital expenditures for pollution abatement was made by establishments in four major industry groups: Chemicals and allied products (major group 28), petroleum and coal products (major group 29), paper and allied products (major group 26), and primary metal industries (major group 33). In 1992, Texas, California, and Louisiana accounted for approximately 38 percent of total new pollution abatement capital expenditures. Texas comprised 18 percent of the total. The table below shows pollution abatement capital expenditures for air, water, solid/contained waste, and nonmedia for the United States.

[In million dollars]

Year	Pollution abatement capital expenditures	Air	Water	Solid waste	Nonmedia
1992	7,866.9	4,403.1	2,509.8	954.0	526.1
1991	7,390.1	3,706.3	2,814.6	869.2	(NA)
1990	6,030.8	2,562.0	2,651.4	817.5	(NA)
1989	4,309.0	1,819.0	1,824.5	665.5	(NA)
1988	3,423.3	1,524.1	1,289.4	609.7	(NA)

Source: U.S. Department of Commerce. Bureau of the Census. "Pollution Abatement Costs and Expenditures, 1992." In *National Economic, Social, and Environmental Data Bank* [CD-ROM]. Prepared by U.S. Department of Commerce, Economics and Statistics Administration. Washington, DC: U.S. Department of Commerce, National Economic, Social, and Environmental Data Bank, Economics and Statistics Administration, Office of Business Analysis, February 1995. *Notes:* Totals may not agree with detail because of independent rounding. "NA" represents "not available."

★ 637 ★
Pollution Abatement and Control

Pollution Abatement Operating Costs in the United States: 1988-1992

Pollution abatement concerns those activities with the primary purpose of protecting the environment by reducing or eliminating unwanted emissions or wastes that are created by the production process. Operating costs related to pollution abatement activities totaled $19,228 million in 1992. Of this amount, $17,466 million was attributable to a particular media: $5,395 million for air; $6,577 million for water; and $5,494 million for solid/contained waste. Spending for nonmedia and other was $1,762 million. Total population abatement media operating costs showed an overall increase of $158 million (1 percent) from 1991, the previous year. Air operating costs increased 9 percent; water operating costs increased 4 percent; solid/contained waste operating costs decreased 9 percent. The table below shows pollution abatement operating control costs for air, water, solid/contained waste, and nonmedia for the United States.

[In million dollars]

Year	Pollution abatement operating costs	Air	Water	Solid waste	Nonmedia
1992	1,7466.4	5,395.0	6,576.9	5,494.4	1,761.6
1991	1,7308.9	4,955.6	6,345.0	6,008.3	(NA)
1990	1,7070.7	5,010.9	6,416.4	5,643.4	(NA)
1989	1,5625.6	4,694.2	5,853.4	5,078.0	(NA)
1988	1,4008.2	4,466.5	5,275.9	4,265.8	(NA)

Source: U.S. Department of Commerce. Bureau of the Census. "Pollution Abatement Costs and Expenditures, 1992." In *National Economic, Social, and Environmental Data Bank* [CD-ROM]. Prepared by U.S. Department of Commerce, Economics and Statistics Administration. Washington, DC: U.S. Department of Commerce, National Economic, Social, and Environmental Data Bank, Economics and Statistics Administration, Office of Business Analysis, February 1995. *Notes:* Totals may not agree with detail because of independent rounding. "NA" represents "not available."

★ 638 ★

Pollution Abatement and Control

Water Pollution Abatement Expenditures: 1972-1991

Table shows water pollution abatement expenditures in constant (1987) dollars. .
Excludes agricultural production of crops and livestock except feedlots.

[In million dollars]

Year	Total[1]	Industrial		Public sewer systems	
		Facilities	Operations[2]	Facilities	Operations[2]
1972	18,667	3,849	2,644	4,801	3,197
1973	19,379	3,739	2,934	5,136	3,510
1974	20,637	3,656	2,922	6,451	3,614
1975	23,530	4,172	3,021	9,426	3,722
1976	25,547	4,827	3,431	9,945	4,032
1977	25,094	4,879	3,764	8,456	4,399
1978	26,370	4,231	3,973	9,508	4,763
1979	26,844	4,095	4,192	9,710	4,997
1980	26,482	3,696	3,988	10,148	5,148
1981	24,251	3,405	4,025	8,270	5,297
1982	23,337	3,284	3,844	7,679	5,616
1983	23,751	2,666	4,264	7,063	5,959
1984	25,382	2,865	4,482	7,791	6,149
1985	26,542	2,879	4,658	8,124	6,550
1987	29,695	2,354	5,383	10,053	7,792
1988	29,107	2,381	5,310	9,376	8,269
1989	30,057	2,802	5,462	9,383	8,803
1990	33,066	4,226	5,935	10,334	9,488
1991	32,589	3,730	5,575	9,839	10,300

Source: 1994 Statistical Abstract of the United States on CD-ROM [machine-readable datafiles]. CD-8A-94. Washington, DC: U.S. Department of Commerce, Economics and Statistics Administration, Bureau of the Census, Data User Services Division, January 1995. Primary source: U.S. Bureau of Economic Analysis. *Survey of Current Business* (May 1993). *Notes:* 1. Includes expenditures for private connectors to sewer systems, by owners of animal feedlots, and by government enterprises. 2. Operation of facilities.

Pollution Abatement and Control, by Industry

★ 639 ★

Pollution Abatement Capital Expenditures for All Industries: 1988-1992

Pollution abatement expenditures are those with the primary purpose of protecting the environment by reducing or eliminating unwanted emissions or wastes that are created by the production process. Pollution abatement capital expenditures (PACE) by manufacturing establishments with 20 employees or more amounted to $8,393 million in 1992. Of this total, $7,867 million was attributable to a particular media: $4,403 million for air; $2,510 million for water; and $954 million for solid/contained waste. Spending for nonmedia and other was $526 million. Approximately 79 percent of the $8,383 million new capital expenditures for pollution abatement was made by establishments in four major industry groups: Chemicals and allied products (major group 28), petroleum and coal products (major group 29), paper and allied products (major group 26), and primary metal industries (major group 33). In 1992, Texas, California, and Louisiana accounted for approximately 38 percent of total new pollution abatement capital expenditures. Texas comprised 18 percent of the total. The table below shows pollution abatement capital expenditures for air, water, solid/contained waste, and nonmedia for all industries.

[In million dollars]

Year	Pollution abatement capital expenditures	Air	Water	Solid waste	Nonmedia
1992	7,866.9	4,403.1	2,509.8	954.0	526.1
1991	7,390.1	3,706.3	2,814.6	869.2	(NA)
1990	6,030.8	2,562.0	2,651.4	817.5	(NA)
1989	4,309.0	1,819.0	1,824.5	665.5	(NA)
1988	3,423.3	1,524.1	1,289.4	609.7	(NA)

Source: U.S. Department of Commerce. Bureau of the Census. "Pollution Abatement Costs and Expenditures, 1992." In *National Economic, Social, and Environmental Data Bank* [CD-ROM]. Prepared by U.S. Department of Commerce, Economics and Statistics Administration. Washington, DC: U.S. Department of Commerce, National Economic, Social, and Environmental Data Bank, Economics and Statistics Administration, Office of Business Analysis, February 1995. *Notes:* Totals may not agree with detail because of independent rounding. "NA" represents "not available."

★ 640 ★

Pollution Abatement and Control, by Industry

Pollution Abatement Capital Expenditures for Chemicals and Allied Products: 1988-1992

Pollution abatement expenditures are those with the primary purpose of protecting the environment by reducing or eliminating unwanted emissions or wastes that are created by the production process. Pollution abatement capital expenditures (PACE) by manufacturing establishments with 20 employees or more amounted to $8,393 million in 1992. Of this total, $7,867 million was attributable to a particular media: $4,403 million for air; $2,510 million for water; and $954 million for solid/ contained waste. Spending for nonmedia and other was $526 million. Approximately 79 percent of the $8,383 million new capital expenditures for pollution abatement was made by establishments in four major industry groups: Chemicals and allied products (major group 28), petroleum and coal products (major group 29), paper and allied products (major group 26), and primary metal industries (major group 33). In 1992, Texas, California, and Louisiana accounted for approximately 38 percent of total new pollution abatement capital expenditures. Texas comprised 18 percent of the total. The table below shows pollution abatement capital expenditures for air, water, solid/ contained waste, and nonmedia for chemicals and allied products.

[In million dollars]

Year	Pollution abatement capital expenditures	Air	Water	Solid waste	Nonmedia
1992	2,120.9	774.5	1,017.3	329.1	194.9
1991	2,066.1	816.4	942.3	307.5	(NA)
1990	1,852.1	596.2	995.0	260.9	(NA)
1989	1,194.8	380.3	598.6	215.9	(NA)
1988	1,095.0	370.7	487.8	236.5	(NA)

Source: U.S. Department of Commerce. Bureau of the Census. "Pollution Abatement Costs and Expenditures, 1992." In *National Economic, Social, and Environmental Data Bank* [CD-ROM]. Prepared by U.S. Department of Commerce, Economics and Statistics Administration. Washington, DC: U.S. Department of Commerce, National Economic, Social, and Environmental Data Bank, Economics and Statistics Administration, Office of Business Analysis, February 1995. *Notes:* Totals may not agree with detail because of independent rounding. "NA" represents "not available."

★ 641 ★

Pollution Abatement and Control, by Industry

Pollution Abatement Capital Expenditures for Electronic and Other Electric Equipment: 1988-1992

Pollution abatement expenditures are those with the primary purpose of protecting the environment by reducing or eliminating unwanted emissions or wastes that are created by the production process. Pollution abatement capital expenditures (PACE) by manufacturing establishments with 20 employees or more amounted to $8,393 million in 1992. Of this total, $7,867 million was attributable to a particular media: $4,403 million for air; $2,510 million for water; and $954 million for solid/contained waste. Spending for nonmedia and other was $526 million. Approximately 79 percent of the $8,383 million new capital expenditures for pollution abatement was made by establishments in four major industry groups: Chemicals and allied products (major group 28), petroleum and coal products (major group 29), paper and allied products (major group 26), and primary metal industries (major group 33). In 1992, Texas, California, and Louisiana accounted for approximately 38 percent of total new pollution abatement capital expenditures. Texas comprised 18 percent of the total. The table below shows pollution abatement capital expenditures for air, water, solid/contained waste, and nonmedia for electronic and other electric equipment.

[In million dollars]

Year	Pollution abatement capital expenditures	Air	Water	Solid waste	Nonmedia
1992	126.6	63.0	45.6	17.9	23.2
1991	233.7	90.7	122.7	20.3	(NA)
1990	177.5	92.8	58.4	26.3	(NA)
1989	188.7	66.6	94.3	27.8	(NA)
1988	154.2	80.6	54.6	19.0	(NA)

Source: U.S. Department of Commerce. Bureau of the Census. "Pollution Abatement Costs and Expenditures, 1992." In *National Economic, Social, and Environmental Data Bank* [CD-ROM]. Prepared by U.S. Department of Commerce, Economics and Statistics Administration. Washington, DC: U.S. Department of Commerce, National Economic, Social, and Environmental Data Bank, Economics and Statistics Administration, Office of Business Analysis, February 1995. *Notes:* Totals may not agree with detail because of independent rounding. "NA" represents "not available."

★ 642 ★

Pollution Abatement and Control, by Industry

Pollution Abatement Capital Expenditures for Fabricated Metal Products: 1988-1992

Pollution abatement expenditures are those with the primary purpose of protecting the environment by reducing or eliminating unwanted emissions or wastes that are created by the production process. Pollution abatement capital expenditures (PACE) by manufacturing establishments with 20 employees or more amounted to $8,393 million in 1992. Of this total, $7,867 million was attributable to a particular media: $4,403 million for air; $2,510 million for water; and $954 million for solid/contained waste. Spending for nonmedia and other was $526 million. Approximately 79 percent of the $8,383 million new capital expenditures for pollution abatement was made by establishments in four major industry groups: Chemicals and allied products (major group 28), petroleum and coal products (major group 29), paper and allied products (major group 26), and primary metal industries (major group 33). In 1992, Texas, California, and Louisiana accounted for approximately 38 percent of total new pollution abatement capital expenditures. Texas comprised 18 percent of the total. The table below shows pollution abatement capital expenditures for air, water, solid/contained waste, and nonmedia for fabricated metal products.

[In million dollars]

Year	Pollution abatement capital expenditures	Air	Water	Solid waste	Nonmedia
1992	103.3	42.4	42.4	18.5	42.1
1991	176.9	80.7	66.4	29.8	(NA)
1990	171.0	52.9	61.1	57.0	(NA)
1989	151.0	50.5	71.3	29.2	(NA)
1988	146.8	45.5	75.3	26.1	(NA)

Source: U.S. Department of Commerce. Bureau of the Census. "Pollution Abatement Costs and Expenditures, 1992." In *National Economic, Social, and Environmental Data Bank* [CD-ROM]. Prepared by U.S. Department of Commerce, Economics and Statistics Administration. Washington, DC: U.S. Department of Commerce, National Economic, Social, and Environmental Data Bank, Economics and Statistics Administration, Office of Business Analysis, February 1995. *Notes:* Totals may not agree with detail because of independent rounding. "NA" represents "not available."

★ 643 ★

Pollution Abatement and Control, by Industry

Pollution Abatement Capital Expenditures for Food and Kindred Products: 1988-1992

Pollution abatement expenditures are those with the primary purpose of protecting the environment by reducing or eliminating unwanted emissions or wastes that are created by the production process. Pollution abatement capital expenditures (PACE) by manufacturing establishments with 20 employees or more amounted to $8,393 million in 1992. Of this total, $7,867 million was attributable to a particular media: $4,403 million for air; $2,510 million for water; and $954 million for solid/ contained waste. Spending for nonmedia and other was $526 million. Approximately 79 percent of the $8,383 million new capital expenditures for pollution abatement was made by establishments in four major industry groups: Chemicals and allied products (major group 28), petroleum and coal products (major group 29), paper and allied products (major group 26), and primary metal industries (major group 33). In 1992, Texas, California, and Louisiana accounted for approximately 38 percent of total new pollution abatement capital expenditures. Texas comprised 18 percent of the total. The table below shows pollution abatement capital expenditures for air, water, solid/contained waste, and nonmedia for food and kindred products.

[In million dollars]

Year	Pollution abatement capital expenditures	Air	Water	Solid waste	Nonmedia
1992	316.8	85.1	202.6	29.1	35.2
1991	481.8	94.6	359.5	27.7	(NA)
1990	249.0	64.6	163.3	21.1	(NA)
1989	260.6	51.7	183.6	25.2	(NA)
1988	211.0	100.2	91.0	19.8	(NA)

Source: U.S. Department of Commerce. Bureau of the Census. "Pollution Abatement Costs and Expenditures, 1992." In *National Economic, Social, and Environmental Data Bank* [CD-ROM]. Prepared by U.S. Department of Commerce, Economics and Statistics Administration. Washington, DC: U.S. Department of Commerce, National Economic, Social, and Environmental Data Bank, Economics and Statistics Administration, Office of Business Analysis, February 1995. *Notes:* Totals may not agree with detail because of independent rounding. "NA" represents "not available."

★ 644 ★

Pollution Abatement and Control, by Industry

Pollution Abatement Capital Expenditures for Furniture and Fixtures: 1988-1992

Pollution abatement expenditures are those with the primary purpose of protecting the environment by reducing or eliminating unwanted emissions or wastes that are created by the production process. Pollution abatement capital expenditures (PACE) by manufacturing establishments with 20 employees or more amounted to $8,393 million in 1992. Of this total, $7,867 million was attributable to a particular media: $4,403 million for air; $2,510 million for water; and $954 million for solid/contained waste. Spending for nonmedia and other was $526 million. Approximately 79 percent of the $8,383 million new capital expenditures for pollution abatement was made by establishments in four major industry groups: Chemicals and allied products (major group 28), petroleum and coal products (major group 29), paper and allied products (major group 26), and primary metal industries (major group 33). In 1992, Texas, California, and Louisiana accounted for approximately 38 percent of total new pollution abatement capital expenditures. Texas comprised 18 percent of the total. The table below shows pollution abatement capital expenditures for air, water, solid/contained waste, and nonmedia for furniture and fixtures.

[In million dollars]

Year	Pollution abatement capital expenditures	Air	Water	Solid waste	Nonmedia
1992	17.9	14.3	0.8	2.8	7.7
1991	23.7	16.2	2.8	4.7	(NA)
1990	23.6	19.0	2.3	2.3	(NA)
1989	14.3	10.8	1.3	2.1	(NA)
1988	27.9	20.4	1.0	6.5	(NA)

Source: U.S. Department of Commerce. Bureau of the Census. "Pollution Abatement Costs and Expenditures, 1992." In *National Economic, Social, and Environmental Data Bank* [CD-ROM]. Prepared by U.S. Department of Commerce, Economics and Statistics Administration. Washington, DC: U.S. Department of Commerce, National Economic, Social, and Environmental Data Bank, Economics and Statistics Administration, Office of Business Analysis, February 1995. *Notes:* Totals may not agree with detail because of independent rounding. "NA" represents "not available."

★ 645 ★

Pollution Abatement and Control, by Industry

Pollution Abatement Capital Expenditures for Industrial Machinery and Equipment: 1988-1992

Pollution abatement expenditures are those with the primary purpose of protecting the environment by reducing or eliminating unwanted emissions or wastes that are created by the production process. Pollution abatement capital expenditures (PACE) by manufacturing establishments with 20 employees or more amounted to $8,393 million in 1992. Of this total, $7,867 million was attributable to a particular media: $4,403 million for air; $2,510 million for water; and $954 million for solid/contained waste. Spending for nonmedia and other was $526 million. Approximately 79 percent of the $8,383 million new capital expenditures for pollution abatement was made by establishments in four major industry groups: Chemicals and allied products (major group 28), petroleum and coal products (major group 29), paper and allied products (major group 26), and primary metal industries (major group 33). In 1992, Texas, California, and Louisiana accounted for approximately 38 percent of total new pollution abatement capital expenditures. Texas comprised 18 percent of the total. The table below shows pollution abatement capital expenditures for air, water, solid/contained waste, and nonmedia for industrial machinery and equipment.

[In million dollars]

Year	Pollution abatement capital expenditures	Air	Water	Solid waste	Nonmedia
1992	150.3	88.8	31.7	29.8	23.9
1991	128.4	88.7	27.6	12.1	(NA)
1990	107.8	46.7	41.3	19.8	(NA)
1989	169.5	99.8	54.8	14.9	(NA)
1988	77.2	21.8	33.2	22.3	(NA)

Source: U.S. Department of Commerce. Bureau of the Census. "Pollution Abatement Costs and Expenditures, 1992." In *National Economic, Social, and Environmental Data Bank* [CD-ROM]. Prepared by U.S. Department of Commerce, Economics and Statistics Administration. Washington, DC: U.S. Department of Commerce, National Economic, Social, and Environmental Data Bank, Economics and Statistics Administration, Office of Business Analysis, February 1995. *Notes:* Totals may not agree with detail because of independent rounding. "NA" represents "not available."

★ 646 ★

Pollution Abatement and Control, by Industry

Pollution Abatement Capital Expenditures for Instruments and Related Products: 1988-1992

Pollution abatement expenditures are those with the primary purpose of protecting the environment by reducing or eliminating unwanted emissions or wastes that are created by the production process. Pollution abatement capital expenditures (PACE) by manufacturing establishments with 20 employees or more amounted to $8,393 million in 1992. Of this total, $7,867 million was attributable to a particular media: $4,403 million for air; $2,510 million for water; and $954 million for solid/contained waste. Spending for nonmedia and other was $526 million. Approximately 79 percent of the $8,383 million new capital expenditures for pollution abatement was made by establishments in four major industry groups: Chemicals and allied products (major group 28), petroleum and coal products (major group 29), paper and allied products (major group 26), and primary metal industries (major group 33). In 1992, Texas, California, and Louisiana accounted for approximately 38 percent of total new pollution abatement capital expenditures. Texas comprised 18 percent of the total. The table below shows pollution abatement capital expenditures for air, water, solid/contained waste, and nonmedia for instruments and related products.

[In million dollars]

Year	Pollution abatement capital expenditures	Air	Water	Solid waste	Nonmedia
1992	89.1	52.7	18.8	17.5	34.1
1991	104.4	27.1	44.3	33.0	(NA)
1990	91.5	57.7	25.5	8.2	(NA)
1989	86.1	33.9	37.8	14.4	(NA)
1988	30.7	15.5	11.8	3.4	(NA)

Source: U.S. Department of Commerce. Bureau of the Census. "Pollution Abatement Costs and Expenditures, 1992." In *National Economic, Social, and Environmental Data Bank* [CD-ROM]. Prepared by U.S. Department of Commerce, Economics and Statistics Administration. Washington, DC: U.S. Department of Commerce, National Economic, Social, and Environmental Data Bank, Economics and Statistics Administration, Office of Business Analysis, February 1995. *Notes:* Totals may not agree with detail because of independent rounding. "NA" represents "not available."

★ 647 ★

Pollution Abatement and Control, by Industry

Pollution Abatement Capital Expenditures for Leather and Leather Products: 1988-1992

Pollution abatement expenditures are those with the primary purpose of protecting the environment by reducing or eliminating unwanted emissions or wastes that are created by the production process. Pollution abatement capital expenditures (PACE) by manufacturing establishments with 20 employees or more amounted to $8,393 million in 1992. Of this total, $7,867 million was attributable to a particular media: $4,403 million for air; $2,510 million for water; and $954 million for solid/contained waste. Spending for nonmedia and other was $526 million. Approximately 79 percent of the $8,383 million new capital expenditures for pollution abatement was made by establishments in four major industry groups: Chemicals and allied products (major group 28), petroleum and coal products (major group 29), paper and allied products (major group 26), and primary metal industries (major group 33). In 1992, Texas, California, and Louisiana accounted for approximately 38 percent of total new pollution abatement capital expenditures. Texas comprised 18 percent of the total. The table below shows pollution abatement capital expenditures for air, water, solid/contained waste, and nonmedia for leather and leather products.

[In million dollars]

Year	Pollution abatement capital expenditures	Air	Water	Solid waste	Nonmedia
1992	8.5	0.9	6.7	0.9	1.1
1991	15.0	1.1	9.6	4.3	(NA)
1990	8.3	0.7	6.5	1.1	(NA)
1989	3.6	0.6	2.9	0.1	(NA)
1988	4.0	1.9	1.6	0.5	(NA)

Source: U.S. Department of Commerce. Bureau of the Census. "Pollution Abatement Costs and Expenditures, 1992." In *National Economic, Social, and Environmental Data Bank* [CD-ROM]. Prepared by U.S. Department of Commerce, Economics and Statistics Administration. Washington, DC: U.S. Department of Commerce, National Economic, Social, and Environmental Data Bank, Economics and Statistics Administration, Office of Business Analysis, February 1995. *Notes:* Totals may not agree with detail because of independent rounding. "NA" represents "not available."

★ 648 ★

Pollution Abatement and Control, by Industry

Pollution Abatement Capital Expenditures for Lumber and Wood Products: 1988-1992

Pollution abatement expenditures are those with the primary purpose of protecting the environment by reducing or eliminating unwanted emissions or wastes that are created by the production process. Pollution abatement capital expenditures (PACE) by manufacturing establishments with 20 employees or more amounted to $8,393 million in 1992. Of this total, $7,867 million was attributable to a particular media: $4,403 million for air; $2,510 million for water; and $954 million for solid/contained waste. Spending for nonmedia and other was $526 million. Approximately 79 percent of the $8,383 million new capital expenditures for pollution abatement was made by establishments in four major industry groups: Chemicals and allied products (major group 28), petroleum and coal products (major group 29), paper and allied products (major group 26), and primary metal industries (major group 33). In 1992, Texas, California, and Louisiana accounted for approximately 38 percent of total new pollution abatement capital expenditures. Texas comprised 18 percent of the total. The table below shows pollution abatement capital expenditures for air, water, solid/contained waste, and nonmedia for lumber and wood products.

[In million dollars]

Year	Pollution abatement capital expenditures	Air	Water	Solid waste	Nonmedia
1992	94.5	50.7	18.9	24.9	8.1
1991	141.2	102.0	13.8	25.4	(NA)
1990	105.1	57.8	10.4	36.9	(NA)
1989	60.0	45.9	6.6	7.5	(NA)
1988	44.5	31.6	7.5	5.4	(NA)

Source: U.S. Department of Commerce. Bureau of the Census. "Pollution Abatement Costs and Expenditures, 1992." In *National Economic, Social, and Environmental Data Bank* [CD-ROM]. Prepared by U.S. Department of Commerce, Economics and Statistics Administration. Washington, DC: U.S. Department of Commerce, National Economic, Social, and Environmental Data Bank, Economics and Statistics Administration, Office of Business Analysis, February 1995. *Notes:* Totals may not agree with detail because of independent rounding. "NA" represents "not available."

★ 649 ★

Pollution Abatement and Control, by Industry

Pollution Abatement Capital Expenditures for Miscellaneous Manufacturing Industries: 1988-1992

Pollution abatement expenditures are those with the primary purpose of protecting the environment by reducing or eliminating unwanted emissions or wastes that are created by the production process. Pollution abatement capital expenditures (PACE) by manufacturing establishments with 20 employees or more amounted to $8,393 million in 1992. Of this total, $7,867 million was attributable to a particular media: $4,403 million for air; $2,510 million for water; and $954 million for solid/contained waste. Spending for nonmedia and other was $526 million. Approximately 79 percent of the $8,383 million new capital expenditures for pollution abatement was made by establishments in four major industry groups: Chemicals and allied products (major group 28), petroleum and coal products (major group 29), paper and allied products (major group 26), and primary metal industries (major group 33). In 1992, Texas, California, and Louisiana accounted for approximately 38 percent of total new pollution abatement capital expenditures. Texas comprised 18 percent of the total. The table below shows pollution abatement capital expenditures for air, water, solid/contained waste, and nonmedia for miscellaneous manufacturing industries.

[In million dollars]

Year	Pollution abatement capital expenditures	Air	Water	Solid waste	Nonmedia
1992	16.6	10.2	(D)	(D)	2.5
1991	13.1	7.3	3.8	2.0	(NA)
1990	17.7	6.6	7.0	4.1	(NA)
1989	10.0	3.3	5.2	1.5	(NA)
1988	11.3	3.6	5.7	2.0	(NA)

Source: U.S. Department of Commerce. Bureau of the Census. "Pollution Abatement Costs and Expenditures, 1992." In *National Economic, Social, and Environmental Data Bank* [CD-ROM]. Prepared by U.S. Department of Commerce, Economics and Statistics Administration. Washington, DC: U.S. Department of Commerce, National Economic, Social, and Environmental Data Bank, Economics and Statistics Administration, Office of Business Analysis, February 1995. *Notes:* Totals may not agree with detail because of independent rounding. "NA" represents "not available." "D" indicates data withheld to avoid disclosing operations of individual companies.

★ 650 ★

Pollution Abatement and Control, by Industry

Pollution Abatement Capital Expenditures for Paper and Allied Products: 1988-1992

Pollution abatement expenditures are those with the primary purpose of protecting the environment by reducing or eliminating unwanted emissions or wastes that are created by the production process. Pollution abatement capital expenditures (PACE) by manufacturing establishments with 20 employees or more amounted to $8,393 million in 1992. Of this total, $7,867 million was attributable to a particular media: $4,403 million for air; $2,510 million for water; and $954 million for solid/ contained waste. Spending for nonmedia and other was $526 million. Approximately 79 percent of the $8,383 million new capital expenditures for pollution abatement was made by establishments in four major industry groups: Chemicals and allied products (major group 28), petroleum and coal products (major group 29), paper and allied products (major group 26), and primary metal industries (major group 33). In 1992, Texas, California, and Louisiana accounted for approximately 38 percent of total new pollution abatement capital expenditures. Texas comprised 18 percent of the total. The table below shows pollution abatement capital expenditures for air, water, solid/contained waste, and nonmedia for paper and allied products.

[In million dollars]

Year	Pollution abatement capital expenditures	Air	Water	Solid waste	Nonmedia
1992	1,004.6	396.7	373.4	234.5	18.0
1991	1,232.6	480.8	552.7	199.0	(NA)
1990	1,075.2	414.0	509.6	151.7	(NA)
1989	808.2	392.4	261.0	154.9	(NA)
1988	417.7	233.4	97.2	87.1	(NA)

Source: U.S. Department of Commerce. Bureau of the Census. "Pollution Abatement Costs and Expenditures, 1992." In *National Economic, Social, and Environmental Data Bank* [CD-ROM]. Prepared by U.S. Department of Commerce, Economics and Statistics Administration. Washington, DC: U.S. Department of Commerce, National Economic, Social, and Environmental Data Bank, Economics and Statistics Administration, Office of Business Analysis, February 1995. *Notes:* Totals may not agree with detail because of independent rounding. "NA" represents "not available."

★ 651 ★

Pollution Abatement and Control, by Industry

Pollution Abatement Capital Expenditures for Petroleum and Coal Products: 1988-1992

Pollution abatement expenditures are those with the primary purpose of protecting the environment by reducing or eliminating unwanted emissions or wastes that are created by the production process. Pollution abatement capital expenditures (PACE) by manufacturing establishments with 20 employees or more amounted to $8,393 million in 1992. Of this total, $7,867 million was attributable to a particular media: $4,403 million for air; $2,510 million for water; and $954 million for solid/contained waste. Spending for nonmedia and other was $526 million. Approximately 79 percent of the $8,383 million new capital expenditures for pollution abatement was made by establishments in four major industry groups: Chemicals and allied products (major group 28), petroleum and coal products (major group 29), paper and allied products (major group 26), and primary metal industries (major group 33). In 1992, Texas, California, and Louisiana accounted for approximately 38 percent of total new pollution abatement capital expenditures. Texas comprised 18 percent of the total. The table below shows pollution abatement capital expenditures for air, water, solid/contained waste, and nonmedia for petroleum and coal products.

[In million dollars]

Year	Pollution abatement capital expenditures	Air	Water	Solid waste	Nonmedia
1992	2,685.0	2,079.8	492.6	112.6	17.8
1991	1,462.5	996.7	373.3	92.5	(NA)
1990	916.8	425.7	400.8	90.3	(NA)
1989	417.6	146.5	230.4	40.7	(NA)
1988	482.8	208.2	203.7	70.8	(NA)

Source: U.S. Department of Commerce. Bureau of the Census. "Pollution Abatement Costs and Expenditures, 1992." In *National Economic, Social, and Environmental Data Bank* [CD-ROM]. Prepared by U.S. Department of Commerce, Economics and Statistics Administration. Washington, DC: U.S. Department of Commerce, National Economic, Social, and Environmental Data Bank, Economics and Statistics Administration, Office of Business Analysis, February 1995. *Notes:* Totals may not agree with detail because of independent rounding. "NA" represents "not available."

★ 652 ★

Pollution Abatement and Control, by Industry

Pollution Abatement Capital Expenditures for Primary Metal Industries: 1988-1992

Pollution abatement expenditures are those with the primary purpose of protecting the environment by reducing or eliminating unwanted emissions or wastes that are created by the production process. Pollution abatement capital expenditures (PACE) by manufacturing establishments with 20 employees or more amounted to $8,393 million in 1992. Of this total, $7,867 million was attributable to a particular media: $4,403 million for air; $2,510 million for water; and $954 million for solid/contained waste. Spending for nonmedia and other was $526 million. Approximately 79 percent of the $8,383 million new capital expenditures for pollution abatement was made by establishments in four major industry groups: Chemicals and allied products (major group 28), petroleum and coal products (major group 29), paper and allied products (major group 26), and primary metal industries (major group 33). In 1992, Texas, California, and Louisiana accounted for approximately 38 percent of total new pollution abatement capital expenditures. Texas comprised 18 percent of the total. The table below shows pollution abatement capital expenditures for air, water, solid/contained waste, and nonmedia for primary metal industries.

[In million dollars]

Year	Pollution abatement capital expenditures	Air	Water	Solid waste	Nonmedia
1992	525.7	342.6	123.5	59.5	34.9
1991	673.4	499.2	131.9	42.2	(NA)
1990	499.1	278.6	166.8	53.7	(NA)
1989	407.0	216.3	138.7	52.1	(NA)
1988	309.8	167.3	100.6	41.8	(NA)

Source: U.S. Department of Commerce. Bureau of the Census. "Pollution Abatement Costs and Expenditures, 1992." In *National Economic, Social, and Environmental Data Bank* [CD-ROM]. Prepared by U.S. Department of Commerce, Economics and Statistics Administration. Washington, DC: U.S. Department of Commerce, National Economic, Social, and Environmental Data Bank, Economics and Statistics Administration, Office of Business Analysis, February 1995. *Notes:* Totals may not agree with detail because of independent rounding. "NA" represents "not available."

★ 653 ★

Pollution Abatement and Control, by Industry

Pollution Abatement Capital Expenditures for Printing and Publishing: 1988-1992

Pollution abatement expenditures are those with the primary purpose of protecting the environment by reducing or eliminating unwanted emissions or wastes that are created by the production process. Pollution abatement capital expenditures (PACE) by manufacturing establishments with 20 employees or more amounted to $8,393 million in 1992. Of this total, $7,867 million was attributable to a particular media: $4,403 million for air; $2,510 million for water; and $954 million for solid/contained waste. Spending for nonmedia and other was $526 million. Approximately 79 percent of the $8,383 million new capital expenditures for pollution abatement was made by establishments in four major industry groups: Chemicals and allied products (major group 28), petroleum and coal products (major group 29), paper and allied products (major group 26), and primary metal industries (major group 33). In 1992, Texas, California, and Louisiana accounted for approximately 38 percent of total new pollution abatement capital expenditures. Texas comprised 18 percent of the total. The table below shows pollution abatement capital expenditures for air, water, solid/ contained waste, and nonmedia for printing and publishing.

[In million dollars]

Year	Pollution abatement capital expenditures	Air	Water	Solid waste	Nonmedia
1992	41.8	32.9	4.5	4.4	6.1
1991	37.2	26.8	6.2	4.2	(NA)
1990	67.8	56.4	4.4	7.0	(NA)
1989	35.1	25.6	2.6	6.9	(NA)
1988	70.0	56.3	4.7	9.0	(NA)

Source: U.S. Department of Commerce. Bureau of the Census. "Pollution Abatement Costs and Expenditures, 1992." In *National Economic, Social, and Environmental Data Bank* [CD-ROM]. Prepared by U.S. Department of Commerce, Economics and Statistics Administration. Washington, DC: U.S. Department of Commerce, National Economic, Social, and Environmental Data Bank, Economics and Statistics Administration, Office of Business Analysis, February 1995. *Notes:* Totals may not agree with detail because of independent rounding. "NA" represents "not available."

★ 654 ★

Pollution Abatement and Control, by Industry

Pollution Abatement Capital Expenditures for Rubber and Miscellaneous Plastics Products: 1988-1992

Pollution abatement expenditures are those with the primary purpose of protecting the environment by reducing or eliminating unwanted emissions or wastes that are created by the production process. Pollution abatement capital expenditures (PACE) by manufacturing establishments with 20 employees or more amounted to $8,393 million in 1992. Of this total, $7,867 million was attributable to a particular media: $4,403 million for air; $2,510 million for water; and $954 million for solid/contained waste. Spending for nonmedia and other was $526 million. Approximately 79 percent of the $8,383 million new capital expenditures for pollution abatement was made by establishments in four major industry groups: Chemicals and allied products (major group 28), petroleum and coal products (major group 29), paper and allied products (major group 26), and primary metal industries (major group 33). In 1992, Texas, California, and Louisiana accounted for approximately 38 percent of total new pollution abatement capital expenditures. Texas comprised 18 percent of the total. The table below shows pollution abatement capital expenditures for air, water, solid/contained waste, and nonmedia for rubber and miscellaneous plastics products.

[In million dollars]

Year	Pollution abatement capital expenditures	Air	Water	Solid waste	Nonmedia
1992	96.7	71.1	18.2	7.3	11.5
1991	81.7	50.8	18.8	12.2	(NA)
1990	93.8	68.9	11.0	13.9	(NA)
1989	78.2	50.3	16.0	12.0	(NA)
1988	40.7	21.7	11.3	7.8	(NA)

Source: U.S. Department of Commerce. Bureau of the Census. "Pollution Abatement Costs and Expenditures, 1992." In *National Economic, Social, and Environmental Data Bank* [CD-ROM]. Prepared by U.S. Department of Commerce, Economics and Statistics Administration. Washington, DC: U.S. Department of Commerce, National Economic, Social, and Environmental Data Bank, Economics and Statistics Administration, Office of Business Analysis, February 1995. *Notes:* Totals may not agree with detail because of independent rounding. "NA" represents "not available."

★ 655 ★

Pollution Abatement and Control, by Industry

Pollution Abatement Capital Expenditures for Stone, Clay, and Glass Products: 1988-1992

Pollution abatement expenditures are those with the primary purpose of protecting the environment by reducing or eliminating unwanted emissions or wastes that are created by the production process. Pollution abatement capital expenditures (PACE) by manufacturing establishments with 20 employees or more amounted to $8,393 million in 1992. Of this total, $7,867 million was attributable to a particular media: $4,403 million for air; $2,510 million for water; and $954 million for solid/ contained waste. Spending for nonmedia and other was $526 million. Approximately 79 percent of the $8,383 million new capital expenditures for pollution abatement was made by establishments in four major industry groups: Chemicals and allied products (major group 28), petroleum and coal products (major group 29), paper and allied products (major group 26), and primary metal industries (major group 33). In 1992, Texas, California, and Louisiana accounted for approximately 38 percent of total new pollution abatement capital expenditures. Texas comprised 18 percent of the total. The table below shows pollution abatement capital expenditures for air, water, solid/contained waste, and nonmedia for stone, clay, and glass products.

[In million dollars]

Year	Pollution abatement capital expenditures	Air	Water	Solid waste	Nonmedia
1992	138.8	93.4	20.2	25.3	15.7
1991	154.4	119.9	22.2	12.3	(NA)
1990	127.5	94.1	19.8	13.6	(NA)
1989	97.3	73.2	17.1	7.0	(NA)
1988	62.3	42.6	13.6	6.1	(NA)

Source: U.S. Department of Commerce. Bureau of the Census. "Pollution Abatement Costs and Expenditures, 1992." In *National Economic, Social, and Environmental Data Bank* [CD-ROM]. Prepared by U.S. Department of Commerce, Economics and Statistics Administration. Washington, DC: U.S. Department of Commerce, National Economic, Social, and Environmental Data Bank, Economics and Statistics Administration, Office of Business Analysis, February 1995. *Notes:* Totals may not agree with detail because of independent rounding. "NA" represents "not available."

★ 656 ★

Pollution Abatement and Control, by Industry

Pollution Abatement Capital Expenditures for Textile Mill Products: 1988-1992

Pollution abatement expenditures are those with the primary purpose of protecting the environment by reducing or eliminating unwanted emissions or wastes that are created by the production process. Pollution abatement capital expenditures (PACE) by manufacturing establishments with 20 employees or more amounted to $8,393 million in 1992. Of this total, $7,867 million was attributable to a particular media: $4,403 million for air; $2,510 million for water; and $954 million for solid/contained waste. Spending for nonmedia and other was $526 million. Approximately 79 percent of the $8,383 million new capital expenditures for pollution abatement was made by establishments in four major industry groups: Chemicals and allied products (major group 28), petroleum and coal products (major group 29), paper and allied products (major group 26), and primary metal industries (major group 33). In 1992, Texas, California, and Louisiana accounted for approximately 38 percent of total new pollution abatement capital expenditures. Texas comprised 18 percent of the total. The table below shows pollution abatement capital expenditures for air, water, solid/ contained waste, and nonmedia for textile mill products.

[In million dollars]

Year	Pollution abatement capital expenditures	Air	Water	Solid waste	Nonmedia
1992	34.3	11.8	18.7	3.9	8.7
1991	56.8	27.8	21.4	7.6	(NA)
1990	45.9	18.7	24.8	2.4	(NA)
1989	29.5	9.7	16.5	3.3	(NA)
1988	18.9	8.0	8.0	2.9	(NA)

Source: U.S. Department of Commerce. Bureau of the Census. "Pollution Abatement Costs and Expenditures, 1992." In *National Economic, Social, and Environmental Data Bank* [CD-ROM]. Prepared by U.S. Department of Commerce, Economics and Statistics Administration. Washington, DC: U.S. Department of Commerce, National Economic, Social, and Environmental Data Bank, Economics and Statistics Administration, Office of Business Analysis, February 1995. *Notes:* Totals may not agree with detail because of independent rounding. "NA" represents "not available."

★ 657 ★

Pollution Abatement and Control, by Industry

Pollution Abatement Capital Expenditures for Tobacco Products: 1988-1992

Pollution abatement expenditures are those with the primary purpose of protecting the environment by reducing or eliminating unwanted emissions or wastes that are created by the production process. Pollution abatement capital expenditures (PACE) by manufacturing establishments with 20 employees or more amounted to $8,393 million in 1992. Of this total, $7,867 million was attributable to a particular media: $4,403 million for air; $2,510 million for water; and $954 million for solid/contained waste. Spending for nonmedia and other was $526 million. Approximately 79 percent of the $8,383 million new capital expenditures for pollution abatement was made by establishments in four major industry groups: Chemicals and allied products (major group 28), petroleum and coal products (major group 29), paper and allied products (major group 26), and primary metal industries (major group 33). In 1992, Texas, California, and Louisiana accounted for approximately 38 percent of total new pollution abatement capital expenditures. Texas comprised 18 percent of the total. The table below shows pollution abatement capital expenditures for air, water, solid/contained waste, and nonmedia for tobacco products.

[In million dollars]

Year	Pollution abatement capital expenditures	Air	Water	Solid waste	Nonmedia
1992	14.5	12.9	(D)	(D)	0.6
1991	5.9	3.8	0.5	1.6	(NA)
1990	5.9	4.0	0.8	1.1	(NA)
1989	10.6	5.6	1.2	3.9	(NA)
1988	7.9	7.4	0.2	0.4	(NA)

Source: U.S. Department of Commerce. Bureau of the Census. "Pollution Abatement Costs and Expenditures, 1992." In *National Economic, Social, and Environmental Data Bank* [CD-ROM]. Prepared by U.S. Department of Commerce, Economics and Statistics Administration. Washington, DC: U.S. Department of Commerce, National Economic, Social, and Environmental Data Bank, Economics and Statistics Administration, Office of Business Analysis, February 1995. *Notes:* Totals may not agree with detail because of independent rounding. "NA" represents "not available." "D" indicates data withheld to avoid disclosing operations of individual companies.

★ 658 ★

Pollution Abatement and Control, by Industry

Pollution Abatement Capital Expenditures for Transportation Equipment: 1988-1992

Pollution abatement expenditures are those with the primary purpose of protecting the environment by reducing or eliminating unwanted emissions or wastes that are created by the production process. Pollution abatement capital expenditures (PACE) by manufacturing establishments with 20 employees or more amounted to $8,393 million in 1992. Of this total, $7,867 million was attributable to a particular media: $4,403 million for air; $2,510 million for water; and $954 million for solid/contained waste. Spending for nonmedia and other was $526 million. Approximately 79 percent of the $8,383 million new capital expenditures for pollution abatement was made by establishments in four major industry groups: Chemicals and allied products (major group 28), petroleum and coal products (major group 29), paper and allied products (major group 26), and primary metal industries (major group 33). In 1992, Texas, California, and Louisiana accounted for approximately 38 percent of total new pollution abatement capital expenditures. Texas comprised 18 percent of the total. The table below shows pollution abatement capital expenditures for air, water, solid/contained waste, and nonmedia for transportation equipment.

[In million dollars]

Year	Pollution abatement capital expenditures	Air	Water	Solid waste	Nonmedia
1992	281.0	179.4	69.2	32.5	40.0
1991	301.4	175.8	94.7	30.8	(NA)
1990	395.3	206.6	142.6	46.1	(NA)
1989	286.8	156.0	84.6	46.2	(NA)
1988	210.2	87.6	80.4	42.2	(NA)

Source: U.S. Department of Commerce. Bureau of the Census. "Pollution Abatement Costs and Expenditures, 1992." In *National Economic, Social, and Environmental Data Bank* [CD-ROM]. Prepared by U.S. Department of Commerce, Economics and Statistics Administration. Washington, DC: U.S. Department of Commerce, National Economic, Social, and Environmental Data Bank, Economics and Statistics Administration, Office of Business Analysis, February 1995. *Notes:* Totals may not agree with detail because of independent rounding. "NA" represents "not available."

★ 659 ★

Pollution Abatement and Control, by Industry

Pollution Abatement Cost Offsets for Chemicals and Allied Products: 1973-1992

Table shows cost offsets in current dollars for pollution abatement. This data measures the amount of pollution abatement costs recovered through the reuse or sale of recovered materials and energy. Cost offsets must be related to production and must be for environmental protection.

[In million dollars]

Year	Cost offsets
1973	83.1
1974	104.5
1975	140.7
1976	188.7
1977	206.4
1978	231.3
1979	230.4
1980	305.9
1981	341.1
1982	345.2
1983	297.4
1984	357.5
1985	268.6
1986	336.4
1988	443.8
1989	395.9
1990	405.7
1991	353.7
1992	511.2

Source: Executive Office of the President of the United States. *Environmental Quality 24: The Twenty-fourth Annual Report of the Council on Environmental Quality.* Prepared by Ray Clark. Written by Carroll Curtis. Edited by Barry Walsh. Washington, DC: U.S. Government Printing Office, 1994, p. 393. Primary source: U.S. Department of Commerce. Bureau of the Census. *Pollution Abatement Costs and Expenditures.* In *Current Industrial Reports.* MA-200. Washington, DC: U.S. Department of Commerce, annual. *Note:* Data for 1987 not available.

★ 660 ★

Pollution Abatement and Control, by Industry

Pollution Abatement Cost Offsets for Electric and Electronic Equipment: 1973-1992

Table shows cost offsets in current dollars for pollution abatement. This data measures the amount of pollution abatement costs recovered through the reuse or sale of recovered materials and energy. Cost offsets must be related to production and must be for environmental protection.

[In million dollars]

Year	Cost offsets
1973	18.5
1974	20.3
1975	14.3
1976	23.7
1977	16.0
1978	12.9
1979	24.1
1980	17.0
1981	22.0
1982	14.2
1983	15.1
1984	18.3
1985	15.2
1986	19.4
1988	39.1
1989	29.3
1990	42.9
1991	32.3
1992	36.4

Source: Executive Office of the President of the United States. *Environmental Quality 24: The Twenty-fourth Annual Report of the Council on Environmental Quality.* Prepared by Ray Clark. Written by Carroll Curtis. Edited by Barry Walsh. Washington, DC: U.S. Government Printing Office, 1994, p. 396. Primary source: U.S. Department of Commerce. Bureau of the Census. *Pollution Abatement Costs and Expenditures.* In *Current Industrial Reports.* MA-200. Washington, DC: U.S. Department of Commerce, annual. *Note:* Data for 1987 not available.

★ 661 ★

Pollution Abatement and Control, by Industry

Pollution Abatement Cost Offsets for Fabricated Metal Products: 1973-1992

Table shows cost offsets in current dollars for pollution abatement. This data measures the amount of pollution abatement costs recovered through the reuse or sale of recovered materials and energy. Cost offsets must be related to production and must be for environmental protection.

[In million dollars]

Year	Cost offsets
1973	9.1
1974	8.2
1975	7.5
1976	6.3
1977	3.5
1978	4.5
1979	13.4
1980	23.9
1981	21.5
1982	13.0
1983	17.7
1984	37.0
1985	15.4
1986	27.1
1988	29.1
1989	21.9
1990	20.0
1991	17.4
1992	45.4

Source: Executive Office of the President of the United States. *Environmental Quality 24: The Twenty-fourth Annual Report of the Council on Environmental Quality.* Prepared by Ray Clark. Written by Carroll Curtis. Edited by Barry Walsh. Washington, DC: U.S. Government Printing Office, 1994, p. 395. Primary source: U.S. Department of Commerce. Bureau of the Census. *Pollution Abatement Costs and Expenditures.* In *Current Industrial Reports.* MA-200. Washington, DC: U.S. Department of Commerce, annual. *Note:* Data for 1987 not available.

★ 662 ★

Pollution Abatement and Control, by Industry

Pollution Abatement Cost Offsets for Food and Kindred Products: 1973-1992

Table shows cost offsets in current dollars for pollution abatement. This data measures the amount of pollution abatement costs recovered through the reuse or sale of recovered materials and energy. Cost offsets must be related to production and must be for environmental protection.

[In million dollars]

Year	Cost offsets
1973	32.6
1974	52.2
1975	62.6
1976	63.7
1977	53.3
1978	57.1
1979	80.3
1980	79.5
1981	91.2
1982	51.1
1983	32.7
1984	43.7
1985	33.4
1986	w/h
1988	110.6
1989	82.0
1990	87.0
1991	71.6
1992	82.2

Source: Executive Office of the President of the United States. *Environmental Quality 24: The Twenty-fourth Annual Report of the Council on Environmental Quality.* Prepared by Ray Clark. Written by Carroll Curtis. Edited by Barry Walsh. Washington, DC: U.S. Government Printing Office, 1994, p. 398. Primary source: U.S. Department of Commerce. Bureau of the Census. *Pollution Abatement Costs and Expenditures.* In *Current Industrial Reports.* MA-200. Washington, DC: U.S. Department of Commerce, annual. *Notes:* Data for 1987 not available. "w/h" indicates "withheld by industry."

★ 663 ★

Pollution Abatement and Control, by Industry

Pollution Abatement Cost Offsets for Industrial Machinery and Equipment: 1973-1992

Table shows cost offsets in current dollars for pollution abatement. This data measures the amount of pollution abatement costs recovered through the reuse or sale of recovered materials and energy. Cost offsets must be related to production and must be for environmental protection.

[In million dollars]

Year	Cost offsets
1973	14.3
1974	11.0
1975	11.9
1976	15.9
1977	17.6
1978	14.8
1979	19.9
1980	17.6
1981	18.1
1982	11.4
1983	18.8
1984	15.8
1985	12.1
1986	12.6
1988	14.7
1989	13.9
1990	19.5
1991	13.0
1992	32.2

Source: Executive Office of the President of the United States. *Environmental Quality 24: The Twenty-fourth Annual Report of the Council on Environmental Quality.* Prepared by Ray Clark. Written by Carroll Curtis. Edited by Barry Walsh. Washington, DC: U.S. Government Printing Office, 1994, p. 396. Primary source: U.S. Department of Commerce. Bureau of the Census. *Pollution Abatement Costs and Expenditures.* In *Current Industrial Reports.* MA-200. Washington, DC: U.S. Department of Commerce, annual. *Note:* Data for 1987 not available.

★ 664 ★

Pollution Abatement and Control, by Industry

Pollution Abatement Cost Offsets for Instruments and Related Products: 1973-1992

Table shows cost offsets in current dollars for pollution abatement. This data measures the amount of pollution abatement costs recovered through the reuse or sale of recovered materials and energy. Cost offsets must be related to production and must be for environmental protection.

[In million dollars]

Year	Cost offsets
1973	2.2
1974	3.5
1975	4.3
1976	11.6
1977	6.1
1978	5.0
1979	15.2
1980	11.8
1981	9.4
1982	10.3
1983	11.2
1984	w/h
1985	10.9
1986	12.0
1988	19.5
1989	19.8
1990	18.8
1991	13.3
1992	13.3

Source: Executive Office of the President of the United States. *Environmental Quality 24: The Twenty-fourth Annual Report of the Council on Environmental Quality.* Prepared by Ray Clark. Written by Carroll Curtis. Edited by Barry Walsh. Washington, DC: U.S. Government Printing Office, 1994, p. 397. Primary source: U.S. Department of Commerce. Bureau of the Census. *Pollution Abatement Costs and Expenditures.* In *Current Industrial Reports.* MA-200. Washington, DC: U.S. Department of Commerce, annual. *Notes:* Data for 1987 not available. "w/h" represents "withheld by industry."

★ 665 ★

Pollution Abatement and Control, by Industry

Pollution Abatement Cost Offsets for Lumber and Wood Products: 1973-1992

Table shows cost offsets in current dollars for pollution abatement. This data measures the amount of pollution abatement costs recovered through the reuse or sale of recovered materials and energy. Cost offsets must be related to production and must be for environmental protection.

[In million dollars]

Year	Cost offsets
1973	7.6
1974	12.8
1975	17.4
1976	25.5
1977	15.3
1978	26.7
1979	28.4
1980	37.6
1981	29.7
1982	16.6
1983	9.0
1984	13.6
1985	10.4
1986	14.7
1988	24.0
1989	19.5
1990	31.6
1991	20.8
1992	18.3

Source: Executive Office of the President of the United States. *Environmental Quality 24: The Twenty-fourth Annual Report of the Council on Environmental Quality.* Prepared by Ray Clark. Written by Carroll Curtis. Edited by Barry Walsh. Washington, DC: U.S. Government Printing Office, 1994, p. 399. Primary source: U.S. Department of Commerce. Bureau of the Census. *Pollution Abatement Costs and Expenditures.* In *Current Industrial Reports.* MA-200. Washington, DC: U.S. Department of Commerce, annual. *Note:* Data for 1987 not available.

★ 666 ★

Pollution Abatement and Control, by Industry

Pollution Abatement Cost Offsets for Paper and Allied Products: 1973-1992

Table shows cost offsets in current dollars for pollution abatement. This data measures the amount of pollution abatement costs recovered through the reuse or sale of recovered materials and energy. Cost offsets must be related to production and must be for environmental protection.

[In million dollars]

Year	Cost offsets
1973	54.6
1974	84.8
1975	112.2
1976	137.6
1977	150.8
1978	175.6
1979	161.5
1980	248.1
1981	298.5
1982	213.7
1983	255.3
1984	118.4
1985	107.3
1986	133.8
1988	245.6
1989	264.9
1990	266.4
1991	170.4
1992	254.6

Source: Executive Office of the President of the United States. *Environmental Quality 24: The Twenty-fourth Annual Report of the Council on Environmental Quality.* Prepared by Ray Clark. Written by Carroll Curtis. Edited by Barry Walsh. Washington, DC: U.S. Government Printing Office, 1994, p. 399. Primary source: U.S. Department of Commerce. Bureau of the Census. *Pollution Abatement Costs and Expenditures.* In *Current Industrial Reports.* MA-200. Washington, DC: U.S. Department of Commerce, annual. *Note:* Data for 1987 not available.

★ 667 ★
Pollution Abatement and Control, by Industry

Pollution Abatement Cost Offsets for Petroleum and Coal Products: 1973- 1992

Table shows cost offsets in current dollars for pollution abatement. This data measures the amount of pollution abatement costs recovered through the reuse or sale of recovered materials and energy. Cost offsets must be related to production and must be for environmental protection.

[In million dollars]

Year	Cost offsets
1973	44.3
1974	83.5
1975	137.7
1976	183.8
1977	238.4
1978	261.8
1979	324.1
1980	506.7
1981	565.6
1982	335.3
1983	524.9
1984	552.8
1985	500.0
1986	498.2
1988	480.0
1989	523.1
1990	562.0
1991	480.5
1992	475.9

Source: Executive Office of the President of the United States. *Environmental Quality 24: The Twenty-fourth Annual Report of the Council on Environmental Quality.* Prepared by Ray Clark. Written by Carroll Curtis. Edited by Barry Walsh. Washington, DC: U.S. Government Printing Office, 1994, p. 393. Primary source: U.S. Department of Commerce. Bureau of the Census. *Pollution Abatement Costs and Expenditures.* In *Current Industrial Reports.* MA-200. Washington, DC: U.S. Department of Commerce, annual. *Note:* Data for 1987 not available.

★ 668 ★

Pollution Abatement and Control, by Industry

Pollution Abatement Cost Offsets for Primary Metals: 1973-1992

Table shows cost offsets in current dollars for pollution abatement. This data measures the amount of pollution abatement costs recovered through the reuse or sale of recovered materials and energy. Cost offsets must be related to production and must be for environmental protection.

[In million dollars]

Year	Cost offsets
1973	51.5
1974	76.9
1975	95.3
1976	100.7
1977	126.3
1978	141.7
1979	241.8
1980	169.5
1981	189.7
1982	148.5
1983	95.4
1984	171.6
1985	136.8
1986	184.6
1988	189.8
1989	190.4
1990	206.3
1991	185.1
1992	164.2

Source: Executive Office of the President of the United States. *Environmental Quality 24: The Twenty-fourth Annual Report of the Council on Environmental Quality.* Prepared by Ray Clark. Written by Carroll Curtis. Edited by Barry Walsh. Washington, DC: U.S. Government Printing Office, 1994, p. 395. Primary source: U.S. Department of Commerce. Bureau of the Census. *Pollution Abatement Costs and Expenditures.* In *Current Industrial Reports.* MA-200. Washington, DC: U.S. Department of Commerce, annual. *Note:* Data for 1987 not available.

★ 669 ★

Pollution Abatement and Control, by Industry

Pollution Abatement Cost Offsets for Rubber and Miscellaneous Plastic Products: 1973-1992

Table shows cost offsets in current dollars for pollution abatement. This data measures the amount of pollution abatement costs recovered through the reuse or sale of recovered materials and energy. Cost offsets must be related to production and must be for environmental protection.

[In million dollars]

Year	Cost offsets
1973	4.6
1974	19.5
1975	12.5
1976	15.8
1977	7.7
1978	8.0
1979	13.6
1980	18.1
1981	14.0
1982	7.0
1983	6.6
1984	9.9
1985	10.0
1986	15.1
1988	18.7
1989	25.6
1990	24.3
1991	29.4
1992	26.7

Source: Executive Office of the President of the United States. *Environmental Quality 24: The Twenty-fourth Annual Report of the Council on Environmental Quality.* Prepared by Ray Clark. Written by Carroll Curtis. Edited by Barry Walsh. Washington, DC: U.S. Government Printing Office, 1994, p. 394. Primary source: U.S. Department of Commerce. Bureau of the Census. *Pollution Abatement Costs and Expenditures.* In *Current Industrial Reports.* MA-200. Washington, DC: U.S. Department of Commerce, annual. *Note:* Data for 1987 not available.

★ 670 ★

Pollution Abatement and Control, by Industry

Pollution Abatement Cost Offsets for Stone, Clay, and Glass Products: 1973-1992

Table shows cost offsets in current dollars for pollution abatement. This data measures the amount of pollution abatement costs recovered through the reuse or sale of recovered materials and energy. Cost offsets must be related to production and must be for environmental protection.

[In million dollars]

Year	Cost offsets
1973	24.5
1974	33.1
1975	41.7
1976	59.3
1977	68.7
1978	74.8
1979	82.4
1980	83.9
1981	91.5
1982	56.0
1983	45.2
1984	46.2
1985	31.5
1986	46.7
1988	103.3
1989	52.3
1990	49.3
1991	49.7
1992	90.3

Source: Executive Office of the President of the United States. *Environmental Quality 24: The Twenty-fourth Annual Report of the Council on Environmental Quality.* Prepared by Ray Clark. Written by Carroll Curtis. Edited by Barry Walsh. Washington, DC: U.S. Government Printing Office, 1994, p. 394. Primary source: U.S. Department of Commerce. Bureau of the Census. *Pollution Abatement Costs and Expenditures.* In *Current Industrial Reports.* MA-200. Washington, DC: U.S. Department of Commerce, annual. *Note:* Data for 1987 not available.

★ 671 ★
Pollution Abatement and Control, by Industry

Pollution Abatement Cost Offsets for Textile Mill Products: 1973-1992

Table shows cost offsets in current dollars for pollution abatement. This data measures the amount of pollution abatement costs recovered through the reuse or sale of recovered materials and energy. Cost offsets must be related to production and must be for environmental protection.

[In million dollars]

Year	Cost offsets
1973	2.8
1974	2.5
1975	w/h
1976	8.4
1977	6.6
1978	w/h
1979	10.5
1980	13.4
1981	18.2
1982	7.6
1983	5.4
1984	5.3
1985	3.3
1986	w/h
1988	10.7
1989	5.8
1990	6.3
1991	4.5
1992	19.7

Source: Executive Office of the President of the United States. *Environmental Quality 24: The Twenty-fourth Annual Report of the Council on Environmental Quality.* Prepared by Ray Clark. Written by Carroll Curtis. Edited by Barry Walsh. Washington, DC: U.S. Government Printing Office, 1994, p. 398. Primary source: U.S. Department of Commerce. Bureau of the Census. *Pollution Abatement Costs and Expenditures.* In *Current Industrial Reports.* MA-200. Washington, DC: U.S. Department of Commerce, annual. *Notes:* Data for 1987 not available. "w/h" represents "withheld by industry."

★ 672 ★

Pollution Abatement and Control, by Industry

Pollution Abatement Cost Offsets for Transportation Equipment: 1973-1992

Table shows cost offsets in current dollars for pollution abatement. This data measures the amount of pollution abatement costs recovered through the reuse or sale of recovered materials and energy. Cost offsets must be related to production and must be for environmental protection.

[In million dollars]

Year	Cost offsets
1973	20.1
1974	13.6
1975	13.4
1976	14.5
1977	13.5
1978	16.6
1979	36.9
1980	24.6
1981	19.3
1982	18.2
1983	22.3
1984	22.7
1985	23.7
1986	28.2
1988	38.7
1989	43.1
1990	41.2
1991	45.9
1992	68.7

Source: Executive Office of the President of the United States. *Environmental Quality 24: The Twenty-fourth Annual Report of the Council on Environmental Quality.* Prepared by Ray Clark. Written by Carroll Curtis. Edited by Barry Walsh. Washington, DC: U.S. Government Printing Office, 1994, p. 397. Primary source: U.S. Department of Commerce. Bureau of the Census. *Pollution Abatement Costs and Expenditures.* In *Current Industrial Reports.* MA-200. Washington, DC: U.S. Department of Commerce, annual. *Note:* Data for 1987 not available.

★ 673 ★

Pollution Abatement and Control, by Industry

Pollution Abatement Operating Costs for All Industries: 1988-1992

Pollution abatement concerns those activities with the primary purpose of protecting the environment by reducing or eliminating unwanted emissions or wastes that are created by the production process. Operating costs related to pollution abatement activities totaled $19,228 million in 1992. Of this amount, $17,466 million was attributable to a particular media: $5,395 million for air; $6,577 million for water; and $5,494 million for solid/contained waste. Spending for nonmedia and other was $1,762 million. Total population abatement media operating costs showed an overall increase of $158 million (1 percent) from 1991, the previous year. Air operating costs increased 9 percent; water operating costs increased 4 percent; solid/contained waste operating costs decreased 9 percent. The table below shows pollution abatement operating control costs for air, water, solid/contained waste, and nonmedia for all industries.

[In million dollars]

Year	Pollution abatement operating costs	Air	Water	Solid waste	Nonmedia
1992	17,466.4	5,395.0	6,576.9	5,494.4	1,761.6
1991	17,308.9	4,955.6	6,345.0	6,008.3	(NA)
1990	17,070.7	5,010.9	6,416.4	5,643.4	(NA)
1989	15,625.6	4,694.2	5,853.4	5,078.0	(NA)
1988	14,008.2	4,466.5	5,275.9	4,265.8	(NA)

Source: U.S. Department of Commerce. Bureau of the Census. "Pollution Abatement Costs and Expenditures, 1992." In *National Economic, Social, and Environmental Data Bank* [CD-ROM]. Prepared by U.S. Department of Commerce, Economics and Statistics Administration. Washington, DC: U.S. Department of Commerce, National Economic, Social, and Environmental Data Bank, Economics and Statistics Administration, Office of Business Analysis, February 1995. *Notes:* Totals may not agree with detail because of independent rounding. "NA" represents "not available."

★ 674 ★

Pollution Abatement and Control, by Industry

Pollution Abatement Operating Costs for Chemicals and Allied Products: 1988-1992

Pollution abatement concerns those activities with the primary purpose of protecting the environment by reducing or eliminating unwanted emissions or wastes that are created by the production process. Operating costs related to pollution abatement activities totaled $19,228 million in 1992. Of this amount, $17,466 million was attributable to a particular media: $5,395 million for air; $6,577 million for water; and $5,494 million for solid/contained waste. Spending for nonmedia and other was $1,762 million. Total population abatement media operating costs showed an overall increase of $158 million (1 percent) from 1991, the previous year. Air operating costs increased 9 percent; water operating costs increased 4 percent; solid/contained waste operating costs decreased 9 percent. The table below shows pollution abatement operating control costs for air, water, solid/contained waste, and nonmedia for chemicals and allied products.

[In million dollars]

Year	Pollution abatement operating costs	Air	Water	Solid waste	Nonmedia
1992	4,425.1	1,026.9	1,946.8	1,451.3	437.1
1991	4,046.9	879.6	1,786.9	1,380.5	(NA)
1990	3,943.4	841.9	1,799.0	1,302.5	(NA)
1989	3,509.2	794.0	1,613.8	1,101.4	(NA)
1988	3,074.9	706.4	1,428.5	940.1	(NA)

Source: U.S. Department of Commerce. Bureau of the Census. "Pollution Abatement Costs and Expenditures, 1992." In *National Economic, Social, and Environmental Data Bank* [CD-ROM]. Prepared by U.S. Department of Commerce, Economics and Statistics Administration. Washington, DC: U.S. Department of Commerce, National Economic, Social, and Environmental Data Bank, Economics and Statistics Administration, Office of Business Analysis, February 1995. *Notes:* Totals may not agree with detail because of independent rounding. "NA" represents "not available."

★ 675 ★

Pollution Abatement and Control, by Industry

Pollution Abatement Operating Costs for Electronic and Other Electric Equipment: 1988-1992

Pollution abatement concerns those activities with the primary purpose of protecting the environment by reducing or eliminating unwanted emissions or wastes that are created by the production process. Operating costs related to pollution abatement activities totaled $19,228 million in 1992. Of this amount, $17,466 million was attributable to a particular media: $5,395 million for air; $6,577 million for water; and $5,494 million for solid/contained waste. Spending for nonmedia and other was $1,762 million. Total population abatement media operating costs showed an overall increase of $158 million (1 percent) from 1991, the previous year. Air operating costs increased 9 percent; water operating costs increased 4 percent; solid/contained waste operating costs decreased 9 percent. The table below shows pollution abatement operating control costs for air, water, solid/contained waste, and nonmedia for electronic and other electric equipment.

[In million dollars]

Year	Pollution abatement operating costs	Air	Water	Solid waste	Nonmedia
1992	657.1	117.9	288.8	250.4	65.0
1991	833.0	22.1r	323.6	409.5	(NA)
1990	787.8	113.1	370.3	304.4	(NA)
1989	729.1	100.9	308.9	319.3	(NA)
1988	659.3	92.2	252.5	314.6	(NA)

Source: U.S. Department of Commerce. Bureau of the Census. "Pollution Abatement Costs and Expenditures, 1992." In *National Economic, Social, and Environmental Data Bank* [CD-ROM]. Prepared by U.S. Department of Commerce, Economics and Statistics Administration. Washington, DC: U.S. Department of Commerce, National Economic, Social, and Environmental Data Bank, Economics and Statistics Administration, Office of Business Analysis, February 1995. *Notes:* Totals may not agree with detail because of independent rounding. "NA" represents "not available."

★ 676 ★

Pollution Abatement and Control, by Industry

Pollution Abatement Operating Costs for Fabricated Metal Products: 1988-1992

Pollution abatement concerns those activities with the primary purpose of protecting the environment by reducing or eliminating unwanted emissions or wastes that are created by the production process. Operating costs related to pollution abatement activities totaled $19,228 million in 1992. Of this amount, $17,466 million was attributable to a particular media: $5,395 million for air; $6,577 million for water; and $5,494 million for solid/contained waste. Spending for nonmedia and other was $1,762 million. Total population abatement media operating costs showed an overall increase of $158 million (1 percent) from 1991, the previous year. Air operating costs increased 9 percent; water operating costs increased 4 percent; solid/contained waste operating costs decreased 9 percent. The table below shows pollution abatement operating control costs for air, water, solid/contained waste, and nonmedia for fabricated metal products.

[In million dollars]

Year	Pollution abatement operating costs	Air	Water	Solid waste	Nonmedia
1992	761.2	130.4	284.3	346.6	108.0
1991	842.6	133.8	301.1	407.6	(NA)
1990	813.8	114.2	343.5	356.1	(NA)
1989	895.7	123.8	389.4	382.4	(NA)
1988	761.9	135.0	316.8	310.1	(NA)

Source: U.S. Department of Commerce. Bureau of the Census. "Pollution Abatement Costs and Expenditures, 1992." In *National Economic, Social, and Environmental Data Bank* [CD-ROM]. Prepared by U.S. Department of Commerce, Economics and Statistics Administration. Washington, DC: U.S. Department of Commerce, National Economic, Social, and Environmental Data Bank, Economics and Statistics Administration, Office of Business Analysis, February 1995. *Notes:* Totals may not agree with detail because of independent rounding. "NA" represents "not available."

★ 677 ★
Pollution Abatement and Control, by Industry

Pollution Abatement Operating Costs for Food and Kindred Products: 1988-1992

Pollution abatement concerns those activities with the primary purpose of protecting the environment by reducing or eliminating unwanted emissions or wastes that are created by the production process. Operating costs related to pollution abatement activities totaled $19,228 million in 1992. Of this amount, $17,466 million was attributable to a particular media: $5,395 million for air; $6,577 million for water; and $5,494 million for solid/contained waste. Spending for nonmedia and other was $1,762 million. Total population abatement media operating costs showed an overall increase of $158 million (1 percent) from 1991, the previous year. Air operating costs increased 9 percent; water operating costs increased 4 percent; solid/contained waste operating costs decreased 9 percent. The table below shows pollution abatement operating control costs for air, water, solid/contained waste, and nonmedia for food and kindred products.

[In million dollars]

Year	Pollution abatement operating costs	Air	Water	Solid waste	Nonmedia
1992	1,312.0	162.7	835.7	313.6	28.1
1991	1,254.2	149.6	788.5	316.1	(NA)
1990	1,108.8	145.9	692.4	270.4	(NA)
1989	1,056.2	137.4	663.5	255.3	(NA)
1988	1,160.0	157.8	673.3	328.9	(NA)

Source: U.S. Department of Commerce. Bureau of the Census. "Pollution Abatement Costs and Expenditures, 1992." In *National Economic, Social, and Environmental Data Bank* [CD-ROM]. Prepared by U.S. Department of Commerce, Economics and Statistics Administration. Washington, DC: U.S. Department of Commerce, National Economic, Social, and Environmental Data Bank, Economics and Statistics Administration, Office of Business Analysis, February 1995. *Notes:* Totals may not agree with detail because of independent rounding. "NA" represents "not available."

★ 678 ★

Pollution Abatement and Control, by Industry

Pollution Abatement Operating Costs for Furniture and Fixtures: 1988-1992

Pollution abatement concerns those activities with the primary purpose of protecting the environment by reducing or eliminating unwanted emissions or wastes that are created by the production process. Operating costs related to pollution abatement activities totaled $19,228 million in 1992. Of this amount, $17,466 million was attributable to a particular media: $5,395 million for air; $6,577 million for water; and $5,494 million for solid/contained waste. Spending for nonmedia and other was $1,762 million. Total population abatement media operating costs showed an overall increase of $158 million (1 percent) from 1991, the previous year. Air operating costs increased 9 percent; water operating costs increased 4 percent; solid/contained waste operating costs decreased 9 percent. The table below shows pollution abatement operating control costs for air, water, solid/contained waste, and nonmedia for furniture and fixtures.

[In million dollars]

Year	Pollution abatement operating costs	Air	Water	Solid waste	Nonmedia
1992	118.5	43.0	14.3	61.2	7.5
1991	136.2	45.9	24.3	66.0	(NA)
1990	140.8	50.5	23.4	66.9	(NA)
1989	132.6	50.4	25.8	56.4	(NA)
1988	118.4	33.8	12.4	72.3	(NA)

Source: U.S. Department of Commerce. Bureau of the Census. "Pollution Abatement Costs and Expenditures, 1992." In *National Economic, Social, and Environmental Data Bank* [CD-ROM]. Prepared by U.S. Department of Commerce, Economics and Statistics Administration. Washington, DC: U.S. Department of Commerce, National Economic, Social, and Environmental Data Bank, Economics and Statistics Administration, Office of Business Analysis, February 1995. *Notes:* Totals may not agree with detail because of independent rounding. "NA" represents "not available."

★ 679 ★

Pollution Abatement and Control, by Industry

Pollution Abatement Operating Costs for Industrial Machinery and Equipment: 1988-1992

Pollution abatement concerns those activities with the primary purpose of protecting the environment by reducing or eliminating unwanted emissions or wastes that are created by the production process. Operating costs related to pollution abatement activities totaled $19,228 million in 1992. Of this amount, $17,466 million was attributable to a particular media: $5,395 million for air; $6,577 million for water; and $5,494 million for solid/contained waste. Spending for nonmedia and other was $1,762 million. Total population abatement media operating costs showed an overall increase of $158 million (1 percent) from 1991, the previous year. Air operating costs increased 9 percent; water operating costs increased 4 percent; solid/contained waste operating costs decreased 9 percent. The table below shows pollution abatement operating control costs for air, water, solid/contained waste, and nonmedia for industrial machinery and equipment.

[In million dollars]

Year	Pollution abatement operating costs	Air	Water	Solid waste	Nonmedia
1992	463.7	65.4	160.5	237.9	60.9
1991	573.9	70.0	165.1	338.8	(NA)
1990	557.7	77.9	159.5	320.3	(NA)
1989	571.9	80.6	170.5	320.8	(NA)
1988	429.6	68.4	139.4	221.8	(NA)

Source: U.S. Department of Commerce. Bureau of the Census. "Pollution Abatement Costs and Expenditures, 1992." In *National Economic, Social, and Environmental Data Bank* [CD-ROM]. Prepared by U.S. Department of Commerce, Economics and Statistics Administration. Washington, DC: U.S. Department of Commerce, National Economic, Social, and Environmental Data Bank, Economics and Statistics Administration, Office of Business Analysis, February 1995. *Notes:* Totals may not agree with detail because of independent rounding. "NA" represents "not available."

★ 680 ★

Pollution Abatement and Control, by Industry

Pollution Abatement Operating Costs for Instruments and Related Products: 1988-1992

Pollution abatement concerns those activities with the primary purpose of protecting the environment by reducing or eliminating unwanted emissions or wastes that are created by the production process. Operating costs related to pollution abatement activities totaled $19,228 million in 1992. Of this amount, $17,466 million was attributable to a particular media: $5,395 million for air; $6,577 million for water; and $5,494 million for solid/contained waste. Spending for nonmedia and other was $1,762 million. Total population abatement media operating costs showed an overall increase of $158 million (1 percent) from 1991, the previous year. Air operating costs increased 9 percent; water operating costs increased 4 percent; solid/contained waste operating costs decreased 9 percent. The table below shows pollution abatement operating control costs for air, water, solid/contained waste, and nonmedia for instruments and related products.

[In million dollars]

Year	Pollution abatement operating costs	Air	Water	Solid waste	Nonmedia
1992	331.9	48.0	89.4	194.5	61.5
1991	280.0	33.3	77.9	168.7	(NA)
1990	247.7	37.4	68.5	141.7	(NA)
1989	239.9	36.2	70.9	132.8	(NA)
1988	197.7	21.7	79.9	96.1	(NA)

Source: U.S. Department of Commerce. Bureau of the Census. "Pollution Abatement Costs and Expenditures, 1992." In *National Economic, Social, and Environmental Data Bank* [CD-ROM]. Prepared by U.S. Department of Commerce, Economics and Statistics Administration. Washington, DC: U.S. Department of Commerce, National Economic, Social, and Environmental Data Bank, Economics and Statistics Administration, Office of Business Analysis, February 1995. *Notes:* Totals may not agree with detail because of independent rounding. "NA" represents "not available."

★ 681 ★

Pollution Abatement and Control, by Industry

Pollution Abatement Operating Costs for Leather and Leather Products: 1988-1992

Pollution abatement concerns those activities with the primary purpose of protecting the environment by reducing or eliminating unwanted emissions or wastes that are created by the production process. Operating costs related to pollution abatement activities totaled $19,228 million in 1992. Of this amount, $17,466 million was attributable to a particular media: $5,395 million for air; $6,577 million for water; and $5,494 million for solid/contained waste. Spending for nonmedia and other was $1,762 million. Total population abatement media operating costs showed an overall increase of $158 million (1 percent) from 1991, the previous year. Air operating costs increased 9 percent; water operating costs increased 4 percent; solid/ contained waste operating costs decreased 9 percent. The table below shows pollution abatement operating control costs for air, water, solid/ contained waste, and nonmedia for leather and leather products.

[In million dollars]

Year	Pollution abatement operating costs	Air	Water	Solid waste	Nonmedia
1992	53.5	3.7	30.6	19.2	0.4
1991	45.9	2.1	28.2	15.6	(NA)
1990	48.9	7.0	26.1	15.7	(NA)
1989	41.6	2.8	23.2	15.6	(NA)
1988	23.1	2.5	11.3	9.3	(NA)

Source: U.S. Department of Commerce. Bureau of the Census. "Pollution Abatement Costs and Expenditures, 1992." In *National Economic, Social, and Environmental Data Bank* [CD-ROM]. Prepared by U.S. Department of Commerce, Economics and Statistics Administration. Washington, DC: U.S. Department of Commerce, National Economic, Social, and Environmental Data Bank, Economics and Statistics Administration, Office of Business Analysis, February 1995. *Notes:* Totals may not agree with detail because of independent rounding. "NA" represents "not available."

★ 682 ★

Pollution Abatement and Control, by Industry

Pollution Abatement Operating Costs for Lumber and Wood Products: 1988-1992

Pollution abatement concerns those activities with the primary purpose of protecting the environment by reducing or eliminating unwanted emissions or wastes that are created by the production process. Operating costs related to pollution abatement activities totaled $19,228 million in 1992. Of this amount, $17,466 million was attributable to a particular media: $5,395 million for air; $6,577 million for water; and $5,494 million for solid/contained waste. Spending for nonmedia and other was $1,762 million. Total population abatement media operating costs showed an overall increase of $158 million (1 percent) from 1991, the previous year. Air operating costs increased 9 percent; water operating costs increased 4 percent; solid/contained waste operating costs decreased 9 percent. The table below shows pollution abatement operating control costs for air, water, solid/contained waste, and nonmedia for lumber and wood products.

[In million dollars]

Year	Pollution abatement operating costs	Air	Water	Solid waste	Nonmedia
1992	243.0	89.3	49.5	104.2	25.0
1991	298.4	91.1	34.8	172.6	(NA)
1990	259.3	86.2	37.1	136.0	(NA)
1989	270.0	88.4	38.6	143.0	(NA)
1988	236.1	84.0	57.6	94.5	(NA)

Source: U.S. Department of Commerce. Bureau of the Census. "Pollution Abatement Costs and Expenditures, 1992." In *National Economic, Social, and Environmental Data Bank* [CD-ROM]. Prepared by U.S. Department of Commerce, Economics and Statistics Administration. Washington, DC: U.S. Department of Commerce, National Economic, Social, and Environmental Data Bank, Economics and Statistics Administration, Office of Business Analysis, February 1995. *Notes:* Totals may not agree with detail because of independent rounding. "NA" represents "not available."

★ 683 ★

Pollution Abatement and Control, by Industry

Pollution Abatement Operating Costs for Miscellaneous Manufacturing Industries: 1988-1992

Pollution abatement concerns those activities with the primary purpose of protecting the environment by reducing or eliminating unwanted emissions or wastes that are created by the production process. Operating costs related to pollution abatement activities totaled $19,228 million in 1992. Of this amount, $17,466 million was attributable to a particular media: $5,395 million for air; $6,577 million for water; and $5,494 million for solid/contained waste. Spending for nonmedia and other was $1,762 million. Total population abatement media operating costs showed an overall increase of $158 million (1 percent) from 1991, the previous year. Air operating costs increased 9 percent; water operating costs increased 4 percent; solid/contained waste operating costs decreased 9 percent. The table below shows pollution abatement operating control costs for air, water, solid/contained waste, and nonmedia for miscellaneous manufacturing industries.

[In million dollars]

Year	Pollution abatement operating costs	Air	Water	Solid waste	Nonmedia
1992	89.7	22.7	21.7	45.3	(D)
1991	74.9	14.5	17.0	43.4	(NA)
1990	114.7	19.2	32.7	62.7	(NA)
1989	124.0	17.7	47.3	58.9	(NA)
1988	76.7	10.1	20.9	45.7	(NA)

Source: U.S. Department of Commerce. Bureau of the Census. "Pollution Abatement Costs and Expenditures, 1992." In *National Economic, Social, and Environmental Data Bank* [CD-ROM]. Prepared by U.S. Department of Commerce, Economics and Statistics Administration. Washington, DC: U.S. Department of Commerce, National Economic, Social, and Environmental Data Bank, Economics and Statistics Administration, Office of Business Analysis, February 1995. *Notes:* Totals may not agree with detail because of independent rounding. "NA" represents "not available." "D" indicates data withheld to avoid disclosing operations of individual companies.

★ 684 ★

Pollution Abatement and Control, by Industry

Pollution Abatement Operating Costs for Paper and Allied Products: 1988-1992

Pollution abatement concerns those activities with the primary purpose of protecting the environment by reducing or eliminating unwanted emissions or wastes that are created by the production process. Operating costs related to pollution abatement activities totaled $19,228 million in 1992. Of this amount, $17,466 million was attributable to a particular media: $5,395 million for air; $6,577 million for water; and $5,494 million for solid/contained waste. Spending for nonmedia and other was $1,762 million. Total population abatement media operating costs showed an overall increase of $158 million (1 percent) from 1991, the previous year. Air operating costs increased 9 percent; water operating costs increased 4 percent; solid/contained waste operating costs decreased 9 percent. The table below shows pollution abatement operating control costs for air, water, solid/contained waste, and nonmedia for paper and allied products.

[In million dollars]

Year	Pollution abatement operating costs	Air	Water	Solid waste	Nonmedia
1992	1,860.7	535.6	822.7	502.4	35.5
1991	1,635.0	400.8	790.7	443.5	(NA)
1990	1,606.8	397.5	788.3	421.0	(NA)
1989	1,449.0	388.1	686.8	374.2	(NA)
1988	1,343.3	372.4	627.7	343.2	(NA)

Source: U.S. Department of Commerce. Bureau of the Census. "Pollution Abatement Costs and Expenditures, 1992." In *National Economic, Social, and Environmental Data Bank* [CD-ROM]. Prepared by U.S. Department of Commerce, Economics and Statistics Administration. Washington, DC: U.S. Department of Commerce, National Economic, Social, and Environmental Data Bank, Economics and Statistics Administration, Office of Business Analysis, February 1995. *Notes:* Totals may not agree with detail because of independent rounding. "NA" represents "not available."

★ 685 ★

Pollution Abatement and Control, by Industry

Pollution Abatement Operating Costs for Petroleum and Coal Products: 1988-1992

Pollution abatement concerns those activities with the primary purpose of protecting the environment by reducing or eliminating unwanted emissions or wastes that are created by the production process. Operating costs related to pollution abatement activities totaled $19,228 million in 1992. Of this amount, $17,466 million was attributable to a particular media: $5,395 million for air; $6,577 million for water; and $5,494 million for solid/contained waste. Spending for nonmedia and other was $1,762 million. Total population abatement media operating costs showed an overall increase of $158 million (1 percent) from 1991, the previous year. Air operating costs increased 9 percent; water operating costs increased 4 percent; solid/contained waste operating costs decreased 9 percent. The table below shows pollution abatement operating control costs for air, water, solid/contained waste, and nonmedia for petroleum and coal products.

[In million dollars]

Year	Pollution abatement operating costs	Air	Water	Solid waste	Nonmedia
1992	2,585.4	1,428.9	742.8	413.7	605.4
1991	2,849.0	1,464.7	793.9	590.4	(NA)
1990	2,704.9	1,472.2	701.9	530.8	(NA)
1989	2,170.0	1,258.2	578.7	333.0	(NA)
1988	2,005.5	1,175.8	561.7	268.0	(NA)

Source: U.S. Department of Commerce. Bureau of the Census. "Pollution Abatement Costs and Expenditures, 1992." In *National Economic, Social, and Environmental Data Bank* [CD-ROM]. Prepared by U.S. Department of Commerce, Economics and Statistics Administration. Washington, DC: U.S. Department of Commerce, National Economic, Social, and Environmental Data Bank, Economics and Statistics Administration, Office of Business Analysis, February 1995. *Notes:* Totals may not agree with detail because of independent rounding. "NA" represents "not available."

★ 686 ★

Pollution Abatement and Control, by Industry

Pollution Abatement Operating Costs for Primary Metal Industries: 1988-1992

Pollution abatement concerns those activities with the primary purpose of protecting the environment by reducing or eliminating unwanted emissions or wastes that are created by the production process. Operating costs related to pollution abatement activities totaled $19,228 million in 1992. Of this amount, $17,466 million was attributable to a particular media: $5,395 million for air; $6,577 million for water; and $5,494 million for solid/contained waste. Spending for nonmedia and other was $1,762 million. Total population abatement media operating costs showed an overall increase of $158 million (1 percent) from 1991, the previous year. Air operating costs increased 9 percent; water operating costs increased 4 percent; solid/contained waste operating costs decreased 9 percent. The table below shows pollution abatement operating control costs for air, water, solid/contained waste, and nonmedia for primary metal industries.

[In million dollars]

Year	Pollution abatement operating costs	Air	Water	Solid waste	Nonmedia
1992	1,993.4	933.1	575.0	485.3	107.7
1991	2,002.6	911.7	564.0	526.9	(NA)
1990	2,025.5	943.7	565.4	516.4	(NA)
1989	1,931.1	883.1	574.3	473.7	(NA)
1988	1,809.0	965.8	516.1	327.2	(NA)

Source: U.S. Department of Commerce. Bureau of the Census. "Pollution Abatement Costs and Expenditures, 1992." In *National Economic, Social, and Environmental Data Bank* [CD-ROM]. Prepared by U.S. Department of Commerce, Economics and Statistics Administration. Washington, DC: U.S. Department of Commerce, National Economic, Social, and Environmental Data Bank, Economics and Statistics Administration, Office of Business Analysis, February 1995. *Notes:* Totals may not agree with detail because of independent rounding. "NA" represents "not available."

★ 687 ★

Pollution Abatement and Control, by Industry

Pollution Abatement Operating Costs for Printing and Publishing: 1988-1992

Pollution abatement concerns those activities with the primary purpose of protecting the environment by reducing or eliminating unwanted emissions or wastes that are created by the production process. Operating costs related to pollution abatement activities totaled $19,228 million in 1992. Of this amount, $17,466 million was attributable to a particular media: $5,395 million for air; $6,577 million for water; and $5,494 million for solid/contained waste. Spending for nonmedia and other was $1,762 million. Total population abatement media operating costs showed an overall increase of $158 million (1 percent) from 1991, the previous year. Air operating costs increased 9 percent; water operating costs increased 4 percent; solid/contained waste operating costs decreased 9 percent. The table below shows pollution abatement operating control costs for air, water, solid/contained waste, and nonmedia for printing and publishing.

[In million dollars]

Year	Pollution abatement operating costs	Air	Water	Solid waste	Nonmedia
1992	239.0	85.6	36.5	117.0	21.0
1991	228.1	87.7	30.3	110.2	(NA)
1990	240.7	70.5	30.6	139.6	(NA)
1989	281.6	67.3	36.2	178.1	(NA)
1988	206.4	72.0	34.2	100.3	(NA)

Source: U.S. Department of Commerce. Bureau of the Census. "Pollution Abatement Costs and Expenditures, 1992." In *National Economic, Social, and Environmental Data Bank* [CD-ROM]. Prepared by U.S. Department of Commerce, Economics and Statistics Administration. Washington, DC: U.S. Department of Commerce, National Economic, Social, and Environmental Data Bank, Economics and Statistics Administration, Office of Business Analysis, February 1995. *Notes:* Totals may not agree with detail because of independent rounding. "NA" represents "not available."

★ 688 ★

Pollution Abatement and Control, by Industry

Pollution Abatement Operating Costs for Rubber and Miscellaneous Plastics Products: 1988-1992

Pollution abatement concerns those activities with the primary purpose of protecting the environment by reducing or eliminating unwanted emissions or wastes that are created by the production process. Operating costs related to pollution abatement activities totaled $19,228 million in 1992. Of this amount, $17,466 million was attributable to a particular media: $5,395 million for air; $6,577 million for water; and $5,494 million for solid/contained waste. Spending for nonmedia and other was $1,762 million. Total population abatement media operating costs showed an overall increase of $158 million (1 percent) from 1991, the previous year. Air operating costs increased 9 percent; water operating costs increased 4 percent; solid/contained waste operating costs decreased 9 percent. The table below shows pollution abatement operating control costs for air, water, solid/contained waste, and nonmedia for rubber and miscellaneous plastics products.

[In million dollars]

Year	Pollution abatement operating costs	Air	Water	Solid waste	Nonmedia
1992	379.6	105.7	73.3	200.5	24.3
1991	440.9	121.0	76.9	243.0	(NA)
1990	427.6	96.6	113.4	217.6	(NA)
1989	403.3	85.3	99.6	218.4	(NA)
1988	277.9	62.5	62.2	153.3	(NA)

Source: U.S. Department of Commerce. Bureau of the Census. "Pollution Abatement Costs and Expenditures, 1992." In *National Economic, Social, and Environmental Data Bank* [CD-ROM]. Prepared by U.S. Department of Commerce, Economics and Statistics Administration. Washington, DC: U.S. Department of Commerce, National Economic, Social, and Environmental Data Bank, Economics and Statistics Administration, Office of Business Analysis, February 1995. *Notes:* Totals may not agree with detail because of independent rounding. "NA" represents "not available."

★ 689 ★

Pollution Abatement and Control, by Industry

Pollution Abatement Operating Costs for Stone, Clay, and Glass Products: 1988-1992

Pollution abatement concerns those activities with the primary purpose of protecting the environment by reducing or eliminating unwanted emissions or wastes that are created by the production process. Operating costs related to pollution abatement activities totaled $19,228 million in 1992. Of this amount, $17,466 million was attributable to a particular media: $5,395 million for air; $6,577 million for water; and $5,494 million for solid/contained waste. Spending for nonmedia and other was $1,762 million. Total population abatement media operating costs showed an overall increase of $158 million (1 percent) from 1991, the previous year. Air operating costs increased 9 percent; water operating costs increased 4 percent; solid/contained waste operating costs decreased 9 percent. The table below shows pollution abatement operating control costs for air, water, solid/contained waste, and nonmedia for stone, clay, and glass products.

[In million dollars]

Year	Pollution abatement operating costs	Air	Water	Solid waste	Nonmedia
1992	491.2	248.5	94.6	148.1	30.3
1991	464.9	220.5	85.1	159.2	(NA)
1990	497.3	247.6	93.1	156.7	(NA)
1989	591.7	328.4	85.0	178.3	(NA)
1988	438.4	247.7	67.7	123.1	(NA)

Source: U.S. Department of Commerce. Bureau of the Census. "Pollution Abatement Costs and Expenditures, 1992." In *National Economic, Social, and Environmental Data Bank* [CD-ROM]. Prepared by U.S. Department of Commerce, Economics and Statistics Administration. Washington, DC: U.S. Department of Commerce, National Economic, Social, and Environmental Data Bank, Economics and Statistics Administration, Office of Business Analysis, February 1995. *Notes:* Totals may not agree with detail because of independent rounding. "NA" represents "not available."

★ 690 ★

Pollution Abatement and Control, by Industry

Pollution Abatement Operating Costs for Textile Mill Products: 1988-1992

Pollution abatement concerns those activities with the primary purpose of protecting the environment by reducing or eliminating unwanted emissions or wastes that are created by the production process. Operating costs related to pollution abatement activities totaled $19,228 million in 1992. Of this amount, $17,466 million was attributable to a particular media: $5,395 million for air; $6,577 million for water; and $5,494 million for solid/contained waste. Spending for nonmedia and other was $1,762 million. Total population abatement media operating costs showed an overall increase of $158 million (1 percent) from 1991, the previous year. Air operating costs increased 9 percent; water operating costs increased 4 percent; solid/contained waste operating costs decreased 9 percent. The table below shows pollution abatement operating control costs for air, water, solid/contained waste, and nonmedia for textile mill products.

[In million dollars]

Year	Pollution abatement operating costs	Air	Water	Solid waste	Nonmedia
1992	256.2	38.1	152.5	65.7	7.9
1991	213.7	36.1	123.5	54.1	(NA)
1990	198.3	26.2	114.7	57.5	(NA)
1989	185.9	25.3	109.4	51.3	(NA)
1988	177.0	30.5	98.8	47.6	(NA)

Source: U.S. Department of Commerce. Bureau of the Census. "Pollution Abatement Costs and Expenditures, 1992." In *National Economic, Social, and Environmental Data Bank* [CD-ROM]. Prepared by U.S. Department of Commerce, Economics and Statistics Administration. Washington, DC: U.S. Department of Commerce, National Economic, Social, and Environmental Data Bank, Economics and Statistics Administration, Office of Business Analysis, February 1995. *Notes:* Totals may not agree with detail because of independent rounding. "NA" represents "not available."

★ 691 ★

Pollution Abatement and Control, by Industry

Pollution Abatement Operating Costs for Tobacco Products: 1988-1992

Pollution abatement concerns those activities with the primary purpose of protecting the environment by reducing or eliminating unwanted emissions or wastes that are created by the production process. Operating costs related to pollution abatement activities totaled $19,228 million in 1992. Of this amount, $17,466 million was attributable to a particular media: $5,395 million for air; $6,577 million for water; and $5,494 million for solid/contained waste. Spending for nonmedia and other was $1,762 million. Total population abatement media operating costs showed an overall increase of $158 million (1 percent) from 1991, the previous year. Air operating costs increased 9 percent; water operating costs increased 4 percent; solid/contained waste operating costs decreased 9 percent. The table below shows pollution abatement operating control costs for air, water, solid/contained waste, and nonmedia for tobacco products.

[In million dollars]

Year	Pollution abatement operating costs	Air	Water	Solid waste	Nonmedia
1992	33.5	11.2	10.8	11.5	(D)
1991	48.4	16.4	13.7	18.3	(NA)
1990	44.8	15.9	13.3	15.6	(NA)
1989	42.4	14.1	13.5	14.9	(NA)
1988	37.6	12.4	14.8	10.4	(NA)

Source: U.S. Department of Commerce. Bureau of the Census. "Pollution Abatement Costs and Expenditures, 1992." In *National Economic, Social, and Environmental Data Bank* [CD-ROM]. Prepared by U.S. Department of Commerce, Economics and Statistics Administration. Washington, DC: U.S. Department of Commerce, National Economic, Social, and Environmental Data Bank, Economics and Statistics Administration, Office of Business Analysis, February 1995. *Notes:* Totals may not agree with detail because of independent rounding. "NA" represents "not available." "D" indicates data withheld to avoid disclosing operations of individual companies.

★ 692 ★

Pollution Abatement and Control, by Industry

Pollution Abatement Operating Costs for Transportation Equipment: 1988-1992

Pollution abatement concerns those activities with the primary purpose of protecting the environment by reducing or eliminating unwanted emissions or wastes that are created by the production process. Operating costs related to pollution abatement activities totaled $19,228 million in 1992. Of this amount, $17,466 million was attributable to a particular media: $5,395 million for air; $6,577 million for water; and $5,494 million for solid/contained waste. Spending for nonmedia and other was $1,762 million. Total population abatement media operating costs showed an overall increase of $158 million (1 percent) from 1991, the previous year. Air operating costs increased 9 percent; water operating costs increased 4 percent; solid/contained waste operating costs decreased 9 percent. The table below shows pollution abatement operating control costs for air, water, solid/contained waste, and nonmedia for transportation equipment.

[In million dollars]

Year	Pollution abatement operating costs	Air	Water	Solid waste	Nonmedia
1992	1,171.7	298.5	347.0	526.2	126.8
1991	1,118.3	254.7	319.6	544.0	(NA)
1990	1,232.0	247.3	373.1	611.6	(NA)
1989	1,000.3	212.2	318.1	470.1	(NA)
1988	974.4	215.7	299.2	459.5	(NA)

Source: U.S. Department of Commerce. Bureau of the Census. "Pollution Abatement Costs and Expenditures, 1992." In *National Economic, Social, and Environmental Data Bank* [CD-ROM]. Prepared by U.S. Department of Commerce, Economics and Statistics Administration. Washington, DC: U.S. Department of Commerce, National Economic, Social, and Environmental Data Bank, Economics and Statistics Administration, Office of Business Analysis, February 1995. *Notes:* Totals may not agree with detail because of independent rounding. "NA" represents "not available."

Pollution Abatement and Control, by State

★ 693 ★

Pollution Abatement Capital Expenditures in Alabama: 1988-1992

Pollution abatement expenditures are those with the primary purpose of protecting the environment by reducing or eliminating unwanted emissions or wastes that are created by the production process. Pollution abatement capital expenditures (PACE) by manufacturing establishments with 20 employees or more amounted to $8,393 million in 1992. Of this total, $7,867 million was attributable to a particular media: $4,403 million for air; $2,510 million for water; and $954 million for solid/contained waste. Spending for nonmedia and other was $526 million. Approximately 79 percent of the $8,383 million new capital expenditures for pollution abatement was made by establishments in four major industry groups: Chemicals and allied products (major group 28), petroleum and coal products (major group 29), paper and allied products (major group 26), and primary metal industries (major group 33). In 1992, Texas, California, and Louisiana accounted for approximately 38 percent of total new pollution abatement capital expenditures. Texas comprised 18 percent of the total. The table below shows pollution abatement capital expenditures for air, water, solid/contained waste, and nonmedia for Alabama.

[In million dollars]

Year	Pollution abatement capital expenditures	Air	Water	Solid waste	Nonmedia
1992	119.4	54.3	48.2	16.9	7.4
1991	316.6	143.0	133.7	39.9	(NA)
1990	195.7	70.6	99.1	26.0	(NA)
1989	104.6	39.8	49.5	15.3	(NA)
1988	58.9	18.0	25.4	15.5	(NA)

Source: U.S. Department of Commerce. Bureau of the Census. "Pollution Abatement Costs and Expenditures, 1992." In *National Economic, Social, and Environmental Data Bank* [CD-ROM]. Prepared by U.S. Department of Commerce, Economics and Statistics Administration. Washington, DC: U.S. Department of Commerce, National Economic, Social, and Environmental Data Bank, Economics and Statistics Administration, Office of Business Analysis, February 1995. *Notes:* Totals may not agree with detail because of independent rounding. "NA" represents "not available."

★ 694 ★

Pollution Abatement and Control, by State

Pollution Abatement Capital Expenditures in Alaska: 1988-1992

Pollution abatement expenditures are those with the primary purpose of protecting the environment by reducing or eliminating unwanted emissions or wastes that are created by the production process. Pollution abatement capital expenditures (PACE) by manufacturing establishments with 20 employees or more amounted to $8,393 million in 1992. Of this total, $7,867 million was attributable to a particular media: $4,403 million for air; $2,510 million for water; and $954 million for solid/contained waste. Spending for nonmedia and other was $526 million. Approximately 79 percent of the $8,383 million new capital expenditures for pollution abatement was made by establishments in four major industry groups: Chemicals and allied products (major group 28), petroleum and coal products (major group 29), paper and allied products (major group 26), and primary metal industries (major group 33). In 1992, Texas, California, and Louisiana accounted for approximately 38 percent of total new pollution abatement capital expenditures. Texas comprised 18 percent of the total. The table below shows pollution abatement capital expenditures for air, water, solid/contained waste, and nonmedia for Alaska.

[In million dollars]

Year	Pollution abatement capital expenditures	Air	Water	Solid waste	Nonmedia
1992	15.3	2.1	11.4	1.8	-
1991	9.3	6.0	(D)	(D)	(NA)
1990	11.1	8.5	(D)	(D)	(NA)
1989	(D)	6.3	(D)	0.2	(NA)
1988	(D)	(D)	(D)	(D)	(NA)

Source: U.S. Department of Commerce. Bureau of the Census. "Pollution Abatement Costs and Expenditures, 1992." In *National Economic, Social, and Environmental Data Bank* [CD-ROM]. Prepared by U.S. Department of Commerce, Economics and Statistics Administration. Washington, DC: U.S. Department of Commerce, National Economic, Social, and Environmental Data Bank, Economics and Statistics Administration, Office of Business Analysis, February 1995. *Notes:* Totals may not agree with detail because of independent rounding. "NA" represents "not available." "D" indicates data withheld to avoid disclosing operations of individual companies. "-" represents zero.

★ 695 ★

Pollution Abatement and Control, by State

Pollution Abatement Capital Expenditures in Arizona: 1988-1992

Pollution abatement expenditures are those with the primary purpose of protecting the environment by reducing or eliminating unwanted emissions or wastes that are created by the production process. Pollution abatement capital expenditures (PACE) by manufacturing establishments with 20 employees or more amounted to $8,393 million in 1992. Of this total, $7,867 million was attributable to a particular media: $4,403 million for air; $2,510 million for water; and $954 million for solid/contained waste. Spending for nonmedia and other was $526 million. Approximately 79 percent of the $8,383 million new capital expenditures for pollution abatement was made by establishments in four major industry groups: Chemicals and allied products (major group 28), petroleum and coal products (major group 29), paper and allied products (major group 26), and primary metal industries (major group 33). In 1992, Texas, California, and Louisiana accounted for approximately 38 percent of total new pollution abatement capital expenditures. Texas comprised 18 percent of the total. The table below shows pollution abatement capital expenditures for air, water, solid/ contained waste, and nonmedia for Arizona.

[In million dollars]

Year	Pollution abatement capital expenditures	Air	Water	Solid waste	Nonmedia
1992	30.8	13.6	16.2	1.1	1.2
1991	24.4	15.6	5.3	3.4	(NA)
1990	18.3	9.7	5.5	3.1	(NA)
1989	48.3	30.9	7.5	10.0	(NA)
1988	(D)	(D)	1.6	3.6	(NA)

Source: U.S. Department of Commerce. Bureau of the Census. "Pollution Abatement Costs and Expenditures, 1992." In *National Economic, Social, and Environmental Data Bank* [CD-ROM]. Prepared by U.S. Department of Commerce, Economics and Statistics Administration. Washington, DC: U.S. Department of Commerce, National Economic, Social, and Environmental Data Bank, Economics and Statistics Administration, Office of Business Analysis, February 1995. *Notes:* Totals may not agree with detail because of independent rounding. "NA" represents "not available." "D" indicates data withheld to avoid disclosing operations of individual companies.

★ 696 ★

Pollution Abatement and Control, by State

Pollution Abatement Capital Expenditures in Arkansas: 1988-1992

Pollution abatement expenditures are those with the primary purpose of protecting the environment by reducing or eliminating unwanted emissions or wastes that are created by the production process. Pollution abatement capital expenditures (PACE) by manufacturing establishments with 20 employees or more amounted to $8,393 million in 1992. Of this total, $7,867 million was attributable to a particular media: $4,403 million for air; $2,510 million for water; and $954 million for solid/contained waste. Spending for nonmedia and other was $526 million. Approximately 79 percent of the $8,383 million new capital expenditures for pollution abatement was made by establishments in four major industry groups: Chemicals and allied products (major group 28), petroleum and coal products (major group 29), paper and allied products (major group 26), and primary metal industries (major group 33). In 1992, Texas, California, and Louisiana accounted for approximately 38 percent of total new pollution abatement capital expenditures. Texas comprised 18 percent of the total. The table below shows pollution abatement capital expenditures for air, water, solid/ contained waste, and nonmedia for Arkansas.

[In million dollars]

Year	Pollution abatement capital expenditures	Air	Water	Solid waste	Nonmedia
1992	75.6	28.3	41.2	6.0	6.4
1991	57.1	17.6	28.4	11.2	(NA)
1990	80.0	34.4	37.8	7.7	(NA)
1989	74.5	54.3	16.8	3.3	(NA)
1988	90.0	62.8	19.9	7.2	(NA)

Source: U.S. Department of Commerce. Bureau of the Census. "Pollution Abatement Costs and Expenditures, 1992." In *National Economic, Social, and Environmental Data Bank* [CD-ROM]. Prepared by U.S. Department of Commerce, Economics and Statistics Administration. Washington, DC: U.S. Department of Commerce, National Economic, Social, and Environmental Data Bank, Economics and Statistics Administration, Office of Business Analysis, February 1995. *Notes:* Totals may not agree with detail because of independent rounding. "NA" represents "not available."

★ 697 ★

Pollution Abatement and Control, by State

Pollution Abatement Capital Expenditures in California: 1988-1992

Pollution abatement expenditures are those with the primary purpose of protecting the environment by reducing or eliminating unwanted emissions or wastes that are created by the production process. Pollution abatement capital expenditures (PACE) by manufacturing establishments with 20 employees or more amounted to $8,393 million in 1992. Of this total, $7,867 million was attributable to a particular media: $4,403 million for air; $2,510 million for water; and $954 million for solid/contained waste. Spending for nonmedia and other was $526 million. Approximately 79 percent of the $8,383 million new capital expenditures for pollution abatement was made by establishments in four major industry groups: Chemicals and allied products (major group 28), petroleum and coal products (major group 29), paper and allied products (major group 26), and primary metal industries (major group 33). In 1992, Texas, California, and Louisiana accounted for approximately 38 percent of total new pollution abatement capital expenditures. Texas comprised 18 percent of the total. The table below shows pollution abatement capital expenditures for air, water, solid/contained waste, and nonmedia for California.

[In million dollars]

Year	Pollution abatement capital expenditures	Air	Water	Solid waste	Nonmedia
1992	547.9	418.7	88.5	40.7	41.9
1991	696.6	443.7	226.4	26.5	(NA)
1990	503.0	286.6	176.1	40.3	(NA)
1989	367.9	141.0	186.9	40.0	(NA)
1988	408.4	243.2	134.9	30.3	(NA)

Source: U.S. Department of Commerce. Bureau of the Census. "Pollution Abatement Costs and Expenditures, 1992." In *National Economic, Social, and Environmental Data Bank* [CD-ROM]. Prepared by U.S. Department of Commerce, Economics and Statistics Administration. Washington, DC: U.S. Department of Commerce, National Economic, Social, and Environmental Data Bank, Economics and Statistics Administration, Office of Business Analysis, February 1995. *Notes:* Totals may not agree with detail because of independent rounding. "NA" represents "not available."

★ 698 ★

Pollution Abatement and Control, by State

Pollution Abatement Capital Expenditures in Colorado: 1988-1992

Pollution abatement expenditures are those with the primary purpose of protecting the environment by reducing or eliminating unwanted emissions or wastes that are created by the production process. Pollution abatement capital expenditures (PACE) by manufacturing establishments with 20 employees or more amounted to $8,393 million in 1992. Of this total, $7,867 million was attributable to a particular media: $4,403 million for air; $2,510 million for water; and $954 million for solid/contained waste. Spending for nonmedia and other was $526 million. Approximately 79 percent of the $8,383 million new capital expenditures for pollution abatement was made by establishments in four major industry groups: Chemicals and allied products (major group 28), petroleum and coal products (major group 29), paper and allied products (major group 26), and primary metal industries (major group 33). In 1992, Texas, California, and Louisiana accounted for approximately 38 percent of total new pollution abatement capital expenditures. Texas comprised 18 percent of the total. The table below shows pollution abatement capital expenditures for air, water, solid/contained waste, and nonmedia for Colorado.

[In million dollars]

Year	Pollution abatement capital expenditures	Air	Water	Solid waste	Nonmedia
1992	13.7	6.5	5.9	1.2	1.4
1991	30.0	7.9	11.0	11.1	(NA)
1990	26.0	9.4	13.0	3.6	(NA)
1989	49.3	8.6	38.5	2.2	(NA)
1988	10.9	2.3	(D)	(D)	(NA)

Source: U.S. Department of Commerce. Bureau of the Census. "Pollution Abatement Costs and Expenditures, 1992." In *National Economic, Social, and Environmental Data Bank* [CD-ROM]. Prepared by U.S. Department of Commerce, Economics and Statistics Administration. Washington, DC: U.S. Department of Commerce, National Economic, Social, and Environmental Data Bank, Economics and Statistics Administration, Office of Business Analysis, February 1995. *Notes:* Totals may not agree with detail because of independent rounding. "NA" represents "not available." "D" indicates data withheld to avoid disclosing operations of individual companies.

★ 699 ★

Pollution Abatement and Control, by State

Pollution Abatement Capital Expenditures in Connecticut: 1988-1992

Pollution abatement expenditures are those with the primary purpose of protecting the environment by reducing or eliminating unwanted emissions or wastes that are created by the production process. Pollution abatement capital expenditures (PACE) by manufacturing establishments with 20 employees or more amounted to $8,393 million in 1992. Of this total, $7,867 million was attributable to a particular media: $4,403 million for air; $2,510 million for water; and $954 million for solid/contained waste. Spending for nonmedia and other was $526 million. Approximately 79 percent of the $8,383 million new capital expenditures for pollution abatement was made by establishments in four major industry groups: Chemicals and allied products (major group 28), petroleum and coal products (major group 29), paper and allied products (major group 26), and primary metal industries (major group 33). In 1992, Texas, California, and Louisiana accounted for approximately 38 percent of total new pollution abatement capital expenditures. Texas comprised 18 percent of the total. The table below shows pollution abatement capital expenditures for air, water, solid/contained waste, and nonmedia for Connecticut.

[In million dollars]

Year	Pollution abatement capital expenditures	Air	Water	Solid waste	Nonmedia
1992	29.3	7.9	13.2	8.2	5.5
1991	70.8	14.4	51.2	5.1	(NA)
1990	41.3	10.9	26.6	3.8	(NA)
1989	51.9	10.0	30.8	11.1	(NA)
1988	25.4	4.6	12.7	8.1	(NA)

Source: U.S. Department of Commerce. Bureau of the Census. "Pollution Abatement Costs and Expenditures, 1992." In *National Economic, Social, and Environmental Data Bank* [CD-ROM]. Prepared by U.S. Department of Commerce, Economics and Statistics Administration. Washington, DC: U.S. Department of Commerce, National Economic, Social, and Environmental Data Bank, Economics and Statistics Administration, Office of Business Analysis, February 1995. *Notes:* Totals may not agree with detail because of independent rounding. "NA" represents "not available."

★ 700 ★

Pollution Abatement and Control, by State

Pollution Abatement Capital Expenditures in Delaware: 1988-1992

Pollution abatement expenditures are those with the primary purpose of protecting the environment by reducing or eliminating unwanted emissions or wastes that are created by the production process. Pollution abatement capital expenditures (PACE) by manufacturing establishments with 20 employees or more amounted to $8,393 million in 1992. Of this total, $7,867 million was attributable to a particular media: $4,403 million for air; $2,510 million for water; and $954 million for solid/contained waste. Spending for nonmedia and other was $526 million. Approximately 79 percent of the $8,383 million new capital expenditures for pollution abatement was made by establishments in four major industry groups: Chemicals and allied products (major group 28), petroleum and coal products (major group 29), paper and allied products (major group 26), and primary metal industries (major group 33). In 1992, Texas, California, and Louisiana accounted for approximately 38 percent of total new pollution abatement capital expenditures. Texas comprised 18 percent of the total. The table below shows pollution abatement capital expenditures for air, water, solid/contained waste, and nonmedia for Delaware.

[In million dollars]

Year	Pollution abatement capital expenditures	Air	Water	Solid waste	Nonmedia
1992	59.8	43.9	(D)	(D)	1.3
1991	60.0	33.0	(D)	(D)	(NA)
1990	25.7	23.0	2.1	0.5	(NA)
1989	22.5	16.0	4.1	2.4	(NA)
1988	12.5	(D)	7.0	(D)	(NA)

Source: U.S. Department of Commerce. Bureau of the Census. "Pollution Abatement Costs and Expenditures, 1992." In *National Economic, Social, and Environmental Data Bank* [CD-ROM]. Prepared by U.S. Department of Commerce, Economics and Statistics Administration. Washington, DC: U.S. Department of Commerce, National Economic, Social, and Environmental Data Bank, Economics and Statistics Administration, Office of Business Analysis, February 1995. *Notes:* Totals may not agree with detail because of independent rounding. "NA" represents "not available." "D" indicates data withheld to avoid disclosing operations of individual companies.

★ 701 ★

Pollution Abatement and Control, by State

Pollution Abatement Capital Expenditures in Florida: 1988-1992

Pollution abatement expenditures are those with the primary purpose of protecting the environment by reducing or eliminating unwanted emissions or wastes that are created by the production process. Pollution abatement capital expenditures (PACE) by manufacturing establishments with 20 employees or more amounted to $8,393 million in 1992. Of this total, $7,867 million was attributable to a particular media: $4,403 million for air; $2,510 million for water; and $954 million for solid/contained waste. Spending for nonmedia and other was $526 million. Approximately 79 percent of the $8,383 million new capital expenditures for pollution abatement was made by establishments in four major industry groups: Chemicals and allied products (major group 28), petroleum and coal products (major group 29), paper and allied products (major group 26), and primary metal industries (major group 33). In 1992, Texas, California, and Louisiana accounted for approximately 38 percent of total new pollution abatement capital expenditures. Texas comprised 18 percent of the total. The table below shows pollution abatement capital expenditures for air, water, solid/contained waste, and nonmedia for Florida.

[In million dollars]

Year	Pollution abatement capital expenditures	Air	Water	Solid waste	Nonmedia
1992	105.9	24.5	74.0	7.4	4.9
1991	90.1	18.6	63.1	8.4	(NA)
1990	130.5	64.3	59.3	6.9	(NA)
1989	82.9	53.0	19.8	10.2	(NA)
1988	64.0	33.9	17.2	12.9	(NA)

Source: U.S. Department of Commerce. Bureau of the Census. "Pollution Abatement Costs and Expenditures, 1992." In *National Economic, Social, and Environmental Data Bank* [CD-ROM]. Prepared by U.S. Department of Commerce, Economics and Statistics Administration. Washington, DC: U.S. Department of Commerce, National Economic, Social, and Environmental Data Bank, Economics and Statistics Administration, Office of Business Analysis, February 1995. *Notes:* Totals may not agree with detail because of independent rounding. "NA" represents "not available."

★ 702 ★

Pollution Abatement and Control, by State

Pollution Abatement Capital Expenditures in Georgia: 1988-1992

Pollution abatement expenditures are those with the primary purpose of protecting the environment by reducing or eliminating unwanted emissions or wastes that are created by the production process. Pollution abatement capital expenditures (PACE) by manufacturing establishments with 20 employees or more amounted to $8,393 million in 1992. Of this total, $7,867 million was attributable to a particular media: $4,403 million for air; $2,510 million for water; and $954 million for solid/ contained waste. Spending for nonmedia and other was $526 million. Approximately 79 percent of the $8,383 million new capital expenditures for pollution abatement was made by establishments in four major industry groups: Chemicals and allied products (major group 28), petroleum and coal products (major group 29), paper and allied products (major group 26), and primary metal industries (major group 33). In 1992, Texas, California, and Louisiana accounted for approximately 38 percent of total new pollution abatement capital expenditures. Texas comprised 18 percent of the total. The table below shows pollution abatement capital expenditures for air, water, solid/contained waste, and nonmedia for Georgia.

[In million dollars]

Year	Pollution abatement capital expenditures	Air	Water	Solid waste	Nonmedia
1992	173.3	146.9	15.8	10.6	12.7
1991	271.0	170.0	86.6	14.4	(NA)
1990	238.3	124.8	98.8	14.7	(NA)
1989	145.4	78.1	51.5	15.7	(NA)
1988	80.7	24.1	36.2	20.5	(NA)

Source: U.S. Department of Commerce. Bureau of the Census. "Pollution Abatement Costs and Expenditures, 1992." In *National Economic, Social, and Environmental Data Bank* [CD-ROM]. Prepared by U.S. Department of Commerce, Economics and Statistics Administration. Washington, DC: U.S. Department of Commerce, National Economic, Social, and Environmental Data Bank, Economics and Statistics Administration, Office of Business Analysis, February 1995. *Notes:* Totals may not agree with detail because of independent rounding. "NA" represents "not available."

★ 703 ★
Pollution Abatement and Control, by State

Pollution Abatement Capital Expenditures in Hawaii: 1988-1992

Pollution abatement expenditures are those with the primary purpose of protecting the environment by reducing or eliminating unwanted emissions or wastes that are created by the production process. Pollution abatement capital expenditures (PACE) by manufacturing establishments with 20 employees or more amounted to $8,393 million in 1992. Of this total, $7,867 million was attributable to a particular media: $4,403 million for air; $2,510 million for water; and $954 million for solid/contained waste. Spending for nonmedia and other was $526 million. Approximately 79 percent of the $8,383 million new capital expenditures for pollution abatement was made by establishments in four major industry groups: Chemicals and allied products (major group 28), petroleum and coal products (major group 29), paper and allied products (major group 26), and primary metal industries (major group 33). In 1992, Texas, California, and Louisiana accounted for approximately 38 percent of total new pollution abatement capital expenditures. Texas comprised 18 percent of the total. The table below shows pollution abatement capital expenditures for air, water, solid/contained waste, and nonmedia for Hawaii.

[In million dollars]

Year	Pollution abatement capital expenditures	Air	Water	Solid waste	Nonmedia
1992	2.8	0.5	2.3	-	(Z)
1991	4.0	1.8	(D)	(D)	(NA)
1990	23.2	12.6	(D)	(D)	(NA)
1989	(D)	(D)	(D)	(D)	(NA)
1988	7.9	3.5	(D)	(D)	(NA)

Source: U.S. Department of Commerce. Bureau of the Census. "Pollution Abatement Costs and Expenditures, 1992." In *National Economic, Social, and Environmental Data Bank* [CD-ROM]. Prepared by U.S. Department of Commerce, Economics and Statistics Administration. Washington, DC: U.S. Department of Commerce, National Economic, Social, and Environmental Data Bank, Economics and Statistics Administration, Office of Business Analysis, February 1995. *Notes:* Totals may not agree with detail because of independent rounding. "NA" represents "not available." "D" indicates data withheld to avoid disclosing operations of individual companies. "-" represents zero. "Z" denotes less than half the unit shown.

★ 704 ★
Pollution Abatement and Control, by State

Pollution Abatement Capital Expenditures in Idaho: 1988-1992

Pollution abatement expenditures are those with the primary purpose of protecting the environment by reducing or eliminating unwanted emissions or wastes that are created by the production process. Pollution abatement capital expenditures (PACE) by manufacturing establishments with 20 employees or more amounted to $8,393 million in 1992. Of this total, $7,867 million was attributable to a particular media: $4,403 million for air; $2,510 million for water; and $954 million for solid/contained waste. Spending for nonmedia and other was $526 million. Approximately 79 percent of the $8,383 million new capital expenditures for pollution abatement was made by establishments in four major industry groups: Chemicals and allied products (major group 28), petroleum and coal products (major group 29), paper and allied products (major group 26), and primary metal industries (major group 33). In 1992, Texas, California, and Louisiana accounted for approximately 38 percent of total new pollution abatement capital expenditures. Texas comprised 18 percent of the total. The table below shows pollution abatement capital expenditures for air, water, solid/contained waste, and nonmedia for Idaho.

[In million dollars]

Year	Pollution abatement capital expenditures	Air	Water	Solid waste	Nonmedia
1992	25.0	14.3	10.3	0.4	0.8
1991	36.5	26.2	9.4	0.9	(NA)
1990	32.2	4.1	26.1	2.1	(NA)
1989	17.3	5.3	6.5	5.5	(NA)
1988	11.2	(D)	(D)	2.7	(NA)

Source: U.S. Department of Commerce. Bureau of the Census. "Pollution Abatement Costs and Expenditures, 1992." In *National Economic, Social, and Environmental Data Bank* [CD-ROM]. Prepared by U.S. Department of Commerce, Economics and Statistics Administration. Washington, DC: U.S. Department of Commerce, National Economic, Social, and Environmental Data Bank, Economics and Statistics Administration, Office of Business Analysis, February 1995. *Notes:* Totals may not agree with detail because of independent rounding. "NA" represents "not available." "D" indicates data withheld to avoid disclosing operations of individual companies.

★ 705 ★

Pollution Abatement and Control, by State

Pollution Abatement Capital Expenditures in Illinois: 1988-1992

Pollution abatement expenditures are those with the primary purpose of protecting the environment by reducing or eliminating unwanted emissions or wastes that are created by the production process. Pollution abatement capital expenditures (PACE) by manufacturing establishments with 20 employees or more amounted to $8,393 million in 1992. Of this total, $7,867 million was attributable to a particular media: $4,403 million for air; $2,510 million for water; and $954 million for solid/contained waste. Spending for nonmedia and other was $526 million. Approximately 79 percent of the $8,383 million new capital expenditures for pollution abatement was made by establishments in four major industry groups: Chemicals and allied products (major group 28), petroleum and coal products (major group 29), paper and allied products (major group 26), and primary metal industries (major group 33). In 1992, Texas, California, and Louisiana accounted for approximately 38 percent of total new pollution abatement capital expenditures. Texas comprised 18 percent of the total. The table below shows pollution abatement capital expenditures for air, water, solid/contained waste, and nonmedia for Illinois.

[In million dollars]

Year	Pollution abatement capital expenditures	Air	Water	Solid waste	Nonmedia
1992	350.5	250.1	81.3	19.1	16.2
1991	207.0	129.8	63.0	14.2	(NA)
1990	273.2	81.0	158.3	33.8	(NA)
1989	179.3	78.4	78.0	22.9	(NA)
1988	146.7	93.0	37.0	16.8	(NA)

Source: U.S. Department of Commerce. Bureau of the Census. "Pollution Abatement Costs and Expenditures, 1992." In *National Economic, Social, and Environmental Data Bank* [CD-ROM]. Prepared by U.S. Department of Commerce, Economics and Statistics Administration. Washington, DC: U.S. Department of Commerce, National Economic, Social, and Environmental Data Bank, Economics and Statistics Administration, Office of Business Analysis, February 1995. *Notes:* Totals may not agree with detail because of independent rounding. "NA" represents "not available."

★ 706 ★

Pollution Abatement and Control, by State

Pollution Abatement Capital Expenditures in Indiana: 1988-1992

Pollution abatement expenditures are those with the primary purpose of protecting the environment by reducing or eliminating unwanted emissions or wastes that are created by the production process. Pollution abatement capital expenditures (PACE) by manufacturing establishments with 20 employees or more amounted to $8,393 million in 1992. Of this total, $7,867 million was attributable to a particular media: $4,403 million for air; $2,510 million for water; and $954 million for solid/contained waste. Spending for nonmedia and other was $526 million. Approximately 79 percent of the $8,383 million new capital expenditures for pollution abatement was made by establishments in four major industry groups: Chemicals and allied products (major group 28), petroleum and coal products (major group 29), paper and allied products (major group 26), and primary metal industries (major group 33). In 1992, Texas, California, and Louisiana accounted for approximately 38 percent of total new pollution abatement capital expenditures. Texas comprised 18 percent of the total. The table below shows pollution abatement capital expenditures for air, water, solid/contained waste, and nonmedia for Indiana.

[In million dollars]

Year	Pollution abatement capital expenditures	Air	Water	Solid waste	Nonmedia
1992	330.9	220.6	94.3	16.0	32.5
1991	364.4	204.5	139.4	20.5	(NA)
1990	246.7	94.2	131.7	20.7	(NA)
1989	175.7	72.3	86.1	17.2	(NA)
1988	116.7	33.4	57.3	26.0	(NA)

Source: U.S. Department of Commerce. Bureau of the Census. "Pollution Abatement Costs and Expenditures, 1992." In *National Economic, Social, and Environmental Data Bank* [CD-ROM]. Prepared by U.S. Department of Commerce, Economics and Statistics Administration. Washington, DC: U.S. Department of Commerce, National Economic, Social, and Environmental Data Bank, Economics and Statistics Administration, Office of Business Analysis, February 1995. *Notes:* Totals may not agree with detail because of independent rounding. "NA" represents "not available."

★ 707 ★

Pollution Abatement and Control, by State

Pollution Abatement Capital Expenditures in Iowa: 1988-1992

Pollution abatement expenditures are those with the primary purpose of protecting the environment by reducing or eliminating unwanted emissions or wastes that are created by the production process. Pollution abatement capital expenditures (PACE) by manufacturing establishments with 20 employees or more amounted to $8,393 million in 1992. Of this total, $7,867 million was attributable to a particular media: $4,403 million for air; $2,510 million for water; and $954 million for solid/contained waste. Spending for nonmedia and other was $526 million. Approximately 79 percent of the $8,383 million new capital expenditures for pollution abatement was made by establishments in four major industry groups: Chemicals and allied products (major group 28), petroleum and coal products (major group 29), paper and allied products (major group 26), and primary metal industries (major group 33). In 1992, Texas, California, and Louisiana accounted for approximately 38 percent of total new pollution abatement capital expenditures. Texas comprised 18 percent of the total. The table below shows pollution abatement capital expenditures for air, water, solid/contained waste, and nonmedia for Iowa.

[In million dollars]

Year	Pollution abatement capital expenditures	Air	Water	Solid waste	Nonmedia
1992	46.9	27.0	14.2	5.7	5.3
1991	39.3	22.1	12.3	4.9	(NA)
1990	30.5	17.6	9.7	3.2	(NA)
1989	35.6	11.5	19.6	4.5	(NA)
1988	27.0	18.2	6.4	2.4	(NA)

Source: U.S. Department of Commerce. Bureau of the Census. "Pollution Abatement Costs and Expenditures, 1992." In *National Economic, Social, and Environmental Data Bank* [CD-ROM]. Prepared by U.S. Department of Commerce, Economics and Statistics Administration. Washington, DC: U.S. Department of Commerce, National Economic, Social, and Environmental Data Bank, Economics and Statistics Administration, Office of Business Analysis, February 1995. *Notes:* Totals may not agree with detail because of independent rounding. "NA" represents "not available."

★ 708 ★

Pollution Abatement and Control, by State

Pollution Abatement Capital Expenditures in Kansas: 1988-1992

Pollution abatement expenditures are those with the primary purpose of protecting the environment by reducing or eliminating unwanted emissions or wastes that are created by the production process. Pollution abatement capital expenditures (PACE) by manufacturing establishments with 20 employees or more amounted to $8,393 million in 1992. Of this total, $7,867 million was attributable to a particular media: $4,403 million for air; $2,510 million for water; and $954 million for solid/contained waste. Spending for nonmedia and other was $526 million. Approximately 79 percent of the $8,383 million new capital expenditures for pollution abatement was made by establishments in four major industry groups: Chemicals and allied products (major group 28), petroleum and coal products (major group 29), paper and allied products (major group 26), and primary metal industries (major group 33). In 1992, Texas, California, and Louisiana accounted for approximately 38 percent of total new pollution abatement capital expenditures. Texas comprised 18 percent of the total. The table below shows pollution abatement capital expenditures for air, water, solid/contained waste, and nonmedia for Kansas.

[In million dollars]

Year	Pollution abatement capital expenditures	Air	Water	Solid waste	Nonmedia
1992	186.1	153.7	23.5	8.9	7.8
1991	85.0	68.9	9.7	6.4	(NA)
1990	35.6	12.8	20.1	2.7	(NA)
1989	24.7	7.9	15.0	1.8	(NA)
1988	14.1	2.8	10.3	1.0	(NA)

Source: U.S. Department of Commerce. Bureau of the Census. "Pollution Abatement Costs and Expenditures, 1992." In *National Economic, Social, and Environmental Data Bank* [CD-ROM]. Prepared by U.S. Department of Commerce, Economics and Statistics Administration. Washington, DC: U.S. Department of Commerce, National Economic, Social, and Environmental Data Bank, Economics and Statistics Administration, Office of Business Analysis, February 1995. *Notes:* Totals may not agree with detail because of independent rounding. "NA" represents "not available."

★ 709 ★

Pollution Abatement and Control, by State

Pollution Abatement Capital Expenditures in Kentucky: 1988-1992

Pollution abatement expenditures are those with the primary purpose of protecting the environment by reducing or eliminating unwanted emissions or wastes that are created by the production process. Pollution abatement capital expenditures (PACE) by manufacturing establishments with 20 employees or more amounted to $8,393 million in 1992. Of this total, $7,867 million was attributable to a particular media: $4,403 million for air; $2,510 million for water; and $954 million for solid/contained waste. Spending for nonmedia and other was $526 million. Approximately 79 percent of the $8,383 million new capital expenditures for pollution abatement was made by establishments in four major industry groups: Chemicals and allied products (major group 28), petroleum and coal products (major group 29), paper and allied products (major group 26), and primary metal industries (major group 33). In 1992, Texas, California, and Louisiana accounted for approximately 38 percent of total new pollution abatement capital expenditures. Texas comprised 18 percent of the total. The table below shows pollution abatement capital expenditures for air, water, solid/contained waste, and nonmedia for Kentucky.

[In million dollars]

Year	Pollution abatement capital expenditures	Air	Water	Solid waste	Nonmedia
1992	180.9	132.4	25.7	22.8	16.6
1991	152.0	86.4	50.6	15.1	(NA)
1990	135.5	60.3	68.4	6.9	(NA)
1989	53.5	30.7	17.5	5.3	(NA)
1988	71.1	31.9	29.1	10.2	(NA)

Source: U.S. Department of Commerce. Bureau of the Census. "Pollution Abatement Costs and Expenditures, 1992." In *National Economic, Social, and Environmental Data Bank* [CD-ROM]. Prepared by U.S. Department of Commerce, Economics and Statistics Administration. Washington, DC: U.S. Department of Commerce, National Economic, Social, and Environmental Data Bank, Economics and Statistics Administration, Office of Business Analysis, February 1995. *Notes:* Totals may not agree with detail because of independent rounding. "NA" represents "not available."

★ 710 ★
Pollution Abatement and Control, by State

Pollution Abatement Capital Expenditures in Louisiana: 1988-1992

Pollution abatement expenditures are those with the primary purpose of protecting the environment by reducing or eliminating unwanted emissions or wastes that are created by the production process. Pollution abatement capital expenditures (PACE) by manufacturing establishments with 20 employees or more amounted to $8,393 million in 1992. Of this total, $7,867 million was attributable to a particular media: $4,403 million for air; $2,510 million for water; and $954 million for solid/ contained waste. Spending for nonmedia and other was $526 million. Approximately 79 percent of the $8,383 million new capital expenditures for pollution abatement was made by establishments in four major industry groups: Chemicals and allied products (major group 28), petroleum and coal products (major group 29), paper and allied products (major group 26), and primary metal industries (major group 33). In 1992, Texas, California, and Louisiana accounted for approximately 38 percent of total new pollution abatement capital expenditures. Texas comprised 18 percent of the total. The table below shows pollution abatement capital expenditures for air, water, solid/contained waste, and nonmedia for Louisiana.

[In million dollars]

Year	Pollution abatement capital expenditures	Air	Water	Solid waste	Nonmedia
1992	1,057.2	477.6	430.8	148.8	33.8
1991	564.2	315.6	184.0	64.5	(NA)
1990	301.9	85.4	144.9	71.6	(NA)
1989	191.3	61.0	100.1	30.2	(NA)
1988	144.5	44.9	58.8	40.8	(NA)

Source: U.S. Department of Commerce. Bureau of the Census. "Pollution Abatement Costs and Expenditures, 1992." In *National Economic, Social, and Environmental Data Bank* [CD-ROM]. Prepared by U.S. Department of Commerce, Economics and Statistics Administration. Washington, DC: U.S. Department of Commerce, National Economic, Social, and Environmental Data Bank, Economics and Statistics Administration, Office of Business Analysis, February 1995. *Notes:* Totals may not agree with detail because of independent rounding. "NA" represents "not available."

★ 711 ★

Pollution Abatement and Control, by State

Pollution Abatement Capital Expenditures in Maine: 1988-1992

Pollution abatement expenditures are those with the primary purpose of protecting the environment by reducing or eliminating unwanted emissions or wastes that are created by the production process. Pollution abatement capital expenditures (PACE) by manufacturing establishments with 20 employees or more amounted to $8,393 million in 1992. Of this total, $7,867 million was attributable to a particular media: $4,403 million for air; $2,510 million for water; and $954 million for solid/contained waste. Spending for nonmedia and other was $526 million. Approximately 79 percent of the $8,383 million new capital expenditures for pollution abatement was made by establishments in four major industry groups: Chemicals and allied products (major group 28), petroleum and coal products (major group 29), paper and allied products (major group 26), and primary metal industries (major group 33). In 1992, Texas, California, and Louisiana accounted for approximately 38 percent of total new pollution abatement capital expenditures. Texas comprised 18 percent of the total. The table below shows pollution abatement capital expenditures for air, water, solid/contained waste, and nonmedia for Maine.

[In million dollars]

Year	Pollution abatement capital expenditures	Air	Water	Solid waste	Nonmedia
1992	62.2	23.8	26.8	11.6	5.0
1991	95.4	21.0	(D)	(D)	(NA)
1990	104.1	25.6	25.1	53.4	(NA)
1989	82.4	26.5	21.0	34.9	(NA)
1988	46.8	22.4	9.8	14.6	(NA)

Source: U.S. Department of Commerce. Bureau of the Census. "Pollution Abatement Costs and Expenditures, 1992." In *National Economic, Social, and Environmental Data Bank* [CD-ROM]. Prepared by U.S. Department of Commerce, Economics and Statistics Administration. Washington, DC: U.S. Department of Commerce, National Economic, Social, and Environmental Data Bank, Economics and Statistics Administration, Office of Business Analysis, February 1995. *Notes:* Totals may not agree with detail because of independent rounding. "NA" represents "not available." "D" indicates data withheld to avoid disclosing operations of individual companies.

★ 712 ★
Pollution Abatement and Control, by State

Pollution Abatement Capital Expenditures in Maryland: 1988-1992

Pollution abatement expenditures are those with the primary purpose of protecting the environment by reducing or eliminating unwanted emissions or wastes that are created by the production process. Pollution abatement capital expenditures (PACE) by manufacturing establishments with 20 employees or more amounted to $8,393 million in 1992. Of this total, $7,867 million was attributable to a particular media: $4,403 million for air; $2,510 million for water; and $954 million for solid/contained waste. Spending for nonmedia and other was $526 million. Approximately 79 percent of the $8,383 million new capital expenditures for pollution abatement was made by establishments in four major industry groups: Chemicals and allied products (major group 28), petroleum and coal products (major group 29), paper and allied products (major group 26), and primary metal industries (major group 33). In 1992, Texas, California, and Louisiana accounted for approximately 38 percent of total new pollution abatement capital expenditures. Texas comprised 18 percent of the total. The table below shows pollution abatement capital expenditures for air, water, solid/contained waste, and nonmedia for Maryland.

[In million dollars]

Year	Pollution abatement capital expenditures	Air	Water	Solid waste	Nonmedia
1992	38.1	16.4	16.2	5.5	7.1
1991	94.6	67.6	21.9	5.2	(NA)
1990	133.1	80.6	45.2	7.3	(NA)
1989	72.9	26.6	41.0	5.3	(NA)
1988	36.9	19.5	11.7	5.7	(NA)

Source: U.S. Department of Commerce. Bureau of the Census. "Pollution Abatement Costs and Expenditures, 1992." In *National Economic, Social, and Environmental Data Bank* [CD-ROM]. Prepared by U.S. Department of Commerce, Economics and Statistics Administration. Washington, DC: U.S. Department of Commerce, National Economic, Social, and Environmental Data Bank, Economics and Statistics Administration, Office of Business Analysis, February 1995. *Notes:* Totals may not agree with detail because of independent rounding. "NA" represents "not available."

★ 713 ★

Pollution Abatement and Control, by State

Pollution Abatement Capital Expenditures in Massachusetts: 1988-1992

Pollution abatement expenditures are those with the primary purpose of protecting the environment by reducing or eliminating unwanted emissions or wastes that are created by the production process. Pollution abatement capital expenditures (PACE) by manufacturing establishments with 20 employees or more amounted to $8,393 million in 1992. Of this total, $7,867 million was attributable to a particular media: $4,403 million for air; $2,510 million for water; and $954 million for solid/contained waste. Spending for nonmedia and other was $526 million. Approximately 79 percent of the $8,383 million new capital expenditures for pollution abatement was made by establishments in four major industry groups: Chemicals and allied products (major group 28), petroleum and coal products (major group 29), paper and allied products (major group 26), and primary metal industries (major group 33). In 1992, Texas, California, and Louisiana accounted for approximately 38 percent of total new pollution abatement capital expenditures. Texas comprised 18 percent of the total. The table below shows pollution abatement capital expenditures for air, water, solid/ contained waste, and nonmedia for Massachusetts.

[In million dollars]

Year	Pollution abatement capital expenditures	Air	Water	Solid waste	Nonmedia
1992	59.5	18.4	35.6	5.5	5.5
1991	55.6	17.5	26.3	11.8	(NA)
1990	69.9	14.5	44.2	11.1	(NA)
1989	44.2	14.8	25.2	4.2	(NA)
1988	37.2	11.0	22.2	4.0	(NA)

Source: U.S. Department of Commerce. Bureau of the Census. "Pollution Abatement Costs and Expenditures, 1992." In *National Economic, Social, and Environmental Data Bank* [CD-ROM]. Prepared by U.S. Department of Commerce, Economics and Statistics Administration. Washington, DC: U.S. Department of Commerce, National Economic, Social, and Environmental Data Bank, Economics and Statistics Administration, Office of Business Analysis, February 1995. *Notes:* Totals may not agree with detail because of independent rounding. "NA" represents "not available."

★ 714 ★
Pollution Abatement and Control, by State

Pollution Abatement Capital Expenditures in Michigan: 1988-1992

Pollution abatement expenditures are those with the primary purpose of protecting the environment by reducing or eliminating unwanted emissions or wastes that are created by the production process. Pollution abatement capital expenditures (PACE) by manufacturing establishments with 20 employees or more amounted to $8,393 million in 1992. Of this total, $7,867 million was attributable to a particular media: $4,403 million for air; $2,510 million for water; and $954 million for solid/ contained waste. Spending for nonmedia and other was $526 million. Approximately 79 percent of the $8,383 million new capital expenditures for pollution abatement was made by establishments in four major industry groups: Chemicals and allied products (major group 28), petroleum and coal products (major group 29), paper and allied products (major group 26), and primary metal industries (major group 33). In 1992, Texas, California, and Louisiana accounted for approximately 38 percent of total new pollution abatement capital expenditures. Texas comprised 18 percent of the total. The table below shows pollution abatement capital expenditures for air, water, solid/contained waste, and nonmedia for Michigan.

[In million dollars]

Year	Pollution abatement capital expenditures	Air	Water	Solid waste	Nonmedia
1992	159.3	99.4	37.9	22.0	24.6
1991	172.9	90.0	49.7	33.1	(NA)
1990	178.9	97.2	52.7	29.1	(NA)
1989	289.0	180.6	80.6	27.9	(NA)
1988	154.4	58.7	67.4	28.4	(NA)

Source: U.S. Department of Commerce. Bureau of the Census. "Pollution Abatement Costs and Expenditures, 1992." In *National Economic, Social, and Environmental Data Bank* [CD-ROM]. Prepared by U.S. Department of Commerce, Economics and Statistics Administration. Washington, DC: U.S. Department of Commerce, National Economic, Social, and Environmental Data Bank, Economics and Statistics Administration, Office of Business Analysis, February 1995. *Notes:* Totals may not agree with detail because of independent rounding. "NA" represents "not available."

★ 715 ★

Pollution Abatement and Control, by State

Pollution Abatement Capital Expenditures in Minnesota: 1988-1992

Pollution abatement expenditures are those with the primary purpose of protecting the environment by reducing or eliminating unwanted emissions or wastes that are created by the production process. Pollution abatement capital expenditures (PACE) by manufacturing establishments with 20 employees or more amounted to $8,393 million in 1992. Of this total, $7,867 million was attributable to a particular media: $4,403 million for air; $2,510 million for water; and $954 million for solid/contained waste. Spending for nonmedia and other was $526 million. Approximately 79 percent of the $8,383 million new capital expenditures for pollution abatement was made by establishments in four major industry groups: Chemicals and allied products (major group 28), petroleum and coal products (major group 29), paper and allied products (major group 26), and primary metal industries (major group 33). In 1992, Texas, California, and Louisiana accounted for approximately 38 percent of total new pollution abatement capital expenditures. Texas comprised 18 percent of the total. The table below shows pollution abatement capital expenditures for air, water, solid/contained waste, and nonmedia for Minnesota.

[In million dollars]

Year	Pollution abatement capital expenditures	Air	Water	Solid waste	Nonmedia
1992	133.1	91.8	29.7	11.6	4.1
1991	64.4	43.9	13.8	6.7	(NA)
1990	92.6	54.6	30.4	7.6	(NA)
1989	46.6	11.3	23.0	12.3	(NA)
1988	47.4	25.4	16.1	5.8	(NA)

Source: U.S. Department of Commerce. Bureau of the Census. "Pollution Abatement Costs and Expenditures, 1992." In *National Economic, Social, and Environmental Data Bank* [CD-ROM]. Prepared by U.S. Department of Commerce, Economics and Statistics Administration. Washington, DC: U.S. Department of Commerce, National Economic, Social, and Environmental Data Bank, Economics and Statistics Administration, Office of Business Analysis, February 1995. *Notes:* Totals may not agree with detail because of independent rounding. "NA" represents "not available."

★ 716 ★

Pollution Abatement and Control, by State

Pollution Abatement Capital Expenditures in Mississippi: 1988-1992

Pollution abatement expenditures are those with the primary purpose of protecting the environment by reducing or eliminating unwanted emissions or wastes that are created by the production process. Pollution abatement capital expenditures (PACE) by manufacturing establishments with 20 employees or more amounted to $8,393 million in 1992. Of this total, $7,867 million was attributable to a particular media: $4,403 million for air; $2,510 million for water; and $954 million for solid/contained waste. Spending for nonmedia and other was $526 million. Approximately 79 percent of the $8,383 million new capital expenditures for pollution abatement was made by establishments in four major industry groups: Chemicals and allied products (major group 28), petroleum and coal products (major group 29), paper and allied products (major group 26), and primary metal industries (major group 33). In 1992, Texas, California, and Louisiana accounted for approximately 38 percent of total new pollution abatement capital expenditures. Texas comprised 18 percent of the total. The table below shows pollution abatement capital expenditures for air, water, solid/contained waste, and nonmedia for Mississippi.

[In million dollars]

Year	Pollution abatement capital expenditures	Air	Water	Solid waste	Nonmedia
1992	112.8	88.3	15.8	8.8	3.0
1991	68.2	43.2	19.0	6.0	(NA)
1990	68.7	27.2	35.1	6.5	(NA)
1989	67.1	32.0	29.8	5.2	(NA)
1988	23.0	10.5	8.4	4.1	(NA)

Source: U.S. Department of Commerce. Bureau of the Census. "Pollution Abatement Costs and Expenditures, 1992." In *National Economic, Social, and Environmental Data Bank* [CD-ROM]. Prepared by U.S. Department of Commerce, Economics and Statistics Administration. Washington, DC: U.S. Department of Commerce, National Economic, Social, and Environmental Data Bank, Economics and Statistics Administration, Office of Business Analysis, February 1995. *Notes:* Totals may not agree with detail because of independent rounding. "NA" represents "not available."

★717★

Pollution Abatement and Control, by State

Pollution Abatement Capital Expenditures in Missouri: 1988-1992

Pollution abatement expenditures are those with the primary purpose of protecting the environment by reducing or eliminating unwanted emissions or wastes that are created by the production process. Pollution abatement capital expenditures (PACE) by manufacturing establishments with 20 employees or more amounted to $8,393 million in 1992. Of this total, $7,867 million was attributable to a particular media: $4,403 million for air; $2,510 million for water; and $954 million for solid/contained waste. Spending for nonmedia and other was $526 million. Approximately 79 percent of the $8,383 million new capital expenditures for pollution abatement was made by establishments in four major industry groups: Chemicals and allied products (major group 28), petroleum and coal products (major group 29), paper and allied products (major group 26), and primary metal industries (major group 33). In 1992, Texas, California, and Louisiana accounted for approximately 38 percent of total new pollution abatement capital expenditures. Texas comprised 18 percent of the total. The table below shows pollution abatement capital expenditures for air, water, solid/ contained waste, and nonmedia for Missouri.

[In million dollars]

Year	Pollution abatement capital expenditures	Air	Water	Solid waste	Nonmedia
1992	65.2	28.5	25.5	11.2	4.5
1991	61.4	39.4	16.6	5.3	(NA)
1990	72.4	22.3	43.8	6.3	(NA)
1989	38.0	13.4	16.3	8.3	(NA)
1988	56.8	29.7	21.5	5.6	(NA)

Source: U.S. Department of Commerce. Bureau of the Census. "Pollution Abatement Costs and Expenditures, 1992." In *National Economic, Social, and Environmental Data Bank* [CD-ROM]. Prepared by U.S. Department of Commerce, Economics and Statistics Administration. Washington, DC: U.S. Department of Commerce, National Economic, Social, and Environmental Data Bank, Economics and Statistics Administration, Office of Business Analysis, February 1995. *Notes:* Totals may not agree with detail because of independent rounding. "NA" represents "not available."

★ 718 ★

Pollution Abatement and Control, by State

Pollution Abatement Capital Expenditures in Montana: 1988-1992

Pollution abatement expenditures are those with the primary purpose of protecting the environment by reducing or eliminating unwanted emissions or wastes that are created by the production process. Pollution abatement capital expenditures (PACE) by manufacturing establishments with 20 employees or more amounted to $8,393 million in 1992. Of this total, $7,867 million was attributable to a particular media: $4,403 million for air; $2,510 million for water; and $954 million for solid/contained waste. Spending for nonmedia and other was $526 million. Approximately 79 percent of the $8,383 million new capital expenditures for pollution abatement was made by establishments in four major industry groups: Chemicals and allied products (major group 28), petroleum and coal products (major group 29), paper and allied products (major group 26), and primary metal industries (major group 33). In 1992, Texas, California, and Louisiana accounted for approximately 38 percent of total new pollution abatement capital expenditures. Texas comprised 18 percent of the total. The table below shows pollution abatement capital expenditures for air, water, solid/contained waste, and nonmedia for Montana.

[In million dollars]

Year	Pollution abatement capital expenditures	Air	Water	Solid waste	Nonmedia
1992	7.1	2.2	(D)	(D)	0.5
1991	18.3	14.7	(D)	(D)	(NA)
1990	9.5	6.0	(D)	(D)	(NA)
1989	4.2	2.4	1.6	0.2	(NA)
1988	(D)	(D)	(D)	(D)	(NA)

Source: U.S. Department of Commerce. Bureau of the Census. "Pollution Abatement Costs and Expenditures, 1992." In *National Economic, Social, and Environmental Data Bank* [CD-ROM]. Prepared by U.S. Department of Commerce, Economics and Statistics Administration. Washington, DC: U.S. Department of Commerce, National Economic, Social, and Environmental Data Bank, Economics and Statistics Administration, Office of Business Analysis, February 1995. *Notes:* Totals may not agree with detail because of independent rounding. "NA" represents "not available." "D" indicates data withheld to avoid disclosing operations of individual companies.

★ 719 ★

Pollution Abatement and Control, by State

Pollution Abatement Capital Expenditures in Nebraska: 1988-1992

Pollution abatement expenditures are those with the primary purpose of protecting the environment by reducing or eliminating unwanted emissions or wastes that are created by the production process. Pollution abatement capital expenditures (PACE) by manufacturing establishments with 20 employees or more amounted to $8,393 million in 1992. Of this total, $7,867 million was attributable to a particular media: $4,403 million for air; $2,510 million for water; and $954 million for solid/contained waste. Spending for nonmedia and other was $526 million. Approximately 79 percent of the $8,383 million new capital expenditures for pollution abatement was made by establishments in four major industry groups: Chemicals and allied products (major group 28), petroleum and coal products (major group 29), paper and allied products (major group 26), and primary metal industries (major group 33). In 1992, Texas, California, and Louisiana accounted for approximately 38 percent of total new pollution abatement capital expenditures. Texas comprised 18 percent of the total. The table below shows pollution abatement capital expenditures for air, water, solid/contained waste, and nonmedia for Nebraska.

[In million dollars]

Year	Pollution abatement capital expenditures	Air	Water	Solid waste	Nonmedia
1992	8.0	3.7	2.6	1.7	4.4
1991	5.6	2.7	2.2	0.7	(NA)
1990	5.8	3.4	1.9	0.4	(NA)
1989	4.3	1.2	2.6	0.5	(NA)
1988	5.6	2.8	(D)	(D)	(NA)

Source: U.S. Department of Commerce. Bureau of the Census. "Pollution Abatement Costs and Expenditures, 1992." In *National Economic, Social, and Environmental Data Bank* [CD-ROM]. Prepared by U.S. Department of Commerce, Economics and Statistics Administration. Washington, DC: U.S. Department of Commerce, National Economic, Social, and Environmental Data Bank, Economics and Statistics Administration, Office of Business Analysis, February 1995. *Notes:* Totals may not agree with detail because of independent rounding. "NA" represents "not available." "D" indicates data withheld to avoid disclosing operations of individual companies.

★ 720 ★
Pollution Abatement and Control, by State

Pollution Abatement Capital Expenditures in Nevada: 1988-1992

Pollution abatement expenditures are those with the primary purpose of protecting the environment by reducing or eliminating unwanted emissions or wastes that are created by the production process. Pollution abatement capital expenditures (PACE) by manufacturing establishments with 20 employees or more amounted to $8,393 million in 1992. Of this total, $7,867 million was attributable to a particular media: $4,403 million for air; $2,510 million for water; and $954 million for solid/contained waste. Spending for nonmedia and other was $526 million. Approximately 79 percent of the $8,383 million new capital expenditures for pollution abatement was made by establishments in four major industry groups: Chemicals and allied products (major group 28), petroleum and coal products (major group 29), paper and allied products (major group 26), and primary metal industries (major group 33). In 1992, Texas, California, and Louisiana accounted for approximately 38 percent of total new pollution abatement capital expenditures. Texas comprised 18 percent of the total. The table below shows pollution abatement capital expenditures for air, water, solid/contained waste, and nonmedia for Nevada.

[In million dollars]

Year	Pollution abatement capital expenditures	Air	Water	Solid waste	Nonmedia
1992	5.3	2.1	2.5	0.8	0.1
1991	2.2	1.0	1.2	(Z)	(NA)
1990	4.1	(D)	(D)	3.1	(NA)
1989	1.3	(D)	0.9	(D)	(NA)
1988	138.0	134.4	3.0	0.5	(NA)

Source: U.S. Department of Commerce. Bureau of the Census. "Pollution Abatement Costs and Expenditures, 1992." In *National Economic, Social, and Environmental Data Bank* [CD-ROM]. Prepared by U.S. Department of Commerce, Economics and Statistics Administration. Washington, DC: U.S. Department of Commerce, National Economic, Social, and Environmental Data Bank, Economics and Statistics Administration, Office of Business Analysis, February 1995. *Notes:* Totals may not agree with detail because of independent rounding. "NA" represents "not available." "D" indicates data withheld to avoid disclosing operations of individual companies. "Z" denotes less than half the unit shown.

★ 721 ★
Pollution Abatement and Control, by State

Pollution Abatement Capital Expenditures in New Hampshire: 1988-1992

Pollution abatement expenditures are those with the primary purpose of protecting the environment by reducing or eliminating unwanted emissions or wastes that are created by the production process. Pollution abatement capital expenditures (PACE) by manufacturing establishments with 20 employees or more amounted to $8,393 million in 1992. Of this total, $7,867 million was attributable to a particular media: $4,403 million for air; $2,510 million for water; and $954 million for solid/contained waste. Spending for nonmedia and other was $526 million. Approximately 79 percent of the $8,383 million new capital expenditures for pollution abatement was made by establishments in four major industry groups: Chemicals and allied products (major group 28), petroleum and coal products (major group 29), paper and allied products (major group 26), and primary metal industries (major group 33). In 1992, Texas, California, and Louisiana accounted for approximately 38 percent of total new pollution abatement capital expenditures. Texas comprised 18 percent of the total. The table below shows pollution abatement capital expenditures for air, water, solid/contained waste, and nonmedia for New Hampshire.

[In million dollars]

Year	Pollution abatement capital expenditures	Air	Water	Solid waste	Nonmedia
1992	(D)	(D)	2.2	(D)	(D)
1991	8.5	2.5	3.6	2.4	(NA)
1990	9.7	3.8	2.9	3.0	(NA)
1989	7.7	2.2	1.4	3.0	(NA)
1988	10.8	(D)	(D)	2.3	(NA)

Source: U.S. Department of Commerce. Bureau of the Census. "Pollution Abatement Costs and Expenditures, 1992." In *National Economic, Social, and Environmental Data Bank* [CD-ROM]. Prepared by U.S. Department of Commerce, Economics and Statistics Administration. Washington, DC: U.S. Department of Commerce, National Economic, Social, and Environmental Data Bank, Economics and Statistics Administration, Office of Business Analysis, February 1995. *Notes:* Totals may not agree with detail because of independent rounding. "NA" represents "not available." "D" indicates data withheld to avoid disclosing operations of individual companies.

★ 722 ★

Pollution Abatement and Control, by State

Pollution Abatement Capital Expenditures in New Jersey: 1988-1992

Pollution abatement expenditures are those with the primary purpose of protecting the environment by reducing or eliminating unwanted emissions or wastes that are created by the production process. Pollution abatement capital expenditures (PACE) by manufacturing establishments with 20 employees or more amounted to $8,393 million in 1992. Of this total, $7,867 million was attributable to a particular media: $4,403 million for air; $2,510 million for water; and $954 million for solid/contained waste. Spending for nonmedia and other was $526 million. Approximately 79 percent of the $8,383 million new capital expenditures for pollution abatement was made by establishments in four major industry groups: Chemicals and allied products (major group 28), petroleum and coal products (major group 29), paper and allied products (major group 26), and primary metal industries (major group 33). In 1992, Texas, California, and Louisiana accounted for approximately 38 percent of total new pollution abatement capital expenditures. Texas comprised 18 percent of the total. The table below shows pollution abatement capital expenditures for air, water, solid/contained waste, and nonmedia for New Jersey.

[In million dollars]

Year	Pollution abatement capital expenditures	Air	Water	Solid waste	Nonmedia
1992	154.0	65.6	70.3	18.0	38.8
1991	245.5	100.3	124.0	21.3	(NA)
1990	152.3	60.3	74.3	17.6	(NA)
1989	121.4	44.8	56.6	20.0	(NA)
1988	84.6	24.2	45.9	14.5	(NA)

Source: U.S. Department of Commerce. Bureau of the Census. "Pollution Abatement Costs and Expenditures, 1992." In *National Economic, Social, and Environmental Data Bank* [CD-ROM]. Prepared by U.S. Department of Commerce, Economics and Statistics Administration. Washington, DC: U.S. Department of Commerce, National Economic, Social, and Environmental Data Bank, Economics and Statistics Administration, Office of Business Analysis, February 1995. *Notes:* Totals may not agree with detail because of independent rounding. "NA" represents "not available."

★ 723 ★

Pollution Abatement and Control, by State

Pollution Abatement Capital Expenditures in New Mexico: 1988-1992

Pollution abatement expenditures are those with the primary purpose of protecting the environment by reducing or eliminating unwanted emissions or wastes that are created by the production process. Pollution abatement capital expenditures (PACE) by manufacturing establishments with 20 employees or more amounted to $8,393 million in 1992. Of this total, $7,867 million was attributable to a particular media: $4,403 million for air; $2,510 million for water; and $954 million for solid/contained waste. Spending for nonmedia and other was $526 million. Approximately 79 percent of the $8,383 million new capital expenditures for pollution abatement was made by establishments in four major industry groups: Chemicals and allied products (major group 28), petroleum and coal products (major group 29), paper and allied products (major group 26), and primary metal industries (major group 33). In 1992, Texas, California, and Louisiana accounted for approximately 38 percent of total new pollution abatement capital expenditures. Texas comprised 18 percent of the total. The table below shows pollution abatement capital expenditures for air, water, solid/ contained waste, and nonmedia for New Mexico.

[In million dollars]

Year	Pollution abatement capital expenditures	Air	Water	Solid waste	Nonmedia
1992	44.3	36.2	(D)	(D)	-
1991	26.0	9.5	(D)	(D)	(NA)
1990	67.3	34.0	32.7	0.7	(NA)
1989	9.9	9.3	0.4	0.1	(NA)
1988	(D)	(D)	(D)	(D)	(NA)

Source: U.S. Department of Commerce. Bureau of the Census. "Pollution Abatement Costs and Expenditures, 1992." In *National Economic, Social, and Environmental Data Bank* [CD-ROM]. Prepared by U.S. Department of Commerce, Economics and Statistics Administration. Washington, DC: U.S. Department of Commerce, National Economic, Social, and Environmental Data Bank, Economics and Statistics Administration, Office of Business Analysis, February 1995. *Notes:* Totals may not agree with detail because of independent rounding. "NA" represents "not available." "D" indicates data withheld to avoid disclosing operations of individual companies. "-" represents zero.

★ 724 ★
Pollution Abatement and Control, by State

Pollution Abatement Capital Expenditures in New York: 1988-1992

Pollution abatement expenditures are those with the primary purpose of protecting the environment by reducing or eliminating unwanted emissions or wastes that are created by the production process. Pollution abatement capital expenditures (PACE) by manufacturing establishments with 20 employees or more amounted to $8,393 million in 1992. Of this total, $7,867 million was attributable to a particular media: $4,403 million for air; $2,510 million for water; and $954 million for solid/ contained waste. Spending for nonmedia and other was $526 million. Approximately 79 percent of the $8,383 million new capital expenditures for pollution abatement was made by establishments in four major industry groups: Chemicals and allied products (major group 28), petroleum and coal products (major group 29), paper and allied products (major group 26), and primary metal industries (major group 33). In 1992, Texas, California, and Louisiana accounted for approximately 38 percent of total new pollution abatement capital expenditures. Texas comprised 18 percent of the total. The table below shows pollution abatement capital expenditures for air, water, solid/contained waste, and nonmedia for New York.

[In million dollars]

Year	Pollution abatement capital expenditures	Air	Water	Solid waste	Nonmedia
1992	128.8	72.9	29.0	26.8	55.7
1991	200.5	88.8	55.4	56.3	(NA)
1990	249.3	121.8	78.9	48.7	(NA)
1989	209.5	96.7	74.0	38.8	(NA)
1988	102.1	45.8	33.0	23.2	(NA)

Source: U.S. Department of Commerce. Bureau of the Census. "Pollution Abatement Costs and Expenditures, 1992." In *National Economic, Social, and Environmental Data Bank* [CD-ROM]. Prepared by U.S. Department of Commerce, Economics and Statistics Administration. Washington, DC: U.S. Department of Commerce, National Economic, Social, and Environmental Data Bank, Economics and Statistics Administration, Office of Business Analysis, February 1995. *Notes:* Totals may not agree with detail because of independent rounding. "NA" represents "not available."

★ 725 ★

Pollution Abatement and Control, by State

Pollution Abatement Capital Expenditures in North Carolina: 1988-1992

Pollution abatement expenditures are those with the primary purpose of protecting the environment by reducing or eliminating unwanted emissions or wastes that are created by the production process. Pollution abatement capital expenditures (PACE) by manufacturing establishments with 20 employees or more amounted to $8,393 million in 1992. Of this total, $7,867 million was attributable to a particular media: $4,403 million for air; $2,510 million for water; and $954 million for solid/contained waste. Spending for nonmedia and other was $526 million. Approximately 79 percent of the $8,383 million new capital expenditures for pollution abatement was made by establishments in four major industry groups: Chemicals and allied products (major group 28), petroleum and coal products (major group 29), paper and allied products (major group 26), and primary metal industries (major group 33). In 1992, Texas, California, and Louisiana accounted for approximately 38 percent of total new pollution abatement capital expenditures. Texas comprised 18 percent of the total. The table below shows pollution abatement capital expenditures for air, water, solid/contained waste, and nonmedia for North Carolina.

[In million dollars]

Year	Pollution abatement capital expenditures	Air	Water	Solid waste	Nonmedia
1992	259.8	97.3	132.2	30.3	21.2
1991	276.3	68.8	181.0	26.5	(NA)
1990	212.3	81.3	110.6	20.4	(NA)
1989	114.7	44.4	46.3	24.0	(NA)
1988	89.3	51.7	30.1	7.6	(NA)

Source: U.S. Department of Commerce. Bureau of the Census. "Pollution Abatement Costs and Expenditures, 1992." In *National Economic, Social, and Environmental Data Bank* [CD-ROM]. Prepared by U.S. Department of Commerce, Economics and Statistics Administration. Washington, DC: U.S. Department of Commerce, National Economic, Social, and Environmental Data Bank, Economics and Statistics Administration, Office of Business Analysis, February 1995. *Notes:* Totals may not agree with detail because of independent rounding. "NA" represents "not available."

★ 726 ★

Pollution Abatement and Control, by State

Pollution Abatement Capital Expenditures in North Dakota: 1988-1992

Pollution abatement expenditures are those with the primary purpose of protecting the environment by reducing or eliminating unwanted emissions or wastes that are created by the production process. Pollution abatement capital expenditures (PACE) by manufacturing establishments with 20 employees or more amounted to $8,393 million in 1992. Of this total, $7,867 million was attributable to a particular media: $4,403 million for air; $2,510 million for water; and $954 million for solid/contained waste. Spending for nonmedia and other was $526 million. Approximately 79 percent of the $8,383 million new capital expenditures for pollution abatement was made by establishments in four major industry groups: Chemicals and allied products (major group 28), petroleum and coal products (major group 29), paper and allied products (major group 26), and primary metal industries (major group 33). In 1992, Texas, California, and Louisiana accounted for approximately 38 percent of total new pollution abatement capital expenditures. Texas comprised 18 percent of the total. The table below shows pollution abatement capital expenditures for air, water, solid/contained waste, and nonmedia for North Dakota.

[In million dollars]

Year	Pollution abatement capital expenditures	Air	Water	Solid waste	Nonmedia
1992	3.7	1.1	2.2	0.3	-
1991	(D)	(D)	(D)	-	(NA)
1990	(D)	(D)	(D)	(D)	(NA)
1989	3.3	1.8	(D)	(D)	(NA)
1988	4.9	(D)	1.4	(D)	(NA)

Source: U.S. Department of Commerce. Bureau of the Census. "Pollution Abatement Costs and Expenditures, 1992." In *National Economic, Social, and Environmental Data Bank* [CD-ROM]. Prepared by U.S. Department of Commerce, Economics and Statistics Administration. Washington, DC: U.S. Department of Commerce, National Economic, Social, and Environmental Data Bank, Economics and Statistics Administration, Office of Business Analysis, February 1995. *Notes:* Totals may not agree with detail because of independent rounding. "NA" represents "not available." "D" indicates data withheld to avoid disclosing operations of individual companies. "-" represents zero.

★ 727 ★
Pollution Abatement and Control, by State

Pollution Abatement Capital Expenditures in Ohio: 1988-1992

Pollution abatement expenditures are those with the primary purpose of protecting the environment by reducing or eliminating unwanted emissions or wastes that are created by the production process. Pollution abatement capital expenditures (PACE) by manufacturing establishments with 20 employees or more amounted to $8,393 million in 1992. Of this total, $7,867 million was attributable to a particular media: $4,403 million for air; $2,510 million for water; and $954 million for solid/contained waste. Spending for nonmedia and other was $526 million. Approximately 79 percent of the $8,383 million new capital expenditures for pollution abatement was made by establishments in four major industry groups: Chemicals and allied products (major group 28), petroleum and coal products (major group 29), paper and allied products (major group 26), and primary metal industries (major group 33). In 1992, Texas, California, and Louisiana accounted for approximately 38 percent of total new pollution abatement capital expenditures. Texas comprised 18 percent of the total. The table below shows pollution abatement capital expenditures for air, water, solid/contained waste, and nonmedia for Ohio.

[In million dollars]

Year	Pollution abatement capital expenditures	Air	Water	Solid waste	Nonmedia
1992	309.1	142.7	127.4	39.0	26.4
1991	290.0	130.9	93.8	65.3	(NA)
1990	298.9	130.8	128.5	39.5	(NA)
1989	240.4	107.0	99.5	33.9	(NA)
1988	172.1	55.4	78.4	38.2	(NA)

Source: U.S. Department of Commerce. Bureau of the Census. "Pollution Abatement Costs and Expenditures, 1992." In *National Economic, Social, and Environmental Data Bank* [CD-ROM]. Prepared by U.S. Department of Commerce, Economics and Statistics Administration. Washington, DC: U.S. Department of Commerce, National Economic, Social, and Environmental Data Bank, Economics and Statistics Administration, Office of Business Analysis, February 1995. *Notes:* Totals may not agree with detail because of independent rounding. "NA" represents "not available."

★ 728 ★
Pollution Abatement and Control, by State

Pollution Abatement Capital Expenditures in Oklahoma: 1988-1992

Pollution abatement expenditures are those with the primary purpose of protecting the environment by reducing or eliminating unwanted emissions or wastes that are created by the production process. Pollution abatement capital expenditures (PACE) by manufacturing establishments with 20 employees or more amounted to $8,393 million in 1992. Of this total, $7,867 million was attributable to a particular media: $4,403 million for air; $2,510 million for water; and $954 million for solid/contained waste. Spending for nonmedia and other was $526 million. Approximately 79 percent of the $8,383 million new capital expenditures for pollution abatement was made by establishments in four major industry groups: Chemicals and allied products (major group 28), petroleum and coal products (major group 29), paper and allied products (major group 26), and primary metal industries (major group 33). In 1992, Texas, California, and Louisiana accounted for approximately 38 percent of total new pollution abatement capital expenditures. Texas comprised 18 percent of the total. The table below shows pollution abatement capital expenditures for air, water, solid/ contained waste, and nonmedia for Oklahoma.

[In million dollars]

Year	Pollution abatement capital expenditures	Air	Water	Solid waste	Nonmedia
1992	41.1	13.9	10.8	16.4	1.5
1991	63.4	28.8	30.4	4.2	(NA)
1990	38.3	18.2	17.3	2.7	(NA)
1989	34.5	19.8	12.1	2.6	(NA)
1988	20.7	13.4	4.7	2.6	(NA)

Source: U.S. Department of Commerce. Bureau of the Census. "Pollution Abatement Costs and Expenditures, 1992." In *National Economic, Social, and Environmental Data Bank* [CD-ROM]. Prepared by U.S. Department of Commerce, Economics and Statistics Administration. Washington, DC: U.S. Department of Commerce, National Economic, Social, and Environmental Data Bank, Economics and Statistics Administration, Office of Business Analysis, February 1995. *Notes:* Totals may not agree with detail because of independent rounding. "NA" represents "not available."

★ 729 ★

Pollution Abatement and Control, by State

Pollution Abatement Capital Expenditures in Oregon: 1988-1992

Pollution abatement expenditures are those with the primary purpose of protecting the environment by reducing or eliminating unwanted emissions or wastes that are created by the production process. Pollution abatement capital expenditures (PACE) by manufacturing establishments with 20 employees or more amounted to $8,393 million in 1992. Of this total, $7,867 million was attributable to a particular media: $4,403 million for air; $2,510 million for water; and $954 million for solid/contained waste. Spending for nonmedia and other was $526 million. Approximately 79 percent of the $8,383 million new capital expenditures for pollution abatement was made by establishments in four major industry groups: Chemicals and allied products (major group 28), petroleum and coal products (major group 29), paper and allied products (major group 26), and primary metal industries (major group 33). In 1992, Texas, California, and Louisiana accounted for approximately 38 percent of total new pollution abatement capital expenditures. Texas comprised 18 percent of the total. The table below shows pollution abatement capital expenditures for air, water, solid/ contained waste, and nonmedia for Oregon.

[In million dollars]

Year	Pollution abatement capital expenditures	Air	Water	Solid waste	Nonmedia
1992	105.8	37.0	63.2	5.6	3.7
1991	74.3	12.9	47.4	14.0	(NA)
1990	51.5	23.2	21.8	6.5	(NA)
1989	39.3	16.5	16.7	6.1	(NA)
1988	36.6	18.4	12.7	5.5	(NA)

Source: U.S. Department of Commerce. Bureau of the Census. "Pollution Abatement Costs and Expenditures, 1992." In *National Economic, Social, and Environmental Data Bank* [CD-ROM]. Prepared by U.S. Department of Commerce, Economics and Statistics Administration. Washington, DC: U.S. Department of Commerce, National Economic, Social, and Environmental Data Bank, Economics and Statistics Administration, Office of Business Analysis, February 1995. *Notes:* Totals may not agree with detail because of independent rounding. "NA" represents "not available."

★ 730 ★

Pollution Abatement and Control, by State

Pollution Abatement Capital Expenditures in Pennsylvania: 1988-1992

Pollution abatement expenditures are those with the primary purpose of protecting the environment by reducing or eliminating unwanted emissions or wastes that are created by the production process. Pollution abatement capital expenditures (PACE) by manufacturing establishments with 20 employees or more amounted to $8,393 million in 1992. Of this total, $7,867 million was attributable to a particular media: $4,403 million for air; $2,510 million for water; and $954 million for solid/contained waste. Spending for nonmedia and other was $526 million. Approximately 79 percent of the $8,383 million new capital expenditures for pollution abatement was made by establishments in four major industry groups: Chemicals and allied products (major group 28), petroleum and coal products (major group 29), paper and allied products (major group 26), and primary metal industries (major group 33). In 1992, Texas, California, and Louisiana accounted for approximately 38 percent of total new pollution abatement capital expenditures. Texas comprised 18 percent of the total. The table below shows pollution abatement capital expenditures for air, water, solid/contained waste, and nonmedia for Pennsylvania.

[In million dollars]

Year	Pollution abatement capital expenditures	Air	Water	Solid waste	Nonmedia
1992	272.4	140.5	63.0	68.9	33.4
1991	340.4	185.9	124.3	30.2	(NA)
1990	206.1	94.1	81.5	30.6	(NA)
1989	166.2	71.5	71.7	23.0	(NA)
1988	119.0	51.3	46.4	21.2	(NA)

Source: U.S. Department of Commerce. Bureau of the Census. "Pollution Abatement Costs and Expenditures, 1992." In *National Economic, Social, and Environmental Data Bank* [CD-ROM]. Prepared by U.S. Department of Commerce, Economics and Statistics Administration. Washington, DC: U.S. Department of Commerce, National Economic, Social, and Environmental Data Bank, Economics and Statistics Administration, Office of Business Analysis, February 1995. *Notes:* Totals may not agree with detail because of independent rounding. "NA" represents "not available."

★ 731 ★

Pollution Abatement and Control, by State

Pollution Abatement Capital Expenditures in Rhode Island: 1988-1992

Pollution abatement expenditures are those with the primary purpose of protecting the environment by reducing or eliminating unwanted emissions or wastes that are created by the production process. Pollution abatement capital expenditures (PACE) by manufacturing establishments with 20 employees or more amounted to $8,393 million in 1992. Of this total, $7,867 million was attributable to a particular media: $4,403 million for air; $2,510 million for water; and $954 million for solid/contained waste. Spending for nonmedia and other was $526 million. Approximately 79 percent of the $8,383 million new capital expenditures for pollution abatement was made by establishments in four major industry groups: Chemicals and allied products (major group 28), petroleum and coal products (major group 29), paper and allied products (major group 26), and primary metal industries (major group 33). In 1992, Texas, California, and Louisiana accounted for approximately 38 percent of total new pollution abatement capital expenditures. Texas comprised 18 percent of the total. The table below shows pollution abatement capital expenditures for air, water, solid/contained waste, and nonmedia for Rhode Island.

[In million dollars]

Year	Pollution abatement capital expenditures	Air	Water	Solid waste	Nonmedia
1992	2.2	0.8	1.3	0.2	3.2
1991	5.9	1.4	4.2	0.2	(NA)
1990	13.6	4.2	5.7	3.7	(NA)
1989	12.1	3.3	5.3	3.6	(NA)
1988	13.4	5.7	5.2	2.5	(NA)

Source: U.S. Department of Commerce. Bureau of the Census. "Pollution Abatement Costs and Expenditures, 1992." In *National Economic, Social, and Environmental Data Bank* [CD-ROM]. Prepared by U.S. Department of Commerce, Economics and Statistics Administration. Washington, DC: U.S. Department of Commerce, National Economic, Social, and Environmental Data Bank, Economics and Statistics Administration, Office of Business Analysis, February 1995. *Notes:* Totals may not agree with detail because of independent rounding. "NA" represents "not available."

★ 732 ★

Pollution Abatement and Control, by State

Pollution Abatement Capital Expenditures in South Carolina: 1988-1992

Pollution abatement expenditures are those with the primary purpose of protecting the environment by reducing or eliminating unwanted emissions or wastes that are created by the production process. Pollution abatement capital expenditures (PACE) by manufacturing establishments with 20 employees or more amounted to $8,393 million in 1992. Of this total, $7,867 million was attributable to a particular media: $4,403 million for air; $2,510 million for water; and $954 million for solid/contained waste. Spending for nonmedia and other was $526 million. Approximately 79 percent of the $8,383 million new capital expenditures for pollution abatement was made by establishments in four major industry groups: Chemicals and allied products (major group 28), petroleum and coal products (major group 29), paper and allied products (major group 26), and primary metal industries (major group 33). In 1992, Texas, California, and Louisiana accounted for approximately 38 percent of total new pollution abatement capital expenditures. Texas comprised 18 percent of the total. The table below shows pollution abatement capital expenditures for air, water, solid/contained waste, and nonmedia for South Carolina.

[In million dollars]

Year	Pollution abatement capital expenditures	Air	Water	Solid waste	Nonmedia
1992	119.9	44.1	64.7	11.1	6.1
1991	99.3	42.8	44.5	12.0	(NA)
1990	127.4	53.6	57.0	16.8	(NA)
1989	100.8	43.6	46.8	10.4	(NA)
1988	47.3	14.9	22.0	10.4	(NA)

Source: U.S. Department of Commerce. Bureau of the Census. "Pollution Abatement Costs and Expenditures, 1992." In *National Economic, Social, and Environmental Data Bank* [CD-ROM]. Prepared by U.S. Department of Commerce, Economics and Statistics Administration. Washington, DC: U.S. Department of Commerce, National Economic, Social, and Environmental Data Bank, Economics and Statistics Administration, Office of Business Analysis, February 1995. *Notes:* Totals may not agree with detail because of independent rounding. "NA" represents "not available."

★ 733 ★

Pollution Abatement and Control, by State

Pollution Abatement Capital Expenditures in South Dakota: 1988-1992

Pollution abatement expenditures are those with the primary purpose of protecting the environment by reducing or eliminating unwanted emissions or wastes that are created by the production process. Pollution abatement capital expenditures (PACE) by manufacturing establishments with 20 employees or more amounted to $8,393 million in 1992. Of this total, $7,867 million was attributable to a particular media: $4,403 million for air; $2,510 million for water; and $954 million for solid/contained waste. Spending for nonmedia and other was $526 million. Approximately 79 percent of the $8,383 million new capital expenditures for pollution abatement was made by establishments in four major industry groups: Chemicals and allied products (major group 28), petroleum and coal products (major group 29), paper and allied products (major group 26), and primary metal industries (major group 33). In 1992, Texas, California, and Louisiana accounted for approximately 38 percent of total new pollution abatement capital expenditures. Texas comprised 18 percent of the total. The table below shows pollution abatement capital expenditures for air, water, solid/contained waste, and nonmedia for South Dakota.

[In million dollars]

Year	Pollution abatement capital expenditures	Air	Water	Solid waste	Nonmedia
1992	(D)	(D)	1.1	0.5	(D)
1991	3.0	2.2	0.2	0.6	(NA)
1990	(D)	(D)	(D)	(D)	(NA)
1989	(D)	(D)	(D)	(D)	(NA)
1988	(D)	(D)	(D)	(D)	(NA)

Source: U.S. Department of Commerce. Bureau of the Census. "Pollution Abatement Costs and Expenditures, 1992." In *National Economic, Social, and Environmental Data Bank* [CD-ROM]. Prepared by U.S. Department of Commerce, Economics and Statistics Administration. Washington, DC: U.S. Department of Commerce, National Economic, Social, and Environmental Data Bank, Economics and Statistics Administration, Office of Business Analysis, February 1995. *Notes:* Totals may not agree with detail because of independent rounding. "NA" represents "not available." "D" indicates data withheld to avoid disclosing operations of individual companies.

★ 734 ★

Pollution Abatement and Control, by State

Pollution Abatement Capital Expenditures in Tennessee: 1988-1992

Pollution abatement expenditures are those with the primary purpose of protecting the environment by reducing or eliminating unwanted emissions or wastes that are created by the production process. Pollution abatement capital expenditures (PACE) by manufacturing establishments with 20 employees or more amounted to $8,393 million in 1992. Of this total, $7,867 million was attributable to a particular media: $4,403 million for air; $2,510 million for water; and $954 million for solid/ contained waste. Spending for nonmedia and other was $526 million. Approximately 79 percent of the $8,383 million new capital expenditures for pollution abatement was made by establishments in four major industry groups: Chemicals and allied products (major group 28), petroleum and coal products (major group 29), paper and allied products (major group 26), and primary metal industries (major group 33). In 1992, Texas, California, and Louisiana accounted for approximately 38 percent of total new pollution abatement capital expenditures. Texas comprised 18 percent of the total. The table below shows pollution abatement capital expenditures for air, water, solid/contained waste, and nonmedia for Tennessee.

[In million dollars]

Year	Pollution abatement capital expenditures	Air	Water	Solid waste	Nonmedia
1992	218.3	163.9	33.5	21.0	3.9
1991	139.2	95.1	28.4	15.7	(NA)
1990	136.3	84.4	39.2	12.7	(NA)
1989	86.1	38.4	32.8	14.9	(NA)
1988	148.1	42.8	78.9	26.5	(NA)

Source: U.S. Department of Commerce. Bureau of the Census. "Pollution Abatement Costs and Expenditures, 1992." In *National Economic, Social, and Environmental Data Bank* [CD-ROM]. Prepared by U.S. Department of Commerce, Economics and Statistics Administration. Washington, DC: U.S. Department of Commerce, National Economic, Social, and Environmental Data Bank, Economics and Statistics Administration, Office of Business Analysis, February 1995. *Notes:* Totals may not agree with detail because of independent rounding. "NA" represents "not available."

★ 735 ★
Pollution Abatement and Control, by State

Pollution Abatement Capital Expenditures in Texas: 1988-1992

Pollution abatement expenditures are those with the primary purpose of protecting the environment by reducing or eliminating unwanted emissions or wastes that are created by the production process. Pollution abatement capital expenditures (PACE) by manufacturing establishments with 20 employees or more amounted to $8,393 million in 1992. Of this total, $7,867 million was attributable to a particular media: $4,403 million for air; $2,510 million for water; and $954 million for solid/contained waste. Spending for nonmedia and other was $526 million. Approximately 79 percent of the $8,383 million new capital expenditures for pollution abatement was made by establishments in four major industry groups: Chemicals and allied products (major group 28), petroleum and coal products (major group 29), paper and allied products (major group 26), and primary metal industries (major group 33). In 1992, Texas, California, and Louisiana accounted for approximately 38 percent of total new pollution abatement capital expenditures. Texas comprised 18 percent of the total. The table below shows pollution abatement capital expenditures for air, water, solid/contained waste, and nonmedia for Texas.

[In million dollars]

Year	Pollution abatement capital expenditures	Air	Water	Solid waste	Nonmedia
1992	1,446.0	777.2	483.5	185.3	45.8
1991	1,055.7	511.4	390.1	154.2	(NA)
1990	895.3	328.7	417.8	148.8	(NA)
1989	481.0	150.1	214.9	116.0	(NA)
1988	365.3	78.4	183.6	103.3	(NA)

Source: U.S. Department of Commerce. Bureau of the Census. "Pollution Abatement Costs and Expenditures, 1992." In *National Economic, Social, and Environmental Data Bank* [CD-ROM]. Prepared by U.S. Department of Commerce, Economics and Statistics Administration. Washington, DC: U.S. Department of Commerce, National Economic, Social, and Environmental Data Bank, Economics and Statistics Administration, Office of Business Analysis, February 1995. *Notes:* Totals may not agree with detail because of independent rounding. "NA" represents "not available."

★ 736 ★

Pollution Abatement and Control, by State

Pollution Abatement Capital Expenditures in Utah: 1988-1992

Pollution abatement expenditures are those with the primary purpose of protecting the environment by reducing or eliminating unwanted emissions or wastes that are created by the production process. Pollution abatement capital expenditures (PACE) by manufacturing establishments with 20 employees or more amounted to $8,393 million in 1992. Of this total, $7,867 million was attributable to a particular media: $4,403 million for air; $2,510 million for water; and $954 million for solid/contained waste. Spending for nonmedia and other was $526 million. Approximately 79 percent of the $8,383 million new capital expenditures for pollution abatement was made by establishments in four major industry groups: Chemicals and allied products (major group 28), petroleum and coal products (major group 29), paper and allied products (major group 26), and primary metal industries (major group 33). In 1992, Texas, California, and Louisiana accounted for approximately 38 percent of total new pollution abatement capital expenditures. Texas comprised 18 percent of the total. The table below shows pollution abatement capital expenditures for air, water, solid/contained waste, and nonmedia for Utah.

[In million dollars]

Year	Pollution abatement capital expenditures	Air	Water	Solid waste	Nonmedia
1992	86.4	74.8	10.0	1.6	0.5
1991	61.9	51.7	8.8	1.4	(NA)
1990	32.2	5.8	21.6	4.7	(NA)
1989	17.9	5.7	11.0	1.3	(NA)
1988	16.4	(D)	(D)	3.9	(NA)

Source: U.S. Department of Commerce. Bureau of the Census. "Pollution Abatement Costs and Expenditures, 1992." In *National Economic, Social, and Environmental Data Bank* [CD-ROM]. Prepared by U.S. Department of Commerce, Economics and Statistics Administration. Washington, DC: U.S. Department of Commerce, National Economic, Social, and Environmental Data Bank, Economics and Statistics Administration, Office of Business Analysis, February 1995. *Notes:* Totals may not agree with detail because of independent rounding. "NA" represents "not available." "D" indicates data withheld to avoid disclosing operations of individual companies.

★ 737 ★

Pollution Abatement and Control, by State

Pollution Abatement Capital Expenditures in Vermont: 1988-1992

Pollution abatement expenditures are those with the primary purpose of protecting the environment by reducing or eliminating unwanted emissions or wastes that are created by the production process. Pollution abatement capital expenditures (PACE) by manufacturing establishments with 20 employees or more amounted to $8,393 million in 1992. Of this total, $7,867 million was attributable to a particular media: $4,403 million for air; $2,510 million for water; and $954 million for solid/contained waste. Spending for nonmedia and other was $526 million. Approximately 79 percent of the $8,383 million new capital expenditures for pollution abatement was made by establishments in four major industry groups: Chemicals and allied products (major group 28), petroleum and coal products (major group 29), paper and allied products (major group 26), and primary metal industries (major group 33). In 1992, Texas, California, and Louisiana accounted for approximately 38 percent of total new pollution abatement capital expenditures. Texas comprised 18 percent of the total. The table below shows pollution abatement capital expenditures for air, water, solid/contained waste, and nonmedia for Vermont.

[In million dollars]

Year	Pollution abatement capital expenditures	Air	Water	Solid waste	Nonmedia
1992	13.7	1.5	9.0	3.2	(D)
1991	3.0	(D)	0.3	(D)	(NA)
1990	(D)	1.4	5.0	(D)	(NA)
1989	6.2	(D)	4.5	(D)	(NA)
1988	4.1	0.7	3.2	0.1	(NA)

Source: U.S. Department of Commerce. Bureau of the Census. "Pollution Abatement Costs and Expenditures, 1992." In *National Economic, Social, and Environmental Data Bank* [CD-ROM]. Prepared by U.S. Department of Commerce, Economics and Statistics Administration. Washington, DC: U.S. Department of Commerce, National Economic, Social, and Environmental Data Bank, Economics and Statistics Administration, Office of Business Analysis, February 1995. *Notes:* Totals may not agree with detail because of independent rounding. "NA" represents "not available." "D" indicates data withheld to avoid disclosing operations of individual companies.

★ 738 ★

Pollution Abatement and Control, by State

Pollution Abatement Capital Expenditures in Virginia: 1988-1992

Pollution abatement expenditures are those with the primary purpose of protecting the environment by reducing or eliminating unwanted emissions or wastes that are created by the production process. Pollution abatement capital expenditures (PACE) by manufacturing establishments with 20 employees or more amounted to $8,393 million in 1992. Of this total, $7,867 million was attributable to a particular media: $4,403 million for air; $2,510 million for water; and $954 million for solid/contained waste. Spending for nonmedia and other was $526 million. Approximately 79 percent of the $8,383 million new capital expenditures for pollution abatement was made by establishments in four major industry groups: Chemicals and allied products (major group 28), petroleum and coal products (major group 29), paper and allied products (major group 26), and primary metal industries (major group 33). In 1992, Texas, California, and Louisiana accounted for approximately 38 percent of total new pollution abatement capital expenditures. Texas comprised 18 percent of the total. The table below shows pollution abatement capital expenditures for air, water, solid/contained waste, and nonmedia for Virginia.

[In million dollars]

Year	Pollution abatement capital expenditures	Air	Water	Solid waste	Nonmedia
1992	217.6	128.0	65.1	24.4	5.2
1991	119.0	60.9	39.3	18.8	(NA)
1990	75.5	24.3	36.6	14.6	(NA)
1989	79.2	36.4	37.1	5.7	(NA)
1988	70.4	29.5	25.7	15.2	(NA)

Source: U.S. Department of Commerce. Bureau of the Census. "Pollution Abatement Costs and Expenditures, 1992." In *National Economic, Social, and Environmental Data Bank* [CD-ROM]. Prepared by U.S. Department of Commerce, Economics and Statistics Administration. Washington, DC: U.S. Department of Commerce, National Economic, Social, and Environmental Data Bank, Economics and Statistics Administration, Office of Business Analysis, February 1995. *Notes:* Totals may not agree with detail because of independent rounding. "NA" represents "not available."

★ 739 ★
Pollution Abatement and Control, by State

Pollution Abatement Capital Expenditures in Washington: 1988-1992

Pollution abatement expenditures are those with the primary purpose of protecting the environment by reducing or eliminating unwanted emissions or wastes that are created by the production process. Pollution abatement capital expenditures (PACE) by manufacturing establishments with 20 employees or more amounted to $8,393 million in 1992. Of this total, $7,867 million was attributable to a particular media: $4,403 million for air; $2,510 million for water; and $954 million for solid/contained waste. Spending for nonmedia and other was $526 million. Approximately 79 percent of the $8,383 million new capital expenditures for pollution abatement was made by establishments in four major industry groups: Chemicals and allied products (major group 28), petroleum and coal products (major group 29), paper and allied products (major group 26), and primary metal industries (major group 33). In 1992, Texas, California, and Louisiana accounted for approximately 38 percent of total new pollution abatement capital expenditures. Texas comprised 18 percent of the total. The table below shows pollution abatement capital expenditures for air, water, solid/contained waste, and nonmedia for Washington.

[In million dollars]

Year	Pollution abatement capital expenditures	Air	Water	Solid waste	Nonmedia
1992	186.7	101.5	41.5	43.7	8.5
1991	389.0	86.2	283.5	19.3	(NA)
1990	127.4	30.7	61.4	35.2	(NA)
1989	104.9	30.9	45.4	28.6	(NA)
1988	56.6	20.4	21.7	14.5	(NA)

Source: U.S. Department of Commerce. Bureau of the Census. "Pollution Abatement Costs and Expenditures, 1992." In *National Economic, Social, and Environmental Data Bank* [CD-ROM]. Prepared by U.S. Department of Commerce, Economics and Statistics Administration. Washington, DC: U.S. Department of Commerce, National Economic, Social, and Environmental Data Bank, Economics and Statistics Administration, Office of Business Analysis, February 1995. *Notes:* Totals may not agree with detail because of independent rounding. "NA" represents "not available."

★ 740 ★

Pollution Abatement and Control, by State

Pollution Abatement Capital Expenditures in West Virginia: 1988-1992

Pollution abatement expenditures are those with the primary purpose of protecting the environment by reducing or eliminating unwanted emissions or wastes that are created by the production process. Pollution abatement capital expenditures (PACE) by manufacturing establishments with 20 employees or more amounted to $8,393 million in 1992. Of this total, $7,867 million was attributable to a particular media: $4,403 million for air; $2,510 million for water; and $954 million for solid/contained waste. Spending for nonmedia and other was $526 million. Approximately 79 percent of the $8,383 million new capital expenditures for pollution abatement was made by establishments in four major industry groups: Chemicals and allied products (major group 28), petroleum and coal products (major group 29), paper and allied products (major group 26), and primary metal industries (major group 33). In 1992, Texas, California, and Louisiana accounted for approximately 38 percent of total new pollution abatement capital expenditures. Texas comprised 18 percent of the total. The table below shows pollution abatement capital expenditures for air, water, solid/ contained waste, and nonmedia for West Virginia.

[In million dollars]

Year	Pollution abatement capital expenditures	Air	Water	Solid waste	Nonmedia
1992	85.1	21.5	33.6	30.0	5.3
1991	51.3	27.4	18.8	5.1	(NA)
1990	51.5	20.8	27.0	3.7	(NA)
1989	40.4	11.2	22.3	6.9	(NA)
1988	68.9	20.1	28.4	20.4	(NA)

Source: U.S. Department of Commerce. Bureau of the Census. "Pollution Abatement Costs and Expenditures, 1992." In *National Economic, Social, and Environmental Data Bank* [CD-ROM]. Prepared by U.S. Department of Commerce, Economics and Statistics Administration. Washington, DC: U.S. Department of Commerce, National Economic, Social, and Environmental Data Bank, Economics and Statistics Administration, Office of Business Analysis, February 1995. *Notes:* Totals may not agree with detail because of independent rounding. "NA" represents "not available."

★ 741 ★

Pollution Abatement and Control, by State

Pollution Abatement Capital Expenditures in Wisconsin: 1988-1992

Pollution abatement expenditures are those with the primary purpose of protecting the environment by reducing or eliminating unwanted emissions or wastes that are created by the production process. Pollution abatement capital expenditures (PACE) by manufacturing establishments with 20 employees or more amounted to $8,393 million in 1992. Of this total, $7,867 million was attributable to a particular media: $4,403 million for air; $2,510 million for water; and $954 million for solid/contained waste. Spending for nonmedia and other was $526 million. Approximately 79 percent of the $8,383 million new capital expenditures for pollution abatement was made by establishments in four major industry groups: Chemicals and allied products (major group 28), petroleum and coal products (major group 29), paper and allied products (major group 26), and primary metal industries (major group 33). In 1992, Texas, California, and Louisiana accounted for approximately 38 percent of total new pollution abatement capital expenditures. Texas comprised 18 percent of the total. The table below shows pollution abatement capital expenditures for air, water, solid/contained waste, and nonmedia for Wisconsin.

[In million dollars]

Year	Pollution abatement capital expenditures	Air	Water	Solid waste	Nonmedia
1992	136.9	63.2	52.2	21.5	10.4
1991	201.1	120.2	50.2	30.7	(NA)
1990	164.2	97.2	40.0	27.0	(NA)
1989	119.2	62.6	28.5	28.1	(NA)
1988	73.9	35.7	15.3	22.9	(NA)

Source: U.S. Department of Commerce. Bureau of the Census. "Pollution Abatement Costs and Expenditures, 1992." In *National Economic, Social, and Environmental Data Bank* [CD-ROM]. Prepared by U.S. Department of Commerce, Economics and Statistics Administration. Washington, DC: U.S. Department of Commerce, National Economic, Social, and Environmental Data Bank, Economics and Statistics Administration, Office of Business Analysis, February 1995. *Notes:* Totals may not agree with detail because of independent rounding. "NA" represents "not available."

★ 742 ★

Pollution Abatement and Control, by State

Pollution Abatement Capital Expenditures in Wyoming: 1988-1992

Pollution abatement expenditures are those with the primary purpose of protecting the environment by reducing or eliminating unwanted emissions or wastes that are created by the production process. Pollution abatement capital expenditures (PACE) by manufacturing establishments with 20 employees or more amounted to $8,393 million in 1992. Of this total, $7,867 million was attributable to a particular media: $4,403 million for air; $2,510 million for water; and $954 million for solid/contained waste. Spending for nonmedia and other was $526 million. Approximately 79 percent of the $8,383 million new capital expenditures for pollution abatement was made by establishments in four major industry groups: Chemicals and allied products (major group 28), petroleum and coal products (major group 29), paper and allied products (major group 26), and primary metal industries (major group 33). In 1992, Texas, California, and Louisiana accounted for approximately 38 percent of total new pollution abatement capital expenditures. Texas comprised 18 percent of the total. The table below shows pollution abatement capital expenditures for air, water, solid/contained waste, and nonmedia for Wyoming.

[In million dollars]

Year	Pollution abatement capital expenditures	Air	Water	Solid waste	Nonmedia
1992	11.8	(D)	6.3	(D)	(D)
1991	13.9	8.7	2.8	2.4	(NA)
1990	13.9	(D)	(D)	(D)	(NA)
1989	5.0	(D)	3.0	(D)	(NA)
1988	(D)	(D)	1.2	0.5	(NA)

Source: U.S. Department of Commerce. Bureau of the Census. "Pollution Abatement Costs and Expenditures, 1992." In *National Economic, Social, and Environmental Data Bank* [CD-ROM]. Prepared by U.S. Department of Commerce, Economics and Statistics Administration. Washington, DC: U.S. Department of Commerce, National Economic, Social, and Environmental Data Bank, Economics and Statistics Administration, Office of Business Analysis, February 1995. *Notes:* Totals may not agree with detail because of independent rounding. "NA" represents "not available." "D" indicates data withheld to avoid disclosing operations of individual companies.

★ 743 ★

Pollution Abatement and Control, by State

Pollution Abatement Operating Costs in Alabama: 1988-1992

Pollution abatement concerns those activities with the primary purpose of protecting the environment by reducing or eliminating unwanted emissions or wastes that are created by the production process. Operating costs related to pollution abatement activities totaled $19,228 million in 1992. Of this amount, $17,466 million was attributable to a particular media: $5,395 million for air; $6,577 million for water; and $5,494 million for solid/contained waste. Spending for nonmedia and other was $1,762 million. Total population abatement media operating costs showed an overall increase of $158 million (1 percent) from 1991, the previous year. Air operating costs increased 9 percent; water operating costs increased 4 percent; solid/contained waste operating costs decreased 9 percent. The table below shows pollution abatement operating control costs for air, water, solid/contained waste, and nonmedia for Alabama.

[In million dollars]

Year	Pollution abatement operating costs	Air	Water	Solid waste	Nonmedia
1992	380.0	136.2	146.7	97.1	21.6
1991	388.5	96.8[1]	156.4	135.3	(NA)
1990	338.8	93.5	138.8	106.5	(NA)
1989	294.0	93.6	125.7	74.7	(NA)
1988	252.3	89.1	106.1	57.2	(NA)

Source: U.S. Department of Commerce. Bureau of the Census. "Pollution Abatement Costs and Expenditures, 1992." In *National Economic, Social, and Environmental Data Bank* [CD-ROM]. Prepared by U.S. Department of Commerce, Economics and Statistics Administration. Washington, DC: U.S. Department of Commerce, National Economic, Social, and Environmental Data Bank, Economics and Statistics Administration, Office of Business Analysis, February 1995. *Notes:* Totals may not agree with detail because of independent rounding. "NA" represents "not available." 1. Revised figure (by 5 percent or more).

★ 744 ★

Pollution Abatement and Control, by State

Pollution Abatement Operating Costs in Alaska: 1988-1992

Pollution abatement concerns those activities with the primary purpose of protecting the environment by reducing or eliminating unwanted emissions or wastes that are created by the production process. Operating costs related to pollution abatement activities totaled $19,228 million in 1992. Of this amount, $17,466 million was attributable to a particular media: $5,395 million for air; $6,577 million for water; and $5,494 million for solid/contained waste. Spending for nonmedia and other was $1,762 million. Total population abatement media operating costs showed an overall increase of $158 million (1 percent) from 1991, the previous year. Air operating costs increased 9 percent; water operating costs increased 4 percent; solid/contained waste operating costs decreased 9 percent. The table below shows pollution abatement operating control costs for air, water, solid/contained waste, and nonmedia for Alaska.

[In million dollars]

Year	Pollution abatement operating costs	Air	Water	Solid waste	Nonmedia
1992	31.4	8.2	14.7	8.5	0.1
1991	45.6	12.8	21.8	11.0	(NA)
1990	32.7	9.8	15.9	7.0	(NA)
1989	21.6	6.9	9.6	5.1	(NA)
1988	18.6	8.4	7.0	3.3	(NA)

Source: U.S. Department of Commerce. Bureau of the Census. "Pollution Abatement Costs and Expenditures, 1992." In *National Economic, Social, and Environmental Data Bank* [CD-ROM]. Prepared by U.S. Department of Commerce, Economics and Statistics Administration. Washington, DC: U.S. Department of Commerce, National Economic, Social, and Environmental Data Bank, Economics and Statistics Administration, Office of Business Analysis, February 1995. *Notes:* Totals may not agree with detail because of independent rounding. "NA" represents "not available."

★ 745 ★

Pollution Abatement and Control, by State

Pollution Abatement Operating Costs in Arizona: 1988-1992

Pollution abatement concerns those activities with the primary purpose of protecting the environment by reducing or eliminating unwanted emissions or wastes that are created by the production process. Operating costs related to pollution abatement activities totaled $19,228 million in 1992. Of this amount, $17,466 million was attributable to a particular media: $5,395 million for air; $6,577 million for water; and $5,494 million for solid/contained waste. Spending for nonmedia and other was $1,762 million. Total population abatement media operating costs showed an overall increase of $158 million (1 percent) from 1991, the previous year. Air operating costs increased 9 percent; water operating costs increased 4 percent; solid/contained waste operating costs decreased 9 percent. The table below shows pollution abatement operating control costs for air, water, solid/contained waste, and nonmedia for Arizona.

[In million dollars]

Year	Pollution abatement operating costs	Air	Water	Solid waste	Nonmedia
1992	129.4	66.4	36.0	27.1	14.0
1991	104.8	61.5	22.0	21.2	(NA)
1990	115.9	68.1	25.1	22.7	(NA)
1989	101.9	59.1	22.9	19.9	(NA)
1988	135.3	100.4	17.1	17.9	(NA)

Source: U.S. Department of Commerce. Bureau of the Census. "Pollution Abatement Costs and Expenditures, 1992." In *National Economic, Social, and Environmental Data Bank* [CD-ROM]. Prepared by U.S. Department of Commerce, Economics and Statistics Administration. Washington, DC: U.S. Department of Commerce, National Economic, Social, and Environmental Data Bank, Economics and Statistics Administration, Office of Business Analysis, February 1995. *Notes:* Totals may not agree with detail because of independent rounding. "NA" represents "not available."

★ 746 ★

Pollution Abatement and Control, by State

Pollution Abatement Operating Costs in Arkansas: 1988-1992

Pollution abatement concerns those activities with the primary purpose of protecting the environment by reducing or eliminating unwanted emissions or wastes that are created by the production process. Operating costs related to pollution abatement activities totaled $19,228 million in 1992. Of this amount, $17,466 million was attributable to a particular media: $5,395 million for air; $6,577 million for water; and $5,494 million for solid/contained waste. Spending for nonmedia and other was $1,762 million. Total population abatement media operating costs showed an overall increase of $158 million (1 percent) from 1991, the previous year. Air operating costs increased 9 percent; water operating costs increased 4 percent; solid/contained waste operating costs decreased 9 percent. The table below shows pollution abatement operating control costs for air, water, solid/contained waste, and nonmedia for Arkansas.

[In million dollars]

Year	Pollution abatement operating costs	Air	Water	Solid waste	Nonmedia
1992	208.1	56.2	92.3	59.5	16.5
1991	174.2	46.7	79.0	48.5	(NA)
1990	161.0	46.2	75.9	39.0	(NA)
1989	179.8	48.3	88.3	43.3	(NA)
1988	140.0	41.4	64.0	34.6	(NA)

Source: U.S. Department of Commerce. Bureau of the Census. "Pollution Abatement Costs and Expenditures, 1992." In *National Economic, Social, and Environmental Data Bank* [CD-ROM]. Prepared by U.S. Department of Commerce, Economics and Statistics Administration. Washington, DC: U.S. Department of Commerce, National Economic, Social, and Environmental Data Bank, Economics and Statistics Administration, Office of Business Analysis, February 1995. *Notes:* Totals may not agree with detail because of independent rounding. "NA" represents "not available."

★ 747 ★

Pollution Abatement and Control, by State

Pollution Abatement Operating Costs in California: 1988-1992

Pollution abatement concerns those activities with the primary purpose of protecting the environment by reducing or eliminating unwanted emissions or wastes that are created by the production process. Operating costs related to pollution abatement activities totaled $19,228 million in 1992. Of this amount, $17,466 million was attributable to a particular media: $5,395 million for air; $6,577 million for water; and $5,494 million for solid/contained waste. Spending for nonmedia and other was $1,762 million. Total population abatement media operating costs showed an overall increase of $158 million (1 percent) from 1991, the previous year. Air operating costs increased 9 percent; water operating costs increased 4 percent; solid/contained waste operating costs decreased 9 percent. The table below shows pollution abatement operating control costs for air, water, solid/contained waste, and nonmedia for California.

[In million dollars]

Year	Pollution abatement operating costs	Air	Water	Solid waste	Nonmedia
1992	1,492.6	490.3	584.1	418.2	145.0
1991	1,717.0	616.4	549.7	550.9	(NA)
1990	1,818.5	673.7	558.2	586.6	(NA)
1989	1,526.6	543.3	463.3	520.0	(NA)
1988	1,363.0	471.9	401.8	489.3	(NA)

Source: U.S. Department of Commerce. Bureau of the Census. "Pollution Abatement Costs and Expenditures, 1992." In *National Economic, Social, and Environmental Data Bank* [CD-ROM]. Prepared by U.S. Department of Commerce, Economics and Statistics Administration. Washington, DC: U.S. Department of Commerce, National Economic, Social, and Environmental Data Bank, Economics and Statistics Administration, Office of Business Analysis, February 1995. *Notes:* Totals may not agree with detail because of independent rounding. "NA" represents "not available."

★ 748 ★

Pollution Abatement and Control, by State

Pollution Abatement Operating Costs in Colorado: 1988-1992

Pollution abatement concerns those activities with the primary purpose of protecting the environment by reducing or eliminating unwanted emissions or wastes that are created by the production process. Operating costs related to pollution abatement activities totaled $19,228 million in 1992. Of this amount, $17,466 million was attributable to a particular media: $5,395 million for air; $6,577 million for water; and $5,494 million for solid/contained waste. Spending for nonmedia and other was $1,762 million. Total population abatement media operating costs showed an overall increase of $158 million (1 percent) from 1991, the previous year. Air operating costs increased 9 percent; water operating costs increased 4 percent; solid/contained waste operating costs decreased 9 percent. The table below shows pollution abatement operating control costs for air, water, solid/contained waste, and nonmedia for Colorado.

[In million dollars]

Year	Pollution abatement operating costs	Air	Water	Solid waste	Nonmedia
1992	83.5	11.3	44.5	27.7	12.0
1991	251.7	28.5	107.3	115.9	(NA)
1990	267.3	22.1	188.2	57.0	(NA)
1989	191.5	20.3	109.3	61.9	(NA)
1988	69.4	12.4	25.4	31.5	(NA)

Source: U.S. Department of Commerce. Bureau of the Census. "Pollution Abatement Costs and Expenditures, 1992." In *National Economic, Social, and Environmental Data Bank* [CD-ROM]. Prepared by U.S. Department of Commerce, Economics and Statistics Administration. Washington, DC: U.S. Department of Commerce, National Economic, Social, and Environmental Data Bank, Economics and Statistics Administration, Office of Business Analysis, February 1995. *Notes:* Totals may not agree with detail because of independent rounding. "NA" represents "not available."

★ 749 ★

Pollution Abatement and Control, by State

Pollution Abatement Operating Costs in Connecticut: 1988-1992

Pollution abatement concerns those activities with the primary purpose of protecting the environment by reducing or eliminating unwanted emissions or wastes that are created by the production process. Operating costs related to pollution abatement activities totaled $19,228 million in 1992. Of this amount, $17,466 million was attributable to a particular media: $5,395 million for air; $6,577 million for water; and $5,494 million for solid/contained waste. Spending for nonmedia and other was $1,762 million. Total population abatement media operating costs showed an overall increase of $158 million (1 percent) from 1991, the previous year. Air operating costs increased 9 percent; water operating costs increased 4 percent; solid/contained waste operating costs decreased 9 percent. The table below shows pollution abatement operating control costs for air, water, solid/contained waste, and nonmedia for Connecticut.

[In million dollars]

Year	Pollution abatement operating costs	Air	Water	Solid waste	Nonmedia
1992	168.5	23.6	52.8	92.1	29.1
1991	213.9	22.8	82.9	108.2	(NA)
1990	249.5	27.8	118.3	103.4	(NA)
1989	219.2	29.4	81.6	108.2	(NA)
1988	160.0	27.8	58.8	73.4	(NA)

Source: U.S. Department of Commerce. Bureau of the Census. "Pollution Abatement Costs and Expenditures, 1992." In *National Economic, Social, and Environmental Data Bank* [CD-ROM]. Prepared by U.S. Department of Commerce, Economics and Statistics Administration. Washington, DC: U.S. Department of Commerce, National Economic, Social, and Environmental Data Bank, Economics and Statistics Administration, Office of Business Analysis, February 1995. *Notes:* Totals may not agree with detail because of independent rounding. "NA" represents "not available."

★ 750 ★

Pollution Abatement and Control, by State

Pollution Abatement Operating Costs in Delaware: 1988-1992

Pollution abatement concerns those activities with the primary purpose of protecting the environment by reducing or eliminating unwanted emissions or wastes that are created by the production process. Operating costs related to pollution abatement activities totaled $19,228 million in 1992. Of this amount, $17,466 million was attributable to a particular media: $5,395 million for air; $6,577 million for water; and $5,494 million for solid/contained waste. Spending for nonmedia and other was $1,762 million. Total population abatement media operating costs showed an overall increase of $158 million (1 percent) from 1991, the previous year. Air operating costs increased 9 percent; water operating costs increased 4 percent; solid/contained waste operating costs decreased 9 percent. The table below shows pollution abatement operating control costs for air, water, solid/contained waste, and nonmedia for Delaware.

[In million dollars]

Year	Pollution abatement operating costs	Air	Water	Solid waste	Nonmedia
1992	145.5	67.9	54.1	23.5	7.9
1991	155.2	64.3	65.1	25.8	(NA)
1990	145.2	58.4	60.9	25.9	(NA)
1989	180.5	88.1	70.3	22.2	(NA)
1988	169.8	84.2	57.4	28.1	(NA)

Source: U.S. Department of Commerce. Bureau of the Census. "Pollution Abatement Costs and Expenditures, 1992." In *National Economic, Social, and Environmental Data Bank* [CD-ROM]. Prepared by U.S. Department of Commerce, Economics and Statistics Administration. Washington, DC: U.S. Department of Commerce, National Economic, Social, and Environmental Data Bank, Economics and Statistics Administration, Office of Business Analysis, February 1995. *Notes:* Totals may not agree with detail because of independent rounding. "NA" represents "not available."

★ 751 ★

Pollution Abatement and Control, by State

Pollution Abatement Operating Costs in District of Columbia: 1988-1992

Pollution abatement concerns those activities with the primary purpose of protecting the environment by reducing or eliminating unwanted emissions or wastes that are created by the production process. Operating costs related to pollution abatement activities totaled $19,228 million in 1992. Of this amount, $17,466 million was attributable to a particular media: $5,395 million for air; $6,577 million for water; and $5,494 million for solid/contained waste. Spending for nonmedia and other was $1,762 million. Total population abatement media operating costs showed an overall increase of $158 million (1 percent) from 1991, the previous year. Air operating costs increased 9 percent; water operating costs increased 4 percent; solid/contained waste operating costs decreased 9 percent. The table below shows pollution abatement operating control costs for air, water, solid/contained waste, and nonmedia for District of Columbia.

[In million dollars]

Year	Pollution abatement operating costs	Air	Water	Solid waste	Nonmedia
1992	1.4	0.3	0.4	0.7	11.9
1991	1.1	(Z)	0.4	0.7	(NA)
1990	1.4	(Z)	0.6	0.8	(NA)
1989	1.6	0.2	(D)	(D)	(NA)
1988	1.9	0.2	0.7	1	(NA)

Source: U.S. Department of Commerce. Bureau of the Census. "Pollution Abatement Costs and Expenditures, 1992." In *National Economic, Social, and Environmental Data Bank* [CD-ROM]. Prepared by U.S. Department of Commerce, Economics and Statistics Administration. Washington, DC: U.S. Department of Commerce, National Economic, Social, and Environmental Data Bank, Economics and Statistics Administration, Office of Business Analysis, February 1995. *Notes:* Totals may not agree with detail because of independent rounding. "NA" represents "not available." "D" indicates data withheld to avoid disclosing operations of individual companies. "Z" denotes less than half of unit shown.

★ 752 ★

Pollution Abatement and Control, by State

Pollution Abatement Operating Costs in Florida: 1988-1992

Pollution abatement concerns those activities with the primary purpose of protecting the environment by reducing or eliminating unwanted emissions or wastes that are created by the production process. Operating costs related to pollution abatement activities totaled $19,228 million in 1992. Of this amount, $17,466 million was attributable to a particular media: $5,395 million for air; $6,577 million for water; and $5,494 million for solid/contained waste. Spending for nonmedia and other was $1,762 million. Total population abatement media operating costs showed an overall increase of $158 million (1 percent) from 1991, the previous year. Air operating costs increased 9 percent; water operating costs increased 4 percent; solid/contained waste operating costs decreased 9 percent. The table below shows pollution abatement operating control costs for air, water, solid/contained waste, and nonmedia for Florida.

[In million dollars]

Year	Pollution abatement operating costs	Air	Water	Solid waste	Nonmedia
1992	304.3	81.6	125.4	97.3	32.4
1991	291.5	88.0	114.5	89.0	(NA)
1990	322.4	97.5	128.8	96.1	(NA)
1989	347.4	100.6	133.0	113.9	(NA)
1988	314.1	123.8	101.6	88.6	(NA)

Source: U.S. Department of Commerce. Bureau of the Census. "Pollution Abatement Costs and Expenditures, 1992." In *National Economic, Social, and Environmental Data Bank* [CD-ROM]. Prepared by U.S. Department of Commerce, Economics and Statistics Administration. Washington, DC: U.S. Department of Commerce, National Economic, Social, and Environmental Data Bank, Economics and Statistics Administration, Office of Business Analysis, February 1995. *Notes:* Totals may not agree with detail because of independent rounding. "NA" represents "not available."

★ 753 ★

Pollution Abatement and Control, by State

Pollution Abatement Operating Costs in Georgia: 1988-1992

Pollution abatement concerns those activities with the primary purpose of protecting the environment by reducing or eliminating unwanted emissions or wastes that are created by the production process. Operating costs related to pollution abatement activities totaled $19,228 million in 1992. Of this amount, $17,466 million was attributable to a particular media: $5,395 million for air; $6,577 million for water; and $5,494 million for solid/contained waste. Spending for nonmedia and other was $1,762 million. Total population abatement media operating costs showed an overall increase of $158 million (1 percent) from 1991, the previous year. Air operating costs increased 9 percent; water operating costs increased 4 percent; solid/contained waste operating costs decreased 9 percent. The table below shows pollution abatement operating control costs for air, water, solid/contained waste, and nonmedia for Georgia.

[In million dollars]

Year	Pollution abatement operating costs	Air	Water	Solid waste	Nonmedia
1992	375.7	118.4	152.3	105.0	21.1
1991	422.3	120.1	191.3	110.8	(NA)
1990	407.8	104.4	187.5	116.0	(NA)
1989	433.6	144.0	163.3	126.3	(NA)
1988	299.4	87.4	131.6	80.4	(NA)

Source: U.S. Department of Commerce. Bureau of the Census. "Pollution Abatement Costs and Expenditures, 1992." In *National Economic, Social, and Environmental Data Bank* [CD-ROM]. Prepared by U.S. Department of Commerce, Economics and Statistics Administration. Washington, DC: U.S. Department of Commerce, National Economic, Social, and Environmental Data Bank, Economics and Statistics Administration, Office of Business Analysis, February 1995. *Notes:* Totals may not agree with detail because of independent rounding. "NA" represents "not available."

★ 754 ★

Pollution Abatement and Control, by State

Pollution Abatement Operating Costs in Hawaii: 1988-1992

Pollution abatement concerns those activities with the primary purpose of protecting the environment by reducing or eliminating unwanted emissions or wastes that are created by the production process. Operating costs related to pollution abatement activities totaled $19,228 million in 1992. Of this amount, $17,466 million was attributable to a particular media: $5,395 million for air; $6,577 million for water; and $5,494 million for solid/contained waste. Spending for nonmedia and other was $1,762 million. Total population abatement media operating costs showed an overall increase of $158 million (1 percent) from 1991, the previous year. Air operating costs increased 9 percent; water operating costs increased 4 percent; solid/contained waste operating costs decreased 9 percent. The table below shows pollution abatement operating control costs for air, water, solid/contained waste, and nonmedia for Hawaii.

[In million dollars]

Year	Pollution abatement operating costs	Air	Water	Solid waste	Nonmedia
1992	12.8	3.3	4.6	4.9	3.4
1991	15.8	(D)	9.0	(D)	(NA)
1990	12.0	3.5	(D)	(D)	(NA)
1989	7.0	3.2	2.5	1.3	(NA)
1988	16.2	4.8	5.9	5.5	(NA)

Source: U.S. Department of Commerce. Bureau of the Census. "Pollution Abatement Costs and Expenditures, 1992." In *National Economic, Social, and Environmental Data Bank* [CD-ROM]. Prepared by U.S. Department of Commerce, Economics and Statistics Administration. Washington, DC: U.S. Department of Commerce, National Economic, Social, and Environmental Data Bank, Economics and Statistics Administration, Office of Business Analysis, February 1995. *Notes:* Totals may not agree with detail because of independent rounding. "NA" represents "not available." "D" indicates data withheld to avoid disclosing operations of individual companies.

★ 755 ★
Pollution Abatement and Control, by State

Pollution Abatement Operating Costs in Idaho: 1988-1992

Pollution abatement concerns those activities with the primary purpose of protecting the environment by reducing or eliminating unwanted emissions or wastes that are created by the production process. Operating costs related to pollution abatement activities totaled $19,228 million in 1992. Of this amount, $17,466 million was attributable to a particular media: $5,395 million for air; $6,577 million for water; and $5,494 million for solid/contained waste. Spending for nonmedia and other was $1,762 million. Total population abatement media operating costs showed an overall increase of $158 million (1 percent) from 1991, the previous year. Air operating costs increased 9 percent; water operating costs increased 4 percent; solid/contained waste operating costs decreased 9 percent. The table below shows pollution abatement operating control costs for air, water, solid/contained waste, and nonmedia for Idaho.

[In million dollars]

Year	Pollution abatement operating costs	Air	Water	Solid waste	Nonmedia
1992	60.4	21.3	23.9	15.2	7.7
1991	37.7	11.1	15.6	11.1	(NA)
1990	44.5	14.1	19.4	10.9	(NA)
1989	41.6	13.7	18.5	9.4	(NA)
1988	43.8	14.7	18.6	10.5	(NA)

Source: U.S. Department of Commerce. Bureau of the Census. "Pollution Abatement Costs and Expenditures, 1992." In *National Economic, Social, and Environmental Data Bank* [CD-ROM]. Prepared by U.S. Department of Commerce, Economics and Statistics Administration. Washington, DC: U.S. Department of Commerce, National Economic, Social, and Environmental Data Bank, Economics and Statistics Administration, Office of Business Analysis, February 1995. *Notes:* Totals may not agree with detail because of independent rounding. "NA" represents "not available."

★ 756 ★

Pollution Abatement and Control, by State

Pollution Abatement Operating Costs in Illinois: 1988-1992

Pollution abatement concerns those activities with the primary purpose of protecting the environment by reducing or eliminating unwanted emissions or wastes that are created by the production process. Operating costs related to pollution abatement activities totaled $19,228 million in 1992. Of this amount, $17,466 million was attributable to a particular media: $5,395 million for air; $6,577 million for water; and $5,494 million for solid/contained waste. Spending for nonmedia and other was $1,762 million. Total population abatement media operating costs showed an overall increase of $158 million (1 percent) from 1991, the previous year. Air operating costs increased 9 percent; water operating costs increased 4 percent; solid/contained waste operating costs decreased 9 percent. The table below shows pollution abatement operating control costs for air, water, solid/contained waste, and nonmedia for Illinois.

[In million dollars]

Year	Pollution abatement operating costs	Air	Water	Solid waste	Nonmedia
1992	896.1	322.5	297.0	276.7	35.9
1991	783.4	261.9	263.7	257.8	(NA)
1990	842.4	287.8	276.7	277.9	(NA)
1989	753.5	273.9	252.4	227.2	(NA)
1988	695.2	227.8	242.2	225.2	(NA)

Source: U.S. Department of Commerce. Bureau of the Census. "Pollution Abatement Costs and Expenditures, 1992." In *National Economic, Social, and Environmental Data Bank* [CD-ROM]. Prepared by U.S. Department of Commerce, Economics and Statistics Administration. Washington, DC: U.S. Department of Commerce, National Economic, Social, and Environmental Data Bank, Economics and Statistics Administration, Office of Business Analysis, February 1995. *Notes:* Totals may not agree with detail because of independent rounding. "NA" represents "not available."

★ 757 ★

Pollution Abatement and Control, by State

Pollution Abatement Operating Costs in Indiana: 1988-1992

Pollution abatement concerns those activities with the primary purpose of protecting the environment by reducing or eliminating unwanted emissions or wastes that are created by the production process. Operating costs related to pollution abatement activities totaled $19,228 million in 1992. Of this amount, $17,466 million was attributable to a particular media: $5,395 million for air; $6,577 million for water; and $5,494 million for solid/contained waste. Spending for nonmedia and other was $1,762 million. Total population abatement media operating costs showed an overall increase of $158 million (1 percent) from 1991, the previous year. Air operating costs increased 9 percent; water operating costs increased 4 percent; solid/contained waste operating costs decreased 9 percent. The table below shows pollution abatement operating control costs for air, water, solid/contained waste, and nonmedia for Indiana.

[In million dollars]

Year	Pollution abatement operating costs	Air	Water	Solid waste	Nonmedia
1992	706.6	255.2	253.2	198.2	45.7
1991	667.5	197.2	240.1	230.2	(NA)
1990	628.5	183.2	257.5	187.9	(NA)
1989	671.3	207.2	276.1	188.1	(NA)
1988	582.9	190.3	239.9	152.7	(NA)

Source: U.S. Department of Commerce. Bureau of the Census. "Pollution Abatement Costs and Expenditures, 1992." In *National Economic, Social, and Environmental Data Bank* [CD-ROM]. Prepared by U.S. Department of Commerce, Economics and Statistics Administration. Washington, DC: U.S. Department of Commerce, National Economic, Social, and Environmental Data Bank, Economics and Statistics Administration, Office of Business Analysis, February 1995. *Notes:* Totals may not agree with detail because of independent rounding. "NA" represents "not available."

★ 758 ★

Pollution Abatement and Control, by State

Pollution Abatement Operating Costs in Iowa: 1988-1992

Pollution abatement concerns those activities with the primary purpose of protecting the environment by reducing or eliminating unwanted emissions or wastes that are created by the production process. Operating costs related to pollution abatement activities totaled $19,228 million in 1992. Of this amount, $17,466 million was attributable to a particular media: $5,395 million for air; $6,577 million for water; and $5,494 million for solid/contained waste. Spending for nonmedia and other was $1,762 million. Total population abatement media operating costs showed an overall increase of $158 million (1 percent) from 1991, the previous year. Air operating costs increased 9 percent; water operating costs increased 4 percent; solid/contained waste operating costs decreased 9 percent. The table below shows pollution abatement operating control costs for air, water, solid/contained waste, and nonmedia for Iowa.

[In million dollars]

Year	Pollution abatement operating costs	Air	Water	Solid waste	Nonmedia
1992	166.9	53.3	60.0	53.6	12.0
1991	149.1	46.4	56.7	46.0	(NA)
1990	140.6	44.3	51.0	45.3	(NA)
1989	147.6	43.1	53.3	51.2	(NA)
1988	126.1	38.8	55.2	32.0	(NA)

Source: U.S. Department of Commerce. Bureau of the Census. "Pollution Abatement Costs and Expenditures, 1992." In *National Economic, Social, and Environmental Data Bank* [CD-ROM]. Prepared by U.S. Department of Commerce, Economics and Statistics Administration. Washington, DC: U.S. Department of Commerce, National Economic, Social, and Environmental Data Bank, Economics and Statistics Administration, Office of Business Analysis, February 1995. *Notes:* Totals may not agree with detail because of independent rounding. "NA" represents "not available."

★ 759 ★
Pollution Abatement and Control, by State

Pollution Abatement Operating Costs in Kansas: 1988-1992

Pollution abatement concerns those activities with the primary purpose of protecting the environment by reducing or eliminating unwanted emissions or wastes that are created by the production process. Operating costs related to pollution abatement activities totaled $19,228 million in 1992. Of this amount, $17,466 million was attributable to a particular media: $5,395 million for air; $6,577 million for water; and $5,494 million for solid/contained waste. Spending for nonmedia and other was $1,762 million. Total population abatement media operating costs showed an overall increase of $158 million (1 percent) from 1991, the previous year. Air operating costs increased 9 percent; water operating costs increased 4 percent; solid/contained waste operating costs decreased 9 percent. The table below shows pollution abatement operating control costs for air, water, solid/contained waste, and nonmedia for Kansas.

[In million dollars]

Year	Pollution abatement operating costs	Air	Water	Solid waste	Nonmedia
1992	107.3	29.0	37.0	41.3	5.7
1991	139.7	47.8	42.2	49.7	(NA)
1990	142.4	41.0	49.5	52.0	(NA)
1989	116.8	33.1	48.1	35.6	(NA)
1988	86.3	18.7	42.2	25.5	(NA)

Source: U.S. Department of Commerce. Bureau of the Census. "Pollution Abatement Costs and Expenditures, 1992." In *National Economic, Social, and Environmental Data Bank* [CD-ROM]. Prepared by U.S. Department of Commerce, Economics and Statistics Administration. Washington, DC: U.S. Department of Commerce, National Economic, Social, and Environmental Data Bank, Economics and Statistics Administration, Office of Business Analysis, February 1995. *Notes:* Totals may not agree with detail because of independent rounding. "NA" represents "not available."

★ 760 ★

Pollution Abatement and Control, by State

Pollution Abatement Operating Costs in Kentucky: 1988-1992

Pollution abatement concerns those activities with the primary purpose of protecting the environment by reducing or eliminating unwanted emissions or wastes that are created by the production process. Operating costs related to pollution abatement activities totaled $19,228 million in 1992. Of this amount, $17,466 million was attributable to a particular media: $5,395 million for air; $6,577 million for water; and $5,494 million for solid/contained waste. Spending for nonmedia and other was $1,762 million. Total population abatement media operating costs showed an overall increase of $158 million (1 percent) from 1991, the previous year. Air operating costs increased 9 percent; water operating costs increased 4 percent; solid/contained waste operating costs decreased 9 percent. The table below shows pollution abatement operating control costs for air, water, solid/contained waste, and nonmedia for Kentucky.

[In million dollars]

Year	Pollution abatement operating costs	Air	Water	Solid waste	Nonmedia
1992	324.8	138.4	102.2	84.1	14.3
1991	331.3	121.4	107.8	102.1	(NA)
1990	327.7	131.2	103.8	92.7	(NA)
1989	295.5	118.1	94.2	83.2	(NA)
1988	237.5	101.9	80.4	55.2	(NA)

Source: U.S. Department of Commerce. Bureau of the Census. "Pollution Abatement Costs and Expenditures, 1992." In *National Economic, Social, and Environmental Data Bank* [CD-ROM]. Prepared by U.S. Department of Commerce, Economics and Statistics Administration. Washington, DC: U.S. Department of Commerce, National Economic, Social, and Environmental Data Bank, Economics and Statistics Administration, Office of Business Analysis, February 1995. *Notes:* Totals may not agree with detail because of independent rounding. "NA" represents "not available."

★ 761 ★

Pollution Abatement and Control, by State

Pollution Abatement Operating Costs in Louisiana: 1988-1992

Pollution abatement concerns those activities with the primary purpose of protecting the environment by reducing or eliminating unwanted emissions or wastes that are created by the production process. Operating costs related to pollution abatement activities totaled $19,228 million in 1992. Of this amount, $17,466 million was attributable to a particular media: $5,395 million for air; $6,577 million for water; and $5,494 million for solid/contained waste. Spending for nonmedia and other was $1,762 million. Total population abatement media operating costs showed an overall increase of $158 million (1 percent) from 1991, the previous year. Air operating costs increased 9 percent; water operating costs increased 4 percent; solid/contained waste operating costs decreased 9 percent. The table below shows pollution abatement operating control costs for air, water, solid/contained waste, and nonmedia for Louisiana.

[In million dollars]

Year	Pollution abatement operating costs	Air	Water	Solid waste	Nonmedia
1992	920.0	317.3	347.6	255.1	49.3
1991	892.4	282.3	366.7	243.4	(NA)
1990	827.0	261.3	328.9	236.7	(NA)
1989	682.9	240.8	278.5	163.7	(NA)
1988	643.8	213.5	257.4	172.9	(NA)

Source: U.S. Department of Commerce. Bureau of the Census. "Pollution Abatement Costs and Expenditures, 1992." In *National Economic, Social, and Environmental Data Bank* [CD-ROM]. Prepared by U.S. Department of Commerce, Economics and Statistics Administration. Washington, DC: U.S. Department of Commerce, National Economic, Social, and Environmental Data Bank, Economics and Statistics Administration, Office of Business Analysis, February 1995. *Notes:* Totals may not agree with detail because of independent rounding. "NA" represents "not available."

★ 762 ★

Pollution Abatement and Control, by State

Pollution Abatement Operating Costs in Maine: 1988-1992

Pollution abatement concerns those activities with the primary purpose of protecting the environment by reducing or eliminating unwanted emissions or wastes that are created by the production process. Operating costs related to pollution abatement activities totaled $19,228 million in 1992. Of this amount, $17,466 million was attributable to a particular media: $5,395 million for air; $6,577 million for water; and $5,494 million for solid/contained waste. Spending for nonmedia and other was $1,762 million. Total population abatement media operating costs showed an overall increase of $158 million (1 percent) from 1991, the previous year. Air operating costs increased 9 percent; water operating costs increased 4 percent; solid/contained waste operating costs decreased 9 percent. The table below shows pollution abatement operating control costs for air, water, solid/contained waste, and nonmedia for Maine.

[In million dollars]

Year	Pollution abatement operating costs	Air	Water	Solid waste	Nonmedia
1992	123.5	21.2	60.7	41.5	6.2
1991	127.3	18.8	59.6	48.9	(NA)
1990	113.5	16.0	56.2	41.2	(NA)
1989	117.8	21.1	63.0	33.6	(NA)
1988	88.5	14.8	46.8	26.9	(NA)

Source: U.S. Department of Commerce. Bureau of the Census. "Pollution Abatement Costs and Expenditures, 1992." In *National Economic, Social, and Environmental Data Bank* [CD-ROM]. Prepared by U.S. Department of Commerce, Economics and Statistics Administration. Washington, DC: U.S. Department of Commerce, National Economic, Social, and Environmental Data Bank, Economics and Statistics Administration, Office of Business Analysis, February 1995. *Notes:* Totals may not agree with detail because of independent rounding. "NA" represents "not available."

★ 763 ★
Pollution Abatement and Control, by State

Pollution Abatement Operating Costs in Maryland: 1988-1992

Pollution abatement concerns those activities with the primary purpose of protecting the environment by reducing or eliminating unwanted emissions or wastes that are created by the production process. Operating costs related to pollution abatement activities totaled $19,228 million in 1992. Of this amount, $17,466 million was attributable to a particular media: $5,395 million for air; $6,577 million for water; and $5,494 million for solid/contained waste. Spending for nonmedia and other was $1,762 million. Total population abatement media operating costs showed an overall increase of $158 million (1 percent) from 1991, the previous year. Air operating costs increased 9 percent; water operating costs increased 4 percent; solid/contained waste operating costs decreased 9 percent. The table below shows pollution abatement operating control costs for air, water, solid/contained waste, and nonmedia for Maryland.

[In million dollars]

Year	Pollution abatement operating costs	Air	Water	Solid waste	Nonmedia
1992	205.6	55.4	80.5	69.7	4.4
1991	212.4	47.6	77.7	87.1	(NA)
1990	194.2	47.6	77.8	68.8	(NA)
1989	192.4	49.9	83.4	59.1	(NA)
1988	216.3	70.1	84.0	62.1	(NA)

Source: U.S. Department of Commerce. Bureau of the Census. "Pollution Abatement Costs and Expenditures, 1992." In *National Economic, Social, and Environmental Data Bank* [CD-ROM]. Prepared by U.S. Department of Commerce, Economics and Statistics Administration. Washington, DC: U.S. Department of Commerce, National Economic, Social, and Environmental Data Bank, Economics and Statistics Administration, Office of Business Analysis, February 1995. *Notes:* Totals may not agree with detail because of independent rounding. "NA" represents "not available."

★ 764 ★

Pollution Abatement and Control, by State

Pollution Abatement Operating Costs in Massachusetts: 1988-1992

Pollution abatement concerns those activities with the primary purpose of protecting the environment by reducing or eliminating unwanted emissions or wastes that are created by the production process. Operating costs related to pollution abatement activities totaled $19,228 million in 1992. Of this amount, $17,466 million was attributable to a particular media: $5,395 million for air; $6,577 million for water; and $5,494 million for solid/contained waste. Spending for nonmedia and other was $1,762 million. Total population abatement media operating costs showed an overall increase of $158 million (1 percent) from 1991, the previous year. Air operating costs increased 9 percent; water operating costs increased 4 percent; solid/contained waste operating costs decreased 9 percent. The table below shows pollution abatement operating control costs for air, water, solid/contained waste, and nonmedia for Massachusetts.

[In million dollars]

Year	Pollution abatement operating costs	Air	Water	Solid waste	Nonmedia
1992	246.2	34.3	106.9	105.1	14.8
1991	247.8	39.1	99.2	109.5	(NA)
1990	249.2	33.7	88.8	126.8	(NA)
1989	268.9	51.3	84.6	133	(NA)
1988	208.9	34.2	74.3	100.4	(NA)

Source: U.S. Department of Commerce. Bureau of the Census. "Pollution Abatement Costs and Expenditures, 1992." In *National Economic, Social, and Environmental Data Bank* [CD-ROM]. Prepared by U.S. Department of Commerce, Economics and Statistics Administration. Washington, DC: U.S. Department of Commerce, National Economic, Social, and Environmental Data Bank, Economics and Statistics Administration, Office of Business Analysis, February 1995. *Notes:* Totals may not agree with detail because of independent rounding. "NA" represents "not available."

★ 765 ★

Pollution Abatement and Control, by State

Pollution Abatement Operating Costs in Michigan: 1988-1992

Pollution abatement concerns those activities with the primary purpose of protecting the environment by reducing or eliminating unwanted emissions or wastes that are created by the production process. Operating costs related to pollution abatement activities totaled $19,228 million in 1992. Of this amount, $17,466 million was attributable to a particular media: $5,395 million for air; $6,577 million for water; and $5,494 million for solid/contained waste. Spending for nonmedia and other was $1,762 million. Total population abatement media operating costs showed an overall increase of $158 million (1 percent) from 1991, the previous year. Air operating costs increased 9 percent; water operating costs increased 4 percent; solid/contained waste operating costs decreased 9 percent. The table below shows pollution abatement operating control costs for air, water, solid/contained waste, and nonmedia for Michigan.

[In million dollars]

Year	Pollution abatement operating costs	Air	Water	Solid waste	Nonmedia
1992	763.0	220.2	290.8	252.0	33.1
1991	692.6	186.1	266.0	240.5	(NA)
1990	739.5	195.9	273.6	270.0	(NA)
1989	703.8	180.0	274.6	249.2	(NA)
1988	713.6	227.0	296.6	190.1	(NA)

Source: U.S. Department of Commerce. Bureau of the Census. "Pollution Abatement Costs and Expenditures, 1992." In *National Economic, Social, and Environmental Data Bank* [CD-ROM]. Prepared by U.S. Department of Commerce, Economics and Statistics Administration. Washington, DC: U.S. Department of Commerce, National Economic, Social, and Environmental Data Bank, Economics and Statistics Administration, Office of Business Analysis, February 1995. *Notes:* Totals may not agree with detail because of independent rounding. "NA" represents "not available."

★ 766 ★

Pollution Abatement and Control, by State

Pollution Abatement Operating Costs in Minnesota: 1988-1992

Pollution abatement concerns those activities with the primary purpose of protecting the environment by reducing or eliminating unwanted emissions or wastes that are created by the production process. Operating costs related to pollution abatement activities totaled $19,228 million in 1992. Of this amount, $17,466 million was attributable to a particular media: $5,395 million for air; $6,577 million for water; and $5,494 million for solid/contained waste. Spending for nonmedia and other was $1,762 million. Total population abatement media operating costs showed an overall increase of $158 million (1 percent) from 1991, the previous year. Air operating costs increased 9 percent; water operating costs increased 4 percent; solid/contained waste operating costs decreased 9 percent. The table below shows pollution abatement operating control costs for air, water, solid/contained waste, and nonmedia for Minnesota.

[In million dollars]

Year	Pollution abatement operating costs	Air	Water	Solid waste	Nonmedia
1992	254.5	72.2	102.5	79.8	7.0
1991	247.3	58.7	87.3	101.3	(NA)
1990	211.9	61.2	77.4	73.3	(NA)
1989	204.2	54.8	73.9	75.5	(NA)
1988	168.5	41.3	72.7	54.4	(NA)

Source: U.S. Department of Commerce. Bureau of the Census. "Pollution Abatement Costs and Expenditures, 1992." In *National Economic, Social, and Environmental Data Bank* [CD-ROM]. Prepared by U.S. Department of Commerce, Economics and Statistics Administration. Washington, DC: U.S. Department of Commerce, National Economic, Social, and Environmental Data Bank, Economics and Statistics Administration, Office of Business Analysis, February 1995. *Notes:* Totals may not agree with detail because of independent rounding. "NA" represents "not available."

★ 767 ★

Pollution Abatement and Control, by State

Pollution Abatement Operating Costs in Mississippi: 1988-1992

Pollution abatement concerns those activities with the primary purpose of protecting the environment by reducing or eliminating unwanted emissions or wastes that are created by the production process. Operating costs related to pollution abatement activities totaled $19,228 million in 1992. Of this amount, $17,466 million was attributable to a particular media: $5,395 million for air; $6,577 million for water; and $5,494 million for solid/contained waste. Spending for nonmedia and other was $1,762 million. Total population abatement media operating costs showed an overall increase of $158 million (1 percent) from 1991, the previous year. Air operating costs increased 9 percent; water operating costs increased 4 percent; solid/contained waste operating costs decreased 9 percent. The table below shows pollution abatement operating control costs for air, water, solid/contained waste, and nonmedia for Mississippi.

[In million dollars]

Year	Pollution abatement operating costs	Air	Water	Solid waste	Nonmedia
1992	269.1	120.9	86.1	62.1	2.8
1991	216.0	101.0	62.6	52.3	(NA)
1990	201.0	92.4	65.0	43.6	(NA)
1989	160.6	62.5	62.2	36.0	(NA)
1988	153.9	53.2	63.7	37.1	(NA)

Source: U.S. Department of Commerce. Bureau of the Census. "Pollution Abatement Costs and Expenditures, 1992." In *National Economic, Social, and Environmental Data Bank* [CD-ROM]. Prepared by U.S. Department of Commerce, Economics and Statistics Administration. Washington, DC: U.S. Department of Commerce, National Economic, Social, and Environmental Data Bank, Economics and Statistics Administration, Office of Business Analysis, February 1995. *Notes:* Totals may not agree with detail because of independent rounding. "NA" represents "not available."

★ 768 ★

Pollution Abatement and Control, by State

Pollution Abatement Operating Costs in Missouri: 1988-1992

Pollution abatement concerns those activities with the primary purpose of protecting the environment by reducing or eliminating unwanted emissions or wastes that are created by the production process. Operating costs related to pollution abatement activities totaled $19,228 million in 1992. Of this amount, $17,466 million was attributable to a particular media: $5,395 million for air; $6,577 million for water; and $5,494 million for solid/contained waste. Spending for nonmedia and other was $1,762 million. Total population abatement media operating costs showed an overall increase of $158 million (1 percent) from 1991, the previous year. Air operating costs increased 9 percent; water operating costs increased 4 percent; solid/contained waste operating costs decreased 9 percent. The table below shows pollution abatement operating control costs for air, water, solid/contained waste, and nonmedia for Missouri.

[In million dollars]

Year	Pollution abatement operating costs	Air	Water	Solid waste	Nonmedia
1992	287.6	79.2	111.6	96.8	11.6
1991	268.4	59.8	115.2	93.4	(NA)
1990	344.2	72.9	160.1	111.2	(NA)
1989	319.6	66.4	137.4	115.8	(NA)
1988	230.4	66.0	82.6	81.7	(NA)

Source: U.S. Department of Commerce. Bureau of the Census. "Pollution Abatement Costs and Expenditures, 1992." In *National Economic, Social, and Environmental Data Bank* [CD-ROM]. Prepared by U.S. Department of Commerce, Economics and Statistics Administration. Washington, DC: U.S. Department of Commerce, National Economic, Social, and Environmental Data Bank, Economics and Statistics Administration, Office of Business Analysis, February 1995. *Notes:* Totals may not agree with detail because of independent rounding. "NA" represents "not available."

★ 769 ★

Pollution Abatement and Control, by State

Pollution Abatement Operating Costs in Montana: 1988-1992

Pollution abatement concerns those activities with the primary purpose of protecting the environment by reducing or eliminating unwanted emissions or wastes that are created by the production process. Operating costs related to pollution abatement activities totaled $19,228 million in 1992. Of this amount, $17,466 million was attributable to a particular media: $5,395 million for air; $6,577 million for water; and $5,494 million for solid/contained waste. Spending for nonmedia and other was $1,762 million. Total population abatement media operating costs showed an overall increase of $158 million (1 percent) from 1991, the previous year. Air operating costs increased 9 percent; water operating costs increased 4 percent; solid/contained waste operating costs decreased 9 percent. The table below shows pollution abatement operating control costs for air, water, solid/contained waste, and nonmedia for Montana.

[In million dollars]

Year	Pollution abatement operating costs	Air	Water	Solid waste	Nonmedia
1992	25.5	17.3	4.8	3.4	(D)
1991	44.5	25.2	11.9	7.4	(NA)
1990	39.9	21.9	11.7	6.4	(NA)
1989	39.6	21.8	12.5	5.3	(NA)
1988	31.3	19.4	8.3	3.6	(NA)

Source: U.S. Department of Commerce. Bureau of the Census. "Pollution Abatement Costs and Expenditures, 1992." In *National Economic, Social, and Environmental Data Bank* [CD-ROM]. Prepared by U.S. Department of Commerce, Economics and Statistics Administration. Washington, DC: U.S. Department of Commerce, National Economic, Social, and Environmental Data Bank, Economics and Statistics Administration, Office of Business Analysis, February 1995. *Notes:* Totals may not agree with detail because of independent rounding. "NA" represents "not available." "D" indicates data withheld to avoid disclosing operations of individual companies.

★ 770 ★

Pollution Abatement and Control, by State

Pollution Abatement Operating Costs in Nebraska: 1988-1992

Pollution abatement concerns those activities with the primary purpose of protecting the environment by reducing or eliminating unwanted emissions or wastes that are created by the production process. Operating costs related to pollution abatement activities totaled $19,228 million in 1992. Of this amount, $17,466 million was attributable to a particular media: $5,395 million for air; $6,577 million for water; and $5,494 million for solid/contained waste. Spending for nonmedia and other was $1,762 million. Total population abatement media operating costs showed an overall increase of $158 million (1 percent) from 1991, the previous year. Air operating costs increased 9 percent; water operating costs increased 4 percent; solid/contained waste operating costs decreased 9 percent. The table below shows pollution abatement operating control costs for air, water, solid/contained waste, and nonmedia for Nebraska.

[In million dollars]

Year	Pollution abatement operating costs	Air	Water	Solid waste	Nonmedia
1992	60.0	12.8	23.6	23.5	2.7
1991	41.1	8.7	14.8	17.6	(NA)
1990	37.9	9.3	14.6	14.0	(NA)
1989	32.9	9.4	12.1	11.4	(NA)
1988	43.9	10.9	18.1	14.9	(NA)

Source: U.S. Department of Commerce. Bureau of the Census. "Pollution Abatement Costs and Expenditures, 1992." In *National Economic, Social, and Environmental Data Bank* [CD-ROM]. Prepared by U.S. Department of Commerce, Economics and Statistics Administration. Washington, DC: U.S. Department of Commerce, National Economic, Social, and Environmental Data Bank, Economics and Statistics Administration, Office of Business Analysis, February 1995. *Notes:* Totals may not agree with detail because of independent rounding. "NA" represents "not available."

★ 771 ★

Pollution Abatement and Control, by State

Pollution Abatement Operating Costs in Nevada: 1988-1992

Pollution abatement concerns those activities with the primary purpose of protecting the environment by reducing or eliminating unwanted emissions or wastes that are created by the production process. Operating costs related to pollution abatement activities totaled $19,228 million in 1992. Of this amount, $17,466 million was attributable to a particular media: $5,395 million for air; $6,577 million for water; and $5,494 million for solid/contained waste. Spending for nonmedia and other was $1,762 million. Total population abatement media operating costs showed an overall increase of $158 million (1 percent) from 1991, the previous year. Air operating costs increased 9 percent; water operating costs increased 4 percent; solid/contained waste operating costs decreased 9 percent. The table below shows pollution abatement operating control costs for air, water, solid/contained waste, and nonmedia for Nevada.

[In million dollars]

Year	Pollution abatement operating costs	Air	Water	Solid waste	Nonmedia
1992	11.0	3.4	4.6	3.0	1.8
1991	9.0	3.1	2.6	3.3	(NA)
1990	7.8	1.4	2.9	3.4	(NA)
1989	9.5	2.1	5.3	2.2	(NA)
1988	11.3	4.6	3.0	3.7	(NA)

Source: U.S. Department of Commerce. Bureau of the Census. "Pollution Abatement Costs and Expenditures, 1992." In *National Economic, Social, and Environmental Data Bank* [CD-ROM]. Prepared by U.S. Department of Commerce, Economics and Statistics Administration. Washington, DC: U.S. Department of Commerce, National Economic, Social, and Environmental Data Bank, Economics and Statistics Administration, Office of Business Analysis, February 1995. *Notes:* Totals may not agree with detail because of independent rounding. "NA" represents "not available."

★ 772 ★

Pollution Abatement and Control, by State

Pollution Abatement Operating Costs in New Hampshire: 1988-1992

Pollution abatement concerns those activities with the primary purpose of protecting the environment by reducing or eliminating unwanted emissions or wastes that are created by the production process. Operating costs related to pollution abatement activities totaled $19,228 million in 1992. Of this amount, $17,466 million was attributable to a particular media: $5,395 million for air; $6,577 million for water; and $5,494 million for solid/contained waste. Spending for nonmedia and other was $1,762 million. Total population abatement media operating costs showed an overall increase of $158 million (1 percent) from 1991, the previous year. Air operating costs increased 9 percent; water operating costs increased 4 percent; solid/contained waste operating costs decreased 9 percent. The table below shows pollution abatement operating control costs for air, water, solid/contained waste, and nonmedia for New Hampshire.

[In million dollars]

Year	Pollution abatement operating costs	Air	Water	Solid waste	Nonmedia
1992	44.1	5.8	20.6	17.7	3.4
1991	49.7	5.2	22.6	21.9	(NA)
1990	51.3	6.3	21.5	23.5	(NA)
1989	51.9	7.3	19.7	24.9	(NA)
1988	36.1	3.1	18.2	14.8	(NA)

Source: U.S. Department of Commerce. Bureau of the Census. "Pollution Abatement Costs and Expenditures, 1992." In *National Economic, Social, and Environmental Data Bank* [CD-ROM]. Prepared by U.S. Department of Commerce, Economics and Statistics Administration. Washington, DC: U.S. Department of Commerce, National Economic, Social, and Environmental Data Bank, Economics and Statistics Administration, Office of Business Analysis, February 1995. *Notes:* Totals may not agree with detail because of independent rounding. "NA" represents "not available."

★ 773 ★

Pollution Abatement and Control, by State

Pollution Abatement Operating Costs in New Jersey: 1988-1992

Pollution abatement concerns those activities with the primary purpose of protecting the environment by reducing or eliminating unwanted emissions or wastes that are created by the production process. Operating costs related to pollution abatement activities totaled $19,228 million in 1992. Of this amount, $17,466 million was attributable to a particular media: $5,395 million for air; $6,577 million for water; and $5,494 million for solid/contained waste. Spending for nonmedia and other was $1,762 million. Total population abatement media operating costs showed an overall increase of $158 million (1 percent) from 1991, the previous year. Air operating costs increased 9 percent; water operating costs increased 4 percent; solid/contained waste operating costs decreased 9 percent. The table below shows pollution abatement operating control costs for air, water, solid/contained waste, and nonmedia for New Jersey.

[In million dollars]

Year	Pollution abatement operating costs	Air	Water	Solid waste	Nonmedia
1992	673.8	146.6	285.7	241.5	111.0
1991	669.5	188.7	244.4	236.4	(NA)
1990	668.9	169.9	273.8	225.3	(NA)
1989	615.5	147.2	231.3	237.0	(NA)
1988	535.4	163.4	185.3	186.8	(NA)

Source: U.S. Department of Commerce. Bureau of the Census. "Pollution Abatement Costs and Expenditures, 1992." In *National Economic, Social, and Environmental Data Bank* [CD-ROM]. Prepared by U.S. Department of Commerce, Economics and Statistics Administration. Washington, DC: U.S. Department of Commerce, National Economic, Social, and Environmental Data Bank, Economics and Statistics Administration, Office of Business Analysis, February 1995. *Notes:* Totals may not agree with detail because of independent rounding. "NA" represents "not available."

★ 774 ★
Pollution Abatement and Control, by State

Pollution Abatement Operating Costs in New Mexico: 1988-1992

Pollution abatement concerns those activities with the primary purpose of protecting the environment by reducing or eliminating unwanted emissions or wastes that are created by the production process. Operating costs related to pollution abatement activities totaled $19,228 million in 1992. Of this amount, $17,466 million was attributable to a particular media: $5,395 million for air; $6,577 million for water; and $5,494 million for solid/contained waste. Spending for nonmedia and other was $1,762 million. Total population abatement media operating costs showed an overall increase of $158 million (1 percent) from 1991, the previous year. Air operating costs increased 9 percent; water operating costs increased 4 percent; solid/contained waste operating costs decreased 9 percent. The table below shows pollution abatement operating control costs for air, water, solid/contained waste, and nonmedia for New Mexico.

[In million dollars]

Year	Pollution abatement operating costs	Air	Water	Solid waste	Nonmedia
1992	63.4	34.2	11.4	17.8	1.8
1991	54.7	29.1	11.5	14.1	(NA)
1990	51.8	31.9	7.3	12.6	(NA)
1989	45.0	26.0	8.0	11.1	(NA)
1988	56.2	(D)	(D)	8.0	(NA)

Source: U.S. Department of Commerce. Bureau of the Census. "Pollution Abatement Costs and Expenditures, 1992." In *National Economic, Social, and Environmental Data Bank* [CD-ROM]. Prepared by U.S. Department of Commerce, Economics and Statistics Administration. Washington, DC: U.S. Department of Commerce, National Economic, Social, and Environmental Data Bank, Economics and Statistics Administration, Office of Business Analysis, February 1995. *Notes:* Totals may not agree with detail because of independent rounding. "NA" represents "not available." "D" indicates data withheld to avoid disclosing operations of individual companies.

★ 775 ★

Pollution Abatement and Control, by State

Pollution Abatement Operating Costs in New York: 1988-1992

Pollution abatement concerns those activities with the primary purpose of protecting the environment by reducing or eliminating unwanted emissions or wastes that are created by the production process. Operating costs related to pollution abatement activities totaled $19,228 million in 1992. Of this amount, $17,466 million was attributable to a particular media: $5,395 million for air; $6,577 million for water; and $5,494 million for solid/contained waste. Spending for nonmedia and other was $1,762 million. Total population abatement media operating costs showed an overall increase of $158 million (1 percent) from 1991, the previous year. Air operating costs increased 9 percent; water operating costs increased 4 percent; solid/contained waste operating costs decreased 9 percent. The table below shows pollution abatement operating control costs for air, water, solid/contained waste, and nonmedia for New York.

[In million dollars]

Year	Pollution abatement operating costs	Air	Water	Solid waste	Nonmedia
1992	650.6	115.5	235.6	299.4	67.9
1991	665.5	106.0	248.2	311.3	(NA)
1990	619.5	109.6	239.9	270.0	(NA)
1989	624.6	111.5	241.9	271.2	(NA)
1988	556.5	87.7	206.8	262.1	(NA)

Source: U.S. Department of Commerce. Bureau of the Census. "Pollution Abatement Costs and Expenditures, 1992." In *National Economic, Social, and Environmental Data Bank* [CD-ROM]. Prepared by U.S. Department of Commerce, Economics and Statistics Administration. Washington, DC: U.S. Department of Commerce, National Economic, Social, and Environmental Data Bank, Economics and Statistics Administration, Office of Business Analysis, February 1995. *Notes:* Totals may not agree with detail because of independent rounding. "NA" represents "not available."

★ 776 ★

Pollution Abatement and Control, by State

Pollution Abatement Operating Costs in North Carolina: 1988-1992

Pollution abatement concerns those activities with the primary purpose of protecting the environment by reducing or eliminating unwanted emissions or wastes that are created by the production process. Operating costs related to pollution abatement activities totaled $19,228 million in 1992. Of this amount, $17,466 million was attributable to a particular media: $5,395 million for air; $6,577 million for water; and $5,494 million for solid/contained waste. Spending for nonmedia and other was $1,762 million. Total population abatement media operating costs showed an overall increase of $158 million (1 percent) from 1991, the previous year. Air operating costs increased 9 percent; water operating costs increased 4 percent; solid/contained waste operating costs decreased 9 percent. The table below shows pollution abatement operating control costs for air, water, solid/contained waste, and nonmedia for North Carolina.

[In million dollars]

Year	Pollution abatement operating costs	Air	Water	Solid waste	Nonmedia
1992	554.4	185.5	213.2	155.6	26.5
1991	433.4	113.5	182.6	137.2	(NA)
1990	431.4	117.7	172.1	141.7	(NA)
1989	411.1	110.2	168.7	132.2	(NA)
1988	344.3	109.2	143.6	91.5	(NA)

Source: U.S. Department of Commerce. Bureau of the Census. "Pollution Abatement Costs and Expenditures, 1992." In *National Economic, Social, and Environmental Data Bank* [CD-ROM]. Prepared by U.S. Department of Commerce, Economics and Statistics Administration. Washington, DC: U.S. Department of Commerce, National Economic, Social, and Environmental Data Bank, Economics and Statistics Administration, Office of Business Analysis, February 1995. *Notes:* Totals may not agree with detail because of independent rounding. "NA" represents "not available."

★ 777 ★

Pollution Abatement and Control, by State

Pollution Abatement Operating Costs in North Dakota: 1988-1992

Pollution abatement concerns those activities with the primary purpose of protecting the environment by reducing or eliminating unwanted emissions or wastes that are created by the production process. Operating costs related to pollution abatement activities totaled $19,228 million in 1992. Of this amount, $17,466 million was attributable to a particular media: $5,395 million for air; $6,577 million for water; and $5,494 million for solid/contained waste. Spending for nonmedia and other was $1,762 million. Total population abatement media operating costs showed an overall increase of $158 million (1 percent) from 1991, the previous year. Air operating costs increased 9 percent; water operating costs increased 4 percent; solid/contained waste operating costs decreased 9 percent. The table below shows pollution abatement operating control costs for air, water, solid/contained waste, and nonmedia for North Dakota.

[In million dollars]

Year	Pollution abatement operating costs	Air	Water	Solid waste	Nonmedia
1992	19.3	4.4	6.8	8.1	(D)
1991	8.7	(D)	3.3	(D)	(NA)
1990	8.0	1.7	2.8	3.5	(NA)
1989	5.3	1.3	2.2	1.8	(NA)
1988	10.2	(D)	4.5	(D)	(NA)

Source: U.S. Department of Commerce. Bureau of the Census. "Pollution Abatement Costs and Expenditures, 1992." In *National Economic, Social, and Environmental Data Bank* [CD-ROM]. Prepared by U.S. Department of Commerce, Economics and Statistics Administration. Washington, DC: U.S. Department of Commerce, National Economic, Social, and Environmental Data Bank, Economics and Statistics Administration, Office of Business Analysis, February 1995. *Notes:* Totals may not agree with detail because of independent rounding. "NA" represents "not available." "D" indicates data withheld to avoid disclosing operations of individual companies.

★ 778 ★

Pollution Abatement and Control, by State

Pollution Abatement Operating Costs in Ohio: 1988-1992

Pollution abatement concerns those activities with the primary purpose of protecting the environment by reducing or eliminating unwanted emissions or wastes that are created by the production process. Operating costs related to pollution abatement activities totaled $19,228 million in 1992. Of this amount, $17,466 million was attributable to a particular media: $5,395 million for air; $6,577 million for water; and $5,494 million for solid/contained waste. Spending for nonmedia and other was $1,762 million. Total population abatement media operating costs showed an overall increase of $158 million (1 percent) from 1991, the previous year. Air operating costs increased 9 percent; water operating costs increased 4 percent; solid/contained waste operating costs decreased 9 percent. The table below shows pollution abatement operating control costs for air, water, solid/contained waste, and nonmedia for Ohio.

[In million dollars]

Year	Pollution abatement operating costs	Air	Water	Solid waste	Nonmedia
1992	1,030.8	271.6	365.9	393.4	139.2
1991	1,031.9	271.0	373.3	387.6	(NA)
1990	1,115.4	283.8	415.0	416.6	(NA)
1989	984.0	280.0	362.3	341.7	(NA)
1988	946.7	255.1	376.5	315.0	(NA)

Source: U.S. Department of Commerce. Bureau of the Census. "Pollution Abatement Costs and Expenditures, 1992." In *National Economic, Social, and Environmental Data Bank* [CD-ROM]. Prepared by U.S. Department of Commerce, Economics and Statistics Administration. Washington, DC: U.S. Department of Commerce, National Economic, Social, and Environmental Data Bank, Economics and Statistics Administration, Office of Business Analysis, February 1995. *Notes:* Totals may not agree with detail because of independent rounding. "NA" represents "not available."

★ 779 ★

Pollution Abatement and Control, by State

Pollution Abatement Operating Costs in Oklahoma: 1988-1992

Pollution abatement concerns those activities with the primary purpose of protecting the environment by reducing or eliminating unwanted emissions or wastes that are created by the production process. Operating costs related to pollution abatement activities totaled $19,228 million in 1992. Of this amount, $17,466 million was attributable to a particular media: $5,395 million for air; $6,577 million for water; and $5,494 million for solid/contained waste. Spending for nonmedia and other was $1,762 million. Total population abatement media operating costs showed an overall increase of $158 million (1 percent) from 1991, the previous year. Air operating costs increased 9 percent; water operating costs increased 4 percent; solid/contained waste operating costs decreased 9 percent. The table below shows pollution abatement operating control costs for air, water, solid/contained waste, and nonmedia for Oklahoma.

[In million dollars]

Year	Pollution abatement operating costs	Air	Water	Solid waste	Nonmedia
1992	117.0	37.5	42.8	36.7	5.7
1991	110.0	31.8	40.6	37.6	(NA)
1990	84.8	22.8	33.0	29.0	(NA)
1989	82.7	18.6	30.0	34.1	(NA)
1988	88.2	18.9	36.5	32.8	(NA)

Source: U.S. Department of Commerce. Bureau of the Census. "Pollution Abatement Costs and Expenditures, 1992." In *National Economic, Social, and Environmental Data Bank* [CD-ROM]. Prepared by U.S. Department of Commerce, Economics and Statistics Administration. Washington, DC: U.S. Department of Commerce, National Economic, Social, and Environmental Data Bank, Economics and Statistics Administration, Office of Business Analysis, February 1995. *Notes:* Totals may not agree with detail because of independent rounding. "NA" represents "not available."

★ 780 ★

Pollution Abatement and Control, by State

Pollution Abatement Operating Costs in Oregon: 1988-1992

Pollution abatement concerns those activities with the primary purpose of protecting the environment by reducing or eliminating unwanted emissions or wastes that are created by the production process. Operating costs related to pollution abatement activities totaled $19,228 million in 1992. Of this amount, $17,466 million was attributable to a particular media: $5,395 million for air; $6,577 million for water; and $5,494 million for solid/contained waste. Spending for nonmedia and other was $1,762 million. Total population abatement media operating costs showed an overall increase of $158 million (1 percent) from 1991, the previous year. Air operating costs increased 9 percent; water operating costs increased 4 percent; solid/contained waste operating costs decreased 9 percent. The table below shows pollution abatement operating control costs for air, water, solid/contained waste, and nonmedia for Oregon.

[In million dollars]

Year	Pollution abatement operating costs	Air	Water	Solid waste	Nonmedia
1992	170.3	48.3	76.8	45.2	12.6
1991	200.4	53.5	70.4	76.5	(NA)
1990	159.4	47.5	55.1	56.8	(NA)
1989	141.9	49.5	47.3	45.1	(NA)
1988	181.1	47.4	61.6	72.1	(NA)

Source: U.S. Department of Commerce. Bureau of the Census. "Pollution Abatement Costs and Expenditures, 1992." In *National Economic, Social, and Environmental Data Bank* [CD-ROM]. Prepared by U.S. Department of Commerce, Economics and Statistics Administration. Washington, DC: U.S. Department of Commerce, National Economic, Social, and Environmental Data Bank, Economics and Statistics Administration, Office of Business Analysis, February 1995. *Notes:* Totals may not agree with detail because of independent rounding. "NA" represents "not available."

★ 781 ★

Pollution Abatement and Control, by State

Pollution Abatement Operating Costs in Pennsylvania: 1988-1992

Pollution abatement concerns those activities with the primary purpose of protecting the environment by reducing or eliminating unwanted emissions or wastes that are created by the production process. Operating costs related to pollution abatement activities totaled $19,228 million in 1992. Of this amount, $17,466 million was attributable to a particular media: $5,395 million for air; $6,577 million for water; and $5,494 million for solid/contained waste. Spending for nonmedia and other was $1,762 million. Total population abatement media operating costs showed an overall increase of $158 million (1 percent) from 1991, the previous year. Air operating costs increased 9 percent; water operating costs increased 4 percent; solid/contained waste operating costs decreased 9 percent. The table below shows pollution abatement operating control costs for air, water, solid/contained waste, and nonmedia for Pennsylvania.

[In million dollars]

Year	Pollution abatement operating costs	Air	Water	Solid waste	Nonmedia
1992	890.9	256.9	295.4	338.6	61.3
1991	867.6	175.8[1]	275.5	416.2	(NA)
1990	880.3	268.8	271.5	340.0	(NA)
1989	833.4	264.6	258.5	310.2	(NA)
1988	778.2	270.6	260.5	247.1	(NA)

Source: U.S. Department of Commerce. Bureau of the Census. "Pollution Abatement Costs and Expenditures, 1992." In *National Economic, Social, and Environmental Data Bank* [CD-ROM]. Prepared by U.S. Department of Commerce, Economics and Statistics Administration. Washington, DC: U.S. Department of Commerce, National Economic, Social, and Environmental Data Bank, Economics and Statistics Administration, Office of Business Analysis, February 1995. *Notes:* Totals may not agree with detail because of independent rounding. "NA" represents "not available." 1. Revised figure (by 5 percent or more).

★ 782 ★

Pollution Abatement and Control, by State

Pollution Abatement Operating Costs in Rhode Island: 1988-1992

Pollution abatement concerns those activities with the primary purpose of protecting the environment by reducing or eliminating unwanted emissions or wastes that are created by the production process. Operating costs related to pollution abatement activities totaled $19,228 million in 1992. Of this amount, $17,466 million was attributable to a particular media: $5,395 million for air; $6,577 million for water; and $5,494 million for solid/contained waste. Spending for nonmedia and other was $1,762 million. Total population abatement media operating costs showed an overall increase of $158 million (1 percent) from 1991, the previous year. Air operating costs increased 9 percent; water operating costs increased 4 percent; solid/contained waste operating costs decreased 9 percent. The table below shows pollution abatement operating control costs for air, water, solid/contained waste, and nonmedia for Rhode Island.

[In million dollars]

Year	Pollution abatement operating costs	Air	Water	Solid waste	Nonmedia
1992	31.0	5.9	12.1	13.0	2.8
1991	34.4	3.9	14.3	16.1	(NA)
1990	62.4	8.9	25.6	27.9	(NA)
1989	63.1	8.5	22.4	32.1	(NA)
1988	59.5	8.6	26.7	24.2	(NA)

Source: U.S. Department of Commerce. Bureau of the Census. "Pollution Abatement Costs and Expenditures, 1992." In *National Economic, Social, and Environmental Data Bank* [CD-ROM]. Prepared by U.S. Department of Commerce, Economics and Statistics Administration. Washington, DC: U.S. Department of Commerce, National Economic, Social, and Environmental Data Bank, Economics and Statistics Administration, Office of Business Analysis, February 1995. *Notes:* Totals may not agree with detail because of independent rounding. "NA" represents "not available."

★ 783 ★
Pollution Abatement and Control, by State

Pollution Abatement Operating Costs in South Carolina: 1988-1992

Pollution abatement concerns those activities with the primary purpose of protecting the environment by reducing or eliminating unwanted emissions or wastes that are created by the production process. Operating costs related to pollution abatement activities totaled $19,228 million in 1992. Of this amount, $17,466 million was attributable to a particular media: $5,395 million for air; $6,577 million for water; and $5,494 million for solid/contained waste. Spending for nonmedia and other was $1,762 million. Total population abatement media operating costs showed an overall increase of $158 million (1 percent) from 1991, the previous year. Air operating costs increased 9 percent; water operating costs increased 4 percent; solid/contained waste operating costs decreased 9 percent. The table below shows pollution abatement operating control costs for air, water, solid/contained waste, and nonmedia for South Carolina.

[In million dollars]

Year	Pollution abatement operating costs	Air	Water	Solid waste	Nonmedia
1992	360.1	104.1	140.7	115.3	19.1
1991	344.4	65.0	141.7	137.7	(NA)
1990	346.2	85.1	146.5	114.5	(NA)
1989	329.1	81.2	133.7	114.2	(NA)
1988	236.2	52.4	109.4	74.4	(NA)

Source: U.S. Department of Commerce. Bureau of the Census. "Pollution Abatement Costs and Expenditures, 1992." In *National Economic, Social, and Environmental Data Bank* [CD-ROM]. Prepared by U.S. Department of Commerce, Economics and Statistics Administration. Washington, DC: U.S. Department of Commerce, National Economic, Social, and Environmental Data Bank, Economics and Statistics Administration, Office of Business Analysis, February 1995. *Notes:* Totals may not agree with detail because of independent rounding. "NA" represents "not available."

★ 784 ★

Pollution Abatement and Control, by State

Pollution Abatement Operating Costs in South Dakota: 1988-1992

Pollution abatement concerns those activities with the primary purpose of protecting the environment by reducing or eliminating unwanted emissions or wastes that are created by the production process. Operating costs related to pollution abatement activities totaled $19,228 million in 1992. Of this amount, $17,466 million was attributable to a particular media: $5,395 million for air; $6,577 million for water; and $5,494 million for solid/contained waste. Spending for nonmedia and other was $1,762 million. Total population abatement media operating costs showed an overall increase of $158 million (1 percent) from 1991, the previous year. Air operating costs increased 9 percent; water operating costs increased 4 percent; solid/ contained waste operating costs decreased 9 percent. The table below shows pollution abatement operating control costs for air, water, solid/ contained waste, and nonmedia for South Dakota.

[In million dollars]

Year	Pollution abatement operating costs	Air	Water	Solid waste	Nonmedia
1992	16.5	2.9	6.3	7.3	(Z)
1991	9.0	1.0	4.8	3.1	(NA)
1990	6.4	0.1	3.5	2.8	(NA)
1989	4.9	0.2	2.3	2.5	(NA)
1988	8.7	4.0	2.9	1.8	(NA)

Source: U.S. Department of Commerce. Bureau of the Census. "Pollution Abatement Costs and Expenditures, 1992." In *National Economic, Social, and Environmental Data Bank* [CD-ROM]. Prepared by U.S. Department of Commerce, Economics and Statistics Administration. Washington, DC: U.S. Department of Commerce, National Economic, Social, and Environmental Data Bank, Economics and Statistics Administration, Office of Business Analysis, February 1995. *Notes:* Totals may not agree with detail because of independent rounding. "NA" represents "not available." "Z" denotes less than half the unit shown.

★ 785 ★
Pollution Abatement and Control, by State

Pollution Abatement Operating Costs in Tennessee: 1988-1992

Pollution abatement concerns those activities with the primary purpose of protecting the environment by reducing or eliminating unwanted emissions or wastes that are created by the production process. Operating costs related to pollution abatement activities totaled $19,228 million in 1992. Of this amount, $17,466 million was attributable to a particular media: $5,395 million for air; $6,577 million for water; and $5,494 million for solid/contained waste. Spending for nonmedia and other was $1,762 million. Total population abatement media operating costs showed an overall increase of $158 million (1 percent) from 1991, the previous year. Air operating costs increased 9 percent; water operating costs increased 4 percent; solid/contained waste operating costs decreased 9 percent. The table below shows pollution abatement operating control costs for air, water, solid/contained waste, and nonmedia for Tennessee.

[In million dollars]

Year	Pollution abatement operating costs	Air	Water	Solid waste	Nonmedia
1992	441.0	99.0	189.8	152.2	33.7
1991	420.8	92.1	183.5	145.2	(NA)
1990	398.6	91.4	179.9	127.4	(NA)
1989	353.0	82.6	153.5	116.9	(NA)
1988	356.0	95.2	149.7	111.0	(NA)

Source: U.S. Department of Commerce. Bureau of the Census. "Pollution Abatement Costs and Expenditures, 1992." In *National Economic, Social, and Environmental Data Bank* [CD-ROM]. Prepared by U.S. Department of Commerce, Economics and Statistics Administration. Washington, DC: U.S. Department of Commerce, National Economic, Social, and Environmental Data Bank, Economics and Statistics Administration, Office of Business Analysis, February 1995. *Notes:* Totals may not agree with detail because of independent rounding. "NA" represents "not available."

★ 786 ★

Pollution Abatement and Control, by State

Pollution Abatement Operating Costs in Texas: 1988-1992

Pollution abatement concerns those activities with the primary purpose of protecting the environment by reducing or eliminating unwanted emissions or wastes that are created by the production process. Operating costs related to pollution abatement activities totaled $19,228 million in 1992. Of this amount, $17,466 million was attributable to a particular media: $5,395 million for air; $6,577 million for water; and $5,494 million for solid/contained waste. Spending for nonmedia and other was $1,762 million. Total population abatement media operating costs showed an overall increase of $158 million (1 percent) from 1991, the previous year. Air operating costs increased 9 percent; water operating costs increased 4 percent; solid/contained waste operating costs decreased 9 percent. The table below shows pollution abatement operating control costs for air, water, solid/contained waste, and nonmedia for Texas.

[In million dollars]

Year	Pollution abatement operating costs	Air	Water	Solid waste	Nonmedia
1992	2,092.2	791.7	753.7	546.8	608.0
1991	2,054.6	739.5	695.3	619.8	(NA)
1990	1,888.0	709.7	606.4	571.9	(NA)
1989	1,584.7	603.3	553.6	427.8	(NA)
1988	1,474.8	594.9	541.5	338.4	(NA)

Source: U.S. Department of Commerce. Bureau of the Census. "Pollution Abatement Costs and Expenditures, 1992." In *National Economic, Social, and Environmental Data Bank* [CD-ROM]. Prepared by U.S. Department of Commerce, Economics and Statistics Administration. Washington, DC: U.S. Department of Commerce, National Economic, Social, and Environmental Data Bank, Economics and Statistics Administration, Office of Business Analysis, February 1995. *Notes:* Totals may not agree with detail because of independent rounding. "NA" represents "not available."

★ 787 ★

Pollution Abatement and Control, by State

Pollution Abatement Operating Costs in Utah: 1988-1992

Pollution abatement concerns those activities with the primary purpose of protecting the environment by reducing or eliminating unwanted emissions or wastes that are created by the production process. Operating costs related to pollution abatement activities totaled $19,228 million in 1992. Of this amount, $17,466 million was attributable to a particular media: $5,395 million for air; $6,577 million for water; and $5,494 million for solid/contained waste. Spending for nonmedia and other was $1,762 million. Total population abatement media operating costs showed an overall increase of $158 million (1 percent) from 1991, the previous year. Air operating costs increased 9 percent; water operating costs increased 4 percent; solid/contained waste operating costs decreased 9 percent. The table below shows pollution abatement operating control costs for air, water, solid/contained waste, and nonmedia for Utah.

[In million dollars]

Year	Pollution abatement operating costs	Air	Water	Solid waste	Nonmedia
1992	123.4	52.4	31.8	39.1	6.3
1991	90.7	45.4	18.1	27.1	(NA)
1990	94.7	29.0	17.8	48.0	(NA)
1989	82.7	29.6	20.7	32.4	(NA)
1988	48.7	18.7	15.6	14.5	(NA)

Source: U.S. Department of Commerce. Bureau of the Census. "Pollution Abatement Costs and Expenditures, 1992." In *National Economic, Social, and Environmental Data Bank* [CD-ROM]. Prepared by U.S. Department of Commerce, Economics and Statistics Administration. Washington, DC: U.S. Department of Commerce, National Economic, Social, and Environmental Data Bank, Economics and Statistics Administration, Office of Business Analysis, February 1995. *Notes:* Totals may not agree with detail because of independent rounding. "NA" represents "not available."

★ 788 ★

Pollution Abatement and Control, by State

Pollution Abatement Operating Costs in Vermont: 1988-1992

Pollution abatement concerns those activities with the primary purpose of protecting the environment by reducing or eliminating unwanted emissions or wastes that are created by the production process. Operating costs related to pollution abatement activities totaled $19,228 million in 1992. Of this amount, $17,466 million was attributable to a particular media: $5,395 million for air; $6,577 million for water; and $5,494 million for solid/contained waste. Spending for nonmedia and other was $1,762 million. Total population abatement media operating costs showed an overall increase of $158 million (1 percent) from 1991, the previous year. Air operating costs increased 9 percent; water operating costs increased 4 percent; solid/contained waste operating costs decreased 9 percent. The table below shows pollution abatement operating control costs for air, water, solid/contained waste, and nonmedia for Vermont.

[In million dollars]

Year	Pollution abatement operating costs	Air	Water	Solid waste	Nonmedia
1992	17.5	2.9	5.9	8.8	2.2
1991	14.7	1.5	6.0	7.2	(NA)
1990	16.6	5.2	4.8	6.7	(NA)
1989	13.8	5.3	3.8	4.7	(NA)
1988	17.3	3.0	7.3	7.1	(NA)

Source: U.S. Department of Commerce. Bureau of the Census. "Pollution Abatement Costs and Expenditures, 1992." In *National Economic, Social, and Environmental Data Bank* [CD-ROM]. Prepared by U.S. Department of Commerce, Economics and Statistics Administration. Washington, DC: U.S. Department of Commerce, National Economic, Social, and Environmental Data Bank, Economics and Statistics Administration, Office of Business Analysis, February 1995. *Notes:* Totals may not agree with detail because of independent rounding. "NA" represents "not available."

★ 789 ★

Pollution Abatement and Control, by State

Pollution Abatement Operating Costs in Virginia: 1988-1992

Pollution abatement concerns those activities with the primary purpose of protecting the environment by reducing or eliminating unwanted emissions or wastes that are created by the production process. Operating costs related to pollution abatement activities totaled $19,228 million in 1992. Of this amount, $17,466 million was attributable to a particular media: $5,395 million for air; $6,577 million for water; and $5,494 million for solid/contained waste. Spending for nonmedia and other was $1,762 million. Total population abatement media operating costs showed an overall increase of $158 million (1 percent) from 1991, the previous year. Air operating costs increased 9 percent; water operating costs increased 4 percent; solid/contained waste operating costs decreased 9 percent. The table below shows pollution abatement operating control costs for air, water, solid/contained waste, and nonmedia for Virginia.

[In million dollars]

Year	Pollution abatement operating costs	Air	Water	Solid waste	Nonmedia
1992	334.4	93.5	139.3	101.6	27.4
1991	271.1	69.3	115.0	86.7	(NA)
1990	271.9	68.8	119.3	83.7	(NA)
1989	259.8	59.4	119.2	81.2	(NA)
1988	268.4	76.6	111.7	80.1	(NA)

Source: U.S. Department of Commerce. Bureau of the Census. "Pollution Abatement Costs and Expenditures, 1992." In *National Economic, Social, and Environmental Data Bank* [CD-ROM]. Prepared by U.S. Department of Commerce, Economics and Statistics Administration. Washington, DC: U.S. Department of Commerce, National Economic, Social, and Environmental Data Bank, Economics and Statistics Administration, Office of Business Analysis, February 1995. *Notes:* Totals may not agree with detail because of independent rounding. "NA" represents "not available."

★ 790 ★

Pollution Abatement and Control, by State

Pollution Abatement Operating Costs in Washington: 1988-1992

Pollution abatement concerns those activities with the primary purpose of protecting the environment by reducing or eliminating unwanted emissions or wastes that are created by the production process. Operating costs related to pollution abatement activities totaled $19,228 million in 1992. Of this amount, $17,466 million was attributable to a particular media: $5,395 million for air; $6,577 million for water; and $5,494 million for solid/contained waste. Spending for nonmedia and other was $1,762 million. Total population abatement media operating costs showed an overall increase of $158 million (1 percent) from 1991, the previous year. Air operating costs increased 9 percent; water operating costs increased 4 percent; solid/contained waste operating costs decreased 9 percent. The table below shows pollution abatement operating control costs for air, water, solid/contained waste, and nonmedia for Washington.

[In million dollars]

Year	Pollution abatement operating costs	Air	Water	Solid waste	Nonmedia
1992	368.2	124.1	132.2	111.9	26.1
1991	387.0	113.4	136.0	137.6	(NA)
1990	374.4	102.8	150.2	121.4	(NA)
1989	328.3	106.2	134.1	88.0	(NA)
1988	313.6	107.0	129.5	77.0	(NA)

Source: U.S. Department of Commerce. Bureau of the Census. "Pollution Abatement Costs and Expenditures, 1992." In *National Economic, Social, and Environmental Data Bank* [CD-ROM]. Prepared by U.S. Department of Commerce, Economics and Statistics Administration. Washington, DC: U.S. Department of Commerce, National Economic, Social, and Environmental Data Bank, Economics and Statistics Administration, Office of Business Analysis, February 1995. *Notes:* Totals may not agree with detail because of independent rounding. "NA" represents "not available."

★ 791 ★
Pollution Abatement and Control, by State

Pollution Abatement Operating Costs in West Virginia: 1988-1992

Pollution abatement concerns those activities with the primary purpose of protecting the environment by reducing or eliminating unwanted emissions or wastes that are created by the production process. Operating costs related to pollution abatement activities totaled $19,228 million in 1992. Of this amount, $17,466 million was attributable to a particular media: $5,395 million for air; $6,577 million for water; and $5,494 million for solid/contained waste. Spending for nonmedia and other was $1,762 million. Total population abatement media operating costs showed an overall increase of $158 million (1 percent) from 1991, the previous year. Air operating costs increased 9 percent; water operating costs increased 4 percent; solid/contained waste operating costs decreased 9 percent. The table below shows pollution abatement operating control costs for air, water, solid/contained waste, and nonmedia for West Virginia.

[In million dollars]

Year	Pollution abatement operating costs	Air	Water	Solid waste	Nonmedia
1992	283.6	75.9	124.1	83.5	23.1
1991	328.0	78.6	118.7	130.7	(NA)
1990	208.9	49.7	94.1	65.1	(NA)
1989	190.6	41.1	89.3	60.3	(NA)
1988	137.5	34.6	64.8	38.1	(NA)

Source: U.S. Department of Commerce. Bureau of the Census. "Pollution Abatement Costs and Expenditures, 1992." In *National Economic, Social, and Environmental Data Bank* [CD-ROM]. Prepared by U.S. Department of Commerce, Economics and Statistics Administration. Washington, DC: U.S. Department of Commerce, National Economic, Social, and Environmental Data Bank, Economics and Statistics Administration, Office of Business Analysis, February 1995. *Notes:* Totals may not agree with detail because of independent rounding. "NA" represents "not available."

★ 792 ★

Pollution Abatement and Control, by State

Pollution Abatement Operating Costs in Wisconsin: 1988-1992

Pollution abatement concerns those activities with the primary purpose of protecting the environment by reducing or eliminating unwanted emissions or wastes that are created by the production process. Operating costs related to pollution abatement activities totaled $19,228 million in 1992. Of this amount, $17,466 million was attributable to a particular media: $5,395 million for air; $6,577 million for water; and $5,494 million for solid/contained waste. Spending for nonmedia and other was $1,762 million. Total population abatement media operating costs showed an overall increase of $158 million (1 percent) from 1991, the previous year. Air operating costs increased 9 percent; water operating costs increased 4 percent; solid/contained waste operating costs decreased 9 percent. The table below shows pollution abatement operating control costs for air, water, solid/contained waste, and nonmedia for Wisconsin.

[In million dollars]

Year	Pollution abatement operating costs	Air	Water	Solid waste	Nonmedia
1992	394.1	83.1	176.1	134.9	10.2
1991	354.0	84.7	142.8	126.5	(NA)
1990	348.4	75.9	150.0	122.5	(NA)
1989	343.8	68.9	146.3	128.5	(NA)
1988	301.4	51.2	146.6	103.7	(NA)

Source: U.S. Department of Commerce. Bureau of the Census. "Pollution Abatement Costs and Expenditures, 1992." In *National Economic, Social, and Environmental Data Bank* [CD-ROM]. Prepared by U.S. Department of Commerce, Economics and Statistics Administration. Washington, DC: U.S. Department of Commerce, National Economic, Social, and Environmental Data Bank, Economics and Statistics Administration, Office of Business Analysis, February 1995. *Notes:* Totals may not agree with detail because of independent rounding. "NA" represents "not available."

★ 793 ★

Pollution Abatement and Control, by State

Pollution Abatement Operating Costs in Wyoming: 1988-1992

Pollution abatement concerns those activities with the primary purpose of protecting the environment by reducing or eliminating unwanted emissions or wastes that are created by the production process. Operating costs related to pollution abatement activities totaled $19,228 million in 1992. Of this amount, $17,466 million was attributable to a particular media: $5,395 million for air; $6,577 million for water; and $5,494 million for solid/contained waste. Spending for nonmedia and other was $1,762 million. Total population abatement media operating costs showed an overall increase of $158 million (1 percent) from 1991, the previous year. Air operating costs increased 9 percent; water operating costs increased 4 percent; solid/contained waste operating costs decreased 9 percent. The table below shows pollution abatement operating control costs for air, water, solid/contained waste, and nonmedia for Wyoming.

[In million dollars]

Year	Pollution abatement operating costs	Air	Water	Solid waste	Nonmedia
1992	28.7	15.5	9.8	3.3	0.1
1991	19.9	6.2	7.0	6.7	(NA)
1990	18.5	4.3	(D)	(D)	(NA)
1989	12.9	5.5	4.2	3.2	(NA)
1988	31.2	25.4	3.4	2.5	(NA)

Source: U.S. Department of Commerce. Bureau of the Census. "Pollution Abatement Costs and Expenditures, 1992." In *National Economic, Social, and Environmental Data Bank* [CD-ROM]. Prepared by U.S. Department of Commerce, Economics and Statistics Administration. Washington, DC: U.S. Department of Commerce, National Economic, Social, and Environmental Data Bank, Economics and Statistics Administration, Office of Business Analysis, February 1995. *Notes:* Totals may not agree with detail because of independent rounding. "NA" represents "not available." "D" indicates data withheld to avoid disclosing operations of individual companies.

Taxes

★ 794 ★

Superfund Tax Liability for Insurers

The Clinton Administration and the House Ways and Means Committee suggested a system of taxes in 1994 to finance a proposed fund to reduce coverage litigation. The Environmental Insurance Resolution Fund would pay part of policyholders' cleanup costs if the policyholders agreed not to see their insurers. The table shows the insurers with the most exposure to the proposed tax. Data are based on insurers' shares of 1993 premiums in combined lines of coverage subject to prospective taxes.

[In percentages]

Insurer	Share
American International Group Inc.	7
Aetna Casualty & Surety Co.	3.8
Chubb Corp.	3.7
Continental Corp.	3.5

Source: Hofmann, Mark A. "Superfund's Tax Burden." *Business Insurance,* 5 September 1994, pp. 2, 42. Primary source: Standard & Poor's.

★ 795 ★

Taxes

Tax Expenditures for Environment-Related Functions: 1993-1996

Table shows tax expenditures for general science and energy items for years ending September 30, except as noted. Tax expenditures are defined as revenue losses attributable to provisions of the federal tax laws that allow a special exclusion, exemption, or deduction from gross income or that provide a special credit, a preferential rate of tax, or a deferral of liability. Represents tax expenditures of $1 billion or more in 1996.

[In million dollars]

Description	1993	1994	1995	1996
General science, space, and technology:				
Expensing of research and development expenditures[1]	2,060	2,230	2,390	2,560
Energy:				
Excess of percentage over cost depletion: Oil and gas	995	1,010	1,035	1,055
Alternative fuel production credit	760	900	970	1,000

Source: 1994 Statistical Abstract of the United States on CD-ROM [machine-readable datafiles]. CD-8A-94. Washington, DC: U.S. Department of Commerce, Economics and Statistics Administration, Bureau of the Census, Data User Services Division, January 1995. Primary source: U.S. Office of Management and Budget. *Budget of the United States Government* (annual). *Note:* 1. Normal Tax method.

Timber and Logging Products

★ 796 ★

Stumpage Prices, by Selected Species: 1980-1992

Table shows stumpage prices for selected species in current and constant dollars. Stumpage prices are based on sales of sawtimber from National Forests.

[In dollars per 1,000 board feet]

Species	1970	1975	1980	1985	1990	1991	1992
Current dollars							
Softwoods:							
Douglas-fir[1]	42	170	432	126	466	395	477
Southern pine[2]	44	57	155	91	127	166	198
Sugar pine[3]	39	99	667	110	285	241	492
Ponderosa pine[4]	32	71	206	101	252	238	292
Western hemlock[5]	21	69	213	51	203	164	165
Hardwoods:							
All eastern hardwoods[6]	27	34	52	65	146	160	167
Oak, white, red, and black[6]	27	30	66	95	188	164	211
Maple, sugar[7]	(NA)	42	70	70	135	121	145
Constant (1982) Dollars[8]							
Softwoods:							
Douglas-fir[1]	114	290	481	122	401	339	407
Southern pine[2]	120	98	173	88	109	143	169
Sugar pine[3]	104	170	742	106	245	207	419
Ponderosa pine[4]	87	122	230	98	217	204	249
Western hemlock[5]	56	118	237	49	175	141	140
Hardwoods:							
All eastern hardwoods[6]	73	58	58	63	126	137	142
Oak, white, red, and black[6]	72	51	73	92	162	140	180
Maple, sugar[7]	(NA)	72	78	68	116	104	123

Source: *1994 Statistical Abstract of the United States on CD-ROM* [machine-readable datafiles]. CD-8A-94. Washington, DC: U.S. Department of Commerce, Economics and Statistics Administration, Bureau of the Census, Data User Services Division, January 1995. Primary source: U.S. Forest Service. *U.S. Timber Production, Trade, Consumption, and Price Statistics* (annual). *Notes:* "NA" represents "not available." 1. Western Washington and western Oregon. 2. Southern region. 3. Pacific Southwest region (formerly California region). 4. Pacific Southwest region (formerly California region). Includes Jeffrey pine. 5. Pacific Northwest region. 6. Eastern and Southern regions. 7. Eastern region. 8. Deflated by the producer price index, all commodities.

★ 797 ★

Timber and Logging Products

Timber Product Producer Price Indexes: 1980-1992

Table shows Producer Price Indexes for selected timber products.

Product	Unit	1980	1985	1990	1991	1992
Lumber and wood products, except furniture	December 1984 = 100	(NA)	100.3	117.0	119.4	129.6
Logging camps and logging contractors	December 1981 = 100	(NA)	94.8	135.6	135.0	151.3
Sawmills and planing mills	December 1984 = 100	(NA)	99.7	113.7	115.3	131.1
Millwork, veneer, and plywood[1]	December 1984 = 100	(NA)	99.9	115.4	118.3	128.3
Softwood plywood	December 1980 = 100	91.4	90.0	102.5	103.5	124.2
Wood containers	June 1985 = 100	(NA)	(NA)	113.9	115.8	123.4
Wood buildings and mobile homes	December 1984 = 100	(NA)	100.6	115.5	118.9	121.4
Particleboard	December 1982 = 100	92.1	110.0	117.1	117.0	121.0
Paper and allied products	December 1984 = 100	(NA)	98.8	121.9	121.1	121.2
Pulp mills	December 1982 = 100	105.5	100.9	153.8	121.8	119.3
Paper mill products except building paper	June 1981 = 100	93.5	109.5	134.0	131.0	126.3
Paperboard mills	December 1982 = 100	97.3	112.0	146.0	140.7	142.8
Converted paper and paperboard products[2]	June 1985 = 100	(NA)	(NA)	111.3	112.9	114.1
Paperboard containers and boxes	December 1984 = 100	(NA)	98.4	117.7	116.6	118.6
Building paper and building board mills	December 1985 = 100	(NA)	(NA)	(NA)	(NA)	(NA)

Source: 1994 Statistical Abstract of the United States on CD-ROM [machine-readable datafiles]. CD-8A-94. Washington, DC: U.S. Department of Commerce, Economics and Statistics Administration, Bureau of the Census, Data User Services Division, January 1995. Primary source: U.S. Bureau of Labor Statistics. *Producer Price Indexes* (monthly). *Notes:* "NA" stands for "not available." 1. Includes structural wood members. 2. Excludes containers and boxes.

Wildlife and Habitat

★ 798 ★

Angler and Hunter Expenditures: 1991

Table shows the expenditures of anglers and hunters for equipment, trips, magazines, membership dues, contributions, land leasing and ownership, licenses, stamps, tags, and other items. Figures by type of fishing and hunting include only expenditures for trips and equipment. An angler or hunter is defined as anyone 16 years old or older who fished or hunted in 1991. Based on the 1991 National Survey of Fishing, Hunting, and Wildlife-Associated Recreation conducted for the U.S. Fish and Wildlife Service by the U.S. Bureau of the Census. See also related tables on anglers and hunters.

[In million dollars]

Type of fishing	Anglers' expenditures	Type of hunting	Hunters' expenditures
Total, all fishing	23,990	Total, all hunting	12,336
All freshwater fishing	15,149	Big game	5,090
Freshwater, except Great Lakes	13,812	Small game	1,550
Great Lakes	1,337	Migratory birds	686
Saltwater	4,992	Other animals	255

Source: *1994 Statistical Abstract of the United States on CD-ROM* [machine-readable datafiles]. CD-8A-94. Washington, DC: U.S. Department of Commerce, Economics and Statistics Administration, Bureau of the Census, Data User Services Division, January 1995. Primary source: U.S. Fish and Wildlife Service. *1991 National Survey of Fishing, Hunting, and Wildlife-Associated Recreation.*

★ 799 ★

Wildlife and Habitat

Sport Fishing and Hunting License Costs: 1970-1992

For fiscal years ending in year shown. Table shows the cost of sport fishing and hunting licenses to anglers and hunters. See also related tables on number of sport fishing and hunting licenses sold.

[In million dollars]

Item	1970	1975	1980	1985	1990	1991	1992
Cost to anglers	91	142	196	282	363	375	398
Cost to hunters	102	155	222	301	422	439	481

Source: *1994 Statistical Abstract of the United States on CD-ROM* [machine-readable datafiles]. CD-8A-94. Washington, DC: U.S. Department of Commerce, Economics and Statistics Administration, Bureau of the Census, Data User Services Division, January 1995. Primary source: U.S. Fish and Wildlife Service. *Federal Aid in Fish and Wildlife Restoration* (annual).

★ 800 ★

Wildlife and Habitat

Wildlife-Associated Recreation Expenditures : 1991

Table shows the expenditures of any person who fished or hunted for sport in 1991.

Type of expenditure	Expenditures (million dollars)				Expenditures per participant (dollars)			
	Total	Fishing	Hunting	Primary noncon-sumptive[1]	Total	Fishing	Hunting	Primary noncon-sumptive[1]
Total[2]	59,027[3]	23,990	12,336	18,104	543[3]	674	877	238
Food and lodging	11,202	4,953	1,824	4,425	103	139	130	58
Transportation	6,748	2,800	1,339	2,609	62	79	95	34
Other trip costs	4,820	4,094	278	448	44	115	20	6
Licenses, stamps, tags and permits	898	487	533	(NA)	22	14	38	(NA)
Special equipment	13,001[3]	5,006	1,250	3,506	120[3]	141	89	46
Equipment	12,727	3,740	3,283	5,704	123	105	233	75
Auxiliary equipment	2,157[3]	619	635	350	20[3]	17	45	5

Source: *1994 Statistical Abstract of the United States on CD-ROM* [machine-readable datafiles]. CD-8A-94. Washington, DC: U.S. Department of Commerce, Economics and Statistics Administration, Bureau of the Census, Data User Services Division, January 1995. Primary source: U.S. Fish and Wildlife Service. *1991 National Survey of Fishing, Hunting, and Wildlife-Associated Recreation. Notes:* "NA" indicates "not available." 1. Observing, photographing, and feeding wildlife. 2. Includes expenditures for magazines, membership dues and contributions, and land leasing and ownership, not shown separately. 3. Includes expenditures not specified by type of activity.

Chapter 10
MARKETS AND COMPANIES

This chapter offers data on environmental and related markets and companies. Tables show information for environmental goods and services, as well as for indirectly associated markets of products with direct impact on the environment—for example, aerosol production. In addition, other business-related issues are covered. Topics include employment and careers, environmental goods and services, industry profiles (featuring companies, earnings, and other information), markets, products, sales and revenue, trade, and transportation.

Much of the corporate information from the Toxic Release Inventory has been provided in the Toxic and Hazardous Substances chapter. Related data on the energy industry may be found in the Energy chapter.

Employment and Careers

★ 801 ★

Environmental Employers: 1994

Table shows the top ten preferred environmental employers as ranked by survey respondents in 1994. Data refer to the proportion of *ENR* readers responding to this survey item with a ranking of "first-," "second-," or "third-best" employer.

[In percentages]

Employer	Respondents
CH2M Hill Cos. Ltd.	18.0
Camp, Dresser & McKee, Inc.	8.2
Bechtel Group	4.7
RUST International Corporation	4.7
Black & Veatch International	3.4
U.S. Environmental Protection Agency	3.2
OHM Corporation	3.2
Fluor-Daniel, Inc.	3.1

[Continued]

★ 801 ★

Environmental Employers: 1994
[Continued]

Employer	Respondents
Woodward-Cycle	2.9
Morrison-Knudson	2.2

Source: "Top 10 Preferred Environmental Employers." *ENR*, 21 November 1994, p. EC5. Primary source: 1994 Environmental Career Survey Results.

★ 802 ★

Employment and Careers

Environmental Regulations and Job Loss: 1987-1990

A study conducted by the Economic Policy Institute suggests that layoffs and plant closures due to environmental regulations are small in number. The study goes on to indicate that environmental regulations actually have a positive effect on employment because "environmental protection requires the intensive use of labor or domestically produced materials in such projects as recycling and construction of sewage facilities" (p. 19). The table below compares impact of various causes of layoffs and job loss.

Reason	1987 Layoff events	1987 Job loss	1988 Layoff events	1988 Job loss	1989 Layoff events	1989 Job loss	1990 Layoff events	1990 Job loss
Automation	9	951	7	737	11	1,378	11	1,688
Bankruptcy	43	7,259	76	16,559	81	18,599	100	26,428
Business ownership change	88	30,955	92	18,973	82	19,147	78	16,989
Contract completion	147	27,696	178	50,822	225	50,971	201	40,167
Domestic relocation	49	10,877	68	12,816	68	1,138	114	18,512
Environment related[1]	4	511	4	388	5	1,304	4	390
Import competition	40	8,328	34	8,222	43	8,310	69	10,028
Labor-management dispute	43	12,592	26	2,824	47	40,387	NA	NA
Material shortages	11	1,872	20	2,169	24	4,318	20	5,859
Model changeover	17	16,441	21	7,186	17	9,089	15	3,039
Overseas relocation	30	4,963	10	1,225	6	1,189	13	3,122
Seasonal work	516	101,168	710	144,522	889	175,970	884	167,287
Slack work	535	94,071	450	69,764	661	102,607	943	142,038
Other (including reorganization)	240	51,207	229	51,744	255	46,778	284	97,474
Not reported	162	23,826	276	45,764	210	53,604	168	24,704
Total, all reasons[2]	2,020	406,887	2,322	450,300	2,764	572,570	3,078	586,690

Source: "Myth That Environmental Regulations Cause Job Loss Is Debunked." *C&EN*, 23 January 1995, p. 19. Primary source: U.S. Department of Labor. *Notes:* "NA" stands for "not available." 1. Includes environmental and safety-related shutdowns. 2. Employer reported.

★ 803 ★

Employment and Careers

Environment-Related Jobs – Salary Survey, by Industry Segment

Table shows average salaries for environmental jobs. Data was compiled from 225 responses of *Environmental Protection* readers.

[In dollars]

Item	Hazardous material	Air	Water	Environ-mental health and safety	Solid waste
Workplace					
Manufacturing	73,675	70,236	56,643	54,333	60,750
Utility	[1]	57,175	63,071	56,000	[1]
Government	51,388	21,582	55,719	49,413	39,160
Academia	[1]	95,000	36,000	41,666	[1]
Pollution Control	92,000	99,500	53,750	[1]	[1]
Other	67,628	65,717	64,211	53,995	49,500
Education					
High School	49,700	49,250	30,500	45,750	53,000
Bachelor's	61,985	64,599	73,686	41,381	48,750
Master's	65,206	62,380	63,943	57,913	43,773
Doctorate	103,000	98,333	66,850	50,250	[1]
Experience (in years)					
0-2	35,360	55,000	43,400	37,860	[1]
3-5	57,566	53,866	48,750	48,881	[1]
6-10	52,820	58,208	44,454	47,375	29,160
11-20	69,417	67,970	88,813	51,741	55,300
21 +	85,895	69,411	69,827	54,700	[1]
People Supervised					
0	14,592	58,016	56,595	50,373	43,580
1-5	81,671	60,756	58,908	51,315	61,500
6-10	58,340	67,248	60,833	74,200	[1]
11-20	86,750	105,606	59,725	42,900	53,000
21-50	80,000	70,525	39,000	100,000	56,000
51 +	[1]	[1]	[1]	100,000	[1]
Region					
Midwest	60,949	76,678	49,479	51,285	[1]
Northeast	64,159	60,928	100,275	47,206	53,000
South	71,125	62,943	63,783	43,025	47,460
West	63,995	61,605	53,075	61,000	46,000

[Continued]

★ 803 ★

Environment-Related Jobs – Salary Survey, by Industry Segment
[Continued]

Item	Hazardous material	Air	Water	Environ-mental health and safety	Solid waste
Gender					
Female	44,941	58,012	45,800	48,977	58,000
Male	69,120	66,541	59,181	53,755	46,970

Source: Neal, Lisa K. "Career Incentives." *Environmental Protection* (April 1994), p. 39. *Notes:* Midwest includes: Illinois, Indiana, Iowa, Kansas, Minnesota, Nebraska, North Dakota, Ohio, South Dakota, Wisconsin; Northeast includes: Connecticut, Delaware, Maine, Maryland, Massachusetts, New Hampshire, New Jersey, New York, Pennsylvania, Rhode Island, Vermont, West Virginia; South includes: Alabama, Arkansas, Florida, Georgia, Kentucky, Louisiana, Mississippi, Missouri, North Carolina, Oklahoma, Puerto Rico, South Carolina, Tennessee, Texas, Virginia; West includes: Alaska, Arizona, California, Colorado, Hawaii, Idaho, Minnesota, Montana, Nevada, Oregon, Utah, Washington, Wyoming. 1. Not applicable from responses.

★ 804 ★

Employment and Careers

Environment-Related Jobs – Salary Survey, by Occupation

Environmental attorney - 160,000
Government regulator - 80,000
Environmental engineer - 65,000
Lab or field technician - 36,000

Chart shows data from column 2.

Entry-level salaries for environmental management jobs average $33,100. Top-level salaries often exceed $78,000. The table below shows starting and senior salaries for selected environmental manager positions.

[In dollars]

Occupation	Salaries	
	Starting	Senior
Environmental attorney	45,000	160,000
Environmental engineer	30,500	65,000
Government regulator	20,000	80,000
Lab or field technician	21,000	36,000

Source: Kulfan, Ted. "Careers 2000: Environmental Manager." *Detroit News*, 20 March 1995, p. 13F.

Environmental Goods and Services

★ 805 ★

Environmental Service Needs of Waste Generators: 1995

According to the source: "These days, industrial waste generators are hiring more environmental service firms, but enjoying it less.... Differences between what owners want and what vendors deliver are widespread.... But efforts are under way to bridge the gaps and develop more lasting relationships " (p. 42). Table shows the demand for environmental services by 531 industrial waste generators. Data show areas identified as most critical.

[In percentages]

Environmental service	Need
Treatment/disposal	29
Clean air compliance	28
Remediation	10
Consulting	9
Wastewater treatment	6
Special waste handling	5
Compliance planning	5

Source: Rubin, Debra K. "Industrial Firms Seek Cleanup Help But Not Everyone Need Apply." *ENR*, 21 November 1994, p. 42. Primary source: BTI Consulting Group Inc.

★ 806 ★

Environmental Goods and Services

Environmental Small Businesses

Stiff competition exists among large federal contractors for small firms equipped to perform site remediation and other federal clean up work. According to the source: "Environmental work falls into a variety of Standard Industrial Classification (SIC) codes, but these set lower revenue ceilings that precluded many firms from small business eligibility" (p. 55). The table below shows current SIC codes and revenue ceilings.

[In million dollars]

Type of work	SIC code	Revenue ceiling
Heavy construction[1]	1629	17
Wrecking and demolition	1795	7
Special trade contractors[1]	1799	7
Local trucking without storage	4212	18.5
Refuse systems	4953	6
Sanitary services[1]	4959	5

[Continued]

★ 806 ★

Environmental Small Businesses
[Continued]

Type of work	SIC code	Revenue ceiling
Engineering services	8711	2.5
Commercial physical/biological research	8731	[2]
Testing laboratories	8734	5

Source: "Environmental Small Businesses, Where They Fit." *ENR,* 21 November 1994, p. 55. Primary source: U.S. Small Business Administration. *Notes:* 1. Covers firms not elsewhere classified. 2. Uses size ceiling of 500 employees.

Industries

★ 807 ★

Electric Utility Industry: 1970-1992

Table shows net generation, net summer capability, generating units, and consumption of fuels. Net generation for calendar years; other data as of December 31.

Item	Unit	1970	1975	1980	1985	1990	1991	1992
Net generation								
Total	Billion kWh	1,532	1,918	2,286	2,470	2,808	2,825	2,797
Average annual change[1]	Percent	7.3	4.5	3.5	0.4	0.9	0.6	-1.0
Net generation, kWh per kW of net summer capability[2]	Rate	4,560	3,904	3,951	3,770	4,064	4,076	4,024
Investor owned	Billion kWh	1,183	1,487	1,783	1,918	2,203	2,213	2,214
Percent of total utilities	Percent	77.2	77.5	78.0	77.7	78.4	78.4	79.2
Publicly owned	Billion kWh	349	431	503	552	606	610	582
Municipal	billion kWh	71	82	87	74	98	97	94
Federal	Billion kWh	186	221	235	233	235	241	225
Cooperatives and other	Billion kWh	91	128	182	245	273	272	263
Source of energy:								
Coal[3]	Percent	46.0	44.6	51.0	57.2	55.5	54.9	56.3
Nuclear	Percent	1.4	9.0	11.0	15.5	20.5	21.7	22.1
Oil	Percent	12.0	15.1	10.8	4.1	4.2	3.9	3.2
Gas	Percent	24.3	15.6	15.1	11.8	9.4	9.4	9.4
Hydro	Percent	16.2	15.6	12.1	11.4	10.0	9.8	8.6
Type of prime mover:[4]								
Hydro	Billion kWh	248	300	276	281	280	276	329
Steam conventional[5]	Billion kWh	1,240	1,414	1,726	1,778	1,919	1,905	1,906
Gas turbine and internal combustion	Billion kWh	22	28	28	16	22	22	21

[Continued]

★ 807 ★

Electric Utility Industry: 1970-1992
[Continued]

Item	Unit	1970	1975	1980	1985	1990	1991	1992
Steam nuclear	Billion kWh	22	173	251	384	577	613	619
Other	Billion kWh	1	3	6	11	11	10	10
Net summer capability								
Total[6]	Million kW	336	491	579	655	691	693	695
Average annual change[1]	Percent	7.2	7.6	3.3	0.6	0.9	0.3	0.3
Hydro	Million kW	64	78	82	89	91	92	93
Steam conventional[7]	Million kW	248	333	397	437	448	447	447
Gas turbine	Million kW	13	37	52	79	46	48	50
Steam nuclear	Million kW	7	37	52	79	100	100	99
Internal combustion	Million kW	4	5	5	5	5	5	5
Geothermal and other	Million kW	(Z)	1	1	2	2	2	2
Number of generating units								
Prime movers, total[8]	Number	9,717	(NA)	11,084	(NA)	10,296	10,260	10,221
Hydro	Number	3,108	(NA)	3,275	(NA)	3,479	3,476	3,497
Steam conventional	Number	2,813	(NA)	2,862	(NA)	2,354	2,284	2,307
Gas turbine	Number	658	(NA)	1,447	(NA)	1,460	1,485	1,501
Steam nuclear	Number	16	(NA)	74	(NA)	111	111	109
Internal combustion	Number	3,118	(NA)	3,410	(NA)	2,847	2,803	2,807
Consumption of fuels								
Net generation by fuel[9]	Billion kWh	1,284	1,618	2,010	2,189	2,525	(NA)	(NA)
Average annual change[1]	Percent	(NA)	3.2	2.1	4.3	0.2	(NA)	(NA)
Coal	Billion kWh	704	853	1,162	1,402	1,560	1,551	1,576
Percent of total	Percent	54.8	52.7	57.8	64.0	61.7	(NA)	(NA)
Petroleum	Billion kWh	184	289	246	100	117	111	89
Gas	Billion kWh	373	300	346	292	264	264	264
Nuclear	Billion kWh	22	173	251	384	577	613	619
Fuel consumed:								
Total energy equivalent	Quadrillion Btu	13.40	15.19	18.57	18.79	20.32	20.06	19.96
Coal	Million short tons	320	406	569	694	774	772	780
Oil	Million barrels	339	507	421	175	200	189	152
Gas	Billion cubic feet	3,932	3,158	3,682	3,044	2,787	2,789	2,765

Source: *1994 Statistical Abstract of the United States on CD-ROM* [machine-readable datafiles]. CD-8A-94. Washington, DC: U.S. Department of Commerce, Economics and Statistics Administration, Bureau of the Census, Data User Services Division, January 1995. Primary sources—1970: U.S. Federal Power Commission. *Electric Power Statistics* and press releases; thereafter: U.S. Energy Information Administration. 1975 and 1980—*Power Production, Fuel Consumption, and Installed Capacity Data* (annual) and unpublished data; thereafter: *Electric Power Annual, Annual Energy Review,* and unpublished data. Notes: "kWh" stands for kilowatt hours. "Btu" denotes British thermal units. "NA" represents "not available." "Z" denotes less that .5 million kilowatts. 1. Change from immediate prior year except for 1970, change from 1960. 2. Net summer capability is the steady hourly output that generating equipment is expected to supply to system load, exclusive of auxiliary power as demonstrated by test at the time of summer peak demand. 3. Includes small percentage (.5%) from wood and waste, geothermal, and and petroleum coke. 4. A prime mover is the engine, turbine, water wheel, or similar machine that drives an electric generator. 5. Fossil fuels only. 6. Includes wind, solar thermal, and photovoltaic, not shown separately. 7. Includes fossil steam, wood, and waste. 8. Each prime mover type in combination plants counted separately. Includes geothermal, wind, and solar, not shown separately. 9. Includes small amounts of wood, waste, wind, geothermal, solar thermal, and photovoltaic.

★ 808 ★

Industries

Energy Producing Companies: 1978-1992

Table shows selected financial and investment indicators for energy-producing companies. Based on data from major publicly owned domestic crude oil producing companies that either had at least one percent of domestic production or reserves of oil, natural gas, coal, or uranium, or at least one percent of refining capacity or petroleum product sales. There were 26 companies during 1978 through 1982; 25 in 1983; 22 during 1984 through 1987; and 23 in 1988 to 1992.

Item	1978	1980	1985	1990	1991	1992
Income statement (billion dollars)						
Operating revenues	294.8	518.6	492.5	510.4	469.3	472.8
Operating expenses	265.0	455.9	444.2	470.1	443.3	449.5
Operating income	29.8	62.7	48.3	40.2	26.0	23.3
Pretax income	30.2	66.9	43.6	37.5	25.1	22.5
Net income	13.9	31.0	17.4	21.6	14.7	1.8[1]
Funds from operations[2]	31.2	59.0	63.5	54.9	47.8	44.8
Balance sheet (billion dollars)						
Net property, plant, and equipment	138.1	188.9	297.7	302.5	305.5	309.7
Net investment in place[3]	148.1	202.6	315.4	319.7	325.6	331.5
Total assets	237.1	333.0	438.4	457.2	447.1	453.6
Ratios (percent)						
Net income to operating revenues	4.7	6.0	3.5	4.2	3.1	0.4
Net income to total assets	5.9	9.3	4.0	4.7	3.3	0.4
Net income to stockholders' equity	12.8	21.1	10.5	12.9	8.8	1.1
Long-term debt to stockholders' equity[4]	35.6	31.5	54.3	53.0	54.3	59.4
Long-term debt to total assets[4]	16.3	13.9	20.5	19.4	20.3	20.6

Source: *1994 Statistical Abstract of the United States on CD-ROM* [machine-readable datafiles]. CD-8A-94. Washington, DC: U.S. Department of Commerce, Economics and Statistics Administration, Bureau of the Census, Data User Services Division, January 1995. Primary source: U.S. Energy Information Administration. *Performance Profiles of Major Energy Producers* (annual). *Notes:* 1. The implementation of the new "Financial Accounting Standard No. 106" greatly reduced the reported profitability of large publicly traded corporations. Net income without these accounting changes would have been $12.5 billion. 2. The sum of net income, depreciation, depletion and amortization, deferred taxes, dry hole expenses, etc. 3. Composed of net property, plant and equipment plus investment and advances to unconsolidated subsidiaries. 4. Long-term debt includes amounts applicable to capitalized leases.

★ 809 ★

Industries

Major Investor-Owned Electric Utilities: 1982-1992

Table shows balance sheet data and income accounts of privately owned companies. Data are as of December 31. As of 1990, covers approximately 180 investor-owned electric utilities that during each of the last 3 years met any one or more of the following conditions: 1 million megawatthours of total sales; 100 megawatthours of sales for resale, 500 megawatthours of gross interchange out, and 500 megawatthours of wheeling for other.

[In billion dollars]

Item	1982	1984	1985	1986	1987	1988	1989	1990	1991	1992
Composite balance sheet										
Assets and other debits	315.0	375.6	404.7	426.1	446.3	454.3	465.7	477.9	487.5	506.4
Electric utility plant[1]	321.2	364.7	396.9	419.5	434.6	449.4	462.4	480.6	497.9	518.8
Depreciation and amortization	67.6	77.1	85.1	93.9	103.2	113.5	125.0	135.7	148.3	160.5
Net electric utility plant	253.6	287.5	311.8	325.6	331.4	335.9	337.5	344.9	349.6	358.3
Other utility plant	16.7	17.6	19.9	21.2	23.1	24.6	26.3	28.5	31.0	33.4
Depreciation and amortization	5.3	6.1	6.5	7.2	7.8	8.5	9.2	9.9	10.8	11.7
Net other utility plant	11.4	12.1	13.4	14.0	15.2	16.1	17.1	18.6	20.2	21.7
Total utility plant	337.9	395.3	431.1	455.9	475.7	493.0	507.9	528.7	548.4	571.9
Depreciation and amortization	72.9	88.0	97.4	107.7	118.7	131.3	144.6	157.4	171.7	185.1
Net total utility plant	265.0	307.3	333.8	348.2	357.0	361.6	363.2	371.3	376.8	386.9
Other property and investments	9.1	10.8	12.1	13.5	15.6	15.2	16.1	17.7	17.4	18.0
Current and accrued assets	31.7	37.9	39.4	38.4	40.9	39.1	41.5	41.5	43.4	43.4
Deferred debits	9.3	19.3	19.4	26.1	32.9	38.3	44.8	47.3	50.0	58.0
Liabilities and other credits[2]	315.0	375.3	404.7	426.1	446.3	454.3	465.7	477.9	487.5	506.4
Capital stock	70.3	79.0	82.8	81.6	79.9	80.7	82.9	83.2	83.6	86.1
Other paid-in capital	27.7	34.0	36.3	38.4	40.3	40.4	39.1	40.5	42.9	44.7
Retained earnings	27.9	37.1	41.1	46.0	48.0	47.1	47.7	48.1	49.0	49.7
Subsidiary earnings[3]	1.6	1.9	2.2	2.3	2.6	2.5	2.8	2.9	3.0	2.7
Long-term debt	124.0	140.6	152.7	157.2	158.4	160.7	162.9	167.9	171.9	174.1
Current and accrued liabilities	28.6	32.0	32.0	34.0	39.3	38.4	42.0	44.3	43.4	45.6
Deferred credits and operating reserves	15.1	19.0	20.9	22.4	25.6	28.1	28.5	28.8	29.2	31.1
Deferred income taxes[4]	19.4	28.1	32.7	39.6	45.9	50.2	53.3	56.5	59.2	65.0
Composite income accounts										
Electric operating revenues	109.3	128.3	135.3	136.3	138.5	143.9	150.9	157.3	166.8	169.5
Electric operating expenses	91.1	105.5	111.1	110.2	111.6	115.3	121.6	127.9	135.9	139.0
Net electric operating revenues	18.1	22.8	24.1	26.1	27.0	28.6	29.4	29.4	30.9	30.5
Other utility operating income	0.9	1.1	1.2	1.1	1.1	1.2	1.2	1.2	1.2	1.3
Total utility operating income	19.1	24.0	25.3	27.2	28.1	29.8	30.6	30.5	32.1	31.8
Other income	5.3	6.8	7.4	7.2	6.6	5.0	5.2	4.1	3.9	2.9
Total income	24.4	30.8	32.7	34.4	34.6	34.8	35.8	34.6	36.0	34.7

[Continued]

★ 809 ★

Major Investor-Owned Electric Utilities: 1982-1992
[Continued]

Item	1982	1984	1985	1986	1987	1988	1989	1990	1991	1992
Income deductions	9.4	11.1	14.0	14.0	15.6	18.8	18.5	17.7	18.1	16.3
Net income[5]	15.0	19.7	18.7	20.4	19.0	16.0	17.3	16.9	16.9	18.4

Source: 1994 Statistical Abstract of the United States on CD-ROM [machine-readable datafiles]. CD-8A-94. Washington, DC: U.S. Department of Commerce, Economics and Statistics Administration, Bureau of the Census, Data User Services Division, January 1995. Primary sources: U.S. Energy Information Administration. 1981-1984, Financial Statistics of Selected Electric Utilities (annual); thereafter, Financial Statistics of Major U.S. Investor-Owned Electric Utilities (annual). Notes: 1. Includes construction work in progress. 2. Includes contributions in aid of construction through 1970. 3. Unappropriated undistributed. 4. Cumulative. 5. Includes net extraordinary income.

★ 810 ★
Industries

Mineral Industries – Employment, Hours, and Earnings: 1985-1993

Item	Unit	1985	1986	1987	1988	1989	1990	1991	1992	1993
All mining:										
All employees	1,000	927	777	717	713	692	709	689	631	599
Production workers	1,000	658	545	511	512	493	509	489	445	423
Average weekly hours	Number	43.4	42.2	42.4	42.3	43.0	44.1	44.4	43.9	44.2
Average weekly earnings	Dollars	520	526	532	541	570	603	630	638	645
Coal mining:										
All employees	1,000	187	176	162	151	144	147	136	126	105
Production workers	1,000	153	144	132	123	116	119	110	102	84
Average weekly hours	Number	41.1	40.6	42.0	42.2	43.4	44.0	44.6	44.0	44.4
Average weekly earnings	Dollars	626	625	662	678	706	735	761	755	766
Oil and gas extraction:										
All employees	1,000	583	450	402	400	381	395	393	350	343
Production workers	1,000	387	287	261	265	248	261	258	226	224
Average weekly hours	Number	44.2	42.6	41.7	41.3	42.0	43.9	44.5	43.8	43.8
Average weekly earnings	Dollars	489	495	481	489	525	568	602	614	619
Metal mining:										
All employees	1,000	46	41	44	50	56	58	56	53	51
Production workers	1,000	34	31	33	39	44	46	44	42	41
Average weekly hours	Number	40.9	41.1	41.9	42.3	42.8	42.8	43.0	42.9	43.1
Average weekly earnings	Dollars	547	542	542	560	581	601	639	655	660
Nonmetallic minerals, except fuels:										
All employees	1,000	110	110	110	112	111	110	105	102	100
Production workers	1,000	84	83	85	85	85	83	78	76	75
Average weekly hours	Number	44.5	44.5	45.4	45.5	45.6	45.3	44.5	44.9	46.1
Average weekly earnings	Dollars	453	462	481	498	513	525	531	551	585

Source: 1994 Statistical Abstract of the United States on CD-ROM [machine-readable datafiles]. CD-8A-94. Washington, DC: U.S. Department of Commerce, Economics and Statistics Administration, Bureau of the Census, Data User Services Division, January 1995. Primary sources: U.S. Bureau of Labor Statistics. Bulletin 2370; Employment and Earnings (March and June issues).

★ 811 ★

Industries

Mineral Industry Lost Workday Injuries and Fatalities: 1980-1992

Excludes office workers. Lost workday injuries are nonfatal occurrences that result in days away from work, days of restricted work activity or a permanent disability. Data for all years include injuries to independent contractors at mine sites. Rates for the noncoal industries are based only on employment and hours worked by mine employees.

Item	Coal Mining				Quarrying & related industries[1]				Metal & nonmetal mining[2]			
	1980	1985	1990	1992	1980	1985	1990	1992	1980	1985	1990	1992
Injuries, total	18,689	9,073	12,226	9,256	3,509	2,545	3,794	2,964	6,877	2,212	3,778	2,847
Fatal	133	68	66	54	42	26	18	18	46	22	26	16
Rate per million work hours:												
Fatal	0.31	0.20	0.22	0.21	0.26	0.19	0.13	0.14	0.18	0.17	0.17	0.11
Nonfatal	43.1	26.6	41.4	35.8	21.4	18.5	28.1	23.7	27.7	16.8	24.5	19.8
Fatalities per 1,000 employed[3]	0.55	0.36	0.41	0.38	0.48	0.37	0.27	0.28	0.34	0.31	0.34	0.22

Source: 1994 Statistical Abstract of the United States on CD-ROM [machine-readable datafiles]. CD-8A-94. Washington, DC: U.S. Department of Commerce, Economics and Statistics Administration Bureau of the Census, Data User Services Division, January 1995. Primary source: U.S. Mine Safety and Health Administration (Denver, CO). Unpublished data. *Notes:* 1. Includes cement. 2. Nonmetal mines exclude extraction of Frasch process sulfur. 3. Average number of persons at work each day mines were active.

★ 812 ★

Industries

Mining Gross Domestic Product: 1977-1991

For 1947-1986, based on 1972 Standard Industrial Classification (SIC); for 1987, estimates are shown first based on the 1972 SIC and then on the 1987 SIC. Estimates thereafter based on 1987 SIC.

[In million dollars, except percentages]

Mining industry	1977	1980	1985	1990	1991
Current dollars, total	54.1	112.6	130.6	103.1	91.8
Metal mining	2.2	4.4	2.5	6.2	5.7
Coal mining	10.3	13.6	13.8	12.7	12.2
Oil and gas extraction	38.0	89.1	108.4	76.9	66.7
Nonmetallic minerals, excluding fuels	3.6	5.5	5.9	7.2	7.2
Constant (1987) dollars, total	83.5	85.0	71.9	91.8	79.9
Metal mining	1.7	1.5	1.6	6.6	1.6
Coal mining	9.5	8.9	8.5	15.3	10.1
Oil and gas extraction	65.7	67.1	54.7	62.9	61.8
Nonmetallic minerals, exc. fuels	6.7	7.5	7.0	7.0	6.4

Source: 1994 Statistical Abstract of the United States on CD-ROM [machine-readable datafiles]. CD-8A-94. Washington, DC: U.S. Department of Commerce, Economics and Statistics Administration, Bureau of the Census, Data User Services Division, January 1995. Primary source: U.S. Bureau of Economic Analysis. *Survey of Current Business* (May and November 1993).

★ 813 ★

Industries

Petroleum and Coal Product Corporations: 1975-1992

Table shows sales, net profits, and profit per dollar of sales for petroleum and coal products corporations. Data represent Standard Industrial Classification (SIC) group 29. Profit rates are averages of quarterly figures at annual rates. Beginning 1986, excludes estimates for corporations with less than $250,000 in assets.

Item	Unit	1975	1980	1985	1990	1991	1992
Sales	Billion dollars	121.8	333.2	320.9	318.5	282.2	278.0
Net profit:							
Before income taxes	Billion dollars	13.3	39.1	17.7	23.3	12.2	2.0
After income taxes	Billion dollars	9.3	25.5	12.7	18.0	10.9	3.2
Depreciation[1]	Billion dollars	5.6	11.6	22.1	18.6	18.0	18.3
Profits per dollar of sales:							
Before income taxes	Cents	10.9	11.7	5.5	7.4	4.3	0.4
After income taxes	Cents	7.6	7.7	4.0	5.7	3.9	0.9
Profits on stockholders' equity:							
Before income taxes	Percent	17.9	30.7	11.7	16.6	8.6	1.5
After income taxes	Percent	12.5	20.0	8.5	12.8	7.7	2.4

Source: 1994 Statistical Abstract of the United States on CD-ROM [machine-readable datafiles]. CD-8A-94. Washington, DC: U.S. Department of Commerce, Economics and Statistics Administration, Bureau of the Census, Data User Services Division, January 1995. Primary sources—through 1981: U.S. Federal Trade Commission; beginning 1982: U.S. Bureau of the Census. *Quarterly Financial Report for Manufacturing, Mining, and Trade Corporations. Notes:* 1. Includes depletion and accelerated amortization of emergency facilities.

★ 814 ★

Industries

Petroleum Industry: 1970-1992

Item	Unit	1970	1975	1980	1985	1990	1991	1992
Crude oil producing wells[1]	1,000	531	500	548	647	602	614	594
Daily output per well	Barrels	18.0	16.8	15.9	13.9	12.2	12.1	12.0
Completed wells drilled, total	1,000	28	39	70	70	30	25	19
Crude oil	1,000	13	17	32	35	12	11	8
Gas	1,000	4	8	17	14	10	9	7
Dry	1,000	11	14	20	21	8	5	4
Crude oil production, total	Million barrels	3,517	3,057	3,146	3,275	2,685	2,707	2,625
Value at wells	Billion dollars	11.2	23.5	67.9	78.9	53.7	44.7	41.8
Average price per barrel	Dollars	3.18	7.67	21.59	24.09	20.03	16.54	15.98
Refinery input of crude oil	Million barrels	3,968	4,541	4,934	4,381	4,895	4,855	4,909
Imports: Crude oil	Million barrels	483	1,498	1,926	1,168	2,151	2,111	2,223
Refined petroleum products	Million barrels	765	712	603	681	775	500	471
Import value	Million dollars	2,740	25,060	74,440	50,370	60,680	50,070	50,530
Crude	Billion dollars	1.26	18.29	61.90	32.90	43.78	36.90	38.54

[Continued]

★ 814 ★
Petroleum Industry: 1970-1992
[Continued]

Item	Unit	1970	1975	1980	1985	1990	1991	1992
Petroleum products	Billion dollars	1.48	6.77	12.54	17.47	16.90	13.17	11.99
Export value	Million dollars	520	1,007	2,870	5,130	4,370	4,680	4,280
Crude	Billion dollars	0.02	(Z)	0.75	0.23	0.14	0.03	0.03
Petroleum products	Billion dollars	0.50	1.01	2.12	4.90	4.23	4.65	4.25
Operable refineries	Number	276	279	319	223	205	202	199
Capacity[2]	Million barrels	4,388	5,461	6,584	5,716	5,683	5,723	5,731
Output	Million barrels	4,421	4,995	5,352	5,019	5,570	5,933	6,050
Utilization rate	Percent	92.6	85.5	75.4	77.6	87.1	86.0	86.6
Proved reserves	Billion barrels	39.0	32.7	29.8	28.4	26.3	24.7	23.7

Source: 1994 Statistical Abstract of the United States on CD-ROM [machine-readable datafiles]. CD-8A-94. Washington, DC: U.S. Department of Commerce, Economics and Statistics Administration, Bureau of the Census, Data User Services Division, January 1995. Primary sources: U.S. Energy Information Administration. *Annual Energy Review, Petroleum Supply Annual; U.S. Crude Oil, Natural Gas,* and *Natural Gas Liquids Reserves. Notes:* "Z" stands for "not available." 1. December 31. 2. January 1.

★ 815 ★
Industries
Timber-Based Industries: 1990 and 1991

Data based on *1987 Standard Industrial Classification Manual*, published by the Office of Management and Budget.

Industry	SIC[1] code	1990 All employees Number (1,000)	1990 All employees Paroll (million dollars)	1990 Value of shipments (billion dollars)	1991 All employees Number (1,000)	1991 All employees Payroll (million dollars)	1991 Value of shipments (billion dollars)
Logging and sawmills	241/242	254.2	5,076	32.2	207.6	4,307	28.9
Logging	2411	83.4	1,647	12.2	78.1	1,561	11.4
Sawmills/planing mills, gen.	2421	138.9	2,913	17.9	129.5	2,747	17.5
Hardwood dimension and flooring mills	2426	29.3	475	1.8	26.1	462	1.7
Special product sawmills, n.e.c	2429	2.5	41	0.2	2.0	36	0.2
Millwork and veneer[2]	243	229.4	4,823	23.2	209.9	4,487	21.4
Millwork	2431	90.5	1,961	9.5	84.9	1,836	9.0
Wood kitchen cabinets	2434	62.8	1,217	4.6	57.1	1,139	4.2
Hardwood veneer and plywood	2435	18.7	335	2.1	17.3	320	1.9
Softwood veneer and plywood	2436	35.6	881	5.0	31.7	810	4.6
Structural wood members, n.e.c.	2439	21.8	429	2.0	18.9	382	1.8
Wood containers	244	41.5	636	2.9	39.8	634	2.9
Nailed and lock corner wood boxes and shook	2441	6.0	98	0.4	6.2	100	0.4
Wood pallets and skids	2448	28.3	417	1.9	27.1	413	2.0
Wood containers, n.e.c	2449	7.2	122	0.5	6.5	120	0.4
Wood buildings and mobile homes	245	61.4	1,217	6.5	54.1	1,106	6.0

[Continued]

★ 815 ★

Timber-Based Industries: 1990 and 1991
[Continued]

Industry	SIC[1] code	1990 All employees Number (1,000)	1990 All employees Paroll (million dollars)	1990 Value of shipments (billion dollars)	1991 All employees Number (1,000)	1991 All employees Payroll (million dollars)	1991 Value of shipments (billion dollars)
Mobile homes	2451	38.8	769	4.2	35.1	714	3.9
Prefab. wood bldgs/components	2452	22.6	448	2.3	19.0	392	2.0
Miscellaneous wood products	249	96.4	1,745	9.6	90.9	1,706	9.5
Wood preserving	2491	13.0	246	2.6	11.7	233	2.6
Reconstituted wood products	2493	22.3	554	3.0	21.0	537	3.0
Wood products, n.e.c	2499	61.1	945	3.9	58.1	936	3.8
Pulp mills	261	16.1	668	6.2	16.8	697	5.3
Paper mills	262	130.1	5,062	35.3	130.3	5,224	33.3
Paperboard mills	263	53.1	2,049	15.9	50.6	2,027	15.0
Paperboard containers and boxes	265	200.3	5,245	30.5	198.6	5,392	30.6
Setup paperboard boxes	2652	8.8	146	0.6	8.7	150	0.6
Corrugated and solid fiber boxes	2653	110.1	2,984	18.6	108.7	3,047	18.0
Fiber cans, tubes, drums, and similar prod.	2655	13.3	341	1.9	12.9	341	1.9
Sanitary food containers, except folding	2656	17.5	392	2.5	17.6	411	2.7
Folding paperboard boxes, including sanitary	2657	50.7	1,382	7.0	50.7	1,443	7.4
Converted paper and paperboard products[3]	267	228.5	5,923	43.5	224.3	6,043	44.6
Packaging paper and plastic film	2671	16.4	489	3.0	15.4	492	3.1
Coated and laminated paper, n.e.c	2672	35.0	985	7.1	34.2	992	7.4
Plastics, foil, and coated paper bags	2673	37.4	870	5.5	35.4	875	5.1
Uncoated paper and multiwall bags	2674	16.9	374	2.8	17.9	398	2.7
Die-cut paper and paperboard and cardboard	2675	16.8	395	2.1	17.0	408	2.3
Sanitary paper products	2676	39.0	1,299	14.7	38.8	1,343	15.6
Envelopes	2677	26.1	648	2.8	24.5	616	2.7
Stationery, tablets, and related products	2678	10.1	203	1.3	10.1	209	1.4
Converted paper and paperboard products, n.e.c	2679	30.7	659	4.1	30.9	711	4.3

Source: 1994 Statistical Abstract of the United States on CD-ROM [machine-readable datafiles]. CD-8A-94. Washington, DC: U.S. Department of Commerce, Economics and Statistics Administration, Bureau of the Census, Data User Services Division, January 1995. Primary sources: U.S. Bureau of the Census. *Census of Manufactures: 1987 Final Industry Series.* MC87-1-24A-D and MC87-1-26A-C; *Annual Survey of Manufactures. Notes:* "n.e.c." stands for "not elsewhere classified." 1. Standard Industrial Classification code. 2. Includes plywood and structural members. 3. Except containers and boxes.

★ 816 ★

Industries

Timber-Based Industries – Employment and Earnings: 1970-1992

Data for production workers. Table shows employment and average hourly earnings in timber-based industries.

Item	SIC[1] code	Employees (1,000)						Earnings (dollars)					
		1970	1980	1985	1990	1991	1992	1970	1980	1985	1990	1991	199
Lumber and wood products[2]	24	564	587	593	605	556	563	2.97	6.57	8.25	9.08	9.24	9.4
Logging	241	(NA)	71	67	70	64	76	(NA)	8.64	10.92	11.22	11.08	11.
Sawmills and planing mills	242	196	190	172	173	160	182	2.84	6.70	8.52	9.22	9.37	9.6
Millwork, plywood, and structural members	243	(NA)	170	195	211	189	245	(NA)	6.44	8.09	9.04	9.27	9.4
Paper and allied products	26	540	519	509	524	518	688	3.44	7.84	10.83	12.31	12.73	13.
Furniture and fixtures	25	362	376	394	401	371	465	2.77	5.49	7.17	8.76	8.76	9.0

Source: 1994 Statistical Abstract of the United States on CD-ROM [machine-readable datafiles]. CD-8A-94. Washington, DC: U.S. Department of Commerce, Economics and Statistics Administration, Bureau of the Census, Data User Services Division, January 1995. Primary sources: U.S. Bureau of Labor Statistics. *Supplement to Employment and Earnings* (July 1991). Bulletin 2370; and *Employment and Earnings* (monthly). *Notes:* 1. 1987 Standard Industrial Classification. 2. Includes other industries, not shown separately.

★ 817 ★

Industries

Uranium Concentrate (U_3O_8) Industry: 1975-1992

Middle demand case.

Item	Unit	1975	1980	1985	1990	1991	1992
Production	1,000 short tons	11.6	21.9	5.6	4.4	4.0	2.8
Net imports (U_3O_8)	1,000 short tons	0.2	-1.1	3.2	12.1	9.80	12.3
Utility and suppliers inventories (U_3O_8 equivalent)	1,000 short tons	(NA)	54.4	68.3[1]	45.6	36.70	(NA)
Price (1988 dollars/pound U_3O_8):							
Long-term contract price	Dollars	36.50	41.4	24.7	(NA)	(NA)	(NA)
Spot market price	Dollars	40.80	45.0	17.0	(NA)	(NA)	(NA)
Delivered price	Dollars	18.10	39.9	33.6[2]	(NA)	(NA)	(NA)
Capital expenditures (1988 dollars)	Million dollars	461	1,107	37	(NA)	(NA)	(NA)
Employment	1,000	9.7	19.9	2.4	1.3	1.0	0.7

Source: 1994 Statistical Abstract of the United States on CD-ROM [machine-readable datafiles]. CD-8A-94. Washington, DC: U.S. Department of Commerce, Economics and Statistics Administration, Bureau of the Census, Data User Services Division, January 1995. Primary sources: U.S. Department of Energy. *Domestic Uranium Mining and Milling Industry* (annual) and *Uranium Industry Annual.* DOE/EIA-0478 (92). *Notes:* "NA" stands for "not available." 1. Includes natural U_3O_8 (uranium oxide), natural UF_6 (uranium hexafluoride), natural UF_6 under usage agreement, UF_6 at enrichment suppliers, enriched UF_6 and fabricated fuel. 2. Average U.S. contract prices and market price settlements.

Markets

★ 818 ★

Coal Market: 1993

Table shows the top ten markets for coal in 1993.

Country	Tonnage (thousands of tons)	Value ($000)
Japan	11,895	484,299
Canada	8,531	287,307
Italy	6,925	307,031
Netherlands	5,562	245,964
Belgium/Luxembourg	5,228	226,018
Brazil	5,191	227,556
United Kingdom	4,110	188,811
Spain	4,061	167,448
France	3,972	167,772
Taiwan	3,435	135,672
Other nations	15,136	617,640
Total	74,044	3,055,520

Source: "Predictions for Coal Included Increases in 1994." *Energy* (June 1994), p. 15.

★ 819 ★

Markets

Compost Market – Dollars

Total potential - 18.6	
Bagged/retail - 8.0	
Field nurseries - 4.0	
Delivered topsoil - 3.7	
Landscapers - 2.0	
Container nurseries - 0.9	

Table shows potential dollar market for compost.

[In millions]

Sector	Cubic yards
Landscapers	2.0
Delivered topsoil	3.7
Bagged/retail	8.0
Container nurseries	0.9
Field nurseries	4.0
Total potential	18.6

Source: "Potential Dollar Market for Compost." *World Wastes* (April 1994), p. CS14. Primary source: The Composting Council.

★ 820 ★

Markets

Compost Market – Penetration

Table shows current penetration of the compost market.

[In millions]

Sector	Cubic yards
Landscapers	<20
Delivered topsoil	<5
Bagged/retail	80
Landfill final cover	<5
Surface mine reclamation	<5
Container nurseries	<50
Field nurseries	<1
Sod production	<1
Silviculture	<1

[Continued]

★ 820 ★

Compost Market – Penetration
[Continued]

Sector	Cubic yards
Agriculture	<1
Total potential	<2

Source: "Current Penetration of Compost Market." *World Wastes* (April 1994), p. CS14. Primary source: The Composting Council.

★ 821 ★
Markets

Compost Market – Volume

Total potential - 1,019.8

Agriculture - 895.0

Silviculture - 104.0

Sod production - 20.0

Landfill final cover - 0.6

Surface mine reclamation - 0.2

Table shows potential volume market for compost.

[In millions]

Sector	Cubic yards
Landfill final cover	0.6
Surface mine reclamation	0.2
Sod production	20.0
Silviculture	104.0
Agriculture	895.0
Total potential	1,019.8

Source: "Potential Volume Market for Compost." *World Wastes* (April 1994), p. CS14. Primary source: The Composting Council.

★ 822 ★

Markets

Environmental Consumer Products Market: 1992

| Cleaning products - 4,500 |
| Health and beauty products - 4,300 |
| Sporting goods and toys - 2,100 |
| Stationery and school supplies - 880 |
| Wheel goods - 228 |

Chart shows data from column 1.

The table below shows 1992 sales estimates for "environmentally friendly" consumer products.

[Sales in million dollars]

Product category	"Green" sales	Percent of total
Cleaning products	4,500	15
Health and beauty products	4,300	11
Sporting goods and toys[1]	2,100	6
Stationery and school supplies	880	15
Wheel goods	228	1

Source: "Market for Environmental Products Is Growing." *Hardware Age* (June 1993), p. 36. Primary source: *Green MarketAlert*, environmental business newsletter (Bethlehem, Connecticut; 1993). *Note:* 1. Nondurable.

★ 823 ★
Markets

Environmental Goods and Services Market

Water/wastewater - 60	
Services - 48	
Waste management - 40	
Air quality control - 30	
Other - 22	

Chart shows data from column 1.

The market for environmental goods and services is global. Canada, Mexico, Brazil, Chile, Asia, and the Pacific Rim have rapidly growing markets. Germany, the United States, and Japan are large exporters of environmental goods and services. According to the source: "Many environmental technology ventures are characterized by growing international interdependence. Companies may license technologies in other countries and own overseas subsidiaries. They may contract locally in the host country for installation materials and assembly while conducting the engineering design at home" (p. 24). The table below shows market revenues and shares for various types of environmental goods and services.

Environmental goods and services	Market revenues (billion dollars)	Market shares (percent)
Water/wastewater	60	30
Services	48	24
Waste management	40	20
Air quality control	30	15
Other	22	11

Source: "What Environmental Goods and Services Sell." *State Government News* (March 1995), p. 24. Primary source: Organization for Economic Cooperation and Development.

★ 824 ★

Markets

Environmental Market in Western Europe: 1990-1995

Table shows the value of environmental market sectors in Western Europe.

[In billion dollars, except as noted]

Market sector	1990	1991	1995	Growth (percent)
Air pollution control	9.6	10.3	12.8	4.3
Waste/wastewater	12.8	13.8	21.3	9.1
Contaminated land	1.0	1.1	2.3	16.1
Waste management	20.9	22.5	28.0	4.5
Total	44.3	47.7	64.4	8.5

Source: "Dirt Busters." Chemistry and Industry, 6 June 1994, p. 398. Primary source: Ecotec.

★ 825 ★

Markets

Environmental Technology Markets: 1990 and 2000

Environmental technology includes those goods and services that reduce or prevent environmental damage. The market for environmental technology is global—and growing. The table below shows environmental technology markets in selected countries.

[In billion dollars, except as noted]

Country	1990	2000	Growth (percent)
North America	84.0	125.0	5.4
Canada	7.0	12.0	7.9
United States	78.0	113.0	5.0
Europe	54.0	78.0	4.9
Asia Pacific	26.2	42.0	6.2
Australia	2.0	2.8	4.4
Austria	1.3	1.8	4.3
Belgium	1.4	2.3	6.4
Denmark	1.0	1.2	2.2
Finland	1.0	1.3	3.3
France	10.0	15.0	5.5
Germany	17.0	23.0	4.0
Greece	0.3	0.5	7.4
Ireland	0.3	0.5	6.5
Italy	5.0	7.7	6.0
Japan	24.0	39.0	6.7
Netherlands	2.7	3.7	4.1
New Zealand	0.2	0.3	5.5
Norway	0.7	1.0	4.4

[Continued]

★ 825 ★

Environmental Technology Markets: 1990 and 2000
[Continued]

Country	1990	2000	Growth (percent)
Portugal	0.4	0.7	8.3
Spain	1.8	3.0	7.4
Sweden	1.5	2.0	3.7
Switzerland	1.9	2.5	3.5
United Kingdom	7.0	11.0	6.3
Organization for Economic Cooperation and Development	164.0	245.0	5.5
Non-Organization for Economic Cooperation and Development	36.0	55.0	5.9
Eastern Europe/Commonwealth of Independent States	15.0	21.0	4.0
Other	21.0	34.0	6.8
Total	200.0	300.0	5.5

Source: "Dirt Busters." *Chemistry and Industry*, 6 June 1994, p. 398. Primary source: Organization for Economic Cooperation and Development.

★ 826 ★

Markets

Farm Fertilizer Market, by Crop: 1993-1994

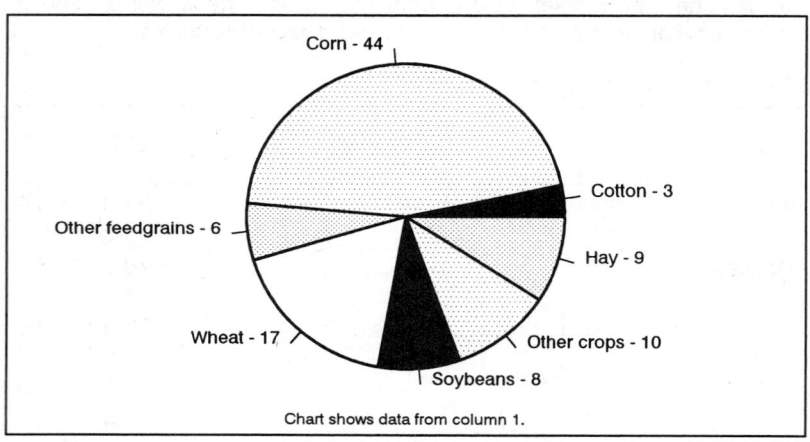

Chart shows data from column 1.

Table shows acreage of U.S. crops and corresponding shares of farm fertilizer market.

[Acreage in millions]

Crop	Percent of farm fertilizer market	Acreage 1993	Percent change from 1992	Acreage 1994	Percent change from 1993
Corn	44	73.7	-7	80.5	+9
Other feedgrains	6	26.7	-8	28.0	+5
Soybeans	8	59.5	-0	61.5	+3
Wheat	17	72.1	-0	71.9	-0

[Continued]

★ 826 ★

Farm Fertilizer Market, by Crop: 1993-1994
[Continued]

Crop	Percent of farm fertilizer market	Acreage 1993	Percent change from 1992	Acreage 1994	Percent change from 1993
Cotton	3	13.7	+3	13.0	-5
Hay	9	60.0	+1	61.5	+2
Other crops	10	14.5	+3	14.5	0

Source: "Crop Pricing Spurs Agchems." *ChemicalWeek*, 5-12 January 1994, p. 42. Primary source: IMC Fertilizer.

★ 827 ★

Markets

Latin American Environmental Market: 1993

According to the source: "The Latin American market was approximately $3.5 billion in 1993 for environmental goods and services in the traditional areas of air and water pollution control, and solid and hazardous waste management" (p. E-11). The table below shows distribution of the 1993 market by Latin American country.

[In percentages]

Country	Distribution
Venezuela and Colombia	2
Argentina	6
Mexico	23
Chile	23
Brazil	34
Other	14

Source: Berkowitz, Joan B., and Alan L. Farkas. "Latin America: Economic Development Aspirations Drive Growing Environmental Markets." *ENR*, 17 October 1994, p. E-11. Primary sources: Farkas Berkowitz & Co.; U.S. Agency for International Development.

★ 828 ★

Markets

Publicly Owned Treatment Works Market, by Product and Region: 1995

```
┌─────────────────────────────────────────────────────┐
│  ┌──────────────────────────────────────────────┐   │
│  │ Total - 1,985                                │   │
│  └──────────────────────────────────────────────┘   │
│  ┌──────────────────────────────┐                    │
│  │ Equipment - 1,016            │                    │
│  └──────────────────────────────┘                    │
│  ┌──────────────────┐                                │
│  │ Services - 551   │                                │
│  └──────────────────┘                                │
│  ┌─────────────┐  Chemicals - 418                    │
│  └─────────────┘                                     │
│                Chart shows data from column 6.       │
└─────────────────────────────────────────────────────┘
```

There are 15,700 publicly owned treatment works (POTWs) in the United States. Sales of equipment, services, and chemicals to POTWs were projected to reach $2 billion in 1995, according to one industry report. The table below shows the POTW market in 1995.

[In million dollars]

Product	Northwest region	Midwest region	Northeast region	Southeast region	Southwest region	Total
Equipment	87	261	278	200	190	1,016
Services	47	126	164	103	111	551
Chemicals	48	81	124	83	82	418
Total	182	468	566	386	383	1,985

Source: "Municipal Wastewater Treatment Market to Increase." *Water Environment & Technology* (May 1994), p. 42. Primary source: 1994-1995 WEF POTW Spending Survey.

★ 829 ★

Markets

Water and Wastewater Services Market Leaders: 1993

Table shows leaders in U.S. water and wastewater services market. Companies are ranked by 1993 revenue from contract water-service business.

[In million dollars]

Company	Parent company location	Revenue
PSG (unit of Cie. Generale des Eaux)	France	76.5
OMI (unit of CH2M Hill)	United States	55
Wheelabrator Technologies (unit of WMX Technologies)	United States	35
Metcalf & Eddy (unit of Air & Water Technologies)	United States	35
Severn Trent	United Kingdom	35
JMM-OSI (affiliate of Lyonnaise des Eaux)	France	18
U.S. Water (unit of North West Water)	United Kingdom	4.5

Source: "French Companies Pour Into U.S. Waterworks Market." *Water Environment & Technology* (May 1994), p. 44. Primary source: *Wall Street Journal*.

Products

★ 830 ★

Aerosol Product Production: 1993

From the source: "The spread of air quality regulations to curb the emission of volatile organic compounds (VOCs) in a wide range of consumer products appears to be having an effect on aerosol production" (p. 64). In 1993, a survey by the Chemical Specialties Mnaufacturers Association (CSMA) found the total number of aerosols filled in the United States (2.94 billion units) decreased 1.6 percent from the previous year. Personal products accounted for 930 million of the units. The table below shows the changes in production for aerosol products based on 1993 production figures.

[In percentages]

Product	Change in production
Personal products	-6.1
Automotive and industrial products	-7.7
Animal products	-25.0
Miscellaneous	-38.0

Source: "VOC Curbs Could Be Factor in Aerosol Downturn." DCI (June 1994), pp. 64-65. Primary source: Chemical Specialties Manufacturers Association. *Pressurized Products Survey. Notes:* Household products, including air fresheners and starches, reported a growth of 6.2 percent. Food products, insecticides, and paints also recorded growth.

★ 831 ★

Products

Chemical Products: 1971-1993

Table shows U.S. production of synthetic organic chemical products.

Product	Year											
	1971	1973	1975	1977	1979	1981	1983	1985	1987	1989	1991	1993
	million kilograms											
Dyes	111	129	93	120	121	104	111	101	116	140	111	154
Pigments	26	31	23	31	40	34	35	37	43	50	51	60
Medical chemicals	101	106	94	109	142	111	106	102	118	129	184	184
Flavors	44	53	46	68	88	75	79	69	57	64	60	93
Rubber	147	182	127	182	179	127	133	118	173	176	155	159
Plasticizers	680	862	635	816	953	862	771	771	907	976	828	963
Pesticides	499	590	726	635	635	649	463	562	472	572	452	644

[Continued]

★ 831 ★

Chemical Products: 1971-1993

[Continued]

Product	Year											
	1971	1973	1975	1977	1979	1981	1983	1985	1987	1989	1991	1993
billion kilograms												
Petroleum[1]	37	41	35	57	55	50	50	47	54	50	54	58
Intermediates[2]	14	16	14	8	22	21	20	21	25	25	24	30
Plastic/resin	10	14	11	16	19	18	20	23	27	26	28	32
Elastomers	2	3	2	3	3	2	2	2	2	2	2	3
Surface agents	2	2	2	2	2	2	2	2	3	3	3	4
Miscellaneous	36	45	39	48	55	53	52	53	44	48	50	77

Source: Executive Office of the President of the United States. *Environmental Quality 24: The Twenty-fourth Annual Report of the Council on Environmental Quality.* Prepared by Ray Clark. Written by Carroll Curtis. Edited by Barry Walsh. Washington, DC: U.S. Government Printing Office, 1994, p. 508. Primary source: U.S. International Trade Commission. *Synthetic Organic Chemicals: United States Production and Sales.* Washington, DC: U.S. International Trade Commission (annual). *Notes:* 1. Primary products from petroleum and natural gas for chemical conversion. 2. Cyclic intermediates that are synthetic organic chemicals derived principally from petroleum and natural gas and from coal-tar crudes produced destructive distillation (pyrolysis) of coal. Most are used in the manufacture of more advance synthetic organic chemicals and finished products, such as dyes, medicinal chemicals, elastomers (synthetic rubber), pesticides, and plastics.

★ 832 ★

Products

Crude Oil and Refined Products: 1973-1993

Data are averages.

[In 42-gallon barrels]

Year	Crude oil (1,000 barrels per day)					Refined oil products (1,000 barrels per day)			Total oil imports[2] (1,000 barrels per day)	Crude oil stocks[3] (million barrels)	
	Input to refineries	Domestic production	Imports totals[1]	Strategic reserve	Exports	Domestic demand	Imports	Exports		Total	Strategic reserve
1973	12,431	9,208	3,244	(X)	2	17,308	3,012	229	6,256	242	(X)
1974	12,133	8,774	3,477	(X)	3	16,653	2,635	218	6,112	265	(X)
1975	12,442	8,375	4,105	(X)	6	16,322	1,951	204	6,056	271	(X)
1976	13,416	8,132	5,287	(X)	8	17,461	2,026	215	7,313	285	(X)
1977	14,602	8,245	6,615	21	50	18,431	2,193	193	8,807	348	7
1978	14,739	8,707	6,356	162	158	18,847	2,008	204	8,363	376	67
1979	14,648	8,552	6,519	67	235	18,513	1,937	236	8,456	430	91
1980	13,481	8,597	5,263	44	287	17,056	1,646	258	6,909	466	108
1981	12,470	8,572	4,396	256	228	16,058	1,599	367	5,996	594	230
1982	11,774	8,649	3,488	165	236	15,296	1,625	579	5,113	644	294
1983	11,685	8,688	3,329	234	164	15,231	1,722	575	5,051	723	379
1984	12,044	8,879	3,426	197	181	15,726	2,011	541	5,437	796	451
1985	12,002	8,971	3,201	118	204	15,726	1,866	577	5,067	814	493
1986	12,716	8,680	4,178	48	154	16,281	2,045	631	6,224	843	512
1987	12,854	8,349	4,674	73	151	16,665	2,004	613	6,678	890	541
1988	13,246	8,140	5,107	51	155	17,283	2,295	661	7,402	890	560
1989	13,401	7,613	5,843	56	142	17,325	2,217	717	8,061	921	580
1990	13,409	7,355	5,894	27	109	16,988	2,123	748	8,018	908	586
1991	13,301	7,417	5,782	0	116	16,714	1,844	885	7,627	893	569

[Continued]

★ 832 ★

Crude Oil and Refined Products: 1973-1993

[Continued]

Year	Crude oil (1,000 barrels per day)					Refined oil products (1,000 barrels per day)			Total oil imports[2] (1,000 barrels per day)	Crude oil stocks[3] (million barrels)	
	Input to refineries	Domestic production	Imports totals[1]	Strategic reserve	Exports	Domestic demand	Imports	Exports		Total	Strategic reserve
1992[4]	13,411	7,171	6,083	10	89	17,033	1,805	861	7,888	893	575
1993[4]	13,610	6,838	6,731	15	98	17,193	1,795	905	8,526	922	587

Source: 1994 Statistical Abstract of the United States on CD-ROM [machine-readable datafiles]. CD-8A-94. Washington, DC: U.S. Department of Commerce, Economics and Statistics Administration, Bureau of the Census, Data User Services Division, January 1995. Primary source: U.S. Energy Information Administration. Monthly Energy Review (March 1994). Notes: "X" represents "not applicable." 1. Includes Strategic Petroleum Reserve. 2. Crude oil (including Strategic Petroleum Reserve imports) plus refined products. 3. End of year. 4. Preliminary.

★ 833 ★

Products

Federal Strategic and Critical Materials

Strategic and critical materials are those items essential to military and industrial requirements in time of national emergency.

[In thousand metric tons, except as indicated]

Item	Tin	silver	Cobalt	Bauxite	Manganese	Tungsten	Zinc	Titanium sponge	Platinum	Chromium	Diamonds industrial	
											Stones	Bort
Production:												
1989	11.0[1]	2.0	1.2[1]	(D)	-	(D)	260	25.2	6,280[2]	99[1]	-	(D)[3]
1990	13.2[1]	2.1	1.2[1]	(D)	-	(D)	263	24.7	7,740[2]	94[1]	-	90.0[3]
1991	13.1[1]	1.9	1.6[1]	(D)	-	(D)	253	13.4	7,780[2]	90[1]	-	90.0[3]
1992	8.8[1]	1.8	1.6[1]	(D)	-	(D)	272	(D)	8,310[2]	95[1]	-	95.0[3]
1993	8.5[1]	1.7	1.6[1]	(D)	-	(D)	255	(D)	8,300[2]	88[1]	-	100.3[3]
Imports:												
1989	34.2	3.3	6.2	11,603	579	7.9	790	0.9	113,278[2]	379	8.8[4]	61.6[4]
1990	33.8	3.4	6.4	12,987	307	6.4	723	1.1	125,354[2]	346	11.0[4]	85.4[4]
1991	29.1	4.2	6.9	12,305	234	7.8	637	0.6	125,661[2]	309	7.6[4]	70.0[4]
1992	27.3	5.0	5.8	11,372	247	2.5	740	0.7	132,006[2]	324	9.8[4]	97.3[4]
1993	33.0	4.5	5.7	11,860	185	2.0	682	1.0	143,000[2]	342	5.5[4]	115.0[4]
Export:												
1989	0.9	1.3	0.9	57	52	0.2	136	13.3[5]	38,301[2]	25	2.8[4]	78.2[4]
1990	0.7	1.8	1.3	64	70	0.1	128	15.8[5]	55,044[2]	14	1.7[4]	71.0[4]
1991	1.0	1.7	1.5	58	66	6	112	12.1[5]	39,624[2]	31	2.9[4]	78.8[4]
1992	1.9	1.8	1.4	68	13	6	120	8.0[5]	57,829[2]	16	5.6[4]	83.6[4]
1993	2.3	1.7	0.9	90	14	6	130	7.3[5]	86,000[2]	18	3.7[4]	96.1[4]
Consumption:												
1989	47.6	5.1[7]	7.2	4,517[8]	559	10.5	1,060	24.9[9]	101,209[2]	452	6.6[4]	75.8[4]
1990	45.5	4.4[7]	7.6	4,570[8]	497	8.4	992	23.2[9]	117,043[2]	439	9.8[4]	112.7[4]
1991	48.7	3.8[7]	7.8	4,609[8]	472	11.8	933	13.6[9]	111,798[2]	377	5.0[4]	89.1[4]
1992	43.6	4.1[7]	6.5	4,863[8]	438	7.5	1,035	14.2[9]	109,469[2]	416	4.3[4]	121.9[4]
1993	45.9	4.0[7]	6.3	4,500[8]	450	6.8	1,120	15.8[9]	112,300[2]	488	1.8[4]	134.4[4]
Net Import reliance, perent:												
1989	77.0	10	83.0	96	100	84.0	61	4.0	90	78	91.0	11
1990	71.0	10	84.0	98	100	81.0	41	11	88	79	95.0	13.0
1991	74.0	10	80.0	100	100	91.0	24	4.0	90	76	94.0	11
1992	80.0	10	75.0	100	100	86.0	30	(D)	87	77	98.0	19.0
1993	81.0	10	75.0	100	100	84.0	26	(D)	88	82	95.0	14.0
Stocks, end of year:												
1989	14.7	8.3	4.6	2,500	470	1.3	91	2.1	32,543[2]	139	(NA)	(NA)
1990	17.3	9.2	3.2	2,300	379	1.1	87	3.3	30,324[2]	125	(NA)	(NA)
1991	13.8	9.4	2.4	2,600	275	1.8	79	2.9	24,313[2]	118	(NA)	(NA)

[Continued]

★ 833 ★

Federal Strategic and Critical Materials
[Continued]

Item	Tin	silver	Cobalt	Bauxite	Mang-anese	Tung-sten	Zinc	Titanium sponge	Platinum	Chromium	Diamonds industrial Stones	Diamonds industrial Bort
1992	10.7	10.1	1.8	2,300	276	0.7	75	1.9	26,946[2]	118	(NA)	(NA)
1993	10.0	9.0	2.2	2,600	260	0.7	77	2.9	24,000[2]	117	(NA)	(NA)
World production:												
1989	233.1	16.0	36.2	103,848	26,389	51.4	6,808	95.7	281,629[2]	14,294	12	55.8[4]
1990	221.7	16.2	35.9	108,609	25,252	51.8	7,184	100.8	291,015[2]	12,968	12	58.8[4]
1991	202.7	15.7	26.8	108,157	21,213	41.9	7,170	56.3	288,338[2]	13,445	12	55.2[4]
1992	179.5	15.3	21.9	103,625	19,929	31.6	7,137	38.6	280,889[2]	10,896	12	55.7[4]
1993	175.0	14.9	17.4	101,000	20,400	25.5	7,000	37.2	273,000[2]	10,000	12	55.7[4]

Source: 1994 Statistical Abstract of the United States on CD-ROM [machine-readable datafiles]. CD-8A-94. Washington, DC: U.S. Department of Commerce, Economics and Statistics Administration. Bureau of the Census, Data User Services Division, January 1995. Primary sources: U.S. Bureau of Mines. *Annual Reports* and *Mineral Commodity Summaries. Notes:* "-" represents or rounds to zero. "D"shows withheld to avoid disclosure of individual company data. "NA" indicates "not available." 1. Production from scrap or secondary production. 2. Kilograms. 3. Manufactured diamond bort, grit, and powder and dust. Million carats. 4. Million carats. 5. All metal forms. 6. Less than 50 metric tons. 7. Apparent demand. 8. Includes alumina. 9. Reported consumtion. 10. Net importer; however, changes in unreported investor stocks preclude calculation of a meaningful net import reliance. 11. Net exporter. 12. Included with bort production; data not separable.

★ 834 ★

Products

Federal Strategic and Critical Materials Inventory: 1980-1992

As of December 31. Covers strategic and critical materials essential to military and industrial requirements in time of national emergency. Market values are estimated current trade values of similar materials and not necessarily amounts that would be realized at time of sale.

Mineral	Unit	Quantity[1] 1980	1985	1990	1991	1992	Value (million dollars) 1980	1985	1990	1991	1992
Tin	1,000 metric ton	200	185	169	163	156	3,158	2,324	962	914	1,034
Silver	1,000 troy ounce	139,500	136,006	92,151	83,951	72,502	2,288	801	374	330	321
Cobalt	Million pound	41	53	53	53	53	1,020	590	443	1,609	798
Bauxite[2]	1,000 long ton	14,333	17,957	18,033	18,033	17,373	583	871	888	827	318
Manganese[3]	1,000 short ton	5,130	4,470	4,017	3,918	3,647	599	520	962	1,000	753
Tungsten[4]	Million pound	97	87	82	82	82	817	369	253	343	225
Zinc	1,000 short ton	380	378	379	379	379	317	268	483	441	388
Titanium	1,000 short ton	43	48	37	37	37	432	405	402	402	236
Platinum	1,000 troy ounce	466	466	453	453	453	215	154	186	162	131
Chromium[5]	1,000 short ton	804	854	1,074	1,121	1,281	773	836	917	924	943
Diamonds: Stones	Carat 1,000	19,224	12,549	7,777	7,777	7,777	349	336	267	267	62
Industrial, bort	Carat 1,000	23,693	22,001	17,353	14,021	5,077	73	39	16	13	11

Source: 1994 Statistical Abstract of the United States on CD-ROM [machine-readable datafiles]. CD-8A-94. Washington, DC: U.S. Department of Commerce, Economics and Statistics Administration, Bureau of the Census, Data User Services Division, January 1995. Primary source: U.S. Defense Logistics Agency. *Statistical Supplement, Stockpile Report to the Congress* (AP-3). *Notes:* 1. Consists of stockpile and nonstockpile grades and reflects uncommitted balances. 2. Consists of abrasive grade, metallic grade Jamaica, metallic grade Suriname, and refractory. 3. Consists of chemical grade, dioxide battery natural, dioxide battery synthetic, electrolytic, ferro-high carbon, ferro-med. carbon, ferro-silicon, and metal. 4. Consists of carbide powder, ferro, metal powder, and ores and concentrates. 5. Consists of ferro-high carbon, ferro-low carbon, ferro-silicon, and metal.

★ 835 ★
Products

Forest Wood Products

In excess of 407 million cubic meters of wood are taken from U.S. forests annually by timber companies. The table below shows use of forest wood products.

[In percentages]

Product	Use
Beams of lumber[1]	44
Paper	29
Fuel	18
Sheets of plywood[2]	9

Source: "How We Use Forest Wood." *Science World*, 9 December 1994, p. 11. Primary source: *Scholastic Environmental Atlas of the United States* (Scholastic Inc., 1993). *Notes:* 1. For building foundations. 2. For furniture and walls.

★ 836 ★
Products

Lumber Consumption, by Species Group and End Use: 1962-1991

In billion board feet, except per capita in board feet. Per capita consumption based on estimated resident population as of July 1.

Item	1962	1970	1976	1986	1991
Species group, total	39.1	39.9	44.7	57.0	54.8
Softwoods	30.8	32.0	36.6	48.0	44.0
Hardwoods	8.5	7.9	8.0	9.0	10.8
Per capita consumption	210	194	205	237	217
End-use					
New housing	14.5	13.3	17.0	19.3	15.0
Residential upkeep and improvement	4.4	4.7	5.7	10.1	11.6
New nonresidential construction[1]	4.2	4.7	4.5	5.3	5.4
Manufacturing	4.5	4.7	4.9	4.8	5.6

[Continued]

★ 836 ★

Lumber Consumption, by Species Group and End Use: 1962-1991

[Continued]

Item	1962	1970	1976	1986	1991
Shipping	4.6	5.7	5.9	6.8	8.2
Other[2]	6.9	6.8	6.7	10.9	8.8

Source: 1994 Statistical Abstract of the United States on CD-ROM [machine-readable datafiles]. CD-8A-94. Washington, DC: U.S. Department of Commerce, Economics and Statistics Administration, Bureau of the Census, Data User Services Division, January 1995. Primary source: U.S. Forest Service. *The 1993 RPA Timber Assessment Update. Notes:* 1. In addition to new construction, includes railroad ties laid as replacements in existing track and lumber used by railroads for railcar repair. 2. Includes upkeep and improvement of non-residential buildings and structures; made-at-home projects, such as furniture, boats, and picnic tables; made-on-the-job items such as advertising and display structures; and miscellaneous products and uses.

★ 837 ★

Products

Lumber Production and Consumption, by Kind of Wood: 1970-1991

Based on sample survey.

[In million board feet, except as indicated]

Item	1970	1975	1980	1985	1990[1]	1991[1]
Total production	34,668	32,619	35,354	36,445	43,466	40,031
Softwoods[2]	27,530	26,747	28,239	30,479	36,224	33,250
Cedar	633	821	722	759	959	863
Douglas fir	7,727	7,329	6,853	7,751	8,831	7,816
Hemlock	1,980	2,020	1,855	(NA)	(NA)	(NA)
Ponderosa pine	3,429	3,544	3,269	3,773	3,645	3,304
Redwood	1,078	1,054	770	1,155	1,077	887
Southern yellow pine	7,063	6,967	8,217	10,230	12,989	12,436
White fir[3]	2,063	2,012	1,643	2,272	3,272	2,900
White pine	898	947	(S)	(NA)	432	437
Hardwoods[2]	7,138	5,872	7,115	5,966	7,242	6,781
Ash	159	124	(S)	218	210	184
Beech	188	136	183	89	82	72
Cottonwood and aspen	229	253	303	216	167	154
Elm	155	117	149	(NA)	(NA)	(NA)
Maple[4]	742	531	225	532	543	517
Oak	3,250	2,724	3,356	2,793	2,615	2,434
Sweet gum[5]	376	245	371	293	219	167
Yellow poplar	606	555	661	544	666	629
Domestic consumption	38,073	36,100	44,536	53,468	54,482	51,134
		16.8	24.4	15.7	15.5	
Percent net imports[6]	12.7	12.2	16.8	24.4	15.7	15.5
Softwoods	31,959	30,466	33,812	44,240	45,003	41,998

[Continued]

★ 837 ★

Lumber Production and Consumption, by Kind of Wood: 1970-1991

[Continued]

Item	1970	1975	1980	1985	1990[1]	1991[1]
Mill stocks, year end	4,340	4,063	4,228	4,765	4,854	4,669
Exports	1,152	1,373	1,956	1,515	2,970	3,090
Imports	5,769	5,711	9,540	14,608	12,148	11,742
Hardwoods	7,910	7,343	10,724	9,228	9,480	9,136
Mill stocks, year end	1,144	875	1,572	1,719	(NA)	(NA)
Exports	138	165	379	397	878	934
Imports	347	224	293	364	55	226

Source: *1994 Statistical Abstract of the United States on CD-ROM* [machine-readable datafiles]. CD-8A-94. Washington, DC: U.S. Department of Commerce, Economics and Statistics Administration, Bureau of the Census, Data User Services Division, January 1995. Primary source: U.S. Bureau of the Census. *Current Industrial Reports.* Series MA-24T (annual). *Notes:* "NA" stands for "not available." 1. New sample, based on the new MA-24T sample. 2. Includes types not shown separately. 3. Beginning 1988, also includes hemfir, and other western truefirs. 4. Includes both hard and soft maple, except data for 1980 excludes hard maple. 5. Includes black, tupelo, and sweet gum. 6. Imports minus exports.

★ 838 ★

Products

Lumber Production, by Geographic Area: 1970-1992

Data based in part on a sample of sawmills and are subject to sampling variability.

[In billion board feet]

Item	1970	1975	1980	1985	1990	1991	1992
United States	34.7	32.6	35.4[1]	36.4	43.5	39.9	40.8
North[2]	4.4	4.1	(NA)	4.2	5.4	5.3	5.4
Hardwood	3.4	3.0	(NA)	3.0	3.7	3.6	3.6
Softwood	1.0	1.1	(NA)	1.2	1.7	1.7	1.8
South[3]	10.8	9.7	(NA)	13.0	16.5	15.5	16.8
Hardwood	3.6	2.7	(NA)	2.7	3.2	2.8	3.0
Softwood	7.2	7.0	(NA)	10.2	13.3	12.7	13.8
West[3]	19.4	18.8	17.2	19.3	21.6	19.1	18.7
Hardwood	0.1	0.1	0.3	0.2	0.4	0.4	0.4
Softwood	19.3	18.6	16.9	19.1	21.2	18.7	18.3
New England	0.7	0.8	1.1	1.1	1.3	1.3	(NA)
Middle Atlantic	0.8	0.7	0.9	0.7	1.0	1.0	(NA)
East North Central	1.2	1.1	1.3	1.3	1.5	1.4	(NA)
West North Central	0.6	0.5	0.6	0.6	0.6	0.6	(NA)
South Atlantic	5.2	4.7	5.2	6.4	8.1	7.6	(NA)

[Continued]

★ 838 ★

Lumber Production, by Geographic Area: 1970-1992
[Continued]

Item	1970	1975	1980	1985	1990	1991	1992
East South Central	3.4	3.0	3.2	4.1	5.3	5.3	(NA)
West South Central	3.2	3.0	2.9	3.1	4.2	3.9	(NA)
Mountain	4.2	3.9	3.8	4.3	4	4	(NA)
Pacific	15.3	14.8	13.4	14.8	21.4	19.0	(NA)

Source: 1994 Statistical Abstract of the United States on CD-ROM [machine-readable datafiles]. CD-8A-94. Washington, DC: U.S. Department of Commerce, Economics and Statistics Administration, Bureau of the Census, Data User Services Division, January 1995. Primary source—Except as noted: U.S. Bureau of the Census. *Current Industrial Reports.* Series MA-24T (annual). *Notes:* "NA" stands for "not available." 1. Includes amounts not specified by division. 2. Source: U.S. Forest Service. Sections are as defined by the Forest Service. Includes Kentucky. 3. Source: U.S. Forest Service. Sections are as defined by the Forest Service.

★ 839 ★

Products

Newsprint: 1970-1992

Table shows newsprint production, stocks, consumption, imports, and price index in North America.

[In thousand metric tons, except price index and imports]

Country and item	1970	1975	1980	1985	1990	1991	1992
Canada:							
Production	7,808	6,966	8,625	8,890	9,068	8,977	8,931
Shipments from mills	7,795	7,010	8,622	8,899	9,074	8,728	9,143
Stocks at mills, end of year	236	86	165	288	315	564	351
United States:							
Consumption, estimate	6,468	8,395	10,088	11,507	12,125	11,381	11,634
Production	3,142	3,348	4,239	4,924	5,997	6,206	6,424
Shipments from mills	3,136	3,347	4,234	4,927	6,007	6,152	6,464
Stocks, end of year: At mills	33	19	21	57	46	98	59
At and in transit to publishers	749	666	732	910	801	932	938
Producer price index (1982=100)	34.1	58.3	88.5[1]	105.3	119.5	120.9	109.9

Source: 1994 Statistical Abstract of the United States on CD-ROM [machine-readable datafiles]. CD-8A-94. Washington, DC: U.S. Department of Commerce, Economics and Statistics Administration, Bureau of the Census, Data User Services Division, January 1995. Primary source—except as noted: U.S. Bureau of Economic Analysis. *Survey of Current Business,* (monthly). Data from American Forest and Paper Association, Inc. (New York, NY) and Canadian Pulp & Paper Association. *Notes:* Imports in short tons. 1. Average for 11 months.

★ 840 ★

Products

Roundwood Production, by Major Product: 1950-1990

[In billion cubic feet]

Year	Lumber	Plywood and veneer	Pulp products	Fuel	Miscellaneous	Total
1950	5.9	0.3	1.5	2.3	0.8	10.8
1955	5.8	0.6	2.2	1.7	0.7	11.0
1960	5.1	0.7	2.6	1.3	0.6	10.2
1965	5.7	1.0	3.1	0.9	0.8	11.5
1970	5.2	1.0	3.8	0.5	1.0	11.6
1975	4.9	1.2	3.5	0.6	1.0	11.1
1980	5.3	1.2	4.4	3.1	1.2	15.2
1985	5.7	1.4	4.2	3.4	1.2	16.0
1990	6.5	1.6	5.1	3.3	1.5	18.0

Source: Executive Office of the President of the United States. *Environmental Quality 24: The Twenty-fourth Annual Report of the Council on Environmental Quality.* Prepared by Ray Clark. Written by Carroll Curtis. Edited by Barry Walsh. Washington, DC: U.S. Government Printing Office, 1994, p. 463. Primary sources: U.S. Department of Agriculture. Forest Service. *U.S. Timber Production, Trade, Consumption, and Price Statistics, 1960-1988.* Washington, DC: U.S. Department of Agriculture, Forest Service, 1991, p. 13; table 4; and unpublished data. *Notes:* Miscellaneous products include log and pulp chip exports and other products not specified. Totals may not agree with detail because of independent rounding.

★ 841 ★

Products

Softwood and Hardwood Timber Stocks: 1952-1991

Table shows volume of softwood and hardwood timber stocks.

[In billion cubic feet]

Year	Farmer and other private		Forest industry		National forest		Other public forests		Total	
	Softwood	Hardwood	Softwood	Hardwood	Softwood	Hardwood	Softwood	Hardwood	Softwood	Hardwood
1952	94.8	133.7	77.4	20.3	204.4	13.6	55.2	16.5	431.8	184.1
1962	104.3	152.5	76.1	25.4	213.7	17.2	55.7	20.7	449.8	215.8
1977	125.3	185.8	74.5	32.3	208.1	21.6	59.0	26.5	467.0	266.1
1986	136.6	220.8	72.8	35.3	186.3	25.1	57.3	31.4	452.9	312.6
1992	143.4	242.3	71.0	34.8	185.6	25.6	50.0	33.0	449.9	335.7

Source: Executive Office of the President of the United States. *Environmental Quality 24: The Twenty-fourth Annual Report of the Council on Environmental Quality.* Prepared by Ray Clark. Written by Carroll Curtis. Edited by Barry Walsh. Washington, DC: U.S. Government Printing Office, 1994, p. 462. Primary source: U.S. Department of Agriculture. Forest Service. *Forest Statistics of the United States, 1992.* General Technical Report RM-234. Washington, DC: U.S. Department of Agriculture, Forest Service, 1993.

★ 842 ★

Products

Timber Stocks: 1952-1991

Table shows annual growth and removal of timber stocks.

[In billion cubic feet]

Year	Farmer and other private		Forest industry		National forest		Other public forests		Total	
	Growth	Removal	Growth	Removal	Growth	Removal	Growth	Removal	Growth	Removal
1952	8.1	6.9	2.6	3.3	2.1	1.1	1.2	0.6	14.0	11.9
1962	9.5	6.4	3.2	3.0	2.5	1.9	1.6	0.7	16.8	12.0
1976	12.6	6.8	4.2	4.2	3.1	2.1	2.0	1.1	21.9	14.2
1986	12.1	8.2	4.3	5.4	3.4	2.3	2.3	1.2	22.1	17.0
1991	12.1	8.0	4.3	5.3	3.3	2.0	1.9	1.0	21.6	16.3

Source: Executive Office of the President of the United States. *Environmental Quality 24: The Twenty-fourth Annual Report of the Council on Environmental Quality.* Prepared by Ray Clark. Written by Carroll Curtis. Edited by Barry Walsh. Washington, DC: U.S. Government Printing Office, 1994, p. 462. Primary source: U.S. Department of Agriculture. Forest Service. *Forest Statistics of the United States, 1992.* General Technical Report RM-234. Washington, DC: U.S. Department of Agriculture, Forest Service, 1993.

★ 843 ★

Products

Wood Product Production: 1970-1990

Item	Unit	1970	1975	1980	1985	1990[1]
Hardwood flooring	Million bd. ft.	307	99	78	122	205
Softwood plywood	Billion sq. ft., 3/8"	14.1	15.1	15.5	19.3	20.7
Insulation boards[2]	1,000 short tons	1,219	1,249	1,051	735	474
Hardboard[2]	Million sq. ft., 1/8"	4,340	5,681	6,140	6,300	5,025
Particleboard	Million sq. ft., 3/4"	1,731	2,503	2,950	3,331	3,806

Source: 1994 Statistical Abstract of the United States on CD-ROM [machine-readable datafiles]. CD-8A-94. Washington, DC: U.S. Department of Commerce, Economics and Statistics Administration, Bureau of the Census, Data User Services Division, January 1995. Primary sources: U.S. Dept. of Commerce. International Trade Administration. *Forest Products Review* (monthly; discontinued April 1983); and unpublished data. Based on reports of U.S. Bureau of the Census, National Oak Flooring Manufacturers Association, and National Particleboard Association. *Notes:* "bd. ft." represents "board feet." "sq. ft." denotes "square feet." 1. Preliminary. 2. Beginning 1982, data are for shipments.

Sales and Revenue

★ 844 ★

Battery Sales: 1993-2004

Table shows total predicted battery sales by type.

[In million 1993 dollars, except as noted]

Market	1993	1994	1999	2004	Average annual growth rate 1994-1999 (percent)	Average annual growth rate 1999-20044 (percent)
Primary						
Zinc-carbon	516	521	521	521	0	0
Alkaline-manganese	1,600	1,648	1,732	1,820	1	1
Mercury oxide	30	27	16	5	-10	-20
Silver oxide	40	38	29	23	-5	-5
Primary lithium	243	253	307	356	4	3
Zinc-air	5	5	6	6	2	2
Specialty	4	4	4	4	0	0
Total primary	2,438	2,496	2,615	2,735	0.93	0.90
Nonautomotive secondary						
Nickel-cadmium	485	500	608	705	4	3
Nickel metal-hydride	25	29	51	78	12	9
Lead-acid	720	730	840	930	3	2
Secondary alkaline	NA	10	75	95	50	5
Secondary specialty	41	42	49	56	3	3
Total secondary	1,271	1,311	1,623	1,864	4.3	2.8
Automotive						
Lead-acid	3,900	3,990	4,590	5,300	2.8	2.9
Total	7,609	7,797	8,828	9,899	2.5	2.3

Source: "U.S. Battery Industry: Not Mature Yet." *Energy* (June 1994), pp. 21-22. Primary source: BCC estimates. *Notes:* "NA" stands for "not available." Specialty batteries include silver-zinc, silver-cadmium, nickel-hydrogen, nickel-zinc, and secondary lithium.

★ 845 ★
Sales and Revenue

Electric Energy Sales, by State: 1970-1992

In billions of kilowatt hours.

Region division, and state	Total[1]	Residential	Commercial	Industrial
1970	1,392.3	466.3	306.7	570.9
1973	1,712.9	579.2	388.3	686.1
1975	1,747.1	588.1	403.0	687.7
1980	2,094.4	717.5	488.2	815.1
1981	2,147.1	722.3	514.3	825.7
1982	2,086.4	729.5	526.4	744.9
1983	2,151.0	750.9	543.8	776.0
1984	2,278.4	777.7	578.3	840.6
1985	2,309.5	791.0	609.0	824.5
1986	2,350.8	817.7	641.5	808.3
1987	2,457.3	850.4	660.4	858.2
1988	2,578.1	892.9	699.1	896.5
1989	2,646.8	905.5	725.9	925.7
1990	2,712.6	924.0	751.0	945.5
1991	2,762.0	955.4	765.7	946.6
1992, total[2]	2,763.3	935.9	761.3	972.7
Northeast	411.8	136.1	142.7	116.9
New England	103.9	37.6	37.9	26.3
Maine	11.5	3.8	2.7	4.8
New Hampshire	9.0	3.4	2.1	3.3
Vermont	4.9	1.9	1.5	1.4
Massachusetts	45.0	15.6	18.6	9.7
Rhode Island	6.4	2.4	2.5	1.4
Connecticut	27.1	10.5	10.5	5.8
Middle Atlantic	307.9	98.5	104.8	90.6
New York	128.5	38.7	46.6	31.0
New Jersey	63.1	20.5	27.4	14.7
Pennsylvania	116.3	39.2	30.8	44.9
Midwest	659.8	204.3	165.8	269.9
East North Central	469.3	136.6	113.8	204.0
Ohio	145.0	39.1	31.8	69.7
Indiana	77.0	22.8	16.1	37.4
Illinois	112.5	32.4	31.5	40.9
Michigan	83.8	25.7	21.2	35.7
Wisconsin	50.9	16.6	13.2	20.4
West North Central	190.5	67.7	52.0	65.9
Minnesota	47.4	14.8	8.3	23.6
Iowa	30.2	10.3	7.0	12.1
Missouri	54.4	21.3	18.8	13.4
North Dakota	7.1	3.0	1.8	1.8
South Dakota	6.5	2.8	1.5	1.8
Nebraska	17.8	6.6	5.3	4.8
Kansas	27.1	8.9	9.4	8.5

[Continued]

★ 845 ★

Electric Energy Sales, by State: 1970-1992

[Continued]

Region division, and state	Total[1]	Residential	Commercial	Industrial
South	1,165.0	428.0	284.8	414.0
South Atlantic	552.8	219.4	159.1	156.6
Delaware	8.5	2.8	2.4	3.2
Maryland	51.0	19.8	10.8	19.8
Dist. of Columbia	10.0	1.5	5.2	3.0
Virginia	76.4	29.8	21.6	16.7
West Virginia	23.8	8.1	5.2	10.4
North Carolina	94.2	34.8	25.1	32.5
South Carolina	58.4	18.9	12.4	26.3
Georgia	83.4	30.5	23.7	28.2
Florida	147.0	73.2	52.6	16.5
East South Central	241.0	80.8	33.7	121.7
Kentucky	67.1	17.8	9.6	37.1
Tennessee	78.6	29.5	6.5	41.7
Alabama	62.2	21.1	10.9	29.5
Mississippi	33.2	12.4	6.7	13.5
West South Central	371.2	127.8	92.0	135.7
Arkansas	28.5	10.4	6.2	11.3
Louisiana	65.1	21.2	13.8	27.5
Oklahoma	38.3	14.3	10.3	11.6
Texas	239.4	81.9	61.7	85.4
West	513.7	163.4	163.5	167.4
Mountain	168.0	51.6	52.7	56.9
Montana	13.1	3.3	2.8	6.4
Idaho	19.0	5.7	5.3	7.6
Wyoming	11.7	1.8	2.4	7.4
Colorado	31.8	10.2	13.9	6.8
New Mexico	14.4	3.8	4.6	4.6
Arizona	43.7	16.2	14.5	11.0
Utah	16.6	4.5	5.0	6.2
Nevada	17.7	6.1	4.2	6.7
Pacific	345.7	111.8	110.8	110.5
Washington	89.3	28.4	18.7	38.3
Oregon	42.9	15.2	11.8	15.1
California	213.4	68.1	80.2	57.1
Alaska	4.3	1.6	2.0	0.5
Hawaii	8.7	2.4	2.4	3.8

Source: 1994 Statistical Abstract of the United States on CD-ROM [machine-readable datafiles]. CD-8A-94. Washington, DC: U.S. Department of Commerce, Economics and Statistics Administration, Bureau of the Census, Data User Services Division, January 1995. Primary source: U.S. Energy Information Administration, *Electric Power Annual. Notes:* 1. Includes other service not shown separately. 2. Preliminary.

★ 846 ★

Sales and Revenue

Electric Utility Sales, by End-Use Sector: 1970-1993

Prior to 1980, covers Class A and B privately owned electric utilities; thereafter, Class A utilities whose electric operating revenues were $100 million or more during the previous year.

[In billion killowatt hours]

Year	Total[1]	Resi- dential	Com- mercial	Indus- trial	Other[2]
1970	1,392	466	307	571	48
1971	1,470	500	329	589	52
1972	1,595	539	359	641	56
1973	1,713	579	388	686	60
1974	1,706	578	385	685	58
1975	1,747	588	403	688	68
1976	1,855	606	425	754	70
1977	1,948	645	447	786	70
1978	2,018	674	461	809	74
1979	2,071	683	473	842	73
1980	2,094	717	488	815	74
1981	2,147	722	514	826	85
1982	2,086	730	526	745	85
1983	2,151	751	544	776	80
1984	2,286	780	583	838	85
1985	2,324	794	606	837	87
1986	2,369	819	631	831	88
1987	2,457	850	660	858	89
1988	2,578	893	699	896	90
1989	2,647	906	726	926	89
1990	2,713	924	751	946	92
1991	2,762	955	766	947	94
1992	2,763	936	761	973	93
1993[3]	2,865	994	790	983	97

Source: 1994 Statistical Abstract of the United States on CD-ROM [machine-readable datafiles]. CD-8A-94. Washington, DC: U.S. Department of Commerce, Economics and Statistics Administration, Bureau of the Census, Data User Services Division, January 1995. Primary source: U.S. Energy Information Administration. *Annual Energy Review. Notes:* 1. Includes other sectors not shown separately. 2. Covers public street and highway lighting, other sales to public authorities, sales to railroads and railways, and interdepartmental sales. 3. Preliminary.

★ 847 ★

Sales and Revenue

Mineral Revenues: 1993

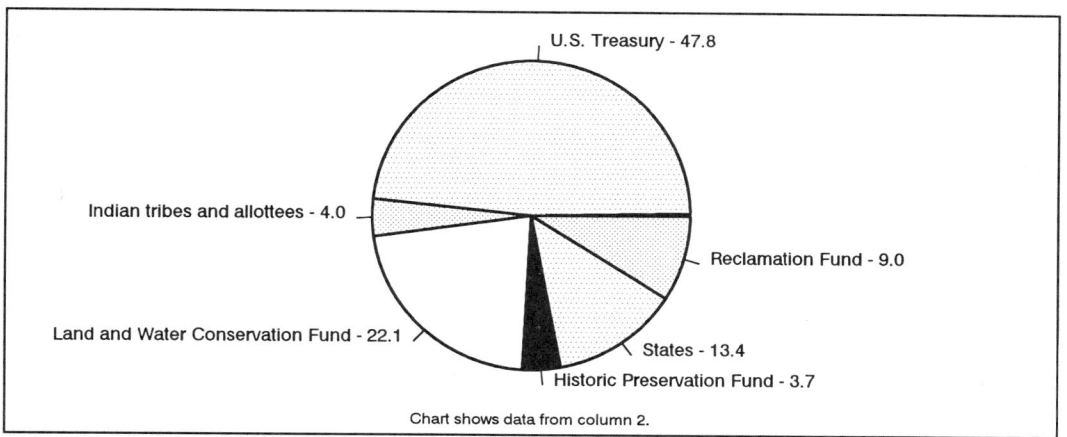

Chart shows data from column 2.

Table shows the disbursement of mineral revenues from federal and Indian leases for the 1993 fiscal year. Disbursements totaled $4,070.4 million.

[In million dollars, except as noted]

Lease	Revenue	Share (percent)
Historic Preservation Fund	150.0	3.7
Indian tribes and allottees	164.4	4.0
Reclamation Fund	366.6	9.0
States	543.7	13.4
Land and Water Conservation Fund	900.0	22.1
U.S. Treasury	1,945.7	47.8

Source: U.S. Department of the Interior. Land and Materials Management. Minerals Management Service. Royalty Management Program. *Mineral Revenues, 1993.* Denver, CO: U.S. Department of the Interior, Land and Minerals Management, Minerals Management Service, Royalty Management Program, 1993, p. 84.

Trade

★ 848 ★

Chemicals in Wastes – Imports, by State: 1992

Table shows states with net imports of Toxic Release Inventory (TRI) chemicals in wastes. Includes transfers received from out of state minus transfers sent out of state.

[In pounds]

State	Transfers to recycling	Transfers to energy recovery	Transfers to treatment	Transfers to disposal	Other[1] off-site transfers	Net imports
Indiana	85,964,439	21,327,684	6,655,857	6,249,895	157,934	120,355,809
Pennsylvania	154,417,132	(15,666,858)	(8,830,856)	(12,609,198)	145,731	117,455,951
Texas	64,726,846	(5,962,694)	1,873,093	5,449,555	29,795	66,116,595
California	39,098,943	(1,010,519)	(1,395,332)	(906,056)	162,410	35,949,446
South Carolina	19,931,403	8,700,872	2,303,211	2,234,057	193,347	33,362,890
Alabama	9,795,356	23,754,958	(5,250,303)	2,082,102	(3,458,881)	26,923,232
Wyoming	23,094,568	(138)	(5,162)	(29,433)	0	23,059,835
Ohio	(38,635,593)	28,975,281	15,468,678	15,415,826	(17,683)	21,206,509
Delaware	18,031,043	(1,373,991)	(704,722)	(10,853)	0	15,941,477
Montana	11,167,420	(117,064)	(10,142)	1,948,042	0	12,988,256
West Virginia	23,312,194	(9,930,309)	(2,289,012)	(428,869)	(14,212)	10,649,792
Illinois	(52,561,182)	(9,303,763)	69,224,720	1,863,416	446,914	9,670,105
District of Columbia	9,444,201	0	750	245	0	9,445,196
Tennessee	16,301,657	(1,343,451)	1,638,460	(7,485,396)	(1,212)	9,110,058
Connecticut	11,479,618	(4,328,565)	(4,257,742)	(438)	(213,797)	2,693,076
Idaho	1,943,180	(302,378)	189,209	188,506	0	2,018,517
Nevada	552,264	(12,769)	29,364	932,909	192	1,501,960
Florida	6,688,746	(1,439,978)	(3,065,471)	(1,047,650)	(463)	1,135,184
Total	404,752,235	31,966,318	71,574,600	13,846,660	(2,569,925)	519,583,888

Source: U.S. Environmental Protection Agency. "Toxic Release Inventory, 1992." In *National Economic, Social, and Environmental Data Bank* [CD-ROM]. Prepared by U.S. Department of Commerce, Economics and Statistics Administration. Washington, DC: U.S. Department of Commerce, National Economic, Social, and Environmental Data Bank, Economics and Statistics Administration, Office of Business Analysis, February 1995. *Notes:* 1. Other transfers are transfers reported with missing or invalid waste management codes. Numbers in parenthesis are negative.

★ 849 ★

Trade

Chemicals in Wastes – Net Exports, by State: 1992

Table shows states with net exports of Toxic Release Inventory (TRI) chemicals in wastes. Includes transfers sent out of state minus transfers received from other states.

[In pounds]

State	Transfers to recycling	Transfers to energy recovery	Transfers to treatment	Transfers to disposal	Other[1] off-site transfers	Net exports
North Carolina	70,558,811	7,493,342	3,595,383	458,998	213,610	82,320,144
Mississippi	60,086,895	3,255,272	608,244	526,005	(41,947)	64,434,469
Missouri	(26,740,202)	1,683,090	71,862,676	666,640	17,564	47,489,768
New Jersey	54,743,917	(4,356,771)	(3,605,702)	610,797	(71,556)	47,320,685
Kentucky	46,681,600	(13,761,716)	3,424,441	458,553	117,624	36,920,502
Arkansas	41,549,182	(3,020,605)	(5,504,556)	971,578	40,476	34,036,075
Utah	30,597,187	327,609	(459,843)	(769,120)	0	29,695,833
Kansas	29,350,853	(3,145,446)	1,173,183	167,976	99,854	27,646,420
Georgia	17,425,126	2,958,397	1,905,447	1,301,559	(57,637)	23,532,892
Louisiana	40,348,607	(5,128,682)	(15,044,604)	(825,279)	(10,088)	19,339,354
New York	4,748,259	7,360,253	5,293,235	904,600	128,604	18,434,951
Iowa	12,734,782	3,558,832	1,015,640	340,600	45,300	17,695,154
Nebraska	12,816,527	1,032,017	216,437	2,440,199	238,790	16,743,970
Arizona	12,859,831	458,392	342,709	38,498	12,540	13,711,970
Virginia	14,712,722	(729,277)	779,198	(1,550,499)	(25,729)	13,186,415
Maryland	11,998,982	642,523	(64,253)	(122,699)	1,580	12,456,133
Oregon	9,156,520	550,640	237,081	1,893,402	4,800	11,842,443
Massachusetts	3,932,935	4,415,969	2,304,444	89,625	(92,577)	10,650,396
Oklahoma	5,409,338	95,440	487,900	4,631,384	3,661	10,627,723
Michigan	(17,188,188)	24,037,520	2,745,754	1,014,872	(65,909)	10,544,049
Rhode Island	8,305,565	386,223	337,496	354,761	6,928	9,390,973
Colorado	6,285,789	(572,098)	1,811,255	32,621	(45,954)	7,511,613
New Hampshire	5,866,515	428,063	531,983	172,438	1,000	6,999,999
Wisconsin	1,643,133	2,406,859	165,267	1,928,970	378,114	6,522,343
Puerto Rico	1,233,240	1,869,068	2,453,101	50,944	3,900	5,610,253
Washington	7,111,581	231,851	(89,826)	(1,769,712)	15,348	5,499,242
Vermont	4,289,285	531,800	121,247	24,997	0	4,967,329
Minnesota	1,963,323	423,455	(665,606)	395,443	17,890	2,134,505
Maine	1,260,877	430,167	255,061	110,743	4,320	2,061,168
South Dakota	228,596	277,083	43,772	6,170	25,344	580,965
New Mexico	287,171	227,060	45,712	4,844	350	565,137
Alaska	242,373	0	(27,374)	(367)	0	214,632
Hawaii	26,749	0	15	159,697	0	186,461
Virgin Islands	703	0	176	57,180	0	58,059
North Dakota	10,953	60,184	34,096	(54,715)	0	50,518
Total	474,539,537	34,426,514	76,329,189	14,721,703	966,200	600,982,543

Source: U.S. Environmental Protection Agency. "Toxic Release Inventory, 1992." In *National Economic, Social, and Environmental Data Bank* [CD-ROM]. Prepared by U.S. Department of Commerce, Economics and Statistics Administration. Washington, DC: U.S. Department of Commerce, National Economic, Social, and Environmental Data Bank, Economics and Statistics Administration, Office of Business Analysis, February 1995. *Notes:* 1. Other transfers are transfers reported with missing or invalid waste management codes. Numbers in parenthesis are negative.

★ 850 ★

Trade

Crude Oil Imports, by Country of Origin: 1970-1993

Table shows crude oil imports into the United States.

[In million barrels]

Country of origin	1970	1975	1980	1985	1990	1991	1992	1993
Total	483	1,498	1,921	1,168	2,151	2,110	2,226	2,457
Canada	245	219	73	171	235	271	292	330
Mexico	0	26	185	261	251	277	288	316
Norway	0	5	53	11	35	27	43	43
Trinidad-Tobago	(Z)	42	42	36	28	26	26	20
United Kingdom	0	(Z)	63	101	57	39	73	111
OPEC	222	1,172	1,410	479	1,283	1,233	1,247	1,339
Algeria	2	96	166	31	23	16	9	9
Ecuador	0	21	6	20	14	19	23	28
Gabon	0	10	9	19	23	31	45	55
Indonesia	26	138	115	107	36	37	26	24
Iran	12	102	3	10	0	12	0	0
Iraq	0	1	10	17	188	0	0	0
Kuwait	12	1	10	1	29	2	14	125
Libya	17	81	200	0	0	0	0	0
Nigeria	17	272	307	102	286	249	243	263
Qatar	0	7	8	0	1	0	0	0
Saudi Arabia	15	256	456	48	436	622	585	466
United Arab Emirates	23	43	63	13	3	1	0	4
Venezuela	98	144	57	112	243	244	302	365
Other	16	34	95	108	264	237	257	298

Source: 1994 Statistical Abstract of the United States on CD-ROM [machine-readable datafiles]. CD-8A-94. Washington, DC: U.S. Department of Commerce, Economics and Statistics Administration, Bureau of the Census, Data User Services Division, January 1995. Primary sources—1970-1972: U.S. Bureau of Mines. *Minerals Yearbooks.* Volume I; thereafter, U.S. Energy Information Administration. *Petroleum Supply Annual.* Volume I. *Notes:* "Z" denotes less than 500,000 or less than .05 percent. Barrels contain 1/2 gallons. "OPEC" stands for Organization of Petroleum Exporting Countries.

★ 851 ★

Trade

Crude Oil – International Flow: 1990

Table shows the daily international flow of crude oil by area.

[In thousand barrels per day]

Exporting area	Total[1]	Importing area							
		North America		Central and South America	Western Europe	Eastern Europe	Middle East and Africa	Japan	Other Far East and Oceania
		U.S.	Canada						
World total	28,077	5,894	546	1,709	9,702	1,662	1,175	3,928	3,560
United States	109	(X)	11	97[2]	-	-	-	-	1
North America, except U.S.	1,920	1,332	12	66	325	-	29	146	10
Central and South America	1,738	934	29	492	170	87	4	8	14
Western Europe	2,655	252	339	61	1,990	7	5	-	(Z)
Eastern Europe and U.S.S.R.	2,170	1	-	34	942	1,052	13	1	97
Middle East	12,521	1,858	80	751	3,411	414	761	2,712	2,533
Africa	4,857	1,235	75	192	2,858	102	333	17	45
Far East and Oceania	2,107	282	-	16	6	-	-	944	859

Source: *1994 Statistical Abstract of the United States on CD-ROM* [machine-readable datafiles]. CD-8A-94. Washington, DC: U.S. Department of Commerce, Economics and Statistics Administration, Bureau of the Census, Data User Services Division, January 1995. Primary source: U.S. Energy Information Administration. *International Energy Annual. Notes:* "-" represents zero. "X" stands for not applicable. "Z" denotes less than 50,000 barrels. 1. Includes stocks at sea, exchanges, transshipments, and other statistical discrepancies not shown separately. 2. Includes shipments to Puerto Rico and Virgin Islands.

★ 852 ★

Trade

Energy Imports and Exports, by Type of Fuel: 1970-1992

Table shows U.S. energy-related imports and exports.

[In quadrillion Btu]

Type of fuel	1970	1975	1980	1985	1990	1991	1992
Net imports:[1]							
Coal	-1.93	-1.74	(2.39)	(2.39)	(2.70)	(2.77)	(2.59)
Natural Gas (dry)	0.77	0.90	0.96	0.90	1.46	1.67	1.84
Petroleum	6.92	12.51	13.50	8.95	15.29	14.22	14.87
Other[2]	-0.04	0.08	0.18	0.41	0.03	0.24	0.30
Imports:							
Coal	(Z)	0.02	0.03	0.05	0.07	0.08	0.10
Natural Gas (dry)	0.85	0.98	1.01	0.95	1.55	1.80	2.09
Petroleum	7.47	12.95	14.66	10.61	17.12	16.35	16.88

[Continued]

★ 852 ★

Energy Imports and Exports, by Type of Fuel: 1970-1992

[Continued]

Type of fuel	1970	1975	1980	1985	1990	1991	1992
Other[2]	0.07	0.16	0.28	0.49	0.25	0.35	0.39
Exports:							
Coal	1.94	1.76	2.42	2.44	2.77	2.85	2.68
Natural Gas (dry)	0.07	0.07	0.05	0.06	0.09	0.13	0.25
Petroleum	0.55	0.44	1.16	1.66	1.82	2.13	2.01
Other[2]	0.11	0.08	0.09	0.08	0.23	0.11	0.09

Source: 1994 Statistical Abstract of the United States on CD-ROM [machine-readable datafiles]. CD-8A-94. Washington, DC: U.S. Department of Commerce, Economics and Statistics Administration, Bureau of the Census, Data User Services Division, January 1995. Primary sources: U.S. Energy Information Administration. *Annual Energy Review; Monthly Energy Review* (March 1994). *Notes:* Btu stands for British thermal units. A Btu is the amount of energy required to raise the temperature of 1 pound of water 1 degree Fahrenheit at or near 39.2 degrees Fahrenheit. "Z" represents less than .005 quadrillion Btu. 1. Net imports equals imports minus exports. Minus sign (-) denotes an excess of exports over imports. 2. Coal coke and small amounts of electricity transmitted across U.S. borders with Canada and Mexico.

★ 853 ★

Trade

Fishery Products – Imports and Exports: 1970-1991

Table shows the quantity and value of edible and nonedible fishery products imported to and exported from the United States. Imports include landings of tuna by foreign vessels at American Samoa.

Year	Imports					Exports				
	Total U.S. value (million dollars)	Fishery products				Total U.S. value (million dollars)	Fishery products			
		Total value (million dollars)	Edible products		Nonedible, value (million dollars)		Total value (million dollars)	Edible products		Nonedible, value (million dollars)
			Quantity (million dollars)	Value (million lb.)				Quantity (million lb.)	Value (million dollars)	
1970	39,756	1,037	1,873	813	225	43,224	118	140	94	24
1980	244,007	3,648	2,145	2,687	962	220,783	1,006	574	904	102
1985	343,553	6,679	2,754	4,064	2,614	213,146	1,084	648	1,010	73
1985	368,657	7,626	2,979	4,813	2,813	217,304	1,356	735	1,290	66
1987	402,066	8,818	3,201	5,711[1]	3,106	252,866	1,660	783	1,577	83
1988	437,140	8,872	2,968	5,442	3,430	320,385	2,275	1,060	2,156	119
1989	472,977	9,604	3,243	5,498	4,107	(NA)	4,707	1,374	2,283	2,424
1990	490,554	9,048	2,885	5,233	3,815	(NA)	5,639	1,910	2,777	2,862
1991	483,028	9,435	3,015	5,672	3,763	(NA)	6,162[1]	2,020[1]	3,037[1]	3,125

Source: 1994 Statistical Abstract of the United States on CD-ROM [machine-readable datafiles]. CD-8A-94. Washington, DC: U.S. Department of Commerce, Economics and Statistics Administration, Bureau of the Census, Data User Services Division, January 1995. Primary source: U.S. National Oceanic and Atmospheric Administration. National Marine Fisheries Service. *Fisheries of the United States* (annual). Compiled from U.S. Bureau of the Census data. *Notes:* "NA" stands for "not available." 1. Record.

★ 854 ★

Trade

Fishery Products – Imports and Exports, by Selected Product: 1985-1992

Table shows the quantity and value of selected fishery products imported and exported by the United States.

Product	Quantity (million pounds)				Value (million dollars)			
	1985	1990	1991	1992	1985	1990	1991	1992
Edible[1]	2,754	2,885	3,015	2,894	4,064	5,233	5,672	5,706
Fresh or frozen[1]	2,229	2,336	2,419	2,345	3,462	4,521	4,859	4,946
Salmon[2]	27	104	107	103	76	253	243	234
Tuna[3]	479	454	496	437	266	339	341	353
Groundfish fillets, blocks[4]	640	442	420	361	655	693	770	581
Other fillets and steaks	231	257	310	276	334	458	533	523
Scallops (meats)	42	40	30	39	147	131	111	160
Lobster, American, spiny	77	74	27	26	465	440	274	276
Shrimp and prawn	343	492	530	586	1,121	1,639	1,836	2,000
Canned[1]	414	458	513	469	466	543	642	580
Sardines and herring[5]	40	42	35	31	30	31	28	26
Tuna	214	285	352	323	209	294	359	309
Oysters	29	14	12	13	30	27	32	37
Pickled or salted	57	45	45	42	53	49	56	60
Cod, haddock, hake, pollock, cusk	35	11	11	10	41	18	22	23
Nonedible scrap and meal	511	239	159	151	62	39	32	35
Canned salmon	48	49	66	78	83	104	134	154
Fish oil, nonedible	279	222	254	177	37	24	35	29

Source: 1994 Statistical Abstract of the United States on CD-ROM [machine-readable datafiles]. CD-8A-94. Washington, DC: U.S. Department of Commerce, Economics and Statistics Administration, Bureau of the Census, Data User Services Division, January 1995. Primary source: U.S. National Oceanic and Atmospheric Administration. National Marine Fisheries Service. *Fisheries of the United States* (annual). Compiled from U.S. Bureau of the Census data. *Notes:* 1. Includes products not shown separately. 2. Excludes fillets. 3. Includes landings of tuna by foreign vessels at American Samoa. 4. Includes cod, cusk, haddock, hake, pollack, Atlantic ocean perch, and whiting. 5. Not in oil.

★ 855 ★

Trade

Mineral and Metal Imports: 1980-1993

Table shows net U.S. imports of selected minerals and metals as percent of apparent consumption and by major foreign sources. Figures based on net imports which equal the difference between imports and exports plus or minus government stockpile and industry stock changes.

[In percentages]

Mineral	1980	1985	1988	1989	1990	1991	1992	1993, est.	Rank of major foreign sources 1989-1992
Columbium	100	100	100	100	100	100	100	100	Brazil, 68%; Canada, 24%; Germany 4%
Manganese	98	100	100	100	100	100	100	100	South Africa, 25%; France, 14%; Brazil, 12%
Mica (sheet)	100	100	100	100	100	100	100	100	India, 63%; Belgium, 21%; Brazil, 3%
Strontium	100	100	100	100	100	100	100	100	Mexico, 91%; Germany, 7%
Bauxite[1]	94	96	97	96	98	100	100	100	Australia, 40%; Jamaica, 19%; Guinea, 18%
Asbestos	78	65	75	90	90	95	95	95	Canada, 98%; South Africa, 1%
Platinum group	87	92	91	90	88	90	87	88	South Africa, 50%; United Kingdom, 15%; Russia, 13%

[Continued]

★ 855 ★

Mineral and Metal Imports: 1980-1993

[Continued]

Mineral	1980	1985	1988	1989	1990	1991	1992	1993, est.	Rank of major foreign sources 1989-1992
Tantalum	90	89	86	86	86	86	85	86	Germany, 37%; Australia, 14%; Canada, 8%
Cobalt	93	94	87	83	84	80	75	75	Zambia, 26%; Zaire, 21%; Canada, 18%
Chromium	91	75	78	78	79	76	77	82	South Africa, 47%; Turkey, 14%; Zimbabwe, 10%
Tungsten	53	68	86	84	81	91	86	84	China, 49%; Bolivia, 8%; Peru, 7%
Nickel	76	71	74	71	69	67	61	64	Canada, 54%; Norway, 16%; Australia, 8%
Tin	79	72	78	77	71	74	80	81	Brazil, 24%; Bolivia, 22%; China, 16%
Barite	44	74	76	77	69	70	52	58	China, 76%; India, 19%; Mexico, 1%.
Potash	65	76	71	65	68	67	67	71	Canada, 92%; Israel, 3%; former U.S.S.R., 2%
Antimony	47	63	65	56	51	53	60	57	China, 60%; Mexico, 10%; South Africa, 10%
Cadmium	55	57	64	48	62	48	49	66	Canada, 34%; Mexico, 17%; Australia, 8%
Selenium	59	(D)	52	55	46	50	48	46	Canada, 37%; Japan, 16%; Belgium, 14%
Petroleum[2]	37	27	38	42	42	40	(NA)	(NA)	(NA)
Zinc	60	70	69	61	41[4]	24[4]	30[4]	26[4]	Canada, 61%; Mexico, 11%; Peru, 6%
Gypsum	35	38	36	35	36	31	31	29	Canada, 70%; Mexico, 23%; Spain, 6%.
Iron ore	25	21	18	22	21	11	12	12	Canada, 52%; Brazil, 24%; Venezuela, 19%
Iron and steel	13	22	19	13	13	12	13	12	European Economic Community, 30%; Canada, 19%; Japan, 18%
Sulfur	14	3	16	1	15	19	20	15	Canada, 60%; Mexico, 36%.
Natural gas[3]	5	5	7	7	8	8	(NA)	(NA)	(NA)
Copper	16[5]	28	13	7[5]	3[5]	5[5]	2	6	Canada, 49%; Chile, 18%; Mexico, 15%
Aluminum	5	16	7	5	5	5	1	16	Canada, 79%; Venezuela, 6%; Mexico, 2%
Silver	7	(NA)	(NA)	(NA)	(NA)	(NA)	(NA)	(NA)	Mexico, 35%; Canada, 27%; United Kingdom, 9%
Mercury	27	(NA)	(NA)	(NA)	(NA)	(NA)	(NA)	(NA)	Spain, 44%; Canada, 42%; Germany, 12%
Titanium	32	(D)	(D)	(D)	(D)	(D)	(D)	(D)	South Africa, 40%; Australia, 39%
Vanadium	35	(D)	(D)	(D)	(D)	(D)	(D)	(D)	South Africa, 35%; European Community, 11%; South America & Mexico, 21%

Source: 1994 Statistical Abstract of the United States on CD-ROM [machine-readable datafiles]. CD-8A-94. Washington, DC: U.S. Department of Commerce, Economics and Statistics Administration, Bureau of the Census, Data User Services Division, January 1995. Primary sources—except as noted: U.S. Bureau of Mines. *Mineral Commodity Summaries*; import and export data from U.S. Bureau of the Census. *Notes:* "D" denotes data withheld to avoid disclosure. "NA" stands for "not available." 1. Includes alumina. 2. Includes crude and products. Sources: Energy Information Administration. *Annual Energy Review* and *Monthly Energy Review*. 3. Sources: Energy Information Administration. *Annual Energy Review* and *Monthly Energy Review*. 4. Effect of sharp rise in exports of concentrates. If calculated on a refined zinc-only basis, reliance would be about the same as pre-1990 level; 1990, 64%; 1991, 60%; and 1992, 63% and 1993, 53%. 5. Net exports.

★ 856 ★

Trade

Mineral Fuels Trade: 1970-1991

Table shows U.S. imports, exports, and net trade in selected mineral fuels.

Mineral fuel	1970	1975	1980	1985	1990	1991
Natural gas						
Imports:						
Billion cubic feet	821	953	985	950	1,532	1,693
Trillion Btu	846	978	1,006	952	1,550	1,713
Exports:						
Billion cubic feet	70	73	49	55	86	122
Trillion Btu	72	74	49	56	88	124
Net trade:						
Billion cubic feet	(751)	(880)	(936)	(894)	(1,446)	(1,571)
Trillion Btu	(774)	(904)	(957)	(896)	(1,462)	(1,589)

[Continued]

★ 856 ★

Mineral Fuels Trade: 1970-1991
[Continued]

Mineral fuel	1970	1975	1980	1985	1990	1991
Crude oil						
Imports:						
Million barrels	483	1,498	1,926	1,168	2,151	2,110
Trillion Btu	2,814	8,721	11,195	6,814	12,764	12,550
Exports:						
Million barrels	5	2	105	75	40	42
Trillion Btu	29	12	609	432	232	244
Net trade:						
Million barrels	(478)	(1,496)	(1,821)	(1,094)	(2,111)	(2,068)
Trillion Btu	(2,785)	(8,708)	(10,586)	(6,381)	(12,532)	(12,306)
Petroleum products						
Imports:						
Million barrels	765	712	603	681	775	655
Trillion Btu	4,656	4,227	3,463	3,796	4,351	3,702
Exports:						
Million barrels	89	74	94	211	273	323
Trillion Btu	520	427	551	1,225	1,594	1,882
Net trade:						
Million barrels	(675)	(638)	(509)	(471)	(502)	(332)
Trillion Btu	(4,136)	(3,800)	(2,912)	(2,570)	(2,757)	(1,820)
Coal						
Imports:						
Thousand short tons	36	940	1,194	1,952	2,699	3,390
Trillion Btu	1	24	30	49	67	85
Exports:						
Thousand short tons	71,733	66,309	91,742	92,680	105,804	108,969
Trillion Btu	1,936	1,761	2,421	2,438	2,772	2,854
Net trade:						
Thousand short tons	71,697	65,369	90,548	90,728	103,105	105,579
Trillion Btu	1,935	1,738	2,391	2,389	2,705	2,769

Source: 1994 Statistical Abstract of the United States on CD-ROM [machine-readable datafiles]. CD-8A-94. Washington, DC: U.S. Department of Commerce, Economics and Statistics Administration, Bureau of the Census, Data User Services Division, January 1995. Primary source: U.S. Energy Information Administration, *Annual Energy Review. Notes:* Btu stands for British thermal unit. Numbers in parentheses [( )] indicate an excess of imports over exports. 1. Beginning 1977, includes strategic petroleum reserve imports.

★ 857 ★

Trade

Petroleum Production and Imports: 1940-1993

Table shows U.S. petroleum production and imports for crude oil and natural gas plant liquids for more than 50 years. Crude oil includes lease condensate. Imports for years 1940 through 1949 cover only crude petroleum products.

[In million barrels per day]

Year	Production			Imports
	Crude oil	NGPL	Total	
1940	3.71	0.15	3.93	0.12
1941	3.84	0.22	4.06	0.14
1942	3.80	0.23	4.03	0.03
1943	4.12	0.24	4.37	0.38
1944	4.60	0.27	4.97	0.12
1945	4.69	0.31	5.00	0.20
1946	4.75	0.32	5.07	0.24
1947	5.09	0.36	5.45	0.27
1948	5.53	0.40	5.94	0.35
1949	5.05	0.43	5.48	0.65
1950	5.41	0.50	5.91	0.85
1951	6.16	0.56	6.72	0.84
1952	6.27	0.61	6.87	0.95
1953	6.46	0.65	7.11	1.03
1954	6.34	0.69	7.03	1.05
1955	6.81	0.77	7.58	1.25
1956	7.15	0.80	7.95	1.44
1957	7.17	0.81	7.98	1.57
1958	6.71	0.81	7.52	1.70
1959	7.05	0.88	7.93	1.78
1960	7.04	0.93	7.96	1.81
1961	7.18	0.99	8.17	1.92
1962	7.33	1.02	8.35	2.08
1963	7.54	1.10	8.64	2.12
1964	7.61	1.16	8.77	2.26
1965	7.80	1.21	9.01	2.47
1966	8.30	1.28	9.58	2.57
1967	8.81	1.41	10.22	2.54
1968	9.10	1.51	10.60	2.84
1969	9.24	1.59	10.83	3.17
1970	9.64	1.66	11.30	3.42
1971	9.46	1.69	11.16	3.93
1972	9.44	1.75	11.18	4.74
1973	9.21	1.74	10.95	6.26
1974	8.77	1.69	10.46	6.11
1975	8.37	1.63	10.01	6.06
1976	8.13	1.61	9.74	7.31
1977	8.24	1.62	9.86	8.81
1978	8.71	1.57	10.27	8.36
1979	8.55	1.58	10.14	8.46
1980	8.60	1.58	10.17	6.91
1981	8.57	1.61	10.18	6.00

[Continued]

★ 857 ★

Petroleum Production and Imports: 1940-1993
[Continued]

Year	Production			Imports
	Crude oil	NGPL	Total	
1982	8.65	1.55	10.20	5.11
1983	8.69	1.56	10.25	5.05
1984	8.88	1.63	10.51	5.44
1985	8.97	1.61	10.58	5.07
1986	8.68	1.55	10.23	6.22
1987	8.35	1.60	9.94	6.68
1988	8.14	1.62	9.76	7.40
1989	7.61	1.55	9.16	8.06
1990	7.36	1.56	8.91	8.02
1991	7.42	1.66	9.08	7.63
1992	7.17	1.70	8.87	7.89
1993	6.84	1.73	8.57	8.53

Source: Executive Office of the President of the United States. *Environmental Quality 24: The Twenty-fourth Annual Report of the Council on Environmental Quality.* Prepared by Ray Clark. Written by Carroll Curtis. Edited by Barry Walsh. Washington, DC: U.S. Government Printing Office, 1994, p. 410. Primary sources: Bureau of the Census. *Historical Statistics of the United States: Colonial Times to 1970.* Series M 143, 138. Washington, DC: U.S. Department of Commerce, Bureau of the Census, 1976; U.S. Department of Energy. Energy Information Administration. *Annual Energy Review, 1993.* DOE/EIA-0384(93). Washington, DC: U.S. Department of Energy, Energy Information Administration, 1994, p. 141, table 5.1. *Notes:* "NGPL" stands for "natural gas plant liquids." Previous year data may have been revised. Current year data are preliminary and may be revised in the future.

★ 858 ★

Trade

Timber Product Imports and Exports: 1970-1992

Table shows U.S. imports and exports of selected timber products.

Item	Unit	1970	1980	1985	1990	1991	1992, prel.
Imports[1]							
Lumber, total[2]	Million board feet	6,114	9,866	14,996	12,159	11,756	13,474
From Canada	Percent	96.0	97.5	97.6	98.5	98.3	98.3
Softwoods	Million board feet	5,778	9,573	14,632	11,927	11,545	13,214
Value	Million dollars	434	1,826	2,898	2,534	2,507	3,310
Hardwoods	Million board feet	337	293	364	232	210	260
Value	Million board feet	62	152	180	141	142	176
Logs, total	Million board feet[3]	144	128	99	28	15	46
From Canada	Percent	79.6	97.4	81.8	67.5	74.5	88.9
Softwoods	Million board feet[3]	107	114	71	18	9	40
Value	Million dollars	9	17	17	7	6	20
Hardwoods	Million board feet[3]	38	13	28	10	6	7
Value	Million dollars	5	3	4	10	6	6
Paper and board[4]	1,000 tons	7,115	8,780	11,522	13,148	12,167	12,543
Value	Million dollars	1,039	3,418	5,698	8,427	7,929	7,899
Woodpulp	1,000 tons	3,518	4,051	4,466	4,893	4,997	5,029

[Continued]

★ 858 ★

Timber Product Imports and Exports: 1970-1992

[Continued]

Item	Unit	1970	1980	1985	1990	1991	1992, prel.
Value	Million dollars	483	1,684	1,521	2,831	2,132	2,094
Plywood	Million square feet[5]	2,049	1,235	1,817	1,687	1,457	1,776
Value	Million dollars	208	409	463	537	457	574
Exports							
Lumber, total[2]	Million board feet	1,243	2,494	1,945	3,802	3,997	3,603
To: Canada	Percent	21.7	25.3	23.7	18.1	15.1	17.3
Japan	Percent	30.8	26.0	32.1	33.5	30.5	30.9
Europe	Percent	24.1	23.8	15.1	19.1	19.6	21.2
Softwoods	Million board feet	1,115	2,007	1,518	2,941	3,055	2,613
Value	Million dollars	163	789	497	1,336	1,358	1,363
Hardwoods	Million board feet	128	487	427	861	942	990
Value	Million dollars	31	272	263	818	879	988
Logs, total	Million board feet[3]	2,741	3,261	3,843	4,262	3,816	3,316
To: Canada	Percent	10.6	9.7	11.6	9.3	11.2	12.6
Japan	Percent	86.3	78.0	49.4	62.5	56.7	62.1
Mainland China	Percent	(NA)	2.7	27.8	8.5	9.7	7.1
Softwoods	Million board feet[3]	2,672	3,109	3,732	4,044	3,532	3,092
Value	Million dollars	320	1,452	1,169	2,170	1,870	1,925
Hardwoods	Million board feet[3]	69	152	111	218	283	224
Value	Million dollars	36	129	91	251	234	238
Paper and board[4]	1,000 tons	2,817	5,214	4,071	6,796	8,331	8,971
Value	Million dollars	602	2,773	2,266	5,035	6,006	6,392
Woodpulp	1,000 tons	3,095	3,806	3,796	5,906	6,337	7,222
Value	Million dollars	464	1,652	1,354	3,156	2,800	3,114
Plywood	Million square feet[5]	172	413	358	1,767	1,552	1,759
Value	Million dollars	16	108	86	338	295	366

Source: 1994 Statistical Abstract of the United States on CD-ROM [machine-readable datafiles]. CD-8A-94. Washington, DC: U.S. Department of Commerce, Economics and Statistics Administration, Bureau of the Census, Data User Services Division, January 1995. Primary source: U.S. Forest Service. *U.S. Timber Production, Trade, Consumption, and Price Statistics: 1960-1989.* Notes: "NA" stands for "not available." 1. Customs value of imports. 2. Includes railroad ties. 3. Log scale. 4. Includes paper and board products. Excludes hardboard. 5. 3/8 inch basis.

★ 859 ★
Trade

U.S. Energy Imports, by Source: 1950-1993

The table shows net energy imports of the United States for more than 30 years. Net energy imports are imports minus exports. Negative values mean that more is exported than imported. British thermal units (Btu) have been used to make solids, gases, and liquids comparable.

[In quadrillion Btu]

Year	Coal	Natural gas	Petroleum	Other[1]	Total
1950	-0.78	-0.03	1.24	0.03	0.47
1955	-1.46	-0.02	1.98	0.04	0.54
1960	-1.02	0.15	3.57	0.04	2.74
1965	-1.37	0.44	5.01	-0.02	4.06
1966	-1.35	0.47	5.21	-0.01	4.32
1967	-1.35	0.50	4.91	-0.02	4.04
1968	-1.37	0.58	5.73	-0.02	4.90
1969	-1.53	0.70	6.42	-0.02	5.56
1970	-1.93	0.77	6.92	-0.04	5.72
1971	-1.54	0.88	8.07	[2]	7.41
1972	-1.53	0.97	9.83	0.05	9.32
1973	-1.42	0.98	12.98	0.14	12.68
1974	-1.57	0.91	12.66	0.19	12.19
1975	-1.74	0.90	12.51	0.08	11.75
1976	-1.57	0.92	15.20	0.09	14.65
1977	-1.40	0.98	18.24	0.20	18.02
1978	-1.00	0.94	17.06	0.33	17.32
1979	-1.70	1.24	16.93	0.27	16.75
1980	-2.39	0.96	13.50	0.18	12.25
1981	-2.92	0.86	11.38	0.33	9.65
1982	-2.77	0.90	9.05	0.28	7.46
1983	-2.01	0.89	9.08	0.36	8.31
1984	-2.12	0.79	9.89	0.40	8.96
1985	-2.39	0.90	8.95	0.41	7.87
1986	-2.19	0.69	11.53	0.36	10.38
1987	-2.05	0.94	12.53	0.49	11.91
1988	-2.45	1.22	14.01	0.37	13.15
1989	-2.57	1.28	15.33	0.14	14.18
1990	-2.70	1.46	15.29	0.03	14.08
1991	-2.77	1.67	14.22	0.24	13.36
1992	-2.59	1.94	14.96	0.32	14.63
1993	-1.77	2.14	16.19	0.31	16.88

Source: Executive Office of the President of the United States. *Environmental Quality 24: The Twenty-fourth Annual Report of the Council on Environmental Quality.* Prepared by Ray Clark. Written by Carroll Curtis. Edited by Barry Walsh. Washington, DC: U.S. Government Printing Office, 1994, p. 414. Primary source: U.S. Department of Energy. Energy Information Administration. *Annual Energy Review, 1993.* DOE/EIA-0384(93). Washington, DC: U.S. Department of Energy, Energy Information Administration, 1994, p. 11, table 1.4. *Notes:* Sum of components may not equal totals because of independent rounding. Previous year data may have been revised. Current year data are preliminary and may be revised in the future. 1. Includes coal coke and small amounts of electricity transmitted across U.S. borders with Canada and Mexico. 2. Less than 0.005 quadrillion Btu.

★ 860 ★

Trade

World Coal Trade: 1975-1990

[In million short tons]

Countries	1975	1980	1985	1990
Exporting countries, total[1]	212.5	277.2	370.2	440.2
United States	66.3	88.7	93.2	105.8
Australia	33.5	46.6	96.6	116.9
South Africa	3.0	30.7	49.8	54.5
Soviet Union	28.8	26.2	26.5	42.7
Germany[2]	16.2	13.8	10.5	6.0
Canada	12.9	16.1	30.3	34.2
Poland	42.4	34.6	39.7	61.8
China: Mainland	0.5	4.2	8.6	19.1
Importing countries, total[1]	212.5	277.2	370.2	440.2
Western Europe/Mediterranean	80.8	126.9	152.3	172.1
Japan	68.5	75.6	103.0	113.9
Eastern Europe	35.1	34.8	39.1	30.6
Canada	16.8	17.4	16.1	15.7

Source: *1994 Statistical Abstract of the United States on CD-ROM* [machine-readable datafiles]. CD-8A-94. Washington, DC: U.S. Department of Commerce. Economics and Statistics Administration, Bureau of the Census, Data User Services Division, January 1995. Primary sources—1975-1984: U.S. Energy Information Administration. *Outlook for U.S. Coal Imports*; thereafter: *Annual Prospects for World Coal Trade. Notes:* 1. Includes areas not shown separately. 2. Includes trade with Japan only.

Transportation

★ 861 ★

Battery-Powered Vehicles

Starting in 1998, 2 percent of each automobile manufacturers' sales in California must be from battery-powered vehicles. The table below shows the number each automaker must sell to reach its quota. Data are based on 1992 California sales.

Manufacturer	Battery-powered vehicles
General Motors	6,600
Ford	6,400
Toyota	3,900
Chrysler	2,700
Honda	2,500

[Continued]

★ 861 ★

Battery-Powered Vehicles
[Continued]

Manufacturer	Battery-powered vehicles
Nissan	1,800
Mazda	900

Source: "Charging up for California." *USA TODAY*, 29 November 1993, p. 1B. Primary source: *Automotive News*.

★ 862 ★

Transportation

Environmental Concerns of New Car Buyers

Table shows items rated as "extremely important" to new car buyers in the United States.

[In percentages]

Item	New car buyers
Freedom from repairs	67
Safety	64
Overall cost of ownership	64
Ease of getting it repaired	61
Quality of workmanship	58
Gas economy	56
Quality of service	53
Enjoyable to drive	51
Riding comfort	47
Low on pollution	34

Source: "Top Priorities." *Detroit Free Press*, 14 April 1994, p. 1E. Primary source: Roper Starch. "The 1994 Starch Automotive Advertising Study" (Mamaroneck, New York).

★ 863 ★

Transportation

Personal Travel: 1969-1990

Table shows the personal travel per household, driver, and mode. Household vehicles include automobiles, station wagons, and vanbuses/mini-buses, and, except for 1969, light pickups and other light trucks. Household vehicles are those that are owned, leased, rented, or company-owned and left at home to be regularly used by household members. They also include vehicles used solely for business purposes or business-owned vehicles if left at home and used for the home-to-work trip (for example, taxicabs and police cars). Average vehicle trip length for 1969 is for automobiles only. Travel to work in 1990 combines automobiles and trucks. Family and personal business includes vehicle trips to school, church, doctor, shop, etc. Social/recreation includes vehicle trips to visit relatives and friends and other types of pleasure driving. Private vehicle modes of travel include automobiles, vans, pick-up trucks, other trucks, camper coaches, and motorcycles. Public transportation includes buses, commuter rail, subways, elevated rail, streetcars, and trolleys. Other includes airplanes, Amtrak, taxis, school buses, mopeds, bicycles, and, except for 1969, walking.

Characteristics of personal travel	Unit	Year			
		1969	1977	1983	1990
Persons per household	Number	3.16	2.83	2.69	2.57
Licensed drivers per household	Number	1.65	1.69	1.72	1.75
Vehicles per household	Number	1.16	1.59	1.68	1.77
Daily vehicle trips per household	Number	3.83	3.95	4.07	4.66
Daily vehicle miles per household	Miles	34.01	32.97	32.16	41.37
Average vehicle occupancy rate	Persons/vehicle	NA	1.90	1.70	1.50
Home to work	Persons/vehicle	NA	1.30	1.30	1.10
Family & personal business	Persons/vehicle	NA	2.00	1.80	1.70
Shopping	Persons/vehicle	NA	2.10	1.80	1.50
Social & recreation	Persons/vehicle	NA	2.40	2.10	1.80
Average vehicle trip length	Miles	8.89	8.34	7.90	8.87
Home to work	Miles	9.40	9.10	8.50	11.00
Family & personal business	Miles	6.50	6.80	6.70	7.40
Shopping	Miles	4.40	5.00	5.30	5.10
Social & recreation	Miles	13.10	10.3	10.5	11.8
Vacation	Miles	160.00	77.90	113.90	114.90
Average distance to work	Miles	9.90	9.20	9.90	10.60
by automobile	Miles	9.40	9.20	9.90	10.40
by truck	Miles	14.20	10.60	11.40	13.00
by bus	Miles	8.70	7.20	8.60	9.30
Average annual travel per driver	1,000 miles	8.69	10.01	10.59	13.18
by male drivers	1,000 miles	11.35	13.40	13.96	16.63
by female drivers	1,000 miles	5.41	5.94	6.38	9.54
Personal travel (average)	1,000 miles	7.12	8.82	8.48	9.53
by private vehicle	1,000 miles	NA	7.59	7.00	8.39
by public vehicle	1,000 miles	NA	0.24	0.51	0.22
by other mode	1,000 miles	NA	0.99	0.98	0.91

Source: Executive Office of the President of the United States. *Environmental Quality 24: The Twenty-fourth Annual Report of the Council on Environmental Quality.* Prepared by Ray Clark. Written by Carroll Curtis. Edited by Barry Walsh. Washington, DC: U.S. Government Printing Office, 1994, p. 502. Primary sources: U.S. Department of Transportation. Federal Highway Administration. *1990 Nationwide Personal Transportation Study: Summary of Travel Trends.* Washington, DC: U.S. Department of Transportation, 1992; U.S. Department of Transportation. Federal Highway Administration. *1990 NPTS Databook: Nationwide Personal Transportation Study.* Vol. 1. Washington, DC: U.S. Department of Transportation, 1993. *Note:* "NA" represents "not available or not applicable."

★ 864 ★

Transportation

Travel and Fuel Consumption: 1966-1993

Table shows vehicle miles of travel and fuel consumption.

[vmt/y in thousands]

Year	Automobiles		Motorcycles		Buses		Trucks			
							2-axle, 4-tire		Trailer combination	
	vmt/y	vmy/g	vmt/y	vmt/g	vmt/y	vmt/g	vmt/y	vmt/g	vmt/y	vmt/g
1966	9.92	14.11	1.28	50.00	14.06	5.42	8.08	9.70	35.99	4.78
1970	10.27	13.52	1.06	50.00	12.04	5.54	8.68	10.01	38.82	4.78
1975	9.69	13.52	1.13	50.00	13.10	5.75	9.83	11.21	41.32	5.40
1980	9.14	15.46	1.79	50.00	11.46	5.95	10.44	12.33	48.47	5.41
1985	9.56	18.20	1.67	50.00	8.22	5.84	11.02	12.86	56.73	5.21
1990	10.55	21.02	2.24	50.00	9.12	6.39	11.99	14.15	59.81	5.52
1991	10.76	21.69	2.20	50.00	9.10	6.65	12.10	14.54	60.46	5.65
1992	11.10	21.68	2.35	50.00	8.93	6.57	12.10	14.28	59.89	5.60
1993	11.09	21.64	2.49	50.00	9.35	6.46	12.16	14.44	59.50	5.55

Source: Executive Office of the President of the United States. *Environmental Quality 24: The Twenty-fourth Annual Report of the Council on Environmental Quality.* Prepared by Ray Clark. Written by Carroll Curtis. Edited by Barry Walsh. Washington, DC: U.S. Government Printing Office., 1994, p. 501. Primary source: U.S. Department of Transportation. Federal Highway Administration. *Highway Statistics.* Washington, DC: U.S. Department of Transportation (annual), table vm-1. *Notes:* "vmt/y" denotes vehicle miles of travel per year; "vmt/g" represents average vehicle miles of travel per gallon of fuel consumed.

Chapter 11
POLITICS, OPINION, LAW

This chapter covers the environmental consciousness of corporations and individuals, law enforcement and legal issues (including legislation), the media, and permits and regulations. Coverage is intended to show general attitudes and views of the general public, the business community, the press, and lawmakers.

Environmental Consciousness of Corporations

★ 865 ★

Corporate Environmental Committees

Table shows Fortune 100 corporate boards with environmental or public policy committees.

[In percentages]

Type of committee	Boards
None	61.0
Public policy	31.0
Environmental	8.0

Source: Muson, Howard. "Winds of Change." *Across the Board* (June 1994), p. 18. Primary source: The Directorship (Westport, Connecticut).

★ 866 ★

Environmental Consciousness of Corporations

Corporate Environmental Initiatives

A survey of Standard & Poor's (S&P) 500 companies and an analysis of government records (1988-1990) show that management at S&P 500 companies is increasing its attentiveness to environmental issues. The table below identifies past and projected environmental initiatives of corporations.

[In percentages]

Environmental initiative	Corporate initiatives	
	Past	Future
Pollution prevention/waste minimization	32	30
Pollution control	-	11
Reuse/recycle	18	10
Management initiatives	15	10
Energy-efficiency	5	-
Other	30	38

Source: Fenn, Scott. "Past Pollution Problems Spur New Management Initiatives." *Water Environment & Technology* (March 1994), p. 38. Primary source: Investor Responsibility Research Center (IRRC) survey. *Note:* "-" indicates data not reported in source.

Environmental Consciousness of Public

★ 867 ★

Environmental Clean Up

Recycling at home - 90

Purchasing biodegradable products - 71

Recycling at work - 62

Contributing money - 37

Table below shows actions reported by Americans helping to clean up the environment through their lifestyles.

[In percentages]

Action	Respondents
Recycling at home	90
Purchasing biodegradable products	71
Recycling at work	62
Contributing money[1]	37

Source: "Who Helps the Environment." *USA TODAY*, 23-24 November 1994, p. 1A. Primary source: Opinion Research Corporation. *Note:* 1. To environmental, conservation, or wildlife preservation groups.

★ 868 ★

Environmental Consciousness of Public

Environmental Concerns in Developing Nations: 1993

The table below shows responses of Gallup poll participants from developing nations. Survey participants were asked their level of personal concern regarding environmental problems. Data represent those indicating "great" or "moderate" concerns in 1993.

[In percentages]

Country	"Great" concern	"Moderate" concern
Philippines	55	94
Nigeria	71	87
Mexico	50	83
Uruguay	38	82
Brazil	53	80
South Korea	22	80
Hungary	32	79

[Continued]

★ 868 ★

Environmental Concerns in Developing Nations: 1993
[Continued]

Country	"Great" concern	"Moderate" concern
Russia	41	78
India	34	77
Chile	30	70
Turkey	12	40
Poland	4	25

Source: "Environmental Concerns Is Global." *Scientific American* (October 1994), p. 120.
Primary source: *Health of the Planet* (George H. Gallup International Institute, 1993).

★ 869 ★
Environmental Consciousness of Public

Environmental Concerns in Industrialized Nations: 1993

The table below shows responses of Gallup poll participants from industrialized nations. Survey participants were asked their level of personal concern regarding environmental problems. Data represent those indicating "great" or "moderate" concerns in 1993.

[In percentage]

Country	"Great" concern	"Moderate" concern
Portugal	46	90
Canada	37	89
United States	38	85
Great Britain	28	81
Norway	18	77
Ireland	22	73
Netherlands	16	71
Japan	23	66
Germany	14	63
Finland	16	63
Denmark	12	53
Switzerland	12	42

Source: "Environmental Concerns Is Global." *Scientific American* (October 1994), p. 120.
Primary source: *Health of the Planet* (George H. Gallup International Institute, 1993).

★ 870 ★

Environmental Consciousness of Public

Environmental Issues

The table below shows environmental issues that Americans reportedly want to see addressed.

[In percentages]

Issue	Responses
Shortages of good drinking water	88
Pollution of lakes, rivers, streams and coastal waters	88
Loss of open areas, woods and natural places	81
Pollution of toxic waste sites	76
Extinction of endangered plants, animals, and insects	74
Air pollution or smog	72
Loss of wetlands	64
Damage of ozone layer	64
Global warming	56
Lack of landfill space	56

Source: "America and the Environment: The Sky Isn't Falling." *Skiing Trade News* (August/September 1994), p. 10. Primary source: Times Mirror Magazines National Environmental Forum Survey, conducted by the Roper Organization.

★ 871 ★

Environmental Consciousness of Public

Environmental Protection, by Group

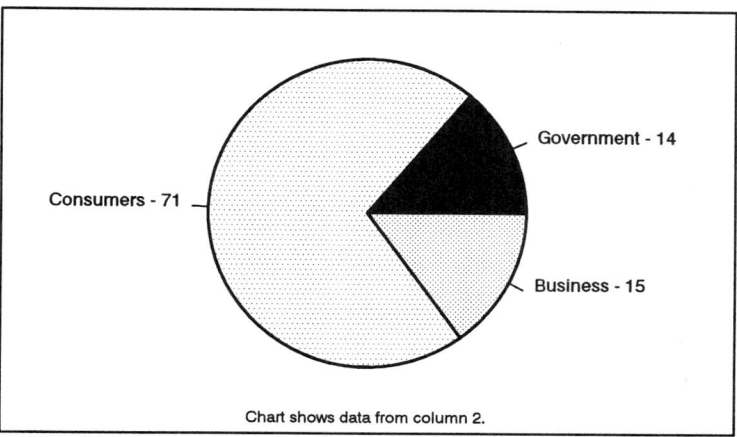

Chart shows data from column 2.

Table show responses of 86 people polled regarding the actions of various groups toward the environment. Data reflect groups whose actions contribute the most of protecting the environment.

[In percentages]

Group	Action	Respondents
Consumers	Choices	71
Business	Operations	15
Government	Laws	14

Source: "Saving the Earth." *USA TODAY*, 29 September 1994, p. 1A. Primary source: Global Futures.

★ 872 ★

Environmental Consciousness of Public

Local Environmental Conditions: 1993

Table below shows National League of Cities ratings for various local conditions, including water and air quality.

[In percentages]

Conditions	"Very good" or "good"	"Fair" or "poor"
Water quality	86	14
Volunteerism/community service	82	18
Police/community relations	78	22
Solid waste management	77	23
Immunization/preventive health care	77	23

[Continued]

★ 872 ★

Local Environmental Conditions: 1993
[Continued]

Conditions	"Very good" or "good"	"Fair" or "poor"
Air quality	72	28
Vitality of neighborhoods	68	32
Health care	68	32
Infrastructure	67	33
City fiscal conditions	65	35
Overall economic conditions	62	38
High school graduation rates	61	39
Quality of education	60	40
Race/ethnic relations	56	44
Housing affordability	54	46
Family stability	51	49
Violent crime	47	53
AIDS	47	53
Unemployment	46	54
Homelessness	46	54
Availability of low income housing	42	58
Gangs	41	59
Poverty	37	63
Cable TV rates and services	36	64
Drugs	32	68
Teen pregnancy	29	71
Impact of unfunded mandates	8	92

Source: "Status of Local Conditions in 1993." *American City & County* (April 1994), p. 16. Primary source: National League of Cities.

Law and Law Enforcement

★ 873 ★

Corporate Legal Needs

Table shows company expectations regarding environment-related legal needs, as well as other areas of law. Data based on a survey of 201 major companies.

[In percentages]

Area of law	Increase
Environmental	68
International	50
Regulatory	47
Labor[1]	47

[Continued]

★ 873 ★

Corporate Legal Needs
[Continued]

Area of law	Increase
Employee benefits[2]	43
Litigation	43
Antitrust	42
Contracts	41
Mergers and acquisitions	32
Securities/finance	28
Labor[3]	28
Patent	23
Tax	23
Bankruptcy	22
Trademark	20
Real estate	19

Source: "Growth Chart." *Wall Street Journal,* 4 February 1994, p. B11. Primary source: Price Waterhouse Law Firm & Law Department Services Group. *1993 Law Department Spending Survey. Notes:* 1. Equal Employment Opportunity Commission (EEOC). 2. Employee Retirement Income Security Act (ERISA). 3. National Labor Relations Board (NLRB).

★ 874 ★
Law and Law Enforcement

Environmental Protection Agency's Criminal Enforcement Efforts: 1989- 1993

The U.S. Environmental Protection Agency (EPA) investigates companies suspected of violating environmental laws. Case loads, staff, and budgets have risen since 1989. The table below outlines criminal enforcement efforts of the EPA.

Fiscal year	Agents	Cases initiated	Referrals for prosecution	Defendants	Convictions	Sentences[1] (years)	Fines[2]
1989	47	120	60	72	NA	27.1	$12.2
1990	51	112	56	100	NA	75.3	$5.5
1991	62	150	81	104	102	80.3	$14.1
1992	72	203	107	150	141	94.6	$37.9
1993	110	410	140	161	110	74.3	$29.7

Source: Litvan, Laura M. "The Growing Ranks of Enviro-Cops." *Nation's Business* (June 1994), p. 30. Primary source: U.S. Environmental Protection Agency. *Notes:* "NA" stands for "not available or applicable." 1. Total years of sentences for all defendants convicted. 2. Total fines for all defendants convicted in millions.

Recycling Laws: 1993

Table shows the states enacting or amending recycling-related laws in 1993. In total, 110 recycling laws were instituted or revised that year.

Issue	1993	1992	Total[1]
Comprehensive recycling	California, Connecticut, District of Columbia, New York, Vermont	2	39
Landfill bans	Arkansas (delay), Georgia, North Carolina, Florida, Minnesota, Oklahoma, Utah, West Virginia (delay)	7	46
Green labeling	Florida, Maine, Oregon, Wisconsin, Minnesota	2	18
SPI coding	Kansas, Texas	1	39
Heavy metals	Florida, Maine, Minnesota, Missouri	4	16
Packaging mandates	California (revised), Florida (revised), Maine (revised), Oregon (revised), Texas, Vermont	7	8
Market and packaging studies	Alabama, Arkansas, California, North Dakota, Minnesota, Nebraska, New Hampshire, Rhode Island, Virginia	2	NA
State purchasing preferences for recycled products	California, Colorado, Connecticut, Florida, Georgia, Hawaii, Maryland, New Hampshire, New Jersey, North Carolina, Ohio, Rhode Island, South Dakota, Virginia	10	43
Tax incentives	Arkansas, California, Hawaii, Maine, Montana, North Dakota, Texas, Virginia, Nevada (all amended only)	3	28
Volume-based fee incentives	Proposed only; local initiatives did pass	2	5
Newsprint mandates	Florida, Colorado, Hawaii Voluntary (14 total)	1	13

[Continued]

★ 875 ★

Recycling Laws: 1993
[Continued]

Issue	1993	1992	Total[1]
Used oil	California, Montana, North Carolina, Oklahoma, Tennessee, Texas, Utah, Virginia	9	NA
Batteries[2]	Arkansas, California, Florida, Hawaii, Maryland, Minnesota, Oklahoma, Rhode Island, Michigan	3	41
Composting	Florida, Hawaii, Indiana, Maine, New Hampshire, Virginia	2	13
Business grants and loans	Arkansas, Illinois, Oregon, Vermont	4	29

Source: "State Laws for 1993 Reflect Recycling Trends." *World Wastes* (March 1994), p. 6. Primary source: Raymond Communications. *Notes:* "NA" stands for "not available or applicable." "SPI" references the U.S. Environmental Protection Agency's Strategic Planning Initiative. 1. Total number of states with laws. 2. Includes landfill bans and 18 states with taxes, take-backs, or deposits on batteries.

★ 876 ★

Law and Law Enforcement

Safe Drinking Water Act Violations: 1991-1992

The Natural Resources Defense Council documented in excess of 250,000 water law violations in 1991 to 1992. Remedies for the "over burdened" and "outdated" water supply infrastructure include more rigid enforcement, more visible notification of violations in the media, adjusted limits for pollutants causing health risks, and state revolving funds for water treatment plant improvements. The table below shows safe Drinking Water Act violations in each state.

State	Excessive contaminants violations	Monitoring, reporting violations
Alabama	55	327
Alaska	223	19,119
Arizona	405	14,886
Arkansas	101	245
California	894	3,396
Colorado	90	782
Connecticut	234	565
Delaware	107	5
District of Columbia	0	2
Florida	521	5,250
Georgia	169	746
Hawaii	34	40
Idaho	464	1,342

[Continued]

★ 876 ★

Safe Drinking Water Act Violations: 1991-1992
[Continued]

State	Excessive contaminants violations	Monitoring, reporting violations
Illinois	730	2,514
Indiana	42	917
Iowa	264	2,359
Kansas	178	291
Kentucky	130	1,461
Louisiana	529	162
Maine	65	154
Maryland	68	264
Massachusetts	113	257
Michigan	155	241
Minnesota	59	469
Missouri	422	850
Mississippi	339	835
Montana	113	1,136
Nebraska	377	70
Nevada	24	367
New York	406	6,174
New Jersey	215	2,819
New Hampshire	335	382
New Mexico	131	473
North Carolina	338	20,054
North Dakota	84	154
Ohio	576	3,085
Oklahoma	532	855
Oregon	309	1,521
Pennsylvania	459	12,897
Rhode Island	29	27
South Carolina	91	1,279
South Dakota	306	1,204
Tennessee	42	250
Texas	822	2,329
Utah	115	613
Vermont	272	892
Virginia	496	1,464
Washington	1,474	7,993
West Virginia	92	817
Wisconsin	164	433
Wyoming	54	482

Source: Tyson, Rae. "Plug Holes in Water Laws, Analysts Say." *USA TODAY,* 27 September 1993, p. 5A. Primary source: Natural Resources Defense Council.

★ 877 ★

Law and Law Enforcement

State Environmental Legislation: 1994

Table shows the type of legislation, number of bills introduced, and number of bills enacted by states during 1994.

Legislation	Bills introduced	Bills enacted
Solid waste programs, funds, studies	35	5
Environmental labeling	24	2
Packaging taxes/fees	22	1
Packaging bans	22	0
Recycled content	16	1
Toxin reduction/control/elimination	15	2
Recycling rates	12	0
Repeals/exemptions of solid waste laws	11	1
Composting	6	0
Source reduction	6	1
Waste-reduction goals	6	0
Incineration	3	0
Landfill bans	3	0
SPI code bans	3	0
Degradability	2	1
SPI code mandates	2	0

Source: "FYI...." *Plastics News*, 20 February 1995, p. 3. Primary source: Foodservice Packaging Institute Inc. *Notes:* "SPI" references U.S. Environmental Protection Agency's Strategic Planning Initiative.

★ 878 ★

Law and Law Enforcement

Waste Incineration Fines

Table show companies cited by the Environmental Protection Agency (EPA) for violating hazardous waste incineration laws. The 10 largest fines proposed by the the EPA are shown.

[In dollars]

Company	Penalty
Lone Star Industries (Greencastle, Indiana)	3,822,056
River Cement (Festus, Missouri)	3,364,388
Chemical Waste Management (Sauget, Illinois)	3,100,000
S.C. Johnson & Sons (Sturtevant, Wisconsin)	1,466,475
Ash Grove Cement (Louisville, Nebraska)	1,274,900
Lafarge Company (Fredonia, Kansas)	1,200,474
Southwestern Portland Cement (Fairborn, Ohio)	1,064,765
Rhone-Poulenc (Institute, West Virginia)	915,125

[Continued]

★ 878 ★

Waste Incineration Fines
[Continued]

Company	Penalty
Holnam (Holly Hills, South Carolina)	838,850
Mayline Company (Sheboygan, Wisconsin)	649,000

Source: Tyson, Rae. "EPA Proposes $20M in Fines for Waste-Burners." *USA TODAY,* 29 September 1993, p. 3A.

Media

★ 879 ★

Environment Reporters

| Very large - 100 |
| Large - 68 |
| Medium - 67 |
| Small newspaper - 38 |
| Local TV - 26 |

A survey of journalists from newspapers, network and local television stations, and leading news magazines found 72 percent of their reporters insufficiently trained to cover complicated environmental issues. Table shows the types of news organizations and the reporters at each specializing in the environment.

[In percentages]

News organization	Reporters specializing in the environment
Small newspaper	38
Medium	67
Large	68
Very large	100
Local TV	26

Source: "More Quantity Than Quality." *Amicus Journal* (winter 1994), p. 41. Primary source: Foundation for American Communications (FACS).

★ 880 ★
Media

Environmental Consciousness of Magazine Executives

According to the source: "Almost two-thirds of the respondents [magazine executives surveyed for a *Folio: Reader Panel Report*] say they would personally spend more to buy a magazine on recycled paper.... Two-thirds of respondents who influence purchasing decisions will support paying more for recycled paper.... A full 65 percent said they would recommend the company pay more—when necessary—to purchase other publishing-related materials, equipment and processes that are more friendly to the environment."

Source: Love, Barbara. "How Do Magazine Executives Rate in Environmental Consciousness?" *Folio: Special Sourcebook Issue* (1994), p. 225. Primary source: *Folio: Reader Panel Report.*

Permits and Regulations

★ 881 ★

Section 404 Applications: 1989-1993

Application withdrawn - 14,950	
Permit issued - 10,499	
Application denied - 1,312	

Chart shows data from column 1.

Section 404 permits are required to alter or destroy wetlands. Many applications for Section 404 permits are withdrawn owing to frustration of applicants, to applicant's need for a different permit, or to applicant's learning that a permit is unnecessary. The table below shows the number and percentage of Section 404 applications processed in fiscal years 1989 through 1993.

Application status	Number	Percent
Application withdrawn	14,950	56
Permit issued	10,499	39
Application denied	1,312	5

Source: "Study Questions 'Myths.'" *ENR*, 18 April 1994, p. 17. Primary source: Corps of Engineers.

★ 882 ★

Permits and Regulations

Water Pollution Permits: 1993

Approximately half of all water pollution permits were expired in 1993. The table below shows the number of water pollution permits and the percent that were expired for each state. Data are ranked by permits expired.

State	Permits	Percent expired
Virginia	2,475	94
New Mexico	175	93
Connecticut	780	86
New Jersey	1,413	85
West Virginia	3,711	83
Nebraska	1,043	83
Alaska	768	81
Hawaii	80	80
Maine	379	78
Massachusetts	561	77
Rhode Island	140	76
Louisiana	1,429	76
New Hampshire	191	75
Washington	655	74
Wisconsin	1,102	73
Delaware	93	73
Ohio	4,478	71
Idaho	276	70
Michigan	1,698	69
Texas	3,122	69
Indiana	1,773	69
California	1,297	67
South Carolina	1,257	64
Maryland	1,017	63
Montana	227	62
Illinois	2,608	54
Nevada	90	54
Minnesota	1,080	54
North Carolina	2,827	53
Oklahoma	675	53
Oregon	1,056	51
Vermont	140	51
Kansas	1,165	50
Pennsylvania	4,882	50
Utah	145	50
Florida	807	48
North Dakota	415	46
Arizona	143	43
Wyoming	862	39
Arkansas	875	37
South Dakota	363	37
Alabama	1,899	37
Colorado	629	37
Missouri	2,375	34

[Continued]

★ 882 ★

Water Pollution Permits: 1993
[Continued]

State	Permits	Percent expired
Iowa	1,702	34
New York	1,959	32
Tennessee	1,584	29
Mississippi	1,481	28
Georgia	1,101	27
Kentucky	2,596	22

Source: "Expired Permits." *Detroit Free Press,* 20 February 1995, p. 6A. Primary sources: Data from U.S. Environmental Protection Agency; computer analysis by Rich Puchalski, Jack Esco, and Laurie Bennett.

Sources

The sources used in *Statistical Record of the Environment,* 3rd edition, are shown below. Sources are arranged alphabetically. Numbers following each listed source refer to table—not page—numbers.

1994 Statistical Abstract of the United States on CD-ROM [machine-readable datafiles]. CD-8A-94. Washington, DC: U.S. Department of Commerce, Economics and Statistics Administration, Bureau of the Census, Data User Services Division, January 1995. Tables: 12-14, 25, 35-36, 38, 40-45, 48, 54, 57-58, 61, 63, 68-112, 114-139, 141-175, 180, 182, 187-196, 208-209, 211, 217-221, 223-229, 233-244, 246-249, 251-252, 277, 280, 282-284, 286, 288-292, 294-297, 305, 319, 322, 323, 325-326, 328-331, 333-334, 336-340, 345-347, 351-352, 354, 356-358, 360-361, 363-365, 367-369, 371-376, 456, 478, 527-529, 531-532, 553, 591, 593-600, 605-606, 608-609, 624-625, 631, 633, 638, 795-800, 807-817, 832-834, 836-839, 843, 845-846, 850-856, 858, 860

"Addressing Pesticide Residues." *Food Review* (October-December 1992). Table: 377

Allman, William F. "Rumblings Coast to Coast." *U.S. News & World Report,* 31 January 1994. Table: 62

"America and the Environment: The Sky Isn't Falling." *Skiing Trade News* (August/September 1994). Table: 870

"Analysis Supports Access to Off-Site Treatment Centers." *World Wastes* (October 1993). Table: 522

Bailey, Jeff. "Recycling Mania Crashes and Burns in California." *Wall Street Journal,* 26 April 1994. Table: 546

Baker, George, and Bart van Aardenne. "CNG: A Fuel for the Future." *Business Mexico* (1993). Table: 23

Barr, Stephen. "Budget and Bureaucracy." *Washington Post,* 8 February 1995. Table: 607

Begley, Ronald. "TRI Releases Down Sixth Year in a Row." *ChemicalWeek,* 20 April 1994. Table: 524

Berkowitz, Joan B., and Alan L. Farkas. "Latin America: Economic Development Aspirations Drive Growing Environmental Markets." *ENR,* 17 October 1994. Table: 827

Berne, Steve. "In-plant Recycling—Responsible Manufacturing." *Prepared Foods* (February 1994). Table: 571

Breslin, Karen. "In Our Own Backyards: The Continuing Threat of Hazardous Waste." *Environmental Health Perspectives* 101, no. 6 (November 1993). Table: 457

Burgert, Phil. "Recycling Programs Evolve in Rural Settings." *World Wastes* (November 1993). Table: 561

"Capital Spending Going Toward Environmental Projects." *ChemicalWeek,* 3 February 1993. Table: 590

"Car Boom Ending?" *USA TODAY,* 1 February 1995, p.1B. Table: 601

"Carbon Dioxide Emissions for Different Fuel Sources." *Technology Review* (January 1995). Table: 17

"Charging up for California." *USA TODAY,* 29 November 1993. Table: 861

"Cities That Failed to Meet Air Quality Standards for Ozone." *Philadelphia Business Journal* 12, no. 18 (5 July 1993). Table: 37

Clary, Mike. "Manatees' Death Rate Alarms Scientists." *Detroit News,* 1 March 1995. Table: 307

"Clearing the Air." *USA TODAY,* 4 January 1995. Table: 15

Cohan, Paul. "Waste-by-Rail: A System That's Been Working on American Railroads." *World Wastes* (December 1993). Table: 565

"Commonly Used Pesticides in Mexico." *Business Mexico* (1993). Table: 381

"Congress Earmarks Grants for Wastewater Projects." *Water Environment & Technology* (January 1995). Table: 628

"Crop Pricing Spurs Agchems." *ChemicalWeek*, 5-12 January 1994. Table: 826

"CRP Enrollment Reaches 36.5 Million Acres." *Agricultural Outlook* (October 1992). Tables: 176-177

"Current Penetration of Compost Market." *World Wastes* (April 1994). Table: 820

Cushman, John H., Jr. "Eagles to Fly Free of the Endangered List." *New York Times,* 30 June 1994. Table: 263

Dana, Amy, and Tom Turner. "Currents of Controversy." *Amicus Journal* 15, no. 2 (summer 1993). Table: 341

"Demand for Pesticides Rising to $34B by '98." *In-Tech* (March 1995). Table: 380

"Dirt Busters." *Chemistry and Industry*, 6 June 1994. Tables: 824-825

"Distribution of National Priority List Sites by States and Territories." *Best's Review-P/C* (May 1994). Table: 458

"Distribution of Treatment Wetlands in the North American Database." *Water Environment & Technology* (February 1994). Table: 259

"Dues and Popular Products Make National Wildlife Thrive." *Money* (December 1994). Table: 317

"Electromagnetic Energy Spectrum." *International Insurance Monitor* (May 1994). Table: 343

"End the Phony 'Asbestos Panic.'" *USA TODAY,* 13 September 1993. Table: 618

"Environmental Compliance Costs (Per Lot)." *Builder* (February 1995). Table: 603

"Environmental Concerns Is Global." *Scientific American* (October 1994). Tables: 868-869

"Environmental Small Businesses, Where They Fit." *ENR*, 21 November 1994. Table: 806

Estes, Ralph. "A Free-Market Model." *Environmental Action* 25, no. 4 (winter 1994). Table: 604

Everly, Steve. "Looking at Firewood's Quality." *Kansas City Star*, 20 November 1994. Table: 344

Executive Office of the President of the United States. *Environmental Quality 24: The Twenty-fourth Annual Report of the Council on Environmental Quality*. Prepared by Ray Clark. Written by Carroll Curtis. Edited by Barry Walsh. Washington, DC: U.S.Government Printing Office, 1994. Tables: 16, 18, 21-22, 24, 26-29, 32-34, 49-51, 53, 55-56, 64-67, 113, 140, 179, 183-186, 197-199, 202, 210, 212, 222, 231-232, 245, 250, 253-258, 265-273, 276, 278, 281, 287, 303, 308-309, 311-316, 320-321, 324, 327, 332, 335, 349, 355, 359, 362, 366, 370, 378-379, 455, 479-499, 530, 533-544, 592, 610, 615-617, 620-623, 632, 634-635, 659-672, 831, 840-842, 857, 859, 863, 864

"Expired Permits." *Detroit Free Press,* 20 February 1995. Table: 882

"The Facts on Electromagnetic Fields." *ABA Journal* (January 1994). Table: 342

Fenn, Scott. "Past Pollution Problems Spur New Management Initiatives." *Water Environment & Technology* (March 1994). Table: 866

"Fires Managed by Agency—1993." *Emergency Medical Services* 24, no. 1 (January 1995). Table: 200

"France: A Nuclear Success Story." *Energy* (June 1994). Table: 353

Freeman, Del. "The Section 1038 Debate on Recycled Roadways." *World Wastes* (March 1994). Table: 556

"French Companies Pour Into U.S. Waterworks Market." *Water Environment & Technology* (May 1994). Table: 829

"FYI...." *Plastics News*, 20 February 1995. Table: 877

"Generation, Recovery, Combustion and Disposal of Municipal Solid Waste, Year 2000." *Nation's Cities Weekly*, 16 November 1992. Table: 526

"German Waste Disposal Evolves Under New Laws." *World Wastes* (September 1993). Table: 552

"Growth Chart." *Wall Street Journal*, 4 February 1994. Table: 873

Harkness, Gregg E., Charles C. Reed, Charles J. Voss, and Curtis I. Kunihiro. "Composting in the Magic Kingdom." *Water Environment & Technology* (August 1994). Table: 516

Harrison, Paul. "Counting Heads, Taking Stock." *The Amicus Journal* (winter 1994). Table: 318

"Hazardous Material: The Top 10 States." *USA TODAY*, 2 December 1994. Table: 449

"Hazardous Waste: Who Generates How Much of What?" *Chemical Engineering* (May 1994). Table: 521

Heinlein, Gary. "Overfishing: A Big Net Loss." *Detroit News*, 5 June 1995. Table: 304

Hofmann, Mark A. "Superfund's Tax Burden." *Business Insurance*, 5 September 1994. Table: 794

"Hold Your Own Earth Summit." *EPA Journal* 19, no. 2 (April-June 1993). Table: 216

Hoversten, Paul. "Toxic Alarm in 10 States." *USA TODAY*, 19 August 1994. Table: 445

"How Does Crop Loss Happen?" *ABA Banking Journal* (January 1994). Table: 181

"How We Use Forest Wood." *Science World*, 9 December 1994. Table: 835

"Indicators." *Far Eastern Economic Review*, 19 October 1992. Table: 348

"Industry Responsible for Generating Waste: Manufacturing Category Details." *Ward's Auto World* 29, no. 7 (July 1993). Table: 523

"Innovative Strategies Needed to Cut Costs, Maintain Services." *Nation's Cities Weekly*, 19 July 1993. Table: 627

"Inundated by Garbage." *Consumers Digest* (May/June 1995). Table: 569

"It's Bad for Weeds—and for Drinking Water." *U.S. News & World Report*, 31 October 1994. Table: 52

Jenkins, David, and Larry L. Russell. "Heavy Metals Contribution of Household Washing Products to Municipal Wastewater." *Water Environment Research* 66, no. 6 (September/October 1994). Table: 46

Johnson, Michael, and Kathleen Parrott. "Recycling: Before You Start." *Journal of Property Management* (July-August 1994). Table: 547

Kanamine, Linda. "An Uneasy Welcome for Gray Wolves." *USA TODAY*, 13 January 1995. Table: 262

Kanamine, Linda. "Gas-Reduction Plan Rooted in Voluntary Efforts." *USA TODAY*, 19 October 1993. Table: 60

Kanamine, Linda. "Support for Controversial Progam Slips." *USA TODAY*, 2 December 1994. Table: 275

Kanamine, Linda. "Whaling Panel Faces 30-Foot, 10-Ton Epic." *USA TODAY*, 23 May 1994. Table: 310

Kulfan, Ted. "Careers 2000: Environmental Manager." *Detroit News*, 20 March 1995. Table: 804

"A Land Trust Sampler." *American City & County* (March 1992). Table: 230

Litvan, Laura M. "The Growing Ranks of Enviro-Cops." *Nation's Business* (June 1994). Table: 874

Love, Barbara. "How Do Magazine Executives Rate in Environmental Consciousness?" *Folio: Special Sourcebook Issue* (1994). Table: 880

Lucas, Allison. "Clinton Proposes Federal R&D Boost, Despite Congressional Opposition." *ChemicalWeek*, 8 March 1995. Table: 614

Lucas, Allison. "CMA Companies Report Reduction in Toxic Releases." *ChemicalWeek*, 22 March 1995. Table: 468

Lucas, Allison. "Report Airs Concerns About Fluorinated Compounds." *ChemicalWeek*, 8 February 1995. Table: 59

Luhan, Michael. "Weather Foils Oil Cleanup." *USA TODAY*, 6 January 1993. Table: 264

"Market for Environmental Products Is Growing." *Hardware Age* (June 1993). Table: 822

Miller, Ken. "Beach Cleanup Finds Litter's Mounting." *USA TODAY*, 22 June 1995. Table: 566

"More Quantity Than Quality." *Amicus Journal* (winter 1994). Table: 879

"Most Developed Countries Say CO$_2$ Emissions to Grow." *C&EN,* 13 March 1995. Table: 19

"MSW Composting." *World Wastes* (April 1994). Table: 517

"Municipal Wastewater Treatment Market to Increase." *Water Environment & Technology* (May 1994). Table: 828

Munson, Dick. "Follow the Money." *Amicus Journal* 15, no. 3 (fall 1993). Table: 613

Muson, Howard. "Winds of Change." *Across the Board* (June 1994). Table: 865

"Myth That Environmental Regulations Cause Job Loss Is Debunked." *C&EN*, 23 January 1995. Table: 802

National Advisory Council on Migrant Health. *1993 Recommendations of the National Advisory Council on Migrant Health.* Rockville, MD: National Advisory Council on Migrant Health, May 1993. Table: 619

"Nationline: Correction." *USA TODAY,* 21 April 1994. Table: 392

"Natural Disasters More Frequent, Costly." *National Consumers League Bulletin* 55, no.5 (September/October 1993). Table: 629

Neal, Lisa K. "Career Incentives." *Environmental Protection* (April 1994). Table: 803

"NREL Identifies Means of Reducing Mercury Emissions." *World Wastes* (September 1993). Table: 525

O'Reilly, James. "PCMI Option May Help Cities Deal With Superfund Liability." *American City & County* (January 1993). Table: 459

Osborn, Tim. "The Conservation Reserve Program: Status, Future, and Policy Options." *Journal of Soil and Water Conservation* (July-August 1993). Table: 178

"Percentage of U.S. Publicly Owned Treatment Works (POTWs) Using Clarifiers for Primary Treatment." *Water Environment & Technology* (March 1994). Table: 559

"Percentage of U.S. Publicly Owned Treatment Works (POTWs) Using Land Spreading, Spraying, or Injection for Biosolids." *Water Environment & Technology* (January 1994). Table: 560

"Plants Are Most Endangered." *USA TODAY,* 29 December 1993. Table: 274

"Potential Dollar Market for Compost." *World Wastes* (April 1994). Table: 819

"Potential Volume Market for Compost." *World Wastes* (April 1994). Table: 821

"Predictions for Coal Included Increases in 1994." *Energy* (June 1994). Table: 818

"Prime Time for Postconsumer Recycling." *Chemical Engineering* (February 1995). Table: 545

"Principal U.S. Aquacultured Species." *Restaurant Business,* 20 May 1994. Table: 279

"Rate Your State." *Science World,* 9 December 1994. Table: 611

"Recycling: Earth Day Legacy." *USA TODAY,* 21 April 1995. Table: 548

"Recycling Gaining Momentum." *AS&U* (September 1994). Table: 562

"Recycling Market Recovers." *ENR,* 6 April 1992. Table: 558

"Recycling Speeds Up Across the Nation." *Editor & Publisher*, 10 April 1993. Table: 551

"Reducing Bycatch." *National Fisherman* (May 1994). Table: 293

Rubin, Debra K. "Industrial Firms Seek Cleanup Help But Not Everyone Need Apply." *ENR,* 21 November 1994. Table: 805

"Safety Has a High Price Tag." *USA TODAY,* 6 December 1993. Table: 602

"Saving the Earth." *USA TODAY,* 29 September 1994. Table: 871

Schneider, Keith. "Incinerators' Users Say Ruling Will Be Costly." *New York Times,* 3 May 1994. Table: 564

Schroeder, Robin L. "The Use of Recycled Materials in Highway Construction." *Public Roads* 58, no. 2 (autumn 1994). Table: 550

Seltzer, Richard. "New Actions to Prevent Chemical Accidents Urged." *C&EN*, 5 September 1994. Tables: 390-391

Sharn, Lori. "Heat Wave's Lethal Accomplice: Human Nature." *USA TODAY*, 24 July 1995. Table: 630

"Sludge Composting." *World Wastes* (April 1994). Table: 518

"Solid Waste Generation." *Wastes Management* (January 1994). Table: 573

"Source-Separated Composting." *World Wastes* (April 1994). Table: 519

"Sources of Ocean Pollution." *ScienceWorld*, 9 December 1994. Table: 47

"State Laws for 1993 Reflect Recycling Trends." *World Wastes* (March 1994). Table: 875

"Status of Local Conditions in 1993." *American City & County* (April 1994). Table: 872

Steuteville, Robert, Jay Freeborne, and Fulton Rockwell. "Trends in Curbside Recycling." *BioCycle* (July 1994). Table: 557

Stevens, William K. "Climate Talks Enter Harder Phase of Cutting Back Emissions." *New York Times*, 11 April 1995. Table: 20

Stevens, William K. "The 25th Anniversary of Earth Day: How Has the Environment Fared?" *New York Times*, 18 April 1995. Table: 285

"Study Questions 'Myths.'" *ENR*, 18 April 1994. Table: 881

"Superfund and the City." *Water Environment & Technology* (August 1994). Table: 460

"Survey of Construction Waste." *Building Design & Construction* (February 1995). Table: 568

"Top 10 Preferred Environmental Employers." *ENR*, 21 November 1994. Table: 801

"Top 10 U.S. Toxic Chemical Air Emissions." *Water Environment & Technology* (March 1995). Table: 31

"Top Industries for Total Release." *Ward's Auto World* 29, no. 7 (July 1993). Table: 477

"Top Priorities." *Detroit Free Press*, 14 April 1994. Table: 862

"Touchstone of an Industrial Revolution." *Financial Times*, 30 June 1994. Table: 589

"The Tragedy of the Oceans." *The Economist*, 19 March 1994. Table: 306

"Trash Talk: Debunking the Mythology." *Wall Street Journal*, 19 January 1995. Table: 570

Tyson, Rae. "EPA Proposes $20M in Fines for Waste-Burners." *USA TODAY*, 29 September 1993. Table: 878

Tyson, Rae. "Plug Holes in Water Laws, Analysts Say." *USA TODAY*, 27 September 1993. Table: 876

"U.S. Battery Industry: Not Mature Yet." *Energy* (June 1994). Table: 844

U.S. Congress. Congressional Budget Office (CBO). *Cleaning Up the Department of Energy's Nuclear Weapons Complex*. A CBO Study. Washington, DC: U.S. Congress, Congressional Budget Office, May 1994. Table: 612

U.S. Department of Agriculture. Forest Service. *1991 National Forest Fire Report*. Prepared by the State and Private Forestry Fire and Aviation Management Staff. Washington, DC: U.S. Department of Agriculture, Forest Service, September 1993. Table: 201

U.S. Department of Agriculture. Forest Service. Forest Pest Management. *Forest Insect and Disease Conditions in the United States, 1992*. Washington, DC: U.S. Department of Agriculture, Forest Service, Forest Pest Management, November 1993. Tables: 203-207

U.S. Department of Agriculture. Forest Service. State and Private Forestry. *Tree Planting in the United States, 1993*. Washington, DC: U.S. Department of Agriculture, Forest Service, State and Private Forestry, 1993. Tables: 213-215

U.S. Department of Commerce. Bureau of the Census. "Pollution Abatement Costs and Expenditures, 1992." In *National Economic, Social, and Environmental Data Bank* [CD-ROM]. Prepared by U.S. Department of Commerce, Economics and Statistics

Administration. Washington, DC: U.S. Department of Commerce, National Economic, Social, and Environmental Data Bank, Economics and Statistics Administration, Office of Business Analysis, February 1995. Tables: 636-637, 639-658, 673-793

U.S. Department of Commerce. National Oceanic and Atmospheric Administration. *Commerce News,* 22 March 1994. Tables: 298-302

U.S. Department of Energy. Energy Information Administration. Office of Coal, Nuclear, Electric, and Alternate Fuels. *Inventory of Power Plants in the United States. 1993.* Washington, DC: U.S. Department of Energy, Energy Information Administration, Office of Coal, Nuclear, Electric, and Alternate Fuels, December 1994. Table: 350

U.S. Department of the Interior. Bureau of Land Management and U.S. Department of Agriculture. Forest Service. *Ninth Report to Congress on the Administration of the Wild Free-Roaming Horse and Burro Act.* Washington, DC: U.S. Department of the Interior, Bureau of Land Management, and U.S. Department of Agriculture, Forest Service, n.d. Table: 261

U.S. Department of the Interior. Land and Materials Management. Minerals Management Service. Royalty Management Program. *Mineral Revenues, 1993.* Denver, CO: U.S. Department of the Interior, Land and Minerals Management, Minerals Management Service, Royalty Management Program, 1993. Table: 847

U.S. Environmental Protection Agency. Risk Reduction Engineering Laboratory. Research and Development. *Waste Minimization Assessment for a Manufacturer of Aerial Lifts.* Prepared by Harry W. Edwards, Michael F. Kostrezewa, and Gwen P. Looby. Environmental Research Brief. EPA/600/S-94/011. Cincinnati, OH: U.S. Environmental Protection Agency, Risk Reduction Engineering Laboratory, Research and Development, September 1994. Table: 574

U.S. Environmental Protection Agency. Risk Reduction Engineering Laboratory. Research and Development. *Waste Minimization Assessment for a Manufacturer of Caulk.* Prepared by Harry W. Edwards, Michael F. Kostrzewa, and Gwen P. Looby. Environmental Research Brief. EPA/600/S-94/017. Cincinnati, OH: U.S. Environmental Protection Agency, Risk Reduction Engineering Laboratory, Re-

search and Development, September 1994. Table: 575

U.S. Environmental Protection Agency. Risk Reduction Engineering Laboratory. Research and Development. *Waste Minimization Assessment for a Manufacturer of Coated Parts.* Prepared by Harry W. Edwards, Michael F. Kostrzewa, and Gwen P. Looby. Environmental Research Brief. EPA/600/S-94/014. Cincinnati, OH: U.S. Environmental Protection Agency, Risk Reduction Engineering Laboratory, Research and Development, September 1994. Table: 576

U.S. Environmental Protection Agency. Risk Reduction Engineering Laboratory. Research and Development. *Waste Minimization Assessment for a Manufacturer of Electrical Rotating Devices.* Prepared by Richard J. Jendrucko, Thomas N. Coleman, and Gwen P. Looby. Environmental Research Brief. EPA/600/S-94/018. Cincinnati, OH: U.S. Environmental Protection Agency, Risk Reduction Engineering Laboratory, Research and Development, September 1994. Table: 577

U.S. Environmental Protection Agency. Risk Reduction Engineering Laboratory. Research and Development. *Waste Minimization Assessment for a Manufacturer of Felt Tip Markers, Stamp Pads, and Rubber Cement.* Prepared by Richard J. Jendrucko, Todd M. Thomas, and Gwen P. Looby. Environmental Research Brief. EPA/600/S-94/013. Cincinnati, OH: U.S. Environmental Protection Agency, Risk Reduction Engineering Laboratory, Research and Development, September 1994. Table: 578

U.S. Environmental Protection Agency. Risk Reduction Engineering Laboratory. Research and Development. *Waste Minimization Assessment for a Manufacturer of Finished Metal and Plastic Parts.* Prepared by Harry W. Edwards, Michael F. Kostrzewa, and Gwen P. Looby. Environmental Research Brief. EPA/600/S-94/005. Cincinnati, OH: U.S. Environmental Protection Agency, Risk Reduction Engineering Laboratory, Research and Development, September 1994. Table: 579

U.S. Environmental Protection Agency. Risk Reduction Engineering Laboratory. Research and Development. *Waste Minimization Assessment for a Manufacturer of Gravure-Coated Metalized Paper and Metalized Film.* Prepared by Richard J. Jendrucko, Thomas N. Coleman, and Gwen P. Looby. Environmental Research Brief. EPA/600/S-94/008. Cincinnati, OH: U.S. Environmental Protection Agency, Risk Reduction Engineering Laboratory, Research and Development, September 1994. Table: 580

U.S. Environmental Protection Agency. Risk Reduction Engineering Laboratory. Research and Development. *Waste Minimization Assessment for a Manufacturer of Microelectronic Components.* Prepared by Harry W. Edwards, Michael F. Kostrzewa, and Gwen P. Looby. Environmental Research Brief. EPA/600/S-94/015. Cincinnati, OH: U.S. Environmental Protection Agency, Risk Reduction Engineering Laboratory, Research and Development, September 1994. Table: 581

U.S. Environmental Protection Agency. Risk Reduction Engineering Laboratory. Research and Development. *Waste Minimization Assessment for a Manufacturer of Mountings for Electronic Circuit Components.* Prepared by Richard J. Jendrucko, Kelly L. Binkley, and Gwen P. Looby. Environmental Research Brief. EPA/600/S-94/012. Cincinnati, OH: U.S. Environmental Protection Agency, Risk Reduction Engineering Laboratory, Research and Development, September 1994. Table: 582

U.S. Environmental Protection Agency. Risk Reduction Engineering Laboratory. Research and Development. *Waste Minimization Assessment for a Manufacturer of Paints and Lacquers.* Prepared by Richard J. Jendrucko, Rebecca A. Bachschmidt, and Gwen P. Looby. Environmental Research Brief. EPA/600/S-94/007. Cincinnati, OH: U.S. Environmental Protection Agency, Risk Reduction Engineering Laboratory, Research and Development, September 1994. Table: 583

U.S. Environmental Protection Agency. Risk Reduction Engineering Laboratory. Research and Development. *Waste Minimization Assessment for a Manufacturer of Parts for Truck Engines.* Prepared by Richard J. Jendrucko, Kelly Binkley, Todd Thomas, Stephanie Wilson, Eric W. Daley, and Gwen P. Looby. Environmental Research Brief. EPA/600/S-94/019. Cincinnati, OH: U.S. Environmental Protection Agency, Risk Reduction Engineering Laboratory, Research and Development, September 1994. Table: 588

U.S. Environmental Protection Agency. Risk Reduction Engineering Laboratory. Research and Development. *Waste Minimization Assessment for a Manufacturer of Pliers and Wrenches.* Prepared by Harry W. Edwards, Michael F. Kostrzewa, and Gwen P. Looby. Environmental Research Brief. EPA/600/S-94/004. Cincinnati, OH: U.S. Environmental Protection Agency, Risk Reduction Engineering Laboratory, Research and Development, September 1994. Table: 584

U.S. Environmental Protection Agency. Risk Reduction Engineering Laboratory. Research and Development. *Waste Minimization Assessment for a Manufacturer of Prewashed Jeans.* Prepared by Richard J. Jendrucko, Thomas N. Coleman, and Gwen P. Looby. Environmental Research Brief. EPA/600/S-94/006. Cincinnati, OH: U.S. Environmental Protection Agency, Risk Reduction Engineering Laboratory, Research and Development, September 1994. Table: 585

U.S. Environmental Protection Agency. Risk Reduction Engineering Laboratory. Research and Development. *Waste Minimization Assessment for a Manufacturer of Screwdrivers.* Prepared by Harry W. Edwards, Michael F. Kostrzewa, and Gwen P. Looby. Environmental Research Brief. EPA/600/S-94/003. Cincinnati, OH: U.S. Environmental Protection Agency, Risk Reduction Engineering Laboratory, Research and Development, September 1994. Table: 586

U.S. Environmental Protection Agency. Risk Reduction Engineering Laboratory. Research and Development. *Waste Minimization Assessment for a Manufacturer of Surgical Implants.* Prepared by Harry W. Edwards, Michael F. Kostrezewa, and Gwen P. Looby. Environmental Research Brief. EPA/600/S-94/009. Cincinnati, OH: U.S. Environmental Protection Agency, Risk Reduction Engineering Laboratory, Research and Development, September 1994. Table: 587

U.S. Environmental Protection Agency. "Toxic Chemical Releases, 1990." In *National Economic, Social, and Environmental Data Bank* [CD-ROM]. Prepared by U.S. Department of Commerce, Economics and Statistics Administration. Washington, DC: U.S. Department of Commerce, National Economic, Social, and Environmental Data Bank, Economics and Statistics Administration, Office of Business Analysis, February 1995. Tables: 393-444

U.S. Environmental Protection Agency. "Toxic Release Inventory, 1992." In *National Economic, Social, and Environmental Data Bank* [CD-ROM]. Prepared by U.S. Department of Commerce, Economics and Statistics Administration. Washington, DC: U.S. Department of Commerce, National Economic, Social, and Environmental Data Bank, Economics and Statistics Administration, Office of Business Analysis, February 1995. Tables: 382-389, 446-448, 450-454, 461-467, 469-476, 500-515, 549, 554, 848-849

"U.S. Sources of River Impairment." *Water Environment & Technology* (September 1994). Table: 39

"VOC Curbs Could Be Factor in Aerosol Downturn." *DCI (June 1994).* Table: 830

"War on Wastes." *Science World*, 9 December 1994. Table: 572

"Warning Sounded on European Emissions Cutback." *Oil & Gas Journal,* 1 August 1994. Table: 30

"Waterways Filled With Trash, Survey Shows." *St. Louis Post-Dispatch*, 8 September 1994. Table: 567

"Wetlands: The Losses Are Slowing." *Builder* (June 1994). Table: 260

"What Environmental Goods and Services Sell." *State Government News* (March 1995). Table: 823

"Where Does Your Garbage Go?" *Science World*, 9 December 1994. Table: 563

"Where Tires Are Retired." *USA TODAY*, 4 October 1993. Table: 555

"Which of the Following Resources Should Municipalities Pursue for Long-Term Funding?" *American City & County* (April 1992). Table: 626

"Who Helps the Environment." *USA TODAY*, 23-24 November 1994. Table: 867

"Yard Waste Composting." *World Waste* (April 1994). Table: 520

Abbreviations and Acronyms

Abbreviations and acronyms used in tables or notes are explained within the context of the data presented whenever possible. The listing below includes abbreviations, acronyms, initialisms, and symbols appearing in *Statistical Record of the Environment,* 3rd edition. Other common abridgements of locations, organization names, government agencies, weights and measures, and items related to *SRE* tables are included as well. Full translations and meanings are provided for each abbreviation. In some cases, explanatory material also has been included for the user's convenience. One abbreviation may represent multiple items. Where more than one use is possible, all explanations of the term are listed. Abbreviations and acronyms appear in alphabetic order.

&	And
$	Dollar
>	Greater than
"	Inches
<	Less than
-	Not applicable
-	Not available
%	Percent
ALCOA	Aluminum Company of America
AMIPFAC	Mexican Association for Pesticide and Fertilizer Industry
AQMD	Air Quality Management District
ATSDR	Agency for Toxic Substances and Disease Registry
Avg.	Average
Bd.ft.	Board feet
BEA	Bureau of Economic Analysis
BLM	Bureau of Land Management

Btu	British thermal unit(s)
BWR	Boiling water reactor
C&D	Construction and demolition
C_2F_6	Perfluoroethane
C_6F_{14}	Perfluorohexane
CD-ROM	Compact disk/read-only memory
CDD	Cooling degree day
CDIAC	Carbon Dioxide Information Analysis Center
CERCLA	Comprehensive Environmental Response, Compensation, and Liability Act of 1980
CERCLIS	Comprehensive Environmental Response, Compensation, and Liability Inventory Sites
CF_4	Perfluoromethane
CFC	Chlorofluorocarbon
c.i.f.	Carriage, insurance, and freight

CMA	Chemical Manufacturers Association	**EPCRA**	Emergency Planning and Community Right-to-Know Act
CMSA	Consolidated Metropolitan Statistical Area	**ERISA**	Employee Retirement Income Security Act
CNG	Compressed natural gas	**est.**	Estimated
CO	Colorado	**FACS**	Foundation for American Communications
Co.	Company		
CO$_2$	Carbon dioxide	**FDA**	Food and Drug Administration
COE	Corps of Engineers	**f.o.b.**	Free on board
Corp.	Corporation	**fyi**	For your information
CPH	Census of Population and Housing	**GDP**	Gross domestic product
CRP	Conservation Reserve Program	**HCB**	Hexachloro benzene
CSMA	Chemical Specialties Manufacturers Association	**HDD**	Heating degree day
		Inc.	Incorporated
D	Depleted	**IRRC**	Investor Responsibility Research Center
DC	District of Columbia		
DCNA	Dichloronitroaniline	**ISTEA**	Intermodal Surface Transportation Efficiency Act ["Ice Tea" Bill]
DCPA	Dichloropropionanilide		
DDE	Dichloro-diphenyl-dichloro ethane and derivatives	**K$_2$O**	Potash
		kg	Kilogram
DDT	Dichloro-diphenyl-trichloro ethane and derivatives	**kg/d**	Kilograms per day
		kW	Kilowatts
DOE	Department of Energy	**kWh**	Kilowatt hours
dol.	Dollar(s)	**lb.**	Pound
DSD	Duales System Deutschland	**LP**	Limited partnership
E	Endangered	**Ltd.**	Limited
EEOC	Equal Employment Opportunity Commission	**LNG**	Liquefied natural gas
		m^3	Cubic meter
EIA	Energy Information Administration	**MA**	Massachusetts
EM	Office of Environmental Restoration and Waste Management	**MA**	Metropolitan area
EPA	Environmental Protection Agency	**MD**	Maryland

Mg	Maghemite		**NOAA**	National Oceanic and Atmospheric Administration
Mg	Magnesium		**n.p.**	No page [of publication]
mG	MilliGauss		**NPL**	National Priority List
mg	Milligram		**NPTS**	Nationwide Personal Transportation Study
mgd	Million gallons per day		**NREL**	National Renewable Energy Laboratory
mil.	Million			
Misc.	Miscellaneous		**NRI**	National Resources Inventory
Mn	Manganese			
MN	Minnesota		**ON**	Ontario
MSA	Metropolitan Statistical Area		**OPEC**	Organization of Petroleum Exporting Countries
MSW	Municipal solid waste		**ORNL**	Oak Ridge National Laboratory
mt	Metric ton		**p.**	Page [of publication]
Mt.	Mount		**PACE**	Pollution abatement capital expenditures
MRF	Material recovery facility			
MWe	Megawatts of electric power		**PCB**	Polychlorinated biphenyl
N	North		**PDSI**	Palmer Drought Severity Index
NA	Not applicable		**pH**	Pouvoir Hydrogene ["hydrogen power," a measure of acidity or alkalinity]
NA	Not available			
NASQAN	National Stream Quality Accounting Network [U.S. Geological Survey]		**PIK**	Payment-in-kind
			PLWR	Pressurized light water reactors
NASS	National Agricultural Statistics		**PM-10**	Particulates with aerodynamic diameter smaller than 10 micrometers
NC	North Carolina			
n.d.	No date [of publication]		**PMSA**	Primary Metropolitan Statistical Area
n.e.c.	Not elsewhere classified			
NGPL	Natural gas plant liquids		**POTW**	Publicly owned treatment work
NLRB	National Labor Relations Board		**PPI**	Producer Price Index
NMFS	National Marine Fisheries Service		**pp.**	Pages [of publication]
no.	Number		**ppm**	Parts per million
			PSI	Pollutant Standards Index

PWR	Pressurized water reactor
R	Range
R&D	Research and development
RMBK	Chernobyl-type nuclear reactor
S&P	Standard & Poor's
SARA	Superfund Amendments and Reauthorization Act
SCS	Soil Conservation Service [U.S. Department of Agriculture]
Sec.	Section
SF$_6$	Sulfur hexafluoride
sh. tons	Short tons
SIC	Standard Industrial Classification
SO$_2$	Sulfur dioxide
SPI	Strategic Planning Initiative [U.S. Environmental Protection Agency]
SPR	Strategic Petroleum Reserve
sq.ft.	Square feet
St.	Saint
Swu	Separative work units
T	Threatened
T	Township
T	Trace
TN	Tennessee

TRI	Toxic Release Inventory
TTPI	Trust Territory of the Pacific Islands (Palau)
TV	Television
TVA	Tennessee Valley Authority
Twp.	Township
U$_3$O$_8$	Uranium oxide
UF$_6$	Uranium hexafluoride
UN	United Nations
U.S.	United States
U.S.A.	United States of America
USDA	U.S. Department of Agriculture
VA	Virginia
vmt/y	Vehicle miles of travel per year
vmy/g	Average vehicle miles of travel per gallon of fuel consumed
VOC	Volatile organic compound
W	West
w/h	Withheld
WMAC	Waste minimization assessment center
WO$_3$	Tungsten concentrate
ZrO$_2$	Zirconium

Keyword Index

The Keyword Index contains references to more than 3,680 subjects, including environmental topics, companies and businesses, place names, personal names, public and private organizations, pollutants, and chemicals mentioned in *Statistical Record of the Environment,* 3rd edition. Locations of corporations, plants, and facilities are included when known to differentiate operating units or subsidiaries of parent companies. Each index citation is followed by page and table reference numbers. Page numbers are preceded by "p." or "pp." Page references do not necessarily identify the page on which a table begins. In cases where tables span two or more pages, references point to the page on which the index term actually appears, which may be the second or subsequent page of a table. Table reference numbers appear in brackets ([]). The index is extensively cross-referenced to direct users to related subjects or terms.

Numbers following p. or pp. are page references. Numbers in [ ] are table references.

Numbers following p. or pp. are page references. Numbers in [ ] are table references.

Keyword Index

Numbers following p. or pp. are page references. Numbers in [ ] are table references.

Keyword Index

Numbers following p. or pp. are page references. Numbers in [ ] are table references.

911

2-phenylphenol continued:
— toxic releases in Michigan, p. 412 [414]
— toxic releases in Missouri, p. 420 [417]
— toxic releases in New Jersey, p. 429 [422]
— toxic releases in Ohio, p. 442 [427]
— toxic releases in Tennessee, p. 461 [435]
— toxic releases in Wisconsin, p. 478 [443]
— treatment or release of chemicals in waste, p. 553 [513]

2,3-dichloropropene
— recycling and energy recovery of chemicals in waste, p. 541 [509]
— releases, p. 349 [382]
— toxic releases in Indiana, p. 392 [406]
— toxic releases in Texas, p. 464 [436]
— treatment or release of chemicals in waste, p. 551 [513]

2,4-d
— pesticide use in Mexico, p. 346 [381]
— recycling and energy recovery of chemicals in waste, p. 540 [509]
— releases, p. 348 [382]
— toxic releases in Alabama, p. 363 [393]
— toxic releases in California, p. 372 [397]
— toxic releases in Florida, p. 381 [401]
— toxic releases in Georgia, p. 383 [402]
— toxic releases in Illinois, p. 389 [405]
— toxic releases in Iowa, p. 395 [407]
— toxic releases in Kansas, p. 397 [408]
— toxic releases in Michigan, p. 412 [414]
— toxic releases in Minnesota, p. 414 [415]
— toxic releases in Mississippi, p. 417 [416]
— toxic releases in Missouri, p. 420 [417]
— toxic releases in Montana, p. 422 [418]
— toxic releases in North Carolina, p. 437 [425]
— toxic releases in Ohio, p. 441 [427]
— toxic releases in Oregon, p. 447 [429]
— toxic releases in Texas, p. 464 [436]
— treatment or release of chemicals in waste, p. 551 [513]

2,4-diaminoanisole
— toxic releases in Mississippi, p. 417 [416]

2,4-diaminoanisole sulfate
— toxic releases in New York, p. 434 [424]

2,4-diaminotoluene
— recycling and energy recovery of chemicals in waste, p. 540 [509]
— releases, p. 348 [382]
— releases of carcinogens, p. 485 [448]
— toxic releases in New Jersey, p. 428 [422]
— toxic releases in New York, p. 434 [424]
— toxic releases in South Carolina, p. 456 [433]
— treatment or release of chemicals in waste, p. 551 [513]

2,4-dichlorophenol
— recycling and energy recovery of chemicals in waste, p. 541 [509]
— releases, p. 349 [382]
— toxic releases in Arkansas, p. 369 [396]
— toxic releases in Michigan, p. 412 [414]
— toxic releases in New York, p. 434 [424]
— toxic releases in Texas, p. 464 [436]

2,4-dichlorophenol continued:
— treatment or release of chemicals in waste, p. 551 [513]

2,4-dimethylphenol
— recycling and energy recovery of chemicals in waste, p. 541 [509]
— releases, p. 349 [382]
— toxic releases in Alabama, p. 363 [393]
— toxic releases in Indiana, p. 392 [406]
— toxic releases in Kansas, p. 397 [408]
— toxic releases in Louisiana, p. 402 [410]
— toxic releases in Minnesota, p. 414 [415]
— toxic releases in Missouri, p. 420 [417]
— toxic releases in New Jersey, p. 428 [422]
— toxic releases in New York, p. 434 [424]
— toxic releases in North Carolina, p. 437 [425]
— toxic releases in Pennsylvania, p. 449 [430]
— toxic releases in Tennessee, p. 461 [435]
— toxic releases in Texas, p. 464 [436]
— toxic releases in Washington, p. 474 [441]
— toxic releases in Wyoming, p. 481 [444]
— treatment or release of chemicals in waste, p. 552 [513]

2,4-dinitrophenol
— recycling and energy recovery of chemicals in waste, p. 541 [509]
— releases, p. 349 [382]
— toxic releases in Mississippi, p. 417 [416]
— toxic releases in New York, p. 434 [424]
— toxic releases in North Carolina, p. 437 [425]
— toxic releases in Pennsylvania, p. 449 [430]
— toxic releases in Tennessee, p. 461 [435]
— toxic releases in Texas, p. 464 [436]
— treatment or release of chemicals in waste, p. 552 [513]

2,4-dinitrotoluene
— recycling and energy recovery of chemicals in waste, p. 541 [509]
— releases, p. 349 [382]
— toxic releases in Florida, p. 381 [401]
— toxic releases in Indiana, p. 392 [406]
— toxic releases in Louisiana, p. 402 [410]
— toxic releases in Mississippi, p. 417 [416]
— toxic releases in New Jersey, p. 428 [422]
— toxic releases in Texas, p. 464 [436]
— toxic releases in Virginia, p. 471 [440]
— toxic releases in West Virginia, p. 476 [442]
— treatment or release of chemicals in waste, p. 552 [513]

2,4,5-trichlorophenol
— recycling and energy recovery of chemicals in waste, p. 544 [509]
— treatment or release of chemicals in waste, p. 554 [513]

2,4,6-trichlorophenol
— recycling and energy recovery of chemicals in waste, p. 544 [509]
— releases of carcinogens, p. 486 [448]
— toxic releases in Michigan, p. 412 [414]
— treatment or release of chemicals in waste, p. 554 [513]

2,6-dinitrotoluene
— recycling and energy recovery of chemicals in waste, p. 541 [509]

Numbers following p. or pp. are page references. Numbers in [ ] are table references.

2,6-dinitrotoluene continued:
— releases, p. 349 [382]
— toxic releases in Louisiana, p. 403 [410]
— toxic releases in Texas, p. 464 [436]
— toxic releases in West Virginia, p. 476 [442]
— treatment or release of chemicals in waste, p. 552 [513]

2,6-xylidine
— recycling and energy recovery of chemicals in waste, p. 544 [509]
— toxic releases in New Jersey, p. 428 [422]
— treatment or release of chemicals in waste, p. 554 [513]

3,3'-dichlorobenzidine
— recycling and energy recovery of chemicals in waste, p. 540 [509]
— releases, p. 349 [382]
— releases of carcinogens, p. 485 [448]
— toxic releases in Illinois, p. 389 [405]
— toxic releases in Michigan, p. 412 [414]
— toxic releases in New Jersey, p. 429 [422]
— treatment or release of chemicals in waste, p. 551 [513]

3,3'-dimethoxybenzidine
— recycling and energy recovery of chemicals in waste, p. 541 [509]
— releases, p. 349 [382]
— releases of carcinogens, p. 485 [448]
— toxic releases in New Jersey, p. 429 [422]
— toxic releases in Pennsylvania, p. 449 [430]
— treatment or release of chemicals in waste, p. 552 [513]

3,3'-dimethylbenzidine
— toxic releases in New Jersey, p. 429 [422]

3M Co.
— air, water, and land toxic releases, p. 515 [475]

3M Co. (Brownwood, Texas)
— decreased air, water, and land releases, p. 507 [469]

3M Co. (Hutchinson, Minnesota)
— air, water, and land toxic releases, p. 513 [473]
— decreased air, water, and land releases, p. 507 [469]

4-aminoazobenzene
— recycling and energy recovery of chemicals in waste, p. 538 [509]
— releases, p. 347 [382]
— releases of carcinogens, p. 485 [448]
— treatment or release of chemicals in waste, p. 549 [513]

4-aminobiphenyl
— recycling and energy recovery of chemicals in waste, p. 538 [509]
— releases, p. 347 [382]
— releases of carcinogens, p. 485 [448]
— treatment or release of chemicals in waste, p. 549 [513]

4-nitrophenol
— recycling and energy recovery of chemicals in waste, p. 543 [509]
— releases, p. 351 [382]
— toxic releases in Illinois, p. 389 [405]
— toxic releases in Louisiana, p. 403 [410]
— toxic releases in Missouri, p. 420 [417]
— toxic releases in New Jersey, p. 429 [422]
— toxic releases in Pennsylvania, p. 449 [430]

4-nitrophenol continued:
— toxic releases in Tennessee, p. 461 [435]
— treatment or release of chemicals in waste, p. 553 [513]

4,4'-diaminodiphenyl ether
— recycling and energy recovery of chemicals in waste, p. 540 [509]
— releases, p. 348 [382]
— releases of carcinogens, p. 485 [448]
— toxic releases in New Jersey, p. 429 [422]
— toxic releases in Ohio, p. 442 [427]
— toxic releases in South Carolina, p. 457 [433]
— treatment or release of chemicals in waste, p. 551 [513]

4,4'-isopropylidenediphenol
— recycling and energy recovery of chemicals in waste, p. 542 [509]
— releases, p. 350 [382]
— toxic releases in Alabama, p. 363 [393]
— toxic releases in California, p. 372 [397]
— toxic releases in Connecticut, p. 377 [399]
— toxic releases in Delaware, p. 379 [400]
— toxic releases in Florida, p. 381 [401]
— toxic releases in Georgia, p. 383 [402]
— toxic releases in Illinois, p. 389 [405]
— toxic releases in Indiana, p. 392 [406]
— toxic releases in Kentucky, p. 399 [409]
— toxic releases in Louisiana, p. 403 [410]
— toxic releases in Maryland, p. 407 [412]
— toxic releases in Massachusetts, p. 409 [413]
— toxic releases in Michigan, p. 412 [414]
— toxic releases in Minnesota, p. 415 [415]
— toxic releases in Missouri, p. 420 [417]
— toxic releases in New Hampshire, p. 426 [421]
— toxic releases in New Jersey, p. 429 [422]
— toxic releases in New York, p. 434 [424]
— toxic releases in Ohio, p. 442 [427]
— toxic releases in Oklahoma, p. 445 [428]
— toxic releases in Pennsylvania, p. 449 [430]
— toxic releases in Rhode Island, p. 454 [432]
— toxic releases in South Carolina, p. 457 [433]
— toxic releases in Tennessee, p. 461 [435]
— toxic releases in Texas, p. 464 [436]
— toxic releases in Wisconsin, p. 478 [443]
— treatment or release of chemicals in waste, p. 552 [513]

4,4'-methylenebis(2-chloro aniline)
— recycling and energy recovery of chemicals in waste, p. 542 [509]
— releases, p. 350 [382]
— releases of bioaccumulators, p. 483 [446]
— releases of carcinogens, p. 486 [448]
— toxic releases in California, p. 372 [397]
— toxic releases in Florida, p. 381 [401]
— toxic releases in Illinois, p. 389 [405]
— toxic releases in Maine, p. 405 [411]
— toxic releases in Maryland, p. 407 [412]
— toxic releases in New York, p. 434 [424]
— toxic releases in Ohio, p. 442 [427]
— toxic releases in Tennessee, p. 461 [435]
— treatment or release of chemicals in waste, p. 553 [513]

Numbers following p. or pp. are page references. Numbers in [ ] are table references.

Keyword Index

913

Numbers following p. or pp. are page references. Numbers in [ ] are table references.

Acetone continued:
— recycling and energy recovery of chemicals in waste, p. 538 [509]
— releases, p. 346 [382]
— total toxic releases, p. 357 [388]
— toxic chemical air emissions, p. 27 [31]
— toxic releases in Alabama, p. 363 [393]
— toxic releases in Alaska, p. 366 [394]
— toxic releases in Arizona, p. 367 [395]
— toxic releases in Arkansas, p. 369 [396]
— toxic releases in California, p. 372 [397]
— toxic releases in Colorado, p. 375 [398]
— toxic releases in Connecticut, p. 377 [399]
— toxic releases in Delaware, p. 379 [400]
— toxic releases in Florida, p. 381 [401]
— toxic releases in Georgia, p. 384 [402]
— toxic releases in Hawaii, p. 386 [403]
— toxic releases in Idaho, p. 388 [404]
— toxic releases in Illinois, p. 389 [405]
— toxic releases in Indiana, p. 392 [406]
— toxic releases in Iowa, p. 395 [407]
— toxic releases in Kansas, p. 397 [408]
— toxic releases in Kentucky, p. 399 [409]
— toxic releases in Louisiana, p. 403 [410]
— toxic releases in Maine, p. 405 [411]
— toxic releases in Maryland, p. 407 [412]
— toxic releases in Massachusetts, p. 409 [413]
— toxic releases in Michigan, p. 412 [414]
— toxic releases in Minnesota, p. 415 [415]
— toxic releases in Mississippi, p. 417 [416]
— toxic releases in Missouri, p. 420 [417]
— toxic releases in Montana, p. 422 [418]
— toxic releases in Nebraska, p. 424 [419]
— toxic releases in Nevada, p. 425 [420]
— toxic releases in New Hampshire, p. 426 [421]
— toxic releases in New Jersey, p. 429 [422]
— toxic releases in New Mexico, p. 432 [423]
— toxic releases in New York, p. 434 [424]
— toxic releases in North Carolina, p. 437 [425]
— toxic releases in North Dakota, p. 440 [426]
— toxic releases in Ohio, p. 442 [427]
— toxic releases in Oklahoma, p. 445 [428]
— toxic releases in Oregon, p. 447 [429]
— toxic releases in Pennsylvania, p. 449 [430]
— toxic releases in Puerto Rico, p. 452 [431]
— toxic releases in Rhode Island, p. 454 [432]
— toxic releases in South Carolina, p. 457 [433]
— toxic releases in South Dakota, p. 459 [434]
— toxic releases in Tennessee, p. 461 [435]
— toxic releases in Texas, p. 464 [436]
— toxic releases in Utah, p. 467 [437]
— toxic releases in Vermont, p. 469 [438]
— toxic releases in Virginia, p. 471 [440]
— toxic releases in Washington, p. 474 [441]
— toxic releases in West Virginia, p. 476 [442]
— toxic releases in Wisconsin, p. 479 [443]
— treatment or release of chemicals in waste, p. 549 [513]
— underground injection, p. 359 [389]

Acetone, evaporated
— waste minimization, pp. 606, 612 [581, 586]
Acetone, spent *See:* Spent acetone
Acetone-wetted rags
— waste minimization, p. 601 [577]
Acetonitrile
— recycling and energy recovery of chemicals in waste, p. 538 [509]
— releases, p. 346 [382]
— total toxic releases, p. 357 [388]
— toxic releases in Alabama, p. 363 [393]
— toxic releases in Arkansas, p. 369 [396]
— toxic releases in California, p. 372 [397]
— toxic releases in Connecticut, p. 377 [399]
— toxic releases in Illinois, p. 389 [405]
— toxic releases in Indiana, p. 392 [406]
— toxic releases in Kentucky, p. 399 [409]
— toxic releases in Louisiana, p. 403 [410]
— toxic releases in Maryland, p. 407 [412]
— toxic releases in Massachusetts, p. 409 [413]
— toxic releases in Michigan, p. 412 [414]
— toxic releases in Mississippi, p. 417 [416]
— toxic releases in Missouri, p. 420 [417]
— toxic releases in New Jersey, p. 429 [422]
— toxic releases in New York, p. 434 [424]
— toxic releases in North Carolina, p. 437 [425]
— toxic releases in Ohio, p. 442 [427]
— toxic releases in Pennsylvania, p. 449 [430]
— toxic releases in Puerto Rico, p. 452 [431]
— toxic releases in South Carolina, p. 457 [433]
— toxic releases in Tennessee, p. 461 [435]
— toxic releases in Texas, p. 464 [436]
— toxic releases in Virginia, p. 471 [440]
— toxic releases in West Virginia, p. 476 [442]
— toxic releases in Wisconsin, p. 479 [443]
— treatment or release of chemicals in waste, p. 549 [513]
— underground injection, p. 359 [389]
Acid rain
— corporate environmental compliance costs, p. 630 [604]
Acid regeneration
— chemical offsite transfers for recycling, p. 533 [503]
Acid solution, spent *See:* Spent acid solution
Acquisitions, corporate *See:* Mergers and acquisitions
Acrolein
— recycling and energy recovery of chemicals in waste, p. 538 [509]
— releases, p. 346 [382]
— toxic releases in Louisiana, p. 403 [410]
— toxic releases in Texas, p. 464 [436]
— treatment or release of chemicals in waste, p. 549 [513]
Acrylamide
— recycling and energy recovery of chemicals in waste, p. 538 [509]
— releases, p. 346 [382]
— releases of carcinogens, p. 485 [448]
— toxic releases in Alabama, p. 363 [393]
— toxic releases in Arkansas, p. 369 [396]
— toxic releases in California, p. 372 [397]

Numbers following p. or pp. are page references. Numbers in [ ] are table references.

Keyword Index

915

Numbers following p. or pp. are page references. Numbers in [ ] are table references.

Numbers following p. or pp. are page references. Numbers in [ ] are table references.

Air continued:

— pollution abatement and control expenditures in Maryland, p. 736 [712]
— pollution abatement and control expenditures in Massachusetts, p. 737 [713]
— pollution abatement and control expenditures in Michigan, p. 738 [714]
— pollution abatement and control expenditures in Minnesota, p. 739 [715]
— pollution abatement and control expenditures in miscellaneous manufacturing industries, p. 673 [649]
— pollution abatement and control expenditures in Mississippi, p. 740 [716]
— pollution abatement and control expenditures in Missouri, p. 741 [717]
— pollution abatement and control expenditures in Montana, p. 742 [718]
— pollution abatement and control expenditures in Nebraska, p. 743 [719]
— pollution abatement and control expenditures in Nevada, p. 744 [720]
— pollution abatement and control expenditures in New Hampshire, p. 745 [721]
— pollution abatement and control expenditures in New Jersey, p. 746 [722]
— pollution abatement and control expenditures in New Mexico, p. 747 [723]
— pollution abatement and control expenditures in New York, p. 748 [724]
— pollution abatement and control expenditures in North Carolina, p. 749 [725]
— pollution abatement and control expenditures in North Dakota, p. 750 [726]
— pollution abatement and control expenditures in Ohio, p. 751 [727]
— pollution abatement and control expenditures in Oklahoma, p. 752 [728]
— pollution abatement and control expenditures in Oregon, p. 753 [729]
— pollution abatement and control expenditures in paper and allied products, p. 674 [650]
— pollution abatement and control expenditures in Pennsylvania, p. 754 [730]
— pollution abatement and control expenditures in petroleum and coal products, p. 675 [651]
— pollution abatement and control expenditures in primary metal industries, p. 676 [652]
— pollution abatement and control expenditures in printing and publishing, p. 677 [653]
— pollution abatement and control expenditures in Rhode Island, p. 755 [731]
— pollution abatement and control expenditures in rubber and miscellaneous plastics products, p. 678 [654]
— pollution abatement and control expenditures in South Carolina, p. 756 [732]
— pollution abatement and control expenditures in South Dakota, p. 757 [733]

Air continued:

— pollution abatement and control expenditures in stone, clay, and glass products, p. 679 [655]
— pollution abatement and control expenditures in Tennessee, p. 758 [734]
— pollution abatement and control expenditures in Texas, p. 759 [735]
— pollution abatement and control expenditures in textile mill products, p. 680 [656]
— pollution abatement and control expenditures in tobacco products, p. 681 [657]
— pollution abatement and control expenditures in transportation equipment, p. 682 [658]
— pollution abatement and control expenditures in United States, p. 660 [636]
— pollution abatement and control expenditures in Utah, p. 760 [736]
— pollution abatement and control expenditures in Vermont, p. 761 [737]
— pollution abatement and control expenditures in Virginia, p. 762 [738]
— pollution abatement and control expenditures in Washington, p. 763 [739]
— pollution abatement and control expenditures in West Virginia, p. 764 [740]
— pollution abatement and control expenditures in Wisconsin, p. 765 [741]
— pollution abatement and control expenditures in Wyoming, p. 766 [742]
— pollution abatement and control operating costs in Alabama, p. 767 [743]
— pollution abatement and control operating costs in Alaska, p. 768 [744]
— pollution abatement and control operating costs in all industries, p. 697 [673]
— pollution abatement and control operating costs in Arizona, p. 769 [745]
— pollution abatement and control operating costs in Arkansas, p. 770 [746]
— pollution abatement and control operating costs in California, p. 771 [747]
— pollution abatement and control operating costs in chemicals and allied products, p. 698 [674]
— pollution abatement and control operating costs in Colorado, p. 772 [748]
— pollution abatement and control operating costs in Connecticut, p. 773 [749]
— pollution abatement and control operating costs in Delaware, p. 774 [750]
— pollution abatement and control operating costs in District of Columbia, p. 775 [751]
— pollution abatement and control operating costs in electronic and other electric equipment, p. 699 [675]
— pollution abatement and control operating costs in fabricated metal products, p. 700 [676]
— pollution abatement and control operating costs in Florida, p. 776 [752]
— pollution abatement and control operating costs in food

Numbers following p. or pp. are page references. Numbers in [ ] are table references.

Numbers following p. or pp. are page references. Numbers in [ ] are table references.

Keyword Index

Numbers following p. or pp. are page references. Numbers in [ ] are table references.

Numbers following p. or pp. are page references. Numbers in [ ] are table references.

Keyword Index

Numbers following p. or pp. are page references. Numbers in [ ] are table references.

Numbers following p. or pp. are page references. Numbers in [ ] are table references.

Numbers following p. or pp. are page references. Numbers in [ ] are table references.

Ammonium nitrate solution continued:
— chemical releases to land, p. 356 [387]
— discharges to surface water, p. 353 [384]
— offsite transfers to publicly owned treatment works, p. 534 [505]
— recycling and energy recovery of chemicals in waste, p. 538 [509]
— releases, p. 347 [382]
— total toxic releases, p. 357 [388]
— toxic releases in Alabama, p. 363 [393]
— toxic releases in Arizona, p. 367 [395]
— toxic releases in Arkansas, p. 369 [396]
— toxic releases in California, p. 372 [397]
— toxic releases in Connecticut, p. 377 [399]
— toxic releases in Florida, p. 381 [401]
— toxic releases in Georgia, p. 384 [402]
— toxic releases in Hawaii, p. 387 [403]
— toxic releases in Idaho, p. 388 [404]
— toxic releases in Illinois, p. 389 [405]
— toxic releases in Indiana, p. 392 [406]
— toxic releases in Iowa, p. 395 [407]
— toxic releases in Kansas, p. 397 [408]
— toxic releases in Kentucky, p. 400 [409]
— toxic releases in Louisiana, p. 403 [410]
— toxic releases in Maine, p. 406 [411]
— toxic releases in Maryland, p. 407 [412]
— toxic releases in Michigan, p. 412 [414]
— toxic releases in Mississippi, p. 417 [416]
— toxic releases in Missouri, p. 420 [417]
— toxic releases in Nebraska, p. 424 [419]
— toxic releases in New Hampshire, p. 427 [421]
— toxic releases in New Jersey, p. 429 [422]
— toxic releases in New York, p. 434 [424]
— toxic releases in North Carolina, p. 438 [425]
— toxic releases in Ohio, p. 442 [427]
— toxic releases in Oklahoma, p. 445 [428]
— toxic releases in Oregon, p. 447 [429]
— toxic releases in Pennsylvania, p. 449 [430]
— toxic releases in South Carolina, p. 457 [433]
— toxic releases in South Dakota, p. 459 [434]
— toxic releases in Tennessee, p. 461 [435]
— toxic releases in Texas, p. 464 [436]
— toxic releases in Utah, p. 467 [437]
— toxic releases in Virginia, p. 471 [440]
— toxic releases in Washington, p. 474 [441]
— toxic releases in Wisconsin, p. 479 [443]
— toxic releases in Wyoming, p. 481 [444]
— treatment or release of chemicals in waste, p. 549 [513]
— underground injection, p. 358 [389]

Ammonium sulfate solution
— air, water, and land toxic releases, p. 355 [386]
— chemical releases to land, p. 356 [387]
— discharges to surface water, p. 353 [384]
— offsite transfers for disposal, p. 531 [501]
— offsite transfers to publicly owned treatment works, p. 534 [505]
— recycling and energy recovery of chemicals in waste, p. 538 [509]

Ammonium sulfate solution continued:
— releases, p. 347 [382]
— total toxic releases, p. 358 [388]
— toxic releases in Alabama, p. 363 [393]
— toxic releases in Arizona, p. 367 [395]
— toxic releases in Arkansas, p. 369 [396]
— toxic releases in California, p. 372 [397]
— toxic releases in Colorado, p. 375 [398]
— toxic releases in Connecticut, p. 377 [399]
— toxic releases in Delaware, p. 379 [400]
— toxic releases in Florida, p. 382 [401]
— toxic releases in Georgia, p. 384 [402]
— toxic releases in Hawaii, p. 387 [403]
— toxic releases in Idaho, p. 388 [404]
— toxic releases in Illinois, p. 389 [405]
— toxic releases in Indiana, p. 392 [406]
— toxic releases in Iowa, p. 395 [407]
— toxic releases in Kansas, p. 397 [408]
— toxic releases in Kentucky, p. 400 [409]
— toxic releases in Louisiana, p. 403 [410]
— toxic releases in Maine, p. 406 [411]
— toxic releases in Maryland, p. 407 [412]
— toxic releases in Massachusetts, p. 410 [413]
— toxic releases in Michigan, p. 412 [414]
— toxic releases in Minnesota, p. 415 [415]
— toxic releases in Mississippi, p. 417 [416]
— toxic releases in Missouri, p. 420 [417]
— toxic releases in Nebraska, p. 424 [419]
— toxic releases in New Hampshire, p. 427 [421]
— toxic releases in New Jersey, p. 429 [422]
— toxic releases in New Mexico, p. 432 [423]
— toxic releases in New York, p. 434 [424]
— toxic releases in North Carolina, p. 438 [425]
— toxic releases in Ohio, p. 442 [427]
— toxic releases in Oregon, p. 447 [429]
— toxic releases in Pennsylvania, p. 449 [430]
— toxic releases in Puerto Rico, p. 453 [431]
— toxic releases in Rhode Island, p. 455 [432]
— toxic releases in South Carolina, p. 457 [433]
— toxic releases in Tennessee, p. 461 [435]
— toxic releases in Texas, p. 464 [436]
— toxic releases in Utah, p. 467 [437]
— toxic releases in Virginia, p. 471 [440]
— toxic releases in Washington, p. 474 [441]
— toxic releases in West Virginia, p. 476 [442]
— toxic releases in Wisconsin, p. 479 [443]
— treatment or release of chemicals in waste, p. 549 [513]
— underground injection, p. 359 [389]

Amoco Oil Co. (Texas City, Texas)
— air, water, and land toxic releases, p. 513 [473]
— increased air, water, and land releases, p. 509 [471]
— increased underground injection, p. 510 [472]
— total toxic releases, p. 514 [474]

Amphibians
— endangered species, pp. 245-246 [276-277]
— threatened species, pp. 246-247 [277-278]

Anadromous fish
— status of assessed fisheries, p. 255 [287]

Numbers following p. or pp. are page references. Numbers in [ ] are table references.

Numbers following p. or pp. are page references. Numbers in [ ] are table references.

Numbers following p. or pp. are page references. Numbers in [ ] are table references.

Keyword Index

Apparel and textile products continued:
— solid waste generation, p. 566 [528]
— toxic release inventory, p. 517 [478]
— Toxic Release Inventory, p. 517 [478]
— Toxic Release Inventory releases, p. 518 [480]
— Toxic Release Inventory releases and transfers, p. 527 [497]
— Toxic Release Inventory transfers, p. 518 [480]
— treatment or release of chemicals in waste, p. 555 [514]
Apparel industry *See:* Apparel and textile products
Appliances *See:* Fixtures and appliances
Appropriations
— national park system, p. 221 [249]
Aquaculture
— catfish production and value, p. 248 [280]
— output, p. 248 [279]
— trout production and value, p. 274 [305]
Aqualon Co. (Hopewell, Virginia)
— increased air, water, and land releases, p. 509 [471]
Aquenous sodium hydroxide
— waste minimization, p. 606 [581]
Aqueous cleaner and rinse water
— waste minimization, p. 601 [577]
Aqueous inorganic treatment
— hazardous waste treatment, p. 562 [522]
Aqueous organic treatment
— hazardous waste treatment, p. 562 [522]
Arab nations
 See also: Organization of Petroleum Exporting Countries; specific countries (e.g., Bahrain)
— crude oil production, p. 333 [367]
Arachnids
— endangered species, pp. 245-246 [276-277]
— threatened species, pp. 246-247 [277-278]
Aransas Bay
— area, p. 44 [43]
Arcadian Fertilizer L.P.
— air, water, and land toxic releases, p. 515 [475]
— total toxic releases, p. 515 [476]
Arcadian Fertilizer L.P. (Geismar, Louisiana)
— air, water, and land toxic releases, p. 512 [473]
— increased air, water, and land releases, p. 509 [471]
— total toxic releases, p. 513 [474]
Arcadian Fertilizer L.P. (Lake Charles, Louisiana)
— decreased air, water, and land releases, p. 507 [469]
Arcadian Fertilizer L.P. (Memphis, Tennessee)
— air, water, and land toxic releases, p. 512 [473]
— increased air, water, and land releases, p. 509 [471]
— total toxic releases, p. 514 [474]
Architectural damage
— corporate environmental compliance costs, p. 630 [604]
Arco Chemical
— environmental spending, p. 617 [590]
Arco Chemical Co. (Channelview, Texas)
— decreased underground injection, p. 508 [470]
Arco Chemical Co. (Pasadena, Texas)
— increased air, water, and land releases, p. 509 [471]
Argentina
— environmental market, p. 845 [827]

Argentina continued:
— natural gas production, p. 333 [368]
— petroleum product prices, p. 623 [597]
Aristech Chemical Corp. (Haverhill, Ohio)
— decreased air, water, and land releases, p. 507 [469]
— decreased underground injection, p. 508 [470]
Arizona
— acreage affected by mountain pine beetle, p. 171 [204]
— area of water bodies, p. 45 [44]
— chemicals used in lettuce production, p. 342 [377]
— electric energy net generation, p. 326 [358]
— electric energy net summer capability, p. 326 [358]
— electric energy sales, p. 859 [845]
— energy consumption, p. 293 [326]
— energy expenditures, p. 621 [594]
— environmental budget, p. 636 [611]
— federal aid to state and local governments, p. 631 [606]
— federally owned land, p. 197 [227]
— hazardous waste sites, p. 492 [456]
— highest point of elevation, p. 183 [217]
— land area, p. 190 [220]
— land cover and use, pp. 199, 201 [228-229]
— lowest point of elevation, p. 185 [218]
— mean elevation, p. 187 [219]
— national forest recreation visitor days, p. 219 [248]
— national forest system land, p. 177 [211]
— National Priority List sites, p. 494 [458]
— net exports of Toxic Release Inventory chemicals, p. 863 [849]
— nonfuel mineral production, p. 214 [242]
— nuclear generating capacity, p. 316 [350]
— nuclear power plants, p. 319 [352]
— pollution abatement and control expenditures, p. 719 [695]
— pollution abatement and control operating costs, p. 769 [745]
— precipitation, p. 72 [71]
— receipt of Toxic Release Inventory chemicals, p. 537 [508]
— recreational use of public lands, p. 223 [251]
— recycling and energy recovery of chemicals in waste, p. 546 [511]
— Safe Drinking Water Act violations, p. 887 [876]
— state parks and recreation areas, p. 224 [252]
— threatened fish species, p. 252 [285]
— total area, p. 190 [220]
— toxic chemical emissions, p. 362 [392]
— toxic chemical releases, p. 367 [395]
— Toxic Release Inventory air, water, and land releases, p. 501 [464]
— Toxic Release Inventory transfers, pp. 503, 530, 548 [466, 500, 512]
— toxic releases in U.S. states and territories, p. 499 [462]
— treatment or release of chemicals in waste, p. 556 [515]
— tree planting on federal land, p. 179 [213]
— tree planting on non-federal land, p. 180 [214]
— tree planting on private land, p. 182 [215]
— waste-by-rail, p. 591 [565]
— water area, p. 41 [40]
— water pollution permits, p. 892 [882]
— water withdrawals and consumptive use, p. 58 [57]

Numbers following p. or pp. are page references. Numbers in [ ] are table references.

Arizona continued:
— western spruce budworm defoliation, p. 173 [207]
Arkansas
— electric energy net generation, p. 326 [358]
— electric energy net summer capability, p. 326 [358]
— electric energy sales, p. 859 [845]
— energy consumption, p. 293 [326]
— energy expenditures, p. 621 [594]
— environmental budget, p. 636 [611]
— federal aid to state and local governments, p. 631 [606]
— federally owned land, p. 197 [227]
— hazardous waste sites, p. 492 [456]
— highest point of elevation in Arkansas, p. 183 [217]
— land area, p. 189 [220]
— land cover and use, pp. 199-200 [228-229]
— lowest point of elevation, p. 185 [218]
— mean elevation, p. 187 [219]
— national forest recreation visitor days, p. 219 [248]
— national forest system land, p. 177 [211]
— National Priority List sites, p. 494 [458]
— net exports of Toxic Release Inventory chemicals, p. 863 [849]
— nonfuel mineral production, p. 214 [242]
— nuclear generating capacity, p. 316 [350]
— nuclear power plants, p. 318 [352]
— pollution abatement and control expenditures, p. 720 [696]
— pollution abatement and control operating costs, p. 770 [746]
— precipitation, p. 73 [72]
— receipt of Toxic Release Inventory chemicals, p. 537 [508]
— recycling and energy recovery of chemicals in waste, p. 546 [511]
— rivers, p. 38 [38]
— Safe Drinking Water Act violations, p. 887 [876]
— southern pine beetle outbreak, p. 172 [205]
— state parks and recreation areas, p. 224 [252]
— state recycling laws, p. 886 [875]
— threatened fish species, p. 252 [285]
— total area, p. 189 [220]
— toxic chemical emissions, p. 362 [392]
— toxic chemical releases, p. 369 [396]
— Toxic Release Inventory air, water, and land releases, p. 501 [464]
— Toxic Release Inventory transfers, pp. 504, 530, 548 [466, 500, 512]
— toxic releases in U.S. states and territories, p. 499 [462]
— treatment or release of chemicals in waste, p. 556 [515]
— tree planting on federal land, p. 179 [213]
— tree planting on non-federal land, p. 180 [214]
— tree planting on private land, p. 182 [215]
— water area, p. 40 [40]
— water pollution permits, p. 892 [882]
— water withdrawals and consumptive use, p. 58 [57]
Arkansas Chemicals Inc. (El Dorado, Arkansas)
— increased underground injection, p. 511 [472]
Arkansas River
— length, discharge, and drainage areas, p. 38 [38]

Arkansas River continued:
— lowest point of elevation in Colorado, p. 185 [218]
Armco Steel Co. L.P. (Middletown, Ohio)
— decreased air, water, and land releases, p. 507 [469]
— increased underground injection, p. 511 [472]
Army Corps of Engineers *See:* U.S. Army Corps of Engineers
Arsenic
— apparent consumption, p. 211 [241]
— average price, p. 648 [625]
— carcinogens released to air, water, land, p. 484 [447]
— exports, p. 211 [241]
— net import reliance, p. 211 [241]
— production, p. 211 [241]
— recycling and energy recovery of chemicals in waste, p. 538 [509]
— releases, pp. 347, 488 [382, 450]
— releases of carcinogens, p. 485 [448]
— toxic releases in Alabama, p. 363 [393]
— toxic releases in Arkansas, p. 369 [396]
— toxic releases in California, p. 372 [397]
— toxic releases in Colorado, p. 375 [398]
— toxic releases in Florida, p. 382 [401]
— toxic releases in Georgia, p. 384 [402]
— toxic releases in Illinois, p. 389 [405]
— toxic releases in Indiana, p. 392 [406]
— toxic releases in Kentucky, p. 400 [409]
— toxic releases in Louisiana, p. 403 [410]
— toxic releases in Massachusetts, p. 410 [413]
— toxic releases in Michigan, p. 412 [414]
— toxic releases in Minnesota, p. 415 [415]
— toxic releases in Mississippi, p. 417 [416]
— toxic releases in New Jersey, p. 429 [422]
— toxic releases in North Carolina, p. 438 [425]
— toxic releases in Ohio, p. 442 [427]
— toxic releases in Oklahoma, p. 445 [428]
— toxic releases in Oregon, p. 447 [429]
— toxic releases in Pennsylvania, p. 449 [430]
— toxic releases in South Carolina, p. 457 [433]
— toxic releases in Tennessee, p. 461 [435]
— toxic releases in Texas, p. 464 [436]
— toxic releases in Virginia, p. 471 [440]
— toxic releases in Washington, p. 474 [441]
— toxic releases in West Virginia, p. 476 [442]
— toxic releases in Wisconsin, p. 479 [443]
— transfers, p. 488 [451]
— treatment or release of chemicals in waste, p. 549 [513]
— wastewater, p. 48 [46]
Arsenic compounds
— chemical releases to land, p. 356 [387]
— recycling and energy recovery of chemicals in waste, p. 539 [509]
— releases, pp. 347, 488 [382, 450]
— toxic releases in Alabama, p. 363 [393]
— toxic releases in Arizona, p. 367 [395]
— toxic releases in Arkansas, p. 369 [396]
— toxic releases in California, p. 372 [397]
— toxic releases in Colorado, p. 375 [398]

Numbers following p. or pp. are page references. Numbers in [ ] are table references.

929

Keyword Index

Numbers following p. or pp. are page references. Numbers in [ ] are table references.

Ash continued:
— waste-by-rail, p. 591 [565]

Ash Grove Cement (Louisville, Nebraska)
— hazardous waste incineration law violations, p. 889 [878]

Asheville, North Carolina
— humidity, p. 125 [151]
— precipitation, p. 86 [102]
— snow and ice pellets, p. 99 [127]
— sunshine, p. 134 [161]
— temperatures, p. 108 [136]
— wind speed, p. 144 [171]

Ashland Chemical
— environmental spending, p. 617 [590]

Ashland, Kentucky
— air quality standard excesses for ozone, p. 34 [36]

Asia
— pesticides, p. 345 [380]

Asia Pacific region
— environmental technology markets, p. 843 [825]

Aspen
— consumption, p. 852 [837]
— production, p. 852 [837]

Asphalt and related bitumens
— construction waste, p. 593 [568]
— production quantities, p. 203 [233]
— production value, p. 205 [234]

Astoria, Oregon
— catch of domestic fisheries, p. 251 [284]
— humidity, p. 124 [150]
— precipitation, p. 88 [106]
— snow and ice pellets, p. 98 [126]
— temperatures, p. 107 [135]
— wind speed, p. 143 [170]

Atchafalaya Bay
— area, p. 44 [43]

Atchafalaya River
— length, discharge, and drainage areas, p. 38 [38]

Athens, Georgia
— humidity, p. 125 [151]
— precipitation, p. 76 [79]
— snow and ice pellets, p. 99 [127]
— temperatures, p. 108 [136]
— wind speed, p. 144 [171]

Atlanta, Georgia
— air quality standard excesses for ozone, p. 33 [36]
— air quality trends, p. 30 [34]
— annual precipitation, p. 69 [68]
— highest temperature, p. 114 [142]
— humidity, p. 125 [151]
— lowest temperature, p. 116 [143]
— maximum temperatures, p. 117 [144]
— minimum temperatures, p. 118 [145]
— normal temperatures, p. 113 [141]
— precipitation, p. 76 [79]
— snow and ice pellets, p. 99 [127]
— sunshine, p. 134 [161]
— temperatures, p. 108 [136]
— trash per person, p. 594 [569]

Atlanta, Georgia continued:
— wind speed, p. 144 [171]

Atlantic City, New Jersey
— air quality standard excesses for ozone, p. 33 [36]
— annual precipitation, p. 70 [68]
— highest temperature, p. 115 [142]
— humidity, p. 121 [148]
— lowest temperature, p. 116 [143]
— maximum temperatures, p. 117 [144]
— minimum temperatures, p. 119 [145]
— normal temperatures, p. 113 [141]
— precipitation, p. 85 [99]
— snow and ice pellets, p. 97 [124]
— sunshine, p. 131 [158]
— temperatures, p. 104 [133]
— wind speed, p. 140 [168]

Atlantic Coast
— area of water bodies, p. 43 [42]
— marine recreational fisheries catch, p. 286 [320]
— population density, p. 228 [257]

Atlantic cod
— domestic catch and value, p. 250 [283]
— population, p. 274 [306]

Atlantic herring
— domestic catch and value, p. 250 [283]
— population, p. 274 [306]

Atlantic Ocean
— lowest point of elevation in Delaware, p. 185 [218]
— lowest point of elevation in Florida, p. 185 [218]
— lowest point of elevation in Georgia, p. 185 [218]
— lowest point of elevation in Maine, p. 185 [218]
— lowest point of elevation in Maryland, p. 185 [218]
— lowest point of elevation in Massachusetts, p. 185 [218]
— lowest point of elevation in New Hampshire, p. 186 [218]
— lowest point of elevation in New Jersey, p. 186 [218]
— lowest point of elevation in New York, p. 186 [218]
— lowest point of elevation in North Carolina, p. 186 [218]
— lowest point of elevation in Puerto Rico, p. 186 [218]
— lowest point of elevation in Rhode Island, p. 186 [218]
— lowest point of elevation in South Carolina, p. 186 [218]
— lowest point of elevation in Virgin Islands, p. 186 [218]
— lowest point of elevation in Virginia, p. 186 [218]
— sea turtles, p. 277 [309]

Atlantic Ocean perch
— catch of principal species, p. 256 [288]
— domestic catch and value, p. 250 [283]
— production and value of fishery products, p. 265 [295]

Atlantic pollack
— domestic catch and value, p. 250 [283]
— production and value of fishery products, p. 265 [295]

Atlantic sea herring *See:* Atlantic herring

Atmospheric pollution
— ocean pollution, p. 49 [47]

Atrazine
— pesticide use in Mexico, p. 346 [381]

Attorneys *See:* Environmental attorneys

Auburn, Maine
— air quality standard excesses for ozone, p. 34 [36]

Numbers following p. or pp. are page references. Numbers in [ ] are table references.

Augusta, Georgia
— humidity, p. 125 [151]
— precipitation, p. 76 [79]
— snow and ice pellets, p. 99 [127]
— temperatures, p. 108 [136]
— wind speed, p. 144 [171]
Austin, Texas
— humidity, p. 128 [154]
— precipitation, p. 90 [112]
— snow and ice pellets, p. 100 [129]
— sunshine, p. 136 [164]
— temperatures, p. 110 [138]
— wind speed, p. 147 [174]
Australia
— carbon dioxide emissions growth, p. 17 [19]
— coal exports, p. 874 [860]
— environmental technology markets, p. 843 [825]
— hydrocarbon emissions, p. 20 [23]
— mineral commodity production, p. 215 [244]
— natural gas production, p. 334 [368]
— petroleum consumption, pp. 306-307 [340]
— petroleum product prices, p. 623 [597]
— U.S. mineral and metal imports, p. 867 [855]
Australian Shrimp Trawl
— bycatch discard rates, p. 263 [293]
Austria
— carbon dioxide emissions growth, p. 17 [19]
— environmental technology markets, p. 843 [825]
— hazardous waste, p. 561 [521]
— petroleum product prices, p. 623 [597]
— sulfur emission targets, p. 26 [30]
Autofluff
— waste-by-rail, p. 591 [565]
Automobiles
— battery-powered vehicles, p. 874 [861]
— cost of safety and emissions equipment, p. 627 [601]
— cost of safety and pollution equipment, p. 628 [602]
— fuel consumption, p. 877 [864]
— personal travel, p. 876 [863]
— pollution abatement and control expenditures, p. 654 [631]
— pollution concerns of car buyers, p. 875 [862]
Automotive and industrial products
— aerosol production, p. 847 [830]
Automotive batteries
— sales, p. 857 [844]
Automotive fuels
— prices, p. 623 [597]
Automotive prime movers
— total horsepower, p. 311 [345]
Avoca, Pennsylvania
— humidity, p. 122 [148]
— snow and ice pellets, p. 97 [124]
— sunshine, p. 132 [158]
— temperatures, p. 105 [133]
— wind speed, p. 141 [168]
Bachelor's degrees
— salaries for environmental jobs, p. 825 [803]

Backbone Mountain
— highest point of elevation in Maryland, p. 184 [217]
Backcountry
— national park system, p. 221 [249]
Bags, multiwall *See:* Uncoated paper and multiwall bags
Bahrain
— natural gas production, p. 334 [368]
Baird Inlet
— area, p. 42 [41]
Bait and animal food
— canned fishery products, p. 267 [297]
— freezings and holdings, p. 268 [298]
Bakersfield, California
— humidity, p. 123 [150]
— precipitation, p. 73 [73]
— snow and ice pellets, p. 98 [126]
— temperatures, p. 106 [135]
— wind speed, p. 142 [170]
Bald eagles
— population, p. 234 [263]
Balloons
— litter on beaches and shorelines, p. 592 [567]
Baltimore, Maryland
— air quality standard excesses for carbon monoxide, p. 31 [35]
— air quality standard excesses for ozone, p. 33 [36]
— air quality trends, p. 30 [34]
— annual precipitation, p. 69 [68]
— highest temperature, p. 114 [142]
— humidity, p. 125 [151]
— lowest temperature, p. 116 [143]
— maximum temperatures, p. 117 [144]
— minimum temperatures, p. 118 [145]
— normal temperatures, p. 113 [141]
— precipitation, p. 80 [89]
— snow and ice pellets, p. 99 [127]
— sunshine, p. 134 [161]
— temperatures, p. 108 [136]
— wind speed, p. 144 [171]
Baltimore oriole
— long- and short-term trends, p. 241 [272]
Bangladesh
— natural gas production, p. 334 [368]
Bankruptcy
— corporate legal needs, p. 884 [873]
Barite
— apparent consumption, p. 211 [241]
— average price, p. 648 [625]
— exports, p. 211 [241]
— net import reliance, p. 211 [241]
— net U.S. imports, p. 868 [855]
— production, p. 211 [241]
— world production, p. 214 [243]
Barite, primary
— production quantities, p. 203 [233]
— production value, p. 205 [234]
Barium
— recycling and energy recovery of chemicals in waste, p. 539

Numbers following p. or pp. are page references. Numbers in [ ] are table references.

932

Keyword Index

Numbers following p. or pp. are page references. Numbers in [ ] are table references.

Basswood
— heat generation, p. 310 [344]
Baton Rouge, Louisiana
— air quality standard excesses for ozone, p. 33 [36]
— humidity, p. 128 [154]
— precipitation, p. 80 [87]
— snow and ice pellets, p. 100 [129]
— temperatures, p. 110 [138]
— unhealthy air pollution levels, p. 37 [37]
— wind speed, p. 147 [174]
Batteries
  See also: specific types; e.g., Alkaline batteries
— market, p. 857 [844]
— state recycling laws, p. 887 [875]
Battery-powered vehicles
— California, p. 874 [861]
Bauxite
  See also: Alumina
— apparent consumption, p. 211 [241]
— average price, p. 648 [625]
— consumption, p. 849 [833]
— exports, p. 211 [241]
— imports, exports, and stocks, p. 849 [833]
— net import reliance, p. 211 [241]
— net U.S. imports, p. 867 [855]
— production, pp. 211, 849 [241, 833]
— production quantities, pp. 206-207 [235-236]
— quantity and value of inventory, p. 850 [834]
— world production, pp. 215-216 [243-244]
Baxter Healthcare Corp. (Johnson City, Tennessee)
— decreased air, water, and land releases, p. 507 [469]
Bay scallops
— commercial harvest of fisheries, p. 249 [281]
Bayer Group
— environmental spending, p. 616 [589]
Beaches and shorelines
— litter, p. 592 [566-567]
Beaked whales
— number and status, p. 275 [308]
Beaufort, North Carolina
— catch of domestic fisheries, p. 251 [284]
Beaumont, Texas
— air quality standard excesses for ozone, p. 33 [36]
Beaver Valley, Pennsylvania
— air quality standard excesses for ozone, p. 35 [36]
Beaverdam Wash
— lowest point of elevation in Utah, p. 186 [218]
Becharof Lake
— area, p. 42 [41]
Bechevin Bay
— area, p. 43 [41]
Bechtel Group
— top ten environmental employers, p. 823 [801]
Beckley, West Virginia
— humidity, p. 125 [151]
— precipitation, p. 94 [119]
— snow and ice pellets, p. 99 [127]
— temperatures, p. 108 [136]

Beckley, West Virginia continued:
— wind speed, p. 144 [171]
Beech
— consumption, p. 852 [837]
— production, p. 852 [837]
Behm Canal
— area, p. 42 [41]
Belarus
— mineral commodity production, p. 215 [244]
Belgium
— coal market, p. 838 [818]
— environmental technology markets, p. 843 [825]
— petroleum consumption, pp. 306-307 [340]
— petroleum product prices, p. 623 [597]
— sulfur emission targets, p. 26 [30]
— U.S. mineral and metal imports, p. 867 [855]
Belle Fourche River
— lowest point of elevation in Wyoming, p. 186 [218]
Benzal chloride
— recycling and energy recovery of chemicals in waste, p. 539 [509]
— releases, p. 347 [382]
— toxic releases in New Jersey, p. 429 [422]
— toxic releases in New York, p. 434 [424]
— toxic releases in Tennessee, p. 461 [435]
— treatment or release of chemicals in waste, p. 550 [513]
Benzene
— air, water, and land toxic releases, p. 355 [386]
— carcinogens released to air, water, land, p. 484 [447]
— recycling and energy recovery of chemicals in waste, p. 539 [509]
— releases, p. 347 [382]
— releases of carcinogens, p. 485 [448]
— total toxic releases, p. 358 [388]
— toxic chemical accidents, p. 360 [390]
— toxic releases in Alabama, p. 364 [393]
— toxic releases in Alaska, p. 366 [394]
— toxic releases in Arizona, p. 367 [395]
— toxic releases in Arkansas, p. 369 [396]
— toxic releases in California, p. 372 [397]
— toxic releases in Colorado, p. 375 [398]
— toxic releases in Connecticut, p. 377 [399]
— toxic releases in Delaware, p. 379 [400]
— toxic releases in Georgia, p. 384 [402]
— toxic releases in Hawaii, p. 387 [403]
— toxic releases in Illinois, p. 390 [405]
— toxic releases in Indiana, p. 392 [406]
— toxic releases in Iowa, p. 395 [407]
— toxic releases in Kansas, p. 397 [408]
— toxic releases in Kentucky, p. 400 [409]
— toxic releases in Louisiana, p. 403 [410]
— toxic releases in Maryland, p. 407 [412]
— toxic releases in Michigan, p. 412 [414]
— toxic releases in Minnesota, p. 415 [415]
— toxic releases in Mississippi, p. 417 [416]
— toxic releases in Missouri, p. 420 [417]
— toxic releases in Montana, p. 422 [418]
— toxic releases in Nevada, p. 425 [420]

Numbers following p. or pp. are page references. Numbers in [ ] are table references.

Benzene continued:
— toxic releases in New Hampshire, p. 427 [421]
— toxic releases in New Jersey, p. 429 [422]
— toxic releases in New Mexico, p. 432 [423]
— toxic releases in New York, p. 434 [424]
— toxic releases in North Carolina, p. 438 [425]
— toxic releases in North Dakota, p. 440 [426]
— toxic releases in Ohio, p. 442 [427]
— toxic releases in Oklahoma, p. 445 [428]
— toxic releases in Oregon, p. 447 [429]
— toxic releases in Pennsylvania, p. 450 [430]
— toxic releases in Puerto Rico, p. 453 [431]
— toxic releases in South Carolina, p. 457 [433]
— toxic releases in Tennessee, p. 461 [435]
— toxic releases in Texas, p. 464 [436]
— toxic releases in Utah, p. 467 [437]
— toxic releases in Virgin Islands, p. 470 [439]
— toxic releases in Virginia, p. 471 [440]
— toxic releases in Washington, p. 474 [441]
— toxic releases in West Virginia, p. 476 [442]
— toxic releases in Wisconsin, p. 479 [443]
— toxic releases in Wyoming, p. 481 [444]
— treatment or release of chemicals in waste, p. 550 [513]
Benzoic trichloride
— recycling and energy recovery of chemicals in waste,
   p. 539 [509]
— releases, p. 347 [382]
— releases of bioaccumulators, p. 483 [446]
— releases of carcinogens, p. 485 [448]
— toxic releases in New York, p. 434 [424]
— toxic releases in Ohio, p. 442 [427]
— toxic releases in Tennessee, p. 461 [435]
— treatment or release of chemicals in waste, p. 550 [513]
Benzoyl chloride
— recycling and energy recovery of chemicals in waste,
   p. 539 [509]
— releases, p. 347 [382]
— toxic releases in California, p. 372 [397]
— toxic releases in Connecticut, p. 377 [399]
— toxic releases in Georgia, p. 384 [402]
— toxic releases in Kansas, p. 397 [408]
— toxic releases in New Jersey, p. 429 [422]
— toxic releases in New York, p. 434 [424]
— toxic releases in Ohio, p. 442 [427]
— toxic releases in Pennsylvania, p. 450 [430]
— toxic releases in Rhode Island, p. 455 [432]
— toxic releases in Tennessee, p. 461 [435]
— toxic releases in Texas, p. 464 [436]
— treatment or release of chemicals in waste, p. 550 [513]
Benzoyl peroxide
— recycling and energy recovery of chemicals in waste,
   p. 539 [509]
— releases, p. 347 [382]
— toxic releases in California, p. 372 [397]
— toxic releases in Colorado, p. 375 [398]
— toxic releases in Connecticut, p. 377 [399]
— toxic releases in Georgia, p. 384 [402]
— toxic releases in Illinois, p. 390 [405]

Benzoyl peroxide continued:
— toxic releases in Indiana, p. 393 [406]
— toxic releases in Kansas, p. 397 [408]
— toxic releases in Kentucky, p. 400 [409]
— toxic releases in Massachusetts, p. 410 [413]
— toxic releases in Michigan, p. 412 [414]
— toxic releases in Missouri, p. 420 [417]
— toxic releases in Nebraska, p. 424 [419]
— toxic releases in New Jersey, p. 429 [422]
— toxic releases in New York, p. 434 [424]
— toxic releases in Ohio, p. 442 [427]
— toxic releases in Pennsylvania, p. 450 [430]
— toxic releases in South Carolina, p. 457 [433]
— toxic releases in Texas, p. 464 [436]
— toxic releases in Virginia, p. 471 [440]
— toxic releases in West Virginia, p. 476 [442]
— treatment or release of chemicals in waste, p. 550 [513]
Benzyl chloride
— recycling and energy recovery of chemicals in waste, p. 539
   [509]
— releases, p. 347 [382]
— toxic releases in California, p. 372 [397]
— toxic releases in Illinois, p. 390 [405]
— toxic releases in Indiana, p. 393 [406]
— toxic releases in Kentucky, p. 400 [409]
— toxic releases in Michigan, p. 412 [414]
— toxic releases in Missouri, p. 420 [417]
— toxic releases in New Jersey, p. 429 [422]
— toxic releases in New York, p. 434 [424]
— toxic releases in North Carolina, p. 438 [425]
— toxic releases in Ohio, p. 442 [427]
— toxic releases in Pennsylvania, p. 450 [430]
— toxic releases in Puerto Rico, p. 453 [431]
— toxic releases in Rhode Island, p. 455 [432]
— toxic releases in South Carolina, p. 457 [433]
— toxic releases in Tennessee, p. 461 [435]
— toxic releases in Texas, p. 464 [436]
— toxic releases in Wisconsin, p. 479 [443]
— treatment or release of chemicals in waste, p. 550 [513]
Bering Sea Rock Sole Trawl
— bycatch discard rates, p. 263 [293]
Bering Sea Sablefish Pot
— bycatch discard rates, p. 263 [293]
Berwick, Louisiana
— catch of domestic fisheries, p. 251 [284]
Beryllium
— recycling and energy recovery of chemicals in waste, p. 539
   [509]
— releases, pp. 347, 488 [382, 450]
— releases of carcinogens, p. 485 [448]
— toxic releases in Georgia, p. 384 [402]
— toxic releases in Michigan, p. 412 [414]
— toxic releases in Ohio, p. 442 [427]
— toxic releases in Pennsylvania, p. 450 [430]
— transfers, p. 488 [451]
— treatment or release of chemicals in waste, p. 550 [513]
Beryllium compounds
— recycling and energy recovery of chemicals in waste, p. 539

Numbers following p. or pp. are page references. Numbers in [ ] are table references.

Numbers following p. or pp. are page references. Numbers in [ ] are table references.

Blackpoll warbler
— long- and short-term trends, p. 241 [272]
Blacktail Creek
— source stream of river, p. 38 [38]
Blast furnace slag
— recycled or reused for highways, p. 580 [550]
Bleach, powder *See:* Powder bleach
Blue Canyon, California
— humidity, p. 123 [150]
— precipitation, p. 73 [73]
— snow and ice pellets, p. 98 [126]
— temperatures, p. 106 [135]
— wind speed, p. 142 [170]
Blue Hill, Massachusetts
— humidity, p. 122 [149]
— precipitation, p. 81 [90]
— snow and ice pellets, p. 97 [125]
— sunshine, p. 132 [159]
— temperatures, p. 105 [134]
— wind speed, p. 141 [169]
Blue whales
— population, p. 278 [310]
Blue-winged ducks
— population, p. 235 [265]
Blue-winged warbler
— long- and short-term trends, p. 241 [272]
Bluefish
— domestic catch and value, p. 250 [283]
Boating
— ocean pollution, p. 49 [47]
— recreational use of public lands, p. 223 [251]
Boats
   See also: specific types; e.g., Fishing craft
— fishing craft, p. 259 [290]
Body wash
— waste minimization, p. 597 [574]
Boeing Wichita (Wichita, Kansas)
— air, water, and land toxic releases, p. 513 [473]
— decreased air, water, and land releases, p. 507 [469]
Boiling water reactors
— nuclear energy and reactors, p. 320 [353]
Boise, Idaho
— annual precipitation, p. 69 [68]
— highest temperature, p. 114 [142]
— humidity, p. 129 [155]
— lowest temperature, p. 116 [143]
— maximum temperatures, p. 117 [144]
— minimum temperatures, p. 118 [145]
— normal temperatures, p. 113 [141]
— precipitation, p. 77 [81]
— snow and ice pellets, p. 101 [130]
— sunshine, p. 137 [165]
— temperatures, p. 111 [139]
— wind speed, p. 148 [175]
Bolivia
— petroleum product prices, p. 623 [597]
— U.S. mineral and metal imports, p. 867 [855]
Bon Secour Bay
— area, p. 44 [43]

Bonito
— catch of principal species, p. 256 [288]
Books and magazines
— environmental consciousness of executives, p. 891 [880]
Borah Peak
— highest point of elevation in Idaho, p. 184 [217]
Borden Chemicals & Plastics (Geismar, Louisiana)
— decreased underground injection, p. 508 [470]
Boron
— apparent consumption, p. 211 [241]
— average price, p. 648 [625]
— exports, p. 211 [241]
— net import reliance, p. 211 [241]
— production, p. 211 [241]
Boron minerals
— production quantities, p. 203 [233]
— production value, p. 205 [234]
Boston, Massachusetts
— air quality standard excesses for carbon monoxide, p. 31 [35]
— air quality standard excesses for ozone, p. 33 [36]
— air quality trends, p. 30 [34]
— annual precipitation, p. 70 [68]
— highest temperature, p. 114 [142]
— humidity, p. 122 [149]
— lowest temperature, p. 116 [143]
— maximum temperatures, p. 117 [144]
— minimum temperatures, p. 118 [145]
— normal temperatures, p. 113 [141]
— precipitation, p. 81 [90]
— snow and ice pellets, p. 97 [125]
— sunshine, p. 132 [159]
— Superfund sites, p. 497 [460]
— temperatures, p. 105 [134]
— trash per person, p. 594 [569]
— wind speed, p. 141 [169]
Botswana
— mineral commodity production, p. 215 [244]
Bottlenose dolphins
— number and status, p. 275 [308]
Bottles
— litter on beaches and shorelines, p. 592 [567]
Bottles, plastic *See:* Plastic soda bottles
Bottom ash *See:* Coal bottom ash and bottom slag
Bottom slag *See:* Coal bottom ash and bottom slag
Bottomfish
— status of assessed fisheries, p. 255 [287]
Boulder, Colorado
— air quality standard excesses for carbon monoxide, p. 32 [35]
Boundary Peak
— highest point of elevation in Nevada, p. 184 [217]
Bowater Inc. (Catawba, South Carolina)
— increased air, water, and land releases, p. 509 [471]
Bowhead whales
— number and status, p. 275 [308]
— population, p. 278 [310]
Box elder
— heat generation, p. 310 [344]

Numbers following p. or pp. are page references. Numbers in [ ] are table references.

Boxes *See:* specific types; e.g., Folding paperboard boxes

BP America
— total toxic releases, p. 515 [476]

BP Chemicals Inc. (Lima, Ohio)
— decreased underground injection, p. 508 [470]
— total toxic releases, p. 514 [474]

BP Chemicals Inc. (Port Lavaca, Texas)
— decreased underground injection, p. 508 [470]
— total toxic releases, p. 514 [474]

Braer tanker
— birds threatened by oil spill, p. 235 [264]

Brant
— population, p. 237 [266]

Brasstown Bald
— highest point of elevation in Georgia, p. 184 [217]

Brazil
— coal market, p. 838 [818]
— environmental concerns, p. 880 [868]
— environmental market, p. 845 [827]
— gas emissions, p. 63 [60]
— mineral commodity production, p. 215 [244]
— petroleum consumption, pp. 306-307 [340]
— petroleum product prices, p. 623 [597]
— U.S. mineral and metal imports, p. 867 [855]

Brazil Shrimp Trawl
— bycatch discard rates, p. 263 [293]

Brazoria, Texas
— air quality standard excesses for ozone, p. 34 [36]

Breeze *See:* Coke and breeze

Breton Sound
— area, p. 44 [43]

Brick
— construction waste, p. 593 [568]

Bridgeport, Connecticut
— humidity, p. 122 [149]
— precipitation, p. 74 [75]
— snow and ice pellets, p. 97 [125]
— temperatures, p. 105 [134]
— wind speed, p. 141 [169]

Bristol, Tennessee
— humidity, p. 121 [147]
— precipitation, p. 90 [111]
— snow and ice pellets, p. 96 [123]
— temperatures, p. 103 [132]
— wind speed, p. 140 [167]

Britain
   See also: Great Britain; United Kingdom
— carbon emissions, p. 18 [20]

British Columbia Cod Trawl
— bycatch discard rates, p. 263 [293]

Broken stone *See:* Crushed and broken stone

Bromine
— domestic production, p. 213 [242]
— production quantities, p. 203 [233]
— production value, p. 205 [234]

Bromine, contained
— apparent consumption, p. 211 [241]
— average price, p. 648 [625]

Bromine, contained continued:
— exports, p. 211 [241]
— net import reliance, p. 211 [241]
— production, p. 211 [241]

Bromochlorodifluoromethane (Halon 1211)
— recycling and energy recovery of chemicals in waste, p. 539 [509]
— releases, p. 347 [382]
— releases of ozone depleters, p. 490 [453]
— releases to air, water, and land, p. 489 [452]
— transfers, p. 490 [454]
— treatment or release of chemicals in waste, p. 550 [513]

Bromoform
— recycling and energy recovery of chemicals in waste, p. 539 [509]
— releases, p. 347 [382]
— toxic releases in Arkansas, p. 369 [396]
— toxic releases in Mississippi, p. 417 [416]
— treatment or release of chemicals in waste, p. 550 [513]

Bromomethane
— recycling and energy recovery of chemicals in waste, p. 539 [509]
— releases, p. 347 [382]
— releases of ozone depleters, p. 490 [453]
— releases to air, water, and land, p. 489 [452]
— toxic releases in Alabama, p. 364 [393]
— toxic releases in Arizona, p. 367 [395]
— toxic releases in Arkansas, p. 369 [396]
— toxic releases in California, p. 372 [397]
— toxic releases in Florida, p. 382 [401]
— toxic releases in Georgia, p. 384 [402]
— toxic releases in Illinois, p. 390 [405]
— toxic releases in Iowa, p. 395 [407]
— toxic releases in Massachusetts, p. 410 [413]
— toxic releases in Michigan, p. 412 [414]
— toxic releases in Mississippi, p. 417 [416]
— toxic releases in Missouri, p. 420 [417]
— toxic releases in Nebraska, p. 424 [419]
— toxic releases in New Jersey, p. 429 [422]
— toxic releases in New York, p. 434 [424]
— toxic releases in North Carolina, p. 438 [425]
— toxic releases in North Dakota, p. 440 [426]
— toxic releases in Pennsylvania, p. 450 [430]
— toxic releases in Puerto Rico, p. 453 [431]
— toxic releases in South Carolina, p. 457 [433]
— toxic releases in Tennessee, p. 461 [435]
— transfers, p. 490 [454]
— treatment or release of chemicals in waste, p. 550 [513]

Bromotrifluoromethane (Halon 1301)
— recycling and energy recovery of chemicals in waste, p. 539 [509]
— releases, p. 347 [382]
— releases of ozone depleters, p. 490 [453]
— releases to air, water, and land, p. 489 [452]
— transfers, p. 490 [454]
— treatment or release of chemicals in waste, p. 550 [513]

Brown-headed nuthatch
— long- and short-term trends, p. 242 [273]

Numbers following p. or pp. are page references. Numbers in [ ] are table references.

Numbers following p. or pp. are page references. Numbers in [ ] are table references.

Numbers following p. or pp. are page references. Numbers in [ ] are table references.

Numbers following p. or pp. are page references. Numbers in [ ] are table references.

Keyword Index

Numbers following p. or pp. are page references. Numbers in [ ] are table references.

Carbaryl continued:
— treatment or release of chemicals in waste, p. 550 [513]
Carbofuran
— pesticide use in Mexico, p. 346 [381]
Carboloy Inc. (Warren, Michigan)
— increased underground injection, p. 511 [472]
Carbon dioxide
— carbon content, p. 63 [61]
— concentrations, p. 13 [16]
— emissions from anthropogenic sources, p. 15 [18]
— gas emissions, p. 63 [61]
— global warming, p. 62 [59]
— production quantities, p. 203 [233]
— production value, p. 205 [234]
Carbon dioxide emissions
— fuel sources, p. 14 [17]
— most developed countries, p. 17 [19]
Carbon disulfide
— air, water, and land toxic releases, p. 355 [386]
— emissions to air, p. 354 [385]
— recycling and energy recovery of chemicals in waste,
   p. 539 [509]
— releases, p. 348 [382]
— total toxic releases, p. 357 [388]
— toxic chemical air emissions, p. 27 [31]
— toxic releases in Alabama, p. 364 [393]
— toxic releases in Arizona, p. 367 [395]
— toxic releases in Arkansas, p. 370 [396]
— toxic releases in California, p. 372 [397]
— toxic releases in Connecticut, p. 377 [399]
— toxic releases in Delaware, p. 379 [400]
— toxic releases in Georgia, p. 384 [402]
— toxic releases in Illinois, p. 390 [405]
— toxic releases in Indiana, p. 393 [406]
— toxic releases in Kansas, p. 397 [408]
— toxic releases in Kentucky, p. 400 [409]
— toxic releases in Louisiana, p. 403 [410]
— toxic releases in Michigan, p. 412 [414]
— toxic releases in Minnesota, p. 415 [415]
— toxic releases in Missouri, p. 420 [417]
— toxic releases in New Jersey, p. 429 [422]
— toxic releases in New York, p. 435 [424]
— toxic releases in Ohio, p. 442 [427]
— toxic releases in Oklahoma, p. 445 [428]
— toxic releases in Pennsylvania, p. 450 [430]
— toxic releases in Puerto Rico, p. 453 [431]
— toxic releases in South Carolina, p. 457 [433]
— toxic releases in Tennessee, p. 461 [435]
— toxic releases in Texas, p. 464 [436]
— toxic releases in Virginia, p. 472 [440]
— toxic releases in Washington, p. 474 [441]
— toxic releases in West Virginia, p. 476 [442]
— toxic releases in Wisconsin, p. 479 [443]
— treatment or release of chemicals in waste, p. 550 [513]
Carbon emissions
— projections, p. 18 [20]
Carbon monoxide
— air pollutant emissions, p. 11 [13]

Carbon monoxide continued:
— air pollutants from gasoline, p. 13 [15]
— air quality, p. 31 [35]
— carbon content, p. 63 [61]
— chemical industries, p. 19 [21]
— electric utilities, p. 19 [21]
— fuel combustion, p. 19 [21]
— gas emissions, p. 63 [61]
— highway vehicles, p. 19 [21]
— industrial fuel combustion, p. 19 [21]
— industrial processes, p. 19 [21]
— metals processing, p. 19 [21]
— national air pollution emissions, pp. 10, 12 [12, 14]
— national ambient air pollution concentrations, p. 21 [25]
— off-highway vehicles, p. 19 [21]
— petroleum industries, p. 19 [21]
— solvent utilization, p. 19 [21]
— storage and transport, p. 19 [21]
— superior air quality levels, p. 29 [33]
— transportation, p. 19 [21]
— waste disposal and recycling, p. 19 [21]
Carbon tetrachloride
— carcinogens released to air, water, land, p. 484 [447]
— recycling and energy recovery of chemicals in waste, p. 539
   [509]
— releases, p. 348 [382]
— releases of carcinogens, p. 485 [448]
— releases of ozone depleters, p. 490 [453]
— releases to air, water, and land, p. 489 [452]
— toxic releases in Alabama, p. 364 [393]
— toxic releases in Arkansas, p. 370 [396]
— toxic releases in California, p. 372 [397]
— toxic releases in Colorado, p. 375 [398]
— toxic releases in Delaware, p. 379 [400]
— toxic releases in Georgia, p. 384 [402]
— toxic releases in Illinois, p. 390 [405]
— toxic releases in Indiana, p. 393 [406]
— toxic releases in Kansas, p. 397 [408]
— toxic releases in Kentucky, p. 400 [409]
— toxic releases in Louisiana, p. 403 [410]
— toxic releases in Maryland, p. 408 [412]
— toxic releases in Michigan, p. 412 [414]
— toxic releases in Minnesota, p. 415 [415]
— toxic releases in Mississippi, p. 417 [416]
— toxic releases in Missouri, p. 420 [417]
— toxic releases in Montana, p. 422 [418]
— toxic releases in New Jersey, p. 429 [422]
— toxic releases in New York, p. 435 [424]
— toxic releases in North Dakota, p. 440 [426]
— toxic releases in Ohio, p. 442 [427]
— toxic releases in Oklahoma, p. 445 [428]
— toxic releases in Pennsylvania, p. 450 [430]
— toxic releases in Tennessee, p. 461 [435]
— toxic releases in Texas, p. 465 [436]
— toxic releases in Virgin Islands, p. 470 [439]
— toxic releases in Virginia, p. 472 [440]
— toxic releases in West Virginia, p. 476 [442]
— transfers, p. 490 [454]

Numbers following p. or pp. are page references. Numbers in [ ] are table references.

Numbers following p. or pp. are page references. Numbers in [ ] are table references.

945

Keyword Index

Numbers following p. or pp. are page references. Numbers in [ ] are table references.

Keyword Index

Numbers following p. or pp. are page references. Numbers in [ ] are table references.

947

Numbers following p. or pp. are page references. Numbers in [ ] are table references.

Numbers following p. or pp. are page references. Numbers in [ ] are table references.

949

Keyword Index

Numbers following p. or pp. are page references. Numbers in [ ] are table references.

Numbers following p. or pp. are page references. Numbers in [ ] are table references.

Numbers following p. or pp. are page references. Numbers in [ ] are table references.

Numbers following p. or pp. are page references. Numbers in [ ] are table references.

Coal

Numbers following p. or pp. are page references. Numbers in [ ] are table references.

954

Keyword Index

Numbers following p. or pp. are page references. Numbers in [ ] are table references.

955

Colorado Springs, Colorado continued:
— temperatures, p. 111 [139]
— wind speed, p. 148 [175]
Columbia, Missouri
— humidity, p. 127 [153]
— precipitation, p. 83 [94]
— snow and ice pellets, p. 100 [128]
— sunshine, p. 136 [163]
— temperatures, p. 109 [137]
— wind speed, p. 146 [173]
Columbia River
— length, discharge, and drainage areas, p. 38 [38]
— source stream of river, p. 38 [38]
Columbia, South Carolina
— annual precipitation, p. 70 [68]
— highest temperature, p. 115 [142]
— humidity, p. 125 [151]
— lowest temperature, p. 116 [143]
— maximum temperatures, p. 117 [144]
— minimum temperatures, p. 119 [145]
— normal temperatures, p. 113 [141]
— precipitation, p. 89 [109]
— snow and ice pellets, p. 99 [127]
— sunshine, p. 134 [161]
— temperatures, p. 108 [136]
— wind speed, p. 144 [171]
Columbian concentrate (Columbium content)
— world production, p. 215 [243]
Columbium
— net U.S. imports, p. 867 [855]
— world production of concentrates, p. 215 [243]
Columbium, contained
— apparent consumption, p. 211 [241]
— average price, p. 648 [625]
— exports, p. 211 [241]
— net import reliance, p. 211 [241]
— production, p. 211 [241]
Columbus, Georgia
— humidity, p. 125 [151]
— precipitation, p. 76 [79]
— snow and ice pellets, p. 99 [127]
— temperatures, p. 108 [136]
— wind speed, p. 144 [171]
Columbus, Ohio
— air quality standard excesses for ozone, p. 34 [36]
— annual precipitation, p. 70 [68]
— highest temperature, p. 115 [142]
— humidity, p. 120 [146]
— lowest temperature, p. 116 [143]
— maximum temperatures, p. 117 [144]
— minimum temperatures, p. 119 [145]
— normal temperatures, p. 113 [141]
— precipitation, p. 87 [104]
— snow and ice pellets, p. 95 [122]
— sunshine, p. 130 [156]
— temperatures, p. 102 [131]
— wind speed, p. 139 [166]
Combustion
— energy recovery, p. 568 [531]

Combustion continued:
— municipal solid waste management, p. 567 [530]
— municipal solid waste projections, p. 565 [526]
Cominco Fertilizers Inc. (Beatrice, Nebraska)
— decreased air, water, and land releases, p. 507 [469]
Cominco Fertilizers Inc. (Borger, Texas)
— decreased underground injection, p. 508 [470]
Commemorative areas See: National commemorative areas
Commerce
— U.S. outlays for physical resources, p. 642 [617]
Commerce, U.S. Department of See: U.S. Department of Commerce
Commercial catch
— size by country, p. 258 [289]
Commercial districts
— National Priority List sites, p. 494 [457]
Commercial establishments
— energy consumption, p. 290 [324]
Commercial fisheries
— corporate environmental compliance costs, p. 630 [604]
Commercial lodgings
— national park system, p. 221 [249]
Commercial physical and biological research
— environmental goods and services, p. 828 [806]
Commercial sector
— average fuel prices, p. 623 [596]
— electric energy sales, p. 858 [845]
— electric utility prices, p. 618 [591]
— electric utility sales, p. 860 [846]
— energy consumption, p. 292 [326]
— energy expenditures, p. 619 [592]
— expenditures, p. 620 [593]
— natural gas consumption, p. 299 [331]
— primary energy consumption, p. 301 [333]
— renewable energy consumption, p. 301 [334]
— solar collectors, p. 312 [346]
— wood energy consumption, p. 305 [338]
Commercial sites
— nuclear waste, p. 574 [543]
Commercial waste
— annual production, p. 595 [570]
— rural recycling programs, p. 588 [561]
Common dolphins
— number and status, p. 275 [308]
Common yellowthroat
— long- and short-term trends, p. 241 [272]
Commonwealth of Independent States
See also: Union of Soviet Socialist Republics (former)
— environmental technology markets, p. 844 [825]
Community and regional development
— U.S. outlays for physical resources, p. 642 [617]
Community relations
— status of local conditions, p. 883 [872]
Community service
— status of local conditions, p. 883 [872]
Compliance costs See: Environmental compliance costs
Compliance planning
— environmental service needs of industrial waste

Numbers following p. or pp. are page references. Numbers in [ ] are table references.

Numbers following p. or pp. are page references. Numbers in [ ] are table references.

Keyword Index

Numbers following p. or pp. are page references. Numbers in [ ] are table references.

958

Keyword Index

Numbers following p. or pp. are page references. Numbers in [ ] are table references.

Numbers following p. or pp. are page references. Numbers in [ ] are table references.

Numbers following p. or pp. are page references. Numbers in [ ] are table references.

Numbers following p. or pp. are page references. Numbers in [ ] are table references.

Numbers following p. or pp. are page references. Numbers in [ ] are table references.

Keyword Index

Numbers following p. or pp. are page references. Numbers in [ ] are table references.

Keyword Index

Numbers following p. or pp. are page references. Numbers in [ ] are table references.

Numbers following p. or pp. are page references. Numbers in [ ] are table references.

Keyword Index

Numbers following p. or pp. are page references. Numbers in [ ] are table references.

Keyword Index

Numbers following p. or pp. are page references. Numbers in [ ] are table references.

969

Numbers following p. or pp. are page references. Numbers in [ ] are table references.

Numbers following p. or pp. are page references. Numbers in [ ] are table references.

Numbers following p. or pp. are page references. Numbers in [ ] are table references.

Numbers following p. or pp. are page references. Numbers in [ ] are table references.

Numbers following p. or pp. are page references. Numbers in [ ] are table references.

Keyword Index

Numbers following p. or pp. are page references. Numbers in [ ] are table references.

Keyword Index

Numbers following p. or pp. are page references. Numbers in [ ] are table references.

Numbers following p. or pp. are page references. Numbers in [ ] are table references.

Numbers following p. or pp. are page references. Numbers in [ ] are table references.

Numbers following p. or pp. are page references. Numbers in [ ] are table references.

Floods
— crop loss, p. 154 [181]
— deaths, p. 654 [630]
— loss of life and property, p. 65 [63]
Flor-Quim Inc. (Patillas, Puerto Rico)
— increased underground injection, p. 512 [472]
Florida
— area of water bodies, pp. 43-45 [42-44]
— chemicals used in lettuce production, p. 342 [377]
— electric energy net generation, p. 325 [358]
— electric energy net summer capability, p. 325 [358]
— electric energy sales, p. 859 [845]
— endangered species, p. 244 [275]
— energy consumption, p. 293 [326]
— energy expenditures, p. 621 [594]
— environmental budget, p. 637 [611]
— federal aid to state and local governments, p. 632 [606]
— federally owned land, p. 197 [227]
— hazardous waste sites, p. 492 [456]
— highest point of elevation, p. 184 [217]
— land area, p. 189 [220]
— land cover and use, pp. 199-200 [228-229]
— lowest point of elevation, p. 185 [218]
— mean elevation, p. 187 [219]
— national forest recreation visitor days, p. 220 [248]
— national forest system land, p. 177 [211]
— National Priority List sites, p. 495 [458]
— net imports of Toxic Release Inventory chemicals, p. 862 [848]
— nonfuel mineral production, p. 214 [242]
— nuclear generating capacity, p. 316 [350]
— nuclear power plants, p. 318 [352]
— pollution abatement and control expenditures, p. 725 [701]
— pollution abatement and control operating costs, p. 776 [752]
— precipitation, p. 75 [78]
— quantity and value of catch for fisheries, p. 260 [291]
— receipt of Toxic Release Inventory chemicals, p. 537 [508]
— recycling and energy recovery of chemicals in waste, p. 546 [511]
— recycling goals, p. 577 [546]
— Safe Drinking Water Act violations, p. 887 [876]
— state parks and recreation areas, p. 224 [252]
— state recycling laws, p. 886 [875]
— threatened fish species, p. 252 [285]
— total area, p. 189 [220]
— toxic chemical accidents, p. 361 [391]
— toxic chemical emissions, p. 362 [392]
— toxic chemical releases, p. 381 [401]
— Toxic Release Inventory air, water, and land releases, p. 501 [464]
— Toxic Release Inventory transfers, pp. 504, 530, 548 [466, 500, 512]
— toxic releases in U.S. states and territories, p. 499 [462]
— treatment or release of chemicals in waste, p. 556 [515]
— tree planting on federal land, p. 179 [213]
— tree planting on non-federal land, p. 180 [214]

Florida continued:
— tree planting on private land, p. 182 [215]
— U.S. territorial expansion and acquisition of land, p. 190 [221]
— water area, p. 40 [40]
— water pollution permits, p. 892 [882]
— water withdrawals and consumptive use, p. 58 [57]
Florida Bay
— area, p. 44 [43]
Flounder
— catch of principal species, p. 256 [288]
— domestic catch and value, p. 250 [283]
— freezings and holdings, p. 269 [301]
— production and value of fishery products, p. 265 [295]
— U.S. catch and value, p. 254 [286]
Fluometuron
— recycling and energy recovery of chemicals in waste, p. 541 [509]
— releases, p. 349 [382]
— toxic releases in Arkansas, p. 370 [396]
— toxic releases in Georgia, p. 385 [402]
— toxic releases in Missouri, p. 421 [417]
— toxic releases in North Carolina, p. 439 [425]
— treatment or release of chemicals in waste, p. 552 [513]
Fluor-Daniel, Inc.
— top ten environmental employers, p. 823 [801]
Fluorescent lamps and lights
— litter on beaches and shorelines, p. 593 [567]
— magnetic field emission levels, p. 309 [343]
— magnetic field emission levels of desk lamps, p. 308 [342]
— mercury in municipal solid waste, p. 564 [525]
Fluorinated compounds
— global warming, p. 62 [59]
Fluorspar
— apparent consumption, p. 211 [241]
— average price, p. 648 [625]
— exports, p. 211 [241]
— net import reliance, p. 211 [241]
— production, p. 211 [241]
— production quantities, p. 203 [233]
— production value, p. 205 [234]
— world production, p. 214 [243]
FMC Corp.
— environmental spending, p. 617 [590]
Foam plastic pieces
— beach litter, p. 592 [566]
Folding paperboard boxes
— employees, p. 836 [815]
— payroll, p. 836 [815]
— value of shipments, p. 836 [815]
Food and kindred products
— aerosol production, p. 847 [830]
— canned animal food fishery products, p. 267 [297]
— canned fish and shellfish, p. 267 [297]
— fishery product imports, p. 266 [296]
— fishery products, p. 266 [296]
— fresh and frozen fish, p. 267 [297]
— hazardous waste, p. 563 [523]
— manufacturing primary energy consumption, p. 298 [330]

Numbers following p. or pp. are page references. Numbers in [ ] are table references.

Numbers following p. or pp. are page references. Numbers in [ ] are table references.

Numbers following p. or pp. are page references. Numbers in [ ] are table references.

Numbers following p. or pp. are page references. Numbers in [ ] are table references.

Gas emissions continued:
— global warming, p. 63 [60]
Gas flaring
— carbon dioxide emissions from anthropogenic
    sources, p. 15 [18]
— greenhouse gas emissions, p. 63 [61]
Gas, natural *See:* Natural gas
Gas turbines
— electric utility industry, p. 828 [807]
— electricity production, p. 326 [359]
Gases
    See also: specific gases
— carbon dioxide emissions from anthropogenic
    sources, p. 15 [18]
Gasoline
— air pollutants, p. 13 [15]
Gasoline blending components
— petroleum balance, p. 340 [376]
Gastonia, North Carolina
— air quality standard excesses for ozone, p. 33 [36]
Geese
— population, p. 237 [266]
Geese, Canadian *See:* Canadian geese
Gelman Sciences Inc. (Ann Arbor, Michigan)
— decreased underground injection, p. 509 [470]
Gemstones
    See also: specific stones; e.g., Diamonds, stones
— apparent consumption, p. 211 [241]
— average price, p. 648 [625]
— domestic production, p. 213 [242]
— exports, p. 211 [241]
— net import reliance, p. 211 [241]
— production, p. 211 [241]
— production quantities, p. 203 [233]
— production value, p. 205 [234]
— quantity, p. 208 [237]
— value of imports and exports, p. 208 [237]
General Electric Co. Plastics (Mount Vernon, Indiana)
— decreased air, water, and land releases, p. 507 [469]
General Motors Corp.
— air, water, and land toxic releases, p. 515 [475]
— battery-powered vehicles, p. 874 [861]
General Motors Corp. (Defiance, Ohio)
— decreased air, water, and land releases, p. 507 [469]
General Motors Corp. (Saginaw, Michigan)
— air, water, and land toxic releases, p. 513 [473]
— decreased air, water, and land releases, p. 507 [469]
General Motors Corp. (Trenton, New Jersey)
— increased underground injection, p. 511 [472]
General plant waste
— waste minimization, p. 611 [585]
General science
— federal outlays, p. 634 [608]
— tax expenditures, p. 818 [795]
Genesolv, evaporated
— waste minimization, p. 614 [588]
Genesolv still bottoms
— waste minimization, p. 614 [588]

Geneva Steel (Orem, Utah)
— decreased air, water, and land releases, p. 507 [469]
Georgia
— area of water bodies, p. 45 [44]
— electric energy net generation, p. 325 [358]
— electric energy net summer capability, p. 325 [358]
— electric energy sales, p. 859 [845]
— energy consumption, p. 293 [326]
— energy expenditures, p. 621 [594]
— environmental budget, p. 637 [611]
— federal aid to state and local governments, p. 632 [606]
— federally owned land, p. 197 [227]
— hazardous waste sites, p. 492 [456]
— highest point of elevation, p. 184 [217]
— land area, p. 189 [220]
— land cover and use, pp. 199-200 [228-229]
— lowest point of elevation, p. 185 [218]
— mean elevation, p. 187 [219]
— national forest recreation visitor days, p. 220 [248]
— national forest system land, p. 177 [211]
— National Priority List sites, p. 495 [458]
— net exports of Toxic Release Inventory chemicals, p. 863
    [849]
— nonfuel mineral production, p. 214 [242]
— nuclear generating capacity, p. 316 [350]
— nuclear power plants, p. 318 [352]
— pollution abatement and control expenditures, p. 726 [702]
— pollution abatement and control operating costs, p. 777 [753]
— precipitation, p. 76 [79]
— quantity and value of catch for fisheries, p. 260 [291]
— receipt of Toxic Release Inventory chemicals, p. 537 [508]
— recycling and energy recovery of chemicals in waste, p. 546
    [511]
— Safe Drinking Water Act violations, p. 887 [876]
— southern pine beetle outbreak, p. 172 [205]
— state parks and recreation areas, p. 224 [252]
— state recycling laws, p. 886 [875]
— threatened fish species, p. 252 [285]
— total area, p. 189 [220]
— toxic chemical emissions, p. 362 [392]
— toxic chemical releases, p. 383 [402]
— Toxic Release Inventory air, water, and land releases, p. 501
    [464]
— Toxic Release Inventory transfers, pp. 504, 530, 548 [466, 500,
    512]
— toxic releases in U.S. states and territories, p. 499 [462]
— treatment or release of chemicals in waste, p. 556 [515]
— tree planting on federal land, p. 179 [213]
— tree planting on non-federal land, p. 180 [214]
— tree planting on private land, p. 182 [215]
— waste-by-rail, p. 591 [565]
— water area, p. 40 [40]
— water pollution permits, p. 893 [882]
— water withdrawals and consumptive use, p. 58 [57]
Georgia-Pacific Corp. (Brunswick, Georgia)
— decreased air, water, and land releases, p. 507 [469]
Georgia-Pacific Corp. (New Augusta, Mississippi)
— increased air, water, and land releases, p. 509 [471]

Numbers following p. or pp. are page references. Numbers in [ ] are table references.

Glycol ethers continued:
— toxic releases in Virginia, p. 472 [440]
— toxic releases in Washington, p. 475 [441]
— toxic releases in West Virginia, p. 477 [442]
— toxic releases in Wisconsin, p. 480 [443]
— toxic releases in Wyoming, p. 481 [444]
— treatment or release of chemicals in waste, p. 552 [513]
Glyphosate
— pesticide use in Mexico, p. 346 [381]
Goats *See:* Sheep and goats
Gold
— domestic production, p. 213 [242]
— prices, p. 647 [624]
— production quantities, pp. 206-207 [235-236]
— world production, pp. 215-216 [243-244]
Gold, contained
— apparent consumption, p. 211 [241]
— average price, p. 649 [625]
— exports, p. 211 [241]
— net import reliance, p. 211 [241]
— production, p. 211 [241]
Gold filters, spent *See:* Spent gold filters
Gold, refined bullion
— quantity, pp. 208-209 [237]
— value of imports and exports, pp. 208-209 [237]
Gold solution, spent *See:* Spent gold solution
Golden-cheeked warbler
— long- and short-term trends, p. 241 [272]
Golden-winged warbler
— long- and short-term trends, p. 241 [272]
Golovnin Bay
— area, p. 43 [41]
Goodland, Kansas
— humidity, p. 126 [153]
— precipitation, p. 79 [85]
— snow and ice pellets, p. 100 [128]
— temperatures, p. 109 [137]
— wind speed, p. 145 [173]
Goose Lake
— area, p. 46 [44]
Government
  See also: specific governments
— capital investment in water resources, p. 635 [609]
— capital investment in water treatment and supply, p. 635 [609]
— environmental protection, p. 883 [871]
— pollution abatement and control expenditures, pp. 656-657 [633-634]
— salaries for environmental jobs, p. 825 [803]
Government, federal
— agency spending on environment, p. 633 [607]
— offshore leasing and exploration, p. 193 [224]
— outlays for environment and natural resources, p. 634 [608]
— pollution abatement and control expenditures, pp. 656-657 [633-634]
— superfunction expenditures on human resources, p. 640 [615]

Government, federal continued:
— superfunction expenditures on national defense, p. 640 [615]
— superfunction expenditures on net interest, p. 640 [615]
— superfunction expenditures on physical resources, p. 640 [615]
— U.S. outlays for natural and environment resources, p. 641 [616]
— U.S. outlays for physical resources, p. 642 [617]
Government, local
— expenditures for natural resources, p. 635 [610]
— expenditures for parks and recreation facilities, p. 635 [610]
— expenditures for sewerage, p. 635 [610]
— expenditures for solid waste management, p. 635 [610]
— national forest system, p. 175 [209]
— pollution abatement and control expenditures, p. 656 [633]
— public service costs, p. 651 [627]
— tree planting, p. 180 [214]
Government regulators
— salaries, p. 826 [804]
Government, state
— environmental budget, p. 636 [611]
— expenditures for natural resources, p. 635 [610]
— expenditures for parks and recreation facilities, p. 635 [610]
— expenditures for sewerage, p. 635 [610]
— expenditures for solid waste management, p. 635 [610]
— pollution abatement and control expenditures, pp. 656-657 [633-634]
Grace & Co., W.R. *See:* W.R. Grace & Co.
Grain Processing Corp. (Muscatine, Iowa)
— increased air, water, and land releases, p. 509 [471]
Grains and grain products
— pesticide residues, p. 644 [621]
Grand Island, Nebraska
— humidity, p. 127 [153]
— precipitation, p. 83 [96]
— snow and ice pellets, p. 100 [128]
— temperatures, p. 109 [137]
— wind speed, p. 146 [173]
Grand Junction, Colorado
— humidity, p. 129 [155]
— precipitation, p. 74 [74]
— snow and ice pellets, p. 101 [130]
— sunshine, p. 137 [165]
— temperatures, p. 111 [139]
— wind speed, p. 148 [175]
Grand Rapids, Michigan
— air quality standard excesses for ozone, p. 34 [36]
— humidity, p. 120 [146]
— precipitation, p. 81 [91]
— snow and ice pellets, p. 95 [122]
— sunshine, p. 130 [156]
— temperatures, p. 102 [131]
— wind speed, p. 138 [166]
Granite City Steel (Granite City, Illinois)
— air, water, and land toxic releases, p. 513 [473]
Granite Peak
— highest point of elevation in Montana, p. 184 [217]
Grant Pass, Oregon
— air quality standard excesses for carbon monoxide, p. 32

Numbers following p. or pp. are page references. Numbers in [ ] are table references.

989

Grant Pass, Oregon continued:
[35]
Grants and loans
See also: Business grants and loans
— government capital investment, p. 635 [609]
— municipal long-term funding, p. 650 [626]
Graphite, crude
— apparent consumption, p. 212 [241]
— average price, p. 649 [625]
— exports, p. 212 [241]
— net import reliance, p. 212 [241]
— production, p. 212 [241]
Graphite moderated reactors
— nuclear energy, p. 320 [353]
Gravel *See:* Sand and gravel
Gravure-coated metalized paper and metalized film
— waste minimization, p. 605 [580]
Gray catbird
— long- and short-term trends, p. 241 [272]
Gray sea trout
— domestic catch and value, p. 250 [283]
Gray whales
— number and status, p. 275 [308]
— population, p. 278 [310]
Grazing
— federal land ownership, leases, and use, p. 192 [223]
— national forest system, p. 175 [209]
Grazing land
— acres, p. 202 [231]
Great Britain
See also: Britain
— environmental concerns, p. 881 [869]
Great-crested flycatcher
— long- and short-term trends, p. 241 [272]
Great Falls, Montana
— annual precipitation, p. 70 [68]
— highest temperature, p. 114 [142]
— humidity, p. 129 [155]
— lowest temperature, p. 116 [143]
— maximum temperatures, p. 117 [144]
— minimum temperatures, p. 118 [145]
— normal temperatures, p. 113 [141]
— precipitation, p. 83 [95]
— snow and ice pellets, p. 101 [130]
— sunshine, p. 137 [165]
— temperatures, p. 111 [139]
— wind speed, p. 148 [175]
Great horned owls
— long- and short-term trends, p. 242 [273]
Great Lakes
See also: specific lakes
— herring gull egg contamination, pp. 238-240 [267-271]
— lake trout contaminant levels, p. 272 [303]
— phosphorus loadings, p. 51 [49]
— population density, p. 228 [257]
— quantity and value of catch for fisheries,1, p. 260 [291]
— sport fishing, pp. 285, 821 [319, 798]
— water area, p. 39 [40]

Great Lakes Chemical Corp.
— environmental spending, p. 617 [590]
Great Lakes Chemical Corp. (El Dorado, Arkansas)
— decreased underground injection, p. 508 [470]
Great Lakes Chemical Corp. (Marysville, Arkansas)
— decreased underground injection, p. 508 [470]
Great northern divers
— threatened by oil spill, p. 235 [264]
Great Salt Lake
— area, p. 45 [44]
Great South Bay
— area, p. 43 [42]
Greater Cincinnati Airport (Ohio)
— humidity, p. 120 [146]
— snow and ice pellets, p. 95 [122]
— sunshine, p. 130 [156]
— temperatures, p. 102 [131]
— wind speed, p. 139 [166]
Greater Connecticut, Connecticut
— air quality standard excesses for ozone, p. 34 [36]
Greater white-fronted geese
— population, p. 237 [266]
Greece
— environmental technology markets, p. 843 [825]
— hazardous waste, p. 561 [521]
— petroleum product prices, p. 624 [597]
— sulfur emission targets, p. 26 [30]
Green Bay (Michigan; Wisconsin)
— area, p. 45 [44]
Green Bay, Wisconsin
— humidity, p. 120 [146]
— precipitation, p. 94 [120]
— snow and ice pellets, p. 96 [122]
— sunshine, p. 130 [156]
— temperatures, p. 102 [131]
— wind speed, p. 139 [166]
Green labeling *See:* Environmental labeling
Green sea turtles
— number of nesting females, p. 277 [309]
Green-winged teal ducks
— population, p. 235 [265]
Greenbrier County, West Virginia
— air quality standard excesses for ozone, p. 34 [36]
Greenhouse gases
See also: Global warming
— carbon dioxide, p. 63 [61]
— carbon monoxide, p. 63 [61]
— chlorofluorocarbons gases, p. 63 [61]
— emissions, p. 63 [61]
— methane, p. 63 [61]
— nitrogen oxide, p. 63 [61]
— nitrous oxide, p. 63 [61]
— nonmethane volatile organic compounds, p. 63 [61]
Greenland turbot
— freezings and holdings, p. 269 [301]
Greensboro, North Carolina
— air quality standard excesses for carbon monoxide, p. 32
[35]

Numbers following p. or pp. are page references. Numbers in [ ] are table references.

Numbers following p. or pp. are page references. Numbers in [ ] are table references.

Keyword Index

Numbers following p. or pp. are page references. Numbers in [ ] are table references.

Numbers following p. or pp. are page references. Numbers in [ ] are table references.

Keyword Index

Numbers following p. or pp. are page references. Numbers in [ ] are table references.

Numbers following p. or pp. are page references. Numbers in [ ] are table references.

Keyword Index

Huron, South Dakota continued:
— snow and ice pellets, p. 100 [128]
— sunshine, p. 136 [163]
— temperatures, p. 109 [137]
— wind speed, p. 146 [173]
Hurricanes
— costs, p. 653 [629]
— deaths, p. 654 [630]
— premature death, p. 643 [618]
Hydraulic oil
— waste minimization, p. 603 [578]
Hydraulic oil, detergent solution
— waste minimization, p. 602 [578]
Hydraulic oil filters
— waste minimization, p. 602 [578]
Hydraulic oil, spent *See:* Spent hydraulic oil
Hydrazine
— recycling and energy recovery of chemicals in waste,
    p. 542 [509]
— releases, p. 350 [382]
— releases of carcinogens, p. 486 [448]
— toxic releases in Alabama, p. 364 [393]
— toxic releases in California, p. 373 [397]
— toxic releases in Connecticut, p. 378 [399]
— toxic releases in Florida, p. 382 [401]
— toxic releases in Illinois, p. 390 [405]
— toxic releases in Kentucky, p. 401 [409]
— toxic releases in Louisiana, p. 404 [410]
— toxic releases in Massachusetts, p. 410 [413]
— toxic releases in Michigan, p. 413 [414]
— toxic releases in Missouri, p. 421 [417]
— toxic releases in New Jersey, p. 430 [422]
— toxic releases in New York, p. 435 [424]
— toxic releases in Ohio, p. 443 [427]
— toxic releases in Pennsylvania, p. 451 [430]
— toxic releases in South Carolina, p. 458 [433]
— toxic releases in Tennessee, p. 462 [435]
— toxic releases in Texas, p. 465 [436]
— toxic releases in Virginia, p. 472 [440]
— toxic releases in West Virginia, p. 477 [442]
— treatment or release of chemicals in waste, p. 552 [513]
Hydrazine sulfate
— recycling and energy recovery of chemicals in waste,
    p. 542 [509]
— releases, p. 350 [382]
— releases of carcinogens, p. 486 [448]
— toxic releases in Louisiana, p. 404 [410]
— toxic releases in Mississippi, p. 418 [416]
— toxic releases in New Jersey, p. 430 [422]
— treatment or release of chemicals in waste, p. 552 [513]
Hydro energy
— carbon dioxide emissions, p. 14 [17]
— electric utility industry, p. 828 [807]
    See also: Hydropower
Hydrocarbon emissions
— transportation sector, p. 20 [23]
Hydrochloric acid
— air, water, and land toxic releases, p. 355 [386]

Hydrochloric acid continued:
— chemical offsite transfers for energy recovery, p. 532 [502]
— chemical offsite transfers for recycling, p. 533 [503]
— chemical offsite transfers for treatment, p. 533 [504]
— discharges to surface water, p. 353 [384]
— emissions to air, p. 354 [385]
— offsite transfers for disposal, p. 531 [501]
— offsite transfers to publicly owned treatment works, p. 534
    [505]
— recycling and energy recovery of chemicals in waste, p. 542
    [509]
— releases, p. 350 [382]
— total toxic releases, p. 357 [388]
— toxic chemical accidents, p. 360 [390]
— toxic chemical air emissions, p. 27 [31]
— toxic releases in Alabama, p. 364 [393]
— toxic releases in Alaska, p. 366 [394]
— toxic releases in Arizona, p. 368 [395]
— toxic releases in Arkansas, p. 370 [396]
— toxic releases in California, p. 373 [397]
— toxic releases in Colorado, p. 376 [398]
— toxic releases in Connecticut, p. 378 [399]
— toxic releases in Delaware, p. 380 [400]
— toxic releases in Florida, p. 382 [401]
— toxic releases in Georgia, p. 385 [402]
— toxic releases in Hawaii, p. 387 [403]
— toxic releases in Idaho, p. 388 [404]
— toxic releases in Illinois, p. 390 [405]
— toxic releases in Indiana, p. 393 [406]
— toxic releases in Iowa, p. 395 [407]
— toxic releases in Kansas, p. 398 [408]
— toxic releases in Kentucky, p. 401 [409]
— toxic releases in Louisiana, p. 404 [410]
— toxic releases in Maine, p. 406 [411]
— toxic releases in Maryland, p. 408 [412]
— toxic releases in Massachusetts, p. 410 [413]
— toxic releases in Michigan, p. 413 [414]
— toxic releases in Minnesota, p. 416 [415]
— toxic releases in Mississippi, p. 418 [416]
— toxic releases in Missouri, p. 421 [417]
— toxic releases in Montana, p. 423 [418]
— toxic releases in Nebraska, p. 424 [419]
— toxic releases in Nevada, p. 426 [420]
— toxic releases in New Hampshire, p. 427 [421]
— toxic releases in New Jersey, p. 430 [422]
— toxic releases in New Mexico, p. 433 [423]
— toxic releases in New York, p. 435 [424]
— toxic releases in North Carolina, p. 439 [425]
— toxic releases in North Dakota, p. 441 [426]
— toxic releases in Ohio, p. 443 [427]
— toxic releases in Oklahoma, p. 446 [428]
— toxic releases in Oregon, p. 448 [429]
— toxic releases in Pennsylvania, p. 451 [430]
— toxic releases in Puerto Rico, p. 453 [431]
— toxic releases in Rhode Island, p. 455 [432]
— toxic releases in South Carolina, p. 458 [433]
— toxic releases in South Dakota, p. 460 [434]
— toxic releases in Tennessee, p. 462 [435]

Numbers following p. or pp. are page references. Numbers in [ ] are table references.

Numbers following p. or pp. are page references. Numbers in [ ] are table references.

Numbers following p. or pp. are page references. Numbers in [ ] are table references.

Keyword Index

Numbers following p. or pp. are page references. Numbers in [ ] are table references.

999

Numbers following p. or pp. are page references. Numbers in [ ] are table references.

Numbers following p. or pp. are page references. Numbers in [ ] are table references.

1001

Numbers following p. or pp. are page references. Numbers in [ ] are table references.

Numbers following p. or pp. are page references. Numbers in [ ] are table references.

Numbers following p. or pp. are page references. Numbers in [ ] are table references.

Keyword Index

Numbers following p. or pp. are page references. Numbers in [ ] are table references.

Numbers following p. or pp. are page references. Numbers in [ ] are table references.

Numbers following p. or pp. are page references. Numbers in [ ] are table references.

Numbers following p. or pp. are page references. Numbers in [ ] are table references.

1009

Keyword Index

Numbers following p. or pp. are page references. Numbers in [ ] are table references.

Numbers following p. or pp. are page references. Numbers in [ ] are table references.

Keyword Index

Numbers following p. or pp. are page references. Numbers in [ ] are table references.

Loans *See:* Business grants and loans; Grants and loans

Lobsters
  See also: specific types; e.g., American lobsters
— frozen seafood products, p. 271 [302]
— U.S. catch and value, p. 254 [286]

Local trucking
— environmental goods and services, p. 827 [806]

Lock corner wood boxes *See:* Nailed and lock corner wood boxes and shook

Lodgings, commercial *See:* Commercial lodgings

Loggerhead sea turtles
— number of nesting females, p. 277 [309]

Logging and sawmills
— average hourly earnings, p. 837 [816]
— employees, p. 835 [815]
— employment, p. 837 [816]
— payroll, p. 835 [815]
— Producer Price Indexes, p. 820 [797]
— value of shipments, p. 835 [815]

Logging camps and logging contractors *See:* Logging and sawmills

Logs
— exports, p. 871 [858]
— imports, p. 871 [858]

Lompoc, California
— air quality standard excesses for ozone, p. 36 [36]

Lone Star Industries (Greencastle, Indiana)
— hazardous waste incineration law violations, p. 889 [878]

Long Beach, California
— humidity, p. 123 [150]
— precipitation, p. 73 [73]
— snow and ice pellets, p. 98 [126]
— temperatures, p. 106 [135]
— wind speed, p. 142 [170]

Long Island, New York
— air quality standard excesses for carbon monoxide, p. 32 [35]
— air quality standard excesses for ozone, p. 35 [36]

Long Island Sound
— area, p. 43 [42]
— lowest point of elevation in Connecticut, p. 185 [218]

Long-tail ducks
— threatened by oil spill, p. 235 [264]

Longmont, Colorado
— air quality standard excesses for carbon monoxide, p. 32 [35]

Lorain, Ohio
— air quality standard excesses for carbon monoxide, p. 31 [35]
— air quality standard excesses for ozone, p. 34 [36]

Los Angeles, California
— air quality standard excesses for carbon monoxide, p. 32 [35]
— air quality trends, p. 31 [34]
— annual precipitation, p. 69 [68]
— catch of domestic fisheries, p. 251 [284]
— cost of natural disasters, p. 653 [629]
— highest temperature, p. 114 [142]

Los Angeles, California continued:
— humidity, p. 123 [150]
— lowest temperature, p. 115 [143]
— maximum temperatures, p. 117 [144]
— minimum temperatures, p. 118 [145]
— normal temperatures, p. 113 [141]
— precipitation, p. 73 [73]
— snow and ice pellets, p. 98 [126]
— sunshine, p. 133 [160]
— Superfund sites, p. 497 [460]
— trash per person, p. 594 [569]
— unhealthy air pollution levels, p. 37 [37]
— wind speed, p. 142 [170]

Los Angeles South Coast Air, California
— air quality standard excesses for ozone, p. 35 [36]

Lost workday injuries
— mineral industries, p. 833 [811]

Louisiana
— area of water bodies, pp. 44-45 [43-44]
— electric energy net generation, p. 326 [358]
— electric energy net summer capability, p. 326 [358]
— electric energy sales, p. 859 [845]
— energy consumption, p. 293 [326]
— energy expenditures, p. 621 [594]
— environmental budget, p. 637 [611]
— federal aid to state and local governments, p. 632 [606]
— federally owned land, p. 197 [227]
— hazardous material, p. 487 [449]
— hazardous waste sites, p. 492 [456]
— herbicide-tainted water, p. 54 [52]
— highest point of elevation, p. 184 [217]
— land area, p. 189 [220]
— land cover and use, pp. 199, 201 [228-229]
— lowest point of elevation, p. 185 [218]
— mean elevation, p. 187 [219]
— national forest recreation visitor days, p. 220 [248]
— national forest system land, p. 177 [211]
— National Priority List sites, p. 495 [458]
— net exports of Toxic Release Inventory chemicals, p. 863 [849]
— nonfuel mineral production, p. 214 [242]
— nuclear generating capacity, p. 316 [350]
— nuclear power plants, p. 318 [352]
— pollution abatement and control expenditures, p. 734 [710]
— pollution abatement and control operating costs, p. 785 [761]
— precipitation, p. 80 [87]
— quantity and value of catch for fisheries, p. 260 [291]
— receipt of Toxic Release Inventory chemicals, p. 536 [508]
— recycling and energy recovery of chemicals in waste, p. 546 [511]
— rivers, p. 38 [38]
— Safe Drinking Water Act violations, p. 888 [876]
— southern pine beetle outbreak, p. 172 [205]
— state parks and recreation areas, p. 224 [252]
— threatened fish species, p. 253 [285]
— total area, p. 189 [220]
— toxic chemical accidents, p. 361 [391]
— toxic chemical emissions, p. 362 [392]

Numbers following p. or pp. are page references. Numbers in [ ] are table references.

Numbers following p. or pp. are page references. Numbers in [ ] are table references.

Keyword Index

Numbers following p. or pp. are page references. Numbers in [ ] are table references.

Numbers following p. or pp. are page references. Numbers in [ ] are table references.

Keyword Index

1017

Numbers following p. or pp. are page references. Numbers in [ ] are table references.

Masonry cement
— domestic production, p. 213 [242]
— production quantities, p. 203 [233]
— production value, p. 205 [234]

Massachusetts
— area of water bodies, p. 43 [42]
— electric energy net generation, p. 325 [358]
— electric energy net summer capability, p. 325 [358]
— electric energy sales, p. 858 [845]
— energy consumption, p. 292 [326]
— energy expenditures, p. 621 [594]
— environmental budget, p. 637 [611]
— federal aid to state and local governments, p. 632 [606]
— federally owned land, p. 196 [227]
— gypsy moth defoliation, p. 171 [203]
— hazardous waste sites, p. 493 [456]
— highest point of elevation, p. 184 [217]
— land area, p. 188 [220]
— land cover and use, pp. 198, 200 [228-229]
— lowest point of elevation, p. 185 [218]
— mean elevation, p. 187 [219]
— national forest recreation visitor days, p. 220 [248]
— national forest system land, p. 177 [211]
— National Priority List sites, p. 495 [458]
— net exports of Toxic Release Inventory chemicals, p. 863 [849]
— nonfuel mineral production, p. 213 [242]
— nuclear generating capacity, p. 316 [350]
— nuclear power plants, p. 318 [352]
— pollution abatement and control expenditures, p. 737 [713]
— pollution abatement and control operating costs, p. 788 [764]
— precipitation, p. 81 [90]
— quantity and value of catch for fisheries, p. 260 [291]
— receipt of Toxic Release Inventory chemicals, p. 537 [508]
— recycling and energy recovery of chemicals in waste, p. 546 [511]
— recycling goals, p. 577 [546]
— Safe Drinking Water Act violations, p. 888 [876]
— state parks and recreation areas, p. 224 [252]
— threatened fish species, p. 253 [285]
— total area, p. 188 [220]
— toxic chemical emissions, p. 362 [392]
— toxic chemical releases, p. 409 [413]
— Toxic Release Inventory air, water, and land releases, p. 501 [464]
— Toxic Release Inventory transfers, pp. 504, 530, 548 [466, 500, 512]
— toxic releases in U.S. states and territories, p. 499 [462]
— treatment or release of chemicals in waste, p. 556 [515]
— tree planting on federal land, p. 179 [213]
— tree planting on non-federal land, p. 180 [214]
— tree planting on private land, p. 182 [215]
— waste-by-rail, p. 591 [565]
— water area, p. 39 [40]
— water pollution permits, p. 892 [882]
— water withdrawals and consumptive use, p. 58 [57]

Master's degrees
— salaries for environmental jobs, p. 825 [803]

Matagorda Bay
— area, p. 44 [43]

Material recovery
— facilities, p. 587 [558]
— municipal, p. 568 [532]
— rural recycling programs, p. 588 [561]

Maui Pineapple Co. Ltd. (Kahului, Hawaii)
— increased underground injection, p. 511 [472]

Mauna Loa, Hawaii
— carbon dioxide concentrations, p. 13 [16]

Mayline Company (Sheboygan, Wisconsin)
— hazardous waste incineration law violations, p. 890 [878]

Mazda
— battery-powered vehicles, p. 874 [861]

McCain Foods Inc. (Presque Isle, Maine)
— increased underground injection, p. 511 [472]

McGrath, Alaska
— humidity, p. 123 [150]
— precipitation, p. 71 [70]
— snow and ice pellets, p. 98 [126]
— temperatures, p. 106 [135]
— wind speed, p. 142 [170]

McNeil River
— source stream of river, p. 38 [38]

Mead Coated Board Inc. (Cottonton, Alabama)
— increased air, water, and land releases, p. 510 [471]

Measurement and photographic instruments
— recycling and energy recovery of chemicals in waste, p. 545 [510]
— Toxic Release Inventory releases and transfers, p. 523 [489]
— treatment or release of chemicals in waste, p. 555 [514]

Meat
— pesticide residues, p. 644 [621]

Medford, Oregon
— air quality standard excesses for carbon monoxide, p. 32 [35]
— humidity, p. 124 [150]
— precipitation, p. 88 [106]
— snow and ice pellets, p. 98 [126]
— temperatures, p. 107 [135]
— wind speed, p. 143 [170]

Media
  See also: specific media; e.g., Television
— environmental consciousness, p. 891 [880]

Medical chemicals
— production, p. 847 [831]

Medicine *See:* Drugs and medicine

Mediterranean
— coal imports, p. 874 [860]

Memphis, Tennessee
— air quality standard excesses for carbon monoxide, p. 32 [35]
— air quality standard excesses for ozone, p. 35 [36]
— annual precipitation, p. 70 [68]
— cost of natural disasters, p. 653 [629]
— highest temperature, p. 115 [142]

Numbers following p. or pp. are page references. Numbers in [ ] are table references.

Numbers following p. or pp. are page references. Numbers in [ ] are table references.

Numbers following p. or pp. are page references. Numbers in [ ] are table references.

Methyl hydrazine continued:
[509]
— releases, p. 350 [382]
— toxic releases in California, p. 373 [397]
— treatment or release of chemicals in waste, p. 553 [513]

Methyl iodide
— recycling and energy recovery of chemicals in waste,
    p. 542 [509]
— releases, p. 350 [382]
— toxic releases in New York, p. 436 [424]
— toxic releases in Tennessee, p. 462 [435]
— toxic releases in Texas, p. 466 [436]
— treatment or release of chemicals in waste, p. 553 [513]

Methyl isobutyl ketone
— air, water, and land toxic releases, p. 355 [386]
— chemical offsite transfers for energy recovery, p. 532 [502]
— recycling and energy recovery of chemicals in waste,
    p. 542 [509]
— releases, p. 350 [382]
— total toxic releases, p. 357 [388]
— toxic releases in Alabama, p. 365 [393]
— toxic releases in Arizona, p. 368 [395]
— toxic releases in Arkansas, p. 370 [396]
— toxic releases in California, p. 373 [397]
— toxic releases in Colorado, p. 376 [398]
— toxic releases in Connecticut, p. 378 [399]
— toxic releases in Delaware, p. 380 [400]
— toxic releases in Florida, p. 382 [401]
— toxic releases in Georgia, p. 385 [402]
— toxic releases in Illinois, p. 391 [405]
— toxic releases in Indiana, p. 393 [406]
— toxic releases in Iowa, p. 396 [407]
— toxic releases in Kansas, p. 398 [408]
— toxic releases in Kentucky, p. 401 [409]
— toxic releases in Louisiana, p. 404 [410]
— toxic releases in Maine, p. 406 [411]
— toxic releases in Maryland, p. 408 [412]
— toxic releases in Massachusetts, p. 411 [413]
— toxic releases in Michigan, p. 413 [414]
— toxic releases in Minnesota, p. 416 [415]
— toxic releases in Mississippi, p. 418 [416]
— toxic releases in Missouri, p. 421 [417]
— toxic releases in Montana, p. 423 [418]
— toxic releases in Nebraska, p. 424 [419]
— toxic releases in New Hampshire, p. 427 [421]
— toxic releases in New Jersey, p. 431 [422]
— toxic releases in New York, p. 436 [424]
— toxic releases in North Carolina, p. 439 [425]
— toxic releases in North Dakota, p. 441 [426]
— toxic releases in Ohio, p. 443 [427]
— toxic releases in Oklahoma, p. 446 [428]
— toxic releases in Oregon, p. 448 [429]
— toxic releases in Pennsylvania, p. 451 [430]
— toxic releases in Puerto Rico, p. 454 [431]
— toxic releases in Rhode Island, p. 455 [432]
— toxic releases in South Carolina, p. 458 [433]
— toxic releases in South Dakota, p. 460 [434]
— toxic releases in Tennessee, p. 462 [435]

Methyl isobutyl ketone continued:
— toxic releases in Texas, p. 466 [436]
— toxic releases in Utah, p. 468 [437]
— toxic releases in Vermont, p. 469 [438]
— toxic releases in Virginia, p. 473 [440]
— toxic releases in Washington, p. 475 [441]
— toxic releases in West Virginia, p. 477 [442]
— toxic releases in Wisconsin, p. 480 [443]
— treatment or release of chemicals in waste, p. 553 [513]

Methyl isobutyl ketone, spent *See:* Spent methyl isobutyl
ketone

Methyl isocyanate
— recycling and energy recovery of chemicals in waste, p. 542
    [509]
— releases, p. 350 [382]
— toxic releases in Montana, p. 423 [418]
— toxic releases in Texas, p. 466 [436]
— toxic releases in West Virginia, p. 477 [442]
— treatment or release of chemicals in waste, p. 553 [513]

Methyl methacrylate
— recycling and energy recovery of chemicals in waste, p. 542
    [509]
— releases, p. 350 [382]
— toxic releases in Alabama, p. 365 [393]
— toxic releases in Arkansas, p. 370 [396]
— toxic releases in California, p. 373 [397]
— toxic releases in Connecticut, p. 378 [399]
— toxic releases in Delaware, p. 380 [400]
— toxic releases in Florida, p. 382 [401]
— toxic releases in Georgia, p. 385 [402]
— toxic releases in Illinois, p. 391 [405]
— toxic releases in Indiana, p. 394 [406]
— toxic releases in Iowa, p. 396 [407]
— toxic releases in Kansas, p. 398 [408]
— toxic releases in Kentucky, p. 401 [409]
— toxic releases in Louisiana, p. 404 [410]
— toxic releases in Maine, p. 406 [411]
— toxic releases in Maryland, p. 408 [412]
— toxic releases in Massachusetts, p. 411 [413]
— toxic releases in Michigan, p. 413 [414]
— toxic releases in Minnesota, p. 416 [415]
— toxic releases in Mississippi, p. 418 [416]
— toxic releases in Missouri, p. 421 [417]
— toxic releases in Nebraska, p. 424 [419]
— toxic releases in New Hampshire, p. 427 [421]
— toxic releases in New Jersey, p. 431 [422]
— toxic releases in New York, p. 436 [424]
— toxic releases in North Carolina, p. 439 [425]
— toxic releases in Ohio, p. 443 [427]
— toxic releases in Oklahoma, p. 446 [428]
— toxic releases in Oregon, p. 448 [429]
— toxic releases in Pennsylvania, p. 451 [430]
— toxic releases in Puerto Rico, p. 454 [431]
— toxic releases in Rhode Island, p. 455 [432]
— toxic releases in South Carolina, p. 458 [433]
— toxic releases in Tennessee, p. 462 [435]
— toxic releases in Texas, p. 466 [436]
— toxic releases in Virginia, p. 473 [440]

Numbers following p. or pp. are page references. Numbers in [ ] are table references.

Keyword Index

1023

Numbers following p. or pp. are page references. Numbers in [ ] are table references.

Numbers following p. or pp. are page references. Numbers in [ ] are table references.

Keyword Index

Numbers following p. or pp. are page references. Numbers in [ ] are table references.

Keyword Index

Numbers following p. or pp. are page references. Numbers in [ ] are table references.

Numbers following p. or pp. are page references. Numbers in [ ] are table references.

Keyword Index

Numbers following p. or pp. are page references. Numbers in [ ] are table references.

Numbers following p. or pp. are page references. Numbers in [ ] are table references.

1031

Keyword Index

Numbers following p. or pp. are page references. Numbers in [ ] are table references.

1032

Numbers following p. or pp. are page references. Numbers in [ ] are table references.

Keyword Index

1033

Numbers following p. or pp. are page references. Numbers in [ ] are table references.

Numbers following p. or pp. are page references. Numbers in [ ] are table references.

Numbers following p. or pp. are page references. Numbers in [ ] are table references.

Numbers following p. or pp. are page references. Numbers in [ ] are table references.

Numbers following p. or pp. are page references. Numbers in [ ] are table references.

Numbers following p. or pp. are page references. Numbers in [ ] are table references.

Numbers following p. or pp. are page references. Numbers in [ ] are table references.

Keyword Index

Numbers following p. or pp. are page references. Numbers in [ ] are table references.

Numbers following p. or pp. are page references. Numbers in [ ] are table references.

Keyword Index

Numbers following p. or pp. are page references. Numbers in [ ] are table references.

1043

Numbers following p. or pp. are page references. Numbers in [ ] are table references.

Numbers following p. or pp. are page references. Numbers in [ ] are table references.

Numbers following p. or pp. are page references. Numbers in [ ] are table references.

Numbers following p. or pp. are page references. Numbers in [ ] are table references.

Numbers following p. or pp. are page references. Numbers in [ ] are table references.

Numbers following p. or pp. are page references. Numbers in [ ] are table references.

Keyword Index

Numbers following p. or pp. are page references. Numbers in [ ] are table references.

Numbers following p. or pp. are page references. Numbers in [ ] are table references.

Numbers following p. or pp. are page references. Numbers in [ ] are table references.

Keyword Index

Numbers following p. or pp. are page references. Numbers in [ ] are table references.

Numbers following p. or pp. are page references. Numbers in [ ] are table references.

Keyword Index

Numbers following p. or pp. are page references. Numbers in [ ] are table references.

Numbers following p. or pp. are page references. Numbers in [ ] are table references.

Numbers following p. or pp. are page references. Numbers in [ ] are table references.

Pink salmon
— freezings and holdings, p. 269 [301]
Pipelines
— chemical spills, p. 482 [445]
Pittsburgh, Pennsylvania
— air quality standard excesses for ozone, p. 35 [36]
— air quality trends, p. 31 [34]
— annual precipitation, p. 70 [68]
— highest temperature, p. 115 [142]
— humidity, p. 122 [148]
— lowest temperature, p. 116 [143]
— maximum temperatures, p. 117 [144]
— minimum temperatures, p. 119 [145]
— normal temperatures, p. 113 [141]
— precipitation, p. 88 [107]
— snow and ice pellets, p. 97 [124]
— sunshine, p. 132 [158]
— temperatures, p. 104 [133]
— wind speed, p. 141 [168]
Planing mills *See:* Sawmills and planing mills
Plant fuel *See:* Lease and plant fuel
Plants
— endangered species, pp. 243, 245-246 [274, 276-277]
— medicinal plants in tropical rainforests, p. 183 [216]
— threatened species, pp. 246-247 [277-278]
Plastic
— beach litter, p. 592 [566]
— construction waste, p. 594 [568]
— municipal solid waste generation and recovery, p. 572 [538]
— municipal solid waste projections, p. 565 [526]
— packaging material recycling in Germany, p. 582 [552]
— production, p. 848 [831]
— recycled or reused for highways, p. 580 [550]
— recycling and energy recovery of chemicals in waste, p. 545 [510]
— solid waste generation, p. 566 [528-529]
— solid waste recovery, p. 568 [532]
— Toxic Release Inventory releases, p. 516 [477]
— Toxic Release Inventory releases and transfers, p. 525 [493]
— treatment or release of chemicals in waste, p. 555 [514]
Plastic caps and lids
— beach litter, p. 592 [566]
Plastic cases, off-specification *See:* Off-specification plastic cases
Plastic containers
— recycling by school districts, p. 589 [562]
Plastic film *See:* Packaging paper and plastic film
Plastic flashing
— waste minimization, p. 601 [577]
Plastic floor covering
— waste minimization, p. 603 [578]
Plastic, foil, and coated paper bags
— beach litter, p. 592 [566]
— employees, p. 836 [815]
— payroll, p. 836 [815]
— value of shipments, p. 836 [815]

Plastic packaging
— recycling, p. 576 [545]
Plastic parts, finished *See:* Finished metal and plastic parts
Plastic pellets
— waste minimization, p. 603 [578]
Plastic products
See also: specific products; e.g., Plastic caps and lids
— hazardous waste, p. 563 [523]
— manufacturing primary energy consumption, p. 298 [330]
— pollution abatement and control expenditures, p. 678 [654]
— pollution abatement and control operating costs, p. 712 [688]
— pollution abatement cost offsets, p. 693 [669]
— toxic release inventory, p. 517 [478]
Plastic runners
— waste minimization, p. 602 [578]
Plastic scrap
— waste minimization, p. 603 [578]
Plastic soda bottles
— recycling, p. 576 [545]
Plastic straws
— beach litter, p. 592 [566]
Plastic stripper, spent *See:* Spent plastic stripper
Plastic wrap
— beach litter, p. 592 [566]
Plasticizers
— production, p. 847 [831]
Plating solution, spent *See:* Spent plating solution
Platinum
— consumption, p. 849 [833]
— imports, exports, and stocks, p. 849 [833]
— prices, p. 647 [624]
— production, p. 849 [833]
— production quantities, pp. 206-207 [235-236]
— quantity and value of inventory, p. 850 [834]
Platinum-group metals
— apparent consumption, p. 212 [241]
— average price, p. 649 [625]
— exports, p. 212 [241]
— net import reliance, p. 212 [241]
— net U.S. imports, p. 867 [855]
— production, p. 212 [241]
— quantity, p. 208 [237]
— value of imports and exports, p. 208 [237]
Pliers and wrenches
— waste minimization, p. 609 [584]
Plymouth Tube Co. (Streator, Illinois)
— decreased underground injection, p. 508 [470]
Plywood and veneer
See also: Millwork, veneer, plywood, and structural members; specific types (e.g., Hardwood veneer and plywood)
— construction waste, p. 594 [568]
— exports, p. 871 [858]
— forest product use, p. 851 [835]
— imports, p. 871 [858]
— production, p. 855 [840]
PM-10 fugitive dust
— agriculture, p. 23 [27]
— construction, p. 23 [27]

Numbers following p. or pp. are page references. Numbers in [ ] are table references.

1060

Numbers following p. or pp. are page references. Numbers in [ ] are table references.

Keyword Index

Numbers following p. or pp. are page references. Numbers in [ ] are table references.

Keyword Index

Numbers following p. or pp. are page references. Numbers in [ ] are table references.

1063

Keyword Index

Numbers following p. or pp. are page references. Numbers in [ ] are table references.

1065

Numbers following p. or pp. are page references. Numbers in [ ] are table references.

Quintozene continued:
[509]
— toxic releases in Arkansas, p. 371 [396]
— toxic releases in Illinois, p. 391 [405]
— toxic releases in Ohio, p. 444 [427]
— treatment or release of chemicals in waste, p. 554 [513]
Rabanco
— waste-by-rail, p. 591 [565]
Race relations
— status of local conditions, p. 883 [872]
Racine, Wisconsin
— air quality standard excesses for ozone, p. 35 [36]
Radiation
— EPA budget requests and appropriations, p. 638 [613]
Radioactivity
— nuclear waste, pp. 574-575 [543-544]
— toxic chemical accidents, p. 360 [390]
Rags *See:* specific types; e.g., Paint filters and rags
Railroads
— chemical spills, p. 482 [445]
— total horsepower of prime movers, p. 311 [345]
— wildfires, p. 169 [201]
Rainbow trout
— freezings and holdings, p. 269 [300]
Rainforests, tropical *See:* Tropical rainforests
Raleigh, North Carolina
— air quality standard excesses for carbon monoxide, p. 32
[35]
— air quality standard excesses for ozone, p. 35 [36]
— annual precipitation, p. 70 [68]
— highest temperature, p. 115 [142]
— humidity, p. 125 [151]
— lowest temperature, p. 116 [143]
— maximum temperatures, p. 117 [144]
— minimum temperatures, p. 119 [145]
— normal temperatures, p. 113 [141]
— precipitation, p. 86 [102]
— snow and ice pellets, p. 99 [127]
— sunshine, p. 134 [161]
— temperatures, p. 108 [136]
— wind speed, p. 144 [171]
Rangeland
— acreage of nonfederal lands, pp. 198, 200 [228-229]
— condition of Bureau of Land Management rangeland,
   p. 203 [232]
— condition of nonfederal rangeland, p. 203 [232]
— sheet and rill erosion, p. 167 [197]
— wind erosion, p. 167 [198]
Rapid City, South Dakota
— humidity, p. 127 [153]
— precipitation, p. 89 [110]
— snow and ice pellets, p. 100 [128]
— sunshine, p. 136 [163]
— temperatures, p. 109 [137]
— wind speed, p. 146 [173]
Raw material drums
— waste minimization, p. 609 [583]
Raw material storage bags
— waste minimization, p. 609 [583]

Raw steel
— world production, p. 215 [243]
Razors, electric *See:* Electric shavers
RBMK
— nuclear energy and reactors, p. 320 [353]
Reading, Pennsylvania
— air quality standard excesses for ozone, p. 35 [36]
Real estate law
— corporate legal needs, p. 884 [873]
Reclaim rubber
— scrap tire utilization, p. 585 [556]
Reclaimed asphalt pavement
— recycled or reused for highways, p. 580 [550]
Reclaimed concrete pavement
— recycled or reused for highways, p. 580 [550]
Reclaimed solvents
— waste minimization, p. 608 [583]
Reclamation, Bureau of *See:* U.S. Bureau of Reclamation
Reclamation Fund
— mineral revenues, p. 861 [847]
Reconstituted wood products
— employees, p. 836 [815]
— payroll, p. 836 [815]
— value of shipments, p. 836 [815]
Recoverable solvent
— waste minimization, p. 605 [580]
Recovery *See:* Reuse and recovery
Recreation
   See also: Parks and recreation facilities
— hunting, p. 821 [798]
— hunting expenditures, p. 822 [800]
— hunting license costs, p. 821 [799]
— hunting license expenditures, p. 822 [800]
— hunting licenses, p. 287 [322]
— national forests, p. 218 [247]
— sport fishing, pp. 285, 821 [319, 798]
— sport fishing expenditures, p. 822 [800]
— sport fishing license costs, p. 821 [799]
— sport fishing license expenditures, p. 822 [800]
— sport fishing licenses, p. 287 [322]
— use of public lands, p. 223 [251]
— wildlife-related activities, p. 287 [321]
Recreation areas *See:* Federal recreation areas
Recreation vehicles
— national park system, p. 221 [249]
Recreation visits
— national park system, p. 221 [249]
Recreational activity impairment
— corporate environmental compliance costs, p. 630 [604]
Recreational resources
— federal outlays, p. 634 [608]
— U.S. outlays for natural resources and environment, p. 641
   [616]
Recycling
— aluminum cans, p. 578 [548]
— bans, p. 889 [877]
— businesses, p. 880 [867]
— carbon monoxide, p. 19 [21]

Numbers following p. or pp. are page references. Numbers in [ ] are table references.

Numbers following p. or pp. are page references. Numbers in [ ] are table references.

Numbers following p. or pp. are page references. Numbers in [ ] are table references.

Numbers following p. or pp. are page references. Numbers in [ ] are table references.

Numbers following p. or pp. are page references. Numbers in [ ] are table references.

Keyword Index

1071

Numbers following p. or pp. are page references. Numbers in [ ] are table references.

Keyword Index

Numbers following p. or pp. are page references. Numbers in [ ] are table references.

Numbers following p. or pp. are page references. Numbers in [ ] are table references.

Numbers following p. or pp. are page references. Numbers in [ ] are table references.

Keyword Index

1075

Numbers following p. or pp. are page references. Numbers in [ ] are table references.

Numbers following p. or pp. are page references. Numbers in [ ] are table references.

Numbers following p. or pp. are page references. Numbers in [ ] are table references.

Numbers following p. or pp. are page references. Numbers in [ ] are table references.

Keyword Index

1079

Numbers following p. or pp. are page references. Numbers in [ ] are table references.

Numbers following p. or pp. are page references. Numbers in [ ] are table references.

Numbers following p. or pp. are page references. Numbers in [ ] are table references.

Keyword Index

Numbers following p. or pp. are page references. Numbers in [ ] are table references.

Numbers following p. or pp. are page references. Numbers in [ ] are table references.

1084

Numbers following p. or pp. are page references. Numbers in [ ] are table references.

1085

Keyword Index

Numbers following p. or pp. are page references. Numbers in [ ] are table references.

1086

Numbers following p. or pp. are page references. Numbers in [ ] are table references.

Keyword Index

Numbers following p. or pp. are page references. Numbers in [ ] are table references.

Numbers following p. or pp. are page references. Numbers in [ ] are table references.

Sweet gum
— consumption, p. 852 [837]
— production, p. 852 [837]
Swimming
— national forests, p. 218 [247]
Switzerland
— carbon dioxide emissions growth, p. 17 [19]
— environmental concerns, p. 881 [869]
— environmental technology markets, p. 844 [825]
— petroleum product prices, p. 624 [597]
— sulfur emission targets, p. 26 [30]
Swordfish
— domestic catch and value, p. 250 [283]
Sycamore
— heat generation, p. 310 [344]
Synthetic gas
— carbon dioxide emissions, p. 14 [17]
Synthetic oil
— carbon dioxide emissions, p. 14 [17]
— waste minimization, p. 603 [578]
Syracuse, New York
— humidity, p. 122 [148]
— precipitation, p. 85 [101]
— snow and ice pellets, p. 97 [124]
— sunshine, p. 132 [158]
— temperatures, p. 104 [133]
— wind speed, p. 140 [168]
Syringes
— litter on beaches and shorelines, p. 593 [567]
Tablets *See:* School supplies; Stationery, tablets, and
   related products
Tacoma, Washington
— air quality standard excesses for carbon monoxide, p. 32
   [35]
— air quality standard excesses for ozone, p. 36 [36]
— annual precipitation, p. 70 [68]
— highest temperature, p. 115 [142]
— lowest temperature, p. 116 [143]
— maximum temperatures, p. 118 [144]
— minimum temperatures, p. 119 [145]
— normal temperatures, p. 114 [141]
— precipitation, p. 93 [118]
Taiwan
— coal market, p. 838 [818]
— petroleum consumption, pp. 306-307 [340]
— petroleum product prices, p. 624 [597]
Talc and pyrophyllite
— apparent consumption, p. 212 [241]
— average price, p. 649 [625]
— domestic production, p. 213 [242]
— exports, p. 212 [241]
— net import reliance, p. 212 [241]
— production, p. 212 [241]
— production quantities, p. 203 [233]
— production value, p. 205 [234]
Talkeetna, Alaska
— humidity, p. 123 [150]
— precipitation, p. 71 [70]

Talkeetna, Alaska continued:
— snow and ice pellets, p. 98 [126]
— temperatures, p. 106 [135]
— wind speed, p. 142 [170]
Tallahassee, Florida
— humidity, p. 124 [151]
— precipitation, p. 75 [78]
— snow and ice pellets, p. 99 [127]
— temperatures, p. 108 [136]
— wind speed, p. 144 [171]
Tampa Bay
— area, p. 44 [43]
Tampa, Florida
— air quality standard excesses for ozone, p. 36 [36]
— humidity, p. 124 [151]
— precipitation, p. 75 [78]
— snow and ice pellets, p. 99 [127]
— sunshine, p. 134 [161]
— temperatures, p. 108 [136]
— wind speed, p. 144 [171]
Tanana River
— length, discharge, and drainage areas, p. 38 [38]
Tangier Sound
— area, p. 43 [42]
Tank barges
— oil polluting incidents, p. 49 [48]
Tankships
— oil polluting incidents, p. 49 [48]
Tantalum
— net U.S. imports, p. 868 [855]
— prices, p. 647 [624]
— world production of concentrates, p. 215 [243]
Tantalum concentrates
— world production, p. 215 [243]
Targeted whitewater assistance
— government capital investment, p. 635 [609]
Taum Sauk Mountain
— highest point of elevation in Missouri, p. 184 [217]
Tax incentives
— state recycling laws, p. 886 [875]
Tax law
— corporate legal needs, p. 884 [873]
Taxes
— energy, p. 818 [795]
— general science, space, and technology, p. 818 [795]
— municipal long-term funding, p. 650 [626]
— Superfund liability of insurers, p. 818 [794]
Technicians *See:* Lab and field technicians
Technology
— federal outlays, p. 634 [608]
— tax expenditures, p. 818 [795]
— U.S. Department of Energy budget, p. 638 [612]
Technology, environmental *See:* Environmental technology
Teen pregnancy
— status of local conditions, p. 883 [872]
Television
— environmental reporters, p. 890 [879]
— magnetic field emission levels, p. 309 [342]

Numbers following p. or pp. are page references. Numbers in [ ] are table references.

Keyword Index

Numbers following p. or pp. are page references. Numbers in [ ] are table references.

Numbers following p. or pp. are page references. Numbers in [ ] are table references.

Numbers following p. or pp. are page references. Numbers in [ ] are table references.

Keyword Index

Numbers following p. or pp. are page references. Numbers in [ ] are table references.

Keyword Index

Numbers following p. or pp. are page references. Numbers in [ ] are table references.

Numbers following p. or pp. are page references. Numbers in [ ] are table references.

Keyword Index

1097

Numbers following p. or pp. are page references. Numbers in [ ] are table references.

Keyword Index

Numbers following p. or pp. are page references. Numbers in [ ] are table references.

Numbers following p. or pp. are page references. Numbers in [ ] are table references.

Numbers following p. or pp. are page references. Numbers in [ ] are table references.

Numbers following p. or pp. are page references. Numbers in [ ] are table references.

Numbers following p. or pp. are page references. Numbers in [ ] are table references.

Numbers following p. or pp. are page references. Numbers in [ ] are table references.

Keyword Index

Numbers following p. or pp. are page references. Numbers in [ ] are table references.

Keyword Index

Numbers following p. or pp. are page references. Numbers in [ ] are table references.

Keyword Index

Numbers following p. or pp. are page references. Numbers in [ ] are table references.

Water continued:
— toxic releases and transfers of chemical companies, p. 506 [468]
— toxic releases of chemicals, p. 355 [386]
— toxic releases of facilities, p. 512 [473]
— toxic releases of parent companies, p. 515 [475]
— withdrawals and consumptive use, p. 58 [57]
— withdrawls and consumptive use., p. 59 [58]
Water and wastewater programs, rural *See:* Rural water and wastewater programs
Water-based coating mixture spills and leaks
— waste minimization, p. 605 [580]
Water-based cutting fluid
— waste minimization, p. 613 [587]
Water-based lubricant
— waste minimization, p. 601 [577]
Water-based recreation
— use of public lands, p. 223 [251]
Water bodies
— area, pp. 41, 43-45, 47 [41-45]
Water, drinking *See:* Drinking water
Water, evaporated
— waste minimization, p. 611 [585]
Water, fresh *See:* Fresh water
Water pollution
— causes of surface water pollution, p. 52 [50]
— corporate environmental compliance costs, p. 630 [604]
— oil polluting incidents, p. 49 [48]
— permits, p. 892 [882]
— pollution abatement and control expenditures, p. 662 [638]
— public opinion, p. 882 [870]
— sources of surface water pollution, p. 52 [51]
— surface water, p. 52 [50-51]
Water power
— developed and undeveloped capacity, p. 313 [347]
Water quality
— EPA budget requests and appropriations, p. 638 [613]
— rivers and streams, p. 56 [54]
— status of local conditions, p. 883 [872]
— U.S. Environmental Protection Agency research budget, p. 639 [614]
Water resources
— government capital investment, p. 635 [609]
— U.S. outlays for natural resources and environment, p. 641 [616]
Water services
— market leaders, p. 846 [829]
Water supply *See:* Water treatment and supply
Water travel
— national forests, p. 218 [247]
Water treatment and supply
— government capital investment, p. 635 [609]
— waterborne disease, p. 646 [623]
Water use
— sources and end-use sectors, p. 56 [55]
Waterborne disease
— water supply systems, p. 646 [623]

Waterloo, Iowa
— humidity, p. 126 [153]
— precipitation, p. 78 [84]
— snow and ice pellets, p. 99 [128]
— temperatures, p. 109 [137]
— wind speed, p. 145 [173]
Weather
See also: specific weather conditions; e.g., Precipitation
— deaths from severe weather, p. 654 [630]
Welfare
— cost to local government, p. 651 [627]
Well drilling
See also: Oil and gas extraction
— crude oil, p. 834 [814]
— crude petroleum and natural gas, p. 324 [357]
— dry, p. 834 [814]
— gas, p. 834 [814]
— offshore exploration, p. 193 [224]
Well production
See also: Oil and gas extraction
— natural gas, p. 332 [366]
West Arctic Ocean
— number and status of marine mammals, p. 275 [308]
West Cote Blanche Bay
— area, p. 44 [43]
West Germany
See also: Germany
— hazardous waste, p. 562 [521]
West North Central United States
See also: specific states and cities
— below freezing temperatures, p. 109 [137]
— electric energy net generation, p. 325 [358]
— electric energy net summer capability, p. 325 [358]
— electric energy sales, p. 858 [845]
— energy consumption, p. 293 [326]
— energy expenditures, p. 621 [594]
— federally owned land, p. 196 [227]
— humidity, p. 126 [153]
— land area, p. 189 [220]
— land cover and use, pp. 199-200 [228-229]
— lumber production, p. 853 [838]
— nonfuel mineral production, p. 213 [242]
— nuclear power plants, p. 318 [352]
— snow and ice pellets, p. 99 [128]
— sunshine, p. 135 [163]
— total area, p. 189 [220]
— water area, p. 40 [40]
— water power, p. 313 [347]
— wind speed, p. 145 [173]
West Palm Beach, Florida
— humidity, p. 125 [151]
— precipitation, p. 75 [78]
— snow and ice pellets, p. 99 [127]
— temperatures, p. 108 [136]
— wind speed, p. 144 [171]
West South Central United States
See also: specific states and cities
— below freezing temperatures, p. 110 [138]

Keyword Index

Numbers following p. or pp. are page references. Numbers in [ ] are table references.

Numbers following p. or pp. are page references. Numbers in [ ] are table references.

Keyword Index

Numbers following p. or pp. are page references. Numbers in [ ] are table references.

Keyword Index

Numbers following p. or pp. are page references. Numbers in [ ] are table references.

Numbers following p. or pp. are page references. Numbers in [ ] are table references.

Numbers following p. or pp. are page references. Numbers in [ ] are table references.